Critical Values of the *t*-Distribution

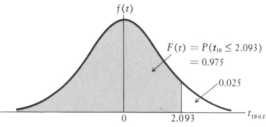

$$\frac{X - \mu}{\sigma / \sqrt{n}}$$

Example: $n = 20$, $v = 19$

$f(t)$

$F(t) = P(t_{19} \le 2.093)$
$= 0.975$

0.025

0   2.093 $t_{19\,d.f.}$

Degrees of freedom v	F .75	.90	.95	.975	.99	.995	.9995
1	1.000	3.078	6.314	12.706	31.821	63.657	636.619
2	.816	1.886	2.920	4.303	6.965	9.925	31.598
3	.765	1.638	2.353	3.182	4.541	5.841	12.941
4	.741	1.533	2.132	2.776	3.747	4.604	8.610
5	.727	1.476	2.015	2.571	3.365	4.032	6.859
6	.718	1.440	1.943	2.447	3.143	3.707	5.959
7	.711	1.415	1.895	2.365	2.998	3.499	5.405
8	.706	1.397	1.860	2.306	2.896	3.355	5.041
9	.703	1.383	1.833	2.262	2.821	3.250	4.781
10	.700	1.372	1.812	2.228	2.764	3.169	4.587
11	.697	1.363	1.796	2.201	2.718	3.106	4.437
12	.695	1.356	1.782	2.179	2.681	3.055	4.318
13	.694	1.350	1.771	2.160	2.650	3.012	4.221
14	.692	1.345	1.761	2.145	2.624	2.977	4.140
15	.691	1.341	1.753	2.131	2.602	2.947	4.073
16	.690	1.337	1.746	2.120	2.583	2.921	4.015
17	.689	1.333	1.740	2.110	2.567	2.898	3.965
18	.688	1.330	1.734	2.101	2.552	2.878	3.922
19	.688	1.328	1.729	2.093	2.539	2.861	3.883
20	.687	1.325	1.725	2.086	2.528	2.845	3.850
21	.686	1.323	1.721	2.080	2.518	2.831	3.819
22	.686	1.321	1.717	2.074	2.508	2.819	3.792
23	.685	1.319	1.714	2.069	2.500	2.807	3.767
24	.685	1.318	1.711	2.064	2.492	2.797	3.745
25	.684	1.316	1.708	2.060	2.485	2.787	3.725
26	.684	1.315	1.706	2.056	2.479	2.779	3.707
27	.684	1.314	1.703	2.052	2.473	2.771	3.690
28	.683	1.313	1.701	2.048	2.467	2.763	3.674
29	.683	1.311	1.699	2.045	2.462	2.756	3.659
30	.683	1.310	1.697	2.042	2.457	2.750	3.646
40	.681	1.303	1.684	2.021	2.423	2.704	3.551
60	.679	1.296	1.671	2.000	2.390	2.660	3.460
120	.677	1.289	1.658	1.980	2.358	2.617	3.373
∞	.674	1.282	1.645	1.960	2.326	2.576	3.291

Statistical Methods for Business and Economics

Statistical Methods for Business and Economics

FOURTH EDITION

Donald L. Harnett
Ashok K. Soni

Indiana University

 Addison-Wesley Publishing Company
Reading, Massachusetts · Menlo Park, California · New York
Don Mills, Ontario · Wokingham, England · Amsterdam
Bonn · Sydney · Singapore · Tokyo · Madrid · San Juan

Front left endpaper: From *Introduction to the Theory of Statistics* by A. M. Mood. Copyright © 1950 by McGraw-Hill Book Company. Used with permission of McGraw-Hill Book Company.

Front right endpaper: This table is abridged from Table III of Fisher & Yates: *Statistical Tables for Biological, Agricultural and Medical Research,* published by Longman Group Ltd. London (previously published by Oliver & Boyd Ltd. Edinburgh) and by permission of the authors and publishers.

Sponsoring Editor: Jerome Grant
Production Supervisor: Marion E. Howe
Production Services: Barbara Pendergast
Text Designer: Nancy Blodget
Copy Editor: Cynthia Benn
Illustrator: Textbook Art Associates
Art Consultant: Dick Morton
Permissions Editor: Mary Dyer
Manufacturing Supervisor: Roy Logan
Cover Designer: Marshall Henrichs

Library of Congress Cataloging-in-Publication Data

Harnett, Donald L.
    Statistical methods for business and economics / Donald L. Harnett, Ashok K. Soni.—
4th ed.
        p. cm.
    Includes bibliographical references and index.
    ISBN 0–201–51395–1
    1. Economics—Statistical methods. 2. Commercial statistics. 3. Statistics. 4. Statistics—Data processing. I. Soni, Ashok K., 1949– . II. Title.
HB137.H376   1991
519.5'025658—dc20
                                                                                            90–23356
                                                                                            CIP

ISBN 0-201-51395-1
ABCDEFGHIJ-DO-943210

To Pam and Sarita

Preface
to the
Fourth
Edition

There has been a tremendous growth in recent years in the role played by quantitative analysis in many academic disciplines, particularly in the social and behavioral sciences. Because of this increasing importance of quantitative skills, college students are being encouraged (and often required) to take more mathematics during their academic career. Many schools now insist that students in business and economics, as well as liberal arts, take a course in college algebra and become familiar with at least the basic elements of calculus. Unfortunately, in the past, too many of these students then elected or were required to take a statistics course whose only prerequisite was high school algebra.

Recently, with more and more students taking mathematics, it has become possible to develop courses in statistics that build on the fundamentals of at least college algebra. Taught in this fashion, statistics can provide a useful synergy: there is an improved understanding of the foundation mathematics as the student learns about the theory and applications of statistics. This book is written for the student who has the equivalent of a course in college algebra, in the hope of achieving this synergy. Although elementary calculus is used in specially marked (optional) sections of the book, calculus is not a prerequisite for the main body of the text.

In general, the student is expected to be familiar with the notation and manipulation of simple mathematical functions. Some of the basic mathematics of functions is reviewed in Appendix A, which also includes a brief review of the calculus used in the optional sections. In the text itself, the use of complicated proofs and mathematical notation has been minimized. Proofs, where necessary, are generally given in a footnote, or in special sections.

While this book is designed as an introductory text, it will also benefit more advanced students who have taken only a course in descriptive statistics.

Because the text provides the instructor with great flexibility in the assignment of topics (including the optional sections), it can be used for a one- or two-semester course at either the undergraduate or the graduate level. The first seven chapters cover basic elements of classical statistical analysis, including descriptive statistics, probability theory, probability distributions, sampling, and estimation. Chapter 8 provides an introduction to quality control, while Chapter 9 covers hypothesis testing. Chapter 10 presents statistical decision theory, and Chapters 11, 12, and 13 cover regression analysis. Chapter 14 is about time series and forecasting, Chapter 15 presents ANOVA, and Chapter 16 describes nonparametric statistics. These last three chapters do not assume knowledge of any of the previous material beyond hypothesis testing.

Revisions to the Fourth Edition

This fourth edition has almost 50 percent new problems, with a particular emphasis on problems of a "real-world" nature. Many of these problems have been taken from the consulting experience of the authors. For this edition, the use of calculus is restricted to footnotes or to sections and problems marked with the □ symbol. Chapter 8, Quality Control, is completely new. As with the previous edition, the Exercises at the end of each chapter are designed to present the student with problems that are a bit more challenging in their level of difficulty, or at least require some independent work involving concepts not covered in the book.

The fourth edition stresses the use of computers in statistics. Numerous computer outputs have been added, using a variety of popular statistical packages, such as Minitab, SAS, and SPSS. Students are encouraged to use the computer to solve problems. Instructors may order a special version of the fourth edition, priced only nominally higher than the regular version, that comes with a statistical package called B-STAT. This statistical package represents a complete, tested, menu-driven program, on a single $3\frac{1}{2}''$ disk. Documentation is included on the disk itself. The instructor's manual (available to instructors by writing to Addison-Wesley, Reading, MA, 01867) also includes a complementary copy of B-STAT. Instructors may make multiple copies of B-STAT for their students, or use B-STAT for a computer lab, as long as adoption of this text continues. Students may wish to purchase the *Student's Solution Manual*, which contains detailed solutions to the odd-numbered problems.

The fourth edition contains a new data set (in Appendix C), a new table in Appendix B (Table IX, for quality control), and the addition of Tables III and VII as endpapers at the beginning of the text. A glossary of symbols is printed on the endpapers at the back of the book.

Acknowledgments

This edition, and the past three, has greatly benefited from the patient assistance and advice of Professor Robert L. Winkler, of Duke University. His most tangible contribution was the authorship of two chapters (Chapters 10 and 15). Equally important were his comments and suggestions during the development of the remaining chapters. Professor Winkler's contribution to this material added greatly to whatever merit is found in these chapters.

In addition to the contributions of Professor Winkler, we received help and encouragement during the preparation of this text from many friends, colleagues, and students, among them Professors William Perkins, Ira Horowitz, Wain Martin, Victor Cabot, William Becker, A. Narayanan, and James Murphy. We are also grateful to the following reviewers who provided important input during the revision process: Dennis Bialaszewski, Ronald Coccari, Darlene Lanier, Terry Seaks, James A. Sullivan, and Marietta Tretter. From Addison-Wesley, Jerome Grant (senior editor), Barbara Pendergast, and Mary Dyer were all most helpful.

We are grateful to the Library Executor of the late Sir Ronald Fisher, F.R.S., to Dr. Frank Yates, F.R.S., and the Longman Group Ltd. London for permission to reprint the Table of Critical Values of the t-Distribution from their book *Statistical Tables for Biological, Agricultural and Medical Research* (6th edition, 1974).

Last, but not least, we owe a debt of gratitude to our wives, Pam and Sarita, to whom we dedicate this book.

Bloomington, Indiana   D.L.H.

                                                                    A.K.S.

Contents

Chapter 4   Discrete Probability Distributions   129

Chapter 5   Continuous Probability Distributions   163

Chapter 6   Sampling and Surveying   195

Chapter 7

Chapter 8

Chapter 9

Chapter 10

Chapter 11   Simple Linear Regression   443

Chapter 12   Simple Linear Correlation   495

Chapter 13   Multiple Regression and Correlation   515

Chapter 14

Time Series, Forecasting, and Index Numbers   573

Chapter 15

Analysis of Variance   623

Chapter 16

Nonparametric Statistics   669

Chapter 1

Introduction and
Descriptive Statistics

*Statistical thinking will one day
be as necessary for efficient
citizenship as the ability to read
and write.*

H. G. WELLS

Statistics and Statistical Analysis

1.1

Statistical techniques are put to use in one form or another in almost all branches of modern science, and in many other fields of human activity as well. As Solomon Fabricant said over 30 years ago, "The whole world now seems to hold that statistics can be useful in understanding, assessing, and controlling the operations of society." Progress in our society can be measured by a variety of numerical indexes. Statistics are used to describe, manipulate, and interpret these numbers.

Beginning Applications of Statistics

Although the origins of statistics can be traced to studies of games of chance in the 1700s, it is only in the past 70 years that applications of statistical methods have been developed for use in almost all fields of science—social, behavioral, and physical. Most early applications of statistics consisted primarily of data presented in the form of tables and charts. This field, known as **descriptive statistics,** soon grew to include a large variety of methods for arranging, summarizing, or somehow conveying the characteristics of a set of numbers.

Today, these techniques account for what is certainly the most visible application of statistics—the mass of quantitative information that is collected and published in our society every day. Crime rates, births and deaths, divorce rates, price indexes, the Dow-Jones average, and batting averages are but a few of the many "statistics" familiar to all of us.

In addition to conveying the characteristics of quantifiable information, descriptive measures provide an important basis for analysis in almost all academic disciplines, especially in the social and behavioral sciences, where human behavior generally cannot be described with the precision possible in the physical sciences. Statistical measures of satisfaction, intelligence, job aptitude, and leadership, for example, serve to expand our knowledge of human motivation and performance. In the same fashion, indexes of prices, productivity, gross national product, employment, free reserves, and net exports serve as the tools of management and government in considering policies directed toward promoting long-term growth and economic stability.

The Use of Statistics in Decision Making

Despite the enlarging scope and increasing importance of descriptive methods over the past several hundred years, these methods now represent only a minor, relatively unimportant portion of the body of statistical literature. The phenomenal growth in statistics since the turn of the century has taken place mainly in the field called **statistical inference** or **inductive statistics.** This field is concerned with the formulation of generalizations, as well as the prediction and estimation of relationships between two or more variables. The terms "inferential" and "inductive analysis" are used here because this aspect of statistics involves drawing conclusions (or "inferences") about the unknown characteristics of certain phenomena on the basis of only limited or imperfect information. Generally, this involves drawing conclusions about a set of data (called a population) based on values observed in a sample drawn from that population. From this sample information, statistical inference can often derive the quantitative information necessary for deciding among alternative courses of action when it is impossible to predict exactly what the consequence of each of these will be.

The process of drawing conclusions from limited information is one familiar to all of us, for almost every decision we face must be made without knowing with certainty the consequences. In deciding to watch television tomorrow rather than study, you may, at least subconciously, be inferring that your grades will not suffer as a result of this decision. You probably have given considerable time and thought to your choice of a major in college, but here again your decision must be made on the basis of the limited amount of information that can be provided by aptitude tests, guidance counselors, and the advice of your parents and friends. If you make a poor choice you may suffer the loss of considerable time and money. Similar problems are faced in business. Should a new product be introduced? What about plant expansion? How much should be spent on advertising? The economic advisor to government policymakers must choose among various alternative recommendations for preventing unemployment, improving the trade balance, dampening inflationary spirals, and increasing production and income. In general the best choices can only be "inferred" from less-than-perfect information about future events. As a result, such decisions often are made under conditions that expose the decision maker to considerable risk. The process of making decisions under these circumstances is usually referred to as decision making under uncertainty, or decision making under risk.*

Statistics as a decision-making tool plays an important role in the areas of research and development, and guidance and control in a wide variety of fields. Both government and industry, for instance, participate in the development, testing, and certification of new drugs and medicines, a process that often requires a large number of statistical tests (and decisions) concerning the safety and effectiveness of these drugs for public use. Similarly, the psychologist, the lawyer, and any person who makes decisions involving uncertain factors such as human behavior often bases decisions on data of a statistical nature. Since complex decision situations almost always call for some type of statistical analysis—formal or informal, explicit or implicit—it is difficult to overemphasize the importance of inferential statistics to the decision maker. In fact, **statistics** is often defined as *the set of methods for making decisions under uncertainty.*

Definition of the Statistical Population

In statistical inference problems, the set of all values under consideration—that is, all pertinent data—is customarily referred to as a **population** or **universe.**

In general, any set of quantifiable data can be referred to as a **population** if that set of data consists of all values of interest.

For example, in deciding on the choice of a major you may want to make inferences about the set of grades you can expect to receive in the courses in a certain field, or perhaps you may want to estimate the salaries being earned by people with degrees in this field. Similarly, a business manager may want to know how many customers might buy a new product considered for possible production, or what increase in sales to expect from the implementation of a particular advertising campaign. A government policymaker may want to estimate the changes in demand for food that would result from increased welfare

---

*Although the two terms "decision making under uncertainty" and "decision making under risk" often are given slightly different interpretations in decision-theory literature, we shall consider them synonymous in this book.

payments to the handicapped or a relaxation of restrictions on imported products. A legislator may need to infer the level of state revenue available from a special excise tax on tobacco products or a sales tax so that a reliable budget can be prepared. In each of these cases that set of all relevant values constitutes a population. Last year's return on common equity for all bonds in the United States could represent a population, as could the return on equity for all *Fortune* 500 companies. Similarly, a population might be the profits of all companies in the service industries, or the monthly level of energy consumed by families with incomes less than $20,000.

In making decisions, we naturally would prefer to have access to as much information as possible about the relevant population or populations. One can avoid the possibility of making an incorrect inference only when all the information about a population is available. Unfortunately, it is usually impossible or much too costly to collect all the information concerning the population associated with a practical problem. Consequently, inferences (and the resulting decisions) must be made on the basis of limited or imperfect information about the population. Statistics aid the decision maker in deciding (1) what information is needed for a particular type of decision, and (2) how this information can best be collected and analyzed for use in making the decision.

In trying to decide what information about a population is necessary for making a decision we shall be referring to certain numerical characteristics that distinguish that population. These numerical characteristics, called parameters, describe specific properties of the population.

Numerical characteristics of populations are referred to as **population parameters,** or simply **parameters.**

For instance, one parameter of the population "executive salaries in the steel industry" is the "average salary in that industry," since this measure describes the central tendency of all salaries in that population. Another parameter would be a measure of the spread or variability of all salaries. A precise definition of these parameters will be given in Sections 1.3 and 1.4. For now, it is important to note that the task of determining the exact value of a population parameter may be quite difficult. This may be due to the inconvenience or impracticality of collecting the necessary data. If we are interested in the population "executive salaries," for example, it may not be possible even to identify all the executives in a given industry, much less their salaries. Suppose that we are interested in executive salaries in the future, say one year from now. The parameters for this population, "executive salaries one year from now," may be impossible to evaluate, not only because of the reluctance of executives to disclose their salaries but also because many of these people may not know what their salaries will be one year from now.

Use of Samples from a Population

Since it is often impossible or impractical to determine the exact value of parameters of a population, the characteristics of a given population are commonly judged by observing a sample drawn from all possible values.

A **sample** is a subset of a population.

The individual values contained in a sample are often referred to as observations, and the population from which they come is sometimes called the **parent population.** We may, for example, take a sample of 100 executives, determine their current salaries, and on the basis of these observations, make statements about different characteristics (parameters) of the population of all executive salaries—such as the average salary, or the variability of salaries in a certain industry, or perhaps the average salary in that industry a year from now.

As another example, a quality-control engineer at Intel is responsible for ensuring the reliability of computer chips produced by a production process. Testing each and every chip may be prohibitively expensive. In some circumstances testing may destroy the item (an example is testing an automobile engine to see if it lasts for the equivalent of 100,000 miles or more). The solution to these problems lies in determining the reliability of all items produced (a population parameter) by inspecting only a subset (a sample) of all items (the population). In order to make decisions about a population on the basis of a sample, we will calculate certain numerical characteristics of a sample.

Numerical characteristics of samples are referred to as **sample statistics,** or simply **statistics.**

If 100 executives are sampled, their average salary is a sample statistic. A measure of the spread of these 100 salaries represents another sample statistic. Figure 1.1 illustrates these relationships. As we will study extensively later in this text, sample statistics are most often used either:

a) to make estimates about population parameters,

b) to test hypotheses (or assumptions) about population parameters,

c) to determine the optimal decision in a context of uncertainty.

In Fig. 1.1 the upper arrow represents the process of estimating population parameters. The lower arrow represents hypothesis testing.

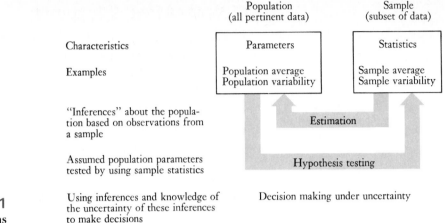

Figure 1.1
Statistical terms

The method for relating populations and samples will be described in greater detail beginning in Chapter 6. Before reaching Chapter 6, however, we will devote considerable attention to the concepts and techniques that form the foundation for these methods. It is important to establish here the major purpose for which these concepts and techniques will be used—to aid in drawing inferences and testing hypotheses about population parameters on the basis of simple statistics, and to make decisions based on knowledge of the reliability of statistical estimates.

In order to be able to discuss the objectives described above, it is necessary to learn more about how a population or a sample can be described. In any statistical problem the researcher must decide if the data gathered (or to be collected) represent all values of interest (a population), or a subset of such values (a sample). In some cases the objective of the analysis may make this distinction. For example, the salaries of all professional women in a particular company may represent a population to be compared with the salaries of all professional males (another population). On the other hand, the salaries of these women could represent a sample of the salaries of all comparable professional women in the United States.

Defining a Population

1.2

Graphical Forms

Graphs and charts, the most popular and often the most convenient means for presenting data, are usually employed when a visual representation of all or a major portion of the information is desired. Although there are many alternative methods for presenting data in this form, only a few will be discussed here. The "pie chart," for example, is a familiar device for describing how a given

SHARE OF U.S. NEW CAR MARKET

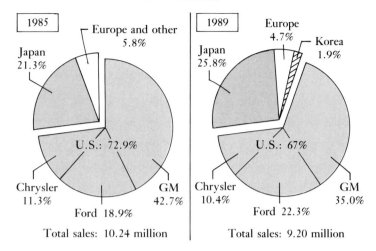

Figure 1.2
Total car sales in the United States. (Reprinted by permission of the Associated Press.)

Notes: Figures for both years as of Nov. 30. U.S. maker shares include "captive imports" (cars built by others and imported for sale under a U.S. nameplate); for foreign makers, shares include cars they build at plants in the U.S. No Korean maker sold cars in the U.S. in 1985.

ASSOCIATED PRESS Pat Lyons

Figure 1.3
U.S. energy demand. (Courtesy of Exxon Company, U.S.A.)

quantity is subdivided. Figure 1.2 presents two pie charts, comparing total U.S. car sales in 1985 to total U.S. car sales in 1989.

Another popular descriptive device is the chart measuring changes over time in some index, such as the U.S. energy demand shown in Fig. 1.3, or the annual steel shipments from U.S. "mini-mills" shown in Fig. 1.4.

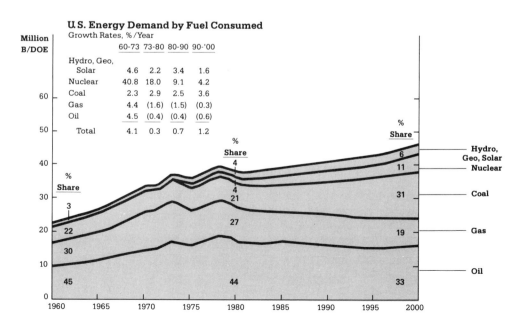

BIG STRIDES AT THE MINI-MILLS

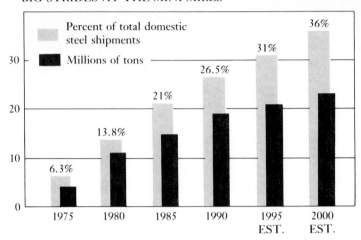

DATA: ECONOMIC ASSOCIATES INC.

Figure 1.4
Annual steel shipments.

Annual steel shipments

Figure 1.5 is derived from an example in Darrel Huff's book *How to Lie with Statistics* (Norton, 1954). This example depicts the increase in the number of cows between 1860 (8 million) and 1936 (24 million). In drawing pictures of cows to represent this growth, one naturally would be inclined to draw the 1936 cow three times as long as the 1860 cow. Of course, a cow three times as long looks rather peculiar unless it is also three times as high. But if the 1936 cow is three times as high and three times as wide, it is nine times as large as the 1860 cow in terms of area. Such a figure would seriously misrepresent the true growth.

Business journals and news magazines often adopt a somewhat whimsical device to avoid this difficulty. Interested primarily in presenting information in a form understandable to the layman (not the statistician), such journals would depict growth in the number of cows by showing one cow to represent 1860 and three cows to represent 1936—thus, each would represent 8 million animals. Similarly, growth in auto production from, let's say, 10 million to 27 mil-

Figure 1.5
Growth in the number of cows.

1860

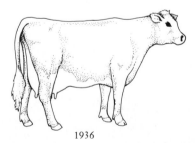

1936

TABLE 1.1   Price/earnings ratios for 50 *Fortune* 500 companies

5.31	4.02	3.17	2.47	5.31	0.49	2.73	4.11	4.79	7.27	3.68
1.56	2.63	3.62	5.21	3.00	1.74	2.19	2.24	1.29	3.51	5.75
1.13	1.70	4.25	2.97	5.32	1.96	3.42	1.40	2.11	1.08	2.06
1.13	4.62	0.05	2.20	2.13	3.09	2.03	2.22	−0.15	2.14	1.95
3.20	4.78	5.34	4.10	2.39	3.17					

lion cars could be indicated by lopping off the motor and front wheels of the third car. This truncation is less gruesome in the case of the car than in the case of the cow.

Frequency Distributions

Although graphs and charts such as those shown in Figs. 1.2 and 1.3 often serve a useful visual function, they are not appropriate for most purposes of statistical analysis and decision making because they provide only a representation of the information and not the actual data themselves. Statistical purposes usually require that the data be presented in a form that gives a more precise indication of the information at hand. Some method is needed that will summarize or describe large masses of data without loss or distortion of the essential characteristics of the information, and also make the data easier to present. One such method is the arrangement of the data into what is called a **frequency distribution** or **histogram.** In constructing a frequency distribution it is first necessary to divide the data into a limited number of different categories or classes, and then to record the number of times (the frequency) an observation falls (or is distributed) into each class. As an illustration of the construction of a frequency distribution, consider the data presented in Table 1.1. These data represent the price/earnings ratio for 50 of the top 500 companies listed by *Fortune*. Figure 1.6 presents the frequency distribution for these data, as constructed by the Minitab statistical computer software package. We will elaborate on how to construct such histograms in the material to follow.

Midpoint	Count	
0	3	***
1	5	*****
2	16	****************
3	9	*********
4	7	*******
5	8	********
6	1	*
7	1	*

Figure 1.6
Histogram for Table 1.1
using Minitab.

Statisticians have developed certain guidelines for the construction of such categories, which can be illustrated in terms of the data from Table 1.1.

1. Classes are generally chosen so that the magnitude of each class, called the **class interval,** is the same for all categories. Otherwise, interpretation of the frequency distribution may be difficult. For example, grouping the data in Table 1.1. into unequal categories such as 0–2, 2–3, 4–8 is ill advised. Comparisons between the number of observations in different categories would be misleading since the size of the categories is not consistent.

2. The number of classes used should probably be fewer than 20 (for ease of handling and to ensure sufficient compacting of the information) and at least 5 (to avoid loss of information due to grouping together widely diverse data).

3. Open-ended intervals should be avoided. Too much information is lost if categories such as " <0 " or " ≥ 5 " (for Table 1.1) are used. If a few extreme values do not conveniently fit into frequency categories they should be listed separately. The best frequency distribution for the other values should be determined after excluding these extremes.

4. Categories should be defined so that no single observation could fall into more than one category. For example, categories such as 0.50–1.50 and 1.50–2.50 for Table 1.1 would be ambiguous, since where to place P/E ratios of exactly 1.50 is not clear. For the P/E data we could let x_i represent the ratios and then define classes as follows:

Class 1:	$-0.50 \leq x_i < 0.50$
Class 2:	$0.50 \leq x_i < 1.50$
Class 3:	$1.50 \leq x_i < 2.50$
Class 4:	$2.50 \leq x_i < 3.50$
Class 5:	$3.50 \leq x_i < 4.50$
Class 6:	$4.50 \leq x_i < 5.50$
Class 7:	$5.50 \leq x_i < 6.50$
Class 8:	$6.50 \leq x_i < 7.50$

    This approach means that class 2, for example, will contain all P/E ratios that are less than 1.50 and equal to or greater than 0.50. In this case it is clear that 1.50 must fall in class 3.

5. The midpoints of each category should be representative of the values assigned to that category. This is important because these midpoints, called **class marks,** will be used in the calculation of summary measures. In Figure 1.6 the midpoints used are 0, 1, 2, 3, 4, 5, 6, and 7. These midpoints are reasonable except perhaps for the first class, where only one of the three data points falls below the midpoint.

To construct Fig. 1.6 Minitab used the eight classes described above, each with width 1.00. The boundaries of each of these classes are referred to as their upper and lower class limits. In this example, the lower class limits are $-0.50, 0.50, \ldots, 6.50$, while the upper class limits are 0.50, 1.50, ..., 7.50. Table 1.2 shows another computer output of the frequency distribution for

TABLE 1.2   Computer output—frequency distribution for ratios in Table 1.1

===CLASS LIMITS===	FREQUENCY	PERCENT	...CUMULATIVE... FREQUENCY	PERCENT
−0.50<0.50	3	6.00	3	6.00
0.50<1.50	5	10.00	8	16.00
1.50<2.50	16	32.00	24	48.00
2.50<3.50	9	18.00	33	66.00
3.50<4.50	7	14.00	40	80.00
4.50<5.50	8	16.00	48	96.00
5.50<6.50	1	2.00	49	98.00
6.50<7.50	1	2.00	50	100.00
TOTAL	50	100.00		

these *P/E* ratios and, in addition, gives the relative and cumulative frequency of each class.

Note in Table 1.2 that the sum of all frequencies must equal the number of observations (50) and the sum of the relative frequencies must equal 100%. **Relative frequency** is determined by dividing frequency of each class by the total number of observations. **Cumulative frequencies** represent the *sum* of the frequencies, from the lowest to the highest. For example, by the end of the third class (at 2.50) the cumulative frequency of *P/E* ratios is 24, which is the sum of the frequencies in the first three classes, or $3 + 5 + 16$. At that point the cumulative frequency of 24 represents 48% of the total observations (24/$50 = 0.48$).

Figure 1.7 presents the histogram for Table 1.1, together with a **frequency polygon.** This polygon, constructed by connecting the midpoints (class marks) of adjacent classes, serves to smooth a set of values. The advantage of using smoothed approximations of discrete data is that working with

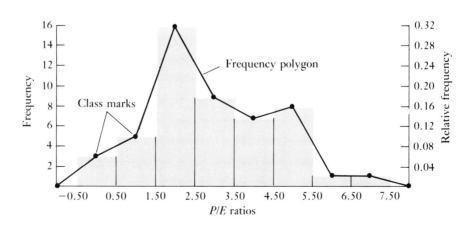

Figure 1.7
Histogram and frequency polygon for Table 1.1.

these approximations is generally much easier. The reader should verify at this point that in Fig. 1.7 the graph of the relative frequencies is the same as that of the absolute frequencies except that the values for the vertical scale are different (relative frequencies are shown on the right side of Fig. 1.7). Note in Fig. 1.7 that the frequency polygon is closed off at either end by extending it to the horizontal axis (midpoint of the next class).

Cumulative Frequency Distributions

Table 1.2 presented the concept of cumulative frequencies. Just as a graph is useful in describing frequencies, a graph of the cumulative frequency or the cumulative relative frequency provides visual information about cumulative values. Note in Fig. 1.8 that cumulative relative frequencies can be smoothed in a fashion similar to smoothing relative frequencies; in this case the polygon is called an **ogive** and the lines are drawn between points at the beginning of each class.

The distributions presented in Figs. 1.7 and 1.8 could provide useful questions for the investor comparing stocks. For example, are there common characteristics of the stocks with low *P/E* ratios? Have the low ratios carried over for more than one or two years? Will these stocks be more likely to rise (or fall) in price over the next year? The same type of statistical analysis used in this example applies to a wide range of very important managerial and governmental decision-making problems.

Summary Measures

Thus far we have concentrated on describing an entire set of observations, either graphically or by means of a frequency distribution. In many cases, however, having one or more descriptive measures that summarize the data in some quantitative form is preferable to working with all observations. In particular, we are usually most interested in the two measures mentioned earlier,

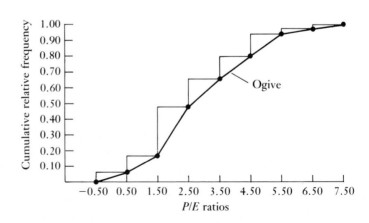

Figure 1.8

Cumulative relative frequency for *P/E* ratios.

TABLE 1.3   Common summary measures

Central location	Variability
Arithmetic mean	Standard deviation
Median	Variance
Mode	Range
Geometric mean	Interquartile range

the central location of the data and the variability or spread of the observations. Such characteristics of a data set are called **summary measures.** As we indicated in Fig. 1.1, when these summary measures apply to an entire population, they are called parameters; when the data represent a sample drawn from a population, they are called statistics. Their usefulness is obvious if one considers the difficulty of making a logical presentation of the meaning and interpretation of a given data set. Simple intuitive or "naked-eyeball" analysis of the values can be misleading and may easily miss some important implications. Furthermore, presenting an analysis of large data sets is tedious and boring for the listener or reader. If the important and most useful information in a data set can be condensed into a few summary measures, then comprehension and comparison of various features of different populations or samples becomes much easier. In decision-making problems (for example, in statistical analysis of pollution abatement systems, or in social welfare programs), summary presentation of this nature is called **data reduction.** All the information in a data set that is useful for a particular purpose is "reduced" into a single measure, such as a reliability measure or an average payment.

As we have said, the two types of summary measures most often used in statistical inference and decision making are the central location and the variability of the data. There are a number of different ways to measure these two characteristics, as is shown in Table 1.3. Some of these terms are perhaps already familiar to you while others are new, technical terms. Although each is useful for certain purposes, this text will emphasize the two most common and useful measures in statistical inference, namely, the arithmetic mean and the standard deviation.

Central Location **1.3**

The single most important measure describing numerical information is the location of the center of the data. The term **central location** may refer to any one of a number of different measures, including the mean, the median, and the mode. Each of these measures is appropriate for certain descriptive purposes, but completely inappropriate for others.

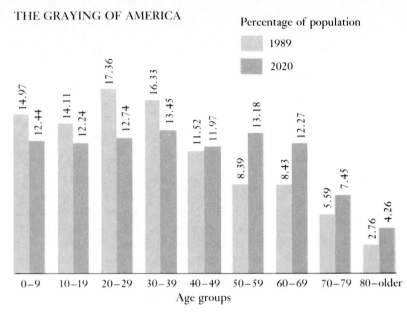

Figure 1.9
Data on the age of
Americans.

SOURCE: U.S. Census Bureau

The Mode

> The **mode** is the value that occurs most often or, equivalently,
> the point (or class) having the highest frequency.

For the *P/E* data shown in Fig. 1.7, the modal class is 1.500 to 2.500, since
there are more observations in this class than any other. Figure 1.9 presents
data on the aging of Americans. Note that the ages projected for the year 2020
in Fig. 1.9 indicate a projected mode at the midpoint of the 30–39 group,
which is different from the 1989 mode of 20–29.

The mode may or may not fall at the middle of a data set; thus it has limited use as a measure of central location for decision making. For descriptive
purposes, however, the mode is useful because it represents the most frequent
value.

The Median

> The **median** is the middle value in a set of numbers arranged in
> order of magnitude.

TABLE 1.4

	Data set A	Data set B	Data set C	Data set D
Observations	2, 2, 3, 4, 8, 10, 13	$-5, 8, 8, 9, 10, 12$	2, 3, 4, 4, 4, 7	11, 9, 26, 11, 10, 11
Median	4	8.5	4	11
Mode	2	8	4	11
Mean	6	7	4	13

When it is desirable to divide the data into two groups, each group containing exactly the same number of values, the median is the appropriate point of division. Finding the median of a set of numbers is not difficult when these numbers are arranged in ascending or descending order. If the number of values in the data set (N) is odd, the middle value can be determined by counting off, from either the highest or lowest value, $(N + 1)/2$ numbers; the resulting number divides the data into the two desired groups and thus represents the median. For example, in a list of five values the median is found by counting down (or up) $(5 + 1)/2 = 3$ values; in a list of seven values, the median is found by counting down (or up) $(7 + 1)/2 = 4$ values.

When N is even, there are two middle values, and the median is usually defined as the number halfway between these two values. The median of six values is thus halfway between the third and fourth numbers. In Table 1.1, for instance, there are 50 numbers, so the median must be halfway between the twenty-fifth and the twenty-sixth number. Remembering that the numbers in Table 1.1 are not arranged in order, we could use a computer to sort these numbers and then could count to find that

$$\text{25th number} = 2.63$$
$$\text{26th number} = 2.73$$

The median is thus $(2.63 + 2.73)/2 = 2.68$.

Note in the examples given in Table 1.4 that no matter how many items there are, the median always has a value such that the number of values on each side of the median is equal when all the values are arranged in numerical order. The only time this rule causes some confusion (but, technically, still holds) is when there are several values equal to the median, as in Examples C and D in Table 1.4.

The Mean

By far the most common measure of central location is the arithmetic mean, commonly referred to as the **average.** Calculating the mean (the word "arithmetic" is usually omitted) of a set of numbers is a relatively straightforward process, one that most of us learned long before knowing anything else about statistics.

The **mean** of a set of numbers is the sum of all values being considered divided by the total number of values in the set.

The symbol μ (the Greek letter mu) is used to represent the mean of a population. The mean of a sample is denoted by the symbol $\bar{x}$, which is read "x-bar." Consider the case of an electrical utility, Public Service Indiana (PSI), which recently formed a holding company. For federal tax purposes, PSI had to determine, or at least estimate, the average price paid for PSI stock by their 54 million shareholders. PSI did not, and does not, know the exact population mean. Let's assume the mean price paid is $\mu = \$14.23$ (it could be some other number in the $14 to $15 range).

Unfortunately, obtaining the exact mean in such a situation may be very difficult, if not impossible. For example, PSI did not know exactly who held the stock in some cases, and other stockholders could not or would not provide this information. Thus, PSI had to rely on a sample of shareholders to estimate the population mean. For example, a survey of 200 shareholders might result in a sample mean relatively close to $14.23 (such as $\bar{x} = \$14.28$), or could yield a sample mean relatively far away (such as $\bar{x} = \$13.85$).

As another example, the average starting salary for all graduating MBAs this year might be $\mu = \$52,328$. But since gathering salary information about all graduating MBAs is almost an impossible task, we must rely on sample data. Such a sample might yield $\bar{x} = \$51,541$, or some other value. Chapter 6 presents more on how to collect samples and how sample means are used to estimate population means. Between now and Chapter 6 we will lay the foundation for the study of samples; to provide that foundation it will be convenient in the intervening chapters to use populations as the reference base. That is, unless specified otherwise, we will assume data sets represent populations rather than samples.

Population Means

A population mean is calculated by summing all relevant values, and then dividing this sum by the number of values. In order to develop a formula for the mean of a population, we denote the number of values in the population by the letter N and let x_1 equal the first value in the population, x_2 equal the second value, and so forth, with x_N equaling the last value. The mean of these N values is their arithmetic sum divided by N, as shown in Formula (1.1).

$$\textit{Population mean: } \mu = \frac{x_1 + x_2 + \cdots + x_N}{N} = \frac{1}{N}\sum_{i=1}^{N} x_i \qquad (1.1)$$

To illustrate the use of Formula (1.1), we will find the mean of the values in Table 1.1. In this case $N = 50$, $x_1 = 5.31$, $x_2 = 4.02$, and $x_N = x_{50} = 3.17$:

$$\mu = \frac{5.31 + 4.02 + \cdots + 3.17}{50} = 2.9576$$

Thus, the average P/E ratio for the 50 companies is 2.9576.

The mean is shown in row 4 for each data set in Table 1.4. Note from these additional examples that the mean may be less than, greater than, or equal to the median. For the data from Table 1.1, the mean (2.9576) is larger than the median (2.68) and larger than the modal class (1.500–2.500). The mean of a data set may be thought of as the point of balance of the data, analogous to the center of gravity for a distribution of mass in physics.

The Mean of a Frequency Distribution

The formula presented for the mean (Formula 1.1) is based on the assumption that each value of the data set is given separately. Often, however, it is much easier to manipulate large amounts of data by grouping them into a frequency distribution. Columns 1 and 2 of Table 1.5 give an example of such a distribution: the starting monthly salaries (reported to the nearest $100) of 250 recent college graduates.

One way to find the mean would be to sum all 250 values separately (8 values of 2700 + 23 values of 2800 + $\cdots$ + 11 values of 3200), and then divide by 250. This is the procedure presented earlier in Formula (1.1). But most of us learned long ago that multiplication is easier than repeated addition; hence, we should take advantage of the fact that there are only six different values in Table 1.5, not 250. In other words, instead of adding 2700 eight times, we can use the product 8(2700) = 21,600. Similar products are used for

TABLE 1.5   Calculating the mean for a frequency distribution of 250 monthly starting salaries

(1)	(2)	(3)	(4)	(5)
			Relative	
Salary (x_i)	Frequency (f_i)	$x_i f_i$	frequency (f_i/N)	$x_i(f_i/N)$
$2700	8	21,600	0.032	86.4
2800	23	64,400	0.092	257.6
2900	75	217,500	0.300	870.0
3000	90	270,000	0.360	1080.0
3100	43	133,300	0.172	533.2
3200	11	35,200	0.044	140.8
Sum	250	742,000	1.000	2968.0

every value of x_i, as shown in column 3 of Table 1.5. The sum of these products for all six values divided by 250 yields the mean, μ.

$$\mu = 742,000/250 = 2968$$

The mean or average starting salary is thus $2968.

To obtain a formula for the above process, let x_i represent the ith value of x_i, and let f_i represent the frequency associated with that value. If there are c different values of x (that is, c different rows), then μ is

$$\text{Population mean for frequency distribution: } \mu = \frac{1}{N} \sum_{i=1}^{c} x_i f_i \qquad (1.2)$$

We must emphasize that Formula (1.2) is merely a more general way of writing Formula (1.1). If each value of x_i occurs with a frequency of $f_i = 1$ (as in Table 1.1), then Formula (1.2) is identical to Formula (1.1), and the value of c will equal the value of N.

It is convenient in view of our forthcoming development of means in Chapter 3 to rewrite the Formula (1.2) in a slightly different (but equivalent) form, placing N inside the sum sign.

$$\text{Population mean for frequency distribution: } \mu = \sum_{i=1}^{c} x_i \left(\frac{f_i}{N}\right) \qquad (1.3)$$

The use of Formula (1.3) is demonstrated by column 5 of Table 1.5. Note that the sum of this column yields $\mu = 2968$, the same mean we calculated above by using Formula (1.2).

Comparison of the Mode, Median, and Mean.

The arithmetic mean is the most widely used measure of central location. Its disadvantage for descriptive purposes is that it is affected more by extreme values than the median or the mode because it takes into account the difference among all values, not merely their rank order (as does the median) or their frequency (as does the mode). A recent cartoon illustrated this problem quite well by depicting a small town worker commenting to a reporter, "The average yearly income in this town is $100,000—there's one person making a million, and ten of us workers making $10,000."

Use of the median requires knowledge not only of the frequency of the values in a data set, but also their ranking, so that these values can be ordered and the middle value obtained. To illustrate, consider the following categories

TABLE 1.6 **Barron's ranking of undergraduate schools**

Group	I	II	III	IV	V	VI
Frequency	36	65	191	678	345	129

used to rank undergraduate colleges and universities in *Barron's Profiles of American Colleges.*

   I   Most competitive

  II   Highly competitive

 III   Very competitive

 IV   Competitive

   V   Less competitive

 VI   Noncompetitive

Table 1.6 shows how the 1444 undergraduate schools in the United States were ranked in a recent edition of *Barron's Profiles.*

For the data in Table 1.6, the mode falls in group IV, because this group has the highest frequency. The median also falls at group IV, as this group contains ranks 722 and 723 (the median being 722.5, which falls between ranks 722 and 723). It would be inappropriate to calculate a mean, since the difference between ranks is not precisely known, nor can these differences be assumed to be equal.

In contrast to the example above, economic and business problems generally involve data in which the differences among values are known—income measures, output quantities, retained profits, prices, and interest rates. The same factor that makes the mean inappropriate for frequency data and ranked data is its special advantage in these cases. It is a more reliable measure of central location because it requires more knowledge about the population, namely the differences between the values in the data set.

In concluding this section, we must point out that the mean, median, and mode are not the only measures of central location. Another type of mean, the geometric mean, is especially useful in certain types of problems in business and economics.* We will not present such measures here, since we wish to emphasize the use of the arithmetic mean.

---

*The geometric mean is a particularly appropriate measure of the central location of data expressed in relative terms, such as rates of change or ratios (such as change in the consumer and producer price indexes). The geometric mean gives equal weight to changes of equal relative importance. For example, if an index is doubled in value, this change is weighted equally to a change that halves the value of the index.

Problems

1.1   What is the difference between descriptive and inferential statistics? Find a newspaper article using descriptive data, and another using data for making inferences.

1.2   If you are examining a data set, how can you tell if the data represent a population or a sample?

1.3   When might the median be a better measure of central location than the mean? Give a specific example.

1.4   What advantage (if any) does the mode have over the mean and the median as a descriptive measure?

1.5   Make up your own (simple) example to demonstrate that Formulas (1.1), (1.2), and (1.3) all yield the same mean for a given data set.

1.6   What happens to Formula (1.3) if $c = N$?

1.7   Find the mean age of the population shown in Fig. 1.9 for the year 2020. Assume the average age of those over 80 is 85 years. What other assumptions must be made to calculate the mean?

1.8   In the figure below, the average of the data set is shown to be 5:49 A.M. Use the data in the pie chart to see if you can come reasonably close (within 5 minutes) of this mean.

EXECS ARE EARLY TO RISE

USA executives wake up at an average time of 5:49 A.M., a new survey shows:

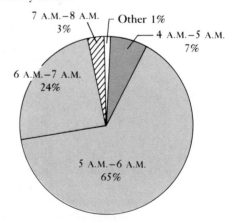

Source: Robert Half Int. Inc. survey of executives from 100 USA corporations

1.9   The following starting salaries for new MBAs graduating from the business schools at these universities were reported in *USA Today.* Consider these data as a population.

Average starting salary

School	1987	1988	Pctg. change
University of Rochester	$37,025	$40,939	+10.6%
Washington University	34,300	36,766	+7.2%
Emory University	35,000	37,500	+7.1%
Duke University	42,000	44,500	+6.0%
Dartmouth College	49,100	51,550	+5.0%
Purdue University	37,400	38,600	+3.2%
University of Michigan	44,700	46,100	+3.1%
University of Virginia	53,159	49,926	−6.1%

Source: USA TODAY research

a) What is the average 1987 and 1988 starting salary?

b) To determine the average percentage change between 1987 and 1988, would you average the "Pctg. change" column, or would you find the percentage change between the average of columns 1 and 2? Do these two methods yield the same percent for these data? Explain why.

c) In your opinion, do these data seem to represent a population or a sample? Explain.

1.10 Consider the data given in the computer output below.

a) How are the classes defined in this output? Do the classes overlap?

b) Calculate the mean for these data.

c) Are the frequencies represented fairly in the histogram? Explain.

d) Do these values look familiar? Explain.

```
                                            ...CUMULATIVE...
===CLASS LIMITS===   FREQUENCY   PERCENT   FREQUENCY   PERCENT
2650.00<2750.00          8        3.20         8        3.20
2750.00<2850.00         23        9.20        31       12.40
2850.00<2950.00         75       30.00       106       42.40
2950.00<3050.00         90       36.00       196       78.40
3050.00<3150.00         43       17.20       239       95.60
3150.00<3250.00         11        4.40       250      100.00
           TOTAL       250      100.00
===CLASS LIMITS===   FREQUENCY .........................
2650.00<2750.00          8 : ==
2750.00<2850.00         23 : =======
2850.00<2950.00         75 : =======================
2950.00<3050.00         90 : ===========================
3050.00<3150.00         43 : =============
3150.00<3250.00         11 : ===
```

1.11 Use the population data given below to determine the mean number of employees in all U.S. companies. Specify any assumption you must make in calculating the mean.

COMPANY SIZE: WHERE AMERICANS WORK

	Number of employees				
	Less than 20	20 to 100	101 to 500	501 to 5,000	5,000 and more
Percentage of all companies	90.1%	8.5%	1.2%	0.2%	less than 0.1%

Source: "The American Economy Poster and Fact Book" by Stephen J. Rose (Pantheon)

NEA GRAPHICS

1.12 In a recent study, the Federal Aviation Administration (FAA) tabulated the ages of 301 adult passengers who were flying with children under 12 years of age.

Age:	18–22	23–27	28–32	33–37	38–42	43–47	48–52	>90
Number:	60	80	50	40	30	20	20	1

a) Draw the histogram for these data, excluding the one 97-year-old person. Draw the frequency polygon.

b) Show the relative frequencies on your histogram in part (a). Draw the frequency polygon.

c) Construct the cumulative relative frequency distribution for the data in part (a). What percent of this population is younger than 33 years? Draw the ogive.

d) In which class does the median fall? (Include the 97-year-old in this case.) Would the midpoint of this class be a good guess for the median? If not, what age would you use as an approximation to the median?

e) What is the mode of this distribution?

f) Calculate a mean for these data, including the 97-year-old. (*Hint:* Use the midpoints 20, 25, . . ., 50 to represent all values in a class.)

1.13 Records were kept on the number of absences of 100 assembly-line workers during a one-month period.

Number of sick days	0	1	2	3	4
Frequency (f)	47	33	14	5	1

a) What are the median and the mode of this population?

b) Find the mean of this population.

c) Sketch the relative frequency distribution and the cumulative relative frequency distribution. Add the frequency polygon and the ogive.

1.14 There are a number of ways to "lie" with statistics when using index numbers. To illustrate, suppose you are preparing a report on how much more it costs now for textbooks and materials for a statistics course, relative to 1980. Let's say that textbook prices have doubled since 1980 and the calculator that you have to buy has halved in price.

a) Assign both the textbooks and calculator an index of 100 for 1980. The present-day indexes will thus be 200 and 50, respectively. Comparing the average index for 1980 versus the present, has the average index increased or decreased?

b) Follow the same procedure as indicated in part (a) except now let the present-day indexes equal 100. Has the average index increased or decreased from 1980 to the present? Comment on why your answer to (a) differs from your answer to (b).

1.15 Publishers Clearing House recently announced a contest in which the following amounts (among others) would be awarded.

Award	$3900	$2600	$1300	$1200	$1000	$500	$250	$100	$ 50
Frequency of award	1	3	5	5	6	72	50	250	500

a) What are the median and the mode of this population?

b) Find the mean of this population.

c) If 1 million people enter this contest, what is the average amount each person will win?

1.16 One line of General Motors cars recently sold 850,000 units. The following table gives the percent of these sales in 10 different categories, each category representing the fuel economy in miles per gallon (mpg) for a particular model.

mpg	20.97	25.39	21.02	20.43	19.94	18.46	17.79	18.92	17.81
% of sales	2.05	25.28	8.42	32.20	3.52	12.99	1.20	8.24	6.10

a) Find the mean fuel economy (mpg) for this line of car.
b) Find the median and mode of this population.

1.17 Sales by the Colgate Palmolive Company for 1978–1980 (in $ millions) are shown below. Comment on why these graphs differ. Which one gives the "true" picture of sales? What possibilities do you see here for "lying" with statistics?

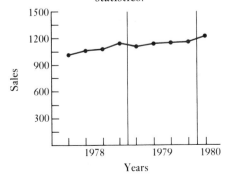

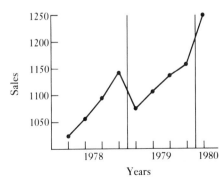

1.18 Draw a pie-chart (comparable to Fig. 1.2) using the following data on the projected energy demand (by consuming sector) for the year 2000.

Sector	New energy	Industrial	Transportation	Residential/ commercial
Percent of demand	8	37	20	35

1.19 A survey recently indicated the percent, by functional field, of MBAs expected to be hired by energy-related companies over the next five years. Present the data given below in the form of a pie-chart.

Accounting:	9.6%	Planning:	8.9%
Finance:	42.4%	Personnel:	5.2%
Marketing:	13.8%	Information systems:	4.9%
Operations management:	8.4%	Other:	6.8%

x	Σf
25	8
26	17
27	24
28	30

1.20 Suppose that a certain gasoline producer sponsors a mileage economy test involving 30 cars. The cumulative frequencies of the number of miles per gallon, x, recorded to the nearest gallon, are given in the table to the left. Find the average miles per gallon for this population by using Formulas (1.2) and (1.3).

1.21 Twenty communities provide information on the vacancy rate for local apartments. Find the mean of the following population of vacancy rates, using both Formula (1.2) and Formula (1.3). (*Hint:* Use the middle value for each vacancy rate.)

Frequency	Vacancy rate
10	3–7%
6	8–12%
4	13–17%

Measures of Dispersion

1.4

Measures of central location usually do not give enough information to provide an adequate description of the data because variability or spread is ignored. An individual who makes a judgment on the mean alone may be compared to the person whose head is in a freezer and whose feet are in an oven declaring, "On the average, I feel fine." Another measure that indicates how spread out or dispersed the data are is needed.

Since there are a number of ways to measure spread, let us consider some of the properties that a good measure should have. A good index of spread should be independent of the central location of the observations; that is, independent of the mean of the data. This property implies, in effect, that if a constant were added to (or subtracted from) each value in a set of observations, this transformation would not influence the measure of spread. In addition, to be most useful, a measure of spread should take into account all observations in its calculation, rather than just a few selected values such as the highest and lowest. Finally, a good measure should reflect the typical spread of the data and it should be convenient to manipulate mathematically.

The Range

One simple example of a measure of spread is the range, which is defined as the absolute difference between the highest and lowest values. The range for the data in Table 1.1 is the absolute difference between the highest value, 7.27, and the lowest value, -0.15, or

$$|7.27 - (-0.15)| = 7.42$$

Similarly, the ranges of the four examples in Table 1.4 are

$$|13 - 2| = 11, \quad |12 - (-5)| = 17, \quad |7 - 2| = 5, \quad \text{and} \quad |26 - 9| = 17,$$

respectively. The range has the advantages of being independent of the measure of central location and being easy to calculate. It has the *disadvantages* of ignoring all but two values of the data set and not necessarily giving a *typical* measure of the dispersion, since a single extreme value changes the range radically.

Deviations About the Mean

We now begin development of a measure of variability that has all the desirable properties mentioned at the beginning of this section. First, recall that we want our measure to be independent of the mean of the data. In other words, the value of μ should have no influence on the value of our measure of variability. This objective is accomplished by working always with data sets that have the *same* mean. That is, if all the populations that we wish to describe have the same mean, then the value of μ cannot influence our measure of variability. It is obvious, of course, that not all data sets have the same mean to begin with. We have to *transform* the values in each set in such a way that the transformed means are all equal.

The transformation used in statistics is designed to yield a data set always having $\mu = 0$. To make $\mu = 0$ is quite simple: merely subtract the mean of the original data set from each value in the set. Each resulting number, called a **deviation** and denoted $(x - \mu)$, indicates how far and in which direction the original number lies from the mean. For example, the deviation $(x - \mu) = 5$ reflects a value of x five units above the mean, and the deviation $(x - \mu) = -7$ indicates a value of x seven units below the mean.

The sum of the deviations $(x - \mu)$ will always equal zero.* Similarly, the average of the deviations $(x - \mu)$ will always equal zero. Consider, for example, the five values in Table 1.7 representing the price per share of five different common stocks. The mean of these prices is $\mu = 10$. If we subtract μ from each value of x, the mean of the new set of values, labeled $x - \mu$, must equal zero. Any set of numbers can be transformed in this fashion into a set of deviations with a mean of zero.

TABLE 1.7

	Deviations	
x	**x − μ**	
4	− 6	
8	− 2	
10	0	
13	+ 3	
15	+ 5	
Sum 50	0	
Mean 10	0	

---

* The fact that the $\sum_{i=1}^{N} (x_i - \mu)$ must equal zero can be proved as follows:

$$\sum_{i=1}^{N} (x_i - \mu) = \sum_{i=1}^{N} x_i - \sum_{i=1}^{N} \mu = \frac{N}{N} \sum_{i=1}^{N} x_i - N\mu = N\mu - N\mu = 0$$

To formalize the above process, consider a population with N values x_i, $i = 1, 2, \ldots, N$, and mean μ. When these N values are transformed into deviations from the mean, the new values are $x_i - \mu$ for $i = 1, 2, \ldots, N$, and the sum of these deviations must be zero. That is,

$$\sum_{i=1}^{N} (x_i - \mu) = 0 \qquad (1.4)$$

Since the transformation $(x_i - \mu)$ gives all sets of data a common central location (i.e., they all have means of zero), measures of dispersion defined in terms of deviations about the mean have the desirable property of being independent of central location.

While the sum of the deviations about μ is advantageous because it takes into account *all* the observations and is independent of the mean, this sum clearly cannot be our measure of variability since its value always equals zero. We will see in the following section that if we *square* each deviation before we sum, the resulting measure no longer equals zero and is relatively easy to manipulate mathematically. If we take the *average* of these squared deviations (i.e., divide their sum by N), our measure also will reflect the typical spread of the data.*

Standard Deviation and Variance

Consider the *average squared deviation* about the mean. Squaring the deviations avoids the problem inherent in ordinary deviations about the mean (namely that their sum always equals zero). Indeed, as we indicated above, this index meets all the properties of a good measure of spread; *thus the* **average squared deviation** *is the traditional method for measuring the variability of a data set.* Since it uses the deviations about the mean, it is independent of central location. It uses every value in the data set and is reasonably easy to compute mathematically. Furthermore, it is very sensitive to any change in the values—even a single change of one value in a set of 100 would result in a different measure of variability.

This "average squared deviation" measure is called the **variance** and is denoted for a population by the symbol σ^2, which is the square of the lower case Greek letter σ. It is defined as follows:

$$\textit{Population variance:} \quad \sigma^2 = \frac{1}{N} \sum_{i=1}^{N} (x_i - \mu)^2 \qquad (1.5)$$

---

*Another possibility for measuring variability is to average the sum of the absolute deviations about the mean, which is

$$\frac{1}{N}\Sigma|x - \mu| = \text{mean absolute deviation}$$

This measure has all of the desirable properties described above, except for the fact that it is not convenient to manipulate mathematically.

TABLE 1.8

x	$x - \mu$	$(x - \mu)^2$
115	-5	25
122	$+2$	4
129	$+9$	81
113	-7	49
119	-1	1
124	$+4$	16
132	$+12$	144
120	0	0
110	-10	100
116	-4	16
Sum 1200	0	436
Mean $120 = \mu$	0	$43.6 = \sigma^2$

To find a variance using Formula (1.5), one first calculates each deviation; these deviations are then squared, the squared deviations are then summed and finally the sum is divided by N.

Very often, the square root of the variance, denoted σ and called the **population standard deviation,** is used in place of (or in conjunction with) the population variance to describe variability. The standard deviation is usually more convenient than the variance for *interpreting* the variability of a data set, since σ^2 is in squared units while σ is in the same units as the original data. The population standard deviation is defined as follows:

$$\text{Population standard deviation: } \sigma = \sqrt{\frac{1}{N} \sum_{i=1}^{N} (x_i - \mu)^2} \qquad (1.6)$$

To illustrate the calculation of a population variance and standard deviation, we will assume that the values of x in Table 1.8 represent the number of tape recorders assembled by 10 different workers on an assembly line over the past month. That is, worker 1 assembled 115 recorders, worker 2 assembled 122 recorders, and so on. The mean number of recorders assembled, at the bottom of the first column, is

$$\mu = \frac{1200}{10} = 120 \text{ (recorders)}$$

The deviations about the mean are shown in the second column. Note that the sum of these deviations equals zero, as it must. The third column of values gives the *squared* deviations about the mean, the sum of which is 436. Hence, the *average squared deviation* (the variance) of this population is

$$Recorders\ variance:\ \ \sigma^2 = \frac{1}{N} \sum_{i=1}^{N} (x_i - \mu)^2 = \frac{436}{10}$$

$$= 43.6\ (recorders)^2$$

While the variance meets the criteria desired for a good measure of dispersion, the standard deviation is a better measure of the typical size of a deviation from the mean because this measure is in the same units as the original data (while, as said earlier, the variance is in squared units). For the data in Table 1.8, the standard deviation is

$$\sigma = \sqrt{variance} = \sqrt{43.6} = 6.60\ (recorders)$$

In general, a precise interpretation of values of σ and σ^2 is difficult because variability depends so highly on the unit of measurement. For instance, variability of income in the United States is certainly larger when measured in dollars than when measured in thousands of dollars. In all cases, as the spread of a population increases, the values of σ^2 (and σ) will also increase. On the other hand, if $\sigma^2 = \sigma = 0$, this means there is no variability at all to the data (all x-values are the same and equal to their mean; that is, x is a constant).

The following rule of thumb often provides a good *approximation* to the spread of a set of observations.

About 68% of all values fall within one standard deviation to either side of the mean, and *about 95%* of all values fall within two standard deviations to either side of the mean.[*]

In other words, the interval from $(\mu - 1\sigma)$ to $(\mu + 1\sigma)$, which we will write as $(\mu \pm 1\sigma)$, often contains about 68% (or about $\frac{2}{3}$) of all population values. Similarly, the interval $(\mu - 2\sigma)$ to $(\mu + 2\sigma)$, that is $(\mu \pm 2\sigma)$, often contains about 95% of all the population values. We must emphasize that these rules are only approximations and do not necessarily hold for any one discrete example. For other examples, the approximations may be quite good. Consider, for instance, the distribution of IQs in the United States measured on the Stanford-Binet test, which has a mean of $\mu = 100$ and a standard deviation of $\sigma = 16$. Studies of this population indicate about 68% of all U.S. IQs fall between 84 and 116 (which is $\mu \pm 1\sigma$) and approximately 95% of all IQs fall between 68 and 132 (which is $\mu \pm 2\sigma$). It is not difficult, for example, to show for the data on tape recorders (Table 1.8) that 60% of the population (6 of the 10 values) falls in the interval $(\mu \pm 1\sigma)$ and 100% of the data fall in the interval $(\mu \pm 2\sigma)$. These intervals are shown in Table 1.9. Recall that $\mu = 120$ and $\sigma = 6.60$.

---

[*]Chapter 5 shows that this rule of thumb is based on the assumption that the population has a symmetrical bell-shaped distribution called the **normal distribution.** A more general rule for such approximations is given in Problem 1.50.

TABLE 1.9

Interval	Values within interval	Actual percent of population within interval	Rule of thumb
$\mu \pm 1\sigma = 120 \pm 6.60$ $= \begin{cases} 113.4 \text{ to} \\ 126.6 \end{cases}$	115, 116, 119, 120, 122, 12	60%	68%
$\mu \pm 2\sigma = 120 \pm 2(6.60)$ $= \begin{cases} 106.80 \text{ to} \\ 133.20 \end{cases}$	110, 113, 115, 116, 119 120, 122, 124, 129, 132	100%	95%

As a final example of the process of calculating and interpreting the variance and standard deviation of a population, consider once again the price/earnings ratios in Table 1.1. We previously calculated the mean of this population to be $\mu = 2.9576$. We now calculate the 50 deviations from this mean so that σ^2 and σ can then be determined:

$$5.31 - 2.9576 = \quad 2.3524$$
$$4.02 - 2.9576 = \quad 1.0624$$
$$\vdots$$
$$2.39 - 2.9576 = \; -0.5676$$
$$3.17 - 2.9576 = \quad 0.2124$$

The mean of these deviations must be zero (since their sum is zero). The value of σ^2 (or variance) is

$$\sigma^2 = \frac{1}{N}\sum(x_i - \mu)^2$$

$$= \frac{1}{50}[(2.3524)^2 + (1.0624)^2 + \cdots + (-0.5676)^2 + (0.2124)^2]$$

$$= 2.4727 \quad (P/E \text{ ratios})^2$$

The standard deviation is the square root of this value,

$$\sigma = \sqrt{2.4727} = 1.5725 \quad (P/E \text{ ratios})$$

If the rule of thumb described earlier holds, then $\mu \pm 1\sigma$ should contain about 68% of the P/E ratios, and $\mu \pm 2\sigma$ should contain about 95% of all these values. Checking these intervals against the values in Table 1.1 gives the following results:

Interval	Percent of values
$\mu \pm 1\sigma = 2.9576 \pm 1(1.5725) = \quad 1.3851 \text{ to } 4.5301$	66%
$\mu \pm 2\sigma = 2.9576 \pm 2(1.5725) = \; -0.1874 \text{ to } 6.1026$	98%

Hence, had we known only that $\mu = 2.9576$ and $\sigma = 1.5725$ for these observations, we could have given a good description of the data's variability as well as central location.

Considering all the measures of central location and dispersion that we have presented, the two measures most often useful in statistical inference and decision making are the mean and the standard deviation. These are common household terms to any statistician, as they are used every day in decisions based on statistical analysis of data sets. The mean is precisely the balance point of all the values. The standard deviation is the typical (or standard) size of the difference (deviation) between the individual values of the population and the mean of the population. As such it provides a good insight into the extent of variability in the data set, especially when the rules of thumb apply. The reader should keep in mind that the variance and the standard deviation do *not* represent two different ways of measuring the variability of a population. Since σ is merely the square root of σ^2, these two measures reflect the *same information* about variability, but are expressed in different units. The standard deviation is easier to interpret because it is not in squared units, but it is more difficult to manipulate mathematically than the variance because of the square-root sign.

Population Variance for a Frequency Distribution

In Formula (1.5) we calculated the variance of a population, assuming that all frequency values were equal to 1 (that is, $f_i = 1$). Formula (1.5) can be generalized to take into account frequencies other than one in exactly the same manner in which the formula for μ was generalized. Again, we assume that there are c different values of x (that is, c rows). A squared deviation $(x_i - \mu)^2$ is calculated for every row. Each squared deviation is then multiplied by its frequency. Dividing the sum of the products by N we get:

Population variance for a frequency distribution:

$$\sigma^2 = \frac{1}{N} \sum_{i=1}^{c} (x_i - \mu)^2 f_i \qquad \text{(1.7)}$$

Formula (1.7) is illustrated by the first four columns of Table 1.10 for our salary example,* which originated in Table 1.5. Using Formula (1.7) and the sum in column 4, we get

$$\sigma^2 = \frac{1}{250} (3,004,000) = 12,016 \, (\text{dollars})^2$$

---

*The inquisitive reader may wonder why the sum of column 3 $[(x_i - \mu)]$ in Table 1.10 does not equal zero, as Formula (1.4) seems to indicate that it should. The reason is that each deviation occurs more than once, according to the frequencies in column 2. If each deviation is multiplied by its frequency and the products are summed, their total will be zero.

TABLE 1.10   Calculating the mean for a frequency distribution of monthly salaries of recent college graduates

(1) Salary x_i	(2) Frequency f	(3) $(x_i - \mu)$	(4) $(x_i - \mu)^2 f_i$	(5) Relative frequency (f_i/N)	(6) $(x_i - \mu)^2 \left(\dfrac{f_i}{N}\right)$
$2700	8	− 268	574,592	0.032	2,298.368
2800	23	− 168	649,152	0.092	2,596.608
2900	75	− 68	346,800	0.300	1,387.200
3000	90	32	92,160	0.360	368.640
3100	43	132	749,232	0.172	2,996.928
3200	11	232	592,064	0.044	2,368.256
2968 = μ	250 = Sum		3,004,000	1.000	12,016.000

As in the case of the formula for computing the mean, it is convenient to modify Formula (1.7) by moving the value ($1/N$) inside the sum sign. This yields the following (equivalent) formula:

> *Population variance for a frequency distribution:*
> $$\sigma^2 = \sum_{i=1}^{c} (x_i - \mu)^2 \left(\frac{f_i}{N}\right)$$

(1.8)

The fact that Formula (1.8) is equivalent to Formula (1.7) can be seen by examining the sum of the values in column 6 in Table 1.10:

$$\sigma^2 = \sum_{i=1}^{c} (x_1 - \mu)^2 \left(\frac{f_i}{N}\right) = 12{,}016 \,(\text{dollars})^2$$

This is the same value obtained previously by using Formula (1.7). The standard deviation is the square root of this value, $\sigma = 109.6$, and it is measured in the original units (dollars).

Other Descriptive Measures

1.5

While the mean and the standard deviation are the most common descriptive measures, there are a number of other measures that give additional information about the characteristics of a data set. This section describes, rather briefly, a few of these measures.

Percentiles, Deciles, and Quartiles

The summary measures discussed thus far all use just a single number to describe certain characteristics of a population. In some circumstances it may be helpful to use more than one number to describe a data set. For example, a company recruiter visiting a college campus may be interested in learning more than just the mean or median grade point average for all graduating seniors. This person may want to know the average of those members of the graduating class who form the upper 10%, the upper 20%, and so forth. Percentiles, deciles, and quartiles are useful in this circumstance in that they divide a data set into a specified number of groups, each containing the same number of values. Percentiles divide the data into 100 equal parts, each representing 1% of all values. The ninetieth percentile, for example, is that value that has 90% of all values below it and 10% above it. Thus, a student scoring higher than 95% and lower than 5% of all students on the college board exams is said to have scored in the ninety-fifth percentile. Percentiles can be *determined exactly* from a table of cumulative relative frequencies of ungrouped data and *approximated* from a table of grouped data. From Table 1.2, for example, we can only estimate that the value of the 50th percentile (the median) is somewhere in class 4, since the end of class 3 ($1.50 \leq x_i < 2.50$) has a cumulative relative frequency of 0.48 and the end of class 4 ($2.50 \leq x_i < 3.50$) has a cumulative relative frequency of 0.62.

The ogive in Fig. 1.8 is useful for approximating the median. Since the median is the 50th percentile, we need to find the point on the horizontal axis corresponding to $\Sigma f/N = 0.50$. Figure 1.10 (a modified version of Fig. 1.8) shows a horizontal line from 0.50 to the ogive; the dotted vertical line from the ogive to the horizontal axis gives an approximation to the median, 2.61(1).

Quartiles and deciles are defined in much the same fashion as percentiles: quartiles divide the data into four equal parts, while deciles divide the data into ten equal parts. The first quartile value (called Q1) is that point

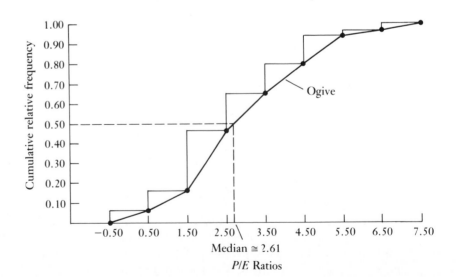

Figure 1.10
Determining a median.

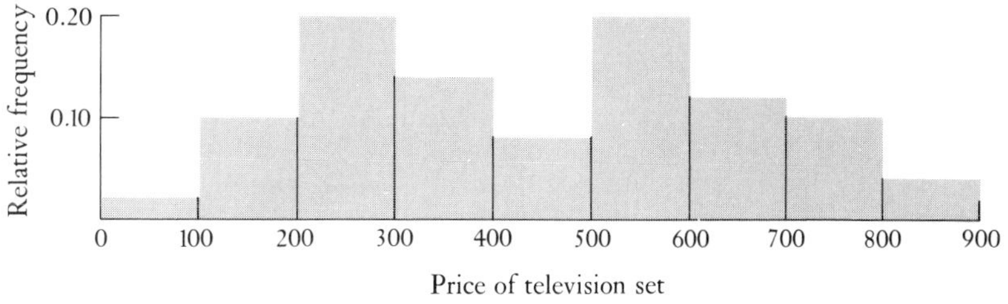

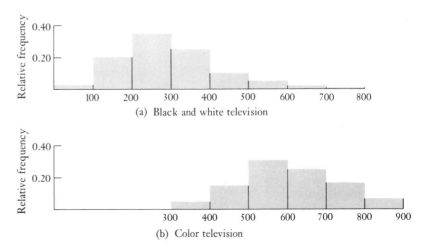

Figure 1.11
Sales of black and white plus color television sets.

which exceeds one-fourth and is exceeded by three-fourths of the observations; similarly, the third quartile value (Q3) exceeds three-fourths and is exceeded by one-fourth. Only three quartile values are necessary to divide the data into four parts. Likewise, nine decile values divide a set of observations into ten equal parts. The fifth decile and the second quartile values are equivalent to the median.

Shapes of Distributions

Having a method for describing the shape of frequency distribution is often more helpful than just being able to describe the central location or spread of a set of values. Most of the distributions representing real-world problems are called **unimodal** distributions, implying that they have only one peak, or mode. A distribution with two peaks is called a **bimodal** distribution. Often, distributions with more than one mode actually reflect the combination of two or more separate kinds of data into a single set of values.

Consider, for example, the frequency distribution shown in Fig. 1.11 representing the frequency of sales of television sets for a large department store, in intervals of $100. What Fig. 1.11 actually represents is two unimodal distributions: one reflecting the sales of black and white television sets, and the other representing the sales of color television sets. If we make this distinction and plot the resulting frequency distributions, the two distributions in Fig. 1.12 are obtained. Note that Fig. 1.12(a) has a fairly long "tail" to the right, a

Figure 1.12
Television set sales.

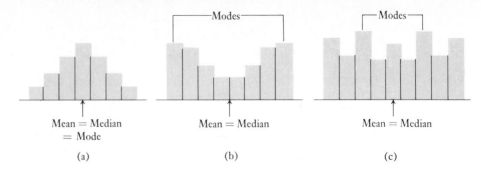

Figure 1.13
Symmetric distributions.

characteristic common to many distributions representing data in the behavioral and social sciences, especially income distributions.

A distribution is symmetric if it has the same shape on both sides of its median. Imagine folding the picture of a distribution in half at its median. To be symmetric, the two halves must match perfectly—they must be "mirror images" of each other. For all symmetric distributions the median equals the mean. The mode also equals the median if the distribution is unimodal. Figure 1.13 shows three symmetric distributions.

A distribution that is not symmetric, but rather has most of its values either to the right or to the left of the mode, is said to be skewed. If most of the values of a distribution fall to the right of the mode, as in Figure 1.12(a), this distribution is said to be skewed to the *right* or **skewed positively.** A distribution with the opposite shape, with most values to the left of the mode, is said to be skewed to the left, or **skewed negatively.** Note in Fig. 1.14 how the lack of symmetry in a distribution affects the relationship between the mean, the median, and the mode. For a completely symmetrical unimodal distribution, such as Fig. 1.13(a), these three values must all be equal. As the distribution becomes skewed positively, the mode remains at the value representing the highest frequency, but the median and the mean move to the right, as in Fig. 1.14.

Figure 1.14
The relationship between the mean, the median, and the mode for a distribution with positive skewness.

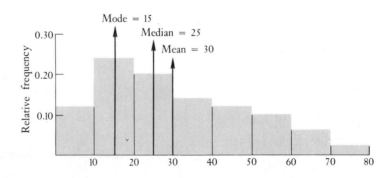

Various memory aids make it easy to remember the direction and the effect of skewness on the measures of central location in a unimodal distribution. Two useful ones are

1. The order of magnitude of the central location measures is *alphabetical* in a *negatively* skewed distribution (mean < median < mode) and *reversed* in a *positively* skewed distribution (such as Fig. 1.14).

2. If a distribution is stretched sideways, the direction of stretch is the direction of skewness. A distribution with its right side stretched out in the positive (increasing numerical value) direction has positive skewness. A distribution with its left tail stretched out in the negative (decreasing numerical value) direction is negatively skewed.

Kurtosis

Another descriptive measure of the shape of a distribution relates to its flatness or peakedness. The term applied to this characteristic of shape is **kurtosis.** The flat distribution with short broad tails illustrated in Fig. 1.15 is called **platykurtic.** A very peaked distribution with long thin tails is called **leptokurtic.** Measures of kurtosis (and skewness) are important to mathematical statisticians in their study of the theoretical properties of distributions. Although summary measures for kurtosis exist, we will not present them in this text, as measures of kurtosis are of relatively little use in elementary applications of statistics.

Figure 1.15
Platykurtic curves have short tails like a platypus, while leptokurtic curves have long tails like kangaroos, noted for "lepping."
(After W. S. Gosset)

Computer Analysis

1.6

Most, if not all, statisticians have easy access to computer programs that make it easy to calculate means, variances, standard deviations, and a large variety of additional statistical measures (many of which will be presented in this text). Our objective in teaching statistics is to have the student understand how to calculate such measures, and to practice on small data sets. Because for most practical data sets the computations are far too burdensome to do by hand, we emphasize the use of standardized computer packages by frequently presenting computer output for interpretations, and at times asking the student to generate his or her own computer output.

To illustrate a typical computer output for descriptive statistics, Table 1.11 presents the output for the data set in Appendix C called SALARIES. These data represent the salaries and work experience for 50 men and 50 women who are computer programmers in the Silicon Valley area of California. Table 1.11, which is a modified version of a Minitab output, shows the mean, the population standard deviation, the minimum (min), maximum (max), and the first and third quartile values of the salary/experience data for both males and females.

Computers are not only useful for describing data, but they are useful for graphical analysis as well. One of the best known graphics packages is called *Harvard Graphics.* The three-dimensional graph in Fig. 1.16, for the SALARIES example, was produced using this package.

The data in Table 1.11 and Fig. 1.16 raise a number of interesting questions to be addressed later in this book. The reader may wish to speculate:

1. Is the difference in salaries large enough to be due to factors other than chance? Since the average female salary is smaller than the average male salary, is this sufficient evidence of a sex bias?

2. How is experience related to salaries? Will the answers above change if experience is taken into account?

Figure 1.16
Distribution of
salaries/experience
for programmers.

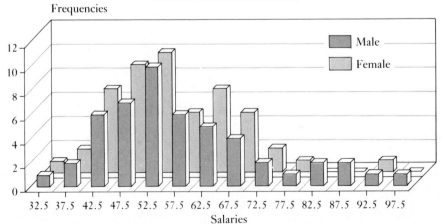

MALE/FEMALE SALARIES

TABLE 1.11   **Descriptive Statistics for SALARIES data**

Sex	N	Mean	Median	STDEV*	Min	Max	Q1	Q3
Salaries								
FEMALE	50	54494	52975	11308	32980	90400	46605	61960
MALE	50	58038	54435	15428	30200	98300	47587	66215
Experience								
FEMALE	50	7.140	6.00	4.539	1	20	4.000	9.000
MALE	50	10.040	8.00	6.296	1	29	6.000	13.000

*Minitab gives *sample* standard deviations; we present the *population* standard deviation.

Problems

1.22 On May 18, 1988, the *Wall Street Journal* reported the following data on the lead time for four recessions.

How Rates Lead Recessions

Interest rate low	Recession's start	Lead time
June 1958	April 1960	22 months
Jan. 1963	Dec. 1969	83 months
Jan. 1972	Nov. 1973	22 months
Jan. 1977	Jan. 1980	36 months
June 1980	July 1981	13 months
---

a) Determine the mean and the variance for these data, assuming the values represent a population.

b) Could this data set be a sample? If so, what is the population?

1.23 a) Use a standardized computer package to replicate the output (or something comparable) to that shown below, which was generated using the data from Problem 1.9.

b) Interpret the output below. Note in this output the variable is called "1988," and there are $N = 8$ population values.

```
        VARIABLE NAME: 1988    N=8
        ARITHMETIC MEAN = 43235.125
     POPULATION STD. DEV. = 5305.777
     POPULATION VARIANCE = 28151272.859

            MINIMUM = 36766
            MAXIMUM = 51550
                SUM = 345881
    SUM OF SQUARES = 15179418453
       DEVIATION SS = 225210182.875
```

1.24 A trainee in the Eli Lilly program for sales representatives scored in the 98th percentile on the final examination.

    a) Interpret this score.

    b) What score would you guess this person had made if the mean on the test was $\mu = 90$, with $\sigma = 2.5$?

    c) What range of scores would you guess for another trainee if you only know this person scored in the third quartile?

1.25 A June 30, 1988, article in the *Wall Street Journal* reported that the median 1987 income for lawyers was $68,922. About one in four lawyers earned over $100,000. Use this information to sketch, as best you can, the distribution of income for lawyers. Is it your guess that this distribution is skewed right, left, or symmetrical? Explain.

1.26 Find the variance and standard deviation for the number of employees presented in Problem 1.11. (Use the same mean and assumptions from that problem.)

1.27 How are the mean, the median, and the mode related in a completely symmetrical and unimodal frequency distribution? How are they related in positively and negatively skewed distributions? Sketch several distributions to illustrate your answer.

1.28 Calculate a mean and a variance for the data given below on zero coupon bonds for 5/31/88 (from *Business Week*). Do these data represent a population or a sample?

ZEROS' EXTRA ZIP

With interest rates up, you can now buy zero coupon bonds for a lot less than at the start of last year. Here are comparisons for a purchase of $10,000 zeros maturing in about 10 years.

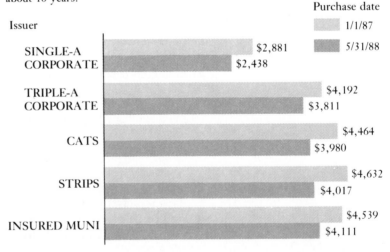

DATA: Merrill Lynch & Co., Prudential-Bache Securities Inc., Drexel Burnham Lambert, Inc.

1.29 Find the variance for the population described in Problem 1.10.

1.30 Find the variance for the population described in Problem 1.12, remembering there is one person aged 97.

1.31 a) Find the variance of the number of absences per worker in Problem 1.13.

b) What percent of the population falls within the intervals $\mu \pm 1\sigma$ and $\mu \pm 2\sigma$?

1.32 a) Find the standard deviation for the population in Problem 1.16.

b) Find the percent of the population that falls within the $\mu \pm 1\sigma$ and $\mu \pm 2\sigma$ intervals.

1.33 The following frequency distribution represents the price-earnings ratios for a population of 20 common stocks.

Class	Frequency	Class Mark
1–5	4	3
6–10	8	8
11–15	3	13
16–20	5	18

a) Find the mean of this population.

b) Find the variance.

1.34 Find the variance for the population in Problem 1.21.

1.35 The Graduate Management Admissions Test (GMAT) is often required for admission to graduate schools of business. Suppose you learn that the population of test scores is bell-shaped and that approximately 95% of all test scores fall between 280 and 680.

a) What value of μ and σ would you estimate for this population based on the information given?

b) What percent of the population would you estimate to fall between 380 and 580? What percent would you estimate to be greater than 580?

1.36 The risk in purchasing a common stock is often measured by the variance of the prices the stock might assume over a specified interval of time. Consider the following stocks, each with a predicted mean and variance for one year from now.

Stock	A	B	C	D
Mean	10	200	100	100
Variance	4	16	50	100

a) Which stock has the largest risk?
Which stock has the lowest risk relative to its price?

b) Based on these estimates, what is the lowest price you might expect for stock B?

1.37 Statistical analysis has become increasingly important in equal employment opportunity litigation. For example, in examining the hiring practices of a company it is often necessary to define characteristics of the population from which workers could be drawn. In one study, the following commuting distances were determined for workers in one metropolitan area.

Distance traveled to work	Fraction of workers
less than 1 mile	0.12
1.0–1.9 miles	0.10
2.0–3.9 miles	0.19
4.0–5.9 miles	0.17
6.0–9.9 miles	0.18
10.0–14.9 miles	0.12
15 miles or more	0.12
Total	1.00

a) Calculate the mean and variance of this population using the midpoint of each class (use 20 miles as the midpoint of the last class).

b) Comment on why this particular classification of distances is not convenient from a statistical viewpoint.

1.38 A leading manufacturer guarantees its quartz watch will be correct within ± 10 seconds each month. Suppose we know that the population of errors by all such watches is bell-shaped, the mean error is zero ($\mu = 0$), and the variance of errors is $\sigma^2 = 100$ (seconds)^2 per month.

a) What percent of the population of watches would you expect to not meet the guarantee?

b) Assume only watches with an error of more than ± 20 seconds will be returned for repair. If 100,000 watches are sold with this guarantee, how many would you expect to be returned for repair?

1.39 Given the following grade distribution on a statistics quiz, find the mean and the variance of x. Use the midvalue of each class (the class mark) as the value of x.

Grade	Frequency	Class mark
96–100	4	98
91–95	5	93
86–90	6	⋮
81–85	5	
76–80	1	
71–75	4	
66–70	2	
61–65	5	

1.40 In a study of discrimination between men and women in the hiring practices of a certain firm, the following starting salaries were paid to nine men and nine women hired for jobs specifying "no previous experience necessary."

	Males	Females	Hourly rate
File clerk	2	7	4.28
Messenger	1	0	4.32
Shipping clerk	2	1	4.41
Assembler—Type I	3	1	4.60
Assembler—Type II	1	0	4.67

a) Find the average wage paid to the men and the average to women. Do you think the difference is large enough to indicate discrimination?

b) Find the average for all 18 new workers.

1.41 The following frequency distribution shows the *cumulative relative* frequency of weekly sales of the British Hat Corporation for last year (52 weeks).

Sales	Cumulative relative frequency
0–$5,999	4/52
$6,000–11,999	10/52
12,000–17,999	20/52
18,000–23,999	36/52
24,000–29,999	48/52
30,000–35,999	52/52

a) Draw the histogram for these data.

b) Compute the mean and the mode.

c) Compute the variance.

d) Sketch the cumulative relative frequency distribution.

1.42 The population "kitchen employees in seven local restaurants" is 2, 9, 1, 3, 10, 3, 2.

a) Find the three quartile values for this population. What is the interquartile range?

b) Calculate σ^2 for these values. Does multiplying the interquartile range by 68/50 yield a good approximation to 2σ?

c) Is this population symmetric or is it skewed? If skewed, is it skewed to the right or left?

1.43 Ten residents of Metropolis report the following incomes:

$30,500 $24,150 $22,505 $26,245 $25,570
$26,600 $34,800 $31,325 $29,170 $39,000

a) Find the mean, standard deviation, and median of these data.

b) Compare the variability and skewness of this distribution with a regional income distribution that reports a mean of $30,000, standard deviation of $3,000, and median of $28,000.

1.44 For Problem 1.43, find the median, the mean, and the mode.

1.45 a) The number of days a certain machine was "down" last year for five different repairs was: 3, 5, 1, 8, and 3. Show that the mean and standard deviations are 4.0 and 2.37, respectively.

b) Assume that another population has the same values given in part (a), plus the two additional values 2 and 6. Find the mean and show that this population has a smaller standard deviation.

1.46 The number of fatal automobile accidents in 10 metropolitan cities for a one-year period was: 35, 14, 6, 18, 14, 27, 19, 7, 12, and 14. Find the mean, mode, median, range, the quartile values, and the interquartile range.

Exercises

1.47 Show by example, or prove mathematically, that

$$\sigma^2 = \frac{1}{N}\sum_i^N x_i^2 - \left(\frac{1}{N}\sum_i^N x_i\right)^2$$

1.48 Throckmorton Jones, manager of A-1 Loan, Inc., has kept a record of the frequency of the *time between arrivals* of customers at his loan office. These data, shown below, indicate that the time interval between consecutive arrivals was between zero and 20 minutes on 50 occasions, between 20 and 40 minutes on 33 different occasions, etc. Since there were 150 customers during this period, there are 150 interarrival times (the time to the first customer is counted as one interarrival time).

Minutes between customers (t)	Frequency (f)
$0 \le t < 20$	50
$20 \le t < 40$	33
$40 \le t < 60$	22
$60 \le t < 80$	15
$80 \le t < 100$	11
$100 \le t < 120$	8
$120 \le t < 140$	5
$140 \le t < 160$	3
$160 \le t < 180$	2
$180 \le t < 200$	1
	150

a) Construct a histogram of relative frequencies and a cumulative relative frequency distribution for the interarrival times. Draw the polygon for these distributions.

b) Find the mode, the median, the mean, and the standard deviation (use class marks of 10, 30, 50, . . .). Use interpolation to find the median.

c) What is the value of the interquartile range? What percent of the observations fall within $\mu \pm 1\sigma$? What percent fall within $\mu \pm 2\sigma$?

d) Based on these data, how many customers would you estimate for A-1 Loan next week if the office is open five days a week, ten hours a day?

1.49 Assume that you are responsible for auditing last month's accounts receivable for the 10,000 credit accounts on the Easy Charge Company. The company has furnished you with the following summary data for this population (this is a slight abstraction of 12,223 actual credit balances).

Balance due	Frequency	Balance due	Frequency
$0–99.99	3123	$600–699.99	180
100–199.99	2085	700–799.99	90
200–299.99	1927	800–899.99	53
300–399.99	1355	900–999.99	25
400–499.99	743	$1000 and over	19
500–599.99	400		

a) Draw the histogram and frequency polygon for these data.

b) As an auditor, are you satisfied with the manner in which the company summarized the data?

c) Use the midpoint of each class and the associated frequencies to calculate the mean of this population. Assume that all 19 values in the eleventh class fall at $1050.

d) Calculate σ and σ^2 for this population. What percent of the population lies within $\mu \pm \sigma$ and $\mu \pm 2\sigma$?

e) Assuming that the population values are evenly spread throughout each class, calculate the median of this population.

f) Is this distribution skewed to the right or left?

1.50 Tchebysheff's Theorem states that at least $(1 - 1/K^2)$ of any population will lie within K standard deviations of their mean, where K is any number ≥ 1.0. For example, using $K = 2$, this theorem says that at least $(1 - \frac{1}{4}) = \frac{3}{4}$ of any population will lie within $\mu \pm 2\sigma$. Similarly, if $K = 3$, then at least $(1 - \frac{1}{9}) = \frac{8}{9}$ of any population will lie within $\mu \pm 3\sigma$. K need not be an integer.

a) What percent of any population will lie between $\mu \pm 4\sigma$?

b) Show, for Problem 1.46, that at least $\frac{3}{4}$ of the population lies between $\mu \pm 2\sigma$.

c) Show, for Table 1.1, that at least $\frac{8}{9}$ of the population lies between $\mu \pm 3\sigma$.

d) Is Tchebysheff's Theorem consistent with the rule of thumb presented in Section 1.4?

1.51 A record was kept of the dollar value of sales over 50 weeks by a person selling surgical supplies (see table at left). Divide each value of x by 1000, and then calculate μ and σ^2. Find the mean and variance of the *original* data using these values of μ and σ^2.

Sales	f
$0–999	11
1000–1999	15
2000–2999	18
3000–3999	6

1.52 Find the median for Problem 1.51 using interpolation.

1.53 The **coefficient of variation** is defined as a standard deviation divided by a mean. This measure indicates the percentage that σ is of μ, and thus permits comparison of the relative variability of one population to the relative variability in another population. For example, if two populations have the same standard deviation, $\sigma = 100$, but $\mu_1 = 1000$ and $\mu_2 = 2000$, then the coefficients of variations are, respectively, $100/1000 = 0.10$, and $100/2000 = 0.05$. The first population has a percentage of variability (10%) twice as large as the second population (5%) even though their standard deviations are the same.

a) If test scores on the Graduate Record Exam (GRE) have $\mu = 500$ and $\sigma = 80$, whereas scores on the Graduate Management Admissions Test have $\mu = 540$ and $\sigma = 100$, do these tests have similar relative variability? Explain.

b) Calculate the coefficient of variation for males and females in Problem 1.40. Is the percentage of variability about equal?

c) Suppose you are trying to decide between three investments that all require the same capital outlay. The average return and variance of returns for the three are

1	2	3
$\mu = 2000$	$\mu = 1000$	$\mu = 1500$
$\sigma = 1200$	$\sigma = 500$	$\sigma = 700$

Using the coefficient of determination as a measure of the "risk" of each investment, which is the most risky? Which is least risky? Which one yields the highest average return?

1.54 The data in Table 1.12 present the 50 companies listed in the food category in the *Fortune* 500 list for 1989.

a) Enter these data into a computer statistical package, and use that package to find the mean and variance for both sales and employees. Make sure the number of employees for Doskocil is treated as missing data, and *not* as a zero.

b) Use your statistical package to construct a frequency distribution for the sales data. Try different class widths before picking the one you believe works best.

c) Does this package assume these data represent a population or a sample? If they are treated as a sample, convert the variances to population variances. (*Hint:* See the formula for a sample variance in Chapter 6.)

TABLE 1.12   The 50 food companies listed in 1989 Fortune 500

Food Companies (Rank)*	Sales ($ Mil.)	Employees
Philip Morris 7	39,069	157,000
Occidental Petroleum 16	20,068	53,500
RJR Nabisco Holdings 24	15,224	48,000
Sara Lee 34	11,738	100,000
Conagra 36	11,340	48,131
Archer Daniels 57	8,057	10,214

TABLE 1.12   The 50 food companies listed in 1989 Fortune 500 (Cont)

Food Companies (Rank)*	Sales ($ Mil.)	Employees
Borden 60	7,593	46,500
Ralston Purina 69	6,712	56,219
Heinz (H.J.) 82	5,832	36,200
General Mills 85	5,798	83,837
Quaker Oats 87	5,724	31,700
Campbell Soup 88	5,710	55,412
CPC International 102	5,129	33,542
Kellogg 108	4,666	17,268
Beatrice 111	4,498	16,400
Whitman 118	4,024	25,188
United Brands 123	3,851	44,000
Agway 140	3,235	15,100
Farmland Industries 151	2,977	6,275
Tyson Foods 174	2,538	42,000
Land O'Lakes 183	2,442	5,836
Hershey Foods 185	2,421	11,800
Hormel (Geo. A.) 190	2,341	8,000
Central Soya 192	2,318	3,474
Holly Farms 214	1,964	18,978
Int'l Multifoods 224	1,883	9,015
Mid-America Dairymen 228	1,798	4,000
Dean Food 240	1,686	7,500
McCormick 299	1,263	7,554
Gold Kist 308	1,216	9,500
Gerber Products 312	1,190	14,691
Doskocil 319	1,148	------
Savannah Foods & Ind. 328	1,097	1,815
IBC Holdings 332	1,080	14,800
Wrigley (Wm. Jr.) 345	1,011	5,750
AG Processing 359	949	608
Ocean Spray 366	873	2,200
Universal Foods 380	837	5,700
Flower Industries 389	789	9,200
Smithfield Foods 395	775	3,900
Amstar 399	766	2,000
Tri Valley Growers 406	747	3,018
Finevest Foods 422	701	2,750
Riceland Foods 429	684	2,041
Imperial Holly 434	668	2,500
Pilgrim's Pride 438	663	7,800
Hudson Foods 453	623	6,262
Thorn Apple Valley 459	613	2,900
Prairie Farms Dairy 481	578	1,829
Sun-Diamond Growers 486	572	2,500

*Abstracted from the *Fortune* 500 list, *Fortune,* April, 1990.

Chapter 2

Probability Theory: Discrete Sample Spaces

The theory of probabilities is nothing more than good sense confirmed by calculations.

PIERRE LAPLACE

Introduction 2.1

As we mentioned in Chapter 1, most problems of statistics involve elements of uncertainty, since it is usually not possible to determine in advance the characteristics of an unknown population or to foresee the exact consequences that will result from each course of action in a decision-making context. A necessary part of an analytical approach to these problems must thus involve evaluations of just how likely it is that certain events have occurred or will occur. "How likely is it that a given sample accurately reflects the characteristics of a certain population?" or "What is the chance that a given consequence will occur following a certain decision?" are examples of inquiries into the probability of an event or set of events of this nature.

Probability Definitions 2.2

The Experiment

An **experiment** *is any situation capable of replication under essentially stable conditions.* The repetitions may be feasible and be performed (such as flipping a coin), or they may be abstract and be theoretically conceivable. For example, investing $1000 in the stock market could be an experiment, even though you intend to do it only once. You could imagine repeating such an investment over and over again many times and consider theoretically the chances that you would make capital gains or losses, or earn a yield of more or less than 10%, or achieve some other result. Hiring a new employee might be considered an experiment. You may hire only one person, but you can imagine, abstractly, many replications of the hiring process under similar circumstances. One interest you might have is the chance the person you hire stays with the company for at least one year.

An experiment is *any situation capable of replication involving uncertainty,* whether it actually recurs many times or whether the repetitions are hypothetical.

Sample Spaces — The Outcomes of an Experiment

The different outcomes of an experiment are often referred to as **sample points,** and the set of all possible outcomes is called the **sample space.** As the following sections explain, sample spaces are often distinguished according to whether they are discrete or continuous. **Continuous** sample spaces generally involve outcomes that are *measured* (such as length, time, weight, mass) and the number of sample points is always infinite. **Discrete** sample spaces contain a finite or an infinite number of points, all of which can be separated and counted.

Suppose an experiment is defined to be "Observe the results of the stock market on a single day." Although we can define numerous sample spaces for this experiment, a simple one uses only two sample points: (market increases, market does not increase). Note that if the experiment is defined to be "Observe two days of the stock market," then the sample space consists of the following pairs of outcomes, where the first outcome represents the first day, and the second represents the second day.

(market increases, market increases)

(market increases, market does not increase)

(market does not increase, market increases)

(market does not increase, market does not increase)

This sample space is *discrete* (because the outcomes can be separated from one another and counted) and *finite* (because the number of outcomes is limited). Suppose, however, we define the experiment as "Observe the stock market until it increases." For this case the number of sample points is infinite, since there is no limit to the number of outcomes. Such a sample space is still discrete because the number of outcomes (that is, the number of days until the stock market increases) can be separated and counted. Thus, a discrete sample space may contain either a finite or an infinite number of outcomes.

Most applications of probability involve experiments with a finite number of outcomes. Usually, however, the number of outcomes is very large, and as a result, it makes little difference (for practical purposes) if the number is assumed to be infinite. When this is the case an experiment with a finite set of discrete outcomes can be approximated by a continuous set. The advantage of such approximations is that they often simplify the derivation of certain statistical results. For example, an experiment involving the number of unemployed workers in the United States would be easier to handle using a continuous approximation even though the number of workers is discrete and finite (although very large).

We hasten to add that it is not always clear from the statement of an experiment exactly what outcomes are relevant. For example, in the experiment "Observe the stock market for two days," the *order* of the outcomes may or may not be important. If order is not important, then the sample space can be defined using three outcomes rather than the four given previously:

(market increases on both days)

(market increases one day, does not increase the other)

(market does not increase on either day)

Examples of discrete sample spaces that contain a finite number of outcomes include the number of minority candidates hired from a list of candidates for a certain job, the number of electronics companies that submit bids on a government contract, or the number of defective items in a shipping lot of a given size. Problems that involve a discrete sample space having an *infinite* number of outcomes include the quoted dollar-value of a common stock (it can vary from zero to infinity, in units of one-eighth of a dollar), or the number of flaws per unit of material from a textile plant (which can be *any* positive integer). The outcomes of an experiment are sometimes grouped into **events**, where an event is some subset of the outcome.

In contrast to a discrete sample space is the concept of a continuous sample space. A sample space is continuous if the number of possible outcomes is infinite and uncountable. An experiment involving the time it takes a light bulb to burn out represents a continous sample space because the outcome of the experiment could be *any* real number from zero to the upper bound (such as 10,000 hours). There is obviously an infinite number of outcomes possible here, and no way to separate and count them. Generally, we are dealing with continuous sample spaces when the data involved are obtained by *measurement* rather than by counting. Thus, a set is continuous if *any* value within an interval can occur, such as any value between 0 and 1, or any value between 200 and 1000, or any value from zero to infinity. The net weight of a box of packaged cereal, the length of a trout caught in a stream, the average speed of the winning car at the Indianapolis 500, or the distance a car can travel on a gallon of gas are all examples of outcomes in a continuous sample space. In working with continuous sample spaces, it may be advantageous to *group* the sample space into a small number of discrete outcomes. For example, in working with the time it takes a light bulb to burn out, we might group the outcomes into the following three sets: (1) time is less than 100 hours, (2) time is between 100 and 1000 hours, and (3) time exceeds 1000 hours. To specify the probabilities associated with a given situation, it is important that the relevant outcomes be carefully defined.

In defining the sample space of an experiment, one must be sure that it is not possible for two or more outcomes to occur in the same replication of the experiment. Outcomes defined in this manner are said to be **mutually exclusive events.** For example, the two outcomes

(stock market increases, stock market does not increase)

are mutually exclusive for the experiment "Observe the stock market one day," but they are not mutually exclusive for the experiment "Observe the stock market for two days." Similarly, the student who defines the outcomes of an accounting exam as "A," "Pass," and "Fail" has not specified a mutually exclusive set of events because both "A" and "Pass" could happen at the same time.

A second requirement in defining the sample space of an experiment is that *the list of outcomes must be* **exhaustive;** that is, no possible outcomes can be omitted. If a flipped coin can stand on its edge, then this outcome must be added to the sample space. If our light bulb could last longer than the specified upper bound (such as 10,000 hours), then this possibility must be added to the sample space. Thus, when defining probabilities it is extremely important that the outcomes associated with the sample space (that is, the sample points) be *both mutually exclusive* and *exhaustive.*

To summarize briefly, we have defined the following terms:

A. Experiment—any situation capable of replication under stable conditions.

B. Sample space—the set of outcomes of an experiment, which may be described as follows.

    1. Discrete (separable and countable outcomes)
        a) Finite (an upper limit on number)
        b) Infinite (no upper limit on numer)
    2. Continuous (nonseparable)—the number of outcomes is infinite.

C. Event—some subset of the outcomes of an experiment.

D. Mutually exclusive and exhaustive events—events with no overlap and that account for (exhaust) all possible outcomes of the experiment.

There are two additional components to every experiment: (1) a random variable, and (2) a probability function. These two components are extremely important in describing the probability of the entire set of events of interest in a given experiment; they will be discussed in detail in Chapter 3.*

---

*Some instructors may wish to cover the portion of Chapter 3 relating to random variables at this point.

Subjective and Objective Probability

2.3

Since there is some disagreement, even among authorities, about the interpretation of probability, it is advisable to begin a discussion of the fundamental concepts of the theory of probability by describing the two major viewpoints or interpretations. Both of these interpretations deal with determining the probability of the occurrence of an event. They differ in the methods they prescribe for determining this probability. The first and more traditional viewpoint is as follows:

Probability is the relative frequency with which an event occurs over the long run.

Probabilities determined by the long-run relative frequency of an event are usually referred to as *frequency probabilities,* or *objective probabilities* (since they are determined by "objective evidence" and would have the same value regardless of who did the determination).

Objective probability: a probability determined by commonly accepted theory or assumptions.

The second interpretation of probability assigns probabilities based on the decision maker's subjective estimates, using prior knowledge, information, and experience as a guide. This approach, in which probabilities are referred to as *subjective* probabilities, recently has gained considerable importance in statistical theory, largely because of the influence of such statisticians as L. J. Savage, R. Schlaifer, and H. Raiffa.

Subjective probability: a probability based on one person's view of the relative frequency of an event

---

Suppose you believe that the chances are 1 in 4 that interest rates will decrease over the next two months, or that the odds are 10 to 1 against a recession in the next year. These are subjective evaluations, in which your personal opinion about the probability of these events need not agree with anyone else's. Although you are entitled to your own opinion, given a sufficient amount of information about the past occurrences of an event, we would expect an individual's subjective opinion to agree fairly closely with the long-run relative frequency of that event.

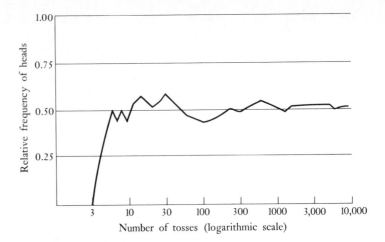

Figure 2.1
Relative frequency of heads
in Kerrick experiment.

The problem (and controversy) in the "frequency" approach to estimating probabilities is that in many real-world problems, there may be little or no historical data available on which to base an estimate of the probability of an event. In such cases, only a subjective probability can be determined; and this probability may differ even among experts who have similar technical knowledge and identical information. For example, various space scientists in 1960 gave different estimates of the probability that humans would walk on the moon within that decade. Different weather forecasters observing the same climatic conditions may give different probabilities that rain will occur on a given day. Fortunately, the rules and operations governing probability theory are the same whether the number itself is generated by an objective or a subjective approach.

A simple example of the concept of probability as a long-run relative frequency is an experiment in which a coin is tossed over and over again, where the outcome of each toss is observed and recorded. For the first few tosses the proportion of heads may fluctuate rather wildly; after a sufficiently large number of tosses, however, it should begin to stabilize about one particular value. The more tosses observed, the closer the proportion of heads approach this long-run or limiting value. Just such an experiment was performed by the statistician J. E. Kerrick during his internment in Denmark during World War II. Kerrick tossed a coin 10,000 times and obtained 5067 heads; the frequency distribution is shown in Fig. 2.1.

Note that in Fig. 2.1 the relative frequency of heads begins to stabilize after quite a few tosses, about one particular value (which in this case appears to be about 0.50). One would expect, as the number of tosses becomes even larger, that the relative frequency of heads will come closer and closer to this particular value until, at the limit (an infinite number of tosses), they are equal. The value at which they are equal, sometimes called the **limit of relative frequency,** represents what we have called long-run relative frequency; and it is this concept of the long-run relative frequency of an event that is generally implied when referring to an "objective probability" or to "the frequency approach to probability." Thus, a probability of heads equal to 0.50 in the Kerrick experiment means that *in the long run* the expected proportion of heads is 50%. In most practical problems, of course, the limit of relative frequency can only be estimated, since it is seldom possible to observe a sufficient number of observations to determine the limit precisely.

Expected Frequency

At times it is convenient to determine another interpretation of probability, that represented by the **expected** or **theoretical long-run relative frequency** of an event. In such cases, the probability of an event depends on assumptions about the conditions underlying the occurrence of this event. For example, if the coin in the experiment by Kerrick had been assumed to be "fair" (that is, not biased to heads or tails), then the theoretical long-run relative frequency of heads for this coin would have been, by definition, 0.50. The underlying conditions or assumptions about an experiment (such as tossing a coin) represent part of what is called the **experimental model.** Making assumptions of this nature is useful in testing to determine if theoretical probability values differ from actual (or observed) probabilities, whether these values are subjective or objective. Notice that Kerrick's observed value differs very little from the theoretical value of 0.50.

Probability Axioms

The set of *all possible outcomes* of interest in an experiment corresponds to what we called a population (all values of interest) in Chapter 1. This set is often referred to as the **sample space** (denoted by the letter S) since it represents the region (or "space") corresponding to all possible sample results.

We can now present the two basic properties necessary for defining the probability of an event. If $P(E_i)$ is the probability of event E_i in a sample space S, then both of the following properties must hold.

$$
\begin{array}{l}
\textit{Property 1. } 1.0 \geq P(E_i) \geq 0 \\
\textit{Property 2. } P(S) = 1.0
\end{array}
\tag{2.1}
$$

It is easy to recognize that these properties are consistent with our previous examples. The first one says that the probability of an event can never be less than 0 (which represents an impossibility) nor greater than 1 (which represents a certainty). The second one says that the events E_i comprising the sample space must be exhaustive—it must be a certainty that one of the mutually exclusive events in the sample space will take place in each replication of the experiment.

Much of the historical development of probability can be traced to analysis of problems in which only a finite number of outcomes may take place, and in which each of these outcomes is assumed to have the same chance of occurring. In such situations, if any one of N "equally likely" outcomes can take place, then the probability of any one outcome occurring is $1/N$. For example, suppose Publishers Clearing House mails out announcements of a contest to 200,000 people, stating that the grand prize winner will be selected "at random" from the list of 200,000 people. Random selection in this context means that each person is equally likely to be selected; the probability of being the grand prize winner is thus

$$P(\text{grand prize winner}) = \frac{1}{200,000} = 0.000005^*$$

When the number of equally likely outcomes in a given problem is relatively small, it is often possible to determine the probability of each outcome by counting the total number of outcomes (N), and then calculating $1/N$. The following special rule holds when all sample points are equally likely.

The probability of an event is the ratio of the number of outcomes comprising this event to the total number of equally likely outcomes in the sample space.

$$P(\text{event}) = \frac{\text{Number of outcomes comprising the event}}{\text{Total number of equally likely outcomes in sample space}}$$

We will give numerous examples of this rule throughout this chapter. For now, let's just consider a simple situation where you would like to determine the probability that a woman will be selected to fill the next Supreme Court vacancy. Suppose there are four female candidates and six male candidates, and all ten people are assumed to have the same chance of being selected. In this situation,

$$P(\text{woman selected}) = \frac{\text{Number of outcomes where "woman selected"}}{\text{Number of equally likely outcomes in the experiment "replace a Supreme Court Judge"}} = \frac{4}{10} = 0.40$$

To further illustrate this rule, consider the procedure followed by a well-known investment service, which rates common stocks in terms of both (1) short-term growth potential and (2) long-term growth potential. Short-term growth is rated as either 1, 2, or 3 while long-term growth is rated as either 1, 2, 3, or 4 (in both cases, higher ratings imply higher potential). The sample space for this experiment, "classify a common stock," can be illustrated as in Fig. 2.2

---

*Probability values can be stated as either fractions or decimals. For the most part, in this chapter the fractional form will be more convenient.

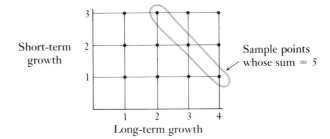

Figure 2.2
The sample space for stock
classifications.

Figure 2.2 illustrates the 12 sample points for classifying a stock. If all 12 sample points are equally likely (they may not be), then the probability of any *one* occurring is $1/N = 1/12$.

Now suppose we define the following two events.

E_5 = sum of two ratings equals 5
E_3 = either long-term ≥ 3 or short-term = 3, or both

To find $P(E_5)$ and $P(E_3)$ we add the equally likely outcomes associated with each one. For example, the three outcomes that sum to five are

$$(4, 1), (3, 2), \text{ and } (2, 3)$$

where the first number in each set corresponds to long-term growth and the second corresponds to short-term growth. Since each one of these sample points is assumed to have a probability of $\frac{1}{12}$,

$$P(E_5) = \frac{3}{12}$$

Similarly, the following eight outcomes comprise the event E_3:

$$(4, 1), (4, 2), (4, 3), (3, 1), (3, 2), (3, 3), (2, 3), \text{ and } (1, 3)$$

Hence, $P(E_3) = \frac{8}{12} = \frac{2}{3}$.

The next several sections elaborate on the rules for computing the probability of an event.

Counting Rules   **2.4**

Many probability experiments involve two or more steps, each of which can result in one of a number of different outcomes. To calculate probabilities in such experiments, we often need to first determine the total number of possible outcomes. For example, suppose three different people are asked whether they own any common stock. Now there are three steps (interviewing three people) and each step has two outcomes [own stock (S) or not own stock

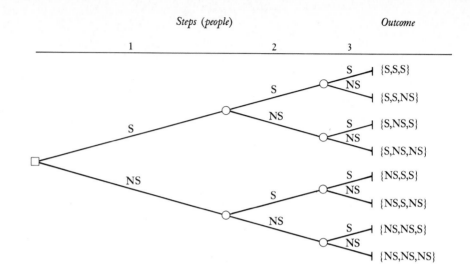

Steps (people)

1   2   3

Outcome

S — {S,S,S}
NS — {S,S,NS}
S — {S,NS,S}
NS — {S,NS,NS}
S — {NS,S,S}
NS — {NS,S,NS}
S — {NS,NS,S}
NS — {NS,NS,NS}

Figure 2.3

Tree diagram for stock/no stock experiment.

(NS)]. The fact that there are eight different outcomes in this experiment is easily seen if we construct a "tree diagram" (Fig. 2.3).

Basic Counting Rule

In the stock survey example above there are three steps (people) and each step has two possible outcomes (S or NS). The total number of outcomes in this experiment (which we denote by the letter N) is

$$N = 2 \times 2 \times 2 = 8$$

To generalize this type of calculation, suppose we denote the number of outcomes in the first step of an experiment as n_1, the number of outcomes in the second step as n_2, and so forth, with n_k denoting the number of outcomes in the last (or kth) step. The **basic counting rule** states that the total number of outcomes (N) equals the product of the number of outcomes in each step.

> *Basic counting rule: Total number of sample points*
> $$N = n_1 \times n_2 \times n_3 \ldots \times n_k$$

(2.2)

In our stock survey example, $n_1 = 2$, $n_2 = 2$, and $n_3 = 2$; hence, $N = n_1 \times n_2 \times n_3 = 2 \times 2 \times 2 = 8$. As another illustration of Formula (2.2), consider a company that is going to select one of four different pricing policies, and then select one of three different advertising packages. In this example, $n_1 = 4$ (pricing) and $n_2 = 3$ (advertising). The total number of outcomes of this experiment is (by Formula 2.2):

$$N = n_1 \times n_2 = 4 \times 3 = 12$$

Problems

2.1 Consider the experiment "Procter & Gamble introduces a new toothpaste."

a) Describe the outcomes of this experiment. (*Note:* Your answer may differ from another person's.) Is this sample space finite or infinite, discrete or continuous?

b) Is the probability $P($new toothpaste earns 10% or more of the market$)$ a subjective or objective probability?

2.2 Describe an experiment for each of the following situations (do not use examples mentioned in the text):

a) the sample space is discrete and finite;

b) the sample space is discrete and infinite;

c) the sample space is continuous.

2.3 Indicate whether the sample space is finite or infinite, discrete or continuous, if the experiment involves:

a) the amount of wheat grown in the United States next year;

b) the number of years before a woman is first elected president of the United States;

c) the percent by which the price of a stock might decrease, if percents are restricted to integer values;

d) the percent by which the price of a stock might decrease, if percents can be any decimal value;

e) the amount of rainfall in New York City in April.

2.4 Indicate whether the following events are (1) mutually exclusive and/or (2) exhaustive:

a) the events "stock market goes up" and "stock market doesn't go up";

b) the events "minority" and "male" in describing a job applicant;

c) the event "unemployment equals 6%" and the "prime rate equals 8%."

2.5 Assume the Publishers Clearing House contest mentioned in Section 2.3 is giving out one grand prize, 500 second prizes, and 1000 third prizes. There are 200,000 people who might win, and no one can win more than one prize. What is the probability you will win if you are one of the 200,000 people?

2.6 Television sets are inspected as they are completed on a production line and classified as either "pass" or "fail." You inspect four sets.

a) Describe the sample space for this experiment. Draw the tree diagram.

b) How many different outcomes are there if it is important which sets pass and which ones fail? How many outcomes are there if one is interested only in the number of passes and failures?

c) If "pass" and "fail" are considered equally likely, what are $P(0$ pass$)$, $P(1$ pass$)$, $P(2$ pass$)$, $P(3$ pass$)$, and $P(4$ pass$)$? Do these values sum to 1.0?

2.7 In one draw from a deck of cards, what is the probability of the event "face card" (an ace is not counted as a face card)?

2.8 You are planning on taking a survey of two of five previously selected local retail establishments.

a) Describe the sample space for the experiment "Select two establishments without replacement." (*Hint:* Label the establishments 1, 2, 3, 4, 5, and list all pairs; note that order is *not* important here.)

b) What is the probability that establishment 1 will be included in the survey?

c) What is the probability that either 1 or 2 will be included in the survey?

2.9 Identify the following as either subjective or objective probabilities:

a) the probability that you will win the grand prize in a Publishers Clearing House sweepstakes;

b) the probability that interest rates will increase next month;

c) the probability that General Motors will decrease car prices next year.

2.10 Prospective employees are classified according to their (1) experience and (2) education. Describe the sample space for a classification involving three levels of experience (1, 2, 3) and two levels of education (1, 2). If all sample points are equally likely, what is the probability of each point? What is the probability, again assuming equally likely outcomes, of having an experience level of at least 2, and an education level of 2?

2.11 An important task of certain business and governmental agencies involves assigning workers to specific tasks (or machines). For example, the Department of Labor assigns Occupational Safety and Health Act (OSHA) inspectors to inspect employer locations for safety. A city has three inspectors and two "first-priority" locations (where a catastrophe or fatality has occurred), and must now assign one inspector to one of the two locations.

a) Draw the decision tree for the experiment "Assign one inspector to one first-priority location." (*Hint:* Label inspectors as A, B, C and the locations as 1, 2.) What is the probability of each sample point, assuming random assignment?

b) Use your decision tree to calculate the probability that A is assigned to 1 (A-1), or B is assigned to 2 (B-2).

Probability Rules   **2.5**

One can often determine the probability of an event from knowledge about the probability of one or more other events in the sample space. In this section we will discuss rules for finding the probability of complementary and conditional events, the probability of the union of two events, and the joint probability of two events.

Basic Definitions.   Before describing these rules we present a few definitions. If we designate A and B as two events of interest in a particular experiment, then the following definitions hold:

1. $P(\overline{A})$ = Probability that A does *not* occur in one replication of the experiment.
$P(\overline{A})$ is called the probability of the *complement* of A.

2. $P(A|B)$ = Probability that A occurs *given that B* has taken place (or will take place).

$P(A|B)$ is called the *conditional probability* of A given B.

3. $P(A$ and $B)$ = Probability that *both A and B* occur in one replication of the experiment.

$P(A$ and $B)$ is called the probability of the *intersection* of A and B or the *joint* probability of A and B.

4. $P(A$ or $B)$ = Probability that *either A* or B or *both* occur in one replication of the experiment.

$P(A$ or $B)$ is called the probability of the *union* of A and B, or called an *additive* probability.

Each of these definitions is elaborated in the sections that follow.

Perhaps the simplest way to form a new event from a given event is to take the *complement* of that event. For example, the complement of the event A, which is denoted by $\overline{A}$ (read A-bar), contains all the points in the sample space that are *not part* of A. If S denotes the total sample space, then $P(\overline{A})$ is defined as follows:

$$\text{\textit{Probability rule for complements: } } P(\overline{A}) = 1 - P(A) \qquad (2.3)$$

To illustrate this rule, suppose the sample space S is the set of points in Fig. 2.2 and E_5 = point whose sum = 5. Then

$$P(\overline{E_5}) = \text{points whose sum does not equal 5}$$
$$= 1 - P(E_5) = 1 - \frac{3}{12} = \frac{9}{12}$$

Similarly, if it is known the probability that a person of age 35 smokes is $P(S) = 0.20$, then the probability of a nonsmoker of this age is

$$P(\overline{S}) = 1 - P(S) = 1 - 0.20 = 0.80$$

Two complementary events must be *exhaustive* because they take into account (or exhaust) all possible events. In addition, complementary events must always be *mutually exclusive* because none of the sample points in A can be a sample point in $\overline{A}$.

Joint, conditional, and additive probabilities can be illustrated using the data in Table 2.1. This is a table of joint probabilities, presenting data from the U.S. Internal Revenue Service (IRS) on the probability a tax filer is audited, depending on the person's income and the tax form used. First look at the first probability in the right margin. This is the probability a tax filer is audited; $P(\text{audited}) = 0.0143$. In other words, 1.43% of all tax returns are audited. The complement of this probability is $P(\text{not audited}) = 0.9857$. Similarly, the probability 0.0373 on the lower right is the probability a filer had an income of more than \$50,000; $P(> \$50,000) = 0.0373$. Note that the sum of the

TABLE 2.1   Joint probabilities from the IRS for being audited

	Short form	Long form	Short form	Long form			
	< $10,000	< $10,000	$10,000– 25,000	$10,000– 25,000	$25,000– 50,000	> $50,000	Total
Audited	0.0010	0.0009	0.0014	0.0031	0.0058	0.0021	0.0143
Not audited	0.2988	0.0953	0.2384	0.1236	0.1944	0.0352	0.9857
Total	0.2998	0.0962	0.2398	0.1267	0.2002	0.0373	1.0000

probabilities across the bottom sum to 1.0000, as these are a set of mutually exclusive and exhaustive events.

To illustrate the joint probabilities in the body of Table 2.1, consider the entry 0.0021 in the first row, in the > $50,000 column. This number represents the joint probability that a randomly selected tax filer has income over $50,000 *and* is audited. That is,

$$P(> \$50,000 \ and \ \text{audited}) = 0.0021$$

Similarly, the entry below this value, 0.0352, is the joint probability that a randomly selected filer reports income greater than $50,000, *and* is not audited. These two joint probabilities sum to the marginal probability 0.0373. The marginal probability 0.0373 is an additive probability, and can be determined by adding the two joint probabilities.

$$P(> \$50,000 \ \text{audited} \ or \ > \$50,000 \ \text{not audited}) = 0.0021 + 0.0352$$
$$= 0.0373$$

This result says there is a 3.73% chance that a randomly selected return will either have an income over $50,000 and be audited, *or* have an income over $50,000 and not be audited.

Conditional probabilities also can be determined using Table 2.1. Suppose we want to know the probability a return will be audited *given that* the income exceeds $50,000. This probability is

$$P(\text{audited} | > \$50,000) = \frac{0.0021}{0.0373} = 0.0563$$

Thus, 5.63% of the > $50,000 returns will be audited.

The following sections describe how to calculate joint, conditional, and additive probabilities, using the rules of probability. The rules for conditional probability are described first.

Conditional Probability

A **conditional probability** is the probability that an event A occurs "given that" or "on the condition that" some other event B has already taken place (or will take place in the future). The "probability of A given B" is thus a conditional probability, which is usually written as $P(A|B)$, where the vertical line is read as "given."

Conditional probabilities are defined as follows:

$$
\text{Conditional probability of } A \text{, given } B: \ P(A|B) = \frac{P(A \text{ and } B)}{P(B)}
$$

$$
\text{Conditional probability of } B \text{, given } A: \ P(B|A) = \frac{P(A \text{ and } B)}{P(A)}
$$

$$(2.4)$$

To illustrate Formula (2.4), consider again the data in Table 2.1, and assume we are interested in the probability a tax filer is audited, given that this person has an income between \$25,000 and \$50,000. Letting A = audited, and B = \$25,000–50,000, from Table 2.1, $P(B) = P(\$25,000–50,000) = 0.2002$ (the sum of $0.0058 + 0.1944$), and $P(\text{audited and } \$25,000–50,000) = P(A \text{ and } B) = 0.0058$. Thus,

$$
P(A|B) = \frac{P(A \text{ and } B)}{P(B)} = \frac{0.0058}{0.2002} = 0.0290
$$

This means that about 3% of the filers with incomes between \$25,000 and \$50,000 will be audited.

As another example of a conditional probability, let's use Fig. 2.2 to calculate a probability studied earlier:

$$
P(\text{short-term} = 2 | \text{long-term} = 3)
$$

From Fig. 2.2 we know there are 12 sample points, hence

$$
P(\text{short-term} = 2 \text{ and long-term} = 3) = 1/12.
$$

Also since there are four long-term categories,

$P(\text{long-term} = 3) = 1/4$, and

$$
P(\text{short-term} = 2 | \text{long-term} = 3) = \frac{P(\text{short-term} = 2 \text{ and long-term} = 3)}{P(\text{long-term} = 3)}
$$

$$
= \frac{1/12}{1/4} = \frac{4}{12} = \frac{1}{3}
$$

This result is easily verified using Fig. 2.2, as there are three (equally likely) outcomes associated with the column corresponding to the event "long-term = 3," one of which is "short-term = 2."

Joint Probabilities

In discussing conditional probabilities in the previous section, we indicated that $P(A$ and $B)$ represents the **joint probability** of A and B —that is, it is the probability that both A and B take place in one replication of an experiment. When A and B occur together in an experiment this is called the **intersection** of A and B. An intersection is pictured in Fig. 2.4.

We now want to develop a formula for a joint probability. To do so, one merely has to solve Formula (2.4) for $P(A$ and $B)$. The resulting formula is called the **general rule of multiplication,** and provides a method for finding a joint probability.

$$\text{General rule of multiplication: } P(A \text{ and } B) = P(A)P(B|A)$$
$$= P(B)P(A|B)$$

(2.5)

The first part of Formula (2.5) can be interpreted as follows: The probability that both A and B take place is given by two occurrences—first, event A takes place, with probability $P(A)$, and then event B takes place *on the condition that A* has already occurred, with probability $P(B|A)$. The probability that both occurrences take place is the product of these two probabilities, or $P(A)P(B|A)$.

To illustrate Formula (2.5), consider a production process where two parts of a particular product are produced simultaneously. Let D_1 denote the fact that the first part is defective and D_2 the fact the second is defective. From past production records it is known that the probability part 1 is defective is $P(D_1) = 0.15$. Also these records indicate that $P(D_2|D_1) = 1/3$. The joint probability $P(D_1$ and $D_2)$ is determined using Formula (2.5):

$$P(D_1 \text{ and } D_2) = P(D_1)P(D_2|D_1) = (0.15)(1/3) = 0.05^*$$

The term "joint probability" implies that the events under consideration take place in the same replication of an experiment. Depending on the nature of the experiment, events that occur jointly do not necessarily take place at identical points in calendar or clock time. For example, in the marketing policy problem, the result of the pricing and advertising decision may be considered a joint occurrence even though the two decisions are not made simultaneously. Similarly, suppose NBC is interviewing two randomly selected U.S. senators. The process of interviewing one senator and then another from the total of 100 senators can be thought of as a joint occurrence even though the two interviews are not simultaneous.

---

*If the values of $P(D_2)$ and $P(D_1|D_2)$ are known, then we can calculate $P(D_2$ and $D_1)$ as follows:

$$P(D_2 \text{ and } D_1) = P(D_2)P(D_1|D_2)$$

This approach must also yield $P(D_2$ and $D_1) = 0.05$.

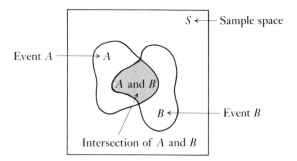

Figure 2.4
The intersection of A and B
(shaded portion).

Let R_1 = Republican on the first interview and R_2 = Republican on the second interview; $P(R_1$ and $R_2)$ is the joint probability that both are Republicans. If the Senate has 48 Republicans and 52 Democrats, then $P(R_1) = 48/100 = 0.48$. After interviewing one Republican senator (who cannot be interviewed again), there remain 99 senators, 47 of whom are Republicans; hence,

$$P(R_2) = \frac{47}{99}$$

and by Formula (2.5),

$$P(R_1 \text{ and } R_2) = P(R_1)P(R_2|R_1) = (48/100)(47/99) = 0.228$$

Because the expressions $P(E_1$ and $E_2)$ and $P(E_2$ and $E_1)$ do not imply any ordering, over time, of the two events E_1 and E_2, but only that these events both occur in a single trial of the experiment, $P(E_1$ and $E_2)$ must equal $P(E_2$ and $E_1)$.

Writing $P(E_2|E_1)$ does not imply that E_1 precedes E_2 in chronological order. For instance, it is just as legitimate to determine the probability that IBM stock went up today given that the stock market went up as it is legitimate to determine the probability that the stock market went up given that IBM stock went up. In general, however, $P(A|B)$ does not equal $P(B|A)$.

Additive Probability, or the Probability of a Union

The **additive probability** of two events A and B, written $P(A$ or $B)$, is the probability that either A occurs, or B occurs, or both A and B take place. This is called the *union* of the events A and B, and is illustrated by Fig. 2.5. The probability $P(A$ or $B)$ is found by identifying the proportion of sample points that are included either in A or in B, or in the intersection of A and B.

To determine the probability $P(A$ or $B)$, we add $P(A) + P(B)$, and then subtract $P(A$ and $B)$ [which would be double-counted in $P(A) + P(B)$]. The result is called the **general rule of addition.**

General rule of addition:
$$P(A \text{ or } B) = P(A) + P(B) - P(A \text{ and } B)$$

(2.6)

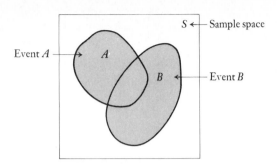

Figure 2.5
The union of A and B
(shaded portion).

Formula (2.6) can be used to find the probability of the union of A and B in our stock-rating problem, where

A = long-term growth is 3 or higher, and
B = short-term growth equals 3

From Fig. 2.2., $P(A) = 2/4$, and $P(B) = 1/3$. Also, from earlier calculations, $P(A \text{ and } B) = 2/12$. Thus,

$$P(A \text{ or } B) = P(A) + P(B) - P(A \text{ and } B)$$
$$= 2/4 + 1/3 - 2/12 = 8/12$$

This probability agrees with the result calculated (less formally) in Section 2.3. This result is shown in Fig. 2.2, where 8 of the 12 sample points have either long-term growth $\geq$ 3 or short-term growth = 3.

Special Case of Independence   **2.6**

Two events are **independent** if the occurrence (or nonoccurrence) of one event cannot influence (or be influenced by) the occurrence (or nonoccurrence) of the other event.

Independence implies that the probability of any given event is unaffected by whether or not another event occurs. Dependence implies just the opposite — that the occurrence of one event *is* influenced by the occurrence of another event (or events). For example, the probability of getting cancer has been reported to be related to (depend on) whether one smokes, the quality of the air one breathes, and even the food one eats. On the other hand, the probability the stock market (the New York Stock Exchange, or NYSE) goes up this week is certainly independent of the event "rain in New York City."

If two events A and B are independent, then the conditional probability of A given B, or $P(A|B)$, must be equal to $P(A)$. This is because the event B can have no influence on the event A, hence knowing that B has (or will) take place does not influence the probability of A. That is,

> *Special conditional probability rule for independent events A and B:*
> $$P(A|B) = P(A)$$

(2.7)

In many statistical problems, it may not be clear whether the events of interest are independent or dependent. In such cases either: (1) it is not important or it is impossible to determine whether the events are independent or dependent, (2) one is trying to *prove* whether the events are independent or dependent, or (3) the experimenter can *assume* that the events are independent because of the way the experiment is defined. These three situations are elaborated on below.

1. When it is not important or it is impossible to determine whether the events are independent or dependent, then the formulas derived thus far [(2.4), (2.5), (2.6)] should be used. *These formulas hold for both independent and dependent events.*

2. In some problems it is important to attempt to *prove* whether events are independent or dependent. In real-world problems, this is important when one is trying to establish the relation between events (such as cigarette smoking and cancer). From a statistical point of view, it is more convenient to work with events that are independent, for then we can use simplified versions of Formulas (2.4), (2.5), and (2.6).

3. In some experiments the events are *assumed* to be independent. For instance, in using polls to determine preference among political candidates the assumption is made that the answer given by any one person interviewed has no influence on (is independent of) the answer given by any other person. In general, sample observations are usually taken "randomly," meaning that one sample observation cannot influence (or be influenced by) any other sample observation.

As an illustration of independent events, consider the data in Table 2.2, representing a study of the age of a population of people who recently purchased a compact disk recorder (CD), and the amount of money spent on the CD. Table 2.2 is a *joint probability table.*

Table 2.2   Joint probability for age and amount spent on a CD

		Amount spent		
		< $200	≥ $200	
Age	< 35	0.22	0.33	0.55
	≥ 35	0.18	0.27	0.45
		0.40	0.60	

The entry in the first cell, 0.22, is the probability that the amount spent is less than \$200, and the age of the consumer is less than 35; that is, $P(<35$ and $<\$200) = 0.22$. A conditional probability of interest might be $P(<35|<\$200)$, which is the probability the consumer is less than 35 *given that* this person spent less than \$200. From Table 2.1,

$$P(<35|<\$200) = \frac{0.22}{0.40} = 0.55$$

Because $P(<35)$ also equals 0.55, this results shows that

$$P(<35|<\$200) = P(<35)$$

which means that the events <35 and $<\$200$ are independent.

Probability Rules for Independent Events

An important effect of independence is that it greatly simplifies the calculation of joint probabilities. This can be shown by substituting Formula (2.7) into the general rule of multiplication Formula (2.5). The result is a special case of the multiplication rule. If A and B are independent, then the joint probability of A and B can be determined by using the following formula:

$$
\boxed{
\begin{array}{c}
\textit{Special case of multiplication rule} \\
\textit{(for independent events):} \\
P(A \text{ and } B) = P(A)\,P(B) = P(B)\,P(A)
\end{array}
}
\qquad (2.8)
$$

Table 2.2 can be used to illustrate Formula (2.8), for we previously determined that the events <35 and $<\$200$ are independent. Because of this fact, $P(<35$ and $<\$200)$ could have been determined using Formula (2.8) as follows:

$$P(<35 \text{ and } <\$200) = P(<35)\,P(<\$200) = (0.55)(0.40) = 0.22$$

Problems

2.12 a) Does the probability $P(A|B) = P(B|A)$? Explain why or why not, and give an example.

    b) Does $P(A \text{ and } B) = P(B \text{ and } A)$? Does $P(A \text{ or } B) = P(B \text{ or } A)$? Explain using examples.

2.13 What does the probability $P(A|B)$ equal if the events A and B are:

    a) mutually exclusive;

    b) independent;

    c) exhaustive.

2.14 Comment on the validity of each part of the statements below, giving an example.

    a) Events that are mutually exclusive must be dependent, but dependent events need not be mutually exclusive.

    b) Events that are not mutually exclusive may be either independent or dependent; however, events that are independent cannot be mutually exclusive.

2.15 How are Formulas (2.5) and (2.4) related to each other?

2.16 Formulate a special version of Formula (2.6) for independent events.

2.17 A study on the probability that a randomly selected person smokes cigarettes divided the U.S. population into three age groups: under 30 (<30), between 30 and 50 ($30-50$), and over 50 (>50). Half of those under 30 were found to smoke.

    a) If $P(<30) = 1/2$, find the probability that a randomly selected person is under 30 and smokes.

    b) If $P(\text{Smokes}|>50) = 1/2$, and $P(\text{Smokes}|30-50) = 1/4$, does this indicate independence or dependence between these events?

    c) If $P(30-50) = 1/4$ and $P(>50) = 1/4$, find $P(S) = P(\text{Smokes})$.

    d) Replace the probability symbols in the following table with their appropriate values.

	<30	$30-50$	>50	
Smokes	$P(S \text{ and} <30)$	$P(S \text{ and } 30-50)$	$P(S \text{ and } >50)$	$P(S)$
Does not smoke	$P(\bar{S} \text{ and } <30)$	$P(\bar{S} \text{ and } 30-50)$	$P(\bar{S} \text{ and } >50)$	$P(\bar{S})$
	$P(<30)$	$P(30-50)$	$P(>50)$	

    e) Find $P(S \text{ or } >50)$

2.18 The following data describe certain characteristics of the employees in a major midwestern corporation.

Work experience	Men	Women	Under 26 years old
Over 4	1325	1100	125
3–4	1200	900	175
2–3	900	850	325
1–2	725	775	950

    a) How many people are represented here?

    b) What is the probability an employee selected "at random" will be a woman?

    c) What is the probability an employee selected "at random" will have over four years of work experience?

d) Calculate $P(1-2$ years exp. and male $)$ and $P(1-2$ years exp.$|$male $)$.

e) Is the event "male" independent of the event "1-2 years exp."?

2.19 The Easy Charge Company of Exercise 1.49 has presented the following table representing a breakdown of customers according to the amount they owe and whether a cash advance has been made.

Amounts owed by customers	Cash advance	No cash advance
$0–99.99	229	2894
$100–199.99	378	1707
$200–299.99	501	1426
$300–399.99	416	939
$400–499.99	260	483
$500 or more	289	478
Total	2073	7927

a) Find $P($Cash advance $)$ and $P(\overline{\text{Cash advance}})$.

b) Find $P($Cash advance$|$Amount owed $< \$100)$.

c) Find $P($Amount owed $< \$100|$Cash advance $)$.

d) Find $P($Amount owed $= \$100-\$199.99$ and $\overline{\text{Cash advance}})$.

e) Find $P($Amount owed $= \$100-\$199.99$ or $\overline{\text{Cash advance}})$.

2.20 In Problem 2.19, are the events "cash advance" and "amount owed $0–$99.99" independent? Explain what your answer means.

2.21 During the 1979 Three Mile Island nuclear crisis, at least three separate problems contributed to the near disaster: (1) a relief valve stuck; (2) a pressurizer gave a false reading; and (3) an auxiliary feedwater pump was left closed when it should have been open. Suppose the probability that each one of these three events occurs is 0.01, and they are assumed to be independent. What is the joint probability that all three will occur jointly? Would you conclude, given these values, the TMI incident was just "bad luck"?

2.22 A machine is known to produce defective components with a probability of 0.05.

a) Defective components are produced independently of one another. If we examine three components, what is the probability that all three will be defective?

b) If you find three defectives, as in part (a), what might you conclude about the machine?

2.23 Consider the pie-chart in Fig. 2.6.

a) According to this chart, what is the probability that a randomly selected person who is unemployed will be either adult or white, $P(W$ or $A)$? What is $P(W$ and $A)$?

b) Given that a person is an adult, what is the probability that this person is white? What is $P(W)$?

c) Is the event W independent of the event A? Explain using your answer to part (b).

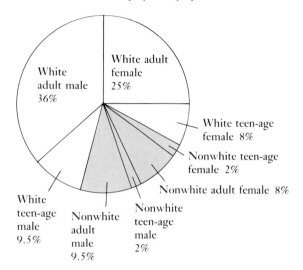

PORTRAIT OF A RECESSION
Percent share of the unemployed in July 1980

Figure 2.6
Portrait of a recession.
(Chart by Nigel Holmes.
Copyright 1980 Time Inc.
Reprinted by permission.)

d) Find the value of $P(A)P(W)$. Use this value and your results from part (a) to determine whether A and W are independent.

2.24 The Management Accounting Examination recently had three multiple-choice questions involving statistics. Each question had four answers.

a) Can the MAE administrators be 99% confident that a student who randomly picks answers will not answer all three questions correctly?

b) What is the probability that a person picking randomly will not get any answers correct?

2.25 A Gallup survey in the *Wall Street Journal* reported on hours worked by 780 chief executive officers (CEOs) as shown in Fig. 2.7.

Figure 2.7
Executive work week.
(Reprinted by permission of
Wall Street Journal. © Dow
Jones & Company, Inc. All
rights reserved.)

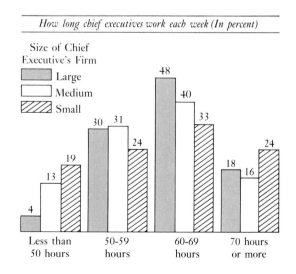

a) Among large firms, what is the probability that a randomly selected executive will be working 60 or more hours per week?

b) Suppose you interview four randomly selected chief executives in small firms. What is the probability that all four will be working less than 50 hours per week, using the data above?

2.26 Consider the data in Fig. 2.7 as a population of 780 CEOs, and assume the survey consisted of 230 executives from large firms, 340 from medium firms, and 210 from small firms. Answer the questions below based on sampling one person, randomly, from this population.

a) What is the probability of a small firm and 60–69 hours?

b) What is the probability of 50–59 hours given a medium firm?

c) What is the probability of either a large firm or less than 50 hours?

d) Is the event large firm independent of the event 70 hours or more?

Marginal Probability

2.7

In a number of circumstances it is convenient to think of a single event as always occurring jointly with other events, where these other events are assumed to influence the probability of the first occurring. For instance, it may be helpful not only to identify defective items produced by a manufacturing line, but also to specify exactly which machines, or which workers, produced these defectives. Insurance companies are interested in not only the amount of damage associated with each automobile accident, but among other things, the city where the accident took place, and the age and sex of the driver. In such situations, the probability of the event in question (for example, the probability of a defective item across all machines and all workers, or the probability of an accident involving at least x dollars across all cities and drivers) may not be known directly, but can be determined using marginal probabilities.

Marginal probabilities were used in an earlier example, when we used Table 2.1 to determine the probability a tax filer will have an income exceeding $50,000. This probability is found in the margin of a table of joint probabilities, and hence is called a **marginal probability.** A marginal probability is the sum of two or more joint probabilities.

To illustrate a marginal probability, Table 2.3 reproduces Table 2.1, but we have changed the column and row headings to keep the notation simpler. There are eight marginal probabilities in the margins of Table 2.3, six across the bottom, and two along the right. The marginal probability, $P(\text{audited}) = P(A)$, can be determined as

$$P(A) = 0.0010 + 0.0009 + 0.0014 + 0.0031 + 0.0058 + 0.0021$$
$$= 0.0143$$

To provide a formula for marginal probabilities, suppose we let A represent the event of interest in a problem (for example, A = audited), and let E_1,

TABLE 2.3   The IRS data reproduced

	E_1	E_2	E_3	E_4	E_5	E_6	Total
A	0.0010	0.0009	0.0014	0.0031	0.0058	0.0021	0.0143
Not A	0.2988	0.0953	0.2384	0.1236	0.1944	0.0352	0.9857
Total	0.2998	0.0962	0.2398	0.1267	0.2002	0.0373	1.0000

$E_2, \ldots, E_j, \ldots E_N$ represent a set of mutually exclusive events, one of which must always occur jointly with A (for example, a tax form and income). The value of $P(A)$ is given by summing the joint probability $P(A \text{ and } E_j)$ over all possible values of j ($0 \leq j \leq N$).

$$\text{\textit{Marginal probability of event A:}}$$
$$P(A) = \sum_{j=1}^{N} P(A \text{ and } E_j) \qquad (2.9)$$

Formula 2.9 is not usually the most convenient form of expressing a marginal probability. Rather, the joint probability $P(A \text{ and } E_j)$ is usually written in its equivalent form given by the general rule of multiplication (Formula 2.5). Using this formula we can write $P(A \text{ and } E_j) = P(E_j) P(A|E_j)$; hence

$$\text{\textit{Marginal probability of event A:}}$$
$$P(A) = \sum_{j=1}^{N} P(A \text{ and } E_j) = \sum_{j=1}^{N} P(E_j)P(A|E_j) \qquad (2.10)$$

Formula (2.10) can be illustrated by calculating $P(A)$ in Table 2.3. To do this we need to use the following formula.

$$P(A) = P(E_1)P(A|E_1) + P(E_2)P(A|E_2) + \cdots + P(E_6)P(A|E_6)$$

The probabilities $P(E_1)$, and $P(E_2), \ldots, P(E_6)$ can be read directly from Table 2.3. The conditional probabilities can also be determined from this table, as follows:

$$P(A|E_1) = \frac{0.0010}{0.2998} = 0.00334, \qquad P(A|E_2) = \frac{0.0009}{0.0962} = 0.00944$$

These probabilities can now be used to determine $P(A)$ using Formula (2.10).

$$\begin{aligned} P(A) &= P(E_1)P(A|E_1) + P(E_2)P(A|E_2) + \cdots + P(E_6)P(A|E_6) \\ &= (0.2998)(0.00334) + (0.0962)(0.00944) + \cdots + (0.0373)(0.0563) \\ &= 0.0143 \end{aligned}$$

Application of Probability Theory: An Example

2.8

Suppose a manufacturer producing delicate electronic components cannot determine whether a component is defective without tearing the component apart and, in the process, destroying the usefulness of that component. However, there is a machine that its makers claim will help detect defective components. This machine, which indicates only that the component appears to be good ($+$) or that it appears to be defective ($-$), is not infallible; that is, it will sometimes indicate positive when the component is defective, and sometimes indicate negative when the component is good. To determine the ability of the machine to distinguish between good and defective items, 800 randomly selected components were first tested on the machine and then torn apart to see whether they were good or defective. The results of this research are shown in Table 2.4. The data in the table can be used to make estimates of a number of different probability values.

TABLE 2.4

		State of component		Marginal totals
		Good	*Defective*	
Result of test	$+$	448	60	508
	$-$	112	180	292
Marginal totals		560	240	800

Intersections.   First note that four joint probabilities representing the *intersection* of two events can be determined directly from the data in Table 2.4: the joint probability of a good item *and* a positive test equals the relative frequency of *both* events occurring together, which is

$$P(\text{Good and Test} +) = \frac{448}{800} = 0.560$$

$$P(\text{Good and Test} -) = \frac{112}{800} = 0.140$$

$$P(\text{Def. and Test} +) = \frac{60}{800} = 0.075$$

$$P(\text{Def. and Test} -) = \frac{180}{800} = 0.225$$

Note that the probabilities of the above four mutually exclusive and exhaustive events sum to 1.

Marginals.   The four probabilities calculated above can now be used to calculate other probabilities in the combined forms of the sets discussed earlier. For instance, although the marginal (unconditional) probability of a good item can be determined from Table 2.4 to be $P(\text{Good}) = 560/800 = 0.700$, its value can also be determined via Formula (2.10):

$$P(\text{Good}) = P(\text{Good and Test} +) + P(\text{Good and Test} -)$$
$$= 0.560 + 0.140 = 0.700$$

The probability $P(\text{Test} +)$ can be determined in a similar fashion:

$$P(\text{Test} +) = P(\text{Good and Test} +) + P(\text{Def. and Test} +)$$
$$= 0.560 + 0.075 = 0.635$$

Unions.   The probability of the union of two events, such as the probability of *either* a good component *or* a positive test, can be determined by using the general rule of addition (Formula 2.6):

$$P(\text{Good or Test} +) = P(\text{Good}) + P(\text{Test} +) - P(\text{Good and Test} +)$$
$$= 0.700 + 0.635 - 0.560 = 0.775$$

The manufacturer in our problem is primarily interested in how well this testing device works — in other words, if it reads + on a given component, how often will the component be good? Similarly, if it reads − , how often will the component be defective? These values can be determined from Table 2.4 by noting that out of the 508 components that tested + , 448 were good; hence

$$P(\text{Good}|\text{Test} +) = \frac{448}{508} = 0.882$$

Similarly, of the 292 components that tested − , 180 were defective, so that

$$P(\text{Def.}|\text{Test} -) = \frac{180}{292} = 0.616$$

These values can formally be determined by using the formula for conditional probability:

$$P(\text{Good}|\text{Test} +) = \frac{P(\text{Good and Test} +)}{P(\text{Test} +)} = \frac{0.560}{0.635} = 0.882$$
$$P(\text{Def.}|\text{Test} -) = \frac{P(\text{Def. and Test} -)}{P(\text{Test} -)} = \frac{0.225}{0.365} = 0.616$$

The value of $P(\text{Good}|\text{Test} -)$ must equal

$$1 - P(\text{Def.}|\text{Test} -) = 1 - 0.616 = 0.384$$

since this event and $P(\text{Def.}|\text{Test} -)$ are complementary.

The results of the machine test in this problem are obviously not independent of the state of the component. If they were independent, $P(\text{Good}|\text{Test} +)$ would have to equal $P(\text{Good})$, and $P(\text{Def.}|\text{Test} -)$ would have to equal $P(\text{Def.})$, which is not the case. But *how much better off* is the manufacturer by knowing the results of the test? The manufacturer is in good shape if the test is positive, as then a guess that the component is good will be correct 88.2% of the time. After a negative indication, however, the manufacturer who guesses the component to be defective will be correct only 61.6% of the time. Fortunately, a positive test will occur most often (with probability 0.635), and a negative test will occur only relatively infrequently (with probability 0.365). Multiplying 0.882 by 0.635 and 0.616 by 0.365, we obtain, as the sum of these products, 0.785. This is the probability of a correct assessment, assuming the manufacturer always accepts the result of the machine test. This weighting is just a common sense use of the formal rule for adding up all the joint occurrences of these events in which the test indicates the correct state of the component:

$$P(\text{Correct}) = P(\text{Good and Test} +) + P(\text{Def. and Test} -)$$
$$= 0.882(0.635) + (0.616)(0.365)$$
$$= 0.785$$

If we now knew how much this machine costs (to buy and operate), and how much the firm's revenue will increase by being better able to distinguish between good and defective components, then we could determine whether the machine is worth purchasing. Without this machine, the manufacturer who presumes all components are good will be correct 70% of the time [since $P(\text{Good}) = 560/800 = 0.70$].

Bayes' Rule   **2.9**

One of the most interesting (and controversial) applications of the rules of probability theory involves estimating unknown probabilities and making decisions on the basis of new (sample) information. Statistical decision theory is a new field of study that has its foundations in just such problems. Chapter 10 investigates the area of statistical decision theory in some detail; this section describes one of the basic formulas of the area, Bayes' rule.

An English philosopher, the Reverend Thomas Bayes (1702–1761), was one of the first to work with rules for reversing probabilities in the light of sample information. Bayes' research, published in 1763, went largely unnoticed for over a century, and only recently has attracted a great deal of attention. His contribution consists primarily of a unique method for calculating conditional probabilities. The so-called Bayesian approach to this problem addresses itself to the question of determining the probability of some event, E_i, *given that* another event, A, has been (or will be) observed; that is, determining the value of $P(E_i|A)$. The event A is usually thought of as sample information, so that Bayes' rule is concerned with determining the probability of an event given certain new information, such as that acquired from a sample, a survey, or a pilot study. For example, a sample output of 3 defectives in 20 trials (event A) might be used to estimate the probability that a machine is not working correctly (event E_i); or you might use the results of your first exam in statistics (event A) as sample evidence in estimating the probability of receiving an "A" in this course (event E_i).

Probabilities before revision by Bayes' rule are called **à priori** or simply **prior probabilities,** because they are determined *before* the sample information is taken into account. Prior probabilities may be either objective or subjective values.

A probability that has undergone revision in the light of sample information (via Bayes' rule) is called a **posterior probability,** since it represents a probability calculated *after* this information is taken into account. Posterior probabilities are always conditional probabilities, the conditional event being the sample information. Thus, by using Bayes' rule, a prior probability, which is an unconditional probability, becomes a posterior probability, which is a conditional probability. In order to calculate such posterior probabilities, we will first derive Bayes' rule for the general problem of determining $P(E_i|A)$.

Recall that earlier in this chapter we indicated that a joint probability can be written in two different conditional forms (see Formula (2.5)). This implies that we can also write the joint probability $P(E_i$ and A) in a similar fashion,

$$P(A)P(E_i|A) = P(E_i \text{ and } A) = P(E_i)P(A|E_i)$$

If this formula holds, then it must also be true that

$$P(A)P(E_i|A) = P(E_i)P(A|E_i)$$

We can now solve for $P(E_i|A)$ directly by dividing both sides by $P(A)$:

$$P(E_i|A) = \frac{P(E_i)P(A|E_i)}{P(A)} \qquad (2.11)$$

The numerator of Formula (2.11) represents the probability that A and E_i will both occur, while the denominator is the probability that A alone will occur. But $P(A)$ can be written in more meaningful terms for this type of problem as a marginal probability. The probability $P(A)$, written as a marginal probability, is given by Formula (2.10) as $P(A) = \sum_{j=1}^{N} P(E_j)P(A|E_j)$. Substituting this value into Formula (2.11) yields Bayes' rule:

$$\textit{Bayes' rule: } P(E_i|A) = \frac{P(E_i)P(A|E_i)}{\displaystyle\sum_{j=1}^{N} P(E_j)P(A|E_j)} \qquad (2.12)$$

$$= \frac{P(E_i)P(A|E_i)}{P(E_1)P(A|E_1) + P(E_2)P(A|E_2) + \cdots + P(E_N)P(A|E_N)}$$

Remember, Bayes' rule is just another way of writing a conditional probability, for its numerator is a form of $P(A \text{ and } E_j)$, and its denominator is $P(A)$. The probabilities $P(E_j)$ are the prior probabilities. It is important to note that the event E_i is *one* specific event contained in the set of all possible events denoted as E_j, where $j = 1, 2, \ldots, N$. In other words, the value of i must be one of the numbers $1, 2, \ldots, N$. The variable j is just an index of summation. Probabilities of the form $P(A|E_j)$ are called *likelihoods* since they indicate how "likely" it is that the specified sample result (A) will occur *given* that the event E_j has taken (or will take) place.

Battery Manufacturer Example.

As an example of Bayes' rule, suppose a manufacturer of automobile batteries produces two types of batteries (regular and heavy-duty) at each of three plants (A, B, and C). Plant A produces 300 batteries a day, 200 of which are regular, and 100 heavy-duty. Plant B produces 200 batteries each day, 50 regular and 150 heavy-duty. Plant C produces 50 batteries of *each* type in a day. What is the probability that a randomly selected heavy-duty battery came from plant B? That is, what is $P(\text{Plant B}|\text{Heavy-duty})$? Table 2.5 shows a diagram of the plants and their production of batteries.

Since we want to calculate $P(\text{Plant B}|\text{Heavy-duty})$, "heavy-duty" represents the sample information (event A) and "plant B" represents the event of interest (E_i). The prior probabilities of all the events E_j (the plants) are

$$P(\text{Plant A}) = \frac{300}{600} = \frac{1}{2}$$

$$P(\text{Plant B}) = \frac{200}{600} = \frac{1}{3}$$

$$P(\text{Plant C}) = \frac{100}{600} = \frac{1}{6}$$

The likelihoods are also easily obtained by looking at Table 2.5.

$$P(\text{Heavy-duty}|\text{Plant A}) = \frac{100}{300} = \frac{1}{3}$$

$$P(\text{Heavy-duty}|\text{Plant B}) = \frac{150}{200} = \frac{3}{4}$$

$$P(\text{Heavy-duty}|\text{Plant C}) = \frac{50}{100} = \frac{1}{2}$$

We can now use this information, and Bayes' rule, to calculate $P(\text{Plant B}|\text{Heavy-duty})$, which we abbreviate as $P(B|HD)$.

$$P(B|HD) = \frac{P(B)P(HD|B)}{P(A)P(HD|A) + P(B)P(HD|B) + P(C)P(HD|C)}$$

$$= \frac{(\frac{1}{3})(\frac{3}{4})}{(\frac{1}{2})(\frac{1}{3}) + (\frac{1}{3})(\frac{3}{4}) + (\frac{1}{6})(\frac{1}{2})} = \frac{1}{2}$$

The posterior probability of plant B is thus $\frac{1}{2}$. This should seem reasonable, since the prior probability was $P(\text{Plant B}) = \frac{1}{3}$, and the sample information (heavy-duty) favors plant B; hence, we would expect its probability to increase. Note that this result is also logical in view of Table 2.5. There are six boxes representing production of heavy-duty batteries, and plant B is associated with three of them; hence, we can see that the posterior probability must be $\frac{1}{2}$. Bayes' rule has merely given us the ratio of the number of events of interest (heavy-duty batteries from plant B) to the total number of sample outcomes (heavy-duty batteries). As an exercise the reader may calculate the other posteriors in this example, such as $P(A|HD), P(C|HD), P(A|\text{Regular})$, etc.

TABLE 2.5

	Regular batteries				Heavy-duty			Total
Plant A	50	50	50	50		50	50	300
Plant B				50	50	50	50	200
Plant C				50		50		100

Total daily plant production   600

Components Example. As a final example of Bayes' rule, let us again consider the problem facing the manufacturer of delicate electronic components. Recall that $P(\text{Good}) = 0.70$ and $P(\text{Def.}) = 0.30$. These are the manufacturer's prior probabilities of a good or a defective component. Once more, we assume that the testing device described in Section 2.8 is being considered. This time, however, we do not want to assume that all the data in Table 2.4 are available. It is perhaps more reasonable to assume that the device has been tested on some components known to be good and some known to be defective. For instance, suppose all we know from Table 2.4 is that 80% of the good components yield a $+$ reading, and 20% yield a $-$ reading. Similarly, for the defective components, all we know is that 75% of the time the test reads $-$, and 25% of the time it reads $+$. That is,

$$P(+\,|\text{Good}) = 0.80 \qquad P(-\,|\text{Good}) = 0.20$$

and

$$P(+\,|\text{Def.}) = 0.25 \qquad P(-\,|\text{Def.}) = 0.75$$

All these values are consistent with those in Table 2.4. They are the likelihoods for this problem.

As we indicated in Section 2.8, the probabilities of interest to the manufacturer are those which indicate *how often* the test is correct — that is, $P(\text{Good}|\,+)$ and $P(\text{Def.}|\,-)$. These values can be calculated by Bayes' rule:

$$P(\text{Good}|\,+) = \frac{P(\text{Good})P(+\,|\text{Good})}{P(\text{Good})P(+\,|\text{Good}) + P(\text{Def.})P(+\,|\text{Def.})}$$

$$= \frac{(0.70)(0.80)}{(0.70)(0.80) + (0.30)(0.25)} = 0.882$$

Similarly,

$$P(\text{Def.}|\,-) = \frac{P(\text{Def.})P(-\,|\text{Def.})}{P(\text{Def.})P(-\,|\text{Def.}) + P(\text{Good})P(-\,|\text{Good})}$$

$$= \frac{(0.30)(0.75)}{(0.30)(0.75) + (0.70)(0.20)} = 0.616$$

The two remaining probabilities in this problem can also be calculated by Bayes' rule. However, it is much easier to find these values by the complementary law of probability.

$$P(\text{Def.}|+) = 1 - P(\text{Good}|+) = 1 - 0.882 = 0.118$$
$$P(\text{Good}|-) = 1 - P(\text{Def.}|-) = 1 - 0.616 = 0.384$$

A good exercise for the reader would be to verify these values by using Bayes' rule.

Problems

2.27 How is Bayes' rule different from a conditional probability?

2.28 What is the difference between a *prior* and a *posterior* probability?

2.29 How is a likelihood different from a posterior probability?

2.30 Indicate whether you agree or disagree with each of the following statements. If you disagree, indicate why.

   a) The denominator of Bayes' rule is a marginal probability.

   b) The numerator of Bayes' rule is a joint probability.

   c) The numerator of Bayes' rule is one of the terms in the denominator of Bayes' rule.

   d) The numerator of Bayes' rule is the product of a conditional probability and a likelihood.

   e) The conditional probabilities on the right-hand side of Bayes' rule are all likelihoods.

2.31 Two hundred marketing strategies were classified as "very effective," "moderately effective," or "not effective" in conjunction with three pricing strategies (I, II, III) as shown below:

Marketing strategies	Pricing strategies			
	I	II	III	Total
Very effective	20	50	30	100
Moderately effective	20	20	20	60
Not effective	20	10	10	40
Total	60	80	60	200

   a) Convert these data into a table showing a joint probability in each cell.

   b) Use Formula (2.10) to calculate the marginal probability $P(\text{Very effective})$.

   c) Use Bayes' rule to calculate the posterior probability $P(\text{Pricing strategy II}|\text{Very effective})$.

2.32 The IRS data in Tables 2.1 and 2.3 present the probability a tax filer will be audited by the IRS. If you know that a person has been audited, what is the probability that this person had an income exceeding $50,000? Use Bayes' rule.

2.33 The data below represent 630 oil and gas wells completed in Texas Railroad Commission's Districts 1, 2, and 3 (data from the *Wall Street Journal*).

District	Oil	Gas	Dry	Total
1 (Southwest Texas)	230	40	100	370
2 (Central Texas Coast)	20	30	40	90
3 (South Texas)	30	90	50	170
Total	280	160	190	630

a) Find $P(\text{oil})$, $P(\text{gas})$, $P(\text{dry})$.

b) Show that $P(\text{oil})$ equals the sum of three joint probabilities.

c) Find $P(\text{oil}|\text{District 1})$ and $P(\text{District 1}|\text{oil})$.

d) Use Bayes' rule to find $P(\text{oil}|\text{District 1})$.

2.34 Consider the data in Fig. 2.6, presenting data on the classes of people unemployed during the 1980 recession. Assume you know that an unemployed person is an adult. Use Bayes' rule to determine the probability that this person is a white female.

2.35 Use the information in Fig. 2.7 to determine the probability an executive was from a large firm given that this person worked 70 hours or more. Use Bayes' rule, and assume that there were 230 CEOs from large firms, 340 from medium firms, and 210 from small firms.

2.36 Use Bayes' rule on the data in Problem 2.17 to calculate the probability that a randomly selected person smokes, given that the person < 30.

2.37 The Easy Charge Company described in Exercise 1.49 has released the following data on the number of customers who were given cash advances last month.

Amounts owed by customers	Cash advance	No cash advance
$0–99.99	229	2894
$100–199.99	378	1707
$200–299.99	501	1426
$300–399.99	416	939
$400–499.99	260	483
Over $500	289	478
Total	2073	7927

a) Use Formula (2.10) to calculate the marginal probability $P(\text{Cash advance})$.

b) Use Bayes' rule to calculate the posterior probability $P(\text{Balance due} < \$100|\text{Cash advance})$.

Exercises

2.38 The data below represent annual deaths per 1000 insured persons (males) of various ages (from *Business Week,* 1988).

Survival of the fittest:			
How insurers see it			
Annual deaths per 1000 insured persons (males)			

Age	Total	**Current rate**	
		Smoker	*Nonsmoker*
35	2.11	2.63	1.69
45	4.55	6.27	3.32
55	10.47	15.14	7.82
65	25.42	36.29	21.13

Source: American Council of Life Insurance

a) Rewrite these values as the probability of death (example, 2.63/1000 = 0.00263). Are they joint or conditional probabilities? Explain. Why do you think *Business Week* chose to report them as deaths per 1000?

b) Is it reasonable to sum the values of 2.63, 6.77, 15.14, and 36.29? Why or why not?

c) If the value 2.11 represents the weighted average of 2.63 and 1.69, what is the population of those expected to die at 35 who are smokers?

d) Are age and the event "smoker" independent or dependent for these data? Explain.

2.39 Given the following table of survey information on a population of salespeople for a clothing company:

Salary ($000)		**Years of college**	
		At least 2	*None*
(A1)	20–29.9	30	50
(A2)	30–39.9	50	40
(A3)	40–49.9	20	10
		100	100

a) Illustrate the use of Bayes' rule by finding the probability of selecting a noncollege respondent, presuming that the one selected is in the highest salary bracket indicated.

b) Are salary and years of college independent in this problem?

2.40 These are two primary types of economic stabilization policies: fiscal policy (controlled by Congress) and monetary policy (controlled by the Federal Reserve Board). Assume the policy decisions made by these two bodies are independent of one another, and that the action of either group is correct 80% of the time and incorrect 20% of the time. Finally, assume that the probabilities that the economy follows a generally stable growth pattern due to (or in spite of) these policy actions are

$P($Stable growth$|$Neither acting correctly$)=0.40;$

$P($Stable growth$|$Both acting correctly$)=0.99;$

$P($Stable growth$|$Only 1 acting correctly$)=0.70.$

a) Use the independence assumption to calculate

$P($Neither acting correctly$)$

$P($Both acting correctly$)$

$P($Only 1 acting correctly$)$

b) You are given the sample information that growth is stable for a particular period. Use Bayes' rule to calculate:

$P($Only 1 acting correctly$|$Stable growth$)$

$P($Both acting correctly$|$Stable growth$)$

$P($Neither acting correctly$|$Stable growth$)$

Check to see if these probabilities sum to 1.0.

2.41 A questionnaire is sent to rural households in Pennsylvania with probability $P(R)=0.50$ and to urban households with probability $P(U)=0.50$, where R stands for "rural" and U for "urban." Households are divided into low-income (L) and high-income (H). Furthermore, the following conditional probabilities are known.

$$P(H|R)=0.20, \qquad P(L|R)=0.80, \qquad P(H|U)=0.40, \qquad P(L|U)=0.60$$

The location code has been omitted on one of the questionnaires received so that it is not known whether it is from a rural or urban household. The analysis of the responses in the questionnaire shows that it was obviously completed by a high-income household. How does this new information affect the probabilistic knowledge of whether it came from a rural or an urban household?

2.42 A training program for middle managers involves 23 people. What is the probability that at least two of these people will have the same birthday (same month and day)? (*Hint:* Approximate the answer using logarithms.)

2.43 Four applicants are under consideration for the position of chief financial officer of a certain company. Two of them are female, three are over 50 years old, and all four are either over 50, or female, or both.

a) What is the probability a candidate is over 50 and female?

b) Given that a candidate is female, what is the probability this person is over 50?

c) Given that the candidate is over 50, what is the probability this person is a female?

2.44 A-1 Loans (from Exercise 1.48) has recorded both the activity level of the local economy (either Hi, Med, or Low) and the mean interval times (0–20 minutes, 20–60 minutes, 60–200 minutes) for its customers over the past 150 weeks.

Time interval between customers		State of economy		
		Hi	*Med*	*Low*
A	0–20	30	12	8
B	20–60	30	21	4
C	60–200	30	12	3

Based on these data:

a) Find $P(\text{Hi})$, $P(\text{Med})$, $P(\text{Low})$, $P(A)$, $P(B)$, and $P(C)$.

b) Find $P(A|\text{Hi})$, $P(A|\text{Med})$, $P(A|\text{Low})$.

c) Use Formula (2.10) to find $P(A)$.

d) Are the events A, B, C independent of the state of the economy?

e) Suppose A-1 would like to revise the probabilities $P(\text{Hi})$, $P(\text{Med})$, $P(\text{Low})$ in light of sample evidence (S). Find $P(\text{Hi}|S)$, $P(\text{Med}|S)$, and $P(\text{Low}|S)$ given that $P(S|\text{Hi})=0.05$, $P(S|\text{Med})=0.10$, and $P(S|\text{Low})=0.40$.

2.45 Prove that if $P(A|B)=P(A)$, then $P(B|A)=P(B)$.

Chapter 3

Probability Theory: Random Variables

Chance favors only the prepared mind.

LOUIS PASTEUR

Introduction **3.1**

Now that we have studied the rules of associating a probability value with a single event, or with a combination of events in an experiment, we can proceed to the next logical problem, that of describing the probability of *all* events in a given experiment. This problem becomes especially important in decision-making contexts; we can seldom properly evaluate a course of action on the basis of one or two outcomes, but should consider all possible consequences of the action. Most of us face problems of this nature regularly; for instance, in deciding whether to take a difficult elective course (or whether to study tonight or watch television), you would certainly want to consider how this decision will affect your chances of receiving not only the grade of "A," but also the grades of "B," "C," "D," or "F." Similarly, the speculator in the stock market should (but does not always) consider the probability of losing significant proportions of the investment, as well as of making a profit.

The outcomes of an experiment are said to take place *randomly*, since they cannot, by definition, occur in any particular order or pattern. Such variables, whose values thus cannot be known in advance by the person conducting the experiment, are called *random variables*. The Dow Jones Industrial Average (DJIA) represents a random variable because we do not know in advance the outcomes of this "experiment." Similarly, the salary you receive upon graduation can be thought of as a random variable because you don't know what this salary will be. On the other hand, the amount of money you earned last year is not (to you at least) a random variable, since presumably you know the exact amount—there is no uncertainty connected with it. However, your income is probably a random variable to your statistics instructor since its value is not known to this person.

Random Variables

Given an experiment and a set of *mutually exclusive* and *exhaustive* outcomes, it is common to consider questions about the probability of the occurrence of any one or more of these outcomes by using the following definition of a random variable.

A **random variable** is a well-defined rule for assigning a numerical value to every possible outcome of an experiment.

This means that the symbols used in Chapter 2 to designate the outcomes of an experiment—males/females, defective/good—are now going to be replaced with numbers. A random variable is a rule designating a number to be associated with each outcome of the experiment.

The outcomes of some experiments readily meet this definition of a random variable because they are already well-defined numbers. For example, the number of hours that a given light bulb might last is a well-defined number; the number of defectives that could occur in a lot of computer chips is a well-defined number; and the potential yield of an investment of $1000 is a well-defined number. In other cases, the outcomes of an experiment may be qualitative. For example, we classified undergraduate programs in Chapter 1 as either I, II, III, IV, V, or VI. Similarly, Moody's ratings for bonds can be Aaa, Aa, A, Baa, or Ba. In these instances the probability model must specify exactly what numerical value corresponds to each qualitative outcome. In the case of Moody's ratings, we might let Aaa = 1, Aa = 2, A = 3, Baa = 4, and Ba = 5. For university grades, usually A = 4, B = 3, C = 2, D = 1, and F = 0.

In working with *continuous* sample space, it is sometimes convenient to reduce the sample space to just a few discrete points. For example, the yield on a $1000 investment might be classified as falling into one of just a small number of intervals (such as 0 to 1.99%, 2.00 to 3.99%, and so forth); and the salaries of all executives in a company might be grouped into classes which are $5000 or $10,000 wide. In all these examples a random variable exists only when numerical values are assigned to the outcomes of the experiment by a well-defined rule.

In making the assignment of numerical values to the outcomes of an experiment, random variables are denoted by *boldface* italic type, such as x, y, z, or sometimes by boldface letters with subscript indexes, such as x_1, x_2, x_3. *Specific* values of each random variable are denoted by letters in lightface italic type, such as x, y, z, or sometimes x_1, x_2, x_3. Thus, the designation $\{x = x\}$ is read as "the random variable x takes on the value x." The following examples illustrate this notation.

1. *Experiment:* Classify candidates for a staff position by sex

> Outcomes: The discrete outcomes male or female
>
> Sample space: Discrete and finite
>
> Random variable: Define $\{x = 1\}$ if female, $\{x = 0\}$ if male

The use of 0 and 1 is convenient in defining random variables. Because we have a well-defined rule for assigning values in this experiment, x is a random variable.

2. *Experiment:* A bond is given a Moody's rating

> Outcomes: Discrete ratings Aaa, Aa, A, Baa, or Ba
>
> Sample space: Discrete and finite
>
> Random variable: Define $\{y = 1\}$ if the rating is Aaa
> $\{y = 2\}$ if the rating is Aa
> $\{y = 3\}$ if the rating is A
> $\{y = 4\}$ if the rating is Baa
> $\{y = 5\}$ if the rating is Ba

The variable y represents a well-defined rule for assigning values to the outcomes of this experiment, hence y is a random variable.

3. *Experiment:* Purchase a lottery ticket

> Outcomes: The dollar values that might be won
>
> Sample space: Discrete (infinite, but countable)
>
> Random variable: Define $z = 0, 1, 2, \ldots$

The random variable z in this case is discrete, and it is also infinite, since there is no limit on the amount won. Realistically, however, there is some upper bound on the value for z, such as $100 million.

4. *Experiment:* Invest $1000 in a common stock

> Outcomes: Values of yield or rate of return
>
> Sample space: Continuous (always infinite)
>
> Random variable: Define x = value of yield $(-\infty < x < \infty)$.

A **continuous random variable** is obtained from a continuous sample space whenever a single value of x is assigned to each outcome in the sample space. For example, because a yield can be *any* positive number (or a negative number), x must be continuous.

5. *Experiment:* Invest $1000 in a common stock

In this example we simplify Experiment 4 somewhat by grouping the various yields into different classes. For example, we might let one class represent all yields between 0 and 1.99%, another represent 2.00% to 3.99%, and so forth.

Outcomes: Class intervals of yields

Sample space: Discrete and infinite (there is no limit on the number of classes)

Random variable: Define x = the midpoint or some representative value (the class mark) of the yields in each class interval.

Assigning values of the random variable so they equal the class marks makes it much easier to find the mean and variance of the probability distribution under study. We will describe the process of finding means and variances of probability distributions later in this chapter. As a final note in this section, we should point out that the numerical value assigned to an outcome in an experiment need not be unique to that outcome. That is, several different outcomes may be assigned the same numerical value.

Probability Distributions

Once an experiment and its outcomes have been clearly stated, and the random variable of interest has been defined, then the probability of the occurrence of any value of the random variable can be specified. As an example, suppose you decide to send out questionnaires to 100 different convenience stores, and you want each store to be a member of one of the top five chains in the United States. From *Business Week* (1988 data), you gather the following information:

No.	Company	No. of Stores
1	Southland	7,450
2	Circle K	4,600
3	Convenience	1,500
4	Dairy Mart	1,200
5	Cumberland Farms	1,190
	Total	15,940

This process of sending questionnaires can be viewed as an experiment in which each questionnaire is sent to a store randomly selected from the 15,940. There are five outcomes, corresponding to the five companies. The sample space is discrete and finite; a random variable x might be defined to have either $x = 1$, $x = 2$, $x = 3$, $x = 4$, or $x = 5$. The probability of each of these outcomes is denoted as $P(x = 1)$, $P(x = 2)$, . . . , $P(x = 5)$, and abbreviated as $P(1), P(2), . . . , P(5)$.

TABLE 3.1

x	$P(x)$
1	0.467
2	0.289
3	0.094
4	0.075
5	0.075

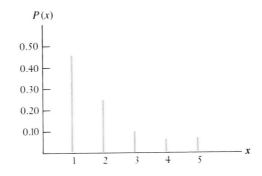

Figure 3.1
Probability distribution for questionnaire example.

Probabilities can be determined by taking the ratio of stores for each company to the total. Thus, the probability a Southland store is selected is

$$P(1) = \frac{7,450}{15,940} = 0.467$$

Similarly, the probability that a questionnaire is sent to a Cumberland Farms' store is

$$P(5) = \frac{1,190}{15,940} = 0.075$$

The probabilities $P(1), P(2), \ldots, P(5)$ taken together form what is called a probability distribution.

A **probability distribution** is a specification (in the form of a graph, a table, or a function) of the probability associated with each value of the random variable.

The sum of all probabilities in the probability distribution must sum to 1.0. Note in Fig. 3.1 and Table 3.1, which present the probability distribution for the convenience store questionnaire problem, that the probabilities do, indeed, sum to one.

The determination of a probability distribution completes the process of describing what is called the **probability model.** Figure 3.2 summarizes this model. First, the experiment must be stated clearly, so that one can specify the relevant sample space. A random variable is then associated with this sample space, which makes it possible to define the probability distribution.

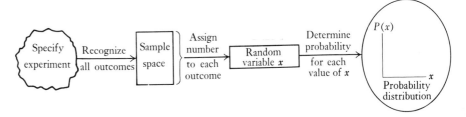

Figure 3.2
The probability model.

Discrete Random Variables

3.2

A probability distribution involving only discrete values of x is usually called a **probability mass function (p.m.f.)**.

A probability mass function (abbreviated p.m.f.) is usually described in one of three ways: (1) by a graph, such as Fig. 3.1, (2) by a table of values, such as Table 3.1, or (3) by a formula.* The name "mass function" derives from the fact that all outcomes associated with the value of a discrete random variable can be represented on a graph by a vertical line whose height (or *mass*) indicates the probability of that value.

To illustrate the concept of describing a mass function by graph, table, and formula, consider the problem of determining how long a certain grocery item might sit on the shelf before being sold. For one relatively low-selling item, the estimate is that there is a 50-50 chance this item is sold on any given day. Suppose we let x = the day on which the item is sold. Since there is a 50-50 chance that the item is sold on the first day, $P(x = 1) = 1/2$. If $\{x = 2\}$, this means the item was not sold on day 1, and *is* sold on day 2. Thus, $P(x = 2) = (1/2)(1/2) = 1/4$. Similarly $P(x = 3) = (1/2)(1/2)(1/2) = 1/8$. A graph of the p.m.f. for this experiment, and a table of its values, are shown in Fig. 3.3 and Table 3.2, respectively.

Using a graph or a table in this problem is inconvenient because of the fact that although x is discrete, an infinite number of x values is possible. That is, the item might not be sold for a very large number of days. Thus, Fig. 3.3 and Table 3.2 are somewhat unsatisfactory because a series of dots is used to indicate the values of x and their probability after $\{x = 5\}$. A formula, on the other hand, can be used to *explicitly* specify how $P(x)$ and x are related for all values of x. In this case the relationship is easily verified to be the following:

$$P(x) = \begin{cases} (1/2)^x & \text{for } x = 1, 2, 3, \ldots, \infty \\ 0 & \text{otherwise} \end{cases}$$

By substituting $x = 1$, $x = 2, \ldots, x = 5$ into this formula, the reader can verify the values in Table 3.2 and Fig. 3.3.

By now the reader should recognize the similarity between the concept of relative frequency, as described in Chapter 1, and the concept of a probability distribution. The difference, technically, is that relative frequencies often are only frequencies based on the outcomes of one or more replications of an experiment, whereas a probability can be viewed as the theoretical long-run relative frequency for all conceivable replications. The same properties defined in Chapter 2 for probability values can now be specified in terms of random variables.

---

*The reader is referred to the review of functions in Appendix A.

TABLE 3.2

x	P(x)
1	1/2
2	1/4
3	1/8
4	1/16
5	1/32
.	.
.	.
.	.

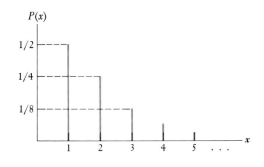

Figure 3.3
Probability mass function for day of sale of grocery item.

Properties of all probability mass functions

Property 1: $0 \le P(x = x) \le 1$
Property 2: $\sum_{\text{All } x} P(x = x) = 1$

Cumulative Mass Function (c.m.f.)

The concept of *cumulative* relative frequency and the graphical representations, which were introduced in Chapter 1, also have their counterparts in the study of probability. A **cumulative mass function (c.m.f.)** describes how probability accumulates in exactly the same fashion as the cumulative column in Table 1.3 describes how relative frequency accumulates—by *summing* all the relative frequency values. The value of the cumulative mass function at any given point x is usually denoted by the symbol $F(x)$, where $F(x)$ is the *sum of values* of the probability mass function for all values of the random variable **x** that are *less than or equal to x.* That is,

$$\boxed{\begin{array}{l} \textit{Cumulative function at the point x:} \\ F(x) = P(x \le x) = \sum_{x \le x} P(x) \end{array}} \qquad (3.1)$$

For our grocery item example, the value of $F(x)$ when $x = 1$ is $F(1) = 0.500$ because $P(x \le 1) = 0.500$. Similarly, $F(2) = 0.750$ because $P(x \le 2) = 0.500 + 0.250 = 0.750$. As with a probability mass function, a cumulative mass function must be defined for *all* values of the random variable. This is usually accomplished by means of either a graph, a table, or a formula. The table and graph for the grocery example are shown in Table 3.3 and Fig. 3.4. A c.m.f. graph will always look like a series of steps (a "step function") going up from zero to one as the value of **x** increases.

Figure 3.4 is perhaps a better way to illustrate the c.m.f. than Table 3.3, as it emphasizes the fact that $F(x)$ is defined for *all* values of **x** from negative

TABLE 3.3

x	$F(x)$
1	0.500
2	0.750
3	0.875
4	0.938
5	0.969
.	.
.	.
.	.

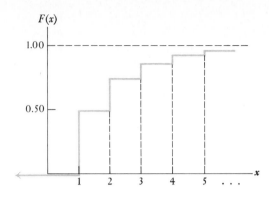

Figure 3.4
The cumulative mass
function for day of sale of a
grocery item.

infinity to positive infinity. That is, the cumulative mass function $F(x)$ is defined for *any* value of x between negative and positive infinity, not just the integer values listed in Table 3.3. As should be clear from Fig. 3.4, $F(x) = 0$ for all values of x from minus infinity up to $x = 1$. At $x = 1$ the value of $F(x)$ becomes 0.50. Similarly, at $x = 2$ the value of the function becomes 0.750. Note that for *any* number between $x = 2$ and $x = 3$, $F(x) = 0.750$. Suppose that we arbitrarily pick a number, say $x = 2.45$. From Fig. 3.4, $F(2.45)$ can easily be seen to be

$$F(2.45) = 0.750$$

The value $F(3) = 0.875$ is interpreted as meaning that there is a probability of 0.875 that this grocery item will be sold in three days or less.

EXAMPLE 1

Many other examples of discrete probability functions can be cited. An article in the *Wall Street Journal* described the possibility of oil at a number of sites in Texas. For five sites, it is known from past experience that an average of two of the wells will be dry, two will not be commercially feasible, and one will be a success. Thus, the experiment "Select a site" has three different outcomes. Let a random variable x assume values of -1, 0, and $+10$ for the three outcomes, respectively. These x-values may affect some management view of the net payoff (or loss) associated with the different outcomes. The values of the probability mass function and the cumulative mass function for this random variable are easily determined; they are given in Table 3.4.

TABLE 3.4   The p.m.f. and c.m.f. for the oil exploration example

Value of x	-1	0	$+10$	All other values
p.m.f. $P(x)$	2/5	2/5	1/5	0
c.m.f. $F(x)$	2/5	4/5	1.0	

As always, $0 \leq P(x) \leq 1.0$, and $F(x)$ is a function of x that never decreases. Only three values of x have positive probabilities, so the random variable is discrete. For any value less than -1, the cumulative value is zero. Now let us consider values larger than $x = -1$. For example,

$$F(4) = \sum_{x \leq 4} P(x)$$

Since the interval $x \leq 4$ includes $x = -1$ and $x = 0$, the nonzero probabilities to be included are

$$F(4) = P(-1) + P(0) = 2/5 + 2/5 = 4/5$$

At the value $x = 4$, we have accumulated four-fifths of the probability values. Indeed, the value of $F(x)$ is $4/5$ for all values, $0 \leq x < 10$. At the point $x = 10$, the value of $F(x)$ steps up to 1.0. ∎

EXAMPLE 2

Inland Container Company sells custom-made boxes. Suppose these boxes must be ordered in units of 1000, 2000, 4000, 6000, or 12,000. In this case we specify the experiment to be that of receiving orders from customers, and let $= \{1, 2, 4, 6, 12\}$, where x is in thousands of boxes. Based on past records, the p.m.f. and the c.m.f. can be described as follows:

x (in 000's)	1	2	4	6	12
$P(x = x)$	0.08	0.27	0.10	0.33	0.22
$F(x) = P(x < x)$	0.08	0.35	0.45	0.78	1.00

We see that for this discrete set of values, $0 \leq P(x) \leq 1.0$ for each x, and

$$\sum_{\text{All } x} P(x) = 1.0$$

so that these values satisfy the two properties of a probability mass function presented earlier. The definition of a cumulative mass function can be used to find a number of probabilities that might be of interest to the management of Inland Container, such as

1. The probability of an order of 4000 or fewer for a given customer

$$P(x \leq 4) = F(4) = 0.45$$

2. The probability of an order of more than 2000, $P(x > 2)$. This probability can be easily determined by using the complementary law of probability,

$$P(x > 2) = 1 - P(x \leq 2)$$

Since $P(x \leq 2) = F(2)$, the solution is

$$P(x > 2) = 1 - F(2) = 1.0 - 0.35 = 0.65$$

3. The probability of an order of more than 1000 but no larger than 6000, $P(1 < x \leq 6)$. As shown in the p.m.f. table,

$$P(x \leq 6) = F(6) = 0.78$$

But, since $F(6)$ *includes* the probability $P(x \leq 1) = F(1)$, we must *subtract* this value from $F(6)$. Hence,

$$P(1 < x \leq 6) = F(6) - F(1) = 0.78 - 0.08 = 0.70$$

4. The probability of an order of 12,000 or *fewer* is

$$P(x \leq 12) = F(12) = 1.0$$

As you can see from these examples, the cumulative mass function is useful in determining probability values for various types of events. Since this function will be used frequently in problems of statistical inference, the student should thoroughly understand this concept and all of the examples and hints for interpretation before proceeding. A good exercise is to sketch the function $F(x)$ for the example of the order of custom-made boxes and determine the answers to items 1 through 4 above by using your graph. ∎

Some Further Questions

Perhaps the reader has become curious about the parameters of the distribution of box orders. Recall from Chapter 1 that the important features of *any* distribution (which we now know includes probability distributions) are the measures of *central location* and *dispersion*. Knowing the mean number of boxes per order, for example, would be of value in deciding how to schedule production.

A measure of the dispersion of sales is also important when one is interested in deviations from the expected or theoretical average payoff. For instance, what is the chance that production facilities will be overburdened because of a succession of orders of 12,000 boxes? For planning purposes, one might want to know how many orders of each type can be expected. These and various other questions necessary for decision making can be posed. In the next section, the measures of central tendency and dispersion for a probability distribution are discussed. To repeat an earlier remark, while the problems and questions used here as examples to guide and motivate your study of statistics may not seem worth the effort, remember that the same concepts, measures, formulas, and methods can be and are applied to important decisions involving millions of dollars, such as choosing investment portfolio holdings, controlling production processes, pricing products for sale in an oligopoly market, and many other significant endeavors. Some of the problems or exercises will illustrate these widespread and important uses.

Expected Value:
The Discrete
Case

3.3

By means of the discussion presented thus far, we can now determine the probability of any single event of an experiment, or describe the probability of the entire set of outcomes associated with a given experiment. Yet this information may not be concise enough for most decision-making contexts. Recall that we had the same problem in Chapter 1, when it was not sufficient merely to present all the data, but in addition several characteristics of these data were given—the most important of which were the mean and the variance. The same type of measures are also useful in describing probability distributions, but in this case we must speak not of an observed mean or an observed variance, but of the mean or variance that would be *expected* to result, on the average, from the random variance under consideration. These values are thus given the name *expectations,* or *expected values.*

The **expected value** of a discrete random variable, x, is found by multiplying each x-value by its probability and then summing over all values of the random variable.

The letter E usually denotes an expected value and must be followed by brackets given the random variable of interest; $E[x]$, for instance, represents the expected value for the random variable x. Using this notation, the expected value of a discrete random variable x is

$$\textit{Expected value of } \pmb{x} \textit{ (discrete case): } E[\pmb{x}] = \sum_{\text{All } x} xP(x) \qquad (3.2)$$

The expected value of a random variable is nothing more than the arithmetic mean of that variable. That is, it is the center of gravity, the balancing point of the values of x "weighted" by their probability. Thus, $E[x]$ is the mean of the population of x values, where the relative frequency of each value of x is $P(x)$ and we can write:

$$\textit{Population mean: } \mu = E[\pmb{x}] = \sum_{\text{All } x} xP(x) \qquad (3.3)$$

Note that this definition of μ corresponds very closely to the definition in Chapter 1 of the mean of a population for grouped data [Formula (1.3)]. The major difference is that in Chapter 1 each value of x was "weighted" by its relative frequency f_i/N; now the weight is the relative frequency $P(x)$. As we pointed out previously, f_i/N is the relative frequency of just one replication (or a few replications) of an experiment, while $P(x)$ can be thought of as the expected relative frequency of an infinite number of replications of the experiment.

As an example of the calculation of an expected value, *Business Week* frequently rates the forecasts of promising stocks by major stockbrokers. In this case the task is to estimate the price at which a certain stock will sell a year from now. A successful broker is asked to let x = price in one year, and to establish a probability mass function. The result is

x = Price in one year	$P(x)$
$80	0.05
85	0.10
90	0.20
95	0.20
100	0.25
105	0.10
110	0.10
	1.00

The typical investor might wish to know what value to expect for x, on the average, in this experiment. In other words, if this experiment were repeated many times, what would be the average of all the x values? What is the *expected value* of x, or $E[x]$?

One method to *approximate* the mean value in any experiment is to replicate the experiment many times, add up the observed numbers, and divide by the number of observations; but such a procedure is often impractical, if not impossible, and gives only an approximation of the desired value. Fortunately, there is no need to replicate an experiment if the probability mass function is known, for we then already know the *expected relative frequency* of each event. For instance, if the experiment above were repeated 100 times, we would expect the price of x = 80 to occur 5 times, since

$$P(x = 80) = 0.05$$

The "weight" we assign to x = 80 is thus 0.05, or equivalently, 5/100. Similarly, the weight for x = 85 is 0.10 (or 10/100) since $P(x = 85) = 0.10$. By substituting the values from our stock example into Formula (3.2), we can calculate the expected price of the stock next year as follows:

$$
\begin{aligned}
E[x] &= \sum xP(x) \\
&= 80\,(0.05) + 85\,(0.10) + 90\,(0.20) + 95\,(0.20) \\
&\quad + 100\,(0.25) + 105\,(0.10) + 110\,(0.10) \\
&= 96.00
\end{aligned}
$$

The expected, or average, price of the stock in one year is thus $96.00. Another way of saying the same thing is to state that the mean (or balance point) of this probability mass function is $96.00.

As another example, reconsider the Inland Container box order situation with x and $P(x)$ defined as in the previous section. What is the expected value of x in this example? That is, what is the balance point of the probability mass function, or the average number of boxes per order? Using Formula (3.2), we obtain

$$E[x] = \sum xP(x)$$
$$= 1(0.08) + 2(0.27) + 4(0.10) + 6(0.33) + 12(0.22)$$
$$= 5.64 \text{ boxes (in 000's)}$$

This means that over an infinite number of sales, the average number of boxes ordered at one time would be 5,640. The expected number of boxes ordered over N orders equals $NE[x]$. For example, in 500 orders, the total number of boxes expected to be sold would be

$$500 \times 5.64 = 2820 \text{ boxes (in 000's)}$$

The number 5.64 represents only a theoretical value (based on an infinite number of orders under similar conditions). Over a finite number of orders, the actual number may deviate from the 5.64 average.

The Variance of a Random Variable

In the same way that the variance of a population was defined in Chapter 1 as the average of the squared deviation of the population values about their mean (μ), so the variance of a random variable x is defined as the expected (average) squared deviation of the values of this random variable (that is, the population values) about their mean ($E[x] = \mu$). The variance of a random variable is often denoted by the symbol $V[x]$, which is defined as follows:

$$V[x] = \sigma^2 = E[(x - \mu)^2]$$

Because an expected value is determined by weighting each deviation about the mean by $P(x)$ and then summing, another equivalent way of defining the variance of a random variable is given by Formula (3.4).

$$\text{Variance of } x\colon V[x] = \sigma^2 = \sum_{\text{All } x} (x - \mu)^2 P(x) \qquad (3.4)$$

Formula (3.4) is the traditional way of defining the variance of a discrete random variable. It can also be used to compute a standard deviation, since the standard deviation, denoted by σ, is always the square root of the variance.

$$\text{Standard deviation of } x\colon \sigma = \sqrt{V[x]} \qquad (3.5)$$

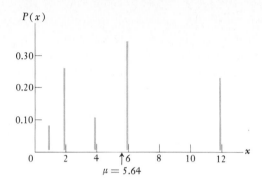

Figure 3.5
Probability mass function for box orders.

In order to illustrate the use of Formula (3.4), suppose we again use the probability distribution of the box-order situation described earlier. The probability mass function for this example is illustrated in Fig. 3.5.

Since we know for this example that the expected value is

$$E[x] = \mu = 5.64$$

we can substitute this value in Formula (3.4) to calculate $V[x]$:

$$V[x] = \sigma^2 = \sum(x - 5.64)^2 P(x)$$
$$= (1 - 5.64)^2\, 0.08 + (2 - 5.64)^2\, 0.27 + (4 - 5.64)^2\, 0.10$$
$$+ (6 - 5.64)^2\, 0.33 + (12 - 5.64)^2\, 0.22$$

Completing these calculations yields

$$V[x] = 14.51 \text{ (boxes squared)}$$

The standard deviation is $\sigma = \sqrt{V[x]} = 3.81$ boxes (in 000's).

The value of $\mu = 5.64$ is the *center* of this probability distribution, in the sense that it is the *expected number of boxes in each order.* The value $\sigma = 3.81$ indicates the expected size of the spread of the distribution of box orders.

It is important to always check the reasonableness of calculations such as $E[x]$ and $V[x]$. For instance, if $E[x]$ is not near where you would expect the center of gravity to be, then double check your calculations. A good way to check the reasonableness of $V[x]$ is to use the rule of thumb for variances presented in Chapter 1. This rule says that if the probability distribution is fairly symmetrical and unimodal, then 68% and 95% represent good approximations to the percent of the distribution falling in the intervals $\mu \pm 1\sigma$ and $\mu \pm 2\sigma$, respectively. For probability distributions, these rules mean that approximately 68% and 95% of the *probability* should be within $\mu \pm 1\sigma$ and $\mu \pm 2\sigma$, respectively. Using the above results for μ and σ, and Fig. 3.5, these intervals can be shown to contain:

Interval	Probability in interval
$\mu \pm 1\sigma = 5.64 \pm 3.81 = 1.83$ to 9.45	$[0.27 + 0.10 + 0.33 = 0.70]$
$\mu \pm 2\sigma = 5.64 \pm 2(3.81) = 0$ to 13.26	$[0.08 + 0.27 + 0.10 + 0.33 + 0.22 = 1.00]$

We see that the actual percentages agree fairly closely with the rule of thumb. The reader should remember, however, that had the distribution been sufficiently asymmetric, the percentages falling into these intervals might have been further from the 68% and 95% values.

Problems

3.1 Information summarized from the *Wall Street Journal* suggests that CEOs of major firms worked the following (average) hours per week:

Hours/week	Proportion of CEOs
45	6%
55	30%
65	46%
75	18%

   a) Specify the probability model for the hours worked by a randomly selected CEO using the data above.

   b) Find the mean and the variance of the probability distribution from part (a).

3.2 A study of the number of different jobs held by business school graduates in the five years since graduation resulted in the following data:

Jobs *(x)*	Proportion
1	48%
2	29%
3	13%
4	8%
5	2%

   a) Specify the probability model of this data.

   b) Find the mean and variance of this probability mass function.

3.3 In 1988 Golden Valley Microwave Foods, Inc., placed a "Jackpop" card in each bag of popcorn. The details on the back of the card give the following values.

Prize	Odds of winning
$5000	1 in 1,875,000
1000	1 in 750,000
1	1 in 375

a) Specify the probability model for this situation.

b) What are the expected winnings per card?

c) Golden Valley states that they have 4 grand prizes ($5000) to award, 10 first prizes ($1000), and 20,000 second prizes ($1). How many cards would you estimate they printed? To determine what the total cost will be to Golden Valley, what additional fact(s) do you need to know?

3.4 What, if any, is the difference between $E[x]$ and μ, and $V[x]$ and σ^2?

3.5 Is it necessary to have both the p.m.f. and the c.m.f. for a probability problem? What difference do these functions provide?

3.6 Describe the similarities and differences between f/N as presented in Chapter 1, and $P(x)$ presented in this chapter.

3.7 Sketch the cumulative mass function of the variable x of the Inland Container box-order example discussed earlier, where x is the number of boxes ordered. What is the median number of boxes ordered?

3.8 A report on sales of Navistar farm equipment estimates that monthly sales of a new grain harvester will be $x = 1, 2, 3,$ or 4 according to the following p.m.f.:

$$P(x) = \begin{cases} 1/10x & \text{for } x = 1, 2, 3, 4 \\ 0 & \text{otherwise} \end{cases}$$

a) Sketch this function and show that it satisfies the two properties necessary if $P(x)$ is to be a p.m.f.

b) Sketch the c.m.f.

c) Find $E[x]$ and $V[x]$ for this function.

3.9 A U.C.L.A. instructor in statistics always announces at the beginning of the quarter that final grades will consist of 20% A's, 30% B's, 30% C's, 10% D's, and 10% F's.

a) Sketch the p.m.f. and c.m.f., letting A = 4, B = 3, C = 2, D = 1, and F = 0.

b) Let x = numerical grade received, and calculate $E[x]$ and $V[x]$.

c) Calculate $\mu \pm 1\sigma$ and $\mu \pm 2\sigma$ for this problem. Is the percentage of values of x within these intervals close to the rule of thumb?

3.10 Champion can ship either 4000 or 12,000 boxes of spark plugs to an automotive outlet in South America. Let x = sales of spark plugs, in units of 1000 boxes. The manufacturer estimates that the following p.m.f. accurately describes sales:

$$P(x) = \begin{cases} 3/x & \text{for } x = 4 \text{ or } 12 \\ 0 & \text{otherwise} \end{cases}$$

a) Sketch this p.m.f., verifying that it meets the two necessary conditions for a mass function.

b) Sketch the c.m.f.

c) Find the mean and the variance of expected sales.

3.11 Reconsider the oil exploration example on page 90.

a) Sketch the p.m.f. and the c.m.f.

b) Find $E[x]$.

c) Find $V[x]$.

3.12 The A & P grocery chain sponsored an "Old Fashioned Bingo" game in which they published the following odds for one visit to an A & P market.

Prize	Odds	Prize	Odds
$1000	1 in 416,666	$5	1 in 1,562
100	1 in 41,666	1	1 in 114
10	1 in 3,125		

a) Find the expected value of the payoff for one visit.

b) What is the probability that a customer will not win a single prize in 20 consecutive visits?

3.13 A large construction company in Philadelphia classifies its laborers as either 3 (unskilled), 2 (semiskilled), or 1 (skilled). Based on past records, they have determined the p.m.f. for rating new workers to be

$$P(x) = \begin{cases} x^2/14 & \text{for } x = 1, 2, 3 \\ 0 & \text{otherwise} \end{cases}$$

a) Sketch this p.m.f. and the corresponding c.m.f. What proportion of workers are classified as unskilled?

b) Find $E[x]$ and $V[x]$.

3.14 Central Hardware of Sioux Falls is participating in a promotion in which each customer receives a card, and each card contains a hidden coin. For every 100 cards, there are 10 nickels, 10 dimes, 15 quarters, 15 half dollars, and 50 souvenir coins (no monetary value).

a) For a customer with one card, what is the probability the coin will be a dime?

b) What is a probability a customer with two coins will have 50 cents or more? Assume that the content of all cards is independent.

c) Sketch the p.m.f. for x = amount won on one card.

d) What is the average amount Central Hardware will give away to each customer?

e) What is the variance of the amount given to each customer?

3.15 The Indiana University Fun Frolic is sponsored by the University's staff to raise money for scholarships. The Planning Committee is considering a booth offering the chance to throw a dart at a balloon. If the balloon is broken, a prize equal to the amount hidden behind the balloon is given. Suppose that each balloon is equally likely to be hit, and that the average chance of a hit is 1/2 for all expected participants. The awards are distributed as follows:

40% have payoff of 5¢   20% have payoff of 25¢
30% have payoff of 10¢   10% have payoff of $1.00

If 15¢ a dart is charged, how much money can the Planning Committee expect to earn if 500 darts are thrown?

Continuous Random Variables

3.4

Probability Density Functions

So far we have examined experiments involving only a discrete set of outcomes, thus limiting ourselves to discrete probability values. As we indicated earlier, however, an outcome set can be continuous as well as discrete; this implies that the random variable in an experiment must be able to assume a continuous form. Continuous random variables are especially convenient to work with, so much so that even when the set of outcomes is discrete it is often advantageous to use a *continuous approximation* to these values. Fortunately, most probability theory is basically the same for discrete and continuous random variables, and the formulas presented in Chapter 2 hold for both cases.

Probability functions defined in terms of a continuous random variable are usually referred to as **probability density functions** (abbreviated p.d.f.), or simply as **density functions.** It is helpful to think of a density function as the frequency polygon for the histogram of a discrete probability function involving a large number of events. Figure 3.6 illustrates what we mean by this, using yearly sales data for a midwestern chain of computer stores.

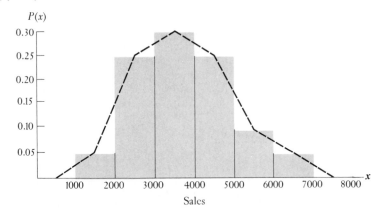

Figure 3.6
Frequency polygon.

Notice how the frequency polygon in Fig. 3.6 serves to smooth the discrete probability values. Now, suppose we decrease the width of the classes, from a class interval of 1000 to a class interval of say 500, or 250, or even to a class interval of 1. In Fig. 3.7, using class intervals of 500 and then of 250, we illustrate the change in the frequency polygon as the width of the interval decreases and the number of intervals increases correspondingly—namely, that it begins to look more and more like a smooth, continuous function. As the width of the class interval goes to zero, the polygon will become a function with no bends or angles.*

---

*For readers with a calculus background, this means that the first derivative exists for all values of x.

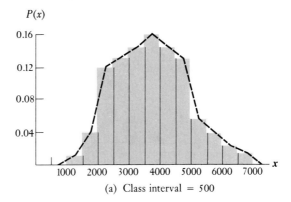

(a) Class interval = 500

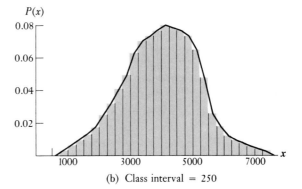

(b) Class interval = 250

Figure 3.7
Frequency polygon for two
different class sizes.

As the width of the class interval goes to zero, the *number* of classes (or events) under consideration must increase until, at the limit (number of classes = ∞), there is an *infinite* number of such events between any two values of x. Because of this fact, one of the important rules of continuous random variables is the following:

For continuous random variables, the probability that any one specific value of x takes place equals zero.

This means that we cannot talk about the probability of a single sample point (it equals zero!); instead, probability must always be defined *over an interval* (between two points). Now, suppose we want to evaluate $P(a \leq x \leq b)$, the probability that the random variable x falls between the two points a and b.* If we had only a finite number of outcomes, this value would be given

---

*Note that, since the probability that any one value of x will occur equals zero, the following is implied:

$$P(a \leq x \leq b) = P(a < x \leq b) = P(a \leq x < b) = P(a < x < b)$$

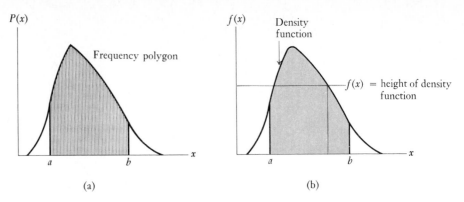

(a)   (b)

Figure 3.8

The continuous approximation to $P(a \leq x \leq b)$.

by summing the probability of each of the events. As the number of events becomes larger and larger, however, the frequency polygon becomes a better approximation to these values (see Fig. 3.8) until, at the limit, it exactly describes the relative frequency of the random variable x. Note in Fig. 3.8 that in using a continuous function to approximate a probability mass function, the sum of the probability "spikes" in part (a) of that figure is approximated by the *area* under the curve in part (b). This curve, which we have labeled $f(x)$, is the probability density function.

The symbol $f(x)$ will be used throughout this book to denote a probability density function, as distinguished from $P(x)$, which represents the probabilities involved in either a density function or a mass function. While the values of $P(x)$ can be specified either by a list of all such values or by means of a formula, the values of $f(x)$ must always be given by a formula since $f(x)$ is a continous function. In this light, the reader is cautioned against making the serious error of interpreting values of $f(x)$ as probabilities. The value of $f(x)$ represents the *height* of the density function at the point x [as shown in Fig. 3.8(b)].

The probability $P(a \leq x \leq b)$ is always given by the total area under the density function $f(x)$ from a to b.*

$$P(a \leq x \leq b) = \left\{ \begin{array}{l} \text{Area under } f(x) \\ \text{from } a \text{ to } b \end{array} \right\}$$

A number of formulas for $f(x)$ will be investigated later in this chapter and in Chapter 4. For now, the diagrams in Fig. 3.9 should suffice to give some insight into the types of functions we will be discussing in detail later in this book. In the first diagram the density function is seen to be a constant, equal to 2.0 for values between $x = 1.0$ and $x = 1.5$, and equal to zero for all other

*From calculus, this area is given by the integral of $f(x)$ from a to b, or $\displaystyle\int_a^b f(x)\,dx$

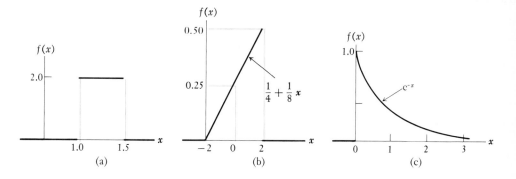

Figure 3.9
Continuous probability functions.

values of x. In this case the random variable x might represent the number of bushels of wheat the USSR buys from the United States in a given year (in millions). Perhaps the United States won't sell less than 1.0 million or more than 1.5 million; hence, $[1.0 \leq x \leq 1.5]$.

In the second diagram, the function $f(x)$ is the straight line $1/4 + (1/8)x$ for values between $x = -2$ and $x = 2$ (and zero otherwise). We might imagine x in this situation to be the error that could occur in certain estimates. For example, in Fig. 3.9(b) x could be the error in estimating the number of cubic yards of concrete needed to complete an office building (there could be an overestimation or underestimation by as much as 2 cubic yards).

In the third diagram, $f(x)$ is a decreasing function for x between zero and infinity.* This type of function is often used in situations where x represents the time between certain events. For example, the time between customers arriving at a retail store, or the time between service needs for certain equipment, often follows the distribution in Fig. 3.9(c).

Probability values determined from a density function must naturally conform to the same probability rules that apply to the values determined from a probability mass function. That is, all probabilities must be greater than or equal to zero, and the total probability must equal one. This means that the function $f(x)$ can never assume a value less than zero, for if it did, the probability (area) associated with the negative range would also be negative, which is not possible. On the other hand, it is not necessary for $f(x)$ always to assume values less than or equal to one; this is because a function whose height is greater than one does not necessarily have a total area greater than one [see Fig. 3.9(a)]. The two properties of a probability density function are thus as follows:

Properties of all probability density functions:

1. $f(x) \geq 0$
2. Area under $f(x)$ equals 1

(3.6)

---

*In Figure 3.9(c), the symbol e denotes the nonrepeating, nonterminating decimal $e = 2.71828\ldots$.

The probability distributions shown in Fig. 3.9 can be *proved* to be proper probability density functions by showing that Properties 1 and 2 both hold. Property 1, which is $f(x) \geq 0$, is easily seen by looking at the graphs in Fig. 3.9. The calculus necessary for Property 2 is shown in the footnote.*

Cumulative Distribution Functions

A cumulative function is convenient for density functions just as it was for mass functions. A **cumulative distribution function** represents the probability that the random variable assumes a value less than or equal to some specified value. As with the discrete case, the symbol $F(x)$ denotes a cumulative function, and is defined as follows.

> *Cumulative distribution function:*
> $$F(x) = P(x \leq x) = \text{area up to } x = x$$

(3.7)

For probability density functions we need a *general* formula for $F(x)$. For example, the formula for $F(x)$ in Fig. 3.9(a) can be shown to be

$$F(x) = \begin{cases} 0 & \text{if } x \leq 1.0 \\ 2x - 2 & \text{if } 1.0 \leq x \leq 1.5 \\ 1.0 & \text{if } x \geq 1.5 \end{cases}$$

Let's check the $2x - 2$ portion of this formula by trying these values: $F(1.0), F(1.25),$ and $F(1.5)$:

$$F(1.0) = 2(1.0) - 2 = 0$$
$$F(1.25) = 2(1.25) - 2 = 0.50$$
$$F(1.5) = 2(1.5) - 2 = 1.0$$

These three values agree with the probability values we know they should assume; thus the general formula appears reasonable.

Formulas for the other two functions in Fig. 3.9 can be calculated in the same manner. We leave it as an exercise for the reader (Problem 3.33) to

---

*a) for $f(x) = \begin{cases} 2 & 1.0 \leq x \leq 1.5 \\ 0 & \text{otherwise} \end{cases}$ $\int_{1}^{3/2} (2)dx = \left[2x \right]_{1}^{3/2} = 1$

b) for $f(x) = \begin{cases} \frac{1}{4} + \frac{1}{8}x & -2 \leq x \leq 2 \\ 0 & \text{otherwise} \end{cases}$ $\int_{-2}^{2} (\frac{1}{4} + \frac{1}{8}x)dx = \left[\frac{1}{4}x + \frac{1}{16}x^2 \right]_{-2}^{2} = 1$

c) for $f(x) = \begin{cases} e^{-x} & 0 \leq x < \infty \\ 0 & \text{otherwise} \end{cases}$ $\int_{0}^{\infty} (e^{-x})dx = \left[-e^{-x} \right]_{0}^{\infty} = 1$

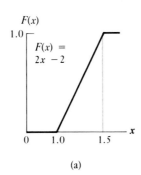 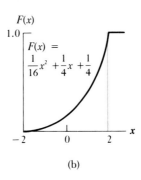 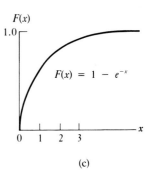

Figure 3.10
Cumulative distribution
functions.

(a) (b) (c)

calculate these general formulas using the definition in the footnote.* The cumulative distribution for all three functions in Fig. 3.9 is graphed in Fig. 3.10.

The function $F(x)$ is especially useful in evaluating the probability that the random variable x falls in the interval between $x = a$ and $x = b$ (where $a < b$). To do this, we use the following rule:

$$P(a \leq x \leq b) = F(b) - F(a) \qquad (3.8)$$

This formula should be intuitively appealing, since $F(b)$ is the probability from minus infinity up to the point $x = b$, and $F(a)$ is the probability from minus infinity up to the point $x = a$. Subtracting the two gives the area between a and b, as shown in Fig. 3.11.

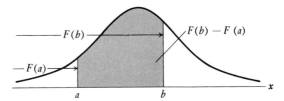

Figure 3.11
Illustrating $P(a \leq x \leq b) = F(b) - F(a)$.

Suppose for the function in Fig. 3.9(a) we want to find $P(1.25 \leq x \leq 1.30)$. This probability can be evaluated as follows:

$$P(1.25 \leq x \leq 1.30) = F(1.30) - F(1.25)$$

Since $F(x) = 2x - 2$ for $1.0 \leq x \leq 1.5$

$$F(1.30) = 2(1.30) - 2 = 0.60, \text{ and}$$
$$F(1.25) = 2(1.25) - 2 = 0.50$$

---

*The definition of $F(x)$ is as follows:

$$F(x) = P(x \leq x) = \int_{-\infty}^{x} f(x)\,dx$$

This means that

$$P(1.25 \leq x \leq 1.30) = 0.60 - 0.50 = 0.10$$

It is important to remember that $f(x)$ is not a probability value, but the height of the density function. On the other hand, $F(x)$ is a probability value, namely, $P(x \leq x)$.

Approximating a Discrete Random Variable by a Continuous Random Variable

3.5

To illustrate the process of approximating discrete probability values with a continuous function, suppose a mail-order book club is interested in a pattern with which its subscribers pay for the books they order. At the same time that a member's order is filled, the customer is sent a bill on which payment is due within five weeks of the shipping date. In analyzing recent records of this book club, it was found that only about 16% of all customers return their payment within the first few weeks; most people wait until weeks 4 or 5 to send in their money. Table 3.5 shows the number of payments received in each of the five weeks for the past 100,000 orders. We will explain column 5 of this table in a moment.

Discrete Case

Suppose we now plot the mass and cumulative functions describing, for each of the five weeks, the probability that a randomly selected customer will make the payment. Figure 3.12 shows the graph of these functions. The tops of the probability lines in this figure form a fairly straight line that has a slope of 0.08

TABLE 3.5

(1) Week payment was received x	(2) Number of payments received f	(3) Relative frequency $f/N = P(x)$	(4) Cumulative relative frequency $F(x)$	(5) $0.08x - 0.04$
1	3,940	0.039	0.039	0.040
2	12,012	0.120	0.159	0.120
3	20,133	0.201	0.360	0.200
4	27,852	0.279	0.639	0.280
5	36,063	0.361	1.000	0.360
Sum	100,000	1.000		

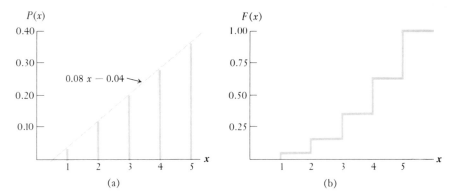

Figure 3.12
Probability functions
representing mail-order
payments.

and a vertical intercept of -0.04. This relationship is shown by the dotted line in Fig. 3.12. An equation that represents the line connecting the tops of the probability values can thus be written as

$$P(x) = 0.08x - 0.04$$

This equation quite accurately describes $P(x)$ for the discrete values $x = 1, 2, 3, 4,$ and 5, as can be seen by comparing columns 3 and 5 in Table 3.5.

Continuous Case

The probabilities shown in Table 3.5 assume that the book club can distinguish only each week ($x = 1, 2, 3, 4,$ or 5) during which a customer's payment was received. But suppose we want a continuous approximation that assumes that a payment can be received at any value of x between 0 and 5. That is, we want to assume that x is a continuous random variable that can assume positive probabilities in the interval $0 \leq x \leq 5$. To make this approximation we need a density function that yields probabilities that are comparable to those in the discrete case—namely, 0.04 that the payment was received *between* the shipping date and the end of the first week [$P(0 \leq x \leq 1) = 0.04$], a probability of 0.12 that the payment was received in the second week [$P(1 \leq x \leq 2) = 0.12$], and so forth, with $P(4 \leq x \leq 5) = 0.36$. Although we omit the details, it is not hard to determine that a function giving this approximation is the following:

$$f(x) = \begin{cases} 0.08x & 0 \leq x \leq 5 \\ 0 & \text{otherwise} \end{cases}$$

The cumulative function formula for this example is

$$F(x) = \begin{cases} 0 & x \leq 0 \\ 0.04x^2 & 0 \leq x \leq 5 \\ 1.0 & x \geq 5 \end{cases}$$

These formulas are shown in Fig. 3.13.

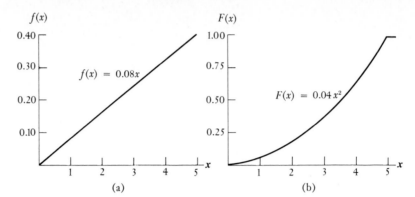

Figure 3.13
Density and cumulative
functions for mail-order
payments.

To show that this density function does, in fact, satisfy our needs, we have calculated the appropriate probabilities as follows:

$$P(0 \leq x \leq 1) = F(1) - F(0) = 0.04 - 0.00 = 0.04$$
$$P(1 \leq x \leq 2) = F(2) - F(1) = 0.16 - 0.04 = 0.12$$
$$P(2 \leq x \leq 3) = F(3) - F(2) = 0.36 - 0.16 = 0.20$$
$$P(3 \leq x \leq 4) = F(4) - F(3) = 0.64 - 0.36 = 0.28$$
$$P(4 \leq x \leq 5) = F(5) - F(4) = 1.00 - 0.64 = 0.36$$

It is also not difficult to show that $f(x) = 0.08x$ satisfies both Properties 1 and 2 for continuous frequency functions, as its value is always positive when $0 \leq x \leq 5$, and $P(0 \leq x \leq 5) = 1.0$.

The Expected Value and Variance of a Linear Transformation (Optional)*

3.6

The Transformation (a + bx)

In statistics a random variable is often transformed into a new variable. One common transformation is $y = a + bx$, where a and b are constants, x is the old random variable, and y is the new variable. This is called a *linear transformation*. When a variable is transformed, we would like to be able to determine the mean and variance of the new variable (y) knowing only the mean and variance of the old variable (x). The following formulas do this for the linear transformation $y = a + bx$.

$$E[y] = E[a + bx] = E[a] + E[bx] = a + bE[x]$$
$$V[y] = V[a + bx] = V[a] + V[bx] = 0 + b^2 V[x] = b^2 V[x]$$

(3.9)

Note: This optional section does not require calculus.

TABLE 3.6   Hours and wages for a computer consultant

(1) Month	(2) Hours	(3) Wages $y = 1000 + 135x$
1	15	3025
2	8	2080
3	10	2350
4	12	2620
5	22	3970
6	17	3295
7	28	4780
8	5	1675
9	0	1000
10	6	1810
11	10	2350
12	14	2890
$E[x] = 12.25$		$E[y] = ?$
$V[x] = 53.854$		$V[y] = ?$

In words, Formula (3.9) says that a linear transformation on x changes the mean by the same linear transformation. The variance of the new variable, y, however, equals the variance of x multiplied by the *square* of the constant b.

To illustrate these two formulas, suppose a computer consultant to a major company charges a retainer of $1000 per month, plus $135/hour. For this person we let x = hours worked, and let $y = 1000 + 135x$ represent total monthly wages. Table 3.6 presents the values of x for the past 12 months, the mean and variance of x, as well as the values of y.

We can find $E[y]$ and $V[y]$ directly, by using the data in column 3. An easier way to determine these values is to use Formula (3.9), as follows.

$$E[y] = E[1000 + 135x] = 1000 + 135E[x] = 1000 + 135(12.25)$$
$$= 2653.75$$
$$V[x] = V[1000 + 135x] = V[1000] + V[135x] = (135)^2 V[x]$$
$$= 18{,}225(53.854) = 981{,}489.15$$

The reader may wish to verify that the mean and variance of column 3 are, indeed, 2653.75 and 981,489.15, respectively (with some rounding error for $V[y]$).

The Transformation $(x - \mu)/\sigma$

A very important special case of the linear transformation $(a + bx)$ occurs when the random variable x is transformed by subtracting μ from each value of *x*, and then by dividing each resulting deviation $(x - \mu)$ by σ. The letter *z* is usually used to denote this transformation. We will write the transformation as $z = (x - \mu)/\sigma$ and call it a "standardization" of the variable *x*.

The standardization $z = (x - \mu)/\sigma$ transforms any variable *x* into a new variable *z*, which has a mean of zero and a variance of one

---

The new variable *z* is important for the comparison of distributions having different means and variances. Chapter 5 describes in detail the usefulness of this standardization. For now, you might think about how the admissions office at your university would compare a candidate with a score of 600 on a test whose average is 500 and variance is 100, with another candidate who has scored 45 on a comparable test where the mean is 40 and the standard deviation is 3.3. Standardization is one way to compare such scores. A standardized value (i.e., a *z* value) indicates how many standard deviations an *x*-value falls above or below the mean.

Our interest in this chapter is merely in demonstrating that the expected value of $z = (x - \mu)/\sigma$ is zero, and its variance is 1.0. It is easy to show that $E[z] = E[(x - \mu)/\sigma] = 0$. Intuitively, we know that the mean is the balance point of any distribution. Some values of *x* are above μ and some are below μ, so that the weighted average of all the values of *x* is μ. Thus, the weighted average of all the differences between the values of *x* and μ must be zero. Since zero divided by any constant, including the standard deviation σ, is still zero, it is reasonable that $E[z] = 0$. For the interested reader, we formally prove $E[z] = 0$ and $V[z] = 1$ in the footnote.* An example illustrating these properties is illustrated below. Consider again the hours-worked data from Table 3.6, and replicated in Table 3.7. In this table we also show the values of $(x - \mu)/\sigma$, in column 4, where $\mu = 12.25$ and $\sigma = \sqrt{53.854} = 7.3385$.

Column 4 represents the standardization of *x*. The reader may wish to verify that, for Column 4, $E[z] = 0$ and $V[z] = 1$. The *z*-values indicate how far away each value of *x* is from the mean (μ), measured in units equal to one standard deviation. For example, note that $\sigma = 7.3385$. The *z*-score for $x = 28$ in Table 3.7 is 2.1462, which indicates that the value of 28 is slightly more than two standard deviations above the mean (of 12.25).

---

*Using the rules presented in Formula (3.9),

$$E[z] = E\left[\frac{x - \mu}{\sigma}\right] = E\left[\frac{x}{\sigma}\right] - E\left[\frac{\mu}{\sigma}\right] = \frac{1}{\sigma}E[x] - \frac{1}{\sigma}E[\mu]$$

$$= \frac{1}{\sigma}(\mu) - \frac{1}{\sigma}(\mu) = 0$$

$$V[z] = V\left[\frac{x - \mu}{\sigma}\right] = V\left[\frac{x}{\sigma}\right] - V\left[\frac{\mu}{\sigma}\right] = \frac{1}{\sigma^2}V[x] - \frac{1}{\sigma^2}V[\mu]$$

$$= \frac{1}{\sigma^2}(\sigma^2) - 0 = 1$$

TABLE 3.7   Calculating z-scores for the hours and wages data

(1) Month	(2) x (hours)	(3) $(x - \mu)$	(4) $(x - \mu)/\sigma = z$
1	15	2.75	0.3747
2	8	− 4.25	− 0.5791
3	10	− 2.25	− 0.3066
4	12	− 0.25	− 0.0341
5	22	9.75	1.3286
6	17	4.75	0.6473
7	28	15.75	2.1462
8	5	− 7.25	− 0.9879
9	0	− 12.25	− 1.6693
10	6	− 6.25	− 0.8517
11	10	− 2.25	− 0.3066
12	14	1.75	0.2385
Mean	12.2500	0	0
Variance	53.8540	53.8540	1
Std. Dev.	7.3385	7.3385	1

□ Expected Value: The Continuous Case (Optional)*

3.7

The formulas on expected value thus far apply only to discrete data. Formulas for the continuous case follow directly from Formulas (3.2) and (3.4) by substituting an integral sign for the summation notation and using $f(x)dx$ instead of $P(x)$. The continuous analogies to Formulas (3.2) and (3.4) are

> *Expected value of x (continuous case):*
> $$E[x] = \mu = \int_{\text{All } x} xf(x)dx$$
> *Variance of x (continuous case):*
> $$V[x] = \sigma^2 = \int_{\text{All } x} (x - \mu)^2 f(x)dx$$

(3.10)

As before, the variance of x is denoted as either σ^2 or $V[x]$, and the standard deviation is denoted as σ, where $\sigma = \sqrt{V[x]}$.

---

*Note: This optional section requires calculus.

We can illustrate the process of using Formula (3.10) by recalling the density function used to approximate the discrete data in the book-club problem:

$$f(x) = \begin{cases} 0.08x & 0 \le x \le 5 \\ 0 & \text{otherwise} \end{cases}$$

$$\mu = E[x] = \int_0^5 x(0.08x)dx = \int_0^5 0.08x^2\, dx = [0.08x^3/3]_0^5$$
$$= 3.33$$

$$\sigma^2 = V[x] = \int_0^5 (x - 3.33)^2(0.08x)dx = 1.41$$

$$\sigma = \sqrt{\sigma^2} = \sqrt{1.41} = 1.19$$

Note that the mean and variance for this density function are not identical to the values $\mu = 3.80$ and $\sigma^2 = 1.36$ obtained in the discrete analysis. The mean is lower and the variance is larger in the continuous case because of the way the data are aggregated: All customers paying within a given week are counted as paying at the *end* of that week in the discrete case, while customers are assumed to be paying *throughout* the five-week period in the continuous case. The discrete probability values begin at $x = 1$, the continuous values at $x = 0$; hence, the latter set of outcomes has a lower mean and is more spread out.

Problems

Note: Those problems or parts of problems marked with a ☐ require some knowledge of calculus.

3.16 Explain, intuitively, why for continuous functions that

    a) $P(x = x) = 0$;

    b) $P(x) \ne f(x)$, in general;

    c) $F(x)$ differs from $f(x)$;

    d) $f(x)$ can be larger than 1.0.

3.17 Verify that the mean is zero and the variance is one for the data in column 4 of Table 3.7.

3.18 The random variance x = time of arrival of the first customer at a certain store (where x is in hours) is defined as follows:

$$f(x) = \begin{cases} 2x & \text{for } 0 \le x \le 1 \\ 0 & \text{otherwise} \end{cases}$$

    a) Sketch the p.d.f. and show that it meets the two properties of all density functions.

    b) What is $P(x \le 1/2)$? Find and interpret $F(1)$.

☐ **3.19 a)** Find $E[x]$ and $V[x]$ for the p.d.f. in Problem 3.18.

    b) Find the median of the function. (*Hint:* Half of the area lies to the left of the median.)

    c) Find the area between $\mu \pm 2\sigma$ and compare this area with the 95% rule of thumb.

3.20 a) For Problem 3.18, $F(x) = x^2$ for $0 \le x \le 1$. Find the value of $F(x)$ for: $x = 0$, $x = 1/2$, $x = 0.707$, $x = 1.0$, $x = 3.7$.

    b) Sketch this cumulative function.

3.21 From phase I to phase II, a glass furnace takes between 1 hour and 1 1/2 hours ($1 \le x \le 3/2$) to reach operating temperature. The actual time required follows the p.d.f.:

$$f(x) = \begin{cases} 2x - 1/2 & 1 \le x \le 3/2 \\ 0 & \text{otherwise} \end{cases}$$

    a) Graph $f(x)$ and show that it meets the two properties of all density functions.

    b) Find $P(5/4 \le x \le 3/2)$ using the graph in (a).

    c) Find the area between $\mu \pm 1\sigma$ and $\mu \pm 2\sigma$ and compare these values to the rule of thumb. Use a graphical approach.

☐ **d)** Find $F(x)$ and graph this function.

☐ **e)** Find $P(5/4 \le x \le 3/2)$ using $F(b) - F(a)$.

☐ **f)** Repeat part (c) using $F(b) - F(a)$.

3.22 With the improved relationship between the United States and the Soviet Union, numerous business opportunities have opened up. An American manufacturer has decided to export a certain type of personal computer to the USSR. The manufacturer estimates that annual demand (d) can be represented by the following p.d.f., where d is in thousands of units:

$$f(x) = \begin{cases} (d - 30)/450 & \text{for } 30 \le d \le 60 \\ 0 & \text{otherwise} \end{cases}$$

    a) Sketch this function and verify that the area under $f(x)$ equals 1.0.

    b) Find $P(d > 45)$ and $F(50)$.

☐ **c)** Find the expected number of sales.

☐ **3.23** Consider the following p.d.f., where x = the square yards of waste (per room) in laying floor tile for a major office complex.

$$f(x) = \begin{cases} 4/3 - x^2 & 0 \le x \le 1 \\ 0 & \text{otherwise} \end{cases}$$

    a) Sketch this p.d.f. and show that it meets the two conditions of all density functions.

    b) What is the probability of more than 1/2 square yards of waste?

3.24 A *Car and Driver* study of the accuracy of automobile speedometers at 50 miles per hour found that they varied from 2 miles per hour too slow to

2 miles per hour too fast. A statistician has used the following p.d.f. to describe the error of a randomly selected speedometer.

$$f(x) = \begin{cases} 1/4 & \text{for } -2 \le x \le 2 \\ 0 & \text{otherwise} \end{cases}$$

a) Sketch this p.d.f. and show that the area is 1.0.

b) What is the probability that a randomly selected speedometer is more than 1 mile per hour (mph) too fast? What percent of the speedometers will be in error by more than 1 mph?

c) Determine a formula for $F(x)$ either intuitively, or by using calculus. Find $F(0)$, $F(-1)$, and $F(2)$ using this formula.

d) Use the formula from part (c) to determine

$$P(-1 \le x \le 1)$$

3.25 An Occupational Safety and Health Administration (OSHA) safety expert has determined that most industrial accidents occur during the last hour of an eight-hour shift. The following p.d.f. accurately describes the time of the accident (x = time, in hours).

$$f(x) = \begin{cases} 3x^2 & 0 \le x \le 1 \\ 0 & \text{otherwise} \end{cases}$$

☐ **a)** Sketch this function, showing that it meets the two p.d.f. conditions.

☐ **b)** Find the formula for $F(x)$. Use this formula to find $F(1/4) = P(x \le 1/4)$.

3.26 The Yarn Basket is a small retail store. The dollar values of daily sales for the first 10 days of the month are 175, 188, 196, 202, 194, 215, 188, 194, 196, and 202.

a) Find the mean of this population (each value has probability 1/10).

b) Find σ^2 and σ.

c) What percentage of the observations fall within $\mu \pm 1\sigma$ and $\mu \pm 2\sigma$?

d) Repeat parts (a) and (b), subtracting 175 from each observation. How does this subtraction affect μ? How does it affect σ^2?

3.27 An entrepreneur is faced with two investment opportunities that each require an initial outlay of $10,000. The estimated return on investment x will be either $40,000, $20,000, or 0, with probabilities of 0.25, 0.50, and 0.25, respectively. For investment y the returns will be $30,000, $20,000, or $10,000 with probabilities of one-third in each case.

a) Compute $E[x]$ and $E[y]$.

b) Check your calculations in (a) by first dividing each value of x and y by 10,000, then calculating the mean of the two new sets of numbers, and finally determining $E[x]$ and $E[y]$ by multiplying the results by 10,000.

c) Compute $V[x]$ and $V[y]$. Try to check your answer by again dividing by 10,000. Determine the relationship between $V[x]$ and $V[x/10,000]$ and $V[x]/10,000$.

3.28 The data in the table at the top of the next page represent the sales of cars for one brand of the major automobile companies for each of the past four years.

x
1,751,000
1,389,000
1,512,000
1,456,000

$E[x] = ?$

a) Calculate the four values of $y = a + bx$, if $a = -1500$ and $b = 1/1000$.

b) Calculate $E[x]$ by calculating $E[y] = E[a + bx]$ first, and then using the following formula:

$$E[x] = \frac{E[a + bx] - a}{b}$$

c) Calculate $V[x]$ by finding $V[a + bx]$ first, and then by solving

$$V[x] = \frac{V[a + bx]}{b^2}$$

3.29 Reconsider the stock market example on page 94. Divide each value of x by 5, and then subtract 15 from each of the resulting values.

a) Calculate $E[y]$ and $V[y]$ for this new variable $(x/5) - 15 = y$.

b) Based on the fact that $E[x] = 96$ and $V[x] = 64$, show how you could have predicted the values in part (a) using the formulas in (3.9).

3.30 Suppose that you are offered the opportunity to participate in an experiment in which a fair coin is tossed until the first tail appears. If a tail appears on the first toss you will be paid $2 for participating. If the first tail appears on the second toss, you will be paid $4 for participating. You will be paid $8 if the first tail appears on the third toss, and $16 if the first tail appears on the fourth toss; in other words, your payment is increased by a factor of 2 for each head that appears, the game ending with the appearance of a tail.

a) How much would you be willing to pay to participate in this game? (If you said less than $2 you don't understand the game.)

b) Determine the expected value for this game. Are you willing to pay more or less than the expected value of the game? Explain why.

3.31 A recent court case in Chicago centered on the hiring of minorities versus nonminorities for clerical positions in a bank. To analyze this type of problem, the applicants can be classified using the random variable $x = 1$ for a minority candidate and $x = 0$ for a nonminority candidate.

a) If $p = 0.30$ that a candidate is a minority, what is the expected value and variance of x?

b) Find a general expression for $E[x]$ and $V[x]$ for any value of p.

3.32 Nurses who work the night shift at a hospital in Atlanta are paid $15 per hour plus a bonus of $12 per day.

a) Describe the linear transformation to convert the hours (x) worked by a nurse on a given night to that day's total wages. If a nurse works 10 nights every two weeks, and x hours, what is the transformation?

b) The payroll for a two-week period included eight nurses, all of whom worked 10 nights, but worked varying hours, as follows: 75, 80, 80, 72, 82, 80, 76, 77. Assume these values represent a random variable x. Find the mean and variance of x.

c) Find the mean and variance of y, where y is the wages for the two-week period.

d) Standardize the values of y in part (c), and show that $E[z] = 0$ and $V[z] = 1$ for these values. Interpret the value of z for $x = 82$.

☐ **3.33** Return to the density functions in Fig. 3.9.

a) For part (b), find a formula for $F(x)$, and then use this formula to find $F(-2), F(0), F(2)$, and $P(-1 \le x \le 1)$.

b) For part (c), verify that $F(x) = 1 - e^{-x}$, when $x \ge 0$. Find $F(0), F(1)$, and $F(\infty)$, and $P(0 \le x \le 2)$.

Discrete Bivariate Probability (Optional)*

3.8

In some situations an experiment involves outcomes that are related to two (or more) random variables. This section covers the theory of such probability functions, which is called **multivariate probability functions.** In this book only the case of **bivariate probability functions** (two variables) will be covered.

The function describing the probability of two random variables is often called a **joint probability function.** For the two random variables x and y, the joint probability that $x = x$ and $y = y$ is written as follows:

> *Joint probability that $x = x$ and $y = y$:*
> $$P(x = x \text{ and } y = y) = P(x, y)$$

As we will show shortly, most of the univariate rules discussed thus far have comparable rules in the bivariate (or multivariate) case. For example, the two properties of all probability functions presented in Section 3.2 have direct counterparts for joint probability functions:

$$\text{Property 1: } 0 \le P(x, y) \le 1$$
$$\text{Property 2: } \sum_{\text{All } x} \sum_{\text{All } y} P(x, y) = 1$$

These and other properties of joint probability functions will be discussed as we progress through this section.

To illustrate a joint probability distribution, let's examine the results of an Indiana University study designed to investigate the relationship between the number of jobs a college graduate holds in the first five years after graduation (x), and the number of promotions (y). Two hundred recent college graduates of comparable age and undergraduate background were surveyed and then classified according to the number of jobs and promotions they received in their first five years out of college. The results of this study are

---

Note: this optional section does not require calculus.

TABLE 3.8   Frequencies for jobs—promotions study

Marginal		Number of promotions (y)				
		1	2	3	4	Total
Number of jobs (x)	1	20	30	24	12	86
	2	10	14	20	10	54
	3	8	4	28	20	60
Marginal total		38	48	72	42	200

given in Tables 3.8 and 3.9. For example, $P(x = 2, y = 3) = P(2, 3)$ is the joint probability that one person drawn randomly from this study had two jobs and was promoted three times in the five years. Table 3.8 shows that 20 people of the total of 200 had these characteristics; hence $P(2, 3) = 20/200 = 0.10$ is the value shown in Table 3.9. Similarly, the probability a person had one job and four promotions is $P(1, 4) = 0.06$.

Analogous to a cumulative probability function for a single random variable is the cumulative joint probability function. This function is denoted as $F(x, y)$ as defined as:

Cumulative joint probability: $F(x, y) = P(x \leq x \text{ and } y \leq y)$

The value of $F(2, 3) = P(x \leq 2 \text{ and } y \leq 3)$ in Table 3.9 can be seen to equal $P(1, 1) + P(1, 2) + P(1, 3) + P(2, 1) + P(2, 2) + P(2, 3) = 0.59$. Note that $F(x, y)$, like $F(x)$, can assume values only between 0 and 1.0.

TABLE 3.9   Probabilities for jobs—promotions study

Marginal		Number of promotions (y)				
		1	2	3	4	Total
Number of jobs (x)	1	0.10	0.15	0.12	0.06	0.43
	2	0.05	0.07	0.10	0.05	0.27
	3	0.04	0.02	0.14	0.10	0.30
Marginal total		0.19	0.24	0.36	0.21	1.00

Marginal Probability

The concept of a marginal probability used here is the same as that discussed in Chapter 2 except that now in using abbreviations we must be careful not to confuse the marginal probability $P(x = x)$ with the marginal probability $P(y = y)$. For instance, it is not clear if $P(2)$ refers to the former or latter case. To make this distinction we will abbreviate $P(x = 2)$ as $P_x(2)$ and abbreviate $P(y = 2)$ as $P_y(2)$. With this notation, and using Formula (2.10) as a reference, we can write the marginal probability of x and y as follows:

> *Marginal probability of x:* $P_x(x) = \sum_{\text{All } y} P(x, y)$
>
> *Marginal probability of y:* $P_y(y) = \sum_{\text{All } x} P(x, y)$

Table 3.9 can be used to illustrate these probabilities.

$$P_x(1) = \sum_{\text{All } y} P(1, y) = P(1, 1) + P(1, 2) + P(1, 3) + P(1, 4)$$
$$= 0.10 + 0.15 + 0.12 + 0.06 = 0.43$$

$$P_y(3) = \sum_{\text{All } x} P(x, 3) = P(1, 3) + P(2, 3) + P(3, 3)$$
$$= 0.12 + 0.10 + 0.14 = 0.36$$

Thus we can conclude that the probability is 0.43 that a person randomly selected from this population will have exactly one job, while 0.36 is the probability a person will have exactly three promotions.

Conditional Probability

A conditional probability for two random variables x and y is defined in the same manner as in Chapter 2, but again we have to be careful about notation. Suppose we let $P_{x|y}(x|y)$ denote the conditional probability $P(x = x|y = y)$, and $P_{y|x}(y|x)$ denote $P(y = y|x = x)$.

> *Conditional probability of x, given y:*
>
> $$P_{x|y}(x|y) = P(x = x|y = y) = \frac{P(x, y)}{P_y(y)}$$
>
> *Conditional probability of y, given x:*
>
> $$P_{y|x}(y|x) = P(y = y|x = x) = \frac{P(x, y)}{P_x(x)}$$

The first formula can be used to calculate $P_{x|y}(2|3)$ from Table 3.9:

$$P_{x|y}(2|3) = P(x = 2|y = 3) = \frac{P(2, 3)}{P_y(3)}$$

Since $P(2, 3) = 0.10$ and $P_y(3) = 0.36$,

$$P_{x|y}(2|3) = \frac{0.10}{0.36} = 0.278$$

In other words, if it is known that a person had three promotions, the probability that this person had exactly two jobs is 0.278.

Independence

Just as we were able in Chapter 2 to determine whether or not two events are independent, so in the present context we can determine whether or not two random variables are independent. The test for independence in the two cases is very similar. In order for two random variables to be independent, all the joint probability values must equal the product of their marginal values. That is, if x and y are independent, then the following relationship must hold for all values of x and y.

> Joint probability of x and y if independent:
> $$P(x, y) = P_x(x) P_y(y)$$ (3.11)

If the above relationship does not hold for *all* possible combinations of x and y, then these variables are not independent. Only one violation is necessary. For the data in Table 3.9, it is easily shown that *none* of the pairs x and y satisfies Formula (3.11). For example, $P(1, 2) = 0.15$, but this value is not equal to the product $P_x(1)P_y(2) = (0.43)(0.24) = 0.1032$. Thus, we can conclude that the number of jobs and promotions a person has had are *not* independent.

Bivariate Expectations (Optional)*

3.9

We have discussed the important measures of the mean, $\mu = E[x]$, and the variance, $V[x] = \sigma^2$, for a single random variable. These same measures can be used to describe similar concepts in bivariate problems. Suppose we write a function of two variables x and y as $g(x, y)$. In general, the expectation of such a function is given as follows:

> Expected value of $g(x, y)$:
> $$E[g(x, y)] = \sum_{\text{All } y} \sum_{\text{All } x} g(x, y) P(x, y)$$ (3.12)

*Note: This optional section does not require calculus.

For example, we may want to find the expected value of the product of x times y, written as $x \cdot y$, in which case $g(x, y) = x \cdot y$ and

$$E[x \cdot y] = \sum_{\text{All } x} \sum_{\text{All } y} (x \cdot y) P(x, y)$$

Similarly, if $g(x, y) = x + y$, then

$$E[x + y] = \sum_{y} \sum_{x} (x + y) P(x, y).$$

We now investigate these two special cases of Formula (3.12).

Expectations of x · y

To illustrate Formula (3.12) when $g(x, y) = x \cdot y$, consider the case of Black Lumber Yard, which sells plywood in two lengths, 4 ft and 8 ft, and in three different widths, 2 ft, 4 ft, and 6 ft. Black Lumber is interested in determining the average amount of paneling sold in terms of area (square feet). That is, they want to determine $E[x \cdot y]$, where x = length and y = width. By the basic permutation rules, there are $(n_1)(n_2) = (2)(3) = 6$ different arrangements of widths and lengths sold. The distributions $P(x)$, $P(y)$, and $P(x, y)$ for the sale of these six combinations, based on company records, are given in Table 3.10. The final column shows that the average square feet of paneling sold is $\mu = 30.80$.

Expectation of x · y when x and y are independent

One special instance of the expectation case of $x \cdot y$ is worth noting: the case in which the variables x and y are independent.

> *Expectation of $x \cdot y$, assuming independence:*
> $E[x \cdot y] = E[x] E[y]$ (3.13)

We will illustrate Formula (3.13) by considering the choices made by a university's faculty and staff involving their Blue Cross/Blue Shield medical

TABLE 3.10   Plywood paneling

x	$P(x)$	$xP(x)$	y	$P(y)$	$yP(y)$	x, y	$P(x, y)$	Area $x \cdot y$	$(x \cdot y)P(x, y)$
4	0.20	0.80	2	0.15	0.30	(4, 2)	0.05	8	0.40
8	0.80	6.40	4	0.55	2.20	(4, 4)	0.05	16	0.80
			6	0.30	1.80	(4, 6)	0.10	24	2.40
						(8, 2)	0.10	16	1.60
						(8, 4)	0.50	32	16.00
						(8, 6)	0.20	48	9.60
Sum	1.00	7.20		1.00	4.30		1.00	$E[x \cdot y] = 30.80$	

insurance plan. This case, slightly modified to make the arithmetic easier, involves asking each employee to select one of three plans: (1) $200 deductible, with high monthly rates, (2) $400 deductible, with moderate monthly rates, or (3) $800 deductible, with low monthly rates. These choices are denoted by $x = 2$, 4, or 8. A second choice available to each employee is the (optional) dental plan. This choice is denoted by $y = 1$ (not select) or $y = 2$ (select). The probability distributions of $P(x)$, $P(y)$, and $P(x, y)$, based on the enrollments through 1990, are given in the matrix below.

		Dental Plan (y)		
		1	2	$P(x)$
	2	0.24	0.16	0.40
Deductible (x)	4	0.12	0.08	0.20
	8	0.24	0.16	0.40
	$P(x)$	0.60	0.40	$1.00 = \Sigma\Sigma P(x, y)$

On the basis of these data, is the choice between a deductible dependent on or independent of the choice of a dental plan? (That is, are they statistically unrelated decisions?) To answer this, note for the matrix above that

$$P(x, y) = P_x(x)P_y(y) \text{ for all } x \text{ and } y$$

For example, in the first cell, $0.24 = (0.40)(0.60)$. Since all such products hold, this means that x and y are independent. This fact can also be demonstrated by using some of the rules of expectations presented earlier in this chapter. Table 3.11 gives the data for the calculations described below. From columns 3 and 6 of Table 3.11, we see that

$$E[x]E[y] = (4.80)(1.40) = 6.72$$

TABLE 3.11 Blue Cross/Blue Shield example

(1) x	(2) $P(x)$	(3) $xP(x)$	(4) y	(5) $P(y)$	(6) $yP(y)$	(7) (x, y)	(8) $P(x, y)$	(9) $(x \cdot y)P(x, y)$
2	0.40	0.80	1	0.60	0.60	(2, 1)	0.24	$(2)(0.24) = 0.48$
4	0.20	0.80	2	0.40	0.80	(2, 2)	0.16	$(4)(0.16) = 0.64$
8	0.40	3.20				(4, 1)	0.12	$(4)(0.12) = 0.48$
						(4, 2)	0.08	$(8)(0.08) = 0.64$
						(8, 1)	0.24	$(8)(0.24) = 1.92$
						(8, 2)	0.16	$(16)(0.16) = 2.56$
Sum 1.00		4.80		1.00	1.40		1.00	$E[x \cdot y] = 6.72$

This is the same result as that given in column 9,

$$E[x \cdot y] = 6.72$$

This result verifies that x and y are, indeed, independent.

Covariance of x and y

At this point we introduce another measure of variation that is very important in most statistical analysis—**the covariance of x and y** (which we denote as $C[x,y]$). The covariance of two random variables is a measure of how they vary together (how they "covary"). If we let

$$\mu_x = E[x] \qquad \text{and} \qquad \mu_y = E[y], \qquad \text{then}$$

Covariance of x and y: $C[x,y] = E[(x - \mu_x)(y - \mu_y)]$ (3.14)

Like a variance, a covariance is somewhat difficult to interpret. If high values of x (high relative to μ_x) tend to be associated with high values of y (relative to μ_y), and low values associated with low values, then $C[x, y]$ will be a large positive number.* If the covariance is a large negative number, this means that low values of one variable tend to be associated with high values of the other, and vice versa. If two variables are independent, then $C[x,y] = 0$ (that is, they are not related).

To calculate the covariance, we could use the definition of $E[g(x,y)]$ in Formula (3.12). Rather than do this, we present an equivalent formula that is much more convenient computationally:

$$C[x,y] = E[x \cdot y] - E[x]E[y] \qquad (3.15)$$

In the formulas dealing with the covariances, if one merely substitutes the variance x wherever the variable y occurs, the result is a variance formula. For example, $C[x, y]$ becomes $C[x, x]$, which by Formulas (3.14) and (3.4), is seen to be exactly the same as $V[x]$.

Now let's use Formula (3.15) to calculate $C[x, y]$ for the data in Table 3.10. From that table, $E[x] = 7.20$, $E[y] = 4.30$, and $E[x \cdot y] = 30.80$:

$$C[x,y] = E[x \cdot y] - E[x]E[y]$$
$$= 30.80 - (7.20)(4.30) = -0.16$$

The covariance in this case is close to zero, which means that the relationship between the length (x) and the width (y) of the lumber sold is not very strong.

If x and y are independent, we know from Formula (3.13) that $E[x \cdot y] = E[x]E[y]$. Substituting this relationship into Formula (3.15) yields a

---

*This is because when $(x - \mu_x)$ is $+$, $(y - \mu_y)$ tends to be $+$, and when $(x - \mu_x)$ is $-$, $(y - \mu_y)$ tends to be $-$; hence the sign of $(x - \mu_x)(y - \mu_y)$ tends to be positive.

result that has already been stated; *when x and y are independent, then their covariance is zero.* *

Covariance when x and y are independent:

$$C[x,y] = E[x]E[y] - E[x]E[y] = 0$$

Expectations of *ax + by*

A special case of $E[g(x,y)]$ of importance is when

$$g(x,y) = ax + by$$

where a and b are constants.

> *Expected value of (ax + by):*
>
> $$E[ax + by] = \sum_y \sum_x (ax + by)P(x,y)$$
> $$= aE[x] + bE[y]$$

(3.16)

We will illustrate Formula (3.16) by considering the special case in which the constants a and b both equal $+1.0$. This makes our algebra easier while still maintaining the essence of the process. Thus, we will demonstrate that

$$E[x + y] = E[x] + E[y]$$

Consider a company that specializes in shipping oranges and grapefruits from their grove and store near Nokomos, Florida. The company is currently trying to analyze the total weight of their packages in order to better control mailing costs. The fruit boxes come in three weights, 5, 10, or 20 pounds, which we denote as $x = \{5, 10, 20\}$. This company always adds a "gift" to each package, randomly selecting either a box of fruit candy or a small jar of orange marmalade. The box of candy weighs 1/2 pound, the marmalade weighs 1 pound. The gifts will be denoted as $y = \{0.5, 1\}$. The company is interested in determining the average weight of each package, or $E[x + y]$, where x = weight of the fruit and y = weight of the gift. The probability distribution of $P(x)$, $P(y)$, and $P(x,y)$, based on sales records, is given in Table 3.12.

From the final column of Table 3.12 we see that the average weight of the packages is 10.50 pounds. This result is also obtained by summing the totals of columns 3 and 6. Thus, we have shown that

$$E[x] + E[y] = E[x + y] = 9.75 + 0.75 = 10.50$$

Generally, it is easier to find $E[x + y]$ by summing $E[x] + E[y]$.

---

*The converse of this relationship does not necessarily hold true.

TABLE 3.12   Package weight example

(1) Weight of fruit (x)	(2) $P(x)$	(3) $xP(x)$	(4) Weight of gift (y)	(5) $P(y)$	(6) $yP(y)$	(7) (x, y)	(8) $P(x, y)$	(9) $(x + y)$	(10) $(x + y)P(x, y)$
5	0.45	2.25	0.5	0.50	0.25	(5, 0.5)	0.20	5.5	1.100
10	0.35	3.50	1.0	0.50	0.50	(5, 1)	0.25	6.0	1.500
20	0.20	4.00				(10, 0.5)	0.15	10.5	1.575
						(10, 1)	0.20	11.0	2.200
						(20, 0.5)	0.15	20.5	3.075
						(20, 1)	0.05	21.0	1.050
Sum	1.00	9.75		1.00	0.75		1.00		10.500

Variance of ($ax + by$)

Our final discussion in this chapter involves calculating $V[ax + by]$, where a and b are constants. Although the formula given below is presented without proof, its derivation is not difficult using the concepts provided in this chapter.

> *Variance of ($ax + by$):* *
> $$V[ax + by] = a^2V[x] + b^2V[y] + 2abC[x, y]$$

(3.17)

We will not try to illustrate Formula (3.17) for various values of a and b, but again will consider the special case where a and b both equal 1.0. That is, we will illustrate the simpler rule,

$$V[x + y] = V[x] + V[y] + 2C[x, y]$$

by applying it to the data in Table 3.10. Although we don't present the calculations, the values of $V[x]$ and $V[y]$ for the data from that table (on page 120) can be shown to be

$$V[x] = 2.56 \quad \text{and} \quad V[y] = 1.71$$

Since we previously calculated $C[x, y] = -0.16$, we can write

$$V[x + y] = V[x] + V[y] + 2C[x, y]$$
$$= 2.56 + 1.71 + 2(-0.16)$$
$$= 3.95$$

---

*The reader should note that variance rule presented on page 108 is merely a special case of Formula (3.17), in which one of the variables is a constant. Also, the sign of the last term in (3.17) will be negative if either a or b is negative (but not both), or if the covariance is negative.

TABLE 3.13   **Bivariate expectation formulas**

Function	Formulas	Special case of independence
1. Mean of $(x \cdot y)$	$E[x \cdot y] = \sum\sum(x \cdot y)P(x, y)$	$E[x]E[y]$
2. Covariance of $(x$ and $y)$	$C[x, y] = E[x \cdot y] - E[x]E[y]$	0
3. Mean of $(ax + by)$	$E[ax + by] = aE[x] + bE[y]$	No change
4. Variance of $(ax + by)$	$V[ax + by] = a^2V[x] + b^2V[y] + 2abC[x, y]$	$a^2V[x] + b^2V[y]$

Independence

As stated earlier, when x and y are independent, then $C[x, y] = 0$; hence

$$Special \; case \; for \; independent \; random \; variables \; x \; and \; y:$$
$$V[ax + by] = a^2V[x] + b^2V[y]$$

(3.18)

Note that Formula (3.18) implies that if $a = 1$ and $b = \pm 1$, then

$$V[x + y] = V[x - y] = V[x] + V[y]$$

Expressed in words, the variance of the sum or difference of the two variables that are independent always equals the *sum* of the two variances calculated separately. The reader can verify this fact by using the data in Table 3.11 to show that

$$V[x + y] = V[x - y] = V[x] + V[y] = 7.36 + 0.24 = 7.60$$

A summary of the bivariate expectation formulas from this section is provided in Table 3.13.

Problems

3.34 A study was conducted to determine if three levels of manual dexterity $(x = 1, 2, 3)$, and three categories of intelligence $\{y = 1, 2, 3\}$ are independent for production workers in an automobile company. The following joint probability table reflects the results of this study.

		x (dexterity)			
		1	**2**	**3**	
	1	0.10	0.05	0.05	0.20
y (I.Q.)	**2**	0.10	0.20	0.10	0.40
	3	0.05	0.15	0.20	0.40
		0.25	0.40	0.35	

a) Find $P_x(2)$, $P_y(2)$, and $P_{x|y}(3|2)$.

b) Would you conclude that x and y are independent or dependent from these data? Explain!

c) Find $E[x]$ and $E[y]$.

d) Find $E[x \cdot y]$ and $E[x + y]$.

e) Find $C[x, y]$.

f) Find $E[5x - 3y]$.

g) Find $V[5x - 3y]$.

3.35 A study involving 46,000 women of childbearing age in the United Kingdom suggested that women who both smoke and use birth control pills run a higher risk of death from diseases of the circulatory system. The following table indicates the annual mortality rate per 100,000 women from such diseases based on this study.

	Number of deaths	
	Pill users	Nonusers
Nonsmokers	13.5	3.0
Smokers	39.5	8.9

a) How many variables are there in this study? Name them.

b) What kinds of probabilities would you want to consider to determine whether smoking increases the risk of death for pill users?

c) What can one conclude from the data in this table about the relationship between using the pill, smoking, and the mortality rate? (Be careful!)

d) What additional data or analysis would you suggest to supplement these data?

3.36 a) For the data of Table 3.11 show that $E[x + y] = 6.20 = E[x] + E[y]$.

b) For the data of Table 3.11 show that $V[x - y] = 7.60 = V[x] + V[y]$.

3.37 a) For the data in Table 3.11, are the variables x and y still independent if the values of x change to $x = [1, 2, 3]$ and the y-values change to $y = \{0, 1\}$? Show your proof or calculations. Find $C[x, y]$.

b) For the data in Table 3.11, are x and y independent for *any* three values of x and two values of y, or does independence depend on the particular values selected? Explain your answer carefully.

3.38 Reconsider the Blue Cross/Blue Shield example on page 121. Divide each value of x by 2, and then subtract 1 from each of the resulting values.

a) Calculate $E[y]$ and $V[y]$ for this new variable $(x/2) - 1 = y$.

b) Based on the fact that $E[x] = 4.80$ and $V[x] = 7.36$ show how you could have predicted the values in part (a) using the formulas of this chapter.

3.39 a) Given a random variable x with mean 10 and variance 9, find the expected value and variance of the random variable y where $y = 12 + 2x$.

b) Given: a random variable x with $E[x] = 5$ and $V[x] = 9$, and another random variable y with $E[y] = 10$ and $V[y] = 25$. The variables x and y are independent.

1. Find $E[x \cdot y]$, $E[x + 2y]$, and $E[13 - 2x]$.

2. Find $V[x - y]$, $V[x + 2y]$, and $V[13 - 2x]$.

3. What is the value of $C[x, y]$?

3.40 Financial analysts and stockbrokers often quote a measure of the risk of a stock or a portfolio called a *beta*. The beta of a stock, for example, is defined as the covariance between the stock's return and some measure of market return, divided by the variance of the market return. That is,

$$\text{Beta} = \frac{C[\text{stock return, market return}]}{V[\text{market return}]}$$

The data given below represent three years of monthly returns for Citicorp, and three years of the monthly return on the 500 stocks for the Standard and Poor's market index. The monthly return on investment is the stock's total gain, expressed as a fraction of the closing price on the last day of the previous month. Find and interpret the beta for these data.

Month	Citicorp	S&P 500	Month	Citicorp	S&P 500
1	0.035	− 0.021	19	− 0.079	− 0.030
2	0.000	− 0.051	20	− 0.007	0.012
3	0.007	− 0.010	21	0.006	0.019
4	0.101	0.043	22	− 0.118	− 0.018
5	− 0.101	− 0.029	23	0.162	0.026
6	− 0.003	− 0.020	24	0.023	− 0.006
7	− 0.025	− 0.021	25	0.024	− 0.007
8	0.077	0.124	26	− 0.039	− 0.036
9	0.059	0.012	27	− 0.054	0.018
10	0.318	0.115	28	− 0.004	0.005
11	0.007	0.049	29	− 0.148	− 0.053
12	− 0.098	0.017	30	0.078	0.022
13	0.085	0.035	31	− 0.029	− 0.018
14	0.039	0.027	32	0.164	0.112
15	0.132	0.035	33	0.076	0.003
16	0.104	0.073	34	− 0.027	0.002
17	− 0.102	0.004	35	0.000	− 0.010
18	− 0.016	0.039	36	0.098	0.024

Exercises

3.41 Prove that a random variable y and a constant k are always statistically independent.

3.42 Construct an example (or a proof) to show that the expectation of x-squared does not equal the expectation of x, squared. That is,

$$E[x^2] \neq (E[x])^2$$

3.43 Construct an example (or a proof) to show that

$$V[x] = E[x^2] - (E[x])^2$$

3.44 In Chapter 4 we will study a mass function called the *Poisson probability distribution.*

$$P(x) = \begin{cases} \dfrac{e^{-\lambda}\lambda^x}{x!} & \text{for } x = 0, 1, 2, \ldots, \infty, \text{ and } \lambda = \text{constant} \geq 0, \\ 0 & \text{otherwise} \end{cases}$$

a) Show that this function meets the two properties of all p.m.f.

$$\left(\text{Hint: } \sum_{x=0}^{\infty} \lambda^x/x! = e^{\lambda} \right)$$

b) Find $E[x]$ and $E[x^2]$, and use these results to find $V[x]$. (See Exercise 3.43.)

3.45 In Chapter 5 we will study a density function called the *exponential function.*

$$f(x) = \begin{cases} \lambda e^{-\lambda x} & \text{for } x \geq 0 \text{ and } \lambda = \text{constant} \geq 0, \\ 0 & \text{otherwise} \end{cases}$$

a) Prove that this function meets the two conditions of all density functions.

b) Find the mean and variance of $f(x)$.

c) Graph the p.d.f. and c.d.f.

3.46 Prove that

$$V[ax + by] = a^2 V[x] + b^2 V[y] + 2abC[x,y]$$

3.47 Use Formula 3.14 to verify that, for the data in Table 3.10, $C[x,y] = -0.16$.

3.48 **a)** Prove that

$$C[x,y] = E[x \cdot y] - E[x]E[y]$$

b) For the following joint probability distribution, show that $C[x,y] = 0$, but that the variables x and y are not independent.

		y		
		-1	0	1
	0	0	0.25	0
x	1	0.25	0	0.25
	2	0	0.25	0

Chapter 4

Discrete Probability Distributions

Lest men suspect your tale untrue,
keep probability in view.

JOHN GAY

Introduction **4.1**

While it is often useful to determine probabilities for a specific random variable, or for more than one random variable, many apparently different situations in statistical inference and decision making involve the same type of probability functions. In such instances it is useful to apply the theory of probability functions described in Chapter 3, to obtain some *general* results about a probability distribution, such as its mean and variance, rather than rederiving these characteristics in each special case that has different numbers. It would be quite discouraging to go through the process of formulating a new mass or density function and deriving its mean and variance every time we are concerned with a slightly different experiment. Fortunately, there are enough similarities between certain types, or families, of apparently unique experiments to make it possible to develop formulas representing the general characteristics of these experiments. We shall discuss three discrete distributions in this chapter, the *binomial,* the *hypergeometric,* and the *Poisson.* Three continuous distributions, the normal, the exponential, and the chi-square distributions, are discussed in Chapter 5. These distributions are among the most widely known and used distributions in statistics. Two other distributions that have applications across a wide variety of fields are discussed in Chapter 6 in the context of sampling theory.

The Binomial Distribution

4.2

Many experiments share the common element that their outcomes can be classified into one of two events. For instance, the experiment "Classify a job applicant as either male or female" has only two outcomes; the experiment "Call a local resident and ask the person to answer marketing research questions" results in a person willing to cooperate, or a person unwilling to cooperate; a production process may turn out items that are either good or defective; and the stock market in general goes either up or down. In fact, it is often possible to describe the outcome of many of life's ventures in this fashion merely by distinguishing only two events, "success" and "failure." Experiments considered as involving just two possible outcomes play an important role in one of the most widely used discrete probability distributions, the **binomial distribution.**

Several generations of the Bernoulli family, Swiss mathematicians of the 1700s, usually receive credit as the originators of much of the early research on probability theory, especially that involving problems characterized by the binomial distribution. Therefore the Bernoulli name has now come to be associated with this class of experiment, and each repetition of an experiment involving only two outcomes (for example, each toss of a coin) is called a **Bernoulli trial.** For the purposes of probability theory, interest centers not on a single Bernoulli trial but rather on a series of *independent, repeated* Bernoulli trials. That is, we are interested in more than one trial. The fact that these trials must be "independent" means that the results of any one trial cannot influence the results of any other trial. In addition, when a Bernoulli trial is "repeated," it means that the conditions under which each trial is held must be an exact replication of the conditions underlying all other trials, implying that the probability of the two possible outcomes cannot change from trial to trial. The status of items from a production process (such as "good" or "defective") could represent a Bernoulli process, as could the responses to a marketing survey (male/female, like/dislike, or purchase/not purchase).

Binomial Parameters

In a binomial distribution the probabilities of interest are those of receiving a certain number of successes, x, in n *independent* trials, each trial having only two possible outcomes and the *same probability, p,* of success.

Note that the two assumptions underlying the binomial distribution, namely independent trials and a constant probability of success, are met by what we have called independent, repeated Bernoulli trials; and so by definition the binomial distribution is appropriate in an experiment involving these trials. The binomial distribution is completely described by the values of n and p, which are referred to as the "parameters" of this distribution. The word "parameter" in this context means the same as it did in Chapter 1—it refers to a characteristic of a population. In the binomial distribution n is the parameter "number of trials," and p is the parameter "probability of success on a single trial." Given specific values of n and p, one can calculate the probability of any specified number of successes, as well as determine other characteristics of the binomial distribution, such as its mean and variance.

To illustrate a situation in which the binomial distribution applies, suppose a production process is producing solid-state components that are classified as either "good" or "defective." When the process is not working correctly, there is a *constant* probability, $p = 0.10$, that a component will be defective. Note in this situation that the definition of "success-defective" does not imply the company is happy with defectives. The number of defectives (x) can range anywhere from zero up to the total number of objects examined (n). The binomial distribution can be used to determine the probability for any specified value of x and n. For example, we may want to ask, "What is the probability that a random sample of four will result in one defective?" or "What is the probability that there will be two or fewer defectives in a sample of four?" The use of the word "random" in this context implies independence among the items sampled. We shall calculate these probabilities later in this section.

The Binomial Formula

We can calculate the probabilities in a binomial situation by using probability rules similar to those developed in Chapter 2. One important relationship is the following:

$$P(\text{Event}) = \left(\begin{array}{c}\text{Number of relevant} \\ \text{occurrences}\end{array}\right) P(\text{One occurrence})$$

In a binomial problem we are interested in calculating the probability of exactly x successes in n repeated Bernoulli trials, each having the same probability of success, p. That is, we want x successes and ($n - x$) failures. To calculate such probabilities, it is necessary to find the probability of *one* occurrence of this type, and then multiply this probability by the number of such occurrences. Since it doesn't make any difference which occurrence we investigate first, let's (arbitrarily) take the one in which the x successes occur first, followed by the ($n - x$) failures. If we let S = success and F = failure, then this particular ordering can be represented as follows:

$$\underbrace{SS \cdots S}_{x \text{ successes}} \underbrace{FF \cdots F}_{\substack{n - x \\ \text{failures}}}$$

To determine the joint probability of this particular sequence of successes and failures, recall that all trials are assumed to be independent. Since the probability of a success is $P(S) = p$ and $P(F) = q$, the following holds.

$$P(\underbrace{SSS \cdots S}_{x \text{ successes}}\ \underbrace{FF \cdots F}_{n-x \text{ failures}}) = P(S)P(S)P(S) \cdots P(S)P(F)P(F) \cdots P(F)$$

$$= (p)(p)(p) \cdots (p)(q)(q) \cdots (q)$$
$$= p^x q^{n-x}$$

We could also show that $p^x q^{n-x}$ represents the probability of *any* sequence of outcomes where there are x successes and $n - x$ failures. Now we need to know how many different occurrences there are of x successes and $n - x$ failures. The answer is the *number of combinations of n objects taken x at a time.* It can be shown that this number is given by the following formula*:

Combinations of n objects taken x at a time: $\dfrac{n!}{x!(n-x)!}$

The product of this formula times $p^x q^{n-x}$ gives the probability of x successes in n trials, with a constant probability of success (p), as shown in Formula (4.1). This is the formula for the binomial distribution.

Binomial distribution:

$P(x \text{ successes in } n \text{ trials}) =$ (4.1)

$$\begin{cases} \dfrac{n!}{x!(n-x)!}\, p^x q^{n-x} & \text{for} \begin{cases} x = 0, 1, 2, \ldots, n \\ n = 1, 2, \ldots \end{cases} \\ 0 & \text{otherwise} \end{cases}$$

To illustrate the use of Formula (4.1), let's answer several of the questions posed earlier in this section about the number of defectives in a sample of $n = 4$ from the output of a production process in which the probability of a defective is $p = 0.10$. Define a success in this case to be the identification of a defective item, so that $x =$ the number of defectives.† The probability that

---

*The notation $n!$ is read as "n-factorial," where
$$n! = (n)(n-1)(n-2) \cdots (1)$$
Similarly $x! = (x)(x-1)(x-2) \cdots (1)$
and $(n-x)! = (n-x)(n-x-1)(n-x-2) \cdots (1)$
By definition, $0! = 1$

†We shall show in a moment that as long as one is consistent throughout the problem, it makes no difference whether $x =$ the number of defectives, or $x =$ the number of good items.

TABLE 4.1   Binomial probabilities for $n = 4, p = 0.10$

x	$\dfrac{n!}{x!(n-x)!}$	$p^x q^{n-x}$	$P(x) = \dfrac{n!}{x!(n-x)!} p^x q^{n-x}$
0	$\dfrac{4!}{0!4!} = 1$	$(0.10)^0(0.90)^4 = 0.6561$	$P(0) = 0.6561$
1	$\dfrac{4!}{1!3!} = 4$	$(0.10)^1(0.90)^3 = 0.0729$	$P(1) = 0.2916$
2	$\dfrac{4!}{2!2!} = 6$	$(0.10)^2(0.90)^2 = 0.0081$	$P(2) = 0.0486$
3	$\dfrac{4!}{3!1!} = 4$	$(0.10)^3(0.90)^1 = 0.0009$	$P(3) = 0.0036$
4	$\dfrac{4!}{4!0!} = 1$	$(0.10)^4(0.90)^0 = 0.0001$	$P(4) = 0.0001$
			Sum = 1.0000

exactly one component will be defective ($x = 1$) out of a sample of four ($n = 4$), when $p = 0.10$ (and hence $q = 0.90$), is

$$P(x = 1) = \frac{x!}{x!(n-x)!} p^x q^{n-x}$$
$$= \frac{4!}{1!3!}(0.10)^1(0.90)^3$$
$$= 0.2916$$

The probability that there are exactly *two* defectives ($x = 2$) in sample of $n = 4$ can be calculated to be

$$P(x = 2) = \frac{4!}{2!2!}(0.10)^2(0.90)^2 = 0.0486$$

Indeed, the probability of any number of defectives from 0 to 4 may be determined in the same way. Table 4.1 presents these values.

From Table 4.1 it is easy to answer our second question posed earlier, concerning the probability of two or fewer defectives when $n = 4$. This value is

$$P(x \le 2) = P(0) + P(1) + P(2)$$
$$= 0.6561 + 0.2916 + 0.0486$$
$$= 0.9963$$

A graph of all the values for $n = 4$ appears in Fig. 4.1.

The calculations in Table 4.1 are not very complex, but the difficulty could readily become overwhelming if n becomes much larger. Consider a more realistic situation where $n = 20$ items are sampled, and the question

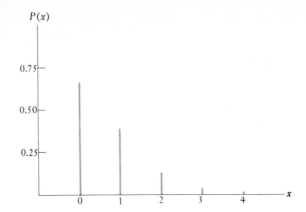

Figure 4.1
Binomial distribution for
$n = 4, p = 0.10$.

posed earlier is now raised again: What is the probability of finding exactly two defectives, when $p = 0.10$? Using Formula (4.1), we have

$$P(x = 2) = \frac{n!}{x!(n - x)!} p^x q^{n-x} = \frac{20!}{2!(18!)}(0.10)^2(0.90)^{18}$$

$$= \frac{20 \times 19 \times (18!)}{2 \times 1 \times (18!)}(0.10)(0.10)\underbrace{(0.90) \cdots (0.90)}_{18 \text{ terms}}$$

Fortunately it is not necessary to carry out such calculations, for tables of binomial probabilities for various values of n and p are readily available. Table I in Appendix B gives the probability for a number of the more commonly referred to values of n, for values of p from 0.01 to 0.99. The probability of $P(x = 2)$ for the preceding problem can be seen to equal 0.2852, by referring to the set of probabilities headed $n = 20$ and finding the values corresponding to $x = 2$ on the left-hand margin and $p = 0.10$ across the top. (The decimal points have all been omitted from Table I.) Note that the entire probability distribution for $n = 20$ and $p = 0.10$ is given in Table I, although probability values smaller than 0.00005 are rounded to 0.0000 in this table.

Figure 4.2 presents the portion of the binomial table in Appendix B relevant for this problem. We have set in color the entry for $n = 20, p = 0.10$, and $x = 2$, which is

$$P(x = 2) = 0.2852$$

Another important fact to notice about Table 1 is its symmetry. Values of p less than 0.51 are found across the top of each set of numbers, while values of p greater than 0.49 are found across the bottom of each set (in which case the values of x are read from the right-hand margin). This symmetry in Table 1 results from the fact that the probability of x successes when p is the probability of success exactly equals the probability of $(n - x)$ failures when the probability of a failure is $(1 - p)$. Thus, in our defective-components example, if $x = $ the number of *good* items in the sample (rather than the number of defectives), and hence the probability of a success equals 0.90 (rather than 0.10), then the probability of 18 good items out of 20 is read from exactly

TABLE 1 Binomial distribution ($n = 20$)

					$n = 20$							
x p	01	02	03	04	05	06	07	08	09	10		
0	8179	6676	5438	4420	3585	2901	2342	1887	1516	1216	20	
1	1652	2725	3364	3683	3774	3703	3526	3282	3000	2702	19	
2	0159	0528	0988	1458	1887	2246	2521	2711	2828	2852	18	
3	0010	0065	0183	0364	0596	0860	1139	1414	1672	1901	17	
4	0000	0006	0024	0065	0133	0233	0364	0523	0703	0898	16	
5	0000	0000	0002	0009	0022	0048	0088	0145	0222	0319	15	
6	0000	0000	0000	0001	0003	0008	0017	0032	0055	0089	14	
7	0000	0000	0000	0000	0000	0001	0002	0005	0011	0020	13	
8	0000	0000	0000	0000	0000	0000	0000	0001	0002	0004	12	
9	0000	0000	0000	0000	0000	0000	0000	0000	0000	0001	11	
	99	98	97	96	95	94	93	92	91	90	p	x

Figure 4.2
Illustrating Table I,
Appendix B.

the same point in the table as was the probability of two defectives, $P(x = 18) = 0.2852$.

Note from Table 4.1 that the binomial distribution for $n = 4$ and $p = 0.10$ satisfies the two properties described in Chapter 3 for all probability mass functions—namely, that*

$$1 \geq P(x) \geq 0 \text{ for all } x$$

and

$$\sum_{\text{All } x} P(x) = 1$$

---

*To show that the function

$$P(x) = \frac{n!}{x!n - x!} p^x q^{n-x}$$

meets the two properties of probability described in Chapter 3 for all values of n and p, first note that

$$\frac{n!}{x!(n-x)!},$$

p^x, and q^{n-x} must all be positive; hence their product will always be positive. To prove that $\Sigma P(x) = 1$, recall the binomial theorem (refer to any good book on algebra), which allows us to state the following:

$$\textit{Binomial theorem:} \sum_{x=0}^{n} \frac{n!}{x!(n-x)!} p^x q^{n-x} = (p + q)^n$$

By substituting $(1 - p)$ for q in the right-hand side of the equation above, we can prove that the second axiom necessary for defining a probability mass function holds true:

$$\sum_{x=0}^{n} \frac{n!}{x!(n-x)!} p^x q^{n-x} = (p + q)^n = [p + (1 - p)]^n = 1$$

Mean and Variance of the Binomial

Since the binomial distribution is characterized by the value of the two parameters, n and p, one might anticipate that the summary measures of the mean and standard deviation also can be determined in terms of n and p. For example, it should appear reasonable that the mean number of successes in any given experiment must equal the number of trials (n) times the probability of successes on each trial (p). If, for example, the probability that a process produces a defective item is $p = 0.10$, then the mean number of defectives in 20 trials is $20(0.10) = 2$; the mean number in 50 trials is $50(0.10) = 5$; and the mean number in 100 trials is $100(0.10) = 10$. Thus, the *mean* number of successes in n trials is np*:

$$\boxed{Binomial\ mean:\ \ \mu = np} \qquad (4.2)$$

The variance (and standard deviation) of the binomial distribution are also functions of the parameters n and p, as follows.

$$\boxed{\begin{array}{l} Binomial\ variance*:\ \ \sigma^2 = npq \\ Binomial\ standard\ deviation:\ \ \sigma = \sqrt{npq} \end{array}} \qquad (4.3)$$

The variance in 20 Bernoulli trials of a process producing defectives with probability $p = 0.10$ is thus

$$npq = 20(0.10)(0.90) = 1.80$$

The standard deviation is

$$\sqrt{npq} = \sqrt{1.80} = 1.34$$

Note from the following table that the intervals $\mu \pm 1\sigma$ and $\mu \pm 2\sigma$ for this problem contain slightly more of the total probability (obtained from Table I) than the rule of thumb given in Chapter 1 (68% and 95%) would indicate.

Interval	Percent of probability
$\mu \pm 1\sigma = 2.00 \pm 1(1.34) = 0.66$ to 3.34	75%
$\mu \pm 2\sigma = 2.00 \pm 2(1.34) = 0$ to 4.68	97%

---

*If x is the number of successes in a binomial problem, then the mean and variance can be written as follows:

$\mu = E[x] = np$
$\sigma^2 = V[x] = npq$

The Shape of the Binomial Distribution

The shape of the binomial distribution depends on its parameters, n and p. It will be useful to consider three different combinations of n and p: (1) When n is small and p is large (that is, $p > \frac{1}{2}$); (2) When n is small and p is also small (that is, $p < \frac{1}{2}$); (3) When $p = \frac{1}{2}$ and/or n is large.

1. **When n is small and $p > \frac{1}{2}$.** To illustrate this case, the distribution for $n = 5, p = 0.80$, is shown in Fig. 4.3. As Fig 4.3 illustrates, the binomial distribution when n is small and $p > \frac{1}{2}$ is skewed to the left, or *negatively* skewed.

2. **When n is small and $p < \frac{1}{2}$.** A typical illustration of this case is the binomial distribution for $n = 4$ and $p = 0.10$, shown in Table 4.1 and pictured in Fig. 4.1. This distribution is skewed to the right, or *positively* skewed, as all binomial distributions will be when n is small and $p < \frac{1}{2}$.

3. **When $p = \frac{1}{2}$ and/or n is large.** When $p = 0.50$, the binomial distribution will always be a symmetrical distribution with its mean equal to its median. This can be seen in a simple example by considering $n = 2$, and $p = 0.50$. The three values of x in this case are

$$P(x = 0) = 0.25, \qquad P(x = 1) = 0.50, \qquad \text{and} \qquad P(x = 2) = 0.25$$

Note that in this example, median = mean = mode = 1 (the mode equals the mean and median when n is even and $p = \frac{1}{2}$). An important fact about the binomial is that even when $p \neq \frac{1}{2}$, the shape of the distribution takes on a more and more symmetrical appearance the larger the value of n. Figure 4.4 illustrates this fact. Note in Fig. 4.4(a) and (b) that even though n is as small as 20, the distributions of $p = 0.20$ and $p = 0.40$ are fairly symmetrical in appearance. For $n = 100$ and $p = 0.30$, shown in Fig. 4.4(c), the distribution has a very symmetrical "bell" shape.

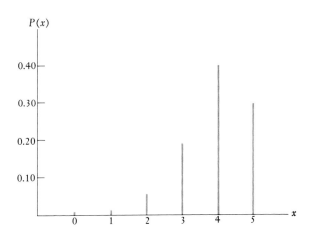

Figure 4.3
Binomial distribution for
$n = 5, p = 0.80$.

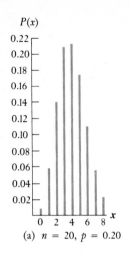

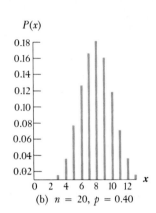

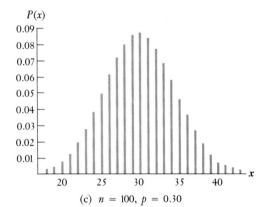

Figure 4.4
The binomial distribution.

Applications of the Binomial Distribution

EXAMPLE 1

Public Service Indiana (PSI) recently needed homeowners to volunteer to participate in an experiment designed to test customer reaction to energy-saving devices installed in their homes (at PSI's expense). Fifty current customers were asked to participate. From past experience in comparable research, PSI expected about 60% of the customers contacted to be willing to volunteer. PSI would like at least 25 customers in the study. They would like to know how many volunteers to expect, the standard deviation for the number of volunteers, and the probability of having at least 25 volunteers.

This is a binomial problem because the experiment (recruiting volunteers) involves just two outcomes (yes or no), and it is reasonable to assume that the n trials ($n = 50$) are independent (one person's decision does not influence any other person's decision) with a constant probability of success ($p = 0.60$).

The expected number of volunteers is

$$E[x] = np = 50(0.60) = 30$$

and the standard deviation is

$$\sigma = \sqrt{npq} = \sqrt{50(0.60)(0.40)} = 3.464$$

Using Table I, Appendix B, for $n = 50$, $p = 0.60$, the probability of 25 or more volunteers is

$$P(x \geq 25) = P(x = 25) + P(x = 26) + P(x = 27) + \cdots + P(x = 50)$$
$$= 0.0405 \quad + 0.0584 \quad + 0.0778 \quad + \cdots + 0.0000$$
$$= 0.9427$$

Thus, PSI can be quite certain of having at least 25 volunteers, given that the assumption of a 60% volunteer rate is correct. ∎

EXAMPLE 2

The binomial distribution is useful as the basis for investigating a number of special problems in statistical inference and decision making. To take a simple example, suppose a U.S. senator is concerned about how to vote on several bills involving unemployment and inflation. One group of concerned citizens claims that 90% of the population considers inflation a more serious problem; another group claims that the population is equally divided, 50% considering inflation more serious and 50% considering unemployment more serious. Since it is impossible or at least impractical for the senator to learn the preferences of the entire population, suppose a small sample is collected by telephoning (at random) 15 households and asking their priorities. Assume that in 10 of these households someone is home, and willing to express a preference, with the following results:

Inflation the more serious	Inflation/unemployment equally serious	Total
7	3	10

We can determine which group's claim seems more reasonable on the basis of this sample by using the binomial distribution. The view of the first group is that $p = 0.90$, as opposed to $p = 0.50$ for the second group. Note that if the first group is correct, the mean number of households indicating inflation as more serious (in a sample of 10) would be $\mu = np = 10(0.90) = 9$. If the second group is correct, the mean would be $\mu = np = 10(0.50) = 5$. The observed result, seven indicating inflation, falls right in the middle of these two means. However, let's calculate the probability of exactly seven successes ($x = 7$ indicating inflation priority) in a sample of $n = 10$ households, using both $p = 0.90$ and $p = 0.50$.

$$\text{If } p = 0.90: \ P(x = 7) = \frac{10!}{7!3!} (0.90)^7 (0.10)^3 = 0.0574$$

$$\text{If } p = 0.50: \ P(x = 7) = \frac{10!}{7!3!} (0.50)^7 (0.50)^3 = 0.1172$$

We thus see that the probability of finding seven households answering inflation is twice as likely if $p = 0.50$ as when $p = 0.90$, indicating that this sample tends to support the equally serious group.

We must quickly point out that our conclusion in the above analysis is very sensitive. Suppose the sample had yielded just one more inflation preference, so that 8 of 10 indicated inflation is a higher priority. In this case $P(x = 8) = 0.1937$ when $p = 0.90$, and $P(x = 8) = 0.0439$ when $p = 0.50$. This means that the inflation claim is more reasonable. To avoid such sensitive results in statistical analysis, larger samples are usually taken. Furthermore, probabilities are usually not calculated for a *single* outcome, such as $x = 7$, but for a *set* of outcomes, such as $P(x \leq 7)$ or $P(x \geq 7)$. For example, the reasonableness of the hypothesis that $p = 0.90$ when $x = 7$ is usually determined by asking how likely it is to have 7 or *fewer* households when $p = 0.90$. This probability is $P(x \leq 7) = 0.0702$. Similarly, the reasonableness of the unemployment claim is determined by asking how likely it is to find 7 *or more* households when $p = 0.50$. This probability is $P(x \geq 7) = 0.1719$. Thus, it is over twice as likely to get seven or more households when $p = 0.50$ as it is to get seven or fewer viewers when $p = 0.90$, indicating again that we should support the claim that unemployment and inflation are equally serious problems. ∎

The following procedure is generally followed in testing hypotheses using a discrete distribution such as the binomial.

If the expected value exceeds the observed value, calculate the probability that x is less than or equal to the observed value [for example, if 9 is expected and 7 is observed, calculate $P(x \leq 7)$]. If the observed value exceeds the expected value, calculate

$$P(x \geq \text{observed value})$$

EXAMPLE 3

As another example of the use of the binomial in decision making, let's assume that the production process described earlier in this chapter is malfunctioning and will require either a minor or a major adjustment. If the defective rate is 10% ($p = 0.10$), then only a minor adjustment is necessary; if the number of defectives has jumped to 25% ($p = 0.25$), then a major adjustment is necessary. The problem at this point is how to decide, on the basis of a random sample of size $n = 20$, whether the process requires a minor or a major adjustment. This decision is not without risks, however, for we assume it is costly to make the wrong decision—that is, to make a minor adjustment to a process needing a major adjustment, or to make a major adjustment to process needing only minor adjustments.

Suppose, for the moment, that *four* defectives is established as the decision point concerning repairs—if there are four or more defectives, then a major adjustment is made; with three or less defectives, minor repairs are made. This decision rule will lead to an *incorrect* decision if $p = 0.10$ and the number of defectives is $x \geq 4$ (since then a major adjustment will be made). Another type of incorrect decision will be made when $p = 0.25$ and the number of defectives is $x \leq 3$ (since then a minor adjustment will be made). To determine how likely it is to make these errors, we need to know the probability of x defectives in a sample of $n = 20$ when $p = 0.10$ and when $p = 0.25$. Table 4.2 provides the appropriate values.

The probability of making the two types of errors is shown in Table 4.2. First, if $p = 0.10$, the probability of receiving four or more defectives is $P(x \geq 4) = 0.1331$; this means that, under this decision rule, the probability of *incorrectly* making a major adjustment (when only a minor one is needed) is

0.1331. The probability of incorrectly making a minor adjustment when $p = 0.25$ is $P(x \leq 3) = 0.2251$.

These probabilities of making an incorrect decision depend on the fact that $x = 4$ was the decision point selected. For example, if the decision point between a major and a minor adjustment is set at $x = 3$ rather than $x = 4$, then the appropriate probabilities can again be determined from Table 4.2.

> Decision point of $x = 3$:
>
> If $p = 0.10$, the probability of incorrectly making a major adjustment is $P(x \geq 3) = 0.3232$.
>
> If $p = 0.25$, the probability of incorrectly making a minor adjustment is $P(x \leq 2) = 0.0912$.

For a given value of n, one of these types of errors (for example, incorrectly making a major or a minor adjustment) can be made smaller only if the other is allowed to become larger. Just what decision rule to use, such as $x = 3$ or $x = 4$, depends largely on the costs associated with making these errors. We shall examine this subject in more detail in Chapters 9 and 10. ■

TABLE 4.2   Binomial probabilities for production process example

Number of defectives (x)	Decision rule		If $p = 0.10$ $P(x) = \left(\dfrac{20!}{x!(20-x)!}\right)(0.10)^x(0.90)^{20-x}$	If $p = 0.25$ $P(x) = \left(\dfrac{20!}{x!(20-x)!}\right)(0.25)^x(0.75)^{20-x}$
0		|	0.1216	0.0032
1	**Minor**		0.2702	0.0211
2	**repairs**		0.2852	0.2251 ⎰ 0.0669
3	**Decision**	|	0.1901	0.1339
4	**point**		0.0898	0.1897
5		|	0.0319	0.2023
6		|	0.0089	0.1686
7		|	0.0020	0.1124
8		|	0.0004	0.0609
9	**Major**	| 0.1331 ⎰	0.0001	0.0271
10	**repairs**	|	0.0000	0.0099
11		|	0.0000	0.0030
12		|	0.0000	0.0008
13			0.0000	0.0002
14–20		|	0.0000	0.0000
		Sum	1.0000	1.0000

Binomial Proportions

4.3

All the binomial problems studied thus far involved the variable x, where x represents the *number* of successes in n Bernoulli trials. In this section, we will show that any one of these problems could have been solved by using the variable x/n, where x/n represents the *proportion* of successes in n Bernoulli trials. For all practical purposes, *it makes no difference in solving a problem whether x is used, or x/n is used.*

To illustrate the statement above, suppose we redo Fig. 4.3, which shows the binomial distribution for $n = 5$, $p = 0.80$. Instead of using x as our horizontal axis, this time (in Fig. 4.5) we use x/n as the horizontal axis.

The important aspect of Fig. 4.5 is that it looks identical to Fig. 4.3 except for the values on the horizontal axis. In other words, dividing each value of x by n doesn't change any of the probability values. The mean and variance of x/n will be different from $\mu = np$ and $\sigma^2 = npq$, but we can easily derive the new values using the algebra of expectations. These new values are

$$
\begin{aligned}
&\textit{Mean of } x/n = E[x/n] = p \\
&\textit{Variance of } x/n = V[x/n] = \frac{pq}{n}
\end{aligned}
$$

Because Table I (in Appendix B) is presented in terms of the *number* of successes (x) rather than the *proportion* of successes (x/n), a problem involving x/n is usually solved by transforming it to the comparable problem involving x. Consider the following problem, which illustrates this point.

A midwestern chemical company was recently in the process of proposing revisions to its stock option plan. For the revision proposed initially, only 40% of the 3275 salaried workers in the company voted in favor of the pro-

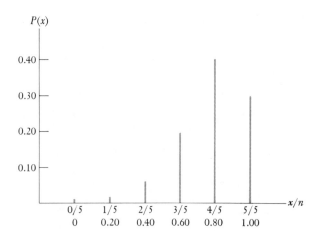

Figure 4.5
Binomial distribution for
$n = 5, p = 0.80$, using x/n as
the variable.

posed changes. Further modifications to the plan were made. To test the assertion that the revisions would make the plan more acceptable, a random sample of 50 employees was taken. Twenty-seven of those sampled were in favor of the new plan. The question is whether 27 of 50, which is 54%, is sufficient evidence to support the claim that the new plan is significantly better than the old.

In problems of this nature we need to calculate the probability of receiving a sample result (such as $x/n = 0.54$) under the assumption that the proportion favoring the new plan has not changed (that is, $p = 0.40$). Recall from Section 4.2 that such probabilities almost always involve a *range* of values (such as ≥ 0.54), rather than a single value (like 0.54). Thus, for this problem we calculate the probability that the proportion is 54% *or larger* (given $n = 50, p = 0.40$), which is written as

$$P\left(\frac{x}{n} \geq 0.54\right) = P(x \geq 27)$$

This problem is easily solved using Table I for $n = 50, p = 0.40$. Be sure to recognize that p in this problem is 0.40 (and not 0.54) because 40% is the assumption we are testing. From Table I

$$P(x \geq 27) = 0.0154 + 0.0084 + \cdots + 0.0001 = 0.0314$$

This result says that in random samples of this nature, only a little over 3% of the time would one expect 27 or more "successes" in 50 trials when $p = 0.40$. The company can thus reasonably conclude that there is more support for the new program.

Would the company reach the same conclusion if only 24 of the 50 (48%) sampled were in favor? In this case the probability of interest is $P(x \geq 24)$, which is (from Table I, $n = 50, p = 0.40$).

$$P\left(\frac{x}{n} \geq 0.48\right) = P(x \geq 24) = 0.1562$$

This result says there is almost a 16% chance that a sample proportion 48% or larger will occur when the population proportion has really remained at 40%. In Chapter 9 we will study the process of trying to decide how low a probability has to be before one can reject the assumption on which it was based. One quite arbitrary rule often used is that *the probability must be less than 0.05 in order to reject the assumption.* Thus, the probability of 0.1562 in this example is not low enough to reject the assumption that $p = 0.40$.

In our stock option plan, the company might have anticipated less support for the new plan. In this case, suppose the sample results in only 22% (11 of 50 people) favoring the new proposal. The appropriate calculation is now for the probability that x/n will be 0.22 *or less.* From Table I, $n = 50$ and $p = 0.40$,

$$P\left(\frac{x}{n} \leq 0.22\right) = P(x \leq 11) = 0.0056$$

There is less than a 1% chance of having 11 or fewer people (of 50) in favor of the revised plan when the true population proportion of people in favor is 40%. Since this probability is quite low (much less than the 5% rule mentioned above), a sample resulting in 22% favoring the new proposal should cause the company to conclude that the proportion in favor of the latest plan is less than the 40% favoring the previous plan.

Computer Programs to Solve Binomial Problems

4.4

Almost without exception, all statistical computer packages provide a procedure for determining binomial probabilities. In most cases the procedure requires the user to input the number of trials (usually designated as either n or N), the probability of success on a single trial (either p, P, or π), and the values of x of interest. The output below uses the notation N, P, and $x1$ (the

TABLE 4.3   Computer output for $n = 50$, $p = 0.40$, $11 \leq x \leq 50$

BINOMIAL DISTRIBUTION
N = 50   P = .4

X	P(X)	CUMULATIVE PROBABILITY	X	P(X)	CUMULATIVE PROBABILITY
11	.00349	.00349	31	.00085	.99728
12	.00756	.01105	32	.00034	.99762
13	.01474	.02579	33	.00012	.99774
14	.02597	.05176	34	.00004	.99779
15	.04155	.09330	35	.00001	.99780
16	.06059	.15389	36	.00000	.99780
17	.08079	.23468	37	.00000	.99780
18	.09874	.33342	38	.00000	.99780
19	.11086	.44428	39	.00000	.99780
20	.11456	.55884	40	.00000	.99780
21	.10910	.66794	41	.00000	.99780
22	.09588	.76382	42	.00000	.99780
23	.07781	.84163	43	.00000	.99780
24	.05836	.90000	44	.00000	.99780
25	.04046	.94046	45	.00000	.99780
26	.02594	.96640	46	.00000	.99780
27	.01537	.98177	47	.00000	.99780
28	.00842	.99019	48	.00000	.99780
29	.00426	.99444	49	.00000	.99780
30	.00199	.99643	50	.00000	.99780

E(X) = 20.00   STD. DEV. = 3.46410   VARIANCE = 12.00

lower limit for x) and $x2$ (the upper limit for x). To illustrate this program, we selected $N = 50$, $P = 0.40$, $x1 = 11$, and $x2 = 50$ so that the reader can verify the probabilities calculated in Section 4.3 for the stock option problem. Note in the computer output in Table 4.3 that in addition to giving $P(x)$, the package also provides cumulative probabilities (which start at $x1 = 11$). The reader should verify the probabilities above using these values.

Problems

4.1   Verify that the mean and the standard deviation printed in the computer output in Section 4.4 are correct using Formulas (4.2) and (4.3).

4.2   A Detroit automobile manufacturer knows from past experience that 40% of its cars will need some kind of repair work (engine or body) before being shipped to the dealer. Six cars are selected at random from this group.

a)   For this problem, what are n and p?

b)   Find $P(x \geq 4)$, $P(x \leq 5)$, and $P(2 < x \leq 5)$.

c)   In 100 cars, what is the expected number of cars needing repair before being shipped? What is the variance?

4.3   The Neybolt Construction Company of Seattle routinely submits bids for major construction projects in western Washington. The company does not win the contract about 80% of the time it bids.

a)   What is the probability Neybolt will win the contract on exactly two of the next four projects, if the results are independent? What does independence mean in this case?

b)   How many contracts would you expect Neybolt to win out of the next 20 bids? What is the highest and lowest number you would expect?

4.4   In a recent court case, two-fifths of the candidates for clerical positions at a Chicago bank were minority candidates. What is the probability that five candidates, randomly selected, will include:

a) exactly four minorities,

b) four or more minorities?

4.5   A panel is being selected for a marketing research study by T.I.M.E., Inc., in Columbus, Ohio. Eight males were invited to attend, but T.I.M.E. knows there is a 60% chance that each male will *not* appear for the panel discussion. Sketch the binomial distribution for the number of males who might show up. Indicate the mean and variance on your sketch. What is $P(x = 7)$? What is $P(x \geq 7)$? Let x = number who show up.

4.6   *Consumer Reports* described a bakery in Los Angeles that was fined for distributing consistently underweight loaves of bread. The bakery claims that in reality 50% of its loaves are either exactly the correct weight, or slightly overweight.

a)   Would you dispute the bakery's claim if 69% of the loaves in a sample of 100 are underweight? Explain.

b) Let y represent the number of loaves that are underweight in a sample of 100. How small does y have to be before you would dispute the bakery's claim?

4.7 A survey by the National Board of Realtors indicated that the average realtor sells one residential dwelling for every 20 homes shown to prospective buyers.

a) If a realtor shows 100 homes, what is the expected number of sales? What is the variance of sales if $n = 100$? Assume sales are independent of one another.

b) What is the probability the realtor in (a) will sell one or fewer homes in 100 showings?

4.8 A *Wall Street Journal* article reported that 14.1% of American married couples can be classified as "DINKs" (double income, no kids).

a) How many DINKs would you expect in a random sample of 300 married couples?

b) What is the smallest and the largest number of DINKs you would reasonably expect to occur in a random sample of 300 couples?

c) How surprised would you be if a random sample of 300 couples resulted in only 24 DINKs? What might you conclude?

4.9 The Big Rivers Electric Cooperative at Henderson, Kentucky, had a new peak demand, in July, of 983 megawatts. Suppose Big Rivers sells power to the Tennessee Valley Authority (TVA) whenever demand is less than 900 megawatts. Big Rivers estimates that demand over the next several months will exceed 900 megawatts only on 5% of the 50 days between July 1 and August 19.

a) What is the average number of days Big Rivers can expect to sell power to TVA, using the binomial distribution? What are the most and fewest days they can expect to sell?

b) Do the assumptions of the binomial appear reasonable in this situation? Explain.

4.10 In an ad in the *Wall Street Journal,* Volvo stated its car is "made well enough to have a life expectancy of 17.9 years in Sweden." If we accept this statement as true, could we further state there is a 50–50 chance that a given Volvo's life expectancy will exceed 17.9 years in Sweden? Explain.

4.11 A study by one automobile manufacturer indicated that one of every four new automobiles required repairs under the company's new-car guarantee, with an average cost of $50 per repair. For 100 cars, what is the expected cost of repairs? What is the highest cost the company might reasonably expect?

4.12 Kroger Supermarket ran a promotional campaign in which customers can win a prize by scratching off a card the one space, out of six, with a prize pictured behind it. One store manager is suspicious of a flaw in the game because there were 24 winners in the last 100 cards. Should the manager be worried?

4.13 Consider the following computer output representing the entire p.m.f. for a binomial problem.

X	P(X)	PROBABILITY	X	P(X)	PROBABILITY
0	.00015	.00015	6	.23598	.60268
1	.00206	.00221	7	.20602	.80888
2	.01259	.01480	8	.12590	.93478
3	.04616	.06096	9	.05129	.98607
4	.11284	.17380	10	.01254	.99861
5	.19308	.36688	11	.00139	1.00000

$E(x) = 6.0500$ STD. DEV. $= 1.6500$ Variance $= 2.72250$

a) What is the value of n for this output? What is p?

b) What is $P(x = 5)$? What is $P(x \geq 5)$?

4.14 A Chicago-based accounting firm proudly advertises that, on the average, three of every five new masters of business administration (MBAs) it hires are still working for the company five years later.

a) This company hired 10 MBAs last year. Sketch the p.m.f. for the number of these MBAs who will still be working for the company in five years, assuming the binomial distribution holds. Indicate the mean and the standard deviation on your sketch.

b) If only three of these MBAs are still working for the company in five years, would you conclude that this company is no longer retaining 60% of the MBA new hires?

4.15 A study of the population of workers available in the Detroit area for certain jobs in the automobile industry indicated that 20% are minorities. If one company hires 100 new workers for these jobs and 12% are minorities, would you conclude the company is discriminating against minorities? What assumptions are necessary?

4.16 American Transair estimates that 60% of the passengers on its Indianapolis-to-Cancun nonstop flight will request a nonsmoking seat.

a) There are 10 seats left to be allocated on a fully booked flight, 5 of which are smoking. What is the probability there will not be a sufficient number of nonsmoking seats if requests are independent?

b) How many seats would you reserve for nonsmokers if you want to honor every nonsmoking request on 99% of all flights? Assume $p = 0.60$, $n = 300$, and independence.

4.17 An article in the *Wall Street Journal* indicated that the percentage of women graduating with a business degree was 37.8%. Suppose a random sample of 500 business students from midwestern universities results in 40.2% women graduates. What is the probability of a proportion this high, or higher, if the midwestern proportion of women is actually $p = 0.378$? What might you conclude from this sample of 500? Use a computer to solve this problem.

Hypergeometric Distribution (Optional)

4.5

The binomial distribution assumes that the value of p is constant from trial to trial. This assumption generally implies that sampling is either with replacement, or from an infinitely large population. *When sampling is without replacement from a finite population the hypergeometric distribution is appropriate.*

The hypergeometric assumes sampling is from a population with k different objects. We will illustrate the hypergeometric only for the case of $k = 2$ objects. Let there be n_1 of the first kind of object, and n_2 of the second kind. The total number of objects is the population size, N, where

$$\text{Population size: } N = n_1 + n_2$$

For this type of problem we are interested in determining the probability of drawing a sample of x_1 of the first kind, and x_2 of the second kind. The hypergeometric formula gives this probability.

Hypergeometric distribution (for $k = 2$):

$$P(x_1 \text{ out of } n_1 \text{ and } x_2 \text{ out of } n_2) = \frac{\dfrac{n_1!}{(n_1 - x_1)\,!x_1!}\dfrac{n_2!}{(n_2 - x_2)!x_2!}}{\dfrac{(n_1 + n_2)!}{(n_1 + n_2 - x_1 - x_2)!(x_1 + x_2)!}} \qquad (4.4)$$

To illustrate the use of the hypergeometric distribution, imagine a production process in which electrical components are produced in lots of 50. If this process is working correctly, there will be no defective items among the 50 produced. Suppose, however, that the process has, in fact, been malfunctioning and exactly five components in a particular lot are defective. What is the probability that exactly one of these defectives will appear in a sample of four randomly selected components? Note that we are sampling without replacement from a finite population ($N = 50$). Hence the hypergeometric distribution is appropriate. Now, what is the probability that a sample of 4 contains exactly 1 defective and 3 good components? The probability that the sample contains $x_1 = 1$ of the $n_1 = 5$ defective components, and $x_2 = 3$ out of the $n_2 = 45$ good components, is given by Formula (4.4).

$$P(1 \text{ defective and 3 good}) = \frac{\dfrac{5!}{4!1!}\dfrac{45!}{42!3!}}{\dfrac{50!}{46!4!}} = 0.308$$

Similarly, one might want to calculate the probability of receiving *two or less* defectives in a sample of 4. Applying Formula (4.4) in the same manner shown above results in

$$P(2 \text{ or less defectives}) = P(0 \text{ def.}) + P(1 \text{ def.}) + P(2 \text{ def.})$$
$$= 0.647 + 0.308 + 0.043 = 0.998$$

TABLE 4.4   Computer Output for the
Hypergeometric Distribution

```
THE POPULATION OF SIZE 50 OBJECTS CONTAINS
              5 POSSIBLE OCCURRENCES
THE SAMPLE SIZE IS 4
                         CUMULATIVE
       X     P(X)     PROBABILITY
       0    .64696      .64696
       1    .30808      .95504
       2    .04299      .99803
       3    .00195      .99998
       4    .00002     1.00000
```

We could have provided a formula for the mean and the variance of the hypergeometric distribution, but these concepts are of limited use for the purposes in this text. The reader may wish to plot the hypergeometric p.m.f. in Table 4.4, noting that all probabilities are between 0 and 1, and the sum of these values is 1.

Computer Programs to Solve Hypergeometric Problems

Hypergeometric problems are generally so tedious to solve, with a great propensity for errors, that computer packages are used whenever possible. This section shows how to use the computer to solve the problem shown above, namely where $N = 50$, $n_1 = 5$, $n_2 = 45$, and the sample size is 4 ($= x_1 + x_2$). Note that if the N (population size) and n_1 (number of possible occurrences of the first kind) are known, then n_2 is also known ($n_2 = N - n_1$). In the computer output in Table 4.4, n_1 is referred to as "the number of possible occurrences."

Table 4.4 provides the probabilities for the example on page 148, namely that there are two or fewer defectives in a sample of 4 when sampling without replacement from 50 objects, where there are 5 of one kind alike (defectives) and 45 of another kind alike (good items). This program also asks for $x1$ and $x2$, the upper and lower limits on the x-values of interest. We have let $x1 = 0$ and $x2 = 4$, so the program prints out all possible values of x (note: x cannot be larger than 4 because the sample size is 4). The reader should verify that the values given in Table 4.4 agree with those determined on page 148.

The Poisson Distribution (Optional)

4.6

Another important discrete distribution, the Poisson distribution, has recently found fairly wide application, especially in the area of operations research. This distribution was named for its originator, the French mathematician S. D. Poisson (1781–1840), who described its use in a paper in 1837. Its rather morbid first applications indicated that the Poisson distribution quite accurately described the probability of deaths in the Prussian army resulting from the kick of a horse, as well as the number of suicides among women and children. More recent (and useful) approximations include many applications involving arrivals at a service facility, or requests for service at that facility, as well as the rate at which this service is provided. A few of the many successful approximations to which the Poisson distribution has been applied include problems involving the number of arrivals or requests for services per unit time at tollbooths on an expressway, at checkout counters in a supermarket, at teller windows in a bank, at runways in an airport, by maintenance men in a repair shop, or by machines needing repair.

In examples of the above nature, the Poisson distribution can be used to determine the probability of x occurrences (arrivals or service completions) per unit time if four basic assumptions are met. First, it must be possible to divide the time interval being used into a large number of small subintervals in such a manner that the probability of an occurrence in each of these subintervals is very small. Second, the probability of an occurrence in *each* of the subintervals must remain constant throughout the time period being considered. Third, the probability of two or more occurrences in each subinterval must be small enough to be ignored. And finally, an occurrence (or nonoccurrence) in one interval must not affect the occurrence (or nonoccurrence) in any other subinterval—that is, the occurrences must be independent.

Consider arrivals at a bank per hour, and suppose we can divide a given hour into intervals of one second, where the probability that a customer arrives during each second is very small and remains constant throughout the one-hour period. Furthermore, assume that only one customer can arrive in a given second (the door is large enough to admit only one person), and that the number of arrivals in a given time period is independent of the number of arrivals in any other time period (customers don't turn away because of long lines). Under these circumstances, the number of arrivals in the one-hour period meets the four basic assumptions, and thus it is not unreasonable to assume the Poisson distribution holds. These assumptions and how they fit the bank example are summarized below.

Assumption	Bank example
1. Possible to divide time interval of interest into many small subintervals.	1. Can divide the hour into subintervals of one second each.
2. Probability of an occurrence remains constant through the time interval.	2. The hour is one for which we have no reason to suspect an uneven flow of customers.
3. Probability of two or more occurrences in a subinterval is small enough to be ignored.	3. Impossible for two or more people to enter the bank simultaneously (in the same second).
4. Independence of occurrences.	4. Arrivals at the bank are not influenced by the length of the lines.

Of these four assumptions, numbers (1) and (3) are general enough to apply to almost any setting involving arrivals over time.* The assumptions that occurrences are constant over time and independent, however, are much less likely to be met in potential applications of the Poisson distribution. Nevertheless, the Poisson does seem to apply in a surprisingly large variety of different situations.

Examples of the Poisson distribution such as those given above are concerned with the probability of x occurrences (arrivals or service completions) *per unit of time.* The only parameter necessary to characterize a population described by the Poisson distribution is the *mean rate* at which events take place in each unit of time. We shall use the Greek letter lambda (λ) for this parameter. Lambda can thus be defined as the mean rate of occurrence for any convenient unit of time, such as one minute, ten minutes, an hour, a day, or even a year. A value of $\lambda = 2.3$, for example, could indicate that there are, on the average, 2.3 requests for service in a particular bank every 10 minutes. For practical applications, the mean rate at which events occur must be determined empirically. That is, λ must be known in advance, such as on the basis of a previous study of the situation. Once λ is known, the frequency function for the Poisson distribution can be used to determine the probability that exactly x occurrences, or events, take place in the specified interval of time. The Poisson distribution is defined as follows:

Poisson distribution:

$$P\left(\begin{array}{c} x \text{ occurrences in a} \\ \text{given time unit} \end{array}\right) = \begin{cases} \dfrac{e^{-\lambda}\lambda^x}{x!} & \text{for} \begin{cases} x = 0, 1, 2, \ldots \\ \lambda > 0 \end{cases} \\ 0 & \text{otherwise} \end{cases} \qquad (4.5)$$

EXAMPLE 1

To illustrate the use of Formula (4.5), suppose the bank in the discussion above knows from past experience that, between 10 A.M. and 11 A.M. each day, the mean arrival rate of customers is $\lambda = 60$ customers (per hour). Since we've assumed that arrivals are constant during a given time interval, this rate is equivalent to an arrival rate of $\lambda = 1$ customer per minute. Now, suppose the bank wants to determine the probability that exactly two customers ($x = 2$) will arrive in a given one-minute time interval between 10 and 11 A.M. Substituting $\lambda = 1$ and $x = 2$ into Formula (4.5) yields

$$P(2 \text{ arrivals}) = \frac{e^{-1}1^2}{2!} = \frac{1}{2}e^{-1}$$

Since $e^{-1} = 0.3679$,

$$P(2 \text{ arrivals}) = 0.3679/2 = 0.1839$$

---

*The Poisson distribution can also be applied to problems involving the number of occurrences of a random variable for a given unit of area, such as the number of typographical errors on a page, the number of white blood cells in a blood suspension, or the number of imperfections in a surface of wood, metal, or paint.

Similarly, they might want to calculate $P(2 \text{ or less arrivals})$:

$$P(2 \text{ or less arrivals}) = P(0) + P(1) + P(2)$$
$$= \frac{e^{-1}1^0}{0!} + \frac{e^{-1}1^1}{1!} + \frac{e^{-1}1^2}{2!}$$
$$= 0.3679 + 0.3679 + 0.1839$$
$$= 0.9197$$

As was the case for the binomial, Poisson probabilities have been extensively tabled, so that one can avoid the task by using Formula (4.5) to calculate such values. Table II in Appendix B gives these probabilities for selected values of λ from $\lambda = 0.01$ to $\lambda = 20.0$. The probability values for the above example are shown in Table II, under the heading $\lambda = 1.0$. These values are graphed in part (a) of Fig. 4.5; parts (b) and (c) of that figure show the probability mass function for $\lambda = 3.8$ and $\lambda = 10.0$. ∎

Characteristics of the Poisson Distribution

As can be seen in the graphs in Fig. 4.6, the Poisson is a discrete mass function which is always skewed to the right (since x cannot be lower than zero, but may be any positive integer). When λ is not too close to zero, however, the shape of the Poisson distribution will often have a very symmetrical appearance, as shown in Fig. 4.6(c).

As we indicated above, λ is the only parameter of the Poisson distribution. Because of this fact, both the mean and the variance of the Poisson must be a function of λ. We know already that the mean number of occurrences in a Poisson distribution is λ. Hence,

$$\boxed{\textit{Mean of Poisson: } \mu = \lambda}$$

Not only is the mean of a Poisson distribution denoted by λ, but the variance of the Poisson distribution also equals λ. That is,

$$\boxed{\textit{Variance of Poisson: } \sigma^2 = \lambda}$$

Thus, if a value of $\lambda = 1.0$ indicates that customers are arriving at a bank at an average rate of 1 customer per minute, then the *variance* of the number of arrivals in each minute is also 1.0.

EXAMPLE 2

As another illustration of the Poisson distribution, suppose a statistical consultant has suggested to the owner of a large supermarket that arrivals at the checkout counters might follow a Poisson distribution during certain periods of time. The owner decides to investigate this possibility by first checking the reasonableness of the four basic assumptions listed earlier, especially assump-

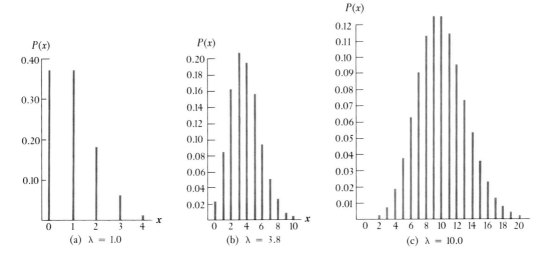

(a) λ = 1.0   (b) λ = 3.8   (c) λ = 10.0

Figure 4.6

The Poission distribution:

$$P(x) = \frac{e^{-\lambda}\lambda^x}{x!}$$

tions number 2 (constant probability) and 4 (independence). Let's assume the owner has decided to use 2 to 4 P.M., Monday–Friday, as the time interval, and all four assumptions appear reasonable for this time interval.

The next step this owner might take is to collect some observations concerning the number of arrivals within the two-hour time from 2 to 4 P.M. Rather than count the number of customers for many different two-hour time periods, the owner has recorded arrivals in each of 100 randomly selected one-minute periods from 2 to 4 P.M. This procedure is reasonable as arrivals are assumed to be constant over the two-hour period; hence it makes no difference, theoretically at least, what time unit is used. The number of customers arriving per minute (x) in this study ranged from 0 to 10, as shown in Table 4.5. For example, the first row indicates that only once did zero customers arrive in the one-minute periods; on eight occasions exactly one customer arrived; on 19 occasions exactly two customers arrived, and so forth.

Recall that, for the Poisson distribution, both μ and σ^2 are equal. Hence, in checking to see if the data in Table 4.5 do follow a Poisson distribution, the owner might first wish to see if $\mu = \sigma^2$. Column 4 in this table gives the appropriate values for calculating μ (use Formula (1.8). We see that $\mu = 3.79$. The variance is shown in column 6 as 3.908. For this population, μ and σ^2 are very nearly equal in value (3.79 vs. 3.908). Theoretically they are supposed to be equal, but in just 100 time periods we would not expect the observed value of either μ or σ^2 to precisely equal the theoretical value.

The closeness of μ and σ^2 in this case is encouraging enough for the store manager to make the most important test, namely, to see if the observed relative frequencies correspond to the theoretical relative frequencies from the Poisson. To make this comparison, suppose that the owner assumes that $\lambda = 3.8$ (note that it is not clear from the data whether $\lambda = 3.79$ or 3.908, or some other value). The choice of $\lambda = 3.8$ is somewhat arbitrary. Now, if the number of arrivals in these 100 one-minute periods does, in fact, follow a Poisson distribution with $\lambda = 3.8$, we would expect the observed frequencies in

TABLE 4.5   Supermarket example

(1) Arrivals (x)	(2) Observed frequency (f)	(3) $\dfrac{f}{N}$	(4) $x\dfrac{f}{N}$	(5) $(x-3.79)^2$	(6) $(x-3.79)^2\dfrac{f}{N}$
0	1	0.01	0.00	14.364	0.144
1	8	0.08	0.08	7.784	0.623
2	19	0.19	0.38	3.204	0.609
3	23	0.23	0.69	0.624	0.144
4	17	0.17	0.68	0.044	0.007
5	15	0.15	0.75	1.464	0.220
6	8	0.08	0.48	4.884	0.391
7	3	0.03	0.21	10.304	0.309
8	3	0.03	0.24	17.724	0.532
9	2	0.02	0.18	27.144	0.543
10	1	0.01	0.10	38.564	0.386
Sum	100	1.00	3.79		3.908

column 3 of Table 4.5 to correspond closely to the probabilities of the Poisson distribution $P(x) = e^{-3.8}(3.8)^x/x!$. These values, shown in Table II, Appendix B, under the heading $\lambda = 3.8$, are reproduced in Table 4.6.

We see in Table 4.6 that the observed relative frequencies correspond quite well to the Poisson values for $\lambda = 3.8$. A good exercise for the reader at this point would be to verify, for the probabilities shown in the last column of Table 4.6, that $\mu = \sigma^2 = 3.8$.

Since the probabilities in the last column in Table 4.6 completely describe the Poisson distribution for $\lambda = 3.8$, we can determine from these values other probabilities that might be of interest. For instance, the probability of *two or fewer* customers arriving in a given one-minute interval is

$$P(x \le 2) = \sum_{x=0}^{2} \frac{e^{-3.8}(3.8)^x}{x!} = 0.2689$$

Similarly, the probability of *eight or more* customers in a one-minute period equals 1 minus the cumulative value of seven or less customers:

$$P(x \ge 8) = 1 - P(x \le 7) = 1 - \sum_{x=0}^{7} \frac{e^{-3.8}(3.8)^x}{x!} = 0.04$$

Probability values such as these might be of use to the supermarket owner and manager in making a number of decisions, especially those concerned with the number of checkout counters to have open during the 2 to 4 P.M. period. ∎

Computer Programs for the Poisson Distribution

Table II in Appendix B is convenient for determining Poisson probability values as long as λ is relatively small. For larger values of λ, computer packages

TABLE 4.6 Observed vs. theoretical Poisson probabilities

Arrivals (x)	Observed relative frequency	Poisson values $P(x) = \dfrac{e^{-3.8}(3.8)^x}{x!}$
0	0.010	0.0224
1	0.080	0.0850
2	0.190	0.1615
3	0.230	0.2046
4	0.170	0.1944
5	0.150	0.1477
6	0.080	0.0936
7	0.030	0.0508
8	0.030	0.0241
9	0.020	0.0102
10	0.010	0.0039
11	0.000	0.0013
12	0.000	0.0004
13	0.000	0.0001
Sum	1.000	1.0000

represent a more convenient method of determining these probabilities. Because λ is the only population parameter necessary for determining the Poisson distribution, Poisson programs need only ask for "the mean number of occurrences," as well as the usual upper and lower x-values of interest ($x1$ and $x2$). The output in Table 4.7 is the Poisson distribution for $\lambda = 3.8$, from $x1 = 0$ to $x2 = 12$. The reader may wish to verify these values with those shown in Table 4.6 and Fig. 4.6(b).

TABLE 4.7 Computer output for Poisson distribution for $\lambda = 3.8$

```
        POISSON DISTRIBUTION
     MEAN RATE OF OCCURRENCE = 3.8
                CUMULATIVE                    CUMULATIVE
    X    P(X)    PROBABILITY    X    P(X)    PROBABILITY
    0   .02237     .02237       7   .05079     .95989
    1   .08501     .10738       8   .02412     .98402
    2   .16152     .26890       9   .01019     .99420
    3   .20459     .47348      10   .00387     .99807
    4   .19436     .66784      11   .00134     .99941
    5   .14771     .81556      12   .00042     .99983
    6   .09355     .90911      13   .00012     .99995
  E(X) = 3.80      STD. DEV. = 1.94936      VARIANCE = 3.80
```

Problems

4.18 The School of Business of the University of Texas was asked to select a grievance committee of six from a list consisting of five men and five women.

a) If the committee is to be chosen by random selection, what is the probability that there will be three men and three women?

b) What is the probability that a majority of the committee will be women?

c) If the committee is picked by one person, what probability value would you use to investigate a claim of biasedness if there are four men and two women?

4.19 A television manufacturer is inspecting a shipment of 10 color television sets. Assume three are defective. A sample of three is to be drawn.

a) What is the probability of receiving *at least* one defective if the samples are drawn with replacement?

b) Repeat part (a) assuming sampling without replacement.

4.20 A market researcher at Bayer Aspirin decides to survey 10 of 100 doctors who are randomly selected from a large population of doctors. If 50% of these 100 doctors actually prefer Bayer, what is the probability that the results of the survey will show that "Nine out of 10 doctors surveyed prefer Bayer"?

4.21 The Department of Defense has announced that it will award a contract to build a prototype of a new military airplane to four companies. Twenty companies have submitted preliminary proposals. You own stock in three of these companies. What is the probability that all three of your companies will be winners if selection is made randomly?

4.22 How does the hypergeometric distribution differ from the binomial distribution? Under what circumstances is each one appropriate?

4.23 Redo Problem 4.21 using the binomial distribution, assuming p is a constant, $p = 4/20$.

4.24 In Problem 2.37, 2073 of the 10,000 customers of the Easy Charge Company received a cash advance during September. You take a random sample of 100 of these customers.

a) Write down the hypergeometric expression representing the probability that 21% of the sample will be customers who received a cash advance.

b) Find the hypergeometric probability for part (a) using a computer package.

4.25 A special congressional committee investigating business ethics was randomly selected from a Senate consisting of 55 Democrats and 45 Republicans. The committee consists of eight people.

a) Write down the hypergeometric expression for the probability the committee will consist of seven Democrats and one Republican.

b) Solve part (a) using a computer package.

c) Sketch the p.m.f. for $x = 0, 1, 2, \ldots, 8$, where x is the number of Republicans. Should the Republicans complain they have been unfairly represented on the committee if seven of the committee members are Democrats? Explain.

4.26 An automobile company recently promoted six assembly line workers to new positions. Ten qualified applicants were considered, four of whom were minorities. One minority candidate was among the six promoted.

a) Use the hypergeometric output shown below to determine the probability that one or fewer of the minority candidates will be promoted, if selection is random.

b) What are the values of N, n_1, n_2, and $x1 + x2$ for this problem?

x	$P(x)$	Cumulative probability
0	.00476	.00476
1	.11429	.11905
2	.42857	.57462
3	.38095	.92857
4	.07143	1.00000

4.27 The CFO at Ross Labs has been asked to form a committee consisting of three people, selected from two departments. Twenty people from the first department are eligible, and 30 people from the second department are eligible. If the CFO selects the three members randomly from the total group of 30 people, what is the probability that the committee will have one from the first department and two from the second?

4.28 Ten percent of a special type of motor produced by Otis Elevator require some reworking after the first inspection at the plant. Assume such problems occur randomly.

a) What is the probability of three or more defectives in a sample of seven?

b) If exactly three items are defective, would you, as a quality control expert, take any action? Why or why not?

4.29 Use a computer to verify for Table 4.6 that $E[x] = 3.79$ and $V[x] = 3.908$.

4.30 When airline baggage is being unloaded at the Philadelphia International Airport, 8.5 pieces of baggage are handled in a typical half minute. What is the probability that exactly 10 pieces of baggage will be handled in such a half minute?

4.31 A textile manufacturing process in Georgia carefully inspects for flaws. Typically, an average of 2 flaws per 10 running yards of material have appeared. What is the probability that a given 10-yard segment will have 0 or 1 defects, if flaws follow a Poisson distribution?

4.32 North Carolina National Bank found that an average of 2.3 calls per minute are made through a central switchboard designed to handle billing problems. If calls follow a Poisson distribution, what is the probability that during a given minute two or more calls will be made?

4.33 A State Farm insurance agent processes an average of 10 claims per working day, a rate that follows a Poisson distribution.

a) Sketch the Poisson p.m.f., indicating on your sketch both the mean and the standard deviation.

    b) Sketch the c.m.f. for $\lambda = 10$.

    c) Find $P(8 \le x \le 12)$.

4.34 a) Determine what percentage of the Poisson distribution lies between $\mu \pm 1\sigma$ and between $\mu \pm 2\sigma$ when $\lambda = 1$. How do these values compare with the rule of thumb given in Chapter 1?

    b) Repeat part (a) for $\lambda = 4$ and $\lambda = 9$ and comment on why you think the percentages are getting closer to the rule of thumb.

4.35 In litigation involving drugs or the exposure to radiation, the question arises as to reasonable expectations about how often abnormalities may occur. For example, in a study of 300 pregnant women taking a drug thought to be harmless, 24 gave birth to a a a premature baby (less than 5 lb 4 oz, or born more than three weeks early). If the national average for premature babies is 6%, would you suspect this drug of being harmful? Explain, using the Poisson distribution.

4.36 Consider the computer output below, which describes the number of arrivals for a 10-minute period, at a grocery store.

    a) What is the value of λ?

    b) What is the probability of two or more successes?

```
POISSON DISTRIBUTION
              CUMULATIVE                    CUMULATIVE
  X    P(X)   PROBABILITY    X    P(X)     PROBABILITY
  0  .00004     .00004      16  .02439       .96835
  1  .00038     .00042      17  .01463       .98299
  2  .00193     .00235      18  .00829       .99128
  3  .00657     .00892      19  .00445       .99573
  4  .01676     .02569      20  .00227       .99800
  5  .03420     .05989      21  .00110       .99910
  6  .05814     .11803      22  .00051       .99961
  7  .08472     .20274      23  .00023       .99984
  8  .10801     .31076      24  .00010       .99994
  9  .12242     .43317      25  .00004       .99998
 10  .12486     .55803
 11  .11578     .67382
 12  .09842     .77223
 13  .07722     .84945
 14  .05626     .90571
 15  .03826     .94396
E(X) = 10.20    STD. DEV. = 3.19374    VARIANCE = 10.20
```

Exercises

4.37 a) Prove that $E[x] = \lambda$ for the Poisson distribution.

    b) Prove that $V[x] = \lambda$ for the Poisson distribution.

4.38 Prove that the Poisson distribution meets the two conditions defining a probability mass function.

4.39 Prove for the binomial distribution that

    a) $E[x/n] = p$

    b) $V[x] = npq$

    c) $V[x/n] = pq$

4.40 Suppose that a baseball player has averaged four official times at bat in each of 150 games and hit 50 home runs. Based on this past performance, what is the probability that in game number 151 this player will hit at least one home run in his first four official times at bat? Are the assumptions of the binomial reasonable for this application? Explain.

4.41 Prove that for a constant value of $\lambda = np$, the Poisson distribution is the limit of the binomial distribution as n approaches infinity. That is,

$$\lim_{n \to \infty} \frac{n!}{x!(n-x)!} p^x q^{(n-x)} = \frac{e^{-\lambda} \lambda^x}{x!}$$

4.42 A classical example of the Poisson distribution resulted from a study of the number of deaths from horse kicks in the Prussian Army from 1875 to 1894. The data for this example are:

Deaths per corps (per year)	Observed frequency
0	144
1	91
2	32
3	11
4	2
5 and over	0
Total	280

    a) Fit a Poisson distribution to these data. (*Hint:* Note that there were 196 deaths from the 280 observations; hence the mean death rate was $\frac{196}{280} = 0.700$.) How good does the Poisson approximation appear to be?

    b) Do the assumptions of the Poisson distribution seem reasonable in this problem?

4.43 **a)** Write a generalization of Formula (4.4) extending the hypergeometric to the problem of determining the probability of x_1 of n_1, x_2 of n_2, ..., and x_k of n_k.

    b) Ten applicants for three identical positions include five from the east, three from the midwest, and two from the west. Assume the positions are filled randomly, and use the formula in part (a) to determine the probability that one person from each area earns the job.

4.44 Consider the data below, representing a random sample of 20 companies selected from the 1989 *Business Week* list of the top 1000 companies in America. For all 1000 companies, the median price/earnings ratio was 15. Use the binomial distribution to determine if a median of 15 is a reasonable assumption for the data below.

Company		P/E Ratio	Company		P/E Ratio
1.	J. C. Penney	9	11.	Hubbell	14
2.	Spiegel	10	12.	F. W. Woolworth	11
3	BankAmerica	8	13.	Lincoln National	9
4.	CPI	13	14.	Tele-Com-USA	22
5.	MBIA	10	15.	Michigan National	7
6.	Safety-Kleen	22	16.	Paccar	10
7.	Atari	9	17.	MCN	8
8.	Lubrizol	11	18.	Bausch & Lomb	14
9.	UNUM	10	19.	Thermo Electron	18
10.	Big Bear	21	20.	A. T. Cross	16

4.45 a) The customers of the A-1 Loan Company (Exercise 1.48) arrive at the loan office at the rate of $\lambda = 12$ customers per day. Graph the probability mass function for all values of x between 5 and 18.

b) What is $P(x \geq 13)$?

c) Suppose the managers at A-1 have noticed that approximately 50 people walk by their office each day. If we assume [from part (a)] that there is a constant probability that each of these people will enter, the binomial distribution can be used to describe the arrival rate.

 1) What is the appropriate value of p if we assume 12 of the 50 people enter? What will μ and σ^2 be for this binomial distribution?

 2) Superimpose on your graph from part (a) the probability mass function of the binomial for values of x between 5 and 18.

4.46 Out of 10 sales representatives, seven (call them group A) make sales on 20% of their calls. The other three (call them group B) make sales on 50% of their calls.

a) What is the average percentage of sales to calls for all 10 sales reps?

b) Suppose the sales manager selects three of these sales representatives at random to assign to a new territory. What is the probability that exactly two of them will be from group A?

c) Suppose we follow one of the sales representatives in group A on her next five calls, each of which is considered independent of any of the others. What is the probability that she makes more than one but fewer than four sales in those five calls?

4.47 The following bridge hand almost broke up the 1955 world championship tournament because it occurred twice in the space of a few hours.

Spades: A, K, 9, 5   Hearts: Q, 8, 4
Diamonds: J, 7, 3   Clubs: 10, 6, 2

a) Write an expression representing the probability of the occurrence of this hand, assuming the cards are dealt randomly.

b) Determine a nonprobabilistic explanation as to why such a bridge hand might have occurred twice in the 1955 world championship.

4.48 A discrete distribution is generated by picking, randomly, an integer between 0 and 9. If each number has a probability of being selected of $\frac{1}{10}$, find $E[x]$ and $V[x]$.

4.49 The Pascal (or negative binomial) distribution is appropriate when one is interested in determining the probability that n Bernoulli trials will be required to produce r successes. This probability is

$$P(n) = \frac{(n-1)!}{(r-1)!(n-r)!} p^r (1-p)^{n-r} \qquad \text{for } n \geq r$$

For example, suppose an advertising agency is trying to evaluate the effects of a television commercial advertising swimming pool chlorine. A caller is assigned to randomly contact residential dwellings in Phoenix, where 40% of the homes have pools.

a) What is the probability that it will take 10 or fewer calls to find exactly five homes with pools (assume all calls are answered politely)?

b) What is the average number of calls required to have five successes if $E[n] = r/p$?

c) What is the variance of the number of calls if $V[n] = r(1-p)/p^2$?

Chapter 5

Continuous
Probability
Distributions

In graphing the data they fell,
In line with a swoop and a swell.
Experimentally normal,
Their pattern was formal,
Their shape emulating a bell.

ROBERT LAMBORN

Introduction **5.1**

This chapter continues presenting a number of the more commonly used probability distributions, but now the discussion includes only continuous distributions. Remember, if a random variable is continuous between two points, then *any* number between these points is at least theoretically possible. For practical purposes, most variables cannot be recorded with very great accuracy. For example, corporate yields (annual dividend divided by stock price) can be, theoretically, any number between zero and infinity. Yields, however, are generally reported only to two decimal points (and usually expressed as a percent). For example, in 1989 the year-end price of General Motors Stock was $44 per share (rounded), and its dividend was $3.00; this means that GM's yield was

$$3.00/44 = 0.0681818 \ldots.$$

The GM yield is never reported this way, but rather rounded, multiplied by 100, and reported as 6.82 (percent). Thus, while some variables are truly continuous (such as yields), even these variables are typically reported in a discrete manner. Nevertheless, because variables such as yield have so many different outcomes (whether you think of them as discrete or continuous), you will see in this chapter that it is convenient to *manipulate* them as continuous variables.

Three continuous variables are discussed in this chapter, the *normal,* the *chi-square,* and the *exponential.* Two additional continuous distributions, the *t*-distribution and the *F*-distribution are discussed in Chapter 6 in the context of sampling theory.

The Normal Distribution

5.2

Scientists in the eighteenth century noted a predictable regularity to the frequency with which certain "errors" occur, especially errors of measurement. Suppose, for example, a machine is supposed to roll a sheet of metal to a width of exactly $\frac{5}{16}$ in.; while this machine produces sheets that are $\frac{5}{16}$ in. wide on the average, some sheets are in "error" by being slightly too wide, others by being slightly too narrow. Experiments producing errors of this nature were found to form a symmetrical distribution that was originally called the "normal curve of errors." The continuous probability distribution that such an experiment approximates is usually referred to as the **normal distribution,** or sometimes the *Gaussian distribution,* after an early researcher, Karl Gauss (1777–1855).

The normal distribution undoubtedly represents the most widely known and used of all distributions. Because the normal distribution approximates many natural phenomena so well, this distribution has developed into a standard of reference for many probability problems. The normal distribution is so important in the theory of statistics that a considerable portion of the sampling, estimation, and hypothesis-testing theory we will study in the rest of this book is based on the characteristics of this distribution.

Characteristics of the Normal Distribution

The normal distribution is a continuous distribution in which x can assume any value between minus infinity and plus infinity ($-\infty < x < \infty$). Two parameters describe the normal distribution, μ, representing the mean, and σ, representing the standard deviation.[*] The normal density function contains two constants, π (where $\pi = 3.1415\ldots$) and e (where $e = 2.7182\ldots$). The normal density function is given by Formula (5.1). Note that in labeling this formula we use the symbol $N(\mu, \sigma^2)$, which is a traditional designation for a normal curve with mean μ and variance σ^2.

---

[*]Beginning students of statistics are sometimes confused by the fact that the normal distribution uses the symbols μ and σ^2 to represent the parameters of this distribution, rather than special ones, such as n and p for the binomial. Also, the term "normal distribution" is typically used to denote what should be more formally called the *normal density function.*

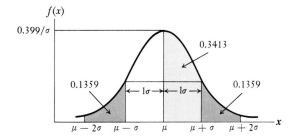

Figure 5.1
Normal distribution with
mean μ and standard
deviation σ.

Normal density function, $N(\mu, \sigma^2)$:

$$f(x) = \frac{1}{\sigma\sqrt{2\pi}} \, e^{-(1/2)[(x-\mu)/\sigma]^2} \qquad \text{for } -\infty < x < \infty. \tag{5.1}$$

The curve described by Formula (5.1) is a completely symmetrical, bell-shaped probability density function, whose graph is shown in Fig. 5.1. The mean of this p.d.f. is designated as μ, and its standard deviation is σ. As is the case for all symmetrical unimodal distributions, the mean = median = mode.

One of the first aspects to notice in Fig. 5.1 is how much of the area (probability) falls within plus or minus one and plus or minus two standard deviations of the mean. These two are illustrated in that graph because they have served as rules of thumb ever since Chapter 1. In effect, we stated that $\mu \pm 1\sigma$ contains "about 68%" of the population, and $\mu \pm 2\sigma$ contains "about 95%" of the population. These rules are based on the normal distribution. To show that, we use Fig. 5.1, and the fact that the normal distribution is symmetrical.

$$P(\mu - 1\sigma \leq x \leq \mu + 1\sigma) = 0.3413 + 0.3413 = 0.6826$$

and

$$P(\mu - 2\sigma \leq x \leq \mu + 2\sigma) = 2(0.3413 + 0.1359) = 0.9544$$

Had we included a few additional values in Fig. 5.1, we could also show that*

$$P(\mu - 3\sigma \leq x \leq \mu + 3\sigma) = 0.9974$$

---

*Since probabilities in the continuous case are given by integrating the p.d.f. in (5.1) over the appropriate intervals, we can thus write:

$$P(\mu - 1\sigma \leq x \leq \mu + 1\sigma) = \int_{\mu-\sigma}^{\mu+\sigma} f(x)\,dx = 0.6826$$

$$P(\mu - 2\sigma \leq x \leq \mu + 2\sigma) = \int_{\mu-2\sigma}^{\mu+2\sigma} f(x)\,dx = 0.9544$$

and

$$P(\mu - 3\sigma \leq x \leq \mu + 3\sigma) = \int_{\mu-3\sigma}^{\mu+3\sigma} f(x)\,dx = 0.9974$$

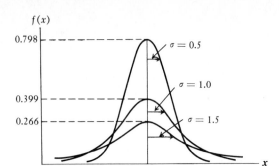

Figure 5.2
Three normal distributions
with different standard
deviations.

It is important to remember that all normal distributions have the same bell-shaped curve pictured in Fig. 5.1, regardless of the values of μ and σ.* The value of μ merely indicates where the center of the "bell" lies, while σ indicates how spread out (or wide) the distribution is. Figure 5.2 illustrates three normal distributions, each having the same mean, but having different standard deviations.

Probabilities such as $P(\mu - 1\sigma \leq x \leq \mu + 1\sigma)$ can be determined using calculus to integrate under the normal density function. Unfortunately, this is not an easy process, so we need to develop a convenient means for determining such probabilities. However, even with the limited information presented thus far about the normal, it is possible to solve certain problems, such as the following one.

Tire-life Example. Suppose the random variable x, representing the tread life (in miles) of a certain new radial tire, is normally distributed with mean, $\mu = 40{,}000$ miles, and standard deviation, $\sigma = 3000$ miles [$N(40{,}000, 3000^2)$]. This information is sufficient to completely determine the probability of any event concerning the values of x. For example, the probability that a randomly selected tire lasts 40,000 miles or more is $P(x \geq 40{,}000) = \frac{1}{2}$, since half of the probability in a normal distribution lies on each side of the mean.

---

*It is easy to see, from Figs. 5.1 and 5.2, that Property 1 of all p.d.f.'s is satisfied for the normal distribution, since $f(x) \geq 0$ for all $-\infty \leq x \leq \infty$. Proving Property 2, that $\int_{-\infty}^{\infty} f(x)\,dx = 1$, is more difficult since it involves switching to polar coordinates. This proof, and proving that $E[x] = \mu$ and $E[(x - \mu)^2] = \sigma^2$ for the normal distribution, are beyond the scope of this book. Note that in Fig. 5.1 the height of the density function at the point $x = \mu$ is $0.399/\sigma$. This fact can be derived from Formula (5.1) by substituting μ for x, and then noting that

$$f(x) = f(\mu) = \frac{1}{\sigma\sqrt{2\pi}}\,e^{-(1/2)[(x-\mu)/\sigma]^2} = \frac{1}{\sigma\sqrt{2\pi}}\,e^0$$

Since $e^0 = 1$ and $1/\sqrt{2\pi} = 0.399$,

$$f(\mu) = \frac{0.399}{\sigma}$$

Thus if $\sigma = 1.0$, then $f(\mu) = 0.399/1.0 = 0.399$. When $\sigma = 0.5$, $f(\mu) = 0.399/0.5 = 0.798$, and if $\sigma = 1.5$, $f(\mu) = 0.399/1.5 = 0.266$. The normal distributions corresponding to these three values of σ are shown in Fig. 5.2.

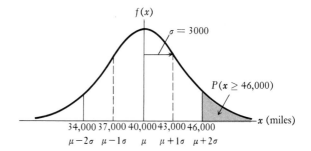

Figure 5.3
Tire-life example.

On the other hand, suppose we calculate the probability that a tire of this model selected at random has a tread life of between 34,000 and 46,000 miles, or $P(34,000 \leq x \leq 46,000)$. We see in Fig. 5.3 that 46,000 is exactly *two standard deviations* above the mean,

$$46,000 - 40,000 = 6000 = 2\sigma$$

Similarly, 34,000 is exactly two standard deviations *below* the mean. The probability $P(34,000 \leq x \leq 46,000)$ is thus equivalent to $P(\mu - 2\sigma \leq x \leq \mu + 2\sigma)$, which we calculated earlier (see Fig. 5.1) to be

$$P(\mu - 2\sigma \leq x \leq \mu + 2\sigma) = 0.9544$$

Now let's move to a slightly more complicated problem—determining the probability that a tire will last at least 46,000 miles, or $P(x \geq 46,000)$.[*] From Fig. 5.3 we see that $P(x \geq 46,000)$ is equivalent to $P(x \geq \mu + 2\sigma)$. But $P(x \geq \mu + 2\sigma)$ is exactly *half* of the area *not* included in $P(\mu - 2\sigma \leq x \leq \mu + 2\sigma)$, since the normal is symmetric. In other words, $P(x \geq \mu + 2\sigma)$ is one-half of the *complement* of $P(\mu - 2\sigma \leq x \leq \mu + 2\sigma) = 0.9544$. That is

$$P(x \geq \mu + 2\sigma) = \tfrac{1}{2}(1.0000 - 0.9544) = \tfrac{1}{2}(0.0456) = 0.0228$$

By the symmetry of the normal distribution, we also know that

$$P(x \leq \mu - 2\sigma) = 0.0228 = P(x \leq 34,000)$$

To carry this analysis one step further, we now have enough information to calculate, directly,

$$P(x \leq 37,000) = P(x \leq \mu - 1\sigma)$$

From Fig. 5.1 we know the probability that x falls between $\mu - 2\sigma$ and $\mu - 1\sigma$ is 0.1359. If we add to this value the probability we calculated above,

$$P(x \leq \mu - 2\sigma) = 0.0228$$

The result is

$$P(x \leq \mu - 1\sigma) = 0.0228 + 0.1359 = 0.1587$$

---

[*]Remember that $P(x > 46,000) = P(x \geq 46,000)$ because $P(x = 46,000) = 0$.

Finally, for this example, suppose we are interested in the probability that tread life will fall between 44,500 and 47,500 miles, or $P(44,500 \leq x \leq 47,500)$. The answer can be determined in two ways. Using calculus, one could integrate the normal p.d.f. with $\mu = 40,000$ and $\sigma = 3000$ from 44,500 to 47,500; or one could use a table of areas already calculated for the precise parameters, $\mu = 40,000$ and $\sigma = 3000$. Both of these methods are unsatisfactory, however; the first one because it is too tedious to evaluate a new integral every time one investigates a different set of parameters or new x-values, and the second one because no such tables exist (there obviously can't be tables listing the infinite number of values of μ and σ).

Standardized Normal

5.3

Values of x for the normal distribution are usually described in terms of *how many standard deviations* they are away from the mean. The value $x = 200$, for example, has little meaning unless we know in what units x was measured (feet, miles, pounds). On the other hand, the statement that x is one standard deviation larger (or smaller) than the mean can be given a very precise interpretation, since it is always meaningful to talk of x being a certain number of standard deviations above (or below) the mean, no matter what value σ assumes or on what scale the variable x is measured. Now, if x is measured in terms of standard deviations about the mean, it is natural to describe probability values in the same terms—that is, by specifying the probability that x will fall within so many standard deviations of the mean. There are three commonly encountered intervals, the first two of which we have referred to often in the last two chapters: $\mu \pm 1\sigma$, $\mu \pm 2\sigma$, and $\mu \pm 3\sigma$.

Treating the values of x in a normal distribution in terms of standard deviations about the mean has the advantage of permitting all normal distributions to be compared to one common or *standard* form. In this standard form, different values of μ and σ no longer generate completely different curves, since x is measured only about μ, and all distances away from μ are in terms of multiples of σ. In other words, it is easier to compare normal distributions having different values of μ and σ if these curves are transformed to one common form, which is called the *standardized normal*. The standardized normal, by definition, has a mean of zero ($\mu = 0$) and a standard deviation of one ($\sigma = 1$). Note that if the standard deviation is one, the variance must also be one since $\sigma^2 = 1.0$ when $\sigma = 1.0$.

This process of standardization gives a hint toward the best method of attack in answering questions concerning a normal probability distribution. Instead of trying to directly solve a probability problem involving a normally distributed random variable x with mean μ and standard deviation σ, an indirect approach is used. We first convert the problem to an equivalent one dealing with a normal variable measured in standard deviation units, called a standardized normal variable. A table of standardized normal values (Table III,

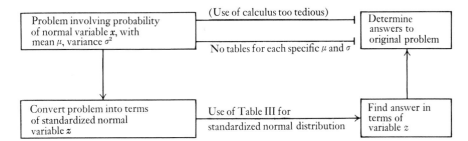

Figure 5.4
Problem-solving tactic using
the standardized normal.

Appendix B) can then be used to obtain an answer in terms of the converted problem. Finally, by converting back to the original units of measurement for *x*, we can obtain the answer to the original problem. Figure 5.4 gives a schematic outline of this method of solving probability problems.

Recall that we discussed in Chapter 3 the process of transforming a random variable *x* (whether normally distributed or not), with mean and standard deviation σ, into a standardized measure with mean zero and standard deviation one. The appropriate transformation was shown to be $z = (x - \mu)/\sigma$. The mean of the variable *z* was shown in Section 3.6 to be $E[z] = 0$ and the variance was shown to be $V[z] = 1.0$.

Although we have used the letter *z* to represent a random variable with mean zero and variance one, this variable traditionally also represents the standardized form of the normal distribution. The letter *z* is thus generally associated with the normal distribution $N(0, 1)$. That is,

$$z = \frac{x - \mu}{\sigma} \quad \text{is} \quad N(0, 1)$$

Standardized normal random variable:
(5.2)

The density function for *z* can be derived by letting $z = (x - \mu)/\sigma$, and $\sigma = 1$ in Formula (5.1). The resulting p.d.f. is denoted as $f(z)$.

Standardized normal density function:

$$f(z) = \frac{1}{\sqrt{2\pi}} e^{-(1/2)z^2}$$
(5.3)

This function is shown graphically in Fig. 5.5. The reader should compare Fig. 5.5 with Fig. 5.1 to verify that the former is merely a special case of the latter, where $\mu = 0$ and $\sigma = 1$.

The interpretation of *z*-values is relatively simple. Since $\sigma_z = 1$, a value of *x* is, for example, two standard deviations away from the mean whenever $z = \pm 2$; likewise, if $z = \pm 1.56$, the corresponding *x*-value is exactly 1.56 standard deviations away from the mean (or $|x - \mu| = 1.56\sigma$).

To illustrate the use of the standardized normal, let's consider the tire-life problem posed at the end of the last section—namely, $P(44,500 \leq x \leq 47,500)$. In transforming this probability into an equivalent one in standard-

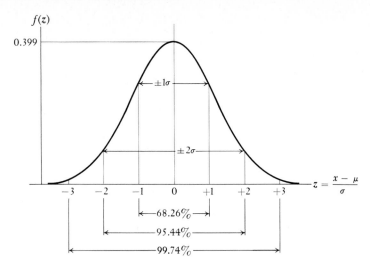

Figure 5.5
Standardized normal
distribution:

$$f(z) = \frac{1}{\sqrt{2\pi}} e^{-(1/2)z^2}.$$

ized-normal form, we need to apply the transformation $z = (x - \mu)/\sigma$ to *each* part of the expression in parentheses. For example, the value 44,500 is transformed into its equivalent form by subtracting $\mu = 40,000$ from it, and then dividing by $\sigma = 3000$; the value 47,500 is transformed in exactly the same manner. Finally, we can think of the variable x being transformed in the same way, since the new variable, z, equals $(x - \mu)/\sigma$. Thus,

$$P(44,500 \le x \le 47,500) = P\left(\frac{44,500 - 40,000}{3000} \le \frac{x - \mu}{\sigma} \le \frac{47,500 - 40,000}{3000}\right)$$

$$= P(1.5 \le z \le 2.5)$$

Figure 5.6 illustrates the equivalence between:

$$P(44,500 \le x \le 47,500) \qquad \text{and} \qquad P(1.5 \le z \le 2.5)$$

As we indicated previously, probabilities involving z-values are usually determined using tables of standardized normal values, such as those shown in Table III, Appendix B. In our discussion of the standardized normal distribution and Table III, we will make use of the cumulative distribution function $F(z) = P(z \le z)$. This function is shown in Fig. 5.7. As we pointed out in Chapter 1, a cumulative function can be used to calculate percentiles. For example, $z = 1$ represents the 84.13th percentile, since $F(1) = 0.8413$. Note that we have plotted z-values only from -3 to $+3$, since very little area lies beyond these limits. At $z = 0$ (the mean of z), the value of $F(z)$ must be 0.50, since $z = 0$ represents the median (as well as the mode and the mean) of the z-values. Most of the other values in Fig. 5.7 should be familiar to you by now. For example, $F(-2) = 0.0228$. This value agrees with the one calculated in the example on tire life, as we saw then that $P(x \le \mu - 2\sigma) = 0.0228$. The value $F(-1) = 0.1587$ should also appear familiar, as this is the same value we calculated in the tire-life problem for $P(x \le \mu - 1\sigma)$.

Since the normal distribution is completely symmetrical, tables of z-values usually include only *positive* values of z. Thus, the lowest value in Table III in Appendix B is $z = 0$, and the cumulative probability at this point is

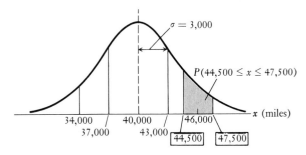

$$P(44,500 \le x \le 47,500)$$

Tire life: $\mu = 40,000$, $\sigma = 3,000$

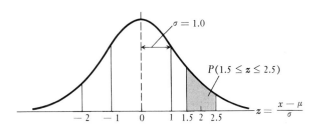

$$P(1.5 \le z \le 2.5)$$

$$z = \frac{x - \mu}{\sigma}$$

Standardized normal: $\mu = 0$, $\sigma = 1.0$

Figure 5.6
Tire-life example.

$F(0) = P(z \le 0) = 0.50$. Table III gives values of z to two decimal points, up to the point $z = 3.49$. The values of z to one decimal are read from the left margin in Table III, while the second decimal is read across the top. The body of the table gives the values of $F(z)$.

To illustrate the use of Table III, we will consider four basic situations. The reader should try to understand (visualize) these examples, *not* memorize them.

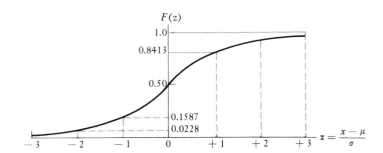

$$z = \frac{x - \mu}{\sigma}$$

Figure 5.7
Cumulative z-values.

EXAMPLE 1   *$P(z \le a)$ is given by $F(a)$ when a is positive.* We can illustrate this situation by determining the probability $P(x \le 45,000)$ in the tire-life problem:

$$P(x \le 45,000) = P\left(\frac{x - \mu}{\sigma} \le \frac{45,000 - 40,000}{3000}\right)$$

$$= P(z \le 1.66) = F(1.66)$$

The value of $F(1.66)$ is found in Table III by looking for 1.6 along the left margin and 0.06 across the top. The intersection of these values shows $F(1.66) = 0.9515$. Thus, $P(x \leq 45,000) = 0.9515$.

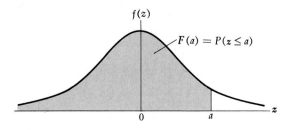

EXAMPLE 2 $P(x \geq a)$ *is given by the complement rule as 1 $- F(a)$.* This example is a direct application of the complement rule of Chapter 2. To illustrate it, consider the tire-life problem in which we calculated $P(x \geq \mu + 2\sigma) = 0.0228$. This probability is equivalent to $P(z \geq 2.0)$, which, by the complement rule, equals $1 - F(2.00)$. From Table III, $F(2.00) = 0.9772$; hence,

$$P(z \geq 2.0) = 1 - 0.9772 = 0.0228$$

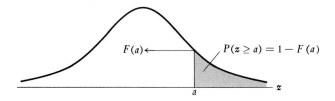

EXAMPLE 3 $P(z \leq -a)$ *is given by 1 $- F(a)$.* Because the normal distribution is completely symmetrical, $P(z \leq -a) = P(z \geq a)$. Since, by Example 2, we know that $P(z \geq a) = 1 - F(a)$, we also know that $P(z \leq -a) = 1 - F(a)$. For example, let's return to the tire-life problem of calculating $P(x \leq 37,000) = P(z \leq -1.00)$. From Table III, $F(1.00) = 0.8413$; hence,

$$P(x \leq 37,000) = P(z \leq -1.00) = 1 - 0.8413 = 0.1587$$

(which agrees with our earlier result).

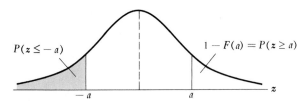

EXAMPLE 4 $P(a \leq z \leq b)$ *is given by F(b) $- F(a)$.* This example is the same as Formula (3.8) in Chapter 3. To illustrate it, suppose we solve the problem at the start of this section, $P(1.5 \leq z \leq 2.5)$. From Table III,

$$F(2.5) = 0.9938 \quad \text{and} \quad F(1.5) = 0.9332$$

Hence,

$$P(1.5 \leq z \leq 2.5) = 0.9938 - 0.9332 = 0.0606$$

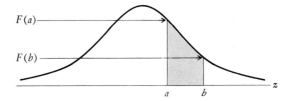

To further illustrate typical calculations involving the normal distribution, we use data from *Standard & Poor's Compustat Services* on the 1989 return on common equity for the top 1000 U.S. Companies (ranked by stock value). This average is $\mu = 15.1$, with a standard deviation of $\sigma = 4.8$. Assuming these returns are (at least approximately) normally distributed, a graph of this distribution would look like Fig. 5.8.

Let's use Fig. 5.8 to determine the probability that a return will be less than 10.0.

$$P(x < 10.0) = P(z < \frac{10.0 - 15.1}{4.8}) = P(z < -1.06)$$

From Table III,

$$P(z < -1.06) = 1 - P(z < 1.06) = 1 - 0.8554$$
$$= 0.1446$$

which means we expect (from the normal distribution) to find 14.46% of the returns to be less than 10.0.

Another type of problem using the normal distribution involves finding an x-value given a probability. For example, suppose in Fig. 5.8 we want to determine a return such that 90 percent of the returns are less than this number. In this problem we first need to find a value a from the Table III such that

$$P(z \leq a) = 0.90$$

From the middle of Table III, a is found to be 1.28, as

$$P(z \leq 1.28) = 0.90 \text{ (approximately)}$$

Figure 5.8

Graph of return on common equity for 1989.

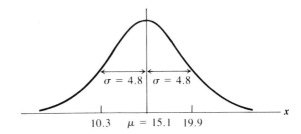

We can now solve for the desired return using this relationship:

$$z = \frac{x - \mu}{\sigma} \qquad \text{or} \qquad 1.28 = \frac{a - 15.1}{4.8}$$

Solving for a yields $a = 21.24$. This means we expect (based on a normal distribution) to find 90% of the returns less than 21.24.

There are many other types of problems that can be solved using the standardized normal distribution. To illustrate several of these problems, we conclude this section with the following example.

Calculating a Probability Interval

Suppose we want to solve a probability problem involving an interval $a \le x \le b$ where both a and b are unknown. For example, in the tire-life problem, one might wish to determine two values a and b such that the probability is 0.95 that a randomly selected tire will fall between these values;

$$P(a \le x \le b) = 0.95$$

It should be readily apparent that there is an infinitely large number of such intervals, depending on how the values of a and b are selected. If our interval is to include 95% of the area under the curve and exclude 5%, we could exclude all 5% above b, or exclude all 5% below a, or exclude part of it below a and part above b. In many cases the best way to split the percent to be excluded among the two tails will be specified in the problem. If it is not specified, then *it is generally agreed* that:

The best way to split the percent to be excluded is in a manner that makes the interval from a to b as small as possible. The smallest interval is obtained by excluding equal amounts in both the upper and lower tails of the distribution.[*]

This result, known as the Neyman–Pearson theorem, is proven in more advanced books on statistics. It tells us that the best way to split our 5% is to have 2.5% in each tail. Let's now use this result to solve the tire-life problem, $P(a \le x \le b) = 0.95$.

To solve this problem let's first standardize it as much as possible, by subtracting $\mu = 40{,}000$ from each term, and then dividing by $\sigma = 3000$.

$$P(a \le x \le b) = P\left(\frac{a - 40{,}000}{3000} \le \frac{x - \mu}{\sigma} \le \frac{b - 40{,}000}{3000}\right) = 0.95$$

---

[*]As we will discuss later, this nontechnical statement is true only for unimodal, symmetrical distributions such as the normal. For other types of distributions, further conditions must be specified.

or

$$P\left(\frac{a - 40{,}000}{3000} \leq z \leq \frac{b - 40{,}000}{3000}\right) = 0.95 \qquad (5.4)$$

We can't solve this expression yet. However, suppose we try to find, using Table III, the appropriate z-values; that is, let us try to find an interval $c \leq z \leq d$ such that

$$P(c \leq z \leq d) = 0.95$$

From Table III, $F(1.96) = 0.9750$, which means that

$$P(z \geq 1.96) = 1.000 - 0.975 = 0.025$$

By symmetry $P(z \leq -1.96) = 0.025$. Since each of the values ± 1.96 excludes an area of 0.025 on the normal distribution, the interval *between* these values must include an area of $1 - 0.025 - 0.025 = 0.95$. That is,

$$P(-1.96 \leq z \leq 1.96) = 0.95 \qquad (5.5)$$

By comparing Formulas (5.4) and (5.5) it is apparent that

$$\frac{a - 40{,}000}{3000} = -1.96 \qquad \text{and} \qquad \frac{b - 40{,}000}{3000} = +1.96$$

Solving for a and b yields $a = 34{,}120$ and $b = 45{,}880$, so we can now write the appropriate intervals as

$$P(34{,}120 \leq x \leq 45{,}880) = 0.95$$

The reader should verify that 34,120 to 45,880 is the *smallest* interval possible, by trying several other possible splits of the 5% to be excluded. Figure 5.9 shows the normal distribution for this example.

Many natural phenomena tend to result in normal distributions, such as length, height, and breadth of animals or plants; medical counts of sugar, white blood cells, incidence of inner ear disease; and behavioral, emotional, or psychological measures of human actions, aptitudes, or abilities. Also, the distribution of measured errors (or degree of perfection) in production processes of many kinds tends to be normal; these include errors from a specified standard in diameters of pistons, widths of computer chips, weight of packaged products, and even lengths of yardsticks.

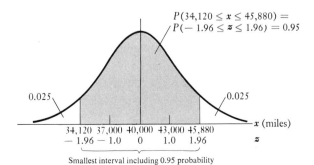

Figure 5.9

However, the family of probability problems where the standardized normal z is useful extends even beyond these many instances. Many other distributions applying to other types of problems tend to be normally distributed under certain conditions. We will make important use of this property in many sections of this book.

Computer Programs for the Normal Distribution

Most problems requiring use of the normal distribution can be solved using Table III in Appendix B. At times, however, the probability or z-value of interest cannot be found in Table III. In these circumstances, interpolating between values may lead to a small amount of error. Fortunately, many statistical packages provide a procedure for determining standardized normal values. In a typical program, the user is asked if the problem is one determining

1. a probability given a z-value, or
2. a z-value given a probability.

There are two computer outputs below. The first (Output 1) illustrates a problem where the user wanted to determine the probability that z is less than -1.58, or $P(z < -1.58)$. Output 1 shows this probability to be $p = 0.0571$, and also shows that $1 - p = 0.9429$. The second output (Output 2) was used to determine the z-value associated with $p = 0.4600$, which is shown to be $z = -0.1004$. User inputs for both outputs are shown in color.

Output (1) The probability for $z=-1.58$	Output (2) The z-value for p=0.4600
NORMAL DISTRIBUTION $z = -1.58$ p=0.0571, 1 - p=0.9429	NORMAL DISTRIBUTION $z = -.1004$ p=0.4600, 1 - p=0.5400

Problems

5.1   Explain what is meant by the phrase "standardization of a variable." Why do we standardize variables?

5.2   RCA offers a service contract to each customer who purchases a new 26-inch color stereo television set. Their experience on repairs to this TV indicates that the time from purchase to the first repair is normally distributed with a mean of 36 months, and a variance of 144 months squared, or $N(36, 144)$.

   a) Sketch this p.d.f.

   b) What is the probability a randomly selected television set will not need a repair for at least four years?

c) What is the probability a repair will be needed within the first 2 1/2 years?

d) Sketch the cumulative distribution function for the TV in part (a).

5.3 *Business Week* annually reports statistics on the leading U.S. corporations in its Investment Outlook Scoreboard. In the January 1, 1990, issue, the (estimated) All-Industry Average for 1988 earnings per share was $\mu = 2.41$. The standard deviation was $\sigma = 2.10$.

a) Is it reasonable to assume that earnings per share are normally distributed? Explain why or why not.

b) If earnings per share are $N(2.41, 4.41)$, then what is the probability a single corporation will have earnings that exceed $6.00? What is the probability earnings will be negative?

c) Find a copy of the 1989 *Business Week* Scoreboard (1/1/90), and look at 50 randomly selected earnings per share for 1988. Count how many of the earnings of 50 randomly selected companies fall within one standard deviation of the mean. Is this number close to 68%? Do the same for two standard deviations, and 95%. Explain what you might conclude from your results.

5.4 New tennis balls are regularly inspected and weighed to determine if their weight falls within the prescribed limits. According to an article in *Tennis* magazine, the mean weight for a population of balls was 2.019 ounces, with a variance of 0.0055.

a) What is the probability a single ball will weigh less than 1.98 ounces?

b) If the weight of two balls is independent, what is the probability that both will weigh more than 2.03 ounces?

c) What lower and upper limit would you place on a single ball if you want its weight to be in the middle 50% of the distribution given above, namely $N(2.019, 0.0055)$?

5.5 The marketing vice president selling the RCA televisions in Problem 5.2 would like to make statistically correct statements about the problem-free period for these 26-inch color sets. Use the information in Problem 5.2 to determine:

a) a time, a, such that the probability is 0.95 that the customer will need a repair before that time, or $P(x \le a) = 0.95$;

b) a value b such that $P(x \ge b) = 0.95$;

c) values a and b such that $P(a \le x \le b) = 0.95$.

5.6 Otis Elevator reported for 1989 that the number of hours per week lost due to employees' illnesses was approximately normally distributed, with a mean of 60 hours and a standard deviation of 15 hours. For a given week, selected at random, what is the probability:

a) that the number of lost hours will exceed 85 hours?

b) the number of lost hours will be between 45 and 55 hours?

c) the number of lost work hours will be exactly 60?

5.7 *Business Week* annually presents the "Corporate Elite," a list of the CEOs of the top 1000 most valuable publicly held U.S. Companies. For 1988 compensation data (salary and bonus), the average reported compensation was $\mu =$ $836,000, with a standard deviation of $\sigma = $244,000.

a) Is it reasonable to assume that the compensation of these CEOs might follow a normal distribution? Explain.

b) If compensation is $N(836, 244^2)$, in thousands, what proportion of the CEOs would be expected to have a compensation of more than $1,500,000? What proportion would be expected to make less than $500,000?

c) Find a copy of the October 20, 1989, *Business Week* special edition listing the compensations described above. Pick 100 randomly selected CEOs and find the mean and standard deviation of their annual compensation. Do your values agree with those given above. If not, why might they differ?

d) What proportion of the 100 CEOs you picked had compensations within one standard deviation of your mean (use your standard deviation)? What proportion was within two standard deviations? Are these proportions close to those expected under the normal distribution? What might you conclude from your data?

5.8 The University of North Carolina Credit Union reports that the average balance on its VISA credit card (for those customers using the card in the past month) is $N($250, 2500)$.

a) Find the probability that a balance is over $300. Find $P(x < $150)$, where x is balance.

b) Find a value of a such that the probability a customer's balance is less than this amount is 0.05.

5.9 A study of the age of the full-time faculty at Cornell University found that population to be $N(45, 64)$.

a) What proportion would you estimate to be over 65? Under 30?

b) Find value of a and b such that $P(a < x < b) = 0.95$.

5.10 Midway through the 1988 Bush-Dukakis presidential campaign, the Harris poll estimated the proportion of voters who intended to vote for Bush as 0.53. A footnote published with this poll indicated the standard deviation was 0.04. Based on this poll, what probability value would you have given (at that time) for Bush winning the election?

5.11 Exxon Oil has a policy of paying recent MBA graduates a starting salary that is within the top 20% of all comparable starting salaries. If the Exxon personnel director estimates that starting salaries this year are $N($46,000, 16,000,000)$, what is the minimum starting salary Exxon should offer? If Exxon wants to be between the 80th and 90th percentile, what salary range is suggested?

5.12 After an intensive three-week training course in Indianapolis, new sales representatives hired by Eli Lilly are given a comprehensive exam. The minimum passing grade is 70.

a) What proportion of the new employees are expected to pass if grades on the exam are $N(84, 26)$? What proportion will "pass with honors" if this distinction requires a grade of 95?

b) A recent class consisted of 32 trainees, four of whom scored below 70. In a class of 32, how many scores would you expect to be less than 70 based on the information in part (a)? What might be concluded in this situation?

5.13 The Graduate Management Admissions Council (GMAC) regularly schedules seminars for minorities interested in MBA programs. The average attendance for these seminars has been $N(435, 1600)$.

a) What is the probability that an auditorium seating 500 people will not seat all who want to attend one of these seminars?

b) GMAC charges a nominal fee for each seminar. If they lose money on 20% of the seminars, what attendance must there be for GMAC to break even? Assume attendance is the only variable.

5.14 The Nielsen rating for a prime-time television show in 1990 indicated a weekly audience of 18 million viewers. The standard deviation is estimated at 3 million viewers. For any given week, what is the lowest number of viewers you would expect to be watching? What is the largest number you would expect to be watching? Assume a normal distribution.

5.15 Some students take the GMAT (Graduate Management Admission Test) while others take the GRE (Graduate Record Exam). In one population, scores on the GMAT were $N(540, 10,000)$, while scores on the GRE were $N(500, 6400)$.

a) Who has scored better, a student with a 600 on the GRE or a student with a 660 on the GMAT?

b) Find values a and b such that $P(a < x < b) = 0.90$ for the GMAT.

c) What percentile should be reported for a student whose score on the GMAT is 640?

5.16 For the standardized normal curve, sketch and then find each of the areas given below:

a) to the left of 1.45   **b)** to the left of -1.60

c) to the left of 0.78   **d)** to the right of -0.95

e) between -1.45 and 1.35   **f)** between -1.90 and -0.85

5.17 Would you be surprised if it were claimed that the following five numbers were generated from a normal distribution with a mean of 100 and a standard deviation of 20: 84, 106, 47, 98, and 120? Explain.

5.18 Find each of the following probabilities, assuming the p.d.f. for x is $N(1000, 100^2)$.

a) $P(x > 1200)$ **b)** $P(x < 850)$

c) $P(775 < x < 1250)$ **d)** $P(700 < x < 950)$

5.19 One airline company recently claimed the average hourly wage of its ground crews is $N(\$15.45, 16.00)$. Would you be surprised if you randomly selected one of these ground crews and found that person's hourly wage to be $24.50? Explain.

5.20 The following list of test scores has an average of 70 and a standard deviation of 10:

59, 72, 61, 84, 67, 49, 78, 64, 85, 67, 57, 69, 57
72, 69, 73, 76, 74, 79, 92, 82, 70, 56, 70, 68

a) What proportion of these scores fall within ± one standard deviation of the mean? Is this percentile close to the proportion you would expect from a normal distribution?

b) Would you be surprised if the next score on the list were 38? Explain.

5.21 Consider a p.d.f. that is $N(100, 10)$

a) What is the height of this p.d.f. when $x = 100$?

b) Sketch this p.d.f.

c) Sketch the c.d.f.

5.22 The 10 random numbers in the left column below were generated by a computer from $N(100, 256)$. The numbers on the right are the equivalent z-values, determined using $\mu = 100$, $\sigma = 16$.

NORMAL NUMBERS	z–VALUES
102.70	0.17
124.36	1.52
88.20	−0.74
98.78	−0.08
95.07	−0.31
86.58	−0.84
79.95	−1.25
110.10	0.63
125.11	1.57
93.33	−0.42

a) Is the mean of the first column $\mu = 100$ and is $\sigma = 16$? Did you expect them to equal 100 and 16? Explain.

b) Verify that the first two z-values are correct. Is the mean of all the z-values $\mu = 0$ and is $\sigma = 1.00$? Did you expect them to equal 0 and 1.00? Explain.

c) Create 10 z-values for the numbers in column 1 that have a mean of zero and a standard deviation of 1.00.

5.23 a) Repeat Problem 5.22 by using a computer to generate your own set of 10 random numbers drawn from $N(100, 256)$.

b) Calculate the 10 z-values equivalent to column 2.

c) Calculate the 10 z-values that have a mean of zero and a variance of 1.00.

5.24 Return to the SALARIES data in Appendix C. Enter the 50 salaries for males into a computer statistical package. Use that program to generate a frequency distribution that starts at $30,000 and has a class interval of $5000. Use the program to determine the mean and standard deviation of the 50 salaries.

a) Does the frequency distribution appear to be approximately normally distributed? Explain.

b) Find the proportion of the salaries falling within one, two, and three standard deviations of the mean. Are these proportions reasonably close to those expected for a normal distribution?

Exponential Distribution (Optional)

5.4

Another important continuous distribution, the *exponential distribution,* is closely related to a discrete distribution discussed previously, the Poisson. Both the Poisson and the exponential distribution have found many applications in operations research, especially in studies of queueing (waiting-line) theory. These two distributions are related in such applications by the fact that if events (such as requests for service or arrivals) are assumed to occur according to a Poisson probability law, then the exponential distribution can be used to determine the probability distribution of the time that elapses *between* such events. For example, if customers arrive at a bank in accordance with a Poisson distribution, the exponential may be used to determine the probability distribution of the time between these arrivals. The time it takes to be serviced (called the service time) in these models is another application of the exponential distribution.

The exponential distribution is a continuous function that has the same parameter, λ, as the Poisson. Lambda, as before, represents the mean rate at which events (arrivals or service completions) occur. Thus a value of $\lambda = 3.0$ might imply that service completions occur, on the average, at the rate of 3.0 per minute (or any other time unit). If a telephone line handles an average of 20 customers per hour, then λ, defined as the mean number of customers being served by the telephone facilities, is $\lambda = 20$ (per hour) or $\lambda = 1/3$ (per minute). Similarly, $\lambda = 3.8$ might imply, as it did in Section 4.6, that on the average 3.8 customers arrive at a checkout counter in a supermarket every minute.

One major assumption necessary for applying the exponential distribution to applications involving service facilities is that the time between arrivals (if λ = the arrival rate) or the time for completing the service (if λ = the service rate) is usually relatively short (for example, our children notwithstanding, phone conversations are usually rather brief). The longer the time interval becomes, the *less* likely it is that the service completion (or the next arrival) will take that long or longer. Suppose we let the random variable T represent the amount of time between service completions, or between arrivals, where $T \geq 0$. As T becomes larger and larger, the value of $f(T)$ for the exponential becomes smaller and smaller. In fact, as can be seen in the graph of the exponential distribution in Fig. 5.10, $f(T)$ approaches zero as T approaches infinity.

Note that the exponential distribution, similar to the Poisson, assumes a value other than zero only when T is greater than or equal to zero and when λ is greater than zero. The vertical intercept of the function shown in Fig. 5.10 is seen to equal λ, which means that $f(0) = \lambda$. These relationships characterize the exponential distribution, whose density function is

$$\textit{Exponential distribution: } f(T) = \begin{cases} \lambda e^{-\lambda T} & \text{for } T \geq 0, \lambda > 0 \\ 0 & \text{otherwise} \end{cases} \qquad (5.6)$$

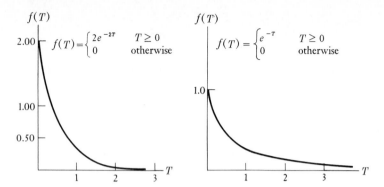

Figure 5.10
The exponential
distribution: $f(T) = \lambda e^{-\lambda T}$

Mean and Variance of the Exponential

Remember that if we interpret λ as the mean arrival (or service) rate, then the exponential gives the probability distribution of the time *between* arrivals (or between service completions).* It should thus not be very surprising to learn that the mean of the exponential distribution is $1/\lambda$. For example, suppose the mean service rate of a cashier in a bank equals one-half customer every minute, or $\lambda = \frac{1}{2}$. Since it takes, on the average, one minute to serve half a customer, it takes two minutes to serve one customer; hence, the mean time between service completions is $1/\lambda = 2$. Similarly, if the mean number of arrivals at a certain airport is $\lambda = 20$ per hour, then the mean time between arrivals will be

$$\frac{1}{\lambda} = \frac{1}{20} = 0.05 \text{ hours}$$

(or one airplane approximately every 3 minutes). As was true for the Poisson, the mean and the variance of the exponential are both functions of λ.

The mean and variance of the exponential are shown in Formula (5.7).

$$
\begin{array}{l}
\textit{Exponential mean}:\ \mu = \dfrac{1}{\lambda} \\[2em]
\textit{Exponential variance}:\ \sigma^2 = \dfrac{1}{\lambda^2}
\end{array}
\qquad (5.7)
$$

Since the exponential and the Poisson distributions can both be applied to problems of arrivals at a service facility, suppose we reconsider the example

---

*To prove that the exponential distribution meets the two axioms defining a probability density function, first note that $f(T)$ is easily seen to be always positive or zero. Showing that the second axiom holds merely requires integrating $f(T)$ from 0 to infinity.

$$\int_{\text{All } T} f(T)dT = \int_0^{\infty} \lambda e^{-\lambda T}dT = \left[-e^{-\lambda T} \right]_0^{\infty} = e^0 = 1$$

in Section 4.6, using the exponential function to describe the time between arrivals at a supermarket where the mean arrival rate is $\lambda = 3.8$. By substituting $\lambda = 3.8$ in Formula (5.6) we get

$$f(T) = 3.8e^{-3.8T}$$

Since $\lambda = 3.8$ for this example, the mean time between arrivals is

$$\frac{1}{\lambda} = \frac{1}{3.8} = 0.263 \text{ (minute)}$$

The variance of the time between arrivals is

$$\frac{1}{\lambda^2} = \frac{1}{(3.8)^2} = 0.069 \text{ (minutes}^2)$$

Now, suppose we want to calculate the probability that the time between arrivals is less than one minute, which is $P(T \leq 1)$. One way to find such a probability is to use calculus.* Fortunately, this approach can be avoided by using a computer, or Table IV in Appendix B. Table IV presents values of $F(T)$ for selected values of λ times T, or λT. For example, if one is interested in determining the probability $P(T \leq 0.5)$ when $\lambda = 3.8$, then it is necessary to first multiply the critical value of $T(= 0.5)$ times the value of $\lambda(= 3.8)$, which is $(0.5)(3.8) = 1.9$. The value of $F(T)$ corresponding to $\lambda T = 1.9$ can then be found in Table IV to be $F(T) = 0.850$. Thus,

$$P(T \leq 0.5) = F(0.5) = 0.850$$

By the complementary rule, we know that $P(T \geq 0.5) = 1 - 0.850 = 0.150$.

Similarly, if one wants to determine the probability that an arrival will occur between one-half and one minute when $\lambda = 3.8$, Table IV can be used to find

$$P(0.5 \leq T \leq 1) = F(1.0) - F(0.5)$$

We already know that $F(0.5) = 0.850$. The value for $F(1.0)$ is found in Table IV under $\lambda(T) = 3.8(1.0) = 3.8$, and equals $F(3.8) = 0.978$. Thus, $P(0.5 \leq T \leq 1.0) = F(1.0) - F(0.5) = 0.978 - 0.850 = 0.128$, which agrees with the value in the footnote. This example is illustrated in Fig. 5.11.

$$*P(T \leq 1) = \int_0^1 3.8e^{-3.8T}dT = \left[-e^{-3.8T} \right]_0^1$$

$$= 1 - e^{-3.8} = 0.978$$

Similarly, one might want to determine the probability that the time between two consecutive arrivals will be between one-half and one minute:

$$P\left(\tfrac{1}{2} \leq T \leq 1\right) = \int_{1/2}^1 3.8e^{-3.8T}dT = \left[-e^{-3.8T} \right]_{1/2}^1$$

$$= 0.150 - 0.022 = 0.128$$

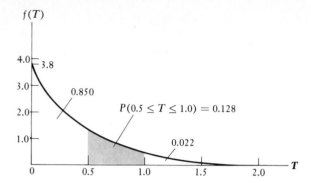

Figure 5.11
Example of exponential
probability problem with
$\lambda = 3.8$.

Calculations of exponential probabilities can be especially useful in the queueing problems mentioned earlier. If, in addition to studying the pattern of arrivals at our supermarket checkout counter, we had also investigated the service time of the cashiers, then we could develop a relationship that indicates the probability that our cashiers will not be busy for a period of T minutes and the probability that the customers will have to wait more (or less) than T minutes. Ideally, such an investigation could lead to an analysis of the benefits of keeping a customer waiting versus the cost of hiring (or firing) another cashier, the result being a staffing policy designed to balance these costs and benefits. (Too often, it seems, the arrival rate *exceeds* the service rate for extended periods of time in many supermarkets.)

Computer Programs for the Exponential Distribution

Although Table IV in Appendix B is useful in determining probabilities for the exponential distribution, readily available statistical packages for the computer provide more flexibility. The computer output below illustrates how to find a probability when the values of λ and T are known, as well as how to find the value of T when λ and a probability are provided. In both outputs shown below, the user has specified that $\lambda = 3.8$ (this is called the "the mean rate of occurrence.") For Output 1 the user specifies that $T = 1.00$, which means that the probability of interest is $P(T \leq 1.00)$. For Output 2, the user inputs $p = 0.8500$, which means that interest is in determining the value of T. This value is seen to be $T = 0.4992$. The reader should compare these values with those shown in Fig. 5.11. In the outputs below, user input is in color.

Output (1) The probability for T=1.00	Output (2) The T-value for p=0.8500
EXPONENTIAL DISTRIBUTION	EXPONENTIAL DISTRIBUTION
Mean rate of occurrence=3.8 T=1.00 P=.9776, 1−p=.0224	Mean rate of occurrence=3.8 T=0.4992 p=.8500, 1−p=.1500

The Chi-Square Distribution (Optional)*

5.5

A number of important probability distributions are closely related to the normal distribution. One of the most widely used of these related distributions is a continuous p.d.f. called the chi-square distribution. The **chi-square distribution** gets its name because it involves the square of normally distributed random variables. The chi-square distribution will be shown (in Chapters 6 and 9) to be particularly useful for problems involving variances (which are squared values). It will also be useful in Chapter 16, when we measure the goodness-of-fit between a set of observed and expected frequencies (again, looking at squared values).

Up to this point we have used examples involving just a single normal variable x. And we saw how this variable can be transformed into an equivalent z-variable in standardized normal form by letting $z = (x - \mu)/\sigma$. Now, let's assume we want to investigate the combined properties of more than just one standardized normal variable, where these variables are assumed to be independent of one another. You might imagine a number of machines (or workers) each producing (independently) a product whose length is normally distributed with μ and variance σ^2 [that is, $N(\mu, \sigma^2)$]. Furthermore, let's assume that the lengths from each machine have been standardized by using the transformation $z = (x - \mu)/\sigma$. The lengths produced by the different machines thus form a set of independent standardized normal variables,

$$z_1 = \frac{x_1 - \mu_1}{\sigma_1}, \qquad z_2 = \frac{x_2 - \mu_2}{\sigma_2}, \qquad \text{and so forth}$$

It will be convenient to denote the *number* of variables in this situation (that is, the number of machines or workers) by the letter ν (the Greek letter nu), and to take the *square* of each of these nu variables. We thus have a set of ν independent variables, as follows:

$$z_1^2 = \frac{(x_1 - \mu_1)^2}{\sigma_1^2}, \qquad z_2^2 = \frac{(x_2 - \mu_2)^2}{\sigma_2^2}, \qquad \ldots, \qquad z_\nu^2 = \frac{(x_\nu - \mu_\nu)^2}{\sigma_\nu^2}$$

You may recall from Chapter 3 that we can form a new random variable by combining two or more random variables. For the present case, we want to take the *sum* of the variables $z_1^2, z_2^2, \ldots, z_\nu^2$. This sum is denoted by the letter χ^2 (the square of the Greek letter chi, or "chi-square"). Usually a subscript is added to the χ^2 symbol to denote the fact that there are ν values being summed. That is,

$$\chi_\nu^2 = z_1^2 + z_2^2 + \cdots + z_\nu^2 = \sum_{i=1}^{\nu} z_i^2$$

The distribution of the random variable χ^2, which is referred to as the chi-square distribution, is important in a number of different contexts. For exam-

---

*This section contains a formal introduction to the chi-square distribution. The material here forms a good introduction to Sections 6.10 and 6.11, but is not a prerequisite to those sections.

ple, if z_i represents a deviation about the mean of the length of a certain product (in standardized units), then z_i^2 is the square of this deviation. And $\chi_{\nu}^2 = \sum_{i=1}^{\nu} z_i^2$ is the sum of the squared deviations of the ν different machines producing this product. Since a variance is also defined in terms of the sum of a set of squared deviations about a mean, it shouldn't surprise you that one of the most important applications of the χ^2 distribution involves variances. We will describe, more completely, this application of the χ^2 distribution in Chapter 6.

Properties of the χ^2 Distribution

The chi-square distribution is a family of density functions having a single parameter, ν, which is called the *number of degrees of freedom*. The degrees of freedom associated with a particular chi-square distribution completely determines the characteristics of its density function, $f(\chi^2)$. For example, the mean and variance of the χ^2 distribution are both related to ν, as follows:

$$\textit{Chi-square mean} = E[\chi_{\nu}^2] = \nu$$

$$\textit{Chi-square variance} = V[\chi_{\nu}^2] = 2\nu$$

The shape of the chi-square distribution is highly skewed to the right when ν is small. Consider, for example, the situation where $\nu = 1$, in which case

$$\chi_1^2 = z_1^2 = \frac{(x_1 - \mu_1)^2}{\sigma_1^2}$$

The mean of this distribution is $E[\chi_1^2] = 1$, and its variance is $V(\chi_1^2) = 2$. Since the values of χ_1^2 will all be positive, and most of them will be relatively close to 1.0 (because we divided by σ_1^2), χ_1^2 has the shape shown in Fig. 5.12 corresponding to $\nu = 1$. The χ^2 distributions for $\nu = 2, 4, 6,$ and 11 are also shown in this figure.

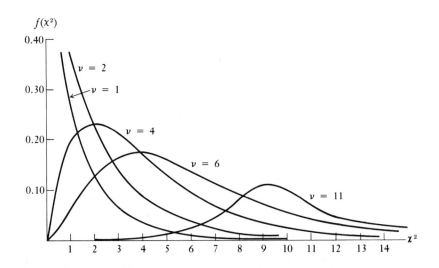

Figure 5.12
The chi-square distribution for various values of ν.

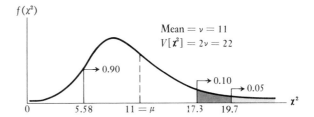

Figure 5.13
Chi-square distribution for
$\nu = 11$.

As ν becomes larger and larger, the shape of the χ^2 distribution becomes more and more symmetrical in appearance. Consider, for example,

$$\chi^2_{11} = z^2_1 + z^2_2 + \cdots + z^2_{11}$$

In this case the mean is $E[\chi^2_{11}] = 11$ and $V[\chi^2_{11}] = 22$. The chi-square distribution for $\nu = 11$ is shown in detail in Fig. 5.13.

We have shown several probability values in Fig. 5.13. For example, we see that when $\nu = 11$,

$$P(\chi^2_{11} \geq 17.3) = 0.10 \qquad \text{and} \qquad P(\chi^2_{11} \geq 19.7) = 0.05$$

Notice in this figure how symmetrical the distribution of χ^2 is for $\nu = 11$, almost like a normal distribution. It can be shown, in fact, that the limit of the χ^2 distribution as $\nu \to \infty$ is the normal.

Use of χ^2 Table—Examples

As was the case with the normal distribution, tables of the χ^2 distribution are readily available. In this case, however, the task of listing values of the distribution is more complicated because the chi-square distribution is different for each value of ν. For this reason it is common to list, in χ^2 tables, only those values of χ^2 which correspond to probabilities most often used. In addition, chi-square tables often give the value of $P(\chi^2 \geq \chi^2)$ rather than values of the cumulative function, as was the case for the normal distribution. The χ^2 table in this book (Table V, Appendix B) lists the values of χ^2 for 10 different probability values (across the top of the table) and for various values of ν up to $\nu = 30$. When $\nu \geq 30$, the formula at the bottom of the table gives the normal approximation to the χ^2 distribution.

EXAMPLE 1

Suppose we want to determine the probability that the value of a chi-square random variable is greater than 18.0 when there are 11 degrees of freedom— that is, find $P(\chi^2_{11} \geq 18.0)$. From Fig. 5.13, we can easily see that $P(\chi^2_{11} \geq 18.0)$ must be larger than 0.05 (since 18.0 is less than 19.7), and it must be smaller than 0.10 (since 18.0 is larger than 17.3). Thus, we can write:

$$0.10 > P(\chi^2_{11} \geq 18.0) > 0.05$$

This relationship also could have been determined by using Table V. First, we need to select the row corresponding to $v = 11$, and then find the columns giving values of χ^2 that bracket the number 18.0. In this case, we see that

$$P(\chi^2_{11} \geq 17.3) = 0.10 \quad \text{and} \quad P(\chi^2_{11} \geq 19.7) = 0.05$$

hence $P(\chi^2_{11} > 18.0)$ must fall between 0.10 and 0.05. In other words, when $v = 11$ a value of χ^2_{11} of 18.0, or larger, will occur between 5% and 10% of the time. ∎

EXAMPLE 2

As a second example, suppose we want to find the narrowest interval where the probability of χ^2 falling within the interval is 0.95, assuming that the number of degrees of freedom is 18. In other words, we want to find values a and b such that $P(a \leq \chi^2_{18} \leq b) = 0.95$. To get the narrowest interval, we exclude an equal probability on the left and the right ends of the distribution, namely, 0.025 on each tail. (This statement is correct only if v is not small ($v \geq 10$); otherwise, the chi-square distribution is quite skewed.) In terms of Table V, this means that we must find values a and b such that:

$$P(\chi^2 \geq b) = 0.025 \quad \text{and} \quad P(\chi^2 \leq a) = 0.025 \quad [\text{or } P(\chi^2 \geq a) = 0.975]$$

Using the row in Table V for $v = 18$, we find $P(\chi^2 \geq b) = 0.025$ when $b = 31.5$, and $P(\chi^2 \geq a) = 0.975$ if $a = 8.23$. Therefore,

$$P(8.23 \leq \chi^2_{18} \leq 31.5) = 0.95$$

and the range of the interval is as narrow as possible while still including 95% of the area under $f(\chi^2_{18})$. Note that the distance from the two endpoints to the mean is not the same, since the chi-square distribution is not symmetric. It is the amount of *area* under $f(\chi^2)$ outside each endpoint (0.025) which is made equal in order to solve the problem. Figure 5.14 shows the χ^2 distribution for this example.

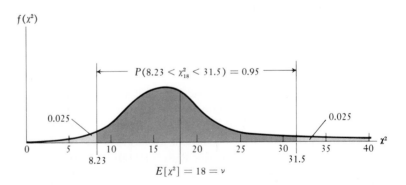

Figure 5.14

Computer Programs for the Chi-Square Distribution

As was the case for the exponential distribution, Appendix B is useful in solving problems, but computer programs provide additional flexibility. Computer packages for the chi-square distribution are generally quite easy to use. The program illustrated below asks the user only for the degrees of freedom, and the chi-square value of interest. For example, if d.f. = 30, and the probability of interest is $P(\chi^2 \geq 40.3)$, then the computer output below is generated, where user input is in color.

CHI-SQUARE DISTRIBUTION

d.f. = 30

CHI-SQUARE = 40.3

p = .9008; 1 − p = .0992

TABLE 5.1   Summary of probability distributions

Probability distribution	Para-meters	Charac-teristics	Function given in formula	Mean	Variance	Reference sections	Probability table
Discrete							
Binomial x	$0 \leq p \leq 1$ $n = 0, 1, 2$ $\cdots$	Skewed unless $p = 0.5$, family of distributions	(4.1)	np	npq	4.2, 4.3	$P(x_{binomial})$ in Table I
Poisson x	$\lambda > 0$	Skewed positively, family of distributions	(4.5)	λ	λ	4.6	$P(x_{Poisson})$ in Table II
Continuous							
Normal x	$-\infty < \mu < \infty$ $\sigma > 0$	Symmetrical, family of distributions	(5.1)	μ	σ^2	5.2	—
Standardized normal z	—	Symmetrical, single distribution	(5.3)	0	1	5.3	$F(z)$ in Table III
Exponential T	$\lambda > 0$	Skewed positively, family of distributions	(5.6)	$1/\lambda$	$1/\lambda^2$	5.4	$F(T)$ in Table IV
Chi-square χ^2	$\nu \geq 1$	Skewed positively, family of distributions	(See Table V)	ν	2ν	5.5	$P(\chi^2 \leq \chi^2)$ in Table V

Problems

5.25 Describe how the Poisson and the exponential distributions are related. What assumptions underlie these distributions? For the following questions, assume an exponential distribution is appropriate, with $\lambda = 3.0$.

   a) Graph the p.d.f. and the cumulative probability distribution.

   b) What is the mean and variance of this function?

   c) What percent of this distribution lies within one standard deviation of the mean? Within two standard deviations?

5.26 A study of five randomly selected customers at Bank One found the following times were needed to service customers by a bank teller: 1/2, 1.00, 1/2, 6.00, 3.00, where all times are in minutes.

   a) What is the mean service time, given these observations?

   b) Graph the exponential distribution for this application.

   c) What is the probability that service will take longer than two minutes? Less than one-half minute?

5.27 A study of the interarrival times at a tollbooth on the Pennsylvania Turnpike found times to have a mean interarrival time of one-half minute.

   a) What is the value of λ for this problem?

   b) What is the variance of interarrival times?

   c) What is the probability that the time between two consecutive arrivals will be between 0 and 1 minute?

   d) What is $P(T > 2.0)$?

5.28 Dreyfus Worldwide Money Fund has a hotline for customers with questions about their account. One line can service, on the average, four customers in a six-minute period, following a Poisson distribution.

   a) What is the probability that this hotline will be able to service six or more customers in a six-minute period?

   b) What is the probability that a customer will take longer than three minutes?

   c) What is the probability that a customer will take between three and six minutes?

5.29 A small store selling cinnamon rolls in Chicago has recorded the number of customers entering the store between 8:00 and 8:30 A.M. Arrivals averaged 10 per morning during this one-half hour, following a Poisson distribution.

   a) What is the probability this store will have exactly 10 customers during this time period on a randomly selected day?

   b) What is the probability that the time between consecutive arrivals (customers) will exceed three minutes?

   c) What is the probability that the time between consecutive customers will fall between 1 1/2 and 3 minutes?

5.30 Machines of a special type in the Bloomington, Indiana, Otis Elevator plant break down at the rate of 1 every 30 days, following a Poisson distribution.

a) What is the probability that the time between consecutive breakdowns will be less than 15 days?

b) What is the probability that the time between consecutive breakdowns will be greater than 45 days?

5.31 Recall the data in Problem 1.48, involving the A-1 Loan Company.

a) Graph the exponential p.d.f. with $\lambda = 0.02$. Compare this graph with the polygon for Problem 1.48. Do they seem to correspond well?

b) Elaborate on your answer to part (a) by finding $P(0 < T < 20)$, $P(20 < T < 60)$, and $P(T > 60)$.

c) What are the mean, median, and standard deviation of an exponential distribution with $\lambda = 0.02$? Are these answers consistent with the values for Problem 1.48?

5.32 Use a computer program to determine the following probabilities.

a) $P(T > 1.23)$ when $\lambda = 0.75$

b) $P(12 < T < 15.50)$ when $\lambda = 0.05$

c) $P(T < 0.22)$ when $\lambda = 40$

5.33 A specialized tool in a machine shop is requisitioned from (and then checked out of) a central tool bin at the rate of five per hour. The manager in charge of the tool bin would like to determine a reasonable minimum and maximum time to be expected between requests for this type of tool. Do this by using a computer program to determine values a and b such that $P(a > T) = 0.05$, and $P(T > b) = 0.05$.

5.34 Sketch the exponential distribution represented by the following computer output.

```
EXPONENTIAL DISTRIBUTION

MEAN RATE OF OCCURRENCE=10
      p=0.90   T=0.23025
      p=0.30   T=0.03566
      p=0.12   T=0.01278
```

5.35 What proportion of the p.d.f. in Problem 5.34 falls within one, two, and three standard deviations of the mean? Do these proportions approximate the values you would expect from a normal distribution? Explain.

5.36 Sketch the chi-square distribution represented by the following computer output.

```
d.f.=35    CHI-SQUARE=30
           p=.2919,  1-p=.7081
           CHI-SQUARE=35
           p=.5318,  1-p=.4682
           CHI-SQUARE=40
           p=.7422,  1-p=.2578
```

5.37 What proportion of the p.d.f. in Problem 5.36 falls within one, two, and three standard deviations of the mean? Do these proportions approximate the values you would expect from a normal distribution? Explain.

5.38 Use a computer program to answer parts (a) through (c).

   a) Find $P(\chi^2 > 40)$ when d.f. $= 42$.

   b) Find $P(38 < \chi^2 < 45)$ when d.f. $= 42$.

   c) Determine the value of a such that $P(\chi^2 > a) = 0.50$ when d.f. $= 42$.

   d) Sketch the chi-square p.d.f. using the values determined above.

5.39 a) What parameter characterizes the chi-square distribution?

   b) What is the mean and variance of a chi-square distribution?

   c) Sketch the chi-square distribution for $\nu = 6$. Indicate on your sketch the region cutting off 5% of the right-hand tail of this distribution.

5.40 Find values of a and b such that $P(a < \chi^2 < b) = 0.95$, assuming that $\nu = 8$. Sketch this area on a graph.

5.41 A random variable is known to be chi-square distributed with parameter $\nu = 24$.

   a) What is the mean and variance of the chi-square distribution for this parameter?

   b) What is the probability that the value of χ^2 will exceed 43.0? What is $P(\chi^2 \geq 33.2)$? What is $P(\chi^2 \geq 9.89)$?

   c) Use your answers to parts (a) and (b) to draw a rough sketch of the chi-square distribution for $\nu = 24$.

   d) Superimpose on your sketch for part (c) a graph of the normal distribution for $\mu = 24$ and $\sigma^2 = 48$. How closely do the two distributions agree?

Exercises

□ **5.42** The *uniform* or *rectangular* distribution can be defined in terms of its cumulative distribution function, as follows:

$$F(x) = \begin{cases} \dfrac{x - a}{b - a} & \text{for } a \leq x \leq b \\ 0 & \text{for } x < a \\ 1 & \text{for } x > b \end{cases}$$

   a) Derive the uniform density function for $a \leq x \leq b$ by differentiating $F(x)$ with respect to x.

   b) Sketch both the density function and the cumulative function for the uniform distribution.

   c) Show that the uniform distribution satisfies the two properties of all probability functions.

   d) Find the mean and the variance of this distribution.

5.43 How many questions would a professor have to put on a multiple-choice exam, where there are four choices for each question, in order to be 99.9% sure that a student who makes a random guess on each question misses at least one-half of the questions? Use the normal to approximate the binomial.

☐ **5.44 a)** Prove that the standardized normal density function reaches its maximum height at $z = 0$. (*Hint:* Set the first derivative equal to zero.)

b) Prove that the points $z = \pm 1$ for the standardized normal density function are inflection points. (*Hint:* Set the second derivative equal to zero.)

5.45 A continuous p.d.f. not presented in this chapter is the *Beta distribution.* This distribution has two parameters, r and n.

$$f(x) = \begin{cases} \binom{n-1}{r-1} x^{r-1}(1-x)^{n-r-1} & 0 \le x \le 1 \\ 0 & \text{otherwise} \end{cases}$$

a) Discuss the similarities and differences between this distribution and the binomial distribution.

b) Graph this distribution for $r = 1, n = 2$.

c) Determine $E[x]$.

d) If $r \le n/2$, will the distribution be positively or negatively skewed?

5.46 In Chapter 6 we will show that the random variable (vs^2/σ^2) follows a χ^2 distribution (that is, $\chi^2 = vs^2/\sigma^2$), where s^2 is a sample variance.

a) If $E[\chi^2] = v$, what is $E[s^2]$?

b) If $V[\chi^2] = 2v$, what is $V[s^2]$?

c) Find the probability that $s^2 \ge 20$, when $\sigma^2 = 10$ and $v = 8$, by calculating

$$P\left(\chi^2 \ge \frac{vs^2}{\sigma^2}\right)$$

5.47 One of the most important characteristics of the exponential distribution is called the "memoryless property." This property states that

$$P(T > a + b | T > a) = P(T > b)$$

where a and b are times. For example, suppose that the average time between arrivals of an empty taxicab at a certain New York City corner is four minutes, following an exponential distribution.

a) If you have been waiting for a cab for three minutes, what is the probability that you will wait at least two more minutes?

b) Prove the memoryless property.

☐ **5.48** Prove, for the exponential distribution, that

a) $E[T] = 1/\lambda$;

b) $V[T] = 1/\lambda^2$.

Chapter 6

Sampling and Surveying

You don't have to eat the whole ox
to know that the meat is tough.

SAMUEL JOHNSON

Introduction   **6.1**

This chapter begins the task of relating the probability concepts studied in the past four chapters to the objectives of statistics stated in Chapter 1: to draw inferences or conclusions about population parameters on the basis of sample information.

Recall from Chapter 1 that a major portion of statistics is concerned with the problem of estimating population parameters, or testing hypotheses about such parameters. If we could take a "census" (that is, examine all items in the population), then the value of the population parameters would be known. Unfortunately, a census of a population is usually not feasible because of monetary and time limitations. Hence, we must rely on observing a subset (or *sample*) of the items in the population, and use this information to make estimates or test hypotheses about the unknown parameters. The process of making estimates is covered in Chapter 7, and the subject of hypothesis testing is described in Chapter 9. In these and subsequent chapters we will usually assume that a sample has been taken. It is therefore important that we describe in this chapter how a sample is taken, and what type of information can be drawn from a sample.

"What is the relevant population?" must be one of the first questions asked in any statistical analysis. No amount of statistical analysis can compensate for sample data generated from the wrong population. To illustrate this point, consider the controversy generated by a 1989 article published in *The New England Journal of Medicine,* reporting on the lack of special benefits of oat bran products in lowering cholesterol. Quaker Oats, which was estimated to have spent at least $20 million to introduce its new ready-to-eat Oat Bran cereal, criticized the study as based on too small a sample (20 men and women) and using subjects not reflecting the general population (they were mostly dieticians). The point here is that it is important to carefully define the population of interest before beginning the process of collecting sample information.

Statisticians distinguish between *cross-sectional* and *longitudinal* data. **Cross-sectional data** are facts and information collected at a single point in time, whereas **longitudinal data** are facts and information taken over a period of time. Longitudinal data are sometimes referred to as *time-series data.* To illustrate, Bristol-Myers' Squibb tracks the prescriptions written for each of its products on a weekly basis. Thus, for any given week the company can determine the number of prescriptions written for products such as Desyrel, BuSpar, and Duricef. This would be cross-sectional data. The firm also wants to track the number of prescriptions written for each of these products over time, say week by week or month by month. This is longitudinal data.

One of the first tasks for the statistician is thus to determine the relevant population. Once this is done, four basic questions must be asked about samples and the process of inference:

1. What are the least expensive methods for collecting samples that best ensure that the samples are representative of the parent population?
2. What is the best way to describe sample information usefully and clearly?
3. How does one go about drawing conclusions from samples and making inferences about the population?
4. How reliable are the inferences and conclusions drawn from sample information?

The next several sections describe some of the many sources for finding data that have already been collected, and various methods for collecting sample data.

Data and Data Collection

6.2

Data for a sample can come from many sources. Clearly, it is easier for the statistician to use existing information sources rather than generate new data. Information on sales patterns, materials costs, advertising expenditures, production schedules, employee wages, performance measures, and so forth, are routinely collected and stored by most companies. Such information is a convenient source of data because it is usually easily accessible (on a computer) by authorized personnel. Corporate data may represent either sample data or census data. For example, payroll records that provide information on all employees in a certain company are a census for that company. Company wages can also be thought of as a sample of all wages in an industry. In some cases, however, information about particular products and market segments may not exist or be accessible, which means the company will need to generate its own data.

Existing Information

There are many other sources for existing data. The following list illustrates only a few of these sources.

1. The U.S. government is a prime resource, publishing volumes of information on a regular basis on a variety of economic measures such as the gross national product, housing starts, exports and imports, wages, and wholesale and retail prices. The U.S. Census Bureau conducts a survey each month to provide information on employment and unemployment. Other governmental agencies routinely publish statistics and conduct surveys.

2. Magazines and trade journals regularly publish the results of sample surveys as well as providing regular information on business activity. For example, once a year *Business Week* publishes a list of the top 1000 companies in the United States and publishes the salaries of the top 500 U.S. business executives. Other commercial products include Standard and Poor's Compustat Service, the Dow-Jones News/Retrieval Service, and Dun & Bradstreet.

3. The National Center for Health Statistics sponsors a survey every year to determine how much money people are spending for different types of medical care.

4. The Gallup Poll and the Harris Survey issue reports periodically, describing national public opinion on a wide range of current issues.

5. Many universities regularly provide information on local and state economic activity.

Collecting Data

Frequently, existing information sources do not provide the type or depth of information necessary to make a certain decision. In this case the sample data must be collected by the decision maker or the statistician. Three of the most popular methods for collecting data are sample surveys, focus groups (or panel studies), and experimentation.

Sample Surveys.   Surveys are used to collect sample data by means of standardized questions. The units sampled may be people, or businesses, or households, or other units, depending on the purpose of the study. For national polls, a sample of about 1500 people can, when properly administered, reflect characteristics of the more than 240 million people living in the United States. How well a sample represents a population is a primary concern for statistical analysis.

Surveys are sometimes classified by their method of data collection, such as by mail, telephone, or personal interview. In other cases surveys are classified by their content; for example, there are factual surveys (the respondent's age, sex, occupation, income, use of a product) and there are opinion surveys (covering local or national issues). The type of questions on a survey may be closed ("Do you approve or disapprove?") or open-ended ("Why do you feel that way?"). Sometimes respondents are asked the same questions repeatedly over a period of time to chart any changes in attitude (such as during the period before a political election).

Focus Groups.   At times data are best collected using a group of people called a *focus group* or a *panel study*. For example, an advertising agency may wish to gather a group of people to view a proposed advertising campaign, or possibly to view several different campaigns. Or perhaps the group is asked to look at several variations of a new product and express their likes and dislikes. At the end of the session the participants (who may have been selected using personal characteristics such as age, sex, and occupation) typically complete a short questionnaire and then participate in a group discussion led by a moderator. This process, which is popular for marketing studies, does not necessarily provide a random sample of opinions, because it depends on gathering participants who have sufficient time and interest to devote to the study. The group interaction may provide data not obtainable in any other manner, however.

Experimentation.   An experiment is a way to gather information under controlled conditions. The designers of a new product may be testing it under a variety of circumstances for durability, safety, and reliability. Or a new type of car tire may be tested for tread life under various weather conditions and driving speeds. In the medical sciences, experiments are often designed to determine if a new drug is beneficial and what possible side effects might be present.

In a "controlled" experiment, scientists attempt to remove or at least take into account any factors that might influence the sample results. Agricultural scientists, for example, test new hybrids by growing them on plots of land with comparable soil characteristics, so that variations in yield cannot be attributed to such differences. As another example, a well-known experiment is the Coca-Cola taste test used in 1985 to determine if customers preferred a new syrup to the old. In that experiment 190,000 volunteers participated in a "blind" test, where participants did not know which syrup they were tasting. The Coca-Cola experiment also controlled for age and geographical differences. This experiment is a prime example of the fact that it is generally impossible to control for all variables, for the results did not take into account the loyalty of many consumers to the old syrup (now Classic Coke). In a "double-blind" test neither the participants nor the experimenters know which group of participants is the experimental group and which is the control.

Economists use experimentation to generate data by means of simulation. For example, econometricians have developed computer models of the

U.S. economy. Such a model might be used to study the effect of a change in the tax laws by generating (simulated) data representing the U.S. economy under various forms of the tax change while other variables (such as interest rates, housing starts, and personal consumption) can be held constant, or varied in a systematic fashion.

Sample Designs **6.3**

A **sample design** is a procedure or plan, specified before any data are collected, for obtaining a sample from a given population.

Throughout most of this book we will assume that the data required for statistical purposes have already been collected. For many decisions, however, statistical analysis requires gathering relevant data; hence it is important for the statistician to understand how to collect data most efficiently and effectively. A sample design is the first step.

Of course, a priority before the collection of any data is determining the purpose for the statistical analysis. In some cases the objective is merely to summarize a set of numbers; other problems require defining a population and collecting a sample from that population. For example, a firm's personnel director may wish to summarize current wages for all hourly workers in the company, a task that may not be difficult, especially if the data are stored in a computer. A more difficult task would be determining how the company's hourly wages compare to those of other companies.

A sample design should answer the following questions:

1. What is the objective of the statistical analysis?
   a. Are there specific questions that need to be answered or decisions that need to be made?
   b. Does the study involve a census (all the population), or a sample from some population? If a sample is to be collected, what is the relevant population, and what population characteristics (parameters) are of interest?
2. How can the relevant data be collected most effectively and efficiently so as to meet the objectives in question 1?
3. What statistical tools will be used on the data in question 2 in order to meet the objectives in question 1?
4. How can the data be summarized and presented to make it understandable to the nonstatistician?

We will attempt to address these and other questions in this chapter and, indeed, throughout the remainder of this book. For now we might describe certain special terms used to designate specific types of sampling objectives. Some of these terms will be elaborated upon when quality control is described in Chapter 8.

Attribute sampling is used when the researcher wants to estimate a population proportion (p). For example, a bank manager concerned with quality control may wish to estimate the proportion of errors made by clerical employees when processing checks.

Variable sampling is used when the objective is to estimate a parameter, such as the population mean (μ). For instance, a market researcher may wish to know the mean dollar amount spent by consumers on camera film each year.

Acceptance sampling is used to determine whether or not an error rate is large enough to reject the entire population. One might want to determine whether the number of defectives in a sample of items is too large to accept the entire lot.

Discovery sampling is a special case of attribute sampling used to locate relatively rare occurrences. For example, an auditor might be looking for critical errors and fraud. This approach is not used for estimating population characteristics.

Nonsampling Errors

The primary requisite for a "good" sample is that it be representative of the population that one is trying to describe. There are, of course, many ways of collecting a "poor" sample. One obvious source of errors of misrepresentation arises when the *wrong population is sampled inadvertently.* The 1936 presidential election poll conducted by the now defunct *Literary Digest* remains a classic example of this problem. *Literary Digest* predicted, on the basis of a sample of over 2 million names selected from telephone directories and automobile registrations, that Alfred Landon would win an overwhelming victory in the election that year. Instead, Franklin D. Roosevelt won by a substantial margin. The sample collected by the *Digest* apparently represented the population of predominantly middle- and upper-class people, who owned telephones and automobiles; it misrepresented the general electorate, however, and Roosevelt's support came from the lower-income classes, whose opinions were not reflected in the poll. Even in modern times telephone surveys can misrepresent certain populations. Estimates indicate that up to 15% of the U.S. adult population either do not have phones or have unlisted numbers.

Modern polls also can be imprecise despite the aid of computers and elaborate interviewing techniques. The George Gallup poll had the largest error factor it has ever had in a presidential election in the 1980 race between Jimmy Carter and Ronald Reagan. The multitude of surveys in the 1988 presidential race predicted everything from a very close win to a runaway for George Bush. Cost is an important factor in major national surveys—a survey of about 1500 people can cost more than $40,000.

Perhaps the most widely publicized poll is the A. C. Nielsen company's rating of television viewing in the United States. The Nielsen organization, which is the largest market research firm in the world, bases its ratings on a sample of television viewers in 3000 homes. This sample is based on a random sample of locations selected from a Census Bureau list so as to give a geographical spread across the country. The ratings, which may have an error of as much as 2.6 points,* can mean life or death for a TV show, and affect billions of advertising dollars a year. Each point in the rating system represents approximately 1 million viewers. Advertising agencies pay as much as $500,000 a year for the Nielsen service, a price that is small when compared to the $300,000 (or more) a minute that is often charged for commercials on top-rated shows, and the $700,000 paid for a commercial during the 1990 Super Bowl.

A potential source of error in sampling, especially in surveys of public opinion, comes from **response bias.** Poorly worded questionnaires or improper interview techniques elicit responses that do not reflect true opinions. Alfred Kinsey's research on sexual practices, for example, received widespread criticism for reporting responses to questions that are sensitive or awkward for most people. Responses to such questions are likely to be distorted from the truth.

Response bias is a problem when the participants in a sample have the option of not answering certain questions or not responding to a questionnaire at all. Perhaps those who do respond are somehow different from those who do not. The television network CNN frequently asks viewers to call in their opinion on a current topic, but is careful to state that the results do not reflect a random sampling of viewers.

The errors described above are called **nonsampling errors.** Nonsampling errors include all kinds of "human errors"—mistakes in collecting, analyzing, or reporting data; sampling from the wrong population; and response bias. A researcher's incorrect addition of a column of numbers represents a nonsampling error just as much as does a failure of the respondent to provide truthful information on a questionnaire.

Sampling Errors

In addition, even in well-designed and well-executed samples, there are bound to be cases in which the sample does not provide a true representation of the population under study, simply because samples represent only a portion of a population. In such cases the information contained in the sample may lead to incorrect inferences about the parent population; that is, an "error" might be made in estimating the population characteristics based on the sample information. Errors of this nature, representing the differences that can exist between a sample statistic and the population parameter being estimated, are called **sampling errors.** Sampling errors obviously can occur in all data-

---

*A Nielsen rating plus or minus 2.6 points brackets the correct rating 95% of the time.

collection procedures except a complete enumeration of the population (a census).

One primary objective in sample design is to minimize both sampling and nonsampling errors. Errors are costly, not only in terms of the time and money spent in collecting a sample, but also in terms of the potential loss implicit in making a wrong decision on the basis of an incorrect inference from the data. An inaccurate public-opinion survey, for instance, can cost a politician votes if a campaign design is based on inferences from these data. Similarly, investment in real estate or stocks might cause an investor to lose a considerable amount of money if the (sample) information that led to a particular investment proved incorrect.

Note that it is the *decisions* resulting from incorrect inferences that may be costly, not the incorrect inferences themselves; hence, it is customary to refer to one objective of sampling as that of *minimizing the cost of making an incorrect decision (error)*. But reducing the costs of making an incorrect decision usually implies increasing the cost of designing and/or collecting the sample. For example, additional effort (or money) devoted to designing a questionnaire, identifying the correct population, or collecting a larger sample usually results in a more representative sample. We can therefore state that the primary objective in sample design is to *balance the costs of making an error and the costs of sampling*.

Designing an optimal sampling procedure may not be easy. For one reason, the elements of a given population may be extremely difficult to locate, gain access to, or even identify. For example, it may be impractical, if not impossible, to identify the population elements of "personal computer owners" in a particular city in the United States. Another obvious difficulty already mentioned is cost; budget constraints, for example, may force one to collect fewer data or to be less careful about collecting these data than ideal designs would dictate. Also, the costs of making an incorrect decision may be very hard to specify. A discussion of all the problems inherent in sample design, especially those concerned with nonsampling errors and the costs of making an incorrect decision, falls outside the scope of this book. Therefore, we shall concentrate our attention on the problem of determining which sample designs most effectively minimize sampling errors.

Probabilistic Sampling

Often, the first criterion for a good sample is that each item in the population under investigation have an *equal and independent chance* to be part of the sample; also, it is often advantageous that each set of n items have an equal probability of being included. Samples in which every possible sample of size n (that is, every combination of n items from the N in the population) is equally likely are referred to as **simple random samples.** These are the types of samples that we have used implicitly throughout our discussion of probability theory to illustrate the use of formulas and probability functions.

Simple random sampling requires that one have access to all items in the population. For a small population of elements that are easy to identify and sample, this procedure normally gives the best results. However, simple random sampling of a large population may be difficult, perhaps even impossible, to implement; at best, it will be quite costly. For this case, a more practical procedure must be designed, even though it will also be more restrictive.

In another popular sampling plan, called **systematic sampling,** a random starting point in the population is selected, and then every kth element encountered thereafter becomes an item in the sample. For example, every 200th name in a telephone directory might be called in order to survey public opinion. This method is *not* equivalent to simple random sampling because every set of n names does not have an equal probability of being selected. Bias will result under systematic sampling if there is a *periodicity* to the elements of the population. For instance, sampling sales in a supermarket every seventh day certainly will result in a sample that represents only the sales of a single day, say Monday, rather than the weekly pattern.

Using Random Numbers to Select a Sample

Designing a sample in which each set of items in the population has an equal probability of being selected usually requires carefully controlled sampling procedures. The stereotype of drawing slips of paper from a goldfish bowl seems to satisfy the requirements of a simple random sample, but there is no practical way to be certain the resulting sample is, indeed, randomly drawn. The 1969 Selective Service draft lottery was highly criticized for using essentially a "goldfish bowl" technique without adequate mixing. A more systematic approach to assuring randomness is to select a sample by using random numbers.

Random numbers are often available in table form; Table VI in Appendix B is a page of random numbers from a book published by the Rand Corporation containing 1 million random digits. Here the term "random" implies that each digit (a number between 0 and 9) occurs with the same probability, and the occurrence of each number is independent of all other numbers. Random digits are usually combined to form numbers of more than one digit. For example, random digits taken in pairs will result in a set of 100 different numbers (00 to 99), each with a probability of occurring of 1/100, and each independent of other numbers formed in the same manner. Table VI contains random digits presented in groups of five.

Random numbers can be used in the following manner to select a simple random sample of n items from a finite population of size N. First, a unique number between 0 and N must be assigned to each of the N items in the population. Then, n random numbers are used to select the items from the population to be included in the sample.

If a table of random numbers is used (like Table VI), then a random selection of a starting point is customary. For example, to select a random sample of four items, ($n = 4$) from a population of 75 elements ($N = 75$), we might arbitrarily start with a number that is the tenth number from the bottom in the first column, 09237. Since each number in the population has only two digits (00 to 99), we need look at only two of the five digits in each set of five digits. In this case it might be convenient to use the first two. Because the first number in the table is 09237, the first element in the sample is item number 09. Reading down, the next three items are 11, 60, and 71 (we skip 79 because there are only 75 elements in the population). Note that if the sample were to contain five items, the number 09 would have occurred again. In most practical situations it may not be possible or desirable to sample the same item twice. Its usefulness may be destroyed by the first sample, as would be the case in testing the tread life of a tire or measuring the yield from a new seed variety. The usual procedure in this situation is to let the next element on the list (for instance, item 63) take its place. When duplicated items are discarded, it must be recognized that sampling is now taking place without replacement, rather than with replacement. Most statistical computer packages have a procedure for generating random numbers.

Sampling with Prior Knowledge

Two important random sampling plans depend on prior knowledge about the population: stratified sampling and cluster sampling.

Stratified Sampling.   The use of stratified sampling requires that a population be divided into homogeneous classes or groups, called *strata*. Each stratum is then sampled according to certain specified criteria. The advantage of this procedure is that if homogeneous subsets of the population can be identified, then only a relatively small number of observations is needed to determine the characteristics of each subset. It can be shown that:

The optimal method of selecting strata is to find groups with a large variability between strata, but with only a small variability within strata.

We illustrate stratified sampling by considering a typical task involved in the annual audit of a business, that of evaluating accounts receivable. If possible, accountants attempt to stratify the accounts receivable, by the size of the receivable, in order to be sure the larger dollar items are given sufficient representation in the sample. A **proportional stratified sample** selects items from each stratum in proportion to the size of that stratum. This procedure ensures that each stratum in the sample is "weighted" by the number of elements it contained. In many cases a **disproportionate stratified sample** may be more efficient. A plan of this nature collects more than a proportionate amount of observations in the most important strata—in those with the greatest variability, or in those strata where being wrong is the most costly. In other words, by allocating a disproportionate amount of effort (time, money, research) to the most important strata, one often obtains a maximum amount of information for a given cost. Similarly, if it is more costly to sample from a particular stratum, one may elect to take fewer items from that stratum.

Cluster Sampling.   Cluster sampling represents a second important sampling plan in which the population is subdivided into groups in an attempt to design an efficient sample. The subdivisions or classes of the population in this case are called *clusters,* where each cluster, ideally, has the same characteristics as the parent population. If each cluster is assumed to be representative of the population, then the characteristics of this population can be estimated by (randomly) picking a cluster and then randomly sampling elements from within this cluster. Sampling within a cluster may take any of the forms already discussed and may even involve sampling from clusters within a cluster (in two-stage cluster sampling). The criterion for the selection of optimal clusters is exactly opposite to that for strata:

There should be little variability between clusters, but a high variability (representative of the population) within each cluster.

Cluster sampling can be illustrated by extending the accounts receivable example and assuming the accountant can identify groups of receivables that are relatively similar to each other. Sampling from one of these groups (or clusters) may provide an adequate representation of the entire population. Within the chosen group the accountant may use simple random sampling, stratified sampling, systematic sampling, or even break the group into smaller clusters. In cluster sampling there is always the danger that a cluster is not representative of the population.

Double, Multiple, and Sequential Sampling

One of the most important decisions in any sampling design involves selecting the *size* of the sample. Usually size is determined in advance of any data collection, but in some circumstances this may not be the most efficient procedure. Consider the problem of determining whether a shipment of 5000 items meets certain specified standards. It would be too expensive to check all 5000 items for their quality, so a sample is drawn and each item in the sample is tested for quality. Rather than take one large sample, of perhaps 100 items, a preliminary random sample of 25 items can be drawn and inspected. It may often be unnecessary to examine the remaining 75 items, for perhaps the entire lot can be judged on the basis of these 25 items. If a high percentage of the 25 components were defective, the conclusion drawn would probably be that the quality of the entire lot may not be acceptable. A low percentage of defectives may lead to accepting the lot. Values other than these extremes may also lead to acceptance or rejection of the entire lot. Nevertheless, there will usually be a range in which there is doubt about the quality of the entire lot. For example, it may be normal to have one or two defectives in a sample of 25; more than three, however, may lead one to suspect the entire lot, but not necessarily to reject it. An additional sample, perhaps the remaining 75 items, could then be taken, and the lot judged on the basis of all 100 items.

Samples in which the items are drawn into different stages, such as in the sequential fashion described above or from a cluster within a cluster, represent a process referred to as *two-stage sampling*. Virtually all important samples, and certainly all large-scale surveys, represent one form or another of multiple-stage sampling, and the sample design is usually not simple to plan. The major advantage of double, multiple, and sequential sampling procedures obviously depends on the savings that result when fewer items than usual must be observed. These procedures are especially appropriate when sampling is expensive, as when inspection destroys the usefulness of a valuable item or when travel expenses of the survey team would be high.

Nonprobabilistic Sampling

In some sense all nonprobabilistic sampling procedures represent *judgment samples,* in that they involve the selection of the items in a sample on the basis of the judgment or opinion of one or more persons. Judgment sampling is usually employed when a random sample cannot be taken or is not practical. It may be that there is not enough time or money to collect a random sample; or perhaps the sample represents an exploratory study where randomness is not too important. Indeed, when the number of population elements is small the judgment of an expert may be better than random methods in picking a truly representative sample. For example, you are using judgment sampling when you ask a friend's opinion about a movie, or about a particular college course. Similarly, "representative" individuals or animals are often chosen to participate in experiments, and accountants frequently select "typical" weeks for auditing accounts.

In *quota sampling,* each person gathering observations is given a specified number of elements to sample. This technique is used often in public-opinion surveys, in which the interviewer is allocated a certain number of people to interview. The decision as to exactly whom to interview is usually left to the individual doing the interview, although certain guidelines are almost always established. With well-trained and trustworthy interviewers, this procedure can be quite effective and can be carried out at a relatively low cost. Great danger exists, however, that procedures left to the interviewer's judgment and convenience may contain many unknown biases not conducive to a representative sample. Quota sampling is used often to obtain market research data or to survey for political preferences. In some of these situations a quota sample can be thought of as a special form of stratified sampling, in which interviewers are sent out and told to obtain a specified number of interviews from each stratum.

The least representative sampling procedure selects observations on the basis of convenience to the researcher, i.e., a *convenience sample.* "Street-corner surveys," in which the interviewer questions people as they go by, seem to be a favorite method of local TV news reporters for collecting public opinions. This method obviously cannot be considered very likely to yield a representative sample; more often, the results are biased and quite unsatisfactory. Convenience sampling is not widely used in circumstances other than preliminary or exploratory studies, or where representativeness is not a crucial factor.

The following table itemizes the sampling procedures described in Section 6.3.

Probabilistic	Nonprobabilistic
Simple random sampling	Judgment sampling
Stratified sampling	Quota sampling
Cluster sampling	Convenience sampling
Multiple/sequential sampling	

Sample Statistics **6.4**

Because the usual purpose of sampling is to learn something about the population being sampled, a primary consideration in selecting a sampling design is the desired degree of accuracy of what is learned from the sample about the population. To be able to assess this accuracy it is important to structure the problem of taking a sample and analyzing the sample results using the probability concepts presented in Chapters 2–5.

Assume the sample design is to take a sample of n observations in order to determine the characteristics of some random variable x. The process of taking a sample from this population can be viewed as an experiment, and the observations that may occur in such an experiment make up the sample space. Suppose the random variables $x_1, x_2, \ldots, x_n$ represent the observations in a sample. That is, the random variable x_1 represents the observation that occurs first in a sample of n observations, x_2 represents the second observation, and so forth. In simple random sampling, every item in the population has an equal chance of being the observation that occurs first, so in this case the sample space for x_1 would be the entire population of x-values. It is important to remember that $x_1, x_2, \ldots, x_n$ are all *random variables,* and each of these variables has a theoretical probability distribution. Under simple random sampling, the probability distribution of each of the random variables $x_1, x_2, \ldots, x_n$ will be identical to the distribution of the population random variable x.

Once we have collected a random sample of n observations, we have one value of x_1, one value of x_2, and so forth, with one value of x_n. We now need to discover how to learn more about the characteristics of the random variable x (the population) by making use of the sample values of $x_1, x_2, \ldots, x_n$. In general, the population parameters of interest are usually those described in Chapter 1—that is, the summary measures such as central location, dispersion, skewness, or kurtosis. It is intuitively appealing (and mathematically provable) that the best estimate of a population parameter is given by a comparable sample measure (a sample *statistic*). For example, we will see that the best estimate of the central location of a population is a measure of the central location of a sample; and the best estimate of the population dispersion is a measure of the dispersion of the sample. *Thus, a sample statistic is used as an estimate of a population parameter.* *

Generally, the population parameters of most interest are the mean and the variance, since these two measures are so useful in describing a distribution and so necessary in decision making. Consequently, the most useful sample statistics are the sample mean and the sample variance. In the development to follow, the reader should bear in mind that a similar development could be presented for sample statistics other than the mean and the variance. In addition, we assume simple random sampling is used.

The Sample Mean and Variance

The mean of a sample is calculated in the same manner as the mean of a population (see Formula 1.2 in Chapter 1), by summing the product of each value of x times its relative frequency. For a sample with n observations the *sample mean* is denoted as $\bar{x}$ (read x-bar) and defined as follows:

$$\text{Sample mean: } \quad \frac{1}{n} \sum_{\text{All } x} x_i f_i \tag{6.1}$$

Recall from Chapter 1 that a mean is not sufficient to describe a population. A variance or standard deviation is needed as well. The same comment holds true for samples, namely that descriptive measures of both location and variability are needed. Again we will use both the variance and the standard deviation to measure variability, recognizing that these two statistics are measuring the same thing, just in different units.

A sample variance is *not* calculated in the same manner as a population variance (Formula 1.5), for two reasons. First, we cannot take the sum of squared deviations about μ, for in most sampling problems μ is an unknown. Instead, we replace μ by our best estimate of μ, which is $\bar{x}$, and take the sum of the squared deviations about $\bar{x}$, or $\sum(x_i - \bar{x})^2$. As was the case for the sample mean in Formula (6.1), each term in the sum must be multiplied by its frequency. This sum is called the sum of squared deviations and is defined as follows:

$$\text{Sum of squared deviations: } \quad \sum_{\text{All } x} (x_i - \bar{x})^2 f_i$$

The second difference in calculating a sample variance is that the sum of squared deviations is *not* divided by the number of observations, but rather by

---

*A sample statistic can be defined as a function of some (or all) of the n random variables x_1, $x_2, \ldots x_n$. That is, a sample statistic is a random variable that is based on the sample values of x_1, $x_2, \ldots, x_n$. This means that there is a theoretical probability distribution associated with every sample statistic.

the sample size minus one, or $(n-1)$. The reason for dividing by $(n-1)$ is that the resulting measure of variability can be shown to satisfy certain desirable properties for making estimates about the (unknown) population variance. This fact will be explained in more detail in Chapter 7, when we discuss estimation procedures. A sample variance is denoted by the symbol s^2.

$$\text{Sample variance:} \quad s^2 = \frac{1}{n-1} \sum_{\text{All } x} (x_i - \bar{x})^2 f_i \qquad (6.2)$$

To demonstrate Formulas (6.1) and (6.2), consider the data in Table 6.1, representing the number of federal grants (such as HUD and TOPICS Programs) to 10 random selected cities with populations ranging from 50,000 to 200,000. In this table x_i is number of grants during the past year, and f_i is the frequency of each value of x_i.

The sample mean can be calculated from columns 2 and 3:

$$\bar{x} = \frac{1}{n} \sum x_i f_i = \frac{1}{10}(28) = 2.8 \quad \text{(grants)}$$

The sample variance is calculated using columns 2 and 6.

$$s^2 = \frac{1}{n-1} \sum (x_i - \bar{x})^2 f_i = \frac{1}{9}(17.60) = 1.955 \quad (\text{grants}^2)$$

Thus, the sample mean of $\bar{x} = 2.8$ is the best guess of the unknown population mean, μ, and the sample variance of $s^2 = 1.955$ is the best guess of the unknown population variance, σ^2.

The sample standard deviation is the square root of the sample variance, and is denoted by the letter s.

$$\text{Sample standard deviation:} \quad s = \sqrt{s^2} \qquad (6.3)$$

TABLE 6.1   **Number of grants to cities with populations 50,000 to 200,000**

(1) x_i	(2) f_i	(3) xf_i	(4) $(x_i - \bar{x})$	(5) $(x_i - \bar{x})^2$	(6) $(x_i - \bar{x})^2 f_i$
1	2	2	-1.8	3.24	6.48
2	3	6	-0.8	0.64	1.92
3	1	3	0.2	0.04	0.04
4	3	12	1.2	1.44	4.32
5	1	5	2.2	4.84	4.84
	10	28			17.60

For the data in Table 6.1, $s = \sqrt{1.955} = 1.398$ grants. Notice that the standard deviation is in the original units (grants), while the variance is in squared units (grants squared).

The Sample Mean and Variance—Grouped Data

The formulas presented above can be used for data that are grouped into classes by letting x_i represent the midpoint of each class. To illustrate the use of Formulas (6.1) and (6.2) for grouped data, consider the salary data in Table 6.2, representing a random sample of the 1988 salaries (plus bonus) of 20 of the top CEOs reported in *Business Week* (May 1989). There are six classes, each class having a width of $300,000 (the data are presented in thousands, which means that 300,000 is shown as 300).

The mean of these data is determined by using Formula (6.1) and midpoints as follows:

$$\bar{x} = \frac{1}{20}[450(3) + 750(4) + \cdots + 2250(1)]$$
$$= 1155 \quad (\text{or } \$1,155,000)$$

The average salary for the sample is thus $1,155,000. If this sample is indeed a random sample from a parent population of CEOs, then our best guess for the population mean is $1,155,000. Of course, we also know that it is highly unlikely the population mean is *exactly* $1,155,000. The population mean may not even be very close to this number. Thus, while a sample mean provides the best estimate of the population mean, some other way is needed to measure the accuracy of such estimates. We will study the process of measuring accuracy in the remainder of this chapter as well as in Chapters 7 and 8.

TABLE 6.2   Sample of salary plus bonus for CEOs

Salary + bonus ($ thousands)	Midpoint	Frequency
300–599	450	3
600–899	750	4
900–1199	1050	5
1200–1499	1350	3
1500–1799	1650	2
1800–2099	1950	2
2100–2399	2250	1
	Total	20

Calculating s^2 and s for Grouped Data

To demonstrate the calculation of a sample variance and standard deviation for grouped data, consider again the data in Table 6.2. These data are repeated in Table 6.3, with the appropriate calculations for determining the sample variance.

The sample variance can be determined using the sum of column 6 in Table 6.3, and Formula (6.2), as follows:

$$\textit{Sample variance: } s^2 = \frac{1}{n-1}\sum(x_i - 1155)^2 f_i = \frac{1}{19}(5269500)$$
$$= 277342.11 \quad \text{(dollars squared)}$$

The sample variance is thus $s^2 = 277{,}342.11$. This sample statistic represents our best guess of the population variance, although we again recognize that the population variance may not be particularly close to this number.

The sample standard deviation is the square root of the variance.

$$\textit{Sample standard deviation: } s = \sqrt{277342.11} = 526.6328 \quad \text{(dollars)}$$

We might check to see if the value $s = 526.6328$ is reasonable by using a rule of thumb comparable to the one used in Chapters 1 and 4: As a rule, about 68% of the observations (based on a normal curve) should fall within plus or minus one standard deviation of the mean. Although this rule is based on the normal distribution, it often provides a good approximation to sample data when the sample distribution is fairly symmetrical. In this case the mean is $\overline{x} = 1155$, and the standard deviation is $s = 526.6328$. Thus,

$$\overline{x} \pm 1s = 1155 + 1(526.6328) \quad \text{or} \quad 628.3672 \text{ to } 1681.6328$$

TABLE 6.3   Calculation of the variance for CEO salary data

(1) **Salary + bonus** **($ thousands)** x_i	(2) f_i	(3) 	(4) $(x_i - \overline{x})$ $(x_i - 1155)$	(5) $(x_i - \overline{x})^2$ $(x_i - 1155)^2$	(6) $(x_i - \overline{x})^2 f_i$ $(x_i - 1155)^2 f_i$
300–599	450	3	− 705	497025	1491075
600–899	750	4	− 405	164025	656100
900–1199	1050	5	− 105	11025	55125
1200–1499	1350	3	195	38025	114075
1500–1799	1650	2	495	245025	490050
1800–2099	1950	2	795	632025	1264050
2100–2399	2250	1	1095	1199025	1199025
Total		20			5269500

TABLE 6.4   Computer output for CEO salary data

VAR NAME	SAMPLE SIZE	MEAN	STD. DEV.	MINIMUM	MAXIMUM
SALARY	20	1155.0000	526.6328	450	2250

===CLASS LIMITS===	FREQUENCY	PERCENT	...CUMULATIVE... FREQUENCY	PERCENT
300 < 600	3	15.00	3	15.00
600 < 900	4	20.00	7	35.00
900 < 1200	5	25.00	12	60.00
1200 < 1500	3	15.00	15	75.00
1500 < 1800	2	10.00	17	85.00
1800 < 2100	2	10.00	19	95.00
2100 < 2400	1	5.00	20	100.00
Total	20	100.00		

The value $s = 526.6328$ seems reasonable since 65% of the 20 sample salaries fall between 628.3672 and 1681.6328 (13 fall between 600 and 1650 if we count one of the two salaries between 1500–1799; 13/20 = 65%).

We conclude from the analysis above that our best guess of the population variance is $s^2 = 277,342.11$, and our best guess of the population standard deviation is $s = 526.6328$.

The computation of these sample statistics may easily be done using a computer. Table 6.4 illustrates a computer output for the CEO salary data. This output gives the same mean (1155) and standard deviation (526.6328) as we calculated above, as well as the minimum and maximum values, and a frequency distribution.

The frequency distribution in Table 6.4 provides both absolute values and cumulative values. As you would expect, the sum of the cumulative frequencies is 20 ($= n$), and the final cumulative percent is 100. A good exercise for the reader at this point is to use a computer program to duplicate Table 6.4.

Perhaps at this point we should reiterate that one of our objectives in calculating a *sample* mean and variance is to be able to make statements about the *population* mean and variance. The population mean and variance are generally unknown because it is too costly and time consuming to take a census. Thus, we must be content to *use sample statistics to estimate the population parameters, and then to make statements about how reliable or accurate such a sample statistic is in describing the population parameter of interest.*

Problems

6.1 a) Under what conditions is nonprobabilistic sampling more appropriate than probabilistic sampling? Give several examples.

b) In designing a sample survey, what factors are most important in establishing the strata in stratified sampling? The clusters in cluster sampling? How will the cost of sampling affect these decisions?

6.2 Distinguish between

a) systematic sampling and simple random sampling;

b) stratified and cluster sampling;

c) single-stage sampling and multistage sampling;

d) judgment, quota, and convenience sampling.

6.3 Assume you have been asked to select 20 of the *Fortune* 500 list of companies to be included in a sample survey. The survey will consist of a questionnaire to be sent to the vice president in charge of marketing to study the company's policy on ethics in advertising.

a) What factors would you want to consider in designing such a study?

b) Decide on several factors from part (a) that you consider most important, and then use these factors to prepare a sample design for selecting 20 companies.

c) Select 20 companies using the design in part (b).

6.4 The pharmaceutical company Eli Lilly wants to gather information on the average number of prescriptions written (per month) by doctors in the United States. Lilly expects to have a sample of at least 1000 doctors.

a) Start the thought process for a sample design by listing the types of doctors Lilly might want to include in this sample, and how (or if) Lilly could find a list of all such doctors.

b) What problems might Lilly encounter in collecting a sample of the prescriptions written by 1000 doctors? Is simple random sampling really feasible? Would cluster or stratified sampling be feasible? How might the number of prescriptions be determined? What response rate would you expect from a questionnaire?

c) Given your thoughts in parts (a) and (b), select a sampling plan for collecting at least 1000 observations on monthly prescriptions written by U.S. doctors.

6.5 **a)** Use Table VI to select a random sample of eight observations from a population of 500 items. Specify where in Table VI you started your process and which are to be included in the sample.

b) Use a computer to generate the eight numbers for part (a).

6.6 Find the mean and the variance of your sample in Problem 6.5.

6.7 The word "random" has been used in several different contexts thus far. Define and distinguish between these uses:

a) random variable;

b) random sample;

c) observations selected "at random."

6.8 Assume the main library at your university has asked you to design a sample of actual and potential users of the library facilities (they have a short questionnaire to administer). They want to sample both user and nonusers of the library, and they want to be sure the sample represents, as best as possible, undergraduates and graduates as well as people from the local community. The library would like a response of at least 200 questionnaires, but they have a limited budget. Construct a sampling design for the library staff.

6.9 Assume you have been commissioned to design a survey of the age, income, and occupation of the customers who patronize a nationwide chain of grocery stores. You have a reasonable, but not unlimited, budget for this project. Construct a sampling design.

6.10 The following 10 random numbers were generated by a computer program. In this case the statistical package was asked to generate 10 random integers between 00 and 99.

Random integers		Random integers	
1	66	6	87
2	17	7	68
3	40	8	56
4	11	9	34
5	48	10	39

a) Find the mean of these 10 numbers. What mean would you expect for 10 such numbers? For a million such numbers?

b) Use a computer to generate your own set of 10 random integers between 00 and 99.

c) Repeat part (a) for the variance.

6.11 Many stockmarket analysts and brokers use shares-traded activity to spot stocks that are suddenly attracting a lot of interest. Listed below is the percentage of outstanding shares traded in a random sample of the top 40 stocks on the New York Stock Exchange, as reported in the *Wall Street Journal.* (Stocks are listed in alphabetical order.)

Company	Pct.	Company	Pct.
Caesars World	1.45	Silicon Systs	2.00
Carson Pirie	5.04	Sun Electric	6.39
Data General	1.75	Tandem Cptr	3.41
IMC Fertilizer	2.00	Williams Cos	1.86
Lands' End	4.64	Zenith	1.54

Find the mean and standard deviation for these sample data (use a computer program, if one is available to you).

6.12 Use a computer program to find the mean and standard deviation for the female salaries presented in Appendix C. Use a frequency distribution to summarize these data, with class widths of $5000 and the first class beginning at $30,000.

6.13 The distribution of the number of defects per square yard of a cotton textile is given as follows:

No. of Defects (x)	Frequency (f)
0	47
1	33
2	14
3	5
4	1
5 or more	0
Total	100

a) Use Formulas (6.1), (6.2), and (6.3) to find the mean and standard deviation of this distribution.

b) Verify your answers to part (a) by using a computer program.

6.14 A 1989 Gallup Survey reported in *USA Today* indicated the following frequency of personal computers in U.S. households, by income, among a sample of 4500 households surveyed.

Income	Frequency of owners
Under $10,000	38
$10,000–$19,000	108
$20,000–$49,000	475
$50,000 or more	199

The headline for this "Snapshot" was that 18% of all U.S. households had personal computers.

a) What sample design would you use for this type of a survey?

b) Show how *USA Today* determined the 18% figure, using these data.

c) Do you agree that it is reasonable to estimate that 18% of U.S. households have personal computers based on this survey. What additional information would you want about 1) how the "sample" was taken and 2) about the distribution of incomes in the United States?

d) Is it possible to use the data in this problem to determine the average income for households with personal computers? Explain.

e) Describe a sampling design you would recommend to determine the proportion of U.S. households with personal computers.

6.15 A telephone survey of 500 customers who had purchased Maytag washing machines within the past 10 years reported that 90% were "happy" with their respective machines. Without knowing anything about this study, what concerns, or at least questions, might you have about these data and how they were collected?

6.16 A company reports that the average weekly wage for all hourly workers is $320. You take a random sample of 100 of these workers, with the results shown in the table to the left. Find the mean of these grouped data. Does this mean equal $320? Did you expect it to equal $320? Explain.

Wages	Frequency
$238–262	4
263–287	15
288–312	20
313–337	30
338–362	15
363–387	10
388–412	6
Total	**100**

6.17 A major computer manufacturer has offered to sell its most popular models of personal computers to students at a 40% discount. They have a stock of these machines in their Lexington, Kentucky, warehouse, and state that the average delivery time is four days (96 hours), with a variance of one day (24 hours). A random sample of the delivery time for four shipments was found to be, in hours, 106, 102, 104, and 108.

a) Find the mean and standard deviation of delivery time for this sample.

b) Is the sample mean close to the population mean? Is the sample standard deviation close to the population standard deviation? Explain your answer.

6.18 A random sample of 20 weeks resulted in the following frequency of repairs needed for the vending machines at a major university. Find the sample mean and variance.

Machines needing repair (x)	Frequency (weeks)
0	1
1	2
2	7
3	9
4	1
5 or more	0

6.19 An article in the January 31, 1990, *Wall Street Journal* presented stock buys by company chairmen in the 1989 fourth quarter as follows.

Company (chairman)	Amount spent (in millions)	Average price (per share)	Number shares
Ask Computer (Kurtzig)	$6.9	$7.89	874,525
Audio Video Affiliates (Rose)	3.3	3.42	964,912
Global Natural Resources (Omara)	1.6	5.25	304,762
Unitil (Tenney)	1.2	36.01	33,324
Sterling Software (Wyly)	1.2	7.37	162,822

a) What is the average number of shares purchased by these five chairmen? Treat these numbers as sample data.

b) Find the mean price of all the shares purchased as listed above.

c) Find the variance of the share prices listed above.

6.20 The following cross-sectional data represent 1989 second quarter sales (in millions) for a sample of eight U.S. Chemical companies, as reported in *Business Week*. Find the mean and the standard deviation.

Company	Sales	Company	Sales
Air Products & Chemical	663.7	Himont	423.5
Dow Chemical	4601.0	Monsanto	2348.0
Ferro	275.4	Pennwalt	279.9
Grace (W. R.)	1510.7	Union Carbide	2277.0

6.21 A headline in the national news stated that "Big 3 Auto Sales up 14.3%." The article then went on to say that G.M. was up 10.2%, Ford and Chrysler were up 15.6% and 17.1%, respectively. Do these figures indicate that sales were up 14.3%? How would you calculate the percentage increase?

6.22 You are tracking the sales for one of the regional representatives in your department. Sales for the past five years were:

Year:	1	2	3	4	5
	126,780	142,150	138,440	159,290	168,650

Find the mean and standard deviation for these data. Do they represent sample or population data? Explain.

Fund category	Gain
Speciality	10.68
Capital Appreciation	12.73
Growth	13.55
Balanced	10.18
Gold-oriented	– 5.39
Income	9.52

6.23 Lipper Analytical Services, Inc. reported on the gain from 1988–89 the sample of six market funds shown at left. Find the mean and standard deviation.

6.24 A random sample of 24 insurance adjusters hired by a large insurance company resulted in the following performance rating on the job (PROJ).

Adjuster	PROJ	Adjuster	PROJ	Adjuster	PROJ
1	394	9	388	17	456
2	104	10	341	18	147
3	455	11	133	19	264
4	283	12	202	20	271
5	203	13	385	21	138
6	135	14	456	22	140
7	204	15	166	23	271
8	313	16	122	24	300

a) Find the mean and standard deviation.

b) Group these data into classes of width 50, starting with 100. Find the mean and standard deviation of the grouped data, and compare these values with those from part (a).

6.25 Describe a sampling plan for the following situations.

a) An auditor wants to estimate the aggregate value of an inventory.

b) A CPA wishes an estimate of the percent of credit card customers who had a cash advance in the last month.

6.26 A classic example of the problems of response bias resulted from a 1989 study, called the Shere Hite report, on the happiness of U.S. married women. This report relied on the responses of 4,500 women, out of approximately 100,000 questionnaires that were distributed nationally to various women's groups, garden circles, and service organizations.

a) Comment on the problems you see in drawing conclusions from the 4,500 responses. Would you be willing to draw *any* conclusions from such a study? Explain.

b) Find a copy of the Hite report, or a summary of its conclusions, and then again answer part (a).

Sampling Distributions

6.5

To establish the reliability or accuracy with which a sample statistic describes a population parameter we form what is called a *sampling distribution*. A sampling distribution is a probability distribution for a sample statistic. Such a distribution gives the probability of each possible value of the sample statistic for some specified population. For example, the *sampling distribution of $\bar{x}$* is presented below.

To illustrate this distribution, imagine taking a large number of random samples from some population, where every sample is of the same size (n). For each sample $\bar{x}$ is calculated. These many values of $\bar{x}$ can be put in the form of a frequency distribution. This frequency distribution will have a certain shape, as well as a mean and a variance. Now, if we take *all possible* samples of size n (the number of samples may be infinite), and determine $\bar{x}$ for each sample, the resulting distribution is the *sampling distribution of $\bar{x}$.*

We could also calculate a *sampling distribution for s^2*, forming a probability distribution from all possible values of s^2 from random samples of a given size n. Other sampling distributions are possible, such as for the median or the range. Sampling distributions are necessary for making probability statements about the reliability and accuracy of sample statistics.

The Sampling Distribution of $\bar{x}$

The *sampling distribution of $\bar{x}$* is the probability distribution of *all possible* values of $\bar{x}$ that could occur when a sample (of size n) is taken from some specified parent population.

TABLE 6.5   All possible samples of size $n = 2$ from the population $x = \{1, 2, 3\}$

Sample	Sample mean ($\bar{x}$)	Sample	Sample mean ($\bar{x}$)
(1, 1)	1.0	(1, 2)	1.5
(2, 1)	1.5	(1, 3)	2.0
(3, 1)	2.0	(2, 2)	2.0
(2, 3)	2.5	(3, 2)	2.5
(3, 3)	3.0		

We will illustrate the concept of the sampling distribution of $\bar{x}$ by considering a very small population and sample size, so that it is possible to list all samples that could occur. The reader should remember that the concepts developed here hold for the much larger populations and sample sizes typically encountered.

Assume Moody's Investors Service is to rate a large number of first-mortgage bonds as either Aaa ($= 3$), or Aa ($= 2$) or A ($= 1$). Furthermore, assume that one-third of the bonds will be rated Aaa, one third as Aa, and one-third as A. That is, the parent population consists of the set $x = \{1, 2, 3\}$, each value of x occurring with probability 1/3. The mean of this parent population is easily seen to be $\mu = 2.0$; i.e., the average bond is classified as Aa. Now, let us assume you do not know how these bonds are classified; in other words, you do not know that the population is $x = \{1, 2, 3\}$. To estimate this population you decide to take a sample of two bonds, and then see how these two are classified. Table 6.5 shows the nine possible samples of size $n = 2$ you could draw from this population of three values. Your sample mean will thus be identical to one of the nine values of $\bar{x}$ in Table 6.5.

Each one of the nine sample means in Table 6.5 has the same probability of occurring, 1/9. However, some of the means are identical—for example, there are three values of $\bar{x} = 2.0$, so

$$P(\bar{x} = 2.0) = 3/9$$

Similarly, $P(\bar{x} = 1.0) = 1/9$, $P(\bar{x} = 1.5) = 2/9$, $P(\bar{x} = 2.5) = 2/9$, and $P(\bar{x} = 3.0) = 1/9$. Note that these six probabilities sum to 1.0. They represent a probability distribution, specifically *the sampling distribution of $\bar{x}$* (for $n = 2$ from the population $x = \{1, 2, 3\}$). This sampling distribution is shown in Fig. 6.1.*

The sampling distribution of $\bar{x}$ is a population. It is a population because it consists of all values of interest, namely all values of $\bar{x}$ that could be drawn in a given situation. As is the case with all populations, we are interested in certain characteristics of this population of $\bar{x}$'s, especially its mean, its variance, and its shape.

---

*We assume, until Section 6.8, that the population is either infinitely large or that sampling is with replacement. However, we note as we proceed that sampling with replacement from a finite population might change our results.

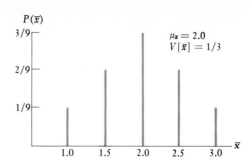

Figure 6.1

The Mean of the Sampling Distribution of $\overline{x}$ (or $\mu_{\overline{x}}$)*

The symbol $\mu_{\overline{x}}$ denotes the mean of all possible sample means, which is the mean of the sampling distribution of $\overline{x}$.

Using the notation of expectations, $\mu_{\overline{x}} = E[\overline{x}]$.

The concept of $\mu_{\overline{x}}$ can be illustrated by calculating its value for Fig. 6.1. That is, what is the average value of $\overline{x}$ when all possible samples of size $n = 2$ are drawn from the population $x = \{1, 2, 3\}$? The mean of these values is calculated in the same manner a mean was calculated in Chapter 3, except that now the variable is $\overline{x}$ and we denote the mean of this variable as $\mu_{\overline{x}}$.

$$\mu_{\overline{x}} = \sum_{\text{All } \overline{x}} \overline{x} P(\overline{x})$$

$$\mu_{\overline{x}} = \sum \overline{x} P(\overline{x}) = (1.0)(\tfrac{1}{9}) + (1.5)(\tfrac{2}{9}) + (2.0)(\tfrac{3}{9}) + (2.5)(\tfrac{2}{9}) + (3.0)(\tfrac{1}{9})$$
$$= 2.00$$

Thus we have shown for this population that $\mu_{\overline{x}} = \mu = 2.00$. The fact that these two means are equal is not a coincidence, as it can be shown that $\mu_{\overline{x}}$ equals μ for *any* parent population and *any* given sample size (and holds for sampling with or without replacement.)

$$E[\overline{x}] = \mu_{\overline{x}} = \mu \tag{6.4}$$

---

*From this point on we will add a subscript to a population parameter or sample statistic whenever it may be unclear which population or sample is being described. For example, s_y refers to the standard deviation of the sample of y-values, while $\mu_{\overline{x}}$ refers to the mean of the population of $\overline{x}$-values. If *no* subscript is used, such as μ or σ or s, these refer to the distribution of x-values under consideration.

The Variance of the Sampling Distribution of $\bar{x}$ (or $\sigma_{\bar{x}}^2$)

In addition to knowing the mean of the sampling distribution of $\bar{x}$ for a given sample size n, we need to know its variance.

The variance of the sampling distribution of $\bar{x}$ is denoted by the symbol $\sigma_{\bar{x}}^2$, or by the symbol $V[\bar{x}]$.

This variance, of the population of all values of $\bar{x}$, is calculated in the same manner the variance of a probability distribution was calculated: subtract the mean ($\mu_{\bar{x}}$ in this case) from each value of the variable ($\bar{x}_i$), square these differences [$(\bar{x}_i - \mu_{\bar{x}})^2$], multiply by the probability $P(\bar{x})$, and then sum all such squared deviations.

$$\boxed{\begin{array}{c} \textit{Variance of the sampling distribution of } \bar{x}: \\ \sigma_{\bar{x}}^2 = \sum(\bar{x}_i - \mu_{\bar{x}})^2 P(\bar{x}) \end{array}} \qquad (6.5)$$

Table 6.6 illustrates the calculation of this (population) variance for the bond example. From the bottom of the last row in Table 6.6 we see that

$$\sigma_{\bar{x}}^2 = \frac{1}{3}$$

To calculate $\sigma_{\bar{x}}^2$ as we did above requires that all possible values of $\bar{x}$ are known. This is impractical if not impossible in the many situations when there is a very large (or infinite) number of values of $\bar{x}$. Fortunately, $\sigma_{\bar{x}}^2$ can be determined much more easily if one knows the variance of the parent population, using the following relationship.

$$\boxed{\begin{array}{l} \text{The variance of } \bar{x} \ (\sigma_{\bar{x}}^2), \text{ assuming each sample consists of } n \\ \text{independent observations, is } 1/n \text{ times the variance of the} \\ \text{parent population } x \ (\sigma^2) \\ \\ \qquad \sigma_{\bar{x}}^2 = \dfrac{1}{n}\sigma^2 \end{array}} \qquad (6.6)$$

Formula (6.6) should appear reasonable in the sense that the variance of the $\bar{x}$'s will always be less than the variance of the parent population (except when $n = 1$) because the chance that a *sample* mean will take on an extreme value is less than the chance a *single* value will take on this same extreme value. For example, in order for a sample mean to be a lot larger than the population mean, most or all of the sample values would have to be much larger than the population mean. This is unlikely since we know that the population mean is the expected value for the $\bar{x}$'s, and it would be very unusual not to draw some middle or very low values. On the other hand, σ^2 represents the

TABLE 6.6   Calculation of the variance for a distribution of sample means

$\overline{x}$	$P(\overline{x})$	$(\overline{x} - \mu_{\overline{x}})$	$(\overline{x} - \mu_{\overline{x}})^2$	$(\overline{x} - \mu_{\overline{x}})^2 P(\overline{x})$
1.0	$\frac{1}{9}$	-1.0	1.00	$\frac{1}{9}$
1.5	$\frac{2}{9}$	-0.5	0.25	$\frac{2}{36}$
2.0	$\frac{3}{9}$	0	0	0
2.5	$\frac{2}{9}$	0.5	0.25	$\frac{2}{36}$
3.0	$\frac{1}{9}$	1.0	1.00	$\frac{1}{9}$

Mean 2.0 $\qquad\qquad\qquad\qquad V[\overline{x}] = \frac{12}{36} = \frac{1}{3}$

variance of *individual* items, and a large single value of x would not be that unusual.*

When $n = 1$, all samples contain only one observation, and the distributions of x and $\overline{x}$ are identical. That is, $\sigma_{\overline{x}}^2 = \sigma^2/1 = \sigma^2$. As n becomes larger ($n \to \infty$) it is reasonable to expect $\sigma_{\overline{x}}^2$ to become smaller and smaller because the sample means will tend to deviate less and less from the population mean $\mu_{\overline{x}}$. When $n = \infty$ (or for finite populations, when $n = N$), all sample means will equal the population mean and the variance of the $\overline{x}$'s will be zero. To illustrate the relationship described by Formula (6.6), let us return to our stock example involving the population (1, 2, 3). The variance of this population is the following:

$$\sigma^2 = \frac{1}{N}\sum(x_i - \mu_{\overline{x}})^2 = \frac{1}{3}[(1-2)^2 + (2-2)^2 + (3-2)^2] = \frac{2}{3}$$

Since we know that the variance of this population is $\frac{2}{3}$ and the sample size is $n = 2$, we can calculate $V[\overline{x}]$ using Formula (6.6):

$$\sigma_{\overline{x}}^2 = \frac{1}{n}\sigma^2 = \frac{1}{2}\left(\frac{2}{3}\right) = \frac{1}{3}$$

---

*Let $x_1, x_2, \ldots, x_n$ be independent random variables, each having the same variance (that is, $V[x_i] = \sigma^2$);

$$V[\overline{x}] = V\left[\frac{1}{n}(x_1 + x_2 + \cdots + x_n)\right] \qquad \text{By definition}$$

$$= \left(\frac{1}{n}\right)^2 V[x_1 + x_2 + \cdots + x_n]$$

$$= \left(\frac{1}{n}\right)^2 [V[x_1] + V[x_2] + \cdots + V[x_n]] \qquad \text{By Formula (3.18)}$$

$$= \frac{n}{n^2}(\sigma^2) = \frac{1}{n}\sigma^2 \qquad \text{Since } V[x_i] = \sigma^2$$

Formulas (6.6) and (6.7) do not hold when sampling without replacement from a finite population (see Section 6.8).

This value of $V[\overline{x}]$ is exactly the same number we calculated in Table 6.6. Thus, we have verified that Formula (6.6) holds for this particular problem.

Standard Error of the Mean

Thus far we have shown that the variance of all possible values of $\overline{x}$ is $\sigma_{\overline{x}_2}^2 = \sigma^2/n$. The square root of $\sigma_{\overline{x}}^2$ is called the *standard error of the mean*.

> The standard deviation of the $\overline{x}$'s, denoted as $\sigma_{\overline{x}}$,
> is called the **standard error of the mean**.
>
> $$\sigma_{\overline{x}} = \sqrt{\sigma^2/n} = \sigma/\sqrt{n}$$

(6.7)

The word "error" in this context refers to sampling error, as $\sigma_{\overline{x}}$ is a measure of the "standard" (or expected) error when the sample mean is used to obtain information or draw conclusions about the unknown population mean.

For our bond example, using the population $x = \{1, 2, 3\}$, we calculated the variance of the $\overline{x}$'s to be $\sigma_{\overline{x}}^2 = 1/3$. The standard error of the mean is the square root of this number.

$$\text{Standard error of the mean: } \sigma_{\overline{x}} = \sqrt{1/3} = 0.577$$

This standard error could have been calculated much more easily by remembering that $\sigma^2 = 2/3$, $n = 2$, and using Formula (6.7) as follows:

$$\sigma_{\overline{x}} = \sqrt{\sigma^2/n} = \sqrt{(2/3)/2} = \sqrt{1/3} = 0.577$$

We emphasize at this point that $\mu_{\overline{x}}$ and $\sigma_{\overline{x}}$ are parameters of the population of all conceivable samples of size n, and these population parameters are *unknown* quantities. In fact, the values of μ, $\mu_{\overline{x}}$, σ, and $\sigma_{\overline{x}}$ are usually *all* unknown quantities, which means that the relationship $\mu_{\overline{x}} = \mu$ and $\sigma_{\overline{x}} = \sigma/\sqrt{n}$ cannot be used to solve for the value of one of these quantities. However, knowledge of the fact that such relationships exist is important in determining how far a sample mean can be expected to deviate from the population mean. The advantage of knowing this information is that we can test *assumptions* about a population by looking at sample results. For example, suppose in our bond example we had *assumed* (but did not know) that the parent population was $x = \{1, 2, 3\}$. If a single sample of size $n = 2$ from this population had yielded $\overline{x} = 1.0$, then we might begin to question our assumption about the population $x = \{1, 2, 3\}$ because $P(\overline{x} = 1.0)$ is only $\frac{1}{9}$ for samples of size 2 from this population. A sample of $(1, 1)$ might in this case lead us to *incorrectly reject the assumption that* $x = \{1, 2, 3\}$. In Chapter 9 we will formally consider this process of testing hypotheses.

Although we have derived the mean and variance of the $\overline{x}$'s, nothing has been said about the *shape* of the sampling distribution of $\overline{x}$. Recall from Chapter 1 that distributions with the same mean and variance may have distinctly different shapes. It is necessary, therefore, to be more specific about the entire distribution of $\bar{x}$'s. To do so, we will first assume that the parent population is normal, and then later drop this assumption.

Sampling Distribution of $\bar{x}$, Normal Parent Population

6.6

We already know the mean and variance of the distribution of $\bar{x}$'s, but what is known about its shape? It is usually not possible to specify the shape of the $\bar{x}$'s when the parent population is discrete and the sample size is small. However, when the sample is drawn from a parent population (x) which is normally distributed, then the shape of the $\bar{x}$'s can be specified. As you might suspect, in this situation, the $\bar{x}$'s are distributed normally. That is,

---

The sampling distribution of $\bar{x}$'s drawn from a normal parent population is a normal distribution.

Using the fact that the mean of the $\bar{x}$'s is $\mu_{\bar{x}} = \mu$ [Formula (6.4)], and that the variance of the $\bar{x}$'s is $\sigma_{\bar{x}}^2 = \sigma^2/n$, we can now specify that the sampling distribution of $\bar{x}$ is $N(\mu_{\bar{x}}, \sigma_{\bar{x}}^2) = N(\mu, \sigma^2/n)$ whenever the parent population is normal.

An illustration of the sampling distribution of $\bar{x}$ can be drawn from an article in *Business Week*, where the average GMAT for selected top MBA programs was (approximately) 600. Let's assume that the population of GMAT scores for this population is normally distributed with a mean of 600 and a variance of 2500, or $N(600, 2500)$. We decide to draw a sample of $n = 20$ students from this population.

Because all normal distributions are continuous, an infinite number of different samples of size 20 could be drawn. For all of these samples a mean, $\bar{x}$, could be calculated. Since the population mean is $\mu = 600$, the mean of the $\bar{x}$'s is $\mu_{\bar{x}} = 600$. Similarly since $\sigma^2 = 2500$, the variance of the $\bar{x}$'s is $\sigma_{\bar{x}}^2 = \sigma^2/n = 2500/20 = 125$. Finally, because x is normal, $\bar{x}$ will also be normally distributed. All this information about $\bar{x}$ can be summarized by the following statement: $\bar{x}$ is $N(600, 125)$.

The standard error of the mean is $\sigma_{\bar{x}} = \sqrt{125} = 11.18$. This means that 68.3% of the sample means will fall within plus or minus one standard deviation of the mean,

$$\mu \pm 1\sigma_{\bar{x}} = 600 \pm 1(11.18) \quad \text{or} \quad 588.82 \text{ to } 611.18$$

95.4% will fall within plus-or-minus two standard deviations of the mean,

$$\mu \pm 2\sigma_{\bar{x}} = 600 \pm 2(11.18) \quad \text{or} \quad 577.64 \text{ to } 622.36$$

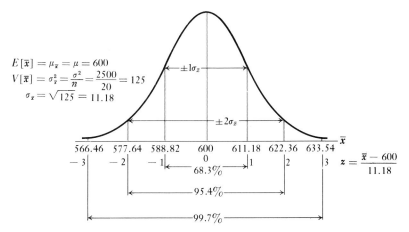

Figure 6.2
Sampling distribution of $\bar{x}$
for sample of $n = 20$ taken
from a population with
distribution $N(600, 2500)$.

and 99.7% of all sample means will fall within plus-or-minus three standard deviations of the mean,

$$\mu \pm 3\sigma_{\bar{x}} = 600 \pm 3(11.18) \quad \text{or} \quad 566.46 \text{ to } 633.54$$

Figure 6.2. shows the sampling distribution of $\bar{x}$ for all possible samples of size 20 taken from a population with the distribution $N(600, 2500)$.

   The following statement summarizes what we now know about the distribution of sample means ($\bar{x}$).

If the parent population (x) is normally distributed, with mean μ and variance σ^2, then the distribution of $\bar{x}$ for a given sample size n will be $N(\mu, \sigma^2/n)$.

The Standardized Form of the Random Variable $\bar{x}$ (σ Known)*

In Chapter 5 we saw that it is usually easier to work with the standard normal form of a variable than to leave it in its original units. The same type of transformation that was made on the random variable x at that point can now be made on the random variable $\bar{x}$. Recall that in Chapter 5 the variable x was transformed to its standard normal form by subtracting the mean from each value, and then dividing by the standard deviation. The resulting variable, $z = (x - \mu)/\sigma$, was shown to have a mean of zero and a variance of one. Although now we are interested in transforming the variable $\bar{x}$ instead of x, and the standard deviation of this variable is $\sigma/\sqrt{n}$ instead of σ, the transfor-

---

*Whenever $\bar{x}$ is normal, the distribution of $\bar{x}$ is $N(\mu, \sigma/\sqrt{n})$ whether or not σ is known. However, in order to make probability statements about $\bar{x}$, we must standardize this variable, and this standardization requires that we know σ.

mation is accomplished in exactly the same fashion. One simply must take care always to subtract the mean and divide by the standard deviation corresponding to the variable being standardized.

$$\text{Standardization of } \overline{x}: \ z = \frac{\overline{x} - \mu_{\overline{x}}}{\sigma_{\overline{x}}} = \frac{\overline{x} - \mu}{\sigma/\sqrt{n}} \tag{6.8}$$

As before, the random variable z has a mean of zero and a variance of one. Since we have said that the distribution of the random variable $\overline{x}$ is normal, it follows that the random variable z must also be normally distributed. Thus:

When sampling from a normal parent population, the distribution of

$$z = \frac{\overline{x} - \mu}{\sigma/\sqrt{n}}$$

will be normal with mean 0 and variance 1.

The standardized normal form of the variable $\overline{x}$ is shown on the z-scale in Fig. 6.2.

The limitations of the preceding discussion should be apparent, for although the normal distribution approximates the probability distribution of many real-world problems, one cannot assume that the parent population is *always* normal. What, for example, will be the shape of the distribution of $\overline{x}$'s when sampling from a highly skewed distribution? We consider this situation in the next section.

Sampling Distribution of $\overline{x}$—Population Unknown, σ Known

6.7

In Section 6.6 the parent population (x) was assumed to be normal. Because of this assumption the sampling distribution of $\overline{x}$ was found to be normally distributed. Now, we focus on the question of the *shape* of the distribution of $\overline{x}$ when x is not normal. As will be discussed, there are two parts to the answer to this question, depending on the size of the sample (n).

1. *When n is small,* the shape of the distribution depends on the shape of the parent population. In general, we cannot easily specify the shape of the $\overline{x}$'s when n is small.

2. *As n becomes larger and larger,* the shape of the sampling distribution of $\overline{x}$ will become more and more like a normal distribution, no matter what the shape of the parent population.

The second statement above is the essence of one of the most important theorems in statistics, called the **central limit theorem.** Stated formally, the central limit theorem (CLT) is

---

The central limit theorem: Regardless of the distribution of the parent population, the distribution of the means of random samples will approach a normal distribution as the sample size n goes to infinity.*

The importance of the CLT to statistics cannot be understated: It permits use of the normal distribution, when n is not small, to solve a wide variety of problems in the many situations when the distribution of the parent population is unknown, or known to be nonnormal. For example, the distribution of incomes is skewed right for many employment sectors. If a reasonably large sample is taken from one of these populations, then the sampling distribution of $\overline{x}$ can be assumed to be normally distributed, and the z distribution used to calculate probabilities.

We will not prove the CLT, but merely show, in Fig. 6.3, graphical evidence of its validity. The first row of diagrams in Fig. 6.3 shows four different parent populations. The next three rows show the sampling distribution of $\overline{x}$ for all possible repeated samples (with replacement) of size $n = 2$, $n = 5$, and $n = 30$, respectively drawn from the populations shown in the first row. Note in the first column that when the parent population is normal, all the sampling distributions are also normal. Also, note that distributions in the same column have the same mean μ, but their variances decrease as $\sqrt{n}$ increases.

The second column of figures in Fig. 6.3 represents what is called a **uniform** (or **rectangular**) **distribution.** We see here that the sampling distribution of $\overline{x}$ is already symmetrical when $n = 2$, and it is quite normal in appearance when $n = 5$. Moving to the third column of figures, the parent population is now a bimodal distribution with discrete values of x (the central limit theorem applies whether x is discrete or continuous). Again, by $n = 2$ the distribution is symmetrical, and by $n = 5$ it is quite bell-shaped. The final parent population is the highly skewed exponential distribution. Here we see that for $n = 2$ and $n = 5$ the distribution is still fairly skewed, although it becomes more symmetrical as n increases. When $n = 30$, however, even such a skewed parent population results in a symmetrical, bell-shaped distribution for $\overline{x}$ which, by the central limit theorem, we know to be approximately normally distributed.

In general, just how large n needs to be for the sampling distribution of $\overline{x}$ to be a good approximation to the normal depends, as we saw in Fig. 6.3, on

---

*The parent population must have a finite mean and variance.

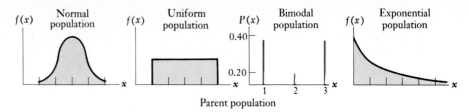

Parent population

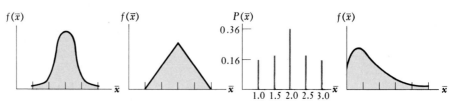

Sampling distribution of $\bar{x}$ for sample size $n = 2$

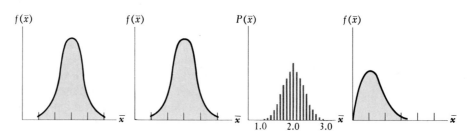

Sampling distribution of $\bar{x}$ for sample size $n = 5$

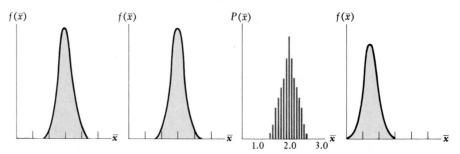

Figure 6.3
Sampling distribution of $\bar{x}$
for various population
distributions when
$n = 2, 5,$ and 30.

Sampling distribution of $\bar{x}$ for sample size $n = 30$

the shape of the parent population. Usually the approximation will be quite good if $n \geq 30$, although the third row of Fig. 6.3 demonstrates that satisfactory results are often obtained when n is much smaller. In Fig. 6.3 the first three distributions in row 3 are fairly symmetrical and bell-shaped.

Example of the Use of the CLT

To illustrate the use of the CLT, consider the case of a midwestern telephone company that recently asked for permission to change to a measured charge, where each residential customer pays for local telephone service by the number of (local) telephone calls made, rather than a flat monthly fee. The estimate provided by the telephone company was that they expect monthly bills under the new system to average $15.30, with a standard deviation of $4.10.

To study this proposal, a random sample was taken of $n = 36$ midwestern customers currently billed under measured charges the same as those proposed by the telephone company. Now, if the surveyed bills come from the same population expected by the telephone company, then we know that

$$\mu_{\bar{x}} = \$15.30 \quad \text{and} \quad \sigma_{\bar{x}} = \sigma/\sqrt{n} = \$4.10/\sqrt{36} = 0.683$$

Furthermore, since the sample size is fairly large, from the CLT we know that the sampling distribution of $\bar{x}$ will be normal. Putting all this together, we know the distribution of $\bar{x}$ for this problem is normally distributed with a mean of $15.30 and a variance of 0.683^2. That is,

$$\bar{x} \text{ is } N(15.30, 0.683^2)$$

Use of this distribution, shown in Fig. 6.4, permits answering a number of probability questions about telephone bills as shown by the following examples.

EXAMPLE 1

Suppose that in the random sample of 36 customers the average phone bill is $14.00. A typical question that might be asked is: What is the probability that a random sample of $n = 36$ will result in an average bill of $14.00 or less, when $\mu_{\bar{x}} = \$15.30$ and $\sigma_{\bar{x}} = 0.683$? Making use of the standard normal transformation, we know that

$$P(\bar{x} \leq 14.00) = P\left(\frac{\bar{x} - \mu_{\bar{x}}}{\sigma_{\bar{x}}} \leq \frac{14.00 - 15.30}{0.683}\right) = P(z \leq -1.90)$$

By the central limit theorem, $\bar{x}$ is approximately normally distributed; hence z is approximately standardized normal and, from Table III,

$$P(z \leq -1.90) = F(-1.90) = 1.0 - F(1.90)$$
$$= 1.0 - 0.9713 = 0.0287$$

The probability that a sample of 36 gives an average no larger than $14.00 is thus 0.0287. The reader should sketch this area on Fig. 6.4.

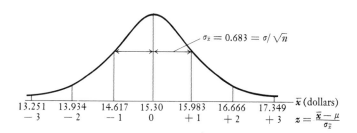

Figure 6.4

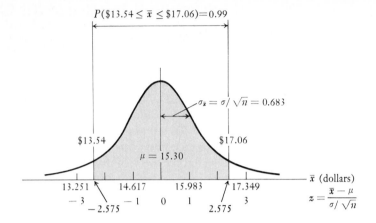

Figure 6.5
Standardized normal form of
the sampling distribution of
$\bar{x}$. Sample mean of monthly
phone charges, μ = \$15.30,
σ = \$4.10, n = 36.

The question we may want to answer from the analysis above is: Can we assume that the sample result $\bar{x}$ = \$14.00 was drawn from the population expected by the phone company? With a probability as low as 0.0287, the answer to this question may well be "no." Chapter 9 discusses this process of drawing conclusions about populations based on sample data; for now the reader should keep such questions in mind to retain a feeling of where we are headed. ∎

EXAMPLE 2

Rather than finding the probability associated with a specific sample result, one often wants to determine values a and b, such that the probability is 0.99 (or some other probability) that the sample mean will fall between these values. Recall that we did a similar calculation in our discussion of the normal distribution in Chapter 5. In the present case we can use the fact that when n = 36, $\bar{x}$ will be approximately normally distributed, with mean $\mu_{\bar{x}}$ = \$15.30, and $\sigma_{\bar{x}} = 4.10/\sqrt{36}$ = 0.683 to find values a and b such that $P\,(a \leq \bar{x} \leq b)$ = 0.99.

As before, we want the smallest interval including 99%, which means that we must exclude half of the remaining probability [or $\frac{1}{2}(0.01)$ = 0.005] in each tail of the distribution of $\bar{x}$. To do this, let us first see what values of the standardized normal distribution exclude 0.005 in each tail. From Table III, $F(z)$ = 0.995 if z = 2.575;* by symmetry, $F(-2.575)$ = $1.0 - F(2.575)$ = 0.0005. Thus,

$$P(-2.575 \leq z \leq 2.575) = 0.99$$

*The reader could determine the value 2.575 by looking for $1 - 0.005$ = 0.995 in the body of Table III. The closest values to $F(0.995)$ are $F(0.9949)$ = 2.57 and $F(0.9951)$ = 2.58. Linear interpolation between these values yields the approximation $F(0.9950)$ = 2.575. A more precise value, taking into account the nonlinear shape of the normal curve, is 2.576.

Finally, we now have to transform the interval $P(-2.575 \leq z \leq 2.575) = 0.99$ into the original units (dollars) by finding values a and b to satisfy $P(a \leq \overline{x} \leq b) = 0.99$. By standardizing the values of a, $\overline{x}$, and b, we get

$$P(a \leq \overline{x} \leq b) = P\left(\frac{a - 15.30}{0.683} \leq z \leq \frac{b - 15.30}{0.683}\right)$$

Thus, $(a - 15.30)/0.683 = -2.575$ and $(b - 15.30)/0.683 = 2.575$. Solving these two equations we find $a = \$13.54$ and $b = \$17.06$; this means that the appropriate interval is $\$13.54$ to $\$17.06$. Figure 6.5 is a diagram of the values in this example.   ∎

Sampling Without Replacement from a Finite Population

6.8

In this chapter the assumption has been made that sampling occurs either with replacement from a finite population, or from an infinite population. But what happens when sampling is not of this type—that is, when samples are drawn from a finite population without replacement? In this case, the formulas developed thus far are not appropriate because the value of $\sigma_{\overline{x}}$ is smaller than $\sigma/\sqrt{n}$. The fact that the standard error is smaller than before can be demonstrated by referring again to Table 6.5, but now assuming that sampling occurs *without* replacement from the finite population $x = \{1, 2, 3\}$. The new sampling distribution for $n = 2$ is shown in Table 6.7.

Table 6.7 shows that $\sigma_{\overline{x}} \cong 0.41$. This standard error is less than the value computed in Section 6.5 for sampling *with* replacement, which was $\sigma/\sqrt{n} = 0.577$. Intuitively, $\sigma_{\overline{x}}$ must be smaller than $\sigma/\sqrt{n}$ when sampling without replacement because $\sigma_{\overline{x}}$ must approach zero as $n \rightarrow N$. For example, if

TABLE 6.7   Samples of $n = 2$ without replacement from $(1, 2, 3)$

Sample	Sample mean $(\overline{x})$	$(\overline{x} - \mu_{\overline{x}})^2$	
$(1, 2)$	1.5	0.25	
$(2, 1)$	1.5	0.25	
$(1, 3)$	2.0	0	$\sigma_{\overline{x}}^2 = \frac{1}{6}(1.00) = \frac{1}{6}$
$(3, 1)$	2.0	0	
$(2, 3)$	2.5	0.25	$\sigma_{\overline{x}} = \sqrt{\frac{1}{6}} \cong 0.41$
$(3, 2)$	2.5	0.25	
		1.00	

each repeated sample consists of the entire population (i.e., $n = N$), then each sample mean $\bar{x}$ will be identical and equal to the population mean μ; thus, $\sigma_{\bar{x}} = 0$. This is not the case for $\sigma/\sqrt{n}$, because it approaches zero as $n \to$ infinity rather than as $n \to N$.

In order for $\sigma/\sqrt{n} \to 0$ as $n \to N$, we multiply $\sigma/\sqrt{n}$ by an adjustment factor called the **finite population correction factor.** This factor, which is based on the hypergeometric distribution, is defined as follows:

$$\textit{Finite population correction factor:} \quad \sqrt{\frac{(N-n)}{(N-1)}}$$

Note that this correction factor will always be a number less than 1.0.

To illustrate this correction factor, let's apply it to the value of $\sigma/\sqrt{n}$ in our problem involving the population (1, 2, 3). Recall that $\sigma/\sqrt{n} = 0.577$, $n = 2, N = 3$:

$$\sigma_{\bar{x}} = \frac{\sigma}{\sqrt{n}} \sqrt{\frac{N-n}{N-1}} = 0.577 \sqrt{\frac{3-2}{2}} \cong 0.41$$

This result agrees with the value of $\sigma_{\bar{x}}$ calculated in Table 6.7.

When n is small relative to N (say 10% or less), the finite population correction factor is sometimes omitted, and $\sigma/\sqrt{n}$ is used as an approximation to $\sigma_{\bar{x}}$. This approach saves some of the tedious calculations involved with the correction factor when this factor will change $\sigma/\sqrt{n}$ only by a relatively small amount. The example below illustrates how little $\sigma/\sqrt{n}$ changes even when n is slightly larger than 10%.

An important use of the finite correction factor occurs when the standardized z-value in Formula (6.8) is calculated. If we include the correction factor, this standardization becomes[*]:

$$\textit{z-standardization:} \quad z = \frac{\bar{x} - \mu}{\frac{\sigma}{\sqrt{n}} \sqrt{\frac{(N-n)}{(N-1)}}} \qquad (6.9)$$

Formula (6.9) can be illustrated by recalling the example in Section 6.7, where a random sample of $n = 36$ telephone customers was taken. Assume now that this sample was taken from a finite population of $N = 300$, without replacement. Since $n/N = 36/300 = 0.12$ (12% of the population is being sampled), the finite population correction factor should be used.

---

[*]When the population size itself is very small, say $N \le 30$, then care must be taken in interpreting this formula, since $\bar{x}$ may not be normally distributed.

We correct the z calculation of page 229 as follows:

$$P\left(\overline{x} \leq 14.00\right) = P\left(\frac{\overline{x} - \mu}{\frac{\sigma}{\sqrt{n}}\sqrt{\frac{N-n}{N-1}}} \leq \frac{14.00 - 15.30}{\frac{4.10}{\sqrt{36}}\sqrt{\frac{300 - 36}{300 - 1}}}\right)$$

$$= P\left(z \leq \frac{-1.30}{0.642}\right)$$

Comparing this result with that on page 229, we see that the denominator has changed from 0.683 to 0.642. Since $-1.30/0.642 = -2.02$, the new probability is

$$P(z \leq -2.02) = F(-2.02) = 1 - F(2.02) = 1 - 0.9783 = 0.0217$$

Problems

6.27 You are told that the distribution of the balance due each month on the MBNA GoldPassage Visa card is a normally distributed random variable with a mean of \$550 and a standard deviation of \$200.

a) Find $P(x \geq 450)$, $P(x \leq 600)$, and $P(450 \leq x \leq 600)$.

b) A random sample of $n = 64$ is taken. Find $P(\overline{x} \leq 560)$, $P(\overline{x} \geq 530)$, and $P(540 \leq \overline{x} \leq 560)$.

c) Sketch the distribution of x and the distribution of $\overline{x}$.

6.28 What is a "sampling distribution"? Why is the knowledge of a sampling distribution of a statistic so important to statistical inference?

6.29 State the central limit theorem. Why is this theorem so important to statistical inference?

6.30 Ameritech took a survey of 121 randomly selected long distance calls and found that the average length of these calls was 5.2 minutes. The population standard deviation is known to be 3/4 minute.

a) What is the probability of a sample mean this large or larger if the true population mean is 5.0 minutes?

b) What is the probability that $\overline{x}$ will be 5.2 or smaller if $\mu = 5.3$?

c) Do your answers to parts (a) and (b) depend on any assumptions about the parent population?

6.31 The distribution of I.Q.'s in the United States, as measured by the Stanford-Binet Test, is reported to be $N(100, 256)$.

a) What proportion of the population have I.Q.'s above 120?

b) What is $P(\overline{x} > 105)$ based on a random sample of 25 people?

c) You take a random sample of the I.Q.'s of 25 hourly workers at RCA and find $\overline{x} = 110$. What is the probability of drawing this sample mean, or one larger, from the population of I.Q.'s described above?

d) What conclusion would you reach based on your sample in part (c)?

6.32 The 1988 all-industry average return on common equity for the top 1000 U.S. companies was reported in *Business Week* to be 15.0. Assume this population has a variance of 55.3.

a) What is the probability a random sample of $n = 40$ of these companies will result in a mean return of 15.5 or larger?

b) What is the probability a single, randomly selected company will have a negative return on equity?

c) Does your answer to part (a) and/or (b) depend on any assumptions about the parent population?

6.33 Funds, Inc. sells bonds maturing in 4, 5, and 9 years. The probability distribution for customers purchasing these bonds is given below.

x	4	5	9	10
$P(x)$	1/2	1/6	1/6	1/6

a) Sketch this probability distribution and find the mean and the standard deviation.

b) Use a computer to generate 20 random samples, each of size $n = 15$, from this population. Use the computer to calculate the mean for each sample. Is the mean of the 20 means close to what you expected? Explain.

c) Calculate the variance of the $\bar{x}$'s in part (b). Is this variance close to what you expected? Explain.

d) Plot the 20 sample means in a frequency distribution, using an appropriate class interval. Is the shape of the distribution close to normal? Did you expect it to be? Explain.

6.34 Use Table VI to collect a random sample of three observations, with replacement, from the population consisting of the digits 0 through 9. Repeat this four more times (for a total of five samples, each of size $n = 3$).

a) Calculate $\bar{x}$ for each of your five samples, and then calculate $\bar{\bar{x}}$, the mean of all five sample means.

b) What is the expected value in the population from which your samples were drawn in part (a)? Is $\bar{\bar{x}}$ close to this value?

c) Calculate the standard deviation of the five sample means about their grand mean ($\bar{\bar{x}}$). What is the standard error of the mean in the population from which you drew samples? Are the two values reasonably close?

6.35 A study of 100 randomly selected salary offers accepted by graduate students using the Indiana University Business Placement Service indicated a mean of $\bar{x} = \$46,982$. A year earlier the average salary was $\mu = \$43,376$, with a standard deviation of $\$5,712$. What is the probability of a mean as high (or higher) than $\$46,982$ if the distribution of salaries did not change from last year to this year? Use the finite population correction factor, assuming that $N = 300$.

6.36 A cereal company checks the weight of each lot of 400 boxes of breakfast cereal by randomly checking 64 of the boxes. This particular brand is packed in 20-ounce boxes.

a) Suppose a particular random sample of 64 boxes yields a mean weight of 19.95 ounces. How often will the sample mean be this low if $\mu = 20$ and $\sigma = 0.10$? Use the finite population correction factor.

b) What is the difference in the standard error after using the finite population correction factor?

6.37 a) List all possible samples of size $n = 2$ that could be drawn with replacement from the population $x = \{4, 5, 9, 10\}$. Draw a graph to illustrate the p.m.f. for the sampling distribution of $\bar{x}$, assuming each value of x occurs with probabilty 1/4.

b) Use your p.m.f. in part (a) to verify that $E[\bar{x}] = \mu$ and $V[\bar{x}] = \sigma^2/n$.

6.38 Sketch the distribution of $\bar{x}$ if one takes an infinite number of samples, all of size $n = 100$, from an exponential distribution with $\lambda = 5$.

6.39 A new bathroom soap comes in a jar that is advertised to dispense liquid soap for an average of 300 uses. A consumer agency tests two jars of this product, and finds 275 and 290 uses. Calculate $\bar{x}$ and s. Comment on this test of the product.

6.40 a) What is the finite population correction factor, and when is it necessary to apply this factor?

b) If $\sigma = 50, n = 25$, and $N = 100$, what is the corrected standard error of the mean?

Sampling Distribution of $\bar{x}$, Normal Population, σ Unknown

6.9

In Section 6.6. we discussed the importance in problem solving of using the following standardization:

$$z = \frac{\bar{x} - \mu}{\sigma/\sqrt{n}}$$

Usually, *our objective in using this type of standardization is to determine the probability of observing some specified value of $\bar{x}$, assuming that the population mean is μ; and then to use this probability in making a decision.* This means we have an assumed value of μ to use in the standardization. But what about the value of σ needed in the denominator? What happens if we do not want to (or cannot) assume a value for σ (that is, if σ is unknown)? In solving a particular problem where σ is unknown, the sample statistic s can be used in place of σ. That is, the standardization now becomes

Standardization of $\bar{x}$ when σ is unknown: $\dfrac{\bar{x} - \mu}{s/\sqrt{n}}$

The substitution of s for σ is reasonable since we can show* that the expected value of s^2 equals σ^2. That is, $E[s^2] = \sigma^2$.

We have shown previously that, when x is normal, the distribution of $(\bar{x} - \mu)/(\sigma/\sqrt{n})$ is $N(0, 1)$. Unfortunately, when s is substituted for σ, the resulting distribution is no longer normally distributed, nor is its variance 1.0. Our next task is thus to determine the distribution of the ratio $(\bar{x} - \mu)/(s/\sqrt{n})$. This distribution can be thought of as being generated by the following process:

1. Collect all possible samples of size n from a normal parent population.
2. Calculate $\bar{x}$ and s for each sample.
3. Subtract μ from each value of $\bar{x}$, and then divide this deviation by the appropriate value of $s/\sqrt{n}$. (Remember, s will be different for each sample.)

This process will generate an infinite number of values of the random variable

$$\frac{\bar{x} - \mu}{s/\sqrt{n}}$$

It is not hard to recognize that the mean of this new distribution still equals zero, since the numerator hasn't changed and it was the numerator that made our original standardization have $E[z] = 0$. The variance of $(\bar{x} - \mu)/(s/\sqrt{n})$ is not equal to 1.0; it is larger than 1.0. This is reasonable when one recognizes that with the ratio $(\bar{x} - \mu)/(s/\sqrt{n})$ one more element of uncertainty (the estimator s) has been added to the standardization. The more uncertainty there is, the more spread out the distribution.

---

*To prove that $E[s^2] = \sigma^2$, we use the expectation rules in Section 3.6.

$$E[s^2] = E\left[\frac{1}{n-1}\sum(x_i - \bar{x})^2\right]$$

$$= \frac{1}{n-1}E\left[\sum\{(x_i - \mu) - (\bar{x} - \mu)\}^2\right]$$
By Formula (3.9) and because $(x_i - \bar{x}) = (x_i - \mu) - (\bar{x} - \mu)$

$$= \frac{1}{n-1}\left\{\sum\left[E[(x_i - \mu)^2] - 2E[n(\bar{x} - \mu)(\bar{x} - \mu)]\right. + \sum E[(\bar{x} - \mu)^2]\right\}$$
By expansion of square term, and $\sum(x_i - \mu)(\bar{x} - \mu) = n(\bar{x} - \mu)(\bar{x} - \mu)$

$$= \frac{1}{n-1}\left(\sum\sigma^2 - 2n\sigma^2/n + \sum\sigma^2/n\right)$$
Since $\sigma^2 = E[(x - \mu)^2]$ and $\sigma^2/n = E[(\bar{x} - \mu)^2]$

$$= \frac{1}{n-1}(n\sigma^2 - 2\sigma^2 + n\sigma^2/n)$$
Since $\sum_{i=1}^{n}(\text{constant}) = n(\text{constant})$

$$= \frac{1}{n-1}\sigma^2(n-1)$$
Collecting terms

$$E[s^2] = \frac{n-1}{n-1}\sigma^2 = \sigma^2$$

If the population is finite, and sampling is *without* replacement, then $E[s^2] \neq \sigma^2$.

Several additional aspects of the distribution of $(\bar{x} - \mu)/(s/\sqrt{n})$ are worth noting. First, we would expect this distribution to be symmetrical, since there is no reason to believe that substituting s for σ will make this distribution skewed either positively or negatively. Second, it should be apparent that the variability of this distribution depends on the size of n, for the sample size affects the reliability with which s estimates σ. When n is large, s will be a good approximation of σ; but when n is small, s may not be very close to σ. Hence, the distribution of $(\bar{x} - \mu)/(s/\sqrt{n})$ is a family of distributions in which variability depends on n.

It should be clear from the above discussion that the distribution of $(\bar{x} - \mu)/(s/\sqrt{n})$ is not normal, but is more spread out than the normal. The distribution of this statistic is called the "t-distribution," and its random variable is denoted as follows:

$$\textit{t-random variable:}\quad t = \frac{\bar{x} - \mu}{s/\sqrt{n}} \tag{6.10}$$

The variable t is a continuous random variable. One of the first researchers to work on determining the exact distribution of this random variable was W. S. Gosset, an Irish statistician. However, the Dublin brewery for which Gosset worked did not allow its employees to publish their research; hence, Gosset wrote under the pen name "Student." In honor of Gosset's research, published in 1908, the t-distribution is often referred to as the "Student's t-distribution." It is not clear from historical records whether Gosset enjoyed the product of his employer, as do many modern "students."

Student's t-Distribution

Since the density function for the t-distribution is fairly complex and not of primary importance at this point, we will not present it but will begin merely by describing the characteristics of this distribution.* As we indicated previously, the t-distribution depends on the size of the sample. It is customary to describe the characteristics of the t-distribution in terms of the sample size minus one, or $(n - 1)$, as this quantity has special significance.

The value of $(n - 1)$ is called the number of **degrees of freedom** (abbreviated d.f.), and represents a measure of the number of independent observations in the sample that can be used to estimate the standard deviation of the parent population.

---

*Mathematically, the random variable t is defined as a standardized normal variable z divided by the square root of an independently distributed chi-square variable, which has been divided by its degrees of freedom; that is, $t = z/\sqrt{\chi^2/\nu}$. The chi-square distribution is discussed in Sections 5.5 and 6.10.

For example, when $n = 1$, there is no way to estimate the population standard deviation; hence there are *no* degrees of freedom ($n - 1 = 0$). There is one degree of freedom in a sample of $n = 2$, since one observation is now "free" to vary away from the other, and the amount it varies determines our estimate of the population standard deviation. Each additional observation adds one more degree of freedom, so that in a sample of size n there are $(n - 1)$ observations "free" to vary, and hence $(n - 1)$ degrees of freedom. The Greek letter ν (nu) is often used to denote degrees of freedom, where $\nu = n - 1$.

A t-distribution is completely described by its one parameter, $\nu = n - 1 =$ degrees of freedom. The mean of the t-distribution is zero, $E[t] = 0$. The variance of the t-distribution, when $\nu \geq 3$, is $V[t] = \nu/(\nu - 2)$.

Because the t-distribution is more spread out than the z, $V[t] \geq 1.0$ for all sample sizes, in contrast to $V[z]$, which is 1.0 no matter what the sample size. For example, when $\nu = 3$ the variance of the t-distribution is $3/(3 - 2) = 3.0$. This distribution and the standardized normal are contrasted in Fig. 6.6.

For small sample sizes, the t-distribution is seen to be considerably more spread out than the normal. Consider a larger sample size, such as $\nu = 30$; then $V[t] = 30/(30 - 2) = 1.07$, which is not much different from $V[z] = 1.0$. As ν gets larger and larger, $V[t] \rightarrow V[z]$. In the limit, as $n \rightarrow \infty$, the t- and z-distributions are identical. Tables of t-values are usually only completely enumerated for $\nu \leq 30$, because for larger samples the normal gives a very good approximation and is easier to use. For this reason it is customary to speak of the t-distribution as applying to "small sample sizes," *even though this distribution holds for any size n.*

Probability questions involving a t-distributed random variable can be answered by using the t-distribution (shown in Table VII). This table gives the values of t for selected values of $P(t \geq t)$, given across the top of the table, and

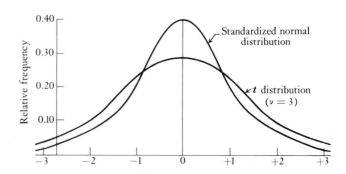

Figure 6.6
The standardized normal and the t-distributions compared.

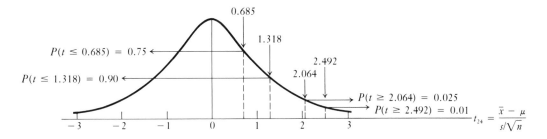

Figure 6.7

Various probabilities for the
t-distribution for $\nu = 24$ d.f.

for degrees of freedom (ν), down the left margin. Figure 6.7 shows the values
of the t-distribution for $\nu = 24$ degrees of freedom, taken from Table VII.
Four different values from Table VII are shown in Fig. 6.7:

$$P(t \le 0.685) = 0.75 \qquad P(t \le 1.318) = 0.90$$

and

$$P(t \ge 2.064) = 0.025 \qquad P(t \ge 2.492) = 0.01$$

Table VII gives probabilities for seven selected t-values for each degree of freedom. More extensive tables are available, and probabilities may be determined
mathematically for any t-value. Computer programs (statistical packages) are
routinely used to determine such probabilities.

Examples of the t-Distribution

As with the normal distribution, the t-distribution is often used to test an
assumption about a population mean based on the standardization of an
observed sample mean.

> The t-distribution is the appropriate statistic for inference on a pop-
> ulation mean whenever the parent population is normally dis-
> tributed and σ is unknown.

EXAMPLE 1

Consider the case of a small finance company which has reported to an auditing firm that its outstanding loans are approximately normally distributed with
a mean of $825; the standard deviation is unknown. In an attempt to verify this
reported value of $\mu = \$825$, a random sample of 25 accounts was taken. This
random sample yields a mean of $\bar{x} = \$780$, with a standard deviation of
$s = 105$. The question facing the auditor is how often might one find a sample
mean of $780 or lower when the true mean is $825? That is, what is $P(\bar{x} \le
\$780)$? This probability cannot be determined exactly since its value depends
on σ, which is unknown. We can approximate it using the t-distribution. To
approximate this probability, we must standardize the values in parentheses. The approximation in this example follows a t-distribution with 24

degrees of freedom because x is normal, σ is unknown, and $n = 25$. Substituting $s = 105$ and $n = 25$ and using Formula (6.10) yields:

$$P(\bar{x} \le \$780) \cong P\left(\frac{\bar{x} - \mu}{s/\sqrt{n}} \le \frac{780 - 825}{105/\sqrt{25}}\right) = P(t \le -2.143)$$

Since the t-distribution is symmetrical, the probability $P(t \le -2.143)$ is equivalent to $P(t \ge +2.143)$. Because the number 2.143 does not appear in Table VII for $\nu = 24$, the exact value of $P(t \ge 2.143)$ cannot be determined from this table. However, we can determine between which two probabilities the value $P(t \ge 2.143)$ lies. From Table VII or Fig. 6.7,

$$P(t \ge 2.064) = 0.025 \quad \text{and} \quad P(t \ge 2.492) = 0.01$$

which means that $P(t \ge 2.143)$ lies between 0.025 and 0.010. Thus, we can write

$$0.01 < P(\bar{x} \le 780) \cong P(t \le -2.143) < 0.025$$

This result says that a sample mean as low as or lower than \$780 will occur (approximately) between 1% and 2.5% of the time when $\mu = \$825$. Faced with such low probabilities, the auditor might well be concerned with the accuracy of the assumption that $\mu = \$825$.

Suppose that in the preceding example, instead of the sample results described there, we found the values $\bar{x} = \$842.60$, and $s = 80.0$. For this result we want to determine the probability that $\bar{x}$ is *greater* than or equal to \$842.60 when $\mu = \$825$.

$$P(\bar{x} \ge \$842.60) \cong P\left(\frac{\bar{x} - \mu}{s/\sqrt{n}} \ge \frac{842.60 - 825}{80/\sqrt{25}}\right) = P(t \ge 1.100)$$

From Table VII, $P(t \ge 1.100)$ lies between $P(t \ge 0.685) = 0.25$ and $P(t \ge 1.318) = 0.10$ when $\nu = 24$. Hence,

$$0.25 > P(\bar{x} \ge \$842.60) \cong P(t \ge 1.100) > 0.10$$

We see from this result that a sample mean of \$842.60 is fairly probable when $\mu = \$825$ and $n = 25$. These values are shown in Fig. 6.8.

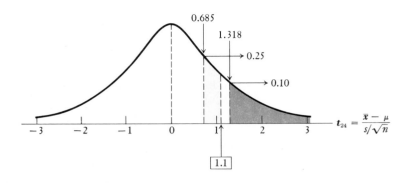

Figure 6.8
t-distribution values for
$\nu = 24$.

EXAMPLE 2

Let us determine an interval (a, b) such that $P(a \leq t \leq b) = 0.95$, assuming $n - 1 = \nu = 8$ degrees of freedom. As before, the smallest interval is found by putting half the excluded area, $\frac{1}{2}(0.05) = 0.025$, in each tail of the distribution. For example, we want $P(t \geq b) = 0.025$. From Table VII for $\nu = 8$, $P(t \geq 2.306) = 0.025$; hence, $b = 2.306$. Now since the t-distribution is symmetrical, the appropriate value for a is merely the negative of the value of b, or $a = -2.306$. Thus,

$$P(-2.306 \leq t \leq 2.306) = 0.95$$

Recall, from our previous examples using the standardized normal distribution, that $P(-1.96 \leq z \leq 1.96) = 0.95$. The critical values for z that exclude 0.025 probability in the upper and lower tails are ± 1.96, as opposed to ± 2.306 for the t-distribution with $\nu = 8$. The difference reflects the fact that the t-distribution is more spread out than the z-distribution. Note in Table VII that by *increasing* the value of ν from 8 to 10, then 20, then 60, then 120, and moving down the column for 0.025, the critical values for t *decrease* from 2.306 to 2.228, then 2.086, then 2.000, then 1.98, respectively. For larger values of ν, the spread of the t-distribution closes in to match the spread of the z-distribution. Indeed, when $n = \infty$, the critical value for t exactly equals the value for z (1.96), as shown by the bottom row in Table VII in Appendix B. ∎

Use of the t-Distribution When the Population Is Not Normal

It must be emphasized at this point that the t-distribution, as well as the chi-square and F-distributions (discussed in the following sections) assume that samples are drawn from a parent population that is normally distributed. Often there is no way to determine the exact distribution of the parent population. In practical problems involving these distributions, the question therefore arises as to just how critical the assumption is that the parent population be exactly normally distributed. Fortunately, the assumption of normality can be relaxed without significantly changing the sampling distribution of the t-distribution. Because of this fact, the t-distribution is said to be quite "robust," implying that its usefulness holds up under conditions that do not conform exactly to the original assumptions.

We should emphasize again that the t-distribution is appropriate whenever x is normal and σ is unknown, despite the fact that many t-tables do not list values higher than $\nu = 30$. For practical problems this does not cause many difficulties; as the reader will note, the t-values in a given column of Table VII change very little after $\nu = 30$. For example, suppose that a sample of size $n = 400$ results in $\bar{x} = 120$ and $s = 200$, and we would like to calculate $P(\bar{x} \geq 120)$. Assume that σ is unknown and $\mu = 100$.

$$P(\bar{x} \geq 120) \cong P\left(\frac{\bar{x} - \mu}{s/\sqrt{n}} \geq \frac{120 - 100}{200/\sqrt{400}}\right) = P(t \geq 2.00)$$

Although $\nu = 399$ is not listed in Table VII, by looking at $\nu = 120$ versus $\nu = \infty$ we can easily determine that

$$0.025 > P(t \geq 2.00) > 0.01$$

Thus, if the appropriate ν is not in Table VII we suggest looking at the table entries for ν above and below the one desired.*

Use of the Computer to Find Probabilities for the t-Distribution

We have made extensive use of Table VII to find t-values and/or to determine the probabilities associated with given t-values. In some problems, determining the probabilities by using Table VII is cumbersome, for we can only approximate the probability for t-values or degrees of freedom not shown in the table. If you have access to a statistical package on a computer, then the process of determining such probabilities is relatively easy.

To illustrate how a computer package is used to determine an exact probability from the t-distribution, consider the problem from the last section, where the probability of interest was that of determining $P(t \geq 2.00)$, for $\nu = 399$. In the computer output below the first input (user input is in color) was the d.f. $= 399$; next, the t-value of interest was input as $t = 2.00$. The computer package then provided the two probabilities, $P(t \leq 2.00) = 0.9769$, and $P(t \geq 2.00) = 0.0231$. Note this probability falls in the range given in the last section (between 0.025 and 0.01).

Probabilities from a Computer Package for $\nu = 399$.

Students t-Distribution:
d.f. $= 399$
$t \quad = 2.00$
$p \quad = 0.9769 \qquad 1 - p = 0.0231$

Problems

6.41 Determine, for each of the following cases, whether the t-distribution or the standardized normal distribution (or neither) is appropriate for answering questions relating to sample means.

a) A small sample from a normal parent population with known standard deviation

---

*Some texts suggest that the normal distribution be used to approximate the t-distribution when $\nu > 30$, since the t- and z- values will then be quite close (the normal value will be slightly smaller than the exact t-value). Because of this procedure, the t-distribution sometimes is referred to *incorrectly* as applying only to "small samples." We prefer to emphasize that the t-distribution is *always* correct whenever σ is unknown.

b) A small sample from a nonnormal population with known standard deviation

c) A small sample from a normal population with unknown standard deviation

d) A small sample from a nonnormal population with unknown standard deviation

e) A large sample from a normal population with unknown standard deviation

f) A large sample from a nonnormal population with unknown standard deviation

Volunteer	New − Old
1	$25.74
2	49.57
3	52.92
4	32.83
5	− 63.33
6	76.59
7	− 80.64
8	− 23.96
9	88.05
10	46.97

6.42 Public Service Indiana conducted an experiment in which customers could save money by volunteering for an experimental rate plan. The plan was designed to reduce electrical use at peak load periods by offering customers a financial incentive to change their use pattern. The data at the left is the 12-month difference between the customer charge under the experimental rate and what they would have been charged under the standard rate (New − Old) for a random sample of 10 of these volunteers.

a) Find the mean, the variance, and the standard error for these sample data.

b) If there is no difference between the new and the old rates, then we would expect the difference (New − Old) to have a mean of zero. What is the probability of getting a mean as large (or larger) as that found in (a) if the population mean is, indeed, equal to zero? The population variance is unknown, but the parent population can be assumed to be normal.

c) What conclusion would you reach on the basis of part (b)?

6.43 a) Explain why the standardized normal distribution does not provide an accurate description of the sampling distribution of $\bar{x}$ for small samples drawn from a normal population when σ is unknown. What distribution is appropriate in this circumstance?

b) Some statistics texts state that when σ is unknown, "the t-distribution is appropriate for small samples and the z-distribution is appropriate for large samples." Comment on the merits of this statement.

6.44 An economist estimates that the number of gallons of gasoline used monthly by each automobile in the United States is a normally distributed random variable with a mean of $\mu = 50$ and unknown variance. A sample of nine observations yields a sample variance of $s^2 = 36$. Use the t-distribution to find the probability that $\bar{x}$ is larger than 54 if $\mu = 50$. Also, find $P(45 \geq \bar{x} \geq 55)$.

6.45 The hourly wages in an automobile factory were reported by the company to be normally distributed with a mean of $15.23. You take a random sample of $n = 25$ of these wages and find a mean of $14.95, and a standard deviation of $5.25. What is the probability of a sample mean this low from the population reported by the company?

6.46 Intelligence quotients in the United States as measured by the Stanford–Binet test are reported to be normally distributed with a mean of 100.

a) A sample of $n = 36$ clerical workers resulted in $\bar{x} = 105$, and $s = 18.4$. What is the probability of a sample mean this large from the overall population, assuming σ is unknown?

b) What would you conclude from the analysis in part (a)?

6.47 A bank has estimated that its tellers provide service to customers following an exponential distribution with $\lambda = 0.3$. Rather than use the formulas from Chapter 5 and this chapter, the bank decides to use simulation to estimate means and standard deviations. Use a statistical package on a computer to generate 100 random samples, each of size $n = 25$, from an exponential distribution with $\lambda = 0.3$. Use a computer to do the following.

a) Find the mean and standard deviation for each of the 100 samples.

b) Construct a frequency distribution for the sample means, using a convenient class interval. Find the mean of this frequency distribution, and its standard deviation. Are these values close to those you expected? Does this distribution have a normal shape? Did you expect it to? Explain in each case.

The Sampling Distribution of s^2, Normal Population* (Optional)

6.10

The only sampling distribution considered thus far has been that of $\bar{x}$, the sample mean. But in many practical problems we need information about the distribution of the sample variance, s^2. That is, we need to investigate the distribution that consists of all possible values of s^2 calculated from samples of size n. The sampling distribution of s^2 is particularly important in problems concerned with the variability in a random sample. For example, the telephone company may just be interested in the variance in length of calls in a random sample as they are in the mean length. Or a manufacturer of steel beams may want to learn just as much about the variance as the mean of tensile strength of the steel beams.

The same statistician who first worked with the t-distribution, W. S. Gosset, was also one of the first to describe the sampling distribution of s^2. First, note that because s^2 must always be positive, the distribution of s^2 cannot be a normal distribution. Rather, the distribution of s^2 is a unimodal distribution that is *skewed* to the right, and looks like the smooth curve in Fig. 6.9. As with the t-distribution, sampling is assumed to be from a normal parent population, and the one parameter is the degrees of freedom, ν. A typical problem in analyzing variances is that of determining the probability that the value of s^2 will be larger (or smaller) than some observed value, given some assumed value of σ^2. For example, suppose that the variance in diameters of steel ball bearings is specified to be $\sigma^2 = 0.0010$ inches. What is the probability that a random sample of $n = 21$ ball bearings will result in a sample variance as large as

---

*This section can be omitted without loss in continuity. Although Section 5.5 provides an excellent introduction to this section, we will not presume 5.5 has been studied.

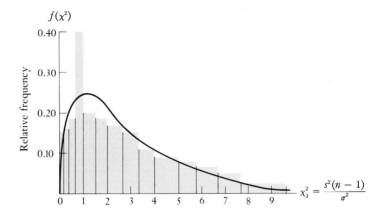

Figure 6.9
Chi-square approximation to
Gosset's data on the heights
of criminals.

$s^2 = 0.0016$ or larger? That is, assuming $\nu = n - 1 = 20$ and $\sigma^2 = 0.0010$, what is

$$P(s^2 \geq 0.0016)$$

Unfortunately, we cannot solve problems like this one directly, but must transform them in a way similar to the standardizations for $\bar{x}$. In this case the transformation is accomplished by multiplying s^2 by $(n - 1)$, and then dividing the product by σ^2. This new variable is denoted by the symbol χ^2, which is the square of the Greek letter chi. This chi-square variable has one parameter, $\nu = n - 1$, which is its degrees of freedom. Thus,

$$\text{Chi-square variable: } \quad \chi^2_{n-1} = \frac{(n-1)s^2}{\sigma^2} \qquad (6.11)$$

In words, this formula says the following:

If s^2 is the variance of random samples of size n taken from a normal population having a variance of σ^2, then the variable $(n - 1)s^2/\sigma^2$ has the same distribution as a χ^2-variable with $(n - 1)$ degrees of freedom.

The subscript on the χ^2 symbol in Formula (6.11) merely serves to remind us of the appropriate degrees of freedom.

Although Gosset was unable to prove Formula (6.11) mathematically, he did demonstrate this relationship in his empirical work. Gosset took the heights of 3000 criminals, calculated the value of σ^2 for these heights, and then grouped these heights into 750 random samples of 4. For each of these 750 samples Gosset, in effect, calculated a value of s^2, multiplied s^2 by $(n - 1) = 3$, and then divided this number by σ^2. The results are plotted in the histogram shown in Fig. 6.9. Note that Gosset's histogram and the chi-square distribution (for $v = n - 1 = 3$) superimposed on it are not in perfect agreement, a fact that Gosset attributed to the particular grouping of heights that he used.

Solving a problem involving s^2 by using Formula (6.11) follows essentially the same process used to solve problems involving $\bar{x}$. For example, let's solve the problem mentioned earlier, $P(s^2 \geq 0.0016)$. Recall for this problem that $v = 20$ and $\sigma^2 = 0.0010$.

$$P(s^2 \geq 0.0016) = P\left(\frac{(n - 1)s^2}{\sigma^2} \geq \frac{(20)(0.0016)}{0.0010}\right) = P(\chi^2_{20} \geq 32)$$

The equivalence between $P(s^2 \geq 0.0016)$ and $P(\chi^2_{20} \geq 32)$ is illustrated in Fig. 6.10.

The number of degrees of freedom in a χ^2-distribution determines the shape of $f(\chi^2)$. Since only squared numbers are involved in calculating χ^2, we know that this variable can never assume a value below zero, but it may take on values up to positive infinity. When v is small, the shape of the density function is highly skewed to the right. As v gets larger, however, the χ^2-distribution becomes more and more symmetrical in appearance, approaching the normal distribution as $n \to \infty$.

The density function for the χ^2-distribution is not of primary importance for our discussion; hence we will not present its formula, but merely concentrate on its characteristics. The mean and the variance of the chi-square distribution are both related to v as follows:*

$$\text{Mean} = E[\chi^2_v] = v$$
$$\text{Variance} = V[\chi^2_v] = 2v$$

Thus, if we have a chi-square variable involved in a problem using random samples of size $n = 21$, then

$$E[\chi^2] = 20 \quad \text{and} \quad V[\chi^2] = 40$$

Chi-Square Examples

Table V in Appendix B gives values of the cumulative χ^2-distribution for selected values of v and gives (at the bottom) a formula for the normal approx-

---

*These relationships are proved below.

$$E[\chi^2] = E\left[\frac{s^2 v}{\sigma^2}\right] = \frac{v}{\sigma^2} E[s^2] \qquad \text{Since } v, \sigma^2 \text{ are constants}$$

$$= \frac{v}{\sigma^2}\sigma^2 = v \qquad \text{Because } E[s^2] = \sigma^2$$

$$V[\chi^2] = V\left[\frac{s^2 v}{\sigma^2}\right] = \frac{v^2}{\sigma^4} V[s^2] \qquad \text{By Section 3.6}$$

$$= \frac{v^2}{\sigma^4}(2\sigma^4/v) = 2v \qquad \text{Since } V[s^2] = 2\sigma^4/v$$

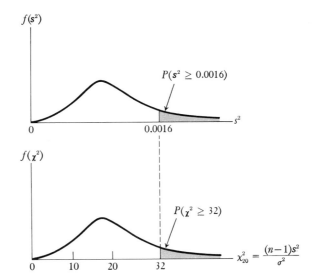

Figure 6.10
Transforming an s^2-value
into an equivalent χ^2-value
with $\nu = n - 1 = 20$.

imation to χ^2 which can be used when $\nu > 30$. To illustrate the use of the χ^2-distribution, we will assume that we have taken all possible random samples of size $n = 21$ from some normal parent population. For each of these random samples we then multiply the value of the sample variance (s^2) by $(n - 1)$ and divide the result by the (assumed) population variance (σ^2). When we have finished this hypothetical task (there is an infinite number of such ratios), we will have calculated all possible values of

$$\chi^2_{20} = \frac{(n - 1)s^2}{\sigma^2} = \frac{(20)s^2}{\sigma^2}$$

The distribution of the statistic given above is the chi-square distribution. We can use Table V in Appendix B to graph a few values of the chi-square distribution for 20 degrees of freedom.

From Fig. 6.11 we see that the ratio $(20)s^2/\sigma^2$ will have a value less than 8.26 only 1% of the time, $2\frac{1}{2}$% of the time it will be less than 9.59, 90% of the

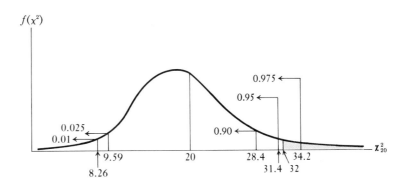

Figure 6.11
The χ^2-distribution for
$\nu = 20$.

time it will be less than 28.4, and so forth. Let us now use this information to solve our previous ball-bearing problem, which was $P(s^2 \geq 0.0016)$ for $n = 21$. We transform each of the values in parentheses by multiplying by $(n - 1)$, and then divide by the assumed population variance, $\sigma^2 = 0.0010$, as follows:

$$P(s^2 \geq 0.0016) = P\left(\frac{(n - 1)s^2}{\sigma^2} \geq \frac{(20)(0.0016)}{0.0010}\right) = P(\chi^2_{20} \geq 32.0)$$

From Fig. 6.11 we see that $P(\chi^2 \geq 32)$ must be between 0.05 and 0.025; that is,

$$0.05 > P(\chi^2 \geq 32.0) = P(s^2 \geq 0.0016) > 0.025$$

A computer statistical package can be used to show the exact probability,

$$P(\chi^2_{20} \geq 32.0) = 0.0433$$

Since a sample variance as high as 0.0016 will occur relatively infrequently when $\sigma^2 = 0.0010$ (less than 5% of the time), we might question this company's statement that $\sigma^2 = 0.0010$.

The F-Distribution (Optional)

6.11

Another important distribution involving variances is the **F**-distribution, named in honor of R. A. Fisher, who first studied it in 1924. The **F**-distribution is particularly useful in problems where one wants to test hypotheses about whether or not two normal populations have the same variance. For example, suppose you are interested in determining whether or not σ^2_1, the variance of some normal population, equals σ^2_2, the variance of a second normal population. Statistically, we can do this by taking a sample from each population, calculating the variance of each sample, and then determining the probability the two sample variances came from populations having equal variances. To determine this probability, let us assume that a random sample from the first population yields a variance of s^2_1, and a random sample from the second population yields a variance of s^2_2. How far the ratio s^2_1/s^2_2 differs from 1.0 can be used to make inferences about whether or not $\sigma^2_1 = \sigma^2_2$. When $\sigma^2_1 = \sigma^2_2$, we would expect the ratio s^2_1/s^2_2 to be close to 1.0. Thus, the more we find that the ratio s^2_1/s^2_2 differs from 1.0, the less confidence we have that $\sigma^2_1 = \sigma^2_2$.

How closely the ratio s^2_1/s^2_2 can be expected to approach 1.0 when $\sigma^2_1 = \sigma^2_2$ depends on the size of the two samples—or, more precisely, on the number of degrees of freedom in each sample. We will denote the number of degrees of freedom in the two samples as ν_1 and ν_2, and the sample sizes as n_1

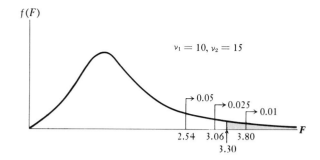

Figure 6.12
The *F*-distribution for $v_1 = 10$, $v_2 = 15$.

and n_2, where $v_1 = n_1 - 1$ and $v_2 = n_2 - 1$. Using this terminology, we can show that:

The ratio of the variances of two independent random samples drawn from normal parent populations having equal variances follows an *F*-distribution* with $v_1 = n_1 - 1$ and $v_2 = n_2 - 1$ degrees of freedom.

$$F_{v_1, v_2} = \frac{s_1^2}{s_2^2}$$

(6.12)

The parameters of the *F*-distribution are v_1 and v_2, the degrees of freedom, and we could show that $E[F]$ and $V[F]$ both depend on these parameters. However, we will not have occasion to use either $E[F]$, $V[F]$, or the density function of the *F*-distribution in this book; hence, these values will not be presented.

Figure 6.12 shows a typical *F*-distribution; this one represents all possible values of s_1^2/s_2^2 when $v_1 = 10$ and $v_2 = 15$. Note that the *F*-distribution is

---

*The *F*-distribution is usually defined as the ratio of two χ^2 variables, each divided by its degrees of freedom. To illustrate, assume s_1^2 and s_2^2 are from random samples drawn from two normal parent populations, each having the same variance, σ^2. Let the two samples have $v_1 = n_1 - 1$ and $v_2 = n_2 - 1$ degrees of freedom, respectively. We know, from Section 6.10, that the variables $v_1 s_1^2/\sigma^2$ and $v_2 s_2^2/\sigma^2$ will both have a χ^2-distribution. If we take the ratio of these two χ^2 variables, each divided by its degrees of freedom, the result is

$$F = \frac{\dfrac{v_1 s_1^2/\sigma^2}{v_1}}{\dfrac{v_2 s_2^2/\sigma^2}{v_2}} = \frac{s_1^2/\sigma^2}{s_2^2/\sigma^2} = \frac{s_1^2}{s_2^2}$$

always positive or zero, and is positively skewed. This is reasonable, since the ratio s_1^2/s_2^2 can never be negative, but can assume *any* positive value. The fact that the F-distribution looks something like a chi-square distribution is not coincidental, since these distributions are closely related. Three particular probabilities are indicated in Fig. 6.12, namely $P(F \geq 2.54) = 0.05$, $P(F \geq 3.06) = 0.025$, and $P(F \geq 3.80) = 0.01$.

To illustrate the use of the F-distribution and Formula (6.12), let's assume that two random samples have been drawn from normal populations, and it is desirable to determine the probability that these two samples were drawn from populations having the same variance. Furthermore, we shall assume that the first sample is of size $n_1 = 11$ and the second is of size $n_2 = 16$. The appropriate F-distribution for this problem has $\nu_1 = 11 - 1 = 10$ degrees of freedom, and $\nu_2 = 16 - 1 = 15$ degrees of freedom, as shown in Fig. 6.12.

Now, let's suppose our first sample of size $n_1 = 11$ yields $s_1^2 = 330$, while the second sample, of size $n_2 = 16$, yields $s_2^2 = 100$. We can calculate the probability that these two samples came from populations having the same variance, by taking the ratio

$$F_{(10,\,15)} = \frac{s_1^2}{s_2^2} = \frac{330}{100} = 3.30$$

From Fig. 6.12 we see that $P(F_{(10,\,15)} \geq 3.30)$ is greater than 0.01, but less than 0.025. Hence, we can write $0.025 > P(F_{(10,\,15)} \geq 3.30) > 0.01$. A computer statistical package can be used to show that the exact probability is

$$P(F \geq 3.30) = 0.0151$$

The values for the F-distribution shown in Fig. 6.12 were taken from Table VIII in Appendix B. Table VIII (a), (b), and (c) give F-values cutting off 0.05, 0.025, and 0.01 in the upper tail of the F-distribution.* The reader should verify that when $\nu_1 = 10$ (the numerator) and $\nu_2 = 15$ (the denominator), then parts (a), (b) and (c) of Table VIII yield the values 2.54, 3.06, 3.80, respectively.

Summary   6.12

Figure 6.13 represents a tree diagram that some students have found useful in deciding when to apply each of these distributions. Table 6.8 provides a summary of the sampling distributions discussed in this chapter.

---

*Rather than calculate lower-tail probabilities, we will assume that s_1^2 and s_2^2 are labeled so that s_1^2/s_2^2 is always greater than 1.0.

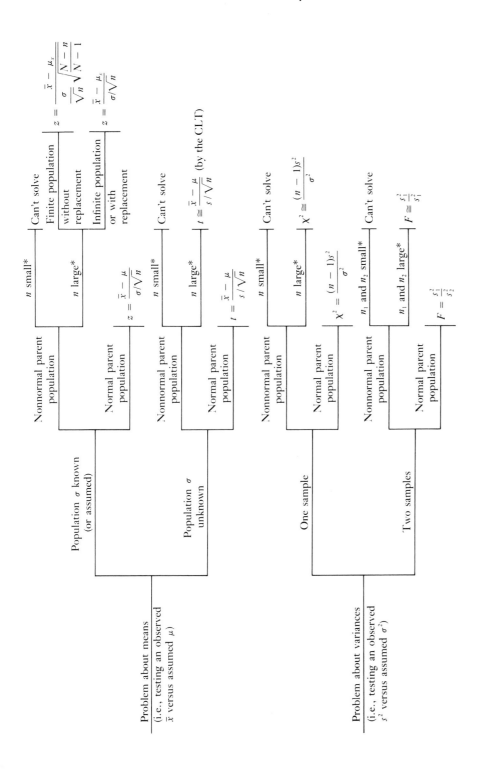

Figure 6.13
Tree diagram for using probability distributions.

*"Large" and "small" may depend on the accuracy desired and the shape of the parent population. For fairly symmetrical distributions, $n \geq 10$ may be sufficient. In almost all cases, $n \geq 30$ is sufficient for "large."

†Remember, the t and χ^2 are fairly "robust," meaning that they work well, even if the parent population is not exactly normally distributed but has some normal characteristics (unimodal and not badly skewed).

TABLE 6.8   Summary of sampling distributions

Random variable	Situation	Reference section	Resulting distribution for problem solving	Mean	Variance
$\bar{x}$	Population normal, σ known, sample size n	6.6	$z = \dfrac{\bar{x} - \mu_{\bar{x}}}{\sigma/\sqrt{n}}$	0	1
$\bar{x}$	Population normal, σ unknown, sample size n*	6.9	$t_\nu = \dfrac{\bar{x} - \mu_{\bar{x}}}{s/\sqrt{n}}$	0	$\nu/(\nu - 2)$ with $\nu = n - 1$ d.f.
$\bar{x}$	Population unknown, σ known, $n > 30$	6.7	$z = \dfrac{\bar{x} - \mu}{\sigma/\sqrt{n}}$	0	1
s^2	Population normal, sample size n	6.10	$\chi_\nu^2 = \dfrac{(n-1)s^2}{\sigma^2}$	ν	2ν with $\nu = n - 1$ d.f.
s_1^2 s_2^2	Populations normal, sample sizes of n_1 and n_2	6.11	$F_{\nu_1, \nu_2} = s_1^2 / s_2^2$	—	— with $\nu_1 = n_1 - 1$ and $\nu_2 = n_2 - 1$ d.f.

*If $n > 30$, $\bar{x}$ will be approximately normal, and s should be close to σ; hence $(\bar{x} - \mu)/(s/\sqrt{n})$ is approximately $N(0,1)$.

Problems

6.48 Suppose you are drawing samples of size $n = 3$ from a normal population with a variance of 8.25. What is the probability that $(n - 1)s^2/\sigma^2$ will exceed 5.99? What is the probability that s^2 will be more than three times as large as σ^2?

6.49 McDonald's is concerned with the variability in its "quarter pounder." The amount of meat in these burgers is supposed to have a variance of no more than 0.2 ounces. A random sample of 20 burgers from one city yields a variance of $s^2 = 0.4$. The parent population is normal.

a) What is the probability that a sample variance will equal or exceed 0.4?

b) Would you suspect that the meat content of the McDonald's quarter pounder from this city varies excessively?

6.50 An economist estimates that the number of gallons of gasoline used monthly by each automobile in the United States is a normally distributed random variable with mean $\mu = 50$ and variance $\sigma^2 = 50$. A sample of $n = 9$ yields $s^2 = 36$. How often will s^2 be this low or lower if the economist's estimates are correct?

6.51 A random variable is known to be chi-square-distributed with parameter $\nu = 24$.

  a) What is the mean and variance of this χ^2-distribution?

  b) What is the probability the value of χ^2 will exceed 43.0? What is $P(\chi^2 \geq 33.2)$? What is $P(\chi^2 \leq 9.89)$?

  c) Use your answers to parts (a) and (b) to draw a rough sketch of the chi-square distribution for $\nu = 24$.

  d) Superimpose on your sketch for part (c) a graph of the distribution for $\mu = 24$ and $\sigma^2 = 48$. How closely do the two distributions agree?

6.52 A manufacturer is testing the strength of a new roofing material. While the mean strength is clearly sufficient, the manufacturer is concerned with weakness due to the variability in strength. Past experience with this material suggests that the variance in strength is $\sigma^2 = 1000$ per square inch. If the population is normal and σ^2 is, in fact, equal to 1000, what is the probability a random sample will yield 2050, 2150, 2270, and 2110?

6.53 The stock market appears to be more volatile after the 1987 crash than before. Study this statement by randomly selecting 30 days in 1986 and 30 days in 1988, recording the change in the DJIA for each day. Calculate the variance for each sample, and then use the F-distribution to determine the probability of receiving these two variances if $\sigma_1^2 = \sigma_2^2$.

6.54 **a)** Sketch the F-distribution for $n_1 = 16$ (the numerator) and $n_2 = 13$ (the denominator).

  b) Two independent random samples are drawn from normal populations. The first, of size $n_1 = 16$, results in $s_1^2 = 250$. The second, of size $n_2 = 13$, yields $s_2^2 = 100$. What is the probability of receiving these two sample variances if $\sigma_1^2 = \sigma_2^2$?

6.55 Calculate, for the salary data in Appendix C, the variance for the males and the variance for the females. Use the F-distribution to determine the probability of receiving these two variances assuming $\sigma_1^2 = \sigma_2^2$.

6.56 One measure of risk inherent in a particular stock portfolio is the variance in expected prices. If a random sample of the expected prices of two different portfolios yields $s_2^2 = 4000$ (based on $n_2 = 31$) and $s_1^2 = 7500$ (based on $n_1 = 61$), how likely is it that s_1^2 will be this much larger than s_2^2 if the two portfolios are equally risky and the populations are normally distributed?

6.57 A public-policy researcher is studying the variance in the amount of money requested by certain government agencies this year relative to five years ago. Random samples, of size $n_1 = 21$ and $n_2 = 25$ resulted in $s_1^2 = (67{,}223)^2$ and $s_2^2 = (37{,}178)^2$. What is the probability that s_2^2 will be this much lower than s_1^2 if the population variances are equal? Assume normal parent populations.

6.58 Suppose an economist is interested in determining the variance of incomes across two communities. Random samples of size $n_1 = 10$ and $n_2 = 11$ result in $s_1^2 = (2400)^2$ and $s_2^2 = (2000)^2$. Assuming that $\sigma_1^2 = \sigma_2^2$ and that the parent

	Chicago	New York
1.	$56,400	$57,200
2.	59,200	54,100
3.	54,999	51,900
4.	51,400	58,300
5.	56,888	55,500
6.	53,100	51,900
7.	60,000	56,900
8.	59,000	57,100
9.	55,500	53,900
10.	54,900	

populations are normal, what is the probability that s_1^2 will be this much higher than s_2^2?

6.59 The random sample shown at left of the starting salaries for MBA finance majors was taken for students starting to work in the Chicago and New York City areas. Would you question the assumption that $\sigma_1^2 = \sigma_2^2$ using these data? Assume the parent populations are normal.

Exercises

6.60 Use a statistical package on the computer to generate 100 random samples of size $n = 25$ each, from the following *uniform distribution.*

$$f(x) = \begin{cases} 1.0 & 0 \le x \le 1.0 \\ 0 & \text{otherwise} \end{cases}$$

a) Calculate $\bar{x}$ and s^2 for each sample.

b) Construct the frequency distribution for the $\bar{x}$'s using some convenient class interval. Compare the shape of this distribution with that predicted by the CLT.

c) For each sample in part (a) calculate the t-value, and then construct the resulting frequency distribution, again using some convenient class interval. Does the distribution of these t-values correspond to that given in Table VII for $v = 24$?

d) Repeat parts (a) and (b) for $n = 4$. What differences did you expect using $n = 4$ rather than $n = 25$?

e) For each sample in part (a), calculate $\chi^2 = 24s^2/\sigma^2$, where $\sigma^2 = 1/12$. Sketch this distribution. Does this sketch correspond to the distribution of χ^2?

6.61 Consult a mathematical statistics text and write the probability density function for the t-distribution and the chi-square distribution. How are these two distributions related?

6.62 a) Construct an example to show that $E[s^2] \ne \sigma^2$ when simple random sampling is done without replacement, from a finite population.

b) Assuming a normal parent population, prove that $V[s^2] = 2\sigma^4/v$ (Hint: Use the fact that $\chi^2 = s^2 v/\sigma^2$ and $V[\chi^2] = 2v$.)

6.63 Research the chi-square distribution and explain what it means to say that this distribution is the sum of the squares of a finite number of independent standardized normal random variables (see Section 5.5).

6.64 Describe how the finite population correction factor and the hypergeometric distribution are related. See if you can justify the fact that the correction factor is $\sqrt{(N - n)/(N - 1)}$.

6.65 Give a brief answer to each of the following questions.

a) If an auditor fails to recognize an error in an account, what type of error is this failure called?

b) As compared to probability sampling, what is the primary disadvantage of judgment sampling?

c) How should a certified public accountant identify strata of a sample in order to determine inventory shrinkage?

d) A sample is drawn from two equal-sized strata. The standard deviation of the first stratum is $45, while the standard deviation of the second is $250. What value (or range of values) would you expect from an unstratified sample from the entire population?

6.66 Write a computer program to demonstrate the central limit theorem. For example, you might consider taking a large number of samples from a Poisson distribution (try $\lambda = 1$). Let the first sample size be $n = 5$, then $n = 15$, then $n = 30$, and show that the resulting distributions of $\bar{x}$ tend to $N(\mu, \sigma^2/n)$ as n gets larger.

6.67 The following data represent a random sample of 30 of the top 1000 companies in America for 1989, as listed in *Business Week*. Pick one of the categories across the top, and then use (some of) the measures of this chapter to describe these data. The mean for all 1000 companies is listed across the bottom.

Company	Mkt value ($ millions)	Sales ($ millions)	Profits ($ millions)	Assets ($ millions)	P/E ratio	1989 earnings per share
Mobil	20434	54877	2038	38820	10	4.93
Am Express	12556	2293	988	142704	13	3.03
May Dept.	5595	11742	503	8144	11	3.74
Con Ed	5173	5109	599.3	9552	9	4.78
Am El Power	5056	4841	693	14262	8	3.16
Whitman	3297	3583	176.7	4039	19	2.09
Merrill Lynch	2842	10547	463.2	62457	7	2.55
Affil. Publi.	2835	534	−80.9	425	55	0.86
Texas Eastern	2676	3481	166.9	4869	16	2.12
UST	2640	619	162.2	598	17	1.68
GR West Finan	2018	2943	248.4	32815	15	2.19
Whirlpool	1836	4421	161.3	3410	11	2.64
Bk-New Eng	1644	3197	319	32220	6	4.41
GAF	1418	962	74.2	481	19	2.64
Northrop	1290	5797	104.2	3139	12	2.80
Williams	1193	494	1673	2185	—	1.71
Greyhound	1141	3305	93.3	3374	12	2.67
Flightsafety	1070	183	50.0	438	21	1.76
Timken	979	1554	65.9	1593	12	1.41
Hasbro	928	1358	72.4	1112	14	1.54
Vista Central	793	794	123.8	493	8	8.92
Service Merch	612	3093	76.5	1711	8	1.91
St. Jude Med	558	114	33.5	143	17	3.40
Nerco	551	662	75.6	1206	7	1.76
Measurex	510	265	37.1	303	14	2.24
Pittway	474	771	37.3	595	13	8.13
New Process	403	418	34.1	157	10	4.20
Wickes	387	3985	−46.1	3918	9	0.93
Symbol Tech	346	93	20.6	140	18	1.32
Atari	339	452	39.4	464	9	1.12
Averages	2391 ($ Mil.)	3,361 ($ Mil.)	200.0 ($ Mil.)	6673 ($ Mil.)	15	3.19

Chapter 7

Estimation

*If the polls are so accurate, why
are there so many polling
companies?*

BILL FOSTER

Introduction **7.1**

In most statistical studies the population parameters are unknown and must be estimated from a sample because it is impossible or impractical (in terms of time and expense) to look at the entire population. Developing methods for estimating as accurately as possible the value of population parameters is thus an important part of statistical analysis. For example, a retail firm wishes to investigate the average sales per week in a particular location by sampling a given number of weeks; or a firm manufacturing electronic components wants to determine the average number of defectives in each batch of 1000 items without inspecting each and every component before shipment. In these cases, a sample statistic used to measure central location, such as the sample mean, can be used as an estimate of the population parameter. Similarly, measures of variability may be of interest, such as the dispersion of defective electronic components from batch to batch or the variability of sales from week to week. Again, the population parameters are estimated from the sample statistics. The objective of this chapter, which deals with similar estimation problems, is two-fold: first, to present criteria for judging how well a given sample statistic estimates the population parameter; and second, to analyze several of the most popular methods for estimating these parameters.

The random variables used to estimate population parameters are called **estimators,** while specific values of these variables are referred to as **estimates** of the population parameters. The random variables $\bar{x}$ and s^2 are thus

257

estimators of the population parameters μ and σ^2. A specific value of $\bar{x}$, such as $\bar{x} = 2500$ is an estimate of μ, just as the specific value $s^2 = 374.5$ is an estimate of σ^2.

It is not necessary that an estimate of a population parameter be one single value; instead the estimate could be a range of values.

Estimates that specify a single value of the population are called **point estimates,** while estimates that specify a range of values are called **interval estimates.**

A point estimate for the average sales per week may be $2500, implying that the best estimate of the population mean is $2500. An interval estimate specifies a range of values, say $2300 to $2700, indicating that we think the mean sales figure for the population lies in this interval.

The choice of an appropriate point estimator in a given circumstance usually depends on how well the estimator satisfies certain criteria. In Section 7.2 we will describe four properties of "good" estimators.

The properties emphasized throughout the remainder of this book are those that have been generally recognized as the most important four properties of a good estimator.

1. *The property of unbiasedness:* On average, the value of the estimate should equal the population parameter being estimated.
2. *The property of efficiency:* The estimator should have a relatively small variance.
3. *The property of sufficiency:* The estimator should take into consideration as much as possible of the information available from the sample.
4. *The property of consistency:* The estimator should approach the value of the population parameter as the sample size increases.

An estimator is a random variable, since it is the result of a sampling experiment. As a random variable, it has a probability distribution with a specific shape, expected value, and variance. Analysis of these characteristics of the distribution of an estimator permits us to specify desirable properties of the estimator.

Four Properties of a "Good" Estimator

7.2

Unbiasedness

Normally, it is preferable that the expected value of the estimator exactly equal, or fall close to the true value of the parameter being estimated. If the average value of the estimator does not equal the actual parameter value, the estimator is said to contain a "bias," or to be a "biased estimator." Under ideal conditions, an estimator has a bias of zero, in which case it is said to be "unbiased." This property thus can be stated as follows:

An estimator is said to be **unbiased** if the expected value of the estimator is equal to the true value of the parameter being estimated. That is,

$$E[\text{estimator}] = \text{population parameter}$$

In determining a point estimate for the population mean, it is certainly not difficult to construct examples of a biased estimator. Simply using the largest observation in a sample of size $n > 1$ to estimate μ, and ignoring the rest of the observations, will yield an estimate whose expected value is larger than μ. This is obviously a poor choice for estimating the population mean, especially when there is a much more appealing choice, that of using $\overline{x}$. The sample mean is the most widely used estimator of all, because one of its major advantages is that it provides an unbiased estimate of μ. The fact that $E[\overline{x}] = \mu$ was presented in Section 6.5. The parameter other than μ most often estimated is σ^2, the population variance. An unbiased estimator for σ^2 is s^2, since $E[s^2] = \sigma^2$, as we showed in Section 6.9.*

Although s^2 is an unbiased estimator of σ^2, it is *not* true that s is an unbiased estimator of σ, that is, $E[s] \neq \sigma$, because the square root of a sum of numbers is not usually equal to the sum of the square roots of those same numbers. To demonstrate this fact, suppose we consider the population discussed in Section 6.5, involving the three elements $(1, 2, 3)$ for the rating of the first-mortgage bonds. We saw, in Table 6.5, that there are nine different samples of size $n = 2$, when sampling with replacement. Table 7.1 shows these nine samples, as well as the mean, variance, and standard deviation of each sample (where $s^2 = \sum(x_i - \overline{x})^2/(n-1)$, and $n = 2$).

The sum of the nine values of s^2 shown in column 5 is 6.00; this means that the average value of s^2 is $E[s^2] = \frac{6}{9} = \frac{2}{3}$. Since the population $(1, 2, 3)$ has a variance of $\frac{2}{3}$, we have shown that $E[s^2] = \sigma^2$.

Now consider the nine values of s shown in column 6 of Table 7.1. If s were an unbiased estimator of σ, the average of these nine values would equal $\sigma = \sqrt{2/3} = 0.817$. The actual average is $5.66/9 = 0.629$; this means that $E[s] \neq \sigma$. In fact, we see that seven of the nine values of s *underestimate* the true population standard deviation of $\sigma = 0.817$.† The bias in this case is $0.817 - 0.629 = 0.188$. *Even though s is not an unbiased estimator of σ, it is still used as an estimator of σ because s^2 is an unbiased estimator of σ^2.*

---

*Recall that $E[s^2] \neq \sigma^2$ when sampling from a finite population without replacement.

†Because the sample standard deviation s usually *underestimates* σ, it follows that the variable $(\overline{x} - \mu)/(s/\sqrt{n})$ will *overestimate* the variable $(\overline{x} - \mu)/(\sigma/\sqrt{n})$. This is one reason the t-distribution is more spread out than the normal distribution.

TABLE 7.1

(1)	(2)	(3)	(4)	(5)	(6)
(x_1, x_2)	$\bar{x}$	$(x_1 - \bar{x})^2$	$(x_2 - \bar{x})^2$	$s^2 = \dfrac{1}{n-1} \sum (x_i - \bar{x})^2$	$s = \sqrt{\dfrac{1}{n-1} \sum (x_i - \bar{x})^2}$
$(1, 1)$	1.0	0.00	0.00	0.00	0.00
$(1, 2)$	1.5	0.25	0.25	0.50	0.71
$(2, 1)$	1.5	0.25	0.25	0.50	0.71
$(1, 3)$	2.0	1.00	1.00	2.00	1.41
$(3, 1)$	2.0	1.00	1.00	2.00	1.41
$(2, 2)$	2.0	0.00	0.00	0.00	0.00
$(2, 3)$	2.5	0.25	0.25	0.50	0.71
$(3, 2)$	2.5	0.25	0.25	0.50	0.71
$(3, 3)$	3.0	0.00	0.00	0.00	0.00
Sum	18.0	3.00	3.00	6.00	5.66

There are correction factors that make *s* an unbiased estimator of σ. These correction factors depend on the form of the population distribution and will not be presented here.

As a final example of the property of unbiasedness, consider the problem of estimating p, the population proportion of successes in a binomial distribution. Recall that in Chapter 4 it was stated that if a sample yields *x* successes in *n* trials, then the ratio x/n is an unbiased estimate of p:

$$E\left[\frac{x}{n}\right] = \frac{1}{n} E[x] = \frac{1}{n}(np) = p$$

The result implies that if, in a random sample of 100 voters, 60 people indicate that they intend to vote for Candidate A, then $\frac{60}{100} = 0.60$ is an unbiased estimate of the population proportion of people who would say they intend to vote for Candidate A.

One weakness of the property of unbiasedness lies in the fact that the criterion requires only that the *average* value of the estimator equal the population parameter. It does not require that most, or even *any* of the values of the estimator be reasonably close to the population parameter, as would seem desirable in a "good" estimator. For this reason, the property of efficiency is important.

Efficiency

For given repeated samples of size n, it is desirable that an estimator have values that are close to each other. That is, it would be comforting in estimating an unknown parameter to believe that the value you computed based on a particular random sample would not be much different from the value you or anyone else would compute based on another random sample of the same size. *The property of efficiency implies that the variance of the estimator should be small.* However, having a small variance doesn't make an estimator a good one, unless this estimator is also unbiased. For example, an estimator that always specifies 200 as its estimate of the population parameter will have zero variance. But this estimate will be biased unless the true population parameter happens to equal 200. In other words, a small variance is desirable, but so is unbiasedness.

The property of efficiency of an estimator is defined by comparing its variance to the variance of all other *unbiased* estimators.

The most efficient estimator among a group of unbiased estimators is the one with the smallest variance.

The most efficient estimator is also called the **best unbiased estimator,** where "best" implies minimum variance. Figure 7.1 illustrates the distributions of three different estimators (labeled 1, 2, and 3) based on samples of the same size. Of the three distributions, 1 and 2 both have expected values equal to the population parameter; that is, they are unbiased. The third distribution has a positive bias, since its mean exceeds the population parameter. The variance of the three estimators decreases in size from 1 to 3. However, the third distribution is not the most efficient estimator among this group because it is not unbiased. Our definition of efficiency requires that the estimator be *unbiased* and have smaller variance than any other unbiased estimator. Thus, estimator 2 is the most efficient of those illustrated. Whether number 2 is the most efficient of *all* possible unbiased estimators has not been shown and is often difficult to prove.

Relative Efficiency

Since it is generally quite difficult to prove that an estimator is the best among all unbiased ones, the most common approach is to determine the **relative**

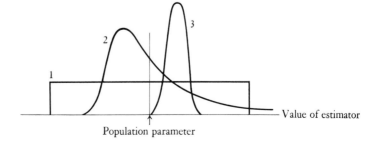

Figure 7.1
Illustration of properties of
unbiasedness and efficiency.

efficiency of two estimators. Relative efficiency is defined as the ratio of the variances of the two estimators.

> *Relative efficiency:* $\dfrac{\text{Variance of first estimator}}{\text{Variance of second estimator}}$

As an illustration of the use of relative efficiency, consider the sample mean versus the sample median as estimators of the mean of a normal population. Both estimators are unbiased when we are sampling from a normal population, since the normal is symmetric. From Section 6.5 we know that the variance of $\bar{x}$ equals σ^2/n. It is also possible to find the variance of an estimator using the sample median to estimate the population mean; this variance is $\pi\sigma^2/2n$*. The ratio of these quantities gives their relative efficiency:

$$\frac{V(\text{median})}{V(\bar{x})} = \frac{\pi\sigma^2/2n}{\sigma^2/n} = \frac{\pi}{2} = 1.57$$

The ratio 1.57 implies that the median is 1.57 times less efficient than the mean in estimating μ. In other words, an estimate based on the median of a sample of 157 observations has the same reliability as an estimate based on the mean of a sample of 100 observations, assuming a normal parent population.

In some problems it is possible to determine precisely the most efficient estimator, that is, the unbiased estimator with the lowest variance. In estimating the mean of a normal population, for example, it can be shown that the variance of any estimator must be greater than or equal to σ^2/n. Since the variance of $\bar{x}$ in this case exactly equals σ^2/n, the sample mean must be the most efficient estimator of μ. In the design of a sample, the most efficient estimator may not always be the best choice because of other factors, such as the time available to collect the sample or the accessibility of the observations. That is, statistical efficiency may have to be sacrificed in order to obtain an estimate in the time allowed; or some other estimator may be less costly to obtain or more meaningful and, therefore, may be preferred over the most efficient one. Many high schools, for example, publish statements about a student's academic performance only in terms of the *rank* relative to the rest of the class (a student is said to "rank tenth in his class," for example). Trying to determine the most efficient estimator in this case (such as the average academic performance) may be difficult and such an estimator may not be as meaningful as a measure based on the ranked performance.

Sufficiency

Unbiasedness and efficiency are desirable properties for an estimator, particularly when one is dealing with small samples. Another property of interest is **sufficiency.**

---

*For further discussion, see reference 12.

> An estimator is said to be **sufficient** if it uses all the information about the population parameter that the sample can provide.

The sufficient estimator somehow takes into account each of the sample observations, as well as all the information that is provided by these observations. The sample median is not a sufficient estimator because it uses only the *ranking* of the observations and ignores information about the distance between adjacent numerical values. The sufficiency property is of importance in that it is a necessary condition for efficiency.

Consistency

Since the distribution of an estimator changes, in general, as the sample size changes, the properties of estimators for large sample sizes (as $n \to \infty$) become important. Properties of estimators based on limits approached as $n \to \infty$ are called **asymptotic properties** and may differ from finite or small-sample properties. The most important of these asymptotic properties is that of **consistency,** which involves the variability of the estimator about the population parameter as the size of n increases:

> An estimator is said to be **consistent** if it yields estimates that converge in probability to the population parameter being estimated as n becomes larger.

To say that an estimator must converge in probability to the parameter being estimated is to imply that, as samples become larger, the expected value of the estimator must approach the true value of the parameter and that the variance of this estimator about the population parameter must become negligible. This requirement is equivalent to specifying that the estimator becomes unbiased and that the variance of the estimator approaches zero as n approaches infinity.

Previously, we showed that $\bar{x}$ is an unbiased estimator of the population mean, and that x/n is an unbiased estimator of the population proportion. It is not difficult to show also that both these estimators are consistent as well as unbiased. We shall prove that x/n is a consistent estimator of p, leaving it to the reader to prove that $\bar{x}$ is also consistent.

$$V[x/n] = \frac{1}{n^2}V[x] \qquad \text{(From Section 3.6)}$$

$$= \frac{1}{n^2}(npq) \qquad \text{(Since } x \text{ is binomially distributed)}$$

$$= \frac{pq}{n}$$

Since the value of pq/n approaches zero as n approaches infinity, and since x/n is an unbiased estimator of p for any sample size, then x/n must be a consistent estimator of p.

While the four properties presented above are certainly all quite desirable, they do not preclude other considerations. We pointed out previously that the inferences (or estimates) made from samples serve as an aid to the process of making decisions, and that samples should be drawn with the objective of minimizing the cost of making an incorrect decision (balanced against the cost of sampling). Since one primary purpose in collecting a sample involves estimating parameters, an estimation procedure should be chosen that will minimize the cost (or loss) of making an incorrect estimate from the sample information. This objective is not necessarily incompatible with any of the properties of good estimators mentioned above; in fact, in many cases, when these properties are satisfied the estimator indeed will minimize the cost of making an error.

Estimating Unknown Parameters

7.3

In the 1920s R. A. Fisher developed the method of maximum likelihood as a means of finding estimators that satisfy some (but not necessarily all) of the criteria discussed previously. This method is popular because maximum-likelihood estimators are usually relatively easy to obtain, and are often efficient and approximately normally distributed for large samples. One disadvantage of the method is that maximum-likelihood estimates are not necessarily unbiased for small samples although they are consistent (large sample property).

The maximum-likelihood method estimates the value of a population parameter by selecting the most likely sample space from which a given sample could have been drawn. In other words, the sample space is selected that would yield the observed sample more frequently than any other sample space. The value of the population parameter corresponding to the generation of this sample space is called the maximum-likelihood estimate; the name **maximum likelihood** is derived from this process of selecting the most likely sample space.

As an illustration of the process of determining a maximum-likelihood estimate, consider the problem of estimating the binomial parameter p. Suppose that, in a sample of 5 trials, 3 successes are observed. What sample space (what binomial population) is most likely to give this particular result; or equivalently, what is the most likely value of p given the observed sample? The most likely population parameter can be determined by calculating the probability of obtaining exactly three successes in five trials for all possible values of the population parameter and selecting that value which yields the highest probability. Table 7.2 examines nine possible values of p, indicating for each

TABLE 7.2

Value of p	Probability of three successes
0.10	0.0081
0.20	0.0512
0.30	0.1323
0.40	0.2304
0.50	0.3125
0.60	0.3456
0.70	0.3087
0.80	0.2048
0.90	0.0729

value the probability of 3 successes in 5 trials; for example, if $p = \frac{1}{10}$, the appropriate probability is (from Table I, in Appendix B):

$$P(3 \text{ successes in 5 trials}) = 0.0081$$

The value of p most likely to yield a sample of 3 successes in 5 trials, as given by Table 7.2, is $p = 0.60$, where the associated probability is 0.3456. The reader will note that this estimate equals the same proportion $x/n = 3/5 = 0.60$. It is often true that the most likely value for a population parameter is the intuitively appealing one, the corresponding measure of the sample. For example, it can be shown that the maximum-likelihood estimator of a population mean is the sample mean. That is, the value of $\bar{x}$ is the most likely value of μ that can be found based on a sample size of n. A proof of this relationship and others involving the derivation of maximum-likelihood estimates is given in Section 7.9.

Problems

7.1 Differentiate between

    a) a point estimate and an interval estimate;

    b) unbiasedness and consistency.

7.2 Given a normal parent population, which of the following estimators are unbiased?

    a) mean   **b)** median   **c)** mode   **d)** x/n

    Explain your answer.

7.3 Elaborate on the four properties of an estimator described in this chapter. Explain why each one is important.

7.4 Consider the population $x = \{5, 15\}$.

a) Calculate μ, σ^2, and σ for this population.

b) Make a list of eight possible samples of size $n = 3$, with replacement [for example, $(5,5,5)$, $(5,15,5)$, $(15,5,15)$]. Calculate $\bar{x}$ for each sample.

c) Show from part (b) that $\bar{x}$ is an unbiased estimate of μ; that is, show $E[\bar{x}] = \mu$.

d) Calculate s^2 for each sample, and then show that $E[s^2] = \sigma^2$.

e) Show that the average of the eight values of s is not equal to σ; that is, show $E[s] \neq \sigma$.

f) Calculate the median for each of the eight samples. Is the average of these values equal to μ; that is, is the median an unbiased estimator in this case?

7.5 Calculate the variance of the median values in Problem 7.4(f). Use this variance and the variance of the values of $\bar{x}$ in Problem 7.5(b) to show that $\bar{x}$ is more efficient than the median as an estimator of μ.

7.6 Repeat Problem 7.4(b), using $n = 2$. Compare the case in which $n = 2$ with that in which $n = 3$, and show that the results support the fact that the mean is a consistent estimator.

7.7 Indicate which of the following statements is incorrect and explain why.

a) Since a point estimator of a population parameter is so precise, it is to be preferred over a confidence interval for the same parameter.

b) When we say that $\bar{x}$ is an unbiased estimator of μ, we are, in effect, saying that $\bar{x} = \mu$.

7.8 An accountant at Banc One, headquartered in Columbus, Ohio, selected a random sample of 100 accounts. The mean balance among these accounts was found to be $842.56. Another accountant then stated that the mean balance must be $842.56 since $\bar{x}$ is an unbiased estimate of μ. Discuss the reasonableness of this assertion.

7.9 Consider the binomial distribution with $n = 4$ and $p = 0.40$. The five possible binomial values of x/n are 0/4, 1/4, 2/4, 3/4, and 4/4.

a) Calculate $E[x/n]$ by multiplying each of the five values by the appropriate probabilities in Table I of Appendix B. Is x/n unbiased; that is, is $E[x/n] = p$?

b) Calculate the variance of the x/n values in part (a). Then calculate the variance of x/n for $p = 0.40$ when $n = 5$. Does the variance decrease from $n = 4$ to $n = 5$, supporting the fact that x/n is consistent?

7.10 Describe, intuitively, what is meant by a maximum-likelihood estimate.

7.11 If a random sample of 100 components in a large production lot yields five defectives, what is the maximum-likelihood estimate of the proportion of defectives in the entire lot?

7.12 Prove that $E[x/n] = p$ for the binomial distribution.

Interval Estimation

7.4

The particular value chosen as most likely for a population parameter is called a **point estimate.** We know that it would be an exceptional coincidence if this estimate were identical to the population parameter (because of sampling error). Thus, even though the best possible value is used as the point estimate, we should have very little confidence that this value is *exactly* correct. One of the major weaknesses of a point estimate is that it does not permit the expression of any degree of uncertainty about the estimate. The most common way to express uncertainty about an estimate is to define, with a known probability of error, an interval or range of values in which the population parameter is likely to be. This process is known as **interval estimation.**

You will recall that on a number of occasions thus far we have determined values a and b so that $P(a \leq \bar{x} \leq b)$ equals some predetermined value. The values a and b were determined from a knowledge about the parent population and its parameters. The interval (a, b) is called a probability interval for $\bar{x}$. For example, if we calculated $P(a \leq \bar{x} \leq b) = 0.90$, based on a random sample of size n drawn from a population with mean μ, we know the random variable $\bar{x}$ will fall in the probability interval (a, b) 90% of the time.

Although it is important to be able to construct probability intervals for $\bar{x}$ based on knowledge of μ, for most practical statistical problems the process must be reversed: It is μ that is the unknown, and we want to construct a confidence interval for μ based on $\bar{x}$. For example, we may want to develop a method for defining an interval based on $\bar{x}$ such that μ is likely to lie in that interval 90% of the times that the method is used—a 90% confidence interval. This means that, on the average, 90 such intervals of every 100 calculated on the basis of means of samples of size n will include the population mean μ.

The use of the future tense in defining a confidence interval is very important because, once such an interval based on a sample is determined, either the true parameter lies in the interval or it does not. The value of μ cannot be said to have a probability of 0.90 of being within the interval because it is not a random variable, but a constant. If it is in a given interval, then the probability that it is in the interval is 1.0; if not, the probability that it is within the interval is 0.0.

To better distinguish between the two types of intervals, consider the outstanding monthly balance for credit card billings for a major credit card at a large bank. Previous analysis has shown that the monthly billings are normally distributed with mean $\mu = \$400$ and $\sigma = \$100$, or $N(400, 100^2)$. Each month, a sample of 16 customers' bills is randomly selected by the bank to check on the billings for the month. The population parameter being investigated here is μ, and we know that in this case $\bar{x}$ has a normal distribution, since x is normal. Because $\sigma/\sqrt{n} = 100/\sqrt{16} = 25$ is the standard deviation of the $\bar{x}$'s, the distribution of $\bar{x}$ is $N(400, 25^2)$.

Figure 7.2 represents the two types of intervals discussed above. This figure shows the mean of 60 different samples (represented by a dot), each of

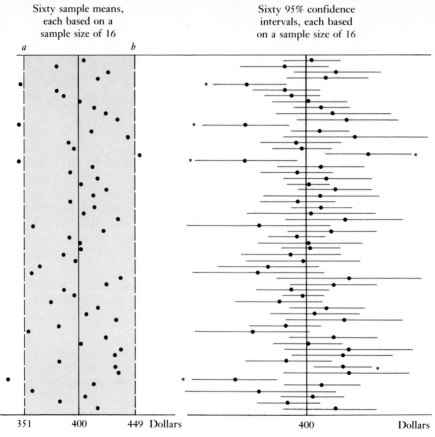

Sixty sample means,
each based on a
sample size of 16

Sixty 95% confidence
intervals, each based
on a sample size of 16

351   400   449 Dollars

400   Dollars

(a) A 95% probability interval
and 60 sample means

(b) Sixty 95% confidence intervals
based on 60 sample means

Figure 7.2
Illustration of probability
interval and of confidence
interval for an unbiased
estimator with a normal
distribution.

which was of size $n = 16$. (These samples were randomly generated from a normal distribution with $\mu = 400$ and $\sigma = 100$ using a computer package.) Part (a) of the figure illustrates a probability interval with its center at the population mean, $\mu = \$400$, and values $a = 351$ and $b = 449$, chosen so that 95% of the values of $\bar{x}$ lie between the endpoints $a = 351$ and $b = 449$. [These endpoints are found, as before, using $z = \pm 1.96$ (Table III in Appendix B) and the process described in Section 6.7.]

In repeated samples of size 16, different values of $\bar{x}$ would be calculated. A 95% probability interval means that on the average, 95 of 100 of these values of $\bar{x}$ should be between a and b. Figure 7.2(a) illustrates 60 different values of $\bar{x}$ calculated from 60 different samples of size 16. Theoretically, 95% (or 57) of these should lie within the interval. Actually, 55 of them do and 5 do not (sample numbers 5, 12, 17, 18, and 55, counting from the top). If a large number of the values of $\bar{x}$ should lie outside the interval, we may conclude that the parameters of the distribution of the billings have changed.

Part (b) of Fig. 7.2 illustrates the 95% confidence intervals based on these same 60 samples of size 16 each. Since each sample of size 16 can have different values, each sample can have a different mean and variance. Each interval depends on these values, so even though the underlying sampling distribution for $\bar{x}$ is the same in each instance, the center and spread of the interval calculated can be different. In Fig. 7.2(b), the center of each interval is at $\bar{x}$; the endpoints depend on s. Each horizontal bar corresponds to a confidence interval for a single sample. When one of these bars intersects the vertical line positioned at $\mu = 400$, the corresponding interval includes the true μ; otherwise, it does not. With a 95% confidence interval, we would expect 95%, or 57 of 60, of the confidence intervals to include μ. Although this does not happen precisely as expected, the results are close to what is predicted: the true population parameter ($\mu = 400$) is included within the horizontal bars in 54 of 60 samples, and excluded in 6 of the 60 samples (sample numbers 5, 12, 17, 18, 53, and 55, counting from the top).

The confidence intervals in Fig. 7.2(b) illustrate the precise meaning of a 95% confidence interval. When we construct such a confidence between the points a and b, we state that the interval from a to b represents a "95% confidence interval for μ." As we stated earlier, this does not mean that μ lies between the points a and b with probability 0.95 but that if we were to use the same procedures to calculate 95% confidence intervals for μ from many different samples, each of size n, the true parameter is expected to be included within these intervals, on the average, in 95 out of 100 such calculations. Since, in practice, we do not know which confidence intervals will contain μ and which will not, we say that we are 95% confident that any particular interval will include μ.

The Probability of an Error, α

It is more convenient to refer to the probability that a confidence interval will *not* include the parameter than to express the probability that it will. The former probability is usually denoted by α (the Greek letter "alpha"). The value of alpha is often referred to as the probability of making an error, since it indicates the proportion of times that one will be incorrect, or "in error," in assuming that the intervals would contain the population parameter. Since α is defined as the probability that a confidence interval will not contain the population parameter, $(1 - \alpha)$ equals the probability that the population parameter will be in the interval. It is customary to refer to confidence intervals as being of size "$100(1 - \alpha)\%$." Thus, if α is 0.05, the associated interval is a $100(1 - 0.05)\%$ or a 95% confidence interval; if a 90% confidence interval is specified, then $\alpha = 1.0 - (\frac{90}{100}) = 0.10$. In the previous example, the credit card billings problem, α equals 0.05, which means that the probability is 0.05 of making an error in saying that the interval contains the parameter when it in fact does not. In other words, on the average, we would be wrong in only 5% of the cases in which we estimate that the interval includes the population parameter.

There is an obvious trade-off between the value of α and the size of the confidence interval: the lower the value of α, the larger the interval must be.* If one need not be very confident that the population parameter will be within the interval, then a relatively small interval will suffice; if one is to be quite confident that the population parameter will be in the interval to be calculated, a relatively large interval will be necessary. The value of α is often set at 0.05 or 0.01, representing 95% and 99% confidence intervals, respectively. This procedure, although widely used, does not necessarily lead to the optimal trade-off between the size of the confidence interval and the risk of making an error.

In general, confidence intervals are constructed on the basis of sample information, so that not only do changes in α affect the size of the interval, but so do changes in n, the sample size. The more observations collected, the more confident one can be about the estimate and, as a result, the smaller the interval needed to assure a given level of confidence. Although it is usually desirable to have as small a confidence interval as possible, the size of the interval must be determined by considering the costs of sampling and how much risk or error one is willing to assume. We shall return several times to this problem of determining the optimal trade-off between the risks of making an error and the sample size. For now we merely caution the reader to be aware that the task of determining an "optimal" trade-off may not be an easy one.

Determining a Confidence Interval

Usually, one of the first steps in constructing a confidence interval is to specify how much confidence one wants to have that the population parameter will fall in the resulting interval, and the size of the sample. In other words, both α and n are usually fixed in advance. It is possible, however, under certain conditions, to consider either α or n as an unknown and to solve for the value of this unknown.

In addition to specifying α in advance, one must also specify what proportion of the probability of making an error is attributable to the fact that the population parameter will sometimes be larger than the upper bound of the confidence interval, and what proportion is attributable to the fact that the population parameter will sometimes be smaller than the lower bound of the confidence interval. As indicated previously, in determining a probability interval, the *smallest* interval is obtained by dividing the probability to be excluded outside the interval *equally* between the upper and lower tails of the distribution (assuming a symmetrical distribution). For a confidence interval, however, the decision on how to divide α into these two parts should depend on how serious or costly it is to make errors on the high side, relative to errors on the low side. Since we normally want to avoid the more costly errors, α should be divided so that these errors occur less frequently. Unfortunately, determining the costs of making an error may be quite difficult, so that the common procedure for determining a confidence interval is the same as for

---

*We assume here that other factors, such as the sample size, are held constant.

the probability intervals — that is, to exclude one-half of α, or $\alpha/2$, on the high side and one-half of α on the low side. Thus, if $\alpha = 0.05$, a value of $\alpha/2 = 0.025$ would be the probability that the population parameter will exceed the upper bound of the confidence interval, and $\alpha/2 = 0.025$ would be the probability that the lower bound will exceed the population parameter. (Such a procedure assumes that errors on the high side are equally as serious as errors on the low side.)

In the discussion thus far we have noted that a given confidence interval will depend on the particular sample values received, on α (and the way α is divided), and on the size of the sample. The final factor influencing the boundaries of a particular confidence interval is the sampling distribution of the statistic used to estimate the population parameter. Normally, the procedure for establishing a confidence interval for a population parameter is *first to find a point estimate* of the parameter. One's uncertainty about this point is then determined by finding that interval of values about the point estimate which, according to the sampling distribution of the statistic used, yields the desired degree of confidence. Since different sampling distributions are used for estimating a population mean, the binomial parameter p, and a population variance, we shall describe in separate sections the process of constructing intervals for each of these cases.

Confidence Intervals for μ with σ Known — 7.5

Suppose that we start by constructing a confidence interval for the population parameter μ based on a random sample drawn from a normal parent population *with known standard deviation*. This section is mainly a building block for the sections to follow, for seldom do we know σ without knowing μ. However, there are some circumstances where σ is known from a previous study, or perhaps does not change over time.

The natural sample statistic for estimating μ is $\bar{x}$, the sample mean, for reasons we discussed in Section 7.2. Recall that the sampling distribution of $\bar{x}$ has a mean of μ and a standard deviation of $\sigma/\sqrt{n}$. Also recall from Section 6.6 that the variable $z = (\bar{x} - \mu)/(\sigma/\sqrt{n})$ has a standardized normal distribution. Now, suppose we let the symbol z_α represent the value of that standardized normal variable z such that the probability of observing values of z greater than z_α is α. That is,

$$P(z \geq z_\alpha) = \alpha$$

Similarly, we will let $-z_\alpha$ equal the point such that

$$P(z \leq -z_\alpha) = \alpha$$

Two such points are illustrated in Fig. 7.3. Their values were derived from Table III in Appendix B.

Figure 7.3

The value of z_α cutting off α percent from the standardized normal distribution.

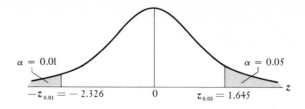

$\alpha = 0.01$

$\alpha = 0.05$

$-z_{0.01} = -2.326$ 0 $z_{0.05} = 1.645$ z

For many problems in the next several chapters, we will be given a value of α, and then will have to find the z-value cutting off *half* of this value $(\alpha/2)$ in each tail of a normal distribution (so that the total area cut off equals α). To distinguish this situation from the one described above, we will let $z_{\alpha/2}$ represent the value such that the probability $P(z \geq z_{\alpha/2}) = \alpha/2$, and let $-z_{\alpha/2}$ equal the point such that $P(z \leq -z_{\alpha/2}) = \alpha/2$. If, for example, $\alpha = 0.05$, then from Table III the value of $z_{\alpha/2}$ satisfying $P(z \geq z_{\alpha/2}) = 0.025$ is seen to be $z_{\alpha/2} = 1.96$. Then the value of $-z_{\alpha/2}$ must be -1.96, since the normal distribution is symmetric. The probability that z falls between the two limits, -1.96 and $+1.96$, is

$$P(-1.96 \leq z \leq 1.96) = 1.0 - 0.05 = 0.95$$

as shown in Fig. 7.4. In more general terms, the probability that z falls between two limits $-z_{\alpha/2}$ and $+z_{\alpha/2}$ can be written in the following form:

$$P(-z_{\alpha/2} \leq z \leq z_{\alpha/2}) = 1 - \alpha$$

Note that the interval $-z_{\alpha/2} \leq z \leq z_{\alpha/2}$ is a $100(1-\alpha)\%$ confidence interval for z. It is also a $100(1-\alpha)\%$ confidence interval for $(\overline{x} - \mu)/(\sigma/\sqrt{n})$, since $z = (\overline{x} - \mu)/(\sigma/\sqrt{n})$. Unfortunately, this is not the confidence interval we originally set out to derive, for we wanted a $100(1-\alpha)\%$ confidence interval for μ, not for $(\overline{x} - \mu)/(\sigma/\sqrt{n})$. The difference is not hard to resolve, however, for by rearranging the terms in the confidence interval for $(\overline{x} - \mu)/(\sigma/\sqrt{n})$, it is possible to find an equivalent expression that represents the confidence interval for μ. That is, by rewriting the inequalities in the expression $-z_{\alpha/2} \leq z \leq z_{\alpha/2}$, we can show that this expression is equivalent to the following inequalities.*

---

*The equivalency is shown as follows:

$-z_{\alpha/2} \leq z \leq z_{\alpha/2}$ is equivalent to $-z_{\alpha/2} \leq \dfrac{\overline{x} - \mu}{\sigma/\sqrt{n}} \leq z_{\alpha/2}$ By substitution

$-z_{\alpha/2} \dfrac{\sigma}{\sqrt{n}} \leq (\overline{x} - \mu) \leq z_{\alpha/2} \dfrac{\sigma}{\sqrt{n}}$ By multiplying each term by $\sigma/\sqrt{n}$

$-\overline{x} - z_{\alpha/2} \dfrac{\sigma}{\sqrt{n}} \leq -\mu \leq -\overline{x} + z_{\alpha/2} \dfrac{\sigma}{\sqrt{n}}$ By adding $(-\overline{x})$ to each term

$\overline{x} + z_{\alpha/2} \dfrac{\sigma}{\sqrt{n}} \geq \mu \geq \overline{x} - z_{\alpha/2} \dfrac{\sigma}{\sqrt{n}}$ By multiplying each term by (-1), thus changing the direction of both inequalities.

Figure 7.4

The value of $z_{\alpha/2}$, cutting off a total area of $\alpha = 0.05$ from the standardized normal distribution, leaving an interval including $100(1 - \alpha)\% = 95\%$ of the probability.

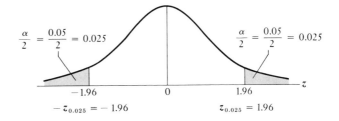

$\dfrac{\alpha}{2} = \dfrac{0.05}{2} = 0.025$ $\qquad$ $\dfrac{\alpha}{2} = \dfrac{0.05}{2} = 0.025$

-1.96 $\qquad$ 0 $\qquad$ 1.96

$-z_{0.025} = -1.96$ $\qquad\qquad$ $z_{0.025} = 1.96$

$100(1 - \alpha)\%$ confidence interval for μ, where σ is known and the parent population is normal (or $n > 30$):

$$\bar{x} - z_{\alpha/2}\frac{\sigma}{\sqrt{n}} \leq \mu \leq \bar{x} + z_{\alpha/2}\frac{\sigma}{\sqrt{n}}$$

(7.1)

To illustrate the use of Formula (7.1), consider the problem of estimating the mean annual starting salary for MBAs graduating from a large midwestern university. Suppose we want to construct a 95% confidence interval for μ on the basis of a random sample of size $n = 25$. Let us assume for now that the population standard deviation of starting salaries is known to be $\sigma = \$3150$, and this population is normally distributed. The random sample of $n = 25$ yields $\bar{x} = \$50,750$. Since we want a 95% confidence interval, the appropriate z-values are $z_{\alpha/2} = 1.96$ and $-z_{\alpha/2} = -1.96$. Substituting these two values, as well as $n = 25$, $\sigma = \$3150$, and $\bar{x} = \$50,750$, into Formula (7.1) gives the desired 95% confidence interval:*

$$\bar{x} - z_{\alpha/2}\frac{\sigma}{\sqrt{n}} \leq \mu \leq \bar{x} + z_{\alpha/2}\frac{\sigma}{\sqrt{n}}$$

$$50,750 - (1.96)\frac{3150}{\sqrt{25}} \leq \mu \leq 50,750 + (1.96)\frac{3150}{\sqrt{25}}$$

$$50,750 - 1234.80 \leq \mu \leq 50,750 + 1234.80$$

$$49,515.20 \leq \mu \leq 51,984.80$$

We can infer from this analysis, with 95% confidence, that the interval is between \$49,515.20 and \$51,984.80. That is, on the average, in 95 out of 100 such samples of size $n = 25$, an interval calculated in this manner will include the true population mean μ. We do not know, of course, whether the above interval contains μ.

---

*For this problem, and the subsequent ones in this chapter, we assume that sampling is from an infinite population, or from a finite population with replacement. When this is not the case, the finite population correction factor must be used—that is, $\sigma/\sqrt{n}$ must be multiplied by $\sqrt{(N - n)}/\sqrt{(N - 1)}$. When $n/N \leq 0.10$, the finite population correction factor may be omitted.

For the confidence interval calculated above, the probability of making an error in assuming that μ is in the specified interval is $\alpha = 0.05$. If one desires a smaller risk of error, α, then a larger confidence interval must be used. For example, in order to have $\alpha = 0.01$ (that is, a 99% confidence interval) the appropriate z-values are interpolated from Table III: $z_{\alpha/2} = 2.576$ and $-z_{\alpha/2} = -2.576$ (for $\alpha/2 = 0.005$). The new confidence interval is thus:

$$50,750 - (2.576)\frac{3150}{\sqrt{25}} \leq \mu \leq 50,750 + (2.576)\frac{3150}{\sqrt{25}}$$
$$50,750 - 1,622.88 \leq \mu \leq 50,750 + 1,622.88$$
$$49,127.12 \leq \mu \leq 52,372.88$$

Since this interval is wider than the previous one, we have greater confidence that it includes the population parameter μ. We could further increase our confidence, and decrease the risk of error, α, by extending the interval even more. Of course, there is a limit to the usefulness of the interval when it gets too large. For example, we have almost 100% confidence that the mean starting salary lies in the interval $40,000 \leq \mu \leq 60,000$, but we probably could have made such a statement without doing any sampling or statistical inference. We sample to get useful information that is more precise. To obtain it, we must be willing to subject our conclusions or inferences to a small controlled level of risk, α.

Relax the Assumption of Normality for the Population

The relationship expressed in Formula (7.1) depends on the assumptions that σ is known and that the parent population is normal. When these assumptions are met, Formula (7.1) holds for any sample size, no matter whether n is large or small. But suppose the parent population is *not normal*. In this case, if the sample size n is small, then the distribution of $(\bar{x} - \mu)/(\sigma/\sqrt{n})$ is not normal, and there is no convenient way to determine a confidence interval. On the other hand, when n is large (usually $n > 30$), we know by the central limit theorem that $(\bar{x} - \mu)/(\sigma/\sqrt{n})$ is *approximately* normally distributed; hence the confidence interval specified by Formula (7.1) is still appropriate.

Suppose in the MBA salary example we now drop the assumption of normality and assume the sample size was $n = 64$ rather than 25. Again, if $\sigma = 3150$ and $\bar{x} = 50,750$, then a 95% confidence interval is

$$50,750 - (1.96)\frac{3150}{\sqrt{64}} \leq \mu \leq 50,750 + (1.96)\frac{3150}{\sqrt{64}}$$
$$50,750 - 771.75 \leq \mu \leq 50,750 + 771.75$$
$$49,978.25 \leq \mu \leq 51,521.75$$

Confidence Intervals for μ, with σ Unknown

7.6

The other assumption we specified at the beginning of the previous section was that the population standard deviation σ is known. This may not be very realistic for many applied problems. When the mean of the population is unknown and must be estimated, it is unlikely that the standard deviation about the unknown mean will be known. Instead, the population standard deviation often must be estimated from the sample standard deviation. Under these circumstances $(\bar{x} - \mu)/(s/\sqrt{n})$ has a t-distribution, with $(n - 1)$ degrees of freedom (assuming that the parent population is normal).

The procedure for determining a $100(1 - \alpha)\%$ confidence interval using the t-distribution follows the same pattern as when the normal distribution holds, except that different limits must be used. The limits are found using t-values from Table VII of Appendix B rather than z values from Table III. Let $t_{(\alpha/2,\nu)}$ represent that value of the t-distribution with $\nu = n - 1$ degrees of freedom that excludes $\alpha/2$ of the probability in the upper tail. That is, $P(t > t_{(\alpha/2,\nu)}) = \alpha/2$; and, by symmetry, $P(t < - t_{(\alpha/2,\nu)}) = \alpha/2$. Then,

$$P(- t_{(\alpha/2,\nu)} \leq t \leq t_{(\alpha/2,\nu)}) = 1 - \alpha$$

or, since $t = (\bar{x} - \mu)/(s/\sqrt{n})$,

$$P(- t_{(\alpha/2,\nu)} \leq (\bar{x} - \mu)/(s/\sqrt{n}) \leq t_{(\alpha/2,\nu)}) = 1 - \alpha$$

Solving the inequalities (as before) for μ, it can be shown that,

$$
\boxed{
\begin{array}{l}
100(1 - \alpha)\% \text{ confidence interval for } \mu, \\
\text{population normal, } \sigma \text{ unknown:} \\[2mm]
\bar{x} - t_{(\alpha/2,\nu)}\dfrac{s}{\sqrt{n}} \leq \mu \leq \bar{x} + t_{(\alpha/2,\nu)}\dfrac{s}{\sqrt{n}}
\end{array}
}
\tag{7.2}
$$

To illustrate the use of the relationship described by Formula (7.2), suppose that we are interested in the fuel efficiency of the new cars manufactured in 1989. One way to measure this efficiency is to calculate the mean highway miles per gallon (MPG) of these cars. Assume that the population mean σ is unknown, and that the MPG for cars is normally distributed. Since σ is unknown and the value of σ has to be estimated from the sample, the t-distribution must be used to develop the confidence interval [as shown in Formula (7.2)].

Table 7.3 shows the MPG of a sample of 18 cars chosen at random from the *1989 Consumer Reports Annual Auto Issue.* Also listed in this table are the weights of these cars. The sample mean, $\bar{x}$, and the sample standard deviation, s^2, have been calculated using the B-STAT package. These are shown in the output in Table 7.4, that is, $\bar{x} = 36.778$, and $s^2 = 7.175$. Thus, the sample variance $s^2 = 51.481$ becomes our estimator for σ^2.

TABLE 7.3   Sample data for highway MPG for 1989 cars

Car model	Weight (lb)	Highway MPG
Acura Integra	2480	36
Ford Festiva	1715	47
Geo Metro	1640	58
Nissan Sentra	2275	38
VW Fox	2160	41
Dodge Daytona	2935	43
Ford Mustang	3310	28
Nissan Pulsar NX	2390	38
Buick Skylark	2640	36
Chevrolet Cavalier	2485	38
Nissan Stanza	2830	34
Volvo 240	2985	31
Chevrolet Celebrity	2850	33
Chrysler Le Baron	2915	34
Dodge Dynasty	3150	35
Sterling 827	3295	30
Saab 900	3065	32
Ford LTD	3790	30

Source: 1989 Consumer Reports Annual Auto Issue

Assume that we wish to obtain a 99% confidence interval for the interval estimate of the MPG. From Table VII for the t-distribution, we have to find the critical values for a 99% confidence interval, $\pm t_{(\alpha/2,\nu)}$. Using the row for $\nu = n - 1 = 17$ degrees of freedom, and the column for $\alpha/2 = 0.01/2 = 0.005$, we obtain $t_{(0.005,17)} = 2.898$. Substituting the appropriate values of $\bar{x}, s, t$, and $\sqrt{n}$ into Formula (7.2) gives

$$\bar{x} - t_{(\alpha/2,\nu)}\frac{s}{\sqrt{n}} \leq \mu \leq \bar{x} + t_{(\alpha/2,\nu)}\frac{s}{\sqrt{n}}$$

$$36.778 - 2.898\frac{7.175}{\sqrt{18}} \leq \mu \leq 36.778 + 2.898\frac{7.175}{\sqrt{18}}$$

$$36.778 - 2.898(1.691) \leq \mu \leq 36.778 + 2.898(1.691)$$

$$36.778 - 4.901 \leq \mu \leq 36.778 + 4.901$$

$$31.877 \leq \mu \leq 41.679$$

TABLE 7.4   B-STAT output for the MPG data

```
NUMBER OF CASES: 18   NUMBER OF VARIABLES: 1
NO   NAME   N    MEAN     STD. DEV.   MINIMUM   MAXIMUM
 1    MPG   18   36.778     7.175      28.0      58.0
```

The interval from 31.877 to 41.679 thus represents a 99% confidence interval for the mean highway MPG for the 1989 new cars. We might be disappointed that the interval is so large. Perhaps we could have guessed that the mean was between 30 and 42. This 99% confidence interval may not be much different from our nonstatistical guess. However, the statistical work has given us a precise method of inference, a precise point estimate of μ, and exact knowledge about the chance of error in assuming that the true mean does lie in this interval, namely, $\alpha = 0.01$. We can decrease the length of the interval in two ways if we wish: Either allow a greater chance of error α, or put more time and effort (cost) into sampling, to increase n.

Determining the Size of *n*

7.7

Thus far we have calculated the width of each confidence interval based on the assumption that the sample size, n, is known. In many practical situations, however, the decision maker does not know what size sample is best. Instead, the decision maker may prefer to specify the width of the interval desired and use this information to solve for n. The conventional approach to this problem of solving for n in these cases is to ask the decision maker two questions:

1. The level of confidence desired, that is, the value of $100(1 - \alpha)$; and
2. The *maximum* difference (D) desired between the estimate of the population parameter and the true population parameter—that is, the value of D is the maximum amount of "error" permitted in estimating the population parameter.

We will consider confidence intervals for both the population mean, μ, and the population proportion, p.

For Statistical Inference on μ

Population Normal, μ Known.   First, we consider the problem of determining n when the decision maker wants a $100(1 - \alpha)\%$ confidence for μ, given that the parent population has a normal distribution with a known standard deviation. In this case, we know the variable

$$z = \frac{\bar{x} - \mu}{\sigma/\sqrt{n}}$$

is $N(0, 1)$. Now if the required level of confidence is $1 - \alpha$, then the above equation results in the following $100(1 - \alpha)\%$ confidence interval for $\bar{x} - \mu$:

$$-z_{\alpha/2}\frac{\sigma}{\sqrt{n}} \leq \bar{x} - \mu \leq z_{\alpha/2}\frac{\sigma}{\sqrt{n}} \tag{7.3}$$

Since the normal distribution is symmetric, we can concentrate on the right-hand inequality, $\bar{x} - \mu \leq z_{\alpha/2}\sigma/\sqrt{n}$. This inequality says that the largest value that $\bar{x} - \mu$ can assume is $z_{\alpha/2}\sigma/\sqrt{n}$. But we also know that our decision maker says that the largest value for $|\bar{x} - \mu|$ to assume is some amount D. Hence, we can write

$$D = z_{\alpha/2}\frac{\sigma}{\sqrt{n}}$$

Solving this relationship for n gives the value of n which will assure the decision maker, with $100(1 - \alpha)\%$ confidence, that $|\bar{x} - \mu|$ will be no larger than D. Solving we get:

> *Optimal sample size:* $n = \dfrac{z_{\alpha/2}^2\, \sigma^2}{D^2}$ (7.4)

To illustrate Formula (7.4), suppose that, in the MBA salary problem of Section 7.5, we wanted to construct a 95% confidence interval for the mean in such a manner that the sample result, $\bar{x}$, and the population mean differ by no more than \$500; that is, $|\bar{x} - \mu| \leq D = 500$. Assuming, as before, that the parent population is normal, and $\sigma = \$3150$, how large should n be to satisfy these conditions?

From Table III, $z_{\alpha/2} = 1.96$ when $\alpha/2 = 0.025$. Substituting this value and $D = 500$, $\sigma = \$3150$, into Formula (7.4) yields the appropriate value for n:

$$n = \frac{(1.96)^2(3150)^2}{(500)^2} = 152.47$$

We always round up in this type of problem, to be assured that the sample size is large enough; hence, a random sample of at least 153 MBAs is needed to be assured that, 95% of the time, the value of $\bar{x}$ will be within \$500 of the true population mean, μ.

Population Not Normal, σ Known.   If the population is not assumed to be normal but the standard deviation is known, the same method as above can be used to determine the minimal sample size necessary to satisfy the conditions of confidence and accuracy. By the central limit theorem, we know that the distribution of sample means approaches the normal distribution. Thus, once the necessary sample size is obtained, we can check to see if that size n exceeds 30, and if it does, then we are confident our method of solution was appropriate.

Population Normal, σ Unknown.   If the population is normal, but the standard deviation is unknown, then the appropriate statistic to use is the t variable, $t = (\bar{x} - \mu)/(s/\sqrt{n})$. Again, the maximum difference for $|\bar{x} - \mu| = D$ is obtained from the decision maker. In this case, we are stuck for a value of s, since s must be calculated from a sample, and we haven't taken a sample yet (the whole purpose is to decide what sample size to take). To make matters worse, the appropriate t value to use in calculating a $100(1 - \alpha)\%$ confidence interval is $t_{(\alpha/2,\nu)}$, which again depends on the unknown sample size. To make a long story short, we conclude this paragraph by saying that the solution for n in this case is not a direct process, but can be achieved by a succession of iterative steps that we will not present here.

Confidence Interval for σ^2 (Optional)*

7.8

Under some circumstances it may be desirable to construct a confidence interval for an estimate of an unknown population variance. As mentioned before, the telephone company is often interested in the *variability* of the length of telephone conversations, and a contractor who is about to purchase some steel girders will probably be interested in the variance of their tensile strengths. A government economist may be just as concerned about the variability of taxes paid among individuals as he is about the average tax paid, because the income redistribution effect of taxation is very important. In these cases it may be important to establish limits on just how large or small σ^2 might be; that is, to determine a confidence interval for the population variance.

To construct a $100(1 - \alpha)\%$ confidence interval for σ^2 when sampling from a *normal* population, recall from Section 6.10 that the variable $(n - 1)s^2/\sigma^2$ has a chi-square distribution with $(n - 1)$ degrees of freedom. Denote the point that cuts off $\alpha/2$ of the area of the right-hand side of a chi-square distribution with $\nu = n - 1$ degrees of freedom as $\chi^2_{(\alpha/2,\nu)}$. That is,

$$P(\chi^2 \geq \chi^2_{(\alpha/2,\nu)}) = \frac{\alpha}{2}$$

Since the chi-square distribution is not symmetrical, $-\chi^2_{(\alpha/2,\nu)}$ does *not* give the appropriate value for cutting off $\alpha/2$ of the left-hand side of this distribution. The point that does give the correct probability is that value of χ^2 that cuts off $1 - \alpha/2$ of the right-hand tail, or $\chi^2_{(1 - \alpha/2,\nu)}$. That is,

$$P(\chi^2 \geq \chi^2_{(\alpha/2,\nu)}) = \frac{\alpha}{2} \quad \text{and} \quad P(\chi^2 \leq \chi^2_{(1 - \alpha/2,\nu)}) = \frac{\alpha}{2}$$

The interval between the points $\chi^2_{(1 - \alpha/2,\nu)}$ and $\chi^2_{(\alpha/2,\nu)}$ thus contains $1 - \alpha$ probability. It is now possible to define a $100(1 - \alpha)\%$ confidence interval for the variable $(n - 1)s^2/\sigma^2$:

$$\chi^2_{(1 - \alpha/2,\nu)} \leq \frac{(n - 1)s^2}{\sigma^2} \leq \chi^2_{(\alpha/2,\nu)} \tag{7.5}$$

*This section, which may be omitted without loss in continuity, presupposes that the reader has covered Section 6.10.

Again, solving these inequalities for the unknown parameter σ^2 gives

> 100(1 − α)% *confidence interval for* σ^2, *with parent population normal:*
>
> $$\frac{(n-1)s^2}{\chi^2_{(\alpha/2,\nu)}} \leq \sigma^2 \leq \frac{(n-1)s^2}{\chi^2_{(1-\alpha/2,\nu)}}$$
>
> (7.6)

It is important to note that, in going from (7.5) to (7.6), the sense of the inequalities has changed. Thus, the larger value of χ^2 now appears in the denominator of the *lower* endpoint for σ^2, while the smaller value of χ^2 is in the denominator of the term that gives the upper endpoint for σ^2.

Consider once again the fuel efficiency example for 1989 cars and assume this time we are interested in estimating the variance of the population (of highway MPG), using the same sample of size $n = 18$ reported in Table 7.3. The best point estimate of σ^2 is s^2, which is computed from this sample to be $s^2 = 51.481$. To achieve an interval estimate for σ^2 with a known level of confidence and a known risk of error, let us compute a 95% confidence interval for σ^2.

Figure 7.5 illustrates the relevant chi-square distribution for $\nu = n - 1 = 17$ degrees of freedom and the cutoff values for $\alpha/2 = 0.025$ and $1 - \alpha/2 = 0.975$. These values are not equidistant from the mean of the chi-square $(E[\chi^2] = \nu = 17)$ because χ^2 is a skewed distribution. The cutoff values from Table V in terms of the chi-square distribution for $\nu = 17$ and $\alpha/2 = 0.025$ and $1 - \alpha/2 = 0.975$ are found to be 30.191 and 7.564, respectively. Thus, $P(7.564 \leq \chi^2_{17} \leq 30.191) = 1 - \alpha = 0.95$.

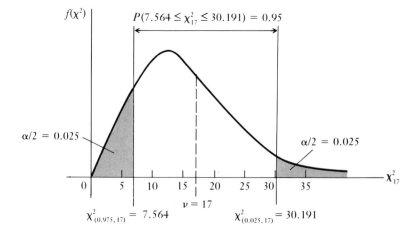

Figure 7.5
The values of $\chi^2_{(\alpha/2, \nu)}$ and $\chi^2_{(1-\alpha/2, \nu)}$ cutting off a total area of $\alpha = 0.05$ from the chi-square distribution with $n = 18$, leaving an interval including 95% of the probability in the middle.

Substituting the values for $\chi^2_{(0.025,\ 17)} = 30.191$ and $\chi^2_{(0.975,\ 17)} = 7.564$, $n - 1 = 17$, and $s^2 = 51.481$ into Formula (7.6) gives

$$\frac{17(51.481)}{30.191} \leq \sigma^2 \leq \frac{17(51.481)}{7.564}$$

$$28.988 \leq \sigma^2 \leq 115.703$$

On the basis of this sample of 18, one can infer with 95% confidence that the population variance lies between 28.988 and 115.703. There is a 2.5% chance of error that the true σ^2 may be greater 115.703 and a 2.5 chance of error that it may be less than 28.988.

□ Appendix (Optional)

7.9

Deriving a Maximum-Likelihood Estimate (MLE)

A maximum-likelihood estimate can be derived in a more rigorous fashion through the use of calculus. Determining a MLE involves finding that value of the population parameter which maximizes the function representing the likelihood of obtaining the sample results. This function is called the **likelihood function** and is denoted by the letter L. In many problems, determining the formula for the likelihood function may not be too difficult, although the notation for describing L may seem formidable. Assume that the random variable x_1 represents all possible values of x that could appear first in a series of sample observations, x_2 represents all possible values of x that could appear second in a series of sample observations, and so forth, x_n representing all possible values of x that could appear last in a series of n sample observations. Now, let x_1 be an observed value of the variable x_1, x_2 be an observed value of x_2, and x_n be an observed value of x_n. If the parent population is discrete with parameter θ, then the probability that a particular sample $x_1, x_2, \ldots, x_n$ will occur is the likelihood function L, where L is conditional on θ:

$$L = P(x_1 = x_1, x_2 = x_2, \ldots, x_n = x_n | \theta)$$

If the parent population x is continuous, L equals the joint density function of $x_1, x_2, \ldots, x_n$, which is $f(x_1, x_2, \ldots, x_n | \theta)$.

Once the function representing L has been determined, the task is to find that value of the population parameter which maximizes this function. Maximizing L can be accomplished in the normal fashion—taking the first derivative with respect to the parameter in question, setting this derivative equal to zero, and then solving for the optimal value of the parameter. In many cases it is easier to maximize the logarithm of L rather than L itself; this transformation does not change the optimal solution, but often makes finding the first derivative much easier.

Perhaps the easiest likelihood function to determine is the one for an experiment generating independent repeated Bernoulli trials. In this case the probability of a sample $x_1, x_2, \ldots, x_n$ depends only on the number of observed successes (and failures), and this probability is given by the binomial distribution. Hence,

$$L = \frac{n!}{x!\,(n-x)!}\,p^x q^{n-x}$$

Determining the MLE for this particular L is a relatively straightforward differentiation problem for anyone familiar with the process of taking the derivative of a logarithm (see Appendix A). That is,

$$\log L = \log\!\left[\frac{n!}{x!\,(n-x)!}\,p^x q^{n-x}\right]$$

$$= \log\frac{n!}{x!\,(n-x)!} + x\log p + (n-x)\log(1-p)$$

$$\partial\log L/\partial p = x\!\left(\frac{1}{p}\right) + (n-x)\!\left[\frac{1}{(1-p)}\right]\!(-1)$$

$$0 = \frac{x}{p} - \frac{(n-x)}{(1-p)}$$

$$p = \frac{x}{n}$$

(Note that p in this case is the estimator and not the population parameter.) The sample proportion was previously shown to be unbiased, consistent, and sufficient. The result proves that, in addition, x/n is the maximum-likelihood estimator of p.

The process described above can be used to find an MLE for the population mean and variance when sampling from a normal population. Assume that n independent observations, $x_1, x_2, \ldots, x_n$, are drawn from a normal population with mean μ and variance σ^2. The probability that these values all occur jointly is $L = f(x_1, x_2, \ldots, x_n)$, and since the n sample values are independent, by the definition of independence presented in Chapter 3 the joint density function can be written as the product of the individual functions, or as $L = f(x_1)f(x_2)\ldots f(x_n)$. For the normal distribution each one of these individual density functions has the following form:

$$f(x_i) = \frac{1}{\sigma\sqrt{2\pi}}\,e^{-(1/2)[(x_i-\mu)/\sigma]^2}$$

Substituting the preceding frequency function for each of the values of i in the formula for L gives the likelihood function for this problem:

$$L = \frac{1}{\sigma\sqrt{2\pi}}\exp\!\left[-\frac{1}{2}\!\left(\frac{x_1-\mu}{\sigma}\right)^2\right]\cdot\frac{1}{\sigma\sqrt{2\pi}}\exp\!\left[-\frac{1}{2}\!\left(\frac{x_2-\mu}{\sigma}\right)^2\right]$$

$$\cdots\frac{1}{\sigma\sqrt{2\pi}}\exp\!\left[-\frac{1}{2}\!\left(\frac{x_n-\mu}{\sigma}\right)^2\right]$$

The formula for L can be simplified by combining the common terms:

$$L = \frac{1}{\sigma^n (2\pi)^{n/2}} \exp\left[-\frac{1}{2} \sum_{i=1}^{n} \left(\frac{x_i - \mu}{\sigma} \right)^2 \right]$$

Maximizing L with respect to μ yields the MLE for the population mean, while maximizing L with respect to σ^2 yields the MLE for the population variance. Again, it is easier to maximize L by first taking the logarithm of L, finding the first derivative of this logarithm, setting the derivative equal to zero, and solving. Note, in the derivation that follows, that natural logarithms (logs to the base e, denoted by the symbol $\ln$,) are used, rather than common logarithms.

$$\ln L = \ln\left[\frac{1}{\sigma^n (2\pi)^{n/2}} e^{-(1/2)\sum[(x_i - \mu)/\sigma]^2} \right]$$

$$= \ln\frac{1}{\sigma^n} + \ln\left(\frac{1}{2\pi} \right)^{n/2} - \frac{1}{2} \sum_{i=1}^{n} \left[\frac{(x_i - \mu)}{\sigma} \right]^2$$

$$= -n \ln \sigma - \left(\frac{n}{2} \right) \ln 2\pi - \frac{1}{2\sigma^2} \sum_{i=1}^{n} (x_i - \mu)^2$$

$$\frac{\partial \ln L}{\partial \mu} = \frac{1}{\sigma^2} \sum_{i=1}^{n} (x_i - \mu) = \left(\frac{1}{\sigma^2} \right)\left(\sum_{i=1}^{n} x_i - n\mu \right)$$

$$0 = \sum_{i=1}^{n} x_i - n\mu$$

$$\mu = \sum_{i=1}^{n} x_i / n = \overline{x}$$

(Note that μ in this case is the estimator and not the population parameter.) This result implies that, given a particular sample $x_1, x_2, \ldots, x_n$, the population mean most likely to produce this sample is $\mu = \overline{x}$. Thus, a value of $\overline{x} = 115$, representing, for example, the mean IQ of a sample of college undergraduates, most likely came from a population with $\mu = 115$.

Instead of differentiating $\ln L$ with respect to μ, the first derivative could have been taken with respect to σ^2, yielding an MLE of the population variance. This analysis leads to a rather interesting result—the MLE of σ^2 is *not* an unbiased estimator. Using $\overline{x}$ to estimate μ, it can be shown that the maximum-likelihood estimate of σ^2 is

$$\left(\frac{1}{n} \right) \sum_{i=1}^{n} (x_i - \overline{x})^2$$

which we know from earlier in this chapter is not an unbiased estimator of σ^2. Thus, if one wants an estimate of the variance of a population that makes the sample appear most likely, then the statistic shown above is the optimal choice. On the other hand, if it seems more desirable to have an estimate that, on the average, equals the true value, then s^2 is the best choice. The cost of making an error in an estimation problem may determine which approach is more appropriate when the sample size is small and the difference between the two is relatively large.

Summary   **7.10**

Table 7.5 summarizes the test statistics and confidence intervals described in this chapter for various situations of statistical inference.

TABLE 7.5   Summary of test statistics and confidence intervals for statistical inference

Unknown parameter	Population characteristics and other description	Reference sections	Test statistic involving the best sample estimator	Endpoints for $100(1\alpha)\%$ confidence interval	Reference formula
Mean μ	Population $N(\mu, \sigma^2)$ or sample size $n \geq 30$, σ known	6.7 7.5	$z = \dfrac{(\bar{x} - \mu)}{(\sigma/\sqrt{n})}$	$\bar{x} \pm z_{\alpha/2}(\sigma/\sqrt{n})$	(7.1)
Mean μ	Population $N(\mu,\sigma^2)$, σ unknown	6.9 7.6	$t_{\nu \, \text{d.f.}} = \dfrac{(\bar{x} - \mu)}{(s/\sqrt{n})}$	$\bar{x} \pm t_{(\alpha/2,\nu)}(s/\sqrt{n})$ where $\nu = n - 1$	(7.2)
Variance σ^2	Population $N(\mu,\sigma^2)$	6.10 7.8	$\chi^2_{\nu \, \text{d.f.}} = \dfrac{(n-1)s^2}{\sigma^2}$	$\dfrac{(n-1)s^2}{\chi^2_{(\alpha/2,\,\nu)}}$ and $\dfrac{(n-1)s^2}{\chi^2_{(1-\alpha/2,\nu)}}$ where $\nu = n - 1$	(7.9)

Problems

7.13 a) What factors must be established before a confidence interval can be constructed?

b) What does the Greek letter α represent? How would you suggest the level of α be established?

7.14 Explain what is meant by a "$100(1 - \alpha)\%$ confidence interval for μ"?

7.15 Find $z_{\alpha/2}$ for each of the following values of α:

a) $\alpha = 0.01$ **b)** $\alpha = 0.05$ **c)** $\alpha = 0.10$ **d)** $\alpha = 0.20$

7.16 a) Write the expression for calculating a $100(1 - \alpha)\%$ confidence interval for μ on the basis of a random sample of size n (large) from a normal population with mean μ and standard deviation σ.

b) Write the expression for calculating a $100(1 - \alpha)\%$ confidence interval for μ on the basis of a random sample of size n (small) from a normal population with mean μ and unknown standard deviation. Would your answer change if the sample size n were larger (> 30)?

7.17 What is the confidence level of each of the following confidence intervals for μ:

a) $\bar{x} \pm 1.96\sigma/\sqrt{n}$ **b)** $\bar{x} \pm 2.576\sigma/\sqrt{n}$

c) $\bar{x} \pm 1.645\sigma/\sqrt{n}$ **d)** $\bar{x} \pm 1.282\sigma/\sqrt{n}$

7.18 What is the confidence level of each of the following confidence intervals for μ:

a) $\bar{x} \pm 1.833s/\sqrt{10}$ **b)** $\bar{x} \pm 2.093s/\sqrt{20}$ **c)** $\bar{x} \pm 2.947s/\sqrt{16}$

7.19 Describe the relationship between the value of $z_{\alpha/2}$ and the width of the confidence interval.

7.20 Based on a survey of 100 people who purchased an IBM PS/2 computer, a marketing analyst for IBM has established a 99% confidence interval for the mean income for all new PS/2 owners to be

$$\$37,458 \leq \mu \leq \$50,542$$

Based on this information and the confidence interval μ, determine whether the following statements are true or false. If a statement is false, explain why it is false.

a) Ninety-nine percent of all people with an income between $37,458 and $50,542 will purchase an IBM PS/2 computer.

b) If an infinite number of such intervals were constructed, IBM would find that 99% of the $\bar{x}$ values would fall between $37,458 and $50,542.

c) If an infinite number of such intervals were constructed using the same procedures, 99% of these intervals, on the average, would contain the population mean income of purchasers of PS/2 computers.

d) Based on this confidence interval, IBM can state that 99% of all purchasers have an income between $37,458 and $50,542.

7.21 Describe the relationship between the size of the sample and the width of the confidence interval.

7.22 Suppose you wish to estimate the mean of a normal population using a 95% confidence interval and σ^2 is known to be equal to 9. To see the effect of the sample size on the length of the confidence interval, calculate the sampling error for $n = 9, 16, 25, 36, 49$, and 64. Plot the sampling error on a graph as a function of the sample size n. What conclusions can you draw from this graph?

7.23 Suppose you wish to estimate a population mean with an 80% confidence interval and a sampling error of 0.5. If you know from prior sampling that the population is normal with σ^2 equal to 2.3, how many observations would you include in your sample?

7.24 According to an article in *The Chronicle of Higher Education,* a survey of university faculty showed that the average yearly salary of faculty members was $35,600. The article stated "the 'confidence interval' for that figure is $624, meaning that there is a 95% probability that the estimated average varies from the true average of the sample population by no more than plus or minus $624." Comment on this interpretation of a confidence interval.

7.25 The admissions office of the graduate school of business administration at a large southern university would like to construct a confidence interval for the average GMAT score of the entering class of 1990. A random sample of 20 students shows that the average GMAT score was 615. The population standard deviation is known to be 52. Construct 90%, 95%, and 99% confidence intervals for the average GMAT score.

7.26 Consider the information in Problem 7.25. Suppose that the sample size was increased to 30 and the average GMAT score was still 615. Construct 90%, 95%, and 99% confidence intervals for the new sample size. Compare the confidence intervals in this problem with the ones in Problem 7.25. Explain the differences between the two sets of intervals.

7.27 A computer manufacturer wants to estimate the mean lifetime of a hard disk. The time to failure is assumed to be normally distributed, with a known standard deviation of $\sigma = 3000$ hours. A random sample of 15 computers resulted in an average time to failure of 27,350 hours. Use this information to construct a 99% confidence interval for μ.

7.28 Every month the AAA Motor Club surveys gasoline prices in various parts of the country. Suppose that a sample of 75 gas stations across Michigan shows that the average price for unleaded premium gas during December 1989 was $0.92 with a standard deviation of $0.02. Construct a 95% confidence interval for the average gasoline price.

7.29 Consider the data in Problem 7.28. Determine how many gas stations would have to be sampled to reduce the length of the 95% confidence interval sampling error to $0.0035.

7.30 Suppose that a random sample of 40 undergraduate accounting majors from the 1990 class shows a mean starting salary of $30,340. If the resulting 95% confidence interval for the mean starting salary of all such accounting majors has length $1580, what can you say about the sample standard deviation, assuming that the confidence interval was formed using the sample standard deviation?

7.31 A loan officer at the First National Bank in Columbia, South Carolina, wishes to determine the mean loan balance for all customers who are currently carrying overdraft loans. A random sample of 20 shows a sample mean $587.25 and a sample standard deviation of $93.76. Construct a 90% confidence interval for μ, assuming that the loan balances are normally distributed.

7.32 Consider the information in Problem 7.31. Determine a 90% confidence interval for σ^2. (Note that this problem requires information from Section 7.8, which is optional.)

7.33 Consider the information in Problem 7.31. Determine how many customers would have to be sampled to reduce the length of the 90% confidence interval sampling error to $25.

7.34 The management of Village Pantry, a chain of convenience stores, wishes to analyze the purchase amounts of customers at one of the stores. A sample of 20 customers shows the following purchase amounts:

| 13.67 | 9.08 | 6.98 | 14.76 | 4.56 | 11.23 | 12.80 | 13.73 | 5.92 | 8.45 |
| 11.74 | 3.45 | 16.54 | 5.80 | 7.75 | 10.50 | 8.15 | 11.76 | 9.82 | 13.87 |

Calculate the sample mean and standard deviation using a computer package. Assuming that the distribution of all purchase amounts is normal, construct a 80% confidence interval for μ.

7.35 Consider the information in Problem 7.34. Using the sample standard deviation, determine a 80% confidence interval for σ^2. (Note that to solve this problem, you will require information from Section 7.8.)

7.36 The yield of a chemical manufactured in a chemical plant varies from day to day. A random sample of 10 days' data gives the following yields in pounds:

674   843   689   764   642   745   714   808   638   792

a) Calculate the sample mean and sample variance (using a computer package), and develop a 95% confidence interval for the mean yield. What assumptions did you make in order to develop this interval?

b) If the population cannot be assumed to be normal, what would you have to do to develop a confidence interval?

c) Determine how many days would have to be sampled to reduce the length of the 95% confidence interval sampling error to 30 lb?

7.37 In Table 7.3 in Section 7.6, the data from the *Consumer Reports Annual Auto Issue* included the weight of each car in the sample. Calculate the sample mean and sample standard deviation and develop a 80% confidence interval for the mean weight of a new 1989 car. What assumption did you make to develop this interval?

7.38 In November 1989 *Business Week* published "The Corporate Elite," the profiles of the chief executives of the 1000 top corporations in the United States. A random sample of 15 executives revealed the information shown in Table 7.6 about their tenure with respective organizations (in years) and their compensation (in thousands of dollars):

TABLE 7.6   Compensation and
tenure data for CEOs

Sample no.	Tenure (years)	Compensation ($)
1	40	585,000
2	35	2,066,000
3	20	838,000
4	30	502,000
5	31	269,000
6	41	537,000
7	22	1,279,000
8	10	470,000
9	14	475,000
10	20	568,000
11	39	549,000
12	14	541,000
13	20	739,000
14	33	1,007,000
15	39	857,000

Source: "The Corporate Elite," *Business Week,* November 1989

TABLE 7.7 New York Stock Exchange share volume (1988)

Date	Volume (millions)
Oct. 17	119.3
Dec. 13	132.3
June 16	161.6
Jan. 26	138.4
May 9	166.3
Mar. 1	200.0
Oct. 27	196.5
Dec. 5	144.7
June 30	227.4
Nov. 1	151.3
Aug. 11	173.0
Feb. 23	192.3

Source: Standard and Poor's Statistical Service, October 1989

a) Determine a 95% confidence interval for the mean tenure, assuming that the population is normally distributed.

b) Also determine a 95% confidence interval for the mean compensation of executives, again assuming that the population is normally distributed.

7.39 Political polls are generally reported using a 95% confidence interval. If a poll reports that the preference for candidate A is 43% with an error of 3%, explain the interpretation of this statement. If in the same poll candidate B is preferred by 39% of the respondents, what statistical inferences can you draw from these results?

7.40 Table 7.7 gives the number of stocks traded daily on the New York Stock Exchange during 1988 for 12 days chosen at random. Using the data from the

TABLE 7.8

Company	Profit margin %	Return on equity %	Dividend yield %	Turnover of shares %
Lubrizol	11.7	21.3	3.65	98.7
Adobe Systems	25.3	47.6	0.38	306.3
Digital Equipment	9.8	16.0	0.00	169.8
Owens Corning	9.0	13.1	3.70	40.6
NY Electric & Gas	12.8	13.5	8.99	64.0
Dean Foods	3.4	16.6	1.99	26.5
Consolidated Edison	11.7	13.3	7.58	41.8
Union Electric	14.4	13.8	8.47	53.9
Foxboro	1.8	5.3	0.32	26.0
Forest Laboratories	22.1	11.5	0.00	87.9
Caterpillar	5.9	15.0	2.09	93.5
NCNB	8.9	13.3	2.78	56.2
Chesapeake	7.2	19.3	2.53	24.5
Precision Castparts	7.3	17.3	0.26	183.1
Inter. Dairy Queen	8.3	34.8	0.00	24.2
TRW	3.7	16.6	3.90	42.5
Omnicom Group	4.4	19.5	4.96	86.2
Equitable Resources	11.6	10.2	3.79	29.8
NWA	2.4	8.4	1.44	180.5
Navistar Inter.	5.8	34.2	0.00	97.9
Capital Holding	9.3	16.5	2.99	39.2
National Medical	5.1	16.8	2.47	62.7
AMP	12.0	21.0	2.79	61.6
Fleetwood Enterprises	4.3	18.0	2.16	62.4
Compaq Computer	12.4	31.3	0.00	330.1
Pepsico	5.9	25.7	1.97	56.0
Stone Container	9.1	35.6	2.40	131.1
Zayre	2.9	10.3	1.59	229.8
Southtrust	10.8	15.2	3.98	21.6
Mercantile Bankshares	14.8	15.5	3.44	302.0

Source: Business Week, The Top 1000, 1989

table, calculate the sample mean and the sample variance, and determine a 90% confidence interval for the mean number of stocks traded daily on the New York Stock Exchange during 1988. What assumptions did you make in developing this confidence interval? Would you consider these assumptions to be reasonable for this problem?

7.41 In July 1989 *Business Week* published its annual list of the top 1000 corporations in the United States. The companies are ranked by stock market value. For each company information about market value, sales, profits, assets, valuation, dividends, and shares is presented. Table 7.8 lists information from this publication for 30 corporations selected at random. Included in this table is data on profit margin, return on equity, dividend yield, and turnover of shares, all in percentage terms.

   a) Use a computer software package to calculate the sample mean and standard deviation for the profit margin.

   b) To develop a 95% confidence interval for the population mean profit margin, what assumptions would you make? Can you make these assumptions with the given information? Explain your answer.

   c) Determine the 95% confidence interval for the population mean profit margin.

   d) What sample size would you require to reduce the length of the 95% sampling error to 1.5?

7.42 Consider the information in Problem 7.41.

   a) Calculate the sample mean and standard deviation for the return on equity and develop a 90% confidence interval for the mean return on equity.

   b) Calculate the sample mean and standard deviation for the dividend yield and develop a 90% confidence interval for the mean dividend yield.

   c) Calculate the sample mean and standard deviation for the turnover of shares. Develop a 90% confidence interval for σ^2.

Chapter 8

Quality Control

*The man who insists on seeing
with perfect clearness before he
decides, never decides.*

HENRI FREDERIC AMIEL

Introduction 8.1

Although methods of quality control were first developed to monitor and
improve the quality of products in manufacturing, the scope of quality control
has expanded beyond this application in recent years. The quality of performance is important for all enterprises, whether they produce goods or services. For example, hospitals and restaurants need to be as concerned with the
quality of the "products" they deliver as are automobile manufacturers, even
though their "products" are classed as services. Quality control techniques are
applied in almost all areas of business. Applications range from monitoring ser-
vice-oriented functions such as financial entries in an accounting system to the
traditional application of monitoring quality of manufactured goods. Quality
control is now increasingly used in the design of new products as well.

The need for quality control became important when mass production
began during the industrial revolution. Quality control techniques evolved
during the 1920s when Walter Shewhart of Bell Labs developed control charts
to identify the causes of variation in manufacturing processes. Unfortunately,
his work had little immediate impact since industry did not, at the time, have
the economic resources to invest in quality control because of the economic
Great Depression. During the Second World War, however, the need to produce reliable weapons and other goods for the war stimulated the use of quality control methods. Many of the concepts of modern quality control
originated during this period.

After the war, quality control no longer seemed as important. Demand for consumer goods rose sharply and the major concern of producers in countries such as the United States and Great Britain became expanding the volume of production to meet this demand. As a result, the use of quality control in these countries declined. A major exception to this decline was Japan, where the American statistician W. Edwards Deming guided a large-scale program of statistical quality control. The success of the Japanese over the past 25 years or so, as measured by their reputation for manufacturing products of a very high quality has, in recent years, renewed interest in the area of quality control.

Many major corporations have initiated quality control programs. For example, all three of the big U.S. automobile manufacturers, General Motors, Ford, and Chrysler, have established elaborate programs to improve quality. Production workers at these companies receive extensive training in the fundamentals of quality control. These programs also extend to their suppliers and dealers. As a result of these initiatives, the quality of cars manufactured in the United States has improved significantly over the past few years. Another industry where quality control programs in manufacturing are well established is the computer industry.

The application of quality control methods is not confined to manufacturing. Its use has increased significantly in the service sector, where applications include banking, insurance, the federal government, state and local governments, health services, transportation, the retail trade, and public utilities. For example, in banking one application of quality control is monitoring the printed quality of checks. Checks are processed using magnetic ink character recognition (MICR) equipment. If the device sensing the magnetic characters fails to read one or more of the magnetic numbers, a check is rejected, resulting in increased costs of processing. The rate of rejection is directly affected by the quality of the checks and typically falls between 0.5% and 1%. Thus, the number of checks rejected allows the monitoring of the quality of the checks.

In the insurance industry, quality control is used to monitor the accuracy of operations processing information, the time to process claims, and audits. Several insurance companies, including United States Fidelity and Guaranty and Blue Cross/Blue Shield, have improved their services because of quality control programs. Quality control programs also exist in many areas of the federal government, ranging from audits for tax returns to surveys of imported goods for customs to monitoring the effectiveness of social services.*

Statistical Process Control

The concept of a process is fundamental to studying quality control. A "process" may be defined as any set of conditions that work together to produce a given result. For example, in building an automobile, each step in the manufacturing line may be considered as a process, with its own input and out-

---

*For more information on applications of quality control in the service sector, see reference 15.

Figure 8.1
A single process.

put (see Fig. 8.1). Thus, attaching automobile body parts such as doors and fenders to the frame would each constitute a separate process, as would preparing the bodywork for painting, applying the primer, spraying the paint, and drying it. Producing a car can then be thought of as a series of individual interrelated processes that make up the manufacturing line, as shown in Fig. 8.2. The quality of the output of these processes can be monitored using statistical methods. Using statistical methods in quality control is called **statistical process control (SPC).**

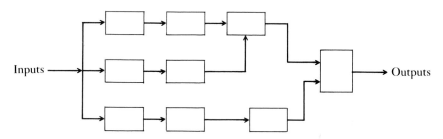

Figure 8.2
A typical series of interrelated processes.

There are two basic approaches to monitoring the quality of an output from a process. The first, called **detection,** is shown in Fig. 8.3. With this approach quality control is used to inspect the final product to screen out items that do not meet the specifications. The flaws in the defective items are then used to determine how to fix the process. Unfortunately, the detection approach focuses on the output of completed processes, and such information may be of limited use in identifying the causes of current problems with the process. For example, it may be difficult to identify, after the fact, such key variables as the quality of batches of materials used, the workers involved, and the equipment used. Thus, it may not be possible to determine exactly which factors were responsible for the defects. Additionally, this approach can be wasteful and uneconomical because it allows effort and materials to be used in products that may not be usable.

The other approach in statistical process control, **prevention,** is shown in Fig. 8.4. With this approach the key variables of a process are monitored

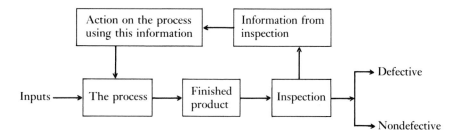

Figure 8.3
The detection approach to quality control.

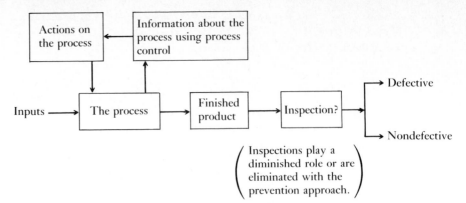

Figure 8.4
The prevention approach to quality control.

while the process is in operation, the objective being to identify potential problems before defective products are manufactured. The goal is to *prevent* the production of defective products.

The traditional approach to manufacturing has been to inspect only the final product, screening out those items not meeting specifications. However, firms are shifting to prevention as the basis of quality control programs. In the prevention approach a process is monitored on a regular basis by tracking the measurements of some of the key variables affecting a process. These measurements are monitored with the help of a control chart. The basic principle is to monitor, individually, all of the many processes involved in producing a product or a service. If observations on any process deviate too far from the expected under "normal" conditions, the process is stopped until the problem is identified and corrected.

Control Charts 8.2

Control charts are plots of data over time that are used to determine if a process has been in statistical control. They are developed by sampling key variables of interest from the process, at regular intervals of time. This sample information is used to calculate control limits for future data obtained from the same process. These control limits are then used to determine if the process is being maintained in a state of statistical control.

Every control chart has a centerline and control limits, as shown in Fig. 8.5. The centerline is the grand average of *all* the sample data plotted and serves as an estimate of the mean of the sampling distribution. The control limits are also estimated from the sample data and are set at three standard deviations above and below the centerline. The control limit above the centerline is called the **upper control limit (UCL);** the one below the centerline is called the **lower control limit (LCL).** Points from the process that fall within the control limits are said to be in control; those outside the limits are out of control.

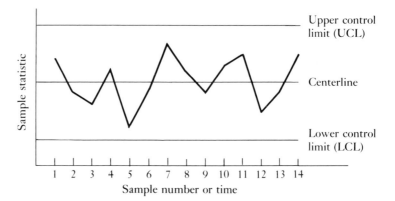

Figure 8.5
A control chart.

Information collected from a process can be either quantitative or qualitative. Quantitative data are those that can be measured, such as temperature, pressure, length, or weight. Qualitative data generally are in binary form; that is, there are only two values, such as accept/reject, pass/fail, conforming/nonconforming. Binary data are called **attribute data.**

Control charts that monitor quantitative data are called **control charts for variables.** The most commonly used control charts for variables monitor the means and ranges of a process. These control charts are referred to as the $\bar{x}$ (pronounced "x bar") and the R charts, respectively. Control charts used to monitor attribute data are called **control charts for attributes.** The most commonly used attribute charts are the p chart and the c chart. The p chart is generally used to track the proportion or the percentage of defectives; the c chart is used to monitor the actual number of defects.

The basic purpose of a control chart is to differentiate between the causes of variation in data resulting from a process. The characteristics of a process may differ because every process contains many possible sources of variability. These differences may be large, or immeasurably small, but they are always present. In process control, variation is classified as due to either *common* (chance) causes or *assignable* (special) causes.

The variation in a process due to common causes is assumed to be the effect of the various random influences that are generally present in all parts of a manufacturing or a service process. This variation could arise for a number of reasons, such as design problems of component parts, inadequate testing of prototypes, inadequate testing of incoming raw materials, specifications that are too stringent or too loose or meaningless, or inadequate training of workers. Variation due to assignable causes arises because of special circumstances. For example, a ball bearing with a 1-inch diameter may, over a period of time, become larger or smaller because of wear and tear in the cutting edge of the machine. Similarly, a machine out of calibration may lead to variation that would be classified as assignable.

A process is said to be in control when common causes are the only source of variation. That is, the variation is solely random. In such cases the variable of interest varies in a random manner. In terms of a control chart, a process is considered to be out of control when one or more data points fall outside the control limits, or when the pattern of these points is nonrandom.

In addition to being in control, the process must also yield results that are within design or engineering specifications. Specification limits, usually set by design engineers, consist of an upper limit, called the **upper specification limit (USL)**, and a lower limit, called the **lower specification limit (LSL).** These specification limits are set so that a product meets certain functional and quality standards. For example, the width of a car door must meet certain specifications in order for it to fit properly. If the width is too small, the door may not fit snugly enough to keep out the wind and the noise. If it is too wide, the door may not close.

A process may be in control but still not meet specifications. Consider the control charts in Fig. 8.6. These charts represent data from three different manufacturing processes. The data in Fig. 8.6(a) show a variable that appears

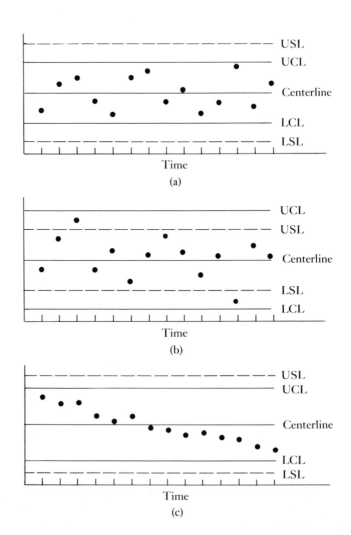

Figure 8.6

(a) Process in control and within specifications.

(b) Process in control but not within specifications.

(c) Process out of control but meeting specifications.

to vary in a random manner within the control limits. Consequently, the process is said to be in control. This process is also producing the products within specifications. Figure 8.6(b) shows points varying in a random manner indicating a process in control; but several of the points exceed the USL/LSL limits, indicating the process may not be meeting specifications. A product that falls outside of the specification limits is said to be **nonconforming.** Figure 8.6(c) shows points within the specifications, but the process seems to be out of control. That is, the data points no longer appear to be random but seem to have a downward trend, indicating an assignable cause of variation.

Control charts only indicate whether the process is in control and by themselves cannot produce control, or identify the cause of the problem. Finding the problem and correcting it is the job of the people responsible for the process. Generally, the discovery of an assignable cause and its removal is the responsibility of someone directly connected with the process, such as an operator or local management. Common causes of variation are problems involving the entire process, and therefore, require management action. One estimate is that only about 15% of all process problems are due to assignable causes, while the rest (85%) result from common cause variation (see reference 7).

Control Charts for Means and Ranges

8.3

Control charts for means and ranges are called the $\bar{x}$ and R charts or the average and the range charts. These charts are the ones most commonly used for variable data and are generally considered to be the most sensitive for diagnosing production problems. The $\bar{x}$ chart monitors the means of samples taken from a process at regular intervals of time whereas the R chart monitors the sample ranges from the same data. The range is the difference between the largest and the smallest values in each sample. Sample sizes for the computation of each mean and range are usually kept small, $n = 3$, 4, or 5 being the most common.

A control chart has the values of $\bar{x}$ or R plotted on the vertical scale and the sequence of the samples through time on the horizontal axis. The $\bar{x}$ chart is usually presented above the R chart with corresponding sampling points (through time) aligned vertically to make interpretation easier. The R chart is always constructed first because the control limits on the $\bar{x}$ chart are calculated by using the centerline, $\bar{R}$, from the R chart. Thus, unless the ranges are first in control, the estimate of $\bar{R}$ is not likely to be reliable. This in turn may cause the control limits for the $\bar{x}$ chart to be computed incorrectly. Thus, in order to obtain reliable estimates of the control limits for the $\bar{x}$ chart, the R chart must first be in control.

The plot of the sample means on a control chart gives a picture of how they vary around their long-run average, $\bar{\bar{x}}$. This $\bar{\bar{x}}$ value also serves as an estimate of $\mu_{\bar{x}}$, the mean of the sampling distribution of the sample means.* Normally the values of $\bar{x}$ in a control chart will exhibit some natural variation around the grand mean $\bar{\bar{x}}$. When the process is in control, the sample means should vary around the grand mean in a random manner, with almost all values falling within three standard deviations of $\bar{\bar{x}}$ (assuming a normal sampling distribution, the probability of falling outside these limits is $1 - 0.9974 = 0.0026$). The limits defined by plus or minus three standard deviations are known as the *three-sigma limits.* Because the probability of falling beyond the three-sigma limits is so low, if one or more of the $\bar{x}$'s deviates beyond these limits we conclude the process is not in control due to assignable causes.

For the population of $\bar{x}$'s, the three-sigma limits are $\mu_{\bar{x}} \pm 3\sigma_{\bar{x}}$. For the population of sample ranges, the three-sigma limits are $\mu_R \pm 3\sigma_R$. Clearly $\mu_{\bar{x}}$, $\sigma_{\bar{x}}$, μ_R, and σ_R are unknown population parameters that will have to be estimated from the sample data. In general, we will designate an estimate of σ with the symbol $\hat{\sigma}$ (sigma hat).† Thus, $\hat{\sigma}_{\bar{x}}$ is an estimate of $\sigma_{\bar{x}}$ and $\hat{\sigma}_R$ is an estimate of σ_R. Also, in making these estimates we need to remember that the sample sizes are generally small; hence the sampling distributions may not be exactly normal.

Constructing an *R* chart

The *R* chart provides a picture of how the range changes from sample to sample (over time). Even for a process in control, the range of one sample may differ from the range of another sample. As with means, we expect ranges to fall in a random pattern within the three-sigma limits around their mean. If the ranges are small, this suggests less variation from item to item. That is, the items tend to be similar to one another. A large range suggests the items are more likely to be different from one another.

An *R* chart is constructed by plotting the ranges (R_i) for each sample taken from the process. A minimum of $k = 25$ samples‡ is recommended for constructing a control chart. The centerline for the *R* chart, $\bar{R}$, is calculated by averaging the *k* sample ranges. That is,

$$\text{Centerline of an R chart: } \bar{R} = \frac{1}{k} \sum_{i=1}^{k} R_i \qquad (8.1)$$

This average, $\bar{R}$, is our estimate of the population parameter μ_R. The parameter σ_R can also be estimated from the sample ranges, but this computation can be

---

*Recall from Chapter 6 that taking a sample of size *n* from a population leads to the sampling distribution of $\bar{x}$, which has the mean, $\mu_{\bar{x}}$, and standard deviation, $\sigma_{\bar{x}}$.

†In earlier chapters, *s* was used to designate an estimate of σ. We change notation in this chapter to correspond with the conventional symbols used in the field of quality control.

‡This number is suggested by several authors. See, for example, reference 8. However, control charts may also be constructed using as few as 20 samples. Generally, the larger the value of *k*, the more reliable the chart will be.

cumbersome and time consuming. For that reason, the quality control specialists traditionally estimate the control limits (UCL_R and LCL_R) using the following short-cut formulas:

$$\boxed{\begin{aligned} \textit{Upper control limit:} \quad & UCL_R = D_4\overline{R} \\ \textit{Lower control limit:} \quad & LCL_R = D_3\overline{R} \end{aligned}}$$

(8.2)

The concept behind Formula (8.2) is that three standard deviations above or below $\overline{R}$ will often be a constant proportion of the value of $\overline{R}$. Thus, D_3 is a constant, which must be less than 1 (since LCL_R is less than $\overline{R}$). The value of D_3 depends on the sample size (n) and the assumption of sampling from a normal parent population. Multiplying $\overline{R}$ by this constant gives an estimate of $\mu_R - 3\sigma_R$. Similarly, multiplying $\overline{R}$ by the constant D_4 (which is greater than 1) gives an estimate of $\mu_R + 3\sigma_R$. Values of D_3 and D_4 for different sample sizes are shown in Table IX, Appendix B.

To illustrate constructing an R chart, consider a manufacturing process that makes precision metal plates used in a clutch assembly for trucks. Engineering design requires the plates have a thickness of 0.500 ± 0.01 inches. That is, the specification limits are USL = 0.510 and LSL = 0.490. These plates are produced at the rate of approximately 100 per hour. To monitor the quality of the process, three plates are randomly sampled every hour and the thickness of each plate is measured. These measurements are shown in columns 2, 3, and 4 of Table 8.1 for 25 different samples. The sample ranges and means for each of the 25 samples are shown in columns 5 and 6, respectively.

The centerline of the control chart is determined first by calculating the mean, $\overline{R}$, of the 25 sample ranges shown in column 5, using Formula (8.1). This mean is equal to 0.0052. Next, the control limits are calculated using Formulas (8.2). For $n = 3$, $D_4 = 2.575$, and $D_3 = 0$.[*] Thus, the control limits are

$$UCL_R = D_4\overline{R} = (2.575)(0.0052) = 0.0134$$
$$LCL_R = D_3\overline{R} = (0)(0.0052) = 0$$

Finally, the 25 sample ranges are plotted in the order in which the samples were taken, as shown in Fig. 8.7. Since none of the ranges falls outside the control limits, the process variation appears to be in control during this time.

Instead of using R charts, process variability can be monitored using control charts based on standard deviations, called s charts. An s chart is more reliable than an R chart because a sample standard deviation uses all the observations in each sample, while a range is calculated from only two observations (the highest and the lowest), resulting in a loss of information. When the sample size n is small (≤ 5), this loss of information is relatively small, so R

---

[*]For sample sizes of 6 or less the lower control limit is negative. Since a negative range is not possible, D_3 is set equal to 0 for those cases.

TABLE 8.1   25 Hourly samples of metal plate thickness, with $n = 3$

(1) Sample	(2) (3) (4) Sample measurements			(5) Sample range, R	(6) Sample mean, $\bar{x}$
1	0.507	0.502	0.508	0.006	0.5057
2	0.502	0.498	0.497	0.005	0.4990
3	0.497	0.499	0.501	0.004	0.4990
4	0.505	0.502	0.497	0.008	0.5013
5	0.502	0.507	0.503	0.005	0.5040
6	0.506	0.500	0.502	0.006	0.5027
7	0.498	0.495	0.497	0.003	0.4967
8	0.495	0.495	0.501	0.006	0.4970
9	0.504	0.506	0.501	0.005	0.5037
10	0.493	0.496	0.497	0.004	0.4953
11	0.495	0.493	0.500	0.007	0.4960
12	0.506	0.501	0.503	0.005	0.5033
13	0.501	0.495	0.496	0.006	0.4973
14	0.500	0.507	0.506	0.007	0.5043
15	0.504	0.503	0.501	0.003	0.5027
16	0.500	0.498	0.499	0.002	0.4990
17	0.499	0.505	0.503	0.006	0.5023
18	0.492	0.498	0.496	0.006	0.4953
19	0.496	0.499	0.500	0.004	0.4983
20	0.503	0.506	0.506	0.003	0.5050
21	0.505	0.505	0.499	0.006	0.5030
22	0.498	0.496	0.502	0.006	0.4987
23	0.499	0.506	0.505	0.007	0.5033
24	0.500	0.495	0.496	0.005	0.4970
25	0.501	0.506	0.500	0.006	0.5023
				$\bar{R} = 0.0052$	$\bar{\bar{x}} = 0.5005$

charts are most often used. The loss is much more serious when n is large, so for large sample sizes ($n > 5$) the standard deviation, rather than the range, should be used to control process variability.

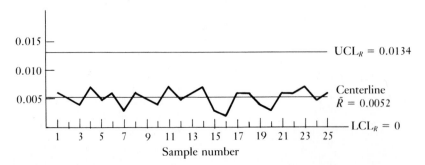

Figure 8.7
R chart for the metal plate thickness.

Constructing an $\bar{x}$ chart

The construction of an $\bar{x}$ chart is very similar to that of an R chart. The centerline, $\bar{\bar{x}}$, is estimated first by averaging all of the k sample means:

$$\text{Centerline of an } \bar{x} \text{ chart: } \bar{\bar{x}} = \frac{1}{k}\sum_{i=1}^{k} \bar{x}_i \qquad (8.3)$$

This average $\bar{\bar{x}}$ is our best estimate of $\mu_{\bar{x}}$, the mean of the sampling distribution of $\bar{x}$. Next, we need to estimate $\sigma_{\bar{x}}$. From Chapter 6 [Formula (6.13)], and using the notation of this chapter, $\hat{\sigma}_{\bar{x}} = \hat{\sigma}_x/\sqrt{n}$, where $\hat{\sigma}_x$ is our estimate of the population standard deviation. One way of making the estimate $\hat{\sigma}_x$ is to calculate the sample standard deviation from the k samples. However, this computation can be tedious and will require a calculator or a computer. An easier computation, used in practice, is to estimate the standard deviation as follows:

$$\text{Estimated standard deviation: } \hat{\sigma}_x = \frac{\bar{R}}{d_2} \qquad (8.4)$$

where $\bar{R}$ is the centerline from the corresponding R chart, and d_2 is a constant obtained from Table IX in Appendix B. The value of d_2 depends on the size of the sample (n). Use of Formula (8.4) assumes the R chart indicates the process is in control. The estimated standard error is thus

$$\hat{\sigma}_{\bar{x}} = \frac{\hat{\sigma}_x}{\sqrt{n}} = \frac{\bar{R}}{d_2\sqrt{n}}$$

This estimate can now be used to determine the three-sigma control limits, as follows:

$$\bar{\bar{x}} \pm 3\hat{\sigma}_{\bar{x}} = \bar{\bar{x}} \pm \frac{3\bar{R}}{d_2\sqrt{n}}$$
$$= \bar{\bar{x}} \pm A_2\bar{R}$$
$$\text{where } A_2 = \frac{3}{d_2\sqrt{n}}$$

Values of A_2 are also tabulated in Table IX in Appendix B for various values of n. Thus, the calculation of the control limits for the $\bar{x}$ chart only requires the computation of $\bar{\bar{x}}$ and $\bar{R}$, and the determination of A_2 from the tables. This procedure makes the computation of the control limits very easy, as shown below.

$$\text{Upper control limit: } \mathrm{UCL}_{\bar{x}} = \bar{\bar{x}} + A_2\bar{R} \qquad (8.5)$$
$$\text{Lower control limit: } \mathrm{LCL}_{\bar{x}} = \bar{\bar{x}} - A_2\bar{R}$$

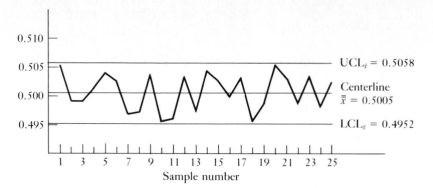

Figure 8.8
$\bar{x}$ Chart for the metal plate thickness.

For the metal plate data in Table 8.1, the sample means have a grand mean of $\bar{\bar{x}} = 0.5005$. Since the R chart indicated the process to be in control, the $\bar{R}$ value may be used in the computation of the control limits for the $\bar{x}$ chart, as shown in Formula (8.4). From Table IX, the value of $A_2 = 1.023$ when $n = 3$. Therefore,

$$UCL_{\bar{x}} = 0.5005 + 1.023(0.0052) = 0.5058$$
$$\text{and } LCL_{\bar{x}} = 0.5005 - 1.023(0.0052) = 0.4952$$

This $\bar{x}$ chart is shown in Fig. 8.8. Since none of the sample means falls outside the control limits and the plot appears to be random, the process is said to be in control.

After the $\bar{x}$ and R charts have been constructed, they may be used to monitor future samples from the process. As the ranges and the means are computed for each sample, they should be plotted on the two charts to compare their values to the control limits. Interpretation of these charts is important to the success of a quality control program. The presence of a point beyond the control limits is evidence of a process not in control. When a point falls outside the control limits, it is usually presumed that a special cause has accounted for the extreme point. Thus, any point outside the control limit should be analyzed immediately to determine its cause.

Even if the sample points all fall within the three-sigma limits, the process may not be in control. Unusual patterns or trends can indicate a change in the process and a loss of control. For example, several points in a row on one side of a centerline, or several points in a row that are consistently increasing (equal to or greater than the preceding points) or consistently decreasing are indications of nonrandom patterns (see, for example, Problems 8.9 and 8.10). Several authors suggest that seven points in a row in either of these patterns is an indication of a process out of control (see, for example, reference 7).

Finally, because of normality assumptions, approximately two-thirds of the data points should lie in the region one sigma on either side of the centerline.* The other one-third should lie between the one sigma line and the control limits. If this is not the case, the statistical control process should be

---

*Recall from Chapter 5 that $\mu \pm 1\sigma$ contains approximately 68% of a normal distribution.

reevaluated (see Problem 8.11). Generally, in such situations either the control limits and/or the plot points have been incorrectly calculated or the measurements used may come from more than one process (that is, the process may have been defined incorrectly).

Problems

8.1   Explain the concept of a process. Give an example of a process and identify its inputs and outputs.

8.2   Give two examples of quality control in the service sector other than those described in this chapter.

8.3   Discuss the differences and similarities between the detection and prevention approaches. What role would the detection approach play in a process where extensive use of control charts is made?

8.4   Distinguish between common variation and assignable variation. Which kind of variation is easily detectable by the use of control charts?

8.5   Consider the following distributions of a variable of interest from two different manufacturing lines making the same product:

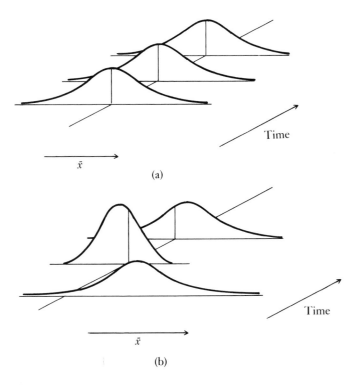

(a)

(b)

What can you say about the variation in these two processes? Which process is in control? Explain.

8.6 Explain the differences between specification limits and control limits.

8.7 Consider the following distributions of a variable of interest from a manufacturing process.

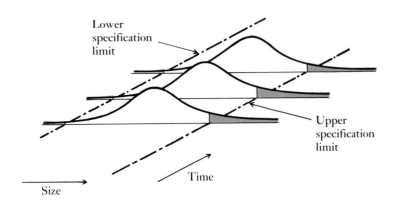

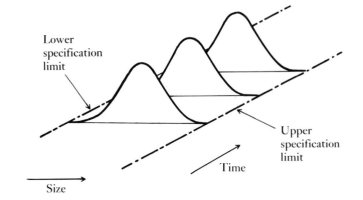

What can you say about this process? Is it in control?

8.8 Explain what is meant by the term *statistical control.* When is a process in statistical control?

8.9 Consider the control charts for ranges shown on the next page. Of these three controls, which one(s) appear to be in control and why? Which one(s) do not appear to be in control and why?

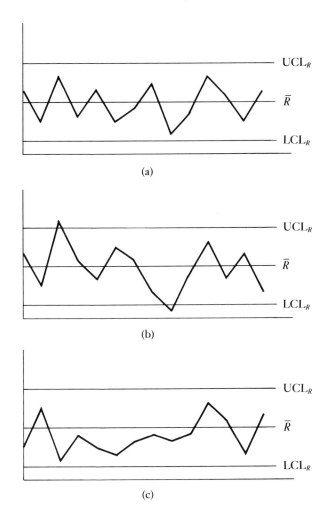

(a)

(b)

(c)

8.10 Consider the following control charts for $\overline{x}$.

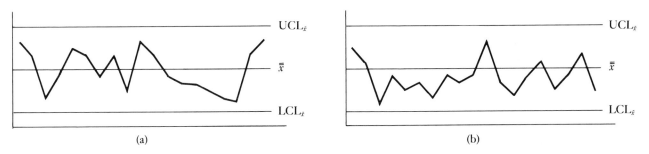

(a)

(b)

Both these processes appear to be out of control. Explain why.

8.11 Consider the following control charts for $\bar{x}$.

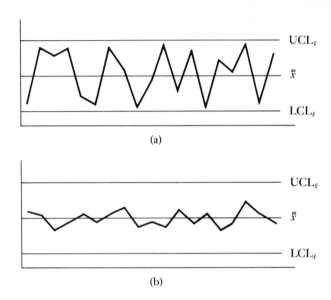

(a)

(b)

What can you say about both these processes? What is a likely explanation and what steps may be taken to correct this situation?

8.12 Describe the construction of an $\bar{x}$ chart. In which two ways can $\sigma_{\bar{x}}$ be estimated? Which one is preferable and why?

8.13 A production process is monitored for two days by randomly sampling $n = 5$ items every hour. The sample information gives $\bar{\bar{x}} = 22.8$ and $\bar{R} = 10.9$.

   a) Use these data to determine the upper and lower control limits for an R chart.

   b) Construct the R chart for this process.

   c) Explain how this chart will be used.

8.14 Refer to the information in Problem 8.13.

   a) Use this information to determine the upper and lower control limits for an $\bar{x}$ chart.

   b) Construct the $\bar{x}$ chart for this process.

   c) Explain how this chart will be used.

8.15 Suppose for this process described in Problem 8.13 that the next 12 hourly observations result in the following sample means:

   23.5,   21.0,   26.5,   25.3,   19.8,   24.5,   25.6,   23.1,   25.7,
   22.4,   23.7,   24.2

Does this process appear to be in control? Explain your answer.

8.16 A manufacturing process is set up to produce fishing line with a 60-lb breaking strength. The specifications require that the actual breaking strength of the line be within 5 lb of that figure. Every shift five samples, each a few inches long, are taken randomly from the spools produced during that shift. For each of these samples the actual breaking strengths are determined. Results from 15 shifts are shown in Table 8.2.

    a) Calculate the sample mean and range for each of the 15 samples.

    b) Construct the R chart for this process. Does the process variation appear to be in statistical control?

    c) Construct the $\bar{x}$ chart for this process. Do the sample means appear to be in control?

8.17 A manufacturing process produces ball bearings. Every hour three bearings are sampled in order to monitor the variation in the diameters. The engineering specifications require that the bearings have a diameter of 0.75 ± 0.01 inches. Table 8.3 shows the diameter measurements from 20 hourly samples.

    a) Calculate the sample mean and range for each of the 20 samples.

    b) Construct the $\bar{R}$ chart for this process.

    c) Construct the $\bar{x}$ chart for this process.

    d) Does the process appear to be in statistical control? Explain your answer.

    e) Do the control limits lie within the specification limits?

TABLE 8.2

Sample number	Sample strength				
	1	2	3	4	5
1	58.4	62.1	59.3	60.7	59.1
2	59.7	62.7	60.3	61.1	60.6
3	60.2	60.3	63.1	60.0	59.3
4	59.3	58.9	60.6	61.2	60.0
5	60.0	59.3	62.0	61.3	60.1
6	58.1	62.2	59.2	60.7	59.9
7	59.7	60.3	58.2	59.2	61.0
8	60.2	62.0	60.6	57.9	60.0
9	62.7	59.8	60.0	60.1	58.5
10	58.9	60.1	59.7	61.6	60.9
11	59.3	60.2	59.6	62.5	61.3
12	60.7	63.1	59.3	58.4	60.2
13	60.1	61.3	57.8	59.3	58.5
14	59.8	59.4	60.3	61.8	60.4
15	58.5	62.4	61.3	60.8	60.3

TABLE 8.3

Sample number	Sample measurements		
	1	2	3
1	0.755	0.748	0.746
2	0.748	0.756	0.752
3	0.743	0.746	0.751
4	0.749	0.753	0.751
5	0.754	0.748	0.750
6	0.752	0.754	0.755
7	0.748	0.753	0.749
8	0.741	0.748	0.747
9	0.750	0.752	0.748
10	0.753	0.749	0.756
11	0.757	0.748	0.750
12	0.743	0.754	0.752
13	0.755	0.753	0.756
14	0.745	0.756	0.752
15	0.750	0.753	0.752
16	0.757	0.753	0.748
17	0.744	0.752	0.751
18	0.756	0.755	0.757
19	0.751	0.748	0.753
20	0.750	0.752	0.752

8.18 The eight samples in Table 8.4 (sample numbers 21–28) were taken the day after the control charts from Problem 8.17 were constructed.

a) Calculate the sample ranges for these eight samples and plot them on the R chart. Does the process variation appear to be in statistical control?

b) Calculate the sample means for these samples and plot them on the $\bar{x}$ chart. Do the sample means still appear to be in control? Explain your answer.

8.19 An insurance company specializing in health insurance would like to monitor the time it takes to process claims. Every week the company samples five claims finalized that week. For each claim the time to process the claim is calculated as the number of days between the receipt of the claim and the mailing of the check. Table 8.5 shows the process time data from 20 weeks.

a) Calculate the sample mean and range for each of the 20 samples.

b) Construct the R chart for this process.

c) Construct the $\bar{x}$ chart for this process.

d) Does the process appear to be within statistical control? Explain your answer.

TABLE 8.4

	Sample measurements		
Sample number	**1**	**2**	**3**
21	0.754	0.753	0.752
22	0.748	0.757	0.753
23	0.752	0.745	0.751
24	0.753	0.754	0.749
25	0.757	0.753	0.755
26	0.748	0.754	0.756
27	0.756	0.753	0.750
28	0.751	0.752	0.749

TABLE 8.5

	Process time				
Week number	**1**	**2**	**3**	**4**	**5**
1	17	25	10	14	14
2	23	15	23	23	19
3	22	22	17	15	24
4	13	14	24	19	12
5	20	18	20	18	18
6	22	19	21	17	18
7	12	13	18	14	13
8	12	11	14	18	17
9	13	25	17	24	13
10	17	19	13	16	19
11	19	10	22	15	16
12	21	16	20	25	19
13	22	11	14	17	12
14	10	23	10	22	25
15	11	17	13	19	16
16	13	12	19	22	11
17	18	25	13	13	19
18	17	14	19	20	15
19	22	21	10	19	14
20	15	24	10	10	24

8.20 Monitoring the process in Problem 8.19 for another 10 weeks (weeks 21–30) gives the results shown in Table 8.6.

   a) Plot both the sample mean and range for each of these 10 weeks on the R and the $\bar{x}$ charts.

   b) What conclusions can you derive from these plots? Does the process variation appear to be in control? Explain your answer.

TABLE 8.6

Week number	Process time				
	1	**2**	**3**	**4**	**5**
21	24	11	17	12	35
22	10	18	23	14	22
23	20	10	15	20	24
24	14	17	14	17	24
25	10	23	11	24	13
26	23	15	15	25	12
27	20	16	17	21	22
28	15	20	23	18	23
29	11	14	24	25	20
30	23	16	11	13	13

Process Capability

8.4

After a process has been brought into a state of statistical control, the question still remains whether the process is "capable." Process capability refers to whether a process is operated in a manner such that the distributions of the key variables, such as $\bar{x}$ and R, lie within the specification limits. For a distribution to lie within the specification limits, the control limits must fall within the specification limits. In other words, a process that is capable must have its lower specification limit (LSL) at or below the lower control limit and the upper specification limit (USL) at or above the upper control limit. For example, in Fig. 8.9(a) the distribution of the sample means lies entirely within the specification limits, whereas the distribution in Fig. 8.9(b) lies partly outside these limits. Therefore, the process in (a) is said to be capable; the process in (b) is noncapable.

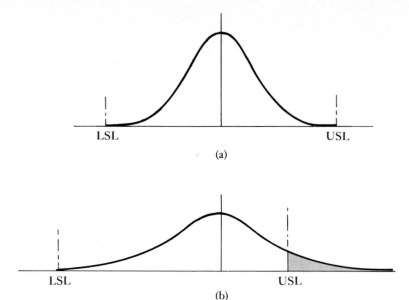

Figure 8.9
(a) A capable process.
(b) A noncapable process.

There are many techniques for assessing the capability of a process that is in statistical control, the most common being **capability indexes.** For this discussion we assume a process output can be represented by a normal distribution. Thus, it follows that almost all of the measurements should fall within a spread of $6\hat{\sigma}$ (representing the three-sigma limits). The first index, called the **process capability index** (C_p), is defined using this range as follows:

$$\text{Process capability index: } C_p = \frac{\text{USL} - \text{LSL}}{6\hat{\sigma}_x} \qquad (8.6)$$

where $\hat{\sigma}_x$ is an estimate of the standard deviation of the process. For example, for an $\bar{x}$ chart, we previously estimated the standard deviation using the equation, $\hat{\sigma}_x = \bar{R}/d_2$.

The process capability index is the ratio of the spread between the specification limits to the spread between the control limits. For a process to be capable, the spread between the specification limits must be greater than the spread between the control limits. Thus, this index may be interpreted as follows: If $C_p \geq 1.0$, the process is said to be capable of meeting its specification limits. When $C_p = 1.0$, the process is said to be just capable. Ideally, we would like the values of C_p to exceed 1.0 because in that range the measurements are more likely to stay within the specifications. When $C_p < 1.0$, the process is not capable of meeting its specifications because one or both control limits will be outside of the specification limits. Figure 8.10 illustrates the values of the C_p index for a distribution of measurement from a process.

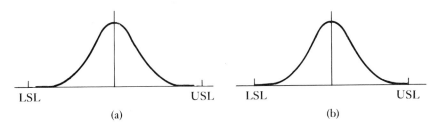

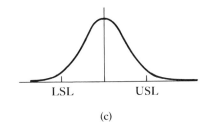

Figure 8.10
Interpretation of the
capability index.
(a) $C_p > 1.0$ (The process
is capable.)
(b) $C_p = 1.0$ (The process
is just capable.)
(c) $C_p < 1.0$ (The process
is not capable.)

To illustrate the C_p index, consider the metal plate data in Table 8.1. These metal plates were required to have a thickness of 0.500 ± 0.01 inches. The $\bar{x}$ and R charts for this process both showed that the process was in statistical control. Thus, it is now possible to measure the process capability using the C_p index.

The required thickness of 0.500 ± 0.01 inches implies that the specification limits are

$$\text{USL} = 0.500 + 0.01 = 0.510$$
$$\text{and} \quad \text{LSL} = 0.500 - 0.01 = 0.490$$

Next, we estimate the variation in the measurements using the equation $\hat{\sigma}_x = \bar{R}/d_2$. For $n = 3$, Table IX (Appendix B) shows that $d_2 = 1.693$. Since $\bar{R} = 0.0052$, $\hat{\sigma}_x$ is

$$\hat{\sigma}_x = \frac{\bar{R}}{d_2} = \frac{0.0052}{1.693} = 0.003071$$

Thus,

$$C_p = \frac{\text{USL} - \text{LSL}}{6\hat{\sigma}_x} = \frac{0.510 - 0.490}{6(0.003071)} = 1.0854$$

Since C_p is greater than 1, this process is capable of staying within its specification limits.

The process capability index, unfortunately, does not take into account the location of the mean of the process; rather, only the spread is used to determine the potential for meeting the specifications. For example, consider a process with $C_p = 1.0$. If the mean of the process is centered midway between the specification limits, there is no problem with the C_p index, as shown in Fig. 8.11(a). However, when the mean of the process is not at the midway point, as in Fig. 8.11(b), the C_p index is misleading.

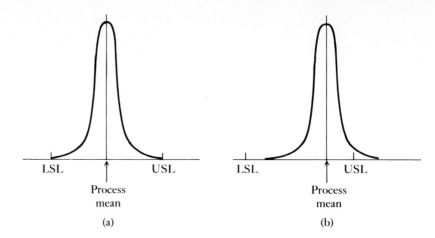

Figure 8.11
Process means. **(a)** Centered
process mean. **(b)** Non-
centered process mean.

An index that *does* take into account the location of the process mean is the C_{pk} index. This index is defined as follows:

$$C_{pk} = \frac{Z_{min}}{3}$$

$$\text{where } Z_{min} = min\left[\frac{USL - \hat{\mu}_x}{\hat{\sigma}_x} \quad , \quad \frac{\hat{\mu}_x - LSL}{\hat{\sigma}_x}\right] \qquad (8.7)$$

Here $\hat{\mu}_x$ and $\hat{\sigma}_x$ are estimates of the mean and the standard deviation of the process of interest. Recall that for an $\bar{x}$ chart, $\hat{\mu}_x = \bar{\bar{x}}$ and $\hat{\sigma}_x = \bar{R}/d_2$. If both USL and LSL are equidistant from μ_x, $(USL - \hat{\mu}_x)/\hat{\sigma}_x = (\hat{\mu}_x - LSL)/\hat{\sigma}_x$. In this case Z_{min} is the number of standard deviations the specification limits are from $\hat{\mu}_x$. If the distances are not the same, the value of Z_{min} will depend on the specification limits closer to $\hat{\mu}_x$. In this case the C_{pk} value is equal to the number of standard deviations between that specification limit and $\hat{\mu}_x$.

When the specification limits are equidistant from the process mean, it can be shown very easily that $C_p = C_{pk}$. If the limits are $\hat{\mu} \pm 3\hat{\sigma}$, $Z_{min} = 3$ and both C_p and C_{pk} will be equal to 1. When the specification limits are not equidistant, the C_{pk} index gives better information about the capability of the process since it is based on the specification limit closer to the process mean. For example, in Fig. 8.11(b), the C_{pk} index is calculated on the basis of the distance from the process mean to the USL, a distance shorter than half the distance between the USL and LSL. Thus, C_{pk} is always less than C_p when the process is not centered between its specification limits. Generally, both C_p and C_{pk} are used together to see how well a process is performing when compared with its specification limits.

As with the C_p index, C_{pk} has to be 1.0 or greater for the process to be capable. The larger the value of C_{pk}, the higher the probability will be of staying within the specification limits. A value of 1.33 is considered very good and is commonly used as a target in many applications (see, for example, reference 4). If the distribution is considered to be approximately normal, a process with the C_{pk} index equal to 1.33 would produce at most 6 of every 100,000 units that do not conform to the specifications, a relatively insignificant proportion (the probability that $Z_{min} \geq 4$ or ≤ -4 is approximately 0.00006).

Earlier, we calculated $C_p = 1.0854$ for the metal plate data. Since C_p is greater than 1, we concluded the process is capable of staying within its limits. More information about the capability of this process may be obtained by calculating the C_{pk} index as follows:

$$Z_{min} = \min \left[\frac{USL - \bar{\bar{x}}}{\hat{\sigma}_x}, \frac{\bar{\bar{x}} - LSL}{\hat{\sigma}_x} \right]$$

$$= \min \left[\frac{0.510 - 0.5005}{0.003071}, \frac{0.5005 - 0.490}{0.003071} \right]$$

$$= \min [3.0935, \quad 3.4191]$$

$$= 3.0935$$

Then,

$$C_{pk} = \frac{3.0935}{3} = 1.0312$$

Since C_{pk} is greater than 1.0, the process appears to be capable of staying within the specification limits. Also, since $C_{pk} < C_p$, it can be concluded that the mean of the process is not centered.

The p Chart   8.5

A p chart monitors the proportion of nonconforming items in a group of items being inspected. After the $\bar{x}$ and the R charts, the p chart is generally considered to be the most sensitive chart for identifying problems with a process. A p chart is monitored in the same way as the $\bar{x}$ and the R charts. We look for the same kinds of patterns as these charts (upward or downward trends, several points on one side of the centerline, and so forth).

A p chart is constructed by taking periodic samples of size n from a process and plotting the proportion of nonconforming items, $\hat{p}$, for each sample. As with the $\bar{x}$ and R charts, a process is said to be in statistical control if the sample proportions fall within the three-sigma limits of the average proportion of defectives, $\bar{p}$. That is, the control limits are $\bar{p} \pm 3\sigma_p$, where σ_p is the population standard deviation and $\bar{p}$ is obtained by averaging the proportion of defectives, $\hat{p}_i$, for the k samples as follows:

$$\text{Average proportion of defectives: } \bar{p} = \frac{1}{k} \sum_{i=1}^{k} \hat{p}_i \qquad (8.8)$$

The average $\bar{p}$ also forms the centerline for the p chart. The sample estimate of the standard deviation ($\hat{\sigma}_p$) is calculated using a formula comparable to one presented in Chapter 4.

$$\hat{\sigma}_p = \sqrt{\frac{\bar{p}(1 - \bar{p})}{n}}$$

The control limits then are

$$
\begin{array}{l}
\textit{Upper control limit:}\ \ \text{UCL}_p = \bar{p} + 3\sqrt{\dfrac{\bar{p}(1 - \bar{p})}{n}} \\[3ex]
\textit{Lower control limit:}\ \ \text{LCL}_p = \bar{p} - 3\sqrt{\dfrac{\bar{p}(1 - \bar{p})}{n}}
\end{array}
\tag{8.9}
$$

If Formula (8.9) results in a negative value of LCL_p, which happens often in practice, the lower control limit is set equal to zero.

A practical problem with p charts is that it may not be possible to choose batches of the same size at each sampling. For example, it is not unusual to use a full day's production to record the proportion of defectives produced each day. Since the number of items produced will most likely be different from day to day, the value of n will vary. If n varies, the control limits will have to be calculated using the equation

$$\bar{p} \pm 3\sqrt{\frac{\hat{p}_i(1 - \hat{p}_i)}{n_i}}$$

where n_i is the size of the ith sample. Thus, the control limits will change as n_i varies. This means that new limits would have to be computed for each different sample size and the resulting control limits would form a "jagged" line. Such control limits are tedious to compute. One way to circumvent this problem is to use an average value of the sample sizes, $\bar{n}$, in place of n in the control limit formulas [Formula (8.9)]. However, this can be done only if the sample sizes do not vary much from each other.

To illustrate the technique for constructing a p chart, consider the data in Table 8.7. These data show the number of items determined to be defective from a process manufacturing automobile windshields over a period of 25 days. A windshield is rejected if it contains scratches, cracks, bubbles, dents, or any other visual imperfections. Since the number of windshields produced and tested varies from day to day, the average sample size method will be used to calculate the control limits. For these data, the average sample size is $\bar{n} = 414$ (rounded). Since $\bar{p} = 0.051$, the limits are calculated using $n = \bar{n} = 414$ and

TABLE 8.7   Data for the windshields tested

Day i	Rejects	Number tested (n_i)	Percent rejects ($\hat{p}_i$)
1	22	425	0.052
2	18	435	0.041
3	17	392	0.043
4	27	421	0.064
5	15	405	0.037
6	29	427	0.068
7	23	397	0.058
8	20	402	0.050
9	24	401	0.060
10	19	430	0.044
11	25	417	0.060
12	17	411	0.041
13	24	404	0.059
14	26	427	0.061
15	15	423	0.035
16	19	398	0.048
17	27	421	0.064
18	22	409	0.054
19	30	438	0.068
20	17	418	0.041
21	27	409	0.066
22	16	422	0.038
23	24	409	0.059
24	14	395	0.035
25	15	422	0.036

$$\bar{n} = 414.32 \qquad \bar{p} = 0.051$$

Formula (8.9) as follows:

$$\text{UCL}_p = \bar{p} + 3\sqrt{\frac{\bar{p}(1-\bar{p})}{n}} = 0.051 + 3\sqrt{\frac{0.051(0.949)}{414}} = 0.0834$$

$$\text{LCL}_p = \bar{p} - 3\sqrt{\frac{\bar{p}(1-\bar{p})}{n}} = 0.051 - 3\sqrt{\frac{0.051(0.949)}{414}} = 0.0186$$

Figure 8.12 is the p chart; it shows control limits for these data. Since none of the points falls outside the control limits, the process appears to be in control.

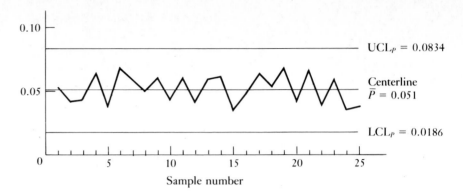

Figure 8.12
The *p* chart for the
windshield data.

The *c* Chart

8.6

Besides monitoring the proportion of defectives produced by a manufacturing process, we may be interested in monitoring the *number* of defects. For example, in the automobile industry it is common to track the number of defects in the paint job of a new car. Similarly, an important variable in textiles is the number of defects per square yard. A defect that is simply a flaw or a nonconformity may not lead to an item being declared unusable, for it is possible to have one or more defects in a product accepted as good. A new car, for example, may have a few minor defects in the paintwork.

The number of defects is monitored using a *c* chart. This chart may be used to control a single type of defect or to control all types of defects without distinguishing between types. The *c* chart requires a constant unit of output that will be sampled at regular intervals of time and examined for defects. This constant unit of output is called an **inspection unit.** It may be specified in any units of measurement. For example, an inspection unit may be defined in terms of an area or volume or weight. Alternatively, an inspection unit may be specified as a single item, or a group of items.

The number of defects per inspection unit is represented by *c*. As with the other control charts presented, a process is said to be in statistical control if the number of defects fall within the three-sigma limits, or within the interval $\hat{\mu}_c \pm 3\hat{\sigma}_c$. For reasons beyond the scope of this chapter, the distribution of *c* is assumed to be Poisson.* This distribution possesses a unique property: its variance is equal to its mean. This implies that $\sigma_c^2 = \mu_c$ or $\sigma_c = \sqrt{\mu_c}$, a fact we will use to estimate σ_c.

The sample mean, $\bar{c}$, is determined as follows:

$$\text{Average number of defects: } \bar{c} = \frac{1}{k}\sum_{i=1}^{k} c_i \qquad (8.10)$$

*This distribution was presented in Chapter 4. The material in this chapter does not assume the reader is familiar with the Poisson distribution.

This average ($\bar{c}$) forms the centerline for the c chart. Because of the special property of the Poisson distribution, the standard deviation of the process can be estimated by the sample mean. That is, $\hat{\sigma}_c = \sqrt{\bar{c}}$, and the control limits are

$$\begin{array}{l} \textit{Upper control limit: } \text{UCL}_c = \bar{c} + 3\sqrt{\bar{c}} \\ \textit{Lower control limit: } \text{LCL}_c = \bar{c} - 3\sqrt{\bar{c}} \end{array}$$

(8.11)

If LCL_c is negative, it is set equal to 0.

To illustrate the construction and use of a c chart consider the data in Table 8.8, representing a carpet manufacturing operation. Rolls of a particular type of carpet are produced in lengths of 30 feet and widths of 12 feet. Defects could arise from a number of causes. The data in Table 8.3 show the number of defects on each roll of carpet, for 40 samples. This company has recently undertaken a new training program for its workers. Samples 25–40 were manufactured by workers trained under this program.

TABLE 8.8   Carpet defects data

Sample i	Number of defects (C_i)	Sample i	Number of defects (C_i)
1	15	21	15
2	11	22	11
3	13	23	13
4	18	24	14
5	16	25	10
6	10	26	9
7	9	27	8
8	15	28	12
9	14	29	11
10	13	30	7
11	11	31	12
12	16	32	13
13	17	33	10
14	12	34	8
15	14	35	12
16	15	36	9
17	11	37	11
18	8	38	10
19	17	39	7
20	16	40	9

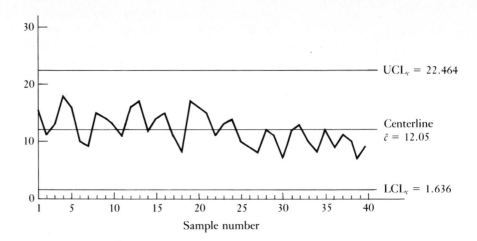

Figure 8.13
The *c* chart for the carpet data.

The average number of defects per roll is calculated using Formula (8.10):

$$\bar{c} = \frac{1}{k}\sum_{i=1}^{k} c_i = \frac{1}{40}(482) = 12.05$$

The control limits are calculated from Formulas (8.11):

$$UCL_c = \bar{c} + 3\sqrt{\bar{c}} = 12.05 + 3\sqrt{12.05} = 22.464$$
$$LCL_c = \bar{c} - 3\sqrt{\bar{c}} = 12.05 - 3\sqrt{12.05} = 1.636$$

Figure 8.13 is the *c* chart for these data. This figure suggests a downward trend beginning around sample number 25. This is a good sign because it shows that the process may be creating fewer defects than normal, and such a change may be a result of the new training program. Since the process appears to have changed, the control limits should be recalculated using the data in Samples 25–40.

Acceptance Sampling   8.7

The focus in this chapter thus far has been on process control, whereby one attempts to detect and correct quality problems as they occur. Another application of quality control is in **acceptance sampling plans.** These plans are used to determine whether to accept or reject either an outgoing or an incoming shipment. Generally, raw materials, components to be used in intermediate products, and finished products, are grouped into lots before being shipped to customers. In acceptance sampling each lot is sampled and inspected. This inspection may be performed by a producer before shipping a lot, or by a customer before accepting a lot. In either case, the sampled items are classified as either defective or nondefective. Based on the number of defectives in the sample, the entire lot is either accepted or rejected.

Acceptance plans have been used extensively in industry. Their use, however, has in recent years, been declining as more organizations shift to control charts and other statistical methods for quality improvement. Many acceptance sampling plans these days are used simultaneously with statistical process control in the initial stages of a quality control program. As the full impact of process control is achieved, the quality levels may improve to the extent that acceptance sampling techniques may no longer be needed.

An acceptance sampling plan is characterized by two numbers: the number of items to include in the sample (n), and the acceptable number of defects allowed in the sample (a) before the lot is rejected. Every item in the sample of n is inspected to determine the total number of defectives, x. If x is less than or equal to a, the lot is accepted. If x is greater than a, the lot is rejected. Every sampling plan is completely specified by these two numbers (n and a). Changing one or both of these numbers changes the sampling plan.

Every lot contains a certain fraction of defectives, p. For the sampling plan to be efficient, the plan must have a high probability of accepting a lot when p is low, and a high probability of rejecting a lot when p is high. For any given acceptance sampling plan the probability of accepting or rejecting a lot is easily computed if p is known. If n is small compared to the number of items in a lot, the number of defectives follows the binomial distribution.* Thus, the probability of accepting a lot may be computed using binomial tables. As an illustration, consider a plan where the sample size is $n = 20$ and the acceptable number is $a = 1$. If $p = 0.05$, then the probability of accepting the lot is computed using Table I in Appendix B as follows:

$$\begin{aligned}
P(\text{Accepting the lot}) &= P(x \leq 1) \\
&= P(x = 0) + P(x = 1) \\
&= 0.3585 + 0.3774 \\
&= 0.7359
\end{aligned}$$

For this acceptance sampling plan, 73.59% of all lots inspected will pass inspection. Similarly, for $p = 0.10$, $n = 20$, the probability of accepting the lot (computed from the binomial table for $n = 20$ and $p = 0.10$) is $P(x \leq 1) = 0.392$. As the value of p increases and n remains the same, the probability of accepting a lot decreases. For example, for $p = 0.20$ and $n = 20$, the probability of acceptance decreases to 0.069. For $p = 0.40$ and $n = 20$, the probability of acceptance is only 0.0006.

To see how well an acceptance sampling plan works, we plot the probability of accepting a lot against the fraction of defectives (p). The resulting graph is called the *operating characteristic (OC) curve* for the sampling plan. There is a unique curve for each possible sample size and acceptance number. Figure 8.14 shows the OC curve for the plan where $n = 20$ and $a = 1$. As the values of n and a change, so do the curves. Figure 8.15 shows the curves for

---

*If n is large relative to the lot size, then the hypergeometric distribution should be used.

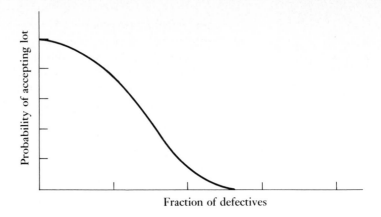

Figure 8.14
OC curve for $n = 20$ and
$a = 1$.

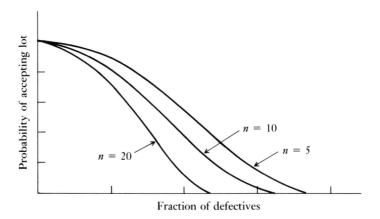

Figure 8.15
OC curve for different values
of n and $a = 1$.

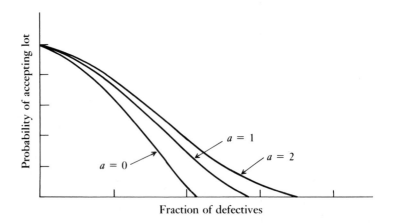

Figure 8.16
OC curves for $n = 20$ and
different values of a.

various sample sizes. Notice that as n increases, the curve becomes steeper. Consequently, the larger the value of n, the better the curve is able to discriminate lots with a high percentage of defectives. For example, when $n = 20$, the probability of accepting lots with only a few defectives is high, while the probability of accepting lots with many defectives is low. Figure 8.16 demonstrates the effect of different acceptance numbers. As the acceptance number increases, the entire curve shifts to the right. This increases the probability of accepting a lot.

In practice, a producer and a consumer first need to agree on a mutually acceptable fraction of defectives to be tolerated in a lot. This fraction is called the **acceptable quantity level (AQL).** For example, they may agree that 5% defectives in a lot is tolerable, but no more than 5%. Without a census the actual proportion of defectives in a lot is unknown. Thus, the sampling plan is of critical importance, especially the choice of acceptable number of defects allowed in the sample (a). Ideally, a sampling plan should be selected that has a high probability of accepting a lot whose fraction of defectives is less than or equal to the AQL, as well as a high probability of rejecting all other lots.

For example, suppose the producer and consumer agree on AQL = 0.05, and a particular lot has 5% defectives. If the sampling plan uses $n = 20$ and, say, $a = 0$, then the probability of accepting this lot (from the binomial table with $n = 20$ and $p = 0.05$) is

$$P(x = 0) = 0.3585$$

This probability means that on the average, 64.15% ($1 - 0.3585 = 0.6415$) of all lots with 5% defectives will be rejected; such a sampling plan is unlikely to be acceptable to the producer.

At the other extreme, suppose there are 10% defectives ($p = 0.10$) and a is set equal to 1. From the binomial table for $n = 20$ and $p = 0.10$,

$$P(x \leq 1) = 0.3918$$

This plan is unlikely to be acceptable to the consumer since approximately 39% of comparable lots will be accepted even though there are 10% defectives. Generally, adjusting the sample size and the acceptable number will lead to a plan agreeable to both the producer and the consumer.

Many different forms of acceptance sampling plans have been developed over the years. One of the most widely used is the Military Standard 105D plan (or MIL-STD-105D in abbreviated form). This plan was developed during the Second World War to control the quality of manufactured war material and has become the standard in many industries, especially those involved in government contract work. The plan consists of a series of tables that tell a user the sample size to employ for a given lot size and the corresponding acceptance number (a) for various AQLs. Thus, it is possible to analyze many different options quickly, thereby making it easy to select a plan that would be acceptable to both the consumer and the producer. For a more detailed treatment of standardized acceptance plans, see reference 17.

Problems

8.21 Explain the interpretation of the C_p index.

8.22 Discuss the relationship between the C_p and the C_{pk} indexes. Explain how these indexes may be used to determine how a process is performing.

8.23 Show that $C_p = C_{pk}$ when the specification limits are equidistant from the process mean.

8.24 In determining whether a machine is capable of meeting the design specifications of a particular operation, it is usual to perform a machine capability analysis. In such analysis, the objective is to determine if the underlying variability of the machine is small enough to accommodate the design specifications. Consider a part whose outside diameter has to be 2.25 ± 0.001 inches. There are five machines that might be used for this operation. Suppose that the inherent accuracy of these machines is known and is expressed as the standard deviation for work of this kind. These standard deviations are as follows:

Machine 1	0.00010 inches
Machine 2	0.00020 inches
Machine 3	0.00025 inches
Machine 4	0.00035 inches
Machine 5	0.00040 inches

Which of these five machines should be used for this operation? Explain your answer.

8.25 A bottling process that is used to fill glass bottles with ketchup is monitored for three days by randomly sampling $n = 5$ bottles every hour. The specifications require that a bottle must contain 16 ± 0.2 oz of ketchup. The sample information gives $\bar{\bar{x}} = 16.05$ and $\bar{R} = 0.15$. Calculate the C_p and the C_{pk} indexes. Is this process capable of meeting its specifications? Explain your answer.

8.26 A production process is monitored for $k = 40$ days by randomly sampling $n = 8$ items per day. From this sample information, we obtain $\bar{\bar{x}} = 25.3$ and $\bar{R} = 2.5$. If this product is designed to produce measurements with the specifications (25 ± 3), is the process capable of meeting its specifications? Use C_p and C_{pk} to measure this capability.

8.27 Refer to Problem 8.16. Recall that the specifications for the breaking strength of the fishing line has to be 60 ± 5 lb. Using the data in Problem 8.16, calculate the C_p and the C_{pk} indexes. Which of the two is a better indicator of the process capability? Explain your answer.

8.28 Refer to Problem 8.17. Calculate the C_p and C_{pk} index and determine if the process is capable of meeting its specifications.

8.29 Explain the difference between a p chart and a c chart. How is each chart used? Give examples of two processes where these charts may be used.

8.30 Samples of $n = 50$ items were selected every shift for 15 days (3 shifts a day). For each sample the proportion of defectives is calculated. The mean of the 45 sample proportions is 0.045.

a) Calculate the upper and the lower control limits for a p chart.

b) Construct a p chart and explain how this chart will be used.

8.31 The entire production of each day of a process making circuit boards for a calculator is tested to determine the proportion of defectives. The production levels vary from day to day. In one 30-day period, the average number of boards tested per day was 323, and the fraction of defectives for this period equaled 0.083. Construct a p chart for the period and explain how this chart will be used.

8.32 A bank records the number of complaints of errors it receives from business clients about billings on purchases made using the bank's credit card. If this information is maintained on a weekly basis and the average number of errors over a 30-week period is 7.4, find the upper and lower control limits for a c chart. Construct a c chart and explain how it may be used by the management.

8.33 The manager of an information system monitors the number of errors in entries to the data base by sampling 100 entries every day. If the sampling over 20 days produced a total of 72 errors, calculate the average number of errors per entry and construct a c chart for this process.

8.34 An electronic manufacturer produces control assemblies for an AM/FM radio receiver. Each assembly is tested individually. It is expected that a certain proportion of these assemblies will be defective and have to be scrapped. The firm produces 1000 assemblies each day. Each assembly is individually tested after manufacture. Tests for a 20-day period resulted in the data given in Table 8.9.

a) Using this information, construct a p chart and determine if the process is in control.

b) Suppose that the next eight days' production results in the following number of defects.

$$17 \quad 26 \quad 24 \quad 62 \quad 35 \quad 39 \quad 18 \quad 27$$

What can you say about the process now? Explain your answer.

TABLE 8.9

Sample number	Number of defectives	Sample number	Number of defectives
1	30	11	36
2	40	12	34
3	34	13	28
4	32	14	37
5	20	15	53
6	33	16	19
7	55	17	26
8	21	18	39
9	48	19	30
10	31	20	25

TABLE 8.10

Day i	Number of defectives	Number tested, N_i	Day i	Number of defectives	Number tested, N_i
1	15	327	16	7	330
2	11	356	17	26	344
3	30	344	18	16	349
4	25	338	19	8	339
5	8	345	20	15	330
6	24	353	21	26	357
7	23	332	22	22	353
8	24	324	23	14	332
9	17	360	24	11	327
10	7	347	25	29	359
11	20	352	26	20	339
12	14	334	27	8	331
13	30	356	28	25	350
14	18	343	29	30	355
15	10	328	30	18	352

8.35 A subcontractor for a computer manufacturer makes graphics circuit boards for microcomputers. Each circuit board is individually tested and classified as either nondefective or defective. A nondefective board is shipped to the manufacturer; a defective board is discarded. The results of these tests for a 30-day period are shown in Table 8.10.

a) Construct a p chart for these data using the average sample size method. Determine if the process is in control.

b) If the control limits were to be determined using the variable size method (Formula 8.13), what would the control chart look like? What are the advantages and the disadvantages of constructing a control chart using this method?

8.36 The management of a weekly news magazine has decided to use quality control techniques to control errors such as misprints, typographical errors, and typesetting errors. Each week, after the magazine has been published, 20 pages are randomly selected and the number of errors are recorded. The results of the procedure for the past 20 weeks are shown below in Table 8.11.

a) Construct a c chart for these data.

b) Suppose that in the next eight weeks the magazine records the following number of errors:

$$3 \quad 6 \quad 8 \quad 12 \quad 13 \quad 14 \quad 12 \quad 15$$

What can you say about this process now?

8.37 Oil filters are sent to an engine assembly plant in large lots. For each shipment, a sample of 50 filters is inspected to determine the number of defectives. A lot is rejected if the number of defectives is greater than or equal to 3. If the actual proportion of defectives is 0.02, what percentage of the lots are rejected with this sampling plan?

TABLE 8.11

Week number	Number of errors	Week number	Number of errors
1	13	11	10
2	7	12	14
3	8	13	7
4	4	14	4
5	12	15	11
6	9	16	11
7	16	17	6
8	10	18	10
9	7	19	14
10	6	20	8

8.38 Consider a sampling plan with sample size $n = 20$ and acceptance number $a = 1$. Calculate the probability of accepting a lot with the following fraction of defectives:

a) $p = 0$ **b)** $p = 0.05$ **c)** $p = 0.10$ **d)** $p = 0.20$

e) $p = 0.40$ **f)** $p = 0.75$ **g)** $p = 1.0$

Graph the operating characteristic curve for this plan.

8.39 Repeat Problem 8.38 for

a) $n = 20$ and $a = 0$

b) $n = 20$ and $a = 2$

c) $n = 20$ and $a = 3$

Graph the operating characteristic curve for the sampling plans in Problem 8.38 and parts (a), (b), and (c) from above on the same graph. What is the effect of increasing the acceptance number a when n is held constant?

8.40 Repeat Problem 8.38 for

a) $n = 10$ and $a = 1$

b) $n = 15$ and $a = 1$

c) $n = 25$ and $a = 1$

Graph the operating characteristic curve for the sampling plans in Problem 8.38 and for parts (a), (b) and (c) of this problem on the same graph. What is the effect of increasing the sample size n when a is held constant?

Exercises

8.41 A manufacturing process makes precision shafts for use in lathes. The engineering specifications require that the length of the shaft be 6.625 ± 0.00125 inches. The process is monitored by randomly selecting $n = 4$ shafts every day. Results of these samples for 20 days are shown in Table 8.12.

a) Calculate the sample mean and range for each of the 20 samples.

b) Construct the $\bar{x}$ and the R charts for this data.

c) Does the process appear to be in control? Explain your answer.

TABLE 8.12

Sample number	Sample measurements			
	1	2	3	4
1	6.6255	6.6251	6.6255	6.6250
2	6.6238	6.6240	6.6250	6.6253
3	6.6248	6.6251	6.6254	6.6255
4	6.6245	6.6247	6.6245	6.6246
5	6.6246	6.6243	6.6244	6.6252
6	6.6246	6.6255	6.6255	6.6248
7	6.6265	6.6256	6.6248	6.6250
8	6.6245	6.6243	6.6253	6.6255
9	6.6250	6.6250	6.6255	6.6251
10	6.6247	6.6257	6.6248	6.6245
11	6.6249	6.6245	6.6243	6.6244
12	6.6250	6.6255	6.6250	6.6240
13	6.6247	6.6248	6.6252	6.6245
14	6.6240	6.6249	6.6245	6.6247
15	6.6260	6.6252	6.6250	6.6255
16	6.6253	6.6253	6.6255	6.6260
17	6.6257	6.6250	6.6257	6.6250
18	6.6250	6.6248	6.6250	6.6250
19	6.6250	6.6252	6.6255	6.6250
20	6.6245	6.6250	6.6249	6.6251

d) Calculate the C_p and the C_{pk} indexes. Is the process capable of meeting its specifications? Explain your answer.

8.42 Refer to the information in Problem 8.41. Suppose that the data for the next eight days gives the results shown in Table 8.13.

a) Calculate the sample mean and range for each sample and plot these on the $\bar{x}$ and the R charts. Does the process appear to be in control over this period? Explain your answer.

TABLE 8.13

Sample number	Sample measurements			
	1	2	3	4
21	6.6253	6.6247	6.6254	6.6246
22	6.6248	6.6254	6.6253	6.6249
23	6.6253	6.6255	6.6250	6.6254
24	6.6246	6.6253	6.6258	6.6255
25	6.6256	6.6253	6.6255	6.6256
26	6.6237	6.6258	6.6258	6.6259
27	6.6255	6.6256	6.6252	6.6250
28	6.6249	6.6248	6.6254	6.6253

b) Suppose the data from Samples 21–28 had given the following sample means:

6.6253   6.6245   6.6248   6.6257   6.6252,   6.6242   6.6240   6.6238

What conclusions can you now derive about the process? Explain your answer.

8.43 A bank processes checks using magnetic ink character recognition (MICR) equipment. This equipment has a sensing device that reads magnetic numbers on checks. If this device fails to read one or more of the magnetic numbers, the check is rejected. The rate of rejection is directly affected by the quality of the checks. In order to monitor the quality of checks, the bank randomly samples 1000 checks each day to determine the number of rejects. The results of the sampling for a 30-day period are shown in Table 8.14.

a) Calculate the proportion of rejects each day.

b) Using the information from part (a), calculate the centerline and the control limits for a p chart.

c) Construct the p chart and determine if the process is in control.

d) Suppose that over the next 10 days (days 31–40), the number of checks rejected were as follows:

10   9   14   16   7   9   20   11   6   12

What can you say about the process now? Explain your answer.

e) Suppose the data from days 31–40 had given the following information:

17   5   4   16   3   18   17   5   16

What conclusions can you now derive about the process? Explain your answer.

TABLE 8.14

Day i	Number of rejects	Day i	Number of rejects
1	6	16	16
2	12	17	13
3	11	18	11
4	10	19	14
5	14	20	12
6	6	21	5
7	10	22	10
8	5	23	13
9	10	24	5
10	8	25	7
11	12	26	11
12	9	27	15
13	8	28	5
14	11	29	7
15	4	30	8

8.44 The data in Table 8.15 represent length dimensions (in inches) of metal speaker screens used in the assembly of television sets at a large international manufacturer of electronics goods. These screens are purchased from a vendor and are measured on an electronic coordinate measuring machine on arrival at the plant. Engineering has specified 6.660 inches as the lower specification limit and 6.690 inches as the upper specification limit. There have been problems with both the quality and failure to meet the specifications. Consequently, the manufacturer has installed a quality control program to monitor these screens. The data in Table 8.15 were collected by taking three samples a day with five parts in each sample.

a) Calculate the sample mean and range for each of the 25 samples.

b) Construct the $\bar{x}$ and the R charts for these data.

c) What conclusions can you derive from these control charts?

d) Calculate the C_p and the C_{pk} indexes. What conclusions can you derive from these indexes? Is the process capable of meeting its specifications? Explain your answer.

e) If you were analyzing this problem, what recommendations would you make to the management of this organization?

TABLE 8.15

| Sample number | Sample measurements | | | | |
	1	2	3	4	5
1	6.700	6.703	6.701	6.702	6.702
2	6.703	6.696	6.707	6.705	6.704
3	6.703	6.703	6.700	6.701	6.703
4	6.697	6.712	6.697	6.690	6.701
5	6.709	6.693	6.693	6.703	6.686
6	6.697	6.701	6.692	6.697	6.700
7	6.699	6.702	6.694	6.698	6.694
8	6.698	6.707	6.706	6.700	6.698
9	6.701	6.704	6.693	6.702	6.696
10	6.700	6.699	6.702	6.698	6.690
11	6.703	6.677	6.703	6.697	6.703
12	6.700	6.706	6.690	6.704	6.703
13	6.703	6.703	6.704	6.705	6.702
14	6.704	6.700	6.703	6.705	6.706
15	6.702	6.701	6.705	6.703	6.703
16	6.705	6.708	6.706	6.706	6.707
17	6.708	6.692	6.698	6.698	6.696
18	6.693	6.700	6.607	6.700	6.694
19	6.700	6.692	6.698	6.696	6.699
20	6.694	6.698	6.703	6.700	6.697
21	6.705	6.704	6.693	6.702	6.699
22	6.705	6.695	6.702	6.700	6.702
23	6.702	6.708	6.705	6.707	6.700
24	6.692	6.697	6.696	6.695	6.696
25	6.701	6.699	6.696	6.697	6.701

Chapter 9

Hypothesis Testing

It is an error to argue in front of your data. You find yourself insensibly twisting them around to fit your theories.

SHERLOCK HOLMES

Introduction and Basic Concepts

9.1

The procedures presented in Chapter 7 describe the process of making both point and interval estimates of population parameters. In this chapter we turn to a class of problems that involves much the same approach as used for interval estimation. However, the objective now is quite different. Previously we used sample statistics to estimate population parameters. Now we are going to make *assumptions* about certain population parameters, then use sample statistics to determine whether these assumptions are reasonable or not. Thus, with estimation the inference is from a sample to a population; for hypothesis testing, the validity of an (assumed) population parameter is tested by looking at the sample results. An assumed value of a population parameter is called a **statistical hypothesis.** Determining the validity of an assumption of this nature is called the *test of a statistical hypothesis,* or simply **hypothesis testing.**

The major purpose of hypothesis testing is *to choose between two mutually exclusive and exhaustive hypotheses about the value of a population parameter.* The process of hypothesis testing brings together many of the previous topics of this book — calculation of sample statistics, random variables, probability distributions, and statistical inference.

To illustrate hypothesis testing, consider a production process designed to produce computer chips for one of the larger suppliers in the United States,

Advanced Micro Devices (AMD). Chips manufactured by this process have to meet rigid quality specifications. Chips not meeting specifications are labeled defective. One common source of defectives is a malfunctioning process, a typical problem occurring when impurities somehow infiltrate the system. When not malfunctioning, the process produces 10% or fewer defectives ($p \leq 0.10$, where p is the proportion of defective chips). When it is malfunctioning, the process typically produces more than 10% defectives ($p > 0.10$). To test hypotheses in this situation means choosing between the mutually exclusive and exhaustive alternatives, $p \leq 0.10$ and $p > 0.10$. A problem of this nature was discussed in Chapter 4 when the binomial distribution was presented.

To decide whether the production process is malfunctioning ($p > 0.10$) or not ($p \leq 0.10$), the quality control staff at AMD plan to take a sample of (n) chips, and determine how many of these chips are defective (x). The sample proportion of defective chips (x/n) is then used to decide between the two conflicting hypotheses. This decision problem is discussed at length in this section. Subsequent sections give other examples in some commonly occurring situations.

Types of Hypotheses

There are simple hypotheses and composite hypotheses. In a **simple hypothesis,** only one value of the population parameter is specified. If the proportion of defectives in a production process is hypothesized to be exactly 10%, $p = 0.10$, this represents a simple hypothesis. A drug company may use the simple hypothesis that the mean time for a drug to take effect is $\mu = 28$ (minutes). If a marketing research analyst specifies that the mean consumer preference for product 1 (μ_1) equals the mean consumer preference for product 2 (μ_2) this hypothesis is written as $\mu_1 - \mu_2 = 0$, and also represents a simple hypothesis.

Composite hypotheses specify a *range* of values that the population parameter might assume. The hypotheses $p \leq 0.10$, $\mu \geq 30$, and $\mu_1 - \mu_2 \neq 0$ all represent composite hypotheses. As you might suspect, assumptions in the form of simple hypotheses are generally easier to test than are composite hypotheses. In the former case we need to determine only whether or not the population parameter equals the specified value, while in the latter case it is necessary to determine whether or not the population parameter takes on any one of what may be a very large (or even infinite) number of values.

The two conflicting (mutually exclusive) hypotheses in a statistical test are referred to as the null hypothesis and the alternative hypothesis. The term **null hypothesis** developed from early work in the theory of hypothesis testing, representing an established or widely held theory the researcher believes does *not* represent the true value of the parameter (hence the word "null," which means invalid, void, or amounting to nothing). In this approach the **alternative hypothesis** generally specifies some new theory, contrary to the established theory, that the researcher believes *does* represent the true value of the population parameter. Thus, this convention, which is widely used in practice and will be used throughout this book, says that the null hypothesis is the "current" or generally accepted theory, and the alternative hypothesis is some "new" theory.*

In testing hypotheses it is most convenient to let the null hypothesis be the one that contains an equal sign, if either one has an equal sign. (*Note:* By an equal sign, we mean either $=$, or $\geq$ or $\leq$). Often the symbol H_0 is used to designate the null hypothesis, and H_a the alternative hypothesis. A colon and then the population assumption always follow these symbols. Thus, to test assumptions about the proportion (p) of defectives in a production process you might establish the following hypotheses:

H_0: $p \leq 0.10$ (null hypothesis, that the population proportion is 10% or less)

H_a: $p > 0.10$ (alternative hypothesis, that the population proportion is greater than 10%)

The null and alternative hypotheses can both be either simple or composite. The simple null hypothesis H_0: $p = 0.10$, for example, may be tested against a simple alternative such as H_a: $p = 0.25$, or against a composite hypothesis such as H_a: $p \neq 0.10$.

Consider an example of a composite null hypothesis involving a single mean. Auditors at Banc One (headquartered in Columbus, Ohio) have been told that the average balance due for the bank's 19,736 Master Card accounts on August 15th was $234. The auditors must establish a test to determine the validity of this statement. They establish the null hypothesis that the population mean is $234 or larger against the alternative that this mean is less than $234. Notice that this approach means the bank's assets are overstated if H_a is true. The test is a composite null versus a composite alternative:

$$H_0: \mu \geq 234 \quad \text{vs.} \quad H_a: \mu < 234$$

A sample (and the sample mean) from the population of 19,736 accounts will be used to decide whether to accept H_0 or accept H_a.

When two variables are involved, the null hypothesis often involves a zero on the right-hand side, indicating that the current theory is that the two variables are unrelated to one another, or have the same mean. To illustrate a test involving two populations, consider the question Public Service Indiana recently was asked (by the Utilities Commission): "Will a different rate structure encourage PSI customers to use less electricity at peak load times?" Without any additional information, the "current" theory here is that the new rate structure would be no better than the old, and maybe even worse than the old. The "new" theory is that mean usage (at peak load time) under the revised plan will, indeed, be better (less) than under the old plan. If we let μ_1 and μ_2

---

*Despite the fact that this convention is widely used in practice, most statisticians prefer *not* to associate any special meaning to the null or alternative hypothesis, but merely let these terms represent two different assumptions about the population(s).

represent the mean electrical usage under the old and new plans, respectively, then the appropriate hypotheses are:

$$H_0: \mu_1 - \mu_2 \leq 0 \quad \text{(null hypothesis that } \mu_1 \leq \mu_2)$$
$$H_a: \mu_1 - \mu_2 > 0 \quad \text{(alternative hypothesis that } \mu_1 > \mu_2)$$

Notice in all these examples that the null hypothesis has an equal sign (either $=$ or $\leq$ or $\geq$) and represents either the current theory or the "zero theory" (zero is included on the right-hand side). Regardless of the form of the two hypotheses, it is extremely important to remember that the true value of the population parameter under consideration *must* be either in the set specified by H_0 or in the set specified by H_a. By testing $H_0: p = 0.10$ against $H_a: p < 0.10$, for example, one is asserting that the true value of p either equals 0.10 or is less than 0.10, and that *no other values are possible* (p cannot be greater than 0.10).

One way to assure that either H_0 or H_a contains the true value of the population parameter is to let these two sets be *complementary*. That is, if the null hypothesis is $H_0: p = 0.10$, then the complementary alternative hypothesis is $H_a: p \neq 0.10$. Similarly, if $H_0: \mu_1 - \mu_2 \leq 0$, then the complementary alternative hypothesis is $H_a: \mu_1 - \mu_2 > 0$. From a statistical point of view, the easiest form to handle is a simple null hypothesis versus a simple alternative hypothesis. Unfortunately, most real-world problems cannot be stated in this form, but instead involve a composite null or a composite alternative hypothesis, or both. If a particular problem cannot be stated as a test between two simple hypotheses, then the next best alternative is to test a simple null hypothesis against a composite alternative. In other words, it is convenient to structure the problem so that the null hypothesis is a simple equality statement.

One- and Two-Sided Tests

If one is fortunate enough to be able to construct the test of hypotheses so that the null hypothesis is simple, then the alternative hypothesis may specify one or more values for the population parameter, and these value(s) may lie entirely above, or entirely below, or on both sides of the one value specified by the null hypothesis. A statistical test in which the alternative hypothesis specifies that the population parameter lies entirely above or entirely below the null hypothesis is called a **one-sided test;** an alternative hypothesis that specifies that the parameter can lie on either side of the value specified by H_0 is called a **two-sided test.** Thus, if Banc One tests $H_0: \mu \geq 234$ against $H_a: \mu < 234$, this is a one-sided test because H_a specifies that μ lies to one side (below) the value in H_0 (234). If the null hypothesis $H_0: \mu = 234$ is tested against $H_a: \mu \neq 234$, this represents a two-sided test, because the alternative value of μ can lie on *either* side of H_0.

The Form of the Decision Problem

The decision problem in hypothesis testing is deciding between two mutually exclusive hypotheses about a population parameter, based on a sample from the relevant population. The decision maker must either accept the null hypothesis or accept the alternative hypothesis. Because these two hypotheses are mutually exclusive and exhaustive, accepting the null hypothesis is equivalent to rejecting the alternative hypothesis. Similarly, accepting H_a is identical to rejecting H_0.

The decision maker has only the sample evidence to use in deciding whether to accept H_0 or H_a. The standard approach to this decision is to first assume that H_0 is true. This is comparable to a court of law, where a person is presumed innocent until proven guilty. Thus, H_0 is presumed true until the evidence suggests it is not (remember, H_0 is the "current" theory). In a court of law innocence is maintained as long as any reasonable doubt about guilt remains. Similarly, in hypothesis testing H_0 is maintained (not rejected) as long as there is a reasonable probability that H_0 is true.

Actually, in hypothesis testing we worry not only about rejecting H_0 when this hypothesis is true, but also about rejecting H_a when this hypothesis is true. Specifically, there are two types of errors in hypothesis testing:

1. The null hypothesis may be rejected incorrectly. This is called a **Type I error.** That is,

$$\text{Type I error} = \text{reject } H_0 \text{ when } H_0 \text{ is true}$$
$$= \text{reject } H_0 \,|\, H_0 \text{ true}$$

2. The alternative hypothesis may be rejected incorrectly. This is called a **Type II error.** That is,

$$\text{Type II error} = \text{reject } H_a \text{ when } H_a \text{ is true}$$
$$= \text{reject } H_a \,|\, H_a \text{ true}$$

There are four possible combinations of decisions and outcomes in hypothesis testing, as shown in Fig. 9.1.

To illustrate the concept of Type I and II errors, recall the example presented earlier about the proportion of defective chips in a production process. We hypothesized H_0: $p \leq 0.10$ (the current theory) versus H_a: $p > 0.10$ (the new theory). Assume for the moment that the process is producing 8% defectives; thus $p = 0.08$ is the actual (population) proportion, which means that H_0 is true. If a sample leads to accepting the hypothesis that $p \leq 0.10$, then the correct decision has been made. If the sample leads to rejecting H_0: $p \leq 0.10$ and accepting H_a: $p > 0.10$, then a Type I error has been made.

Figure 9.1
The four possible decision outcomes in hypothesis testing.

Action

	The true situation is	
	H_0 is true	H_a is true
Reject H_0 (Accept H_a)	Type I error	Correct decision
Reject H_a (Accept H_0)	Correct decision	Type II error

Now suppose that the actual proportion of defectives is 13%, which means that p is greater than 0.10% and H_a: $p > 0.10$ is true. If the sample leads to rejecting the alternative hypothesis in this case, then a Type II error has been made.

As another example of Type I and II errors, consider again the PSI example, where the mean electrical usage under a new rate plan (μ_2) was tested against the mean usage under the old rate (μ_1) with the following hypotheses:

$$H_0: \mu_1 - \mu_2 \leq 0 \quad \text{(new rate mean greater than or equal to the old)}$$
$$H_a: \mu_1 - \mu_2 > 0 \quad \text{(new rate mean is lower)}.$$

If a sample *incorrectly* leads to the conclusion the new rate is better (that is, reject H_0 when it is true), this is a Type I error; if the sample *incorrectly* leads to the conclusion the new rate is not better (reject H_a when it is true), then a Type II error is being made.

To illustrate Type I and II errors, recall again the analogy between a court of law and hypothesis testing. Figure 9.1 could be drawn as shown in Fig. 9.2 for the law case. In this situation the Type I error is generally considered far more serious, that of finding an innocent person guilty.

As indicated earlier, probabilities are involved in deciding whether to accept or reject H_0. Specifically, we would like to determine the probability of making a Type I error as well as the probability of making a Type II error. The probability theory from Chapters 4–6 can be used to determine these probabilities. The probabilities of Type I and II errors are conditional probabilities, as the former depends on the condition that H_0 is true, and the latter on the condition that H_a is true. The probability of a Type I error is denoted by the Greek letter α (alpha), and is called the **level of significance.**

$$\text{Level of significance: } \alpha = P(\text{Type I error})$$
$$= P(\text{reject } H_0 \mid H_0 \text{ true})$$

The level of significance of a statistical test is comparable to the probability of an error (also called α) as discussed in Chapter 7.

The probability of a Type II error is denoted by the Greek letter β (beta).

$$\beta = P(\text{Type II error})$$
$$= P(\text{reject } H_a \mid H_a \text{ true})$$

	The true situation is	
	Not guilty (H_0)	**Guilty (H_a)**
Jury finds guilty (Accept H_a)	Type I error	Correct decision
Jury finds not guilty (Accept H_0)	Correct decision	Type II error

Action

Figure 9.2
The four decision outcomes in the court of law.

Rather than refer to β, statisticians sometimes use $1 - \beta$, which is called the **power of a statistical test.** The power of a test is the complement of a Type I error. As such, it represents the ability (or "power") of a test to correctly reject a false null hypothesis.

$$Power\ of\ a\ test = 1 - \beta = 1 - P(\text{reject } H_a \,|\, H_a \text{ true})$$

The power of a test is discussed in Section 9.8 of this chapter.

Because decision makers want to avoid making *any* kind of error, one objective in hypothesis testing is to make *both* α and β as small as possible. But this is not as easy as it sounds, for (in general) as α is increased, β decreases, and vice versa (if n remains unchanged). Furthermore, a one-unit decrease (increase) in α does not imply a one-unit increase (decrease) in β, for these probabilities are *not* complementary. If n is increased, it is possible for both α and β to decrease because sampling error is potentially decreased. Since increasing n usually costs money, the researcher must decide just how much additional money should be spent on increasing the sample size in order to reduce the sizes of α and β.

A typical approach to hypothesis testing is to first establish a value for α. The rationale behind this procedure is that it is important to establish beforehand the risk that one wants to assume of incorrectly rejecting a true null hypothesis. In other words, the size of the Type I error in this approach is viewed as so much more important than the size of the Type II error that α is set without much regard for β. The practice of setting α in this manner stems from the approach to hypothesis testing whereby the null hypothesis represents a "current opinion" on an issue and the alternative hypothesis represents a viewpoint of the researcher contrary to that commonly accepted.

The value of α, (the level of significance), indicates the importance (the significance) that a researcher attaches to the consequences associated with incorrectly rejecting H_0. A researcher who uses a level of significance of $\alpha = 0.05$ is willing to accept a 5% chance of being wrong when rejecting H_0. For most statistical problems in the social sciences α is set, rather arbitrarily, as either 0.05 or 0.01. However, in the medical sciences α is set much lower, perhaps as low as 0.005 or 0.001. Medical science has to be *very* concerned about accepting an incorrect hypothesis. Although α is seldom set higher than $\alpha = 0.10$, and values such as $\alpha = 0.05$, $\alpha = 0.01$, and $\alpha = 0.001$ are used frequently, there is no reason any other value may not be used. If α is set at some predetermined level, then it is extremely important that this value be specified before any data are collected.

In testing a new drug, such as a cure for cancer, the drug must be assumed to be of no benefit, or even harmful, until it is proved otherwise. The alternative hypothesis is that the drug is indeed beneficial. A serious Type I error would be made if a harmful drug (H_0 true) were certified as beneficial. Another example of the costs of making a Type I error involves the controversy in 1989 surrounding an announcement by two chemists that they had discovered a method for "cold fusion" of atoms. Subsequent investigation and the inability to replicate the experiment suggested they had not really achieved fusion, although errors in their technique made it appear they had. Thus, decision makers often approach hypothesis testing by initially establishing α, so the probability of rejecting a true "current" theory is predetermined.

The discussion thus far should have been useful in deciding which hypothesis to designate as the null and which the alternative. Although theoretically it should make no difference, the widespread practice of setting α at some predetermined level gives an automatic "boost" to the null hypothesis (because of our reluctance to reject H_0 unless we are convinced it is not true). As we suggested above, the traditional approach is to designate as H_0 the current theory (or perhaps the more "conservative" hypothesis—the hypothesis that best protects the general public, for instance). Thus, in testing a new theory of relativity, we would let Einstein's theory of relativity be H_0, as the current theory. Similarly, we would let H_0 be the assumption that there is no cure for the common cold, and let H_0 represent the hypothesis that there is no way to achieve cold fusion.

Balancing the Risks and Costs of Making a Wrong Decision

When α is set at some predetermined level, the value of β is automatically established (for a given sample size). Most modern statisticians do not condone the indiscriminate use of setting α without regard for β. First, it is not always good statistical practice to establish H_0 as the hypothesis the researcher is trying to disprove. Such a convention may give an artificiality to the research that distorts its true purpose or hinders the effectiveness of the testing procedure. In addition, setting α at some predetermined level does not consider the associated level of β. While it is not incorrect to set α at some predetermined level, this value should be established by considering the risks of *both* Type I and Type II errors. To be more specific, the researcher should find the optimal balance between α and β in order to minimize the *costs* of making an error.

As pointed out in Chapter 6, the objective of sampling can be stated as one of minimizing the cost of making an incorrect decision (including sampling costs). Unfortunately, in many circumstances, there may be no easy way even to determine what these costs are, much less to try to balance them. In medical research, for example, it may be difficult if not impossible to assess the costs associated with an incorrect decision involving a new drug or surgical technique. But even if these costs could somehow be assessed, how does one go about balancing costs that may include pain, suffering, and even loss of life? On the other hand, if it is possible to identify the relevant costs and express them in terms of some comparable basis, such as dollars, then we may be able to balance these costs quite explicitly. Section 9.7 features an example of cost balancing.

The Standard
Format of
Hypothesis
Testing

9.2

There are many different population parameters, many different potential forms of hypotheses, and many different sample statistics, random variables, and probability distributions that may be involved in testing hypotheses. It is not, therefore, feasible to catalog all such tests. However, they all follow a similar procedure, which can be learned and then applied to different situations as they arise. This procedure can be summarized by the following five steps, each of which will be elaborated on in following sections.

1. Determine the relevant population and state the null and alternative hypotheses.
2. Determine the appropriate test statistic (such as a z-test, a t-test, or a binomial test).
3. Collect the sample and compute a probability value (p-value).
4. Either accept/reject H_0 based on a given value of α, or "report" the p-value.
5. Interpret the accept/reject decision or the p-value.

We will illustrate these five steps by the example involved with the production of computer chips. A production process at Advanced Micro Devices is malfunctioning. When the process is malfunctioning, AMD knows there will be either 10% ($p = 0.10$) or 25% ($p = 0.25$) defective chips. It is critical to AMD to know which is the case, for only minor repairs are needed if $p = 0.10$, whereas major repairs are needed if $p = 0.25$. Typically, a random sample of $n = 20$ is taken from the process, and the number of defects in this sample is used to determine if the process is judged to need minor repairs or major repairs. The five steps necessary for performing this test are described below.

Step 1. Determine the Relevant Population and State the Null and Alternative Hypotheses

In every hypothesis-testing problem the first step is to determine what population is under investigation, and then clearly state the two conflicting hypotheses. Defining the population is important because there may be confusion about what information is relevant to test a specific hypothesis, and how to collect a random sample from this population. The example in Chapter 6 regarding the 1936 presidential election poll conducted by the *Literary Digest* is classic in that the population sampled did not represent the general electorate. As another example, market research surveys frequently are taken at malls, gathering the opinion of passing shoppers. There is serious question whether such opinions reflect shoppers in general, or even reflect the opinion of all shoppers in that particular mall.

It is most convenient to formulate the null and alternative hypotheses as simple hypotheses, although it is not necessary to do so. We will use the convention that the null hypothesis *always* contains an equal sign (= , or ≤ , or ≥), and that H_0 represents either the "current" theory or the "zero" theory (a zero on the right-hand side). In all cases the two conflicting hypotheses must be formulated so that the true value of the population parameter is included in either the null or the alternative hypothesis (it is not possible for *both* hypotheses to be false).

For our production-process example, the assumption is that either $p = 0.10$ or $p = 0.25$, and that *no other values of p are possible.* In this case either value of p could be the null hypothesis; from past records, however, the company is known to prefer to assume the current theory to be minor repairs rather than major repairs. Hence,

$$H_0: \ p = 0.10 \quad \text{(minor repairs needed)}$$
$$H_a: \ p = 0.25 \quad \text{(major repairs needed)}$$

One of these hypotheses must be true, the other false. In this case we assume the relevant population to be all chips currently produced by the process.

Step 2. Determine the Appropriate Test Statistic

The second step in hypothesis testing is to determine which test statistic (a random variable) is appropriate to determine whether to accept or reject H_0. The random variables presented thus far include the standardized normal, the *t,* the *F,* the chi-square, and the binomial. If the population parameter being tested involves means, then the random variable will usually involve the normal distribution (z-test) or the t-distribution. If the population parameter involves variances, then the chi-square or F-distribution is usually appropriate. For problems involving two discrete outcomes, such as in the present example with good or defective items in a production process, then the correct distribution is typically the binomial.

A **test statistic** is a random variable used to determine how close a specific sample result falls to the null hypothesis.

The following test statistics are examples of the many we will present in this chapter.

$$z = \frac{\overline{x} - \mu}{\sigma/\sqrt{n}} \qquad \text{(test statistic for } \mu \text{ when } \sigma \text{ is known)}$$

$$t = \frac{\overline{x} - \mu}{s/\sqrt{n}} \qquad \text{(test statistic for } \mu \text{ when } \sigma \text{ is unknown)}$$

x successes in n trials   (proportions test for p, using the binomial distribution)

Step 3. Collect the Sample and Compute a Probability Value (p-value)

The sample is taken using the random sampling techniques described in Chapter 6. The next step is then to calculate the sample statistic used to estimate the population parameter being tested. For hypotheses about μ, the statistic $\overline{x}$ is calculated. For tests about σ^2, s^2 is calculated. For tests about a binomial proportion (p), the number of successes (or failures) in the sample is used (x).

After the sample statistic is calculated, then we calculate a *probability-value*, or *p-value*. The p-value is a probability that (essentially) indicates how far away the sample statistic is from the value (of this statistic) expected under the null hypothesis. A low p-value, such as $p = 0.003$, indicates the sample statistic is quite far from that expected under H_0. In fact, a p-value of $p = 0.003$ indicates that such a sample result would occur only 3 times in 1000 replications of the experiment, when H_0 is true. On the other hand, a high p-value, such as $p = 0.40$, indicates there is a high probability (40 times in 100) the given sample result will occur when H_0 is true. This suggests that the sample result is *not* particularly far from that expected under H_0.

A p-**value** is the probability of observing a given sample result, or one more extreme, assuming that H_0 is true.

To illustrate calculating a p-value, consider again Advanced Micro Devices' production problem, where a random sample of $n = 20$ chips is taken, and each chip is examined to determine if it is good or defective. The number of defective chips in this sample, labeled as x, can be any number from 0 to 20. To determine the p-value we need to know the probability distribution for all possible sample outcomes, *assuming H_0: $p = 0.10$ is true*. Thus, we need to know the (binomial) probability distribution for $n = 20$, $p = 0.10$. Table 9.1 represents a computer output using the statistical package Minitab, in which we asked for binomial values when $p = 0.10$ and $n = 20$.*

Suppose, for the moment, that the random sample of $n = 20$ results in $x = 4$ defectives. This result is used to calculate the p-value, which is the probability of receiving a sample of $x = 4$ defectives, or a sample of a more extreme value, assuming $p = 0.10$. Samples that are "more extreme" are those farther away from the expected value assuming the null hypothesis is true (which is 0.10 for this problem). In a sample of $n = 20$, the null hypothesis predicts $np = 20(0.10) = 2$ defectives. Hence, for this problem, $x = 5$ is a more

---

*The Minitab commands for producing Table 9.1 are

MTB > PDF;
SUBC > BINOMIAL n = 20 p = 0.10.

TABLE 9.1   Minitab output for the binomial, $n = 20, p = 0.10$

BINOMIAL WITH $n = 20$, $p = 0.10$

K	$P(x = K)$
0	0.1216
1	0.2702
2	0.2852
3	0.1901
4	0.0898
5	0.0319
6	0.0089
7	0.0020
8	0.0004
9	0.0001
10	0.0000
	$E[x] = 2$

Note: Probabilities not shown, such as $P(x = 11)$, all equal 0.

extreme result, as is $x = 6, x = 7$, and so forth, up to $x = 20$. Thus, the p-value is the sum $P(x \geq 4)$.

$$p\text{-value} = P(x = 4) + P(x = 5) + \cdots + P(x = 20)$$

From Table 9.1, this probability is

$$
\begin{aligned}
P(x \geq 4) &= P(x = 4) + P(x = 5) + \cdots + P(x = 20) \\
&= 0.0898 \quad + 0.0319 \quad + \cdots + 0.0000 \\
&= 0.1331
\end{aligned}
$$

The p-value is thus 0.1331. As we will discuss in Step 4, this probability means there is a 13.31% chance of receiving four or more defectives when $p = 0.10$ (that is, when H_0 is true). We will give many examples of the calculation and interpretation of p-values throughout the remainder of not only this chapter, but most of the remaining chapters as well.

p-Values for Two-Sided Tests.

In the chip problem described above, the alternative hypothesis, H_a: $p = 0.25$, is one-sided, because it specifies a value entirely on one side of the null hypothesis, H_0: $p = 0.10$. Thus, our test was a one-sided test. If the alternative hypothesis specifies values on *both* sides of H_0, then the test is a two-sided test. For example, the hypotheses

$$H_0: p = 0.10 \quad \text{versus} \quad H_a: p \neq 0.10$$

represent a two-sided test. A two-sided test means the researcher is much less certain about the alternative hypothesis, which implies that the p-value will have to be comparably larger than for a one-sided test. For a two-sided test, the p-value is twice the size of the probability for a one-sided test.

TABLE 9.2   Minitab output for the binomial, $n = 100, p = 0.10$

BINOMIAL WITH $n = 100$ $p = 0.10$			
K	P(x=K)	K	P(x=K)
0	0.0000	12	0.0988
1	0.0003	13	0.0743
2	0.0016	14	0.0513
3	0.0059	15	0.0327
4	0.0159	16	0.0193
5	0.0339	17	0.0106
6	0.0596	18	0.0054
7	0.0889	19	0.0026
8	0.1148	20	0.0012
9	0.1304	21	0.0005
10	0.1319	22	0.0002
11	0.1199	23	0.0001
			E[x] = 10

When a two-sided test is used, the p-value is exactly double the probability calculated as if the test were one-sided.[*]

Let's use the two-sided test above to illustrate this doubling, namely H_0: $p = 0.10$ versus H_a: $p \neq 0.10$. Now assume a random sample of $n = 100$ items was taken from the production process, and $x = 4$ of these are defective. Table 9.2 shows the Minitab printout of the binomial distribution for the first 20 values of x when $n = 100, p = 0.10$.

Notice at the bottom of Table 9.2 that the expected value of x is $E[x] = 10$. This is the average value expected under the null hypothesis, and equals $np = 100(0.10) = 10$. The p-value is the probability of our sample result, $P(x = 4)$, *plus the probability of all the more extreme sample results.* All the more extreme results are those farther away (than $x = 4$) from the expected value (of 10). Thus, $x = 3$, $x = 2$, $x = 1$, and $x = 0$ are all more extreme results. Therefore, the probability we need to calculate is $P(x \leq 4)$. From Table 9.2,

$$P(x \leq 4) = P(x = 4) + P(x = 3) + P(x = 2) + P(x = 1) + P(x = 0)$$
$$= 0.0159 \quad + 0.0059 \quad + 0.0016 \quad + 0.0003 \quad + 0.0000$$
$$= 0.0237$$

---

[*]There are some special modifications to this rule that we will describe as the occasion arises. The reader should be careful *not* to double a p-value that is greater than 0.50, for the resulting value will exceed 1.0, and not be a probability.

The probability 0.0237 is the p-value for a one-sided test. Since H_a is two-sided, the p-value is *twice* this probability. That is,

$$p\text{-value} = 2(0.0237) = 0.0474$$

Procedure When H_0 Is Composite.   What happens if H_0 is not simple, but composite? For example, both the following hypotheses are composite:

$$H_0: p \leq 0.10 \quad \text{versus} \quad H_a: p > 0.10$$

For a composite null there is no one single value of H_0 (for example, there are many values of p that are ≤ 0.10). The most common approach in this situation is to *determine the p-value using the most conservative value possible under the null hypothesis.* The most conservative value is generally the one closest to the alternative hypothesis. Thus, if the alternative hypothesis is $H_a: p > 0.10$, then the closest value specified by the null hypothesis is $p = 0.10$. The p-value can now be calculated by testing the null hypothesis as if it were $H_0: p = 0.10$ versus $H_a: p > 0.10$. This is a one-sided test. If we had the sample result $x = 17$, with $n = 100$, then the reader should use Table 9.2 to verify that the

$$p\text{-value} = 0.0206$$

Step 4. Either Accept/Reject H_0 Based on a Given Value of α, or "Report" the p-value

As we have indicated, the risk of most concern in classical hypothesis testing is that of incorrectly rejecting a true null hypothesis. Essentially, a p-value is the "risk" involved, based on a specific sample result, of incorrectly rejecting a true null hypothesis. We will call this "the risk the decision maker *has* to take." The level of significance (α), on the other hand, is "the risk the decision maker is *willing* to take" of incorrectly rejecting a true null hypothesis. To make a decision to accept/reject H_0 we compare these two risks. *If the risk the decision maker is willing to take is greater than the risk this person has to take, then H_0 should be rejected. Otherwise, accept H_0.* This rule is easily specified if α is known.

If α is greater than the p-value, reject H_0.
If α is less than or equal to the p-value, accept H_0.

Suppose α is specified in advance to be $\alpha = 0.05$, and the p-value $= 0.0206$, as it was in our last example (a one-sided test). In this case $\alpha > p$-value, which means that we reject H_0. In fact, any α that exceeds 0.0206 leads to rejection of H_0.

Now suppose the test is two-sided, H_a: $p \neq 0.10$. In this case the p-value $= 2(0.0206) = 0.0412$. All values of $\alpha \leq 0.0412$ in this situation lead to acceptance of H_0.

Reporting a p-value. When the decision maker is someone other than the person carrying out the research (the statistician), then the level of significance (α) may not be known. Or perhaps the statistician is writing a report in which each of the various readers may be thought of as potential decision makers, all with possibly different α's. In these circumstances a common procedure is to report the p-value. This reporting permits the decision maker to compare the α-level with the p-value, and then make the decision to accept or reject H_0. Some people call this "passing the buck."

Step 5. Interpret the Accept/Reject Decision or the p-value

The statistician frequently has to interpret the results of a statistical analysis to people who may not be familiar with statistical terminology. Thus, it is important for the researcher to summarize or interpret the conclusions reached to the layman, *in terms of the original problem.* For example, suppose in the production process example, the sample leads to rejecting H_0: $p \leq 0.10$ in favor of H_a: $p > 0.10$, with a p-value of 0.0206. In this case the researcher may wish to state something like the following: "The sample results do not support the hypothesis that the proportion of defectives is 10% or less. We reject this hypothesis, but recognize in doing so that there is some risk (about 2%) that this conclusion is not correct."

Calculating Critical Regions

9.3

In some circumstances the decision maker may wish to decide to reject/accept H_0 by determining a *critical region* based on the value of α. This approach leads to *exactly* the same result as that described above; it is merely an alternative approach to deciding whether to accept or reject the null hypothesis.

The **critical region** is those values of the sample statistic that lead to rejection of H_0, based on a given value of α.

To illustrate a critical region, return to the binomial probabilities in Table 9.2, and suppose we know that $\alpha = 0.05$. In this problem the sample size is $n = 100$ and the null and alternative hypotheses are

$$H_0: p \leq 0.10 \quad \text{versus} \quad H_a: p > 0.10$$

The critical region is the set of values of the test statistic (x) that would lead to rejection of H_0 when $\alpha = 0.05$. To show how to find the critical region for the problem above, we have reproduced in Fig. 9.3 the probabilities from Table 9.2. Because H_a specifies that the proportion of defectives must be *greater* than 10%, the set of x-values leading to rejection of H_0 must be greater than 10 (representing the expected number of defectives when $n = 100$ and $p = 0.10$). That is, no values of x less than 10 could possibly lead to rejecting H_0: $p \leq 0.10$; hence the critical region must lie above $x = 10$.

The critical region must be constructed such that the probability of falling in this region is as large as possible, *but no larger than α* (equal to α is ideal). The critical region in Fig. 9.3, $x \geq 16$, was determined by finding a set of x-values in the upper tail whose total probability is as large as possible, but still not larger than $\alpha = 0.05$. From Table 9.2 the probability of falling in the critical region $x \geq 16$ is

$$P(x \geq 16) = P(x = 16) + P(x = 17) + \cdots + P(x = 23)$$
$$= 0.0193 \quad + 0.0106 \quad + \cdots + 0.0001$$
$$= 0.0399$$

The critical region $x \geq 15$ is not possible because the probability $P(x \geq 15) = 0.0718$ is *larger* than $\alpha = 0.05$; the critical region $x \geq 17$ is not appropriate because $x \geq 16$ has a higher probability. Thus, $x \geq 16$ is the correct critical region.

For one-sided tests, the critical region is always in one tail (in the direction predicted by H_a). For two-sided tests, the critical region will consist of two parts, one part in the upper tail, and one part in the lower tail.

Two-Tailed Critical Regions

In the example above the critical region was in one tail of the binomial distribution. Now suppose the alternative hypothesis is two-sided, such as

$$H_0: p = 0.10 \quad \text{versus} \quad H_a: p \neq 0.10$$

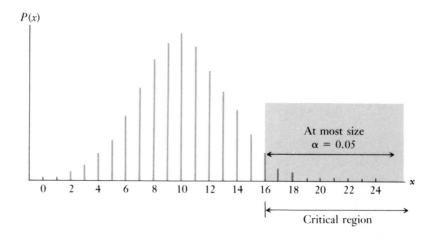

Figure 9.3
Illustration of a one-tailed critical region.

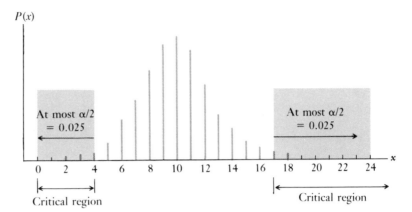

Figure 9.4
Illustration of a two-tailed
critical region.

The critical region for this two-sided test must lie in both tails of the binomial distribution. Generally, half of α is allocated to each tail (just as we did for confidence intervals). Thus, if $\alpha = 0.05$, then $\alpha/2 = 0.025$ must be allocated to each tail. Figure 9.3 is reproduced in Fig. 9.4, showing this time two parts to the critical region, $x \leq 4$, and $x \geq 17$.

The value $x = 4$ was selected to begin the lower part of this critical region because $P(x \leq 4) = 0.0237$ is not greater than $\alpha/2 = 0.025$, and $P(x \leq 5) = 0.0576$ is too large a probability. Similarly, the value $x = 17$ was selected because $P(x \geq 17) = 0.0206$ is as large as possible but not greater than $\alpha/2 = 0.025$. The reader may note that for this problem the *actual* size of α is $0.0237 + 0.0206 = 0.0443$, rather than 0.05. This is as close as we can get to $\alpha = 0.05$ for this binomial problem without being larger than 0.05.

Problems

9.1 **a)** Which is more serious: a Type I or a Type II error? Why?

   b) Why is it necessary to be concerned with the *probability* of Type I and Type II errors?

   c) What is meant by the phrase "the costs of making an incorrect decision"? How are these costs related to the problem of balancing the risks of making an incorrect decision?

   d) Think of a potential hypothesis-testing problem in a business situation. Describe the relevant population and establish an appropriate null and alternative hypothesis. Specify the costs of making a Type I and II error.

9.2 *Consumer Reports* described a Los Angeles bakery that was fined $1200 for selling loaves of bread that were underweight. The stated weight of each loaf of bread is 24 oz. A sample of 1861 loaves was taken, and each one weighed.

   a) What null and alternative hypothesis would you establish as an attorney for the City of Los Angeles?

b) Describe, in words, what a Type I and II error would be in this circumstance. What would you guess to be the consequences of each type of error in this situation?

c) What test statistic is appropriate here?

d) If the p-value $= 0.0013$, how would you interpret this value for a nonstatistician? What conclusion would you expect in this circumstance?

9.3 A spokesperson for Ford Motor Company claims that more customers are "very pleased" with their new Fords this year than were last year, when 70% of the population gave this (highest) rating. In sample of 50 randomly selected customers this year, 39 gave this rating.

a) As the first step in the survey process, what is the relevant population and what hypotheses would you have established? Is this a one- or two-sided test?

b) What test statistic is appropriate here? How did you know?

c) Calculate the p-value associated with your test statistic in part (b).

d) Interpret the p-value in part (c).

e) If you had known that $\alpha = 0.05$, what critical region would you have established?

9.4 A nationally known insurance company has been advertising on television that "Nine out of ten claims are in the return mail two days after receipt." You are suspicious of this proportion, and decide to take a random sample of 100 of the firm's returns to see if the proportion may, in fact, be lower. What null and alternative hypotheses would you establish? Specify the costs of making a Type I and II error.

9.5 Some federal highway money may be withheld from a state if the proportion of cars exceeding the speed limit in that state is judged to be higher than the national average. The national average is estimated to be 20% exceeding the speed limit. Complete all five steps of hypothesis testing in this circumstance, assuming a random sample of 50 cars in the state finds 16 to be exceeding the speed limit.

9.6 Specify the relevant population and establish the null and alternative hypotheses in each of the following circumstances. Specify in each case whether the alternative hypothesis is one- or two-sided.

a) The average face value of a grocery coupon was 38 cents in 1988 according to the Manufacturer's Coupon Control Center. What hypotheses would be appropriate to determine if the average face value has changed?

b) The report in part (a) indicated that 3.2% of the coupons were redeemed. What hypotheses are appropriate now?

c) A Farm Bureau study of rural incomes is designed to determine if county A's income differs significantly from county B's.

d) In a national television advertisement, randomly selected consumers were asked to taste two types of beer and then indicate which one they preferred, type A or type B. Type B was the beer sponsoring the ad.

e) A study by the American Bankers Association survey of 453 commercial banks indicated that 40% of all credit-card holders paid their balance in full each month in 1987; a similar study of 429 banks indicated 35% paid in full in 1988. What hypotheses would have been appropriate for this study?

f) Procter and Gamble is trying to determine if the proportion of people using Crest toothpaste is different in Indiana, where it was developed, than it is in Ohio, where P&G has its headquarters.

9.7 What is meant by the term "level of significance"? Give an example not presented in the book.

9.8 **a)** What is the difference (if any) between using p-values in hypothesis testing, and the approach that uses critical regions?

b) What advantage does reporting a p-value have over using an α-value to accept or reject the null hypothesis?

9.9 Why do we say that the null hypothesis has a "built-in advantage"? Is this approach optimal? Why is it used?

9.10 T.I.M.E., Inc., a marketing research company headquartered in Columbus, Ohio, was asked to collect a sample to compare Campbell's vegetable soup with Rax's vegetable soup. In this study 135 randomly selected soup eaters were asked to rate the two brands of soup, rating each one on a scale from 1 to 10. What hypotheses would you establish here? What do you think is the relevant population?

9.11 Is a one-sided alternative hypothesis better than a two-sided alternative? What effect does a two-sided alternative have on the p-value?

9.12 The two Kroger supermarkets in a midwestern city have agreed to advertise in the newspaper of a neighboring town if it can be established that more than 15% of the people in the town shopped at one of the two stores at least once in the past year.

a) What null and alternative hypotheses should be established by the newspaper? What is the population?

b) What sample statistic is appropriate?

c) A random sample of size $n = 156$ is collected, and $\alpha = 0.05$. Use the computer output in Table 9.3 to determine what critical region the newspaper should establish to decide whether to advertise.

TABLE 9.3

BINOMIAL DISTRIBUTION

$n = 156$ $p = .15$

X	P(X)	CUMULATIVE PROBABILITY	X	P(X)	CUMULATIVE PROBABILITY	X	P(X)	CUMULATIVE PROBABILITY
7	.00002	.00002	20	.07026	.26277	33	.00955	.98520
8	.00007	.00009	21	.08029	.34307	34	.00609	.99129
9	.00019	.00028	22	.08695	.43002	35	.00375	.99504
10	.00050	.00078	23	.08940	.51941	36	.00222	.99727
11	.00117	.00195	24	.08742	.60683	37	.00127	.99854
12	.00250	.00445	25	.08146	.68829	38	.00070	.99924
13	.00489	.00934	26	.07243	.76072	39	.00038	.99962
14	.00881	.01816	27	.06154	.82226	40	.00019	.99981
15	.01472	.03288	28	.05003	.87229	41	.00010	.99991
16	.02290	.05578	29	.03897	.91126	42	.00005	.99996
17	.03327	.08905	30	.02911	.94038	43	.00002	.99998
18	.04534	.13440	31	.02088	.96126		$E[X] = 23.40$	
19	.05812	.19252	32	.01440	.97565			

d) Thirty-one people respond that they have shopped at least once in the past year. What p-value would you report? What decision should be made if $\alpha = 0.05$?

9.13 A report in *USA Today* suggested that the proportion of the U.S. population preferring domestic cars to imports is now greater than 50% (H_a), whereby previously it had been running about 50% (H_0). Fifty randomly selected people were asked their preference.

a) Specify the relevant population and the appropriate hypotheses.

b) If the researcher uses $x \geq 31$ as the critical region, what is the assumed value of α?

c) If the researcher switches to a two-sided test, $H_a: p \neq 0.50$, what critical region is appropriate if $\alpha = 0.05$?

9.14 a) What is the power of a test? Is it always desirable to use the most powerful test available?

b) Describe a situation where the power of a test would be very important to a researcher.

9.15 A 1989 *Wall Street Journal* article reported on returns for the first quarter of 1989 relative to returns the previous year for 12 fund categories. What hypotheses would you establish for this problem? What is the relevant population?

9.16 An April 6, 1989, article in the *Wall Street Journal* reported on a Chicago case where a federal court ruled against a company for racial discrimination. Magistrate Elaine E. Bucko said that hiring statistics supplied by both the EEOC and the company "showed a significant disparity between availability and hire rates for black clericals" and that "chance alone cannot account for the discrepancy." What is the relevant population here? What hypotheses should have been established?

One-Sample Tests on μ

9.4

One of the most common tests in hypothesis testing involves μ, the mean of a population. In general, there are two types of tests involving μ, one in which σ is assumed to be known, and the other in which σ is assumed to be unknown. In the former case the z-distribution is the appropriate test statistic. In the latter case the t-distribution is the appropriate test statistic, although the z is used commonly even in these cases, provided that n is large (where "large" generally means over 30). Both the z- and the t-tests for μ are discussed in this section.

The z-Test for μ When σ Is Known

To illustrate a test on means, let's return to the example in Chapter 6, where a midwestern telephone company is considering changing to measured service. Company records indicate that current charges for basic service average

$15.30, and are normally distributed with a standard deviation of $4.10. That is, $\mu = 15.30$, $\sigma = 4.10$, and charges are normally distributed. Recall such a distribution is abbreviated as $N(\$15.30, 4.10^2)$.

The telephone company claims that charges under the new measured service will result in an average bill that is less than the current average of $15.30. Opponents state that the average will be equal to or higher than $15.30. In this case it is not obvious which hypothesis should be H_0 and which H_a. However, since the company is claiming something "new" (from current rates), and the opponent's theory has the equal sign, we make $\mu \geq \$15.30$ the null hypothesis and $\mu < \$15.30$ the alternative. This is a one-sided test.

$$H_0: \mu \geq 15.30 \quad \text{versus} \quad H_a: \mu < 15.30$$

If n is large ($n \geq 30$), or the parent population is normally distributed, then the appropriate test statistic is

> *Test statistic for μ when σ is known:* $z_c = \dfrac{\overline{x} - \mu_0}{\sigma/\sqrt{n}}$ (9.1)

In Formula (9.1) the symbol z_c stands for a *calculated* value of z. This is to distinguish it from a value of z that is determined by searching Table III in Appendix B. The symbol μ_0 represents the *hypothesized* value, under H_0, of the population parameter μ. Thus, $\mu_0 = 15.30$ for our current example. For now we assume the population standard deviation, σ, and n, are both known.

The next step is to take the sample. As in Chapter 6, a random sample size of $n = 36$ is taken, and this sample results in a mean of $14.00 ($\overline{x} = 14.00$). Since the sample size is greater than 30, the hypotheses can be tested using a value of z_c calculated from Formula (9.1) without assuming a normal parent population.

$$z_c = \frac{\overline{x} - \mu_0}{\sigma/\sqrt{n}} = \frac{14.00 - 15.30}{4.10/\sqrt{36}} = -1.90$$

(This is the same value calculated on page 229.)

Recall that a p-value is the probability of obtaining the computed value of the test statistic, or a more extreme value. For the example above, "more extreme" means values of z less than or equal to -1.90, because $z = 0$ is expected under the null hypothesis. Thus,

$$p\text{-value} = P(z \leq -1.90)$$
$$= 0.0287 \quad (\text{From Table III})$$

Either this p-value can be "reported," or a decision can be made to accept/reject H_0 if α is known. For example, if $\alpha = 0.05$, then we reject H_0 since the p-value $< \alpha$. In this case the interpretation might be as follows: "The sample mean of $\overline{x} = \$14.00$ will occur less than 3% of the time when the true mean is $15.30 or larger, thus casting serious doubt on the current assumption that average charges will be $15.30 or larger under the new plan." In statistical

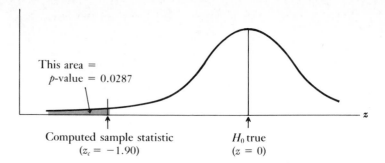

Figure 9.5
Illustrating the
determination of a p-value.

terms, we say that this sample mean is "significantly different" from the mean of $15.30 specified by H_0, assuming $\alpha = 0.05$.

Any $\alpha > 0.0287$ will lead to rejection of H_0. Any $\alpha \leq 0.0287$ will lead to acceptance of H_0. Figure 9.5 illustrates this p-value.

The approach described in Section 9.3, that of using a critical region, can be used in the current situation. For this type of problem the critical region can be expressed either in terms of the original sample statistic $(\bar{x})$, or expressed in standardized terms (z). The two approaches are equivalent, and since the latter (z-value) approach is much easier, we will use it.

The critical region is those values of the **z**-distribution which lead to rejection of H_0, for a given α. If $\alpha = 0.05$, and the test is a one-sided, the appropriate z-value cuts off 5% of the area in one of the two tails of the normal distribution. From Table III, we can see that the value $z = -1.645$ cuts off 5% in the lower tail (the lower tail is used because H_a is one-sided on the lower side). Figure 9.6 illustrates the critical region and the p-value together.

Because the sample falls in the critical region H_0 should be rejected. This is exactly the same conclusion reached by comparing the p-value with α — rejecting H_0 because the value of α (0.05) is greater than the p-value (0.0287). The reader may wish to redo the analysis above assuming the test is two-sided, using H_0: $\mu = 15.30$ versus H_a: $\mu \neq 15.30$. We will illustrate the two-sided approach in the next example.

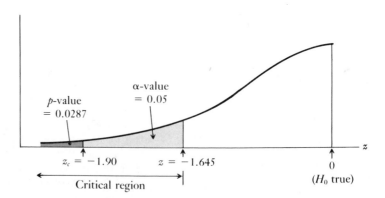

Figure 9.6
The critical region and
p-value for H_0: $\mu \geq 15.30$
versus H_a: $\mu < 15.30$ when
$\alpha = 0.05$.

The t-test for μ When σ Is Unknown

In many circumstances it is unreasonable to assume that σ is known, for when the population mean (μ) is unknown, the population standard deviation often is unknown also (since σ depends on the size of the squared deviations about μ). When σ is unknown, the z-test statistic is no longer exactly correct.

Recall from Chapter 6 that in order to solve problems involving μ when σ is unknown, the t-distribution is appropriate (if the parent population is normal). The test statistic is

---

Test statistic when σ is unknown:

$$t_c = \frac{\bar{x} - \mu_0}{s/\sqrt{n}}$$

with $\nu = n - 1$ degrees of freedom

(9.2)

EXAMPLE 1

Automobile manufacturers typically offer an extended warranty on new automobiles. Chevrolet, for example, currently offers a three-year or 50,000 miles bumper-to-bumper warranty on new cars. A change is proposed, extending the warranty to four years or 60,000 miles. Past experience suggests that repairs under this warranty are normally distributed and average \$400/car. However, this \$400 figure is under dispute. Repair costs have increased, but recent advances in quality control have resulted in fewer repairs. The following hypotheses are established:

$$H_0\colon \mu = 400 \quad \text{versus} \quad H_a\colon \mu \neq 400$$

In this situation we assume the population standard deviation is unknown, and the population is normal. Hence, the test statistic given by Formula (9.2) is appropriate. A random sample of $n = 27$ cars is taken, and $\bar{x} = \$439.64$, $s = 120.60$. The calculated t-value is

$$t_c = \frac{\bar{x} - \mu_0}{s/\sqrt{n}} = \frac{439.64 - 400}{120.60/\sqrt{27}} = 1.708$$

To determine the p-value we first calculate the probability that a t-value will be this large (1.708) or larger (more extreme) when d.f. $= n - 1 = 26$. More extreme means farther away from the value of t expected under the null hypothesis, which is $t = 0$. Thus, we first determine $P(t \geq 1.708)$.

$$P(t \geq 1.708) = 0.05 \quad \text{(from Table VII, for } \nu = 26)$$

Remember, if the test is two-sided, a probability such as $P(t \geq 1.708)$ must be doubled. This means that the p-value is *twice* the 0.05 value determined above. That is,

$$p\text{-value} = 2(0.05) = 0.10$$

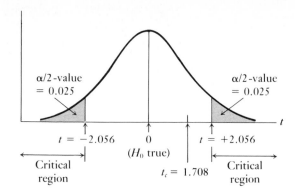

Figure 9.7

The critical region and t_c for
H_0: $\mu = 400$ versus
H_a: $\mu \neq 400$ when $\alpha = 0.05$.

Since most traditional levels of significance (α-levels) are less than 0.05, a p-value as large as the current one (0.10) will generally lead to accepting H_0 (since $\alpha < p$). In this case the conclusion could be: Although the sample mean of \$439.64 falls above the assumed population mean of \$400, for the sample size of $n = 27$ this difference is not large enough to reject the assumption that the population mean is still \$400. In statistical terms, we would say the sample result $\bar{x} = \$439.64$ is "not significantly different" from $\mu = \$400$. At this point the company may wish to consider extending the warranty on the basis of the \$400 figure, or perhaps taking a larger sample.

The critical t-values for the problem above can be determined from Table VII (remembering that $\alpha = 0.05$, $\nu = 26$) to be $t = -2.056$ and $t = +2.056$ (because 95% of the t-distribution falls between these two numbers when $\nu = 26$). Figure 9.7 shows the (two-sided) critical region when $\alpha = 0.10$ as well as the calculated test statistic, $t_c = 1.708$. Since $t_c = 1.708$ does not fall in the critical region, H_0 should be accepted. This is the same conclusion reached by comparing α (0.05) with the p-value (0.10), noting that $\alpha < p$. ∎

EXAMPLE 2

In many problems the exact value of t_c cannot be found in Table VII, Appendix B, either because the degrees of freedom is not among the set given in that table, or because t_c falls between the critical values listed. Often in these cases it is possible to determine at least a *range* of probabilities that includes the p-value. This is done by looking at the numbers in a given row, or by looking at a nearby row when the degrees of freedom cannot be found in Table VII.

For example, suppose $\nu = 45$, and $t_c = 1.831$ for a one-sided test. The probability $P(t \geq 1.831)$ cannot be found directly from Table VII, since 45 d.f. is not on the table. We move to $\nu = 40$ as the closest d.f., and then note that $t_c = 1.831$ falls between the values $t = 1.684$ (for $\alpha = 0.05$) and $t = 2.021$ (for $\alpha = 0.025$). Thus, our range of p-values would be

$$0.05 > p\text{-value} > 0.025$$

If this range had been a *two-sided* alternative hypothesis, then the range of p-values would have been *double* the above probabilities:

$$0.10 > p\text{-value} > 0.05$$

Using a Computer to Test Hypotheses

For students with access to a computer, it is relatively easy to determine the p-value $= P(t \geq 1.831)$ for $\nu = 45$. The following computer output, from the statistical package Interactive Data Analysis (IDA), shows this p-value $= 0.0369$. This is the one-sided p-value, as the IDA output indicates by the statement $PR(ABS(T) > ABS(L)) = 0.0369$, which says the probability given (0.0369) is the probability (PR) that the absolute value of t [ABS(T)] exceeds the absolute value of the limiting value $L = 1.831$ [ABS(L)]. Notice that this p-value of 0.0369 falls in the one-sided range determined above, as it must. User input is in color.

```
IDA COMPUTER OUTPUT
  STUDENTS t DISTRIBUTION
  *INTERVAL OR TAIL PROBABILITY:
  *GIVE DEGREES OF FREEDOM FOR STUDENT-T VARIABLE:
  *GIVE LOWER LIMIT L FOR T VALUE:  1.831
   PR (ABS (T) >ABS (L)) =0.0369
```

EXAMPLE 3

Statistical packages on the computer make the process of testing hypotheses even easier. For example, the data in Appendix C on salaries was placed in a computer file called SALARIES. This file was used to test the (alternative) hypothesis that the mean salary of the males in this data set (observations 1–50) is larger than $50,000. That is, the hypotheses are

$$H_0: \mu \leq \$50,000 \quad \text{versus} \quad H_a: \mu > \$50,000$$

Because the population standard deviation is unknown, and the parent population can be assumed to be normal, the appropriate test statistic is the t-test given by Formula (9.2).

For this analysis we used the Minitab statistical package. The value of μ_0 is $50,000. The Minitab output is shown in Table 9.4.*

TABLE 9.4   Minitab output for testing SALARIES data

	N	MEAN	STDEV	SE MEAN	T	P VALUE
MALES	50	58037.60	15402.45	2178.24	3.69	0.0003

In Table 9.4 SE MEAN (standard error of the mean) is the denominator of the t-test in Formula (9.2). The p-value $= 0.0003$. This result, for most levels

---

*The Minitab commands, assuming the salaries are in column 1 of the file called SALARIES, are

```
MTB  > RETRIEVE 'SALARIES'
MTB  > TTEST of mu = 50000 using the data in c1;
SUBC > ALTERNATIVE is upper tailed = +1.
```

of significance, would lead to rejection of the null hypothesis that salaries are $50,000 or less. Because we told the Minitab program that the alternative hypothesis is one-sided toward the upper tail (see footnote), the package prints out the t-value for a one-sided test; this probability would be doubled had we specified to Minitab that the test is two-sided (ALTERNATIVE = 0). ■

Two-Sample Tests About μ

9.5

Instead of testing the results of a *single* sample against a hypothesized mean, one may wish to see if *two* different independent (random) samples came from populations having equal means. This approach is quite common in testing for the effect of different treatments on two groups, where one group is often a "control" group and the other is given a special treatment (such as a new drug), a new approach to learning, or a product manufactured in a different manner. In all these cases the objective is to determine whether the mean of one population differs from the mean of some other population.

Specifying the Hypotheses

As was suggested in Section 9.2, the first step is specifying the null and alternative hypotheses. Suppose μ_1 represents the mean of the first population, and μ_2 represents the mean of the second population. For most problems the null hypothesis is that the two populations have the same mean, or that $\mu_1 = \mu_2$. This is equivalent to

Null hypothesis: H_0: $\mu_1 - \mu_2 = 0$ (no difference in means)

The alternative hypothesis in this situation can be either one-sided (in which case the right-hand side is ≥ 0 or ≤ 0) or two-sided (in which case the right-hand side is $\neq 0$). Let's assume the alternative hypothesis is two-sided:

Alternative hypothesis: H_a: $\mu_1 - \mu_2 \neq 0$ (means are not equal)

Determining the Test Statistic

As was the case in Section 9.4, the test-statistic is either a z-test, or a t-test, in this case depending on whether the *two* population standard deviations are known or unknown. In either case the test statistic uses the following standardization, which is the same form used for the z- and t-test statistics.

$$\text{Test statistic} = \frac{\text{Point estimate} - \text{hypothesized mean}}{\text{Standard error of the point estimator}}$$

(9.3)

Test When Both Population Variances Are Known

If the denominator of the standardization in Formula (9.3) involves known values of σ_1^2 and σ_2^2, then the test statistic is that shown in Formula (9.4).

$$
\boxed{
\begin{array}{c}
\textit{Test statistic when } \sigma_1^2 \textit{ and } \sigma_2^2 \textit{ are known:} \\[4pt]
z_c = \dfrac{(\bar{x}_1 - \bar{x}_2) - (\mu_1 - \mu_2)}{\sqrt{\dfrac{\sigma_1^2}{n_1} + \dfrac{\sigma_2^2}{n_2}}}
\end{array}
}
\qquad (9.4)
$$

In Formula (9.4) the hypothesized mean is $(\mu_1 - \mu_2)$. This value, which is the right-hand side of the null hypothesis, is usually set equal to zero (but it need not be). The point estimate of $(\mu_1 - \mu_2)$ is $(\bar{x}_1 - \bar{x}_2)$, where $\bar{x}_1$ is the sample mean from the first population and $\bar{x}_2$ is the sample mean from the second population. The denominator is the standard error of the point estimator $(\bar{x}_1 - \bar{x}_2)$, assuming samples of size n_1 and n_2 from the two populations.* Note the similarity of this formula to the z-test in Formula (9.2). As was the case in Formula (9.2), the point estimate has to be normally distributed. It can be shown that if both $\bar{x}_1$ and $\bar{x}_2$ are normally distributed, then $(\bar{x}_1 - \bar{x}_2)$ will also be normal.

We will not illustrate Formula (9.4) because of its limited usefulness — few practical problems have known variances. A much more important test statistic is the t-test described below, which assumes the variances are unknown.

The t-Test for Two Independent Samples (s_1^2 and s_2^2 Unknown but Assumed Equal)

The t-test described in this section assumes that both populations being sampled (x_1 and x_2) are normally distributed. If x_1 and x_2 are not normally distributed, but both n_1 and n_2 are reasonably large (each one ≥ 15), then again the t-distribution can be used. In addition, the t-test assumes that the variances of the two populations are equal ($\sigma_1^2 = \sigma_2^2$), although there is a t-test that will be described shortly that does not require this assumption. Fortunately, the test described below is a fairly "robust" distribution, meaning that deviations from the above assumptions may not destroy the usefulness of this approach. This test assumes "independent samples"; that is, the observations in each sample are taken randomly.

---

*The variance of the difference, $V[\bar{x} - \bar{x}_2]$, can be derived as follows, assuming that the samples are drawn independently:

$$
\begin{aligned}
V[\bar{x}_1 - \bar{x}_2] &= V[\bar{x}_1] + V[-\bar{x}_2] \\
&= V[\bar{x}_1] + (-1)^2 V[+\bar{x}_2] \\
&= \frac{\sigma_1^2}{n_1} + \frac{\sigma_2^2}{n_2} \quad \text{(Since } V[\bar{x}] = \sigma^2/n)
\end{aligned}
$$

The t-test for two independent samples has the same format as the test statistic described in Formula (9.4). Because the two population variances are assumed to be equal (and unknown), there is only one population variance to be estimated. But since we have two sample variances, s_1^2 and s_2^2, the denominator must be a pooled or weighted estimate using both of these two sample variances. By a **pooled estimate,** we mean the two sample variances are weighted by their degrees of freedom as follows:

$$\text{Weighted average of } s_1^2 \text{ and } s_2^2:$$

$$\frac{(n_1 - 1)}{n_1 + n_2 - 2} s_1^2 + \frac{(n_2 - 1)}{n_1 + n_2 - 2} s_2^2$$

Each sample variance has $(n - 1)$ degrees of freedom, and the total number of degrees of freedom is $\nu = (n_1 - 1) + (n_2 - 1) = n_1 + n_2 - 2$. The reader should verify that the "weights" shown above always sum to 1.00. The square root of this weighted average is called the **pooled standard deviation.**

Let us now rewrite Formula (9.4) by letting σ^2 denote the two equal variances (that is, $\sigma_1^2 = \sigma_2^2 = \sigma^2$). Factoring σ^2 out of the denominator of (9.4) permits rewriting Formula (9.4) as follows:

$$\frac{(\bar{x}_1 - \bar{x}_2) - (\mu_1 - \mu_2)}{\sqrt{\sigma^2 \left(\dfrac{1}{n_1} + \dfrac{1}{n_2} \right)}}$$

Substituting the weighted-average formula for σ^2 from above yields the appropriate t-test statistic:

Two-sample t-test statistic for testing $\mu_1 - \mu_2$ assuming equal variances in normal parent populations:

$$t_c = \frac{(\bar{x}_1 - \bar{x}_2) - (\mu_1 - \mu_2)}{\sqrt{\left(\dfrac{(n_1 - 1)s_1^2}{n_1 + n_2 - 2} + \dfrac{(n_2 - 1)s_2^2}{n_1 + n_2 - 2} \right) \left(\dfrac{1}{n_1} + \dfrac{1}{n_2} \right)}} \qquad (9.5)$$

with $\nu = n_1 + n_2 - 2$ degrees of freedom

EXAMPLE 1

The t-test in Formula (9.5) can be illustrated by applying it to the male and female SALARIES data in Appendix C. The following hypotheses were formulated (before seeing the data):

$H_0: \mu_1 - \mu_2 = 0$ (mean of male salaries $=$ mean of female salaries)
$H_a: \mu_1 - \mu_2 \neq 0$ (mean of male salaries $\neq$ mean of female salaries)

For the salary data, $\bar{x}_1 = \$58{,}037.60$, $s_1^2 = (15{,}402.45)^2$, $\bar{x}_2 = \$54{,}493.60$, and $s_2^2 = (11{,}422.99)^2$. In this case the sample sizes $(n_1 = n_2 = 50)$ are fairly large; hence the assumption of normal parent populations is not critical. We still need to assume, however, that the two population variances are equal. Plugging the values from page 356 into Formula (9.5) gives

$$t_c = \frac{(58037.6 - 54493.6) - 0}{\sqrt{\left(\dfrac{(50-1)((15402.45)^2}{50+50-2} + \dfrac{(50-1)(11422.99)^2}{50+50-2}\right)\left(\dfrac{1}{50} + \dfrac{1}{50}\right)}}$$

$$= \frac{3544}{2711.9} = 1.3068$$

The calculations above are somewhat tedious, hence it is easier to let the computer complete the arithmetic. Table 9.5 uses the Minitab statistical package to do this for the SALARIES data.*

TABLE 9.5   Minitab computer output for two-sample SALARIES analysis

```
TWOSAMPLE T FOR MALES VS FEMALES

            N     MEAN    STDEV   SE MEAN
  MALES    50    58038    15402    2178
FEMALES    50    54494    11423    1615

TTEST MU MALES = MU FEMALES (VS NE): T = 1.31   P = 0.19   DF = 98

POOLED STDEV = 13560
```

The last line of this output gives the pooled standard deviation, which is the first part of the denominator in Formula (9.5). The line above it states that the test involves the null hypothesis that the population mean (MU or μ) of males equals the population mean of females, versus the alternative they are not equal (NE). The p-value for this two-sided test is shown in Table 9.5 as P = 0.19. For any reasonable α-level this relatively high p-value would *not* lead to rejection of the null hypothesis that male and female salaries are equal, in the population. Thus, for these data, the mean male and female salaries are not significantly different. The reader should note that if the alternative hypothesis had been one sided (such as H_a: $\mu_1 - \mu_2 > 0$) then the p-value would have been $1/2(0.19) = 0.095$. ∎

The t-test above assumes the sample variances are to be pooled. There is another test that is not presented here that does not make this assumption. Also, some statistics texts recommend using a normal approximation to the t-distribution when the degrees of freedom $(n_1 + n_2 - 2)$ is relatively large (such as ≥ 30). We have not emphasized that process (although it is quite

---

*The Minitab commands, assuming the appropriate data are in 'MALE' and 'FEMALE' columns of the file SALARIES, are

MTB > RETRIEVE 'SALARIES'
MTB > TWOSAMPLE 'MALES' 'FEMALES';
SUBC > ALTERNATIVE = 0.

straightforward), but rather remind the reader that the *t*-distribution is *always* the correct distribution when σ_1^2 and σ_2^2 are unknown.

Matched Pairs *t*-Test

There is another way to test for significant differences between two samples involving small values of *n* that does *not* use the assumption that the variances of the two populations are equal. In this test it is necessary that the observations in the two samples be collected in the form called **matched pairs.** With this approach each observation in one sample must be paired with an observation in the other sample in such a manner that these observations are somehow "matched" or related, in an attempt to eliminate extraneous factors that are not of interest in the test.

Often, when people are involved, we match subjects in terms of such variables as age, sex, race, socioeconomic background, experience, weight, and any other criterion that needs to be controlled for in studying the variable of interest. One of the most common methods of forming matched pairs is to let a subject "serve as his own control," in which case the person is matched with himself at different points in time, or in a "before-and-after" treatment study.

Matched pairs could have been used in the SALARIES example if the difference between the male and female salaries might have occurred because the males are (for example) considerably older than the females and/or have more work experience. When we want to control for (or eliminate) the effect of such differences, then a sample needs to be taken where each male is carefully matched with a comparable female — in terms of age, experience, undergraduate major, or any other criterion that might affect salary.

If observations can be collected in the form of matched pairs, then a *t*-test for differences between the two samples can be constructed on the basis of the **difference score** for each matched pair. This score is calculated by subtracting the score or value associated with the one person or object in each pair from the score or value of the other person or object in that pair. The *t*-test assumes that these difference scores are normally distributed and independent. If we denote the average difference in scores between the two populations by the capital Greek letter (Δ), then the hypothesis being tested is

$$H_0\text{: }\Delta = k$$

where *k* is the hypothesized difference between the two populations. If the set of difference scores is denoted by *D*, then the average difference is $\overline{D}$, and the standard deviation of the difference scores is s_D. The appropriate test statistic is

---

Test statistic for matched pairs:

$$t_c = \frac{\overline{D} - \Delta}{s_D/\sqrt{n}}$$

with $\nu = n - 1$ (*n* = number of matched pairs)

(9.6)

TABLE 9.6   Ten matched pairs taken from SALARIES data

Pair	Males	Experience	Females	Experience	Difference
1	$73,500	14	$70,880	14	$2,620
2	54,990	8	59,550	8	−4,560
3	58,980	9	68,110	9	−9,130
4	39,800	3	40,100	3	−300
5	49,320	10	60,600	10	−11,280
6	45,750	11	63,740	11	−17,990
7	68,430	14	67,220	14	1,210
8	78,100	12	60,470	12	17,630
9	64,400	8	52,850	8	11,550
10	52,560	6	52,380	6	180

Mean $\overline{D} = -\$1,007.00$

Standard Deviation $s_D = 10,528.05$

To illustrate Formula (9.6), we have matched the first 10 males in the SALARIES data in Appendix C with 10 females, by using experience as the matching criteria (picking the first female to match each male on experience). The 10 matched pairs are shown in Table 9.6. The hypotheses in this problem are

H_0: $\mu_M - \mu_F = 0$ or H_0: $\Delta = 0$ (male salaries = female salaries)

H_a: $\mu_M - \mu_F \neq 0$ or H_0: $\Delta \neq 0$ (male salaries ≠ female salaries)

The $\overline{D} = -\$1007$ in the last column is the average difference between male and female salaries — that is, the males earned slightly over $1000 *less* than the females, on the average. Substituting these values into Formula (9.6) yields

$$t_c = \frac{\overline{D} - \Delta}{s_D/\sqrt{n}} = \frac{-1007 - 0}{10528.05/\sqrt{10}} = \frac{-1007}{3329.26} = -0.3025$$

For this problem we used the statistical package B-STAT, whose output is shown in Table 9.7. (Note that the results agree with those calculated above.)

TABLE 9.7   Matched pairs t-test for 10 pairs of SALARIES data

```
DIFFERENCE BETWEEN MEANS: PAIRED OBSERVATIONS
NUMBER OF CASES: 10    NUMBER OF VARIABLES: 2
HYPOTHESIZED DIFF. =        .0000
              MEAN = -1007.0000
         STD. DEV. = 10528.0515
        STD. ERROR =  3329.2622
              N = 10
    t = -.3025    (D.F. = 9)        GROUP 1: Males
  PROB. = 0.3846                    GROUP 2: Females
```

The p-value, shown in the last line of Table 9.7, is 0.3846. Since this value is quite large, we cannot reject the null hypothesis, and thus conclude that the two sample means do not differ significantly.

Two-Sample Test for Proportions

In Section 9.2 we presented a one-sample test involving the binomial parameter p. The comparable test in this section is designed to distinguish between two population proportions, p_1 and p_2. One illustration of this type of situation is the marketing researcher attempting to determine if a company's market share in one location (or at one point in time) differs from the market share in another location (or another point in time). A similar example is the quality control expert attempting to determine if the proportion of defectives is significantly different between two machines, or between two plants.

The usual null hypothesis in testing two population proportions is that p_1 and p_2 are equal; that is,

$$H_0: p_1 - p_2 = 0$$

The alternative hypothesis can take any of the forms used previously, such as

$$H_a: p_1 - p_2 \neq 0 \quad \text{or} \quad H_a: p_1 - p_2 > 0 \quad \text{or} \quad H_a: p_1 - p_2 < 0$$

The test statistic appropriate in this case is the z-distribution, provided that both n_1 and n_2 are sufficiently large. If we let (x_1/n_1) and (x_2/n_2) represent the sample proportion from the first and second populations, respectively, and $(p_1 - p_2)$ represent the hypothesized difference in the proportions, then the appropriate formula for z is Formula (9.7).

Test statistic for testing $p_1 - p_2$:

$$z_c = \frac{\left(\dfrac{x_1}{n_1} - \dfrac{x_2}{n_2}\right) - \left(p_1 - p_2\right)}{\sqrt{\left(\dfrac{x_1 + x_2}{n_1 + n_2}\right)\left(1 - \dfrac{x_1 + x_2}{n_1 + n_2}\right)\left(\dfrac{1}{n_1} + \dfrac{1}{n_2}\right)}}$$

(9.7)

To illustrate this test we take data from a study used to determine if Pittsburgh, Pennsylvania, and St. Louis, Missouri, differ in terms of the proportion of new homes built using electricity as the primary source of heat. A random sample of $n_1 = 400$ new homes taken from Pittsburgh found $x_1 = 38$ using electricity; a sample of $n_2 = 300$ new homes in St. Louis found $x_2 = 49$ built with electricity. The relevant hypotheses are

$$H_0: p_1 - p_2 = 0 \quad \text{versus} \quad H_a: p_1 - p_2 \neq 0$$

Substituting the appropriate values in Formula (9.7) gives z_c:

$$z_c = \frac{(38/400 - 49/300) - 0}{\sqrt{\left(\dfrac{38 + 49}{400 + 300}\right)\left(1 - \dfrac{38 + 49}{400 + 300}\right)\left(\dfrac{1}{400} + \dfrac{1}{300}\right)}}$$

$$= \frac{0.095 - 0.1633}{\sqrt{0.00063}} = -2.71$$

The p-value is first determined by finding

$$P(z \le -2.71) = 0.0034 \quad \text{(from Table III)}$$

Because the alternative hypothesis is two-sided, we double this probability.

$$p\text{-value} = 2(0.0034) = 0.0068$$

Thus, any significance level (α-value) above 0.0068 leads to rejection of the null hypothesis that the population proportion is the same in the two cities. Since this p-value is quite low, for most α-levels the conclusion would be that the proportion of new houses using electricity as the primary heat source differs significantly between the two cities.

Table 9.11 provides a summary of the test statistics in this chapter.

Problems

(*Note*: The reader is encouraged to solve as many as possible of the following problems using a computer.)

9.17 When testing hypotheses about means, the appropriate test statistic may be a z-test or a t-test. In general, when is the z-test appropriate and when is the t-test appropriate? Are there circumstances when these two tests are roughly comparable? Explain.

9.18 A financial analyst wants to determine if there is any difference between the 1989 return on common equity between banks in the East and banks in the Midwest. Use the following random sample from *Business Week* to complete all five steps of hypothesis testing.

Return on common equity (%)

Eastern banks		Midwestern banks	
1. Chase Manhattan	23.9	1. Banc One	17.2
2. Bank of Boston	16.4	2. Norwest	19.0
3. Bank of New York	16.5	3. Society	14.7
4. Keycorp	14.2	4. Firstar	20.6
5. Baybanks	16.2	5. Indiana National	14.2
6. First Pennsylvania	20.7	6. Northern Trust	27.4
7. U.S. Trust	15.7	7. First Chicago	26.4
8. Mercantile Bankshares	15.5		

9.19 Use the SALARIES data in Appendix C to determine if the proportion of males with less than 10 years' work experience is significantly different from the proportion of females with less than 10 years' work experience.

9.20 A random sample was collected of 30 companies from the top 400 in the *Business Week* top 1000 company listing, and 30 companies from the bottom 400 companies. The 1987 actual earnings per share was entered in a computer file. These data were then tested using a statistical computer program, where the test was a pooled variance test for the difference between means. Complete all five hypothesis testing steps, using the following Minitab output.

```
TWOSAMPLE T FOR TOP 400 VS BOTTOM 400
             N     MEAN    STDEV   SE MEAN
TOP400      30   3.1547   1.6802  0.3067
BOT400      30   1.6483   1.3381  0.3009
TEST MU TOP400 = MU BOT400 (VS NE): T = 3.84 P = 0.0002 DF = 58
POOLED STDEV = 0.3922
```

9.21 Repeat Problem 9.20, collecting your own sample of 60 companies, 30 selected at random from the top 400, and 60 from the bottom 400 listed in the *Business Week* top 1000 companies. In this case let your variable be each company's "return on common equity."

9.22 Repeat Problem 9.20, collecting your own sample from the *Business Week* list of top 1000 companies. For your sample use a matched pairs approach, matching 30 companies from the top 400 with 30 companies from the bottom 400. Match on at least the variable "Industry Group," plus any other reasonable variables.

9.23 Recently Public Service Indiana was asked to design a study to determine if residential customers could be induced to switch their use of electricity at peak load times by a rate incentive. PSI conducted a two-year study using a sample of matched pairs, where group I had the new rate plan, and group II kept the old plan. Each house in group I was carefully matched with a house in group II. Matching was accomplished using geographical location, age of house, type of heating system, existence of air conditioning, and past history of electrical use. The results of this study (slightly modified for this problem) are shown in the computer output below. Interpret this output by going through all five steps of hypothesis testing.

```
              HYPOTHESIS TESTS FOR MEANS
       NUMBER OF CASES: 60    NUMBER OF VARIABLES: 2
       DIFFERENCE BETWEEN MEANS: PAIRED OBSERVATIONS
       HYPOTHESIZED DIFF. = .0000
                    MEAN = -.0648
              STD. DEV. = 1.0238
              STD. ERROR = .1322
                       N = 60
       T = -0.4905 (D.F. = 59)   GROUP 1: EXPERIMENTAL
                                 GROUP 2: CONTROL
          PROB = 0.3128
```

9.24 T.I.M.E., Inc., a market research company headquartered in Columbus, Ohio, has interviewed 100 randomly selected shoppers who were classified as having rural backgrounds. Sixty said they prefer to purchase cameras in discount stores. In a comparable study involving 250 shoppers with urban backgrounds, 50% said they prefer the discount stores. Complete the five hypotheses-testing steps to determine if the two population proportions are different. Report a p-value.

9.25 A report by the National Coupon Association in 1989 indicated that the average value of all coupons was 38 cents. A study a year later of 1347 random selected coupons resulted in a sample mean of 38.7 cents, with a standard deviation of 22 cents. Complete all five steps of hypothesis testing.

9.26 A report by *Nielsen Marketing Research* stated that in 1989 51% of U.S. supermarkets were open 24 hours per day.

  a) What hypotheses would you establish to determine if the percentage of supermarkets open 24 hours has changed since 1989?

  b) Design a study to test the hypotheses in part (a). Explain carefully how you would collect your sample.

  c) Suppose you collect a random sample of 156 supermarkets, and find that 86 are open 24 hours. Report a p-value. Would you recommend accepting or rejecting H_0?

9.27 A manufacturer of steel rods considers the process to be working properly if the mean length of the rods is 8.6 inches. The standard deviation of these rods always runs about 0.3 in. The manufacturer would like to see if the process is working correctly by taking a random sample of size $n = 36$. There is no indication of whether the rods may be too long or too short.

  a) Establish H_0 and H_a for this problem. Determine the p-value if the sample yields an average length of 8.7 inches. Interpret this p-value.

  b) What values of z form the critical region if $\alpha = 0.04$? Would you accept or reject H_0?

9.28 In a study of family income levels, nine households in a certain rural county are selected at random. The incomes in these households are known to be normally distributed with $\sigma = 2400$. An average income of \$21,617 is reported from this sample survey. Use a statistical test to decide if the null hypothesis, $\mu = \$22,000$, can be rejected in favor of H_a, which states that the true average income is less than \$22,000. Use an 0.05 level of significance.

9.29 A manufacturer of rope produces 22,500 ft of rope a day, in lengths of 50 ft each. Each day, 16 of the 50-ft lengths are tested for tensile strength. The variance of tensile strength is always approximately $\sigma^2 = 256$. The mean tensile strength of one sample of 16 observations was 340 lb.

  a) What probability value would you report if the null hypothesis H_0: $\mu = 350$ is tested against H_a: $\mu \neq 350$? How will your answer change if the alternative is H_a: $\mu < 350$? Assume that tensile strength is normally distributed.

  b) Rework part (a), assuming that the population variance is unknown, and that the sample of $n = 16$ yields $s^2 = 298$. What are the critical values for t, assuming $\alpha = 0.05$ when 1) the test is a two-sided test, and 2) the test is one-sided?

9.30 An industrial firm that manufactures small battery-powered toys periodically purchases a large number of flashlight batteries for use in testing the toys. The policy of the company has been never to accept a shipment of batteries unless it is possible to reject, at the 0.05 level of significance, the hypothesis that the batteries have a mean life of 50 or fewer hours. The standard deviation of the life of all shipments has typically been 3 hours.

a) What null and alternative hypotheses should be established to implement the company policy?

b) Should the company accept a shipment from which a sample of 64 batteries results in a mean life of 50.5 hours?

c) What is the minimum mean life that this company should accept in a sample of 64 batteries?

9.31 A manufacturer claims that its new radial tire will last, on the average, more than 70,000 miles.

a) Should the null hypothesis be H_0: $\mu \geq 70,001$ or H_0: $\mu \leq 70,000$? Which hypothesis would the manufacturer prefer? Explain.

b) Assume H_0: $\mu \leq 70,000$ and H_a: $\mu > 70,000$. Describe the consequences of a Type I and Type II error.

c) Suppose $\sigma = 10,000$. What p-value would you report if a sample of $n = 100$ results in $\bar{x} = 71,250$?

d) Assume that σ is unknown and that $s = 9,758$. What is the p-value now?

9.32 A statistician is investigating the charge that a minority group of workers is paid less-than-average wages. The population for all comparable workers has a mean wage of $24,500.

a) Establish H_0 and H_a. Describe possible consequences of a Type I error and a Type II error.

b) What test statistic is appropriate if σ is unknown and the population is normal?

c) What p-value would you report if $n = 9$, $\bar{x} = \$24,300$, and $s = \$200$?

9.33 You are interested in a site for a new restaurant, and a real estate developer claims that, on the average, residents of your community eat at least eight meals out per week (lunch plus dinner). To test this claim, you randomly select 20 residents, and determine the times they have eaten out in the last week. The results are: 6, 5, 7, 4, 8, 6, 9, 2, 10, 8, 0, 7, 6, 4, 14, 1, 4, 7, 4, 10. Test, using $\alpha = 0.01$, whether the sample mean is significantly different from the hypothesized value of 8. Assume the population is normal.

9.34 Ornamental, Inc. packages deluxe ornamental matches for fireplace use by a process designed to place 18 matches in each box. The process was started and allowed to produce 400 boxes. A sample of 16 boxes was then drawn. On the basis of this sample, the number of matches per box averaged 17, and the sample standard deviation was 2. Would a one-sided test suggest rejecting H_0 if $\alpha = 0.05$, assuming a normal parent population?

9.35 A local branch of RCA assembles television sets. The number of finished units per day is normally distributed and has a scheduled average of 85 units. Twenty-five days are selected at random, and the output for each day is observed. The average output calculated from this sample is 81 units, with a standard deviation of 9 units.

a) Write the hypotheses as a one-sided test, and report a p-value assuming a one-sided test. Why might a one-sided test be appropriate here?

b) Repeat part (a) assuming a two-sided test.

9.36 The city of Bellevue, Washington, recently attempted to determine the average number of cars parked during the day at a local grocery store. The following nine random observations were drawn: 25, 17, 18, 22, 21, 27, 19, 15, 25.

a) Test the null hypothesis that the average is 24 cars, using a two-sided test. Assume a normal distribution, and report a p-value.

b) Repeat part (a) assuming: H_a: $\mu < 24$.

9.37 A power shovel was designed to remove 31.5 cubic feet of earth per scoop. On a test run, some 25 sample scoops were made; the mean of the samples was 29.3 cubic feet. The standard deviation, as derived from the sample information, was three cubic feet. Test whether the design specification for this equipment should be revised on the basis of the sample information. Use $\alpha = 0.05$, and assume a normal population. Describe the two types of error possible in this test.

9.38 Two groups of new cars were tested for gas mileage. One group, consisting of 36 cars, averaged 34.0 mpg while the other, consisting of 72 cars, averaged 32.5 mpg.

a) Establish H_0 and H_a to determine if the groups differ.

b) Determine a p-value assuming $s_1 = 1.22$ and $s_2 = 1.41$.

c) Is it necessary to assume that x_1 and x_2 are normally distributed?

d) Suppose the manufacturer of the first type of car had claimed that its average gas mileage was at least 1 mpg better than that for the cars in the second group. Is this claim supported by the data?

9.39 Assume for the SALARIES data in Appendix C that the salary population standard deviations are known: $\sigma_1 = 15,100$, and $\sigma_2 = 11,750$.

a) If $\alpha = 0.05$, do the male and female salaries differ significantly? Show all five steps in hypothesis testing.

b) Sketch the critical region for z, and show where on your graph the calculated value of the test statistic falls.

9.40 Two groups of managers participated in different seminars on how to use spreadsheets. Each seminar was rated on a scale of 1 to 100 on its effectiveness. The first seminar resulted in a mean rating of 82, with a standard deviation of 6. The second seminar resulted in an average rating of 84, with a standard deviation of 4. The first seminar was of size $n = 60$, and the second of size $n = 40$.

a) Establish the appropriate hypotheses to determine if the effectiveness differs significantly across the two samples.

b) What test statistic is appropriate?

c) Report a p-value, and interpret this value.

9.41 A union representative from city A is trying to determine the difference, if any, in fringe benefits between hourly workers, for the same company, in two different cities. The company claims that benefits in city A are more than

$1.00/hr higher than city B because of the cost of living in city A. The following data are collected.

	City A	City B
Sample size	30	42
Sample mean	$4.87	$3.69
Sample std. dev.	$.42	$.38

Complete the five steps in hypothesis testing for this situation.

9.42 A Center County farm agent has experimented with eight acres of land. Half of the acreage is treated with fertilizer x, and half with fertilizer y. The average difference in yield between paired acres is 10 bushels. The standard deviation of the difference is 4. Would you conclude there is a significant difference between the two differently fertilized tracts? Assume normally distributed differences, and let $\alpha = 0.01$.

9.43 A random sample of doctors was taken by Bristol-Myers Squibb to determine if the number of prescriptions written differs between midsize and small cities, with the following results.

Sample	Sample size	Mean	Standard deviation
Midsize	46	123.5	15.1
Small	38	108.2	13.7

Determine if the sample means differ significantly (using $\alpha = 0.05$) by completing the 5 steps of hypothesis testing.

9.44 New sales representatives for Eli Lilly must pass a test to determine their knowledge of various company products. A group of new sales reps is given classroom instruction, while another group is given released time for self-study. The test scores are as follows:

    Classroom study: 65, 68, 72, 82, 85, 87, 91, 95

    Self-study: 50, 59, 71, 80

a) What assumptions about the parent population are necessary to test hypotheses here?

b) Complete the five steps of hypothesis testing.

9.45 Can the pooled estimate of the population variance for a two-sample t-test be larger than the larger value of s^2 or smaller than the smaller value of s^2? Explain.

9.46 The production department at a large eastern company compared two different spreadsheets relative to their efficiency in solving complex scheduling problems. The time it took to solve each scheduling problem was carefully monitored. Program A is the more expensive, and supposed to be faster. Six different problems were used to test the two programs, with each problem being run on the two spreadsheets. Use the data below to complete the five steps in hypothesis testing.

Time required to solve (minutes)

	Program A	Program B
Problem 1	30.7	31.1
2	28.7	35.4
3	40.6	48.3
4	15.1	14.9
5	39.5	50.3
6	21.2	34.6

9.47 A professor of Human Performance at The University of Tennessee, Knoxville, matched 40 people according to age and experience before each one took a manual-dexterity test. The scores are summarized below. Group A represents athletes, and Group B represents nonathletes (20 in each group).

Mean difference (Group A − Group B):   33.75
Standard deviation of difference: 63.77

Complete the five steps of hypothesis testing.

9.48 Nine students in two introductory statistics classes at the University of Minnesota were carefully matched according to age, sex, grade point average, and SAT scores. The two groups were then taught statistics by two different methods (but with the same instructor). Their scores on the (same) final exam are shown below.

Pair	Group A	Group B
1	76	83
2	92	91
3	83	72
4	84	93
5	65	75
6	71	87
7	60	75
8	81	79
9	72	74

Write down and then test the hypotheses that these two samples differ significantly. Use $\alpha = 0.05$.

9.49 A University of Florida medical researcher testing the effectiveness of a new drug found that 70% of a random sample of 280 patients improved under this drug. In a control group, 140 patients were given a placebo (a harmless, inert substance that *looked* like the drug). Fifty percent of these patients improved. Would you conclude that the new drug is more effective than the placebo? Use $\alpha = 0.01$.

9.50 General Mills will switch to a new TV advertising campaign if the new campaign will "significantly increase" the proportion of viewers who rate the ad as "highly attractive." In a random sample of 400 viewers, 23% rated the current campaign as "highly attractive." After viewing the new campaign, 35% of a random sample of 100 viewers rated the new campaign as "highly attractive." Would you recommend that General Mills switch if $\alpha = 0.02$?

Example Showing the Calculation of α and β (Optional)

9.6

The purpose of this section is to illustrate the calculation of both α and β, using the (binomial) production problem presented earlier in this chapter and in Chapter 4. In that problem a process producing computer chips needed either minor repairs ($p = 0.10$) or major repairs ($p = 0.25$). The null and alternative hypotheses were established to be:

$$H_0: p = 0.10 \quad \text{(needs minor repairs)}$$
$$H_a: p = 0.25 \quad \text{(needs major repairs)}$$

TABLE 9.8   (Table 4.2 Reproduced)

Binomial probabilities for production example

Number of defectives (x)	Decision rule		If $p = 0.10$ $P(x)$	If $p = 0.25$ $P(x)$
0		↑	0.1216	0.0032
1	Minor		0.2702	0.0211
2	repairs		0.2852 $\beta = 0.2251$	0.0669
3	Critical	↓	0.1901	0.1339
4	Value	↑	0.0898	0.1897
5			0.0319	0.2023
6			0.0089	0.1686
7			0.0020	0.1124
8			0.0004	0.0609
9	Major $\alpha = 0.1331$		0.0001	0.0271
10	repairs		0.0000	0.0099
11			0.0000	0.0030
12			0.0000	0.0008
13			0.0000	0.0002
14–20		↓	0.0000	0.0000
		Sum	1.0000	1.0000

To decide between these two hypotheses a random sample of $n = 20$ items is taken from the process. The critical region, which represents those outcomes leading to rejecting H_0, is selected to be $x < 4$. That is, H_0 is accepted if $x < 4$, and H_a is accepted if $x \geq 4$. The value $x = 4$ is called the **critical value.**

We now have enough information to calculate α and β. Since α is the probability of accepting H_a: $p = 0.25$ when H_0: $p = 0.10$ is true, and we accept H_a when $x \geq 4$, $\alpha = P(x \geq 4 \mid p = 0.10)$. Similarly, since β is the probability of accepting H_0 when H_a: $p = 0.25$ is true, and H_0 is accepted when $x < 4$, $\beta = P(x < 4 \mid p = 0.25)$. Both these probabilities can be calculated from the binomial values under $n = 20$ in Table I of Appendix B. In fact, we calculated their value in Chapter 4 in our discussion of binomial probabilities. Table 4.2 from Chapter 4, which is reproduced here (as Table 9.8), with the notation of this chapter, gives these probabilities. Thus, for this particular critical value, the probability is $\alpha = 0.1331$ of accepting H_a: $p = 0.25$ when H_0: $p = 0.10$ is true (a Type I error) and $\beta = 0.2251$ of accepting H_0: $p = 0.10$ when H_a: $p = 0.25$ is true (a Type II error). Figure 9.8 is a graph of these probabilities.

We must emphasize that the values of α and β need not add up to 1, as these two probabilities are not complementary. They are conditional probabilities based on different conditions. The value of α is conditional on the fact that H_0 is true, while the value of β is conditional on the fact that H_a is true. Thus, a one-unit change in α does not imply a corresponding one-unit change in β, or vice versa. However, since both α and β represent probabilities of events from the same decision problem, they are not independent of each other or of the sample size (n). When α is lowered, β normally rises, and vice versa (if n remains unchanged). The values of α and β also depend on the particular critical value selected (which was $x = 4$ in this case).

Figure 9.8
Critical region to test
H_0: $p = 0.10$ versus
H_a: $p = 0.25$.

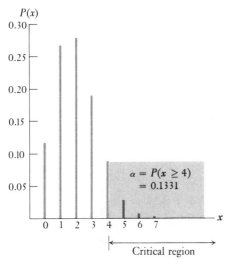

(a) H_0 true $(p = 0.10)$

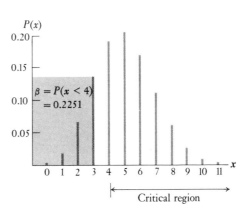

(b) H_a true $(p = 0.25)$

It is important to recognize from our production-process example that the value of α and β could not have been calculated if we had not first specified the size of the sample and a decision rule for accepting or rejecting the null and alternative hypotheses. This will always be the case, for α cannot be calculated until the circumstances are specified under which H_a will be accepted, and β cannot be calculated until the circumstances which lead to the acceptance of H_0 are specified. Different decision rules and sample sizes will lead to different values of α and β. For instance, suppose we change the number of defectives required for a major adjustment from $x = 4$ to $x = 5$, in our production-process example. The value of α and β can again be calculated from Table 9.8, and in this case can be shown to equal

$$\alpha = P(x \geq 5 | H_0 \text{ true}) = 0.0433$$

and

$$\beta = P(x < 5 | H_a \text{ true}) = 0.4148$$

The change in our decision rule has decreased α by 0.0898 (from 0.1331 to 0.0433), while increasing β by 0.1897 (from 0.2251 to 0.4148). The probability of a Type I error has thus decreased, and the probability of a Type II error has increased. Whether or not the trade-off is beneficial in this case, and in general how one goes about balancing the risks associated with a Type I error against the risks associated with a Type II error, are problems we shall discuss in the next section.

To illustrate the effect of sample size on the probability of making Type I and Type II errors, suppose, in the above example, that the sample size could be increased to $n = 50$. Usually a change in sample size means a change in the critical region. Let's rather arbitrarily choose $x \geq 10$ as the critical region for this sample of 50. That is, we will accept H_a: $p = 0.25$ if the number of defectives is greater than or equal to 10, and accept H_0: $p = 0.10$ if $x < 10$. From Table I in Appendix B (under $n = 50$) we can calculate α and β:

$$\alpha = P(x \geq 10 | p = 0.10) = 0.0245$$
$$\beta = P(x < 10 | p = 0.25) = 0.1636$$

The important point to note is that by increasing the sample size from $n = 20$ to $n = 50$, we have *decreased* the probability of making *both* types of errors. The trade-off in this case is between the increase in cost associated with increasing the sample size, and the reduction in the cost of making an error because α and β are now both smaller.

Balancing the Risks and Costs of Making a Wrong Decision (Optional)

9.7

We now focus on the important problem of how to choose the "best" critical region to balance off the risks and costs associated with making a Type I error against those associated with making a Type II error. As was pointed out earlier, the objective of sampling can be stated as one of minimizing the cost of

Percent defectives
$p = 0.10$ $p = 0.25$
H_0 is true H_0 is false

	H_0 is true	H_0 is false
Accept H_0 make minor adjustment	Correct decision	$200
Reject H_0 make major adjustment	$500	Correct decision

Decision

Figure 9.9
Costs of making an incorrect
decision.

making an incorrect decision, including sampling costs. The example in this section demonstrates that it is possible to balance the risks of making an error if the relevant costs are known and can be expressed in dollar values.

This example, an extension of the quality control problem in Section 9.6, finds the critical region that minimizes the expected cost of making an incorrect decision. The first part of the example assumes the sample size to be fixed at $n = 20$; later this assumption is relaxed and $n = 50$ is considered. To begin the process we assume that all possible costs associated with an incorrect decision (loss in profit, goodwill, and so on) are those shown in Fig. 9.9. A correct decision is assumed to result in no loss in profit or goodwill.

For each possible critical region we can calculate the expected cost (per sample of 20) that will result if the process is (1) producing 10% defectives or (2) producing 25% defectives. These expected costs are calculated by multiplying the probability of making each type of error *times* the cost of making that error. We have calculated these values for two critical regions, the one used in Fig. 9.8 of $x \geq 4$, and an alternate one, $x \geq 5$, which gives a smaller α at the expense of a larger β.

a) *Critical region* $x \geq 4$ ($\alpha = 0.1331$ and $\beta = 0.2251$)

1. $p = 0.10$
Expected cost $= P(\text{Type I error}) \times \text{Cost of a Type I error}$
$= 0.1331(\$500) = \$66.55$

2. $p = 0.25$
Expected cost $= P(\text{Type II error}) \times \text{Cost of a Type II error}$
$= 0.2251(\$200) = \$45.02$

b) *Critical region* $x \geq 5$ ($\alpha = 0.0433$ and $\beta = 0.4148$)*

1. $p = 0.10$
Expected cost $= P(\text{Type I error}) \times \text{Cost of a Type I error}$
$= 0.0433(\$500) = \$21.65$

---

*The reader can quickly calculate these probabilities of errors from Table 9.8 by moving the decision line down one row and recalculating the sum of terms included in the brackets. Table I for the binomial with $n = 20$, $p = 0.25$, may, of course, be used directly to get the same values.

2. $p = 0.25$
Expected cost = $P(\text{Type II error}) \times$ Cost of a Type II error
$$= 0.4148(\$200) = \$82.96$$

The expected costs given above are *conditional values,* in that each one was calculated by assuming that either $p = 0.10$ or $p = 0.25$. In order to be able to determine which of these critical regions is better, we need to know how often the process is expected to be producing 10% defectives, relative to the number of times it will be producing 25% defectives. Suppose that if an adjustment is required, the probability that it will be a minor adjustment is 0.70, while the probability that a major adjustment is necessary is 0.30. The *total* expected costs associated with each of the two critical regions can now be calculated by taking the product of the expected costs determined above times the probability that each of these costs will be incurred.

a) *Critical region $x \geq 4$*
Total expected cost = $P(\text{Major adj. needed}) \times$ Exp. cost of an error
$\qquad\qquad\qquad\qquad + P(\text{Minor adj. needed}) \times$ Exp. cost of an error
$$= 0.30(\$45.02) + 0.70(\$66.55)$$
$$= \$60.09$$

b) *Critical region $x \geq 5$*
Total expected cost = $P(\text{Major adj. needed}) \times$ Exp. cost of an error
$\qquad\qquad\qquad\qquad + P(\text{Minor adj. needed}) \times$ Exp. cost of an error
$$= 0.30(\$82.96) + 0.70(\$21.65)$$
$$= \$40.04$$

Thus, when the process is malfunctioning, the total expected cost for each sample of 20 equals \$60.09 if the critical region is $x \geq 4$ and \$40.04 if the critical region is $x \geq 5$. We leave it as an exercise for the reader to determine that $x \geq 5$ is, in fact, the *optimal* critical region for this problem, with total expected cost smaller than any other critical region.

Changing the Sample Size

Suppose in the example above that the sample size could have been increased to $n = 50$ at a cost of \$10. The discussion of trade-offs between α, β, and n in Section 9.7 suggests that this increase in sample size can lead to a decrease in both α and β if an appropriate critical region is used. The question is whether or not the decreased probability of making an error is worth the increased sampling costs of \$10. In order to answer this question, let us select a critical region for the new situation (with $n = 50$), and then determine α and β and the total expected cost for this critical region. This total expected cost can then be compared with the preceding optimal of \$40.04.

Since n has increased 2.5 times from 20 to 50, let us arbitrarily try a new boundary value which is 2.5 times the previous old one ($x = 4$); that is, $x = 10$. [We leave it as a good exercise for the reader to determine if a better critical region than $x \geq 10$ could be found — perhaps by using $x \geq 12$ or $x \geq$

13 (which are approximately 2.5 times the previous optimal value of $x = 5$).]
The probability of observing a specific number of defectives when $n = 50$
under the two hypotheses, $H_0: p = 0.10$ and $H_a: p = 0.25$, is shown in Table
9.9. From these values the probabilities of Type I and Type II errors are seen to
be $\alpha = 0.0245$ and $\beta = 0.1636$. We thus see that increasing n from 20 to 50
has *reduced* both α and β (see Table 9.9).

Critical region $x \geq 10$

1. $p = 0.10$:
   Expected costs $= P(\text{Type I error}) \times \text{Cost of a Type I error}$
   $$= 0.0245(\$500) = \$12.25$$

2. $p = 0.25$
   Expected cost $= P(\text{Type II error}) \times \text{Cost of a Type II error}$
   $$= 0.1636(\$200) = \$32.72$$

Total expected cost $= P(\text{Major adj. needed}) \times \text{Exp. cost of an error}$
$$+ P(\text{Minor adj. needed}) \times \text{Exp. cost of an error}$$
$$= 0.30(\$32.72) + 0.70(\$12.25)$$
$$= \$18.39$$

Thus, if we have to choose between a sample of 20 and critical region $x \geq 5$
(with $\alpha = 0.0433$ and $\beta = 0.4142$), in which the costs will average \$40.04,
and a sample of 50 and critical region $x \geq 10$ (with $\alpha = 0.0245$ and
$\beta = 0.1636$), in which the costs will average \$18.39 for the incorrect deci-
sions and \$10.00 for the additional observations, it would be better to take the

TABLE 9.9 Determining α and β when $n = 50$ and the critical region is $x \geq 10$

x	Decision	$p = 0.10$ $P(x)$		$p = 0.25$ $P(x)$
0		0.0052		0.0000
1	Accept H_0,	0.0286		0.0000
2	make minor	0.0779	$\beta = 0.1636$	0.0001
⋮	adjustment	⋮		⋮
8		0.0643		0.0463
9		0.0333		0.0721
10		0.0152		0.0985
11		0.0061		0.1194
12	Reject H_0	0.0022	$\alpha = 0.0245$	0.1294
⋮	make major	⋮	Critical	⋮
24	adjustment	0.0000	region	0.0002
25		0.0000		0.0001
26–50		0.0000		0.0000
	Sum	1.0000		1.0000

larger sample. It may be, of course, that some other critical region will be even better than $x \geq 10$, or that some other sample size gives a lower expected cost. Given information on the cost of all possible sample sizes, the "optimal" sample size and its associated critical region could be determined for this problem. (Again, parts of this task are left as an exercise for the reader.) In Chapter 10 we shall return to an extended version of this problem and study in more detail the question of sample size.

The Power Function of a Critical Region (Optional)

9.8

The examples thus far have involved only simple hypotheses, largely because the problem of calculating and balancing the risks of Type I and Type II errors is considerably more difficult when the null or alternative hypothesis, or both, is *composite.* The difficulty stems from the fact that there is a *different* probability that a given sample falls in the critical region for *each one* of the values specified by a composite hypothesis, so that no one number can express the risk associated with making an incorrect decision.

The different probability values for β that occur when H_a is composite can be presented in a table, graphed, or described by a functional relationship. Often, however, it is more useful to present the values of $(1 - \beta)$. A function describing such probabilities is called a **power function,** since it indicates the ability (or "power") of the test to correctly reject a false null hypothesis. In general, test statistics and critical regions having the highest power are preferred. Although it is beyond the scope of this book to examine the concepts involved in finding a power function for most statistical tests, we must emphasize that the tests presented thus far have made use of these concepts in that we have always selected the *most powerful critical region.* The complexity involved in finding the power of a statistical test again emphasizes the rationale for making the null hypothesis a simple test. If H_0 were a composite hypothesis, then we would also have to use a function to describe all the values of α, or be satisfied with just a single value associated with the most conservative value in H_0.

The power function also indicates the probability that the null hypothesis will be rejected when H_0 is true. The advantage of calculating various power functions for a given statistical test is that by this means it may be possible to eliminate *obviously inferior* critical regions, and perhaps even to decide on an *optimal* critical region. The *ideal power function* is one in which the probability of rejecting H_0 is 1.0 when H_0 is false and 0.0 when H_0 is true. Figure 9.10 shows the ideal power function for a test in which the null hypothesis states that θ is less than or equal to some value θ_0, H_0: $\theta \leq \theta_0$, while the alternative hypothesis states that θ is greater than this value, H_a: $\theta > \theta_0$.

To illustrate the calculation of β [or $(1 - \beta)$] and the trade-offs between α, β, and the sample size, we will consider a firm that manufactures rubber

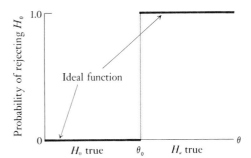

Figure 9.10

Ideal power function for testing H_0: $\theta \le \theta_0$ versus H_a: $\theta > \theta_0$.

bands. Control over the number of rubber bands placed in each box is kept by sampling and testing hypotheses, rather than by a counting procedure. When the production process is working correctly, the number (x) of good bands placed in each box has a mean of $\mu = 1000$, with a standard deviation of 37.5. This variable x is presumed to have an approximately normal distribution; that is, x is $N(1000, 37.5^2)$.

In this case the company wants to test H_0: $\mu = 1000$ against H_a: $\mu \ne 1000$, and the appropriate test statistic is $z = (\bar{x} - \mu_0)/(\sigma/\sqrt{n})$. A Type I error occurs whenever the test results suggest that the process is out of control ($\mu \ne 1000$), when it actually *is* in control ($\mu = 1000$). A Type II error occurs whenever the process is judged to be in control ($\mu = 1000$) and it actually is out of control ($\mu \ne 1000$). In constructing a test of these hypotheses, let us assume that the company periodically selects a random sample of size $n = 9$ boxes, and the company policy is to let $\alpha = 0.05$. For these values the boundary points of the critical region are

$$\mu_0 \pm z_{\alpha/2} \frac{\sigma}{\sqrt{n}} = 1000 \pm 1.96 \left(\frac{37.5}{\sqrt{9}}\right) = 1000 \pm 24.5$$

The critical regions are shown in Fig. 9.11.

The question we turn to now is how to calculate β for this problem. Since β is a conditional probability that depends on the value of μ, we will assume that $\mu = 990$. We can now write

$$\beta = P(\text{Accept } H_0: \mu = 1000 | \mu = 990)$$

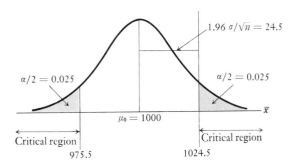

Figure 9.11

Critical regions for test of H_0: $\mu = 1000$ against H_a: $\mu \ne 1000$, $\sigma = 37.5$, $n = 9$, and $\alpha = 0.05$.

From Fig. 9.11 we see that H_0 is accepted whenever $\bar{x}$ lies between 975.5 and 1024.5. Hence, $\beta = P(975.5 \leq \bar{x} \leq 1024.5 | \mu = 990)$. This probability can be determined by using the same procedure we learned in Chapter 6 in working with $z = (\bar{x} - \mu)/(\sigma/\sqrt{n})$. First, we transform the problem to standardized normal terms by letting $\mu = 990$, $\sigma = 37.5$, and $\sqrt{n} = \sqrt{9}$, and then we use Table III to find the appropriate probabilities.

$$P(975.5 \leq \bar{x} \leq 1024.5) = P\left(\frac{975.5 - 990}{37.5/\sqrt{9}} \leq \frac{\bar{x} - \mu}{\sigma/\sqrt{n}} \leq \frac{1024.5 - 990}{37.5/\sqrt{9}}\right)$$

$$= P(-1.16 \leq z \leq 2.76) = F(2.76) - F(-1.16)$$

$$= 0.9971 - 0.1230 = 0.8741$$

Thus, $P(\text{Type II error}) = 0.8741$, as shown in Fig. 9.12. This means that our test procedure is such that when $\mu = 990$, we will *incorrectly* accept H_0: $\mu = 1000$ as being true 87.41% of the time. The *power* of this test is $1 - \beta = 0.1259$, which means that this test will *correctly* recognize this false null hypothesis 12.59% of the time when $\mu = 990$.

Instead of using the value $\mu = 990$ to calculate β, we might have used $\mu = 1010$. These two values of μ are both an equal distance (10 units) away from H_0: $\mu = 1000$, so it should not be surprising to learn that the value of β is the same in both cases ($\beta = 0.8741$). Figure 9.13(a) shows the area corresponding to β for $\mu = 1010$, while parts (b) and (c) of this figure show the area for β corresponding to $\mu = 970$ and $\mu = 950$, respectively. The calculation of β when $\mu = 970$ is shown below:

$$P(\text{Type II error} | \mu = 970) = P(975.5 \leq \bar{x} \leq 1024.5 | \mu = 970)$$

$$= P\left(\frac{975.5 - 970}{37.5/\sqrt{9}} \leq z \leq \frac{1024.5 - 970}{37.5/\sqrt{9}}\right)$$

$$= P(0.44 \leq z \leq 4.36)$$

$$= F(4.36) - F(0.44)$$

$$= 1.000 - 0.670 = 0.3300$$

Note that in Fig. 9.13 the size of β decreases as the value of μ gets farther away from $\mu = 1000$. That is, the more incorrect H_0 is, the lower will be the value of β [and the higher $(1 - \beta)$]. This fact is shown in Table 9.10 where we

Figure 9.12
Probability of β for the critical region shown in Fig. 9.11 if the true mean is $\mu = 990$.

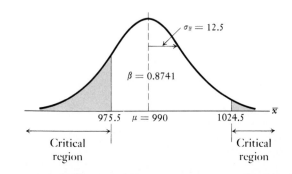

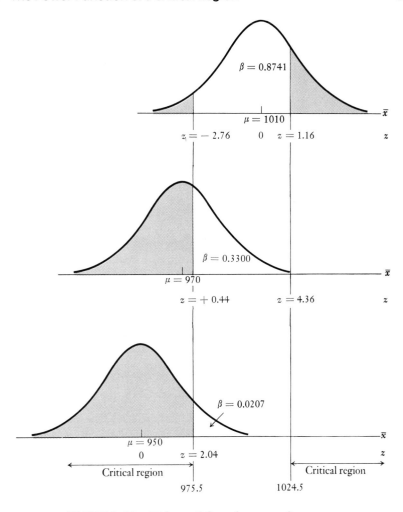

Figure 9.13
Values of β for different μ's, $\alpha = 0.05$, $n = 9$, $\sigma = 37.5$.

TABLE 9.10 Value of β and power for given true values of μ

μ	$P(\text{Accept } H_0) = \beta$	$P(\text{Reject } H_0) =$ Power $= 1 - \beta$
950	0.0207	0.9793
970	0.3300	0.6700
980	0.6406	0.3594
990	0.8741	0.1259
1000	$1 - \alpha = 0.95$	$\alpha = 0.05$
1010	0.8741	0.1259
1020	0.6406	0.3594
1030	0.3300	0.6700
1050	0.0207	0.9793

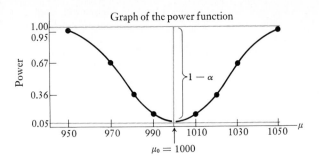

Figure 9.14

present the value of β and $(1 - \beta)$ for eight different values of μ. The row corresponding to $\mu = 1000$ is placed in a box to emphasize that this is the one case in which H_0 is true; hence β is not defined for $\mu = 1000$. Figure 9.14 is a graph of the power function $(1 - \beta)$.

In comparing the power functions of a number of different tests, we look for tests where the power function rises quickly as the value of μ differs by small amounts from μ_0. The most powerful test would be the one with the steepest ascending power function. In other words, we desire a test such that the probability of recognizing a false null hypothesis increases rapidly, even for rather small differences between the hypothesized value of the parameter and the true value.

The Trade-offs Between α and β

We have emphasized that when the sample size is fixed, α and β have an inverse relationship. To illustrate this trade-off, we will use the same production-

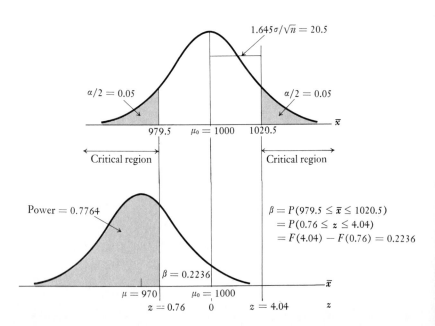

Figure 9.15

Critical region for
H_0: $\mu = 1000$ against
H_a: $\mu \neq 1000$ given
$\sigma = 37.5$, $n = 9$, $\alpha = 0.10$;
and the representation of β
given that the true mean is
$\mu = 970$.

process example described above, but we now will change α from 0.05 to 0.10. Since α has increased, the critical region has become larger.

The effect of the increase in α should be a reduction of β. Figure 9.15 shows the new critical regions, calculated by letting $z_{\alpha/2} = z_{0.05} = 1.645$. In this situation, the null hypothesis is accepted if $979.5 \leq \bar{x} \leq 1020.5$. The result is that the size of β is reduced from 0.3300 (shown in Table 9.10) to the new value, $\beta = 0.2236$. The power of the test has increased correspondingly. These values are shown in Fig. 9.15.

If we calculated additional values of the power function, we would find all of them larger when $\alpha = 0.10$ than when $\alpha = 0.05$. As we increase α, we increase the critical region, and hence make our test more powerful. Similarly, if we decrease the value of α, then the critical region gets smaller, β will rise, and the power of the test will drop. Thus, the size of α is related inversely to the size of β and directly to the size of the power, but the trade-off is not one-to-one. In this example, α was increased by 0.05 (0.05 to 0.10), but β decreased by more than twice this amount (0.3300 to 0.2236).

Decreasing α and β by Increasing n

Until now our discussion has been based on the assumption that the size of the sample is fixed in advance. If n is changed, however, the size of both α and β may be changed, because the size of n affects the location of the critical regions. To illustrate this effect, suppose we return α to its previous level of 0.05, and increase n from 9 to 36. The new critical region for our test, and the determination of β when the true value of μ is 970, are shown in Fig. 9.16.

Figure 9.16
Critical region for the test on H_0: $\mu = 1000$ against H_a: $\mu \neq 1000$, $\sigma = 37.5$, $n = 36$, $\alpha = 0.05$; and the representation of β when the true mean is $\mu = 970$.

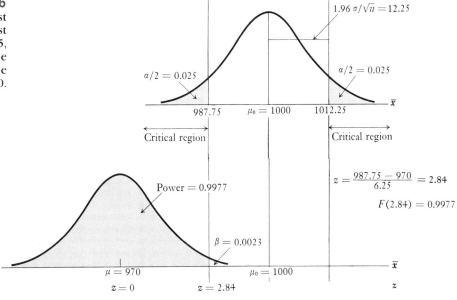

We see that the increased sample size makes our test more sensitive in distinguishing between H_0 and H_a; the standard error of the mean, $\sigma/\sqrt{n}$, is now half its former value (from $37.5/\sqrt{9} = 12.5$ to $37.5/\sqrt{36} = 6.25$). The null hypothesis will be accepted in this test if $987.75 < \bar{x} \leq 1012.25$. The probability that H_0 will be accepted given that $\mu = 970$ is now only $\beta = 0.0023$. By comparing Figs. 9.15 and 9.16 we see that we have reduced α from 0.10 to 0.05 and reduced β from 0.2236 to 0.0023 merely by increasing n from 9 to 36. Unfortunately, obtaining larger samples is more time-consuming and is often quite costly, so the researcher is faced with the task of balancing the costs of making incorrect decisions against the costs of sampling. We will return to this consideration in Chapter 10.

Problems

(*Note:* The reader is encouraged to solve as many as possible of the following problems using a computer).

9.51 Explain why, in testing H_0: $\mu = 20$ versus H_a: $\mu \neq 20$, we can calculate a single value of α for a given critical region, but we cannot calculate a single value of β.

9.52 Explain why most users of statistics set a level for α and then ignore the value of β. Similarly, why do most researchers have such a difficult time setting α and β so as to balance the costs of making an incorrect decision?

9.53 Reconsider Problem 9.2, assuming that the true weight of the loaves of bread in this population is 23.90 oz and $\sigma = 1.0$. What is the value of β if $\alpha = 0.01$? What is the power of the test if $\mu = 23.90$? Using words a "nonquantitative" person might understand, interpret the meaning of the values of α and β in this problem.

9.54 A fast-food chain has been averaging about $5000 worth of business on a typical weekday. To determine if sales are slipping the manager establishes the hypotheses H_0: $\mu = 5000$ versus H_a: $\mu < 5000$.

  a) What is the value of β if $n = 4$ and $\alpha = 0.05$ and the true value of $\mu = \$4900$? What is the power of the test?

  b) Repeat part (a) assuming that the true values are $4800, $4700, $4600, and $4500. Construct a graph of the power function, using these values.

9.55 Return to Problem 9.30, in which the sample size was $n = 64$ and $\alpha = 0.05$.

  a) Find β if $\mu = 51$.

  b) Show that for the hypotheses and critical region presented in part (a), the values of both α and β decrease if n is increased to 100.

9.56 Suppose you are testing the hypotheses H_0: $\mu = 1.2$ versus H_a: $\mu \neq 1.2$, using $\alpha = 0.01$ and $n = 100$. The standard deviation is known to be $\sigma = 0.4$. Sketch the power function assuming the true values of μ are 0.90, 0.95, 1.00, 1.05 and 1.10.

9.57 It was shown in Section 9.7 that, for the production process under investigation, a sample size of 50 results in a lower expected cost than a sample of 20 if the additional observations only cost an extra $10. Suppose that we now have the opportunity to buy 50 more observations (for a total of n of 100) for $15 more (that is, sampling cost of $25). Estimate, as best you can, the optimal critical region for this size of sample. Is the total expected cost in this case lower or higher than the cost when $n = 50$?

9.58 In the discussion in Section 9.7, we calculated the probability of making an incorrect decision concerning adjustments to a production process. The values of α and β were determined for the critical region $x \geq 4$ and for the critical region $x \geq 5$, assuming a sample size of 20.

   a) Calculate α and β for this problem for the critical region $x \geq 6$.

   b) Calculate the expected cost associated with this critical region when the probability of a defective is 0.10. Do the same thing for the probability of a defective equal to 0.25. Calculate the total expected cost, assuming $P(\text{minor}) = 0.70$ and $P(\text{major}) = 0.30$.

   c) Is the cost that you determined in part (b) better or worse than the cost calculated in Section 9.7 for the critical region $x \geq 5$? What do you think is the best critical region for this sample size? Explain why, and then try to draw a graph relating the location of the critical region to the total expected costs. (Let the horizontal axis be the lower bound of the critical regions.)

9.59 A survey is made to determine if one make of automobile is preferred to another using $n = 50$ randomly selected people. Assume the proportion preferring Make A is either $p = 0.50$ (H_0) or $p = 0.75$ (H_a).

   a) Using a critical region of $x \geq 31$, find α and β.

   b) Describe the two types of error that could be made and their consequences.

   c) If a Type I error is judged equally serious as a Type II error, would the critical region $x \geq 31$ be appropriate? If not, suggest a better one.

9.60 IDS Financial Services spent about $120,000 in 1989 to have the Yankelovich Group survey 1400 people nationally about their retirement goals and financial problems.

   a) What might be the purposes of such a survey? Name some hypotheses you could imagine IDS postulating.

   b) IDS found, for example, that 403 of the "baby boomers" sampled (523 people) expected to have to reduce their standard of living when they retire. In contrast, 308 of a sample of older Americans (447) had a similar pessimistic outlook. Complete the five hypothesis testing steps using these data.

Exercises

Note: Some of the tests necessary to solve the following exercises involve sample statistics not specifically described in this chapter—that is, the χ^2 and the F. Their properties are described in Chapter 6.

9.61 What assumption is necessary for using the F-test to test the null hypothesis H_0: $\sigma_1^2 = \sigma_2^2$?

9.62 In solving Problem 9.20 it is necessary to assume that $\sigma_1^2 = \sigma_2^2$. Use an F-test to determine whether or not this assumption is reasonable when $\alpha = 0.10$. What p-value would you report if α is unknown?

9.63 The Chamber of Commerce in a small town in Colorado is having a war of words with a small town in Hawaii as to which town enjoys better weather in the summer. Both locations have an average temperature of 85°, and both claim to have less variability in temperatures.

   a) What null and alternative hypotheses would you establish in this situation? What is the appropriate test statistic?

   b) Assume that you have been given a grant to take a random sample of weather in both locations. You spend two months in Hawaii, and calculate the variance of temperature over these 61 days to be $s_1^2 = 16$. A 31-day stay in Colorado yields $s_2^2 = 9$. Assuming that these are random samples, would you accept H_0 or H_a if $\alpha = 0.10$? What p-value would you report?

   c) Comment on how "random" you think these samples really are.

9.64 The telephone company is continually studying the duration of phone calls, as well as the variability in durations. Suppose that the national population variance of calls is $\sigma^2 = 4$ minutes. The telephone company wants to test whether a certain community's calls differ in variability from the national value. The duration of calls is assumed to be normally distributed.

   a) What null and alternative hypotheses would you establish for the test described above?

   b) What critical region(s) would you use for this test if $\alpha = 0.05$ and $n = 25$? Assume a normal parent population.

   c) Would you accept or reject H_0 if the sample of $n = 25$ resulted in $s^2 = 2.5$?

9.65 Basketball players sometimes are rated on how consistent they are at scoring (some are consistently bad). One "expert" has suggested that a good scorer should have a variance in the number of points scored of no more than $\sigma^2 = 25$. Suppose that State U.'s leading scorer made the following number of points in the first five games: 21, 14, 26, 9, and 15. On the basis of this sample (OK, perhaps it is not random) would you accept H_0: $\sigma^2 \leq 25$ or H_a: $\sigma^2 > 25$? [*Hint:* Make H_0 a simple hypothesis.] Use $\alpha = 0.05$. What probability value would you report? Assume that the parent population is normal.

9.66 Suppose that you are convinced that Harvard MBAs have high IQs, but you also believe that there is a higher variability among these people than the national average of $\sigma^2 = 256$.

   a) What null and alternative hypotheses would you use to test your assertion?

b) What test statistic is appropriate if all IQs are assumed to be normally distributed?

c) What critical region is appropriate if $\alpha = 0.025$ and $n = 31$?

d) Would you accept H_0 or H_a if the sample result is $s^2 = 350$?

e) What p-value would you report?

9.67 A sample survey firm is contracted by an advertising agency to determine whether or not the average income in a certain large metropolitan area exceeds $27,500. The agency wants the results of this survey to reject the null hypothesis H_0: $\mu = \$27,500$ in favor of H_a: $\mu > \$27,500$ at the $\alpha = 0.05$ level of significance when the true mean is as small as $27,600. If the population standard deviation of incomes in this area is assumed to be $1000, how large a sample will the survey firm have to take in order to meet the requirements of the advertising agency?

9.68 Suppose that, in Exercise 9.67, the survey firm charges $5 for each observation it collects for the advertising agency. How much more will it cost the agency to be able to reject H_0: $\mu = \$27,500$ at the $\alpha = 0.01$ level rather than at the $\alpha = 0.05$ level?

9.69 It has been estimated that most families in the United States spend approximately 90% of their yearly income and save no more than 10% of their yearly income. Suppose that a random sample of 100 families with high incomes (exceeding $80,000) shows that 60% of these people save more than 10% of their income.

a) Does this sample support the hypothesis that a majority of families with incomes exceeding $80,000 save more than 10% of their income? What is the null hypothesis in this case? Given these sample results, what is the probability that the null hypothesis is true?

b) Would you conclude from the sample in this problem that families with high incomes will tend to save more than families with more average incomes? Why or why not?

9.70 A public-policy researcher is studying the variance in the amount of money requested by certain government agencies. The alternative hypothesis is that the variance this year (σ_1^2) is larger than the variance five years ago (σ_2^2). Random samples, of size $n_1 = 21$ and $n_2 = 25$, yielded variances of $s_1^2 = (67,233)^2$ and $s_2^2 = (37,178)^2$. Assume that the two populations are normally distributed. Test, at $\alpha = 0.01$, the hypothesis H_0: $\sigma_1^2 = \sigma_2^2$. What p-value would you report if α is unknown?

9.71 A sample of 10 fibers treated with a standard technique has average strength of 10, with a standard deviation of 3.2. Another sample of 17 fibers treated with a new technique has an average strength of 20 and standard deviation of 3.0. Test at the 0.05 level of significance to see whether the new technique can be expected to produce a population of fibers with average strength *at least* 5 greater than the population of fibers treated with the standard technique. Assume that the populations are normal.

9.72 Go to Table VI in Appendix B and collect two random samples in which each observation is a two-digit number. The first sample should be of size $n_1 = 4$, and the second of size $n_2 = 6$. Calculate $\bar{x}_1, \bar{x}_2, s_1^2$, and s_2^2. Assume that you do not know that these samples came from the same population.

a) Use an F-test to test H_0: $\sigma_1^2 = \sigma_2^2$ versus H_a: $\sigma_1^2 \neq \sigma_2^2$, setting $\alpha = 0.01$. Are the assumptions necessary for use of the F-test met in this case?

b) Use a t-test to test H_0: $\mu_1 - \mu_2 = 0$ versus H_a: $\mu_1 - \mu \neq 0$, setting $\alpha = 0.01$. Are the assumptions required for use of the t-test met in this case?

9.73 Suppose you are given the following probability density function:

$$f(x) = \begin{cases} 1/\theta & \text{for } 0 \leq x \leq \theta \\ 0 & \text{otherwise} \end{cases}$$

a) You decide to test the null hypothesis H_0: $\theta = 1$ against the alternative H_a: $\theta = 2$ by means of a single observation. What is the value of α and β if you select the interval $x \leq 0.50$ as the critical region? Sketch this density function under both the null and alternative hypotheses, and indicate the critical region on this graph.

b) What is the value of α and β if you select 0.75 as the critical region?

c) Which of these two critical regions would be more appropriate if a Type II error is more serious than a Type I error?

9.74 An intersection has had an accident every 50 days, on the average, over the past 15 years. A new stoplight is hypothesized to reduce the number of accidents by one-fourth (to one accident every 200 days). The following hypotheses were formulated on the assumption that the exponential distribution is used as the test statistic.

$$H_0: 1/\lambda = 50 \quad \text{versus} \quad H_a: 1/\lambda = 200$$

Use the exponential distribution to determine the probability of a Type I and Type II error assuming that x = number of days until the next accident (after the light is installed), and H_0 will be rejected if $x \geq 150$.

9.75 Prove that Formula (9.4) and Formula (9.5) yield identical values of t and z when $n_1 = n_2$, $s_1^2 = \sigma_1^2$, $s_2^2 = \sigma_2^2$.

9.76 Suppose that you decide to test the null hypothesis that the probability of a 6 on each toss of a single die is 0.17. You intend to toss this die 100 different times, and will reject the null hypothesis if fewer than 10 sixes or more than 24 sixes appear.

a) For the critical region described above, and using Table I in Appendix B, what is the probability of making a Type I error?

b) Use a computer package to answer part (a).

c) What is the probability of a Type I error if the critical region is defined to be the occurrence of 22 or more sixes (a one-tailed test)?

d) If the alternative hypothesis is H_a: $p = 0.25$, and the critical region in part (c) is used, what is the probability of a Type II error?

9.77 (This problem incorporates concepts from Chapters 6, 7, and 9.) Assume you are working for Delta Airlines, and are concerned with the time it takes for a 727 to fly from Indianapolis to Atlanta. The time has obvious implications for fuel consumption estimates as well as scheduling departures and arrivals. A random sample of 10 flights resulted in the following times (in minutes): 84, 86, 90, 72, 81, 80, 78, 83, 77, 79. Assume the population is normally distributed. The following questions all refer to this sample.

a) Find an unbiased estimate of μ and σ^2.

b) Construct a 95% confidence interval for μ.

c) You are very concerned with the proportion of times a flight exceeds 85 minutes. Construct a 99% confidence interval for this proportion.

d) Test H_0: $\mu = 85$ versus H_a: $\mu = 80$ using $\alpha = 0.05$. What p-value would you report if α were unknown?

e) What is β for part (d) using $\alpha = 0.05$, and assuming that $\sigma^2 = 50$?

f) Does it appear reasonable that this random sample was drawn from a population with $\sigma^2 = 50$? Explain.

g) What size sample should have been taken if you had wanted an error in part (b) of no more than 1 minute? Assume $\sigma^2 = 50$.

h) Test H_0: $p = \frac{1}{2}$ versus H_a: $p < \frac{1}{2}$, where p is the proportion of flights over 85 minutes, using $\alpha = 0.03$.

TABLE 9.11 **Summary of tests of hypotheses**

Unknown parameter	Population description	Reference section	Test statistic
Mean μ	Population $N(\mu, \sigma^2)$ or $n \geq 30$, σ known	9.4	$z = \dfrac{\bar{x} - \mu_0}{\sigma/\sqrt{n}}$
Mean μ	Population $N(\mu, \sigma^2)$, σ unknown	9.4	$t = \dfrac{\bar{x} - \mu_0}{s/\sqrt{n}}$
Difference $\mu_1 - \mu_2$	Both populations normal, or n_1 and $n_2 \geq 25$, and σ_1^2 and σ_2^2 known	9.5	$z = \dfrac{(\bar{x}_1 - \bar{x}_2) - (\mu_1 - \mu_2)}{\sqrt{(\sigma_1^2/n_1) + (\sigma_2^2/n_2)}}$
Difference $\mu_1 - \mu_2$	Both populations normal, σ_1^2 and σ_2^2 are unknown, but must be equal	9.5	$t = \dfrac{(\bar{x}_1 - \bar{x}_2) - (\mu_1 - \mu_2)}{\sqrt{\left(\dfrac{(n_1 - 1)s_1^2}{n_1 - n_2 - 2} + \dfrac{(n_2 - 1)s_2^2}{n_1 + n_2 - 2}\right)\left(\dfrac{1}{n_1} + \dfrac{1}{n_2}\right)}}$
Difference $\mu_1 - \mu_2$ (matched pairs)	Both populations normal	9.5	$t = \dfrac{\bar{D} - \Delta}{s_D/\sqrt{n}}$
Difference $p_1 - p_2$	Both n_1 and n_2 are "large."	9.5	$z = \dfrac{[x_1/n_1) - (x_2/n_2)] - (p_1 - p_2)}{\sqrt{\left(\dfrac{x_1 + x_2}{n_1 + n_2}\right)\left(1 - \dfrac{x_1 + x_2}{n_1 + n_2}\right)\left(\dfrac{1}{n_1} + \dfrac{1}{n_2}\right)}}$

Chapter 10

Statistical
Decision
Theory

I was a trembling because I'd got to decide forever betwixt two things, and I knowed it. I studied for a minute, sort of holding my breath, and then say to myself, "All right, then, I'll go to hell."

HUCK FINN

Introduction **10.1**

As noted earlier, one purpose of statistical analysis is to aid in the process of *making decisions under uncertainty.* In Chapters 7 and 8 the process of making inferences based on sample information was discussed. In this chapter we go one step further—from making inferences to making decisions. Life is a constant sequence of decision-making situations. Most decisions are made intuitively without even thinking about them. For example, consider the decision facing you when you want to cross a busy street. You must decide when to attempt to cross the street, keeping in mind how much of a hurry you are in and how heavy the traffic is. The consequence of a "bad" decision here could be quite serious—you could be hit by a car and be killed. Yet you probably do not consciously think of this possibility because you have faced the situation many times in the past. Other decisions may require some thought, but can still be made intuitively. An example might be the choice of a main dish from a menu at a restaurant. You consciously evaluate the various choices, taking into consideration your tastes and the prices, and you make a judgmental decision and give the waiter your order.

Some decisions are not as easy to make as these two examples, however. For instance, consider the decision to purchase common stock. There are many stocks to choose from, and the decision involves the "outlook" for the various stocks, the investor's attitude toward risk, and many other considerations. Complex decisions faced by organizations, such as whether or not to build a new plant or how many units of a given item to produce, are also difficult decisions. It is for decisions such as these that the formal decision-theory procedures to be discussed in this chapter should be useful. Applying the formal models of decision theory may not always be easy, as we shall see, but for important decisions it should prove worthwhile.

As with any statistical procedure, applying decision theory is a modeling problem in which the statistician attempts to build a model that is a reasonable approximation to the real-world decision-making problem of interest but is not so complex that it is difficult to work with. First, it is necessary to carefully identify the problem and to prepare a list of possible decisions, or actions. Next, it is necessary to define the possible events, or states of the world, that seem to have an important bearing on the outcome of the decision. As we shall see, it is desirable to *assign probabilities* to these events, and these probabilities should represent the decision maker's uncertainty concerning the events. Thus, some of the previous material in this book regarding probability will be useful in decision theory. The other key input to problems of decision making under uncertainty involves the *potential consequences* of the various actions that are being considered. These consequences might be measured in terms of monetary payoffs or losses, or they might involve nonmonetary considerations, as we shall see when we discuss utility.

Once all of the inputs have been determined, the decision-making problem can be solved by using the techniques that will be developed in this chapter. Topics discussed include decision-making criteria, the role of probability and utility in decision-making problems, the value of information, the distinction between inference and decision, and a few related topics. The primary emphasis is placed on the mechanics of combining inputs appropriately to determine a decision that is "optimal" according to some criterion. You should keep in mind, however, that the initial modeling of a problem is also very important. Often this modeling process is iterative, since the model-building process may lead to the consideration of new actions or events that had previously been ignored.

Certainty vs. Uncertainty

10.2

Before we present the theory of making decisions under the condition of uncertainty, it should be useful to discuss the difference between certainty and uncertainty. Formally, a **consequence,** or a **payoff** to the decision maker, is the result of the interaction of two factors:

1. The *decision,* or the *action,* selected by the decision maker; and

2. The actual *state of the world which occurs.*

For example, suppose that you are faced with a decision concerning the purchase of common stock. For the sake of simplicity, we shall assume that you intend to invest exactly $1000 in a single common stock and hold the stock for exactly one year, at which time you will sell it at the market price. Furthermore, assume that you are considering only three stocks, A, B, and C, each of which currently sells for $10 a share. Thus, you intend to buy 100 shares of *one* of the three stocks. Your selection of a single stock from the three constitutes your *decision,* or *action.* The prices of the three stocks one year from now constitute the *state of the world.* The combination of your action and the state of the world determines your payoff. Suppose that at the end of one year, the prices of stocks A, B, and C are $15, $5, and $10. The payoffs for the three possible actions are then + $500, − $500, and $0, respectively. For this state of the world, the best decision is to buy stock A, for this results in the highest payoff. If we know the state of the world with certainty, the decision can be made in this manner, and this is called decision making *under certainty.* In our example, if we know what the prices of the stocks will be in one year, then we simply buy the stock that will give us the maximum payoff—that is, the stock that will increase in value the most during the coming year.

Of course, the assumption that we know what the prices of stocks will be one year hence is not at all realistic. We probably have some ideas regarding the prices, ideas that may be based on our impressions of the economy in general, various industries, and various firms within industries. Our knowledge may be due to a careful study of the stock market, or it may be due to a hot tip from a friend. At any rate, we have knowledge, but not perfect knowledge. As a result, we are no longer operating under the condition of certainty. Instead, we are faced with a problem of decision making *under uncertainty.* In this example, it is clear that the decision-making problem is considerably more difficult under uncertainty than it is under certainty.

It should be pointed out that in many situations, decision making under certainty is by no means easy. Often the problem is complex enough to make it very difficult to determine the best action even though all of the relevant factors are known for certain. For example, suppose that a manufacturer must ship a certain product from a number of factories to a number of warehouses. Each factory produces a certain number of units of the product, and each warehouse requires a certain number of units. Furthermore, the cost of shipping from any given factory to any given warehouse depends on the amount shipped, the particular factory, and the particular warehouse. The decision-making problem is this: What shipping pattern minimizes the total transportation costs? That is, what is the least expensive way to transport the product from the factories to the warehouses? In this problem there is no uncertainty;

the amounts produced at the various factories, the amounts needed at the various warehouses, and the costs of shipping are all known. Even under certainty, this decision-making problem is clearly not trivial to solve, although it becomes much more complex if uncertainty is introduced. Under certainty, the problem can be solved by a technique known as linear programming. Other decision-making problems under certainty require the use of different types of mathematical optimization procedures that often are classified under the heading *operations research.* We are concerned with the case of uncertainty rather than certainty, so operations-research procedures are not discussed here, but you should recognize that decision making under certainty includes many important and by no means mathematically trivial problems.

Criteria for Decision Making Under Uncertainty

10.3

In the certainty case, the payoffs for each potential action are determined, and the action resulting in the highest payoff is then chosen. Under uncertainty, however, the payoffs cannot be determined for certain simply because the state of the world is not known for certain. For each action, then, there are various possible payoffs corresponding to the various possible states (we shall use the terms "state" and "state of nature" interchangeably with "state of the world"). For example, consider the common-stock example once again, with the assumption that there are only two possible states of nature. In the first state (state I), the prices of the stocks A, B, and C at the end of one year are, respectively, $15, $5, and $10. In the second state (state II), the prices are $8, $14, and $12. This results in the payoff table given in Table 10.1, where the payoffs are expressed in dollars. It is not obvious from the payoff table that any one of the three actions is clearly the "best" action. If state of nature I occurs, then A gives the greatest payoff; if state of nature II occurs, then B gives the greatest payoff. An argument can also be made for buying C, for this eliminates the possibility of a negative payoff. This argument is put forth by those supporting the following decision-making criterion: for each action, find the smallest

TABLE 10.1 Payoff table for stock example

		State of nature	
		I	II
	Buy A	+ 500	− 200
Actions	**Buy B**	− 500	+ 400
	Buy C	0	+ 200

possible payoff and choose the action for which this smallest possible payoff is largest. In this case the smallest possible payoffs for the three actions are -200, -500, and 0. Clearly zero is the largest of these three numbers, so according to this criterion, the "best" action is to buy stock C. This criterion is called the **maximin** (maximization of minimum gain) criterion.

The maximin criterion can be criticized on two grounds. First, it considers only the smallest payoff for each action and fails to take into account the *largest* payoff. By choosing to buy stock C in the above example, we are avoiding the possibility of a large loss, but at the same time we are giving up a chance for a larger gain. The best we can do with C is to gain $200, whereas with A it would be possible to gain $500. A second criticism of the maximin criterion is that it fails to take into consideration the relative likelihoods of the two possible states of nature. These likelihoods can be represented by probabilities, $P(\text{I})$ and $P(\text{II})$, which must sum to one because of the assumption that I and II are the only possible states of nature. If, for example, $P(\text{I}) = 0.90$ and $P(\text{II}) = 0.10$, we might feel that the odds in favor of state I are high enough to warrant the purchase of stock A, which results in a $+$ $500 payoff if state I occurs.

Before considering the introduction of the probabilities, $P(\text{I})$ and $P(\text{II})$, which represent our uncertainty about the state of nature, let us consider one more possible criterion. This criterion, which we shall label the **maximax** criterion, involves finding the largest possible payoff for each action and choosing the action for which this largest possible payoff is the greatest. In our example, the largest possible payoffs are, respectively, $+500$, $+400$, and $+200$, so the maximax criterion leads to the purchase of stock A. The maximax criterion amounts to trying to attain the highest payoff in the entire payoff table, and as such it is a risk-taking strategy, for it ignores the possibilities of large losses. In the same way, the *maximin* criterion is a risk-avoiding strategy, for it attempts to avoid large losses, even at the sacrifice of possible large gains. Since the maximax criterion considers only the largest entry in each row of the payoff table and does not take $P(\text{I})$ and $P(\text{II})$ into consideration, it can be criticized on the same grounds as the maximin criterion.

In order to make use of the probabilistic nature of the situation, it is necessary to use the concept of *expected value,* which was introduced in Chapter 3. For each action, it is possible to compute an expected payoff, and the best action would be the one with the highest expected payoff. If payoffs are expressed in terms of money, as in the stock example, we shall call this criterion the **EMV (expected monetary value)** criterion. In our example,

$$\text{EMV (Buy A)} = (\$500)P(\text{I}) + (-\$200)P(\text{II})$$
$$\text{EMV (Buy B)} = (-\$500)P(\text{I}) + (\$400)P(\text{II})$$

and

$$\text{EMV (Buy C)} = (\$0)P(\text{I}) + (\$200)P(\text{II})$$

Suppose $P(\text{I}) = 0.90$ and $P(\text{II}) = 0.10$. Then the three EMV's are, respectively, $430, $-$410, and $20. In this case, the EMV criterion leads to the purchase of stock A. If, on the other hand, the probabilities are $P(\text{I}) = 0.30$ and $P(\text{II}) =$

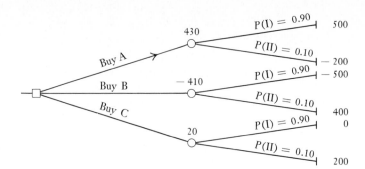

Figure 10.1
Decision tree for stock
example.

0.70, the EMV's would be $10, $130, and $140, and the best action would be to buy stock C. With the EMV criterion, then, the payoffs alone do not determine the best action; it is necessary to take into consideration the probabilities representing the uncertainty about the state of nature. The EMV then represents the expected value, or the average payoff, for the different actions.

An alternative way of presenting a decision-making problem involves making tree diagrams. The use of tree diagrams is often preferred to the use of payoff tables because the tree diagrams make it easier to see the general structure of decision-making problems, particularly in the case of somewhat complex problems. Tree diagrams are particularly helpful in problems that involve buying additional information, as we shall see in Sections 10.5 and 10.6. In Fig. 10.1 a tree diagram for the stock-purchasing example is presented. The point at the left-hand side of the diagram represents the initial position, and the three branches of the tree emanating from that point represent the three actions in the problem. Thus, the left fork is called a decision fork, or an action fork. At the end of each of the three branches representing the possible actions, there is another fork with two branches. These two branches represent the two states of nature, or events, and as a result these forks are called event forks, or chance forks. All forks in a decision tree are either **decision forks** (involving possible actions) or **event forks** (involving possible events). This particular tree is quite simple, with only one decision fork and one event fork for each possible action. The numbers on the event branches are the probabilities of the events, and the numbers on the right-hand side of the tree diagram are the payoffs. For example, if the decision maker buys stock A and event I occurs, then the payoff is $500.

To solve a decision-making problem that is expressed in the form of a decision tree, we start at the right-hand side of the diagram and work "backward" to the initial point. Hence, the solution procedure is often called **backward induction.** In working backward, there are only two rules to follow:

1. At chance forks, find expected values (EMV's). Following conventional notation, we will denote chance forks with a circle, ○.

2. At decision forks, choose the action with the highest EMV. Decision forks will be designated with a box symbol, ☐.

For the tree in Fig. 10.1, EMV's are calculated for each of the three chance forks on the right-hand side of the diagram. These EMV's, which turn out to be $430, − $410, and $20, as calculated previously, are written at the "starting points" of the three chance forks. At the action fork, then, we simply compare these three numbers, note that the largest is $430, corresponding to the purchase of stock A, and put an arrow on the branch marked "Buy A" to indicate that this is the optimal action. As you will find later in the chapter, more complicated decision trees require more calculations, but they do not necessitate any procedures different from the procedures used to solve the simple problem represented by this tree diagram.

For another example, consider a contractor who is about to submit a bid for the construction of a new office building. It will cost the contractor $400,000 to build the proposed building, and he must decide how much to bid. The larger the bid, the more profit the contractor will earn if he wins the bid. However, the contract is awarded to the low bidder, and the contractor knows that some of his competitors will also be submitting bids on this job. After giving the matter serious thought, the contractor decides that the job is not worth his while if he earns less than $100,000, so the lowest bid he will consider is $500,000. Furthermore, it is a waste of time to bid more than $600,000, for he is certain that the low bid will not be above $600,000. He finally decides to consider bids of $500,000, $525,000, $550,000, and $575,000. After considering his knowledge about the bidding strategies of his competitors, he decides that the chances of winning the bid are one in two if he bids $500,000, one in three if he bids $525,000, one in four if he bids $550,000, and one in ten if he bids $575,000. This decision-making problem is represented in Fig. 10.2, and we see that the optimal action is to bid $500,000. In this problem, the probability of winning the bid goes down rapidly as the bid increases; had the probability not gone down so rapidly, one of the other bids might have turned out to be optimal.

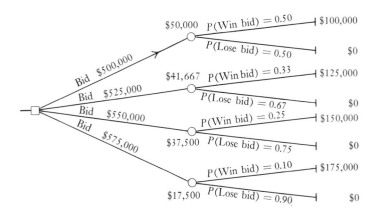

Figure 10.2
Decision tree for bidding example.

The Revision of Probabilities

10.4

One important input to the decision-making procedure that has not been discussed in detail is the set of probabilities for the various possible states of nature. This section shows how probabilities can be revised on the basis of sample information. In order to do this we shall have to recall Bayes' rule from Chapter 2 and restate it in the terminology of decision making.

Bayes' rule: If $\theta_1, \theta_2, \ldots, \theta_k$ represent the possible states of nature, with probabilities $P(\theta_i)$, $i = 1, \ldots, k$, and x is some other event, then

$$P(\theta_i|x) = \frac{P(x|\theta_i)P(\theta_i)}{\sum_{j=1}^{k} P(x|\theta_j)P(\theta_j)} \qquad i = 1, \ldots, k$$

In this form, Bayes' rule provides a means of revising probabilities on the basis of sample evidence. The probabilities $P(\theta_i)$ are the probabilities of the various states of nature *prior to seeing the sample information.* These probabilities may represent a person's judgments (that is, they may be subjective), or they may represent past sample information (in this sense, they may be regarded as objective). In general, we shall assume that the probabilities are subjective. The event x represents some sample information, and the probabilities $P(\theta_i|x)$ are the probabilities of the various states of nature *after seeing the sample information.* We shall call the $P(\theta_i)$ **prior probabilities** and the $P(\theta_i|x)$ **posterior probabilities.** The other probabilities appearing in Bayes' rule, which are of the form $P(x|\theta_i)$, will be called **likelihoods,** for they represent the probability, or the likelihood, of the observed sample results *given that* a particular state of nature occurs. The function $P(x|\theta_i)$ is essentially identical to the likelihood function encountered in the appendix to Chapter 7.

The example presented in Chapter 2 concerning a component that is produced by a certain process should help to clarify the preceding concepts. From past data, it is known that, of the components resulting from the production process, about 70% have been good and about 30% have been defective. (Furthermore, there is no reason to believe that there has been any change in the process that would alter these percentages.) However, management must make a decision as to whether to reject or accept individual components, so some information is desired about the individual components. To provide this information, a testing device is used. The testing device will read positive (+) if it appears that the component is good, and it will read negative (−) if the component appears defective. A large number of components were run through the testing device to check its accuracy, with the following results:

1. Among the good components, 80% had a positive reading and 20% had a negative reading.
2. Among the defective components, 25% had a positive reading and 75% had a negative reading.

Thus, the testing device is *more likely* to give a positive reading if the component is good, but the device is by no means perfect.

From the information in the preceding paragraph, Bayes' rule can be used to determine the posterior probabilities that a component is good or defective after the component is tested. Given no information other than the historical data, the prior probabilities are

$$P(\text{Good}) = 0.70 \quad \text{and} \quad P(\text{Defective}) = 0.30$$

If the test yields a positive reading, the likelihoods are

$$P(+\,|\text{Good}) = 0.80 \quad \text{and} \quad P(+\,|\text{Defective}) = 0.25$$

On the other hand, if the test yields a negative reading, the likelihoods are

$$P(-\,|\text{Good}) = 0.20 \quad \text{and} \quad P(-\,|\text{Defective}) = 0.75$$

Suppose that a particular component is tested and yields a positive reading. Bayes' rule is then applied as follows:

$$P(\text{Good}|+) = \frac{P(+\,|\text{Good})P(\text{Good})}{P(+\,|\text{Good})P(\text{Good}) + P(+\,|\text{Defective})P(\text{Defective})}$$

$$= \frac{(0.80)(0.70)}{(0.80)(0.70) + (0.25)(0.30)} = 0.882$$

and

$$P(\text{Defective}|+) = \frac{P(+\,|\text{Defective})P(\text{Defective})}{P(+\,|\text{Good})P(\text{Good}) + P(+\,|\text{Defective})P(\text{Defective})}$$

$$= \frac{(0.25)(0.30)}{(0.80)(0.70) + (0.25)(0.30)} = 0.118$$

The positive reading increases the probability that the component is good from 0.70 to 0.882, and decreases the probability that the component is defective accordingly. This is intuitively reasonable, since a positive reading is more likely for a good component than for a defective component.

Since the probabilities of the various states of nature in a decision-making problem are supposed to represent the state of uncertainty, we can think of Bayes' rule as a technique for taking into account new information and suitably revising probabilities. The prior probabilities represent the state of uncertainty *prior* to seeing any sample, and the posterior probabilities represent the state of uncertainty *after* seeing a particular sample. The terms *prior* and *posterior,* then, relate only to a particular sample. In the example given above, suppose that the component is tested a second time. Assuming that the two tests are independent and that the testing device essentially "has no memory," the likelihoods given in the previous paragraph are still valid for the second test. The probabilities 0.882 and 0.118, the probabilities posterior to the first sample, now represent the state of uncertainty *prior to the new sample.* Suppose that the second test yields a positive reading, just as the first test did. Applying Bayes' rule a second time,

$$P(\text{Good}|+,+) = \frac{P(+|\text{Good})P(\text{Good}|+)}{P(+|\text{Good})P(\text{Good}|+) + P(+|\text{Defective})P(\text{Defective}|+)}$$

$$= \frac{(0.80)(0.882)}{(0.80)(0.882) + (0.25)(0.118)} = 0.960$$

and

$$P(\text{Defective}|+,+) = \frac{P(+|\text{Defective})P(\text{Defective}|+)}{P(+|\text{Good})P(\text{Good}|+) + P(+|\text{Defective})P(\text{Defective}|+)}$$

$$= \frac{(0.25)(0.118)}{(0.80)(0.882) + (0.25)(0.118)} = 0.040$$

The revised probabilities are now 0.960 and 0.040. The second positive reading has increased still more the probability that the component is good, as would be expected. If more tests were made, the probabilities could be revised again.

One nice feature of Bayes' rule is that if we have a sample of more than one trial, it makes no difference whether the probabilities are revised trial by trial, as in the previous example, or revised just once after the completion of *all* the trials. In this case, starting with prior probabilities of 0.70 and 0.30 and observing two positive readings on two tests, we could apply Bayes' rule as follows:

$$P(\text{Good}|+,+) = \frac{P(+,+|\text{Good})P(\text{Good})}{P(+,+|\text{Good})P(\text{Good}) + P(+,+|\text{Defective})P(\text{Defective})}$$

$$= \frac{(0.80)^2(0.70)}{(0.80)^2(0.70) + (0.25)^2(0.30)} = 0.960$$

and

$$P(\text{Defective}|+,+) = \frac{P(+,+|\text{Defective})P(\text{Defective})}{P(+,+|\text{Good})P(\text{Good}) + P(+,+|\text{Defective})P(\text{Defective})}$$

$$= \frac{(0.25)^2(0.30)}{(0.80)^2(0.70) + (0.25)^2(0.30)} = 0.040$$

This application of Bayes' rule makes use of the fact that the two trials were independent. By independence,

$$P(+,+|\text{Good}) = P(+|\text{Good})P(+|\text{Good}) = (0.80)^2$$

and

$$P(+,+|\text{Defective}) = P(+|\text{Defective})P(+|\text{Defective}) = (0.25)^2$$

Note that the resulting probabilities are identical to those obtained by applying Bayes' rule twice, once after each test.

Bayes' rule, then, can be used to revise probabilities as new information is obtained. In this manner we can determine probabilities that represent our current state of uncertainty at the time a decision is to be made. Sometimes no sample information is available, and decisions must be based on prior probabilities that represent the subjective judgments of the decision maker. In still other cases, no prior information is available, and decisions must be based solely on the sample information. This corresponds to the situation where the prior probabilities for the various states of nature are all equal.

Problems

10.1 Distinguish between making an inference and making a decision.

10.2 Suppose that a friend of yours loves to gamble, and he offers a bet on the toss of a coin. He will pay you $10 if the coin comes up heads, and you will pay him $1 if the coin comes up tails. You can use a coin from your pocket (so as to be sure that your friend is not slipping in a "loaded" coin) and you can do the tossing.

    a) What are the two possible actions available to you?

    b) What are the two possible events of interest?

    c) What are the probabilities for these events?

    d) For each combination of an action and an event (for example, you take the bet and the coin comes up heads), what is the consequence, or payoff, to you?

10.3 In Problem 10.2, if you take the bet and the coin comes up tails, does this mean that you made a bad decision? Explain your answer.

10.4 Explain the difference between decision making under certainty and decision making under uncertainty.

10.5 It is sometimes said that we are living in an increasingly uncertain world. List some major uncertainties facing managerial decision makers today.

10.6 Give an example of a decision-making problem under certainty.

10.7 Discuss the relative merits of the maximin, maximax, and EMV criteria for decision making.

10.8 Explain the terms "prior probability" and "posterior probability."

10.9 Suppose that you have some judgments about whether the economy will fall into a recession during the next year, and you quantify those judgments, deciding that the probability is 0.30 that a recession will occur. Then you see some new economic figures: they cause you to revise your judgments, and therefore your probability as well. The figures are somewhat pessimistic, so your probability of a recession becomes 0.50. Finally, a well-known economic forecaster is quoted as saying that she is virtually certain there will be no recession for at least the next 18 months. This causes you to adjust the probability of a recession to 0.20. Is the probability of 0.50 a prior probability or a posterior probability?

10.10 Express Problem 10.2 in the form of a tree diagram. Which action is "optimal" according to the maximin criterion? The maximax criterion? The EMV criterion?

10.11 A firm must decide whether or not to initiate a special advertising campaign for a certain product. The firm feels that a competitor might introduce a competing product, and that if such a new product is introduced, sales of the firm's own product would greatly decrease unless an advertising campaign

TABLE 10.2

	State of nature	
	Competitor introduces new product	**Competitor does not introduce new product**
No advertising	100,000	700,000
Minor ad campaign	300,000	600,000
Major ad campaign	400,000	500,000

Action {

for the product was in progress. The three actions under consideration are "no advertising," "minor ad campaign," and "major ad campaign." Taking into account the cost of advertising and its anticipated effect on sales, the decision maker determines the payoff table (Table 10.2).

a) What should the firm do if the maximin criterion is used?

b) What should the firm do if the maximax criterion is used?

c) On the basis of currently available information concerning the actions of the competing firm, it is decided that the probability is 0.60 that the new product will be introduced. What should the firm do if the EMV criterion is used?

10.12 A company has $100,000 available to invest. The company can either expand production, invest the money in stocks, or put the money in the bank at a fixed 8% interest. If there is no recession, the company expects to make 14% if production is expanded and 12% if stocks are purchased. If there is a recession, however, expansion will lead to a 6% loss and stocks will provide a 2% loss. The decision will be reevaluated in one year, so that only the first year's return is of interest now.

a) Draw a tree diagram for this problem.

b) Find the action that is best according to the maximin criterion.

10.13 In Problem 10.12, suppose that the company wants to maximize EMV. If the probability of a recession is 0.2, what should the company do? How large would the probability of a recession have to be before the company would put the money in the bank?

10.14 During a study of past records, it was found that 10% of the coats manufactured by a particular firm had an imperfection. As a result, an inspector was hired to closely inspect the coats before they leave the factory. Of course, the inspector is not infallible. If a coat has an imperfection, the probability that the inspector will classify it as imperfect is 0.80. If a coat has no imperfection, on the other hand, the probability that the inspector will classify it as imperfect is 0.10.

a) If a coat has been classified as imperfect, what is the probability that it really is imperfect?

b) If a coat has been classified as good, what is the probability that it really is imperfect?

10.15 When someone applies for a loan, a bank gathers information about the applicant and applies a credit rating system to label the applicant either a "good risk," a "moderate risk," or a "bad risk." The bank will lend money to good or moderate risks, but not to bad risks. About 5% of the people borrowing money from the bank fail to repay the loan. Moreover, the bank's records show that 10% of those who failed to repay had been rated as good risks, while 60% of those who *did* repay had been rated as good risks.

a) Without using the credit rating system, what is the probability that an applicant will fail to repay a loan?

b) If the credit rating system labels an applicant a good risk, what is the probability that the applicant will fail to repay?

c) If the credit rating system labels an applicant a moderate risk, what is the probability that the applicant will fail to repay?

10.16 A security analyst feels that daily price changes of a particular security are independent and that the probability that the security's price increases on any given day is either $0.4, 0.5$, or 0.6. If it is 0.4, the security is classified as a poor investment; if $p = 0.5$ it is classified as an average investment: and if $p = 0.6$ it is classified as a good investment. The security analyst feels that the security is equally likely to be an average investment or a good investment, and that it is twice as likely to be a good investment as it is to be a bad investment.

a) Find $P(p = 0.4), P(p = 0.5)$, and $P(p = 0.6)$, where p is the probability that the price of the security increases on any given day.

b) The analyst observes the security in question for one day, and on that particular day the price of the security goes up. Use this new information to revise the analyst's distribution of p.

c) The security is observed for a second day and on that day the price goes up again. Once again, revise the analyst's distribution of p.

10.17 In the component-testing example in Section 10.4, suppose that a new test is available. This test gives positive readings to 90% of the good components and 15% of the bad components.

a) If a component receives a positive reading on the new test, what is the probability that it is defective?

b) If a component receives a negative reading on the new test, what is the probability that it is defective?

c) If both tests are run on a component, with positive results from both tests, what is the probability that the component is defective?

10.18 In Problem 10.17, if the old test and the new test cost the same to use, which one would you prefer to use? Explain your answer.

The Value
of Perfect
Information

10.5

The term "information" has been used in discussing the state of uncertainty facing the decision maker. The more information he or she has regarding the states of nature, the better off we would expect the decision maker to be. The extreme example is that of perfect information, which corresponds to what

TABLE 10.3   Payoff table for component example

		State of the world	
		Component good	Component defective
Action	Market component	3	− 5
	Scrap component	− 1	− 1

has previously been labeled certainty. The decision maker with perfect information simply chooses the act that results in the largest payoff—there is no uncertainty. In the production-process example, suppose that the decision maker must decide whether to accept or reject a component. If the component is accepted, it will be marketed. Of course, there is still a chance that it might be defective, and any components that are sold and later found to be defective are replaced immediately with an alternative component that costs more but is guaranteed to be good. The additional cost is borne by the producer (the decision maker, in the example) in order to keep from losing the business of dissatisfied customers. If the component is rejected, it is scrapped. This is clearly a problem of decision making under uncertainty, for the decision maker is not sure whether the component is good or defective yet must decide whether to market it or scrap it. After taking into account the various costs, the decision maker arrives at the payoff table given in Table 10.3. All payoffs are expressed in dollars.

Prior to testing the component, the decision maker's prior probabilities are $P(\text{Good}) = 0.70$ and $P(\text{Defective}) = 0.30$, and the EMV's for the two actions are

$$\text{EMV(Market)} = 3(0.70) + (-5)(0.30) = 0.60$$

and

$$\text{EMV(Scrap)} = -1(0.70) + (-1)(0.30) = -1.00$$

The optimal decision is to market the component, since this action has the larger of the two EMV's.

What if the decision maker could obtain perfect information? That is, what if it were possible to find out *for sure* whether the component is good or defective? (In this example, it is possible to conceive of a test that could determine for sure whether a component is good or defective, although such a test might be quite expensive. Usually, however, it is not even *possible* to obtain perfect information in decision-making problems. Nevertheless, it is useful to investigate the value of perfect information and to consider it as an *upper bound* on the value of less-than-perfect information.) With perfect information, the decision maker could obtain a payoff of $3 for certain if the component is good and a payoff of − $1 for certain if the component is defective. But according to the prior probabilities determined from historical data,

$$P(\text{Good}) = 0.70 \quad \text{and} \quad P(\text{Defective}) = 0.30$$

Thus, *before* obtaining the perfect information (but knowing that it will be obtained), the decision maker knows that there is a 0.70 chance of receiving $3 and a 0.30 chance of losing $1. The corresponding EMV, called the expected payoff under perfect information, is

$$\text{EMV}(\text{Perfect information}) = (\text{Highest payoff if good})P(\text{Good})$$
$$+ (\text{Highest payoff if defective})P(\text{Defective})$$
$$= 3(0.70) + (-1)(0.30) = 1.80$$

Before actually obtaining perfect information, then, the decision maker can compute the expected payoff under perfect information, and the expected value of perfect information, denoted by EVPI, is

$$\text{EVPI} = \text{EMV}\left(\begin{array}{c}\text{Perfect}\\\text{information}\end{array}\right) - \text{EMV}\left(\begin{array}{c}\text{Optimal action}\\\text{under prior information}\end{array}\right)$$

Thus, EVPI simply represents how much better off the decision maker expects to be if the decision can be made with perfect information instead of on the basis of current probabilities. For the example, the best EMV under the decision maker's present state of information is $0.60, and the difference between EMV (Perfect information) and $0.60 represents the expected value of perfect information:

$$\text{EVPI} = \$1.80 - \$0.60 = \$1.20$$

Therefore, if the decision maker could purchase perfect information, he or she should be willing to pay up to $1.20 for it.

The consideration of perfect information is illustrated in decision-tree form in Fig. 10.3. Note that the first fork is a decision fork, with the decision being whether to purchase perfect information before making a final decision

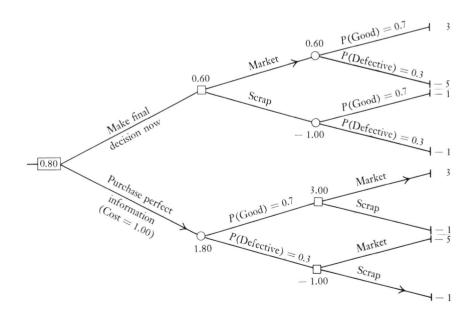

Figure 10.3
Decision tree for component example.

regarding the component or to make the final decision *without* obtaining additional information. If the decision is made without additional information, the EMV is \$0.60, whereas if the decision is made with perfect information, the EMV is \$1.80. Comparing the top portion of the tree in Fig. 10.3 with the bottom portion of the tree, it can be seen that with perfect information, the branches corresponding to whether the item is good or defective come *before* the branches corresponding to the decision whether to market or scrap.

Of course, if the perfect information costs something, its cost must be subtracted from the \$1.80 figure. For example, on the decision tree, the perfect information costs \$1, in which case the *net* EMV with perfect information is \$1.80 − \$1 = \$0.80. This is still better than \$0.60, so the optimal strategy is to purchase the perfect information before making the final decision regarding the component.

Now suppose that the decision maker observes two tests of the component, with positive readings on both tests. Applying Bayes' rule as in the previous section, the posterior probabilities are 0.960 and 0.040. The EMV's are then

$$EMV(\text{Market}| + , +) = 3(0.96) + (- 5)(0.04) = 2.68$$

and

$$EMV(\text{Scrap}| + , +) = - 1(0.96) + (- 1)(0.04) = - 1.00$$

Using the posterior probabilities, the EMV under perfect information is now

$$3(0.96) + (- 1)(0.04) = 2.84$$

Therefore, the expected value of perfect information is now

$$\$2.84 - \$2.68 = \$0.16$$

The decision maker is now willing to pay only up to \$0.16 for perfect information, whereas previously he or she would have been willing to pay up to \$1.20. It appears that observing the sample information (the results of the two tests) has improved his lot somewhat. After the two positive readings, the probability that the component is good is very high, so it is very unlikely that perfect information will change the decision. If, on the other hand, the decision maker had observed one positive reading and one negative reading, he or she would not be so certain about whether the component was good or defective, and the expected value of perfect information would not be so low.

The Value of Sample Information

10.6

From the expected value of perfect information, the decision maker knows how much perfect information is worth—that is, how much he or she should be willing to pay for perfect information. In most real-world decision-making problems, however, perfect information is not available. Even in the component example, it is unlikely that the decision maker can find out for certain whether a component is good or defective without either destroying the component or conducting a prohibitively expensive examination of the component. The expected value of perfect information is still useful as an upper bound to the amount the decision maker should be willing to pay for imperfect information, or *sample* information. Given the prior probabilities in the component example, if the expected value of perfect information is $1.20, the decision maker surely should not pay any more than that for less than perfect information.

Ideally, of course, it is desirable to compute exactly the expected value of sample information. After a sample is observed, the decision maker revises probabilities and recomputes EMV's for the actions under consideration. *Before* the sample is observed, he or she needs to decide whether or not to take the sample. After all, samples usually have some cost, and the decision maker wants to know if the sample is expected to be worth the cost involved.

In our example, suppose that the decision maker has not observed any sample information, but is contemplating running the test discussed in the previous section. To determine the expected value of sample information, it is necessary to consider all possible sample outcomes and to compute the posterior probabilities and posterior EMV's under each possible sample outcome. We already know that if the test yields a positive reading, the posterior probabilities are

$$P(\text{Good}|+) = 0.882 \quad \text{and} \quad P(\text{Defective}|+) = 0.118$$

The corresponding expected payoffs are

$$\text{EMV}(\text{Market}|+) = 3(0.882) + (-5)(0.118) = 2.06$$

and

$$\text{EMV}(\text{Scrap}|+) = -1(0.882) + (-1)(0.118) = -1.00$$

Using Bayes' rule, the posterior probabilities following a negative reading are

$$P(\text{Good}|-) = 0.384 \quad \text{and} \quad P(\text{Defective}|-) = 0.616$$

and the expected payoffs are

$$\text{EMV}(\text{Market}|-) = -1.93 \quad \text{and} \quad \text{EMV}(\text{Scrap}|-) = -1.00$$

Thus, if the test yields a positive reading, the optimal action is to market the component, and the EMV of this optimal action is $2.06. If the test yields a negative reading, the optimal action is to scrap the component, and the EMV of this optimal action is $-$ $1.00.

The probabilities for the two possible results of the test, as calculated before the test is run, can be determined as follows:

$$P(+) = P(+|\text{Good})P(\text{Good}) + P(+|\text{Defective})P(\text{Defective})$$
$$= (0.80)(0.70) + (0.25)(0.30) = 0.635$$

and

$$P(-) = P(-|\text{Good})P(\text{Good}) + P(-|\text{Defective})P(\text{Defective})$$
$$= (0.20)(0.70) + (0.75)(0.30) = 0.365$$

Therefore, the overall expected payoff *with* the test, as calculated before the test is run, is

$$\text{EMV}\left(\begin{array}{c}\text{Sample}\\\text{Information}\end{array}\right) = \left(\begin{array}{c}\text{Highest}\\\text{EMV after }+\end{array}\right)P(+) + \left(\begin{array}{c}\text{Highest}\\\text{EMV after }-\end{array}\right)P(-)$$

$$= 2.06(0.635) + (-1.00)(0.365) = 0.94$$

Before the sample is actually observed, then, the expected payoff under sample information can be computed, and the expected value of sample information, denoted by EVSI, is

$$\text{EVSI} = \text{EMV}\left(\begin{array}{c}\text{Sample}\\\text{information}\end{array}\right) - \text{EMV}\left(\begin{array}{c}\text{Optimal action}\\\text{under prior information}\end{array}\right)$$

EVSI tells the decision maker how much better off he or she can expect to be if the choice is made to obtain sample information before making the final decision. For the example, the best EMV under the decision maker's present state of information is $0.60, and the EVSI is

$$\text{EVSI} = \$0.94 - \$0.60 = \$0.34$$

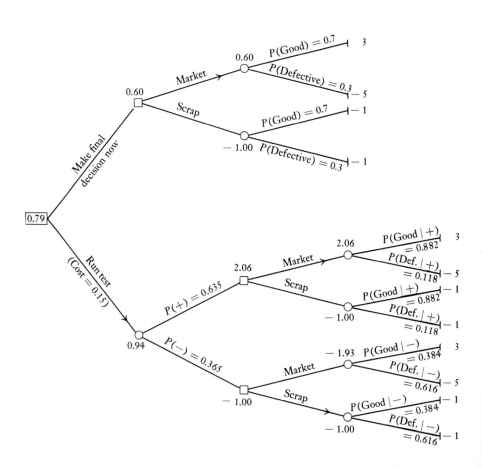

Figure 10.4
Decision tree for test of component.

Thus, the decision maker should be willing to pay up to $0.34 to observe the proposed test.

Suppose that it costs $0.15 to run the test. This is less than the expected value of the sample information, so the decision maker should run the test. Formally, a decision as to whether or not to run the test should be based on the expected net gain from sample information, denoted by ENGS:

$$ENGS = EVSI - CS$$

where CS represents the cost of sampling. For the example,

$$EVSI = \$0.34 \qquad \text{and} \qquad CS = \$0.15$$

so

$$ENGS = \$0.34 - \$0.15 = \$0.19$$

Since the ENGS is positive, the test should be run.

The preceding analysis is illustrated in decision-tree form in Fig. 10.4. The left fork represents the decision regarding the running of the test. If the test is not run, the decision to market or scrap is based on the prior probabilities, and this portion of the tree is identical to the top portion of the tree given in Fig. 10.3. If the test is run, the next fork is a chance fork corresponding to the result of the test, a positive reading or a negative reading. If a positive reading is observed, the optimal action is to market and the EMV is $2.06, whereas if a negative reading is observed, the optimal action is to scrap and the EMV is $-$ $1.00. The expected value of sample information is $0.94 $-$ $0.60 = $0.34, and since the test costs $0.15, it costs less than it is worth to the decision maker.

Note that even though this tree is much more complex than the simple trees presented in Section 10.3, it can still be solved using only the two simple rules given in that section: Find expected values at chance forks, and choose the action with the largest EMV at decision forks.

Determining the Optimal Sample Size (Optional)

10.7

In the preceding section, the procedure for determining the EVSI and the ENGS for a particular experiment was presented and illustrated for a situation in which the experiment consisted of a test of a component produced by a certain process. The choice facing the decision maker was whether or not to conduct the experiment. Often the situation is a bit more complicated, with several potential experiments being considered by the decision maker. In the example, there might be several different tests that could be performed on the component in an attempt to obtain more information about whether the component is good or defective. In a market-research study, a number of different experiments might be contemplated to obtain more information about consumers' reactions to a new product. In auditing, different ways of obtaining more information about a firm's "books" might be considered. In each of these situations, the choice is not just between running an experiment and not running the experiment; the decision maker must choose among no experimentation, experiment A, experiment B, experiment C, and so on. If the ENGS can be computed for each experiment, then the optimal experiment is simply the one with the largest ENGS, provided that the ENGS is positive. If the ENGS is negative for all experiments, then it is optimal not to experiment at all.

A situation of particular interest in statistics is that in which the only difference among the experiments that are being considered is a difference in sample size. In the production-process example, for instance, suppose that the testing device discussed in previous sections is the only testing device available to the decision maker. However, there is nothing to prevent the decision maker from running the same component through the testing device several times. Thus the choice is among the following experiments: Do not use the testing device at all; test the component once; test the component twice; and so on. Similarly, a market researcher may have decided on the basic design for a study of consumers' reactions to a new product. The only question now is how many consumers to include in the experiment. The problem here is to find the optimal sample size, and the procedure is simply to compute the EVSI and ENGS for each sample size and to choose the sample size that yields the largest ENGS. (If $n = 0$ yields the largest ENGS, of course, no sample will be taken.)

Returning to the production-process example, suppose that a component can be run through the testing device any number of times, and that the successive tests on the same component can be regarded as independent. In the previous section, the EVSI and ENGS for a sample of size 1 were computed; now consider a sample of size 2. For $n = 2$, there are three possible sample outcomes: two positive readings; one positive reading and one negative reading; and two negative readings. In Section 10.4 it was pointed out that for samples of more than one trial, it is not necessary to revise the probabilities after each trial. Instead, we can simply wait until all trials have been observed and *then* determine the revised probabilities. In that section, we computed the posterior probabilities for a sample of size two with two positive readings,

$$P(\text{Good}| + , +) = 0.960 \quad \text{and} \quad P(\text{Defective}| + , +) = 0.040$$

Using these posterior probabilities, the expected payoffs for the two actions are

$$\text{EMV}(\text{Market}| + , +) = 3(0.960) + (- 5)(0.040) = \$2.68$$

and

$$\text{EMV}(\text{Scrap}| + , +) = - 1(0.960) + (- 1)(0.040) = - 1.00$$

Thus, the optimal decision following two positive readings is to market, and the corresponding EMV is $2.68.

Next, consider a sample with one positive reading and one negative reading. There are two ways to obtain this result (+ , − and − , +), so the likelihoods needed for the application of Bayes' rule are

$$P(+, - \text{ or } -, + |\text{Good}) = P(+, - |\text{Good}) + P(-, + |\text{Good})$$
$$= 0.80(0.20) + 0.20(0.80) = 0.320$$

and

$$P(+, - \text{ or } -, + |\text{Defective}) = P(+, - |\text{Defective}) + P(-, + |\text{Defective})$$
$$= 0.25(0.75) + 0.75(0.25) = 0.375$$

The posterior probabilities are

$$P(\text{Good}| +, - \text{ or } -, +) = \frac{P(+, - \text{ or } -, + |\text{Good})P(\text{Good})}{P(+, - \text{ or } -, + |\text{Good})P(\text{Good}) + P(+, - \text{ or } -, + |\text{Defective})P(\text{Defective})}$$
$$= \frac{0.320(0.70)}{0.320(0.70) + 0.375(0.30)} = 0.666$$

and

$$P(\text{Defective}| +, - \text{ or } -, +) = \frac{P(+, - \text{ or } -, + |\text{Defective})P(\text{Defective})}{P(+, - \text{ or } -, + |\text{Good})P(\text{Good}) + P(+, - \text{ or } -, + |\text{Defective})P(\text{Defective})}$$
$$= \frac{0.375(0.30)}{0.320(0.70) + 0.375(0.30)} = 0.334$$

From these posterior probabilities, the expected payoffs are

$$\text{EMV}(\text{Market}| +, - \text{ or } -, +) = 3(0.666) + (-5)(0.334) = 0.33$$

and

$$\text{EMV}(\text{Scrap}| +, - \text{ or } -, +) = -1(0.666) + (-1)(0.334) = -1.00$$

The optimal decision is to market, and the corresponding EMV is 0.33.

Finally, consider the other possible sample result, two negative readings. Revising the probabilities on the basis of two negative readings yields

$$P(\text{Good}| -, -) = \frac{P(-, - |\text{Good})P(\text{Good})}{P(-, - |\text{Good})P(\text{Good}) + P(-, - |\text{Defective})P(\text{Defective})}$$
$$= \frac{(0.20)^2(0.70)}{(0.20)^2(0.70) + (0.75)^2(0.30)} = 0.142$$

and

$$P(\text{Defective}| -, -) = \frac{P(-, - |\text{Defective})P(\text{Defective})}{P(-, - |\text{Good})P(\text{Good}) + P(-, - |\text{Defective})P(\text{Defective})}$$
$$= \frac{(0.75)^2(0.30)}{(0.20)^2(0.70) + (0.75)^2(0.30)} = 0.858$$

and the expected payoffs are

$$\text{EMV}(\text{Market}| -, -) = 3(0.142) + (-5)(0.858) = -3.86$$

and

$$\text{EMV}(\text{Scrap}| -, -) = -1(0.142) + (-1)(0.858) = -1.00$$

The optimal action following two negative readings is to scrap the component, and the EMV is -1.00.

The optimal EMV following each possible sample result has been calculated, and only the probabilities of the three possible sample results are needed to compute EMV (Sample information). These probabilities are

$$P(+,+) = P(+,+|\text{Good})P(\text{Good}) + P(+,+|\text{Defective})P(\text{Defective})$$
$$= (0.80)^2(0.70) + (0.25)^2(0.30) = 0.46675,$$
$$P(+,-\text{ or }-,+) = P(+,-\text{ or }-,+|\text{Good})P(\text{Good})$$
$$+ P(+,-\text{ or }-,+|\text{Defective})P(\text{Defective})$$
$$= 0.320(0.70) + 0.375(0.30) = 0.33650$$

and

$$P(-,-) = P(-,-|\text{Good})P(\text{Good}) + P(-,-|\text{Defective})P(\text{Defective})$$
$$= (0.20)^2(0.70) + (0.75)^2(0.30) = 0.19675$$

Therefore, the overall expected payoff with a sample of size two, as calculated before the sample is actually taken, is

EMV(Sample information)
$$= (\text{Highest EMV after } +,+)P(+,+)$$
$$+ (\text{Highest EMV after } +,-\text{ or }-,+)P(+,-\text{ or }-,+)$$
$$+ (\text{Highest EMV after } -,-)P(-,-)$$
$$= 2.68(0.46675) + 0.33(0.33650) + (-1.00)(0.19675)$$
$$= 1.16$$

The expected value of sample information is

EVSI = EMV(Sample information)
$$- \text{EMV(Optimal action under prior information)}$$
$$= 1.16 - 0.60 = 0.56$$

Thus, the sample of size two is expected to improve the decision maker's EMV by \$0.56. If the cost of sampling is \$0.15 per test, as given in the preceding section, the cost of two tests is \$0.30, so the ENGS is

$$\text{ENGS} = \text{EVSI} - \text{CS} = \$0.56 - \$0.30 = \$0.26$$

TABLE 10.4   EVSI, CS, and ENGS for the production-process example

n	EVSI	CS	ENGS
1	0.34	0.15	0.19
2	0.56	0.30	0.26
3	0.72	0.45	0.27
4	0.83	0.60	0.23
5	0.91	0.75	0.16
6	0.95	0.90	0.05

Recall, from Section 10.6, that the ENGS for a single test was calculated as \$0.19. Therefore, testing the component twice yields a larger ENGS than testing it only once. What about the possibility of testing it more than twice? We will not take the space here to present the computations for larger sample sizes. (As you might guess, the computations become more burdensome as the sample size increases, but that is not a serious problem since it is quite easy in many situations to write a computer program to compute EVSI.) For the production-process example, EVSI, CS, and ENGS for sample sizes up to 6 are given in Table 10.4 and shown graphically in Fig. 10.5. Note that the EVSI increases fairly rapidly at first and then begins to level off. For this example, EVPI = \$1.20, so we know that EVSI can never be greater than \$1.20. The cost of sampling is just a linear function of n, $0.15n$. The ENGS rises at first, but when the incremental gain from a larger sample size levels off and is surpassed by the incremental cost of the larger sample size, the ENGS drops. For the

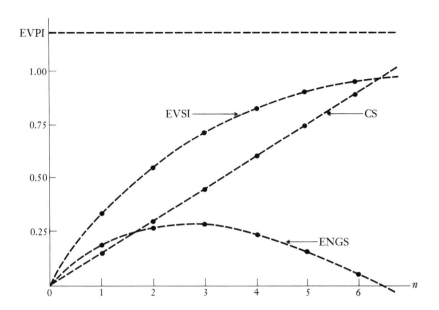

Figure 10.5
EVSI, CS, and ENGS for
production-process example.

example, the optimal sample size is 3; the decision maker should test the component three times before deciding whether to market it or scrap it.

The preceding analysis implies that the decision maker has more than one decision to make. The first is to decide whether or not to purchase sample information. Then, at the point at which the decision maker has decided to seek no more sample information, he or she must make the *terminal decision* between the potential actions available. We are primarily concerned with the terminal decision in this chapter. The decision regarding sampling is also important, however. The criterion for this decision is the same as the criterion for the terminal decision: maximize EMV. By comparing the EMV's for different experiments with each other and with the EMV if *no* experiment is run, the decision regarding sampling can be made. Of course, once a sample has been taken, it is still possible to determine whether or not to seek *more* sample information. It is only after a decision has been made *not* to seek more sample information that a terminal decision is made.

Decision Making Under Uncertainty: An Example   **10.8**

In this section we attempt to apply the concepts that have been developed in this chapter to a slightly more complicated problem involving information seeking. Even this problem will seem to be a somewhat simplified representation of the real world, but such simplification is often unavoidable. If every possible factor entering into a problem were included in the formal decision-

theory analysis, the analysis would be much too cumbersome. If we can identify the *most important* factors, the formal analysis should be of value even if it
is somewhat of a simplification.

A firm is considering the marketing of a new product. For convenience,
suppose that the events of interest are simply θ_1 = "new product is a success"
and θ_2 = "new product is a failure." The prior probabilities determined by the
firm's top management are

$$P(\text{Success}) = 0.3 \quad \text{and} \quad P(\text{Failure}) = 0.7$$

If the product is marketed and is a failure, the firm will suffer a loss of
$300,000. On the other hand, if the product is a success, the firm will earn a
net profit of $500,000. If the product is not marketed, the firm will suffer no
loss, nor will it earn any profit. This is a relatively simple, straightforward problem with only two actions and two states of nature. It can be represented on a
tree diagram, as in Fig. 10.6, and the expected payoffs of the two actions are

$$\text{EMV}(\text{Market}) = 500{,}000(0.3) + (-300{,}000)(0.7) = -60{,}000$$

and

$$\text{EMV}(\text{Don't market}) = 0(0.3) + 0(0.7) = 0$$

It appears, therefore, that on the basis of the current information, as represented by the prior probabilities, $P(\text{Success}) = 0.3$ and $P(\text{Failure}) = 0.7$, the
firm should *not* market the product.

Although it looks as though the *optimal decision* is not to market the
product, there is a considerable amount of uncertainty concerning the even-
tual success or failure of the product. Therefore, additional information might
be useful to the firm. Perfect information is not available; the only way to tell
for sure whether the product will succeed is to go ahead and market it. Nevertheless, the expected value of perfect information is easy to calculate and
serves as a convenient benchmark, in the sense that it is an upper bound for
the expected value of sample information. With perfect information, the firm
will market the product and earn $500,000 if they are assured that the product
will be successful; if the perfect information indicates that the product will not

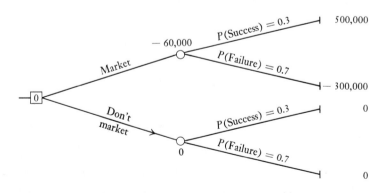

Figure 10.6
Tree diagram for marketing
problem.

succeed in the marketplace, the firm will not pursue the matter and will wind up with a payoff of $0. *Before* the firm sees the perfect information, then, the expected payoff under perfect information is

$$\text{EMV(perfect information)} = 500{,}000(0.3) + 0(0.7) = 150{,}000$$

Since the optimal action under the prior information is not to market, and this action has an EMV of $0, the expected value of perfect information (EVPI) is simply

$$\text{EVPI} = \text{EMV(Perfect information)} - \text{EMV}\left(\begin{array}{c}\text{Optimal action under}\\ \text{prior information}\end{array}\right)$$

$$= 150{,}000 - 0 = 150{,}000$$

Thus, the firm should be willing to pay up to $150,000 for perfect information concerning the success or failure of the product.

As we can see from our calculations of EVPI in this problem and from the intuitively reasonable notion that decision making is much less risky under certainty, a clairvoyant who was "genuine" in the sense of always being able to predict perfectly could earn large sums of money! In the absence of any such clairvoyant, decision makers have the option to make their decisions without additional information, or to purchase information that is less than perfect. In our example, suppose that the firm is considering the purchase of additional information in the form of a market survey. The market-research department of the firm proposes two possible surveys, labeled A and B. The result of each survey will be an indication of "favorable," "neutral," or "unfavorable." If the product will actually be successful in the marketplace, there is a 0.60 chance that survey A will give a favorable indication, a 0.30 chance of a neutral indication, and a 0.10 chance of an unfavorable indication. If the product will not be successful, there is a 0.10 chance of favorable indication from survey A, a 0.20 chance of a neutral indication, and a 0.70 chance of an unfavorable indication. Survey A costs $20,000 to conduct.

Before going on to survey B, we shall determine the expected value of sample information from survey A. Recalling that Bayes' rule is of the form

$$\text{Posterior probability} = \frac{(\text{Prior prob.})(\text{Likelihood})}{\sum(\text{Prior prob.})(\text{Likelihood})}$$

where the sum is taken over the possible states of nature, we can present the calculations of the posterior probabilities in tabular form. The first column in Table 10.5 gives the possible sample outcomes—favorable (F), neutral (N), and unfavorable (U). The second column gives the two states of nature, success and failure of the product. The third column gives the prior probabilities for θ_1 and θ_2, the states of nature, and the fourth column gives the likelihoods. From the information given above, for example, the likelihood of a favorable indication from survey A given that the product will be successful is 0.60. The fifth column is the product of the prior probabilities and the likelihoods, and the last column gives the posterior probabilities. In each case, this is the value

TABLE 10.5   Posterior probabilities after survey A

(1) Sample outcome	(2) θ	(3) Prior prob.	(4) Likelihood	(5) (3) × (4)	(6) Posterior prob.
Favorable	θ_1	0.30	0.60	0.18	18/25
	θ_2	0.70	0.10	0.07	7/25
				0.25	
Neutral	θ_1	0.30	0.30	0.09	9/23
	θ_2	0.70	0.20	0.14	14/23
				0.23	
Unfavorable	θ_1	0.30	0.10	0.03	3/52
	θ_2	0.70	0.70	0.49	49/52
				0.52	

in the fifth column divided by the sum of all of the elements in the fifth column for a given sample result. This last operation serves to *normalize* the posterior probabilities—to make them sum to one. From the values computed in Table 10.5, we see that the posterior probability that the product will be successful is 18/25 if survey A yields a favorable indication, 9/23 if survey A yields a neutral indication, and 3/52 if survey A yields an unfavorable indication.

Figure 10.7 is a tree diagram for the calculation of the expected value of sample information from survey A. Observe that if the survey is taken, the branches marked F, N, and U represent the three possible results from the survey. The probabilities on the event branches following these survey results are the posterior probabilities calculated in Table 10.5. Because the portion of the tree following the "Make decision now" branch was presented in Fig. 10.6, we simply put the EMV of this action in Fig. 10.7 instead of reproducing that entire portion of the tree. Looking at the lower portion of the tree once again and working backward from the right-hand side of the tree, we see that the expected payoff of marketing the product, if the survey indication is favorable, is

$$500,000\left(\frac{18}{25}\right) + (-\,300,000)\left(\frac{7}{25}\right) = \frac{6,900,000}{25}$$

If the survey is neutral, we have

$$500,000\left(\frac{9}{23}\right) + (-\,300,000)\left(\frac{14}{23}\right) = \frac{300,000}{23}$$

and if the survey is unfavorable, we have

$$500,000\left(\frac{3}{52}\right) + (-\,300,000)\left(\frac{49}{52}\right) = -\,\frac{13,200,000}{52}$$

We now know what the firm should do after any sample: If the survey indication is favorable or neutral, the firm should market the product (since the EMV

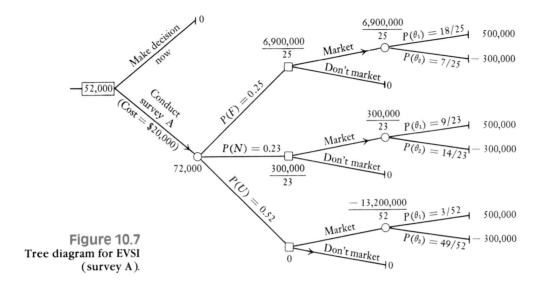

Figure 10.7
Tree diagram for EVSI
(survey A).

is positive, while the EMV for not marketing is zero); if the survey indication is unfavorable, the firm should not market the product. Incidentally, the EMV's are left in fractional form to simplify the calculations at the next step. For instance, when multiplying 6,900,000/25 by 0.25, the computation is much easier than it would be if the actual division 6,900,000/25 were carried out before multiplying by the 0.25 figure. The probabilities for the three survey outcomes, as determined from Table 10.5, are the sums of the relevant figures in the fifth column of the table—they are 0.25, 0.23, and 0.52. Continuing to work backward, we see that the overall EMV of the "Conduct survey A" branch is

$$(0.25)\left(\frac{6,900,000}{25}\right) + (0.23)\left(\frac{300,000}{23}\right) + (0.52)(0) = 72,000$$

Since the EMV of the "Make decision now" branch is 0, the expected value of sample information (EVSI) for survey A is

$$\text{EVSI(survey A)} = \text{EMV(survey A)} - \text{EMV}\left(\begin{array}{c}\text{Optimal action under} \\ \text{prior information}\end{array}\right)$$
$$= 72,000 - 0 = 72,000$$

Therefore, the firm should be willing to pay up to $72,000 for survey A. But the cost of survey A is $20,000, so the expected net gain from survey A is $72,000 − $20,000 = $52,000.

Next, we shall consider survey B, which costs $30,000. If the product will be successful, there is a 0.80 chance that survey B will give a favorable indication, a 0.10 chance of a neutral indication, and a 0.10 chance of an unfavorable indication. If the product will not be successful, there is a 0.10 chance of a favorable indication, a 0.40 chance of a neutral indication, and a 0.50 chance of an unfavorable indication. The calculation of posterior probabilities following each of the possible outcomes from survey B is presented in Table 10.6, and the tree diagram in Fig. 10.8 enables us to calculate the EVSI for survey B. Observe that after survey B is conducted, the optimal decision is to market if a favorable indication is obtained, but not to market otherwise. A neutral indication here leads to not marketing, whereas in survey A it led to marketing. The overall EMV of the "Conduct survey B" branch is $99,000, so the expected value of sample information from survey B is

$$\text{EVSI(survey B)} = \text{EMV(survey B)} - \text{EMV}\left(\begin{array}{c}\text{Optimal action under}\\\text{prior information}\end{array}\right)$$
$$= 99,000 - 0 = 99,000$$

Therefore, the firm should be willing to pay up to $99,000 for survey B. But the cost of survey B is only $30,000, so the expected net gain from survey B is $99,000 − $30,000 = $69,000.

Summarizing the results of the analysis to this point, we see that the EMV of making a marketing decision without additional information is $0, since the optimal action under the prior probabilities is not to market the product. Perfect information has an expected value of $150,000, but perfect information is not available to the firm in this situation. Survey A has an expected value of $72,000 and it costs $20,000 to conduct, so its net expected value is $52,000. Survey B has an expected value of $99,000, which is almost two-thirds of EVPI, and the cost of survey B is $30,000, so the net expected gain from survey B is $69,000. At this point, it appears that the best strategy for the firm to follow is to conduct survey B. From Figure 10.8, the firm should market the product only if survey B yields a favorable indication.

Thus, we have compared three information-seeking options: survey A, survey B, and the option *not* to seek any more information. Of these three options, survey B is the best choice. Of course, the firm may wish to consider yet other surveys, although it must be kept in mind that survey B has an EVSI

TABLE 10.6   Posterior probabilities after survey B

(1) Sample outcome	(2) θ	(3) Prior prob.	(4) Likelihood	(5) (3) × (4)	(6) Posterior prob.
Favorable	θ_1	0.30	0.80	0.24	24/31
	θ_2	0.70	0.10	0.07	7/31
				0.31	
Neutral	θ_1	0.30	0.10	0.03	3/31
	θ_2	0.70	0.40	0.28	28/31
				0.31	
Unfavorable	θ_1	0.30	0.10	0.03	3/38
	θ_2	0.70	0.50	0.35	35/38
				0.38	

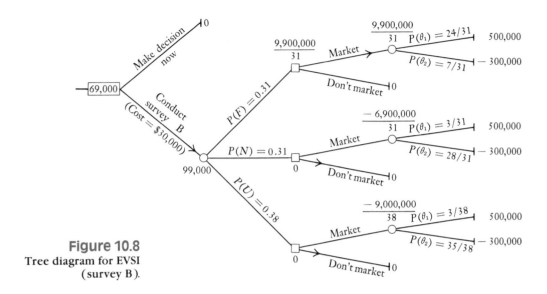

Figure 10.8
Tree diagram for EVSI
(survey B).

that is just about two-thirds of EVPI. The EVSI of any other survey can be at best only

$$\$150,000 - \$99,000 = \$51,000$$

better than the EVSI of survey B, and any survey that yields an EVSI that is very close to EVPI might be expected to be quite expensive. One option that can be evaluated quickly is the possibility of conducting *both* survey A *and* survey B. Assuming that the two surveys can be considered to be independent, the likelihoods for conducting both surveys are simply the products of the likelihoods of the individual surveys. Since each survey has three possible outcomes, there are $3(3) = 9$ possible combinations of outcomes. We will not present the calculations, because this example is already quite lengthy; but it turns out that the EVSI for the combination of both samples is $102,300. This EVSI is only slightly better than the EVSI of survey B alone, and the cost is $20,000 greater than the cost of survey B alone, so the combination of both surveys is not the best course of action.

Often a sequential information-seeking strategy can be advantageous. In our example, the firm might conduct survey A and then consider whether or not to conduct survey B. If survey A yields relatively conclusive results, it is probably not worthwhile to continue and take survey B, but if the results are somewhat inconclusive, survey B might prove valuable. We will not present the calculations, but the expected net gain from this sequential plan is $73,900, which is $4900 greater than the expected net gain from survey B alone. If survey A yields a favorable indication, the best strategy is to make a final decision to market the product; if survey A yields an unfavorable indication, the best strategy is to make a final decision not to market the product. However, if survey A yields a neutral indication, the best strategy is to conduct survey B, marketing the product if survey B is favorable and not marketing it otherwise. Proceeding sequentially rather than deciding in advance to use both surveys has the advantage of avoiding the cost of the second survey when it appears on the basis of the results of the first survey that the second survey is not worthwhile.

This example illustrates the comparison of different sampling plans. In comparing such plans, the plan with the highest net expected gain should be chosen, provided, of course, that this net expected gain is greater than zero. If all net expected gains are less than zero, then the decision maker should make a final decision without obtaining any additional information.

Problems

10.19 a) Carefully distinguish betwen the expected *payoff* under perfect information and the expected *value* of perfect information. Calculate both of these values for Problem 10.2.

b) In decision-making problems under uncertainty, is perfect information typically available to the decision maker?

10.20 Suppose that a firm is deciding whether to sell bonds to raise money. A decision tree is constructed, and one of the uncertainties concerns the rate of inflation. Additional information can be obtained: an economist's forecast as to whether the inflation rate will be high, moderate, or low. After performing the necessary calculations, the analyst finds that with a forecast of high inflation, the firm can maximize EMV by selling bonds. However, the same result is obtained with a forecast of moderate inflation or a forecast of low inflation. What can the analyst say about the EVSI associated with the forecast? Would the EVSI for this inflation forecast necessarily be the same for a different firm faced with a different decision-making problem?

10.21 a) What is the relationship, if there is any, between the expected value of perfect information and the expected value of sample information?

b) If information is free, is it ever better to obtain sample information instead of perfect information? If information is not free, is sample information ever preferred to perfect information? Explain your answers.

10.22 In Fig. 10.5, the EVSI increases quite rapidly at first and then levels off. Can you think of a different type of scenario where the EVSI is virtually zero for small sample sizes but then increases at a relatively rapid pace for moderate sample sizes before finally leveling off again? Explain.

10.23 How much should you be willing to pay for perfect information in the stock example in Fig. 10.1 if $P(I) = 0.30$?

10.24 A store must decide whether or not to stock a new item. The decision depends on the reaction of consumers to the item, and the payoff table (in thousands of dollars) is shown in Table 10.7. If $P(0.10) = 0.2$, $P(0.20) = 0.3$, $P(0.40) = 0.1$, and $P(0.50) = 0.1$, what decision should be made? For this problem, determine the expected value of perfect information.

TABLE 10.7

		Proportion of consumers purchasing the item				
		0.10	**0.20**	**0.30**	**0.40**	**0.50**
	Stock 1000	− 10	− 2	12	22	40
Decision	**Stock 500**	− 4	6	12	16	16
	Don't stock	0	0	0	0	0

10.25 In Problem 10.12, suppose that the probability of recession is 0.4. What is your optimal action, and what is the EMV associated with that action? Next, suppose that you could find out for certain whether or not a recession will occur during the coming year. Before obtaining this information, what is your EMV (perfect information)? What is the expected value of the information?

10.26 A corporation considers two levels of investment in a real estate development, a low participation (A_1) or a high participation (A_2). Two states of nature are deemed possible, a partial success (B_1) or a complete success (B_2). The payoff matrix (in thousands of dollars) is estimated to be:

	B_1	B_2
A_1	− 200	400
A_2	− 500	1000

a) How large does the *à priori* probability of B_1 have to be in order to make action A_1 the better choice?

b) Suppose that the states of nature are presumed initially to occur with probabilities $P(B_1) = 0.4, P(B_2) = 0.6$. Then a more careful study is made, which leads to the conclusion that the project will be only a partial success. In previous relevant studies, this same conclusion was obtained in 8 of 10 cases when similar projects were partial successes. Also, this conclusion was obtained in 4 of 12 cases when similar projects were *complete* successes. Find the revised probabilities of the states of nature, and determine which investment level is appropriate.

10.27 Joe Doakes is considering flying from New York City to Boston in the hope of making an important sale to P. J. Bety, president of NOCO, Inc. If Joe makes this sale he will earn a commission of $1100. Unfortunately, Joe figures there is a 50–50 chance that Bety will be called out of town at the last moment and he will have no chance at a sale. Even if he goes to see Bety, Joe estimates that he has only one chance in five of making the sale. The trip will cost Joe $100, whether or not he gets to see Bety.

a) Draw the tree diagram for Joe, and determine whether Joe should fly to Boston or not.

b) Joe was heard to remark, "I'd give my right arm to know if Bety will be in town." How much does he value his right arm?

c) Suppose an information service offers to tell Joe, before he decides to fly, whether or not they think Bety will be in town. The record of this company is such that if they say Bety will be in, the probability that he will, in fact, be in is 0.70; that is, the posterior probability is $P(\text{in}|\text{say in}) = 0.70$. If they say he will be out, they will be correct 90% of the time; i.e., $P(\text{out}|\text{say out}) = 0.90$. If this service costs \$10, and Joe figures that the probability that they will say Bety is in is $\frac{2}{3}$, should he buy the service? Draw the tree diagram. Find ENGS.

10.28 For the component example, find the expected value of sample information for the new test in Problem 10.17. Compare this with the EVSI found in the text for the other test, and discuss any difference in the EVSI figures for the two tests.

10.29 In Problem 10.14, each coat costs \$80 to produce (not including inspection costs) and is sold to a distributor for \$100. Imperfect coats that are shipped out are returned and repaired at a cost of \$30. If a coat is sent back for repairs before being shipped out, the cost is only \$10. Any imperfections are found and fixed in the repairing process. The cost of inspection is \$1 per coat.

a) If no inspection is made, should each coat be shipped out or put through the repairing process before being sent out?

b) If the inspector classifies a coat as imperfect, should it be shipped out? What is the EMV?

c) If the inspector does not classify a coat as imperfect, should it be shipped out? What is the EMV?

d) What is EMV (sample information) for an inspection?

e) Find the EVSI and ENGS for an inspection.

10.30 In Problem 10.11, suppose that the firm finds out that its competitor is building a new plant. It is likely that the new plant is intended to produce the new product mentioned in that problem, although it could also be used to produce other items. If the competitor really does intend to introduce the new product, the chances are very good (probability 0.8) that a new plant would be built. On the other hand, if the competitor does not intend to introduce the new product, the probability is only 0.3 that a new plant would be built. On the basis of the information that the plant is being built, revise the probabilities concerning the new product and find the optimal decision for the firm by using the revised probabilities.

10.31 In Problem 10.30, suppose that the firm does not yet know whether the competing firm is building a new plant. It may be possible to find out, at some cost, whether the new plant is being built. What is the maximum amount the firm should be expected to pay for such information?

10.32 For the component example, suppose that the new test in Problem 10.17 will be used on each item n times. Find EVSI when $n = 1$, when $n = 2$, and when $n = 3$. If the cost of the test is \$0.15, like the other test, find the ENGS values for the new test with $n = 1$, $n = 2$, and $n = 3$.

10.33 In Problem 10.24, suppose that sample information is available in the form of a random sample of consumers. For a sample of size 1,

a) Find the posterior distribution if the one person sampled will purchase the item, and find the posterior EMV's and the optimal action under the posterior distribution.

b) Find the posterior distribution if the one person sampled will not purchase the item, and find the posterior EMV's and the optimal action under the posterior distribution.

c) Calculate the expected value of sample information for this sample of size 1.

d) Draw the decision tree.

10.34 In Problem 10.33, suppose that a sample of two consumers is being contemplated.

a) List the possible sample outcomes and find the posterior distribution following each possible outcome.

b) Find the optimal action under each of the posterior distributions found in part (a).

c) Find the expected value of sample information for a sample of two consumers.

d) Draw the decision tree.

10.35 For the situation described in Problem 10.24, compare the EVPI (as calculated in that problem), the EVSI for a sample of one consumer (as calculated in Problem 10.33), and the EVSI for a sample of two consumers (as calculated in Problem 10.34). Explain any differences among these three values.

10.36 a) Assume that for the example in Section 10.8, a third survey, survey C, indicates either favorable or unfavorable (there is no "neutral" indication). The probability of a favorable indication is 0.9 if the product will be successful and 0.3 if the product will not be successful. Find the EVSI for survey C.

b) Show that the EVSI for the combination of both surveys in the Section 10.8 example is $102,300, as claimed in the text.

10.37 The Dixon Corporation makes picture tubes for a large television manufacturer. Dixon is concerned because approximately 30% of their tubes have been defective. When the television manufacturer encounters a defective tube, Dixon is charged a $20 penalty cost (to pay for repairs and lost time). One way Dixon can avoid this penalty cost is to reexamine and fix each defective tube before shipping. This would cost an extra $7 per tube. Or they can rent a testing device that costs $1 for each tube tested. Since this device is not infallible, its effectiveness was tested by running through it a large number of tubes, some known to be good, and others known to be defective. The results of this study determined the following likelihoods.

		State of tube	
		Good	Defective
Test results	Good	0.75	0.20
	Def	0.25	0.80
		1.00	1.00

Draw the decision tree for Dixon, assuming that they must decide between shipping directly, reexamining each tube, or testing each tube. Calculate ENGS and EVSI.

10.38 The Techno Corporation is considering making either minor or major repairs to a malfunctioning production process. When the process is malfunctioning, the percentage of defective items produced seems to be a constant, with either $p = 0.10$ (indicating minor repairs necessary) or $p = 0.25$ (indicating major repairs necessary). Defective items are produced randomly, and there is no way Techno can tell for sure whether the machine needs minor or major repairs. If minor repairs are made when $p = 0.25$, the probability of a defective is reduced to 0.05. If minor repairs are made when $p = 0.10$, or major repairs made when $p = 0.10$ or $p = 0.25$, then the proportion of defectives is reduced to zero. Techno has recently received an order for 1000 items. This item yields them a profit of \$0.50 per unit, except that they have to pay a \$2.00 penalty cost for each item found defective. Major repairs to the process cost \$100 while minor repairs cost \$60. No adjustment can be made to the production process once a run has started. Prior to starting the run, however, Techno can sample items from a "trial" run, at a cost of \$1.00 per item. The prior probabilities are $P(\text{major}) = 0.3$, $P(\text{minor}) = 0.7$.

a) Find the optimal action for Techno if they are trying to decide between not sampling at all and sampling one item. Draw the decision tree.

b) Find the optimal action for Techno if they are willing to consider a sample of either one or two items. Draw the decision tree. Calculate ENGS and EVSI.

□ Bayes' Rule for Normal Distributions (Optional)

10.9

In Chapters 7 and 8, the importance of the normal distribution in statistics was clearly demonstrated. Most of the confidence intervals and tests of hypotheses discussed in those chapters involved the use of the normal distribution, and these techniques are widely applicable (especially for large samples, due to the Central Limit Theorem). In this chapter we present a method for incorporating prior information as well as sample information in the inferential and decision-making process. Unfortunately, only the discrete case is considered in Section 10.4. The procedures of Section 10.4 can be applied in the continuous case if the continuous distributions of interest are approximated by discrete distributions. Moreover, Bayes' rule is also applicable if the variable of interest is continuous rather than discrete:

Bayes' Rule for Continuous Distributions

If $f(\theta)$ is the prior density function of a parameter θ and $\ell\,(\text{Sample}|\theta)$ is the likelihood function, then the posterior density function of θ is

$$f(\theta|\text{Sample}) = \frac{f(\theta)\,\ell\,(\text{Sample}|\theta)}{\int f(\theta)\,\ell\,(\text{Sample}|\theta)d\theta}$$

Note that this is very similar to Bayes' rule for discrete distributions, presented in Section 10.4. In the discrete case, the prior probabilities are multiplied by the appropriate likelihoods and the resulting numbers are divided by their sum, so that they will sum to one. In the continuous case, the prior density function is multiplied by the likelihood function and the resulting function is divided by its integral over all values of θ, so that the posterior density function will integrate to one (recall that a continous variable must have a density function with a total area of one under the graph of the function).

As previously presented, Bayes' rule is applicable to any choice of a prior distribution and likelihood function. We are particularly interested in the normal distribution, however, so let us consider this special case. Suppose that we are sampling from a normal population with *known* variance σ^2, that we are interested in making inferences about μ (the mean of the population), and that the following two conditions are satisifed:

1. The prior distribution of μ is a normal distribution with mean m and variance v.
2. A sample of size n is observed, with sample mean $\bar{x}$.

Under these conditions, the posterior distribution of μ is a normal distribution with mean

$$M = \frac{(m/v) + (n\bar{x}/\sigma^2)}{(1/v) + (n/\sigma^2)}$$

and variance

$$V = 1/[(1/v) + (n/\sigma^2)]$$

For example, suppose that $\sigma^2 = 144$ and the prior distribution of μ has mean 60 and variance 48 (assuming, of course, that it is a normal distribution). A sample of size 4 is taken, with an observed sample mean of 70. The posterior distribution is then a normal distribution with mean

$$M = \frac{(60/48) + 4(70)/144}{(1/48) + (4/144)} = 65.71$$

and variance

$$V = 1/[(1/48) + (4/144)] = 20.57$$

The numerical example illustrates a number of interesting features of Bayes' rule as applied to normal distributions. The most important feature is the fact that if the prior distribution is normal and the sample comes from a normal population with known variance, then the posterior distribution is also normal. Remember that if we have a series of samples, Bayes' rule can be applied successively to each sample, thus continually revising the probabilities. In this special case, the posterior distribution is normal, which implies that if another sample is taken, the same procedure can be repeated, using the posterior distribution following the first sample as the prior distribution prior to the second sample (this is possible because all of the conditions given above are still satisfied).

A second point of interest is that the posterior mean lies between the prior mean and the sample mean. This result is intuitively appealing, since the use of Bayes' rule is nothing more than a combination of prior information and sample information. It will always be true that the posterior mean will lie between the prior mean and the sample mean.

A third feature of Bayes' theorem for normal distributions is that the variance of the posterior distribution is smaller than the variance of the prior distribution (in the example, $V = 20.57$ and $v = 48$). This is reasonable, for the new information obtained in the sample should reduce our uncertainty concerning μ and hence reduce the variance, just as an increase in sample size reduces the variance of the sample mean.

In the Bayesian approach to statistics, the posterior distribution should be used instead of the sampling distribution or the likelihood function in making inferences. If we want to estimate μ, for example, we might take M, the mean of the posterior distribution of μ, rather than the estimator $\bar{x}$, which is based solely on sample information. Similarly, confidence intervals and tests of hypotheses should be based on the posterior distribution.

For a slightly more realistic example of Bayes' rule for normal distributions, suppose that an accountant in the credit department of a department store is concerned with μ, the average outstanding balance for the store's charge accounts. It is known from historical data that the standard deviation of outstanding balances is 5 (all values are expressed in dollars). Furthermore, the accountant's judgments about the average balance can be represented by a normal distribution with a mean of $m = 12$ and a variance of $v = 4$. This implies, for example, that she feels that there is approximately a 0.95 probability that μ is between

$$12 - 2\sqrt{4} = 8 \quad \text{and} \quad 12 + 2\sqrt{4} = 16$$

In order to obtain additional information, the accountant randomly selects a sample of 25 accounts; the average balance on these accounts is 9. Assuming that the population distribution of outstanding balances can be approximated by a normal distribution (this might be questionable in this situation because of a large number of zero balances and a small number of very large balances), the accountant's posterior distribution for μ is a normal distribution with mean

$$M = \frac{(12/4) + 25(9)/25}{(1/4) + (25/25)} = 9.6$$

and variance

$$V = 1/[(1/4) + (25/25)] = 0.8$$

Thus, after seeing the sample information, the accountant's posterior point estimate for μ is 9.6 and the probability is approximately 0.95 that μ is between

$$9.6 - 2\sqrt{0.8} = 7.81 \quad \text{and} \quad 9.6 + 2\sqrt{0.8} = 11.39$$

If the accountant is interested in the hypotheses

$$H_0: \mu \geq 10 \quad \text{and} \quad H_a: \mu < 10$$

she can calculate the posterior probabilities of these hypotheses:

$$P(H_0) = P(\mu \geq 10) = P\left(z \geq \frac{10 - 9.6}{\sqrt{0.8}}\right) = P(z \geq 0.45)$$
$$= 0.3264$$

and

$$P(H_a) = P(\mu < 10) = P\left(z < \frac{10 - 9.6}{\sqrt{0.8}}\right) = P(z < 0.45)$$
$$= 0.6736$$

Thus, on the basis of the posterior distribution H_a appears to be $0.6736/0.3264 = 2.06$ times as likely as H_0.

These examples illustrate the ease with which Bayes' rule can be applied when the population of interest is normally distributed with unknown mean and known variance, and when the prior distribution of the population mean μ is a normal distribution. In this situation, the normal prior distribution is said to be a **natural conjugate distribution** with respect to the normal population. In working with Bayes' rule for continuous distributions, the analysis is greatly simplified if the prior distribution is a member of the family of distributions that is a natural conjugate family with regard to the population or data-generating process of interest. Otherwise, it is necessary to carry out the integration in the denominator of Bayes' rule for continuous distributions, and this integration can sometimes be quite difficult. Using natural conjugate prior distributions means that the application of Bayes' rule can be expressed in a few simple formulas such as the formulas given above for M and V in the normal case. The combination of a normal prior distribution and a normal population is but one example of a natural conjugate relationship. If we are dealing with a Bernoulli process, for example, as discussed in Chapter 4, the natural conjugate family of prior distributions for p, the Bernoulli parameter, is the family of beta distributions; for the Poisson process, also discussed in Chapter 4, the natural conjugate family for λ, the Poisson parameter, is the family of gamma distributions. We will not discuss these families of distributions here. For a relatively nontechnical discussion of the notion of natural conjugate prior distributions, see R. L. Winkler, *An Introduction to Bayesian Inference and Decision.* A more advanced treatise on the subject is H. Raiffa and R. Schlaifer, *Applied Statistical Decision Theory.*

Inference and Decision

10.10

In a way, statistical inference is closely related to statistical decision theory. The theory of estimation is concerned with deciding on an estimate, and the theory of hypothesis testing involves a choice between two actions: accepting or rejecting a hypothesis. As we have seen, a formal theory has been developed to determine estimates and to test hypotheses; and this theory, together with probability theory, forms the backbone of the traditional, or "classical," approach to statistics. Decision theory represents an extension of the classical theory in the sense that it includes the same inputs as the classical theory (likelihoods) and allows other inputs (prior probabilities, payoffs). The decision-theory approach to statistics has, for an obvious reason, been labeled "Bayesian statistics." In this view, the use of prior probabilities and payoffs is extended to estimation and hypothesis-testing procedures. In estimation, for example, the costs of *overestimation* and *underestimation* are introduced into the analysis. In hypothesis testing, the prior probabilities of each of the hypotheses under consideration are included (see the example in the preceding section), as well as the costs of Type I and Type II errors.

An example should serve to demonstrate how estimation can be thought of as a decision-making problem. Suppose that an appliance dealer must place an order for television sets and that this is his last chance to order the current model. Next month's order will be for the manufacturer's new model, and any current-model televisions still in stock at that time will be sold by the appliance dealer at a reduced price. The television sets cost the appliance dealer $400 each, and he sells them for $500. Any leftover current models will be sold for $350, however. In a sense, we can think of the number of sets ordered as an estimate of the demand for the sets. Moreover, unlike previous estimation problems we have considered, the costs of overestimating and underestimating can be determined in this problem from the information given above. If too many sets are ordered, the appliance dealer will suffer a loss because he will have to sell leftover sets at a loss of $50 per set. If too few sets are ordered, the appliance dealer will be forgoing a chance to make additional profits of $100 per set. In addition, a complete analysis of this problem might include consideration of the cost of carrying inventory, the cost due to unsatisfied customers who come in to buy television sets and find that there are none in stock, and so on. We ignore these considerations in this example.

Suppose that the appliance dealer is sure that the demand for television sets between now and the time the new models appear will be between 6 and 10 sets. Moreover, on the basis of his past experience with demand near the end of a model year, he feels that the probability distribution of demand is as follows:

θ (**Demand**)	$P(\theta)$
6	0.10
7	0.25
8	0.30
9	0.25
10	0.10

Clearly, then, he will not order fewer than 6 sets or more than 10 sets. From the information given in the preceding paragraph, a payoff table can be

TABLE 10.8   **Payoff table for television example**

		Demand				
		6	7	8	9	10
Action	**6**	600	600	600	600	600
(Number of	**7**	550	700	700	700	700
television sets	**8**	500	650	800	800	800
ordered)	**9**	450	600	750	900	900
	10	400	550	700	850	1000

determined for this problem, and the payoff table is given in Table 10.8. For instance, if 8 sets are ordered and the demand is only 7, the appliance dealer makes a profit of $700 on the 7 sets that are sold but loses $50 on the one set that is left over and must be sold at a reduced price of $350. Thus, his overall payoff is $700 − $50 = $650. The expected payoff for the first action, ordering 6 sets, is

$$EMV(\text{Order } 6) = 600(0.10) + 600(0.25) + 600(0.30)$$
$$+ 600(0.25) + 600(0.10)$$
$$= 600$$

Similarly,

$$EMV(\text{Order } 7) = 685$$
$$EMV(\text{Order } 8) = 732.5$$
$$EMV(\text{Order } 9) = 735$$

and

$$EMV(\text{Order } 10) = 700$$

Hence, the optimal action for the appliance dealer is to order 9 television sets.

Observe, from the probability distribution for demand, that the mean of the distribution is 8 sets. Yet in a decision-theoretic sense, the best estimate of demand is 9 sets. This is because the cost of underestimating demand is $100 per set (the lost profits due to not having enough sets on hand), whereas the cost of overestimating demand is only $50 per set (the loss due to selling left-over sets at a reduced price). Since the cost of overestimation is less than the cost of underestimation, the optimal strategy is to increase the estimate in order to avoid the highest cost of underestimation. If the two costs were equal, then by symmetry the best estimate would be the median, 8 sets. In this case, the asymmetry in the costs causes the appliance dealer to order one additional set. In general, the optimal estimate in this type of problem is the

$$\frac{100k_{\text{u}}}{(k_{\text{u}} + k_{\text{o}})}$$

percentile of the probability distribution, where k_{u} is the cost of underestimation and k_{o} is the cost of overestimation. In the example, $k_{\text{u}} = 100$ and $k_{\text{o}} = 50$, so we want the $100(100)/(100 + 50) = $ 67th percentile. For the given distribution, 9 is the 67th percentile.

In order to illustrate the use of continuous distributions in decision-making problems, consider a modification of the example. Suppose that the appliance dealer owns a very large chain of appliance stores and that he must place a single order for television sets for the entire chain of stores. The appliance dealer feels that the total demand for television sets in the chain of stores between now and the time the new models appear is approximately normally distributed, with a mean of 140 sets and a standard deviation of 16 sets. All the other details of the example are unchanged. As noted above, in order to maximize EMV, the appliance dealer should order a number of sets equal to the 67th percentile of the distribution of demand. But from the table of normal probabilities, the 67th percentile of a standard normal distribution is 0.75, so the 67th percentile of a normal distribution with mean 140 and standard deviation 16 is

$$140 + 0.75 (16) = 152$$

Thus, 152 sets should be ordered, and in the sense of maximizing EMV, 152 is the optimal estimate of demand.

The main advantage of this approach to statistics is that it enables the statistician to include all relevant information, including prior information and information concerning payoffs or losses, in the formal statistical model. Some statisticians object to the inclusion of such information because it is often of a "subjective" nature; objections like this are essentially philosophical rather than practical. From a practical viewpoint, a disadvantage of the Bayesian approach is that it is not always easy to determine the necessary inputs to the formal model. Assessing a prior distribution is not always easy, and information concerning relevant payoffs and losses is often somewhat vague. Nevertheless, for important problems it is worthwhile to consider an analysis of the sort suggested in this chapter, particularly when there is a considerable amount of prior information and the potential payoffs and losses are quite serious.

Utility   # 10.11

Payoffs and Utilities

In this chapter we have used the EMV criterion to make decisions in the face of uncertainty. This criterion states that the action with the highest EMV should be chosen. There are situations in which maximizing EMV is not an appealing strategy, however. In this section you will discover why maximizing EMV does not always seem to be a good approach, and we shall discuss briefly a more general criterion: *maximization of expected utility.*

One weakness of the EMV criterion is that it considers only the expected payoff, or the mean payoff, and not the variability in payoffs. For example, sup-

TABLE 10.9   Payoff table for bet on die

| | **State of nature—face coming up on toss of die** | |
	1, 2, or 3	**4, 5, or 6**
Bet A	− \$1	+ \$1
Bet B	− \$10,000	+ \$10,500

pose that you were offered the bets given in Table 10.9 concerning a single toss of a fair six-sided die. The EMV's of bets A and B are as follows (assuming the die is fair):

$$\text{EMV(bet A)} = (-\$1)(0.50) + (\$1)(0.50) = \$0$$

and

$$\text{EMV(bet B)} = (-\$10,000)(0.50) + (\$10,500)(0.50) = \$250$$

According to the EMV criterion, you should prefer bet B to bet A. Yet if you were forced to choose between the two in an actual betting situation, which bet would you choose? Because of the potential loss of \$10,000 in bet B, most people would choose bet A, even though it has a smaller EMV. This is because most of us would be put in deep financial difficulty if faced with a sudden debt of \$10,000. If this is the case, there must be factors involved in this example which are not formally considered by the EMV criterion.

For a more practical example, consider an investor who has, say, \$10,000 to invest. He is considering three alternatives:

1. A savings account that will yield a fixed amount, 5%;

2. A conservative stock that has a normally distributed return with mean 7% and standard deviation 5%;

3. A speculative stock that has a normally distributed return with mean 10% and standard deviation 15%.

According to the EMV criterion, the investor should look only at the expected returns of the three investments, in which case he will invest all of his money in the investment with the highest return. The three expected returns are 5%, 7%, and 10%, respectively, for the savings account, the conservative stock, and the speculative stock. Therefore, the EMV criterion would have the investor invest everything in the speculative stock. For most investors, however, the risk associated with the investments would be a relevant consideration. The savings account is a risk-free investment, while both of the stocks have an element of risk. The speculative stock, of course, is the riskiest of the three investments. In reality, the investor's decision will probably depend not just on the expected returns, but also on this person's attitude toward risk. To avoid risk at any cost, the investor should put all of the money into the savings account. The investor who is completely indifferent to risk will put all of the money into the speculative stock. Most likely, the investor will attempt to achieve some sort of compromise by *diversifying*. That is, the investor will buy some of the speculative stock in the hope of obtaining a high return; but to reduce the overall risk, the investor will also put some money in the savings account, and may also buy some of the conservative stock. If the EMV criterion is rigidly followed, such diversification is not possible. Thus, the fact that diversification is common in real-world investing suggests that many investors are not willing to act strictly in accordance with the EMV criterion.

If EMV is not always a good criterion for decision making under uncertainty, how can we determine a better criterion, one that will take into account the decision maker's preferences for various consequences or payoffs? The theory of utility prescribes such a criterion: the *maximization of expected utility,* or the EU criterion. In order to understand this criterion, it is first necessary to discuss briefly the concept of **utility.**

Essentially, the theory of utility makes it possible to measure the *relative* value to a decision maker of the payoffs, or consequences, in a decision problem. First of all, it is necessary to determine what we consider to be the most preferable and least preferable payoffs. These can be assigned utility values of 1 and 0, respectively. The choice of 1 and 0 is arbitrary; we could just as easily have chosen 234 and -101, but 1 and 0 simplify the calculations somewhat. Let us call the most preferable payoff M and the least preferable payoff L. Then suppose there is another payoff, P, the utility of which we would like to determine. We can do this in the following manner. Consider the following betting situation:

Bet I—Receive P for certain

Bet II—Receive M with probability p

Receive L with probability $1 - p$

According to the EU criterion, the bet with the highest expected utility should be selected. But we can calculate the expected utilities, where the utility of a consequence C is denoted by $U(C)$:

$$EU(\text{bet I}) = U(P)$$
$$EU(\text{bet II}) = p(U(M)) + (1 - p)(U(L))$$
$$= p(1) + (1 - p)(0) = p$$

Thus, if $U(P) < p$, bet II should be chosen; if $U(P) > p$, bet I should be chosen; and if $U(P) = p$, we are indifferent between the two bets. We shall exploit this last property to determine the utility of P. If we can determine a probability p which makes us *indifferent* between the two bets, then the utility of P is equal to this value, p. In this manner, we can determine the utility of any consequence, or payoff, once the most and least preferable consequences, M and L, have been determined. Note that it is not necessary for the consequences to be stated in terms of dollars, as it is when we are using EMV. Because of this, it is possible to take into consideration both monetary and *non*monetary factors in determining the utility of a consequence. In many business decisions, nonmonetary factors (for example, factors involving labor, such as working conditions; factors involving prestige, such as the size and design of office buildings; and

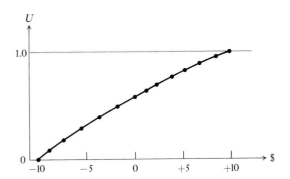

Figure 10.9
A utility function for money.

factors involving business ethics) can be quite important, and it is useful to be able to consider these factors in the analysis.

Although nonmonetary factors may be of some importance, it is of interest to determine the relationship between money and utility. Suppose that we are interested in this relationship over a range of monetary values from $- \$10$ to $+ \$10$. Then $M = + \$10$ and $L = - \$10$. If we use the above analysis, we can determine the utility of any amount between L and M. For example, suppose we decide that we are indifferent between (1) receiving $5 for certain and (2) receiving M with probability 0.80 and receiving L with probability 0.20. Then U($5) = 0.80. If we assess U($0), U($1), U($- \$1$), etc., in a similar manner, we can plot the resulting points on a graph, as shown in Fig. 10.9. After several points are determined, it is possible to draw a rough curve through them. This curve is a **utility function for money.** It is important to note that different persons have different utility functions, and that any single individual may have different utility functions at different points in time. It is not possible to make interpersonal comparisons of utility, however, because of the arbitrary scale (0 to 1) used for utilities.

Types of Utility Functions

Several types, or classes, of utility functions for money can be distinguished, although there are utility functions not falling in any of the classes to be described. In Fig. 10.10 three utility curves are presented. Curve A represents the utility curve of a risk avoider, curve B represents the curve of a risk taker, and curve C represents the curve of a person who is neither a risk taker nor a risk avoider (but **risk neutral**). To see why these labels apply to the three curves, consider the following bet: win $10 with probability $\frac{1}{2}$ and lose $10 with probability $\frac{1}{2}$. This can be thought of as a bet of $10 on the toss of a fair coin. In terms of EMV, a person should be indifferent about the bet, since it has an EMV of zero. In terms of EU, however, the situation varies with the three curves presented in Fig. 10.10. The gains in utility for the three curves if the bet is won are w_A, w_B, and w_C. The corresponding losses in utility if the bet is lost are l_A, l_B, and l_C.

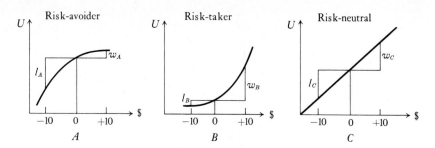

Figure 10.10
Three types of utility
functions.

The expected utility of this bet to the three types of individuals can be calculated by multiplying the probability of winning times the gain in utility from winning, and then subtracting the probability of losing times the loss in utility if the bet is lost. Thus, the expected utility to individuals A, B, and C is

$$\text{EU}(A) = \tfrac{1}{2}w_A - \tfrac{1}{2}l_A = \tfrac{1}{2}(w_A - l_A)$$
$$\text{EU}(B) = \tfrac{1}{2}w_B - \tfrac{1}{2}l_B = \tfrac{1}{2}(w_B - l_B)$$

and

$$\text{EU}(C) = \tfrac{1}{2}w_C - \tfrac{1}{2}l_C = \tfrac{1}{2}(w_C - l_C)$$

From curve A we can see that this "fair" bet is unfavorable to the risk avoider since the amount of utility he can gain, w_A, is less than the amount of utility he can lose, l_A, and as a result $\text{EU}(A) < 0$. The risk avoider represented by curve A would thus be expected to *reject* the bet in question since he prefers to avoid the risk of a bet with EMV = 0; in fact, we could find some bets with *positive* EMV's that A would consider unfavorable. The individual represented by curve B, on the other hand, would be expected to *accept* this bet, as his potential gain in utility, w_B, exceeds the potential loss, l_B, so that $\text{EU}(B) > 0$. In other words, this type of person prefers to take the risk associated with a bet of EMV = 0, and we could, in fact, find some bets with *negative* EMV's that B would consider favorable. And finally, the individual represented by curve C is indifferent regarding the bet, as this person's utility function for money is linear; that is,

$$w_C = l_c \qquad \text{and} \qquad \text{EU}(C) = 0$$

When a person's utility function for money is linear, then choosing the action with the highest EU is equivalent to choosing the action with the highest EMV. To prove this, note that if the curve is linear, it can be written in the form

$$U = a + b(\text{MV})$$

where b must be greater than zero since more money is always preferred to less money. But a and b are constants, so, by the laws of expected values,

$$E(U) = a + bE(\text{MV})$$

EU is then at a maximum when EMV is at a maximum, so the two criteria are equivalent in this case.

The curves presented in Fig. 10.10 are by no means the only possible forms for utility functions. Several other forms, which we shall not describe, have been proposed; and still other forms, many of which are not mathematically tractable (that is, they cannot be represented by a simple mathematical function), exist. Most utility curves for individuals probably are similar to curve *A*. It is an interesting exercise to select a range of values (say, − $100 to + $100) and attempt to determine your own utility curve.

Maximizing Expected Utility

Once a utility function for money is determined, the EU criterion is easy to apply. Simply take each value in the payoff table for the decision-making problem of interest and use the utility function to convert the payoff to a utility. In this fashion, the entire payoff table can be converted into a utility table. If a tree diagram is used, all of the payoffs at the right-hand side of the tree must be converted to utilities *before* the backward-induction procedure is started. It is very important to remember that the conversion from payoffs to utilities must occur *before* any expected values are calculated. To calculate expected payoffs and *then* convert to utilities is an invalid procedure.

For an example of the use of a utility function in a decision-making problem, consider an investor who wants to invest $10,000. She is considering three investments: a savings account, a conservative stock, and a speculative stock. To simplify the problem, assume that she has decided to invest the entire $10,000 in a single investment—that is, she has *ruled out* the possibility of diversification. The assessor thinks about her preferences and contemplates various bets in order to assess a utility function, and it turns out that the resulting utility function can be represented quite well by the function

$$U(M) = 10 - \left(\frac{2000 - M}{500}\right)^2 \quad \text{for } M \le 2000$$

where *M* represents dollars. This function, which is graphed in Fig. 10.11, illustrates the use of a mathematical function to represent a decision maker's utility

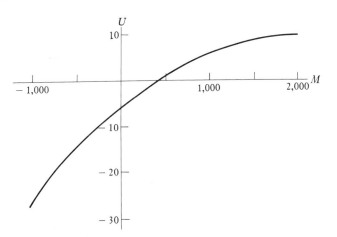

Figure 10.11
Investor's utility function.

function. This particular function is a quadratic function; other mathematical functions that are frequently used to represent utility functions are exponential and logarithmic functions (in addition to linear functions, of course). Observe from the graph that the investor's utility function takes on both positive and negative values and that a utility of zero does *not* correspond to a dollar value of zero. Earlier in the section we discussed utility functions with values from zero to one, but not all utility functions are so restricted.

The investor feels that her payoff from the investment during the coming year will depend on whether the stock market goes up or down. In either case, the savings account will yield a return of 5%, so her payoff will be $500 for the year. Furthermore, the investor judges that the conservative stock will yield her a profit of $1000 if the market goes up but $0 if the market goes down, and the speculative stock will yield her a profit of $2000 if the market goes up but a loss of $1000 if the market goes down. The payoff table, expressed in dollars, is given in Table 10.10. Now suppose that the investor feels that the probability that the market will go up is 0.60. The EMV's are 500 for the bank account, 600 for the conservative stock, and 800 for the speculative stock. Therefore, if her utility function were linear, so that she could use the EMV criterion, it would be optimal for the investor to buy the speculative stock.

Since the investor's utility function is not linear with respect to money, we need to convert the payoff table from dollars into utility values. We can do this by reading values from the graph, but since the utility function is expressed as a mathematical function, it is more accurate to simply use this function to determine the utility corresponding to each payoff in Table 10.10. For instance, if the investor chooses the savings account and the market goes up, the payoff is $500, and the utility corresponding to $500 is

$$U(\$500) = 10 - \left(\frac{2000 - 500}{500}\right)^2 = 1$$

Similarly, all of the values in the payoff table can be converted to utilities, and the resulting table of utilities is given in Table 10.11. The expected utilities of the three actions are

$$EU(\text{Savings account}) = 1(0.60) + 1(0.40) = 1$$
$$EU(\text{Conservative stock}) = 6(0.60) + (-6)(0.40) = 1.2$$

and

$$EU(\text{Speculative stock}) = 10(0.60) + (-26)(0.40) = -4.4$$

TABLE 10.10   Payoff table for investor

		State of nature	
		Market up	**Market down**
Action (Investment)	Savings account	500	500
	Conservative stock	1000	0
	Speculative stock	2000	− 1000

TABLE 10.11 Utility table for investor

		State of nature	
		Market up	Market down
Action (Investment)	Savings account	1	1
	Conservative stock	6	−6
	Speculative stock	10	−26

Thus, the optimal action, according to the EU criterion, is to buy the conservative stock. In this case, the speculative stock was risky enough and the investor was **risk averse** enough so that, even though the speculative stock had the highest EMV, the conservative stock had the highest EU (and the savings account was not far behind!). This does not mean that risk avoiders will avoid risks. In this example, even the conservative stock has a risk of a return of zero, which is much less than the sure return from the savings account.

Important decisions should be based on the EU criterion rather than on the EMV criterion. For simplicity, however, we assumed in much of this chapter that utility was linear with respect to money. This assumption allowed us to use EMV as a decision-making criterion, since maximizing EMV is equivalent to maximizing EU. You should keep in mind, however, that this is a simplifying assumption that may not be realistic in many decision-making situations.

Problems

10.39 Discuss some potential advantages and disadvantages of the Bayesian approach to statistics.

10.40 In applying Bayes' rule for normal distributions, what can you say about the posterior mean M in relation to the prior mean m and the sample mean $\bar{x}$, and what can you say about the posterior variance V in relation to the prior variance v and the variance of the sample mean, σ^2/n? Do these relationships seem intuitively reasonable?

10.41 In an estimation problem such as that faced by the appliance dealer in the example in Section 10.10, where would you expect the "best" estimate to lie in relation to the median if the cost of overestimation is greater than the cost of underestimation?

10.42 Why is the maximization of EMV not always a reasonable criterion for decision making? What problems does this create for an analyst who is trying to model a decision-making problem using the techniques discussed in this chapter?

10.43 Attempt to determine your own utility function for money in the range from − $500 to + $500.

10.44 Would you anticipate that wealthy individuals would be less risk averse, more risk averse, or about the same in terms of risk aversion when compared with poor people? How about wealthy individuals compared with middle-income people?

10.45 A production manager is interested in the mean weight of items turned out by a particular process. He feels that the weight is normally distributed with standard deviation 2, and his prior distribution for μ is a normal distribution with mean 110 and variance 0.4. He randomly selects five items from the process and weighs them, with the following results: 108, 109, 107.4, 109.6, 112. What is the production manager's posterior distribution?

10.46 You are attempting to assess a prior distribution for the mean of a process, and you decide that the 25th percentile of your distribution is 160 and the 60th percentile is 180. Assuming that your prior distribution is normal, determine the mean and variance.

10.47 In assessing a distribution for μ, the mean height of a certain population of college students, a physical education instructor decides that the distribution is normal, the median is 70 inches, and the 20th percentile is 67 inches. The instructor is interested in

$$H_o: \mu \geq 71 \qquad \text{versus} \qquad H_a: \mu < 71$$

Taking a random sample of 80 students, the instructor observes $\bar{x} = 71.2$ inches. Assume (from previous studies) that $\sigma = 5.6$ inches is the population standard deviation. Find the posterior odds ratio of H_o to H_a.

10.48 Since the deregulation of the airline industry, airlines find that their personnel are swamped with calls and that many customers are unable to reach a reservation clerk by telephone without a long holding period. The holding time is thought to be normally distributed with mean μ and variance 4, and the prior distribution of μ is normal with $P(\mu < 3.5) = 0.067$ and $P(\mu > 6) = 0.16$. A call is selected at random and it results in a holding time of 1.2 minutes. Find the posterior distribution of μ.

10.49 In Problem 10.45, find a 95% interval estimate for μ and determine $P(\mu > 110)$

a) from the prior distribution,

b) from the posterior distribution.

10.50 A contractor must decide how many houses to build in a new subdivision. All houses built in this subdivision must use solar energy for heating, and the contractor is not sure how strong the demand is for such expensive houses. Each house costs the contractor $160,000 to build and sells for $200,000. However, to build the houses, the contractor must take a loan from the local bank, and the terms of the loan state that any houses unsold at the end of six months will be bought by the bank at $144,000 per house. The contractor's distribution of θ, the number of houses that can be sold within six months, is as follows:

θ	4	5	6	7	8	9	10	11
$P(\theta)$	0.05	0.13	0.22	0.28	0.15	0.09	0.06	0.02

10.51 The manager of a bookstore in a college community must decide how many copies of a particular book to order for the coming semester. Based on the anticipated enrollment of the course in which the book is being used and the number of competing bookstores in town, the manager feels that the demand for the book at the store is normally distributed, with mean 120 and variance 100. The book costs the bookstore $30 and retails for $36. Since the course is being phased out of the curriculum, the book will not be used again, so any unsold copies will be returned to the publisher. The publisher will repurchase the books at $27 per copy, and the bookstore's cost for postage and handling on returned copies amounts to $0.75 per copy. How many copies of the book should be ordered?

10.52 The manager of a grocery store must decide how many gallons of milk to order for the coming week. The milk costs the store $1.50 per gallon and retails for $1.60, but any milk unsold at the end of the week must be thrown out. The cost due to loss of goodwill when customers try to buy milk and find that it is sold out is judged to be $0.20 per gallon. From past sales data, it appears that weekly sales of milk are approximately normally distributed with a mean of 820 gallons and a standard deviation of 60 gallons. How much milk should the manager order?

10.53 On April 1, a car dealer in a small town has five new cars on hand and is preparing to place an order for more cars. The additional cars will arrive in a week, and the *next* order of new cars won't arrive until May 1. The dealer feels that the process "generating" car purchases at the dealership can be treated as a Poisson process with an average intensity of 10 cars per month. The cars cost the dealer $8000 and sell for $8500, and the dealer suffers an opportunity loss of $200 (due to loss of goodwill and possible loss of a sale) if a customer wants to buy a car but the dealer has none in stock. For each car unsold at the end of a month, the dealer suffers a "carrying cost" of $150. How many cars should the dealer order?

10.54 Suppose that you are contemplating drilling an oil well, with the following payoff table in terms of thousands of dollars:

		State of the world	
		Oil	No oil
Action	Drill	100	−40
	Don't drill	0	0

If after consulting a geologist you decide that $P(\text{Oil}) = 0.30$, would you drill or not drill according to the

a) maximin criterion?

b) maximax criterion?

c) EMV criterion?

d) EU criterion, where $U(0) = 0.40$, $U(100) = +1$, and $U(-40) = 0$?

Explain the differences in the results in parts (a) through (d).

10.55 In Problem 10.11, suppose that $U(M) = 50 - (8 - M)^2$, where M represents the payoff in units of $100,000. Graph U and discuss the behavior implied by such a utility function. What should the firm do if the objective is to maximize expected utility?

10.56 In Problem 10.12, suppose that the company wants to maximize expected utility. The firm's utility function is

$$U(M) = \begin{cases} M + 5 & \text{if } M \geq 5 \\ 2M & \text{if } M < 5 \end{cases}$$

where M represents the payoff in thousands of dollars. If the probability of a recession is 0.3, what should the company do?

10.57 In Problem 10.56, how large would the probability of a recession have to be before the company would put the money in the bank?

10.58 Compare your answers to Problem 10.57 and 10.13. Explain any differences.

Exercises

10.59 A coin lying on a table is either two-headed or a fair coin. You are asked to guess whether or not the coin is two-headed. If you guess correctly you win $2. If you guess incorrectly, you lose $1. You can't see the coin, but you do have the opportunity of having an impartial observer flip the coin and tell you if it came up heads or tails. This flip costs you $0.20. Draw a decision tree and use it to determine your optimal action and the value of ENGS and EVSI.

10.60 In Problem 10.59, suppose you can elect to buy either two flips or one flip, at a cost of $0.20 per flip. Draw the decision tree for this problem, and calculate ENGS. Assume you must decide before the first flip whether or not you wan the second flip.

10.61 For Problem 10.60, assume that the cost per flip is $0.10. Write and run a computer program to determine the optimal sample size.

10.62 a) Redo Problem 10.60, assuming that you can decide whether or not to purchase a second flip *after* viewing the first flip.

b) Redo Problem 10.61 with the same assumption as given above.

10.63 Consider a bookbag filled with 100 poker chips. You know that either 70 of the chips are red and the remainder blue, or that 70 are blue and the remainder red. You must guess whether the bookbag is (70R, 30B) or (70B, 30R). If you guess correctly, you win $5. If you guess incorrectly, you lose $3. Your prior probability that the bookbag contains (70R, 30B) is 0.40.

a) If you had to make your guess on the basis of the prior information, what would you guess?

b) If you could purchase perfect information, what is the most that you should be willing to pay for it?

c) If you could purchase sample information in the form of one draw from the bookbag, how much should you be willing to pay for it? Draw the decision tree.

d) If you could purchase sample information in the form of three draws (with replacement) from the bookbag, how much should you be willing to pay for it? Draw the decision tree.

10.64 Do Problem 10.63 with the following payoff table in dollars:

		State of the world	
		(70R, 30B)	(70B, 30R)
Your guess	(70R, 30B)	6	−2
	(70B, 30R)	−6	10

10.65 Write a computer program to calculate EVSI for any size sample from $n = 1$ to $n = 50$ in Problem 10.63(d). What is the optimal sample size if each sample draw costs $0.25?

10.66 An investor is contemplating an investment having the potential payoffs shown in Table 10.12. The investor assesses utility for values from − $30,000 to $50,000 in increments of $10,000 as shown in the table below.

a) Graph the utility function and interpret the shape of the curve.

b) Should the investor make the investment or not?

TABLE 10.12

Payoff	Probability
− $30,000	0.2
− $10,000	0.1
$5,000	0.1
$20,000	0.4
$50,000	0.2

M	$U(M)$	M	$U(M)$	M	$U(M)$
− $30,000	0	$0	0.60	$30,000	0.90
− $20,000	0.28	$10,000	0.72	$40,000	0.96
− $10,000	0.45	$20,000	0.82	$50,000	1.00

10.67 A construction firm wants to choose between bidding on the construction of either a dam or an airport. The firm can bid on only one of these jobs, since its engineers don't have time to analyze both jobs in order to determine an appropriate bid. Preliminary estimates of construction costs from the projects are $10,000,000 from the airport and $18,000,000 from the dam. In addition, the out-of-pocket costs for preparing the bids are $500,000 for the airport and $1,000,000 for the dam. Moreover, the firm has a choice of using its standard bidding procedure or trying to bid lower than usual to increase the chances of winning the job. The standard bids would be approximately $12,500,000 for the airport and $23,000,000 for the dam, and the lower bids are $11,500,000 for the airport and $21,000,000 for the dam. According to the maximin criterion, what should the firm do? According to the maximax criterion, what should the firm do?

10.68 In Problem 10.67, the chances of winning the bid are 0.4 for the airport and 0.3 for the dam if standard bids are used, but the chances are 0.7 for the airport and 0.5 for the dam if lower bids are used. What should the firm do?

10.69 An importer has an option to buy 100,000 tons of scrap iron from a foreign firm for $5 per ton. The market price in the United States for scrap iron is $8 per ton. The importer must decide immediately whether to purchase the scrap iron, but a license must be obtained later, before the material can be imported. Because of an increasing tendency to protect U.S. business by restricting imports, the importer feels that there is a 50–50 chance that the government will refuse to grant an import license, in which case the contract will be annulled and the importer will have to pay a penalty of $1 per ton to the foreign government. Should the importer purchase the scrap iron if this person wants to maximize EMV?

10.70 A contractor must decide whether to buy or rent equipment for a job up for bid. Because of lead-time requirements in getting the equipment, she must decide before knowing whether the contract is won. If she buys, a contract would result in a net profit of $120,000; but failing to win the contract means that the equipment will have to be sold at a $40,000 loss. By renting, her profit from the contract is only $50,000 if she wins it, but there will be no loss of money if the job is not won. The probability that she will win the job is 0.4. What should the contractor do?

10.71 An insurance company's records reveal that in a one-year period, approximately 20% of drivers under age 21 submit a claim as a result of an accident. Further investigation shows that 30% of those submitting claims are students, while 60% of those not submitting claims are students. What is the probability that a person randomly chosen from the under-age-21 students insured by the company will submit a claim as a result of an accident in the next year?

10.72 In Problem 10.16, suppose that the security analyst observes the security for a total of 15 days, and the price increases on 9 of those days. The analyst could revise her probability distribution each day, but suppose that she decides to wait until the end of the 15-day period. Is there an easy way to determine the relevant likelihoods for the entire 15-day period? (*Hint:* The likelihoods are of the form

$$P\left(\begin{matrix}\text{Security price goes up on} \\ \text{9 days in a sample of 15 days}\end{matrix}\middle|\begin{matrix}\text{Probability of price going} \\ \text{up on any given day is } p\end{matrix}\right)$$

From Chapter 4, try to find a distribution that can be used to calculate probabilities of this form.) After the 15-day period, what is the analyst's probability that the security is an average investment? Also find the probabilities for "poor investment" and "good investment" after the information from the 15-day sample.

10.73 In Problem 10.69, how much would the importer pay to learn, before deciding about the purchase of the scrap iron, whether the import license would be approved?

10.74 In Problem 10.70, find the EVPI.

10.75 It is felt by a market-research group that the total time elapsed between the development of a new product and the time the product reaches the market is normally distributed with mean μ and variance 7.5. The prior distribution of μ is a normal distribution with mean 6 and variance 0.5. A sample of 26 new products results in an average "time to market" of 5.8 months. What is the posterior distribution of μ following this sample?

10.76 In Problem 10.75, find a 95% interval estimate for μ

a) from the prior distribution,

b) from the sample,

c) from the posterior distribution.

10.77 Envisioning a potentially large new market, a U.S. manufacturer agrees to export food processors to China. The manufacturer will send a shipment of the current year's models to China, and no additional shipments will be made for one year, at which time next year's models will be available. The expected demand for food processors during the first year they are sold in China is normally distributed with mean 12,000 and standard deviation 3000. The net profit for each food processor sold in China is $10, and any left unsold at the end of the first year will be shipped elsewhere to be sold at a loss of $15 per unit. How many food processors should be sent in the first year's shipment?

10.78 In Problem 10.70, what is the best strategy if the contractor's utility function is $U(M) = \sqrt{M + 40,000}$, where M represents dollars?

10.79 A very small electronics company produces and sells minicomputers and assorted computer hardware and software. The firm is relatively new, and all of its sales have been domestic. Recently a French firm learned of the company's products, and the firm now has offered to purchase several minicomputers and other items. The proposed contract calls for full payment in French francs at the time of delivery, which is to be no later than six months from the date the contract is offered. The amount is 2,400,000 francs.

This is by far the largest order the company has received in its short lifetime. The six-month deadline can be met, but it will be necessary to put off other orders to do so. The president estimates that if the French order is accepted, the company will have to forgo other sales that would lead to a net profit of about $260,000. The cost of filling the French order, including shipping, is expected to be $200,000.

At the time the payment of 2,400,000 francs is received, the company will need cash, and the francs will have to be converted into dollars immediately. Because of recent fluctuations of the dollar vis-à-vis the franc and other currencies, the president is unsure about how many dollars will be received. After some brief consultations with bankers and economists, the president comes up with the following probability distribution for θ, the exchange rate (in dollars per French franc) six months from now, shown in Table 10.13. Given the current state of the world economy, such a wide range of values of θ is not surprising. Nevertheless, it makes the president very nervous.

One option that is available is to obtain further information about the dollar/franc exchange rate. For $2000, an econometric forecasting firm will forecast whether the dollar is expected to be weak or strong in the next six months. The chances of a forecast of a weak dollar are 0.70 if θ will end up at 0.18 in six months, 0.60 if θ will be 0.20, 0.50 if θ will be 0.22, 0.40 if θ will be 0.24, and 0.30 if θ will be 0.26. The corresponding chances of a forecast of a strong dollar are 0.30 (for $\theta = 0.18$), 0.40, 0.50, 0.60, and 0.70 (for $\theta = 0.26$).

In talking with some friends, the president learns that it might be possible to remove the uncertainty caused by the need to convert francs to dollars in six months. At a cost of $25,000, an insurance policy will guarantee a rate no lower than 0.22 dollars/franc for the changing of 2,400,000 francs six

TABLE 10.13

θ	$P(\theta)$
0.18	0.10
0.20	0.20
0.22	0.30
0.24	0.30
0.26	0.10

months from now. That is, if $\theta < 0.22$, the insurance company will purchase the francs at a rate of 0.22, while if $\theta \geq 0.22$, the company will change the francs at the market rate, θ. Alternatively, the firm can obtain a "futures" contract, agreeing to deliver 2,400,000 French francs six months from now at a rate of 0.21 dollars per franc.

a) Assuming that the president is risk-neutral, what course of action would you advise?

b) Suppose that the president's utility function for M, payoffs in units of $100,000, is

$$U(M) = 9 - (5 - M)^2.$$

Also, the econometric forecasting firm just went out of business. Now what course of action would you advise?

10.80 The Delaney-Bryce Corporation is a major manufacturer of specialized soap and detergent products. It currently controls 31 subsidiary companies that manufacture disinfecting detergent powder primarily for use by hospitals, linen suppliers, diaper services, and other large institutional laundry facilities. Each of the 31 subsidiaries sells in its own region, and together they serve a large portion of the United States.

Delaney-Bryce established the Ohio Valley Detergent Corporation in Indianapolis last year. Since that time Ohio Valley has captured a larger market share in each of the three quarters its plant has been in operation. The directors expect that the company will have reached maturity sometime in the next three years, and that the rapid growth in sales it has been experiencing during the present start-up period will begin to level off. The warehouse that Ohio Valley has been using for the past year is rapidly becoming inadequate to serve the company's growing sales volume. The directors, knowing that such rapid changes in requirements would occur in the company's first stages, leased the present warehouse facilities for only 18 months. This lease will expire soon and the directors and officers now wish to negotiate another. Now that Ohio Valley is approaching maturity they wish to acquire warehouse space for a period of three years. Leasing facilities on this long-term basis will save the company money both as a result of lower monthly rent payments and by avoiding the need to regularly renegotiate lease terms.

There are only two warehouse facilities in Indianapolis that the directors of Ohio Valley feel may be adequate. Both contain the necessary equipment and other features that the company's operation requires. The location of each warehouse is also suitable to the directors. But the sizes of the facilities differ, one being 16,500 square feet, the other, 21,000 square feet. The decision must be made, then, as to which of these two different-sized warehouses Ohio Valley Detergent Corporation should lease in order to minimize its expected cost. But before such a decision can be made it will be necessary for the directors to have some reliable prediction of the level of sales the company can expect to maintain over the period covered by the lease. Kenneth Rein, a member of the board, has predicted that over the next three years Ohio Valley will sell about 10.83 million pounds of detergent annually, and that this prediction of sales comes from a normal distribution with a standard deviation of 1.18 million pounds. The 16,500 square-foot warehouse will hold a maximum of 1,835,000 pounds of detergent. Likewise, the

21,000-square-foot warehouse can be used to store at most 2,300,000 pounds.

The company plans to keep on hand at any one time a two-month supply of its product. This means that if Ohio Valley should sell exactly the predicted amount of 10.83 million pounds, it would want always to keep in storage $(\frac{1}{6})(10.83) = 1,805,000$ pounds of detergent. Note that, for this prediction for two months of sales, the standard deviation is 196,666 pounds, which is one-sixth of the error associated with the prediction of full-year sales (that is, $\frac{1}{6} \times 1,180,000$).

In addition to this information on warehouse utilization, Rein has given you the following guidelines concerning the costs involved in leasing each of the two warehouses available. As Ohio Valley is most concerned here with avoiding unnecessary expenses, Rein tells you to consider that, for this decision, the cost will be zero if the company leases the smaller warehouse and, for the duration of the lease, requires no more than the space that the smaller warehouse can provide. The cost is also assumed to be zero if Ohio Valley leases the larger facility and requires over the years more space than the smaller warehouse could have provided. If the company leases the smaller warehouse and sales are at a higher level than can be supplied by this facility, high-cost short-term facilities will have to be leased to supplement the main warehouse. Rein estimates that this added cost, combined with costs of reduced efficiency due to the resulting lack of centralization, will be approximately $500,000 over the entire period of the lease. If the company leases the larger warehouse and sales over the lease years prove to be low enough so that it actually needs only the smaller warehouse, the extra expense will be $325,000 over the life of the lease (lease terms prohibit subleasing of unused space).

Ohio Valley has recently learned that they can purchase a sample survey for $5000. This survey's outcomes will be either "favorable" (meaning large sales) or "unfavorable" (meaning moderate sales). Judging from past records, Ohio Valley estimates that if sales ≤ 1,835,000 is the true state of nature, the survey will result in the "unfavorable" outcome about 77% of the time. Conversely, if sales > 1,835,000 is the true state of nature, the survey will result in the "favorable" outcome about 66% of the time. On the basis of this information, draw the decision tree, and calculate EVSI and ENGS.

Chapter 11

Simple Linear Regression

If a problem has really big numbers in it, the answer is always "one million."

PEPPERMINT PATTY, IN *PEANUTS*

Introduction 11.1

In the past several chapters we have discussed the process of using sample information to make inferences, test hypotheses, or modify beliefs about the characteristics of a population. In this chapter and the next we turn to a related problem, solving two or more variables—making inferences about how changes in one set of variables are related to changes in another set. A description of the nature of the relationship between two or more variables is called **regression analysis,** while investigation into the strength of such relationships is called **correlation analysis.**

Sir Francis Galton, an English expert on heredity in the late 1800s, was one of the first researchers to work with the problem of describing one variable on the basis of one or more other variables. Galton's work centered on the heights of fathers compared to the heights of their sons. He found a tendency toward the mean: Exceptionally short fathers tend to have sons of more average height (taller than their fathers), while just the opposite is true for unusually tall fathers. Galton said that the heights of the sons "regressed" or reverted to the mean, and thus originated the term "regression." Nowadays **regression** means, more generally, the description of the nature of the relationship between two or more variables.

Regression analysis is concerned with the problem of describing or estimating the value of one variable, called the **dependent variable,** on the basis of one or more other variables, called **independent variables.** Suppose, for example, that a manager is trying to predict sales for next month (the dependent variable) on the basis of indexes of disposable income, price levels, or any of numerous other independent variables; or perhaps this person is trying to predict the performance of one product under certain conditions of stress or at various temperatures; similarly the decision maker may be using one or more of a battery of tests in trying to evaluate the ability of prospective employees for new jobs. In these cases, regression analysis is being used in an attempt to describe the relationship between known values of two or more variables. An economist may use it for this purpose as an aid in understanding the relationship between historical observations over a specified time span, such as the relation of consumption to current and past levels of income and wealth, or the relationship between any one or more of a number of economic indicators and prices, or profits, or sales in a given industry.

No matter whether regression analysis is used for descriptive or predictive purposes, one cannot expect to be able to estimate or describe the exact value of sales, or profits, or consumption, or any other dependent variable of this nature. Many factors can cause variations in the dependent variable for a given value of the independent variables, such as fluctuations in the stock market, changes in the weather, a passing fact, or just differences in human ability and motivation. Because of these possible variations, we shall for the most part be interested in determining the average relationship between the dependent variable and the independent variables. That is, we will want to be able to estimate the mean value of a dependent variable for any given value of the independent variable. Although regression analysis can involve one or more independent variables, in this chapter analysis is confined to only one independent variable. This is known as **simple linear regression.** Multiple linear regression is presented in Chapter 13.

The Regression Model

For most regression analysis, the average population relationship between the dependent variable (which is usually denoted by the letter y) and the independent variable (denoted by the letter x) is assumed to be linear.* A linear function is used because it is mathematically simple and has been shown to provide either a sufficiently close approximation to many real-world relationships or a very good first step in a multiple regression.

In regression we are interested in determining the mean value of y for a given value of x. This is represented mathematically as the conditional expectation $E[y|x]$. Another symbol often used to denote this expectation is $\mu_{y \cdot x}$, which is read as "the mean of the y values for a given x value." By assuming that

---

*In this chapter the variable x is not, technically, a random variable. Hence we will not denote this variable by boldface type. Specific values of x will be denoted by the symbol x_i.

y and x are linearly related, we are saying that all possible conditional means ($E[y|x] = \mu_{y \cdot x}$) that can be calculated (one for each possible value of x) must be on a single straight line. This line is called the **population regression line.** To specify this line (or any straight line), we need to know its slope and intercept.

If we let α represent the y-intercept and β the slope of the line, this line is written as follows*

$$\text{Population regression line:} \quad \mu_{y \cdot x} = E[y|x] = \alpha + \beta x \qquad (11.1)$$

To illustrate this population regression line, consider the relationship between the number of housing starts in a year and the average mortgage interest rate over that year. As the interest rates increase, we would expect the number of housing starts to decline. Similarly, we would expect the number of housing starts to increase with a decline in the mortgage rate. If y represents the number of housing starts (in thousands) in a year and x the mortgage interest rate, $\mu_{y \cdot x}$ then is the mean number of housing starts for some given mortgage interest rate. When an exact value of x is specified, this value is customarily denoted as x_i. Then $\mu_{y \cdot x_i}$ represents the mean of the y values for that specific value of x. For example, if $x_i = 11\%$, then

$$\mu_{y \cdot x_i} = \mu_{y \cdot 11} = \alpha + \beta(11)$$

would be the mean number of housing starts when the mortgage interest rate is equal to 11%. Thus, when speaking of a specific value of x, we merely substitute x_i for x in Equation (11.1).

In addition to estimating the mean value $\mu_{y \cdot x_i}$, we also make statements about the actual value of y for a given value of x_i. This value is denoted as y_i and is usually not equal to $\mu_{y \cdot x_i}$. For example, the number of housing starts 1975 in one year, when the mortgage interest rate is $x_i = 11\%$ might be 1800 in another year (y_i), and 2250 in a third year (note that the y_i values are presented in thousands). The mean number of housing starts ($\mu_{y \cdot x_i}$) with a mortgage interest rate of 11% may be 2000 (thousand) over many years. The difference between y_i and $\mu_{y \cdot x_i}$ depends upon the accuracy of the regression model in depicting the real-world situation, and by the accuracy with which the variables x and y are measured. It also depends on the predictability of the underlying behavior of the persons, businesses, or governments involved in the model. Any changes in human or institutional behavior could also cause such differences.

The point of the preceding discussion is that the difference between y_i and $\mu_{y \cdot x_i}$, is the unpredictable element in regression analysis. For this reason, this difference is usually called the **random error,** and denoted by the symbol ϵ_i. That is,

$$\epsilon_i = y_i - \mu_{y \cdot x_i} \qquad \text{or} \qquad y_i = \mu_{y \cdot x_i} + \epsilon_i \qquad (11.2)$$

---

*The meaning of the Greek letters α and β as used in this chapter has no relationship to the meaning of these same letters used in Chapter 9 to describe the probability of Type I and Type II errors.

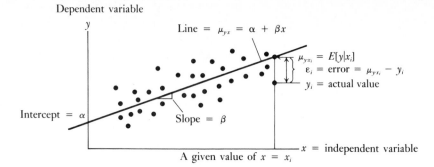

Figure 11.1

The population regression model.

For example, if a mortgage interest rate of 11% for a certain year leads to a y value of 1800, then the error would be

$$\epsilon_i = 1800 - 2000 = -200$$

We can now use Formula (11.2) to describe what is called the "population regression model." This model consists of all the terms that, when added together, sum to y_i. Substituting $y_i = \mu_{y \cdot x_i} + \epsilon_i$ into (11.1) we get

> *Population regression model:* $y_i = \alpha + \beta x_i + \epsilon_i$ **(11.3)**

An example of this model is shown in Fig. 11.1. When values of x and y are plotted in this fashion, the diagram is called a **scatter diagram.**

As illustration of a problem in which regression might be used to estimate an unknown population relationship, consider the problem facing the management of an executive placement agency. One of the important services this agency provides is the negotiation of salaries for their clients with the hiring corporations. The process of deciding the salary levels is a difficult one, in which most hiring companies presumably attempt to relate this level to a large variety of factors such as past experience, education, recommendations, and age. In general, the only way to determine the nature of such a (population) relationship is on the basis of past data (sample information). If it can be determined that certain of these factors have been related to some definition of success in the past, then this information may be helpful in determining the potential salary level. One of the key variables, for example, is likely to be the past experience. Thus, the relationship between the salary level of a newly hired executive and the number of years experience is likely to be an important one.

Let us denote by x the experience (in years) and by y the salary level. For ease of presentation, the salary levels are in thousands. Thus, y equals 70 for a salary of $70,000. The population in this case might be considered to be all the executives placed by this agency in a specified period of time. Once again it must be pointed out that use of the term "population relationship" does not imply that there is necessarily an exact relationship, which always holds true, between two variables. The variables salary and experience are obviously not related exactly, as more experience will not always lead to a higher salary; still, one would expect to find a positive relationship between mean values of salary and experience. It is therefore meaningful to attempt to determine how changes in the independent variable influence the mean value of a dependent variable. The methods of this chapter enable us to estimate the parameters of the population regression model by using sample data.

We can illustrate the characteristics of a population regression model by assuming (for the moment) that the population parameters for this salary–experience relationship are known quantities. For example, let's assume $\alpha = 40.0$ and $\beta = 2.0$. This means that the population regression line is

$$\textit{Population regression line: } \mu_{y \cdot x} = 40.0 + 2.0x$$

and the population regression model is

$$\textit{Population regression model: } y_i = 40.0 + 2.0x_i + \epsilon_i$$

This regression model is diagrammed in Fig. 11.2, where each dot represents one observation (one executive) in the population. The value of $\alpha = 40$ represents the point at which the line **intercepts** or cuts through the y-axis; that is, when $x = 0$. The value of $\beta = 2.0$ represents the **slope** of the line; it is the amount of increase (or decrease if β is negative) in the mean value of y for every one unit increase in x. This implies that α is measured in the same units as y (thousands of dollars in this example) and β is measured in the units of y divided by the units of x (thousands of dollars per year of experience).

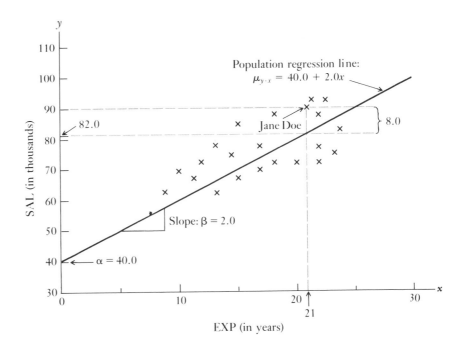

Figure 11.2

Population regression line for the salary example.

In Fig. 11.2 the population mean value when $x = 21$ is seen to be

$$E[y|21] = \mu_{y \cdot 21} = 82.0$$

In other words, the average salary for all executives with an experience of 21 years is \$82,000. This value is easily derived by substituting $x_i = 21$ into the population regression line, as follows:

$$\mu_{y \cdot 21} = 40.0 + 2.0(21) = 82.0$$

Now, let's assume one executive in this population, "Jane Doe," had 21 years of experience, and she earned a starting salary of $y_i = 90$ (\$90,000). For her the value of the error ϵ_i is

$$\epsilon_i = y_i - \mu_{y \cdot 21} = 90.0 - 82.0 = 8.0$$

Our assumption that α and β are known is, of course, an unrealistic one. Usually, α and β can only be estimated on the basis of sample data. For example, we might use as sample data salary and experience values of all executives placed by this agency in the past six months. The discussion in the following section introduces the sample regression model as the basis for estimating α and β.

The Sample Regression Model

To estimate the population regression line, we generally take a sample and develop a line from these sample points. This is called the **sample regression line** and has the same form as the population regression line (Formula 11.1):

$$\boxed{\text{Sample regression line: } \hat{y} = a + bx} \qquad (11.4)$$

Here a is the best estimate for α; b the best estimate for β; and $\hat{y}$ the resulting estimate of $\mu_{y \cdot x}$. The values a and b are called the **regression coefficients.**

Just as we did for the population regression line, we can add the subscript i to these variables to indicate specific values. Thus, if x_i is a specific value of x, then $\hat{y}_i = a + bx_i$ is the equation for finding $\hat{y}_i$, which is the best estimate of $\mu_{y \cdot x_i}$ for this value of x. We can also specify a sample regression model just as we specified a population regression model. Again we need to define an error term, which in this case is the difference between the predicted value $\hat{y}_i$ and the actual value y_i. This error term is denoted as e, which means that the sample regression error e_i is an estimate of the population error ϵ_i. The errors e_i are often called **residuals.**

$$\text{Residuals: } e_i = y_i - \hat{y}_i \qquad \text{or} \qquad y_i = \hat{y}_i + e_i$$

If we substitute the value $y_i = \hat{y}_i + e_i$ into Formula (11.4), we get the sample regression model:

$$\boxed{\textit{Sample regression model: } y_i = a + bx_i + e_i} \qquad (11.5)$$

Suppose we illustrate the concept of a sample regression model by assuming that the placement agency in our salary example has selected a random sample of executives placed, one of whom is Jane Doe. Figure 11.3 shows these observations in a scatter diagram; the line drawn through these points is the sample regression line (we will explain later how this line was derived). From Fig. 11.3 we see that

$$a = 39.4057 \qquad \text{and} \qquad b = 2.0513$$

and the sample regression line is

$$\hat{y} = 39.4057 + 2.0513x$$

Note that, on the basis of our sample regression line, we predict that the mean salary of all executives with an experience of 21 years will be

$$\hat{y}_i = 39.4057 + 2.0513(21) = 82.483$$

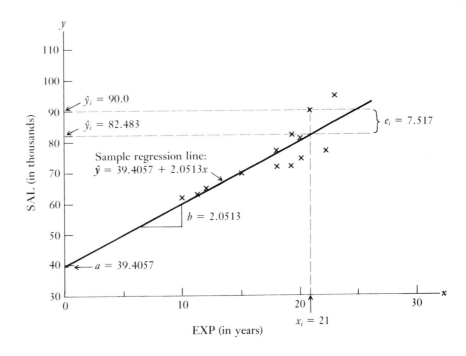

Figure 11.3

Sample scatter diagram of observed values for y and x.

We can also determine the amount of "error" in predicting Jane Doe's salary by recalling that her salary was $y_i = 90$ (\$90,000). The value of ϵ_i is therefore

$$e_i = y_i - \overset{\wedge}{y_i} = 90.0 - 82.483 = 7.517$$

Thus, the value of $a = 39.4057$ is an estimate of $\alpha = 40.0$; $b = 2.0513$ is an estimate of $\beta = 2.0$; and for Jane Doe, the error $e_i = 7.517$ is an estimate of the true error $\epsilon_i = 8.0$.

Now that we have specified the sample and population regression model, we need a procedure for determining values of a and b that provide the best estimates of α and β. The procedure for finding such estimates is called the **method of least squares.**

Estimating the Values of α and β by Least Squares

11.2

A first step in finding a sample regression line of best fit is to plot the data in a scatter diagram. Such a plot allows us to visually determine whether a straight-line approximation to the data appears reasonable, and to make rough estimates of a and b by freehand drawing. Although this approach often yields fairly satisfactory results, there are at least two reasons for having a more systematic approach to finding the best straight-line fit to the data. First, different people are likely to find slightly different values for a and b by this method. Second, the freehand estimation procedure provides no way of measuring the sampling errors, which are always important in forming confidence intervals or doing tests of hypotheses on population parameters.

What we need is a mathematical procedure for determining the sample regression line that best fits the sample data. The difficulty in establishing such a mathematical procedure to give the line of best fit is in determining the criterion to use in defining "best fit." Perhaps the most reasonable criterion is to find values a and b so that the resulting values of $\hat{y}$ (in the equation $\hat{y} = a + bx$) are as close as possible to the actual values y_i. That is, we want to minimize the values of e_i, where $e_i = y_i - \overset{\wedge}{y_i}$ (which, in Fig. 11.3, is seen to be the vertical distance from $\overset{\wedge}{y_i}$ to y_i).

The approach almost universally adopted to find the line of best fit in regression analysis is to determine the values of a and b which minimize the sum of the squared errors. This procedure is known as the **method of least squares.** Since $e_i = y_i - \overset{\wedge}{y_i}$, this method is defined as follows:

Method of least-squares estimation:

$$\text{Minimize } \sum_{i=1}^{n} e_i^2 = \sum_{i=1}^{n} (y_i - \overset{\wedge}{y_i})^2 \tag{11.6}$$

By minimizing the sum of the squared errors (the vertical deviations), the method of least squares is assuming, in effect, that the values of the independent variable are fixed quantities, known in advance, and that the only random element is the value of the dependent variable. That is why we have defined the population regression line as the conditional distribution of y, given x. Suppose that we are testing a new type of automobile engine for the length of time it takes a certain part to wear out, relative to the speed at which the engine is run. The regression relationship in this case might logically be tested by running the engine at a number of predetermined speeds, say 30, 40, 50, and 60 miles per hour, and noting the time to failure. Controlled experiments such as this are common in agricultural research, in studying the effect of certain predetermined levels of various types of fertilizers on crop yields. In other cases, however, it is not obvious that the independent variable can always be treated as a fixed quantity. In determining the relationship between the height and weight of college freshmen, for instance, both variables should probably be considered as random variables. Fortunately, the assumption that the values of x are fixed quantities (rather than a random variable) is not a crucial one in least-squares regression analysis, so that it is possible to apply the technique even when both x and y are random variables.

Determining the least-squares regression line requires finding those values of a and b that minimize $\sum_{i=1}^{n} (y_i - \hat{y}_i)^2$, which is equivalent to minimizing

$$\sum_{i=1}^{n} [y_i - (a + bx_i)]^2$$

since $\hat{y}_i$ is defined to be equal to $a + bx_i$. For convenience, let

$$G = \sum_{i=1}^{n} (y_i - a - bx_i)^2$$

Then, in order to minimize G, it is necessary to take the partial derivative of G with respect to the variables of concern, set each of these partials equal to zero, and then solve the resulting equations, simultaneously. The reader must take care to understand the fact that the variables in this problem are a and b (not x and y), since it is these two values that are free to vary (x and y are fixed by the data). Hence, it is necessary to set the derivatives equal to zero, and then solve for a and b. Solving yields*

$$\sum_{i=1}^{n} y_i = na + b \sum_{i=1}^{n} x_i \qquad (11.7)$$

---

*Solving first for $\partial G/\partial a$ yields

$$\frac{\partial G}{\partial a} = \sum_{i=1}^{n} 2(y_i - a - bx_i)(-1)$$

$$0 = -2 \sum_{i=1}^{n} (y_i - a - bx_i)$$

which is equivalent to (11.7).
   The same process is followed for $\partial G/\partial b$:

$$\frac{\partial G}{\partial b} = \sum_{i=1}^{n} 2(y_i - a - bx_i)(-x_i)$$

$$0 = -2 \sum_{i=1}^{n} (y_i - a - bx_i)(x_i)$$

which is equivalent to (11.8).

and

$$\sum_{i=1}^{n} x_i y_i = a \sum_{i=1}^{n} x_i + b \sum_{i=1}^{n} x_i^2 \qquad (11.8)$$

Formulas (11.7) and (11.8) are called the **normal equations.** The solution to these two equations for a and b gives the line of "best fit" to the sample data—that is, the regression line that minimizes $\sum_{i=1}^{n}(y_i - \hat{y}_i)^2$. Solving these equations results in the following values for a and b:*

Slope of least-squares line:

$$b = \frac{\dfrac{1}{n-1}\sum_{i=1}^{n}(x_i - \bar{x})(y_i - \bar{y})}{\dfrac{1}{n-1}\sum_{i=1}^{n}(x_i - \bar{x})^2} \qquad (11.9)$$

Intercept of least-squares line:
$$a = \bar{y} - b\bar{x}$$

Two features of the sample regression line should be noted from Formula (11.9). First, note that if we substitute $a = \bar{y} - b\bar{x}$ into the equation $\hat{y} = a + bx$, we get $\hat{y} = \bar{y} + b(x - \bar{x})$. This means that, whenever $x = \bar{x}$, then $\hat{y} = \bar{y}$; hence, the regression line always goes through the point $(\bar{x}, \bar{y})$. Secondly, in minimizing $\sum e_i^2$, the least-squares method automatically sets $\sum e_i = 0$. Thus, the line estimating the average relationship between y and x passes through the point of average $(\bar{x}, \bar{y})$, and splits the scatter diagram of observed points so that the positive residuals (underestimates of the true points) always exactly cancel the negative residuals (overestimates of true points). Such a sample regression line therefore correctly (unbiasedly) estimates the population regression line.

---

*A simpler formula for b may be obtained as follows:

Solving first for a using Formula (11.7) yields

$$a = \frac{1}{n}\sum_{i=1}^{n} y_i - b\left(\frac{1}{n}\right)\sum_{i=1}^{n} x_i$$

Substituting for a in Formula (11.8) gives

$$\sum_{i=1}^{n} x_i y_i = \left[\frac{1}{n}\sum_{i=1}^{n} y_i - b\left(\frac{1}{n}\right)\sum_{i=1}^{n} x_i\right]\sum_{i=1}^{n} x_i + b\sum_{i=1}^{n} x_i^2$$

Finally, solving for b gives

$$b = \frac{\sum_{i=i}^{n} x_i y_i - \frac{1}{n}\sum_{i=1}^{n} x_i \sum_{i=1}^{n} y_i}{\sum_{i=1}^{n} x_i^2 - \frac{1}{n}\left(\sum_{i=1}^{n} x_i\right)^2}$$

This formula for b is known as the computational formula. Although it is simpler to use than (11.9) for hand calculations, it is expected that a computer package will be used to compute the values of a and b.

TABLE 11.1 **Sample points for salary (y_i) and experience (x_i) and calculation of their means and variances**

(1) (x_i)	(2) (y_i)	(3) $(x_i - \bar{x})$	(4) $(y_i - \bar{y})$	(5) $(x_i - \bar{x})(y_i - \bar{y})$	(6) $(x_i - \bar{x})^2$
10	62	−8.083	−14.5	117.204	65.335
12	65	−6.083	−11.5	69.955	37.003
18	72	−0.083	−4.5	0.374	0.007
15	70	−3.083	−6.5	20.040	9.505
20	81	1.917	4.5	8.627	3.675
18	77	−0.083	0.5	−0.042	0.007
19	72	0.917	−4.5	−4.127	0.841
22	77	3.917	0.5	1.959	15.343
20	75	1.917	−1.5	−2.876	3.675
21	90	2.917	13.5	39.380	8.509
19	82	0.917	5.5	5.044	0.841
23	95	4.917	18.5	90.965	24.177
Sum 217	918	0		346.503	168.917

Mean $\bar{x} = 18.0833$
Mean $\bar{y} = 76.5$

To illustrate the technique of finding a least-squares regression line, consider again the salary example. Suppose we now use the method of least squares to determine a and b for a random sample of 12 observations (that is, 12 executives). Columns 1 and 2 in Table 11.1 give the data for these executives. We will use the rest of the data in Table 11.1 in a moment.

The first step in analyzing the data in the first two columns of Table 11.1 is to construct a scatter diagram, to see if the assumption of linearity is a reasonable one in this case. Figure 11.4 indicates that it is. Also, the plot indicates a positive relationship, which implies that the slope of the regression line, b, will be positive. An inverse (negative) relationship leads to a negative slope.

The sums in columns 5 and 6 of Table 11.1 give the information necessary to calculate a and b. Using Formula (11.9), we can determine b as follows:

$$b = \frac{\dfrac{1}{n-1}\sum_{i=1}^{n}(x_i - \bar{x})(y_i - \bar{y})}{\dfrac{1}{n-1}\sum_{i=1}^{n}(x_i - \bar{x})^2} = \frac{346.503/11}{168.917/11} = 2.0513$$

Using this value of b and the means of y and x shown in columns 1 and 2 of Table 11.1, the value of a is calculated using (11.9) as follows:

$$a = \bar{y} - b\bar{x} = 76.5 - 2.0513(18.0833) = 39.4057$$

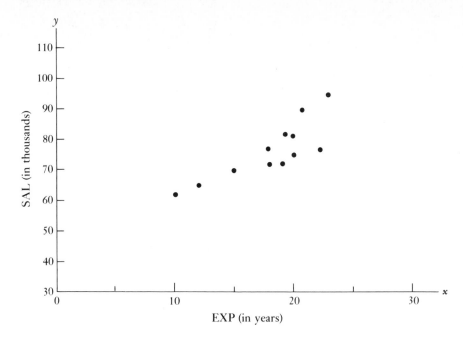

Figure 11.4
Scatter diagram for the
salary–experience sample
values.

Hence, the least-squares regression line for this example (rounded-off to four decimal places) is

$$\hat{y} = 39.4057 + 2.0513x \qquad (11.10)$$

Figure 11.5 illustrates this sample regression line. Since the line in Fig. 11.5 was determined by the method of least squares, there is no other line that could be drawn such that the sum of the squared residuals between the points and the line (measured in a vertical direction) could be smaller than for this line. The residuals and the estimated mean values of y_i for all 12 sample points are given in Table 11.2. Note that the sum of errors is equal to -0.001, and not zero, due to rounding-off errors.

At this time the reader should check on how well the least-squares regression line is understood by verifying that the point of mean $(\overline{x}, \overline{y})$ does lie on the line, and by examining the corresponding values of the errors (or **residuals** as they are often called) in Table 11.2. Note from Fig. 11.5 that a positive residual such as $e_5 = 0.568$ means that the point (x_5, y_5) lies above the line and therefore, $\hat{y}_5$ underestimates y_5. On the other hand, a negative residual such as $e_7 = -6.380$ corresponds to an overestimation of y_7 by $\hat{y}_7$, in that the point (x_7, y_7) lies below the regression line.

Further Discussion of the Estimators *a* and *b*

The least-squares regression line described by Formula (11.10) serves several related purposes. First, the regression coefficients provide point estimates of the population parameters, 39.4057 being an estimate of α, and 2.0513 an estimate of β. These point estimates, and the interval estimates that can be derived

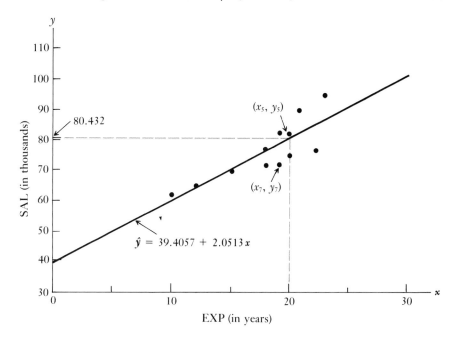

Figure 11.5
The least-squares regression
line $\hat{y} = 39.4057 + 2.0513x$.

**TABLE 11.2   Observed, estimated and residual values for
the least-squares regression shown in Fig. 11.5**

x_i	Observed value (y_i)	Predicted value $(\hat{y}_i = 39.4057 + 2.0513x_i)$	Residual $e_i = (y_i - \hat{y}_i)$
10	62	59.919	2.081
12	65	64.021	0.979
18	72	76.329	− 4.329
15	70	70.175	− 0.175
20	81	80.432	0.568
18	77	76.329	0.671
19	72	78.380	− 6.380
22	77	84.534	− 7.534
20	75	80.432	− 5.432
21	90	82.483	7.517
19	82	78.380	3.620
23	95	86.586	8.414
Sum 217	918		− 0.001

from them, serve a variety of research needs. Economists, for example, use regression analysis in an attempt to test various assumptions about population characteristics of economic concepts, such as marginal propensity to consume, the price elasticity of demand, and the factor shares of labor and capital in production, and to study the effect of changes in one variable (such as a tax change) on one or more other variables (such as consumption). Knowing the regression line also enables us to use the values of $\hat{y}$ to estimate the conditional mean of the dependent variable, $\mu_{y \cdot x}$, for specific values of x. Perhaps most important, the regression line permits prediction of the actual values of the dependent variable, given a value of the independent variable.

For example, suppose an executive has 20 years' experience ($x_i = 20$) and we would like to predict the salary (y_i) that this person will earn. The best estimate of y_i, using Formula (11.10), is given by $\hat{y}_i$, which in this case is

$$\hat{y}_i = 39.4057 + 2.0513(20) = 80.432$$

This value of $\hat{y}_i$ is shown in Fig. 11.5.

In using a regression line to make predictions about the dependent variable, special care must be taken when the value of the independent variable falls outside the range of past experience (historical data), since it may be that these values cannot be represented by the same equation.

Additional precaution in using regression is needed in order to avoid the **regression fallacy.** This fallacy occurs when one attempts to relate the values of a variable at one point in time to the comparable values of that same variable at some other point in time. The problem in using regression or correlation in this circumstance arises because of the tendency for unusually high or low values of a random variable to be followed by more average values. For example, students scoring abnormally high or low on a midterm exam tend to have more average grades on the final. A corporation earning exceptionally high or low profits in one year is likely to have more nearly average profits the next year. This is not to imply that these observations are not related—students do tend to make consistently high or low exam scores, and the profits a corporation earns in one period are related to those in another period. The random fluctuations in such variables, however, will produce a spurious convergence that will often cause the regression line to have a slope less than would be expected. For example, in Galton's research relating the heights of fathers to the heights of their sons, he found that the regression line had a slope of less than the expected 45° line, as shown in Fig. 11.6. This inclination below the 45° should not interpreted as a "regression to mediocrity," but rather the convergence of chance variations to the mean.

Several aspects of the method of least squares need to be emphasized at this point. First, this method is just a curve-fitting technique, and as such it requires no assumptions about the distribution of x or y. It is only when probability statements about the parameters of the population are desired that such assumptions are necessary. Second, the method of least squares can be adapted to apply to nonlinear populations. Although the formulas necessary for applying the method of least squares to a nonlinear relationship will naturally differ from those used for linear relationships, the objective in fitting the curve

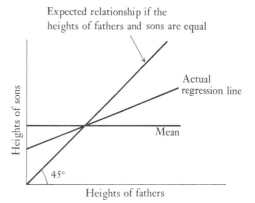

Figure 11.6
The regression fallacy.

is the same in the two cases—to find the line minimizing the sum of the squared residuals. Nonlinear regression models, which are often quite complex, will be discussed briefly in Chapter 13.

When certain assumptions are made about the population, then the resulting estimators a and b can be shown to be unbiased, consistent, and efficient. Furthermore, these assumptions permit us to construct the confidence intervals and test the hypotheses that are so crucial to regression analysis. In other words, the assumptions provide the rationale behind the widespread use of the least-squares approach. In every regression-analysis problem, the researcher must therefore be satisfied that such assumptions are reasonable. The assumptions are concerned with the random variable ϵ, for this variable describes how well $\mu_{y \cdot x_i}$ estimates y_i. Making assumptions about the mean and the variance of ϵ enables us to make inferences about this variable on the basis of the sample values of e.

Assumptions and Estimation

11.3

Many possible sets of assumptions about the distribution of the variables in the population regression model can be formulated. Five assumptions are commonly used because they yield relatively simple estimators possessing many desirable properties, and they result in test statistics that follow commonly known distributions. The following section describes these five assumptions of simple linear regression.

The Five Assumptions

Assumption 1. The random variable ϵ is assumed to be statistically independent of the values of x.

This means that the values of the independent variable are not related to the corresponding error terms. This assumption will be true necessarily when x is

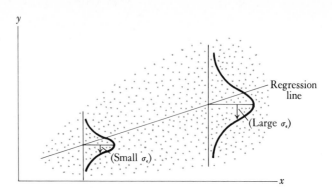

Figure 11.7
Violation of assumption 1
(and assumption 5).

a fixed variable with values known in advance, rather than a random variable with values drawn from an underlying sampling distribution.* When x is a fixed variable, it must be independent of the random variable ϵ. When x is a random variable, this assumption may be violated. Suppose that the errors are a percentage of the values of x because of measurement error. For example, let y be aggregate consumption and x be national income measured over time. Since these values have increased by a factor of 10 since World War II, it is likely that the size of typical errors of measurement has also increased. Thus, the random variable ϵ is larger today than it was in 1946. In this case, the probability of observing larger errors increases as the size of the variable x increases, as shown in Fig. 11.7.

Other violations of assumption 1 may occur when an important variable is omitted from the regression analysis. Let us consider the problem of estimating demand for U.S. compact cars where the quantity demanded is y and the price of compacts is x. For simplicity, suppose that we assume that the only variable of importance omitted from this model is the price of the substitute good, import compacts. If the price of U.S. compacts increases, we would expect a lower demand for U.S. compacts, assuming that all other factors are equal. But all other factors are not equal, as demand also depends on the price of imports. If, as the price of U.S. compacts increases, it becomes more and more difficult to predict demand (that is, the errors increase because we do not know what will happen to the price of imports), then assumption 1 is violated. Figure 11.8 illustrates this situation by a diagram showing errors on the y-axis.

Many other examples can be cited in which behavior is fairly exact for moderate values of the independent variable, but erratic for extreme high or low values of x. These also correspond to violations of assumption 1. Suppose that y is investment expenditures by firms and x is annual growth in sales. If sales growth is 5% to 10%, firms might make corresponding investment

---

*Both of these interpretations about x are commonly used in regression analysis. With proper handling, the calculational and interpretive results presented in this chapter can be used when x is a random variable as well as when it is a fixed variable.

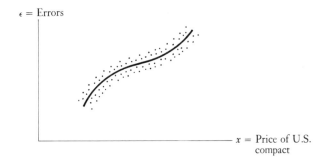

Figure 11.8
Illustration of how larger
values of *x* may lead to
larger errors.

expenditures to replace worn-out equipment and buy some new goods to allow for some expansion of production. This behavioral response would be quite consistent across firms. However, suppose that sales growth for a group of firms was 75% to 100%. More variation in response could be expected. Some might feel very optimistic and make large investment expenditures to double their output. Others might be very cautious and feel that the sales growth was a one-time increase. They might save the extra revenues temporarily and not expand at all. They might not even replace what wears out, and use the current sales figures as motivation to sell out at a good price. Large variations in investment decisions could also be expected in response to a sudden downturn indicated by a negative growth in sales. Thus, the errors ϵ would be quite large in estimating investment at a high (or low) level of sales growth because the behavior predicted in the model is not systematic under these circumstances. The error ϵ and the sales growth *x* are not independent because the relation fits much better (small ϵ) in the range of *x* where investment behavior is consistent, and fits much worse (large ϵ) in the ranges of *x* where firms make widely different decisions on investment expenditures. Figure 11.9 represents this situation.

Assumption 2. The random variable ϵ is assumed to be normally distributed.

Since ϵ_i is a composite of many factors (such as errors of measurement, errors in specifying the model, or irregular errors such as economic, political, social, and business fluctuations), it is reasonable to expect that many of these

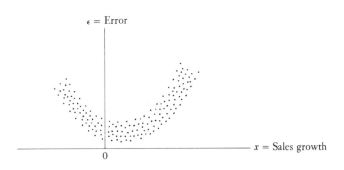

Figure 11.9
Illustration of errors
dependent on sales growth.

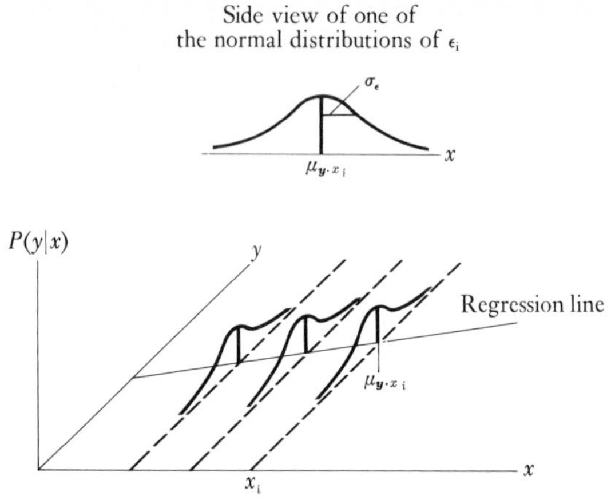

Figure 11.10
Normally distributed errors
ϵ_i about $\mu_{y \cdot x_i}$, for any value x_i
(given that assumptions 3
and 5 also hold).

factors tend to offset each other so that large values of ϵ_i are much less likely than small values of ϵ_i. Indeed, if many of these factors are unrelated, a form of the central limit theorem guarantees that their joint effect (represented by ϵ_i) will be approximately normally distributed. Figure 11.10 illustrates the meaning of this assumption by showing the normal distribution of errors ϵ_i about the population straight-line relationship between y and x.

> **Assumption 3.** The variable ϵ is assumed to have a mean of zero; that is, $E[\epsilon] = 0$.

Assumption 3 means that, for a given x_i, the differences between y_i and $\mu_{y \cdot x}$ are sometimes positive, sometimes negative, but on the average are zero. Thus, the distribution of ϵ_i about the population regression line $\mu_{y \cdot x}$ (as shown in Fig. 11.10) is always centered at the value $\mu_{y \cdot x_i}$ for any given x_i. Assumption 3 establishes the estimability of α. That is, only when $E[\epsilon] = 0$ can one get an unbiased estimate of α using the method of least squares.

> **Assumption 4.** Any two errors, ϵ_k and ϵ_j, are assumed to be statistically independent of each other.

Assumption 4 means that the error of one point in the population cannot be related systematically to the error of any other point in the population. In other words, knowledge about the size or sign of one or more errors does not help in predicting the size or sign of any other error. For example, knowing that the error in describing the salary of one (or more) executive is positive does not give you any help in determining whether or not the error for another executive will also be positive.

This assumption is violated most commonly when observations are drawn periodically over time (time-series data). A simple graph of the values of ϵ over time that indicates such a violation is shown in Fig. 11.11. Figure 11.11(a), for example, might represent long-term changes in the prime inter-

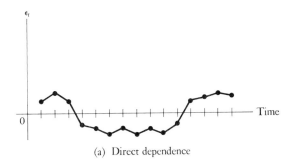

(a) Direct dependence

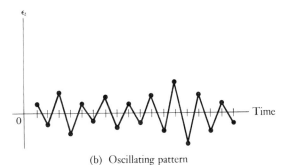

(b) Oscillating pattern

Figure 11.11
Time-sequence plots of
errors ϵ.

est rate, where time is measured in months or years. Figure 11.11(b), on the other hand, could represent fluctuations in the amount of electrical usage in a city, where time is measured in 12-hour periods.

Assumption 5. The random variables ϵ_i are assumed to have a finite variance σ_ϵ^2 that is constant for all given values of x_i.

This means that the dispersion or variability of points in the population about the population regression line must be constant. In Fig. 11.10 this constant variance of ϵ_i is represented by depicting all the normal distributions about $\mu_{y \cdot x}$ as having the same standard deviation. No one distribution is more spread out or more peaked than another for a different value of x.

Assumption 5 is violated in data measured over time as well as at the same point of time (cross-sectional data). For example, in a study relating per capita income and state monies allocated for highway repair across the United States, assumption 5 might be violated because of differing state legal codes, climate, or political interests. Similarly, a study relating educational attainment and household income might be affected by differing races or locations (urban, suburban, rural). Figure 11.12 illustrates a case in which the distribution of errors is more spread out (has a large variance of ϵ) for higher values of x than for lower values of x.

When assumption 1 is violated because of proportional errors in measuring x, assumption 5 (constant variance) will be violated. Thus, Fig. 11.7 is also an illustration of the violation of assumption 5, because the distribution of errors is more spread out (has larger variances) for higher values of x than for

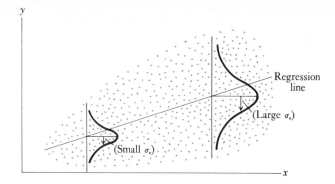

Figure 11.12
Increasing variance of ϵ as x increases (reproduction of Fig. 11.7).

lower values of x. Usually, assumption 5 is referred to as the assumption of **homoscedasticity**. Populations that do not have a constant variance are called **heteroscedastic**.

Properties of the Regression Coefficients

As indicated previously, the five assumptions presented above provide the rationale for the widespread use of the least-squares procedure. Given assumption 2, it can be shown that the estimators of x, β, and $\mu_{y \cdot x_i}$ obtained by using the least-squares criterion are identical to the estimators that would result using the principle of maximum likelihood estimation. Such estimators have a number of desirable properties (such as consistency).

A second important result related to the least-squares estimators is called the Gauss–Markov theorem. This classical result of linear estimation was formulated by the German mathematician and astronomer Karl F. Gauss (1777–1855) in his early works published in 1807 and 1821. Since these involved applications in physics and planetary motion, they generally remained unknown to social scientists and business executives until they were restated in a more modern context by A. A. Markov in 1912, in a study of linear processes. In the 1930s the work of Markov was extended and applied directly to least-squares estimation in several ways, and the Gauss-Markov theorem assumed the identity it has today:

Gauss–Markov theorem   If assumptions 1, 3, 4, and 5 hold true, then the estimators of α, β, and $\mu_{y \cdot x}$ determined by the least-squares criterion are best linear unbiased estimators (BLUE).

In this context, the term "linear" means that the estimators are straight-line functions of the values of the dependent variable y. They are unbiased because their expected value is equal to the population value (given that assumptions 1 and 3 are true). They are best in the sense of being efficient (if assumptions 4 and 5 are true). That is, the least-squares estimators have a variance smaller than that of any other linear unbiased estimator. Thus, the importance of the Gauss–Markov theorem is that if assumptions 1, 3, 4, and 5 hold, then the least-squares estimators have the desirable properties of unbiasedness and efficiency.

Problems

11.1 **a)** Describe what is meant by the method of least squares. What is a least-squares regression line?

  b) What assumptions about the parent population are necessary to fit a least-squares regression line to a set of observations?

  c) What assumptions about the parent population are necessary to make interval estimates on the basis of a least-squares regression line?

11.2 Explain why a disturbance term ϵ is included in the population regression line.

11.3 If the variables x and y have a positive relationship, what would the scatter diagram of the x and y values look like? What would it look like if they had a negative relationship?

11.4 In a population regression equation $\mu_{y \cdot x} = \alpha + \beta x$, explain the interpretation of α and β.

11.5 A random sample of 15 new 1990 model cars gives the following relationship between the fuel efficiency, as measured by the miles per gallon (MPG), and the size of the engine (ENG) in cubic inches: MPG = 43.946 − 0.1068ENG.

  a) Interpret the values of the intercept and the slope.

  b) What would the MPG of a car with an engine size of 94.0 cubic inches be?

  c) Two cars chosen at random have engine sizes of 96.0 and 145.0 cubic inches. What would the expected difference in the MPG of these two cars be?

11.6 Table 11.3 lists the Graduate Management Admission Test (GMAT) scores and the subsequent performance, as measured by the grade point average (GPA), of a sample of 10 MBAs taken at graduation in 1990 at a large midwestern university.

  a) Draw a scatter diagram for these data. Fit a straight line by the freehand method. Does a linear relationship seem appropriate?

  b) Find the least-squares regression line for predicting the GPA for an MBA student on the basis of the GMAT score.

  c) Interpret the slope and the intercept of the regression line from part (b).

11.7 Refer to the information in Problem 11.6. Using the least-squares line from part (b), calculate the fitted values and the residuals for the GPA–GMAT example.

TABLE 11.3

GMAT Score	GPA
480	3.18
515	3.26
523	3.22
534	3.30
570	3.50
582	3.15
588	3.70
590	3.60
610	3.75
640	3.70

11.8 Refer again to the information in Problem 11.6.

    a) Using the least-squares line from part (b), what GPA would you predict for a student with a GMAT score of 575? 675?

    b) How would you interpret the GPA for a GMAT score of 800?

    c) For what approximate range of GMAT scores would you consider this regression line to be appropriate? Explain your answer.

11.9 Table 11.4 lists the number of people employed (in millions) in manufacturing industries and the total sales (in billions of constant 1976 dollars) of these companies in the United States from 1976 to 1986.

TABLE 11.4

Year	No. of employees (millions)	Total yearly sales (billions of 1976 dollars)
1976	18.99	1209.00
1977	19.65	1247.52
1978	20.51	1305.36
1979	21.04	1366.20
1980	20.29	1310.53
1981	20.17	1352.52
1982	18.85	1202.52
1983	18.68	1207.90
1984	19.55	1279.71
1985	19.37	1233.51
1986	19.09	1153.11

Sources: Statistical abstract of the United States, 1988, and Standard and Poor's Current Statistics, May 1988.

    a) Draw a scatter diagram of the total sales (on the y-axis) against the number of employees (on the x-axis). Does a linear relationship seem appropriate?

    b) Find the least-squares regression line for predicting the total sales (in billions) for manufacturing on the basis of the number of manufacturing employees.

    c) Interpret the slope of the regression line.

    d) Using the least-squares line from part (b), calculate the fitted values and the residuals.

11.10 Refer to the information in Problem 11.9. Using the least-squares line from part (b), what would you predict for total sales (in constant 1976 dollars) if the number of employees in 1987 decreased to 19 million? Increased to 19.5 million?

11.11 Prove that a least-squares regression line always passes through the point $(\bar{x}, \bar{y})$.

The Standard Error of the Estimate

11.4

The Components of Variability

Presentation of the standard error of the estimate will be more easily understood if we first examine some of the components of variability in regression analysis.

In regression analysis the difference between y_i and the mean of the y values $(\bar{y})$ is often called the total deviation of y; that is, it represents the total amount by which the ith observation deviates from the mean of all y values. Now it is not too hard to show that this total deviation can be written as the sum of two other deviations, one of which is $(y_i - \hat{y}_i)$, and the other is $(\hat{y}_i - \bar{y})$. Since the deviation $(\hat{y}_i - \bar{y})$ is the part of total deviation that is "explained" (accounted for by the regression line), this term is called **explained deviation.** On the other hand, the deviation $(y_i - \hat{y}_i)$ is the error for the ith sample observation, and since we have no basis for explaining why it occurred, this term is called **unexplained deviation.** That is,

$$
\begin{array}{ccccc}
\text{Total} & & \text{Unexplained} & & \text{Explained} \\
\text{deviation} & = & \text{deviation} & + & \text{deviation} \\
(y_i - \bar{y}) & = & (y_i - \hat{y}_i) & + & (\hat{y}_i - \bar{y})
\end{array}
\tag{11.11}
$$

This relationship is illustrated in Fig. 11.13 in the context of the salary–experience example for the sample point $x_i = 21$ and $y_i = 90$ (see Table 11.2). For $x_i = 21$, the regression line gives $\hat{y}_i = 82.483$. With $\bar{y} = 76.5$, the total deviation $(y_i - \bar{y})$ is 13.5. Of this, the unexplained deviation $(y_i - \hat{y}_i)$ is 7.517 and the explained deviation $(\hat{y}_i - \bar{y})$ is 5.983.

Because the two parts of total deviation shown in Formula (11.13) are independent, it can be shown* that this same relationship holds when we square each deviation, and sum over all n observations. That is,

$$
\sum_{i=1}^{n} (y_i - \bar{y})^2 = \sum_{i=1}^{n} (y_i - \hat{y}_i)^2 + \sum_{i=1}^{n} (\hat{y}_i - \bar{y})^2
\tag{11.12}
$$

---

*To prove this statement, observe that

$$
\begin{aligned}
\sum (y_i - \bar{y})^2 &= \sum [(y_i - \hat{y}_i) + (\hat{y}_i - \bar{y})]^2 \\
&= \sum [(y_i - \hat{y}_i)^2 + 2(y_i - \hat{y}_i)(\hat{y}_i - \bar{y}) + (\hat{y}_i - \bar{y})^2] \\
&= \sum (y_i - \hat{y})^2 + \sum 2(y_i - \hat{y}_i)(\hat{y}_i - \bar{y}) + \sum (\hat{y}_i - \bar{y})^2
\end{aligned}
$$

If the middle term of this last expression equals zero, then we have proved (11.12). By a little manipulation, we can write

$$
\sum 2(y_i - \bar{y}_i)(\hat{y}_i - \bar{y}) = 2b \sum (x_i - \bar{x})(y_i - \hat{y}_i)
$$

The right-hand side was set equal to zero when solving $\partial G/\partial b$ for the least-squares estimate on page 451.

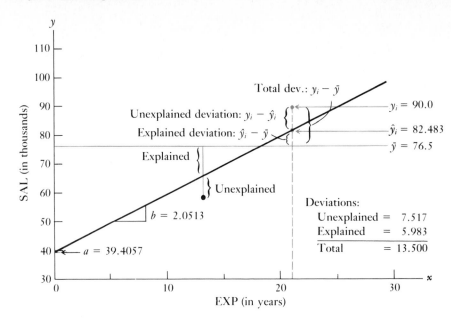

Figure 11.13
Explained and unexplained
variation (see Table 11.2).

The left-hand side of Formula (11.12) is referred to as the total variation, or as the **sum of squares total (SST)**. The first term on the right is the unexplained variation, or equivalently, the **sum of squares error (SSE)**. You should recognize SSE as $\sum e_i^2$, the term that was minimized in finding the least-squares regression line. The last term in (11.12), which is the sum of squares of the values of $\hat{y}$ about $\bar{y}$, is called the explained variation, or the **sum of squares regression (SSR)**. Thus, we can rewrite (11.12) as follows:

$$
\begin{array}{lcccc}
SST & = & SSE & + & SSR \\
\textit{Total} & = & \textit{Unexplained} & + & \textit{Explained} \\
\textit{variation} & & \textit{variation} & & \textit{variation} \\
\sum_{i=1}^{n} (y_i - \bar{y})^2 & = & \sum_{i=1}^{n} (y_i - \hat{y}_i)^2 & + & \sum_{i=1}^{n} (\hat{y}_i - \bar{y})^2
\end{array}
\tag{11.13}
$$

The advantage of breaking total variation into these two components is that we can now talk about goodness of fit in terms of the size of SSE. For example, if the line is a perfect fit to the data, then SSE = 0. Usually, however, the line is not a perfect fit; hence, SSE ≠ 0.

We can calculate SST, SSE, and SSR for the salary example from the data in Tables 11.1 and 11.2. First, SST can be derived by squaring the values in column 4 of Table 11.1. These values are shown in column 1 of Table 11.5. The value of SSE is derived by squaring the errors $e_i = (y_i - \hat{y}_i)$ shown in the final column of Table 11.2. These squares (rounded to three decimals) are shown in

TABLE 11.5   Calculation of SST, SSE, and SSR

(1) y_i	(2) $(y_i - \bar{y})^2$	(3) $(y_i - \hat{y}_i)^2$	(4) $(\hat{y}_i - \bar{y})$	(5) $(\hat{y}_i - \bar{y})^2$
62	210.25	4.332	−16.581	274.940
65	132.25	0.959	−12.479	155.720
72	20.25	18.741	−0.171	0.029
70	42.25	0.031	−6.325	40.003
81	20.25	0.323	3.932	15.458
77	0.25	0.451	−0.171	0.029
72	20.25	40.710	1.880	3.536
77	0.25	56.766	8.034	64.550
75	2.25	29.503	3.932	15.459
90	182.25	56.505	5.983	35.796
82	30.25	13.102	1.880	3.536
95	342.25	70.802	10.086	101.719

Mean = 76.5   SST = 1003.00   SSE = 292.225   SSR = 710.775

column 3 of Table 11.5. Finally, we can calculate SSR $= \sum(\hat{y}_i - \bar{y})^2$ by subtracting $\bar{y} = 76.5$ from each value of $\hat{y}$ in column 3 of Table 11.2, and then squaring these differences. These values are shown in column 5 of Table 11.5. We thus see that

$$SST = SSE + SSR$$
$$1003 = 292.225 + 710.775$$

Standard Error of the Estimate

The measure of the variability about the regression line is the value of SSE divided by its degrees of freedom. Since SSE is the sum of the squared errors, this measure is thus the sample variance of the values of e_i.* The number of degrees of freedom in this measure is $n - 2$, because two sample statistics (a and b) must be calculated before the values of $\hat{y}$ can be computed (since $\hat{y} = a + bx$). Hence,

$$\textit{Variance of errors: } s_e^2 = \frac{1}{n - 2} \sum_{i=1}^{n} (y_i - \hat{y}_i)^2 = \frac{1}{n - 2}(SSE)$$

Since standard deviations are usually easier to interpret than are variances, the usual measure of goodness of fit for regression analysis is the square root of

---

*Recall from Chapter 6 that an unbiased sample variance is calculated by dividing the sum of squared deviations by the degrees of freedom.

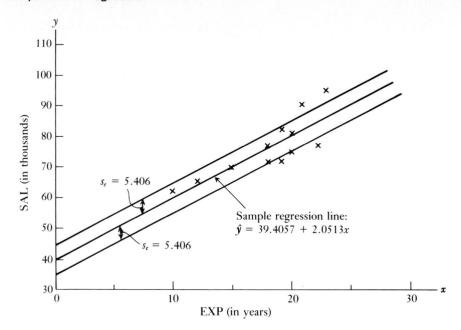

Figure 11.14
A band of one s_e about the regression line.

s_e^2, which is called the **standard error of the estimate** (denoted by the symbol s_e).

$$\textit{Standard error of the estimate:}$$
$$s_e = \sqrt{\frac{1}{n-2}\sum(y_i - \hat{y}_i)^2} = \sqrt{\frac{\text{SSE}}{n-2}} \qquad (11.14)$$

To illustrate the calculation of s_e for the salary example, we need to recall from column 3 of Table 11.5 that $\sum e_i^2 = \text{SSE} = 292.225$. Since $n = 12$ for that example, the value of s_e is

$$s_e = \sqrt{\frac{\text{SSE}}{n-2}} = \sqrt{\frac{292.225}{10}} = 5.406$$

The value of s_e can be interpreted in a manner similar to the sample standard deviation of the values of x about $\bar{x}$. That is, given that assumption 2 holds (the ϵ_i are normal, with mean of zero), then approximately 68.3% of the observations will fall within $\pm 1s_e$ units of regression line, 95.4% will fall within $\pm 2s_e$ units of this line, and 99.7% will fall within $\pm 3s_e$ units of it.* Using this information gives one a good indication of the fit of the regression line to the sample data. In our example, a range of $\pm 3s_e$ would be $\pm 3(5.406) = 16.218$, which means the potential error in estimating salary on the basis of experience

---

*Technically, this interpretation of s_e should be used only when the sample size is relatively large, as it gives an approximation to the correct interval (see Section 11.6). For present purposes, however, we will ignore this distinction.

usually will be less than $16,218. This might be considered a rather large potential error. This is partly due to a small sample size. On the other hand, we see that 7 of the 12 "errors" in the graph shown in Fig. 11.14 fall within one standard error. Also, the largest error is only 8.414.

Test of the
Significance of
the Sample
Regression Line

11.5

We have presented a way of estimating the best regression line fitting the linear relation between y and x, and we have discussed measures of the strength of the linear relationship. However, we have not given any rules or guidelines to help determine whether knowledge of the independent variable x is useful in predicting the values of y_i. Suppose the population relationship is such that $\beta = 0$. This means that the population regression line must be a horizontal straight line, where $\hat{y} = \bar{y}$. Since $\hat{y}$ is a constant whenever $\beta = 0$, the values of x are of no use in predicting y. If β is not equal to zero, then the values of x are meaningful in predicting y. Thus, to determine whether or not the estimation of the y values is improved by using the regression line, we need to test the null hypothesis that $\beta = 0$.

Test on the Slope: A t-Test

Suppose the null hypothesis is

$$H_0: \beta = 0$$

Rejecting H_0 in this case means concluding, on the basis of the sample information given, that β does not equal zero, and hence that the regression line improves our estimate of the dependent variable. The alternative hypothesis for this test might take on a number of different forms. For example, we could use the one-sided alternative that the slope is greater than zero ($H_a: \beta > 0$), or the two-sided alternative would be to hypothesize merely that the slope does not equal zero ($H_a: \beta \neq 0$).

Although these hypotheses are by far the most common forms used, the hypothesized value need not be zero. To illustrate a problem where β is not assumed to be equal to zero, suppose that it is desirable to test the null hypothesis that the slope of the regression line relating personal income and consumption (that is, marginal propensity to consume) has not deviated from some historical value, such as $\beta = 0.90$. If we assume that the alternative hypothesis is two-sided, then the appropriate test is $H_0: \beta = 0.90$ against $H_a: \beta \neq 0.90$. The assumed value of β in such a test is usually denoted as β_0; a two-sided alternative would thus be

$$H_0: \beta = \beta_0 \qquad \text{vs.} \qquad H_a: \beta \neq \beta_0$$

A t-test is used to test the null hypothesis $H_0: \beta = \beta_0$. This test is very similar to the t-test about a population mean, as we are again testing a mean

(β), the population is assumed to be normal (the ϵ_i's), and the population standard deviation is unknown. In the present case, the sample statistic is b (rather than $\bar{x}$), the hypothesized population value is β_0 (rather than μ_0), and the sample standard error is s_b (rather than $s_{\bar{x}}$), where s_b is defined as follows:

Standard error of the regression coefficient b:

$$s_b = s_e \sqrt{\frac{1}{\sum\limits_{i=1}^{n} (x_i - \bar{x})^2}} \tag{11.15}$$

The value of s_b is a measure of the amount of sampling error in the regression coefficient b, just as $s_{\bar{x}}$ was a measure of the sampling error of $\bar{x}$. We can now test the null hypothesis $H_0: \beta = \beta_0$ by subtracting the hypothesized value β_0 from b and dividing by the standard error of the regression coefficient.

Statistic for testing H_0: $\beta = \beta_0$:

$$t = \frac{b - \beta_0}{s_b} \tag{11.16}$$

This statistic follows a t-distribution with $(n - 2)$ degrees of freedom.*

To illustrate the use of Formula (11.16), suppose in our salary example that the null hypothesis $H_0: \beta = 0$ is tested against $H_a: \beta \neq 0$. First, we need to calculate s_b by substituting into Formula (11.15) the previously determined values $s_e = 5.406$ and $\sum (x_i - \bar{x}) = 168.917$. We obtain

$$s_b = 5.406 \sqrt{\frac{1}{168.917}} = 0.4159$$

Therefore,

$$t = \frac{b - \beta_0}{s_b} = \frac{2.0513 - 0}{0.4159} = 4.932$$

For $n - 2 = 10$ degrees of freedom, the probability that t is larger than 4.932 is less than 0.0005 (see Table VII in Appendix B). Thus, the p-value < 0.001, and it is highly unlikely that a slope of $b = 2.0513$ will occur by chance when $\beta = 0$; we can conclude that the regression line does seem to improve our ability to estimate the dependent variable (that is, we reject H_0).

In addition to being able to test hypotheses about β, it is possible to construct a $100(1 - \alpha)\%$ confidence interval for β. Since the regression coeffi-

---

*A similar test statistic could be used to test hypotheses about the population y-intercept α_0, based on the sample estimate a and its standard error (S_a):

$$S_a = \sqrt{S_e^2 \sum_{i=1}^{n} x_i^2 \Big/ \sum_{i=1}^{n} (x_i - \bar{x})^2}$$

The proper t-statistic with $(n - 2)$ degrees of freedom is $t = (a - \alpha_0)/S_a$.

cient b follows a t-distribution with $n - 2$ degrees of freedom and standard deviation s_b, the desired interval is

$$100\,(1 - \alpha)\%\ \text{confidence interval for } \beta:$$
$$b - t_{(\alpha/2,\,n-2)}\,s_b \leq \beta \leq b + t_{(\alpha/2,\,n-2)}\,s_b \tag{11.17}$$

A 95% confidence interval given that $n = 12$,

$$t_{(\alpha/2,\,n-2)} = t_{(0.025,\,10)} = 2.228$$

and $s_b = 0.4159$ would be

$$2.0513 - (2.228)(0.4159) \leq \beta \leq 2.0513 + (2.228)(0.4159)$$
$$1.125 \leq \beta \leq 2.978$$

On the basis of our sample of 12 executives we would thus expect an increase of between \$1125 and \$2978 in average starting salary for each additional year of experience. This is rather a wide interval for any precise forecasting of salaries, but again we must point out that the sample is very small.

Test on the Slope: The *F*-test

There is still another way of testing the null hypothesis H_0: $\beta = 0$, this one using the measures of unexplained and explained variation. This test is commonly referred to as the "overall F-test" and is particularly important because it can be generalized to problems involving more than just one independent variable (it can be generalized to the multiple regression case). This use is discussed in Chapter 13.

Recall that SST = SSE + SSR. You may also recall that the degrees of freedom associated with SST is $n - 1$ (since only $\bar{y}$ needs to be calculated before SST can be computed), while the degrees of freedom for SSE is $n - 2$ (both a and b need to be calculated before computing SSE). Since the degrees of freedom for SST must equal the sum of those for SSE and SSR, we see by subtraction that the degrees of freedom for SSR = 1 [because $(n - 1) = (n - 2) + (1)$]. Now, a sum of squares divided by its degrees of freedom is called a mean square. The two mean squares we will need are mean square error (MSE) and mean square regression (MSR).

$$\text{Mean square error: } \text{MSE} = \frac{\text{SSE}}{n - 2} = s_e^2$$
$$\text{Mean square regression: } \text{MSR} = \frac{\text{SSR}}{1} \tag{11.18}$$

It is customary to present information about MSE and MSR in what is called an **analysis-of-variance (ANOVA) table,** such as Table 11.6. One word

TABLE 11.6   ANOVA table for simple regression

Source of variation	Sum of squares	Degrees of freedom	Mean square
Regression	SSR	1	SSR/1
Error (or residual)	SSE	$n - 2$	SSE/$(n - 2)$
Total	SST	$n - 1$	

of caution is necessary here: Although the sums of squares and the degrees of freedom are additive, it is not true that the mean-square terms are additive. Note, in the analysis-of-variance table, that no MS term is given in the row labeled Total. The SST and the degrees of freedom total are given in the table, so that it can be verified that elements in the body of the table do sum to these values.

To illustrate the use of an analysis-of-variance table, let's construct such a table for the salary example. Recall, from Section 11.4, that

$$SST = 1003 \qquad SSE = 292.225 \qquad SSR = 710.775$$

Hence,

$$MSR = \frac{SSR}{1} = \frac{710.775}{1} = 710.775$$

and

$$MSE = \frac{SSE}{(n - 2)} = \frac{292.225}{10} = 29.223$$

Table 11.7 shows the analysis-of-variance table for this example.

Now we return to our new test of $H_0: \beta = 0$. If the value of MSR is high relative to the value of MSE, then a large proportion of the total variability of y is being explained by the regression line, implying that we should reject this null hypothesis. If, however, MSR is small relative to the MSE, then the regression line does not explain much of the variability in the sample values of y, and the null hypothesis would not be rejected. Thus, the null hypothesis $H_0: \beta = 0$

TABLE 11.7   Analysis of variance for the regression of salary on experience

Source	Sum of squares	Degrees of freedom	Mean square
Regression	710.775	1	710.775
Error	292.225	10	29.223
Total	1003.000	11	

can be tested by using the ratio of the mean squares, MSR/MSE. This ratio can be shown to have an F-distribution with 1 and $(n - 2)$ degrees of freedom.*

> *Statistic for testing: $H_0: \beta = 0$:*
>
> $$F = \frac{\text{MSR}}{\text{MSE}}$$
>
> (11.19)

We can now use the data in Table 11.7 to test the hypothesis $H_0: \beta = 0$. If we choose a significance level of $\alpha = 0.01$, the critical value (from Table VIII(a) in Appendix B) is $F = 10.00$. The decision rule should thus be to reject H_0 if the calculated value of F based on our sample exceeds the value of 10.0.

Using Formula (11.19) and Table 11.7, we calculate the value of F as

$$F = \frac{\text{MSR}}{\text{MSE}} = \frac{710.775}{29.223} = 24.322$$

Since the sample value of F exceeds the critical value of 10.0, we reject the null hypothesis and conclude that the linear relationship does help explain the variation in SAL. Alternatively, a p-value ($p < 0.01$) can be reported.

We see from the above discussion that the F-test is comparable to the t-test for $H_0: \beta = 0$, in that they are both measures of the strength of the relationship in linear regression. In fact, it can be shown that the t-test on β and the F-test are equivalent tests for the significance of the linear relationship between the two variables. The calculated value of F should always equal the square of the calculated value of t. In our example,

$$t^2 = (4.932)^2 = 24.325$$

which differs from $F = 24.322$ only due to rounding errors. The advantage of the F-test is that it can be generalized to a test of significance when there is more than one independent variable, while the t-test cannot. The t-test is more flexible since it can be used for one-sided alternatives while the F-test cannot.

Constructing a Forecast Interval (Optional)

11.6

One of the important uses of the sample regression line is to obtain forecasts of the dependent variable, given some value of the independent variable. The estimated value $\hat{y}_i = a + bx_i$ is the best estimate we can make of both $\mu_{y \cdot x_i}$ (the mean value of y, given a value of x_i) and of y_i (the actual value of y that

---

*Recall that the ratio of two chi-square variables each divided by their degrees of freedom follows the F-distribution. In this case, both SSR and SSE can be shown to be chi-square distributed.

corresponds to the given value x_i). Forecasts of both types are frequently desired. Economists may desire to forecast the average or expected level of unemployment, given assumed values of independent variables under policy control. From such forecasts, they might argue which variables should be affected by policy, by how much, and in what direction, so that unemployment can be expected to be reduced toward a certain policy goal, say, 4% unemployed. In other cases, the forecast of the actual value of the dependent variable may be desired, as, for example, in making predictions of the level of unemployment that will occur in the second quarter of the next year, or of the price of General Motors common stock at the end of this year, or of the total yield of this year's corn crop.

Point Estimates of Forecasts

To obtain the best point estimate for forecasts of both the mean value and the actual value of y, the given value of the independent variable (call it x_g) is substituted into the estimating equation to obtain the forecast value (called $\hat{y}_g$):

$$\hat{y}_g = a + bx_g$$

Thus, $\hat{y}_g$ is an estimate of both $\mu_{y \cdot x_g}$ and y_g.

Suppose that in the salary example we wish to forecast the salary for an executive with $x_g = 25$ years of experience. Using the estimated regression coefficients $a = 39.4057$ and $b = 2.0513$, we obtain

$$\hat{y}_g = a + bx_g = 39.4057 + 2.0513(25) = 90.688$$

Thus, our best estimate for an executive who has 25 years' experience is $\hat{y}_g = 90.688$ ($90,688).

Similarly, our estimate for the mean of all executives having 25 years' experience is also $\hat{y}_g = 90.688$ ($90,688). Although these estimates both equal the same value, we must emphasize that they are interpreted differently. This difference is important for making interval estimates. The confidence interval for estimating a single value is always a lot larger than the confidence interval for estimating the mean value because the former always has a larger standard error.

Interval Estimates of Forecasts

Recall that an interval estimate uses a point estimate as its starting point, and then uses the standard error of the point estimate to find the endpoints of the interval. From the discussion above we know that the starting point is always the same value, $\hat{y}_g$. And, as we pointed out in Section 11.4, the standard error s_e can be used to form the endpoint of the interval when estimating the actual sample value y_g based on the regression estimate, $\hat{y}_g$. For estimates based on values of x not included in the original data, the value of s_e is actually only an approximation to the appropriate standard error. The appropriate standard error is usually called the **standard error of the forecast,** which we will denote as s_f. We write the formula for s_f below in terms of s_e:

$$s_f = s_e \sqrt{1 + \frac{1}{n} + \frac{(x_g - \overline{x})^2}{\Sigma(x_i - \overline{x})^2}} \qquad (11.20)$$

Note that s_f is always larger than s_e since the term under the square root is always greater than 1. Also, note that s_f depends on the particular value of x_g of interest. Finally, we see that if n is large and if the new sample value of x_g is close to $\overline{x}$ (the mean of the previous sample values), then the term under the square root is close to 1.0; hence, s_e and s_f are approximately equal. This result should not be too surprising, for we know that the larger the sample, and the less that a given value x_g deviates from $\overline{x}$, the more faith we have in the sampling results and in the subsequent forecast.

We can now use our point estimate, $\hat{y}_g$, and the standard error s_f, to construct a $100(1 - \alpha)\%$ confidence interval for y_g. The appropriate test statistic in this case is the t-distribution with $(n - 2)$ degrees of freedom.

> *Endpoints of a* $100(1 - \alpha)\%$ *forecast interval for* y_g:
>
> $$\hat{y}_g \pm t_{(\alpha/2,\, n-2)}\, s_f \qquad (11.21)$$

Suppose we want to construct on the basis of our sample of $n = 12$, a 95% forecast interval for the salary of an individual executive with 25 years of experience. From Table VII the value of $t_{(0.025,\, 10)} = 2.228$, and we know from our previous analysis that

$$\hat{y}_{25} = 90.688, \qquad s_e = 5.406, \qquad \overline{x} = 18.083,$$
$$\text{and } \Sigma(x - \overline{x})^2 = 168.917$$

Substituting these values into Formula (11.21), and using the definition of s_f in Formula (11.20), we get the following endpoints for the forecast interval:

$$90.688 \pm 2.228(5.406)\sqrt{1 + \frac{1}{12} + \frac{(25 - 18.083)^2}{168.917}}$$

$$= 90.688 \pm 2.228(5.406)(1.169)$$
$$= 90.688 \pm 14.08$$
$$= 76.608 \text{ and } 104.768$$

We can thus assert, with 95% confidence, that the salary of an executive with 25 years' experience will fall between $76,608 and $104,768.

Now we turn to the problem of constructing a forecast interval for $\mu_{y \cdot x_g}$, the mean of the y-values. In this case the appropriate standard error is denoted by the symbol $s_{\overline{y}}$, where

$$s_{\overline{y}} = s_e \sqrt{\frac{1}{n} + \frac{(x_g - \overline{x})^2}{\Sigma(x_i - \overline{x})^2}} \qquad (11.22)$$

As was the case for s_f, $s_{\bar{y}}$ depends on n, x_g, and s_e. The value for $s_{\bar{y}}$, however, will always be smaller than s_f, since s_f contains one additional positive term under the square-root sign. Again, the appropriate test statistic is the *t*-distribution, with $(n - 2)$ degrees of freedom. The endpoints of a $100(1 - \alpha)\%$ interval are thus

$$
\boxed{
\begin{array}{l}
\textit{Endpoints for a } 100(1 - \alpha)\% \\
\textit{forecast interval for } \mu_{y \cdot x_g}: \\[4pt]
\hat{y}_g \pm t_{(\alpha/2,\, n - 2)}\, s_{\bar{y}}
\end{array}
}
\qquad (11.23)
$$

Substituting the appropriate values in (11.22) for $s_{\bar{y}}$, and using Formula (11.23) for $s_{\bar{y}}$, we obtain the following endpoints:

$$
90.688 \pm 2.228(5.406)\sqrt{\frac{1}{12} + \frac{(25 - 18.083)^2}{168.917}}
$$

$$
= 90.688 \pm (2.228)(5.406)(0.605)
$$
$$
= 90.688 \pm 7.287
$$
$$
= 83.401 \text{ and } 97.975
$$

The interval 83.401 to 97.975 thus represents a 95% forecast interval for the mean salary of all executives with an experience of 25 years ($\mu_{y \cdot 25}$).

Figure 11.15 shows the forecast interval for values of x from $x_g = 10$ to $x_g = 30$ for both $\mu_{y \cdot x_g}$ (the narrow band) and for y_g' (the wide band). As indi-

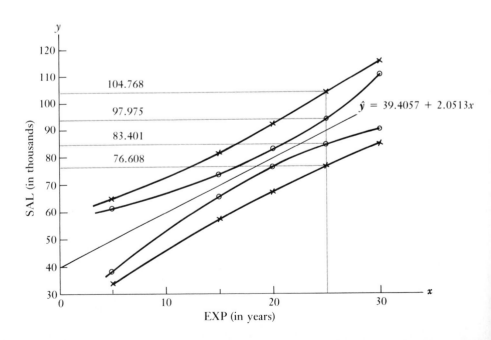

Figure 11.15

Ninety-five percent forecast interval (FI) for $\mu_{y \cdot x_g}$ (narrow band) and y_g (wide band).

cated before, the forecast interval is wider for y_g than for $\mu_{y \cdot x_g}$ because predicting the salary for an individual involves a lot more variability than predicting for an average over many such individuals (that is, s_f is larger than $s_{\bar{y}}$). Note that both bands become increasingly wider for values of x_g farther away from $\bar{x}$. This reflects the fact that the least-squares estimating line is most accurate at the point of means $(\bar{x}, \bar{y})$, since it is a representation of the average relationship between x and y.

Simple Linear Regression: An Example

11.7

The previous sections presented the basic steps in applying the simple linear regression model. In this section we put these steps together by applying them to an example. For this, consider the data in Table 11.8 relating the number of housing starts in the United States to the mortgage interest rates for the period 1977 to 1986.

To carry out the regression analysis for this problem we first hypothesize a model to relate the number of units started y (in thousands) to the mortgage interest rate, x (in percent). We hypothesize the straight-line model presented in the beginning of this chapter

$$\mu_{y \cdot x} = \alpha + \beta x$$

One simple way to verify if this model is reasonable is to plot a scatter diagram (a scattergram) of the y values against the x values. For this data the plot in Fig.

TABLE 11.8 Housing starts vs. mortgage rates

Year	Mortgage interest rate x	Number of new units started (in thousands) y
1977	8.95	1,987
1978	9.68	2,020
1979	11.15	1,745
1980	13.95	1,292
1981	16.52	1,084
1982	15.79	1,062
1983	13.43	1,703
1984	13.80	1,750
1985	12.28	1,742
1986	10.07	1,805

Sources: Bureau of Census, *Statistical Abstract of the United States,* 1985 and 1988.

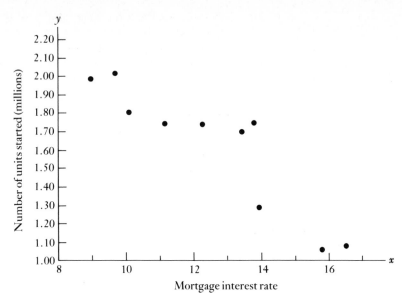

Figure 11.16
Sample scatter diagram of
observed x and y values.

11.16 shows that a linear relationship between these two variables does seem appropriate. Next, the unknown parameters, α and β, are estimated from the sample data using the equations in (11.9). In order to use these equations we first require the following calculations:

$$\bar{x} = 12.562$$
$$\bar{y} = 1619$$

$$\frac{1}{n-1}\sum_{i=1}^{n}(y_i - \bar{y})(x_i - \bar{x}) = -7295.32/9 = -810.5911$$

$$\frac{1}{n-1}\sum_{i=1}^{n}(x_i - \bar{x})^2 = 59.93416/9 = 6.65935$$

Then, the least-squares estimates of the intercept α, given by a, and the slope β, given by b, are

$$b = \frac{-810.59110}{6.65935} = -121.722$$

$$a = \bar{y} - b\bar{x} = 1619 - (-121.722)(12.562) = 3148.072$$

And the least-squares regression equation is

$$\hat{y} = 3148.072 - 121.722x$$

This equation is shown in Fig. 11.17, along with a plot of the data points.

Having calculated the regression equation, we now check the usefulness of the hypothesized model. That is, whether a knowledge of the mortgage interest rates is useful in predicting the number of housing starts in a year. To do this, we test the hypothesis $H_0: \beta = 0$ against the alternative hypothesis $H_a: \beta \neq 0$. That is, the null hypothesis is that no linear relationship exists between mortgage interest rates and the number of housing starts, and the alternative hypothesis is that the slope β is less than zero ($\beta < 0$, implying that the

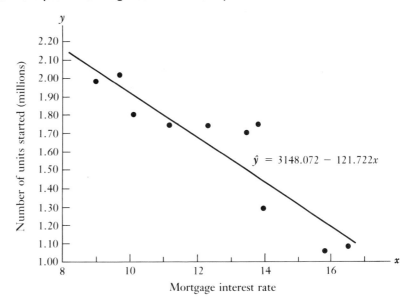

Figure 11.17
The least-squares
regression line
$\hat{y} = 3148.072 - 121.722x$.

estimate of the y value is improved by using the regression line). This test on the slope may be carried out by using either the t-distribution or the F-distribution.

To test these hypotheses using an F-test, we first presented the following quantities, calculated from the data in Table 11.8.

$$\text{SST} = 1,089,446 \qquad \text{SSR} = 888,002.7 \qquad \text{SSE} = 201,443.3$$

Next, we construct the ANOVA table as follows:

Source	SS	d.f.	Mean square
Regression	888002.7	1	888002.70
Error	201443.3	8	25180.42
Total	1089446.0	9	

This leads to the calculation of the F value as

$$F = \frac{\text{MSR}}{\text{MSE}} = \frac{888002.70}{25180.42} = 35.266$$

This F value has 1 degree of freedom in the numerator and 8 degrees of freedom in the denominator, and has a p-value of less than 0.01. A probability as small as this implies that it is highly unlikely that β is equal to 0, and that the alternative hypothesis is true. In other words, the linear relationship does help explain the variation in the number of housing starts.

To test the hypothesis using a t-test, we first need to calculate the standard error of the regression coefficient, s_b, using Formula (11.15). In order to calculate s_b, we require a value for s_e, the standard error of the estimate. s_e^2 is calculated by dividing the SSE by the degrees of freedom for the errors. That is,

$$s_e^2 = \frac{\text{SSE}}{n-2} = \frac{201443.3}{8} = 25180.42$$

$$s_e = \sqrt{25180.42} = 158.683$$

Then,

$$s_b = s_e \sqrt{\frac{1}{\sum\limits_{i=1}^{n}(x_i - \bar{x})^2}}$$

$$= 158.683\sqrt{\frac{1}{59.9342}} = 20.4971$$

This leads to the following t statistic,

$$t_8 = \frac{b - 0}{s_b} = \frac{-121.7220}{20.4971} = 5.938$$

For 8 degrees of freedom, the probability that t is larger than 5.938 is less than 0.0005 (see Table VII in Appendix B). Thus, it is highly unlikely that a slope of $b = -121.722$ will occur by chance when $\beta = 0$. That is, we can conclude that the regression line does seem to improve our ability to estimate the dependent variable.

In addition to being able to test the hypotheses about β with the t-distribution, it is possible to construct a $100(1 - \alpha)\%$ confidence interval for β. Since the regression coefficient b follows a t-distribution with 8 degrees of freedom and standard deviation $s_b = 20.4971$, a 95% interval would be

$$b - t_{(0.025,8)}\, s_b \leq \beta \leq b + t_{(0.025,8)}\, s_b$$

$$-121.722 - 2.306(20.4971) \leq \beta \leq -121.722 + 2.306(20.4971)$$

$$-168.988 \leq \beta \leq -74.456$$

That is, on the basis of our sample of 10 years we would expect a decrease of between 74,456 and 168,988 in the average number of housing starts for each 1% increase in the mortgage interest rate.

We are now in position to use the least-squares model to make forecasts. Suppose we wish to forecast the number of housing starts in a year when the mortgage interest rate is 12%; that is, $x_g = 12$. The predicted value is

$$\hat{y}_g = a + bx_g = 3148.072 - 121.722(12) = 1687.408$$

Thus, our best estimate for the number of housing starts with a mortgage interest rate is $\hat{y}_g = 1,687,408$. A 95% prediction interval for this value is

$$\hat{y}_g + t_{(\alpha/2,\, n-2)}\, s_e \sqrt{1 + \frac{1}{n} + \frac{(x_g - \bar{x})^2}{\sum(x_i - \bar{x})^2}}$$

$$= 1687.408 \pm 2.306(158.683)\sqrt{1 + \frac{1}{10} + \frac{0.31584}{59.9342}}$$

$$= 1687.408 \pm 2.306(158.683)(1.0513)$$

$$= 1687.408 \pm 384.695 = 1302.713 \text{ and } 2072.103$$

That is, with 95% confidence, we can say that the number of housing starts in a year when the mortgage interest rate is 12% will fall between 1,302,713 and 2,072,103.

In addition to the above interval, we can also construct a forecast interval for $\mu_{y \cdot x_g}$, the mean of the y-values. In this case a 95% confidence interval is given by

$$\hat{y}_g \pm t_{(\alpha/2,\, n-2)}\, s_e \sqrt{\frac{1}{n} + \frac{(x_g - \overline{x})^2}{\Sigma(x_i - \overline{x})^2}}$$

$$= 1687.408 \pm 2.306\,(158.683)\sqrt{\frac{1}{10} + \frac{0.31584}{59.9342}}$$

$$= 1687.408 \pm 2.306(158.683)(0.3245)$$

$$= 1687.408 \pm 118.742$$

$$= 1568.666 \text{ and } 1806.150$$

In other words, the interval from 1568.666 (1,568,666 starts) to 1806.150 (1,806,150 starts) represents, with 95% confidence, the number of housing starts for all years when the mortgage interest rate is 12%.

Note of Caution: Caution must be exercised in applying a regression model outside the range of the observations that have been used to estimate the model's parameters and verify its validity. In the above example, we fitted the regression model to observations where the mortgage interest rate was between 8.9% and 16.5%. While the fit appears to be satisfactory for these observations, it is not possible to predict the validity of this model outside this range of $8.9 \leq x \leq 16.5$. Thus, it may not be advisable to use this model for x values less than 8.9% or greater than 16.5%.

Computer Analysis for Simple Linear Regression

11.8

The examples that have been presented in this chapter for simple linear regression have required tedious calculations. Even with a hand calculator, the process is laborious and time-consuming. Thus, much of the computational work for such analysis is performed on the computer using statistical software packages. In this section we present the analysis for the housing starts problem from Section 11.7 using two different statistical computer software packages, B-STAT and Minitab. The B-STAT output for this problem is shown in Fig. 11.18 and the Minitab output in Fig. 11.19. Even though there are many different packages currently on the market, most produce very similar outputs, as illustrated by these two packages. Generally, these outputs differ only in format and labeling. Thus, it should be relatively easy to analyze outputs from other packages. Some of these will be used in Chapters 12 and 13 and also in the problems following this section.

The output from B-STAT for simple linear regression consists of five sets of analysis. The first set consists of the descriptive measures of the data and appears at the top. Here the mean and the standard deviation for each variable in the data are given. For this problem the mean of the x values is 12.562 with a standard deviation of 2.5806 and the mean of the y values is 1619 with a standard deviation of 347.9218. In the second set of analysis we find the estimates of the intercept, a, and the slope, b, along with the t-test for the hypothesis H_0: $\beta \neq 0$. The values for a and b are found under the column titled Regression Coefficient. These are $a = 3148.0747$ and $b = -121.7222$. (Note that the

Figure 11.18
B-STAT printout for simple regression analysis.

INDEX	NAME	MEAN	STD.DEV.
1	x	12.5620	2.5806
DEP. VAR.:	y	1619.0000	347.9218

DEPENDENT VARIABLE. y

VAR.	REGRESSION COEFFICIENT	STD. ERROR	T(DF = 8)	PROB.
X	− 121.7222	20.4972	− 5.938	.00035
CONSTANT	3148.0747			

STD. ERROR OF EST. = 158.6834

r SQUARED = .8151
r = − .9028

ANALYSIS OF VARIANCE TABLE

SOURCE	SUM OF SQUARES	D.F.	MEAN SQUARE	F RATIO	PROB.
REGRESSION	888002.67	1	888002.67	35.266	3.464E−04
RESIDUAL	201443.33	8	25180.42		
TOTAL	1089446.00	9			

	OBSERVED	CALCULATED	RESIDUAL	STANDARDIZED RESIDUALS −2.0 0 2.0
1	1987.00	2058.661	− 71.6607	*
2	2020.00	1969.803	50.1965	*
3	1745.00	1790.872	− 45.8718	*
4	1292.00	1450.050	− 158.0495	*
5	1084.00	1137.223	− 53.2234	*
6	1062.00	1226.081	− 164.0806	*
7	1703.00	1513.345	189.6549	*
8	1750.00	1468.308	281.6921	*
9	1742.00	1653.326	88.6743	*
10	1805.00	1922.332	− 117.3318	*

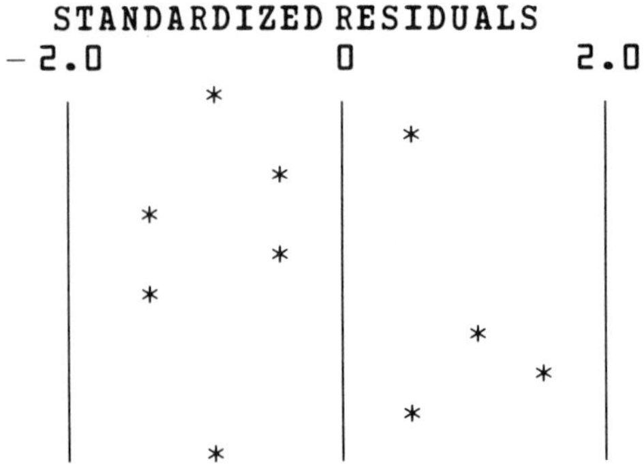

value of a differs from the computation in Section 11.7 only because of rounding errors.) The standard error listed here, equal to 20.4972, refers to the standard error of the regression coefficient, s_b. The values of b and s_b lead to the computation of the t statistic of -5.938. To determine which hypothesis this test statistic supports, we can set up a rejection region using the t table. However, the printout from the package makes this unnecessary because the p-value corresponding to the t statistic (equal to 0.00035) is shown directly to the right of the t statistic under the column heading Prob. Such a low p-value would certainly lead to rejection of H_0.

In the next part of the output we find the standard error of the estimate, s_e, the coefficient of determination, r^2, and the correlation coefficient, r. The r and the r^2 values will be discussed in Chapter 12. The s_e value is shown to be 158.6834. This corresponds to the value that we calculated in Section 11.7.

The analysis-of-variance table appears next. Here we find the SSR, SSE, and SST values under the column heading Sum of Squares and across the row labels Regression, Residual, and Total. The output shows that SSR = 888002.67, SSE = 201443.33, and SST = 1089446.00. The values of SSR and SSE divided by their degrees of freedom lead to the MSR and MSE computations of 888002.67 and 25180.42, respectively. The other figures shown in this table are the F statistic (equal to 35.266) and the p-value that corresponds to this statistic. Note that this p-value rounded off also equals 0.00035.

The final set of analysis in the printout consists of the predicted values (under the column heading Calculated), the error terms (under the column heading Residual) and a plot of the standardized residuals. The predicted values are obtained by substituting the x values (the mortgage interest rates) into the regression equation, $\hat{y} = 3148.0747 - 121.7222x$. The residuals are the difference between the observed y values and the predicted values. Standardized residuals, discussed in Chapter 13, are determined by s_e.

Most statistical packages are very similar in that they essentially perform the same set of analysis. Generally, the only difference between them is in their command structure. Additionally, as mentioned earlier, the outputs from these packages are also very similar. To illustrate this point, we have included an output from Minitab for the problem shown in Fig. 11.18. This is shown in Fig. 11.19. As this figure shows, the output from Minitab is very similar to the output from B-STAT. Thus, it should be relatively easy to interpret regression output from other packages. The major advantage of using a package is that the package alleviates much of the computational burden of regression analysis. This enables us to concentrate more on the model-building and the interpretation of the model. Thus, it is very important that every student learn to use a statistical package for regression analysis.

The reader should verify that Figs. 11.8 and 11.19 give the same results, subject to rounding errors. Also, students with access to Minitab may wish to duplicate Fig. 11.19 by using the data in Table 11.8, and the following commands (assuming C1 contains x and C2 contains y).

MTB > BRIEF OUTPUT LEVEL 3
MTB > REGRES 'C2' ON 1 PREDICTOR IN 'C1'

The regression equation is y = 3148 - 122x

```
Predictor     Coef    Stdev   t-ratio      p
Constant     3148.1   262.3    12.00     0.000
x            -121.72   20.5    -5.94     0.000

s = 158.7   R-sq = 81.5%   R-sq (adj.) = 79.2%
```

Analysis of Variance

```
SOURCE        DF      SS       MS        F       p
Regression     1    888003   888003    35.27   0.000
Error          8    201443    25180
Total          9   1089446
```

```
Obs.    x       y       Fit    Stdv.Fit  Residual  St.Resid
 1     8.9   1987.0   2058.7    89.4      -71.7      -0.55
 2     9.7   2020.0   1969.8    77.5       50.2       0.36
 3    11.1   1745.0   1790.9    57.9      -45.9      -0.31
 4    13.9   1292.0   1450.0    57.7     -158.0      -1.07
 5    16.5   1084.0   1137.2    95.4      -53.2      -0.42
 6    15.8   1062.0   1226.1    83.0     -164.2      -1.21
 7    13.4   1703.0   1513.3    53.2      189.7       1.27
 8    13.8   1750.0   1468.3    56.2      281.7       1.90
 9    12.3   1742.0   1653.3    50.5       88.7       0.59
10    10.1   1805.0   1922.3    71.6     -117.3      -0.83
```

Figure 11.19

Minitab printout for simple regression analysis.

Some of the output in Fig. 11.19 contains concepts we have not yet discussed, but will cover later [e.g., R-Sq, (adj.)]. Also, note that the values of x are rounded to one decimal for this output.

Problems

11.12 Consider the 10 points shown in the table below:

x	5	10	15	20	25	30	35	40	45	50
y	8	21	29	43	47	57	73	80	87	102

a) Find the least-squares line for y against x.

b) Calculate SSE, s_e^2, and s_e.

c) Calculate SSR and SST. What percentage of the variability in y is explained by the values of x?

d) Construct a 95% confidence interval for β.

11.13 It has been claimed that people with more education earn more on the average. The U.S. Bureau of Census reported the following data for 1985:

No. of years of education	Mean income (in dollars)
<8	13,749
8	16,305
9–11	16,935
12	19,543
13–15	22,885
16	30,391
>16	38,707

No. of years of education	Approximate mean
<8	6
8	8
9–11	10
12	12
13–15	14
16	16
>16	18

a) If the approximate mean number of years in each category is as shown in the table to the left draw a scatter diagram of the mean income (on the y-axis) against the approximate mean number of years of education (on the x-axis). Does a linear relationship seem appropriate?

b) Find the least-squares line for income against mean number of years of education.

c) Interpret the slope of this regression line.

11.14 Refer to the information in Problem 11.13.

a) Find SSE, SSR, and SST for this problem.

b) What percentage of the variability in the mean income is explained by the number of years of education?

c) Calculate the s_e value. Explain the interpretation of this value.

11.15 Refer to the information in Problem 11.13.

a) Estimate the mean income for someone with (a) 11 years of education, and (b) 15 years of education. In each case construct a 95% confidence interval.

b) Would it be possible to use the regression line to predict the salary of a person with only 5 years of education? Explain your answer.

11.16 Define or describe each of the following:

a) standard error of the estimate;

b) standard error of the forecast;

c) standard error of the regression coefficient.

11.17 What is the hypothesis of no linear regression? Describe two methods for testing this hypothesis.

11.18 Show that solving the normal equations does, in fact, lead to Formula (11.9).

TABLE 11.9

Size of house (in square feet)	Price ($ thousands)
x	y
3800	242.8
3250	218.5
3740	260.0
2700	185.0
3100	199.0
4250	265.0
2900	191.0
3450	224.0
2500	167.0
2950	204.0

11.19 Table 11.9 lists the prices and the sizes of 10 new houses selected at random from two new subdivisions in Bloomington, Indiana, in September 1989.

   a) Draw a scatter diagram of the prices of the new houses (on the y-axis) against the size of the houses (on the x-axis). What can you say about the relationship between these two variables?

   b) Find the least-squares line for the price of the houses against the size of the houses.

   c) Interpret the value of the slope.

11.20 Refer to the information in Problem 11.19.

   a) Find SSE, SSR, and SST for this problem.

   b) Calculate the s_e and s_b values.

   c) What percentage of the variability in y is explained by the values of x?

11.21 Refer to the information in Problems 11.19 and 11.20.

   a) From the information given in these examples, test the null hypothesis $H_0: \beta = 0$ against $H_a: \beta \neq 0$ by means of an **F**-test.

   b) Calculate the value of **t** necessary for testing the hypothesis of no linear regression. How is this value of **t** related to the value of F you calculated in part (a) above? Show that they both lead to rejection of the null hypothesis at the same level of significance.

11.22 Refer again to the information in Problems 11.19 and 11.20.

   a) Using this information, construct a 95% confidence interval for the value of β.

   b) Using the least-squares line, predict the cost of a new house if the size is equal to 3400 square feet. Construct a 95% interval for this forecast.

   c) Could you use this equation to predict the price of a new house in Chicago? Explain your answer.

11.23 Assume a least-squares regression line was fitted to crop yields from 22 randomly selected acres of land in Nebraska. The relationship between yield (y)

and the amount of fertilizer applied (x, in hundreds of pounds) was $\hat{y} = 16.9 + 1.225x$. For this example SST was determined to be 785. The coefficient of determination (r^2) was calculated to be 0.75.

a) Using this information, complete the following ANOVA table:

Source	Sum of squares	d.f.	Mean square	F-ratio
Regression				
Error				
Total				

b) Test the hypothesis H_0: $\beta = 0$ against H_a: $\beta \neq 0$ using the F-test at $\alpha = 0.05$. What p-value would you report for this test?

11.24 Refer to the data in Problem 11.23. Calculate the value of s_b, the standard error of the regression coefficient. Construct a 95% confidence interval for β.

11.25 A simple linear regression with 11 observations yielded the following ANOVA table:

Source	Sum of squares	d.f.	Mean square
Regression			
Error			1500
Total	2500		

a) Complete this ANOVA table.

b) Test the hypothesis H_0: $\beta = 0$ against H_a: $\beta \neq 0$ using the F-test at $\alpha = 0.05$.

c) What p-value would you report?

11.26 The least-squares analysis shown in the table to the left resulted from a regression relating the beginning salaries of graduating MBA students (y, in thousands) and the number of years of work experience of each student (x).

$\hat{y} = 41.65 + 2.445x$

Source	Sum of squares	d.f.
Regression	1440	1
Error	342	38

a) What was the sample size in this problem? What is SST?

b) Use an F-test to accept or reject the hypothesis H_0: $\beta = 0$ against H_a: $\beta \neq 0$. What p-value would you report?

11.27 Refer to the data in Problem 11.26. Calculate the value of s_e, the standard error of the estimate. Use this information to construct a 95% confidence interval for y if (i) $x = 3.0$ and (ii) $x = 5.0$.

TABLE 11.10

Year	Crude oil price x (\$/barrel)	Gasoline price y (¢/gallon)
1978	9.00	62.6
1979	12.64	85.7
1980	21.59	119.1
1981	31.77	133.1
1982	28.52	122.2
1983	26.19	115.7
1984	25.88	112.9
1985	24.09	111.5
1986	12.66	85.7

Sources: Bureau of Census, *Statistical Abstract of the United States,* 1988, and *Standard and Poor's Current Statistics,* May 1988

11.28 Over the past decade, the price of crude oil has fluctuated dramatically on the world market because of political and market forces. As a result, the price of gasoline at the pump has also fluctuated. Table 11.10 lists the average price for a gallon of regular gasoline and the average price of a barrel of crude oil for the period 1978 to 1986.

a) Draw a scatter diagram of gasoline prices (on the y-axis) against crude oil prices (on the x-axis). What can you say about the relationship between these two variables?

b) Find the least-squares line that describes the relationship between the price of a gallon of gasoline and the price of a barrel of crude oil.

c) What percentage of the variability in y is explained by the values of x?

11.29 Refer to the data in Problem 11.28.

a) From the information given in this example, test the null hypothesis H_0: $\beta = 0$ against H_a: $\beta \neq 0$ using an F-test. What p-value would you report?

b) Repeat the above test of no linear regression using a t-test.

11.30 Refer again to Problem 11.28.

a) Using the information in this problem, forecast the price of a gallon of gasoline if the price of crude oil was \$20 per barrel. Construct a 95% confidence interval for this forecast.

b) Construct a 95% confidence interval for $\mu_{y \cdot x_g}$.

Exercises

11.31 The four data sets in Table 11.11 were presented by F. J. Anscombe in an article in the *American Statistician:*

a) Find the least-squares regression line for each of the four data sets.

TABLE 11.11

I		II		III		IV	
x	y	x	y	x	y	x	y
10.0	8.04	10.0	9.14	10.0	7.46	8.0	6.58
8.0	6.95	8.0	8.14	8.0	6.77	8.0	5.76
13.0	7.58	13.0	8.74	13.0	12.74	8.0	7.71
9.0	8.81	9.0	8.77	9.0	7.11	8.0	8.84
11.0	8.33	11.0	9.26	11.0	7.81	8.0	8.47
14.0	9.96	14.0	8.10	14.0	8.84	8.0	7.04
6.0	7.24	6.0	6.13	6.0	6.08	8.0	5.25
4.0	4.26	4.0	3.10	4.0	5.39	19.0	12.50
12.0	10.84	12.0	9.13	12.0	8.15	8.0	5.56
7.0	4.82	7.0	7.26	7.0	6.42	8.0	7.91
5.0	5.68	5.0	4.74	5.0	5.73	8.0	6.89

b) Examine the residuals for each data set. Comment on your findings.

c) Construct a scatterplot for each data set. Did you anticipate the difference between the sets on the basis of the residuals? Is a linear model appropriate in all four data sets? Explain why or why not for each data set.

11.32 In recent years, the value of the dollar has fluctuated considerably against the major currencies. One result of these fluctuations has been in the number of tourists traveling abroad. Generally, when the dollar is strong, more people travel overseas. The reverse is true when the dollar is weak. Table 11.12 lists the number of visitors from the United States to Western Europe and the exchange rates for the French franc, the German mark, and the British pound for the period 1979 to 1986.

a) Draw a scatter diagram of the number of visitors to Western Europe (on the y-axis) against each of these three currencies. What can you say about the relationship between the number of visitors and these exchange rates?

TABLE 11.12

Year	No. of visitors (in 000's)	Francs per U.S. dollar	Marks per U.S. dollar	Pounds per U.S. dollar
1979	4,068	4.2566	1.8342	0.4712
1980	3,934	4.2250	1.8175	0.4302
1981	3,931	5.4396	2.2631	0.4940
1982	4,144	6.5793	2.4280	0.5731
1983	4,780	7.6203	2.5539	0.6597
1984	5,760	8.7355	2.8454	0.7482
1985	6,457	8.9799	2.9419	0.7708
1986	5,126	6.9256	2.1704	0.6813

Sources: Statistical Abstract of the United States, 1988, and *Standard and Poor's Statistical Service, Current Statistics,* May 1988.

b) Find the least-squares line that describes the relationship between the number of visitors and the exchange rate for (i) the British pound, and (ii) the French franc.

11.33 Refer to the information in Problem 11.32. For part (b), test the null hypothesis $H_0: \beta = 0$ against $H_a: \beta \neq 0$ for both the pound and the franc using the t-test. What p-value would you report for each case?

11.34 Refer to the data in Problem 11.32.

a) If we now create a composite exchange rate for Western Europe by adding the exchange rates for the franc, the mark, and the pound, find the least-squares line that describes the relationship between the number of visitors (y) and this composite exchange rate (x). What can you say about this relationship?

b) What percentage of the variability in y is explained by the values of x?

c) Test the null hypothesis $H_0: \beta = 0$ against $H_a: \beta \neq 0$ using an F-test. What p-value would you report?

11.35 Refer to the information in Problems 11.32 and 11.34. Forecast the number of visitors expected to visit Western Europe if the composite exchange rate was (i) 10, and (ii) 8.5. In each case construct a 95% confidence interval for the forecast.

11.36 Table 11.13 lists the quarterly figures for personal consumption expenditures and personal disposable income in the United States for the period Quarter 1, 1985, to Quarter 1, 1988. Both of these are measured at an annual rate in billions of dollars:

a) Draw a scatter diagram of personal consumption expenditures (on the y-axis) against personal disposable income (on the x-axis). What can you say about the relationship between these two variables?

TABLE 11.13

Year	Quarter	Personal consumption expenditures	Personal disposable income
1985	1	2531.0	2755.5
	2	2576.0	2832.0
	3	2627.1	2882.2
	4	2667.9	2828.0
1986	1	2737.9	2966.0
	2	2765.8	3022.4
	3	2837.1	3038.2
	4	2858.6	3061.6
1987	1	2893.8	3125.9
	2	2943.7	3130.6
	3	3011.3	3195.3
	4	3022.6	3275.0
1988	1	3068.7	3320.2

Source: Standard and Poor's Statistical Service, *Current Statistics,* June 1988.

b) Find the least-squares line that describes the relationship between personal consumption and personal disposable income.

c) What percentage of the variability in consumption expenditures is explained by the personal disposable income?

d) Do these analyses provide evidence that personal disposable income contributes information for predicting the personal consumption expenditures?

e) Explain the interpretation of the regression coefficient, β, in the context of this problem.

f) Develop a 95% confidence interval for β. Does this support the conclusion reached in part (d)?

11.37 Refer to the data in Problem 11.36.

a) Using this information, forecast the personal consumption expenditures if the personal disposable income is $3500 billion. Construct a 95% confidence interval for this forecast.

b) Now construct a 95% confidence interval for $\mu_{y \cdot x_g}$.

11.38 The Ohio Valley Detergent Company has 30 subsidiaries in the United States. In an effort to relate the sales of each subsidiary to the surrounding population, a regression was run using the SPSS package with sales as the dependent variable and population as the independent variable. The following partial output was generated from the 30 subsidiaries (the data for this is given in Problem 13.40):

VARIABLE	B	STD ERROR B	F
			SIGNIFICANCE
POP	.53339673	.50520918E-01	111.47006
			.000
(CONSTANT)	1386969.3	883403.06	2.4649940
			.128

a) Write the least-squares regression equation.

b) What is the s_b value? Use this value to construct a t-test for $H_0: \beta = 0$ against $H_a: \beta \neq 0$ at a level of significance equal to 0.05.

c) Interpret the value 111.47006 in the last column of the output. What does the .000 below it represent? How are these values related to your answers to part (b)?

d) What value of sales would you predict if the population is 19.66 million?

e) Use a different computer package on the sales and population data in Problem 13.36 to verify the output given above.

11.39 Refer to the data for the price of oil and gasoline prices in Problem 11.28. The table on the following page consists of the regression printout from the B-STAT package for this problem. The variable "cbar" represents the cost of a barrel of oil whereas the variable "cgal" refers to the price of a gallon of gasoline.

```
INDEX     NAME     MEAN     STD.DEV.
1         cbar     21.371    8.026
DEP.VAR.  cgal    105.389   22.486
```

DEPENDENT VARIABLE: cgal

```
                 REGRESSION
       VAR.     COEFFICIENT   STD.ERROR   T(DF=7)    PROB.
       cbar        2.686         .301      8.924     .00005
     CONSTANT     47.989
```

STD.ERROR OF EST. = 6.833
r SQUARED = .919
r = .959

ANALYSIS OF VARIANCE TABLE

```
SOURCE        SUM OF SQUARES   D.F.   MEAN SQUARE   F RATIO    PROB.
REGRESSION       3717.986       1      3717.986     79.638   4.507E-05
RESIDUAL          326.802       7        46.686
TOTAL            4044.789       8
```

a) Write the least-squares regression equation.

b) What is the interpretation of the regression coefficient, b, in the context of this problem?

c) What percentage of the variability in y is explained by the values of x?

d) What is the value of s_b? Show how this value is used to construct the t-test for $H_0: \beta = 0$ against $H_a: \beta \neq 0$.

e) Show how the F ratio of 79.638 is calculated.

f) Calculate the fitted values and the residuals.

11.40 Refer to the sales-employment data for manufacturing employees from Problem 11.9. The following table consists of the regression printout from the Minitab package for this problem. The variable "emp" represents the number of employees (in millions) and the variable "sales" represents the yearly sales in billions.

```
Predictor     Coef    Stdev     t-ratio        p
Constant    -314.7    253.9       -1.24    0.247
emp          80.16    12.91        6.21    0.000

s = 31.01   R-sq = 81.1%   R-sq(adj) = 79.0%
```

Analysis of Variance

```
SOURCE       DF      SS      MS       F       p
Regression    1   37077   37077   38.55   0.000
Error         9    8657     962
Total        10   45734
```

a) Draw the scatter diagram of the total sales against the number of employees.

b) Find the least-squares line and plot it on the scatter diagram.

c) What is the s_b value? Show how this value is used to carry out the t-test for no linear regression.

d) What are the number of degrees of freedom associated with the t value in part (c)? What p-value would you report for this test?

e) Find the s_e value. Construct a 95% confidence interval for y.

f) Forecast the sales if the number of employees were equal to 19.75 million. Construct a 95% confidence interval for this forecast.

11.41 Refer to the exchange rate data from Problem 11.32. The following table consists of the regression printout from the Interactive Data Analysis (IDA) package for this problem. The variable "Mark" represents the exchange rate for the German Mark against the U.S. dollar and the variable "visito" represents the number of visitors (in thousands) from the United States to Western Europe.

COMMAND> **** ANOV ****

SOURCE	SS	DF	MS	F
REGRESSION	4.13743E+06	1	4.13743E+06	11.81
RESIDUALS	2.10277E+06	6	3.50462E+05	
TOTAL	6.24020E+06	7	8.91457E+05	

COMMAND> **** SUMM ****

	MULTIPLE R	R-SQUARE
UNADJUSTED	0.8143	0.6630
ADJUSTED	0.7790	0.6069

STD. DEV. OF RESIDUALS = 5.9200E+02
N = 8

COMMAND> **** COEF ****

VARIABLE	B(STD.V)	B	STD.ERROR(B)	T
MARK	0.8143	1.8322E+03	5.3325E+02	3.436
CONSTANT	0	4.5683E+02	1.2741E+03	0.359

---

a) Write down the least-squares regression equation.

b) What is the interpretation of the regression coefficient in the context of this problem?

c) What is the value of s_b? What is the value of s_e?

d) Show how the F value of 11.81 was calculated. Perform the F-test for H_0: $\beta = 0$ against H_a: $\beta \neq 0$ at a level of significance equal to 0.05. What p-value would you report for this test?

e) Show that the *t*-test also results in the same *p*-value.

f) What will your forecast for the number of visitors be if the exchange rate for the mark is 2.0? Construct a 95% confidence interval for this forecast.

11.42 One measure of the risk of a stock or a portfolio is called a *beta*. One definition of beta was given in Problem 3.40. Another definition is:

Beta = slope of stock return (y) vs. market return (x)

a) Use the data in Problem 3.40 to find the beta for Citicorp.

b) Verify that your answer to (a) corresponds to the answer to Problem 3.40.

Chapter 12

Simple Linear Correlation

I have a great subject (statistics) to write upon, but feel keenly my literary incapacity to make it easily intelligible without sacrificing accuracy and thoroughness.

SIR FRANCIS GALTON

Introduction 12.1

The discussion of linear regression in Chapter 11 concentrated on describing the nature of the relationship between two or more variables. We now turn to a very closely related problem, that of determining the strength of the linear relationship between these variables. The word "strength" in this context refers to the degree of association (or the closeness of fit) between variables: for example, how close do two variables come to following an exact straight-line relationship, given that a linear function best approximates the population relationship? If the values of two variables form a perfect straight line, then the closeness of the fit, or the strength of the linear relationship, between these two variables is said to be "perfect," because the value of one variable can always be determined from a knowledge of the other. In other words, in determining the strength of the relationship between variables, we are measuring how well the value of one variable can be estimated (or described) on the basis of a knowledge of the other variables.

There are a number of ways to measure strength of association, several of which were presented in Chapter 11. The standard error of the estimate, for instance, provides some information about the strength of the relationship between variables; but this measure is difficult to interpret because it depends

495

so highly on the units used to measure the variables. Testing regression coefficients for significant differences from zero also gives evidence about the closeness of fit between variables; yet this method still does not provide a single indicator measuring the relative strength of association. This chapter presents a measure that does provide such an indicator, the correlation coefficient.

Just as Chapter 11 investigated simple linear regression, describing the nature of the relationship between two variables related by a linear function, this chapter investigates simple linear correlation, describing the strength of association between two variables assumed to be linearly related. Our objective is to develop a measure that indicates the strength of the tendency for high (or low) values of one variable to be associated with high (or low) values of the other: that is, to formulate a measure of how well two variables, x and y, "vary together."

The Simple Linear Correlation Model

12.2

One measure of variation between two variables, x and y, is their **covariance.** The population covariance of two random variables, denoted as $C[x, y]$ is a measure of how these variables vary together and is given by

$$\text{Covariance of } x \text{ and } y: \quad C[x, y] = E[(x - \mu_x)(y - \mu_y)]$$

A covariance is somewhat difficult to interpret. If high values of x (high relative to the mean of x, μ_x) tend to be associated with high values of y (relative to the mean of y, μ_y), and low values associated with low values, then $C[x, y]$ will be a large positive number.* If the covariance is a large negative number, this means that low values of one variable tend to be associated with high values of the other, and vice versa. If two variables are independent, then $C[x, y] = 0$ (that is, they are not related). Although the covariance has many important statistical uses, in general this measure is not a good indicator of the relative strength of the relationship between two variables because its magnitude depends so highly on the units used to measure the variables. For example, the covariance between two measures of length x and y will be much smaller if x is scaled in feet than if x is scaled in inches. For this reason it is necessary to "standardize" the covariance of two variables in order to have a good measure of fit. This standardization is accomplished by dividing $C[x, y]$

---

*This is because, when $(x - \mu_x)$ is positive, $(y - \mu_y)$ tends to be positive, and when $(x - \mu_x)$ is negative, $(y - \mu_y)$ tends to be negative; hence, the sign of $(x - \mu_x)(y - \mu_y)$ tends to be positive.

by σ_x and σ_y. The resulting measure is called the **population correlation coefficient** and is denoted by the Greek letter ρ (rho):

$$
\begin{array}{l}
\textit{Population correlation coefficient:} \\[2mm]
\rho = \dfrac{\text{Covariance of } x \text{ and } y}{(\text{Std. dev. of } x)(\text{Std. dev. of } y)} = \dfrac{C[x,y]}{\sigma_x \sigma_y}
\end{array}
\tag{12.1}
$$

Three values of ρ serve as benchmarks for interpretation of a correlation coefficient. First, let's consider the population where the values of x and y all fall on a single straight line that has a positive slope. In this case, which is referred to as a "perfect positive linear relationship" between x and y, the value of $C[x,y]$ exactly equals the values of σ_x times σ_y: hence, ρ equals $+1$.

When the relationship between x and y is a perfect negative linear relationship, all values of x and y lie on a straight line with a negative slope. This situation results in a value of $C[x,y]$ that exactly equals $-(\sigma_x)(\sigma_y)$. Thus, in this case, ρ will equal -1.

If x and y are not linearly related (that is, if the slope of the regression line equals zero), then the value of the correlation coefficient will be zero, since in this case $C[x,y]=0$, which means that $\rho = C[x,y]/\sigma_x \sigma_y = 0$. Thus, ρ measures the strength of the linear association between x and y. Values of ρ close to zero indicate a weak relation; values close to $+1.0$ indicate a strong "positive" correlation, and values close to -1.0 indicate a strong "negative" correlation. Figure 12.1 presents scatter diagrams for some selected values of ρ.

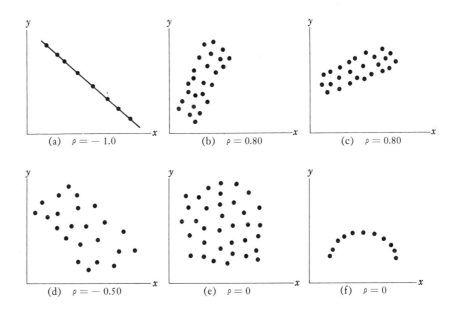

Figure 12.1
The population correlation coefficient.

(a) $\rho = -1.0$ (b) $\rho = 0.80$ (c) $\rho = 0.80$

(d) $\rho = -0.50$ (e) $\rho = 0$ (f) $\rho = 0$

Figure 12.2
The bivariate normal
distribution for $\rho = 0$ and
$\rho = 0.50$.

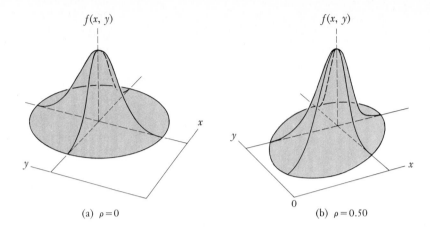

(a) $\rho = 0$ (b) $\rho = 0.50$

Note, from Figs. 12.1(b) and 12.1(c), that two populations that appear quite different can have the same correlation coefficient. Figures 12.1(c) and 12.1(d) show the difference between positive and negative correlation. The last two diagrams show different examples of a population with zero correlation. In Fig. 12.1(f), x and y are perfectly related in a nonlinear fashion, yet ρ still equals zero, which emphasizes the fact that ρ measures the strength of the linear relationship.

A legitimate question might be raised at this point as to exactly what population characteristic the parameter ρ represents. First, we should point out that the calculation of ρ does not require any assumption about the (joint) distribution of x and y. As was the case for regression analysis, however, it is necessary to make assumptions about the population in order to make inferences on the basis of sample data. In this case we need only to make a single assumption, namely, that both x and y are normally distributed random variables. Under this assumption, if x and y are independent ($\rho = 0$), their distribution is the perfectly symmetrical bell-shaped curve shown in the first diagram in Fig. 12.2.* If x and y are normal, but are not independent, then the joint distribution of the two variables becomes more and more elongated as ρ moves away from zero. Figure 12.2(b) shows the joint distribution of x and y for $\rho = 0.50$. From these diagrams, it can be seen that ρ measures the degree of symmetry in the joint distribution of x and y, perfect symmetry occurring when $\rho = +1$ or -1.

We indicated before that, in making inferences from correlation analysis, it is usually necessary to assume that both x and y are normally distributed random variables. As has been the case for many of the measures studied thus far, the fact that the assumption of normality is not exactly met in practical problems does not destroy the usefulness of this technique.

---

*The symmetrical shape will be circular only if $\sigma_x = \sigma_y$.

12.3

The Sample Correlation Coefficient

As in all estimation problems, we use a sample statistic to estimate a population parameter. In this case, the population parameter is ρ: the sample statistic is called the **sample correlation coefficient,** and is denoted by the letter r. The value of r is defined in the same way as ρ, except that we substitute for each population parameter its best estimates based on the sample data. For instance, the best estimate of $C[x,y]$ in Formula (12.1) is the sample covariance, which is denoted by the symbol s_{xy}, where

$$\textit{Sample covariance: } s_{xy} = \frac{1}{n-1}\sum_{i=1}^{n}(x_i - \overline{x})(y_i - \overline{y})$$

We already know from Chapter 6 that the best estimate of σ_x^2 is the sample variance $s_x^2 = (1/(n-1))\sum(x_i - \overline{x})^2$, and the best estimate of σ_y^2 is the sample variance $s_y^2 = (1/(n-1))\sum(y_i - \overline{y})^2$. Substituting these estimates in Formula (12.1) yields the following formula for r.

$$\textit{Sample correlation coefficient:}$$
$$r = \frac{s_{xy}}{s_x\, s_y} = \frac{\text{Sample covariance of } x \text{ and } y}{(\text{Std. dev. of } x)(\text{Std. dev. of } y)}$$

$$= \frac{\dfrac{1}{n-1}\sum(x_i - \overline{x})(y_i - \overline{y})}{\sqrt{\dfrac{1}{n-1}\sum(x_i - \overline{x})^2}\ \sqrt{\dfrac{1}{n-1}\sum(y_i - \overline{y})^2}}$$

(12.2)

This correlation coefficient is often referred to as the **Pearson product-moment correlation coefficient,** in honor of early research by Karl Pearson.

A sample correlation coefficient is interpreted in the same manner as ρ, except that it measures the strength of the sample data (rather than of the population values). For example, when $r = \pm 1$, there is a perfect straight-line fit between the sample values of x and y; hence, they are said to have a **perfect correlation.** If the sample values of x and y have little or no relationship, then r will be close to or equal to zero.*

To illustrate the determination of the sample correlation coefficient, once again consider the data for the salary example from Chapter 11. The data necessary for calculating r are given in Table 12.1. We see that the sample data in this example have a correlation of 0.8418, indicating a fairly strong linear relationship. This result agrees with the result of our t-test on the same data in Chapter 11 (see page 470).

---

*This assumes that the joint distribution of x and y is bivariate normal.

TABLE 12.1

(1) (x_i)	(2) (y_i)	(3) $(x_i - \bar{x})$	(4) $(y_i - \bar{y})$	(5) $(y_i - \bar{y})(x_i - \bar{x})$	(6) $(x_i - \bar{x})^2$	(7) $(y_i - \bar{y})^2$
10	62	-8.083	-14.5	117.204	65.335	210.25
12	65	-6.083	-11.5	69.955	37.003	132.25
18	72	-0.083	-4.5	0.374	0.007	20.25
15	70	-3.083	-6.5	20.040	9.505	42.25
20	81	1.917	4.5	8.627	3.675	20.25
18	77	-0.083	0.5	-0.042	0.007	0.25
19	72	0.917	-4.5	-4.127	0.841	20.25
22	77	3.917	0.5	1.959	15.343	0.25
20	75	1.917	-1.5	-2.876	3.675	2.25
21	90	2.917	13.5	-39.380	8.509	182.25
19	82	0.917	5.5	5.044	0.841	30.25
23	95	4.917	18.5	90.965	24.171	342.25

Sum 217   918   0   0   346.503   168.917   1003.00

Mean $\bar{x} = 18.083$

Mean $\bar{y} = 76.5$

$$r = \frac{\frac{1}{n-1}\sum (x_i - \bar{x})(y_i - \bar{y})}{\sqrt{\frac{1}{n-1}\sum(x_i - \bar{x})^2}\ \sqrt{\frac{1}{n-1}\sum(y_i - \bar{y})^2}} = \frac{346.503/11}{\sqrt{(168.917/11)}\ \sqrt{(1003/11)}} = 0.8418$$

The Coefficient of Determination

In most correlation problems, the value of r may be somewhat difficult to interpret. For example, what do we mean when we say that $r = 0.8418$ indicates a "fairly strong linear relationship"? What we need is a measure permitting us to interpret the strength of fit implied by a particular value of r. Such a measure is given by the square of r, that is, r^2. This is called the **coefficient of determination.**

We can explain the logic behind the interpretation of the coefficient of determination by presenting this measure in terms of SST, SSR, and SSE. Suppose in the relationship SST = SSE + SSR we divide each term by SST, as follows:

$$\frac{SST}{SST} = \frac{SSE}{SST} + \frac{SSR}{SST}$$

Since SSE is the unexplained variation in y, the ratio SSE/SST is the proportion of total variation that is unexplained by the regression line. Similarly, the ratio

SSR/SST is the proportion of total variation that is explained by the regression line. This last ratio, SSR/SST, is thus a relative measure of the goodness of fit of the sample points to the regression line.

Now, let's explore the relationship between r^2 and SSR/SST. It is not difficult to show that

$$\frac{\text{Variation explained}}{\text{Total variation}} = \text{Coefficient of determination:}$$

$$\frac{\text{SSR}}{\text{SST}} = r^2$$

Thus, the coefficient of determination is the square of the correlation coefficient. The advantage of the coefficient of determination is that it is easier to interpret, as we illustrate in the following examples.

Once the value of r^2 is calculated in a regression analysis, we have a measure of goodness of fit for the sample. For example, if $r^2 = 0.70$, this means that 70% of total variation in the sample y values is explained by the best fitting linear function to the sample values of x and y. Similarly, if $r^2 = 0.50$, then 50% of the variation in y is explained by x. If the regression line perfectly fits all the sample points, then all residuals will be zero, which means that SSE will be zero; hence, SSR/SST $= r^2$ would equal 1.0. In other words, a perfect straight-line fit always yields $r^2 = 1$. As the level of fit becomes less accurate, less and less of the variation in y is explained by the relation with x (that is, SSR decreases), which means that r^2 must decrease. The lowest value of r^2 is 0, which will occur whenever SSR $= 0$. A value of $r^2 = 0$ thus means that none of the sample variation in y is explained by the sample values x.

To further illustrate the concept of a coefficient of determination, let's calculate r^2 in our salary–experience example. From page 467 in Chapter 11, we know that SSR $= 710.775$ and SST $= 1003$. Hence,

$$r^2 = \frac{\text{SSR}}{\text{SST}} = \frac{710.775}{1003} = 0.7086$$

Since we earlier found

$$r = 0.8418 \qquad r^2 = (0.8418)^2 = 0.7086$$

we see that this definition of r^2 is consistent with our definition of r. The interpretation of this result is that 70.86% of the total sample variation in y (salary) is explained by the values of x (experience). The remaining 29.14% of the variation in y is still unexplained. Probably some other factors omitted from our regression model could help determine some additional percent of the variation. If these other factors could be measured and included as additional independent variables, we would have a multiple regression model. Such an extension is considered in Chapter 13.

The Relationship Between Correlation and Regression

12.4

Simple linear correlation is quite closely related to simple linear regression and can, in fact, be considered as just another way of looking at the problem of describing the relationship between two or more variables. As we have pointed out, the objectives of these two approaches are different, regression describing the nature of the relationship between variables, correlation describing the strength of this relationship. Although both correlation and regression can be applied to any set of observations without making any assumptions about the parent population, it is necessary to make certain assumptions about the underlying model if we want to construct confidence intervals or test hypotheses. In regression analysis it is necessary to assume that the dependent variable is a normally distributed random variable, while in correlation analysis it is usually necessary to assume that both the independent and dependent variables are normally distributed random variables. In addition, when certain inferences are desired, it is necessary to assume, in regression analysis, that the values of the independent variable are not randomly distributed, but are fixed quantities, known in advance. Fortunately, for most problems this assumption that the x's are fixed quantities is not crucial, and so it is possible to use the techniques of regression in problems where x, rather than being fixed, is a random variable, and to compare the results of a correlation analysis with the results of a regression analysis on the same data.

We can explore the connection between the value of r and the value of the slope b by comparing Formulas (12.2) and (11.9), which are reproduced below:

$$r = \frac{s_{xy}}{s_x s_y} \qquad \text{and} \qquad b = \frac{\frac{1}{n-1}\sum(x-\bar{x})(y-\bar{y})}{\frac{1}{n-1}\sum(x-\bar{x})^2}$$

The numerator of this expression for b is the sample covariance of x and y, which is denoted as s_{xy}. Also, the denominator is the sample variance of x. Thus, we may represent the expression for b as

$$b = \frac{\text{Sample covariance of } x \text{ and } y}{\text{Sample variance of } x} = \frac{s_{xy}}{s_x^2}$$

Now if we substitute $s_{xy} = bs_x^2$ into the formula for r, we get

$$r = b\frac{s_x}{s_y} \tag{12.3}$$

Since s_x and s_y are never negative, a positive correlation always corresponds to a regression line with a positive slope, and a negative r corresponds to a negative slope. That is, the sign of r and b will always be the same. Note also that if $b = 0$, then r must equal 0.

We can confirm that the relationship shown in (12.3) holds by multiplying the expression for b given by Formula (11.9) by the ratio of s_x/s_y, and noting that the result is equivalent to Formula (12.2). To illustrate the use of (12.3) for the data in Table 12.1, recall from Chapter 11 that $b = 2.0513$,

$s_x = \sqrt{168.917/11}$, and $s_y = \sqrt{1003/11}$. Hence, from (12.3):

$$r = \frac{2.0513\sqrt{168.917/11}}{\sqrt{1003/11}} = 0.8418$$

which agrees with the value of r calculated earlier.

It is important to note, at this point, that the value of the correlation coefficient does not depend on which variable is designated as x and which as y. The distinction is important in regression analysis, however, for the conditional distribution of y, given x, results in a different regression line than the conditional distribution of x, given y. Formula (12.3) holds only if the numerator is b multiplied by the standard deviation of the independent variable.

A note of caution must be added to anyone attempting to infer cause and effect from correlation or regression analysis, because a high correlation (or a good fit to a regression line) does not imply that x is "causing" y, nor that x will provide a good estimate of y in the future. For example, the weekly Dow-Jones stock index was reported to have an 0.84 correlation with the number of points scored by a New York City basketball team, and liquor consumption in the United States is supposed to be highly correlated with teachers' salaries. In the latter case, the high correlation undoubtedly results because of the presence of one or more additional influences on both variables, such as increases in the general economic well-being.

The preceding discussion should not be interpreted to mean that one cannot, or should not, draw inferences or conclusions from regression or correlation analysis, but only that care must be taken in assuming cause and effect. As an example, economists make frequent use of regression techniques in attempts to determine cause-and-effect relationships, especially those that might prove useful in predicting the future of the economy. These techniques form the basis for the field of econometrics.

Tests on the Correlation Coefficient

12.5

When $\beta = 0$, then the correlation between y and x must be zero (that is, $\rho = 0$). Thus, testing $H_0: \rho = 0$ is exactly equivalent to testing $H_0: \beta = 0$. In Chapter 11, we presented two formulas for testing $H_0: \beta = 0$, one of which was a t-test (Formula 11.16) and the other an F-test (Formula 11.19). There is a t-test that is equivalent to Formula (11.16) but uses the value of r rather than b. The following t-distributed random variable, with $(n - 2)$ d.f., can be used:

> *t-statistic for testing $H_0: \rho = 0$:*
>
> $$t_{(n-2)} = \frac{r\sqrt{n - 2}}{\sqrt{1 - r^2}}$$

(12.4)

To illustrate how this ratio can be used to test the hypothesis H_0: $\rho = 0$, we again use the salary example from Chapter 11, in which $r = 0.8418$. For the same reason that we used the alternative H_a: $\beta > 0$, we now use the alternate hypothesis H_a: $\rho > 0$ (because we expect salary and experience to be positively related). To determine the probability that a value such as 0.8418 would occur by chance, given that $\rho = 0$ and $n = 12$, we use Formula (12.4) to obtain:

$$t_{10} = \frac{0.8418\sqrt{12 - 2}}{\sqrt{1 - 0.8418^2}} = 4.932$$

This is (and must be) exactly the same t-value obtained when we used (11.16) to test H_0: $\beta = 0$ for the same salary–experience data. As we did then, we reject the null hypothesis that x and y are not related at a level of significance of less than 0.0005 (from Table VII in Appendix B) for $n - 2 = 10$ d.f.

A number of additional significance tests are available for use in linear correlation. For example, it is possible to test for a significant difference between two (or more) regression coefficients. The methods for these tests are described in a number of statistics textbooks* and will not be discussed here.

Simple Regression and Correlation Analysis: An Example

12.6

Having specified all the concepts and formulas essential for both simple regression and correlation analysis, we now review these in an application using the software package Minitab. In this application we analyze aggregate investment levels in the United States.

One of the important decisions faced by business managers is the amount of investment they should make in new plant and equipment, and in maintenance and repair of existing capital goods. Economists are also interested in the level of aggregate investment over all private business in the United States as this value is an important factor in determining national income and potential for growth in an economy. Basic economic principles suggest theoretical relations between investment and such variables as the existing amount of plant and equipment that is depreciating, current and past levels of profits, the interest rates, and so forth. Generally, it is recognized that the level of investment depends on the availability of funds for investment and on the need for expanding production capacity. Thus, any variables that reflect these supply and demand factors might be appropriate in explaining or predicting changes in levels of investment.

---

*See, for example, *Applied Regression Analysis and Other Multivariable Methods*, by D. G. Kleinbaum, L. L. Kupper, and K. E. Muller (Boston: PWS-Kent, 1988).

To specify such a relationship, suppose we hypothesize the relationship $y = \alpha + \beta x + \epsilon$, where x represents a composite price index for 500 common stocks during a given period, and y represents the amount of aggregate investment during the following time period. We might postulate such a relationship because we believe that stock market prices are indicative of the general level of business expectations for the future. For this example, we will estimate the population regression line on the basis of 20 quarterly observations. The data, shown in Table 12.2, represent investment measured at an annual rate in billions of dollars.

The printout for this problem from Minitab is shown in Fig. 12.3. This analysis shows the relationship between the dependent variable investment (y = invest) and the independent variable stock index (x = stock). The first information given in Fig. 12.3 provides us the regression equation

$$\text{invest} = 3.86 + 0.123 \text{ stock}$$

This regression equation is determined from the second set of figures, where the value of the constant is shown to be 3.855 and the value of the variable, stock, is 0.12347. The standard error of the regression coefficient, s_b, is 0.01296. The b and s_b values give us the t-ratio of 9.53, enabling us to test the null hypothesis H_0: $\rho = 0$ (or H_0: $\beta = 0$). That same line of output gives the p-value for the test, $p = 0.000$.

The next part of the output shows the standard error of the estimate and the coefficient of determination. The standard error, s_e, is given by $s = 10.28$. The r^2 value is given by R–sq = 83.4%. That is, 83.4% of the variation is being explained by the regression line. The other value shown here is the R-sq (adj) value equal to 82.5%. This r^2 value takes into account the number of independent variables in the model and will be discussed in more detail in Chapter 13.

The ANOVA table appears next. This table gives further information for testing the strength of the linear relationship. The F-value of 90.74 also leads

TABLE 12.2   Data for estimating the investment equation

Observ.	Investment y	Stock index x	Observ.	Investment y	Stock index x
1	62.30	398.4	11	84.30	581.8
2	71.30	452.6	12	85.10	707.1
3	70.30	509.8	13	90.80	776.6
4	68.50	485.4	14	97.90	875.3
5	57.30	445.7	15	108.70	873.4
6	68.80	539.8	16	122.40	943.7
7	72.20	662.8	17	114.00	830.6
8	76.00	620.0	18	123.00	907.5
9	64.30	632.2	19	126.20	905.3
10	77.90	703.0	20	137.00	927.4

```
The Regression Equation is

invest = 3.86 + 0.123 stock

Predicator      Coef     Stdev    t-ratio        p
Constant       3.855     9.220       0.42    0.681
stock        0.12347   0.01296       9.53    0.000

s = 10.28   R-sq = 83.4%   R-sq (adj.)= 82.5%

Analysis of Variance

SOURCE        DF        SS       MS       F       p
Regression     1     9584.4   9584.4   90.74   0.000
Error         18     1901.3    105.6
Total         19    11485.7
```

to a p-value equal to 0.000. Both the t-test and the F-test imply that there is virtually no chance of committing a Type I error; that is, concluding there is some linear correlation (or regression) when this is not the case. In other words, if stock prices do reflect business expectations, then this data supports the theory that business firms are more willing to expand their plants and equipment when they foresee "good times" ahead. Here, either this F-test or the t-test presented earlier can be used to test H_0: $\rho = 0$.

Problems

12.1 Explain what relationship you would infer between the x and y values in the sample for the following sample correlation coefficients:

    a) $r = 1$ **b)** $r = -1$ **c)** $r = -0.10$ **d)** $r = 0.70$

    e) $r = 0$ **f)** $r = -0.90$

12.2 In a simple regression and correlation analysis based on 72 observations, we find $r = 0.8$ and $s_e = 10$.

    a) Find the amount of unexplained variation.

    b) Find the proportion of unexplained variation to the total variation.

    c) Find the total variation of the dependent variable.

12.3   **a)** In a simple regression, explain the importance of r^2 and s_e, and differentiate between them.

    b) A large-scale national survey relating health habits to length of life reported a high negative correlation between the number of breakfasts a person skips and the length of life. Would you be willing to infer from this study that eating breakfast regularly will help prolong one's life? Explain.

12.4   Refer to the information in Problem 11.6 about the GPA–GMAT scores:

    a) Find the value of r.

    b) Show that $r = b(s_x/s_y)$.

    c) Test H_0: $\rho = 0$ against H_a: $\rho \neq 0$. What p-value would you report?

12.5   What is the difference between regression analysis and correlation analysis? When should each be used? What assumptions about the parent population are necessary for making inferences about ρ?

12.6   Define or describe briefly each of the following:

    a) Sample covariance (s_{xy})

    b) Coefficient of determination

    c) Pearson product-moment correlation coefficient

12.7   If two variables are highly correlated, does this imply a "cause-and-effect" relationship? Explain your answer.

12.8   In a regression of y on x based on 11 observations, the value of the coefficient of determination is 0.36.

    a) Does this indicate a significant correlation between y and x at the 0.05 significance level if proper normality assumptions are made? Let H_a be two-sided.

    b) What is the proportion of variation left unexplained in this regression?

12.9   Through a simple regression based on 32 observations, it is found that $r = 0.60$ and $s_e = 10$.

    a) Find SST, SSR, and SSE.

    b) Do an analysis-of-variance test to determine whether a linear relationship is significant at the 0.01 level.

12.10   Refer to the information in Problem 11.9 about manufacturing employees:

    a) Find the value of r.

    b) Test the hypothesis H_0: $\beta = 0$ against H_a: $\beta \neq 0$ using a t-test. What p-value would you report?

    c) Now test the hypothesis H_0: $\rho = 0$ against H_a: $\rho \neq 0$ using a t-test. What p-value would you report? Does this value agree with your answer in part (b)?

12.11   A fast-food restaurant wishes to determine how its sales in a given week are related to the number of coupons it prints in the local newspaper during the week. Data from eight randomly selected weeks are shown below:

Number of coupons	Sales ($)
5	12,560
8	16,250
6	14,800
3	12,100
9	17,250
10	17,900
7	15,800
6	15,000

a) Draw a scatter diagram of the sales against the number of coupons.

b) Find the least-squares regression line for predicting the sales on the basis of the number of coupons.

c) What is the interpretation of the intercept for this problem?

d) Calculate the r value. Use a t-test to accept or reject the hypothesis H_0: $\rho = 0$ at $\alpha = 0.05$.

e) Calculate the r^2 value. Interpret this value.

12.12 The following table lists the number of deaths due to automobile accidents and the tobacco consumption (lb/capita) in the United States from 1978 to 1985:

Year	Number of auto deaths	Tobacco consumption
1978	52,653	8.1
1979	53,786	8.3
1980	45,284	8.0
1981	44,000	7.6
1982	39,092	7.5
1983	37,976	7.2
1984	39,631	6.9
1985	39,195	6.8

Source: Statistical Abstract of the United States, 1984 and 1985

a) Plot the scatter diagram of the number of auto deaths against the tobacco consumption. What conclusions can you draw from this graph?

b) Calculate the correlation coefficient, r. Can you infer a causal relationship from this analysis? Explain your answer.

12.13 Suppose that, in analyzing the relationship between 26 observations of two variables, you find that SST $= 1200$ and SSE $= 500$. The slope of the regression line is positive.

a) What is the value of r for this problem? What percentage of the sample variation has been explained?

b) Use a t-test to test the hypothesis H_0: $\rho = 0$ against H_a: $\rho \neq 0$ at $\alpha = 0.05$. What p-value would you report?

12.14 Refer to the information in Problem 11.13 about the education levels and salaries:

a) Find the value of r for this problem. Show that $r = b(s_x/s_y)$.

b) What percentage of the sample variation has been explained?

c) Use a t-test to test H_0: $\rho = 0$ against H_a: $\rho \neq 0$.

12.15 The following table lists the percentage of games won, the team batting average, and the team earned run average (ERA) for all the baseball teams in the National League in 1987.

Team	Percentage of wins	Team batting average	Team ERA
San Francisco	.556	.260	3.68
Los Angeles	.451	.252	3.72
Houston	.469	.254	3.84
New York	.568	.268	3.84
St. Louis	.586	.263	3.91
Montreal	.562	.265	3.92
Philadelphia	.494	.254	4.18
Pittsburgh	.494	.264	4.20
Cincinnati	.519	.266	4.24
San Diego	.401	.260	4.27
Chicago	.472	.264	4.55
Atlanta	.429	.258	4.63

Source: The Sporting News Official Baseball Guide (1988)

a) À priori, what would you expect the relationship to be between the percentage of wins and the team batting average? Between the percentage of wins and the team ERA? Explain your answers.

b) Draw a scatter diagram of the percentage of wins (y-axis) against the team batting average (x-axis). Is the plot consistent with your answer in part (a)?

c) Find the least-squares line for the percentage of wins against the team batting average. Graph the least-squares line on your scatter diagram. Does this regression line seem to fit the points on the scatter diagram?

d) Calculate the r^2 value for this regression line. What conclusions can you draw from this analysis?

12.16 Refer to the data in Problem 12.15.

a) Draw a scatter diagram of the percentage of wins against the team ERA.

b) Find the least-squares line for the percentage of wins against the team ERA. Graph this regression line on your scatter diagram.

c) Calculate the r^2 value for this regression line.

d) What conclusions can you draw from these analyses?

e) Which of the two statistics, the team batting average and the team ERA, is a better predictor of wins? Explain your answer.

12.17 Refer to the information in Section 11.7 on the housing starts and mortgage interest rates.

a) Find the correlation between the number of housing starts and the mortgage interest rates.

b) Test the null hypothesis H_0: $\rho = 0$ against the alternative hypothesis H_a: $\rho \neq 0$ by means of a t-test at $\alpha = 0.05$. What p-value would you report?

12.18 Assume a least-squares regression line was fitted to 17 pairs of observations of x and y. The correlation coefficient was determined to be 0.81.

a) If SSR equals 504.3, complete the following ANOVA table:

Source	Sum of squares	d.f.	Mean square	F-ratio
Regression				
Error				
Total				

b) What p-value would you report for this test?

c) Calculate the s_e value.

12.19 A simple linear regression with 22 observations yielded the following ANOVA table:

Source	Sum of squares	d.f.	Mean square	F-ratio
Regression				
Error			50	
Total				

a) If the correlation coefficient, r, is equal to 0.9, complete this ANOVA table.

b) Test the hypothesis H_0: $\beta = 0$ against H_a: $\beta \neq 0$ at a significance level of 0.05. What p-value would you report for this test?

12.20 The following table lists the number of cable subscribers (in thousands) and the cable revenues (in billions of constant 1978 dollars) for the period 1978 to 1985.

Year	No. of subscribers (thousands)	Revenues (billions)
1978	13,400	1424
1979	15,000	1630
1980	17,500	1929
1981	21,500	2500
1982	25,400	3175
1983	29,450	3795
1984	32,800	4645
1985	35,444	5249

Source: Bureau of Census, *Statistical Abstract of the United States*, 1988

a) Draw a scatter diagram of the revenues against the number of subscribers.

b) Find the least-squares regression line for predicting the cable revenues on the basis of the number of subscribers.

c) Calculate the r and r^2 values for this regression line. Interpret these values.

d) Use a t-test to accept or reject the hypothesis H_0: $\rho = 0$ against H_a: $\rho \neq 0$. What p-value would you report?

e) If the number of subscribers increased to 37 million, what would be the revenues in 1978 dollars? Construct a 95% confidence interval for this forecast.

12.21 The Census Bureau in 1988 reported the following figures for the U.S. population (in thousands) in the age group 18–21 and the number of freshmen (in thousands) in each of the years from 1977 to 1985.

Year	Population (18–21)	Freshmen
1977	17,225	2394
1978	17,406	2390
1979	17,505	2503
1980	17,531	2588
1981	17,432	2595
1982	17,284	2505
1983	16,890	2444
1984	16,369	2352
1985	15,813	2292

Source: Bureau of Census, *Statistical Abstract of the United States,* 1988

a) Calculate the correlation coefficient, r.

b) Test the hypothesis H_0: $\rho = 0$ against H_a: $\rho \neq 0$.

c) What p-value would you report for this test?

12.22 Refer to the data in Problem 12.21.

a) Find the least-squares regression line for predicting the total number of freshmen on the basis of the population between the ages of 18 and 21.

b) Calculate the r^2 and the s_e values for this regression line.

c) Use the regression equation to forecast the number of freshmen if the population in the 18 to 21 group during 1986 dropped to 15,500.

d) Develop a 95% confidence interval for the forecast in part (c).

12.23 The following table lists the number of visitors from the United States to Canada (in thousands) and the exchange rate for the Canadian dollar against the U.S. dollar for the period 1979 to 1986.

Year	Visitors (thousands)	Exchange rate
1979	1599	1.1603
1980	1817	1.1693
1981	2070	1.1990
1982	1936	1.2344
1983	2160	1.2325
1984	2416	1.2953
1985	2694	1.3658
1986	3242	1.3896

a) Find the least-squares regression line for predicting the number of U.S. visitors to Canada on the basis of the exchange rate.

b) Calculate the r and the r^2 values.

c) Use the t-test to accept or reject the hypothesis H_0: $\beta = 0$.

d) Use the regression equation to forecast the number of visitors if the exchange rate was 1.25. Also, if it was 1.30.

e) For each forecast in part (d), develop a 95% confidence interval.

12.24 Refer to the GMAT-GPA data from Problem 11.6. The following table represents the regression printout from the Minitab package.

```
Predictor          Coef        Stdev   t-ratio        p
Constant         1.2652       0.4687      2.70    0.027
GMAT         0.0039431    0.0008509      4.63    0.000

s = 0.1377   R-sq = 72.9%   R-sq(adj) = 69.5%

Analysis of Variance

SOURCE        DF        SS         MS        F        p
Regression     1   0.40740    0.40740    21.48    0.000
Error          8   0.15176    0.01897
```

a) Construct the scatter diagram for this data.

b) Find the least-squares line and plot it on the scatter diagram.

c) Find the r^2 value.

d) What is the s_b value? Show how this value is used to carry out the t-test for no linear regression.

12.25 Refer to the data in Problem 11.36. The following table consists of the B-STAT printout of the regression analysis for this problem. The variable 'consum' represents personal expenditures and the variable 'pdi' represents the personal disposable income.

```
INDEX        NAME         MEAN    STD.DEV.
1            pdi      3033.3000   176.3433
DEP. VAR.:   consum   2810.8846   176.5466
```

```
DEPENDENT VARIABLE:  consum

VAR.         REGRESSION COEFFICIENT   STD. ERROR   T(DF = 8)   PROB.
pdi                       .9841          .0554      17.765     .0000
CONSTANT              -174.3311

STD. ERROR OF EST. = 33.8420
        r SQUARED = .9663
              r = .9830
```

ANALYSIS OF VARIANCE TABLE

SOURCE	SUM OF SQUARES	D.F.	MEAN SQUARE	F-RATIO	PROB.
REGRESSION	361426.2724	1	361426.2724	315.570	1.898E-09
RESIDUAL	12598.0645	11	1145.2786		
TOTAL	374024.3369	12			

a) Write the least-squares regression equation.

b) What is the interpretation of the regression coefficient, b, in the context of this problem?

c) What is the value of s_b? Show how this value is used to carry out the t-test for no linear regression.

d) What p-value would you report for the t-test in part (b)?

e) What is the correlation coefficient, r? Test the hypothesis H_0: $\rho = 0$ against H_a: $\rho \neq 0$. What p-value would you report for this test? Compare this with the answer you get in part (d).

f) Calculate the fitted values and the residuals.

Chapter 13

Multiple Regression and Correlation

There are three types of liars: liars, damn liars, and statisticians.

BENJAMIN DISRAELI

In Chapters 11 and 12 we presented the methods for simple linear regression and correlation. In this chapter, we extend these analyses by presenting the methods for relating a dependent variable to two or more independent variables. Multiple regression is presented first, followed by multiple linear correlation.

Multiple Linear Regression: The Population

13.1

As was the case for simple linear regression, we first need to specify certain population relationships. Suppose that there are m independent variables, x_1, $x_2, \ldots, x_m$, where $m \geq 1$, and again let y be the dependent variable. Also, let

$$E[y|x_1, x_2, \ldots, x_m] = \mu_{y \cdot x_1, x_2, \ldots, x_m}$$

denote the conditional mean of the y values, given specific values of the m independent variables. We now need to specify the relationship between $\mu_{y \cdot x_1, x_2, \ldots, x_m}$ and the values of $x_1, x_2, \ldots, x_m$. This relationship could take on many different forms, most of which would be extremely difficult to handle in a regression analysis. For example, although certain nonlinear relationships can be solved by an extension of the methods of this chapter (see Section 13.6), for the most part we will assume that the variables are all linearly related. By this we mean that the relationship between y and each one of the independent variables is linear. Assuming linearity, and letting α equal the y-intercept, β_1 equal the slope of the relationship between y and x_1, β_2 equal to the slope between y and x_2, and so forth, the equation relating $\mu_{y \cdot x_1, x_2, \ldots, x_m}$ to the independent variables is called the

---

Population multiple linear regression equation:

$$\mu_{y \cdot x_1, x_2, \ldots, x_m} = \alpha + \beta_1 x_1 + \beta_2 x_2 + \ldots + \beta_m x_m$$

(13.1)

The coefficients $\beta_1, \beta_2, \ldots, \beta_m$ are called the partial regression coefficients, because they indicate the (partial) influence of each independent variable on y, with the influence of all the remaining variables held constant.

To illustrate a regression equation, consider the salary example from Chapter 11. Suppose that the placement agency would now like to expand the analysis by considering, in addition to experience, the number of employees supervised, education, or a variety of other factors that might be useful in predicting the dependent variable (salary). For example, suppose we designate experience as x_1, the number of employees supervised as x_2, and assume the mean salary ($\mu_{y \cdot x_1, x_2}$) is related to these variables as follows:

$$\mu_{y \cdot x_1, x_2} = 35.0 + 1.5\,x_1 + 0.1 x_2$$

(13.2)

This multiple regression equation is shown graphically in Fig. 13.1. The value of $\beta_1 = 1.5$ in this case indicates that, if we eliminate or take into account the effect of all other variables (that is, hold them constant), a one-unit increase in x_1 (experience) will increase the mean value of y (salary) by 1.5 units ($\$1500$). Similarly, a one-unit increase in x_2 (number of employees supervised) will increase the mean y (salary) by 0.1 units ($\$100$), since $\beta_2 = 0.1$. Note that the fact that β_1 is larger than β_2 does not mean that experience is more important in determining salary than is the number of employees. The value of the partial regression coefficients assumed depends so highly on the choice of units to measure x that it is usually difficult, if not impossible, to make any direct comparisons.

As was the case for simple linear regression, we also want to specify the population regression model used to predict the specific values y_i. To do this, we again need to add an error term (ϵ) to the regression equation, and put the subscript i on each variable (to indicate the relationship represents the ith observation in the population).

Population regression model:

$$y_i = \alpha + \beta_1 x_{1i} + \beta_2 x_{2i} + \ldots + \beta_m x_{mi} + \epsilon_i$$

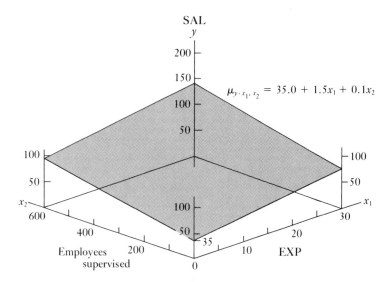

Figure 13.1
The population regression
plane $\mu_{y \cdot x_1, x_2} =$
$35.0 + 1.5x_1 + 0.1x_2$

The process of using sample information to estimate the parameters of a multiple linear regression equation involves the same least-squares technique used in the simple linear regression case.

Multiple Least-Squares Estimation

13.2

This section presents the sample regression model and the least-squares estimate of the population parameters. Suppose we have a sample consisting of n observations for each of the m variables. The problem is to find the sample regression equation that provides the "best fit" to these data, and to use the coefficients of that equation as estimates of the parameters of the population regression equation. This sample regression equation has the following form:

$$
\begin{array}{|l|}
\hline
\textit{Sample regression equation:} \\
\hat{y} = a + b_1 x_1 + b_2 x_2 + \ldots + b_m x_m \\
\hline
\end{array}
\qquad (13.3)
$$

where the value of $\hat{y}$ is the estimate of the mean value for a given set of values of $x_1, x_2, \ldots, x_m$ (that is, $\hat{y}$ is an estimate of $\mu_{y \cdot x_1 \cdot x_2, \ldots, x_m}$), a is the estimate of α and $b_1, b_2, \ldots, b_m$ are the estimates of the partial regression coefficients $\beta_1, \beta_2, \ldots, \beta_m$.

The sample regression model follows the same pattern: adding the subscript i to each x value, and adding the sample error term e_i, as an estimate of ϵ_i yields:

$$
\begin{array}{|l|}
\hline
\textit{Sample regression model:} \\
\hat{y}_i = a + b_1 x_{1i} + b_2 x_{2i} + \ldots + b_m x_{mi} + e_i \\
\hline
\end{array}
\qquad (13.4)
$$

The values of the estimators $a, b_1, b_2, \ldots, b_m$ can be obtained by a direct extension of the least-squares approach presented in Chapter 11. Assuming a sample of n observations (that is, $i = 1, 2, \ldots, n$), it is again necessary to minimize the sum of the squared deviations of the individual values y_i about the predicted values $\hat{y}_i$:

$$\text{Min } G = \sum_{i=1}^{n} (y_i - \hat{y}_i)^2 = \sum_{i=1}^{n} (y_i - a - b_1 x_{1i} - b_2 x_{2i} - \ldots - b_m x_{mi})^2$$

The procedure for minimizing G is similar to the simple linear process, except that now partial derivatives must be taken for $(m + 1)$ variables instead of just two. In other words, derivatives need to be taken with respect to a, and with respect to the m variables $b_1, b_2, \ldots b_m$. Setting these $(m + 1)$ partials equal to zero and solving yields $(m + 1)$ normal equations.*

The number of normal equations $(m + 1)$ always exceeds the number of independent variables by 1. When the normal equations involve only one or two independent variables (that is, two or three equations), then, solving these equations for a and b_1, or a, b_1 and b_2, is usually relatively simple.† Solving more than three normal equations, or solving when the number of observations is large, requires tedious arithmetic. Thus, such systems of equations are solved using computer packages.

To illustrate the use of multiple linear regression, suppose that the placement agency has calculated the following least-squares multiple linear regres-

---

*The normal equations are

$$na + b_1 \sum x_{1i} + b_2 \sum x_{2i} + \ldots + b_m \sum x_{mi} = \sum y_i \tag{13.5}$$

$$a \sum x_{1i} + b_1 \sum x_{1i}^2 + b_2 \sum x_{1i} x_{2i} + \ldots + b_m \sum x_{1i} x_{mi} = \sum x_{1i} y_i \tag{13.6}$$

$$a \sum x_{2i} + b_1 \sum x_{1i} x_{2i} + b_2 \sum x_{2i}^2 + \ldots + b_m \sum x_{2i} x_{mi} = \sum x_{2i} y_i \tag{13.7}$$

$$\vdots \qquad \vdots \qquad \vdots \qquad \qquad \vdots \qquad \vdots$$

$$a \sum x_{mi} + b_1 \sum x_{1i} x_{mi} + b_2 \sum x_{2i} x_{mi} + \ldots + b_m \sum x_{mi}^2 = \sum x_{mi} y_i \tag{13.8}$$

These equations are not as forbidding as they may at first appear. Formula (13.5) can be viewed as a generalization of Formula (11.7), while Formulas (13.6) to (13.8) can be viewed as generalizations of Formula (11.8), with different values of the first subscript of x. Thus, Formula (13.6) is similar to (11.8), except that (13.6) sums x_{1i} instead of x_i. Likewise, (13.7) is similar to (11.8) except that it sums x_{2i} instead of x_i. Note that (13.6) can be derived by multiplying both sides of (13.5) by x_{1i} and summing; (13.7) can be derived by multiplying both sides of (13.5) by x_{2i} and summing; and so forth.

†For example, when there are two variables and 12 observations, as in the salary example, the three normal equations to be solved are

$$na + b_1 \sum_{i=1}^{12} x_{1i} + b_2 \sum_{i=1}^{12} x_{2i} = \sum_{i=1}^{12} y_i$$

$$a \sum_{i=1}^{12} x_{1i} + b_1 \sum_{i=1}^{12} x_{1i}^2 + b_2 \sum_{i=1}^{12} x_{1i} x_{2i} = \sum_{i=1}^{12} x_{1i} y_i$$

$$a \sum_{i=1}^{12} x_{2i} + b_1 \sum_{i=1}^{12} x_{1i} x_{2i} + b_2 \sum_{i=1}^{12} x_{2i}^2 = \sum_{i=1}^{12} x_{2i} y_i$$

sion equation for y (salary in thousands), x_1 (experience), and x_2 (number of employees supervised):

$$\hat{y} = 33.7033 + 1.371x_1 + 0.0914x_2 \qquad (13.9)$$

This equation then provides estimates for α, β_1, and β_2. Thus, an estimate of α is equal to 33.7033, an estimate of β_1 equal to 1.371, and an estimate of β_2 equal to 0.0914. The value of $\hat{y}$ that results from substituting specific values of x_1 and x_2 into this equation is an estimate of $\mu_{y \cdot x_1, x_2}$. For example, suppose we want an estimate of the mean salary for all executives who have an experience of 20 years and who will supervise 150 employees. Substituting $x_1 = 20$ and $x_2 = 150$ into the equation given above yields the following estimate:

$$\hat{y} = 33.7033 + 1.371(20) + 0.0914(150) = 74.833$$

Now, suppose we want to predict the salary of an individual executive, and this executive has 20 years' experience and will supervise 150 employees. Our best estimate in this case is the same as before. That is, the estimate of an individual salary, given $x_1 = 20$ and $x_2 = 150$ is

$$\hat{y}_i = 33.7033 + 1.371(20) + 0.0914(150) = 74.833$$

Even though these two estimates are equal, we must again point out that we have much less confidence in the estimate of a single value ($\hat{y}_i$) than we do in the estimate of the mean value ($\hat{y}$). To be more precise about the degree of confidence one has for the estimates in multiple linear regression, we need to again present the assumptions (about the errors ϵ_i) that are necessary for interpreting the estimators of the ($m + 1$) parameters (estimators of α and m values of β).

Assumptions for the Multiple Regression Model

13.3

Again we must emphasize that the least-squares procedure does not require any assumptions about the population, since this procedure is merely a curve-fitting technique. However, in order to be able to test the goodness of fit of a sample regression equation, it is once more necessary to make certain assumptions about the error term (ϵ) in the population regression model. The first five of these assumptions are parallel to those specified in Section 11.2 for the simple regression model. We repeat them below for the multiple regression case:

Assumption 1. The error term ϵ is independent of each of the m independent variables $x_1, x_2, \ldots, x_m$.

Assumption 2. The errors ϵ_i for all possible sets of given values of $x_1, x_2, \ldots, x_m$ are normally distributed.

Assumption 3. The expected value of the errors is zero for all possible sets of given values $x_1, x_2, \ldots, x_m$. That is, $E[\epsilon_i] = 0$ for $i = 1, 2, \ldots, n$.

Assumption 4. Any two errors ϵ_k and ϵ_j are independent. Their covariance is zero; $C[\epsilon_k, \epsilon_j] = 0$ for $k \neq j$.

Assumption 5. The variance of the errors is finite, and is the same for all possible sets of given values for $x_1, x_2, \ldots, x_m$. That is, $V[\epsilon_i] = \sigma_\epsilon^2$ is a constant for $i = 1, 2, \ldots, n$.

In addition to these five assumptions, two additional conditions are necessary to obtain least-squares estimates in the multiple regression equation.

Condition 1. None of the independent variables is an exact linear combination of the other independent variables.

This means that no one variable x_i is an exact multiple of any other independent variable. Further, if $m \geq 2$, this assumption means that no one variable x_i can be written as

$$x_i = a_1 x_1 + a_2 x_2 + \cdots + a_{i-1} x_{i-1} + a_{i+1} x_{i+1} + \cdots + a_m x_m$$

where the a's are constants. This assumption is a weak condition, since it requires only that the variables not be perfectly related to each other in a linear function. In practice, the independent variables often are partially linearly related to each other, or related to each other in some nonlinear way. Although least-squares estimates can be calculated in these situations, problems sometimes arise in their interpretation.

Condition 2. The number of observations (n) must exceed the number of independent variables (m) by at least two (that is, $n \geq m + 2$).

Since, in the multiple regression equation, there are $m + 1$ parameters to be estimated, the number of degrees of freedom is $n - (m + 1)$. This condition merely specifies that there be at least one degree of freedom (that is, $n - (m + 1) \geq 1$). In practice, the sample size must be quite a bit larger than this value; otherwise, any measure of goodness of fit may be more a consequence of having only a small amount of data, rather than of having an accurately specified explanatory model.

Standard Error of the Estimate

13.4

Just as for simple linear regression, the total variation in a regression problem, $\text{SST} = \Sigma(y_i - \bar{y})^2$, can be divided into the sum of $\text{SSE} = \Sigma(y_i - \hat{y}_i)^2$ and $\text{SSR} = \Sigma(\hat{y}_i - \bar{y})^2$. And once again the standard error of the estimate is defined as

$$s_e = \sqrt{\frac{(\text{Unexplained variation})}{(\text{Degrees of freedom})}} = \sqrt{\frac{\text{SSE}}{\text{d.f.}}}$$

In the present case there are $(m + 1)$ parameters to be estimated before the errors can be calculated; hence the d.f. associated with SSE is $n - (m + 1) = n - m - 1$. Thus,

Multiple standard error of the estimate:

$$s_e = \sqrt{\frac{SSE}{n - m - 1}} = \sqrt{\frac{1}{n - m - 1}\sum_{i=1}^{n} e_i^2}$$

(13.10)

For the salary example from Chapter 11, total variation is $SST = \sum(y_i - \bar{y})^2 = 1003$. When both x_1 (experience) and x_2 (number of employees supervised) are included in the analysis, then it can be shown that:

$$SSE = \sum(y_i - \hat{y}_i)^2 = 134.437$$

and

$$SSR = \sum(\hat{y}_i - \bar{y})^2 = 868.563$$

Note that SSE and SSR sum to SST, as they must. The data used in these computations are shown in Fig. 13.2 on page 525.

We can now calculate s_e by remembering that $m = 2$ (two independent variables) and $n = 12$ (observations in the sample).

$$s_e = \sqrt{\frac{SSE}{n - m - 1}} = \sqrt{\frac{134.437}{12 - 2 - 1}} = 3.8649$$

As before, we know that when n is large, about 68% of all sample points should lie within one standard error of the estimated value $\hat{y}_i$, and about 95% should be within two standard errors.

The reader may recall from Chapter 11 that the standard error with only one independent variable (experience) is $s_e = 5.406$, which is larger than the comparable value of 3.8649 when there are two independent variables (x_1 and x_2). In general, s_e may either increase or decrease with the addition of new variables. When new variables are added, SSE can never increase; but since an extra d.f. is lost with each new variable, in some cases s_e will increase.

Tests for Multiple Linear Regression

13.5

A variety of test procedures have been developed for the parameters of a multiple regression model. Not all these tests will be discussed here, because their complexity is better handled in a more advanced text. The usual questions in a multiple linear relationship are the overall goodness of fit, as well as the significance of the partial regression coefficients.

The *F*-Test

In multiple linear regression, one of the most commonly held null hypotheses is that there is no linear regression at all in the population—all the β values are equal to zero:

$$H_0: \beta_1 = \beta_2 = \cdots = \beta_m = 0$$

The alternative hypothesis is that at least one of the regression coefficients, $\beta_i (i = 1, m)$, is nonzero. That is,

$$H_a: \text{At least one } \beta_i \neq 0$$

Thus, this test attempts to establish whether the independent variables, as a whole, are useful in explaining the dependent variable y.

If the null hypothesis is true, then we would expect SSE to be relatively large and SSR to be relatively small. If each of these sums is divided by its degrees of freedom, then a mean square is obtained. The ratio of the mean-square regression (MSR) to the mean-square error (MSE) can be shown to follow an F-distribution (just as it did in Chapter 11).

As we indicated previously, the d.f. associated with SSE is $n - (m + 1)$, because $(m + 1)$ parameters are being estimated (one d.f. is lost for each parameter estimated). The d.f. for SSR is the same as the number of independent variables (m). Note that these d.f. sum to the total degrees of freedom, which must be $(n - 1)$. These values are summarized in the analysis-of-variance table, Table 13.1. The form of the ANOVA table is identical to those in Chapter 11 except that the degrees of freedom are different.

The appropriate statistic to test the null hypothesis is given by the ratio of MSR to MSE, which follows an F-distribution with m and $(n - m - 1)$ d.f.:

Statistic for testing H_0: $\beta_1 = \beta_2 = \ldots = \beta_m = 0$:

$$F = \frac{\text{SSR}/m}{\text{SSE}/(n - m - 1)} = \frac{\text{MSR}}{\text{MSE}}$$

TABLE 13.1

Source	SS	d.f.	Mean square
Regression	SS regression	m	SS regression/m = MSR
Error	SS error	$n - (m + 1)$	SS error/$(n - m - 1)$ = MSE
Total	SS total	$n - 1$	

We illustrate this test by referring again to the salary example. Since we know that SST = 1003, SSR = 868.563, SSE = 134.437, and the degrees of freedom are $m = 2$ and $(n - m - 1) = (12 - 2 - 1) = 9$,

$$F = \frac{868.563/2}{134.437/9} = \frac{434.2815}{14.9374} = 29.073$$

From Table VIII in Appendix B we see that this value will occur less than 1% of the time by chance when the null hypothesis of no linear regression is true (that is $p < 0.01$). Hence, we can probably safely accept the alternative hypothesis that our equation is useful in describing the values of y.

Tests on Values of β_i

To determine the significance of an individual coefficient (β_i) in the regression model, a test is used that is similar to that for the slope in simple linear regression. (Note that this t-test would be carried out only if the F-test for overall regression is significant, that is, if we accept the hypothesis that the equation is useful in explaining the values of y.) The null hypothesis H_0: $\beta_i = 0$ means that the variable x_i has no linear relationship with y, holding the effect of the other independent variables constant. The best linear unbiased estimate of β_i is the sample partial regression coefficient b_i. Under the assumption that the (unknown) error is normally distributed, then the test for this null hypothesis follows the t-distribution with $(n - m - 1)$ d.f.:

Statistic for testing H_0: $\beta_i = 0$:

$$t = \frac{b_i - 0}{s_{b_i}}$$

The value of s_{b_i} is the estimated standard error of the estimate b_i. Calculation of s_{b_i} is quite tedious, but it is always shown in the output from a regression analysis package. Thus, the determination of t in a practical application is simply done by forming the ratio of the coefficient to its estimated standard error. When the calculated value of t exceeds the critical value of t determined from Table VII, then the null hypothesis of no significance can be rejected. It is then concluded that the variable x_i does have an important influence on the dependent variable y, even after accounting for the influence of all other independent variables included in the model.

For our example, the estimated standard errors of the coefficients b_1 and b_2 of the variables x_1 and x_2 are $s_{b_1} = 0.3637$ and $s_{b_2} = 0.0281$, respectively. Since $n = 12$ and $m = 2$ in this case, the critical value for a one-sided test on either coefficient (using a significance level of $\alpha = 0.01$) is $t_{(\alpha, n-m-1)} = t_{(0.01, 9)} = 2.821$. Thus, the critical region for a one-sided test when H_0: $\beta_1 = 0$ (or H_0: $\beta_2 = 0$) is all values of t that are greater than or equal to 2.821. We choose a one-sided test because our *à priori* theoretical propositions were that both x_1 and x_2 were positively related to y.

For the test on β_1,

$$t = \frac{b_1}{s_{b_1}} = \frac{1.3710}{0.3637} = 3.770$$

and for the test on the significance of β_2,

$$t = \frac{b_2}{s_{b_2}} = \frac{0.09136}{0.02811} = 3.250$$

Because both of these t-values exceed the critical value of 2.821, we conclude that both variables, x_1(experience) and x_2 (number of employees supervised), are significantly related to y (salary). Alternatively, we could have reported p-values for both x_1 and x_2. These are 0.0022 for x_1 and 0.005 for x_2. The variable x_1 is the more influential of the two, since it has the higher t value (or alternatively, a smaller p-value).

Although we have shown how to carry out this analysis using formulas, multiple regression analyses are generally carried out on a computer. The analysis for this problem was run on the Minitab package. The output from this analysis is shown in Fig. 13.2. Note that this output contains two different r^2 values. These will be explained in Section 13.7. (The Minitab output in Fig. 13.2 shows p-values that are twice the ones above because Minitab assumes a two-sided hypothesis test.)

Now that we have found that both regression coefficients provide a good fit for the data, we can proceed to the next logical task, that of determining the best point forecast based on the previous relationships between y and x_1 and x_2. In doing so, we must remember that, even if the regression equation has been shown to fit well, and has all very significant coefficients, such results may not hold for future data. The relationship for new placements may differ due to changes in the social, political, or economic environment. However let's be courageous and assume that the past relationship (Formula 13.9) will hold for executives currently applying for positions. If the given values of the independent variables for one such executive are $x_1 = 25$ and $x_2 = 200$, then the forecast value is

$$\hat{y} = a + b_1 x_1 + b_2 x_2$$
$$= 33.7033 + 1.371(25) + 0.0914(200)$$
$$= 86.2583$$

The estimated salary for this executive is thus 86.2583 ($86,258.30).

It is important to recognize that we have presented only part of the analysis possible in our regression model. We could have constructed a confidence interval for y_i and $\mu_{y \cdot x_1, x_2}$, or we might have added other independent variables and then performed the same F-test (for the overall relationship) and t-test (for the individual coefficients) for the new data.

The least-squares approach works for two or more independent variables. Now we need to make the comparable extension of simple linear correlation. This extension is begun in Section 13.7.

```
y    x1    x2
62   10   175
65   12   150
72   18   135
70   15   175
81   20   150
77   18   200
72   19   180
77   22   225
75   20   175
90   21   275
82   19   225
95   23   300
```

The Regression Equation is

$y = 33.70 + 1.37\ x1 + 0.09\ x2$

```
Predictor    Coef    Stdev    t-ratio         p

Constant    33.703
x1           1.371   0.364    3.770      0.0044
x2           0.0914  0.028    3.250      0.0100

s = 3.8649   R-sq = 86.60%   R-sq(adj) = 83.62%
```

Analysis of Variance

```
SOURCE        DF        SS        MS        F        p
Regression     2    868.563   434.282   29.073   0.000
Error          9    134.437    14.937
Total         11   1003.000
```

Figure 13.2
Partial output from Minitab
for the salary multiple
regression example.

□ Nonlinear Relationships (Optional)

13.6

In many circumstances it may not be reasonable to assume a linear relationship between the dependent variable and the independent variables. This fact often becomes obvious when constructing a scatter diagram for the sample observations; for this reason such diagrams are very useful. If the relationship between two variables is not linear, then it may be possible to 1) transform the data so that it takes on a linear form, or 2) find a curvilinear function which provides a good fit to the data. (A third method that employs a number of short straight lines to approximate small portions of a curved line is also used. This method, called piecewise linear approximation, will not be discussed here, but can be found in a number of intermediate texts.)

A large number of functions exist for transforming a set of observations into linear form. In some cases, the appropriate transformation can be decided upon after viewing the scatter diagram. Under these circumstances it is often helpful to plot the data on semilogarithmic graph paper, using the log scale for either variable, or on a double-logarithmic graph. If the observations on any one of these graphs follow approximately a straight line, then a logarithmic transformation can be used. For instance, if the relationship is linear when x is plotted on the log scale, then $\hat{y} = a + b \log x$ is the appropriate form; when y is plotted on the log scale, the $\log \hat{y} = a + bx$ is appropriate. When the relationship is linear on a double-logarithmic graph, the appropriate equation is $\log \hat{y} = a + b \log x$. Although a logarithmic transformation on x or y is a common form, many other transformations may give the desired linear relationship. To name just a few others, y may have a linear relationship with the reciprocal of x, $\hat{y} = a + b/x$, or with the square of x, $\hat{y} = a + bx^2$, or perhaps even with a polynomial function of x, such as $\hat{y} = a + bx + cx^2$. In this latter case, x^2 can be treated as if it were a new variable, say, $x_2 = x^2$. If we now call the original variable x_1, and let $b = b_1$ and $c = b_2$, then the parabola $\hat{y} = a + bx + cx^2$ can be written as $\hat{y} = a + b_1 x_1 + b_2 x_2$. The relationship between x and y in this form can be handled by the techniques of multiple linear regression that were described in Section 13.2. In fact, this method of transforming a parabola is, in general, applicable to any higher-order polynomials.

Rather than pick a suitable transformation for x and y on the basis of a scatter diagram, the researcher may often have an *à priori* rationale for selecting one transformation over another or may want to try several "models" and simply determine which one provides the best fit to the sample data (which one gives the lowest standard error of the estimate). For example, suppose the relationship between x and y is estimated by an exponential function of the form $\hat{y} = ae^{bx}$. Taking the logarithm to the base e of both sides yields a linear function between $\ln y$ and x:

$$\hat{y} = ae^{bx},$$
$$\ln \hat{y} = \ln(ae^{bx}) = \ln a + bx$$

The estimates provided by a regression line based on this relationship could be compared with the estimates provided by some other fit to the data, to see which one gives the best fit. Unfortunately, transformations like those may cause problems in regression analysis, especially in the error terms.

Instead of transforming the data into a linear form, it may be possible in some circumstances to directly determine a least-squares estimate of the population parameters for a curvilinear function relating two or more variables. Consider once again the parabolic relationship described above, $\hat{y} = a + bx + cx^2$. To minimize the sum of the squared errors, again let

$$G = \sum_{i=1}^{m} (y_i - \hat{y}_i)^2$$

and minimize

$$G = \sum_{i=1}^{m} (y_i - a - bx_i - cx_i^2)^2$$

by taking the partial derivative of G with respect to a, b, and c.* Now that we have presented the analysis for extending simple linear regression ($m = 1$) to multiple regression ($m > 1$), in Section 13.7 we make the comparable extension of simple correlation to multiple linear correlation.

Problems

13.1 Discuss the usefulness and value of the extension of regression analysis to include more than one explanatory factor.

13.2 Explain the difference in meaning between the simple regression coefficient in a simple regression analysis and a partial regression coefficient in a multiple regression analysis.

13.3 Describe the difference between the population regression equation and the population regression model.

13.4 In multiple regression analysis:

a) What measures are used to determine whether the equation fits the data well and may be useful for forecasting?

b) How can you determine which of the explanatory factors included in the model has the most significance in explaining the variation of the dependent variable y?

13.5 A multiple linear regression with three independent variables and $n = 16$ yielded the following ANOVA table:

Source	Sum of squares	d.f.	MS
Regression			1250
Error			
Total	5000		

---

*The resulting normal equations are

$$na + b \sum_{i=1}^{n} x_i + c \sum_{i=1}^{n} x_i^2 = \sum_{i=1}^{n} y_i$$

$$a \sum_{i=1}^{n} x_i + b \sum_{i=1}^{n} x_i^2 + c \sum_{i=1}^{n} x_i^3 = \sum_{i=1}^{n} x_i y_i$$

$$a \sum_{i=1}^{n} x_i^2 + b \sum_{i=1}^{n} x_i^3 + c \sum_{i=1}^{n} x_i^4 = \sum_{i=1}^{n} x_i^2 y_i$$

The equations shown here have the same form as the normal equations for multiple linear regression [see Eqs. (13.8)]. The variable x_1 in Formula (13.8) corresponds to the variable x in the present case, x_2 corresponds to x^2, and the constants b_1 and b_2 correspond to b and c. The three equations above can be solved in the same way as in the multiple regression case to yield the least-squares regression line.

    a) Complete the ANOVA table.

    b) Test the null hypothesis that there is no linear regression. Use $\alpha = 0.01$.

    c) What p-value would you report?

13.6 In a multiple regression equation with $m = 3$ and $n = 32$, the MSE value is equal to 42.56 and the SST value is equal to 4387.22. Use the F-test to test the null hypothesis that there is no linear regression. What p-value would you report?

13.7 A multiple regression problem yields the following partial ANOVA table:

Source	Sum of squares	d.f.
Regression	1500	4
Error	1000	35

    a) How many independent variables are there? What is the sample size?

    b) Test the null hypothesis that there is no linear regression. Use $\alpha = 0.01$. What p-value would you report?

    c) Calculate the standard error of the estimate, s_e.

13.8 In a multiple regression equation involving two independent variables, the following estimates of the regression coefficients and their standard deviations were obtained:

$$b_1 = 5.543 \qquad s_{b_1} = 2.145$$
$$b_2 = 0.259 \qquad s_{b_2} = 0.167$$

Test the significance of each of these variables using $\alpha = 0.05$. What p-values would you report?

13.9 Keller Building Supply, a lumber yard in St. Louis, Missouri, has developed the sample regression line $\hat{y} = a + b_1x_1 + b_2x_2$ to predict the firm's monthly lumber orders. Here y is the monthly lumber orders in thousands of board feet, x_1 the number of building permits issued for the market region, and x_2 the interest rate on conventional first mortgages. The B-STAT package was used to fit the sample regression line to data from the past 18 months. The partial output is shown in Table 13.2.

    a) What are the estimates for a, b_1, and b_2? Write the least-squares equation.

    b) Find SSE and MSE. Calculate the standard error of the estimate, s_e.

    c) Test the null hypothesis that there is no linear regression. Use $\alpha = 0.05$. What p-value would you report?

    d) Test the hypothesis H_0: $\beta_1 = 0$ against H_a: $\beta_1 \neq 0$. Use $\alpha = 0.05$. What p-value would you report?

    e) Of the two independent variables, x_1 and x_2, which is the more important in explaining the variation in the sales of lumber?

13.10 Explain how the use of the t-distribution differs from the use of the F-distribution in testing hypotheses in multiple linear regression.

TABLE 13.2

DEPENDENT VARIABLE: y

VAR.	REGRESSION COEF.	STD. ERROR	T(DF = 16)	PROB.
x1	14.261	1.406		
x2	−3.663	1.317		
CONSTANT	24.052			

STD. ERROR OF EST. =

R SQUARED = .8337
MULTIPLE R = .9131

ANALYSIS OF VARIANCE TABLE

SOURCE	SUM OF SQUARES	D.F.	MEAN SQUARE	F RATIO	PROB.
REGRESSION	880.6067	2			
RESIDUAL					
TOTAL	1056.2980	17			

13.11 A chain of electronic discount stores has developed a multiple regression model to predict their average weekly sales. Data from 15 branch locations was used to fit the sample regression line

$$\hat{y} = a + b_1x_1 + b_2x_2 + b_3x_3$$

using the Minitab package. Here y is the average weekly sales (in thousands of dollars), x_1 the population within a five-mile radius (in thousands), x_2 the mean personal disposable income, and x_3 the number of competitors within a five-mile radius. The partial output obtained is shown in Table 13.3.

TABLE 13.3

Predictor	Coef	Stdev	t-ratio	p
Constant	115.625		8.98	0.000
x1	14.752	2.403		
x2	0.013	0.003		
x3	−16.873	2.198		

s = 8.935   R−sq = 93.7%

Analysis of Variance

SOURCE	DF	SS	MS	F	p
Regression	3	11367.3			
Error	11	759.1			
Total	14				

a) Write down the least-squares equation.

b) Test the null hypothesis that there is no overall linear regression. Use $\alpha = 0.01$. Explain the results of this test.

c) Test the hypothesis $H_0: \beta_1 = 0$ against $H_a: \beta_1 \neq 0$. Use $\alpha = 0.05$. What p-value would you report?

d) Explain the differences between the two tests in parts (b) and (c).

13.12 In a multiple regression based on 25 observations, the following results are obtained:

$$\hat{y} = 18.456 + 6.235x_1 - 2.665x_2 + 7.34x_3 + 4.897x_4$$

The standard errors for b_1, b_2, b_3, and b_4 are 1.561, 2.057, 3.142 and 1.034, respectively.

a) Explain the meaning of the coefficient for x_1.

b) Using the two-sided t-test, determine which of the independent variables are the most significant.

c) Explain what you would do if a variable is determined to be insignificant.

13.13 The following multiple regression model

$$y = \alpha + \beta_1 x_1 + \beta_2 x_2 + \epsilon$$

is used to determine the annual household food expenditures in the United States in 1990 where y is the food expenditures (in thousands of dollars), x_1 the household income (in thousands of dollars) and x_2 the number of persons in the household. A random sample of 40 households in the Chicago area gave the following sample regression line:

$$\hat{y} = 1.533 + 0.0101x_1 + 0.355x_2$$

The estimates for the standard errors of the regression coefficients b_1, and b_2 are 0.00297 and 0.0316, respectively.

a) Calculate the values of the t-statistic for one-sided tests of the significance of each individual estimate of the regression coefficients, and find the critical value for such tests if $\alpha = 0.05$. What p-values would you report?

b) Determine which independent variable is more important for explaining the variation in the dependent variable. Explain your answer.

13.14 In Problem 11.13 we presented the data shown in the table to the left relating the educational levels and the mean income in the United States in 1985.

a) Determine the least-squares regression line, $\hat{y} = a + bx$ for these data. Calculate the standard error of estimate, s_e.

b) Now fit the model $y = \alpha + \beta_1 x + \beta_2 x^2 + \epsilon$ to these data. Calculate the standard error of estimate, s_e.

c) Of these two models, which provides the better fit? Explain your answer. Does a lower s_e value always mean a better fit? Under what circumstances will the model in part (b) be worse than the model in part (a)?

13.15 The table at the top of the next page lists the percentage of games won (PERC), the team batting average (TBA), and the team earned run average (ERA) for all the baseball teams in the American League in 1987.

Approximate years of education x	Mean income (in dollars) y
6	13,749
8	16,305
10	16,935
12	19,543
14	22,885
16	30,391
18	38,707

Source: U.S. Census Bureau

Team	Percentage of wins	Team BA	Team ERA
Detroit	.605	.272	4.02
Toronto	.593	.269	3.74
Milwaukee	.562	.276	4.62
New York	.549	.262	4.36
Boston	.481	.278	4.77
Baltimore	.414	.258	5.01
Cleveland	.377	.263	5.28
Minnesota	.525	.261	4.63
Kansas City	.512	.262	3.86
Oakland	.500	.260	4.32
Seattle	.481	.272	4.49
Chicago	.475	.258	4.30
Texas	.463	.266	4.63
California	.463	.252	4.38

Source: The Official Baseball Guide, *The Sporting News*, St. Louis, Mo., 1988.

a) *À priori,* what would you expect the relationship to be between the percentage of wins and the team batting average? Between the percentage of wins and the team ERA?

b) If we hypothesize the following multiple regression model

$$PERC = \alpha + \beta_1(TBA) + \beta_2(ERA) + \epsilon$$

Determine the least-squares equation from the above data.

c) Test the null hypothesis that there is no linear regression. Use $\alpha = 0.05$. What p-value would you report?

d) Determine which of the two explanatory factors, TBA and ERA, has the most significance in explaining the variation of the dependent variable, PERC.

13.16 In Problem 11.6 we developed a regression equation to predict the GPA of an MBA based on the GMAT scores. Suppose we now expand the analysis by including the undergraduate grade point average (UGG) in addition to the GMAT scores. This means that the regression equation will now be

$$\hat{GPA} = a + b_1(GMAT) + b_2(UGG)$$

Given the information in the table to the left for a sample of 10 MBAs:

GMAT Score	UGG	GPA
480	3.25	2.95
490	3.45	3.10
500	3.30	3.15
520	3.40	3.30
530	3.35	3.10
550	3.20	3.15
575	3.55	3.70
590	3.42	3.60
610	3.70	3.75
640	3.52	3.70

a) Fit a multiple least-squares regression line to the above observations in order to predict the GPA using the independent variables GMAT and UGG.

b) Test the null hypothesis that there is no linear regression. Use $\alpha = 0.05$. What p-value would you report?

c) Determine which of the two explanatory variables, GPA and UGG, is the more significant in explaining the variation in GPA. Explain your answer.

Test I Score (x_1)	Test II Score (x_2)	Rating y
74	40	91
59	41	72
83	45	95
76	43	90
69	40	82
88	47	98
71	37	80
69	36	75
61	34	74
70	37	79

13.17 A corporation gives its prospective managers two tests during the year in order to judge their potential. At the end of the year the company evaluates the managers for their effectiveness. The evaluations result in a job effectiveness rating. For a sample of 10 managers, the data are as shown in the table to the left.

a) Fit a multiple regression line to the above observations using x_1 and x_2 as the independent variables.

b) How would you interpret b_1, the regression coefficient of x_1? How would your answer differ if you had estimated the equation with just one independent variable, x_1?

c) Test the null hypothesis that there is no linear regression. Use $\alpha = 0.01$. What p-value would you report?

d) Which of the two independent variables is more useful in predicting the variation in the value of y?

Multiple Linear Correlation

13.7

Coefficient of Multiple Correlation

Multiple linear correlation bears the same relationship to simple linear correlation as multiple linear regression does to simple linear regression; that is, it represents an extension of the techniques for handling the relationship between only two variables to the set of methods for handling the relationship between more than two variables. In multiple linear correlation, the objective is to estimate the strength of the relationship between a variable y and a group of m other variables, $x_1, x_2, \ldots, x_m$. The measure usually used for this purpose is an index of the strength of the relationship of the sample data, which we call the coefficient of multiple correlation and denote by the expression $R_{y \cdot x_1, x_2, \ldots, x_m}$. This measure can be interpreted in a manner similar to r, as a multiple linear correlation coefficient represents the simple linear correlation coefficient between the sample values y_i and estimates of these values provided by the multiple regression equation. The value of a multiple coefficient R lies between zero and one, because it is not possible to indicate the sign of each of the regression coefficients that relate y to the variables $x_1, x_2, \ldots, x_m$ by a single plus or minus sign. Since $R_{y \cdot x_1, x_2, \ldots, x_m}$ is merely a generalization of the formula for r^2 on page 501, it is defined in precisely the same manner:

> *Coefficient of multiple correlation:*
>
> $$R_{y \cdot x_1, x_2, \ldots, x_m} = \sqrt{\frac{\text{SSR}}{\text{SST}}}$$

(13.11)

As before, the square of a correlation coefficient is much easier to interpret than the coefficient itself. The square of a coefficient of multiple correlation is called the **multiple coefficient of determination,** and is defined as follows:

$$
\text{Multiple coefficient of determination:} \\
R^2_{y \cdot x_1, \ldots, x_m} = \frac{\text{SSR}}{\text{SST}}
$$

(13.12)

We see from Formula (13.12) that R^2 is interpreted exactly like r^2, in that it measures the proportion of total variation that is explained by the regression line.

To illustrate the use of Formulas (13.11) and (13.12), recall that SST = 1003 in the salary example, and with x_1 and x_2 in the analysis, that

$$\text{SSE} = 134.437 \quad \text{and} \quad \text{SSR} = 868.563$$

Given these values, we can calculate the coefficient of multiple correlation between y_i and $\hat{y}$, which is $R_{y \cdot x_1, x_2}$, as follows:

$$R_{y \cdot x_1, x_2} = \sqrt{\frac{\text{SSR}}{\text{SST}}} = \sqrt{\frac{868.563}{1003}} = 0.9306$$

Since the square of the coefficient of multiple regression is $R^2_{y \cdot x_1, x_2} = 0.9306^2 = 0.866$, this result indicates that 86.6% of the variability of y (salary) is explained by differences in experience and differences in the number of employees supervised. Because 70.86% of SST was originally explained using x_1 (experience) values alone ($r^2 = 0.8418^2 = 0.7086$), the addition of x_2 (number of employees supervised) to the analysis explains an additional 15.74% of the variability in y.

When two variables are independent, the additional amount of variability explained is not affected by the order in which they enter the analysis. If the two variables are correlated, then adding one of these variables to the analysis automatically explains some of the variability in y that could have been explained by the other variable. Adding variables to a regression analysis can never decrease SSR; hence, R must always either increase or stay the same as more independent variables are included in the model.

The value of R measures the degree of association between the dependent variable and all of the variables $x_1, x_2, \ldots, x_m$ taken together. One may, however, be more interested in the degree of association between y and one of the variables $x_1, x_2, \ldots, x_m$ with the effect of all the other variables removed, or equivalently, held constant. The measure of strength of association in this case is called a **partial correlation coefficient.**

Partial Correlation Coefficient

Partial correlation analysis measures the strength of the relationship between y and one independent variable, in such a way that variations in the other independent variables are taken into account. Thus, a partial correlation coefficient is analogous to a partial regression coefficient, in that all other factors are "held constant." Simple correlation, on the other hand, ignores the effect of all other variables, even though these variables might be quite clearly related to the dependent variable, or to one another.

Partial correlation measures the strength of the relationship between y and a single independent variable by considering the relative amount that the unexplained variance is reduced by including this variable in the regression equation. For instance, in the salary example, we might want to calculate the partial correlation between y and x_2, where the linear effect of x_1 is held constant (that is, eliminated). This partial correlation is denoted by the symbol $r_{y,x_2 \cdot x_1}$, where the variables before the dot indicate those variables whose correlation is being measured (y and x_2), and the variable(s) after the dot (x_1) indicate those whose influence is being held constant.

As before, the square of a correlation coefficient is usually easier to interpret than the coefficient itself. In the case of a partial regression coefficient, this square is called a partial coefficient of determination. A partial regression coefficient of determination measures the proportion of the unexplained variation in y that is additionally explained by the variable not being held constant. Using this definition, we can now interpret $r^2_{y,x_2 \cdot x_1}$ as

$$r^2_{y,x_2 \cdot x_1} = \frac{\text{Extra variation in } y \text{ explained by the additional influence of } x_2}{\text{Variation in } y \text{ unexplained by } x_1 \text{ alone}}$$

To illustrate the calculation of $r^2_{y,x_2 \cdot x_1}$, recall that in the salary example the total variation in y (salary) is $\sum(y_i - \bar{y})^2 = 1003$. Based on the simple relationship between y and x_1 (experience), the amount of unexplained variation in y was SSE = 292.225. When x_2 is added to the analysis, SSE decreases to 134.437. This means that the extra variation explained by x_2 is $292.225 - 134.437 = 157.788$. These values are shown in Fig. 13.3.

Using the values in Fig. 13.3, we can now calculate $r^2_{y,x_2 \cdot x_1}$:

$$r^2_{y,x_2 \cdot x_1} = \frac{\text{Extra explained variation with } x_2}{\text{Unexplained variation with } x_1 \text{ alone}}$$

$$= \frac{157.788}{292.235} = 0.5399$$

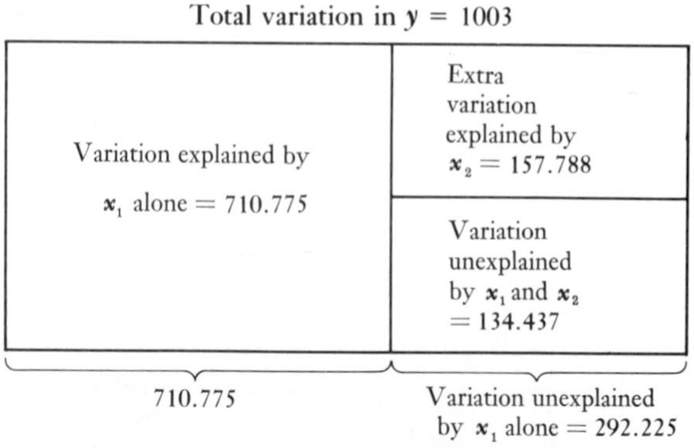

Total variation in $y = 1003$

| Variation explained by x_1 alone = 710.775 | Extra variation explained by $x_2 = 157.788$ |
| | Variation unexplained by x_1 and x_2 = 134.437 |

710.775 | Variation unexplained by x_1 alone = 292.225

Figure 13.3
The elements of variation in determining $r^2_{y,x_2 \cdot x_1}$.

In other words, 53.99% of the unexplained variability in y (after considering x_1) is now explained by the addition of x_2 (number of employees supervised). The square root of this value gives the partial correlation coefficient between x_1 and x_2, holding y constant: $r_{y, x_2 \cdot x_1} = \sqrt{0.5399} = 0.735$.*

The value $r_{y, x_2 \cdot x_1}$ represents the partial correlation coefficient for x_2, holding x_1 constant. We could just as easily calculate the partial correlation coefficient for x_1, holding x_2 constant, if the value of SSE (x_2) is known. If we were interested in the effect of adding a third variable, x_3, to the analysis, holding x_1 and x_2 constant, the appropriate partial correlation coefficient would be

$$r_{y, x_3 \cdot x_1, x_2} = \frac{\text{Extra variation in } y \text{ explained by additional influence of } x_3}{\text{Variation in } y \text{ unexplained by } x_1 \text{ and } x_2 \text{ alone}}$$

Notice the similarities in the definition of a partial correlation coefficient and the definition of a multiple correlation coefficient, in Formula (13.11). That is, a partial correlation coefficient measures reductions in the unexplained variation of y, while a multiple correlation coefficient measures reductions in the total variation of y.

Multicollinearity   **13.8**

We return now to a consideration of special problems that arise when one of the conditions specified in Section 13.3 is violated. This section deals with the violation or near violation of condition 1, which specifies that none of the independent variables can be an exact linear combination of the other independent variables. If the independent variables, $x_1, x_2, \ldots, x_m$ are perfectly linearly related to each other, then they are linearly dependent. In this case, no estimates of the partial regression coefficients can be obtained, since the normal equations will not be solvable; that is, the method of least squares breaks down and no estimates can be calculated. Perfect dependence seldom occurs in practice, because most investigators are careful not to include in the regression model two or more explanatory variables that represent the same influence on the dependent variable y. Indeed, even if an investigator did accidentally include two or more such variables, it is unlikely that the sample observations representing measures of these variables would be perfectly related, because some slight errors of measurement and sampling are almost inevitable.

Sometimes, however, special problems do occur, when two or more of the independent variables are strongly (but not perfectly) related to one another. This situation is known as multicollinearity. When multicollinearity occurs, it is possible to calculate least-squares estimates, but difficulty arises in the interpretation of the strength of the effect of each variable.

---

*In this case we would have to know, in advance, that the sign of $r_{y, x_2 \cdot x_1}$ is positive rather than negative. Or, we could define $r_{y, x_2 \cdot x_1}$ as the ordinary correlation of y^* and x_2^*, where the asterisk represents residuals from linear regression on x_1.

Detection of a Multicollinearity Problem

From the foregoing discussion we see that a high correlation between any pair of explanatory variables x_i and x_j may be used to help identify multicollinearity. It is possible, however, for all independent variables to have relatively small mutual correlations and yet to have some multicollinearity among three or more of them. Sometimes it is possible to detect these higher-order associations by using a multiple correlation coefficient that deals only with the explanatory variables. Suppose that we use the symbol R_j to denote the multiple correlation coefficient of variable x_j with all the other $(m-1)$ independent variables, $x_1, x_2, \ldots, x_{j-1}, x_{j+1}, \ldots, x_m$. Such a measure can be determined for each of the independent variables. Generally, if one or more of these values, $R_1, R_2, \ldots, R_j, \ldots, R_m$, is approximately the same size as the multiple correlation coefficient $R_{y \cdot x_1 \ldots x_m}$, then multicollinearity is a problem. In other words, if the strength of the association among any of the independent variables is approximately as great as the strength of their combined linear association with the dependent variable, then the amount of overlapping influence may be substantial enough to make the interpretation of the separate influence difficult and imprecise.

To illustrate, we present a model with four independent variables,

$$y = \alpha + \beta_1 x_1 + \beta_2 x_2 + \beta_3 x_3 + \beta_4 x_4 + \epsilon$$

The multiple correlation coefficient for this model is

$$R_{y \cdot x_1 x_2 x_3 x_4} = 0.90$$

To check for multicollinearity, first calculate the six simple correlations between pairs of independent variables

$$r_{x_1 x_2}, \quad r_{x_1 x_3}, \quad r_{x_1 x_4}, \quad r_{x_2 x_3}, \quad r_{x_2 x_4}, \quad r_{x_3 x_4}$$

If one of these is close to unity, then imprecise estimation will result. The next step is to calculate the multiple correlation coefficients of each independent variable with the other three:

$$R_{x_1 \cdot x_2 x_3 x_4}, \quad R_{x_2 \cdot x_1 x_3 x_4}, \quad R_{x_3 \cdot x_1 x_2 x_4}, \quad \text{and} \quad R_{x_4 \cdot x_1 x_2 x_3}$$

If any of these are as large as

$$R_{y \cdot x_1 x_2 x_3 x_4} = 0.90$$

then the problem of multicollinearity may be substantial. There is really no statistical method for testing whether these values indicate high multicollinearity or not, since this is not a problem of statistical inference about the population, but merely a property of sample observations. There are other, more complex methods for detecting multicollinearity, but they will not be detailed here (see, for example, reference 13).

Effects of Multicollinearity

When multicollinearity occurs, the least-squares estimates are still unbiased and efficient. The problem is that the estimated standard error of the coefficient (say, s_{b_i} for the coefficient b_i) tends to be inflated. This standard error tends to be larger than it would be in the absence of multicollinearity because the estimates are very sensitive to any changes in the sample observations or in the model specifications. In other words, including or excluding a particular variable or certain observations may greatly change the estimated partial coefficient. When s_{b_i} is larger than it should be, then the t-value for testing the significance of β_i is smaller than it should be. Thus, one is likely to conclude that a variable x_i is not important in the relationship when it really is.

If one is interested primarily in the forecasts of y_i, or $\mu_{y \cdot x_1, x_2, \ldots, x_m}$, rather than in the significance of the separate coefficients $b_1, b_2, \ldots, b_m$, then multicollinearity may not be a problem. Suppose that the combined fit for the regression equation is very good. If the observed linear relationships among all the independent variables can be expected to remain true for some new observations, then the regression model should also give a close fit for the new sample values even if multicollinearity is present.

Correction of Multicollinearity

When multicollinearity in a regression model is severe, and more precise estimates of the coefficients are desired, one common procedure is to select the independent variable most seriously involved in the multicollinearity and remove it from the model. The difficulty with this approach is that the model now may not correctly represent the population relationship, and all estimated coefficients would contain a specification bias. It would be better to try to replace the multicollinear variable with another that is less collinear but may still measure the same theoretical construct. For example, if the theoretical variable "business expectations" is measured by a stock price index that is highly collinear with retained earnings, then it may be possible to replace the stock index with some other measure, perhaps an index of business expectations obtained by surveying executives in the 500 largest corporations. In this way, the multicollinearity is reduced while the theoretical base for the model is still retained.

Violation of Assumption 4 or 5

13.9

Recall that assumption 5 states that each ϵ_i has the same variance ($V[\epsilon_i] = \sigma_\epsilon^2$), and assumption 4 states that the covariance between any two disturbance variables ϵ_k and ϵ_j is zero. That is,

$$C[\epsilon_k, \epsilon_j] = 0$$

We mentioned that these two assumptions are crucial in obtaining simple least-squares estimates of the regression coefficients that are efficient. This means that these estimators have a smaller variance than any other linear unbiased estimator that might be devised. If one or both of these assumptions is violated, then the estimator calculated by the method of least squares would not have the smallest variance; some other estimator that uses more information would be the efficient one. This loss in efficiency occurs whenever either of two problems is encountered: heteroscedasticity or autocorrelation. These terms are defined below.

> *Heteroscedasticity* occurs when assumption 5 is violated. It means that the variance of the disturbances ϵ_i is not constant, but changing.

> *Autocorrelation* occurs when assumption 4 is violated. It means that there is a correlation between the error terms.

The effect of either of these problems is a least-squares estimate of the regression coefficient for which the standard error of the coefficient is not minimized. Thus, tests of hypotheses or confidence intervals based on this property will not be correct.

Detection of Heteroscedasticity

To detect a situation where the variance of the errors is not constant, it is often useful to plot each $\hat{y}$-value against its corresponding residual $(y_i - \hat{y}_i)$. For example, the V-shaped slope of the boundary lines for the scatter of points in Fig. 13.4(a) suggests an increasing variance of the residuals as the value $\hat{y}$ increases. Such a plot may indicate that the fit of the model is not uniform and that the disturbances may not have a constant variance. A changing variance can also be indicated if the boundary lines approximate an inverted V or if they are close together at some points and wider apart at others, as, for example, in Fig. 13.4(b). Assumption 5, constant variance, does not seem to be violated if the boundary lines are approximately parallel, as in Fig. 13.4(c). If the variance of ϵ is suspected to be related to the size of a particular independent variable, such as x_j = time, then we may plot e_i against the specific x-variable rather than against $\hat{y}$.

Figure 13.4

Plotting residuals against $\hat{y}$ to detect heteroscedasticity.

Frequently, the assumption of constant variance is not seriously violated when using economic or business data measured over time, unless some signif-

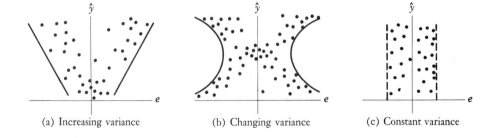

(a) Increasing variance   (b) Changing variance   (c) Constant variance

icant structural change occurs to affect the observations, such as a new law, a war, a major policy change, or some natural disaster. More often, the problem of heteroscedasticity arises when cross-sectional data is used,* such as employment or production data across firms, or tax and revenue data across states. In these cases, the disturbances may not have constant variances because of differing factors related to the size or the legal code of the different cross-sectional entities. For example, large corporations have different structures and operate under different tax laws than do small business firms. Thus, one would expect a specified model to represent one of these types better than the other. The variance of disturbances for the one type that it fits best will be smaller than the variance of disturbances for observations of the other type.

Detection of Serial Correlation or Autocorrelation[†]

Violations of assumption 4 tend to occur most frequently when the observations for the variables are taken at periodic intervals over time. If some underlying factors not specified in the model exert an influence on the fit of the model over several time periods, then the disturbances tend to be correlated to each other. Consider a change in corporate tax laws that might affect both the amount of investment (due to investment tax credit or depreciation write-offs) and the amount of retained earnings (due to taxes on profits). This legal factor may not be represented in the model, but its effect may be seen in the errors of the regression equation. For example, the average relationship estimated may give values too high before the tax-law change and too low afterward. The residuals would then tend to be all negative for observations taken before the tax changes and all positive for observations made after the change. Thus, the residuals would not be occurring at random but would systematically be related to each other, or **autocorrelated**.

The most frequently considered form of autocorrelation is the linear association of successive residuals. If we denote a residual at time period t by e_t and the previous residual by e_{t-1}, then first-order autocorrelation refers to the simple linear correlation of e_t and e_{t-1} over the entire set of observations, $t = 2, 3, 4, \ldots, n$. A measure of this correlation is given by the correlation coefficient between these two variables, $r_{e_t e_{t-1}}$. A geometric representation can be obtained by making a scatter diagram of the points corresponding to each pair (e_t, e_{t-1}). Figure 13.5 illustrates three cases: positive autocorrelation (a); negative autocorrelation (b); and no autocorrelation (c). When the points are predominantly in the positive quadrants (a), this means that successive residuals tend to have the same sign. If most points lie in the negative quadrants (b), then successive residuals tend to have opposite signs. If the scatter of

---

*There are two major types of data: time series data and cross-sectional data. Data measured over time at regular intervals are called **time-series data.** Data that measure the characteristics of a population at a given point in time are referred to as **cross-sectional data.**

†The terms **serial correlation** and **autocorrelation** often are used to refer to the same phenomenon, namely, the correlation of a variable with a lagged version of itself. Correlation of residuals from cross-sectional data, when it occurs, is called **spatial correlation.**

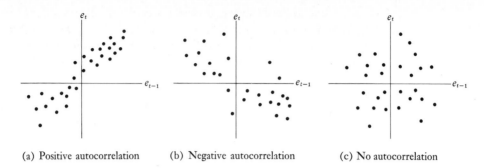

(a) Positive autocorrelation   (b) Negative autocorrelation   (c) No autocorrelation

Figure 13.5
Plots of successive residuals.

points is spread over all quadrants (c), successive residuals tend to be independent, or not correlated.

Autocorrelation of higher orders may also exist. For example, second-order autocorrelation refers to the simple linear correlation of e_t and e_{t-2} over the entire set of observations, $t = 3, 4, 5, \ldots, n$. However, in this book we restrict the treatment of autocorrelation to first-order autocorrelation only.

Although autocorrelation clearly exists in both Fig. 13.5(a) and (b), it is generally difficult to determine whether autocorrelation is present merely by using a scatter diagram. Hence, we need a test statistic to determine whether or not to accept the null hypothesis of independence (no autocorrelation) among successive error terms. The test used most often for this purpose is called the Durbin–Watson test.

The Durbin–Watson Test

The Durbin–Watson (D–W) test is designed to test the null hypothesis that there is no first-order autocorrelation among the error terms. The alternative hypothesis is that first-order autocorrelation does exist. To be more precise, let us suppose that the relationship between the population errors ϵ_t and ϵ_{t-1} can be expressed as follows:

$$\epsilon_t = \rho\epsilon_{t-1} + v_t$$

where ρ is the population autocorrelation coefficient between ϵ_t and ϵ_{t-1}. The v_t are the error terms and they satisfy assumptions 1–5 as applied to this model. When $\rho = 0$, no autocorrelation exists; the further ρ is away from zero toward $+1.0$ or -1.0, the greater the autocorrelation.

The test statistic for autocorrelation is the value of d determined by the following equation:

$$Durbin\text{–}Watson\ statistic:\ d = \frac{\sum\limits_{t=2}^{n}(e_t - e_{t-1})^2}{\sum\limits_{t=1}^{n}e_t^2} \qquad (13.13)$$

The value of d always falls between zero and four: $0 \leq d \leq 4$. If no auto-correlation exists, the value of d is expected to be the number 2. When posi-tive autocorrelation is present, the difference between e_t and e_{t-1} tends to be relatively small [see Fig. 13.5(a)], and d tends toward zero. With negative auto-correlation [see Fig. 13.5(b)], the difference between e_t and e_{t-1} tends to be relatively large and d tends toward the value 4.0. Thus, the null hypothesis of no autocorrelation will be rejected for relatively low values of d, which indi-cate positive autocorrelation, as well as for relatively large values of d, which indicate negative autocorrelation.

The test statistic d was developed in 1950 by two Englishmen, a statisti-cian and a social scientist, for use in tests of hypotheses about the existence of first-order autocorrelation. The contribution of Durbin and Watson was to determine the distribution of the test statistic d and to develop a table of criti-cal values for testing the null hypothesis, H_0: $\rho = 0$: no autocorrelation exists. The form of this table (Table X in Appendix B) includes two critical values, a d-upper (d_U) and a d-lower (d_L) for specified sample sizes n, for the number of independent variables in the regression model, $m = 1, 2, 3, 4$, or 5, and for two significance levels, $\alpha = 0.01$ or 0.05. The testing process that they proposed is slightly different from the ones we have used thus far, since the d-statistic leads to one of four conclusions, instead of the usual two. The possible conclusions are: no autocorrelation, positive autocorrelation, negative autocorrelation, or "don't know." The reason for this inconclusive region in the test result is that the distribution of the test statistic d depends to some extent on the particular characteristics of the interrelationships among the independent variables in each particular problem, and no generalizations of these characteristics can be found that unambiguously restrict the d-distribution. Figure 13.6 illustrates the possible values of the d-statistic and the conclusions associated with them.

Figure 13.6
Alternate conclusions based
on the Durbin–Watson
d-statistic.

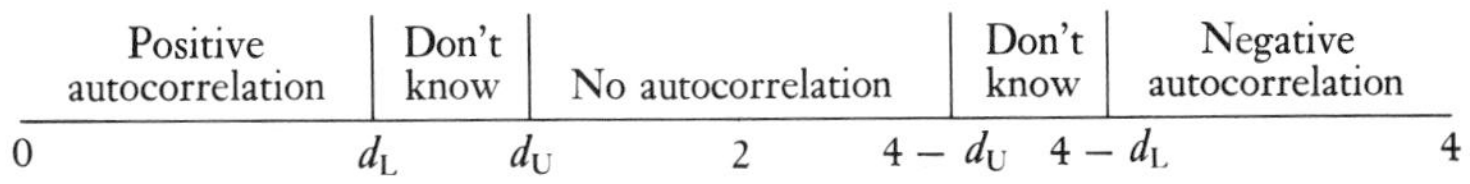

The following examples will show the reader how to use Table X and Fig. 13.6 to detect the problem of autocorrelation.

EXAMPLE 1

Suppose that we suspect the presence of positive autocorrelation in a particu-lar regression problem involving $m = 3$ independent variables, $n = 45$ obser-vations, and a calculated d-value, from Formula (13.15), of $d_c = 1.31$. Using the portion of Table X for $\alpha = 0.05$, we find $d_L = 1.38$ and $d_U = 1.67$. Since our computed value d_c is below d_L, we conclude that positive autocorrelation is a problem. We have in our model a significant violation of assumption 4. ∎

EXAMPLE 2

Suppose that we suspect the presence of negative autocorrelation in a particu-lar regression problem where $m = 4$ independent variables, $n = 79$,

$d_c = 2.94$, and $\alpha = 0.01$. Using the portion of Table X for $\alpha = 0.01$, we find $d_L = 1.34$ and $d_U = 1.58$. Since we are testing for negative autocorrelation and Table X gives values only for the test on positive autocorrelation, we must transform the d-statistic, using the property of symmetry. We find that the transformed critical values are $4 - d_L = 2.66$ and $4 - d_U = 2.42$. Since our computed value $d_C = 2.94$ lies above $4 - d_L$, we conclude that a significant problem of negative autocorrelation exists.   ∎

Most commonly, one does not know, before calculating d from Formula (13.13) or before looking at a plot of successive residuals as in Fig. 13.5, whether to be suspicious of positive or negative autocorrelation (although positive correlation occurs much more frequently in business and economic applications of regression analysis). In this case, one really is using a two-sided test and should realize that the proper significance level is found by doubling the values of 0.05 or 0.01 given in Table X.

Finally, recent research on the distribution of d and on alternate new statistics for detecting autocorrelation indicate that the inconclusive region in the D–W test may usually be reduced in the direction of d_U. That is, a single critical value separating the no-autocorrelation region from the positive-autocorrelation region seems closer to d_U than to d_L (and $4 - d_U$ is the better value in the negative autocorrelation test). Therefore, current users of the d-statistic would use the d_U- and d_L-values as indexes of the severity of the problem, replacing the original conclusions in Fig. 13.6 as follows:

$d < d_L$: serious problem of positive autocorrelation that requires correction

$d_L < d < d_U$: weaker problem of positive autocorrelation for which a correction is probably worthwhile

$d_U < d < 4 - d_U$: no problem of autocorrelation worth correcting

$4 - d_U < d < 4 - d_L$: weaker problem of negative autocorrelation for which correction is probably worthwhile

$4 - d_L < d$: serious problem of negative autocorrelation that requires correction

EXAMPLE 3

Suppose that we wish to test for autocorrelation in a particular regression problem with $m = 2$ independent variables, $n = 100$, and $d_c = 1.60$. Using the table for $\alpha = 0.01$, we find $d_c > d_U = 1.58$. Thus, we accept the condition of no autocorrelation (along with the possibility of some unknown Type II error—that we are accepting this when it is false). Using the table for $\alpha = 0.05$, we find that $d_c < d_L = 1.63$. In this case, we would conclude that positive autocorrelation is a problem (accepting a potential Type I error of 0.10, since we must double the α-value in a two-sided test for which we did not know *à priori* whether the computed d_c would lie above or below the value 2.0). In this example the test conclusion is critically affected by the choice of the significance level $\alpha = 0.01$ or 0.05.   ∎

Correction of Heteroscedasticity or Autocorrelation

As indicated previously, when either assumption 4 or assumption 5 is violated, the ordinary least-squares (OLS) estimators that we have described are not efficient. Another estimating procedure exists which also gives linear unbiased estimates and in which the variance of the estimators is smaller than that of OLS estimators. This procedure corrects for violations of assumption 4 or 5 by using a more complete estimating procedure, called generalized least squares (GLS), which explicitly uses information about the variances and covariances of the error terms ϵ_i in the calculation. This information is usually determined from an analysis of the residuals ϵ_i obtained from a first OLS estimation of the regression model. The purpose in using this information is to generate a new model situation in which the new error terms are free of the violations of assumptions 4 and 5.

For example, if the problem is a first-order positive autocorrelation of the errors, then a method is needed whereby the data or the model can be transformed so that the revised errors are free of autocorrelation. If the problem is heteroscedasticity, then this information about the way the variance increases or decreases (as depicted in Fig. 13.4(a) or (b)) should be used to weight the original observations before determining the least-squares estimates. In general, those observations for which the variance of the errors is smallest should be the more reliable, and therefore should be weighted more heavily. Since these methods are more complex, they will not be detailed here (for details see reference 9).

Dummy Variables in Regression Analysis

13.10

Thus far, the variables we have used in regression problems have been "quantitative variables," which means that they represent variables that are either measured or counted. In some types of problems it is desirable to use another type of variable, called a **qualitative variable,** which merely indicates whether or not an object belongs to a particular category or possesses a particular quality. For example, in a regression analysis in which the dependent variable is the consumption expenditures of families in the United States, one may be interested not only in relating y to family income (x_1) but also to whether or not the family lives in an urban or rural community (x_2). The variable x_1 is a quantitative variable (it measures income) while the variable x_2 is a qualitative variable (it indicates whether or not the family is classified as rural or urban). A variable such as x_2 often is called a **dummy variable.** To construct such a variable, we might let $x_2 = 0$ if the family lives in a rural community, and let $x_2 = 1$ if they live in an urban community.

The introduction of a dummy variable does not change the multiple regression process described thus far. That is, all computations are made in the same way as for a regression analysis involving only quantitative variables. One characteristic of the addition of a dummy variable, x_2, is that we know that its value in the regression equation is either zero or one. Hence, we can write two regression equations, one using $x_2 = 0$, and the other using $x_2 = 1$. To illustrate this, we present the following least-squares regression line where $x_2 = $ dummy variable:

$$\hat{y} = a + b_1 x_1 + b_2 x_2$$

If $x_2 = 1$, then substituting $x_2 = 1$ into this equation yields

$$E[y \mid x_2 = 1] = a + b_1 x_1 + b_2(1) = (a + b_2) + b_1 x_1$$

Since $x_2 = 1$ indicates an urban family, this equation represents the regression line for urban families. If we substitute $x_2 = 0$ in the original regression line, we get the regression line for rural families.

$$E[y \mid x_2 = 0] = a + b_1 x_1 + b_2(0) = a + b_1 x_1$$

Thus, we have derived two regression lines from the original regression model, as shown in Fig. 13.7.

In this example the distinction between rural and urban families shifts the regression intercept from a to $(a + b_2)$. (The graph shows a positive value for b_2.) Note that the slope of both straight lines is the same (b_1).

If we wished to allow for a different slope in the relation between consumption and income for rural versus urban families, the specification of the model that includes the dummy variable would be different. We would then specify the regression model as

$$\hat{y} = a + (b + cx_2)x_1$$

where $x_2 = $ dummy variable. Then, if $x_2 = 1$ for an urban family, the line is

$$E[y \mid x_2 = 1] = a + (b + c)x_1 \quad \text{with a slope of } (b + c)$$

When $x_2 = 0$ for a rural family, the line is

$$E[y \mid x_2 = 0] = a + bx_1 \quad \text{with a slope of } b$$

A positive value of c would indicate that urban families have a higher propensity to consume out of extra income received than do rural families, who would have a higher propensity to save extra income. A negative value of c

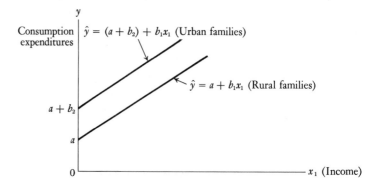

Figure 13.7
Two regression lines
resulting from the use of a
dummy variable.

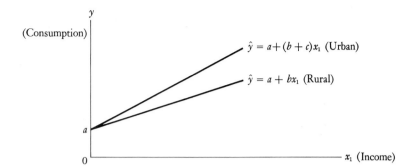

Figure 13.8
Two regression lines
resulting from the use of a
dummy slope variable.

would give evidence of the converse. In both cases, the intercept is the same value. Figure 13.8 illustrates the situation of a dummy slope variable. The reader should recognize the dummy variables may be used to allow for both different intercepts and different slopes in the same model.

An Example Using a Single Dummy Variable

To illustrate the use of dummy variables, we will present two examples: one involving a single dummy variable, and a second involving three dummy variables. In each example dummy variables will be used for intercepts, since the algebra is simpler. Dummy variables used for different slopes would be similar. The data for these examples are presented in Table 13.4.

TABLE 13.4

	Quarter	Retail sales y	GNP x_1	Increase variable x_2	Quarter variable x_3	x_4	x_5
1972	1	978	1112.5	0	1	0	0
	2	1123	1143.0	0	0	1	0
	3	1125	1169.3	0	0	0	1
	4	1260	1204.7	0	0	0	0
1973	1	1121	1248.9	0	1	0	0
	2	1275	1277.9	0	0	1	0
	3	1257	1308.9	0	0	0	1
	4	1381	1344.0	1	0	0	0
1974	1	1172	1358.8	1	1	0	0
	2	1368	1383.8	1	0	1	0
	3	1382	1416.3	1	0	0	1
	4	1454	1430.9	1	0	0	0
1975	1	1260	1416.6	1	1	0	0
	2	1462	1440.9	1	0	1	0

Source: Survey of Current Business

Table 13.4 presents quarterly data, measured at an annual rate, on retail sales of cars (in millions of dollars) as the dependent variable (y) and gross national product (in billions of dollars) between 1972 and mid-1975 as x_1. Now, suppose that we want to investigate the effect on retail sales of cars of a huge oil price increase initiated by the OPEC countries in October, 1973. To do this, we introduce the dummy variable x_2, and let $x_2 = 1$ for any period after the price increase, and $x_2 = 0$ before the price increase. A least-squares regression using these variables yields (the standard errors are in parentheses):

$$\hat{y} = -242.11 + 1.2346x_1 - 42.456x_2$$
$$\qquad\qquad (0.4122) \quad (89.61)$$

By substituting $x_2 = 0$ into this equation, we get the regression equation for the period before the price increase,

$$\hat{y} = -242.11 + 1.2346x_1 - 42.456(0)$$
$$= -284.566 + 1.2346x_1$$

The short-run impact of the oil price increase, as represented by these data, was to dampen retail sales by about \$42 million per year. Perhaps a shift in sales from large, expensive cars to cheaper, gas-saving cars accounted for much of this.

As is the case with all regression variables, we are interested in whether or not the coefficient of a dummy variable differs significantly from zero. In the present example, we might have hypothesized that the sign of the coefficient b_2 will be negative due to a shift from "gas-guzzlers" to "gas-sippers"; that is, we might be testing

$$H_0: \beta_2 = 0 \qquad \text{versus} \qquad H_a: \beta_2 < 0$$

The calculated value of t for these hypotheses is

$$t = \frac{b_2}{s_{b_2}} = \frac{-42.456}{89.61} = -0.474$$

Since the value $t = -0.474$ is not in the critical region for $(n - m - 1) = (14 - 2 - 1) = 11$ d.f. for any reasonable α, we must accept the null hypothesis $H_0: \beta_2 = 0$. Therefore, our conclusion must be that the price increase did not significantly affect retail sales. The size of the apparent change in sales is not uncommon even during periods of no change in oil prices.

An Example Using Multiple Dummy Variables

Again, we will use Table 13.4 to illustrate how two or more dummy variables can be used simultaneously. Suppose that we decide that there may be consistent differences in retail sales related to the quarters of the year (winter, spring, summer, fall). To include the quarter of the year as a variable in the problem we must add three dummy variables to the analysis, as shown in the final three columns of Table 13.4. If $x_3 = 1$ (and $x_4 = x_5 = 0$), this indicates the first (or winter) quarter; when $x_4 = 1$ (and $x_3 = x_5 = 0$), this indicates the second (or spring) quarter; for the third (or summer) quarter, $x_5 = 1$ (and

$x_3 = x_4 = 0$). Note that we only need three dummy variables to indicate four quarters, for the fourth quarter (fall) is designated by the absence of a 1 in the x_3, x_4, or x_5 columns (that is, $x_3 = x_4 = x_5 = 0$). In general, if the model includes an intercept term a, then the number of dummy variables needed to specify b different categories or levels is $b - 1$. Thus, to indicate two different categories (such as rural versus urban, or before price change by the Organizi-ation of Petroleum Exporting Countries (OPEC) versus after), only one dummy variable is needed.

The least-squares regression analysis for the data in Table 13.4 (omitting variable x_2) is shown in the Minitab output in Fig. 13.9. The regression equa-tion is

$$\hat{y} = 76.023 + 0.972x_1 - 191.115x_3 - 43.295x_4 - 82.770x_5$$

When the appropriate values of x_3, x_4, and x_5 are substituted, the above equa-tion yields the four different regression lines shown in Fig. 13.10. For example, the equation for the first quarter is derived by setting $x_3 = 1$, $x_4 = 0$, and $x_5 = 0$:

$$\hat{y} = 76.023 + 0.972x_1 - 191.115(1) - 43.295(0) - 82.770(0)$$
$$= -115.092 + 0.972x_1$$

The values of $\hat{y}$ for the other three quarters are

$$\hat{y} = \quad 32.728 + 0.972x_1 \quad \text{(second quarter)},$$
$$\hat{y} = -6.747 + 0.972x_1 \quad \text{(third quarter)},$$
$$\hat{y} = \quad 76.023 + 0.972x_1 \quad \text{(fourth quarter)}.$$

```
The Regression Equation is

y = 76.02 + 0.97 x1 - 191.12 x3 - 43.30 x4 - 82.77 x5

Predictor        Coef     Stdev    t-ratio        p
Constant       76.023
x1              0.972     .0503     19.313    0.000
x3           -191.115   15.6141    -12.240    0.000
x4            -43.295   15.4868     -2.796    0.021
x5            -82.770   16.5976     -4.987    0.001

s = 20.253   R-sq = 98.60%   R-sq(adj) = 97.98%

Analysis of Variance

SOURCE         DF        SS         MS         F         p

Regression      4    259719.9   64930.0    158.30    0.0000
Error           9      3691.5     410.2
Total          13    263411.4
```

Figure 13.9

Minitab output for the data in Table 13.4

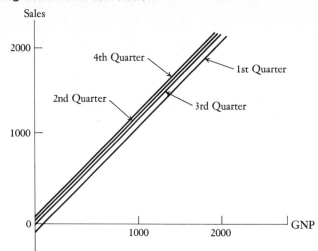

Figure 13.10
Testing the joint effect of a subgroup of variables

From Fig. 13.10 we see that the regression lines do appear to differ from quarter to quarter. At this point we could use a t-test to determine whether each of the coefficients b_3, b_4, and b_5 is significantly different from zero. Perhaps a more meaningful test, however, would be to test the explanatory contribution of all three dummy variables simultaneously, as follows:

H_0: The joint effect of the dummy variables is not significant.
   versus
H_a: The dummy variables as a group do contribute to the explanation of the variation in y.

A test statistic useful in this circumstance is derived by comparing the amount of unexplained variation (SSE) when all the variables are in the equation (GNP and the three dummy variables) with the amount of unexplained variation when the dummy variables are not included, labeled as SSE_s for the sum of squares of the errors in the "shorter" or "smaller" form of the model (including only GNP). If there are j dummy variables, the following F-test is appropriate:

$$F = \frac{(SSE_s - SSE)/j}{SSE/(n - m - 1)}$$

(13.14)

For our retail data, $SSE_s = 75955.8$, and $SSE = 3691.4$, $j = 3$, and $(n - m - 1) = (14 - 4 - 1) = 9$. Substituting these values into (13.14) yields

$$F = \frac{(75955.8 - 3691.4)/3}{3691.4/9} = \frac{24088.1}{410.16} = 58.729$$

Since this value of F exceeds the critical value of 6.99 when $\alpha = 0.01$, we can reject the null hypothesis that seasonal factors do not affect retail sales, and conclude that the quarterly dummy variables are useful in explaining variation in retail sales.

As a final note, we add that Formula (13.14) is useful in any situation where one is considering the inclusion of one or more additional variables (not necessarily dummy variables) in a multiple regression analysis. One way to do this is to fit a regression equation twice to the same data, once with all variables included in the analysis, and once excluding all variables with coefficients that are hypothesized to equal zero. The results of the original run will yield SSE, while the second run will yield SSE_s. Then Formula (13.14) can be used with j = number of independent variables in the subgroup excluded, and m = total number of independent variables.

Multiple Linear Regression: An Example

13.11

Suppose that a leading securities firm, Cabot, Perkins, and Winston, has decided to compete in the sealed bidding on a new $10 million series of first-mortgage bonds. These bonds, which must be purchased as a single unit, are to be awarded to the highest bidder. Bids are to be in terms of a percentage of the par value of the issue. Moody's Investors Service rates the bonds as Aa, the second highest rating.

In the process of determining a bid price, the analysts at Cabot learn that there will be only a single competitor bidding against them for the bonds, the firm of Martin and Wainwright. Furthermore, they find in their files a complete record of the 20 previous occasions in which Cabot and Martin were both bidding on the same issue. These records show Martin's bid for the issue, the par value of the issue, the number of bidders participating, and the Moody's rating. After examining this information, shown in Table 13.5, the analysts at Cabot decide to use linear regression analysis in an attempt to better assess what Martin might bid for the current issue.

Before calculating a linear regression equation for the data in Table 13.5, we first plot the relationship between the dependent variable (Martin's bid) and each of the three independent variables (par value, number of bidders, and Moody's rating) in order to visually check whether or not the relationship in these three cases is approximately linear. Before doing so it is necessary to attach a numerical value to the Moody's ratings. Suppose we give the highest rating, Aaa, a value of 1, the second highest rating, Aa, a value of 2, A a value of 3, Baa a value of 4, and the lowest rating, Ba a value of 5. The scatter diagrams in Fig. 13.11 show the relationship between Martin's bid price and each of the three independent variables. Note that a linear approximation is not unreasonable for the first two relationships, but that Martin's bid and the Moody's rating follow a curvilinear pattern rather than a linear one. Although it may not be apparent from the scatter diagram, it is possible to show (by some procedures not discussed here) that Martin's bid price is related to percent changes in the Moody's rating rather than absolute changes measured on a scale from 1 to 5.

TABLE 13.5

Martin's bid (% of par) y	Par value (millions) x_1	Number of bidders[a] x_2	Moody's rating x_3
97.682	13.0	2	A
98.424	6.0	5	A
101.435	9.0	5	Aa
102.266	5.5	7	Aaa
97.067	7.0	3	Baa
97.397	9.5	2	Ba
99.481	17.0	2	Aa
99.613	12.5	5	A
96.901	13.5	2	Ba
100.152	12.5	3	Aaa
98.797	13.0	4	Baa
100.796	7.5	6	Aa
98.750	7.5	2	Aa
97.991	12.0	3	Ba
100.007	14.0	4	Aaa
98.615	11.5	6	Ba
100.225	15.0	2	Aa
98.388	8.5	6	Baa
98.937	14.5	7	A
100.617	9.5	5	Aaa

[a]Including Cabot and Martin.

Fortunately, this type of curvilinear relationship can be transformed into a linear one by taking the logarithm of each value of the independent variable: that is, let the rating $Aaa = \log_{10}1 = 0$, $Aa = \log_{10}2 = 0.301$, $A = \log_{10}3 = 0.477$, $Baa = \log_{10}4 = 0.602$, and $Ba = \log_{10}5 = 0.699$. A scatter diagram of Martin's bid price plotted against $\log_{10}$ (Moody's rating) is seen in Fig. 13.12 to approximate the desired linear form.

Figure 13.11
Scatter diagrams.

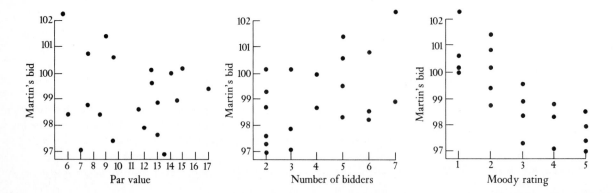

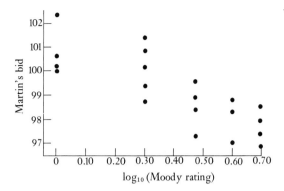

Figure 13.12
Scatter diagram of
Martin's bid and $\log_{10}$
(Moody's rating).

Stepwise Regression Analysis Using SAS

As stated earlier, multiple linear regression equations are generally determined using statistical packages. One of the most widely used packages for regression analysis is SAS. We will use the stepwise multiple regression function in this package to analyze the data in Table 13.5.

As this name implies, the program computes the multiple regression equation in steps. The first step is to compute the simple regression line between the dependent variable and that particular independent variable that will reduce SSE to its smallest value. In other words, the program chooses, from the set of all independent variables specified, the one explaining the most variation in y, and then calculates the regression equation between y and this variable. In each succeeding step, one additional variable is added to the equation, the variable added always being the one which results in the greatest reduction in SSE. We present the output from SAS in a modified form in Figs. 13.13. through 13.16.

Figure 13.13 shows the simple correlation coefficient (r) between each of these variables. For the purposes of this example, the variables are defined as follows: y = MARTIN for Martin's bid, x_1 = PAR for par value, x_2 = BIDDERS for the number of bidders, and x_3 = MRLOG for $\log_{10}$ of the Moody's ratings. The correlation matrix gives the simple correlation coefficient between each pair of variables, the diagonal elements all being equal to 1 because a variable is always perfectly correlated with itself. Note that the highest correlation is

CORRELATION MATRIX

VARIABLE	MARTIN	PAR	BIDDERS	MRLOG
MARTIN	1.000	− 0.133	0.483	− 0.799
PAR	− 0.133	1.000	− 0.372	0.057
BIDDERS	0.483	0.483	1.000	− 0.160
MRLOG	− 0.799	0.057	− 0.160	1.000

Figure 13.13
SAS output for correlation.

```
STEP 1   VARIABLE MRLOG ENTERED   R SQUARE = 0.62094

             DF   SUM OF SQUARES   MEAN SQUARE        F    PROB > F

REGRESSION   1       25.9630         25.9630       31.74   0.0001
ERROR        18      14.7246          0.8180
TOTAL        19      40.6876

             B VALUE    STD ERROR                    F    PROB > F
INTERCEPT    101.0469
MRLOG        - 4.6655     0.8281                    31.74   0.0001
```

Figure 13.14

Partial SAS output, step 1.

between the variables MARTIN (Martin's bid) and MRLOG ($\log_{10}$ of the Moody's ratings), equaling -0.799. From the definition of a correlation coefficient given by Formula (13.11), the variable explaining the most variability in y will be that independent variable most highly correlated with y. In a stepwise procedure this variable should thus be the first one entered in the regression equation, and we see in the output given in Fig. 13.14 that it is.

The term labeled INTERCEPT represents the value of a. Thus, $a = 101.0469$. Following this term, the program prints out the value of the regression coefficient, which is $b = -4.6655$. Since $y = $ MARTIN (Martin's bid price) and $x_3 = $ MRLOG ($\log_{10}$ of the Moody ratings), the regression equation is

$$\hat{y} = 101.0469 - 4.6655x_3$$

The remaining values in the computer output provide additional information about the variables, the regression coefficients, and the fit of the regression equation to the sample observations. The analysis-of-variance table, for example, indicates that the ratio MSR/MSE is $F = 31.74$. Since the p-value of $F = 31.74$ with 1,18 d.f. is less than 0.0001, we can reject the null hypothesis of no linear regression. Missing from this output is a direct computation of the standard error of the estimate. However, this may easily be computed by taking the square root of MSE. Thus, $s_e = \sqrt{0.8180} = 0.9044$. The standard error of the regression coefficient is $s_{b_3} = 0.8281$.

Step 2 in SAS

The variable added in step 2 of the regression is BIDDERS (the number of bidders). This is shown in Fig. 13.15.

We can now see that adding the variable, BIDDERS, to the regression equation increases the multiple coefficient of determination to

$$R^2 = 0.7672$$

which means that about 76.72% of the variability in Martin's previous bid prices has now been explained. The standard error of the estimate is again cal-

```
STEP 2   VARIABLE BIDDERS ENTERED    R SQUARE = 0.7672

                  DF      SUM OF SQUARES   MEAN SQUARE       F   PROB>F

REGRESSION         2         31.2135        15.6068      28.01   0.0001
ERROR             17          9.4741         0.5573
TOTAL             19         40.6876

              B VALUE       STD ERROR                       F   PROB>F

INTERCEPT     99.7060
MRLOG         -4.3246        0.6925                      39.00   0.0001
BIDDERS        0.2974        0.0969                       9.42   0.0069
```

Figure 13.15
SAS output, step 2.

culated as $s_e = \sqrt{MSE}$ and is $\sqrt{0.5573} = 0.7465$. This is a reduction from Step 1. Since BIDDERS $= x_2$, the multiple regression is

$$\hat{y} = 99.706 + 0.2974x_2 - 4.3246x_3 \qquad (13.15)$$

where x_3 = MRLOG ($\log_{10}$ of Moody's ratings).

At this point the question is whether or not PAR (par value) should be entered into the regression equation. The question of when to stop adding variables is comparable to the choice of an α-level in hypothesis testing, and as such it will depend on the risk the researcher is willing to incur of including a variable in the regression equation which has a β-value of zero. Recall that adding an additional variable can never increase the amount of unexplained variation in a given problem but may decrease SSE by such a small amount that when dividing this sum by the number of degrees of freedom in order to compute the mean square error, the one extra degree of freedom lost may result in an increase of the standard error of the estimate. Such a result occurs in the present case, when adding the variable par value, as shown in the final output from SAS for this example (Fig. 13.16). Note that the standard error of b_1,

$$s_{b_1} = 0.0578$$

is larger than the value of the coefficient itself, as $b_1 = 0.0232$. Thus, even a 68% confidence interval will include the value $\beta_1 = 0$, and one cannot have much confidence that the value of β_1 differs from zero.

To complete this example, let's assume that Cabot has decided to use the output from step 2 of SAS, since x_1 (par value) does not appear to aid their predictive ability. From Formula (13.15) we know that the appropriate regression equation is

$$\hat{y} = 99.706 + 0.2974x_2 - 4.3246x_3$$

where x_2 = BIDDERS (number of bidders) and x_3 = MRLOG ($\log_{10}$ of Moody's ratings). Since, in the present case, there are two bidders and the Moody's rat-

STEP 3   VARIABLE PAR ENTERED   R SQUARE = 0.7695

	DF	SUM OF SQUARES	MEAN SQUARE	F	PROB > F
REGRESSION	3	31.3080	15.6068	17.80	0.0001
ERROR	16	9.3796	0.5862		
TOTAL	19	40.6876			

	B VALUE	STD ERROR		F	PROB > F
INTERCEPT	99.3883				
MRLOG	− 4.3239	.7103		37.06	0.0001
BIDDERS	0.3131	0.1069		8.59	0.0098
PAR	0.0232	0.0578		0.16	0.6934

Figure 13.16
SAS output, step 3.

ing is Aa, we substitute $x_2 = 2$ and $x_3 = \log_{10}2 = 0.301$ into this equation to get the expected bid for Martin:

$$\hat{y} = 99.706 + 0.2974(2) - 4.3246(0.301) = 98.999$$

From this result and the output of step 2 of SAS, Cabot can now construct a probability distribution for the bid they expect from Martin. The mean of this distribution is $\hat{y} = 98.999$, and its standard deviation is (calculated as the square root of SSE) $s_e = 0.7456$, as shown in Fig. 13.17. If we knew the profit Cabot expects to make for each possible bid, we could use the probability distribution in Fig. 13.17 to find the bid that would maximize expected profits.

It is possible in using SAS to have the computer print the error of prediction, $y_i - \hat{y}_i$, for each set of observations in the sample. These errors, usually given in a "list of residuals," can be examined to check on the assumptions of linearity and homoscedasticity. In fact, most regression programs allow for the option of having the computer plot a scatter diagram showing the relationship between residual values and each of the independent variables or alternatively, between the residual values and the fitted values. This process of constructing scatter diagrams in regression analysis is an important one, for it is all too easy, especially when using the computer, to compute a regression line and not check the assumptions of linearity, independence, uniform variance, and, for small samples, normality. For this example the plot of the errors

Figure 13.17

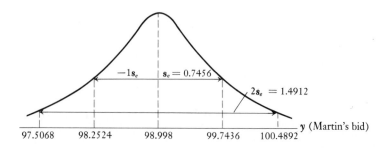

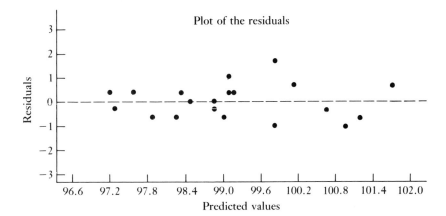

Figure 13.18
SAS plot of the fitted values against the residuals.

against the fitted values from the SAS program is shown in Fig. 13.18. This plot seems to indicate randomly distributed residuals. One conclusion that we can draw is that these data do not seem to have heteroscedasticity problems.

A Note of Caution   In using multiple regression analysis, care must be exercised to ensure that the equation has face validity. By this we mean that the variables included in the equation make intuitive sense. We strongly recommend that the analyst use his or her own judgment to screen out the independent variables in advance, discarding those variables that can not be intuitively explained. This is particularly true in stepwise regression, where one is often tempted to throw into the regression a long list of potential independent variables and then let stepwise regression screen out the ineffective variables. With this approach there is always a possibility that some variables that are not linearly related to the dependent variable may be included in the equation. To avoid this, a careful evaluation of the potential independent variables must be done in advance to discard such variables.

Problems

13.18 Explain the meaning of multicollinearity, and specify one of its effects that you think is important.

13.19 Calculate the fitted values and the residuals for the regression equation in Fig. 13.14 (see Table 13.5). Plot the fitted values against the residuals. Does your plot indicate any problems of heteroscedasticity? Explain your answer.

13.20 Refer to the residuals calculated in Problem 13.19. Assume that these observations represent a variable measured over time. Calculate the value of the Durbin–Watson statistic d and interpret the result. Let $\alpha = 0.02$, $m = 2$, and use a two-sided alternative hypothesis.

13.21 Assume the following regression model was fit

$$y = \alpha + \beta_1 x_1 + \beta_2 x_2 + \beta_3 x_3 + \beta_4 x_4 + \beta_5 x_5 + \epsilon$$

to 40 data points with the results.

$$s_e^2 = 4.589 \quad \text{and} \quad R^2 = 0.88$$

a) Do the values of s_e^2 and R^2 suggest that the model provides a good fit to the data? Explain your answer.

b) Test the hypothesis H_0: $\beta_1 = \beta_2 = \beta_3 = \beta_4 = \beta_5 = 0$ versus H_a: At least one β_i ($i = 1, 5$) $\neq 0$. Use $\alpha = 0.05$. What p-value would you report?

13.22 Assume the following regression model was fit

$$y = \alpha + \beta_1 x_1 + \beta_2 x_2 + \epsilon$$

to 22 data points with the results

$$\sum(y_i - \hat{y}_i)^2 = 6.286 \quad \text{and} \quad \sum(y_i - \bar{y})^2 = 14.697$$

a) Construct the analysis of variance table for this regression analysis, using Table 13.1 as a model.

b) Calculate the F-ratio and test the hypothesis that there is no linear regression. Use $\alpha = 0.05$. What p-value would you report?

c) Calculate the s_e and the R^2 values.

13.23 Recently a study of corn yields on several midwestern farms was conducted by agricultural experts. The following information was collected for one of the farms in the study:

y = average yield in bushels of corn per acre;
x_1 = amount of summer rainfall measured at a nearby weather station;
x_2 = average daily use in machine hours of tractors on the farm;
x_3 = amount of fertilizer used per acre.

The sample for this study includes observations for ten crop years. Based on this sample, a multiple regression model was developed, resulting in the following equation:

$$\hat{y} = 16.21 + 75.13x_1 + 5.90x_2 + 48.28x_3$$
$$(10.3) \quad (25.1) \quad (4.3) \quad (8.2)$$

The number in parentheses are the standard errors of the regression coefficients. Additionally, the analysis gave the following information:

$$s_e = 20.12 \text{ bushels} \qquad s_y = 39.92 \text{ bushels,}$$
$$r^2_{y, x_1 \cdot x_2 x_3} = 0.60$$

Based on this information answer the following questions:

a) What are the degrees of freedom for t-distributed test statistics for regression?

b) Explain which variable appears to be the most important in explaining the variation of yield.

c) From the regression results, is it proper to argue that more machine hours of tractor use causes more yield, or that more yield requires more machine hours of tractor use? Explain.

d) Find the multiple coefficient of determination, $R^2_{y \cdot x_1 x_2 x_3}$.

e) Account for the different values of

$$R^2_{y \cdot x_1 x_2 x_3} \text{ and } r^2_{y, x_1 \cdot x_2 x_3}$$

by explaining the different meanings of the two coefficients.

13.24 Using 12 observations, a model $y = \alpha + \beta_1 x_1 + \beta_2 x_2 + \beta_3 x_4 + \epsilon$ is estimated by the method of least squares. Here SST = 400, SSE = 170, and the amount of variation explained jointly by x_1, x_2, and x_3 is 200.

a) Find $r^2_{y, x_4 \cdot x_1 x_2 x_3}$ and explain what it means.

b) Do an ANOVA test with $\alpha = 0.05$ to determine whether this linear relationship is significant. What p-value would you report?

13.25 Consider a linear-regression model, $y = \alpha + \beta_1 x_1 + \beta_2 x_2 + \epsilon$, where

y = learning by grade 12, as measured by an academic test score composite, with mean 300 and standard deviation 150, for the entire population of 12th-graders;

x_1 = school expenditures per pupil during 3 years of high school (in hundreds of dollars);

x_2 = an index of socioeconomic status of the individual, with mean 10 and standard deviation 2, for the entire population of 12th graders.

Based on a sample of 25 twelfth-grade-level individuals who were arrested on drug possession charges, the following results (Table 13.6) are obtained. Analyze, interpret, and explain these data in the way you think most appropriate and meaningful.

TABLE 13.6

Variable	Mean	Standard deviation
y	306.67	175.98
x_1	12.58	9.31
x_2	11.17	8.95

Correlations:
$r_{yx_1} = 0.83$ $r_{yx_2} = 0.35$ $r_{x_1 x_2} = 0.10$

Coefficient	Estimate	Standard error	t-value
a	10.16	11.90	0.85
b_1	17.60	0.62	28.30
b_2	4.30	2.90	1.48

Multiple $R = 0.92$; $s_e = 3.015$

Analysis of variance	SS	d.f.	Mean square
Regression	1090	2	545.00
Residual	200	22	9.09

13.26 Suppose the variation in y is 500 units and the model

$$\hat{y} = a + b_1x_1 + b_2x_2$$

leaves 240 units unexplained (based on 15 observations). Extending the model to include variable x_3 explains 80 more units of variation in y. Find $R^2_{y \cdot x_1x_2x_3}$ and $r^2_{y,\,x_3 \cdot x_1x_2}$.

13.27 Consider a multiple regression model, $\hat{y} = a + b_1x_1 + b_2x_2 + b_3x_3$ based on 24 observations on each variable. Suppose that the total variation, SST, equals 300, the unexplained variation is 60, and the amount of variation explained by variables x_1 and x_2 together is 160.

a) Calculate the value of the multiple coefficient of determination and interpret its meaning.

b) Prepare a diagram similar to Fig. 13.3 to explain the meaning and value of $r^2_{y,\,x_3 \cdot x_1x_2}$.

c) Complete an analysis-of-variance table to test the significance of the linear relation. What p-value would you report?

13.28 A grocery chain uses two forms of advertising to promote sales of certain lines of food products every week. The first promotion is through advertising in the local daily newspaper(s). The second is through the distribution of discount coupons. These coupons appear in the Sunday papers for use in the following week. Coupons are also available at the store during the week of the promotion. Management wishes to study the effects of these two types of promotional expenditures. They have selected at random 12 supermarkets where a certain product line was recently promoted using both forms of promotions. Shown below is the output from the Minitab package for this problem.

```
Predictor      Coef    Stdev    t-ratio        p
Constant     5.5957
madv        15.5804   1.3399      11.63    0.000
coupons      4.1866   0.9450       4.43    0.002

s = ?                R-sq = 94.4%    R-sq (adj) = 93.1%

Analysis of Variance

SOURCE          DF         SS          MS         F        p
Regression       2   2024.0266   1012.0133   75.548    0.000
Error            9    120.5609     13.3957
Total           11   2144.5875
```

a) What are the sample estimates of α, β_1, β_2?

b) What is the standard error of the estimate, s_e? What is the standard error of the regression coefficient of the variable "madv" (media advertising)?

c) Does the analysis provide sufficient evidence to support the hypothesis that sales increase with these two forms of promotions? Explain your answer.

d) Does the regression show that sales increase with promotion through coupons? Explain your answer.

e) Of the two independent variables, which is more important for explaining the variation in the dependent variable?

13.29 A time-series study used annual data for the period 1962–1987 on the demand for money as a function of the current interest rate, last period's interest rate, and the change in the interest rate from year to year. Last period's interest rate reflects habit and inertia, and the change in interest rates reflects expectations of change based on recent changes. The regression model is

$$y_t = \alpha + \beta_1 x_{1t} + \beta_2 x_{2t} + \beta_3 x_{3t} + \epsilon$$

where

y_t is the money supply at time t,
x_{1t} is the interest rate at time t,
x_{2t} is the interest rate at time $t - 1$,
x_{3t} is the change in the interest rate from last period, $x_{1t} - x_{2t}$.
The Durbin–Watson statistic is 1.1, $R^2 = 0.95$, and $n = 26$.

a) Using a 5% level of significance, test the hypothesis of no positive autocorrelation against the alternative of positive autocorrelation.

b) Based on your answer to (a), either test the hypothesis that the regression does not explain the demand for money against the alternative that it does, or explain why such a test is inappropriate in this case.

13.30 Given the following multiple-regression results (Tables 13.7–13.9), where $n = 12$,

a) Which independent variable is most important in determining y?

b) Find the residual for the twelfth observation if the observed values for x_1 and x_2 are 8 and 9, respectively.

c) What is the number of degrees of freedom for the **F**-test on the multiple linear association represented by this estimated model?

d) What percentage of the total variation in y has been explained by this regression?

e) Using a plot, comment on the validity of the assumption of homoscedasticity in this model.

TABLE 13.7

Variable	Mean	Standard deviation		
y	306.67	174.98	r_{xy_1}	$= 0.9348$
x_1	12.58	9.31	r_{yx_2}	$= 0.3501$
x_2	11.17	8.95	$r_{x_1 x_2}$	$= 0.0096$

TABLE 13.8

Coefficient	Estimator	Standard deviation		
b_1	17.61	0.623	$R_{y \cdot x_1 x_2}$	$= 0.995$
b_2	6.70	0.647		
a	10.17	11.972	s_e	$= 19.220$

TABLE 13.9

Observation	Observed y	Residual
1	650	−1.63
2	80	11.99
3	120	−18.46
4	180	+32.34
5	360	17.79
6	140	−21.07
7	450	7.11
8	550	11.43
9	280	−14.37
10	300	−16.30
11	350	−17.43
12	220	

f) Using a plot, comment on the validity of the assumption of no autocorrelation in this model.

g) Do you think multicollinearity is a problem in this estimation? Explain your answer.

h) If new observations on x_1 and x_2 are obtained, a corresponding value y can be predicted by using the regression equation. Discuss the accuracy of such a prediction if x_1 and x_2 are 20 and 30, respectively, as compared to the prediction of $\hat{y}$ if x_1 and x_2 are 10 and 12, respectively.

13.31 Let y = individual income for persons selected from among full-time workers in manufacturing, and let x = age. A simple regression model is written $y = \alpha + \beta x + \epsilon$.

a) Suppose you wish to include in the model the factor of sex. Specify and interpret the dummy variable to be included in order to differentiate levels of income depending on sex as well as on age.

b) Suppose that now you wish to allow for different impacts of age on income, depending on whether or not the person completed college. Specify a dummy slope variable to be added to the model, and explain the separate regression lines that can be derived.

c) Make a sketch with income and age on the axes, and illustrate the different potential regression lines you have implied in parts (a) and (b).

d) Finally, add a set of dummy variables to the model to allow for different income levels for five different areas of the county: northeast, midwest, southeast, southwest, and west. In your model specify the difference in the intercepts for females in the northeast compared to males in the west.

13.32 Consider the following partial output from the BMDO2R statistical package for a stepwise regression problem:

Step 2

```
SOURCE       SS       DF   MS      F-ratio
Regression   105.26    2   52.63    10.40
Residual     328.74   65    5.06
```

(Constant 17.321)

Variables in equation			Variables not in equation	
Variable	Coeff.	Std. error	Variable	Partial corr.
x4	−2.317	0.157	x1	−0.2314
x1	4.539	1.128	x3	0.1788

a) Write the least-squares equation at this step.

b) Determine the standard error of the estimate.

c) Find the value of multiple R.

d) Test the H_0: $\beta_i = 0$ vs. H_a: $\beta_i \neq 0$ for both β_2 and β_4.

e) Test H_0: $\beta_2 = \beta_4 = 0$ vs. H_a: β_2 or β_4 or both $\neq 0$.

f) Which variable will enter next in the stepwise procedure? How much will SSE be reduced by this new variable?

13.33 Consider the following correlation matrix from the B-STAT package:

	y	x1	x2	x3
y	1.000			
x1	.563	1.000		
x2	−.673	.884	1.000	
x3	.324	.264	.398	1.000

a) Does it appear that a multiple regression equation for y with x_1, x_2, and x_3 as the independent variables will be successful? Explain your answer.

b) Can you foresee any problems in obtaining accurate estimates of the regression coefficients? Explain your answer.

c) In a stepwise multiple regression procedure, which variable would enter first? Why?

13.34 Suppose you are trying to decide how many independent variables to include in a multiple regression analysis.

a) Can adding additional variables ever decrease R?

b) Can additional variables ever decrease the value of F?

c) Can adding additional variables ever increase the value of $\sum (y - \hat{y})^2$? Will s_e ever decrease? Explain your answers.

13.35 A multiple regression equation was developed to predict the salaries of senior executives from the pharmaceutical industry with SAL (salary in thousands) as the dependent variable and, EXPR (experience in years) and AGE (age of the executives) as the independent variables. The following partial output of the analysis was obtained from the Minitab package:

```
The Regression Equation is

sal = -60.48 - 1.70 expr + 4.86 age

Predictor       Coef   Stdev   t-ratio       p

Constant      -60.479
expr           -1.704   2.438   -0.699    0.497
age             4.864   2.139    2.274    0.041

s = 13.083   R-sq = 80.49%   R-sq(adj) = 77.49%

Analysis of Variance

Source       DF       SS       MS       F       p
Regression    2   9179.97   4589.99  26.818   0.000
Error        13   2225.01    171.15
Total        15  11405.98
```

a) Consider the information on the regression coefficients. Do the signs of the regression coefficients make intuitive sense? Explain your answer.

b) Consider the F-test from the ANOVA table. What conclusions can you derive from this test?

c) Now consider the t-tests on the regression coefficients. What conclusions can you derive from these tests? Are the results of these t-tests different from the results of the F-test? If so, what is the most likely explanation? How much confidence do you have in the accuracy of the estimates of the regression coefficients.

13.36 A chain of discount stores specializing in electronic goods has analyzed the stores' sales using multiple regression analysis. To carry out these analyses they collected data from stores in 15 different locations for the following four variables:

SALES   = average weekly sales (in thousands of dollars)

POP   = target population within a three-mile radius (in thousands)

INC   = annual per capita income of the target population

COMPT = number of competitors in the area

Analysis of the data using the B-STAT package resulted in the following correlation matrix:

	SALES	POP	INC	COMPT
SALES	1.000			
POP	0.577	1.000		
INC	0.562	0.513	1.000	
COMPT	−0.471	0.293	0.240	1.000

a) Are all the signs of the correlation coefficients (positive or negative) what you would expect? Explain your answer.

b) If a simple linear regression is performed with SALES as the dependent variable and INC as the independent variable, what percentage of the variability would be explained by the regression equation?

c) If a stepwise regression analysis is performed with SALES as the dependent variable and POP, INC, and COMPT as the independent variables, which independent variable will enter the equation first? Explain your answer.

13.37 Refer to the information in Problem 13.36. In this problem the stepwise analysis resulted in the following partial output from the B-STAT package:

```
STEP 1.    VARIABLE: POP ENTERED

DEPENDENT VARIABLE: SALES

VARIABLE   REGR.COEFF.   STD.ERROR
POP            .1506         .0591
CONSTANT    114.6938

ANALYSIS OF VARIANCE TABLE

SOURCE          SUM OF SQUARES   D.F.
REGRESSION         4154.3433      1
RESIDUAL           8302.9900     13

VARIABLES NOT IN THE EQUATION

NAME     PARTIAL r^2
INC         .1444
COMPT       .6738
```

a) Write the least-squares equation.

b) Determine the multiple R value.

c) Test the hypothesis $H_0: \beta_1 = 0$ versus $H_a: \beta_1 \neq 0$ using a t-test where $x_1 = $ POP. What p-value would you report?

d) Which variable will enter the equation in step 2 of the stepwise procedure? How much will SSE be reduced by the new variable?

e) What will the multiple R value in step 2 be after the second variable has entered the equation?

f) What will the standard error of the estimate be in step 2 of the stepwise procedure?

g) Test the hypothesis H_0: $\beta_1 = \beta_2 = 0$ versus H_a: β_1 or β_2 or both $\neq 0$ for step 2. What p-value would you report?

13.38 In golf putting is considered one of the harder parts of the game. Generally, the longer the putt, the harder it is to make it. The information in the table to the left regarding putting performances of professional golf players on the PGA Tour was reported in *Sports Illustrated* (March 27, 1989).

Length of putt (in feet)	Proportion of putts made
2.0	.9330
3.0	.8310
4.0	.7410
5.0	.5890
6.0	.5480
7.0	.4630
8.0	.4650
9.0	.3180
10.0	.3350
11.0	.3160
12.0	.2570
13.0	.2400
14.0	.3100
15.0	.1680
16.0	.1340
18.0	.1730
19.0	.1360
20.0	.1580

a) Plot a scatter diagram of the proportion of putts made (y) against the length of the putt (x). Does a linear relationship seem appropriate?

b) Find the least-squares sample regression line $\hat{y} = a + bx$. Calculate the R^2 and the s_e values.

c) Fit the sample regression line $\hat{y} = a + b(\ln x)$ to this data set. Calculate the R^2 and the s_e values.

d) Fit the sample regression line $\hat{y} = a + b_1x + b_2x^2$ to this data set. Calculate the R^2 and the S_e values.

e) Of the three regression lines in parts (b), (c) and (d), which one provides the better fit? Explain your answer.

13.39 Consider the information in Problem 13.38. Select the best regression equation and calculate the fitted values and the residuals. Plot the fitted values against the residuals. Comment on the validity of the assumption of homoscedasticity in this equation.

13.40 The Ohio Valley Detergent Corporation produces and markets laundry detergent throughout the United States. The firm would like to develop a regression equation to predict sales for their marketing regions. In order to do that the firm has collected data from 30 of the regions for 1990 for four variables: population, unemployment rate, advertising expense, and the number of competitors. This information is shown in Table 13.10.

a) Use a statistical package to develop a multiple regression equation to predict sales with unemployment rate, advertising, number of competitors, and population as the independent variables. Interpret each part of the output.

b) Test the significance of the coefficient of each independent variable using the p-values. Would you include all four of the independent variables? Explain your answer.

c) Plot sales against each of the four independent variables. Is there any evidence that a transformation may improve the fit for any of these four variables?

d) Transform each of the independent variables using a log transformation. Rerun the multiple regression analysis using the original variables and the

TABLE 13.10

Population		Unemployment rate	Advertising expense	Competition	Sales
1.	750,000	5.1	59,000	0	5,170,000
2.	871,000	6.3	62,500	1	5,780,000
3.	1,000,000	4.7	61,000	1	4,840,000
4.	745,000	5.4	61,000	1	6,000,000
5.	867,000	5.4	6,100	1	6,000,000
6.	1,100,000	7.2	12,500	1	6,120,000
7.	1,318,000	5.8	35,800	1	6,400,000
8.	1,381,000	5.9	59,900	1	7,100,000
9.	1,443,000	6.2	57,200	2	8,500,000
10.	1,000,000	5.5	35,800	1	7,500,000
11.	1,321,000	6.8	27,900	1	9,300,000
12.	1,710,000	6.2	24,100	2	8,800,000
13.	1,512,000	6.3	27,700	2	9,960,000
14.	1,870,000	5.0	24,000	3	9,830,000
15.	2,020,000	5.5	57,200	3	10,120,000
16.	1,500,000	5.8	44,300	3	10,700,000
17.	1,760,000	7.1	49,200	4	10,450,000
18.	1,980,000	7.5	23,000	4	11,320,000
19.	1,440,000	8.2	62,700	2	11,870,000
20.	2,035,000	7.8	55,800	2	11,910,000
21.	1,890,000	6.2	50,000	3	12,600,000
22.	2,160,000	7.1	47,600	4	12,600,000
23.	2,525,000	4.0	43,500	4	14,240,000
24.	2,750,000	4.2	55,900	5	14,410,000
25.	2,100,000	7.0	51,200	4	13,730,000
26.	1,970,000	6.4	76,600	3	13,760,000
27.	2,415,000	5.0	63,000	3	13,775,000
28.	1,765,000	8.5	68,100	4	14,920,000
29.	2,230,000	7.1	74,400	5	15,280,000
30.	2,400,000	8.0	70,100	5	14,410,000

transformed variables. Do these transformed variables provide a better fit? Explain your answer.

13.41 Consider the information in Problem 13.40. For the regression equations developed in parts (a) and (d), calculate the residuals and the fitted values. Plot the fitted values against the residuals. What conclusions can you derive from this plot? Explain your answer.

13.42 Use your best equation from Problem 13.40 to predict the sales for Ohio Valley's Central Indiana region for the next year. The population of this region is 1,225,000, the unemployment rate 6.2%, and the firm has three competitors. Ohio Valley plans to spend $35,000 on advertising.

Exercises

13.43 Give an argument that explains why any one of the standard assumptions for regression analysis would be violated, in each of the following situations, for a simple model of the form $y = \beta x + \epsilon$. Also, suggest how the violation of this assumption would affect the properties of the ordinary least-squares (OLS) estimators.

a) y measures the wealth of an individual and x measures this person's age.

b) Observations on y and x are daily stock averages and volume of trading, respectively.

13.44 Consider the information in Table 13.11 regarding 1989 model cars. This data was collected by randomly sampling 18 cars from the 1989 *Consumer Reports*.

a) Use a computer package to develop a regression equation to predict the fuel efficiency of 1989 cars in terms of highway miles per gallon (MPG) based on the variables WEIGHT (the weight of the car in pounds), ENGINE (the engine size in cubic inches) and REVS (the engine revolutions per mile).

b) Test the significance of the coefficient for each independent variable using p-values. What conclusions can you derive from this analysis?

TABLE 13.11

Model	Weight (lb)	Engine size (cu in)	Engine revs/mile (RPG)	Highway miles/gal (MPG)
Acura Integra	2480	97	2940	36
Ford Festiva	1715	81	3150	47
Geo Metro	1640	61	3755	58
Nissan Sentra	2275	97	3285	38
VW Fox	2190	109	2765	41
Dodge Daytona	2935	135	2565	43
Ford Mustang	3310	302	1495	28
Nissan Pulsar NX	2390	97	3210	38
Buick Skylark	2640	151	2405	36
Chevrolet Cavalier	2485	121	2690	38
Nissan Stanza	2830	120	2470	34
Volvo 240	2985	141	2210	31
Chev Celebrity	2850	151	2380	33
Chrysler LeBaron	2915	153	2535	34
Dodge Dynasty	3150	153	2465	35
Sterling 827	3295	163	2300	30
Saab 900	3065	121	2535	32
Ford LTD	3790	302	1415	30

c) Are there any significant multicollinearity problems in this equation? If so, what steps would you take, if any, to correct this problem. Explain your answer.

d) Calculate the residuals and the fitted values. Plot the residuals against the fitted values to check for heteroscedasticity. What conclusions can you derive from this plot?

e) Suppose we now want to determine if there is any difference between the fuel efficiencies of domestic and foreign cars. Explain how you would carry out this analysis.

13.45 Classic Cars Inc., a car rental company based in Orlando, operates a fleet of rental cars in Florida. In the past few years, the company has purchased some diesel cars because it had been claimed that they were more economical to operate. Management would like to review the maintenance costs of their fleet. In particular, they would like to determine the maintenance cost differences between diesel and gasoline powered cars. A random sample of 15 cars gives the following information for 1990:

Car	Maintenance expenses	Miles driven	Age in years	Power[a] type
1	852.10	24,070	1	d
2	1035.25	25,650	2	d
3	924.25	20,750	2	d
4	938.13	19,600	3	d
5	979.75	21,650	3	d
6	996.40	21,230	3	d
7	896.50	23,110	1	g
8	907.60	22,380	1	g
9	924.25	23,590	1	g
10	935.35	21,710	2	g
11	952.00	22,140	2	g
12	910.38	20,044	2	g
13	1007.50	20,990	3	g
14	985.30	20,200	3	g
15	946.45	20,750	3	g

[a] d = diesel; g = gasoline

a) Develop a regression equation to determine the maintenance costs of a car based on the miles driven, age of the car and whether the car is diesel or gasoline powered.

b) Test the significance of the coefficient for each independent variable using p-values. Would you include all three independent variables? Explain your answer.

c) Are there any significant differences between diesel and gasoline powered cars? Explain your answer.

d) Calculate the residuals and the fitted values. Plot the residuals against the fitted values to check for heteroscedasticity. What conclusions can you derive from this plot?

13.46 An article in the *San Francisco Chronicle* suggested that female computer programmers employed in California's "Silicon Valley" are paid less than males for programming positions. The *Chronicle* article indicated that the average annual salary for females may be as much as $3000 to $5000 less than the average salary for males. Several males have suggested that the reverse is true; that is, it is the males who have been discriminated against. In order to gain more information regarding this salary controversy, a random sample of 50 male and 50 female programmers currently working in the area was taken. The data for each person is shown in Appendix C, and includes the salary for that person, the programming experience in years, and the person's sex (male = 1, female = 0). Use regression analysis to analyze these data and determine if there is any validity to either of the two claims of discrimination. Explain your answer.

13.47 The observations below represent 50 months of industrial electrical usage (in kilowatt hours, or KWH) in Indiana, from January 1976. Beginning about December 1978 (month = 36) there was considerable pressure for cutbacks in electrical use throughout the state. In March of 1979 (month = 39) there was a coal strike in Indiana, forcing many industries to shut down or to cut back severely on use of electricity.

Use a computer package to construct a regression model for these data, using a dummy variable. What KWH does your model predict for month = 51? Construct a 95% confidence interval (C.I.) for this prediction. The actual value for month = 51 was 513928. What is the "error" for your prediction? Does your C.I. contain the true value?

MON	KWH	MON	KWH	MON	KWH
1	372504	18	461558	35	501996
2	384161	19	419596	36	438065
3	357089	20	447663	37	430685
4	356367	21	465072	38	444128
5	369023	22	465127	39	358485
6	367648	23	455987	40	445464
7	361958	24	456709	41	493822
8	404673	25	427442	42	505066
9	418914	26	451918	43	492880
10	407881	27	453020	44	519381
11	407895	28	486727	45	529790
12	394314	29	493094	46	542049
13	375347	30	492569	47	528507
14	416543	31	465602	48	523019
15	437404	32	465602	49	509574
16	431884	33	507530	50	534515
17	446431	34	495298		

13.48 In November 1989, *Business Week* published its annual edition on the Corporate Elite, a profile of the CEOs of the top 1000 corporations in the United States. Shown below is a partial profile of a random sample of 26 CEOs and the corporations they lead:

Company	Experience in years	Market value	Profits	Salary
Albany Int	37	554	36	417,000
American Pres	40	561	81	729,000
Arvin Industries	34	372	16	474,000
Bowater	34	1100	164	674,000
Cinci Gas & Elec	30	1400	227	305,000
Continental Bank	29	1100	316	1,100,000
Eastman Kodak	39	15700	1400	1,252,000
Fed Nat Mortgage	20	7900	507	1,000,000
First Union Bank	24	2700	297	900,000
The Gap	40	1900	74	1,374,000
General Signal	25	1000	25	860,000
IBP	28	805	62	3,476,000
Int Multifoods	20	419	35	383,000
Lyondell Petro	26	1800	543	678,000
Meredith	35	679	37	482,000
Old Kent	30	685	77	557,000
Pfizer	40	11500	792	1,371,000
Raychem	42	1300	125	1,000,000
Rockwell	30	6000	812	1,240,000
Stone Container	32	1900	342	1,181,000
American Express	29	15600	988	2,764,000
Comdisco	28	1300	92	836,000
Delta	26	3900	307	457,000
Greyhound	26	1400	93	1,711,000
Mattel	36	924	36	564,000
Wells Fargo	34	4300	513	1,330,000

Develop a regression model that explains the salary of the CEOs based on their experience, their corporation's market value and the profit margins. Are these variables useful in explaining the salaries? Of these three variables, which one is the most useful in explaining salaries. What other variables are likely to be useful in developing a model to explain salaries of CEOs? Collect the data on these additional variables and rerun the regression analysis with these variables.

13.49 The *Herald Telegraph* is the major daily newspaper in a fast growing medium-sized metropolitan area. The number of subscribers has been increasing steadily over the past two years. In order to budget cash flow, management has asked the circulation manager to forecast the number of subscribers for the next six months. She suspects that circulation is influenced by four factors—the population of the metropolitan area, the income of the population, the subscription rate, and the amount of advertising by the newspaper to promote sales. Advertising is done mainly on local radio and television. Circulation could also be a function of past circulation levels, because readers develop a loyalty to their daily newspaper or get into the habit of reading a certain paper.

In an attempt to develop a model to forecast the number of subscribers, the circulation manager has developed the data for 24 months shown in the following table. The notation used in the table is as follows:

SUB = Number of subscribers (in thousands)

POP = Metropolitan population (in thousands)

ADV = The advertising budget

INC = The median income

RATE = The monthly subscription rate

MONTH	SUB	POP	ADV	INC	RATE
1	57.15	509.27	2000	10580	9.00
2	57.00	509.77	2500	10650	9.00
3	57.45	510.45	2500	10640	9.00
4	57.00	510.98	2000	10700	9.00
5	57.60	511.76	2000	10780	9.10
6	57.90	512.95	1600	10810	9.10
7	58.20	514.21	1600	10900	9.40
8	56.80	515.11	900	10950	9.40
9	56.50	516.32	800	10980	9.40
10	56.95	517.53	1400	11050	9.40
11	57.25	517.87	2000	11075	9.20
12	58.05	517.99	2000	11120	9.20
13	59.25	520.12	2600	11120	9.20
14	59.70	523.40	2600	11300	9.20
15	60.15	525.55	2100	11305	9.20
16	60.75	525.80	2100	11375	9.20
17	60.45	526.77	1600	11360	9.20
18	61.35	527.20	1600	11390	9.30
19	60.75	527.79	800	11450	9.30
20	61.50	528.55	800	11505	9.30
21	61.50	528.84	600	11570	9.30
22	62.40	530.22	1400	11620	9.30
23	62.70	530.57	1900	11650	9.30
24	63.75	532.69	2700	11740	9.30

Month	Budget
25	$2,200
26	2,400
27	2,000
28	3,000
29	2,750
30	3,000

a) Develop a multiple regression equation that the *Herald Telegraph* can use to predict subscription levels for the next six months. Note that several different equations could be developed for this problem. Some of these equations may have autocorrelation or multicollinearity problems or both. Thus, special attention needs to be paid to these problems. Also, additional independent variables can be created by lagging.

b) Use your equation from part (a) to predict the number of subscribers for the next six months (months 25 to 30). The rate is scheduled to be increased in month 27 to $9.40. The advertising budget for the next six months has been set as shown in the table to the left.

The population and income estimates are not available but may be estimated from past data.

13.50 The following data represent quarterly sales (in millions of dollars) for the ten stores in Texas of a large departmental chain of retail stores for the period 1978 to 1989. Also shown are the dollar amounts (in thousands of dollars) spent quarterly on advertising by these stores in Texas.

	Quarter							
	I		**II**		**III**		**IV**	
Year	**Sales**	**Adv.**	**Sales**	**Adv.**	**Sales**	**Adv.**	**Sales**	**Adv.**
1978	66.96	162	73.32	210	85.08	357	110.28	656
1979	72.84	206	79.80	220	92.64	380	124.80	725
1980	81.48	228	83.76	254	98.76	414	130.56	748
1981	82.92	253	91.68	279	104.40	460	136.44	817
1982	90.24	274	96.24	298	116.64	483	164.40	897
1983	94.20	288	100.56	323	121.20	518	167.40	966
1984	96.12	320	102.12	331	116.28	520	169.56	1081
1985	118.08	322	124.56	334	136.80	552	181.20	1410
1986	123.00	345	132.96	358	148.68	548	193.44	1116
1987	129.00	351	138.00	358	154.08	552	203.52	1150
1988	138.60	362	151.80	369	163.56	564	204.12	1160
1989	135.36	380	152.76	390	173.76	603	228.24	1165

Develop a multiple regression equation that management could use to forecast their sales in Texas for each of the four quarters in 1990. There are several possible equations that could be developed. Note that the time series has both a trend upward and seasonality by quarters. Dummy variables may be used to control for seasonality. Also, it may be possible to use lags to develop additional independent variables. Since this is time series data, problems with autocorrelation may arise.

Chapter 14

Time Series, Forecasting, and Index Numbers

Statistics are the heart of democracy.

SIMEON STRUNSKY

Introduction to Time Series

14.1

Recording observations of a variable periodically over time results in a set of numbers called a **time series.** Most data in business and economic publications take the form of time series. The monthly sales receipts in a retail store, the annual gross national product (GNP) of the United States, the Dow Jones Industrial Average, and indexes of consumer and wholesale prices are just a few examples. The analysis of time-series data in such circumstances is either descriptive or inferential. **Descriptive analysis** uses graphical and numerical methods to obtain an understanding of the time series. **Inferential analysis** attempts to estimate the factors (or **components,** as they are called) that produce the pattern in the series and uses these estimates to forecast the future behavior of the series. For example, for an inferential analysis of the Dow Jones Average, we may first graph the time series in order to estimate the past and the present trends of the average. Once we have an understanding of these trends, we may then want to forecast the future trends in order to make decisions about buying and selling stocks.

This chapter first discusses methods for describing and summarizing time series using index numbers and moving averages. This is followed by estimating the components of the time series and the forecasting implications provided by these estimates. Our approach will emphasize economic time series because of their central importance in the planning function performed by many businesses and government agencies.

Index Numbers   **14.2**

Index numbers represent one of the most common techniques for characterizing and summarizing large masses of data. An **index number** relates the values of a dependent variable (such as sales or price) to an independent variable (such as time, income, or interest rates). Although index numbers are used in many areas of the behavioral and social sciences, their main application involves describing business and economic activity.

There are two important types of indexes in business and economic applications: price and quantity indexes. Price indexes are used to measure changes in the price of a commodity or group of commodities over a period of time. The **consumer price index** (CPI) is an example of a price index. The CPI measures price changes of a group of commodities that represent typical purchases by American consumers. On the other hand, a **quantity index** measures the changes in output of a quantity. The **index of industrial production (IIP)**, which measures changes in manufacturing output, is a quantity index.

The primary purpose of an index number is to provide a value useful for comparing aggregated magnitudes to each other, and to measure the changes in these magnitudes over time. Consequently, many different indexes have been developed for special uses, ranging from the very simple to some very complex indexes. The next three sections provide details on the calculation, uses, and interpretation of several different types of index numbers.

Simple Index Numbers   **14.3**

A **simple index number** is based on the price or quantity of a single commodity. It is determined by calculating the ratio (in percentage terms) of the variable of interest in a given period to the value of that variable in another period (called the **base period**). To illustrate a simple index number, consider the average retail gasoline prices shown in Table 14.1. To construct an index to describe the relative changes in the gasoline prices, a base year is first selected. The value of the index in the base period is set at 100.00. The selection of the base year is somewhat arbitrary, but very important. If the year selected has extreme values of the variable of interest, then all other values of the index will be affected.

The index number for a particular year is calculated by dividing that year's price by the price for the base year and then multiplying the result by

TABLE 14.1   Average retail gasoline prices (excluding taxes), 1974–1987

Year	Gasoline prices (cents per gallon)
1974	40.4
1975	45.4
1976	47.5
1977	50.7
1978	53.0
1979	87.8
1980	121.7
1981	133.4
1982	122.5
1983	115.7
1984	112.9
1985	111.5
1986	85.7
1987	89.7

Source: Standard and Poor's Statistical Service, *Standard and Poor's Basic Statistics: Power and Fuels,* 1985, and *Current Statistics,* April 1988

TABLE 14.2 Simple index numbers for gasoline prices, 1974–1987

Year	Index
1974	88.99
1975	100.00
1976	104.63
1977	111.67
1978	116.74
1979	193.39
1980	268.06
1981	293.83
1982	269.82
1983	254.85
1984	248.68
1985	245.59
1986	188.77
1987	197.58

TABLE 14.3   Producer prices and simple index numbers for electrolytic copper, 1974–1987

Year	Price (¢ per lb)	Index
1974	77.06	119.42
1975	64.53	100.00
1976	69.62	107.89
1977	66.72	103.39
1978	66.53	103.10
1979	92.75	143.73
1980	102.19	158.36
1981	85.59	132.64
1982	74.56	115.54
1983	78.33	121.39
1984	68.77	106.57
1985	68.85	106.69
1986	67.91	105.24
1987	84.80	131.41

Source: American Metal Market, *Metal Statistics,* 1987

100. To illustrate this calculation, let's assume for Table 14.1 that the base year is 1975; the gasoline price index for 1980 is thus:

$$1980 \text{ index number} = \frac{(1980 \text{ gasoline price})}{(1975 \text{ gasoline price})} \times 100$$
$$= \frac{121.7}{45.4} \times 100 = 268.06$$

Similarly, the index number for 1985 is

$$1985 \text{ index number} = \frac{(1985 \text{ gasoline price})}{(1975 \text{ gasoline price})} \times 100$$
$$= \frac{111.5}{45.4} \times 100 = 245.59$$

The 1980 index number indicates there was a 168.06 percentage increase in the gasoline price between 1975 and 1980 (268.06 − 100.0 = 168.06). Between 1975 and 1985 there was a 145.59 percentage increase. The complete set of index numbers for the gasoline prices between 1974 and 1987 is shown in Table 14.2.

One important application of the simple index is the comparison of relative price (or quantity) changes of different commodities. For example, consider the producer prices of electrolytic copper from 1974 to 1987, as shown in Table 14.3. If we now calculate index numbers using 1975 as the base year,

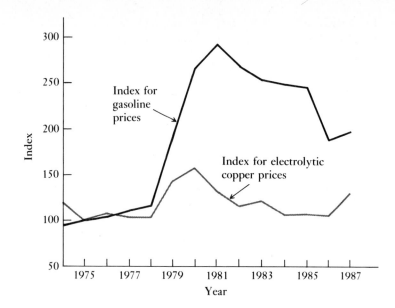

Figure 14.1
Comparison of the simple
indexes for gasoline and
electrolytic copper prices.

it is possible to compare the relative changes in the prices of copper and gasoline over the period 1974 to 1987 (see Fig. 14.1) even though the units of measurement are different (cents per gallon and cents per pound). This comparison reveals that during the period 1974 to 1987 the gasoline prices escalated more rapidly than copper prices.

Aggregate Index Numbers

14.4

An **aggregate index number** represents combinations of prices or quantities of several commodities. For example, suppose we want to construct an index for a portfolio that includes investing in three precious metals: silver, gold, and platinum. The prices for these metals are shown in Table 14.4. One way to construct this index is to add the prices of these metals for the given year and divide this total by the total of the prices in the base year. This **simple aggregate price index** is calculated as follows:

$$\text{Simple aggregate price index: } I_n = \frac{\sum P_{n,i}}{\sum P_{0,i}} \times 100 \qquad (14.1)$$

Here $P_{n,i}$ is the price of commodity i in year n and $P_{0,i}$ is the price of commodity i in the base year. For example, if the base year for the precious

TABLE 14.4 Commodity prices of silver, platinum, and gold

Year	Silver $/oz.	Platinum $/oz.	Gold $/oz.
1973	2.560	152.18	97.81
1974	4.708	184.98	161.08
1975	4.420	169.87	161.49
1976	4.354	168.39	124.77
1977	4.623	167.71	148.31
1978	5.400	237.08	193.55
1979	11.090	351.83	307.59
1980	20.683	436.77	612.51
1981	10.481	475.00	459.61
1982	7.950	328.32	375.94
1983	11.439	423.14	423.83
1984	8.141	383.88	360.23
1985	6.192	291.33	317.31
1986	5.476	465.31	369.60
1987	7.021	485.90	447.90

Source: 1987 CRB Commodity Yearbook

TABLE 14.5
Simple aggregate index for silver, platinum, and gold

Year	Index
1973	75.21
1974	104.46
1975	100.00
1976	88.60
1977	95.49
1978	129.86
1979	199.69
1980	318.65
1981	281.46
1982	212.11
1983	255.65
1984	224.03
1985	183.11
1986	250.28
1987	280.19

Source: 1987 CRB Commodity Yearbook

metals portfolio is set at 1975, the simple aggregate index for 1978 is calculated as

$$I_{1978} = \frac{(\text{Sum of 1978 prices})}{(\text{Sum of 1975 prices})} \times 100$$
$$= \frac{(5.40 + 237.08 + 193.55)}{(4.420 + 169.87 + 161.49)} \times 100$$
$$= \frac{436.03}{335.78} \times 100 = 129.86$$

This value indicates that the prices of these commodities have increased collectively by 29.86% between 1975 and 1978. The index numbers for the other years are calculated similarly using the base price of 335.78. These are shown in Table 14.5.

The simple aggregate price index has a major disadvantage: It fails to consider the quantity of the commodities purchased. For example, if more silver had been purchased than gold or platinum, the weighting of silver in the simple aggregate index is inappropriate. This weakness can be overcome by considering the relative importance of the commodities in the index using a weighted index number. Typically, a weighted index is constructed by multiplying the quantity consumed of each commodity by the price. Since the quantities purchased may change from one time period to the next, the choice of which time period's quantities to use is an important one. One method uses the base-period quantities (labeled q_0) as weights. The resulting index is called a **Laspeyres price index:**

$$\text{Laspeyres price index: } I_n = \frac{\sum p_n q_0}{\sum p_0 q_0} \times 100 \qquad (14.2)$$

If the quantity q_n purchased in a *given* year n is used to weight prices, the resulting index is called a **Paasche price index:**

$$\text{Paasche price index: } I_n = \frac{\sum p_n q_n}{\sum p_0 q_n} \times 100 \qquad (14.3)$$

Note the only difference between these two indexes is that the first uses the base-year quantities (q_0) as weights while the second uses the given-year quantities (q_n) as weights.

To illustrate these indexes, assume the base year for the precious metals portfolio is 1975, and in 1975 the portfolio consisted of 1000 oz of silver, 20 oz of platinum, and 20 oz of gold. The Laspeyres index is calculated using these quantities as the base weights; the Paasche index uses the quantities in each

TABLE 14.6   The Laspeyres and Paasche index numbers for the precious metals portfolio

	Quantity in Portfolio (oz)			Laspeyres	Paasche
Year	Silver	Platinum	Gold	index	index
1973	1000	20	20	68.43	68.43
1974	1000	20	20	105.27	105.27
1975	1000	20	20	100.00	100.00
1976	1000	30	30	92.49	91.56
1977	800	30	30	99.06	97.79
1978	500	30	30	128.84	128.54
1979	500	30	30	219.77	208.44
1980	500	20	50	377.19	363.27
1981	500	20	30	264.08	272.95
1982	500	20	20	199.46	204.37
1983	1000	20	20	256.88	256.88
1984	1000	20	20	208.41	208.41
1985	1000	10	20	166.24	165.28
1986	1000	30	20	200.72	210.48
1987	1000	30	20	232.61	239.73

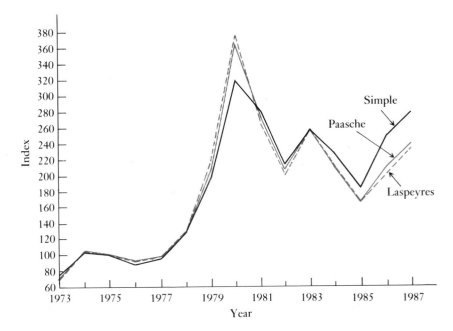

Figure 14.2
Comparison of the simple
and the weighted indexes
for the precious metals
portfolio.

year to weight the prices. If, for example, the portfolio in 1980 consisted of 500 oz of silver, 20 oz of platinum, and 50 oz of gold, the Laspeyres index is

$$1980 \text{ Laspeyres index} = \frac{1000(20.683) + 20(436.77) + 20(612.51)}{1000(4.420) + 20(169.87) + 20(161.49)} \times 100$$
$$= 377.19$$

The Paasche index is

$$1980 \text{ Paasche index} = \frac{500(20.683) + 20(436.76) + 50(612.51)}{500(4.420) + 20(169.87) + 50(161.49)} \times 100$$
$$= 363.27$$

The index numbers for other years are calculated similarly, and are shown in Table 14.6. A comparison of the simple, the Laspeyres, and the Paasche index numbers is presented in Fig. 14.2.

As Fig. 14.2 indicates, there are differences between the Laspeyres and the Paasche indexes. Typically, the Laspeyres index is more appropriate when the base quantities are reasonable approximations of quantities purchased in subsequent periods. This index has two major advantages. First, the quantities need to be estimated only once, in the base period. Second, the indexes from this formula use the same base and are therefore directly comparable. If, however, the purchased quantities change significantly from those in the base period, the index can be misleading. The Paasche index, on the other hand, is more appropriate if the objective is to compare current prices to the base-period prices with purchased quantities at the current levels. There are, however, two major disadvantages to using this index. First, it requires that the purchase quantities be updated every period. This process may be costly. Second, the indexes for different periods (with the same base period) are not directly comparable because they are based on different quantities. For example, for the precious metals portfolio, the Paasche index numbers are 97.79 for 1977 and 128.54 for 1978. Although this may appear to represent an increase of 30.75% in the value of the portfolio from 1977 to 1978, the comparison is not meaningful since these two indexes are determined using different quantities.

Additionally, both these indexes tend to reflect a slight bias when reporting price changes. Under the usual conditions of a downward sloping demand schedule, when people tend to purchase more of low-priced items and less of high-priced items, the numerator of the Laspeyres index will be somewhat higher than it should be, resulting in an overestimation of price increases. At the same time, the numerator of the Paasche index tends to be lower than it should be, resulting in an underestimation of price increases.

Economic Indexes and Their Limitations

14.5

We have presented a brief introduction to the topic of index numbers. In practice, the process of constructing and updating an index can become quite involved. Before leaving the subject, we shall describe a number of the more widely used indexes and some of their limitations.

The consumer price index (CPI) and the producer price index (formerly the wholesale price index), both published by the U.S. Department of Labor's Bureau of Labor Statistics (BLS), are the two best known price indexes. These two indexes represent excellent examples of attempts to summarize large masses of data in a single price index. The **CPI** is a modified Laspeyres index with 1967 as the base year and is a measure of the cost of living for a "typical" family in the United States. It is based on approximately 400 different items in such expenditure classes as foods, fuels, apparel, housing, and transportation. Since 1978 BLS has published two CPIs, CPI-Urban and CPI-Wage Earners. **CPI-Urban (CPI-U)** is a new index and measures the price changes in a constant "market basket" of goods and services that are representative of the purchases of all urban residents. This group represents approximately 80% of the U.S. population. CPI-U is the index typically reported in the media. The **CPI-Wage Earners (CPI-W)** is based on the price changes in a constant basket of goods and services typically purchased by urban wage earners and clerical workers (approximately 50% of the U.S. population) and is the index used for labor contracts and government benefit programs.

The CPI is reported monthly. The computation of this index is a complex procedure. The basis of this computation is an extensive survey undertaken every 10 years or so by the BLS of the buying habits of thousands of households in 56 cities; the most recent occurred between 1982 and 1984. Based on this survey BLS constructs a market basket of about 2000 goods and services. Thereafter, each month BLS surveys 20,000 stores in these 56 cities to collect current price data on approximately 400 of these goods and services. These prices are then used to compute the CPI for the month.

The **producer price index** provides an indication of prices received in primary markets (not retail) of the United States by producers in all stages of processing. It includes price movements of goods in manufacturing, agriculture, forestry, fishing, mining, gas, electricity and public utilities, and for finished goods, intermediate goods, and raw materials. This index is computed monthly from about 10,000 price quotations for approximately 2800 commodities.

There are two major economic quantity indexes: (1) the Index of Industrial Production (IIP), published by the Federal Reserve Board, and (2) the Export and Import Indexes, published by the U.S. Department of Commerce. The Export and Import Indexes calculate quantity changes in both exports and imports. As discussed earlier, the IIP measures changes in manufacturing output.

The limitations of economic indexes follow directly from the problems suggested earlier in the construction of an index. First, the useful and meaningful application of an index often depends on what year is selected as the base. For example, if prices in the base year are abnormally low, the index in future years will be inflated. Thus, it is important to use as a base a period with "normal" or "average" economic activity. Sometimes the base-year value can be the average price or quantity of several years rather than a single year. Second, the items included in the index have an important bearing on the validity of the index. For example, in the case of the CPI, the market basket changes every few years. Finally, over a period of time, the quality of products changes. Some items fall out of use completely, and others appear that had no earlier counterpart. Thus, it is difficult, if not impossible, to compare the prices of many of today's goods with those of an earlier period.

This inability to compare goods, and consequently prices, over time has led to charges that price indexes exaggerate the real increase in prices, and that the CPI, in particular, exaggerates the change in the cost of living because the indexes do not take into account the improvement in the quality of goods. Even though the Bureau of Labor Statistics attempts to factor out all the quality changes that can be detected in the items used in computing the CPI, it is extremely difficult to measure the worth of these increases to consumers. The economist Lloyd G. Reynolds illustrates this problem quite well with the following scenario: Give a family à 1975 Sears Roebuck Catalog and a 1990 Sears Catalog and $1000, and allow consumers to make up an order list from either the 1975 or the 1990 catalog, but not from both. Most families would probably use the 1990 catalog, which must mean that they consider the higher 1990 prices more than offset by new products and improved quality. This implies that there was no real increase in consumer prices between 1975 and 1990, even though the CPI indicated a sizable increase.

Because there are so many difficulties in constructing meaningful price indexes, they should be used only as guides and indicators of price movements, and should not be quoted as indisputable facts. Also, one should remember that they represent prices of some "average" person with "average" tastes and preferences. Whether or not they are relevant to a particular person or group must always be questioned before they are applied.

Problems

Year	Beer output	Year	Beer output
1975	160.7	**1982**	196.2
1976	163.7	**1983**	195.4
1977	170.5	**1984**	192.2
1978	179.1	**1985**	193.3
1979	184.2	**1986**	196.5
1980	194.1	**1987**	195.4
1981	193.7	**1988**	197.7

Source: Standard and Poor's Statistical Service, annual editions, various years, and *Current Statistics,* November 1989

14.1 Explain (in words) how you would construct the following indexes:

    a) Simple aggregate index

    b) Laspeyres index

    c) Paasche index

14.2 What is the weakness of the Laspeyres index? Of the Paasche index?

14.3 The table to the left (top) lists the beer output (in millions of barrels) in the United States over the period 1975–1988. Construct a simple index for this series using 1977 as the base year.

14.4 The table to the left (below) lists the annual retail sales (in billions of dollars) in the United States during the period 1975–1988.

    a) Construct a simple index for this series using 1977 as the base year.

    b) Interpret the 1981 and 1982 values for this index.

14.5 The monthly closing prices of Procter & Gamble stock, and Eli Lilly stock for the period 1986 to 1987 are shown in the following table.

Year	Sales ($ billions)
1975	588.15
1976	657.38
1977	722.50
1978	804.15
1979	896.77
1980	957.31
1981	1038.65
1982	1069.28
1983	1171.19
1984	1298.37
1985	1379.62
1986	1454.41
1987	1507.10
1988	1622.40

Source: U.S. Department of Commerce

Month	1986		1987	
	P&G	**Eli Lilly**	**P&G**	**Eli Lilly**
Jan.	65.88	54.50	88.00	86.50
Feb.	69.00	60.00	86.75	94.38
Mar.	74.88	75.50	92.00	91.50
Apr.	73.50	67.38	84.75	91.00
May	77.88	75.75	91.50	88.00
June	80.13	80.88	98.00	93.88
July	77.38	75.25	93.13	96.00
Aug.	80.00	78.00	102.88	98.25
Sept.	67.75	65.38	101.00	96.25
Oct.	75.00	75.00	88.25	77.00
Nov.	77.75	75.13	81.38	67.00
Dec.	76.38	74.25	85.38	78.00

Source: New York Stock Exchange, *Daily Stock Record,* 1986–87

    a) Using January 1986 as the base period, construct the simple index for the monthly closing prices of each stock for 1986 and 1987.

b) If your portfolio consisted of these two stocks, construct the simple aggregate index for the closing monthly prices of these stocks for 1986 and 1987 using January 1986 as the base period.

14.6 Refer to the data in Problem 14.5. Suppose you purchased 100 shares of Eli Lilly stock and 200 shares of Procter & Gamble stock in January 1986. Over the period 1986 and 1987 you sold some of these shares and purchased additional ones. After each transaction the remaining shares left in your portfolio are as follows:

	Number of Eli Lilly Shares	Number of P&G Shares
Mar. 1986	100	150
May 1986	150	200
Aug. 1986	100	200
Dec. 1986	75	150
Jan. 1987	175	200
Aug. 1987	100	100
Dec. 1987	50	50

a) Using the stock prices from Problem 14.5 construct the Laspeyres index for this stock portfolio with January 1986 as the base period.

b) Using the same data, construct the Paasche index.

14.7 Refer to the data and the simple indexes constructed in Problem 14.5(a). Plot the two indexes on a graph.

a) If you had purchased 10 shares each of Procter & Gamble stock and Eli Lilly stock in January 1986 and sold these in December 1987, which stock would have given a better return?

b) If you sold these in October 1987 (right after the October 19 stock market collapse), which stock would have given a better return?

14.8 Refer to the simple aggregate index constructed in Problem 14.5(a) and the Paasche and the Laspeyres indexes constructed in Problem 14.6(a). Plot these indexes on the same graph. Compare and contrast these indexes. Of these three indexes, which one, in your opinion, represents most accurately the changes in this portfolio?

14.9 Consider the values of cost-of-living index shown in the table to the left for all items for the period 1975 to 1988 (base 1967). Using the data from Problem 14.4 and the cost-of-living index, adjust the values of each year's retail sales for inflation to reflect the changes in real terms. Compare the values of the actual retail sales with the inflation-adjusted figures by plotting both on a graph. What conclusions can you derive from this analysis?

Year	Cost-of-living index
1975	161.2
1976	170.5
1977	181.5
1978	195.4
1979	217.4
1980	246.8
1981	270.4
1982	289.1
1983	298.4
1984	311.1
1985	322.2
1986	328.4
1987	339.7
1988	354.4

Source: U.S. Bureau of Labor Statistics

14.10 The following table lists the weekly average earnings (in dollars per week) of workers in manufacturing industries and of workers in gas and electrical utilities from January 1987 to December 1988.

Month	1987		1988	
	Manufacturing workers	**Utility workers**	**Manufacturing workers**	**Utility workers**
Jan.	401.1	652.6	412.9	697.1
Feb.	401.1	669.1	409.9	695.4
Mar.	402.5	677.9	412.3	696.7
Apr.	398.8	671.8	414.5	689.7
May	403.3	677.1	415.7	686.8
June	406.1	678.4	418.6	699.3
July	401.1	679.3	414.3	687.2
Aug.	403.3	670.4	414.1	694.3
Sept.	406.8	613.4	423.3	710.6
Oct.	409.8	653.4	422.9	729.7
Nov.	414.4	691.4	427.5	731.4
Dec.	421.3	708.9	433.5	739.5

Source: Standard and Poor's Statistical Service, *Current Statistics,* November 1989

Using January 1987 as the base period, construct the simple index of average weekly earnings for both manufacturing workers and utility workers.

14.11 Refer to the information in Problem 14.10. Plot both indexes on a graph and compare the changes in the earnings of these workers over this two-year period. Which workers had the greater percentage change in earnings?

14.12 The following table lists the average monthly value of the Dow Jones Industrial Average and the Financial Times (London Stock Exchange) Shares Average over the period January 1987 to December 1988.

Month	1987		1988	
	Dow Jones	**Financial Times**	**Dow Jones**	**Financial Times**
Jan.	2158.0	1392.6	1958.2	1418.1
Feb.	2224.0	1530.5	2071.6	1397.4
Mar.	2304.7	1596.2	1988.1	1368.3
Apr.	2286.4	1554.4	2032.3	1418.7
May	2291.6	1667.1	2031.1	1428.6
June	2418.5	1760.4	2141.7	1468.8
July	2572.1	1857.3	2128.7	1488.3
Aug.	2663.0	1757.5	2031.7	1473.2
Sept.	2596.3	1804.1	2112.9	1429.5
Oct.	1993.5	1649.9	2148.7	1492.7
Nov.	1833.6	1299.8	2114.5	1479.5
Dec.	1938.8	1326.0	2168.6	1439.1

Source: Standard and Poor's Statistical Service, *Current Statistics,* November 1989

a) Using January 1987 as the base period, construct the simple index for both the Dow Jones and the Financial Times averages.

b) Explain the sharp changes in both these indexes.

c) Plot both these indexes on a graph. Compare the performance of the two stock markets using this graph. Are the trends similar? Of the two, which stock exchange performed better over this two year period?

Moving Averages 14.6

Smoothing with Moving Averages

As you saw in the previous sections, index numbers are very useful for describing trends and changes in time series. However, some time series may have irregular or random fluctuations to the extent that trends are difficult to describe. In such cases it may be easier to estimate the movement of the time series if the effects of these fluctuations are removed from the data. Methods for removing these effects are usually referred to as **smoothing techniques**.

The most commonly used technique for smoothing data is called the **method of moving averages. A moving average** is actually a series of averages, where each average is the mean value of the time series over a fixed interval of time, and where all possible averages of this time length are included in the analysis. A 12-month moving average, for example, must include the mean value for each 12-month period in the series. These averages represent a new series that has been smoothed to eliminate fluctuations that occur within a 12-month period.

To illustrate the process of calculating a moving average, consider the time series consisting of the closing monthly price of Procter & Gamble stock from 1986 to 1987 (see Table 14.7). As shown in Fig. 14.3, the price of this stock fluctuates considerably. Suppose we want to calculate a five-month moving average (5-M MA). To do this, we first determine the mean value for the initial five months, January 1986 to May 1986. This value, which equals

$$(1/5)(65.88 + 69.00 + 74.88 + 73.50 + 77.88) = 72.23$$

is "centered" on the middle month of the five months being averaged, March 1986. Similarly, the next moving average, 75.08, is computed from the values corresponding to February 1986 to June 1986 and centered on the middle month, April 1986. This process continues until the last observation is included. Thus, the last moving average is for the months August 1987 to December 1987. This is equal to 91.78 and is centered at October 1987. The entire moving-averages time series is shown in Table 14.7. These values, when compared to the original values, tend to reduce the variation and represent a smoothed version of the time series. The comparison between the original time series for the Procter & Gamble stock prices and its representation by the moving average values is shown in Fig. 14.3. Note that the long-term trend of

TABLE 14.7   Monthly closing prices (in $/share) of Procter & Gamble stock and its five-month moving average with equal weights and different weights

	Stock price	5-M MA (equal wts)	5-M MA (weighted)
Jan. 1986	65.88	—	—
Feb.	69.00	—	—
Mar.	74.88	72.23	74.13
Apr.	73.50	75.08	76.76
May	77.88	76.75	77.53
June	80.13	77.78	78.61
July	77.38	76.63	75.27
Aug.	80.00	76.05	74.73
Sept.	67.75	75.58	75.29
Oct.	75.00	75.38	75.56
Nov.	77.75	76.98	79.77
Dec. 1986	76.38	80.78	83.03
Jan. 1987	88.00	84.18	86.77
Feb.	86.75	85.58	86.96
Mar.	92.00	88.50	88.77
Apr.	84.75	90.50	91.93
May	91.00	91.78	92.81
June	98.00	93.95	96.51
July	93.13	97.20	98.86
Aug.	102.88	96.65	95.88
Sept.	101.00	93.33	90.79
Oct.	88.25	91.78	88.14
Nov.	81.38	—	—
Dec. 1987	85.38	—	—

Source: New York Stock Exchange, *Daily Stock Record*, 1986–87

the stock prices is easier to follow with the moving averages than with the original time series.

One problem with the use of a moving average is the choice of its length, denoted by n, the number of consecutive values used in the averages. The larger the value of n, the more the moving average smooths out the original data. But as n increases so does $(n - 1)$, which is the total number of observations at the beginning and end of the data for which no moving-average value can be determined. Using the five-period moving average, we see from Table 14.7 that a total of four observations are lost in the moving-average series, two at the beginning and two at the end. If the time series contains certain fluctuations or cycles that tend to recur, the number of periods to include in a moving

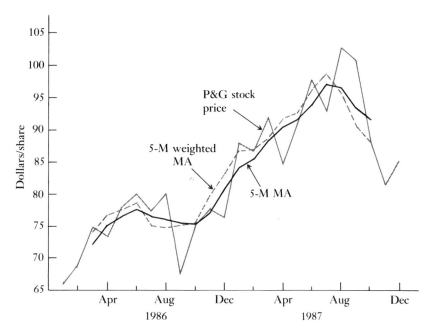

Figure 14.3
Moving averge series for
Procter & Gamble stock.

average should equal the period of this cycle. However, most business and economic time series do not contain simple or regular cycles, making it difficult to determine n. Ideally n should be chosen so that it is large enough for smoothing purposes but small enough to retain sufficient observations. In practice, however, we generally choose n by trying several values until one meets this criterion.

The moving-average procedure gives equal weight to all five observations in calculating each mean value. Sometimes, one may wish to increase the relative importance of one or more observations by using a weighted moving average. To calculate a weighted moving average, each observation being averaged is given a weight that reflects its relative importance. In a five-month weighted moving average, for example, the weights might be 1, 2, 3, 4, 5, based on the assumption that the most recent values in a series of observations should have the largest weight to reflect the latest trends. Thus, under this scheme a weight of 5 is given to the most recent observation, a weight of 4 to the next most recent observation and so on. Using this weighting system on the Procter & Gamble stock, we obtain a weighted moving average centered at March 1986 equal to

$$\frac{1(65.88) + 2(69.00) + 3(74.88) + 4(73.50) + 5(77.88)}{15}$$
$$= 74.13$$

That is, the sum of the weighted observations is divided by the sum of the weights. Using this scheme the most recent observation accounts for 33.33% (5/15) of the weighted average, followed by weights of 26.67%, 20%, 13.33%, and 6.67% for the other four observations. By continuing this process of weighted averaging, we can derive the entire series for the weights 1, 2, 3, 4, 5, as shown in Table 14.7. By applying a heavier weighting to the most recent observations, the resulting weighted moving-average time series responds more quickly to changing trends, as shown in Fig. 14.3. Had we used some other weighting system, an entirely different moving average would have emerged. In general, the weights used depend on the degree to which the analyst wishes to emphasize particular values.

Forecasting with Moving Averages

So far, we have shown how to use the method of moving averages to describe the underlying movement of a time series. This method may also be used to obtain simple short-term forecasts of the future values of the time series. To make these forecasts, we calculate the moving averages as before. However, for forecasting, the mean of the n periods becomes the forecast for the period immediately following the n periods in the average. For instance, in the Procter & Gamble stock price example, the first five-month moving average of 72.23 (for the period January to May1986) will form the forecast for June 1986. Similarly, the second moving average of 75.08 (for the period February to June 1986) becomes the forecast for July 1986 and so on. Under this scheme the forecast for January 1988 will be 91.78, the moving-average value for the period August 1987 to December 1987.

Although this method provides easy-to-calculate forecasts, it makes several simplifying assumptions, the most important of which is that the patterns of the past will hold for the future. However, if there are rapidly changing trends, the moving-average time series tends to lag behind the original time series, resulting in poor forecasts. One way to respond to changing trends is to use weighted moving averages. However, as we discuss later, other techniques such as decomposition and exponential smoothing (which is based on the principle of weighted moving averages) tend to be more efficient computationally.

Components of a Time Series

14.7

The preceding sections described techniques to analyze the behavior of a time series. We now expand our analysis and present a number of forecasting techniques that enable us to predict future values of the time series. To forecast from a time series, it is often useful to separate the fluctuations in an economic time series into four different components: trend (T), seasonal variation (S), cyclical variation (C), and irregular or random variation (I). Figure 14.4 presents a graphical view of these four components. In each case the dependent variable y_t is expressed as a function of the independent variable t (time). These graphs are based on hypothetical data to show the patterns clearly.

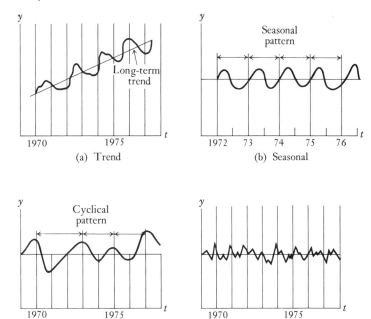

Figure 14.4
The four components of a
time series.

However, real time series are seldom this well behaved. Thus, the procedures
to analyze the components of a time series are quite involved.

Trend is the long-term movement in a time series. Gross national
product, for example, has grown at a rate of approximately 3% to 4% per year
over the past 20 years. The tendency toward increasing production output per
hour and increasing price levels over the past several decades also illustrate
long-term movements, or trends. Long-term trend is also known as the **secular
trend. Seasonal variation** represents fluctuations that repeat themselves
within a fixed period of less than one year. Many economic series have seasonal highs or lows due to changes in the supply of certain inputs (youth
employment in the summer, food harvests in the fall), or in demand for certain
products (ski equipment in the winter, toys before Christmas, gardening supplies in the spring), or in marketing factors (seasonal changes in clothing, new
car models in the fall). The **cyclical component** of a time series represents a
pattern repeated over periods of differing length, usually longer than one year.
Business cycles, with their stages of prosperity, recession, and recovery are an
important example of such cyclical movements.

The movements in a time series generated by trend and by seasonal and
cyclical variation are assumed to be based on systematic causes. That is, these
movements do not occur merely by chance, but reflect factors that have a
more or less regular influence. Exactly the opposite holds true for **random** or
irregular variation, which is, by definition, fluctuation that is unpredictable,
or takes place at various points in time, by chance or randomly. Floods, strikes,
and fads illustrate the irregular component of a time series.

Now that we have specified the components of a time series, the problem becomes one of estimating each of these components for a given series. That is, we want to be able to estimate what portions of the value of the variable of interest, y_t, for any given year are attributable respectively to trend, seasonal factors, cyclical factors, or random or irregular variation. In order to separate these values, we must make some assumptions about how these components are related in the population under investigation. These assumptions are referred to as the **time-series model.**

Time-series models usually fall into one of two categories, depending on whether their components are expressed as sums or products. The first of these, called the **additive model,** assumes that the value of y_t equals the sum of the four components.

$$\textit{Additive model: } y_t = T + S + C + I \qquad\qquad \textbf{(14.4)}$$

By assuming that the components of a time series are additive we are, in effect, assuming that these components are independent of one another. Thus, for example, trend can affect neither seasonal nor cyclical variation, nor can these components affect trend.

The other major type of relationship between the components expresses y_t in the form

$$\textit{Multiplicative model: } y_t = T \times S \times C \times I \qquad\qquad \textbf{(14.5)}$$

This is called the **multiplicative model.** A model of this form assumes that the four components are related to one another, yet still allows for the components to result from different basic causes. Note that one can transform a multiplicative model into a linear (additive) model by taking the logarithm of both sides:

$$\log y_t = \log T + \log S + \log C + \log I \qquad\qquad \textbf{(14.6)}$$

Other models also exist in addition to the additive and multiplicative ones. These models usually take the form of combinations of additive and multiplicative elements.

For the purpose of estimating each of the components of a time series, models normally treat S, C, and I as deviations from the underlying trend. In other words, trend is usually estimated first, and the variation that can be attributed to trend is eliminated from the values of y_t. The variation remaining in y_t must then be due to either seasonal, cyclical, or irregular factors. Each of these components of the time series can be isolated by other statistical techniques. While some of these methods are excessively tedious, the basic concepts are similar to the simple methods to be discussed in this chapter. Once all the components of a time series are estimated, then forecasts of the value of the time series at some future point in time can be made by estimating first the value of the trend component at that point, and then modifying this trend value by an adjustment that takes into account the seasonal and cyclical components.

Estimation of Trend

14.8

The first step in analyzing a time series is usually estimation of the trend component, T. As was true in regression analysis, the first decision usually must be whether or not the trend can be assumed to be linear. Several linear methods will be presented before we discuss (briefly) various methods for estimating nonlinear trends.

Linear Trends

Often a graph of the time-series data can indicate quite well whether or not a linear relationship provides a good approximation to the long-term movement of the series. If a linear relationship is appropriate, then there are several methods for roughly approximating T. A fairly accurate approximation can often be obtained by merely drawing the line that, by free-hand estimation, seems to represent best the long-run movement of the points. A more systematic approach is to use simple linear regression. Here, a straight line is fitted relating the time series, y_t, to time t. The regression line is written as $y_t = a + bt$, where t is the time. This least-squares line represents trend.

To illustrate this, let's consider the data in Table 14.8. These data represent the consumer installment debt (in billions of dollars) for the period 1986 to 1987. A plot of the data (Fig. 14.5) shows that this debt increases gradually over time. By fitting a least-squares line to the data, we get the regression equation $\hat{y}_t = 531.8 + 3.358t$. (The variable t is time in months, with January 1986 as $t = 1$ and December 1987 as $t = 24$.) This regression line (also shown in Fig. 14.5) implies that consumer installment debt is increasing by approximately \$3.358 billion per month. Thus, we may use this equation to project the consumer installment debt into the future. For example, for January 1988 ($t = 25$) the forecast will be

$$\hat{y}_{25} = 531.8 + 3.358(25) = 615.75$$

Similarly, the forecast for February 1988 ($t = 26$) will be

$$\hat{y}_{26} = 531.8 + 3.358(26) = 619.11$$

Generally, such projections are only made for short-term forecasts.

Nonlinear Trends

So far we have discussed fitting a linear trend line to a time series. However, all time-series data may not be best represented by a linear model. The problem of fitting a trend line to a nonlinear time series is essentially the same problem

TABLE 14.8 Consumer installment debt ($ billions)

Month	1986	1987
Jan.	529.1	578.3
Feb.	534.2	580.4
Mar.	531.6	579.5
Apr.	542.5	582.8
May	546.8	583.0
June	551.8	586.7
July	558.1	591.3
Aug.	563.7	595.8
Sept.	571.3	602.2
Oct.	579.6	606.3
Nov.	577.6	607.7
Dec.	577.8	612.6

Source: Standard and Poor's Statistical Service, *Current Statistics*, April 1988

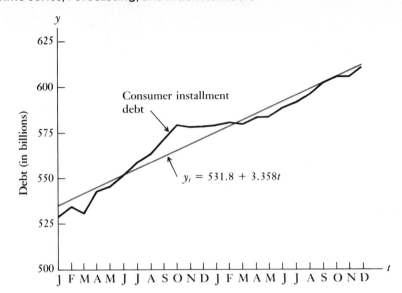

Figure 14.5

Monthly consumer installment debt, 1986 to 1987 ($ billions).

mentioned in Chapter 13 concerning nonlinear regression—that of finding an equation that best describes the relationship between an independent variable (time, in this case) and the dependent variable (the time-series values). As is true in fitting a regression line, it is not sufficient merely to find an equation that provides a good fit to the data; it also is necessary to find a model that is justifiable in terms of the underlying economic nature of the series. In estimating the trend in a time series there are a number of nonlinear equations that can be justified under a wide variety of circumstances. Of interest here are two such nonlinear equations, the exponential curve and the modified exponential curve.

The exponential curve is generally used to approximate those time series that increase or decrease at a constant proportion over time. Examples of such series include population growth, the sales of a new product, and the spread of a highly communicable disease. The exponential curve is represented by the equation:

$$\text{\textit{Exponential curve: } } y_t = ab^t \qquad (14.7)$$

The form of the exponential curve depends on the values of a and b. If b is between zero and one, then the value of y_t will decrease as t increases. When b is larger than one, y_t will increase as t increases. The value of a gives the y-intercept of the curve, as shown in Fig. 14.6.

Note that by taking the logarithm of both sides of Formula (14.4), we can transform the exponential curve into a linear relationship. That is,

$$\log y_t = \log (ab^t) = \log a + t \log b \qquad (14.8)$$

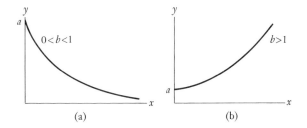

Figure 14.6
The exponential curve
$y_t = ab^t$.

(a)   (b)

Our model is now linear, and the least-squares approach can be used to find the line of best fit.

In a number of circumstances it is desirable to allow for more flexibility in deciding on the position of the trend line than is provided by the exponential curve, without altering the basic form of this curve. One way to accomplish this objective is to modify the exponential curve by adding a constant to the equation. Suppose we add the constant c. The resulting equation is called the **modified exponential curve.**

TABLE 14.9
Sales of VCRs
in the United States,
1975–1986
($ millions)

Year	Sales
1975	34
1976	65
1977	180
1978	326
1979	389
1980	621
1981	1127
1982	1303
1983	2162
1984	3585
1985	4789
1986	5258

Source: Bureau of Census, *Statistical Abstract of the United States,* 1988

$$\text{Modified exponential curve: } y_t = c + ab^t \qquad (14.9)$$

The modified exponential, like the exponential itself, can assume many different forms depending on the values of a, b, and in this case c. Although the addition of the constant c merely serves to shift the exponential curve up or down by a constant amount, such a shift is convenient in describing a time series with values that approach an upper or lower limit, as shown in Fig. 14.7. Finding the best fit to a modified exponential curve is not as easy as in the case of the exponential curve, because there is no simple transformation that makes the equation linear, and finding the best least-squares fit directly is a fairly difficult task. However, fitting curves to data can be accomplished using packages such as Minitab and SAS.

To illustrate the process of fitting a nonlinear line to a time series, we use the data shown in Table 14.9. These data represent the sales (in millions of dollars) of video cassette recorders (VCRs) in the United States (y_t) over the period 1975 to 1985. VCRs were introduced in 1974 and displayed a rapid increase in sales over the next few years, as shown in Fig. 14.8. This sales graph closely resembles the exponential curve in Fig. 14.6(b). Thus the exponential curve may be used to represent the sales of VCRs. To fit the exponential curve

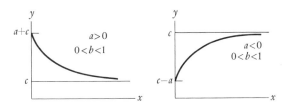

Figure 14.7
The modified exponential
curve $y_t = c + ab^t$.

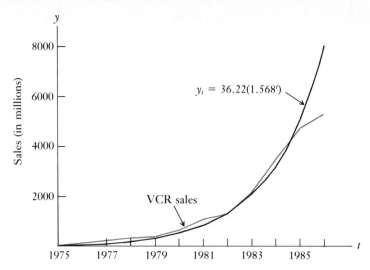

Figure 14.8
Sales of VCRs in the United States, 1975–1986.

to these data, we use Equation (14.8) by first finding the logarithm of the y_t values and then determining the least-squares fit for $\log y_t = \log a + t \log b$. (The variable t is time in years, with 1975 $t = 1$ and 1986 $t = 12$.) Using this approach results in $a = 36.22$ and $b = 1.568$, and thus

$$y_t = 36.22(1.568^t)$$

This exponential curve yields $r^2 = 0.97$, representing a very good fit to sales over the period 1975 to 1986.

The exponential curve is only one of many functions available for use in finding a fit to nonlinear data. The problem of deciding which nonlinear equations to use in estimating trend in a given circumstance is often difficult. It is not unusual, in fitting the commonly used mathematical curves to a set of time-series observations, to find that two or more equations provide approximately the same closeness of fit, so that for the purpose of merely describing the data there is little to choose between these curves. The problem arises when such curves are used to predict future values of the time series (extrapolations into the future), for the curves tend to diverge rather quickly, and unacceptably large divergences may result from even a small extrapolation. For instance, in the VCR example, the rapid increase in sales seems to be slowing down in 1985 and 1986, from an annual increase of about 65% in both 1983 and 1984 to only 32% in 1985 and 11% in 1986. If the fitted exponential curve is used to predict the 1985 and 1986 sales, we get a forecast of $5102 millions for 1985 and $8000 millions for 1986. The actual sales for 1985 and 1986 are only $4739 and $5258 millions, respectively. Thus, as pointed out earlier in this section, it is not sufficient to merely find a trend line providing a "good fit" to the data. It is necessary to fit a curve that can be justified by a general assessment of the underlying nature of the series.

Estimation of Seasonal Components

14.9

Until now we have been concerned with estimating only trend. Often, however, it may be just as (or even more) important to be able to estimate the seasonal component in a time series. The seasonal component of a time series is usually expressed by a number, called a **seasonal index number.** This index expresses the value of the seasonal fluctuation in each period as a percentage of the trend value expected for that period. A value of 104 thus means that, because of seasonal factors, the time-series value is expected to be 4% above the trend value. If the index number is 93, then the time-series value is expected to be 7% less than the trend value. Because of seasonal variation, special care must be taken in forecasting the time-series value for any given period, or in comparing these values between periods. Such forecasts or comparisons are usually made by first removing the effects of seasonality from the data using a seasonal index. This is called "deseasonalizing" the data.

To illustrate this type of index, we will assume that bicycle sales for a given manufacturer have averaged 50,000 units a month for the past five years. The average sales in each month are not always equal to 50,000. In February, for example, sales over the past five years have averaged 30,000 units. Similarly, May has averaged 50,000 units, and December, 80,000 units. Since February has averaged only 60% of the overall average sales of 50,000, the seasonal index for February is $S_{\text{Feb.}} = 60.0$. Similarly, the indexes for May and December would be $S_{\text{May}} = 100.0$ and $S_{\text{Dec.}} = 160$.

In deseasonalizing a time-series value, we first divide the value by the seasonal index, and then multiply it by 100. That is,

$$\text{Deseasonalized value} = \frac{(\text{Original value})}{(\text{Seasonal index})} \times 100 \qquad (14.10)$$

This formula can be used to deseasonalize values in our bicycle problem. Suppose that the actual sales for February and December this year were 32,000 and 84,000, respectively. These values are then deseasonalized as follows:

$$\text{Deseasonalized February sales} = \frac{32,000}{60} \times 100 = 53,333$$

$$\text{Deseasonalized December sales} = \frac{84,000}{160} \times 100 = 52,500$$

Note how this process of deseasonalizing a time-series value makes the comparison of sales between the two months very easy. In this case February sales were slightly better than December sales on a seasonally adjusted basis.

Finding a Seasonal Index

In order to determine seasonal index numbers, it is necessary to estimate the seasonal component of a time series. Suppose that a given time series can be represented by the multiplicative model $y_t = T \times S \times C \times I$. One method for estimating the seasonal component in this model is called the **ratio–to–moving averages method.** For this discussion we will assume a monthly time series, with seasonality. The first step in this approach is to smooth the data by using a 12-month moving average. If we disregard the irregular component, the causes and occurrences of which are unknown, the smoothed series will contain fluctuations attributable only to T and C, since a 12-month moving average will remove seasonal variations. In terms of the multiplicative model we have, in effect, divided y_t by S, so that the new series is $y_t/S = T \times C$. If the original time-series values, y_t, are now divided by this newly calculated series containing only T and C, the result is

$$y_t/(T \times C) = (T \times S \times C)/(T \times C) = S \qquad (14.11)$$

Thus, by a rather roundabout route, we have isolated S and determined a seasonal index in which the variations attributable to T and C have been removed.

To illustrate how this process works, we use the data from Table 14.10 (also shown in Fig. 14.9). These data represent the monthly U.S. retail sales (in billions of dollars) for the period 1984 to 1987. Analysis of the data shows that this time series has both an increasing trend (indicated by the successive yearly totals) and seasonal patterns (as shown by the peaks and valleys for the same months, in Fig. 14.9). To remove the seasonal fluctuations, we first calculate a 12-month moving average over all months in the series. This moving average is shown in columns 3 and 6 of Tables 14.11(a) and 14.11(b). Since the number of months in this average is even, the average is placed between

TABLE 14.10   Monthly U.S. retail sales, 1984–1987 ($ billions)

Month	1984	1985	1986	1987
Jan.	92.4	98.8	106.7	106.4
Feb.	93.2	95.7	100.5	105.8
Mar.	103.8	110.2	114.9	120.4
Apr.	104.1	113.2	116.3	125.4
May	111.3	120.5	126.1	129.0
June	111.7	115.1	121.0	129.0
July	106.3	115.8	121.4	129.9
Aug.	110.6	121.4	124.7	131.0
Sept.	103.4	114.5	125.4	123.8
Oct.	109.0	116.5	123.8	127.2
Nov.	112.7	118.7	121.4	125.4
Dec.	130.9	139.3	152.1	154.8
Totals	1289.4	1379.71	1454.3	1508.1

Source: Standard and Poor's Statistical Service, *Current Statistics*, April 1988

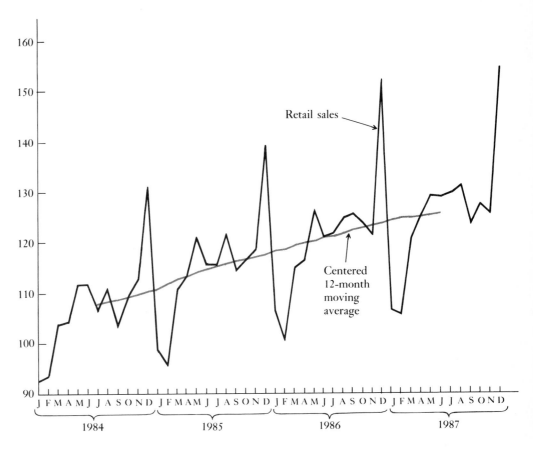

Figure 14.9
Monthly U.S. retail sales,
1984–1987 ($ billions).

the sixth and seventh month of each moving average. To associate the moving-average values with the middle of each month, these values are further "adjusted" by taking the average of the moving-average values for each two adjacent months. For example, the first moving average, 107.5, lies in the middle between June and July. Effectively it is centered at the end of June. Similarly, the second value, 108.0, is centered at the end of July. Thus, the average of these two moving average values, 107.8, will be centered in the middle of July. Similar computations give us a new time series of moving averages centered in the middle of each month. These values are shown in columns 4 and 7 of Tables 14.11(a) and 14.11(b) and are also plotted in Fig. 14.9. They represent $T \times C$ and some parts of I. That is, using this process we have now eliminated S and some parts of I from the series.

Next, we find the "raw" seasonal indexes by dividing the original time-series values [columns 2 and 5 in Tables 14.11(a) and 14.11(b)] by the corresponding 12-month centered moving-average values (columns 4 and 7). For example, the first seasonal index determined will be for July 1984. This is calculated as

$$S_{\text{July 84}} = 106.3/107.8 = 98.6$$

TABLE 14.11(a)

(1) Month	(2) 1984 sales	(3) 12-month MA	(4) Centered 12-month MA	(5) 1985 sales	(6) 12-month MA	(7) Centered 12-month MA
Jan.	92.4			98.8	111.3	110.9
Feb.	93.2			95.7	112.2	111.8
Mar.	103.8			110.2	113.2	112.7
Apr.	104.1			113.2	113.8	113.5
May	111.3			120.5	114.3	114.1
June	111.7	107.5		115.1	115.0	114.7
July	106.3	108.0	107.8	115.8	115.6	115.3
Aug.	110.6	108.2	108.1	121.4	116.0	115.8
Sept.	103.4	108.7	108.5	114.5	116.4	116.2
Oct.	109.0	109.5	109.1	116.5	116.7	116.6
Nov.	112.7	110.3	109.9	118.7	117.2	117.0
Dec.	130.9	110.5	110.2	139.3	117.6	117.4

TABLE 14.11(b)

(1) Month	(2) 1986 sales	(3) 12-month MA	(4) Centered 12-month MA	(5) 1987 sales	(6) 12-month MA	(7) Centered 12-month MA
Jan.	106.7	118.1	117.9	106.4	124.4	124.1
Feb.	100.5	118.4	118.3	105.8	125.0	124.7
Mar.	114.9	119.3	118.9	120.4	124.8	124.9
Apr.	116.3	119.9	119.6	125.4	125.1	125.0
May	126.1	120.1	120.0	129.0	125.5	125.3
June	121.0	121.2	120.7	129.0	125.7	125.6
July	121.4	121.2	121.2	129.9		
Aug.	124.7	121.6	121.4	131.0		
Sept.	125.4	122.1	121.9	123.8		
Oct.	123.8	122.8	122.5	127.2		
Nov.	121.4	123.1	123.0	125.4		
Dec.	152.1	123.7	123.4	154.8		

Similarly, the second index calculated, for August 1984, is

$$S_{\text{Aug. }84} = 110.6/108.1 = 102.3$$

If this division is now carried out for the rest of the data, we get three separate index numbers for each month of the year, as shown in Table 14.12. These index numbers represent the seasonal component. The seasonal indexes computed using this method may still contain some random variation. One way to eliminate this is to calculate the median (or mean) of the three seasonal indexes for each month. In Table 14.12 we used the median, and these median values become our seasonal indexes.

A final step that is often necessary in the construction of seasonal indexes is called **leveling the index** or **normalizing** the index. The need for leveling may arise because in the ratio–to–moving averages method we obtained the seasonal index values by calculating the median value for each month. This process was done without any restrictions as to what the average of these "medians" must be over the entire year. However, the average of the raw seasonal indexes must be 100 if the index is to alter only the pattern but not the level of the raw data series when deseasonalizing the series. For example, if the average over the year of the raw seasonal indexes were 90, the use of the raw seasonal indexes would raise the average level of the deseasonalized series by $[(100/90)] - 1]$ or about 11% above the average level of the raw data series. Clearly, this is an unintended result of deseasonalizing the series.

To level an index we first find the average of the raw seasonal indexes. Next, we adjust each raw seasonal index by dividing it by this average and multiplying by 100. For this example, the raw seasonal indexes averaged 99.78. If we adjust each seasonal index by this average, the net effect is an increase in each value of the raw seasonals. For example, for January we adjust the raw

TABLE 14.12   Seasonal index numbers

Month	1984	1985	1986	1987	Median index	Level indexes
Jan.	—	89.1	90.5	85.7	89.1	89.3
Feb.	—	85.6	85.0	84.8	85.0	85.2
Mar.	—	97.8	96.6	96.4	96.6	96.8
Apr.	—	99.7	97.2	100.3	99.7	99.9
May	—	105.6	105.1	103.0	105.1	105.3
June	—	100.3	100.2	102.7	100.3	100.5
July	98.6	100.4	100.2	—	100.2	100.4
Aug.	102.3	104.8	102.7	—	102.7	102.9
Sept.	95.3	98.5	102.9	—	98.5	98.7
Oct.	99.9	99.9	101.1	—	99.9	100.1
Nov.	102.5	101.5	98.7	—	101.5	101.7
Dec.	118.8	118.7	123.3	—	118.8	119.1

index of 89.1 as 89.1/99.78 × 100 = 89.3. These computations make the average of the leveled indexes exactly 100 over the year. Note that if the average of the raw seasonal indexes had been greater than 100, the result of leveling would have been a decrease in the values of the raw seasonal indexes.

Cyclical Variations

14.10

The previous two sections focused on procedures to identify and calculate the trend and the seasonal components of a time series. The final systematic component is the cyclical component. In some analyses, it is desirable to isolate the cyclical component so that turning points as well as peaks and troughs can be studied. If a stable cyclical pattern, such as a 3.4-year business cycle or a 20-year housing construction cycle, could be isolated, it would greatly aid in determining the underlying causes and in forecasting future movements. However, the cyclical components in business and economic series generally tend to vary in both duration and amplitude from one cycle to the next, making it very difficult to analyze these variations. Although a wide variety of complicated methods have been proposed for studying the cyclical component, we present a simple roundabout computational procedure to isolate C.

Given a time series $y_t = T \times C \times S \times I$, the seasonal component S is first determined by the ratio–to–moving averages method. The values of y_t are then divided by the seasonal index S to obtain $y_t \times 100/S = T \times C \times I$. Next, we estimate the trend component from $T \times C \times I$ by a least-squares fit, using the most appropriate linear or nonlinear curve. Dividing $T \times C \times I$ by the values of $\hat{y}_t$ obtained from this least-squares analysis leaves us with only the components $C \times I$. Finally, to eliminate I we can use a number of methods. One way is to compute a weighted moving average of three or five periods using $C \times I$ data. If a longer moving average were used, the cycles might be smoothed out too much and partially eliminated also.

The best type of weights to use are large weights for the center values and much smaller weights for the values farther away from the center. If the weights are constructed so that their sum is equal to 1, then no division by the sum of the weights is necessary. For example, in a five-period moving average, the weights might be 0.1, 0.2, 0.4, 0.2, and 0.1. The advantage of this extra computation using weights is that it produces a smoother curve for the cyclical component C. At the same time it is also more sensitive to the original fluctuations, because it preserves the amplitude of the cycles more faithfully. Using the odd-period moving average is convenient for centering the resulting values (which constitute the component C). For example, based on the monthly data for our retail sales problem, the cyclical component for April would be

$$C_{\text{April}} = 0.1(C \times I)_{\text{Feb.}} + 0.2(C \times I)_{\text{Mar.}} + 0.4(C \times I)_{\text{Apr.}} + 0.2(C \times I)_{\text{May}} + 0.1(C \times I)_{\text{June}}$$

Values of C for other months may be found in a similar way.

Problems

14.13 What is the difference between the seasonal and the cyclical components of a time series? Why is the cyclical component more difficult to estimate than the seasonal component?

14.14 Describe the effect of using three periods and seven periods in computing a moving average. Of these two, which will produce a smoother series? Which responds to trends better? Explain your answer.

14.15 The following table lists the closing monthly prices (in dollars per share) of IBM stock for the period 1985 to 1987.

	1985	1986	1987
Jan.	136.38	151.50	128.75
Feb.	134.00	150.88	139.50
Mar.	127.00	149.13	150.13
Apr.	126.50	156.25	160.13
May	128.63	152.38	160.00
June	123.75	146.50	162.50
July	131.38	132.50	161.00
Aug.	126.63	138.75	168.38
Sept.	123.88	134.50	150.75
Oct.	129.88	123.63	122.50
Nov.	139.75	127.13	110.75
Dec.	155.50	120.00	115.50

Calculate the three-month and five-month moving averages for this time series.

14.16 Refer to the information in Problem 14.15. Plot the time series of the IBM stock, and its three-month and five-month moving averages on a graph. Which of the two moving-average series defines the underlying trend more clearly?

14.17 Refer to the information in Problem 14.12.

a) Calculate a three-month and a five-month moving average for both the Dow Jones and the Financial Times average for the period 1987–88.

b) Plot the Dow Jones average and its three-month and five-month moving average series on a graph. Which of the two moving averages describes the underlying trend better?

14.18 Refer to the information in Problem 14.15 about IBM shares. Using the data from October 1986 onward, develop a three-month moving average to forecast the price of IBM stock for each month in 1987. Compare the forecasted values against the actuals by computing the absolute error (the absolute difference between the actual and the forecasted values) for each month.

14.19 Redo Problem 14.18 by calculating a three-month weighted moving average with a weight of three attached to the most recent month, a weight of 2 to the middle month and a weight of 1 to the oldest month. Does this method do a better job of forecasting?

14.20 The following table lists the civilian employment figures (in thousands) from 1974 to 1987.

Year	Civilian labor force	Year	Civilian labor force
1974	86,794	1981	100,397
1975	85,846	1982	99,526
1976	88,752	1983	100,834
1977	92,017	1984	105,005
1978	96,048	1985	107,150
1979	98,824	1986	109,600
1980	99,303	1987	112,400

Source: Standard and Poor's Statistical Service, *Current Statistics,* April 1988

a) Plot this time series. Does a linear trend seem reasonable for this time series?

b) Let $t = 1$ correspond to 1974. Fit a least-squares line to these data. How good is this regression line in estimating the trend?

14.21 Because of inflation and other factors, the value of the dollar has dropped consistently over the years. For example, the value of the dollar in 1988 as measured against the 1967 dollar is worth only about 29 cents. The following table lists the value of the dollar for the period 1974 to 1987 as measured against the 1967 dollar.

Year	Value of dollar (in cents)	Year	Value of dollar (in cents)
1974	67.8	1981	36.7
1975	62.1	1982	34.6
1976	58.7	1983	33.5
1977	55.1	1984	32.1
1978	51.2	1985	31.0
1979	46.0	1986	30.1
1980	40.5	1987	29.2

Source: U.S. Bureau of Labor Statistics

a) Plot this time series.

b) Does a linear trend seem reasonable for this series? Would an exponential curve do a better job?

c) Let $t = 1$ correspond to 1974. Fit both a linear trend line and an exponential curve to these data. Which one of these two lines fits the data better? Explain your answer.

14.22 The U.S. Department of Commerce reported the following data for monthly retail sales (in billions of dollars) of durable goods in the United States over the period 1983 to 1987.

	1983	1984	1985	1986	1987
Jan.	25.09	32.18	35.68	39.45	37.77
Feb.	25.46	34.08	35.55	37.79	40.16
Mar.	32.43	37.94	41.63	43.09	47.54
Apr.	31.82	38.56	43.95	56.38	49.84
May	34.28	42.27	47.34	50.19	50.69
June	36.73	42.72	44.77	49.10	53.12
July	34.48	39.84	45.22	48.58	52.21
Aug.	34.67	40.44	46.22	49.03	52.71
Sept.	33.81	36.89	45.51	54.81	49.65
Oct.	34.65	40.20	43.27	48.48	48.60
Nov.	35.09	39.57	41.62	44.47	42.26
Dec.	39.43	42.69	47.02	56.69	54.85
Totals	397.94	467.38	517.98	568.06	579.40

a) Fit a linear trend line to these data using the yearly totals. Determine an approximate monthly trend from the annual trend line.

b) Using the data for 1984 to 1987 only, calculate the 12-month moving averages and the centered moving averages.

c) Using the ratio–to–moving averages method, calculate the monthly seasonal indexes.

14.23 a) Refer to the information in Problem 14.21. Using the linear trend line from part (b), forecast the civilian employment for 1988 and 1989.

b) Find the actual values for 1988 and 1989 and compare these values with your forecast.

14.24 a) Refer to Problem 14.22. Using the monthly linear trend line from part (a), and the seasonal indexes from part (c), forecast the monthly retail sales of durable goods for the period January 1988 to June 1988.

b) Find the actual values for the period January 1988 to June 1988 and compare these actuals with your forecasted values from part (a).

Exponential Smoothing Models

14.11

In Section 14.6 moving averages were used to smooth time series and obtain simple forecasts. We now examine another smoothing method used to develop forecasting models called **exponential smoothing.** These models are generally used for situations where forecasts for many different time series are required on a frequent and periodic basis. For example, in the management of manufacturing inventories, monthly demand forecasts for thousands of different stock items may be required for procurement and production decisions. Efficient inventory cost control can only be achieved if reliable forecasts are easily obtained. Exponential smoothing models are easy to use and can be computerized for analyzing large amounts of data. Thus, they are well suited for providing such forecasts. Exponential smoothing models have been successfully applied in a variety of different settings in addition to inventory management. In this section we present two exponential smoothing models, the simple exponential smoothing model and Winters' model.

The Simple Exponential Smoothing Model

The **simple exponential smoothing model** is used for time series in which neither trend nor seasonal components are present. That is, the only variation in this series is due to random fluctuations. A time series of this kind is called a **stationary time series.** To forecast a stationary time series using exponential smoothing, we first smooth the time series using weighted averages. The smoothed values from this process in turn form a time series. This new time series then represents the underlying mean level of the stationary time series and may be projected into the future to obtain forecasts.

The exponential smoothing model calculates the smoothed value in period t, denoted by S_t, as a weighted average of the current observation, y_t, with weight α, and the smoothed value from the preceding period $t - 1, S_{t-1}$, with weight $1 - \alpha$.

$$\textit{Smoothed value: } S_t = \alpha y_t + (1 - \alpha) S_{t-1} \qquad \textbf{(14.12)}$$

The weight α (alpha) is called a **smoothing constant** and lies between 0 and 1. This smoothing process, represented by Formula (14.12), removes the random fluctuations from the original time series. If the time series is expected to remain stationary in future periods, the smoothed value in the current period, S_t, provides an appropriate estimate of the underlying mean of the future values of the time series. Thus, S_t may be used to forecast the time series n periods into the future.

$$\textit{Forecasted value: } F_{t+n} = S_t \qquad \textbf{(14.13)}$$

Exponential smoothing using (14.12) is a special form of weighted moving averages. It calculates the smoothed value (S_t) as a weighted average of past observations. To show this let's expand Equation (14.13) by calculating and substituting for S_{t-1}. Going back to the preceding period, $t - 1, S_{t-1}$ is calculated using (14.12) as follows:

$$S_{t-1} = \alpha y_{t-1} + (1 - \alpha) S_{t-2} \qquad \textbf{(14.14)}$$

If this expression for S_{t-1} is now substituted in Equation (14.12), we get

$$S_t = \alpha y_t + \alpha(1-\alpha)y_{t-1} + (1-\alpha)^2 S_{t-2} \qquad (14.15)$$

Repeating this process and substituting first for S_{t-2}, then for S_{t-3} and so on, we find that the formula for S_t expands to

$$S_t = \alpha y_t + \alpha(1-\alpha)y_{t-1} + \alpha(1-\alpha)^2 y_{t-2} + \cdots$$
$$+ \alpha(1-\alpha)^{t-1}y_1 + (1-\alpha)^t S_0 \qquad (14.16)$$

where S_0 is the starting smoothed value.

Equation (14.16) shows that S_t, the smoothed value in period t, is a weighted average of the past observations $y_t, y_{t-1}, \cdots, y_1$. The weights are determined by α. For example, if $\alpha = 0.5$, the current observation, y_t, is given a weighting of 0.5. The next most recent observation, y_{t-1}, (for period $t-1$) is given a weighting of $\alpha(1-\alpha) = 0.25$. This is followed by a weight of $\alpha(1-\alpha)^2 = 0.125$ for period $t-2$, of $\alpha(1-\alpha)^3 = 0.0625$ for period $t-3$ and so on. As we go farther back into the past, the weight is reduced by 50% for each period. If α has been set equal to 0.10, the observation for the current period would be given a weight equal to 0.10. The weight for each subsequent observation in the past is reduced by 10%. The weights for $\alpha = 0.1$ and $\alpha = 0.5$ are shown in Fig. 14.10. This figure shows how the weights decline exponentially for previous data points; hence the name "exponential smoothing."

The selection of the smoothing constant, α, controls the smoothness of S_t and is critical to the responsiveness and performance of the model as a forecasting tool. A low value of α places more emphasis on past values of the time series and therefore yields a smoother series. High values of α give more

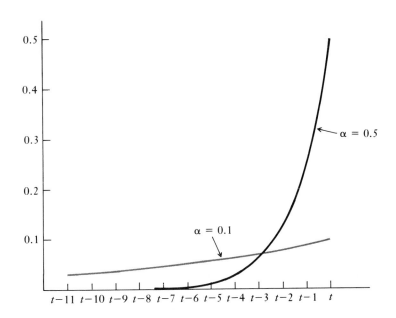

Figure 14.10
Weights for $\alpha = 0.1$ and $\alpha = 0.5$.

weighting to recent observations. If α is too large, it may not smooth out the random fluctuations effectively. On the other hand, if α is too small, the model may respond too slowly to any changes in the underlying mean level of the series. Thus, the choice of α must strike a balance between these two extremes. In practice α is usually chosen in the range from 0.1 to 0.5.

A value for S_0, the starting smoothed value, is necessary to begin an exponential smoothing model. For a stationary time series, the value of S_0 may be set equal to the average of several observations from periods prior to the starting period. If no past observations are available, the average of the first few observations of the time series may be used instead.

To illustrate how this model works, consider the data shown in columns 2 and 5 of Table 14.13. These data represent the monthly U.S. exports in billions of dollars. A plot of these data (Fig. 14.11) reveals that the time series seems to be stationary in 1986, with an upward trend in 1987. To analyze this time series using the simple exponential model requires an initial estimate for S_0. This may be obtained by averaging the figures for several months from 1985 (not shown here). If we use October, November, and December 1985, the initial estimate of S_0 is $(17.87 + 17.74 + 17.48)/3 = 17.70$. We use it to start the model in January 1986. We calculate two smoothed series, one with $\alpha = 0.1$ and the other with $\alpha = 0.5$. For example, with $\alpha = 0.1$, the smoothed value for January 1986 is calculated as

$$S_1 = \alpha y_1 + (1 - \alpha) S_0 = 0.1(17.04) + 0.9(17.70) = 17.63$$

Similarly, the smoothed value for February 1986 is

$$S_2 = \alpha y_2 + (1 - \alpha) S_1 = 0.1(17.40) + 0.9(17.63) = 17.61$$

TABLE 14.13   Simple exponential smoothing: Monthly U.S. exports ($ billions)

(1) Month	(2) 1986 exports	(3) Smoothed estimate $\alpha = 0.1$	(4) Smoothed estimate $\alpha = 0.5$	(5) 1987 exports	(6) Smoothed estimate $\alpha = 0.1$	(7) Smoothed estimate $\alpha = 0.5$
Jan.	17.04	17.63	17.37	16.76	17.80	17.63
Feb.	17.40	17.61	17.39	19.36	18.04	18.49
Mar.	18.58	17.71	17.98	21.78	18.42	20.14
Apr.	18.00	17.73	17.99	20.50	18.62	20.32
May	18.27	17.79	18.13	20.78	18.84	20.55
June	19.09	17.92	18.61	21.13	19.07	20.84
July	17.35	17.86	17.98	21.01	19.27	20.92
Aug.	16.90	17.77	17.44	20.22	19.36	20.57
Sept.	17.53	17.74	17.49	20.99	19.52	20.78
Oct.	19.56	17.92	18.52	21.75	19.75	21.27
Nov.	18.41	17.97	18.47	—	—	—
Dec.	18.52	18.03	18.49	—	—	—

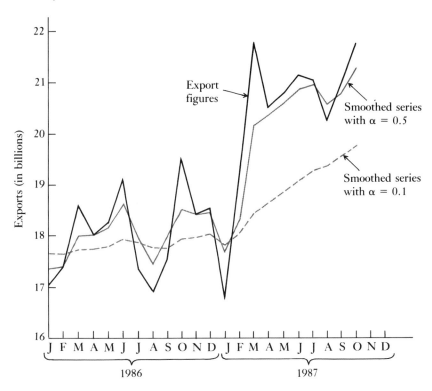

Figure 14.11
Exponential smoothed series
of monthly U.S. exports.

The entire smoothed series for both smoothing constants ($\alpha = 0.1$ and $\alpha = 0.5$) are shown in Table 14.13.

A plot of the two smoothed series is presented in Fig. 14.11. For the stationary part of the original series (1986), the smoothing constant $\alpha = 0.1$ does a better job of tracking the underlying mean level of the series. However, when a trend is present (1987), the smoothed values lag behind. This smoothing constant does not respond as well to changing trends. A higher value of α, $\alpha = 0.5$, does not do as good a job of smoothing out the random fluctuations for the stationary data but does a much better job of responding to changing trends. Thus, the selection of the value of α is very important. If the series is expected to stay stationary, a low value of α (close to 0.1) is used. If there are any changes in the underlying mean level of the series, a higher value of α (closer to 0.5) is more appropriate. Values of α greater than 0.5 are generally not used for the simple model. If a value greater than 0.5 gives better results, it is often the case that a different model would be more appropriate.

Winters' Exponential Smoothing Model

The simple model works well only when the time series is stationary. If a time series contains trend and seasonality components, this model is no longer appropriate. For such series we now extend our simple model to allow for trend and seasonality. This model is called **Winters' model** (in honor of its originator).

Winters' model consists of three smoothing equations. The first equation updates the overall mean level of the series (S_t) at the end of each period t. This mean level is the underlying mean of the series without the trend and seasonality components. The second equation updates the trend estimate, T_t. The third equation updates the seasonal indexes. Seasonal indexes in this model, denoted by Q_t, are expressed as fractions (to the base 1) rather than percentages. For example, a seasonal index of 105 in percentage terms is expressed as 1.05. Similarly, an index of 95 is expressed as 0.95. Additionally, for this model we need to define L, the number of periods in the seasonal cycle. Thus, for quarterly data $L = 4$. For monthly data $L = 12$.

The smoothing equation for S_t is a weighted average of two different estimates of the current mean level of the series. It is represented by the following formula (where α is again a number between 0 and 1):

$$\textit{Smoothed value: } S_t = \alpha\, \frac{y_t}{Q_{t-L}} + (1 - \alpha)(S_{t-1} + T_{t-1}) \qquad \textbf{(14.17)}$$

The first estimate, y_t/Q_{t-L}, is obtained by dividing the current observation (y_t) by Q_{t-L} (the seasonal index for period $t - L$). This index is the best estimate of the seasonal index for the current period. For example, if t is January 1988 in a monthly time series with $L = 12$, then $t - L$ corresponds to January 1987, the last period in which the January seasonal index was updated. Thus, y_t/Q_{t-L} is the deasonalized observation for the current period.

The second estimate needed to determine S_t in Formula (14.17) is $(S_{t-1} + T_{t-1})$. Note that S_{t-1} is the smoothed value of the series calculated in period $t - 1$; T_{t-1} is the trend estimated in period $t - 1$. Since T_{t-1} is the expected one period change due to trend and both T_{t-1} and S_{t-1} are deseasonalized, $(S_{t-1} + T_{t-1})$ is simply an estimate of the overall mean level of the series for period t without any current seasonal adjustment. This estimate is given a weight of $1 - \alpha$.

The trend component is the amount by which we expect the series to increase or decrease (if trend is negative) in one period without taking into account any seasonal effects. The smoothing equation for trend is also a weighted average of two different estimates of the trend component. Trend in Winters' model is calculated using the smoothing constant beta (where $0 \leq \beta \leq 1$) as follows:

$$\textit{Trend value: } T_t = \beta(S_t - S_{t-1}) + (1 - \beta)T_{t-1} \qquad \textbf{(14.18)}$$

The first estimate, $(S_t - S_{t-1})$, is a measure of the trend due to the change in the smoothed series between periods $t - 1$ and t. This estimate reflects the trend component of the most recent observation, (y_t), and is given a weight equal to β. The other estimate of trend is T_{t-1}, the estimated trend component from the preceding period. It is given a weight equal to $1 - \beta$.

The final smoothing equation in Winters' model updates the seasonal index using the smoothing constant gamma (where $0 \leq \gamma \leq 1$) as follows:

$$\text{Seasonal value: } Q_t = \gamma \frac{y_t}{S_t} + (1 - \gamma)Q_{t-L} \qquad (14.19)$$

As before, this seasonal index is a weighted average of two different estimates of the seasonal index. The first (y_t/S_t) is a measure of how much the current observation (y_t) differs from the expected deseasonalized mean level of the series (S_t). The other estimate, Q_{t-L}, is the seasonal index for the current period based on the index from L periods (or one year) ago. The first estimate is given a weight equal to γ while the second is weighted $1 - \gamma$. Note that these seasonal indexes may have to be leveled if the average of the seasonal indexes for the current seasonal cycle does not equal 1. (The procedure for leveling is the same discussed in Section 14.9.)

Having updated the values for S_t, T_t, and Q_t, the time series may be projected n periods into the future using Formula (14.20).

$$\text{Forecasted value: } F_{t+n} = (S_t + nT_t)Q_{t-L+n} \qquad (14.20)$$

In this equation ($S_t + nT_t$) is a projection of the deseasonalized series n periods into the future. This projected level of the series is then adjusted for seasonality by multiplying it by Q_{t-L+n}, the seasonal index that corresponds to period $t + n$.

To evaluate these equations beginning with period 1, we need initial estimates for the mean level of the series (S_0), the trend (T_0), and L seasonal factors, one for each season in the seasonal cycle. We label these initial seasonal indexes from Q_{-L+1} to Q_0. For example, the seasonal indexes for quarterly data would be labeled Q_{-3} to Q_0. For monthly data these would be Q_{-11} to Q_0. These starting values for the seasonal indexes are generally computed from past observations. For example, if enough historical data are available, it may be possible to use the method of ratio–to–moving averages. Similarly, S_0 and T_0 are also computed from past observations. For example, the value of S_0 may be set equal to the average of several deseasonalized observations from periods preceding period 1. There are several ways of estimating T_0. One possibility is to calculate the trend component for several periods prior to period 1 using deseasonalized observations and then averaging these trend values.

The choice of the smoothing constants α, β, and γ is critical to the performance of the model. As in the stationary model, there are no simple rules that govern the selection of these values. In general, the values of these constants are chosen in the range from 0.1 to 0.5. However, for most applications several combinations may be tried in order to determine the one that provides the best forecasts. One way of measuring whether one combination of smoothing constants is better than another is to use some measure of forecast accuracy. Two popular measures of forecast accuracy are the mean absolute deviation (MAD) and the root mean squared error (RMSE) of the forecasts. The **mean absolute deviation** calculates the average of the absolute values of the forecast errors and is defined in Formula (14.21), where N = number of periods.

$$\text{Mean absolute deviation: } \text{MAD} = \frac{\sum |E_t|}{N} = \frac{\sum |y_t - F_t|}{N} \qquad (14.21)$$

The **root mean squared error** calculates the square root of the mean squared differences between the forecasts and the actual values and is defined as follows:

$$\text{Root mean squared error: } \text{RMSE} = \sqrt{\frac{\sum\limits_{t=1}^{N} (y_t - F_t)^2}{N}} \qquad (14.22)$$

Care must be taken in assessing forecast accuracy using these criteria. The number of periods used in the evaluation will be critical to the selection of the model. Also, the number of time periods to be forecasted into the future will play an important role in the selection.

To illustrate the computational procedure of the Winters' model, we use the data from Table 14.14. These data represent the number of passenger miles (in billions) flown within the United States in the period 1984 to 1988. As we would expect, this time series is seasonal, rising in the summer months and falling in the winter months. There is also an upward trend, as indicated by the successive yearly totals.

To analyze these data using Winters' model, we first require estimates of the starting values of the mean level, the trend and the seasonal indexes. In general the older data are used for estimating these initial values. For this model we will use the 1984 data to do the initial computations. These values can be calculated in several different ways. For example, to estimate S_0 one possible method is to use the average of the twelve observations in 1984. Another is to calculate the seasonal indexes first and then use the deseasonalized value for December. For this analysis, we will use the 1984 average of 16.211 as the initial estimate for S_0. T_0 can also be computed using several different approaches. One way is to use the average monthly increase between 1984 and 1985. Alternatively, T_0 may be determined by fitting a regression line to the 1984 and 1985 values. We will use the former approach, setting T_0 equal to 0.205. (This is done by finding the difference between the average monthly figures for 1984, 16.211, and 1985, 18.666 and dividing this difference by 12 to arrive at the monthly trend.)

TABLE 14.14   U.S. Domestic passenger miles flown (billions)

Month	1984	1985	1986	1987	1988
Jan.	14.46	17.41	18.19	20.68	21.70
Feb.	13.85	15.67	17.41	21.29	21.93
Mar.	16.82	20.49	21.71	26.56	26.55
Apr.	16.05	19.25	20.27	24.65	24.70
May	16.28	19.14	20.94	25.34	25.09
June	17.64	19.25	22.00	25.30	26.18
July	17.63	21.16	23.66	27.26	27.51
Aug.	18.83	21.58	25.31	28.16	29.05
Sept.	15.32	16.38	19.64	21.53	22.74
Oct.	16.49	17.73	21.01	23.08	24.73
Nov.	15.56	16.51	19.87	22.93	23.22
Dec.	15.60	19.42	22.12	22.93	23.47
Total	194.53	223.99	252.13	281.81	296.87

Source: Standard and Poor's Statistical Service, *Current Statistics,* November 1989

As discussed earlier, seasonal indexes may also be determined in several different ways. One possibility is to use the ratio–to–moving averages method. An easier way, however, is to compute these indexes directly from the 1984 data by indexing each month's value to the 1984 average of 16.211. For example, the index for January (Q_{-11}) is determined as $14.46/16.211 = 0.892$. Similarly, the index for February (Q_{-10}) will be $13.85/16.211 = 0.854$. Using this procedure the other initial seasonal indexes are $Q_{-9} = 1.038$, $Q_{-8} = 0.990$, $Q_{-7} = 1.004$, $Q_{-6} = 1.088$, $Q_{-5} = 1.088$, $Q_{-4} = 1.162$, $Q_{-3} = 0.945$, $Q_{-2} = 1.017$, $Q_{-1} = 0.960$, and $Q_0 = 0.962$.

Having estimated these initial values for S_0, T_0, and Q_{-11} to Q_0, we now evaluate the smoothing equations for January 1985 (which is period 1). These computations are shown using the following the smoothing constants: $\alpha = 0.30$, $\beta = 0.10$, and $\gamma = 0.25$. (These values produced relatively efficient forecasts on a computerized version of this model.) Given these values, S_1 is calculated as follows:

$$\begin{aligned} S_1 &= \alpha(y_1/Q_{-11}) + (1 - \alpha)(S_0 + T_0) \\ &= 0.30(17.41/0.892) + 0.70(16.211 + 0.205) \\ &= 17.346 \end{aligned}$$

Next, the value of T_1 is updated as

$$\begin{aligned} T_1 &= \beta(S_1 - S_0) + (1 - \beta)T_0 \\ &= 0.10(17.346 - 16.211) + 0.90(0.205) \\ &= 0.298 \end{aligned}$$

Finally, the seasonal index, Q_1, is updated using the expression

$$Q_1 = \gamma(y_1/S_1) + (1 - \gamma)Q_{-11}$$
$$= 0.25(17.41/17.346) + 0.75(0.892)$$
$$= 0.924$$

Having updated these values, we are now in a position to make a forecast for period 2 (February 1985).

$$F_2 = (S_1 + T_1)Q_{-10}$$
$$= (17.346 + 0.298)0.854$$
$$= 15.07$$

Here Q_{-10} is the most recent seasonal index for February. Note that the actual observation for period 2, 15.67, is higher than the forecasted value, 15.07, by 0.60.

Winters' model tracks a time series by updating the values of S_t, T_t, and Q_t for each period using the smoothing equations. The estimates for S_t, T_t, and Q_t for the rest of the series are shown in Tables 14.15, 14.16, and 14.17. Using

TABLE 14.15   Smoothed levels (S_t)

Year	Jan.	Feb.	Mar.	Apr.	May	June	July	Aug.	Sept.	Oct.	Nov.	Dec.
1985	17.347	17.856	18.645	19.141	19.383	19.132	19.440	19.392	18.963	18.643	18.313	18.945
1986	19.300	19.705	20.115	20.351	20.682	20.821	21.253	21.651	21.708	21.662	21.616	22.047
1987	22.282	23.122	23.896	24.330	24.891	24.802	25.053	25.069	24.765	24.463	24.568	24.300
1988	24.121	24.427	24.601	24.723	24.865	24.943	25.093	25.248	25.280	25.342	25.246	24.962

TABLE 14.16   Trends (T_t)

Year	Jan.	Feb.	Mar.	Apr.	May	June	July	Aug.	Sept.	Oct.	Nov.	Dec.
1985	.298	.319	.366	.379	.365	.304	.304	.269	.199	.147	.100	.153
1986	.173	.196	.218	.219	.231	.221	.242	.258	.238	.210	.184	.209
1987	.211	.274	.324	.341	.357	.313	.306	.277	.219	.167	.161	.118
1988	.088	.110	.116	.117	.119	.115	.119	.122	.113	.108	.088	.051

TABLE 14.17   Seasonal indexes (Q_t)

Year	Jan.	Feb.	Mar.	Apr.	May	June	July	Aug.	Sept.	Oct.	Nov.	Dec.
1985	.920	.860	1.053	.994	1.000	1.068	1.088	1.150	.925	1.001	.945	.978
1986	.926	.866	1.060	.994	1.003	1.065	1.094	1.155	.920	0.993	.939	.984
1987	.926	.880	1.073	.998	1.007	1.054	1.093	1.147	.907	0.981	.937	.974
1988	.920	.884	1.074	.999	1.007	1.053	1.094	1.148	.905	0.979	.933	.966

TABLE 14.18   Actuals, forecasts, and forecast errors, 1987–88

| | 1987 | | | 1988 | | |
| | Actuals | Forecasts | Errors | Actuals | Forecasts | Errors |
Month	y_t	F_t	E_t	Y_t	F_t	E_t
Jan.	20.68	20.61	0.07	21.70	22.61	− 0.91
Feb.	21.29	19.48	1.81	21.93	21.30	0.63
Mar.	26.56	24.80	1.76	26.55	26.33	0.22
Apr.	24.65	24.07	0.58	24.70	24.67	0.03
May	25.34	24.75	0.59	25.09	25.01	0.08
June	25.30	26.89	− 1.59	26.18	26.33	− 0.15
July	27.26	27.48	− 0.22	27.51	27.39	0.12
Aug.	28.16	29.29	− 1.13	29.05	28.92	0.13
Sept.	21.53	23.32	− 1.79	22.74	23.01	− 0.27
Oct.	23.08	24.81	− 1.73	24.73	24.91	− 0.18
Nov.	22.93	23.13	− 0.20	23.22	23.85	− 0.63
Dec.	22.93	24.33	− 1.40	23.47	24.68	− 1.21

these estimates for each period t, a forecast for the following period, $t + 1$, can easily be constructed. For example, in Table 14.18 we show the forecasts obtained from this model for 1987 and 1988. These forecasts when compared with the actual observations show that the model provides very reliable forecasts.

The forecast errors range from a minimum of 0.02 (April 1988) to a maximum of 1.82 (February 1987). The maximum percentage error (from the actual observation) occurs in February 1987 and is equal to 8.50% (1.81/ 21.29 × 100). One precise measure of the accuracy of the forecasts, however, is determined from the MAD value. This is calculated by finding the average of the absolute errors for the period January 1987 to December 1988. That is,

$$\text{MAD} = \frac{0.07 + 1.81 + 1.76 + \cdots + 0.18 + 0.63 + 1.21}{24}$$
$$= 0.73$$

In other words, the average absolute forecast error is 0.73 per month, or on the order of approximately 2.99% (calculated as a percentage of the average monthly value of 24.44).

Computational Analysis

14.12

Most of the techniques presented in this chapter require a lot of computational work to arrive at the forecasts in spite of the simplicity of these models. For larger time series, such as the airline data in Section 14.11, the arithmetic operations involved make it difficult to operate these models using hand computations. Thus, the computational work for models such as these is generally carried out on a computer. Many standard statistical packages for computers include forecasting and time-series analysis options. Many of these programs are very sophisticated, but an accessible yet powerful alternative for these computations is a spreadsheet program such as Lotus 1-2-3. Most spreadsheets not only enable the user to carry out the computations easily but also provide "what-if" flexibility and graphics. In this section we present a method that enables us to do the computational work for these forecasting models on Lotus 1-2-3. This procedure is illustrated for the Winters' model using the airline data from Table 14.14 in Section 14.11. It is assumed that the reader has a working knowledge of Lotus 1-2-3.

To create the Winters' model on Lotus 1-2-3, we first assign the following cells and columns for storage and computations:

Column A   Period numbers

Column B   The actual observations (y_t)

Column C   The forecasts (F_t)

Column D   The smoothed values (S_t)

Column E   The trend values (T_t)

Column G   The absolute deviations ($|y_t - F_t|$)

Cell D4 α

Cell D5 β

Cell D6 γ

Cell F5   MAD

Using these cells and columns, the Lotus 1-2-3 model for 1985–86 is shown in Fig. 14.12. To save space, the data for 1987–88 are *not* shown in Fig. 14.12. The MAD value, however, is calculated using *only* the 1987–88 data (as shown in Table 14.18). The cells D4, D5, and D6 contain the smoothing constants and are designated absolute location cells. The computation of the MAD value is carried out in cell F5. The columns are either used for storing data (columns A and B) or for carrying out the computations within the model (columns C to G). To set up the model in Fig. 14.12 requires the following six-step procedure:

Step 1:   Enter labels, period numbers, and the data. The period numbers range from -11 to 48 and are entered in cells A12 to A71. The data entered include

(i) the actual observations (y_t) from January 1985 to December 1988 (periods 1 to 48) entered in cells B24 to B71,

(ii) the initial smoothed value (S_0), entered in cell D23,

(iii) the initial trend value (T_0), entered in cell E23, and

(iv) the 12 initial seasonal indexes (Q_{-11} to Q_0) entered in cells F12 to F23. (Note that the period numbers from -11 to 0 are entered specifically for these initial seasonal indexes.)

Step 2:   Enter the smoothing constants as follows: alpha ($\alpha = 0.30$) in cell D4, beta ($\beta = 0.10$) in cell D5, and gamma ($\gamma = 0.30$) in cell D6.

Step 3:   Enter the updating formulas for S_t, T_t, and Q_t in the cells indicated below:

Cell	Formula
D24	$+ \$D\$4*(B24/F12)+(1-\$D\$4)*(D23+E23)$
E24	$+ \$D\$5*(D24-D23)+(1-\$D\$5)*E23$
F24	$+ \$D\$6*(B24/D24)+(1-\$D\$6)*F12$

Copy each of these formulas to row 71.

Step 4:   Enter the formula to forecast for the next period in cell C24 as follows:

$$(D23+E23)*F12$$

(Note that this forecast is for period 1 and is made at the end of period 0.) Copy the formula to row 71.

Step 5:   Enter the formula to calculate the absolute deviation in cell G24 as follows:

$$@ABS(B24-C24)$$

Copy the formula to row 71.

Step 6:   Enter the equation to calculate the MAD value for January 1987 to December 1988 (periods 25 to 48) in cell F5 as

$$@AVG(G48..G71)$$

(The MAD figure using this equation results in the same value shown in Section 14.11.)

Having created the Winters' model on Lotus 1-2-3, it is now possible to fine-tune the model. The process of fine-tuning involves the selection of values for the three smoothing constants α, β, and γ. As discussed earlier, these values determine how accurate the forecasts will be. The measure of this accuracy is the MAD figure. Generally, the lower the MAD value, the more accurate the model. The easiest method for determining the values of the smoothing constants is to use a systematic search on the spreadsheet by varying one smoothing constant at a time. On the Lotus model, this involves changing the smoothing constant in either cell D4 or D5 or cell D6, and monitoring the MAD figure in cell F5. Alternatively, it is possible to use a what-if table to determine the α, β, and γ values. This procedure offers a more objective way of choosing these values. (Details of this method may be obtained from the Lotus manual.) Using either method makes it possible to easily determine a good set of values for α, β, and γ.

Another advantage of a spreadsheet such as Lotus 1-2-3 is the graphics capability. Graphs allow a visual assessment of the accuracy of the model by plotting the forecasted values against the actual observations. For this model, such a graph is presented in Fig. 14.13. This graph shows the forecasted values against the actuals for the airline data from January 1987 to December 1988

		A	B	C	D	E	F
1		WINTERS' MODEL FOR DOMESTIC PASSENGER MILES					
2							
3		SMOOTHING CONSTANTS					
4			ALPHA =		0.30		
5			BETA =		0.10	MAD =	0.73
6			GAMMA =		0.25		
7							
8							
9		PERIOD	ACTUAL	Ft	St	Tt	Qt
10		======	======	====	====	====	====
11							
12		-11.00					0.89
13		-10.00					0.85
14		-9.00					1.04
15		-8.00					0.99
16		-7.00					1.00
17		-6.00					1.09
18		-5.00					1.09
19		-4.00					1.16
20		-3.00					0.95
21		-2.00					1.02
22		-1.00					0.96
23		0.00			16.21	0.21	0.96
24		1.00	17.41	14.64	17.35	0.30	0.92
25		2.00	15.67	15.07	17.86	0.32	0.86
26		3.00	20.49	18.87	18.64	0.37	1.05
27		4.00	19.25	18.82	19.14	0.38	0.99
28		5.00	19.14	19.60	19.38	0.37	1.00
29		6.00	19.25	21.49	19.13	0.30	1.07
30		7.00	21.16	21.15	19.44	0.30	1.09
31		8.00	21.58	22.94	19.39	0.27	1.15
32		9.00	16.38	18.58	18.96	0.20	0.92
33		10.00	17.73	19.49	18.64	0.15	1.00
34		11.00	16.51	18.04	18.31	0.10	0.95
35		12.00	19.42	17.71	18.94	0.15	0.98
36		13.00	18.19	17.57	19.30	0.17	0.93
37		14.00	17.41	16.75	19.71	0.20	0.87
38		15.00	21.71	20.96	20.11	0.22	1.06
39		16.00	20.27	20.21	20.35	0.22	0.99
40		17.00	20.94	20.57	20.68	0.23	1.00
41		18.00	22.00	22.33	20.82	0.22	1.06
42		19.00	23.66	22.90	21.25	0.24	1.09
43		20.00	25.31	24.71	21.65	0.26	1.15
44		21.00	19.64	20.26	21.71	0.24	0.92

Figure 14.12
Partial Lotus output for the airline data (1985–86).

Note: **This spreadsheet was computed using three decimal places. The values above use two decimal places, and thus are subject to rounding errors.**

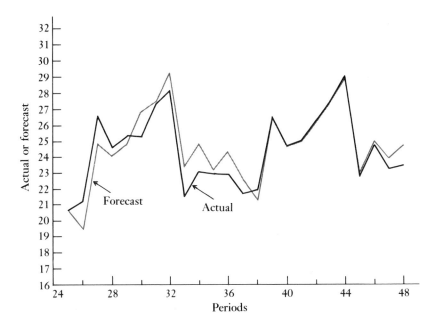

Figure 14.13
Lotus graph of forecasted against actuals.

(periods 25 to 48) for the data in Table 14.18. As this graph shows, the model does an excellent job of predicting the movement of this time series.

This analysis shows that a spreadsheet is a very powerful tool for operating these forecasting models. As mentioned earlier, several statistical packages such as IDA, SAS, and SPSS also provide the capability to do time-series analysis and forecasting. Each package differs in the type of analysis that may be carried out. However, it is highly recommended that the reader learn and understand these techniques before utilizing the standard packages.

	1986	1987
Jan.	110.7	80.6
Feb.	103.4	84.8
Mar.	89.4	85.6
Apr.	81.5	87.9
May	85.2	88.8
June	88.5	90.6
July	82.2	92.1
Aug.	77.8	94.6
Sept.	79.7	94.0
Oct.	77.1	93.1
Nov.	76.2	92.8
Dec.	76.4	91.2

Source: Standard and Poor's Statistical Service, *Current Statistics,* April 1988

Problems

14.25 Describe the effect of using a small value of the smoothing constant α as opposed to a large value in the simple exponential smoothing model. Under what circumstances would a higher value of α be used in the simple model?

14.26 If $\alpha = 0.2$, calculate the weights that would be applied to the five most recent observations in a simple exponential smoothing model. Compare these weights to the weights applied when $\alpha = 0.5$.

14.27 Explain why the Winters' model is considered a better model than the simple model? Under what circumstances would the simple model be used?

14.28 The table to the left lists the average retail gasoline prices (in cents per gallon) for the period 1986 to 1987.

    a) Let $t = 1$ correspond to January 1986. If $S_0 = 112$ and $\alpha = 0.2$, use the simple model to calculate the S_t values for every month in 1986.

b) Use the S_t values to forecast the gasoline prices for January 1986 to December 1986. Calculate the MAD value for these 12 months.

14.29 a) Refer to the gasoline prices data in Problem 14.28. Let $t = 13$ correspond to January 1987. Using S_{12} from Problem 14.28 (a) and $\alpha = 0.2$, forecast the gasoline prices for January 1987 to December 1987. Calculate the MAD and the RMSE values for these 12 months.

b) Repeat part (a) with $\alpha = 0.4$. Of these two smoothing constants, which does a better job of forecasting gasoline prices?

14.30 The following data list the quarterly retail sales (in billions of dollars) in the United States over the period 1984 to 1986.

Quarter	1984	1985	1986	1987
1	289.4	304.7	322.1	332.6
2	327.1	348.8	363.4	383.4
3	320.3	351.7	371.5	384.7
4	352.6	374.5	397.3	407.4

a) Plot this time series. Do these data show seasonality? Explain your answer.

b) Using the 1984 and 1985 data, estimate the initial seasonal indexes for each quarter by using the average quarterly sales figure for each year.

c) If the first period to be forecasted is fiscal quarter 1, 1986, determine the estimates for S_0, the initial base value, and T_0, the initial trend value using the data from 1984 and 1985. Explain your procedures for determining these values.

14.31 Refer to the data and the initial estimates of S_0, T_0, and the seasonal indexes in Problem 14.30. Using Winters' model with $\alpha = 0.2$, $\beta = 0.3$, and $\gamma = 0.5$, determine the forecasts for retail sales for all four quarters in 1986. Also determine the forecast errors for each quarter and calculate the MAD and the RSME values for these four quarters.

14.32 Using the data and the information from Problems 14.30 and 14.31, complete the following table for 1987:

Quarter	Actual sales	Forecast	Forecast error
1	332.6		
2	383.4		
3	384.7		
4	407.4		

14.33 The following data list the quarterly U.S. figures for beer consumption (in millions of barrels) for the period 1985 to 1988.

Quarter	1985	1986	1987	1988
1	40.70	41.66	42.66	43.00
2	49.67	49.71	48.67	48.76
3	46.25	47.06	47.17	46.75
4	38.51	39.96	39.37	39.63

Source: Standard and Poor's Statistical Service, *Current Statistics,* November 1989

a) Plot this time series. What exponential smoothing model would be the most appropriate for these data? Explain your answer.

b) If the Winters' model is to be used with January 1987 as period 1, estimate the values for S_0, T_0 and the initial seasonal indexes. Explain your procedures for calculating these values.

c) Will low values (closer to 0.1) or higher values (closer to 0.5) of the smoothing constants produce better forecasts for this time series? Discuss each smoothing constant separately.

14.34 Refer to the data and the information in Problem 14.33. Using Winters' model with $\alpha = 0.3$, $\beta = 0.2$ and $\gamma = 0.3$, forecast the beer consumption for each quarter in 1987 and 1988. Compare these forecasts against the actual values by calculating the forecast errors and the MAD value for these two years.

Exercises

14.35 The following table lists the monthly foreign exchange rates, in U.S. cents per unit of foreign currency, over 1986 and 1987 for three currencies: the Swiss franc, the Japanese yen, and the German mark.

	1986			1987		
	Swiss franc	Japanese yen	German mark	Swiss franc	Japanese yen	German mark
Jan.	48.62	.5010	41.09	64.56	.6493	54.22
Feb.	51.58	.5443	43.09	65.01	.6520	54.88
Mar.	52.04	.5575	43.78	64.85	.6578	54.33
Apr.	52.83	.5734	44.16	66.57	.6965	55.02
May	54.28	.6034	45.00	67.58	.7090	55.69
June	54.33	.6559	44.78	66.58	.6956	55.19
July	57.47	.6302	46.56	65.31	.6679	54.26
Aug.	60.18	.6491	48.48	64.41	.6719	53.52
Sept.	60.59	.6492	49.02	66.03	.6916	54.85
Oct.	61.10	.6426	49.99	67.07	.7003	55.58
Nov.	59.48	.6152	49.42	73.07	.7379	59.48
Dec.	60.02	.6155	50.28	75.27	.7794	61.16

a) Calculate a simple index for each of these three currencies using January 1986 as the base period.

b) Plot all three indexes on a graph and compare the performances of these currencies against the U.S. dollar. Which of these three currencies has gained the most in value against the U.S. dollar?

14.36 Refer to the currency exchange rate data in Problem 14.35. Calculate a simple aggregate index using January 1986 as the base year. Does this index accurately reflect the changes in the data? If not, how would you calculate an index that accurately represents the changes?

14.37 Refer to the data in Problem 14.35.

a) Plot the time series for the exchange rates for the German mark. Does a linear-trend model seem appropriate for these data?

b) If so, fit a least-squares line to these data. Using this regression line, determine the forecasts of the exchange rate for the German mark for each month in 1987. Determine the accuracy of these forecasts by calculating the MAD value.

c) Use the regression line from part (b) to forecast the exchange rates for January, February, and March 1988. Compare these forecasts with the actuals of 60.62 for January, 58.98 for February, and 59.56 for March.

14.38 Refer again to the exchange rate data for the German mark. Now use a three-month moving average to forecast the exchange rates for each month in 1987. Compare the accuracy of these forecasts with that of the linear trend model by calculating the MAD figure for this procedure. Also use the moving average method to forecast for January, February, and March 1988 and compare these forecasts with the ones obtained from the least-squares line.

14.39 The following table lists the monthly figures for the civilian labor force (in millions) for the period 1984 to 1987.

	1984	1985	1986	1987
Jan.	114.0	116.6	115.4	117.7
Feb.	114.4	116.8	115.7	118.0
Mar.	114.6	117.2	116.3	118.4
Apr.	114.9	117.1	116.3	118.3
May	115.4	117.1	117.2	119.7
June	115.3	116.5	119.6	121.2
July	115.6	116.6	120.3	122.1
Aug.	115.8	117.5	119.5	121.6
Sept.	115.5	116.7	118.2	119.9
Oct.	115.7	115.9	118.7	120.7
Nov.	115.8	116.1	118.6	120.6
Dec.	116.2	115.8	118.0	120.2
Avg.	115.3	116.7	117.8	119.9

Source: Standard and Poor's Statistical Service, *Current Statistics,* May 1988.

Use the ratio-to-moving averages method to estimate the seasonal indexes for these data.

14.40 Refer to the data and the seasonal indexes in Problem 14.39.

a) Using the yearly totals, estimate a linear trend line for these data. Use this to estimate a monthly linear trend line.

b) Using the monthly trend line and the seasonal indexes, determine the forecasts of the civilian labor force for 1987. Compare these forecasts with the actual values by calculating the MAD value. Also, forecast the civilian labor force for the period January–June 1988 and compare these with the actual values of 119.7, 119.9, 120.0, 120.3, 120.8, and 123.0.

14.41 The following table lists the automotive retail sales (in billions of dollars) in the United States for the period 1984 to 1987.

	1984	1985	1986	1987
Jan.	19.76	21.91	23.84	20.90
Feb.	21.68	22.47	23.26	24.05
Mar.	24.03	26.51	26.04	29.18
Apr.	24.10	27.64	28.05	30.41
May	26.13	29.65	30.36	30.22
June	26.25	27.56	29.51	32.31
July	24.27	27.95	28.80	31.65
Aug.	24.09	28.41	29.06	32.09
Sept.	21.20	28.48	35.04	29.63
Oct.	23.87	24.99	28.07	28.04
Nov.	22.47	23.14	24.22	25.47
Dec.	21.01	23.16	29.54	26.49
Total	278.86	311.87	355.79	340.44

Source: Standard and Poor's Statistical Service, *Current Statistics,* May 1988

a) Plot this time series. Do these data have stable seasonality? That is, do the peaks and the valleys occur in the same months every year? Explain your answer.

b) Are there any unusual months where the sales are different from the established patterns? If so, explain some possible reasons for this.

c) Using the ratio–to–moving averages method, estimate the seasonal indexes for these data. Given your answer from part (a), do these seasonal indexes accurately represent the seasonal patterns across all four years?

14.42 Refer to the data and the seasonal indexes from Problem 14.41.

a) Develop a monthly linear trend line for the automotive retail sales.

b) Using the monthly trend line and the seasonal indexes, determine the forecasts of the retail sales for automotive products for 1986 and 1987.

14.43 Refer again to the data and information from Problem 14.41.

a) Use the 1984 and 1985 data to develop initial estimates of the seasonal indexes by indexing each month's figure to the corresponding yearly average. Compare these indexes to the indexes developed in Problem 14.41(b). Which method is likely to be more reliable? Explain your answer.

b) Using these seasonal indexes, deseasonalize the 1985 data and calculate the initial estimates for S_0 and T_0 if period 1 is to be January 1986. Explain the method used to determine these initial estimates.

c) Use a spreadsheet, such as Lotus 1-2-3, to develop the Winters' exponential smoothing model with $\alpha = 0.1$, $\beta = 0.2$ and $\gamma = 0.5$, and determine the forecasts for automotive sales for 1986 and 1987. Compare these forecasts with the actual values by calculating the forecast errors, and the MAD and the RMSE values.

14.44 Use the spreadsheet model from Problem 14.43(c) to determine a more efficient set of smoothing constants using the MAD value as the criterion. Compare these forecasts with the forecasts from the time-series model (Problem 14.42). Which of these two models is better at forecasting the automotive sales for 1986 and 1987? (Use the MAD figure for this comparison.)

14.45 The following table lists the number of persons employed in the construction business in the United States over the period 1984 to 1987. The construction business is seasonal with more people employed during the warmer months.

Construction employment (in millions)

	1984	1985	1986	1987
Jan.	3.78	4.14	4.48	4.68
Feb.	3.77	4.03	4.35	4.56
Mar.	3.79	4.18	4.44	4.60
Apr.	4.06	4.53	4.74	4.84
May	4.30	4.61	4.95	5.04
June	4.52	4.84	5.16	5.21
July	4.62	4.97	5.29	5.31
Aug.	4.67	5.03	5.36	5.37
Sept.	4.65	5.02	5.32	5.29
Oct.	4.65	5.01	5.27	5.29
Nov.	4.57	4.90	5.14	5.21
Dec.	4.41	4.72	4.93	5.04

Source: Standard and Poor's Statistical Service, annual edition, various years, and *Current Statistics,* November 1988

a) Use the time-series model to determine forecasts for 1987. Compute the forecast errors and the MAD value to determine the accuracy of these forecasts.

b) Use the time-series model to forecast the construction employment over the period January 1988 to June 1988 and compare the forecasts to the following actuals: January, 4.64; February, 4.62; March, 4.80; April, 5.08; May, 5.29; and June, 5.50.

c) Now use a spreadsheet to develop the Winters' model. Use this model to determine an efficient set of smoothing constants and forecast the construction employment for 1987. Also, use this model to forecast construction employment over the period January to June 1988. Compare the forecasts from the Winters' model with those from the time-series model.

Chapter 15

Analysis
of
Variance

*A single death is a tragedy, a
million deaths is a statistic.*

JOSEPH STALIN

Introduction   **15.1**

In Chapter 9, tests of hypotheses concerning the means of two populations were discussed. Of particular interest was the test of

$$H_0: \ \mu_1 - \mu_2 = 0$$

(which is equivalent to $H_0: \ \mu_1 = \mu_2$) against the alternative hypothesis

$$H_a: \ \mu_1 - \mu_2 \neq 0$$

(which is equivalent to $H_a: \ \mu_1 \neq \mu_2$). In other words, we take samples from each of the populations and use these samples to see if there are any significant differences between the population means. This type of test is widely applied; we may want to compare the output of two production processes, the gasoline mileage of two automobiles, the academic performance of two groups of students, and so on. In many situations we may be interested in more than two populations; there may be three production processes of interest, five automobiles, or four groups of students. It is a computationally burdensome and statistically improper practice to run the test for the difference between two means on all possible pairs of populations. If there are 15 populations, for example,

623

there are $15!/2! \, 13! = 105$ possible pairs. If each pair is tested at the 0.10 significance level, say, then we would expect to get approximately 10 "significant" results purely by chance, making it difficult to interpret the results. What is needed is a method for *simultaneously* investigating the differences among the means of several populations, and the body of statistical procedures which is called "analysis of variance" is such a method.

The analysis of variance is a method of estimating how much of the total variation in a set of data can be attributed to certain assignable causes of variation and how much can be attributed to chance. In the simplest model, the total variation in a set of J samples (from J populations) is divided into two parts: (1) the variation *between* the J samples, and (2) the variation *within* the J samples. The latter variance is attributable only to chance, while the former variance is attributable in part to chance and in part to any differences which may exist among the means of the J populations. By comparing these variances, we can investigate for differences among the J means. After discussing this simple model, which is called a **one-factor model,** we will turn to a **two-factor model** in which each observation is classified on each of two factors. In this model, variation not attributable to chance alone may be caused by the first factor, the second factor, or interactions between the two factors. As in the simple one-factor model, the study of these effects is carried out through comparisons of variances. If certain variances are larger than might be expected through chance, then we may infer that particular effects do in fact exist.

The Simple One-Factor Model

15.2

Suppose that we are interested in comparing the means of J different populations, and that we therefore have J samples, one from each population. Furthermore, suppose that the sample size of the jth sample is n_j ($j = 1, \ldots, J$). Now we are ready to state a model for the composition of any observed value y_{ij}, corresponding to the ith observation in the jth sample. The model used is a simple linear model:

$$y_{ij} = \mu + \tau_j + \epsilon_{ij}, \qquad \text{with } j = 1, 2, \ldots, J$$
$$i = 1, 2, \ldots, n_j \qquad (15.1)$$

According to this model, an observation is the sum of three components:

1. the grand mean μ of the "combined" populations,
2. a treatment effect τ_j associated with the particular population from which the observation is taken,
3. a random-error term ϵ_{ij}.

The treatment effects can be thought of as deviations from the grand mean. In general, we assume that the proportional representation of the various treatment groups in the experiment is the same as the proportional representation of the groups in the combined population. This condition can be expressed in the form

$$\sum_{j=1}^{J} n_j \tau_j = 0$$

The random-error terms reflect variability within each of the J populations. Although it is not necessary to introduce distributional assumptions at this point (such assumptions will be necessary in the next section), the random-error terms are generally taken to be independent and normally distributed, with mean zero and variance σ^2. Note that there is a similarity between the simple one-factor analysis-of-variance model given by Formula (15.1) and the linear regression model presented in Chapter 11; we shall discuss this similarity later in this chapter.

An alternative way to write the one-factor model is

$$y_{ij} = \mu_j + \epsilon_{ij} \tag{15.2}$$

where μ_j is the mean of the jth population. This is equivalent to 15.1, for the mean μ_j is simply the sum of the grand mean μ and the treatment effect τ_j. Recall that we want to compare the means of the J populations, so that the following hypothesis is of interest:

$$H_0\text{: } \mu_1 = \mu_2 = \cdots = \mu_J$$

But if the J means are equal, each mean μ_j is equal to the grand mean μ, and then there are no "treatment effects," so this hypothesis can be rewritten as follows:

$$H_0\text{: } \tau_1 = \tau_2 = \cdots = \tau_J = 0$$

To illustrate the model, consider a simple situation in which three drugs are being tested in order to investigate their effects on an individual's pulse rate. Six individuals participate in the study involving the drugs, and they are randomly assigned to the three treatments (the three drugs) such that two individuals are in each treatment group. Thus, $J = 3$ and $n_1 = n_2 = n_3 = 2$. For each subject, the difference between the pulse rate 10 minutes after taking the drug and the pulse rate just before taking the drug is measured. Suppose that the grand mean is 20 and that the treatment effects and error terms are all zero. Then each subject's pulse rate would increase by exactly 20, and our data would look like Table 15.1.

Now, in addition, suppose that the treatment effects are nonzero:

$$\tau_1 = +4$$
$$\tau_2 = -6$$
$$\tau_3 = +2$$

TABLE 15.1

and

Drug 1	Drug 2	Drug 3
20	20	20
20	20	20

The first drug tends to increase the pulse rate 4 units more than the grand mean, the second drug tends to increase the pulse rate 6 units less than the grand mean, and the third drug tends to increase the pulse rate 2 units more than the grand mean. The data are then as shown in Table 15.2.

TABLE 15.2

Drug 1	Drug 2	Drug 3
$20 + 4 = 24$	$20 - 6 = 14$	$20 + 2 = 22$
$20 + 4 = 24$	$20 - 6 = 14$	$20 + 2 = 22$

Observe that there are now differences *between* the three samples, or treatments, due to the nonzero treatment effects. *Within* each sample, however, the observations are identical, because the random-error terms are all zero. According to the model presented in this section, the only variability within samples is attributable to chance (random error). It is highly unrealistic to assume no random variability, so let us add some nonzero error terms to the data of the drug example and see what the data might look like (Table 15.3).

The increase in pulse rate for a particular individual now depends on the grand mean, on the specific treatment effect associated with the particular drug, and on random variation. There are not only differences *between* samples (attributable both to differences in treatment effects and to random error), but there are also differences *within* each sample (attributable solely to random error).

The preceding example should serve to explain the model that is represented by Formulas (15.1) or (15.2). Of course, the model assumes that the grand mean, the treatment effect, and the random error term corresponding to any observation are additive. Although the model is reasonably simple, it should be adequate to describe numerous situations in which there are several samples.

Naturally, in applications we shall not be given the values of μ, τ_j, and ϵ_{ij} and asked to construct the raw data. Instead, the data will be given and the objective will be to estimate treatment effects and the grand mean and to test for differences among the J population means (that is, test to see if any of the estimated treatment effects is significantly different from zero). To estimate μ, we simply take the grand sample mean,

$$\bar{y} = \frac{\displaystyle\sum_{j=1}^{J} \sum_{i=1}^{n_j} y_{ij}}{\displaystyle\sum_{j=1}^{J} n_j}$$

TABLE 15.3

Drug 1	Drug 2	Drug 3
$20 + 4 + 3 = 27$	$20 - 6 + 1 = 15$	$20 + 2 - 2 = 20$
$20 + 4 - 2 = 22$	$20 - 6 - 3 = 11$	$20 + 2 + 3 = 25$

The sample means are used to estimate the corresponding population means. Thus, an estimator of μ_j is

$$\bar{y}_j = \frac{\displaystyle\sum_{i=1}^{n_j} y_{ij}}{n_j}$$

To estimate the treatment effects, then, the estimated grand mean is subtracted from each of the estimated population means:

$$\hat{\tau}_j = \bar{y}_j - \bar{y}$$

(Recall that it is assumed that the random error terms have zero mean and are independent.)

For example, suppose that a production manager is interested in comparing the output of three machines. He conducts an experiment, running each machine under identical conditions (or as nearly identical as possible) and recording the output per minute. This is done for 5 minutes for Machine 1, 10 minutes for Machine 2, and 6 minutes for Machine 3, so that $n_1 = 5$, $n_2 = 10$, and $n_3 = 6$. The data are given in Table 15.4. The estimated treatment effects are thus

and

$$\hat{\tau}_1 = \bar{y}_1 - \bar{y} = 8.4 - 8.2 = 0.2$$
$$\hat{\tau}_2 = \bar{y}_2 - \bar{y} = 6.7 - 8.2 = -1.5$$
$$\hat{\tau}_3 = \bar{y}_3 - \bar{y} = 10.7 - 8.2 = 2.5$$

TABLE 15.4

Machine 1	Machine 2	Machine 3
10	6	11
6	7	8
8	9	13
12	4	10
6	6	10
	10	12
	5	
	6	
	8	
	6	

$$\sum_{i=1}^{5} y_{i1} = 42 \quad \sum_{i=1}^{10} y_{i2} = 67 \quad \sum_{i=1}^{6} y_{i3} = 64 \quad \sum_{j=1}^{3}\sum_{i=1}^{n_j} y_{ij} = 173$$

$$\bar{y}_1 = 8.4 \qquad \bar{y}_2 = 6.7 \qquad \bar{y}_3 = 10.7 \qquad \bar{y} = 8.2$$

Problems

15.1 In order to compare the average tread life of three brands of radial tires, random samples of six tires of each brand are selected. A machine that simulates road conditions is used to find the tread life (in thousands of miles) of each tire. If all three brands have identical distributions of tread life, would you expect the 18 tires to last exactly the same number of miles? To what would you attribute differences in tread life among the 18 tires?

15.2 In the experiment in Problem 15.1 suppose that we observe six tires with tread lives of 36 (thousand miles), six with tread lives of 40, and six with tread lives of 42. Consider the following two cases:

Case 1: For each brand, we see two tires with tread lives of 36, two with 40, and two with 42.

Case 2: The six brand A tires have tread lives of 36, the six brand B tires have tread lives of 42, and the six brand C tires have tread lives of 40.

For these two extreme cases, compare the variation between the three brands with the variation within the three brands.

15.3 To investigate a claim that the Scholastic Aptitude Test (SAT) used by many colleges in their admissions process is biased against low-income students, the test is administered to random samples of 20 low-income students, 20 middle-income students, and 20 high-income students from a community. Let $j = 1$ for the low-income students, $j = 2$ for the middle-income students, and $j = 3$ for the high-income students. Interpret the following in the context of this example: $y_{72}, y_{13}, \tau_1, \epsilon_{53}, \mu_3, n_2,$ and μ. For the third student in the low-income sample, explain in words the expression of this student's SAT score in terms of Formulas (15.1) and (15.2).

15.4 If in fact there are nonzero treatment effects in the situation described in Problem 15.3, would you expect that the variability of SAT scores within income levels would be less than, about the same as, or greater than the variability of SAT scores between different income levels? Explain your answer.

15.5 A firm wishes to compare four programs for training workers to perform a certain manual task. Twenty new employees are randomly assigned to the training programs, with five in each program. At the end of the training period, a test is conducted to see how quickly trainees can perform the task. The number of times the task is performed per minute is recorded for each trainee, with the following results:

```
Program 1:    9   12   14   11   13
Program 2:   10    6    9    9   10
Program 3:   12   14   11   13   11
Program 4:    9    8   11    7    8
```

Estimate the treatment effects for the four programs.

15.6 In Problem 15.1, the observed tread lives are as follows:

```
Brand A:   38   44   37   39   41   37
Brand B:   41   48   46   42   47   46
Brand C:   40   35   36   32   39   37
```

Estimate the population mean tread lives and the treatment effects for the three brands.

15.7 A number of company presidents were sampled at random from the United States, and the annual income of each president sampled was recorded, as was the region where the company's headquarters were located. The incomes (in thousands of dollars) shown in Table 15.5 were observed in the sample. Find estimates for the mean income of company presidents in the United States and the mean income of company presidents in each of the six regions. Also, assuming that the sample sizes accurately reflect the corresponding population sizes (for example, there are twice as many companies with headquarters in the Northeast as in the Northwest), estimate the treatment effects associated with the different regions.

TABLE 15.5

Southeast	Southwest	Northeast	Northwest	Midwest	Far West
84	89	98	118	93	120
117	128	116	103	86	131
110	84	91	91	138	91
91	123	117	86	131	96
114	82	95	114	122	100
89	127	114		103	95
89	87	111		112	
113	91	95			
86	124	92			
	130	109			

15.8 In the experiment in Problem 15.3, the SAT scores are given in Table 15.6. Estimate the mean SAT score in the entire population of low-income students, the mean SAT score in the population of middle-income students, and the mean SAT score in the population of high-income students. Assuming that each of the income groups constitutes about one-third of the community, estimate the treatment effects and the mean SAT score for the entire community.

TABLE 15.6

Low		Middle		High	
736	729	773	881	873	1127
1065	839	784	1060	1071	704
667	850	912	941	1246	809
840	972	1259	922	1049	1139
448	708	791	932	774	986
579	1082	556	630	1002	926
800	599	929	977	785	655
1031	1008	706	961	644	989
744	692	1030	1047	1033	634
1234	1005	1135	742	958	787

The *F*-Test in the Analysis Variance

15.3

In the previous section we presented the simple one-factor model for the analysis of variance and determined estimates of the grand mean and treatment effects. We mentioned that the hypothesis of interest for comparing the means of the J populations is

$$H_0: \tau_1 = \tau_2 = \cdots = \tau_J = 0$$

In this section we shall discuss a test of this hypothesis against the alternative hypothesis that one or more of the treatment effects is nonzero.

The sample variance of the entire set of data (all J samples pooled together) can be written in the following form:

$$s^2_{\text{Total}} = \frac{\displaystyle\sum_{j=1}^{J} \sum_{i=1}^{n_j} (y_{ij} - \bar{y})^2}{\displaystyle\sum_{j=1}^{J} n_j - 1} \tag{15.3}$$

This is the usual form for a sample variance; the numerator is the sum of the squared deviations about the grand sample mean, and the denominator is the total sample size minus 1. It is convenient to consider the numerator and denominator of Formula 15.3 separately. The numerator is a sum of squares (SS), and will be called SS Total. The denominator can be thought of as the number of degrees of freedom associated with s^2_{Total}.

In order to conduct an analysis of variance, it is necessary to break s^2_{Total} into two parts, the first representing the variability within the samples (treatments) and the second representing the variability between the sample (treatment) means. To find the sum of squares *within* the jth sample, simply calculate $\sum_{i=1}^{n_j} (y_{ij} - \bar{y}_j)^2$. Summing this over all samples gives us

$$\text{SS Within} = \sum_{j=1}^{J} \sum_{i=1}^{n_j} (y_{ij} - \bar{y}_j)^2$$

There are $n_j - 1$ degrees of freedom associated with each individual sample, so the total number of degrees of freedom "within" is

$$\sum_{j=1}^{J} (n_j - 1) = \sum_{j=1}^{J} n_j - J$$

The sum of squares between the sample means is

$$\text{SS Between} = \sum_{j=1}^{J} n_j (\bar{y}_j - \bar{y})^2$$

and, since there are J samples, there are $J - 1$ degrees of freedom associated with SS Between.

The partition of total variance into two sources is such that the sum of d.f. between and d.f. within equals the total degrees of freedom, for

$$(J-1) + \left(\sum_{j=1}^{J} n_j - J \right) = \sum_{j=1}^{J} n_j - 1$$

In addition to the fact that the number of degrees of freedom *between* samples and the number of degrees of freedom *within* samples sum to the total number of degrees of freedom, it can be shown that the sum of SS Between and SS Within equals SS Total.* That is,

$$\text{SS Total} = \text{SS Within} + \text{SS Between}$$

or

$$\sum_{j=1}^{J} \sum_{i=1}^{n_j} (y_{ij} - \bar{y})^2 = \sum_{j=1}^{J} \sum_{i=1}^{n_j} (y_{ij} - \bar{y}_j)^2 + \sum_{j=1}^{J} n_j (\bar{y}_j - \bar{y})^2$$

It is convenient to arrange the preceding terms as shown in Table 15.7, in an analysis-of-variance table comparable to that used in Chapter 11. Note that the total variation has been separated into two sources, between samples and within samples. For each of these sources, the sum of squares and degrees of freedom can be calculated, and these are used to determine the mean square between (MS Between) and mean square within (MS Within). Each MS is determined by dividing the appropriate SS by the degrees of freedom. Note, incidentally, that when $J = 2$, MS Within is identical to the pooled estimate of σ^2 given in the two-sample case in Chapter 9.

---

*To prove this statement, observe that

$$\text{SS Total} = \sum_j \sum_i (y_{ij} - \bar{y})^2 = \sum_j \sum_i [(y_{ij} - \bar{y}_j) + (\bar{y}_j - \bar{y})]^2$$

$$= \sum_j \sum_i (y_{ij} - \bar{y}_j)^2 + \sum_j \sum_i (\bar{y}_j - \bar{y})^2 + 2 \sum_j \sum_i (y_{ij} - \bar{y}_j)(\bar{y}_j - \bar{y})$$

But for any j, $(\bar{y}_j - \bar{y})$ is the same for all values of i, so that the last term can be written as follows:

$$2 \sum_j \sum_i (y_{ij} - \bar{y}_j)(\bar{y}_j - \bar{y}) = 2 \sum_j (\bar{y}_j - \bar{y}) \sum_i (y_{ij} - \bar{y}_j)$$

Now, for any j,

$$\sum_i (y_{ij} - \bar{y}_j) = \sum_i y_{ij} - \sum_i \bar{y}_j = \sum_i y_{ij} - n_j \bar{y}_j = 0$$

Therefore,

$$2 \sum_j \sum_i (y_{ij} - \bar{y}_j)(\bar{y}_j - \bar{y}) = 0$$

and

$$\text{SS Total} = \sum_j \sum_i (y_{ij} - \bar{y}_j)^2 + \sum_j \sum_i (\bar{y}_j - \bar{y})^2$$

$$= \text{SS Within} + \sum_j \sum_i (\bar{y}_j - \bar{y})^2$$

Finally, for any j, $(\bar{y}_j - \bar{y})^2$ is a constant with respect to the index of summation i, so that

$$\sum_j \sum_i (\bar{y}_j - \bar{y})^2 = \sum_j n_j (\bar{y}_j - \bar{y})^2 = \text{SS Between}$$

and thus

$$\text{SS Total} = \text{SS Within} + \text{SS Between}$$

TABLE 15.7   Analysis of variance with unequal sample sizes

Source of Variation	SS	d.f.	MS = SS/d.f.
Between samples (treatments)	$\sum_{j=1}^{J} n_j(\bar{y}_j - \bar{y})^2$	$J - 1$	SS Between/$J - 1$
Within samples	$\sum_{j=1}^{J} \sum_{i=1}^{n_j} (y_{ij} - \bar{y}_j)^2$	$\sum_{j=1}^{J} n_j - J$	SS Within$\left/ \sum_{j=1}^{J} n_j - J \right.$
Total	$\sum_{j=1}^{J} \sum_{i=1}^{n_j} (y_{ij} - \bar{y})^2$	$\sum_{j=1}^{J} n_j - 1$	

Frequently the sample sizes for the various samples, or treatments, are equal. In this case, we can let n denote the sample size for each sample (that is, $n_j = n$ for $j = 1, \ldots, J$). Using equal sample sizes has the advantage of minimizing adverse effects of violations of the assumption that the J populations have the same variance. The analysis-of-variance table for the special case of equal sample sizes is presented in Table 15.8.

In order to test the hypothesis that the treatment effects are all zero, it is necessary to make some distributional assumptions. Thus, we will invoke the assumptions mentioned in the previous section concerning the random-error terms:

1. For each sample (for each $j = 1, 2, \ldots, J$), the random-error terms ϵ_{ij} are normally distributed with mean zero and variance σ^2, and the variance σ^2 is the same for all samples.

2. The random-error terms are independent.

In addition, of course, it is assumed that the linear model given by (15.1) is applicable. That is, it is assumed that the three factors affecting y_{ij} (the grand mean, the treatment effect, and a random-error term) behave in an additive

TABLE 15.8   Anova with equal sample sizes

Source of variation	SS	d.f.	MS = SS/d.f.
Between samples (treatments)	$n\sum_{j=1}^{J} (\bar{y}_j - \bar{y})^2$	$J - 1$	SS Between/$J - 1$
Within samples	$\sum_{j=1}^{J} \sum_{i=1}^{n} (y_{ij} - \bar{y}_j)^2$	$J(n - 1)$	SS Within/$J(n - 1)$
Total	$\sum_{j=1}^{J} \sum_{i=1}^{n} (y_{ij} - \bar{y})^2$	$Jn - 1$	

fashion. Under these assumptions, it can be shown that the expectations of the mean squares are

$$E(\text{MS Between}) = \sigma^2 + \frac{\sum_{j=1}^{J} n_j \tau_j^2}{J - 1} \qquad (15.4)$$

and

$$E(\text{MS Within}) = \sigma^2 \qquad (15.5)$$

Observe that under the null hypothesis of zero treatment effects, $E(\text{MS Between}) = E(\text{MS Within}) = \sigma^2$. Furthermore,

$$\frac{(J - 1)(\text{MS Between})}{\sigma^2}$$

has a chi-square distribution with $J - 1$ degrees of freedom, and

$$\frac{\left(\sum_{j=1}^{J} n_j - J\right)(\text{MS Within})}{\sigma^2}$$

has a chi-square distribution with $\sum_{j=1}^{J} n_j - J$ degrees of freedom. That these two variables have chi-square distributions follows from the fact that if we have a sample from a normally distributed population, $\nu S^2/\sigma^2$ has a chi-square distribution with ν degrees of freedom. Also, the two variables are independent.

In Chapter 6 we pointed out that the ratio of two independent χ^2 variables divided by their degrees of freedom has an F-distribution. Taking the ratio of the two chi-square variables given above (each divided by its d.f.) gives the following result:

$$F = \frac{\text{MS Between}}{\text{MS Within}}.$$

Thus, the ratio of MS Between to MS Within has an F-distribution with $J - 1$ and $\sum_{j=1}^{J} n_j - J$ degrees of freedom, respectively, provided that the null hypothesis of zero treatment effects is true. This F-statistic can be used to test the hypothesis that the treatment effects are all zero. From (15.4), any nonzero treatment effects will tend to increase MS Between, and thus the null hypothesis should be rejected only for large values of F; the right hand tail of the F-distribution should be used.

An Example 15.4

For an example illustrating the use of analysis of variance, suppose that a marketing manager is interested in the effect of different types of packaging on the sales of a particular new item. Three different types of packaging have been suggested for the item. The manager draws a random sample of 60 stores from the population of stores that would stock the item. The three different types of packaging are each used at 20 of the stores, with the stores assigned randomly to the three "treatments." The sales of the item at each of the stores are carefully recorded for a period of one month, with the results given in Table 15.9.

For example, the first store in group A (the stores with type A packaging) sold 52 items during the month of the experiment, the second store sold 48 items, and so on down to the last store in group C, which sold 17 items. Here we have three samples ($J = 3$), with each sample size equal to 20 ($n_1 = n_2 = n_3 = 20$).

The formulas given in Section 15.3 for sums of squares can be difficult to apply. Computational formulas that are much easier to deal with when computing by hand or by calculator are available. Ideally, of course, we should let a computer perform the computations. Thus, rather than use the formulas from Section 15.3 to compute sums of squares and to generate an analysis-of-variance table for the packaging example, we will present output from three different statistical packages: SAS, ISP, and Statgraphics.

TABLE 15.9   Sales (by type of packaging)

Type A	Type B	Type C
52	28	15
48	35	14
43	34	23
50	32	21
43	34	14
44	27	20
46	31	21
46	27	16
43	29	20
49	25	14
38	43	23
42	34	25
42	33	18
35	42	26
33	41	18
38	37	26
39	37	20
34	40	19
33	36	22
34	35	17

$$\sum_{i=1}^{20} y_{i1} = 832 \qquad \sum_{i=1}^{20} y_{i2} = 680 \qquad \sum_{i=1}^{20} y_{i3} = 392 \qquad \sum_{j=1}^{3}\sum_{i=1}^{20} y_{ij} = 1904$$

TABLE 15.10   Output from SAS for sales example

```
                              SAS
                GENERAL LINEAR MODELS PROCEDURE
                    CLASS LEVEL INFORMATION
CLASS                   LEVELS                VALUES
PACKAGE                    3                  TYPEA TYPEB TYPEC

             NUMBER OF OBSERVATIONS IN DATA SET = 60
                              SAS
                GENERAL LINEAR MODELS PROCEDURE

DEPENDENT VARIABLE: SALES
SOURCE                   DF    SUM OF SQUARES       MEAN SQUARE
MODEL                     2    4994.13333333       2497.06666667
ERROR                    57    1457.60000000         25.57192982
CORRECTED TOTAL          59    6451.73333333

MODEL F =                97.65                  PR > F = 0.0001

                         MEANS
                PACKAGE        N        SALES
                TYPEA         20     41.6000000
                TYPEB         20     34.0000000
                TYPEC         20     19.6000000
```

The analysis-of-variance table from the SAS printout is presented in Table 15.10, along with the mean sales for the three types of packaging. SAS uses slightly different terminology: Where we say "between," SAS uses the term "model," and where we say "within," SAS says "error." This is because the only source of variation within the treatments is the error term, and any additional variation between treatments is explained by the treatment effects in the analysis-of-variance model in Formula (15.1).

Note from Table 15.10 that the mean square between (model) is much larger than the mean square within (error), indicating that the packaging is an important source of variability. This is reflected in the extremely large F-value of 97.65 (with 2 and 57 degrees of freedom), which is significant far beyond the 0.01 level. The p-value for the test of the hypothesis that the treatment effects are all zero is 0.0001, as shown on the output in Table 15.11. The marketing manager can feel very confident in asserting that the type of packaging does have some effect on the sales of the item in question.

Output from ISP and Statgraphics for this example is shown in Tables 15.11 and 15.12, respectively. Software vary slightly in the number of significant digits retained and in exactly what is presented. However, the basic results are the same in Tables 15.10–15.12.

TABLE 15.11   Output from ISP for sales example

One-Way Analysis of Variance

Source	Sum of Squares	d.f.	Mean Square	Computed F-value	F-value alpha = .05	p-value
Between groups	4994.13	2	2497.07	97.65	3.16	.000
Error (within groups)	1457.60	57	25.5719			
Totals	6451.73	59				

	n	Means	Estimated Effects
VAR1	20	41.6000	9.86667
VAR2	20	34.0000	2.26667
VAR3	20	19.6000	-12.1333
Grand mean		31.7333	

TABLE 15.12   Output from Statgraphics for sales example

One-Way Analysis of Variance

Source of variation	Sum of Squares	d.f.	Mean Square	F-ratio	sig. level
Between groups	4994.1333	2	2497.0667	97.649	.0000
Within groups	1457.6000	57	25.5719		
Total (corrected)	6451.7333	59			

The marketing manager may want to estimate the effect of each type of packaging. The estimated grand mean is

$$\bar{y} = \frac{1904}{60} = 31.7$$

and the three sample means (also given in the output in Tables 15.10 and 15.11), are

$$\bar{y}_1 = \frac{832}{20} = 41.6$$

$$\bar{y}_2 = \frac{680}{20} = 34.0$$

$$\bar{y}_3 = \frac{392}{20} = 19.6$$

and

Thus, the estimated treatment effects of types A, B, and C are, respectively,

$$\hat{\tau}_1 = \bar{y}_1 - \bar{y} = 41.6 - 31.7 = 9.9$$
$$\hat{\tau}_2 = \bar{y}_2 - \bar{y} = 34.0 - 31.7 = 2.3$$

and
$$\hat{\tau} = \bar{y}_3 - \bar{y} = 19.6 - 31.7 = -12.1$$

These estimates, which are also provided in the output in Table 15.11, indicate that type A packaging produces the greatest sales. If the marketing manager must decide on a single type of packaging for the product, type A would surely be his best bet on the basis of the experimental results. Incidentally, this suggests a situation in which the results of the *F*-test in the analysis of variance may be of absolutely no importance to the statistician. In the packaging example, suppose that the marketing manager must choose a single type of packaging and that the costs of the three types are identical. In this case, he should choose the type of packaging with the greatest estimated treatment effect, regardless of whether the difference between the treatment effects is statistically "significant" according to the *F*-test. Even if the differences are very small and "insignificant," as long as he must choose one type of packaging, he might as well choose the one which looks the best in light of the experiment. Of course, if the statistician is not primarily interested in a decision-making problem, but just wants to make inferences about differences in the treatment effects, then the *F*-test is of interest.

At this point, it should be useful to review the procedure and the rationale for the analysis of variance. The basic idea is to determine whether all of the variation in a set of data is attributable to random error (chance) or whether some of the variation is attributable to chance and some is attributable to differences in the means of the *J* populations of interest. First, the sample variance for the entire set of data is computed and is seen to be composed of two parts: the numerator, which is a sum of squares, and the denominator, which is the degrees of freedom. The total sum of squares can be partitioned into SS Between and SS Within, and the total degrees of freedom can be partitioned into d.f. Between and d.f. Within. By dividing each sum of squares by the respective d.f., MS Between and MS Within are determined; these represent the sample variability between the different samples and the sample variability within all of the samples, respectively. But the variability *within* the samples must be due to random error alone, according to the assumptions of the one-factor model. The variability *between* the samples, on the other hand, may be attributable both to chance and to any differences in the *J* population means. Thus, if MS Between is significantly greater than MS Within (as measured by the *F*-test), then the null hypothesis of zero treatment effects must be rejected. Thus, the analysis of variance is a procedure for a *simultaneous* comparison of a number of means (as opposed, for example, to a series of paired comparisons of the possible pairs of means which can be chosen from the entire set of means of interest).

Multiple Comparisons

15.5

The F-test developed in Section 15.3 enables us to test the hypothesis that the treatment effects are all zero—that there are no differences among the means of the J treatments, or populations, that are being investigated. If the F-test leads to rejection of the null hypothesis at a given significance level, this is an indication that there *are* differences among the J population means. Such a result does not, however, provide any information regarding differences between *pairs* of populations chosen from the J populations. A significant value of F indicates that at least one of these pairwise differences is significant, but it does not indicate which differences are significant and which are not significant.

Sometimes the difference between two particular treatment effects is of interest. For instance, in the example of the previous section, the marketing manager might want to investigate $\tau_1 - \tau_2$, the difference in the effects of type A packaging and type B packaging. A $100(1 - \alpha)\%$ confidence interval for this difference is given by

$$(\hat{\tau}_1 - \hat{\tau}_2) \pm t_{\alpha/2, \Sigma n_j - J} \sqrt{\text{MS Within} \left(\frac{1}{n_1} + \frac{1}{n_2} \right)}$$

Here, MS Within is being used to estimate σ^2 (from Formula 15.5), $E(\text{MS Within}) = \sigma^2$). For example, a 95% confidence interval for $\tau_1 - \tau_2$ is

$$(9.9 - 2.3) \pm 2.00\sqrt{25.57(2/20)}$$

or

$$(4.4, 10.8)$$

Since this confidence interval does not "cover" zero (that is, zero is not included in the interval), $\tau_1 - \tau_2$ is said to be significantly different from zero at the $1 - 0.95 = 0.05$ level of significance.

It is possible, of course, to compute such an interval estimate for each possible pair of treatments. Unfortunately, this leads to the same difficulty noted in Section 15.1 regarding the use of tests for the difference between two means on all possible pairs of populations. Techniques are available, however, for simultaneously determining confidence intervals for all possible differences. One such technique, developed by Henry Scheffe, is called the **S-method.** The S-method can be used to simultaneously handle all possible *contrasts* involving the treatment effects, where a contrast is a linear combination of the form $\sum_{j=1}^{J} c_j \tau_j$, with $\sum_{j=1}^{J} c_j = 0$. We are interested in a special set of contrasts: differences between pairs of treatment effects. Note that the difference $\tau_1 - \tau_2$, for instance, is simply a contrast with $c_1 = 1$, $c_2 = -1$, and $c_3 = c_4 = \cdots = c_j = 0$.

The differences $\tau_k - \tau_l$ and $\tau_l - \tau_k$ are equivalent since one is simply the negative of the other. Thus, there are $J(J - 1)/2$ possible pairwise comparisons from a set of J populations. Using the S-method, the probability is at least α that all the $J(J - 1)/2$ differences $\tau_k - \tau_l (k \neq l)$ *simultaneously* satisfy

$$(\hat{\tau}_k - \hat{\tau}_l) \pm \sqrt{(J - 1) F_{(\alpha, J - 1, \Sigma n_j - J)} (\text{MS Within}) \left(\frac{1}{n_k} + \frac{1}{n_l} \right)}$$

Here $\hat{\tau}_k$ and $\hat{\tau}_l$ are simply the estimated treatment effects of population k and population l; $F_{(\alpha, J - 1, \Sigma n_j - J)}$ is the critical value of the F-distribution, which can be found in Table VIII of Appendix B for $\alpha = 0.05$, $\alpha = 0.025$, and $\alpha = 0.01$; and MS Within is used once again to estimate σ^2. For the marketing example, the following three intervals hold simultaneously, with a 95% level of confidence:

$$(9.9 - 2.3) \pm \sqrt{2(3.15)(25.57)(2/20)} \quad \text{or} \quad (3.6, 11.6) \text{ for } \tau_1 - \tau_2$$
$$(9.9 + 12.1) \pm \sqrt{2(3.15)(25.57)(2/20)} \quad \text{or} \quad (18.0, 26.0) \text{ for } \tau_1 - \tau_3$$
$$\text{and} \quad (2.3 + 12.1) \pm \sqrt{2(3.15)(25.57)(2/20)} \quad \text{or} \quad (10.4, 18.4) \text{ for } \tau_2 - \tau_3$$

In general, an interval computed via the S-method for a particular difference is wider than the corresponding interval computed as though that difference were the only difference of interest. A 95% confidence interval for $\tau_1 - \tau_2$ was computed as $(4.4, 10.8)$, whereas the corresponding interval computed from the S-method is $(3.6, 11.6)$. For the former interval, of course, the "95% confidence" refers to that interval alone, whereas in the S-method, it refers to an entire set of intervals.

Since we are simultaneously comparing pairs of treatment effects, or populations, in the S-method, such a procedure is often called a **multiple-comparisons** procedure. In fact, the confidence intervals can be used to simultaneously test all possible differences. If a given interval does not include zero, then that difference is said to be significant. The F-test simply tells us whether there are any significant differences among the populations or not. Methods of multiple comparisons enable us to identify the particular differences that are significant at any given level of significance. In some instances, we are simply interested in the presence or absence of differences among the populations, and the F-test provides the information of interest. In other cases, we are concerned with pairwise comparisons, in which case a multiple-comparisons procedure should be used following an F-test with significant results.

Problems

15.9 Compute SS total, SS between, and SS within for the two cases in Problem 15.2. Compare the two cases. Can you see why these are called "extreme" cases?

15.10 In the F-test in the one-factor model for the analysis of variance, why is the null hypothesis of equal means rejected only for large values of F? Discuss the sources of variation contributing to the mean square terms in the numerator and denominator of F.

15.11 See if you can prove, without consulting the text, that

$$\text{SS Total} = \text{SS Between} + \text{SS Within}$$

15.12 If MS Between and MS Within turn out to be equal in an analysis of variance, what is implied about the treatment effects? Is it ever possible for MS Within to be larger than MS Between? If not, why not? If so, how would you interpret the results?

15.13 In the example in Section 15.5, a confidence interval of $(4.4, 10.8)$ was computed for $\tau_1 - \tau_2$. Then, when all possible differences between treatment effects were of interest, the S-method was used to compute a different confidence interval for $\tau_1 - \tau_2$: $(3.6, 11.6)$. Explain why the interval computed from the S-method is wider than the other interval.

15.14 For the data given in Problem 15.5, find the total sum of squares, the sum of squares between programs, and the sum of squares within programs, using the formulas from Section 15.3. Construct an analysis-of-variance table for this experiment. Test the hypothesis of equality among the means of the four programs, using $\alpha = 0.05$.

15.15 Do Problem 15.14 using any statistical computer package to which you have access. (Check to make sure that the package handles analysis-of-variance problems.)

15.16 Construct an analysis-of-variance table showing sums of squares, degrees of freedom, and mean squares for the data given in Problem 15.6. Test the hypothesis of zero treatment effects at the $\alpha = 0.01$ level.

15.17 For the example concerning the output of three machines with the data given in Table 15.4, find SS total, SS between machines, SS within machines, MS between machines, and MS within machines. At the $\alpha = 0.05$ level, can the production manager reject the hypothesis of equal mean output for the three machines?

15.18 An experiment concerning the output per hour of four machines gave the results shown in Table 15.13. Construct an analysis-of-variance table and test the hypothesis of equality among the four population means, using $\alpha = 0.01$.

15.19 Given the following output from ISP for the data on SAT scores in Table 15.6, test at the $\alpha = 0.05$ level to see whether the effects of different income levels on SAT scores are zero or not.

TABLE 15.13

A	B	C	D
160	134	104	86
155	139	175	71
170	144	96	112
175	150	83	110
152	156	89	87
167	159	79	100
180	170	84	105
154	133	86	93
141	128	83	65

One-Way Analysis of Variance

Source	Sum of Squares	d.f.	Mean Square	Computed F-value	F-Value alpha = .05	p-value
Between groups	71471.6	2	35735.8	1.06	3.16	.354
Error (within groups)	.192417E+07	57	33757.4			
Totals	.199565E+07	59				

15.20 Conduct an analysis-of-variance for the data in Problem 15.7 using $\alpha = 0.05$ for the **F**-test. Can you conclude that there are regional differences in incomes of company presidents?

15.21 To investigate differences among four industries (aerospace, telecommunications, electronics, and chemicals) in terms of research and development (R & D) expenses, samples of seven firms were taken from each industry. For these firms, R & D expenses as a function of sales were recorded. (*Source: Business Week,* June 20, 1988.) The data are given in Table 15.14, along with output from Statgraphics. What is the p-value for the test of the hypothesis of equal R & D expenses (as percentages of sales) in these four industries?

TABLE 15.14

Aerospace	Telecommunications	Electronics	Chemicals
5.4	9.3	4.8	2.7
1.4	3.1	3.3	3.7
3.6	4.0	1.5	2.3
4.9	8.2	6.7	1.8
2.7	4.1	2.7	5.7
5.2	11.4	7.8	2.3
3.4	5.7	3.5	3.9

One–Way Analysis of Variance

Analysis of Variance

Source of Variation	Sum of Squares	d.f.	Mean Square	F-ratio	Sig. level
Between groups	44.64964	3	14.883214	3.162	.0429
Within groups	112.95143	24	4.706310		
Total (corrected)	157.60107	27			

0 missing value(s) have been excluded.

15.22 Use the S-method to find a set of interval estimates for all possible pairwise differences between programs in Problem 15.5 with a confidence level of 95%.

15.23 Carry out the multiple-comparisons procedure at the 99% confidence level for the data in Table 15.4. At this confidence level, are any of the pairwise differences between machines significant?

15.24 Instead of using the multiple-comparisons procedure in Problem 15.23, compute interval estimates separately for each pairwise difference at the 99% confidence level. Compare the resulting intervals with those found in Problem 15.23 and explain why they are not identical.

15.25 In Problem 15.18, estimate the treatment effects and use the S-method to find simultaneous confidence intervals at the 95% confidence level for the six possible pairwise differences between machines.

**The Two-Factor
Model**

15.6

In the one-factor model, we worked with a set of J samples, or treatments, and attempted to investigate possible differences between them. In some situations, the statistician may want to investigate simultaneously *two* sets of treatments. In the marketing example, suppose that in addition to the type of packaging, a second factor of interest is advertising. For this factor, assume that there are two treatments (or two levels of the factor), advertising and no advertising. Interest is now focused on two distinct experimental factors, the type of packaging and the advertising, either or both of which possibly influence sales. A random sample of 60 stores is selected, with 10 assigned randomly to each of the *six* possible treatment *combinations.* That is, 10 stores have type A packaging and no advertising; 10 have type A and advertising; 10 have type B and no advertising; and so on. This experiment represents an instance where two different sets of experimental treatments are completely crossed: each category or level of one factor (packaging) occurs with each level of the other factor (advertising). Since there are three levels of packaging and two levels of advertising, there are six distinct sample groups, each with a particular combination of the two factors. Furthermore, this experiment is said to be *balanced,* since each of these six groups has the same sample size.

In this experiment, the marketing manager is interested in three questions:

1. Are there systematic effects due to type of packaging alone (irrespective of advertising)?
2. Are there systematic effects due to advertising alone (irrespective of type of packaging)?
3. Are there systematic effects due neither to type of packaging alone, nor to advertising alone, but attributable only to the *combination* of a particular type of packaging with a particular level of advertising?

Note that the experiment can be viewed as two separate experiments carried out on the same set of stores: (a) there are three groups of 20 stores each, differing in type of packaging; and (b) there are two groups of 30 stores each, differing in level of advertising. The third question cannot, however, be answered by the comparison of types of packaging alone or by the comparison of levels of advertising alone, but is a question of *interaction,* the unique effects of combinations of treatments. This is an important feature of the two-factor analysis-of-variance model: We shall be able to examine *main effects* of the separate experimental variables or factors just as in the one-factor model (a "main effect" is the variability due to different levels of a *single* variable) as well as *interaction effects,* differences apparently due only to the unique *combinations* of treatments.

In order to present the two-factor model formally, suppose that there are J levels of the first factor and K levels of the second factor, and that there are n observations for each combination of one level from each factor. If y_{ijk} denotes the ith observation in the group with level j on the first factor and level k on the second factor, then the model may be written as follows:

$$y_{ijk} = \mu + \tau_j + \lambda_k + (\tau\lambda)_{jk} + \epsilon_{ijk}$$

with $i = 1, \ldots, n$, $j = 1, \ldots, J$, and $k = 1, \ldots, K$. The observation is thought of as the sum of five components: the grand mean μ over the entire population; a treatment effect τ_j associated with the particular level (the jth level) of the first factor: a treatment effect λ_k associated with the particular level (the kth level) of the second factor; an interaction effect $(\tau\lambda)_{jk}$ associated with the particular combination of the jth level of the first factor and the kth level of the second factor; and finally, a random error term ϵ_{ijk}. It is assumed that the sum of the treatment effects for the first factor is zero, that the sum of the treatment effects for the second factor is zero, and that for any given level of either of the two factors, the sum of the interaction effects across the other factor is zero. Furthermore, in order to make inferences concerning the parameters of the model, the random-error terms are assumed to be independent and normally distributed, with means of zero and identical variances. Observe that just as there is a similarity between the simple one-factor model and the bivariate linear regression model, there is also a similarity between the above model and the multiple regression model discussed in Chapter 13.

To illustrate the two-factor model, suppose, in the marketing example, that the grand mean is 30 and that all other terms are zero; each observation in the experiment should equal 30. Alternatively, suppose that the treatment effects for type of packaging are $+4$, -3, and -1, respectively. Then the observations will look like this (only one observation is presented for each group, since all observations within a group will be equal because the random-error term is zero):

	Type of packaging		
	A	**B**	**C**
Advertising	$30 + 4 = 34$	$30 - 3 = 27$	$30 - 1 = 29$
No advertising	$30 + 4 = 34$	$30 - 3 = 27$	$30 - 1 = 29$

On the other hand, it might turn out that nonzero effects exist only for advertising (not for type of packaging), with the effects of *advertising* and *no advertising* being $+3$ and -3:

	Type of packaging		
	A	**B**	**C**
Advertising	$30 + 3 = 33$	$30 + 3 = 33$	$30 + 3 = 33$
No advertising	$30 - 3 = 27$	$30 - 3 = 27$	$30 - 3 = 27$

Now suppose that there are *both* packaging and advertising effects:

	Type of packaging		
	A	**B**	**C**
Advertising	$30 + 4 + 3 = 37$	$30 - 3 + 3 = 30$	$30 - 1 + 3 = 32$
No advertising	$30 + 4 - 3 = 31$	$30 - 3 - 3 = 24$	$30 - 1 - 3 = 26$

Observe that the linear model specifies that the effect of a combination of levels of the two factors is the sum of the individual effects and an interaction effect (which has been assumed to be zero). Finally, let us add interaction effects:

	Type of packaging		
	A	**B**	**C**
Advertising	$30 + 4 + 3 - 2 = 35$	$30 - 3 + 3 + 7 = 37$	$30 - 1 + 3 - 5 = 27$
No advertising	$30 + 4 - 3 + 2 = 33$	$30 - 3 - 3 - 7 = 17$	$30 - 1 - 3 + 5 = 31$

The effect associated with a combination of treatments is no longer the simple sum of the two individual treatment effects, because there are nonzero interaction effects. Of course, in an actual experiment there will also be nonzero random-error terms, and the observations within a particular group will no longer be identical. For example, assuming a sample size of three for each combination of factors, the data might look something like Table 15.15.

TABLE 15.15

	Type of packaging		
	A	**B**	**C**
Advertising	33	37	29
	36	33	34
	40	39	36
No advertising	30	12	34
	34	19	29
	34	18	33

Inferences in the Two-Factor Model

15.7

Just as in the one-factor model, the basic idea in the two-factor model is to determine how much of the total variation in the data can be attributed to chance and how much can be attributed to certain "effects." In the two-factor model, three effects of interest are those associated with the first factor (Factor τ), those associated with the second factor (Factor λ), and interaction effects. The total sum of squares is partitioned into four components:

$$\text{SS Columns (Factor } \tau) = \sum_j Kn(\bar{y}_j - \bar{y})^2 \tag{15.6}$$

$$\text{SS Rows (Factor } \lambda) = \sum_k Jn(\bar{y}_k - \bar{y})^2 \tag{15.7}$$

$$\text{SS Error} = \sum_i \sum_j \sum_k (y_{ijk} - \bar{y}_{jk})^2 \tag{15.8}$$

and

$$\text{SS Interaction} = \sum_j \sum_k n(\bar{y}_{jk} - \bar{y}_j - \bar{y}_k + \bar{y})^2 \tag{15.9}$$

The number of observations in treatment combination jk (level j of τ, level k of λ) is n, the total number of observations for level j of τ is Kn, and the total number of observations for level k of λ is Jn. The sample mean for the n observations in treatment combination jk is denoted by $\bar{y}_{jk}$, the sample mean for the Kn observations in factor level j of τ is $\bar{y}_j$, the sample mean for the Jn observations in factor level k of λ is $\bar{y}_k$, and the grand sample mean is $\bar{y}$. The sum of the four SS terms above is simply

$$\text{SS Total} = \sum_i \sum_j \sum_k (y_{ijk} - \bar{y})^2 \tag{15.10}$$

Using Formulas (15.6) through (15.10), the analysis-of-variance table for the two-factor model is given in Table 15.16.

The assumptions in the two-factor model are similar to those in the one-factor model:

1. For each treatment combination jk, the random error terms ϵ_{ijk} are normally distributed with mean zero and variance σ^2, and the variance σ^2 is the same for all treatment combinations.
2. The random error terms are independent.

TABLE 15.16

Source	SS	d.f.	MS
Columns (Factor τ)	SS Columns	$J - 1$	SS Columns/$(J - 1)$
Rows (Factor λ)	SS Rows	$K - 1$	SS Rows/$(K - 1)$
Interaction	SS Interaction	$(J - 1)(K - 1)$	SS Interaction/$(J - 1)(K - 1)$
Error	SS Error	$JK(n - 1)$	SS Error/$JK(n - 1)$
Total	SS Total	$JKn - 1$	

Under these assumptions, the expectations of the mean squares can be calculated:

$$E(\text{MS Columns}) = \sigma^2 + \frac{Kn \sum_j \tau_j^2}{J - 1}$$

$$E(\text{MS Rows}) = \sigma^2 + \frac{Jn \sum_k \lambda_k^2}{K - 1}$$

$$E(\text{MS Interaction}) = \sigma^2 + \frac{n \sum_j \sum_k (\tau\lambda)_{jk}^2}{(J - 1)(K - 1)}$$

and
$$E(\text{MS Error}) = \sigma^2$$

There are several tests of interest in this model. First, consider the hypothesis that the effects of the J levels of Factor τ are all zero:

$$H_0: \tau_1 = \tau_2 = \cdots = \tau_J = 0$$
$$H_a: \text{at least one } \tau_j \neq 0$$

If H_0 is true, $E(\text{MS Columns}) = \sigma^2$, and, by the same line of reasoning used to develop the *F*-test in the one-factor model,

$$F = \frac{\text{MS Columns}}{\text{MS Error}}$$

has an *F*-distribution with $J - 1$ and $JK(n - 1)$ degrees of freedom. This *F*-statistic can be used to test H_0; the null hypothesis will be rejected for large values of *F*.

A second hypothesis of interest is the hypothesis that the effects of the K levels of Factor λ are all zero:

$$H_0: \lambda_1 = \lambda_2 = \cdots = \lambda_K = 0$$
$$H_a: \text{at least one } \lambda_k \neq 0$$

Under the null hypothesis,

$$E(\text{MS Rows}) = \sigma^2$$

and

$$F = \frac{\text{MS Rows}}{\text{MS Error}}$$

has an *F*-distribution with $K - 1$ and $JK(n - 1)$ degrees of freedom. Finally, we might also be interested in the hypothesis that all interaction effects are zero:

$$H_0: (\tau\lambda)_{jk} = 0 \quad \text{for all } j = 1,\ldots,J \quad \text{and} \quad k = 1,\ldots,K$$
$$H_a: (\tau\lambda)_{jk} \neq 0 \quad \text{for at least one combination } (j, k)$$

The statistic used to test this hypothesis is

$$F = \frac{\text{MS Interaction}}{\text{MS Error}}$$

which has an *F*-distribution with $(J - 1)(K - 1)$ and $JK(n - 1)$ degrees of freedom.

To illustrate the two-way analysis of variance, suppose that the experiment discussed in Section 15.4 involving the influence of type of packaging and advertising on sales were actually carried out, with the results shown in Table 15.17. Some output from SAS for an analysis of this data set is given in Table 15.18. Here the second factor is listed as "promote," with two levels: advertising and no advertising.

For the hypothesis that there are no interaction effects, we have

$$F = \frac{MS \text{ Interaction}}{MS \text{ Error}} = \frac{810.13/2}{643.20/54} = 34.01$$

TABLE 15.17

	Type of packaging		
	A	**B**	**C**
Advertising	52	28	15
	48	35	14
	43	34	23
	50	32	21
	43	34	14
	44	27	20
	46	31	21
	46	27	16
	43	29	20
	49	25	14
	$\sum_i y_{i11} = 464$	$\sum_i y_{i21} = 302$	$\sum_i y_{i31} = 178$	$\sum_j \sum_i y_{ij1} = 944$
No advertising	38	43	23
	42	34	25
	42	33	18
	35	42	26
	33	41	18
	38	35	26
	39	37	20
	34	37	19
	33	40	22
	34	36	17
	$\sum_i y_{i12} = 368$	$\sum_i y_{i22} = 378$	$\sum_i y_{i32} = 214$	$\sum_j \sum_i y_{ij2} = 960$
	$\sum_k \sum_i y_{i1k} = 832$	$\sum_k \sum_i y_{i2k} = 680$	$\sum_k \sum_i y_{i3k} = 392$	$\sum_k \sum_j \sum_i y_{ijk} = 1904$

TABLE 15.18

```
                              SAS
               GENERAL LINEAR MODELS PROCEDURE
                  CLASS LEVEL INFORMATION
                  CLASS      LEVELS      VALUES
                  PACKAGE      3         TYPEA TYPEB TYPEC
                  PROMOTE      2         AD NOAD
               NUMBER OF OBSERVATIONS IN DATA SET = 60

                              SAS
               GENERAL LINEAR MODELS PROCEDURE
DEPENDENT VARIABLE: SALES

    SOURCE                DF      SUM OF SQUARES      F VALUE      PR > F
    PACKAGE                2      4994.13333333       209.64       0.0001
    PROMOTE                1         4.26666667         0.36       0.5520
    PACKAGE*PROMOTE        2       810.13333333        34.01       0.0001
    ERROR                 54       643.20000000
            TOTAL         59      6451.73333333

                              MEANS
              PACKAGE          N                  SALES
              TYPEA           20               41.6000000
              TYPEB           20               34.0000000
              TYPEC           20               19.6000000

              PROMOTE          N                  SALES
              AD              30               31.4666667
              NOAD            30               32.0000000

         PACKAGE        PROMOTE         N             SALES
         TYPEA          AD             10          46.4000000
         TYPEA          NOAD           10          36.8000000
         TYPEB          AD             10          30.2000000
         TYPEB          NOAD           10          37.8000000
         TYPEC          AD             10          17.8000000
         TYPEC          NOAD           10          21.4000000
```

with 2 and 54 d.f., which is much greater than the critical value corresponding to $\alpha = 0.05$. The p-value for this test is 0.0001.

Thus, the marketing manager may conclude with considerable confidence that there are nonzero interaction effects. For the tests concerning column effects (packaging) and row effects (advertising), the statistics are

$$F = \frac{\text{MS Columns}}{\text{MS Error}} = \frac{4994.13/2}{643.20/54} = 209.64$$

with 2 and 54 d.f. and

$$F = \frac{\text{MS Rows}}{\text{MS Error}} = \frac{4.27/1}{643.20/54} = 0.36$$

with 1 and 54 d.f. The former statistic is highly significant (p-value $= 0.0001$), whereas the latter is clearly not significant (p-value $= 0.5520$). The following assertions can be made:

1. There is apparently little or no effect of advertising *alone* on sales.
2. The type of packaging alone *does* seem to affect sales.
3. There is apparently an interaction between advertising and type of packaging, meaning that the magnitude and the direction of the effects of type of packaging differ for the two different advertising levels.

In short, the type of packaging makes a difference in sales, but the kind and extent of the difference depends on the level of advertising.

It should be mentioned that as a result of the fact that the interaction effect was found to be statistically significant, the outcomes of the other two *F*-tests were of less importance than would be the case if the interaction effect had not been found significant. The statistician is usually interested in whether a particular factor (such as advertising) has an effect on the variable of primary interest (such as sales), although he or she may not care whether the factor has a significant effect by itself or only through the interaction term. In our example, advertising apparently does have an effect on sales through its interaction with type of packaging, so the marketing manager will have to consider advertising in making decisions on the basis of the given data. However, had the interaction term not been significant, the other two tests would be of much greater interest.

Given the preceding results, the marketing manager is interested in estimating the packaging effects and the interaction effects. The effects of packaging can be estimated by subtracting the grand sample mean from the respective column means:

$$\hat{\tau}_1 = 41.6 - 31.7 = 9.9$$
$$\hat{\tau}_2 = 34.0 - 31.7 = 2.3$$

and $$\hat{\tau}_3 = 19.6 - 31.7 = -12.1$$

To estimate interaction effects, subtract the appropriate row and column sample means from the grand sample mean and add the sample mean for the particular combination of interest. For example,

$$\text{Est. } (\tau\lambda)_{32} = \frac{1904}{60} - \frac{392}{20} - \frac{960}{30} + \frac{214}{10} = 1.5$$

All six interaction effects can be estimated in this manner. The rationale behind this procedure is quite simple: from the sample mean for the combination of interest, we would like to subtract the row and column effects and the grand mean. In subtracting the appropriate row and column means, we are subtracting the row and column effects and at the same time subtracting the grand mean twice. Therefore, we have to add back the grand mean. In other words, we have

$$\text{Est. } (\tau\lambda)_{jk} = \bar{y}_{jk} - \bar{y}_j - \bar{y}_k + \bar{y}$$

But

$$\hat{\tau}_j = \bar{y}_j - \bar{y}$$

so

$$\bar{y}_j = \bar{y} + \hat{\tau}_j$$

Similarly,

$$\bar{y}_k = \bar{y} + \hat{\lambda}_k$$

Therefore, we have

$$\text{Est. } (\tau\lambda)_{jk} = \bar{y}_{jk} - \bar{y} - \hat{\tau}_j - \bar{y} - \hat{\lambda}_k + \bar{y}$$

$$= \bar{y}_{jk} - \hat{\tau}_j - \hat{\lambda}_k - \bar{y}$$

which is exactly what we wanted in the first place.

Although the linear analysis-of-variance model is believed to be quite widely applicable, there are admittedly many situations in which the assumptions concerning the error terms are not satisfied. Therefore it is of some interest to investigate the "robustness" of the analysis-of-variance procedure to violations of these assumptions. The least important of the assumptions is that of normality: nonnormality of the error terms usually has little effect on the results, particularly if the sample size is reasonably large. The assumption that the error terms all have the same variance is somewhat more important, especially when the various samples or groups have unequal sample sizes. If it is suspected that the variance might not be constant, it is a good idea to make the sample sizes equal. Finally, violations of the last assumption (independence of the error terms) are quite serious and may affect the results of the analysis quite severely.

Problems

15.26 Construct examples of two-factor experiments in which

    a) row effects only are present;

    b) row and column effects, but no interaction effects, are present;

    c) row, column, and interaction effects are all present.

15.27 In the marketing example in Section 15.6, suppose that the row effects for advertising are zero. Does this mean that advertising has no impact upon sales?

15.28 In an analysis-of-variance, an attempt is made to estimate how much of the total variation in the data can be attributed to certain assignable causes of variation and how much can be attributed to chance. If row, column, and interaction effects are all present in a two-factor experiment, how can the variation due to chance be estimated?

15.29 The interaction effect for the combination of advertising and type A packaging in the marketing example in Section 15.6 is -2, while the interaction effect for the combination of advertising and type B packaging is $+7$. How can you interpret these figures?

15.30 In a study of the amount of air pollution in a city, the two factors of interest are the day of the week (Monday, Tuesday, Wednesday, Thursday, Friday) and the time of day (morning, afternoon). The study reveals nonzero effects for each factor individually and a nonzero interaction effect. Explain what each of these effects represents.

15.31 For the data in Table 15.15,

    a) find the grand sample mean, the sample mean for each row, the sample mean for each column, and the sample mean for each of the six treatment combinations;

    b) compute SS Columns, SS Rows, SS Interaction, SS Error, and SS Total;

    c) determine the mean squares for columns, rows, interaction, and error;

    d) construct an analysis-of-variance table;

    e) conduct F-tests with $\alpha = 0.05$ for nonzero column effects, row effects, and interaction effects.

15.32 A consumer research firm wants to compare three brands of radial tires in terms of tread life over different road surfaces. Random samples of four tires of each brand are selected for each of three surfaces (asphalt, concrete, gravel). A machine that can simulate road conditions for each of the road surfaces is used to find the tread life (in thousands of miles) of each tire. The data are shown in Table 15.19. Construct an analysis-of-variance table and conduct F-tests with $\alpha = 0.05$ for the presence of nonzero brand effects, road surface effects, and interaction effects.

TABLE 15.19

		Brand					
		A		**B**		**C**	
	Asphalt	36	39	42	40	32	36
		39	38	39	42	35	34
Road	Concrete	38	40	42	45	37	33
surface		41	40	48	47	33	34
	Gravel	34	32	34	34	36	35
		34	35	30	31	35	33

15.33 Determine estimates for the six interaction effects in the marketing example in Section 15.7.

15.34 In Problem 15.8, suppose that the experiment was designed so that of the 20 students in each income group, 10 were male and 10 were female. When the scores are arrayed by sex as well as income, we have the results shown in Table 15.20 along with output from ISP. Test (at the 0.01 level) for significant income effects, sex effects, and interaction effects.

TABLE 15.20

		Income				
		Low		**Middle**		**High**
Male	736	729	773	881	873	1127
	1065	839	784	1060	1071	704
	667	850	912	941	1246	809
	840	972	1259	922	1049	1139
	448	708	791	932	774	986
Female	579	1082	556	630	1002	926
	800	599	929	977	785	655
	1031	1008	706	961	644	989
	744	692	1030	1047	1033	634
	1234	1005	1135	742	958	787

Two-Way Analysis of Variance

Source	Sum of Squares	d.f.	Mean Square	Computed F-value	F-value alpha = .05	p-value
Columns (FACTOR A)	71471.6	2	35735.8	1.09	3.17	.344
Rows (FACTOR B)	16236.2	1	16236.2	.49	4.02	.485
Row X Col Interactions	133933.	2	66966.5	2.04	3.17	.140
Error (within cells)	.177401E+07	54	32851.9			
Totals	.199565E+07	59				

15.35 Determine estimates for any effects that are significant in Problem 15.34. What conclusions can be drawn from the experimental results insofar as the relationships between SAT scores and sex or income are concerned?

15.36 A manufacturer frequently sends small packages to a customer in another city via air freight, and in many cases it is important for a package to reach the customer as soon as possible. Three different firms offer air freight service, including pickup and delivery, on a 24-hour basis. The head of the manufacturer's shipping department would like to know if the firms differ in speed of service and if the time of day makes any difference. An experiment is designed to investigate these issues. Packages are sent at random times, and the air freight firm used for each package is also randomly chosen. The customer records the time that each package arrives so that the time elapsed during shipment can be determined. These times are rounded to the nearest hour; the experimental results for a total of 54 packages are shown in Table 15.21. Analyze these data by constructing an analysis-of-variance table, conducting *F*-tests, and determining estimates for the treatment effects.

15.37 A consumer research group is interested in how the price of the leading brand of aspirin varies, if it varies at all, across different regions of a metropolitan area and across different types of retail outlets. The area is divided into four regions: center city, lakefront, west side, and north suburbs. Three types of retail outlets are considered: drugstores, discount stores, and

TABLE 15.21

| | | **Firm** | | |
		Speedy Air Freight	**ABC Shipping**	**Eagle Air Freight**
	Morning	8, 6, 6, 12, 7, 8	11, 11, 9, 10, 8, 11	7, 4, 6, 4, 9, 7
Time	**Afternoon**	7, 10, 8, 11, 9, 11	10, 13, 10, 12, 11, 10	10, 8, 6, 5, 8, 6
	Night	13, 11, 14, 11, 15, 12	12, 16, 15, 15, 10, 17	8, 11, 9, 9, 9, 10

grocery stores. For each region and each type of store, four stores are chosen at random and the price of a large bottle of aspirin is recorded (in dollars). The prices observed are shown in Table 15.22. Using the output in Table 15.23, carry out an analysis of variance, including appropriate tests and estimates, and provide an interpretation of the results of the analysis.

TABLE 15.22

| | **Region** | | | |
	Center city	**Lakefront**	**West side**	**North suburbs**
Drugstore	2.46 2.63 2.52 2.42	2.85 2.61 2.73 2.68	2.44 2.29 2.48 2.37	2.65 2.73 2.51 2.60
Discount store	2.27 2.39 2.24 2.30	2.34 2.30 2.43 2.28	2.35 2.19 2.28 2.37	2.36 2.27 2.43 2.30
Grocery store	2.81 2.68 2.63 2.72	2.70 2.64 2.79 2.62	2.68 2.76 2.59 2.65	2.78 2.74 2.95 2.84

TABLE 15.23

Two-Way Analysis of Variance

Source	Sum of Squares	d.f.	Mean Square	Computed F-value	F-value alpha = .05	p-value
Columns (FACTOR A)	.159440	3	.531465E-01	8.04	2.87	.000
Rows (FACTOR B)	1.32874	2	.664369	100.57	3.26	.000
Row X Col Interactions	.142379	6	.237298E-01	3.59	2.37	.007
Error (within cells)	.237825	36	.660625E-02			
TOTALS	1.86838	47				

Experimental Design

15.8

The discussion of sampling theory in Chapter 6 demonstrated that there is often more to taking a sample than just determining the sample size, n. First, there is the problem of carefully defining the population of interest. Once this is done, various sampling plans, such as simple random sampling, stratified sampling, and so on, must be considered. Once a sampling plan is chosen, the actual items to be sampled can be determined. This procedure falls under the general heading of "sample design," and the overall objective in designing a sample is to get the greatest possible precision for a given cost, or to attain some given level of precision in the least costly manner.

In sampling theory, it is presumed that the sample consists of observations on an *existing* population; that is, some members of the population are observed and the desired information about these members is recorded. This contrasts with the idea of a *controlled experiment,* which is widely encountered in scientific research. In a controlled experiment, instead of merely observing an existing population, the statistician attempts to control, or to modify, certain factors of interest and then observes the effect of these modifications on the results of the experiment. Rather than observing the proportion of defective items in a sample from a production process, the experimental statistician might try a modification of the process and observe the proportion of defectives, both with and without the modification. The statistician must do this carefully, however, to ensure that all factors other than the one being varied remain constant. In terms of the production example, the statistician attempts to make the conditions under which the process is run *with* and *without* the modification as similar as possible. If the modification is used during the night shift but not during the day shift, then any differences that appear may be caused by the different sets of personnel rather than by the modification. Unfortunately, it is often quite difficult, if not impossible, to hold such factors constant in actual problems. In the marketing example used to illustrate the analysis of variance, for instance, the various stores in the experiment will obviously differ in some respects (location, number and type of customers). In business and the social sciences it is not as easy to control extraneous factors as it is in the physical sciences.

The marketing example illustrated the idea of experimental design. First, the factors of interest were determined (type of packaging and advertising), each with a certain number of "levels" (three types of packaging, two levels of advertising). The total sample size was chosen and the 60 experimental units (stores) were selected. The next problem was the allocation of stores to the six possible treatment combinations. This was done randomly, thus invoking the principle of randomization, which is an important principle in experimental statistics. The use of randomization permits the experimenter to make inferential statements from the observed data.

This example should give you an idea of what experimental design is all about. Of course, the example was purposely made simple in order to illustrate a particular analysis-of-variance model, the two-factor model with interaction.

A textbook example such as this may give the impression that an experiment is "forced" to fit a certain model. In practice, however, various models are generally considered, and the model that seems to best fit the situation at hand is chosen. Experimental design proceeds from the problem situation to the model, not vice versa. In the marketing example, the marketing manager may decide that factors such as "type of store" may cause a great deal of variation and that it would be desirable to somehow reduce this variation. A generalization of the one-factor model called a **randomized blocks** model allows the experimenter to allow for some of this extraneous variation separately instead of including it in the estimated random variation. For example, if there are five different types of stores, three stores of each type could be selected and the three types of packaging could be randomly assigned to these three stores. The types of stores are the "blocks," and the experimental assignment of treatments to stores within each block is random—hence the term "randomized blocks." Of course, a similar extension could be used in the two-factor situation with combinations of type of packaging and advertising—no advertising assigned randomly to stores, within each type of store.

In some instances, of course, more than two factors are of interest. In general, experimental designs involving several factors are called **factorial** designs and, conceptually at least, there is no limitation on the number of factors that can be considered. As the number of factors increases, the experimental design becomes more complex and the analysis more difficult. If there are four factors and each has four levels (four possible treatments within each factor), then there are 4^4, or 256 combinations of factor levels. If the design is complete in the sense that all combinations are included and if the samples sizes are identical for all combinations, then the overall sample size will be a multiple of 256. By carefully considering the situation at hand, it may be possible to reduce the number of combinations. For instance, some interaction effects, particularly higher-order interaction effects, might be eliminated from consideration *a priori* by the experimenter. Alternatively, various models are available that allow the experimenter to reduce the overall sample size. For example, in a design known as a *Latin square* design, only one level of a third factor is used with each possible combination of levels of the first two factors. Two other types of designs that lead to reductions in the overall sample size are *incomplete block* designs and *fractional factorial* designs.

As we have pointed out, there is a difference between "sample design" and "experimental design," and there are also some similarities. In both cases, the statistician is attempting to obtain as much information as possible for the smallest cost. The results should be as precise as possible. Of course, precision can be increased by increasing sample size, but this may be quite costly in terms of both time and money. Another way to obtain more precise results is to design the experiment or sampling plan more carefully. For instance, it is often possible to increase the precision of estimates obtained from a sample without increasing the sample size by adopting, say, a stratified sampling plan instead of simple random sampling. The same idea holds in experimental design. Designs such as those mentioned in the previous paragraph may enable an experimenter to greatly reduce the number of experimental units needed to make inferences in certain situations. Complex experimental designs such as these are beyond the scope of this book; the student who is interested in pursuing this subject further should see references 3 and 19.

Regression and Analysis of Variance: The General Linear Model

15.9

At various points in this chapter we have noted the similarity between the linear analysis-of-variance model and the linear regression model. The bivariate linear regression model is similar to the simple one-factor analysis-of-variance model, and the multiple regression model is similar to a two-(or more-) factor analysis-of-variance model without the interaction terms. Even the assumptions concerning the random-error terms are the same in the two models. The discussion of regression analysis in Chapters 11 and 13 included terms like "sum of squares." Therefore, such terms should not have been new to you in this chapter.

Suppose that, in a simple one-factor model, the J treatment categories correspond to J values of the independent variable, x, and that we want to investigate the linear regression of a second variable, y, on x. The linear regression model can be written as follows:

$$y_{ij} = \alpha + \beta x_j + \epsilon_{ij}$$

There are J levels of the factor x, and a sample of size n_j is taken in the jth level. On the basis of the entire sample (which is of size $\sum_j n_j$), the parameters α and β are estimated by using the least-squares criterion, and the estimated linear regression is

$$y_{ij} = a + bx_j + e_{ij}$$

or

$$y_{ij} = \hat{y}_j + e_{ij}$$

Here y_{ij} is the observed value of y and $\hat{y}_j$ is the value predicted by the estimated linear regression.

Using the model above, the deviation of an observed value y_{ij} from the grand mean $\hat{y}$ can be thought of as the sum of two parts:

$$y_{ij} - \bar{y} = (y_{ij} - \hat{y}_j) + (\hat{y}_j - \bar{y})$$

The first term on the right-hand side of this equation is simply the deviation of the particular observation from the predicted value for its group or treatment level. The second term is the deviation of the predicted value itself from the grand mean.

By an argument like that used earlier in this chapter and in Chapter 11, it can be shown that over all observations in all groups, the total sum of squares can be partitioned into SS Error and SS Linear Regression, which reflect, respectively, random error and the "linear regression effect." The formula for SS Total is

$$SS\ Total = \sum_j \sum_i (y_{ij} - \bar{y})^2$$

and for SS Linear Regression,

$$SS\ Linear\ Regression = \sum_j n_j(\hat{y}_j - \bar{y})^2$$

The analysis-of-variance table is given in Table 15.24.

In practice, the usual computational formula used to determine SS Total is

$$SS\ Total = \sum_j \sum_i y_{ij}^2 - \frac{\left(\sum_j \sum_i y_{ij}\right)^2}{\sum_j n_j}$$

The sums of squares associated with the linear regression can be expressed in terms of the sample correlation coefficient and the sample variance of y:

$$SS\ Linear\ Regression = \left(\sum_j n_j\right)r^2 s_y^2$$

Finally, SS Error is found by subtracting SS Linear Regression from SS Total. The statistic used to test the hypothesis that there is no linear regression effect is

$$F = \frac{MS\ Linear\ Regression}{MS\ Error}$$

which has an F-distribution with 1 and $\sum_j n_j - 2$ degrees of freedom, respectively.

This section demonstrates the fact that a linear regression model can be thought of as a simple analysis-of-variance model. Both linear regression analysis and the analysis of variance fall under the heading of the *general linear model*. In multivariate statistical problems the general linear model is of great value, both because it is often a realistic model and because nonlinear models are very difficult to work with when there are many variables.

TABLE 15.24

Source	SS	d.f.	MS
Linear Regression	SS Linear Regression	1	SS Linear Regression/1
Error	SS Error	$\sum_j n_j - 2$	$SS\ Error \Big/ \left(\sum_j n_j - 2\right)$
Total	SS Total	$\sum_j n_j - 1$	

Problems

15.38 Try to explain in your own words exactly what the term "experimental design" encompasses.

15.39 Carefully explain the difference between the terms "sample design" and "experimental design."

15.40 Discuss the role of randomization in experimental statistics.

15.41 In Problem 15.5, 20 new employees are randomly assigned to the training programs. Would it affect the experiment if some other assignment procedure were used? For example, what if the first five employees to be hired were put in the first program, the next five in the second program, and so on? What if the personnel director decided which employees should be assigned to each program?

15.42 A linear regression is used to predict yearly oil consumption in the United States as a function of the year. The data were analyzed on the computer using SAS, and some of the output is presented in Table 15.25. Interpret these results. At the 0.05 level of significance, test the hypothesis that there is no linear regression effect against the alternative that there is such an effect.

TABLE 15.25

SAS

DEP VARIABLE: CONSUMP

ANALYSIS OF VARIANCE

SOURCE	DF	SUM OF SQUARES	MEAN SQUARE	F VALUE	PROB > F
MODEL	1	80.51212121	80.51212121	501.681	0.0001
ERROR	8	1.28387879	0.16048485		
C TOTAL	9	81.79600000			

ROOT MSE	0.4006056	R-SQUARE	0.9843	
DEP MEAN	13.72	ADJ R-SQ	0.9823	
C.V.	2.919866			

PARAMETER ESTIMATES

VARIABLE	DF	PARAMETER ESTIMATE	STANDARD ERROR	T FOR H0: PARAMETER=0	PROB > |T|
INTERCEP	1	-958.84667	43.42177903	-22.082	0.0001
YEAR	1	0.49393939	0.02205261	22.398	0.0001

15.43 For the data in Problem 11.6, find the SS Total and SS Linear Regression and complete the analysis-of-variance table for the regression.

15.44 A production manager knows that a particular task can be completed faster if more workers are used. To investigate the relationship between the time required to finish the task and the number of workers assigned to the task, an experiment is conducted. The experimental results are as follows:

Number of Workers:	1	2	3	4
Time required to finish task (minutes)	15, 18, 10, 14, 16	12, 10, 15, 14, 12	12, 8, 8, 9, 9	6, 4, 4, 7, 5

The total sample size is 20, with a sample of five for each choice of number of workers. Find the analysis-of-variance table and conduct an F-test with $\alpha = 0.05$ for the presence of a linear regression effect.

15.45 Construct an analysis-of-variance table for the regression of personal consumption on disposable income in Problem 11.36.

Exercises

15.46 Discuss the general rationale behind the analysis of variance. Since the hypotheses of interest involve means, why does the analysis of variance focus on variances?

15.47 Explain the advantage, if any, of a comparison of J means ($J > 2$) by an analysis of variance and an F-test over the practice of carrying out a t-test separately for each pair of means.

15.48 Suppose that four randomly selected groups of five observations each were used in an experiment. Furthermore, imagine that the overall sample mean was 60. What would the data be like if the F-test resulted in $F = 0$? What would the data be like if $F \rightarrow \infty$? If the hypothesis of equality of the means for the four groups were true, how large should we expect F to be?

15.49 In a two-way analysis of variance as described in Section 15.6, there are n observations for each combination of one level of each factor. In other words, there are n observations in each cell of the two-way table of data. Would the inferential procedures developed in Section 15.6 still be appropriate if we had only one observation per cell (that is, if $n = 1$)? Discuss.

15.50 Students registering for a review course in accounting in preparation for a CPA examination were randomly divided into three sections of twelve students each. In the first section, the students spent all their time in class working various types of accounting problems. The second section emphasized accounting concepts and was taught primarily in a lecture format. The third section represented a mixture of lectures concerning concepts and practice with actual problems. At the end of the course, the 36 students took the CPA examination, and their scores were as follows:

Section 1:   72, 58, 81, 70, 68, 60
            74, 56, 64, 67, 66, 71

Section 2:   52, 78, 64, 69, 73, 55
            56, 62, 58, 67, 61, 70

Section 3:   68, 76, 82, 80, 91, 84
            77, 71, 79, 85, 82, 66

    a) Perform an analysis-of-variance on these data and discuss the results.

    b) Determine a set of interval estimates for all possible pairwise differences, using a 95% confidence coefficient. From these interval estimates, which differences are significant?

15.51 An experiment was designed to investigate differences in the life of light-bulbs from three different manufacturers. Five lightbulbs were randomly selected from each of three large shipments of bulbs from the different manufacturers. For each bulb, the number of hours until failure was recorded:

    Manufacturer I: 120, 90, 105, 100, 125

    Manufacturer II: 100, 130, 125, 140, 120

    Manufacturer III: 110, 75, 100, 90, 100

Table 15.26 provides some output from Statgraphics for this data set.

TABLE 15.26

Analysis of Variance

Source of variation	Sum of Squares	d.f.	Mean Square	F-ratio	Sig. level
Between groups	1963.3333	2	981.66667	4.888	.0280
Within groups	2410.0000	12	200.83333		
Total (corrected)	4373.3333	14			

0 missing value(s) have been excluded.

---

    a) Interpret the computer output and indicate whether significant effects due to the manufacturers seem to be present.

    b) Determine an estimate of σ^2, the error variance.

    c) Use the S-method for multiple comparisons to investigate the differences between I and II, between II and III, and between I and III, in terms of the life of their lightbulbs.

15.52 There are many small firms in a particular industry. Some of the firms are unionized under union A, some are unionized under union B, and others are not unionized. A random sample of firms reveals the following average pay increases (in percentage terms) over the past year:

    Union A: 12, 16, 13, 10, 8, 14, 17, 11

    Union B: 8, 13, 7, 9, 11, 6, 8, 8

    Nonunion: 10, 12, 8, 11, 7, 9, 10, 8

Carry out an analysis-of-variance, including an *F*-test for equality of means and a set of interval estimates for pairwise differences in means with a 95%

confidence coefficient. What can you conclude about the impact of the two unions and of the lack of a union on pay increases?

15.53 A new type of pill that, when taken daily, is intended to reduce the chance of catching a cold has been developed in the research laboratory of a drug manufacturer. In order to test the drug, an experiment is designed. Forty-five people are randomly divided into three groups of 15 each. Each experimental subject takes one pill per day, with one group receiving the new pill, one group receiving vitamin C, and one group receiving a placebo (a pill containing no medication or vitamins). The subjects do not know which of the pills they are receiving. The experiment is conducted for six months, and the number of days with colds is recorded for each subject, with the following results:

New pill:	4, 15, 8, 6, 9, 8, 18, 0, 12, 6, 7, 10, 11, 2, 6
Vitamin C:	13, 7, 2, 0, 11, 8, 5, 3, 10, 9, 8, 8, 4, 7, 1
Placebo:	9, 12, 17, 13, 5, 19, 6, 8, 10, 11, 2, 14, 15, 1, 12

Output from the analysis-of-variance routine of ISP is shown in Table 15.27.

TABLE 15.27

One-Way Analysis of Variance

Source	Sum of Squares	d.f.	Mean Square	Computed F-value	F-value alpha = .05	p-value
Between groups	112.533	2	56.2667	2.66	3.22	.082
Error (within groups)	888.267	42	21.1492			
TOTALS	1000.80	44				

a) Estimate the treatment effects.

b) Are these treatment effects significantly different from zero at the $\alpha = 0.01$ level of significance?

c) Interpret the results of the experiment.

d) The experimenter could just skip the placebo with the third group and tell the subjects which groups they are in. Would that make any difference?

15.54 One year ago, a contractor built and sold houses with three different types of heating in a new subdivision. The three heating systems utilize gas, electricity, and solar energy, respectively. The contractor is planning an addition to the subdivision, and he must decide what heating systems to use in the new houses that are to be built. The impact of the heating system on the initial cost of the house is an important consideration, as is the anticipated cost of heating the house. To obtain more information on operating costs, the contractor finds the heating costs for the past winter for the houses sold last year. These heating costs, in hundreds of dollars, are as follows:

Gas heat	Electric heat	Solar heat
6.1	8.2	5.2
7.2	7.5	6.1
5.4	8.7	5.7
5.8	7.4	5.4
6.3	7.8	6.2
6.7	9.2	
7.4		
6.4		

a) Estimate the population means and the treatment effects for the three heating systems.

b) Construct an analysis-of-variance table for this example.

c) Are the costs different for the three heating systems at the 0.05 level of significance?

15.55 The director of a medical insurance plan is concerned about the length of time patients spend in the hospital. From records of patients with a certain type of illness, six male patients and six female patients are chosen at random from each of three hospitals. The number of days spent in the hospital by each patient is given in Table 15.28. Carry out an analysis of variance, testing for and estimating hospital effects, sex effects, and interaction effects.

TABLE 15.28

	Hospital A		Hospital B		Hospital C	
	29	36	14	5	22	25
Male patients	35	33	8	7	20	30
	28	38	10	16	23	32
	25	35	3	5	18	7
Female patients	31	32	8	9	15	11
	26	34	4	6	8	10

15.56 In Problem 15.5, suppose that the firm was interested in the effect of age as well as the effect of the training program. New employees are divided into "below 30" and "30 or older" age groups, and four from each age group are randomly assigned to each program. After the program, the number of times the task is performed per minute is recorded for each trainee, with the results shown in Table 15.29. At the $\alpha = 0.01$ level, test for nonzero program effects, age effects, and interaction effects.

TABLE 15.29

		Program 1	Program 2	Program 3	Program 4
Age	Below 30	11, 13, 10, 14	10, 0, 7, 9	12, 10, 13, 10	6, 11, 8, 8
	30 or over	10, 9, 12, 10	9, 11, 6, 8	8, 11, 10, 11	9, 7, 7, 6

15.57 To compare the air pollution in different cities and at different times of day, air samples are taken at four randomly selected points within each city. Each sample is analyzed, and an air pollution index is used to indicate the overall degree of pollution in the sample (a larger number means more pollution). Results are shown in Table 15.30, along with output from ISP. Carry out an analysis of variance, with appropriate tests and estimates.

TABLE 15.30

	City 1	City 2	City 3
9 a.m.	14, 20 28, 22	27, 31 18, 25	6, 12 13, 10
12:30 p.m.	21, 25 19, 32	22, 26 28, 24	12, 15 11, 9
4 a.m.	20, 34 22, 24	19, 27 23, 29	28, 20 25, 23

```
                 Two-Way Analysis of Variance

                   Sum of            Mean   Computed  F-value
Source            Squares   d.f.    Square   F-value  alpha=.05  p-value

Columns (FACTOR A)  637.722     2   318.861    15.26     3.36       .000
Rows    (FACTOR B)  206.889     2   103.444     4.95     3.36       .015
Row X Col interactions 285.611  4    71.4028    3.42     2.73       .022
Error (within cells)  564.000  27    20.8889

TOTALS             1694.22     35
```

15.58 A linear regression with sales as the dependent variable and population as the independent variable resulted in the output from SAS that is shown in Table 15.31. Does this indicate a significant linear relationship at the $\alpha = 0.05$ level?

TABLE 15.31

SAS

DEP VARIABLE: SALES

ANALYSIS OF VARIANCE

SOURCE	DF	SUM OF SQUARES	MEAN SQUARE	F VALUE	PROB > F
MODEL	1	255090333	255090333	111.470	0.0001
ERROR	28	64075763.94	2288420.14		
C TOTAL	29	319166097			

ROOT MSE	1512.753	R-SQUARE	0.7992	
DEP MEAN	10246.33	ADJ R-SQ	0.7921	
C.V.	14.76384			

PARAMETER ESTIMATES

VARIABLE	DF	PARAMETER ESTIMATE	STANDARD ERROR	T FOR H0: PARAMETER = 0	PROB > |T|
INTERCEP	1	1386.96925	883.40306	1.570	0.1276
POP	1	0.53339673	0.05052092	10.558	0.0001

15.59 In Problem 15.58, SAS was used for a linear regression predicting sales as a function of population. Some output is given in Table 15.32 relating sales to the unemployment rate. Is there a significant linear relationship at the $\alpha = 0.05$ level?

TABLE 15.32

SAS

DEP VARIABLE: SALES

ANALYSIS OF VARIANCE

SOURCE	DF	SUM OF SQUARES	MEAN SQUARE	F VALUE
MODEL	1	31166985.41	31166985.41	3.030
ERROR	28	287999111	10285682.54	
C TOTAL	29	319166097		

15.60 The information in Table 15.33 was generated by computer for the multiple regression predicting sales as a function of the other four variables in Problem 15.58 (population, unemployment rate, advertising expense, competition). Is there a significant multiple linear regression effect at the $\alpha = 0.05$ level?

TABLE 15.33

SOURCE	DF	SUM OF SQUARES
MODEL	4	284350772
ERROR	25	34815324.84
C TOTAL	29	319166097

15.61 A division of a large multinational food products corporation produces bakery goods, including frozen cakes that are sold under the "Pastry Shop" label in supermarkets throughout the United States, Canada, and in some foreign countries as well. A new cake is being developed by the division, and there is some disagreement about the sweetening agent to be used in the cake. Top management feels that sugar should be used because any other sweetener will hurt the reputation of the "Pastry Shop" label. However, cost estimates indicate that corn syrup would be considerably cheaper, and members of the marketing research group point out that a switch from sugar to corn syrup in another of the division's products met with favorable response in test marketing and did not lead to a reduction in sales when implemented on a regular basis. The director of the research laboratory, however, thinks that a switch from sugar to corn syrup is not a good idea because an artificial sweetener would be even cheaper and, with recent developments, tastes more like sugar than does corn syrup. The proponents of sugar and corn syrup are united in their stand against artificial sweeteners, pointing out that the government has banned certain artificial sweeteners from time to time and that the public is becoming increasingly wary of foods with artificial ingredients. The laboratory director disagrees, blaming poor taste for lack of acceptance of previous artificial sweeteners. The new artificial sweetener has been well received in taste tests and has been approved for use by the government.

In order to gain more information about consumer response to the new cake, a taste-testing experiment is conducted. A random sample of consumers is taken, and each person in the sample is asked to taste various items and to rate each one on a scale from 1 to 5, with 1 representing "tastes awful" and 5 representing "tastes great." One of the items is the new cake, and other items are included to gather information about them as well as to prevent the subjects from focusing just on the new cake. The results for the new cake in terms of the frequencies of the different ratings are shown in Table 15.34. From these figures, the average rating is 2.83 with sugar, 2.55 with corn syrup, and 2.39 with artificial sweetener. Are the differences among these sample means large enough to be attributable to something other than chance (use $\alpha = 0.05$)?

In the experiment, sugar comes out on top. But the average rating for the new cake with sugar is still disappointing. Some of the company's current products were also included in the experiment, and they all received average ratings in the neighborhood of 3.5. Top management's first response to the taste test is to scrap the plans for the new cake altogether. When someone

TABLE 15.34

Rating	Sugar	Corn syrup	Artificial sweetener
1	14	16	19
2	30	35	42
3	26	32	22
4	19	12	15
5	11	5	2

points out that a similar cake marketed by a competitor is very successful, the president decides that further investigation is warranted before dropping the project. The investigation reveals that the argument about the sweetener distracted attention from another change. To cut costs, vegetable oil had been substituted for butter, which is used in all of the company's other cakes. The president becomes very upset at this news and demands a replication of the experiment with butter used in place of vegetable oil. The results are shown in Table 15.35.

TABLE 15.35

Rating	Sugar	Corn syrup	Artificial sweetener
1	3	4	10
2	12	10	23
3	31	28	36
4	32	37	23
5	22	21	8

Analyze the experimental data (treat the two sets of data as a single experiment). Indicate what you think should be done about the new cake, and justify your recommendations.

15.62 The management of "Nightlife" magazine is studying the sensitivity of sales to subscription price. In one part of this study 27 subscribers were asked to indicate the maximum amount they would pay for a one-year subscription. These 27 people were classified according to their level of education and according to their degree of extroversion. The results of this study are shown in Table 15.36, with amounts given in dollars.

TABLE 15.36

		Level of extroversion		
		Ambivert	**Extrovert**	**Introvert**
Highest level of education	**Secondary school**	22, 23, 20	24, 27, 23	18, 15, 17
	Some college	20, 24, 25	25, 26, 29	16, 17, 19
	College grad	25, 24, 21	28, 24, 27	19, 17, 16

A SAS program for a two-way analysis of variance was used to analyze these data. What conclusions can "Nightlife" draw from the SAS output given in Table 15.37?

TABLE 15.37

```
                              SAS
                GENERAL LINEAR MODELS PROCEDURE
                   CLASS LEVEL INFORMATION
          CLASS     LEVELS VALUES
          EDUC        3         COLLEGE GRAD SCHOOL
          LEVEL       3         AMBI EXTRO INTRO

        NUMBER OF OBSERVATIONS IN DATA SET = 27
                              SAS

                GENERAL LINEAR MODELS PROCEDURE
DEPENDENT VARIABLE: PRICE
```

SOURCE	DF	SUM OF SQUARES	F VALUE	PR > F
EDUC	2	10.66666667	1.43	0.2662
LEVEL	2	354.88888889	47.44	0.0001
EDUC*LEVEL	4	1.77777778	0.12	0.9740
ERROR	18	67.33333333		3.74074074
TOTAL	26	434.66666667		

Chapter 16

Nonparametric Statistics

It ain't so much the things we don't know that get us in trouble. It's the things we know that ain't so.

ARTEMUS WARD

Introduction **16.1**

Most of the statistical tests considered thus far have specified certain properties of the parent population that must hold before these tests can be used. A *t*-test, for example, requires that the observations come from a normal population; and if this test is used in testing for differences between means, the two populations must have equal variances. The same type of assumption is necessary in the analysis-of-variance tests presented in Chapter 15, and we assumed a bivariate normal distribution in making probability statements about correlation coefficients. Although most of these tests are quite "robust," in the sense that the tests are still useful when the assumptions about the parent population are not exactly fulfilled, there are still many circumstances when the researcher cannot or does not want make such assumptions. The statistical methods appropriate in these circumstances are called **nonparametric tests** because they do not depend on any assumptions about the parameters of the parent population.

In addition to not requiring assumptions about the parameters of the parent population, most nonparametric tests do not require a level of measurement as strong as that necessary for parametric tests. By "measurement" we mean the process of assigning numbers to objects or observations, the level of measurement being a function of the rules under which the numbers are assigned. The problem of measurement is so important to a discussion of nonparametric statistics that we begin this chapter by first studying the most common levels of measurement.

Measurement 16.2

The measurement of quantifiable information usually takes place on one of four levels, depending on the strength of the underlying scaling procedure used. The four major levels of measurement are represented by nominal, ordinal, interval, and ratio scales.

The weakest type of measurement is given by a **nominal scale,** which merely sorts objects into categories according to some distinguishing characteristic and gives each category a "name" (hence, *nominal*). Since classification on a nominal scale does not depend on the label or symbol assigned to each category, these symbols can be interchanged without affecting the information given by the scale. Classifying automobiles by makes constitutes a nominal scale, as does distinguishing Republican from Democratic voters, or apples from oranges. No quantitative characteristics may differentiate these objects; if it is necessary to permit quantitative distinctions, a measurement stronger than nominal must be assumed. In most nominal measurement, one is concerned with the number (or frequency) of observations falling in each of the categories.

An **ordinal scale** offers the next highest level of measurement, one expressing the *relationship of order.* Objects in an ordinal scale are characterized by relative rank, so that a typical relationship may be "higher," "greater," or "preferred to"; only the relations "greater than," "less than," or "equal to" have meaning in ordinal measurement. When a school of business is "ranked" nationally, for example, such a measurement implies an ordinal scale if it is impossible (or meaningless) to say how *much* better or worse this school is compared to others. Most subjective attributes of objects or persons (flavor, beauty, honesty) are difficult (if not impossible) to consider on a scale higher than the ordinal. Distinguishing service personnel by rank (captain, major) is another example of ordinal measurement.

A third type of scale is given by **interval measurement,** sometimes called **cardinal measurement.** Measurement on an interval scale assumes an exact knowledge of the quantitative difference between objects being scaled. That is, it must be possible to assign a number to each object in such a manner that the relative difference between them is reflected by the difference in the numbers. Any size of unit may be used in this type of measurement, as long as a one-unit change on the scale always reflects the same change in the object being scaled. The choice of a zero point (origin) for the data also can be made arbitrarily. Temperature measured on either a Celsius or a Fahrenheit scale represents interval measurement, as the choice of origin and unit for these scales is arbitrary. Temperature measured on an absolute scale, however, does not represent interval measurement, because this scale has a natural origin (the zero point is that at which all molecular motion ceases). As another example, most IQ measures represent interval scales, since there is no natural origin (zero intelligence?), and the choice of a unit can be made arbitrarily. The name "interval measurement" is used because this type of scale is concerned primarily with the distance *between* objects, that is, the "interval" between them.

The strongest type of measurement is represented by **ratio scales,** or scales that have all the properties of an interval scale *plus* a natural origin— only the unit of measurement is arbitrary. Fixing the origin (the zero point) permits comparisons not only of the intervals between objects, but of the absolute value of the numbers assigned to these objects. Hence, in this type of scale, "ratios" have meaning, and statements can be made to the effect that "*x* is twice the value of *y*." Profits, number of employees, and sales all represent ratio measurement since these scales have a common origin (the zero point).

Parametric vs. Nonparametric Tests

16.3

In addition to assuming some knowledge about the characteristics of the parent population (for example, normality), parametric statistical methods require measurement equivalent to at least an interval scale. That is, to find the means and variances necessary for these tests, one must be able to assume that it is meaningful to compare intervals. It makes no sense to add, subtract, divide, or multiply ordinal-scale values because the numbers on an ordinal scale have no meaning except to indicate rank order. There is no way to find, for example, the average between a captain and a major in terms of military rank.

To avoid the parametric assumptions normally required for tests based on interval or ratio scales, most nonparametric tests assume only nominal or ordinal data. That is, such tests ignore any properties of a given scale except ordinality. This means that if the data are, in fact, measurable on an interval scale, nonparametric tests waste (by ignoring) this knowledge about intervals. By wasting data such tests gain the advantage of not having to make parametric assumptions, but sacrifice power in terms of using all available information to reject a false null hypothesis. Nonparametric tests, for example, typically involve medians rather than means, because determining a mean requires interval data while determining a median requires only ordinal data.

We have already studied one type of nonparametric test in Chapters 4 and 9, when applications of the binomial distribution were presented. As we indicated then, the binomial distribution can be applied in an experiment in which all outcomes fall into one of two categories, and where there is a constant probability that an observation will fall into these two categories on each of a series of independent trials. The numbers of successes and failures resulting from Bernoulli trials represent measurement on only a nominal scale because these numbers reflect not the quantitative characteristics of any variable, but only the frequency of observations falling into two arbitrarily defined categories. In addition, the assumption of independence in these trials does not represent a parametric assumption. The binomial distribution is also useful in several types of nonparametric tests, as we will discuss in the following section.

In the sections to follow, we have divided the discussion of nonparametric techniques into the following headings:

1. Tests equivalent to the *t*-test for independent samples
2. Tests equivalent to the *t*-test for matched pairs
3. Goodness-of-fit tests
4. The chi-square test for independence
5. Correlation measures for ranked data

This grouping is rather arbitrary, since the tests involved could be (and often are) classified under many different headings. Also, we have presented only a few of the numerous nonparametric tests available. The reader interested in a more detailed description of the techniques in this area is referred to references 14 and 15.

Most statistical computer packages include options for calculating nonparametric test statistics. A number of these options are illustrated in the sections below. In other cases we have elected not to present the computer analysis because the process is either trivial or more complicated than it is worth. For example, to calculate a nonparametric correlation coefficient (Spearman's rho), the nonparametric approach is merely to convert the two variables to ranks and then use the Pearson product-moment measure (from Chapter 12).

Tests Equivalent to the *t*-Test for Independent Samples

16.4

Recall that in Chapter 9 we used the *t*-distribution to test for the difference between the means of two independently drawn samples (Section 9.5). There are a number of nonparametric equivalents to this test that can be used for data weaker than interval scaling, or when the researcher wishes to avoid the assumptions of the *t*-distribution. We will present two tests which can be used in such circumstances, the *Mann–Whitney U-test,* and the *Wald–Wolfowitz runs test.*

Mann–Whitney *U*-test

The Mann–Whitney *U*-test is one of the most powerful nonparametric tests, and is a useful alternative to the two-sample *t*-test described in Section 9.5. This test is designed to determine whether or not two samples were drawn from the same population. Thus, the null hypothesis is that the two populations are identical, and the alternative hypothesis is that they are not the same.

The first step in the Mann–Whitney *U*-test is to consider all the scores representing the two samples as a single set of observations, and to rank this entire group from the lowest to the highest score. If the null hypothesis that the two samples were drawn from the same population is true, then the observations from the two samples will be fairly well scattered throughout this ranking of both groups. If the two samples do not come from the same population, then the observations of one sample will tend to be bunched together, either at the low end of the rankings or at the high end of the rankings. Such patterns can be detected by calculating a value of *U,* which is the statistic for the Mann–Whitney test. The statistic *U* for the Mann–Whitney test is calculated by counting the number of times the values from one sample precede the values in the other sample. If the count is quite large or quite small relative to the value expected under the null hypothesis, then the two samples may not be randomly interspersed, but one set of observations may have come from a different population than the other.

To illustrate the Mann–Whitney *U*-test, suppose a stock analyst is interested in determining whether the price/earnings (*P/E*) ratio of small growth companies is related to the way such companies were rated in a *Business Week* article. The data in Table 16.1 represent a sample of 12 companies taken from the highest rated companies (group A) in the *Business Week* article, and 10 lower rated (group B) companies in this article. (Price was not a factor in the *Business Week* ratings.) The analyst has hypothesized that the *P/E* ratios for group B should be lower than those for group A (a one-sided test).

To calculate the value of the statistic *U* for these data, we need to determine the total number of times an observation in the *A* group precedes each

TABLE 16.1 *P/E* ratios for two groups of small companies

Group A (high rating)	Group B (lower rating)
12	5
12	5
13	7
13	7
13	8
14	10
17	11
22	15
23	18
24	101
28	
30	

TABLE 16.2

P/E ratio	5	5	7	7	8	10	11	12	12	13	13
Group	B	B	B	B	B	B	B	A	A	A	A
Rank	1	2	3	4	5	6	7	8	9	10	11

P/E ratio	13	14	15	17	18	22	23	24	28	30	101
Group	A	A	B	A	B	A	A	A	A	A	B
Rank	12	13	14	15	16	17	18	19	20	21	22

value in the B group. Suppose we call this number T_A. The format for calculating T_A is given in Table 16.2, where the values from A and B groups are arranged in ascending order in a single set of observations.

To calculate T_A, focus on each B-value and count the number of A-values lower than this value. For example, in Table 16.2, the first B-value is 5, and there are no A-values lower than 5. In fact, there are no A-values lower than the first seven B-values in Table 16.2. The eighth B-value has a P/E value of 15, and there are six A-values lower than 15. The next B-score is 18, and there are seven A-values lower than 18. Finally, the last B-value (of 101) is higher than all 12 A-values. Adding these values together gives T_A:

$$T_A = 0 + 0 + 0 + 0 + 0 + 0 + 0 + 6 + 7 + 12 = 25$$

To complete the Mann–Whitney U-test we also need to calculate the T_B, which is the total number of times a total value in the B group precedes each value in the A group. A good exercise for the reader would be to verify that

$$T_B = 7 + 7 + 7 + 7 + 7 + 7 + 8 + 9 + 9 + 9 + 9 + 9 = 95$$

The value of the Mann–Whitney statistic U is defined to be the minimum of the two values T_A, T_B. Thus, for this example,

$$U = \min \{T_A, T_B\} = \min \{25, 95\} = 25$$

Defining U this way means that the more similar the two samples are, the higher the value of U. Hence, H_0 should be rejected when U is relatively small. Since the value of U depends only on the ranks of the values in the two groups, it is possible to determine the probability of various values of U for specific sample sizes. For small samples these probabilities have been tabulated and are available in several sources (see reference 4 or 18). For instance, in our example, where $N_A = 12$ (group A) and $N_B = 10$ (group B), the critical region for a one-sided test using $\alpha = 0.025$, is $U \leq 29$; that is, $P(U \leq 29) = 0.025$. The fact that the observed value of U was 25 means the null hypothesis that the two populations do not differ can be rejected at the $\alpha = 0.025$ level of significance.

For large sample sizes the above procedure for calculating T_A and T_B can become quite tedious. Fortunately, however, these two values can be determined quite easily by using the combined ranking of all $n_A + n_B$ observations. If r_A = the sum of the ranks of the values from the A group, and r_B the sum of the ranks from the B group, then

$$T_A = n_A n_B + \frac{n_A(n_A + 1)}{2} - r_A$$

and

$$T_B = n_A n_B - T_A$$

We should point out that these formulas can be used for *any* values of n_A and n_B (not just large samples), and that it makes no difference which sample is labeled A and which one is labeled B. In our present example, the sums of the ranks of the A group are seen in Table 16.2 to be

$$r_A = 8 + 9 + 10 + 11 + 12 + 13 + 15 + 17 + 18 + 19 + 20 + 21$$
$$= 173$$

This means that

$$T_A = (12)(10) + (12)(13)/2 - 173 = 25$$

and

$$T_B = (12)(10) - 25 = 95$$

Tables of the critical values of U are available for sample sizes up to about 20. When n_A or n_B is larger than 20, and the two sample sizes are not too different in size, then the sampling distribution of U can be approximated with the following normal distribution:

Standardization of U for Mann–Whitney test: $z = \dfrac{U - E[U]}{\sigma_U}$

where

$$E[U] = \frac{n_A n_B}{2}$$

and

$$\sigma^2_{U} = \frac{n_A n_B(n_A + n_B + 1)}{12}$$

When ties occur in the Mann–Whitney test, they are usually treated by assigning the *average* of the ranks of those observations which are tied. Suppose, for example, that the observations corresponding to ranks two and three are identical. In this case, both observations would be given a rank of 2.5, which is the average of the ranks 2.0 and 3.0.

Using the Computer for the Mann–Whitney U-Test

The computer programs used to determine the Mann–Whitney U value are typically quite simple to use. Most programs assume the data are represented by a single variable, and the observations from the two groups are ranked as if

TABLE 16.3 The combined rankings for groups A and B (from Table 16.2)

P/E Ratio	Group	Rank	P/E Ratio	Group	Rank
12	A	8.5	5	B	1.5
12	A	8.5	5	B	1.5
13	A	11	7	B	3.5
13	A	11	7	B	3.5
13	A	11	8	B	5
14	A	13	10	B	6
17	A	15	11	B	7
22	A	17	15	B	14
23	A	18	18	B	16
24	A	19	101	B	22
28	A	20			
30	A	21			

they were a single group. Statistical programs can be used to rank the data. The data in Table 16.3 represent the file used to run the Mann–Whitney test. These data are the same as those shown in Table 16.2, using ranks. For example, the first two observations in group A have the value 12. In Table 16.2 the number 12 is ranked 8th and 9th; hence its average ranking is 8.5.

The computer output for using these data is shown below. Note that the program generates a z-statistic, and its associated p-value. The user must decide if the sample size is large enough to justify use of z-value. (In this case the "prob $= 0.0105$" is consistent with the p-value we found above, $p \leq 0.025$, even though the sample size is probably too small to use a normal approximation.)

Mann–Whitney U-Test

```
VARIABLE TESTED: GROUP A
SUM OF RANKS, GROUP 1 = 173   N1 = 12
SUM OF RANKS, GROUP 2 =  80   N2 = 10
U = 25
Z = -2.308, PROB. = .0105
```

The Wald–Wolfowitz Runs Test

Another test that can be used in place of the t-test for independent samples is the *Wald–Wolfowitz runs test*. Although this test is not as powerful as the Mann–Whitney U-test, it is useful in some situations where that test may not be appropriate. The null hypothesis in this test is the same as in the Mann–Whitney test—namely, that the two samples were drawn from the same population. Again, the alternative hypothesis is that the two populations differ in some respect. To test for differences between two samples, the observations from both samples are placed in a single group, and then ranked (just as they were in the Mann–Whitney test). The number of runs in this ranking can now be counted, where a run is a sequence of the ranked observations all of which come from the same sample. An indication of whether or not the two samples come from the same population is given by the total number of runs. A large number of runs will occur when the ranks corresponding to the two samples are fairly randomly intermixed, and hence in this case it is reasonable to accept H_0, that they came from the same population. A small number of runs will occur whenever there is some systematic difference between the two samples. For example, if the ranks corresponding to one sample are consistently lower than those in the other sample, this suggests that the central location of the two samples differs. Similarly, if one sample has a smaller *spread* than the other sample, then the ranks corresponding to this first sample will bunch in the center of the array, resulting in a low number of runs. Tables are available to determine whether a given total number of runs is small enough to reject H_0 (see Table XI in Appendix B).

To illustrate the Wald–Wolfowitz runs test, consider again the problem presented earlier, that of determining if the *P/E* ratios of two groups of stocks differ. As before, all 22 observations are arranged in order from lowest to highest (see Table 16.2). The number of runs in this array is shown below to be seven.

Value	5	5	7	7	8	10	11	12	12	13	13	13	14
Group	B	B	B	B	B	B	B	A	A	A	A	A	A
Run				1							2		

Value	15	17	18	22	23	24	28	30	101
Group	B	A	B	A	A	A	A	A	B
Run	3	4	5			6			7

From Table XI we see that the critical region for $\alpha = 0.05$, when $n_A = 12$ and $n_B = 10$, is $r \leq 7$, where r = the number of runs. Since our sample result of seven runs falls in this critical region, we can reject the null hypothesis that these two samples were drawn from the same population.

Table XI presents critical values *only* for small values of n_A and n_B. When both sample sizes are fairly large (greater than 20, for example), then the following normal approximation can be used:

Standardization of r for runs test: $z = \dfrac{r - E[r]}{\sigma_r}$

where

$$E[r] = \frac{2n_A n_B}{n_A + n_B} + 1$$

TABLE 16.4   Residuals from 40 months of industrial electrical use in Indiana

Month	KWH	Run	Month	KWH	Run	Month	KWH	Run
1	−7921	1	15	20679	6	29	40071	10
2	1143	2	16	12567	6	30	36953	10
3	−28521	3	17	24521	6	31	7393	10
4	−31836	3	18	37055	6	32	4800	10
5	−21773	3	19	−7499	7	33	44135	10
6	−25741	3	20	17975	8	34	29311	10
7	−34023	3	21	32791	8	35	33416	10
8	6098	4	22	30253	8	36	−33107	11
9	17746	4	23	18520	8	37	−43080	11
10	4120	4	24	16649	8	38	−32229	11
11	1542	4	25	−15209	9	39	−120465	11
12	−14631	5	26	6673	10	40	−36079	11
13	−36191	5	27	5182	10			
14	2411	6	28	36296	10			

and

$$\sigma_r^2 = \frac{2n_A n_B (2n_A n_B - n_A - n_B)}{(n_A + n_B)^2 (n_A + n_B - 1)}$$

When ties occur in this test, the usual procedure is to assign ranks so as to make the number of runs as large as possible (that is, ranks are assigned in a manner least favorable to rejecting H_0).

As another example of the runs test, recall the problem from Chapters 11 and 13 of testing the assumption that successive residuals in a regression analysis are uncorrelated. In this case we want to determine the number of runs of positive and negative residuals. The data in Table 16.4 represent the residuals from a simple least squares analysis of 40 months of industrial use of kilowatt hours (KWH) of electricity (in Indiana). Because these data were not corrected for seasonality, we might expect positive autocorrelation.

The computer output for these data, shown below, indicates that the null hypothesis of no autocorrelation can be rejected at $p = 0.001371$.

```
         WALD–WOLFOWITZ RUNS TEST
     VARIABLE TESTED : RESIDUALS
     CASES BELOW = 15   CASE ABOVE = 25
     RUNS BELOW =   6   RUNS ABOVE =  5
            TOTAL RUNS = 11
     Z = −2.995,   PROB. = 1.371E−03
```

16.5

The tests presented in this section represent the nonparametric alternatives to the matched-pairs *t*-test discussed in Section 9.5. Again, we must point out that these tests are not the only ones available for this purpose, nor is our way of classifying them the only way they can be grouped. Two tests are presented here, the sign test, and the Wilcoxon test.

Sign Test

A **sign test** is designed to determine whether significant differences exist between two samples that are related in such a manner that each observation from one sample can be matched with a specific observation from the other sample. For example, one may wish to study the behavior of identical twins under two "treatments," the "before and after" effect of a certain drug, or the attitudes of husbands in contrast to the attitudes of their wives. In the sign test, ordinal data is assumed, so that it is meaningful to rank the observations from one sample (for example, the husbands) only as higher than, equal to, or lower than their corresponding value in the other sample (the wife group). An easy way to record which sample has the higher value for each matched pair (husband versus wife) is to give each of these pairs a "sign," either a plus (+) sign representing the fact that the first sample has the higher value, or a minus (−) sign representing the fact that the second sample has the higher value. The null hypothesis is usually that the two samples were drawn from populations with the same median, so that the probability of a plus sign (p) or a minus sign (q) for each matched pair is $p = q = \frac{1}{2}$. This hypothesis can be tested, by using the binomial distribution, as illustrated in the following example.

Educators throughout the country are interested in determining if recent emphasis on SAT scores increased average scores during the 1980s. The data in Table 16.5 represent the average SAT scores in 1978 and 1988 in a sample of 10 states. To use the sign test we have assigned a "+" if the 1988 average is higher than 1978, and a "−" if the 1988 average is lower.

TABLE 16.5   Average SAT scores, by state, in 1978 and 1988

State	1978 Ave.	1988 Ave.	Sign	State	1978 Ave.	1988 Ave.	Sign
NH	932	933	+	NJ	870	893	+
OR	906	923	+	FL	889	890	+
AL	943	916	−	NY	902	889	−
VT	907	909	+	HA	866	888	+
CA	893	908	+	SC	787	838	+

Source: The College Board.

The null hypothesis (H_0: $p = 1/2$) is that the two years have the same median. The alternative hypothesis (H_0: $p > 1/2$) is that the 1988 median is higher. To use the binomial distribution to test these hypotheses we calculate a p-value in the manner presented in Chapter 9. For the sample in Table 16.5 the sample size is $n = 10$, $p = 1/2$, and the observed number of successes ($+$ signs) is $x = 8$. Thus, the appropriate p-value is $P(x \geq 8 | n = 10, p = 1/2)$. From Table I in Appendix B, this probability is 0.0547. If the decision maker has an α-level of 0.0547 or lower, then H_0 must be accepted; in other words, this may not be enough information to conclude that SAT scores have improved.

The computer output for this problem, shown below, gives the same p-value, 0.05469.

```
       BINOMIAL DISTRIBUTION
          N = 10          P = .5
                        CUMULATIVE
       X      P(X)     PROBABILITY

       8    .04395       .04395
       9    .00976       .05371
      10    .00098       .05469
```

As in the binomial test, the null hypothesis in the sign test need not specify that $p = q = \frac{1}{2}$. Suppose a random sample of 10 people have been interviewed and asked to rate each of two products (A and B) on a scale from 0 to 100. We might have hypothesized that the probability of A being preferred to B is not $\frac{1}{2}$, but some other value, say $\frac{3}{4}$ (that is, $P(A > B) = \frac{3}{4}$), the alternative to this hypothesis being that $P(A > B) < \frac{3}{4}$. The sample results of the ten interviews are given in Table 16.6.

TABLE 16.6

Consumer	Product A score	Product B score	Sign
1	75	58	+
2	85	92	−
3	61	69	−
4	55	50	+
5	82	71	+
6	88	84	+
7	45	78	−
8	90	79	+
9	63	69	−
10	71	80	−

Under the null hypothesis, the probability of five (or fewer) +'s is (from Table I, Appendix B)

$$P(x \leq 5) = 0.078$$

It is not possible, on the basis of this sample, to reject the null hypothesis H_0: $p = \frac{3}{4}$ at levels of significance less than 0.078.

One of the problems that might occur in a sign test is that there may be one (or more) matched pairs in which the two scores are identical (a tie). In the case of a tie, the usual procedure is to drop that matched pair from the analysis, and simply work with the smaller sample size. Note that the sign test does not require knowledge about the *magnitude* of the difference between the matched pairs, as does the *t*-test. If these differences *are* known, then a more powerful nonparametric test is the Wilcoxon test.

The Wilcoxon Test

The **Wilcoxon test** has the same null hypothesis as the sign test—namely, that the median difference between two populations equals zero. The test in this case, however, takes into account the magnitude of the difference between each matched pair. These magnitudes are first ranked according to their *absolute* value. Then each of these ranks is given either a (+) sign or a (−) sign, depending on whether sample A was larger than B (the plus sign) or sample B larger than A (the minus sign). Now, if the null hypothesis is true, we would expect the sum of those ranks with + signs to be about equal to the sum of those ranks with minus signs. If the two sums differ by very much, we would infer that the two populations are not identical.

Suppose we let T_+ equal the sum of the positive ranks and T_- equal the sum of the *absolute value* of the negative ranks. The Wilcoxon test is based on the statistic T, which is defined to be the *minimum* of T_+ and T_-; that is, $T = \min\{T_+, T_-\}$. Critical values of T for small samples are given in Table XII in Appendix B.

To illustrate the Wilcoxon test, consider the data in Table 16.7 representing a bank where two different systems were under study for processing checks. Eleven clerks used to determine if one of the two methods (labeled A and B) permitted faster processing of checks. Table 16.7 presents the number of checks processed by each clerk in the time period allocated.

Note in the final column of Table 16.7 that we assigned the average of the two ranks to the difference scores that are tied (a difference of 3). If some difference score had been 0, this matched pair would be dropped from the analysis. For the present data, the value of T_+ is

$$T_+ = 10 + 2.5 + 11 + 5 + 2.5 + 1 + 7 + 8 + 9 = 56$$

and

$$T_- = 4 + 6 = 10$$

TABLE 16.7   Checks processed under two methods

Clerk	Method A	Method B	Difference	Rank of difference	Signed rank
1	129	115	14	10	+10
2	111	108	3	2.5	+2.5
3	118	123	−5	4	−4
4	120	104	16	11	+11
5	116	110	6	5	+5
6	101	98	3	2.5	+2.5
7	107	106	1	1	+1
8	127	119	8	7	+7
9	105	95	10	8	+8
10	123	130	−7	6	−6
11	113	101	12	9	+9

Hence, $T = \min \{56, 10\} = 10$. From Table XII the critical region when $\alpha = 0.05$ for $n = 11$ matched pairs is $T \leq 11$ (assuming a two-sided alternative); that is, we reject H_0 whenever T is 11 or smaller. Since our calculated value is $T = 10$, we reject the null hypothesis of no difference between the two populations.

When the number of matched pairs (n) is not small (for example, $n > 8$), then the distribution of T can be shown to be approximately normally distributed:

$$\text{Standardization of } T \text{ for Wilcoxon test: } z = \frac{T - E[T]}{\sigma_T}$$

where

$$E[T] = \frac{n(n + 1)}{4} \quad \text{and} \quad \sigma_T^2 = \frac{n(n + 1)(2n + 1)}{24}$$

Problems

16.1 Distinguish between parametric and nonparametric statistical tests. Under what circumstances is each type most appropriate? Give several specific examples of problems where a nonparametric test would be more appropriate than a parametric test.

16.2 Briefly describe and distinguish between the four levels of measurement—nominal, ordinal, interval, and ratio—giving several examples of each type of scale.

16.3 Identify each of the following numbers as representing measurement on either nominal, ordinal, interval, or ratio scales:

a) the numbers designating years (such as 1991, 1992, 1993);

b) the numbers representing zip codes;

c) the Dow-Jones Industrial Average;

d) social security numbers.

16.4 Two groups of managers were given a test on communications skills. There were 10 students in the first group (A) and eight in the second (B). Their scores are shown below:

$$A: \quad 25, 30, 42, 44, 58, 59, 75, 79, 87, 90$$
$$B: \quad 45, 49, 62, 63, 68, 69, 69, 71$$

a) Use these data to calculate the statistic U of the Mann–Whitney test. What null hypothesis is being tested in this case? Can H_0 be rejected if the critical value for $n_1 = 10$, $n_2 = 8$ is 17 at the 0.05 level of significance (a two-tailed test)?

b) Use the runs test to determine whether the null hypothesis that the samples came from the same population can be rejected.

c) Use a computer program to solve parts (a) and (b) of this problem.

16.5 A study was conducted using the Mann–Whitney U-test on the number of days absent from work for a group of smokers (group A) and a group of non-smokers (group B). In this sample $n_A = n_B = 40$, and the calculated value of $U = 300$, with the smoking group having more absences. Use a normal approximation to determine whether or not these samples can be considered to be drawn from the same population.

16.6 When the Wald–Wolfowitz runs test was applied to the data of Problem 16.5, the result was a total of 30 runs. Use a normal approximation to test the hypothesis that the samples can be considered to be drawn from the same population.

16.7 An in article the *Wall Street Journal* presented both the 1982 and the 1987 percentage of operating expenses spent by major airlines on direct maintenance. These percentages are shown in the table to the left. Use a sign test to test the null hypothesis at $\alpha = 0.05$ that the 1982 percentages are no different from the 1987 percentages. At what level of significance can H_0 be rejected for a two-sided test? At what level can H_0 be rejected if we had hypothesized that the 1987 percentages would be higher?

16.8 **a)** Use the Wilcoxon test on the data in Problem 16.7. Use Table XII of Appendix B to accept or reject H_0, assuming a two-sided alternative.

b) Use the normal approximation to the Wilcoxon test to test the same hypothesis as in part (a). Do your answers agree?

16.9 A *Wall Street Journal* advertisement gave overall customer satisfaction with five 386 PCs and five 286 PCs. The models ranked included IBM PS/2, Zenith

Maintenance: Percentage of operating expenses

	1987	1982
Eastern	7.8	4.6
Northwest	7.3	5.2
Continental	6.9	4.0
USAir	6.5	6.6
Piedmont	6.4	5.1
TWA	6.1	4.6
American	6.1	3.8
United	6.0	3.3
Pan Am	4.6	2.9
Delta	4.3	3.4

Source: Department of Transportation Studies

Model-Z, Dell System, AST Premium, and Compaq Deskpro. Without identifying vendors, the satisfaction scores were as follows:

Vendor	286 score	386 score
1	83	84
2	78	81
3	78	79
4	75	78
5	80	78

a) Use a sign test to determine whether customer satisfaction differs across the two systems, using $\alpha = 0.05$. Specify H_0 and H_a and report a p-value.

b) Repeat part (a) using a t-test for matched pairs (see Chapter 9).

16.10 In the 1988 presidential election an October poll by one of the major television networks surveyed 1500 randomly selected people who indicated they intended to vote. Of this number, 780 said they intended to vote for George Bush.

a) Use a computer program to determine the p-value for rejecting H_0: $p = 1/2$ in favor of H_a: $p > 1/2$, where p = proportion who will vote for Bush.

b) Use the computer output below to determine the critical value for testing H_0: $p = 0.52$ against the alternative H_a: $p > 0.52$ at the 0.01 level of significance.

```
               BINOMIAL DISTRIBUTION
            n = 1500            P = .52
             CUMULATIVE                      CUMULATIVE
  X    P(X)   PROBABILITY    X    P(X)   PROBABILITY
 824  .00155   .00155       838  .00023   .01099
 825  .00138   .00293       839  .00020   .01119
 826  .00122   .00415       840  .00017   .01135
 827  .00108   .00522       841  .00014   .01149
 828  .00095   .00617       842  .00012   .01162
 829  .00083   .00700       843  .00010   .01172
 830  .00073   .00773       844  .00009   .01180
 831  .00064   .00837       845  .00007   .01197
 832  .00055   .00892       846  .00006   .01194
 833  .00048   .00941       847  .00005   .01199
 834  .00042   .00982       848  .00004   .01203
 835  .00036   .01018       849  .00003   .01206
 836  .00031   .01049       850  .00003   .01209
 837  .00027   .01076
```

16.11 A company is considering a sales promotion where customers receive a $2.00 rebate with a proof-of-purchase receipt. One estimate is that approximately 10% of the customers purchasing the product will ask for a rebate. In a test involving 100 randomly selected customers, 20 customers asked for the rebate. Is this sample evidence sufficient to reject the null hypothesis H_0: $p = 0.10$ in favor of H_a: $p \geq 0.10$?

16.12 A company advertising on national television claims that taste tests indicate their product is preferred by a 3:1 ratio over the leading competitor. In a sample of 100 randomly selected people conducted by the Consumer Protection Agency, 62 rated this product better than the other brand.

a) Formulate the appropriate null and alternative hypotheses.

b) Report a p-value using a computer. Would you reject H_0 if $\alpha = 0.01$?

c) Does the computer output below agree with your answer to part (b)? If not, explain why.

```
     BINOMIAL DISTRIBUTION
        N = 100        P = .75
                     CUMULATIVE
     X    P (X)     PROBABILITY
     55   .00001      .00001
     56   .00002      .00002
     57   .00004      .00006
     58   .00008      .00014
     59   .00018      .00032
     60   .00036      .00068
     61   .00071      .00140
     62   .00135      .00274
```

16.13 Adverse publicity regarding airline flights not arriving on time resulted in better performance by some airlines. The data below were published by the U.S. Department of Transportation.

a) Use a sign test to determine if August and September differ significantly using $\alpha = 0.05$. Write the hypotheses being tested and report a p-value.

b) Repeat part (a) using the Wilcoxon test.

Percentage of flights arriving within 15 minutes of scheduled time

Airline	Aug.	Sept.
America West	91.5	92.9
Eastern	80.8	90.5
Southwest	90.5	89.3
Delta	86.9	88.0
American	85.9	87.8
Alaska	83.7	86.9
Continental	86.8	86.3
United	81.0	84.0
USAir	75.0	83.7

16.14 In a report by the major real estate broker Coldwell Banker, office vacancy rates for the second quarter of 1988 were compared with the vacancy rates for the second quarter of 1987.

Area	2nd quarter 1987	2nd quarter 1988
Atlanta	18.0%	17.5%
Cincinnati	14.8	14.0
Dallas	27.9	28.2
Hartford	14.9	13.4
Indianapolis	16.0	20.4
Los Angeles	16.9	15.5
Nashville	21.0	18.9
New Orleans	26.8	25.9
Philadelphia	12.8	14.8
St. Louis	16.4	15.1
Seattle	15.6	13.7
Tucson	28.0	24.4

a) Use a sign test to determine if the vacancy rate decreased between these two years. Write the hypotheses, and then report a p-value. Would you accept or reject H_0 using $\alpha = 0.05$?

b) Repeat part (a) using the Wilcoxon test.

16.15 Use a runs test on the errors shown in Table 14.18 for domestic passenger miles. Specify the null and alternative hypotheses.

16.16 According to the Committee for the Study of the American Electorate, voter turnout for the 1988 election was significantly less than for the 1984 election. A random selection of eight states resulted in the percentage of voters listed below. Do these data support the committee's conclusions? Use a sign test and a computer program, if a program is available to you; otherwise use Table I.

Percentage of voters		
	1984	1988
Ariz.	45.2	43.9
Ill.	57.1	52.4
Miss.	52.2	48.9
N.H.	53.0	53.7
Ore.	61.8	53.3
Pa.	54.0	49.4
Texas	47.2	49.4
Wis.	63.5	61.3

TABLE 16.8

	RESIDUAL		RESIDUAL		RESIDUAL		RESIDUAL
1	−28331	9	−8452	17	18013	25	−12002
2	−16582	10	16904	18	28437	26	−20328
3	−28264	11	−3179	19	18534	27	−44464
4	−1258	12	11576	20	−16006	28	−16333
5	9656	13	16106	21	−28371	29	6097
6	22419	14	15509	22	8742	30	19747
7	9382	15	12973	23	−10764	31	22465
8	4398	16	−3626	24	−2908		

WALD–WOLFOWITZ RUNS TEST
CASES BELOW = 15   CASES ABOVE = 16
RUNS BELOW = 6   RUNS ABOVE = 6
TOTAL RUNS = 12
Z = −1.640,   PROB. = .0505

16.17 The values in Table 16.8 represent the residuals from a regression analysis involving 31 months of a time series describing electrical usage.

a) Count the number of runs. Does there appear to be a problem with auto-correlation? Explain.

b) Interpret *all* parts of the computer output following the data. Would you reject the null hypothesis that the residuals are random?

c) Run a computer program to duplicate the Wald–Wolfowitz output in Table 16.8.

Goodness-of-Fit
Tests

16.6

The tests presented thus far represent nonparametric procedures designed to see how closely two *sample* probability distributions correspond to one another in order to test the hypothesis that they came from the same *population* probability distribution. In many statistical problems the researcher is interested in a closely related problem, that of determining how closely an observed (sample) probability distribution fits some theoretical probability distribution. In this section, we will present two tests designed for this purpose, called *goodness-of-fit tests.*

We have already studied one type of goodness-of-fit test in our applications of the binomial distribution. The binomial distribution is a goodness-of-fit test, in the sense that it compares the frequency of sample observations in two categories with the frequency of observations expected under the null hypothesis. The binomial distribution is used to determine how "good" the fit is: for close fits we accept H_0; otherwise H_0 is rejected. In addition to being able to use the binomial test on problems of this nature, it is possible to use a statistical test based on the chi-square distribution. This test, called the **chi-square test,** has the advantage (over the binomial) of being generalizable to problems involving more than just the two nominal categories used in a binomial test. When there are just two categories, however, the binomial test is preferred because it is more powerful.

The Chi-Square Test

The chi-square variable is used in this situation to test how closely a set of observed frequencies corresponds to a given set of expected frequencies. The expected frequencies can be thought of as the average number of values expected to fall in each category, based on some theoretical probability distribution. For example, one probability distribution that is often useful is to assume that the expected frequencies in the various categories will all be equal. The observed frequencies can be thought of as a *sample* of values from some probability distribution. The chi-square variable can be used to test whether the observed and expected frequencies are close enough so we can conclude they represent the same probability distribution. For this reason the test is called a "goodness-of-fit" test.

   Suppose we assume there are c categories ($c > 1$) and the expected frequency in each of these categories is denoted as $E_1, E_2, \ldots, E_c$, or equivalently, $E_i (i = 1, 2, \ldots, c)$. Similarly, the c observed frequencies will be denoted as $O_1, O_2, \ldots, O_c$, or $O_i (i = 1, 2, \ldots, c)$. To test the goodness of fit of the observed frequencies (O_i) to the expected frequencies (E_i), we use the following statistic, which can be shown to be approximately a chi-square variable with ($c - 1$) degrees of freedom.*

$$\text{Test statistic for goodness of fit: } \chi^2_{(c-1 \text{ d.f.})} = \sum_{i=1}^{c} \frac{(O_i - E_i)^2}{E_i} \qquad (16.1)$$

   Formula (16.1) measures the goodness of fit between the values of O_i and E_i as follows: When the fit is good (that is, when O_i and E_i are generally close), then the numerator of (16.1) will be relatively small; hence the value of χ^2 will be low. Conversely, if O_i and E_i are not close, then the numerator of (16.1) will be relatively large, and the value of χ^2 will also be large. Thus, the critical region for the test statistic given by (16.1) will always be in the *upper* tail of the χ^2 distribution because we want to reject the null hypothesis whenever the difference between E_i and O_i is relatively large. For example, suppose in a particular problem involving 16 categories, the fit between the 16 values of O_i

---

*Technically, the chi-square distribution is only an approximation to the distribution of the test statistic (16.1).

TABLE 16.9   Monthly new car sales

	Months						Total
	Jan.	Feb.	Mar.	Apr.	May	June	
Expected sales (E_i)	25	25	25	25	25	25	150
Observed sales (O_i)	27	18	15	24	36	30	150

and E_i from Formula (16.1) yields $\chi^2 = 30.0$. From Table V in the row corresponding to $c - 1 = 15$. d.f., we find that $P(\chi^2 \geq 25) = 0.05$. Because the calculated value (of 30) exceeds the critical value (of 25), we can reject the null hypothesis that the observed values came from the same distribution as the expected values.

To illustrate the use of the chi-square test, suppose that an automobile dealer, in trying to arrange vacations for the salespersons, decides to test the (null) hypothesis that the sales of new cars were equally distributed over the first six months of last year. The expected frequency distribution thus specifies that $E_1 = E_2 = \cdots = E_6$. The alternative hypothesis is that sales were *not* equally distributed over the six months. If we assume that the dealership sold 150 new cars in this period, the expected frequency under the null hypothesis would be 25 cars sold in each month. The expected and observed sales are given in Table 16.9.

The null and alternative hypotheses are

$$H_0: E_1 = E_2 = \cdots = E_5 = 25$$
$$H_a: \text{The frequencies are not all equal}$$

The chi-square statistic for this example has $c - 1 = 5$ degrees of freedom. If we let $\alpha = 0.025$, then the appropriate critical region, shown in Fig. 16.1, is derived from the row $\nu = 5$ in Table V. From this figure we see that the

Figure 16.1
Chi-square critical region for $\nu = 5$, $\alpha = 0.025$.

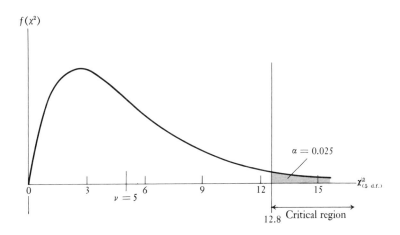

null hypothesis will be rejected in favor of the alternative hypothesis of unequal frequencies in monthly sales if the calculated value χ^2 exceeds 12.8.

The value of χ^2 can now be calculated as follows:

$$\chi^2 = \frac{(27-25)^2}{25} + \frac{(18-25)^2}{25} + \frac{(15-25)^2}{25}$$
$$+ \frac{(24-25)^2}{25} + \frac{(36-25)^2}{25} + \frac{(30-25)^2}{25}$$
$$= 12.0$$

Thus, at the significance level of $\alpha = 0.025$, we *fail to reject* the null hypothesis that all monthly sales are equal (that deviations from sales equal to 25 are due to random occurrences). However, from Table V, note that for $c - 1 = 5$ degrees of freedom and $\alpha = 0.05$, the critical value for the test would be 11.1. Therefore, if $\alpha = 0.05$ had been selected as the level of significance for rejecting H_0, then the null hypothesis *would* have been rejected. In this case, the choice of the α-level is crucial to the decision. The costs of having too many or too few salespersons on hand in a given month should be given more consideration before setting α at an arbitrary level. A larger number of past months may be sampled if the sales pattern is presumed not to have changed. For example, the sum of sales for the past three years in the month of January, and February, and March, and so on, might be used to test for equal monthly sales.

In using the chi-square distribution in these circumstances, one must be careful not to use categories having small expected frequencies. The rule of thumb in chi-square tests is generally that the expected frequency should be at least *five;* recent research, however, has indicated that an expected value of *one or more* in each category is usually sufficient. The easiest way to increase the expected frequencies in a chi-square test is by collapsing two or more adjacent categories, as the following example illustrates.

Consider again the supermarket example from Chapter 4 (Section 4.6). The observed and expected frequencies shown in Table 16.10 are derived from Table 4.6, except that now we have collapsed the categories 9, 10, 11, 12, 13 into a single category labeled ≥ 9. This ensures that all expected frequencies are ≥ 1. For example, from the probabilities in column 3 of Table 4.6, we know that the probability of 0 arrivals is 0.0224. Over 100 observations, the theoretical or expected frequency would be $100(0.0224) = 2.24$. Similarly, from Table 4.6 the probability $P(x \geq 9) = 0.0159$; hence, the expected frequency for the category ≥ 9 is $100(0.0159) = 1.590$. All such theoretical frequencies are shown in Table 16.10.

From the last column in Table 16.10, we see that

$$\chi^2 = \frac{\sum (O_i - E_i)^2}{E_i} = 4.2130$$

For this problem, there are $c - 1 = 9$ d.f.; the critical value from Table V for $\alpha = 0.05$ is thus 16.9. Since our observed value 4.2130 is less than 16.9, we

TABLE 16.10   Calculating chi-square

Arrivals	Observed frequency (O_i)	Expected frequency (E_i)	$(O_i - E_i)^2/E_i$
0	1	2.240	0.6864
1	8	8.500	0.0294
2	19	16.150	0.5029
3	23	20.460	0.3153
4	17	19.440	0.3063
5	15	14.770	0.0036
6	8	9.360	0.1976
7	3	5.080	0.8517
8	3	2.410	0.0695
≥ 9	3	1.590	1.2503
	100	100.000	4.2130

conclude that the sample probability distribution is a close fit to the theoretical distribution; that is, we accept H_0 (that these distributions are the same).

The Kolmogorov–Smirnov Test

We showed above how the χ^2 test can be used to measure goodness of fit when the data is in nominal form (categories). When the data is in at least *ordinal* form, then the **Kolmogorov–Smirnov** test can be used. This test has the advantage over the χ^2 test in that it is generally more powerful, it is easier to compute, and it does not require a minimum expected frequency in each cell.

The Kolmogorov–Smirnov test involves a comparison between the theoretical and sample *cumulative* frequency distributions. To make this comparison, the data is put into classes (or categories) that have been arrayed from the lowest class to the highest class. Suppose we use the symbol F_i to denote the cumulative relative frequency for each category of the theoretical distribution, and S_i to denote the comparable value for the sample frequency. The Kolmogorov-Smirnov test is based on the maximum value of the absolute difference between F_i and S_i. If we denote the statistic for this test as D, then

> *Statistic for Kolmogorov–Smirnov test:* $D = \underset{i}{\text{Max}} \left| F_i - S_i \right|$

The decision to reject the null hypothesis (that the sample was drawn from the theoretical distributions) is based on the value of D: the larger D is, the more confidence we have that H_0 is false. Note that this is a one-tail test, since the value of D is always positive, and we reject H_0 for large values of D. Table XIII in Appendix B gives the critical values of D for various probability values.

To illustrate the Kolmogorov–Smirnov test, let's once again consider the supermarket data from Chapter 4. In this case, we repeat the data from Table 4.6, which shows the relative frequencies for both the observed and theoretical (Poisson) distribution. Table 16.11 repeats these values and includes the cumulative values F_i and S_i, and each difference $|F_i - S_i|$.

From the last column in Table 16.11, we see that the maximum value of $|F_i - S_i|$ is $D = 0.0365$. Since the sample size in the example is $n = 100$, the last column of Table XIII in Appendix B gives the appropriate critical values of D: for $\alpha = 0.01$, $1.63/\sqrt{n} = 1.63/\sqrt{100} = 0.163$. Because $D = 0.0365$ is less than this critical value, we do not reject H_0. As we found before, the agreement between the *observed* and *theoretical* values is sufficiently close for us to believe they represent the same distribution.

Note that the Kolmogorov–Smirnov test uses the *ordinal* nature of the classes, while the χ^2 test makes use of only the *nominal* properties of this data. We should also point out that the Kolmogorov–Smirnov test can also be used for testing the goodness of fit between two *sample* cumulative relative frequency distributions. In this case, the procedure is exactly the same as before, except that the statistic D has a different distribution (which we shall not present).

TABLE 16.11

Arrivals	Observed relative frequency	Cumulative observed frequency (S_i)	Poisson values (theoretical relative frequency)	Cumulative relative frequency (F_i)	$|F_i - S_i|$
0	0.010	0.0100	0.0224	0.0224	0.0124
1	0.080	0.0900	0.0850	0.1074	0.0174
2	0.190	0.2800	0.1615	0.2689	0.0111
3	0.230	0.5100	0.2046	0.4735	0.0365
4	0.170	0.6800	0.1944	0.6679	0.0121
5	0.150	0.8300	0.1477	0.8156	0.0144
6	0.080	0.9100	0.0936	0.9092	0.0008
7	0.030	0.9400	0.0508	0.9600	0.0200
8	0.030	0.9700	0.0241	0.9841	0.0141
9	0.020	0.9900	0.0102	0.9943	0.0043
10	0.010	1.0000	0.0039	0.9982	0.0018
11	0.000	1.0000	0.0013	0.9995	0.0005
12	0.000	1.0000	0.0004	0.9999	0.0001
13	0.000	1.0000	0.0001	1.0000	0.0000

**Chi-Square
Test for
Independence**

16.7

In the chi-square test of Section 16.6, a set of *observed* values, classified into *c* categories according to a *single* attribute, were tested for goodness of fit against a set of *expected* values. At this time, we extend that analysis by assuming that more than one attribute is under investigation, and we want to determine whether or not these attributes are independent. For example, instead of investigating automobile sales relative to the single attribute "months of the year," we might wish to construct a test to determine if the attributes "car model" (such as sedans versus hatchbacks) and the attribute "months of the year" are *independent* in their effect on sales. Similarly, in the supermarket example, we might have been interested in determining whether or not the pattern of arrivals per minute is independent of the attribute "days of the week."

  In examples of this type, a direct extension of the chi-square test of Section 16.6 can be used to test the null hypothesis that the attributes under investigation are independent. For such problems there is generally no "theory" available to use in determining the expected frequency for each category. However, we can use the observed data to calculate expected frequencies, under the assumption that the null hypothesis (of independence) is true. For example, suppose in our car-sales example that 20% of the total number of sales fall in the month of June. If the null hypothesis is true, namely, that car model (sedan, hatchback) and months of the year are independent, then we would expect about 20% of all sedan sales to fall in June, and 20% of all hatchback sales to fall in June. The same relationship should hold for all six months under study. If the alternative hypothesis is true (these attributes are not independent), then we would expect to find differences in the proportion of sedan and hatchback sales across the six months.

  To continue the example, let's assume that out of the 150 cars sold over the six-month period, 50 were sedans and 100 were hatchbacks. Since June sales represented 20% of this total, if H_0 is true, the dealer would thus "expect" 20% of the 50 sedan sales to occur in June, which would be $0.20(50) = 10$ cars. Similarly, he would "expect" 20% of the 100 hatchback sales to occur in June, or $0.20(100) = 20$ cars. Note that he expects to sell 10 sedans plus 20 hatchbacks, for a total of 30 cars, which is exactly 20% of the 150 cars sold. Also, notice that he expects in June to sell hatchbacks and sedans in a ratio of 2 to 1. This ratio exactly agrees with his total sales ratio of 100 hatchbacks to 50 sedans (or 2 to 1). The entire set of expected frequencies (E_{ij}) and observed frequencies (O_{ij}) for this problem are given in Table 16.12. In each cell the expected frequency is in the upper left corner and the observed frequency is in the lower right corner, thus:

TABLE 16.12   Observed and expected sales of automobiles

	Jan.	Feb.	Mar.	Apr.	May	June	Total
Month							
Sedans	9 / 3	6 / 3	5 / 4	8 / 12	12 / 16	10 / 12	50
Hatchbacks	18 / 24	12 / 15	10 / 11	16 / 12	24 / 20	20 / 18	100
Totals	27	18	15	24	36	30	150

We perform the chi-square test for this type of problem exactly as we did before, except that we now sum over all cells in *two* rows rather than just one.

$$\chi^2 = \sum_{i=1}^{2} \sum_{j=1}^{6} \frac{(O_{ij} - E_{ij})^2}{E_{ij}}$$

$$= \frac{(3-9)^2}{9} + \frac{(3-6)^2}{6} + \cdots + \frac{(18-20)^2}{20}$$

$$= 14.15$$

The number of degrees of freedom for this problem is 5, for if the marginal totals in Table 16.12 are considered fixed, then only 5 of the 12 cells are free to vary at any one time. The probability $P(\chi_5^2 > 14.15)$ for $\nu = 5$ degrees of freedom lies between 0.025 and 0.01 (see Table V). Thus, for any level of significance higher than 0.025, the null hypothesis that the attributes "car model" and "months of the year" are independent is rejected and we conclude that the proportion of sedans to hatchbacks *does* vary from month to month. If α had been known in advance, then the calculated value of $\chi^2 (= 14.15)$ is compared to the critical value in Table V.

The chi-square test illustrated above can be used for problems involving any number of categories for each attribute. If there are c columns and r rows in a problem, then the appropriate chi-square statistic is given by Formula (16.2).

> *Chi-square statistic for independence:*
>
> $$\chi^2_{(r-1)(c-1)} = \sum_{i=1}^{r} \sum_{j=1}^{c} \frac{(O_{ij} - E_{ij})^2}{E_{ij}}$$ (16.2)

The number of degrees of freedom for this χ^2 statistic can be determined by noting that in calculating the expected frequency for each cell we must assume that the marginal totals are fixed quantities. This means that one degree of freedom is lost for each row and each column, so that the total number of degrees of freedom is $(r - 1)(c - 1)$.

Calculating the expected frequency E_{ij} for any cell follows the same process used above; that is, the total for the row involved is multiplied by the total for the column involved, and this product is divided by the total number of observations. For example, in Table 16.12 the expected frequency for row 2, column 3 $(E_{2,3} = 10)$ is determined by multiplying the row 2 total (= 100) by the column 3 total (= 15), and then dividing this product by the grand total (= 150):

$$E_{2,3} = (\text{row 2 total})(\text{col. 2 total})/\text{grand total} = (100)(15)/150$$
$$= 10$$

We remind the reader of the rule of thumb that the expected frequency in each cell must be at least 1.0. If necessary, adjacent cells should be combined to assure that $E_{ij} \geq 1.0$.

Using the Computer to Solve Chi-Square Problems

To illustrate both Formula (16.2) as well as the use of the computer for chi-square problems, consider the problem of trying to determine whether the prices of certain stocks on the New York Stock Exchange are independent of the industry to which they belong. Using *Business Week* data, four categories of industries are investigated (I = automotive, II = banks, III = electrical and electronics, and IV = manufacturing); the stock prices in these industries are classified into one of three categories ("high," "medium," and "low"). The observed frequencies in each cell from this analysis are shown in Table 16.13.

TABLE 16.13   Observed frequencies for stock problem

	Industry				
	I	II	III	IV	Total
High	15	8	10	12	45
Medium	20	16	12	12	60
Low	5	6	3	11	25
Total	40	30	25	35	130

A chi-square computer program will easily generate the expected frequencies for these data, as well as the χ^2 test statistic. Table 16.14 shows such an output. In Table 16.14,

1. the first entry in each cell is the expected frequency;
2. the second entry is the expected frequency expressed as a percentage of the total frequency;

TABLE 16.14   Expected values for stock example

```
-------------CROSSTAB / CHI-SQUARE TESTS------------
EXPECTED VALUES (Cell format: count/ percent:total/ percent:row/ percent:col)
                    |   1  |   2  |   3  |   4  | Total
              ------------------------------------------------
                    | 13.85| 10.38|  8.65| 12.12| 45.00
                1   | 10.65|  7.99|  6.66|  9.32| 34.62
                    | 30.77| 23.08| 19.23| 26.92|
                    | 34.62| 34.62| 34.62| 34.62|
                    |      |      |      |      |
              ------------------------------------------------
                    | 18.46| 13.85| 11.54| 16.15| 60.00
                2   | 14.20| 10.65|  8.88| 12.42| 46.15
                    | 30.77| 23.08| 19.23| 26.92|
                    | 46.15| 46.15| 46.15| 46.15|
                    |      |      |      |      |
              ------------------------------------------------
                    |  7.69|  5.77|  4.81|  6.73| 25.00
                3   |  5.92|  4.44|  3.70|  5.18| 19.23
                    | 30.77| 23.08| 19.23| 26.92|
                    | 19.23| 19.23| 19.23| 19.23|
                    |      |      |      |      |
              ------------------------------------------------
            Total | 40.00| 30.00| 25.00| 35.00| 130.00
                    | 30.77| 23.08| 19.23| 26.92| 100.00
        CHI-SQUARE = 6.743,    D.F. = 6,    PROB. = .3452
```

3. the third entry is the expected frequency expressed as a percentage of the row total; and

4. the final entry is the expected frequency expressed as a percentage of the column total.

The chi-square statistic of $\chi^2 = 6.743$, with $(r-1)(c-1) = (2)(3) = 6$ degrees of freedom, results in a p-value of 0.3452. Hence we cannot reject the null hypothesis that industry and price are independent.

Nonparametric Measures of Correlation

16.8

Contingency Coefficient

The Pearson product–moment method of correlation described in Chapter 12 assumes that the variable under consideration can be measured on an interval scale. But as we have pointed out in this chapter, interval measurement may be inappropriate or even impossible in a variety of circumstances. If only nominal data are available, then the value of χ^2 can be used to provide a measure of the degree of association between two variables. When there is no association between two variables, then the observed frequency in each cell of a chi-square table should closely correspond to the expected frequency in that cell, because expected frequencies are calculated under the assumption (the null hypothesis) that the two variables are not related. The higher the degree of association between the variables, the larger will be the discrepancy between the observed and expected cell frequencies, and hence the larger the value of χ^2. It is convenient, in defining a nonparametric measure of correlation, to have a statistic that equals zero when there is no association between the variables and one that approaches 1.0 as the amount of association increases. One such statistic, called the **contingency coefficient** and denoted by the letter *C*, is defined as follows:

$$\text{Contingency coefficient:} \quad C = \sqrt{\frac{\chi^2}{(n + \chi^2)}}$$

In Section 16.6 we calculated the value of χ^2 for testing the association between months of the year and observed sales of new cars, and found it to be 12.0 for $n = 150$. The contingency coefficient for this example is thus:

$$C = \sqrt{12.0/(150 + 12.0)} = 0.27$$

Determining whether a contingency coefficient significantly differs from zero is equivalent to the χ^2 test for the difference between the observed and expected frequencies. We saw, in Section 16.6, that a value of $\chi^2 = 12.00$ permits rejection of the null hypothesis at a level of significance smaller than 0.05 and larger than 0.025. Thus, the null hypothesis that the contingency coefficient for this example equals zero can be rejected at a probability between 0.05 and 0.025.

The contingency coefficient is not appropriate when ordinal data are available since in that case we need a method of **rank correlation.** There are two important methods available for correlating ordinal data, *Spearman's rank-correlation* method and *Kendall's rank-correlation* approach, both of which will be presented in this section.

Spearman's Rho

Research published by C. Spearman in 1904 led to development of what is perhaps the most widely used nonparametric measure of correlation. This measure, usually denoted either by the letter *r* or by the Greek word rho, has thus become known as Spearman's rho, or r_S. Spearman's rank correlation coefficient r_S is the ordinary correlation coefficient using ranks as the original data. A perfect positive correlation ($r_S = +1$) means that the two samples rank each object identically, while a perfect negative correlation ($r_S = -1$) means that the ranks of the two samples have an *exactly inverse* relationship. Values of r_S between -1 and $+1$ denote less than perfect correlation. To measure correlation, Spearman's test squares the difference between the rank of an object in one sample and its rank in the second sample. If this squared difference is denoted as d_i^2 for the ith pair of observations, then the sum of these squared differences over a set of n pairs of observations is $\sum_{i=1}^{n} d_i^2$. The value of $\sum_{i=1}^{n} d_i^2$ is used as a measure of the distance between the ranks in the two samples*:

$$
\begin{array}{l}
\textit{Spearman's rank-correlation coefficient:} \\[2mm]
r_S = 1 - \dfrac{6\sum_{i=1}^{n} d_i^2}{n^3 - n}
\end{array}
\qquad (16.3)
$$

EXAMPLE 1

To illustrate the use of Spearman's rho, suppose that we calculate the rank correlation between the number of checks processed by the 11 clerks in Table 16.7. The information in that table is reproduced in Table 16.15, together with the ranking of each method, and the appropriate d-values. From Table 16.15 the value of r_S is seen to be 0.755.

TABLE 16.15

Clerk	Method A	Rank	Method B	Rank	d_i	d_i^2
1	129	11	115	8	3	9
2	111	4	108	6	−2	4
3	118	7	123	10	−3	9
4	120	8	104	4	4	16
5	116	6	110	7	−1	1
6	101	1	98	2	−1	1
7	107	3	106	5	−2	4
8	127	10	119	9	1	1
9	105	2	95	1	1	1
10	123	9	130	11	−2	4
11	113	5	101	3	2	4
						Sum = 54

$$
r_S = 1 - \frac{6\sum d_i^2}{n^3 - n} = 1 - \frac{6(54)}{11^3 - 11} = 0.755
$$

In order to test the whether a given value of r_S differs significantly from zero, it is necessary to determine the probability that a given value of r_S will

---

*Formula (16.3) is equivalent to Formula (12.2) applied to ranks (except when there are ties).

occur under the null hypothesis. This probability depends on the number of permutations of the two variables that give rise to the particular value of r_S. Tables are available that give the critical values of r_S for small values of n. For example, the $r_S = 0.755$ value is significant at the 0.01 level when $n = 11$. When n is large ($n \geq 10$), the significance of an obtained value of r_S under the null hypothesis of no rank correlation can be determined using the following t-variable*:

$$\text{Test statistic for Spearman's rho:} \quad t = r_S \sqrt{\frac{n-2}{1-r_S^2}}$$

This statistic can be shown to follow the t-distribution with $(n-2)$ degrees of freedom. To illustrate, suppose we had used this formula for the check processing problem in Table 16.5. In this case $r_S = 0.755$, $n = 11$, and the computed value of t is

$$t = 0.755\sqrt{(11-2)/(1-0.755^2)} = 3.454$$

From the t table in Appendix B, the value $t = 3.454$ indicates that $r_S = 0.755$ is significantly different from zero at the 0.005 level of significance. [Note that we have assumed that a one-tailed test is appropriate in this example. That is, the alternative hypothesis is H_a: $\rho > 0$. If a two-tailed test had been used (that is, H_a: $\rho \neq 0$), then the significance level would be $2(0.005) = 0.01$ rather than 0.005.]   ■

EXAMPLE 2

Suppose we are interested in determining the rank correlation between the amount a company spends on research and development (R&D), and R&D as a percentage of sales. A sample of eight companies yielded the data in Table 16.16. In this case the rank correlation is $r_S = 0.143$.

Recall that the Spearman's rho is the equivalent for ranked data to the Pearson product-moment correlation coefficient. A good exercise is to verify that the methods of Chapter 12 lead to the same correlation (0.143) found for the ranked data above.   ■

Kendall's Tau

An alternative method for determining a rank correlation coefficient is to calculate Kendall's correlation coefficient. This statistic, developed by the statistician M. G. Kendall, is denoted by the Greek letter τ (tau), and called Kendall's tau. Although Kendall's tau is suitable for determining the rank correlation of the same type of data for which Spearman's rho is useful, the two methods use different techniques for determining this correlation, so their values will not

*Note that this t-statistic is directly comparable to the t-statistic used for r in Chapter 12 (Formula 12.4).

TABLE 16.16   **Research and development spending ($ millions)**

Company	R&D spending	Rank	R&D: % of sales	Rank	d_i	d_i^2
Shell Oil	254.0	8	1.2	8	0	0
Boeing	409.0	2	3.0	6	-4	16
NCR	299.1	6	6.9	4	2	4
Procter & Gamble	400.0	3	3.1	5	-2	4
Eli Lilly	369.8	4	11.3	2	2	4
GTE	313.0	5	2.0	7	-2	4
Upjohn	284.1	7	14.1	1	6	36
Kodak	976.0	1	9.2	3	-2	4
					Sum $=$	72

$$r_S = 1 - \frac{6(72)}{8^3 - 8} = 1 - 0.857 = 0.143$$

Source: Inside R&D, Technical Insights

normally be the same. Spearman's rho is perhaps more widely used, but Kendall's tau has the advantage of being generalizable to a partial correlation coefficient.

The rank correlation coefficient τ is determined by first calculating an index that indicates how the ranks of one set of observations, *taken two at a time,* differ from the ranks of the other set of observations. The easiest way to determine the value of this index is to arrange the two sets of rankings so that one of them, say the first sample, is in ascending order, from the lowest score (rank) to the highest score (rank). The other set, representing the other sample, will not be in ascending order unless the ranks of the two samples agree perfectly. Now, consider all possible combinations of the **n** ranks in this second sample, taken two at a time (all pairs); assign a value of $+1$ to each pair in which the two ranks are in the same (ascending) order as they are in the first sample, and a value of -1 to each pair in which the two ranks are not in the same (ascending) order as they are in the first sample. The sum of these $+1$ and -1 values is an indication of how well the second set of rankings agrees with the first set. Since there are $n!/x!(n - x)!$ combinations of n objects taken two at a time, this sum (or index) can assume any value between

$$-\frac{n!}{x!(n - x)!} \quad \text{and} \quad +\frac{n!}{x!(n - x)!}$$

Kendall's tau is defined as the ratio of the computed value of this index to the maximum value it can assume [which is $n!/x!(n - x)!$]:

> *Kendall's rank-correlation coefficient:*
> $$\tau = \frac{\text{Computed index}}{\text{Maximum index}}$$

(16.4)

When there is perfect positive correlation, τ will equal $+1$, since the computed index and the maximum index will both equal $n!/x!\,(n-x)!$; if there is a perfect negative correlation, the computed index will equal -1.

EXAMPLE 1

Consider once again the R & D data presented in Table 16.16. To calculate τ we first place one of the groups in ascending rank order. Table 16.17 arranges spending in this order.

Now look at pairs of ranks in the last column to see if each pair is in ascending order ($+1$) or descending order (-1). For example, the first pair is Kodak and Boeing, with ranks 3 and 6, respectively, in the final column. Since 3 and 6 are in ascending order, a $+1$ is assigned to this pair. The next pair is Kodak and Procter & Gamble, with ranks 3 and 5; again a $+1$ is assigned. For the next pair, Kodak and Eli Lilly, the ranks (3 and 2) are in descending order, so this pair is assigned a -1. Continuing in this manner yields $8!/(2!)(6!) = 28$ different pairs. Of these 28 pairs, 15 lead to a $+$ sign, and 13 to a $-$ sign, as shown in Table 16.18. The numerator of Kendall's tau (the computed index) is thus $15 - 13 = 2$, and

$$\tau = \frac{\text{Computed index}}{\text{Maximum index}} = \frac{2}{28} = 0.071$$

TABLE 16.17   Research and development spending ($ millions)

Company	R&D Spending	Rank	R&D: % of Sales	Rank
Kodak	976.0	1	9.2	3
Boeing	409.0	2	3.0	6
Procter & Gamble	400.0	3	3.1	5
Eli Lilly	369.8	4	11.3	2
GTE	313.0	5	2.0	7
NCR	299.1	6	6.9	4
Upjohn	284.1	7	14.1	1
Shell Oil	254.0	8	1.2	8

Source: Inside R&D, Technical Insights

TABLE 16.18   Assigning values for Kendall's tau

Pair	Sign	Pair	Sign	Pair	Sign	Pair	Sign	Pair	Sign
3vs6	$+1$	6vs5	-1	5vs2	-1	2vs7	$+1$	4vs1	-1
3vs5	$+1$	6vs2	-1	5vs7	$+1$	2vs4	$+1$	4vs8	$+1$
3vs2	-1	6vs7	$+1$	5vs4	-1	2vs1	-1	1vs8	$+1$
3vs7	$+1$	6vs4	-1	5vs1	-1	2vs8	$+1$		
3vs4	$+1$	6vs1	-1	5vs8	$+1$	7vs4	-1		
3vs1	-1	6vs8	$+1$			7vs1	-1		
3vs8	$+1$					7vs8	$+1$		

■

EXAMPLE 2   Let's calculate τ for the data in Table 16.15, representing the number of checks processed by 11 clerks under two methods. This table is repeated in Table 16.19, with the ranks under the A method placed in ascending order.

In this problem, there are 55 paired comparisons. A good exercise for the reader would be to verify that 42 of the 55 comparisons in the method A column are in the same order as in the method B column ($+1$) and 13 are in the reverse order (-1). The calculated index for Kendall's tau thus is $42 - 13 = 29$, and τ is

$$\tau = \frac{29}{55} = 0.527$$

Note that Kendall's tau in the two examples we have considered (0.071 and 0.527) is considerably less than the comparable value of Spearman's rho (0.143 and 0.755). Both coefficients, however, utilize the same amount of information about the association between two variables, and for a given set of observations both will reject the null hypothesis that two variables are unrelated in the population at the same level of significance. For small examples, tables are available for determining the probability of a given value of t under the null hypothesis. Since τ and r_s must both reject the null hypothesis at the same level of significance, $\tau = 0.527$ for $n = 11$ must be significant at the 0.01 level as was $r_s = 0.755$. When $n \geq 10$, the statistic τ may be considered to be normally distributed with mean $\mu_\tau = 0$, and standard deviation:

$$s_\tau = \sqrt{\frac{2(2n + 5)}{9n(n - 1)}}$$

The distribution of τ can thus be transformed into the following z-variable:

> *Standardization of τ for Kendall's tau:* $z = \dfrac{\tau - \mu_\tau}{s_\tau}$

TABLE 16.19

Clerk	Method A	Rank	Method B	Rank
6	101	1	98	2
9	105	2	95	1
7	107	3	106	5
2	111	4	108	6
11	113	5	101	3
5	116	6	110	7
3	118	7	123	10
4	120	8	104	4
10	123	9	130	11
8	127	10	119	9
1	129	11	115	8

In our example, the sample of $n = 11$ resulted in a value of Kendall's tau of $\tau = 0.527$. The standard deviation of a sample of this size is

$$s_\tau = \sqrt{2(2 \times 11 + 5)/9 \times 11(11 - 1)} = 0.234$$

The standardized normal value is thus

$$z = \frac{0.527}{0.234} = 2.252$$

Since $P(z > 2.252) = 0.0122$, we can reject H_0 when $\alpha \geq 0.0122$ for a one-sided test, and when $\alpha \geq 2(0.0122) = 0.0244$ for a two-sided test.

Problems

16.18 A *Lotto Guide* is published weekly in Florida. The February 1, 1989, issue reported on the frequency of occurrence of the digits 0 to 9. These frequencies are shown below. Use a chi-square test to determine if the null hypothesis of randomness can be rejected. If you were betting on a digit, would you bet on one that occurs more frequently or one that occurs less frequently? Explain why.

Number	Frequency	Number	Frequency
0	65	5	64
1	85	6	76
2	20	7	82
3	71	8	72
4	80	9	76

16.19 Identify the level of measurement required for the following tests:
   a) the binomial test
   b) the chi-square test
   c) the runs test
   d) the sign test
   e) the Mann–Whitney U-test
   f) Kendall's tau and Spearman's rho
   g) the contingency coefficient
   h) Kolmogorov–Smirnov test

16.20 Universities are often criticized for having hired less than a proportional number of members of minority groups for faculty positions. Suppose that a national survey indicates that of all earned doctorates, 20% belong to females, 10% belong to male minorities, and 70% belong to white males. A random sample of 1000 faculty positions yields the following breakdown:

White males	Women	Minority males
800	150	50

a) Calculate the expected frequency for each cell, using the populations 70%, 20%, and 10%. Use the χ^2 test to determine whether the observed and expected frequencies differ significantly. Specify the hypotheses and use $\alpha = 0.01$.

b) What p-value would you report?

16.21 In one of his classical experiments on heredity, Gregor Mendel observed the color of the plants bred from a purple-flowered and a white-flowered hybrid. Of 929 plants observed, 705 had a purple flower and 224 had a white flower.

a) Test the hypothesis that the probability of observing a purple-flowered plant is 3/4, using the chi-square test and letting $\alpha = 0.05$.

b) Repeat the test above using the binomial test.

16.22 An airline decides to stock three different entries to offer passengers on a transatlantic flight: steak, chicken, and fish. Based on previous flights, the airline expects 40% of the passengers to order steak, 30% chicken, and 30% fish. On the most recent flight, there were 87 orders for steak, 79 orders for chicken, and 74 orders for fish. Does this flight represent sample data that differs significantly from the orders expected by the airline? Use $\alpha = 0.05$.

16.23 Return to Problem 4.42 and once again determine the Poisson approximation to the frequencies for deaths from the kick of a horse in the Prussian army. Use the χ^2 test to determine whether the observed frequencies differ significantly from the expected frequencies under the Poisson distribution. At what level of significance can H_0 be rejected?

16.24 A study investigated whether or not the *order* in which a person's name appears on a political ballot has any influence on that person's chance of being elected. Ninety-two elections were observed, with each having four candidates. The results are shown below.

	Position on ballot				
	1	2	3	4	Total
Number of wins	29	21	17	25	92

a) Use the Kolmogorov–Smirnov test to examine the relationship between these data and the distribution one would expect if the probability of winning were equal for all four positions. Is H_0 accepted or rejected?

b) Use the chi-square test to accomplish the same purpose as part (a).

16.25 One measure of the health of the banking industry is the return on equity. The suggestion has been that for 1988 about 20% of the banks would have a return on equity less than 20%, 30% would fall between 10% and 15%, 30% would be between 15% and 20%, and 20% would be above 20%. Use the chi-square test to determine if the following sample of 50 banks supports this suggestion.

1988 Return on equity— banks

	<10%	10–15%	15–20%	>20%
Frequency	9	21	14	6

Source: Standard & Poor's Compustat Services

16.26 The *Business Week* Investment Outlook Scoreboard estimated an overall (all-industry) average earnings per share for 1989 of 3.22. A random sample of 20 chemical companies, for 1989, resulted in the following frequencies:

P/E Ratio < 3.22	*P/E* Ratio > 3.22
15	5

a) Does a chi-square test indicate that you can reject the hypothesis that half of the chemical companies will exceed the industry average and half will fall below it?

b) Use another statistical test appropriate for testing the hypothesis in part (a).

c) If the all–industry average *P/E* ratio is, in fact 3.22, does this necessarily mean that half the industry *P/E* ratios will exceed 3.22? Explain.

16.27 Use the SALARIES data in Appendix C to construct a 2 × 4 contingency table by counting the frequency of male/female salaries falling in the following work experience categories: 1–4 years, 5–9 years, 10–14 years, and over 15 years. Does a chi-square test indicate a significance difference between males and females in terms of work experience?

16.28 Use the SALARIES data in Appendix C to construct a 2 × 4 contingency table by counting the frequency of male/female salaries falling in the following salary ranges: 30,000–39,999, 40,000–49,999, 50,000–59,999, and 60,000–69,999. Would you conclude that the male and female salaries differ significantly? Explain.

16.29 Use the Kolmogorov–Smirnov test to measure the goodness-of-fit for the data in Problem 4.42. Is H_0 accepted or rejected?

16.30 A manufacturing facility has kept track of employee absences by age and shift, as follows:

Employee absences by age and shift

		Shift 1	Shift 2	Shift 3
Age	<35	15	5	10
	>35	5	10	15

a) Determine the expected frequency in each cell. What null hypothesis is being tested with a chi-square test?

b) How many degrees of freedom are there? At what level of significance can H_0 be rejected?

16.31 What is meant by the phrase "goodness-of-fit"? How is the chi-square distribution used to make this test?

16.32 Use all 100 observations for the SALARIES data in Appendix C to answer the following questions.

a) Find the mean and the standard deviation.

b) Find the number of salaries falling in the six intervals below (all measured in standard deviations).

1) ≤ -2.00 2) between -1.99 and -1.00
3) between -0.99 and 0   4) between 0 and 0.99
5) between 1.00 and 1.99   6) ≥ 2.00.

c) Determine the expected frequency for each of the 6 intervals in part (b) assuming a normal distribution with $\mu = \$56,000$ and $\sigma = \$12,000$.

d) Use a chi-square test to determine whether to accept or reject the hypothesis that the salary data are drawn from the normal population in part (c).

e) Use the Kolmogorov–Smirnov test to answer part (d).

16.33 Calculate the contingency coefficient for Problem 16.30.

16.34 Use the data in Problem 16.21 to find the value of C, the contingency coefficient.

16.35 Standard & Poor's Compustat Services was used to categorize the 1988 market value change (%) for a group of stocks in three industry groups (Service, Manufacturing, and Nonbank financial) using three classes of change (less than -5%, -5% to $+5\%$, greater than 5%). The following frequencies resulted.

Percentage change in 1988 market value

		$< -5\%$	-5% to $+5\%$	$> 5\%$
	Service	8	5	11
Industry	Manufacturing	3	13	10
	Nonbank financial	5	3	16

a) Use the computer output in Table 16.20 to determine if the percentage increase in value is independent of the industry categories. Explain the meaning of each number in cell (1, 1).

b) Generate a computer output of your own comparable to the one in Table 16.20 using these same data.

16.36 The top 10 companies for 1988 according to *Business Week* and *Forbes* are given in Table 16.21. These rankings differ because of differences in the market values used ($ billions). Find both Spearman's rho and Kendall's tau for these data.

16.37 A 1989 *Wall Street Journal* article reported on returns for the first quarter of 1989 relative to the previous year for 12 fund categories, as shown in Table 16.22. Find Spearman's rho and Kendall's tau.

16.38 Surveys in *Business Week* and *U.S. News and World Report* have recently rated the top MBA programs in the United States. Suppose you wish to compare the relative ranking of five programs, labeled schools A, B, C, D, and E. Find Spearman's rho and Kendall's tau.

Rank	*Business Week*	*U.S. News*
1	A	B
2	B	C
3	C	A
4	D	E
5	E	D

TABLE 16.20

```
         CROSSTAB / CHI-SQUARE TESTS
  EXPECTED VALUES (Cell format:count/
  percent: total percent:row percent/: col)
          Service  Manuf  Nonbank
             1       2       3     TOTAL
```

	Service 1	Manuf 2	Nonbank 3	TOTAL
<-5%	5.19	6.81	12.00	24.00
	7.01	9.20	16.22	32.43
	21.62	28.38	50.00	
	32.43	32.43	32.43	
-5% to 5%	5.62	7.38	13.00	26.00
	7.60	9.97	17.57	35.14
	21.62	28.38	50.00	
	35.14	35.14	35.14	
>5%	5.19	6.81	12.00	24.00
	7.01	9.20	16.22	32.43
	21.62	28.38	50.00	
	32.43	32.43	32.43	
TOTAL	16.00	21.00	37.00	74.00
	21.62	28.38	50.00	100.00

CHI-SQUARE = 11.758,   D.F. = 4,   PROB. = .0192

TABLE 16.21

	Business Week rank	Market value	*Forbes* rank	Market value
IBM	1	$66.3	1	$71.8
Exxon	2	59.9	2	56.7
GE	3	40.5	3	40.4
AT&T	4	34.4	4	30.9
Philip Morris	5	27.0	7	23.5
GM	6	25.8	5	30.8
Merk	7	25.6	8	22.9
Ford	8	24.5	6	24.1
Dupont	9	24.3	9	21.1
Amoco	10	20.8	10	19.4

TABLE 16.22   Total return by fund category

Fund category	First quarter 1989	Previous year
Health/biotechnology	+11.04	+11.89
Natural resources	+8.63	+10.68
Speciality	+7.97	+16.30
Small company growth	+7.66	+12.73
Capital appreciation	+6.90	+12.42
Growth	+6.87	+13.55
Growth and income	+5.89	+14.18
Equity income	+5.27	+14.07
Service and technology	+4.82	+7.12
Convertible securities	+4.54	+10.04
Option income	+4.41	+13.28
Gold-oriented	+4.28	−5.39

Exercises

16.39 Discuss the similarities and differences between the χ^2 (goodness-of-fit) test (Section 16.6) and the χ^2 test of Independence (Section 16.7). Are they two different tests, or merely different versions of the same test?

16.40 Show that Spearman's rho is the rank-order equivalent of the correlation coefficient presented in Chapter 12.

16.41 There is a test called a one-sample runs test that can be used to test the hypothesis that the observations in a sample are random. For example, during one stretch of 23 days last April, the weather in Boston was classified as either "sunny" or "cloudy." The following pattern was observed, where S = sunny and C = cloudy.

S S C C S S S C C C S S S S S S C C C C S S S S

Suggest how a runs test similar to the Wald–Wolfowitz test can be used to test for randomness here. What kinds of patterns would suggest nonrandomness? Would H_0 be rejected only when the number of runs is small?

16.42 An April 6, 1989, article in the *Wall Street Journal* reported on a Chicago case where a federal court ruled against a company for racial discrimination. Magistrate Elaine E. Bucko said that hiring statistics supplied by both the EEOC and the company "showed a significant disparity between availability and hire rates for black clericals" and that "chance cannot account for the discrepancy."

a) Design a sample survey that could have been used to provide "hiring statistics" to Magistrate Bucko. What nonparametric statistics would be appropriate here?

b) Use one of the nonparametric tests from this chapter to determine if the salary data in Appendix C supports sex discrimination.

Appendix A

Subscripts, Summations, Variables and Functions, Calculus Review

Education is . . . hanging around
until you've caught on.

ROBERT FROST

Subscripts and Summations

A.1

Throughout this book we use certain symbols to distinguish between the numbers in a set of data, and to indicate the sum of such numbers. For example, we may wish to distinguish between the monthly sales of a certain business, and then sum these monthly sales to get the yearly sales. To do this, suppose that we let the symbol x denote the monthly sales of this firm. Furthermore, we will add a subscript to this symbol to denote which month is being represented. Thus, x_1 = sales in the first month, x_2 = sales in the second month, and so forth, with x_{12} = sales in the twelfth month. That is, if sales in the sixth month were 120 units, then we would write $x_6 = 120$. The notation x_i thus stands for "sales in the ith month," where i can be any number from 1 to 12; that is, $i = 1, 2, \ldots, 12$. The dots in this last expression are used to indicate "and so on."

Now, assume that we want to sum the sales for all 12 months in a year, which is

$$x_1 + x_2 + \cdots + x_{12}$$

Another way of writing this sum is to use the Greek letter $\sum$ (capital sigma). This symbol is read as "take the sum of." At the bottom of this $\sum$ sign we usually place the first value of i that is to be included in the sum. The last value of i to be summed is usually placed at the top of the sum sign. Thus,

$$\sum_{i=1}^{12} x_i$$

is read as "sum the values of x_i starting from $i = 1$ and ending with $i = 12$." That is,

$$\sum_{i=1}^{12} x_i = x_1 + x_2 + \cdots + x_{12}$$

Similarly, suppose that we want the sum of only the last seven months in the year. This sum is written as follows:

$$\sum_{i=6}^{12} x_i = x_6 + x_7 + \cdots + x_{12}$$

In statistics we often do not know in advance what the final value in a summation will be. For example, we know that we want to sum a set of sales values, but we do not know how many values there are to be summed. To designate this situation, we will let the symbol n represent the last number in the sum (where n can be any integer value, such as 1, 2, 3, . . .). The notation

$$\sum_{i=1}^{n} x_i = x_1 + x_2 + \cdots + x_n$$

is thus read as "the sum of n numbers, where the first number is x_1, the second is x_2, and the last is x_n." In summing monthly sales over a year, we would thus let $n = 12$, so that $\sum_{i=1}^{n} x_i = \sum_{i=1}^{12} x_i$.

Perhaps we should mention that, in some chapters in this book, we have sometimes omitted the limits of summation, and simply written $\sum x_i$. This notation should be interpreted to mean "sum all relevant values of x_i." In these instances we have made sure that the reader always knows what the relevant values of x_i are. Also, we might point out that the choice of symbols in designating a sum of numbers is often quite arbitrary. For example, we might have used the letter y to denote monthly sales (instead of x), and used the letter j as a subscript (instead of i). In this case $\sum_{j=1}^{12} y_j$ would denote the sum of the 12 monthly values.

Double Summations

In a number of chapters in this book we have found it convenient to use *two* subscripts instead of just one. In these instances the first subscript indicates one characteristic under study, and the second subscript some other characteristic. For example, suppose that we let x_{ij} = sales in the ith month by the jth salesman. The notation $x_{6,2} = 15$ would indicate that in the sixth month

($i = 6$), salesman number 2 ($j = 2$) sold 15 units. Using the same procedure as described above, we can denote the total sales over 12 months by the jth salesman as the sum of x_{1j} (sales in the 1st month by the jth salesman) plus $x_{2j}, \ldots,$ plus $x_{12,j}$ (sales in the 12th month by the jth salesman). That is,

$$\text{Total sales by salesman } j: \sum_{i=1}^{12} x_{ij} = x_{1j} + x_{2j} + \cdots + x_{12j}$$

Another example of a similar type of sum is the sum of sales in the ith month (where i is some number between 1 and 12) by all the sales representatives in the company. If we let m = total number of sales reps, then this sum is x_{i1} (sales in month i by sales rep 1) plus $x_{i2}, \ldots,$ plus x_{im} (sales in month i by sales rep m). That is,

$$\text{Total sales in month } i: \sum_{j=1}^{m} x_{ij} = x_{i1} + x_{i2} + \cdots + x_{im}$$

Finally, we might wish to sum over all months ($i = 1, 2, \ldots, 12$) and all salesmen ($j = 1, 2, \ldots, m$). This sum could be written as

$$\text{Total sales over all months and all salesmen:}$$

$$\sum_{\text{All } j} \sum_{\text{All } i} x_{ij} = \left\{ \begin{array}{l} x_{11} + x_{12} + \cdots + x_{1m} \\ + x_{21} + x_{22} + \cdots + x_{2m} \\ \vdots \\ + x_{12,1} + x_{12,2} + \cdots + x_{12,m} \end{array} \right\}$$

Variables and Functions

A.2

Variables

Variables and the relationship between variables represent an important part of statistics. Hence, it is important that we define these concepts carefully.

A **variable** is a quantity that may assume any one of a set of values. For example, we might describe the worth of a common stock by the variable "current worth on the stock market." The values of this variable are the different prices the stock can assume. Or, we might be interested in describing how well a specific brand of alkaline battery works by defining the variable "the length of time before failure when in constant use." The values of this variable are the various times it might take before the battery fails.

Variables are often classified according to whether their values are *discrete* or *continuous*. The values of a discrete variable are individually distinct; that is, they are separable from one another. The price of a common stock, for instance, represents a discrete variable because the prices a stock can assume are all separate values, distinguishable from one another. The following examples also represent discrete variables:

1. the number of defectives in a production lot,

2. the amount of advertising expenditure a certain company plans for next year,

3. the amount of federal income tax owed by an individual.

Most discrete variables represent some quantity that can be "counted."

The values of a **continuous** variable are not separable from one another; each value is immediately adjacent to and indistinguishable from the next. Quantities that are *measured* are usually continuous variables; for example, measures of time, weight, length, and area typically represent continuous variables. Thus, in our earlier example, the time it takes a battery to fail represents a continuous random variable. There are always an infinite number of values of a continuous variable.* The following variables also are continuous:

1. the percentage increase in the consumer price index last month,

2. the amount of gasoline available in the United States next year,

3. the quality of the air in Los Angeles yesterday, measured in a way so as to include all numbers from 0 to 100.

One of the practical difficulties with continuous variables is that the devices used to measure such variables usually are read only in a discrete manner. For example, the variable "amount of gasoline needed to fill a car" is clearly a continuous random variable, since this amount may be *any* value between zero and the capacity of the gas tank. From a *practical* point of view, however, this variable is discrete because most gas pumps cannot be read (at least accurately) beyond a few decimal points (usually $\frac{1}{10}$ of a gallon). *For most statistical analysis it makes little difference if we treat such variables as discrete or continuous, although a continuous variable is often easier to manipulate than is a discrete variable with many different values.*

Functions

If a unique value of some variable y is associated with every possible value of another variable x, then the variable y is said to be "a function of" the variable x. To illustrate a functional relationship, we will let x represent the number of gallons of gasoline you purchase at a service station, and let y be the amount of money you must pay for this gasoline. In this case y is a function of x [written $y = f(x)$] because the exact (unique) amount (y) you will be charged for every possible gasoline purchase (x) is known (assuming the price doesn't change before you get there).

There are three commonly used methods for describing a functional relationship: (1) a table, (2) a graph, and (3) an equation. As shown below, the first two of these methods work well for discrete functions, while the latter two work well for continuous functions.

---

*The number of values of a discrete variable may be either finite or infinite.

TABLE A.1

Miles per hour (x)	Miles per gallon $[y = f(x)]$
$x = 10$	$y = f(10) = 21.6$
$x = 20$	$y = f(20) = 26.1$
$x = 30$	$y = f(30) = 27.8$
$x = 40$	$y = f(40) = 25.3$
$x = 50$	$y = f(50) = 19.5$

Discrete Functions.   A **discrete function** is the function in any situation where x is a discrete variable. If x is discrete, then y must be discrete as well. To illustrate a discrete function, we propose that the Environmental Protection Agency (EPA) is testing a new car to determine its gas mileage (y) at various speeds (x). This car was tested at $x = 10, 20, 30, 40,$ and 50 miles per hour (MPH). The miles per gallon (MPG) at these speeds were $y = 21.6, 26.1, 27.8, 25.3,$ and 19.5, respectively. This information is shown in Table A.1.

Note that the variable x is discrete, since all possible values of this variable are distinguishable from one another—that is, they are individually distinct. It is important to understand the symbolic notation in writing functions. For example, the notation $f(10) = 21.6$ means that when $x = 10$, the value of $f(x)$ is $y = 21.6$. Similarly, $f(50) = 19.5$ means that $y = 19.5$ when $x = 50$. Figure A.1 is a graph of the function relating MPH (x) and MPG (y).

We must resist the temptation to connect the points in Fig. A.1 with a line, since such a line might incorrectly lead a viewer to assume that the function is defined for speeds other than $x = 10, 20, 30, 40,$ and 50 MPH. It may be possible to define a function that relates additional values of x to y, but in this example the function is defined only for five x-values. When the number of x-values is large, a formula is often useful to describe a functional relationship. Chapter 4 gives several examples of such formulas.

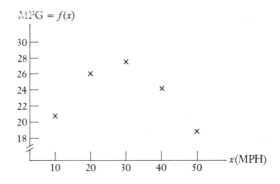

Figure A.1
Graph of the function relating x = MPH and y = MPG.

Continuous Functions. When the random variable x is continuous, then the functional relationship between x and y usually must be expressed as a formula, or in a graph. Consider a simple example, where the variable x is temperature measured on the Fahrenheit scale, and the variable y is temperature measured on the Celsius scale. For converting values from the Fahrenheit scale (x) to the Celsius scale (y), the following functional relationship is used*:

$$y = \frac{5}{9}x - \frac{160}{9}$$

This relationship represents a function because a unique value of y is specified for each value of x. The function is continuous, since the values of x are indistinguishable. Now, suppose that we want to graph this function. First, we recognize that it is a straight line, since the exponent of the variable x is 1. To graph a straight line we need only two points. The easiest two points to take are usually the one where $x = 0$ and the one where $y = 0$. When $x = 0$,

$$y = \frac{5}{9}(0) - \frac{160}{9} = -17.78$$

Similarly, when $y = 0$ we can solve for x as follows:

$$0 = \frac{5}{9}x - \frac{160}{9}$$

$$\frac{5}{9}x = \frac{160}{9}$$

so

$$x = \frac{160}{9} \cdot \frac{9}{5} = \frac{160}{5} = 32$$

We now have two points on our function, $(0, -17.78)$ and $(32, 0)$. This function is graphed, in Fig. A.2, by connecting these two points.

From either the straight line in Fig. A.2, or the function itself, we can solve for any additional point. For example, most of us are familiar with the boiling point of water at 212 degrees Fahrenheit, $x = 212$. The comparable value of y is $f(212)$:

$$y = f(212) = \frac{5}{9}(212) - \frac{160}{9}$$

or

$$y = f(212) = 100$$

which is the Celsius temperature for the boiling point of water. We could have solved for any one of the infinite number of different y-values in a similar manner.

---

*We could have written this formula as

$$f(x) = \frac{5}{9}(x - 32)$$

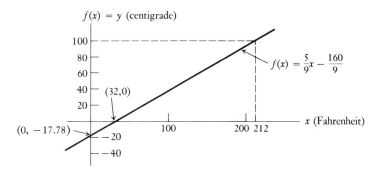

Figure A.2
A graph of
$y = f(x) = \frac{5}{9}x - \frac{160}{9}$.

Calculus Review

A.3

Introduction

This text does not require a background in calculus. However, using calculus does help one's understanding of some of the foundations of statistics. For this reason, we have, in specially marked sections and in some footnotes, incorporated use of the basic elements of calculus. The brief review in this appendix may help the reader already familiar with calculus to recall enough of this material so as to make the special sections and footnotes meaningful.

The study of calculus is usually divided into two distinct, though related, parts: differential calculus and integral calculus. Differential calculus is concerned primarily with the slope of a function or curve at any given point on that function; that is, the rate of change. Once the slope of a curve is known, it is usually possible to determine certain important characteristics of the curve, such as where it reaches a maximum or minimum. In statistical analysis, integral calculus is usually associated with the process of finding the area under a curve—that is, between a curve and the x-axis. As is the case for differential calculus, integral calculus provides information extremely useful for describing certain characteristics of a function or a curve.

Differential Calculus

The slope of a function, or curve, representing the relationship between an independent variable x and a dependent variable y is merely "the rate of change of y divided by the rate of change of x." The slope of a line thus describes how a change in x affects the variable y. If a positive change in x results in a positive change in y, the slope will have a positive sign; when a positive increment in x produces a *negative* change in y, the slope is negative. For different values of x, the slope may vary.

The usual notation representing slope is dy/dx (or $df(x)/dx$), which is the *first derivative* (rate of change *or* slope) of y with respect to x. Higher derivatives just represent the process of taking the derivative of a derivative: the rate of change *of the slope.* The second derivative therefore represents the derivative of the slope of a function. Sometimes prime marks are used to designate derivatives: $f'(x)$ thus stands for the first derivative, $f''(x)$ the second derivative, and so forth.

Maximum or minimum points of a function can often be determined by finding the values of x for which the function has a slope of zero. These values can be found by setting the first derivative equal to zero and solving for x. When the first derivative equals zero, the value of the second derivative describes whether the function is a maximum or a minimum. A negative second derivative indicates a relative maximum, while a positive second derivative indicates a relative minimum. If the second derivative equals *zero,* the curve has an inflection point at the value of x.

Partial differentiation is the process of finding the rate of change (slope) between two variables whenever the dependent variable (y) is a function of more than one variable. For partial differentiation, all variables except y and the dependent variable of interest are treated as constants and differentiated accordingly. The symbol $\partial y/\partial x$ [or $\partial f(x)/\partial x$] represents the partial derivative of y with respect to x.

It should be noted that the *letters* used to denote the variables in differentiation or integration problems are not significant—the relationship could just as easily be $r = f(t)$ with the derivative dr/dt, or $x = f(y)$ and dx/dy, etc. Throughout most of this book, however, we shall assume y to be the dependent variable, and $y = f(x_1, x_2, \ldots, x_n)$, where $x_1, x_2, \ldots, x_n$ are the independent variables.

Differentiation Formulas

There are many rules to aid the process of finding derivatives. We shall present only a few of the most widely used rules, stressing those with particular applications in this book.

1. $y = k; \quad \dfrac{dy}{dx} = 0$

The derivative of a constant (horizontal straight line) is zero.

2. $y = ax + b; \quad \dfrac{dy}{dx} = a$

The derivative of any straight line, $y = ax + b$, is a constant.

3. $y = f(x) \pm g(x); \quad \dfrac{dy}{dx} = \dfrac{df(x)}{dx} \pm \dfrac{dg(x)}{dx}$

The derivative of the sum (difference) of two functions is the sum (difference) of the derivatives.

4. $y = f(x)g(x); \quad \dfrac{dy}{dx} = f(x)\dfrac{dg(x)}{dx} + g(x)\dfrac{df(x)}{dx}$

The derivative of a product of two functions is the first function times the derivative of the second plus the second function times the derivative of the first.

5. $y = e^{f(x)}; \quad \dfrac{dy}{dx} = e^{f(x)}\dfrac{d[f(x)]}{dx}$

The derivative of the constant e, to a power that is a function of x, $f(x)$, is $e^{f(x)}$ times the derivative of the exponent.

6. $y = [f(x)]^{n}; \quad \dfrac{dy}{dx} = n[f(x)]^{n-1}\dfrac{df(x)}{dx}$

The derivative of a function raised to a power, n, is n times the function raised to the $(n-1)$ power times the derivative of the function.

7. $y = \log_{e}x; \quad \dfrac{dy}{dx} = \dfrac{1}{x}$

The derivative of the natural logarithm of x is $1/x$.

Exercises

A.1 Find $\dfrac{dy}{dx}$ for each of the following functions:

a) $y = x^{3}$ [Ans.: $3x^{2}$]

b) $y = 20 + 5x^{2}$ [Ans.: $10x$]

c) $y = 5e^{-2x}$ [Ans.: $-10e^{-2x}$]

d) $y = (x^{2} - 1)^{2}$ [Ans.: $4x(x^{2} - 1)$]

e) $y = 2\log_{e}x$ $\left[\text{Ans.: } \dfrac{2}{x}\right]$

f) $y = x\log_{e}x$ [Ans.: $1 + \log_{e}x$]

g) $y = x^{2}e^{2x^{2}}$ [Ans.: $2xe^{2x^{2}} + 4x^{3}e^{2x^{2}}$]

A.2 Find $\dfrac{\partial G}{\partial a}$ and $\dfrac{\partial G}{\partial b}$ for each of the following functions:

a) $G = 5a^{2} + 6bx + 7b^{2}$ $\left[\text{Ans.: } \dfrac{\partial G}{\partial a} = 10a\right.$

$\left. \dfrac{\partial G}{\partial b} = 6x + 14b\right]$

b) $G = \sum(y - a - bx)^{2}$ $\left[\text{Ans.: } \dfrac{\partial G}{\partial a} = \sum(y - a - bx)(-2)\right.$

$\left. \dfrac{\partial G}{\partial b} = \sum(y - a - bx)(-2x)\right]$

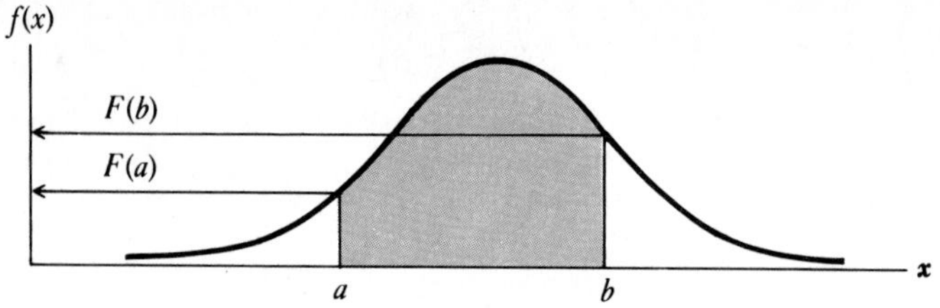

$f(x)$

Figure A.3
Area from a to b equals
$F(b) - F(a)$.

A.3　Find the maximum and minimum for the following functions:

a) $y = 2x^3 + 3x^2 - 12x + 2$　　[*Ans.*: $x = -2$ is a max
　　　　　　　　　　　　　　　　　　　$x = +1$ is a min]

b) $y = (x^2 - 1)^2$　　　　　　　　[*Ans.*: $x = 0$ is a max
　　　　　　　　　　　　　　　　　　　$x = \pm 1$ are mins]

Integral Calculus

Integral calculus is most useful in statistics for finding the area under a curve. If $f(x)$ is a continuous function, and we want to find the area under this function from the point a to the point b, this area can be determined as follows:

$$\left(\begin{matrix}\text{Area under } y = f(x) \text{ from} \\ \text{point } a \text{ to point } b\end{matrix}\right) = \left(\begin{matrix}\text{Integral} \\ \text{from } a \text{ to } b\end{matrix}\right) = \int_a^b f(x)\,dx$$

The notation $F(a)$ is often used to represent the integral from minus infinity up to the point a. Thus,

$$F(a) = \left(\begin{matrix}\text{Area from minus} \\ \text{infinity to the point } a\end{matrix}\right) = \int_{-\infty}^a f(x)\,dx$$

The notation $[F(x)]_a^b$ is used to represent the evaluation of an integral from a to b — the area between a and b. In other words, if we take the area from minus infinity up to the point b, and subtract from it the area from minus infinity up to the point a, then we are left with the area between the points a and b.

$$\text{Area from } a \text{ to } b = [F(x)]_a^b = F[b] - F[a] = \int_a^b f(x)\,dx$$

Figure A.3 shows the area from a to b under the curve $f(x)$.

Integration Formulas

1. $\displaystyle\int_a^b dx = [x]_a^b = b - a$

2. $\displaystyle\int_a^b kf(x)\,dx = k\int_a^b f(x)\,dx$

3. $\displaystyle\int_a^b [f(x) \pm g(x)]\,dx = \int_a^b f(x)\,dx \pm \int_a^b g(x)\,dx$

4. $\displaystyle\int_a^b x^n dx = \left[\frac{x^{n+1}}{n+1}\right]_a^b = \frac{b^{n+1}}{n+1} - \frac{a^{n+1}}{n+1}$

5. $\displaystyle\int_a^b e^{g(x)}\frac{d[g(x)]}{dx}dx = \left[e^{g(x)}\right]_a^b = e^{g(b)} - e^{g(a)}$

6. $\displaystyle\int_a^b \frac{dx}{x} = \left[\log_e x\right]_a^b = \log_e b - \log_e a$

Exercises

Integrate the following functions:

A.4 $\displaystyle\int_1^5 4dx$ [*Ans.:* 16]

A.5 $\displaystyle\int_0^{10} \frac{x}{2}\,dx$ [*Ans.:* 25]

A.6 $\displaystyle\int_4^{16} \frac{\sqrt{x}}{50}dx$ $\left[\textit{Ans.:}\ \frac{56}{75}\right]$

A.7 $\displaystyle\int_0^{\infty} ke^{-kx}dx$ [*Ans.:* 1]

A.8 $\displaystyle\int_2^5 \frac{3}{x}dx$ [*Ans.:* $3(\log_e 5 - \log_e 2)$]

A.9 $\displaystyle\int_0^4 (2x^2 + x)dx$ [*Ans.:* $50\frac{2}{3}$]

Appendix B:
Tables

TABLE I   Binomial Distribution

From Robert Schlaifer, *Analysis of Decisions Under Uncertainty* (New York: McGraw-Hill Book Co., Inc., Preliminary Edition, Volume II, 1967) by specific permission of the President and Fellows of Harvard College, who hold the ocpyright.

The following table gives values of the binomial mass function defined by

$$P(x) = {_nC_x}p^x(1 - p)^{n-x}$$

$$= \frac{n!}{x!(n - x)!} p^x(1 - p)^{n-x}.$$

This is the probability of exactly x successes in n independent Bernoulli trials with probability of success on a single trial equal to p. The values of x at the left of any section are to be used in conjunction with the values of p at the top of that section; the values of x at the right of any section are to be used in conjunction with the values of p at the bottom of that section.

Example: To evaluate $P(x)$ for $n = 5$, $x = 3$, and $p = 0.83$, locate the section of the table for $n = 5$, the column for $p = 0.83$, and the row for $x = 3$, and read

$$P(x) = 0.1652.$$

$n = 1$

x	p	01	02	03	04	05	06	07	08	09	10		
0		9900	9800	9700	9600	9500	9400	9300	9200	9100	9000		1
1		0100	0200	0300	0400	0500	0600	0700	0800	0900	1000		0
		99	98	97	96	95	94	93	92	91	90	p	x

x	p	11	12	13	14	15	16	17	18	19	20		
0		8900	8800	8700	8600	8500	8400	8300	8200	8100	8000		1
1		1100	1200	1300	1400	1500	1600	1700	1800	1900	2000		0
		89	88	87	86	85	84	83	82	81	80	p	x

x	p	21	22	23	24	25	26	27	28	29	30		
0		7900	7800	7700	7600	7500	7400	7300	7200	7100	7000		1
1		2100	2200	2300	2400	2500	2600	2700	2800	2900	3000		0
		79	78	77	76	75	74	73	72	71	70	p	x

x	p	31	32	33	34	35	36	37	38	39	40		
0		6900	6800	6700	6600	6500	6400	6300	6200	6100	6000		1
1		3100	3200	3300	3400	3500	3600	3700	3800	3900	4000		0
		69	68	67	66	65	64	63	62	61	60	p	x

x	p	41	42	43	44	45	46	47	48	49	50		
0		5900	5800	5700	5600	5500	5400	5300	5200	5100	5000		1
1		4100	4200	4300	4400	4500	4600	4700	4800	4900	5000		0
		59	58	57	56	55	54	53	52	51	50	p	x

(Continued)

Appendix B

TABLE I Binomial Distribution ($n = 2$)

$$n = 2$$

x	p	01	02	03	04	05	06	07	08	09	10		
0		9801	9604	9409	9216	9025	8836	8649	8464	8281	8100		2
1		0198	0392	0582	0768	0950	1128	1302	1472	1638	1800		1
2		0001	0004	0009	0016	0025	0036	0049	0064	0081	0100		0
		99	98	97	96	95	94	93	92	91	90	p	x

x	p	11	12	13	14	15	16	17	18	19	20		
0		7921	7744	7569	7396	7225	7056	6889	6724	6561	6400		2
1		1958	2112	2262	2408	2550	2688	2822	2952	3078	3200		1
2		0121	0144	0169	0196	0225	0256	0289	0324	0361	0400		0
		89	88	87	86	85	84	83	82	81	80	p	x

x	p	21	22	23	24	25	26	27	28	29	30		
0		6241	60f4	5929	5776	5625	5476	5329	5184	5041	4900		2
1		3318	3432	3542	3648	3750	3848	3942	4032	4118	4200		1
2		0441	0484	0529	0576	0625	0676	0729	0784	0841	0900		0
		79	78	77	76	75	74	73	72	71	70	p	x

x	p	31	32	33	34	35	36	37	38	39	40		
0		4761	4624	4489	4356	4225	4096	3969	3844	3721	3600		2
1		4278	4352	4422	4488	4550	4608	4662	4712	4758	4800		1
2		0961	1024	1089	1156	1225	1296	1369	1444	1521	1600		0
		69	68	67	66	65	64	63	62	61	60	p	x

x	p	41	42	43	44	45	46	47	48	49	50		
0		3481	3364	3249	3136	3025	2916	2809	2704	2601	2500		2
1		4838	4872	4902	4928	4950	4968	4982	4992	4998	5000		1
2		1681	1764	1849	1936	2025	2116	2209	2304	2401	2500		0
		59	58	57	56	55	54	53	52	51	50	p	x

(Continued)

TABLE I   **Binomial Distribution ($n = 3$)**

$n = 3$

x	p	01	02	03	04	05	06	07	08	09	10		
0		9703	9412	9127	8847	8574	8306	8044	7787	7536	7290		3
1		0294	0576	0847	1106	1354	1590	1816	2031	2236	2430		2
2		0003	0012	0026	0046	0071	0102	0137	0177	0221	0270		1
3		0000	0000	0000	0001	0001	0002	0003	0005	0007	0010		0
		99	98	97	96	95	94	93	92	91	90	p	x

x	p	11	12	13	14	15	16	17	18	19	20		
0		7050	6815	6585	6361	6141	5927	5718	5514	5314	5120		3
1		2614	2788	2952	3106	3251	3387	3513	3631	3740	3840		2
2		0323	0380	0441	0506	0574	0645	0720	0797	0877	0960		1
3		0013	0017	0022	0027	0034	0041	0049	0058	0069	0080		0
		89	88	87	86	85	84	83	82	81	80	p	x

x	p	21	22	23	24	25	26	27	28	29	30		
0		4930	4746	4565	4390	4219	4052	3890	3732	3579	3430		3
1		3932	4014	4091	4159	4219	4271	4316	4355	4386	4410		2
2		1045	1133	1222	1313	1406	1501	1597	1693	1791	1890		1
3		0093	0106	0122	0138	0156	0176	0197	0220	0244	0270		0
		79	78	77	76	75	74	73	72	71	70	p	x

x	p	31	32	33	34	35	36	37	38	39	40		
0		3285	3144	3008	2875	2746	2621	2500	2383	2270	2160		3
1		4428	4439	4444	4443	4436	4424	4406	4382	4354	4320		2
2		1989	2089	2189	2289	2389	2488	2587	2686	2783	2880		1
3		0298	0328	0359	0393	0429	0467	0507	0549	0593	0640		0
		69	68	67	66	65	64	63	62	61	60	p	x

x	p	41	42	43	44	45	46	47	48	49	50		
0		2054	1951	1852	1756	1664	1575	1489	1406	1327	1250		3
1		4282	4239	4191	4140	4084	4024	3961	3894	3823	3750		2
2		2975	3069	3162	3252	3341	3428	3512	3594	3674	3750		1
3		0689	0741	0795	0852	0911	0973	1038	1106	1176	1250		0
		59	58	57	56	55	54	53	52	51	50	p	x

(Continued)

Appendix B

TABLE I Binomial Distribution ($n = 4$)

						$n = 4$							
x	p	01	02	03	04	05	06	07	08	09	10		
0		9606	9224	8853	8493	8145	7807	7481	7164	6857	6561		4
1		0388	0753	1095	1416	1715	1993	2252	2492	2713	2916		3
2		0006	0023	0051	0088	0135	0191	0254	0325	0402	0486		2
3		0000	0000	0001	0002	0005	0008	0013	0019	0027	0036		1
4		0000	0000	0000	0000	0000	0000	0000	0000	0001	0001		0
		99	98	97	96	95	94	93	92	91	90	p	x
x	p	11	12	13	14	15	16	17	18	19	20		
0		6274	5997	5729	5470	5220	4979	4746	4521	4305	4096		4
1		3102	3271	3424	3562	3685	3793	3888	3970	4039	4096		3
2		0575	0669	0767	0870	0975	1084	1195	1307	1421	1536		2
3		0047	0061	0076	0094	0115	0138	0163	0191	0222	0256		1
4		0001	0002	0003	0004	0005	0007	0008	0010	0013	0016		0
		89	88	87	86	85	84	83	82	81	80	p	x
x	p	21	22	23	24	25	26	27	28	29	30		
0		3895	3702	3515	3336	3164	2999	2840	2687	2541	2401		4
1		4142	4176	4200	4214	4219	4214	4201	4180	4152	4116		3
2		1651	1767	1882	1996	2109	2221	2331	2439	2544	2646		2
3		0293	0332	0375	0420	0469	0520	0575	0632	0693	0756		1
4		0019	0023	0028	0033	0039	0046	0053	0061	0071	0081		0
		79	78	77	76	75	74	73	72	71	70	p	x
x	p	31	32	33	34	35	36	37	38	39	40		
0		2267	2138	2015	1897	1785	1678	1575	1478	1385	1296		4
1		4074	4025	3970	3910	3845	3775	3701	3623	3541	3456		3
2		2745	2841	2933	3021	3105	3185	3260	3330	3396	3456		2
3		0822	0891	0963	1038	1115	1194	1276	1361	1447	1536		1
4		0092	0105	0119	0134	0150	0168	0187	0209	0231	0256		0
		69	68	67	66	65	64	63	62	61	60	p	x
x	p	41	42	43	44	45	46	47	48	49	50		
0		1212	1132	1056	0983	0915	0850	0789	0731	0677	0625		4
1		3368	3278	3185	3091	2995	2897	2799	2700	2600	2500		3
2		3511	3560	3604	3643	3675	3702	3723	3738	3747	3750		2
3		1627	1719	1813	1908	2005	2102	2201	2300	2400	2500		1
4		0283	0311	0342	0375	0410	0448	0488	0531	0576	0625		0
		59	58	57	56	55	54	53	52	51	50	p	x

(*Continued*)

TABLE I   Binomial Distribution ($n = 5$)

$n = 5$

x	p	01	02	03	04	05	06	07	08	09	10		
0		9510	9039	8587	8154	7738	7339	6957	6591	6240	5905		5
1		0480	0922	1328	1699	2036	2342	2618	2866	3086	3280		4
2		0010	0038	0082	0142	0214	0299	0394	0498	0610	0729		3
3		0000	0001	0003	0006	0011	0019	0030	0043	0060	0081		2
4		0000	0000	0000	0000	0000	0001	0001	0002	0003	0004		1
		99	98	97	96	95	94	93	92	91	90	p	x

x	p	11	12	13	14	15	16	17	18	19	20		
0		5584	5277	4984	4704	4437	4182	3939	3707	3487	3277		5
1		3451	3598	3724	3829	3915	3983	4034	4069	4089	4096		4
2		0853	0981	1113	1247	1382	1517	1652	1786	1919	2048		3
3		0105	0134	0166	0203	0244	0289	0338	0392	0450	0512		2
4		0007	0009	0012	0017	0022	0028	0035	0043	0053	0064		1
5		0000	0000	0000	0001	0001	0001	0001	0002	0002	0003		0
		89	88	87	86	85	84	83	82	81	80	p	x

x	p	21	22	23	24	25	26	27	28	29	30		
0		3077	2887	2707	2536	2373	2219	2073	1935	1804	1681		5
1		4090	4072	4043	4003	3955	3898	3834	3762	3685	3601		4
2		2174	2297	2415	2529	2637	2739	2836	2926	3010	3087		3
3		0578	0648	0721	0798	0879	0962	1049	1138	1229	1323		2
4		0077	0091	0108	0126	0146	0169	0194	0221	0251	0283		1
5		0004	0005	0006	0008	0010	0012	0014	0017	0021	0024		0
		79	78	77	76	75	74	73	72	71	70	p	x

x	p	31	32	33	34	35	36	37	38	39	40		
0		1564	1454	1350	1252	1160	1074	0992	0916	0845	0778		5
1		3513	3421	3325	3226	3124	3020	2914	2808	2700	2592		4
2		3157	3220	3275	3323	3364	3397	3423	3441	3452	3456		3
3		1418	1515	1613	1712	1811	1911	2010	2109	2207	2304		2
4		0319	0357	0397	0441	0488	0537	0590	0646	0706	0768		1
5		0029	0034	0039	0045	0053	0060	0069	0079	0090	0102		0
		69	68	67	66	65	64	63	62	61	60	p	x

x	p	41	42	43	44	45	46	47	48	49	50		
0		0715	0656	0602	0551	0503	0459	0418	0380	0345	0313		5
1		2484	2376	2270	2164	2059	1956	1854	1755	1657	1562		4
2		3452	3442	3424	3400	3369	3332	3289	3240	3185	3125		3
3		2399	2492	2583	2671	2757	2838	2916	2990	3060	3125		2
4		0834	0902	0974	1049	1128	1209	1293	1380	1470	1562		1
5		0116	0131	0147	0165	0185	0206	0229	0255	0282	0312		0
		59	58	57	56	55	54	53	52	51	50	p	x

(*Continued*)

Appendix B

TABLE I Binomial Distribution ($n = 6$)

$n = 6$

x	p	01	02	03	04	05	06	07	08	09	10		
0		9415	8858	8330	7828	7351	6899	6470	6064	5679	5314		6
1		0571	1085	1546	1957	2321	2642	2922	3164	3370	3543		5
2		0014	0055	0120	0204	0305	0422	0550	0688	0833	0984		4
3		0000	0002	0005	0011	0021	0036	0055	0080	0110	0146		3
4		0000	0000	0000	0000	0001	0002	0003	0005	0008	0012		2
5		0000	0000	0000	0000	0000	0000	0000	0000	0000	0001		1
		99	98	97	96	95	94	93	92	91	90	p	x

x	p	11	12	13	14	15	16	17	18	19	20		
0		4970	4644	4336	4046	3771	3513	3269	3040	2824	2621		6
1		3685	3800	3888	3952	3993	4015	4018	4004	3975	3932		5
2		1139	1295	1452	1608	1762	1912	2057	2197	2331	2458		4
3		0188	0236	0289	0349	0415	0486	0562	0643	0729	0819		3
4		0017	0024	0032	0043	0055	0069	0086	0106	0128	0154		2
5		0001	0001	0002	0003	0004	0005	0007	0009	0012	0015		1
6		0000	0000	0000	0000	0000	0000	0000	0000	0000	0001		0
		89	88	87	86	85	84	83	82	81	80	p	x

x	p	21	22	23	24	25	26	27	28	29	30		
0		2431	2252	2084	1927	1780	1642	1513	1393	1281	1176		6
1		3877	3811	3735	3651	3560	3462	3358	3251	3139	3025		5
2		2577	2687	2789	2882	2966	3041	3105	3160	3206	3241		4
3		0913	1011	1111	1214	1318	1424	1531	1639	1746	1852		3
4		0182	0214	0249	0287	0330	0375	0425	0478	0535	0595		2
5		0019	0024	0030	0036	0044	0053	0063	0074	0087	0102		1
6		0001	0001	0001	0002	0002	0003	0004	0005	0006	0007		0
		79	78	77	76	75	74	73	72	71	70	p	x

x	p	31	32	33	34	35	36	37	38	39	40		
0		1079	0989	0905	0827	0754	0687	0625	0568	0515	0467		6
1		2909	2792	2673	2555	2437	2319	2203	2089	1976	1866		5
2		3267	3284	3292	3290	3280	3261	3235	3201	3159	3110		4
3		1957	2061	2162	2260	2355	2446	2533	2616	2693	2765		3
4		0660	0727	0799	0873	0951	1032	1116	1202	1291	1382		2
5		0119	0137	0157	0180	0205	0232	0262	0295	0330	0369		1
6		0009	0011	0013	0015	0018	0022	0026	0030	0035	0041		0
		69	68	67	66	65	64	63	62	61	60	p	x

x	p	41	42	43	44	45	46	47	48	49	50		
0		0422	0381	0343	0308	0277	0248	0222	0198	0176	0156		6
1		1759	1654	1552	1454	1359	1267	1179	1095	1014	0937		5
2		3055	2994	2928	2856	2780	2699	2615	2527	2436	2344		4
3		2831	2891	2945	2992	3032	3065	3091	3110	3121	3125		3
4		1475	1570	1666	1763	1861	1958	2056	2153	2249	2344		2
5		0410	0455	0503	0554	0609	0667	0729	0795	0864	0937		1
6		0048	0055	0063	0073	0083	0095	0108	0122	0138	0156		0
		59	58	57	56	55	54	53	52	51	50	p	x

(*Continued*)

TABLE I   Binomial Distribution ($n = 7$)

							$n = 7$						
x	p	01	02	03	04	05	06	07	08	09	10		
0		9321	8681	8080	7514	6983	6485	6017	5578	5168	4783		7
1		0659	1240	1749	2192	2573	2897	3170	3396	3578	3720		6
2		0020	0076	0162	0274	0406	0555	0716	0886	1061	1240		5
3		0000	0003	0008	0019	0036	0059	0090	0128	0175	0230		4
4		0000	0000	0000	0001	0002	0004	0007	0011	0017	0026		3
5		0000	0000	0000	0000	0000	0000	0000	0001	0001	0002		2
		99	98	97	96	95	94	93	92	91	90	p	x
x	p	11	12	13	14	15	16	17	18	19	20		
0		4423	4087	3773	3479	3206	2951	2714	2493	2288	2097		7
1		3827	3901	3946	3965	3960	3935	3891	3830	3756	3670		6
2		1419	1596	1769	1936	2097	2248	2391	2523	2643	2753		5
3		0292	0363	0441	0525	0617	0714	0816	0923	1033	1147		4
4		0036	0049	0066	0086	0109	0136	0167	0203	0242	0287		3
5		0003	0004	0006	0008	0012	0016	0021	0027	0034	0043		2
6		0000	0000	0000	0000	0001	0001	0001	0002	0003	0004		1
		89	88	87	86	85	84	83	82	81	80	p	x
x	p	21	22	23	24	25	26	27	28	29	30		
0		1920	1757	1605	1465	1335	1215	1105	1003	0910	0824		7
1		3573	3468	3356	3237	3115	2989	2860	2731	2600	2471		6
2		2850	2935	3007	3067	3115	3150	3174	3186	3186	3177		5
3		1263	1379	1497	1614	1730	1845	1956	2065	2169	2269		4
4		0336	0389	0447	0510	0577	0648	0724	0803	0886	0972		3
5		0054	0066	0080	0097	0115	0137	0161	0187	0217	0250		2
6		0005	0006	0008	0010	0013	0016	0020	0024	0030	0036		1
7		0000	0000	0000	0000	0001	0001	0001	0001	0002	0002		0
		79	78	77	76	75	74	73	72	71	70	p	x
x	p	31	32	33	34	35	36	37	38	39	40		
0		0745	0672	0606	0546	0490	0440	0394	0352	0314	0280		7
1		2342	2215	2090	1967	1848	1732	1619	1511	1407	1306		6
2		3156	3127	3088	3040	2985	2922	2853	2778	2698	2613		5
3		2363	2452	2535	2610	2679	2740	2793	2838	2875	2903		4
4		1062	1154	1248	1345	1442	1541	1640	1739	1838	1935		3
5		0286	0326	0369	0416	0466	0520	0578	0640	0705	0774		2
6		0043	0051	0061	0071	0084	0098	0113	0131	0150	0172		1
7		0003	0003	0004	0005	0006	0008	0009	0011	0014	0016		0
		69	68	67	66	65	64	63	62	61	60	p	x
x	p	41	42	43	44	45	46	47	48	49	50		
0		0249	0221	0195	0173	0152	0134	0117	0103	0090	0078		7
1		1211	1119	1032	0950	0872	0798	0729	0664	0604	0547		6
2		2524	2431	2336	2239	2140	2040	1940	1840	1740	1641		5
3		2923	2934	2937	2932	2918	2897	2867	2830	2786	2734		4
4		2031	2125	2216	2304	2388	2468	2543	2612	2676	2734		3
5		0847	0923	1003	1086	1172	1261	1353	1447	1543	1641		2
6		0196	0223	0252	0284	0320	0358	0400	0445	0494	0547		1
7		0019	0023	0027	0032	0037	0044	0051	0059	0068	0078		0
		59	58	57	56	55	54	53	52	51	50	p	x

(*Continued*)

Appendix B

TABLE I   Binomial Distribution ($n = 8$)

$n = 8$

x	p	01	02	03	04	05	06	07	08	09	10		
0		9227	8508	7837	7214	6634	6096	5596	5132	4703	4305		8
1		0746	1389	1939	2405	2793	3113	3370	3570	3721	3826		7
2		0026	0099	0210	0351	0515	0695	0888	1087	1288	1488		6
3		0001	0004	0013	0029	0054	0089	0134	0189	0255	0331		5
4		0000	0000	0001	0002	0004	0007	0013	0021	0031	0046		4
5		0000	0000	0000	0000	0000	0000	0001	0001	0002	0004		3
		99	98	97	96	95	94	93	92	91	90	p	x

x	p	11	12	13	14	15	16	17	18	19	20		
0		3937	3596	3282	2992	2725	2479	2252	2044	1853	1678		8
1		3892	3923	3923	3897	3847	3777	3691	3590	3477	3355		7
2		1684	1872	2052	2220	2376	2518	2646	2758	2855	2936		6
3		0416	0511	0613	0723	0839	0959	1084	1211	1339	1468		5
4		0064	0087	0115	0147	0185	0228	0277	0332	0393	0459		4
5		0006	0009	0014	0019	0026	0035	0045	0058	0074	0092		3
6		0000	0001	0001	0002	0002	0003	0005	0006	0009	0011		2
7		0000	0000	0000	0000	0000	0000	0000	0001	0001	0001		1
		89	88	87	86	85	84	83	82	81	80	p	x

x	p	21	22	23	24	25	26	27	28	29	30		
0		1517	1370	1236	1113	1001	0899	0806	0722	0646	0576		8
1		3226	3092	2953	2812	2670	2527	2386	2247	2110	1977		7
2		3002	3052	3087	3108	3115	3108	3089	3058	3017	2965		6
3		1596	1722	1844	1963	2076	2184	2285	2379	2464	2541		5
4		0530	0607	0689	0775	0865	0959	1056	1156	1258	1361		4
5		0113	0137	0165	0196	0231	0270	0313	0360	0411	0467		3
6		0015	0019	0025	0031	0038	0047	0058	0070	0084	0100		2
7		0001	0002	0002	0003	0004	0005	0006	0008	0010	0012		1
8		0000	0000	0000	0000	0000	0000	0000	0000	0001	0001		0
		79	78	77	76	75	74	73	72	71	70	p	x

x	p	31	32	33	34	35	36	37	38	39	40		
0		0514	0457	0406	0360	0319	0281	0248	0218	0192	0168		8
1		1847	1721	1600	1484	1373	1267	1166	1071	0981	0896		7
2		2904	2835	2758	2675	2587	2494	2397	2297	2194	2090		6
3		2609	2668	2717	2756	2786	2805	2815	2815	2806	2787		5
4		1465	1569	1673	1775	1875	1973	2067	2157	2242	2322		4
5		0527	0591	0659	0732	0808	0888	0971	1058	1147	1239		3
6		0118	0139	0162	0188	0217	0250	0285	0324	0367	0413		2
7		0015	0019	0023	0028	0033	0040	0048	0057	0067	0079		1
8		0001	0001	0001	0002	0002	0003	0004	0004	0005	0007		0
		69	68	67	66	65	64	63	62	61	60	p	x

x	p	41	42	43	44	45	46	47	48	49	50		
0		0147	0128	0111	0097	0084	0072	0062	0053	0046	0039		8
1		0816	0742	0672	0608	0548	0493	0442	0395	0352	0312		7
2		1985	1880	1776	1672	1569	1469	1371	1275	1183	1094		6
3		2759	2723	2679	2627	2568	2503	2431	2355	2273	2187		5
4		2397	2465	2526	2580	2627	2665	2695	2717	2730	2734		4
5		1332	1428	1525	1622	1719	1816	1912	2006	2098	2187		3
6		0463	0517	0575	0637	0703	0774	0848	0926	1008	1094		2
7		0092	0107	0124	0143	0164	0188	0215	0244	0277	0312		1
8		0008	0010	0012	0014	0017	0020	0024	0028	0033	0039		0
		59	58	57	56	55	54	53	52	51	50	p	x

(*Continued*)

TABLE I   Binomial Distribution ($n = 9$)

$n = 9$

x	p	01	02	03	04	05	06	07	08	09	10		
0		9135	8337	7602	6925	6302	5730	5204	4722	4279	3874		9
1		0830	1531	2116	2597	2985	3292	3525	3695	3809	3874		8
2		0034	0125	0262	0433	0629	0840	1061	1285	1507	1722		7
3		0001	0006	0019	0042	0077	0125	0186	0261	0348	0446		6
4		0000	0000	0001	0003	0006	0012	0021	0034	0052	0074		5
5		0000	0000	0000	0000	0000	0001	0002	0003	0005	0008		4
6		0000	0000	0000	0000	0000	0000	0000	0000	0000	0001		3
		99	98	97	96	95	94	93	92	91	90	p	x

x	p	11	12	13	14	15	16	17	18	19	20		
0		3504	3165	2855	2573	2316	2082	1869	1676	1501	1342		9
1		3897	3884	3840	3770	3679	3569	3446	3312	2169	3020		8
2		1927	2119	2295	2455	2597	2720	2823	2908	2973	3020		7
3		0556	0674	0800	0933	1069	1209	1349	1489	1627	1762		6
4		0103	0138	0179	0228	0283	0345	0415	0490	0573	0661		5
5		0013	0019	0027	0037	0050	0066	0085	0108	0134	0165		4
6		0001	0002	0003	0004	0006	0008	0012	0016	0021	0028		3
7		0000	0000	0000	0000	0000	0001	0001	0001	0002	0003		2
		89	88	87	86	85	84	83	82	81	80	p	x

x	p	21	22	23	24	25	26	27	28	29	30		
0		1199	1069	0952	0846	0751	0665	0589	0520	0458	0404		9
1		2867	2713	2558	2404	2253	2104	1960	1820	1685	1556		8
2		3049	3061	3056	3037	3003	2957	2899	2831	2754	2668		7
3		1891	2014	2130	2238	2336	2424	2502	2569	2624	2668		6
4		0754	0852	0954	1060	1168	1278	1388	1499	1608	1715		5
5		0200	0240	0285	0335	0389	0449	0513	0583	0657	0735		4
6		0036	0045	0057	0070	0087	0105	0127	0151	0179	0210		3
7		0004	0005	0007	0010	0012	0016	0020	0025	0031	0039		2
8		0000	0000	0001	0001	0001	0001	0002	0002	0003	0004		1
		79	78	77	76	75	74	73	72	71	70	p	x

x	p	31	32	33	34	35	36	37	38	39	40		
0		0355	0311	0272	0238	0207	0180	0156	0135	0117	0101		9
1		1433	1317	1206	1102	1004	0912	0826	0747	0673	0605		8
2		2576	2478	2376	2270	2162	2052	1941	1831	1721	1612		7
3		2701	2721	2731	2729	2716	2693	2660	2618	2567	2508		6
4		1820	1921	2017	2109	2194	2272	2344	2407	2462	2508		5
5		0818	0904	0994	1086	1181	1278	1376	1475	1574	1672		4
6		0245	0284	0326	0373	0424	0479	0539	0603	0671	0743		3
7		0047	0057	0069	0082	0098	0116	0136	0158	0184	0212		2
8		0005	0007	0008	0011	0013	0016	0020	0024	0029	0035		1
9		0000	0000	0000	0001	0001	0001	0001	0002	0002	0003		0
		69	68	67	66	65	64	63	62	61	60	p	x

x	p	41	42	43	44	45	46	47	48	49	50		
0		0087	0074	0064	0054	0046	0039	0033	0028	0023	0020		9
1		0542	0484	0431	0383	0339	0299	0263	0231	0202	0176		8
2		1506	1402	1301	1204	1110	1020	0934	0853	0776	0703		7
3		2442	2369	2291	2207	2119	2027	1933	1837	1739	1641		6
4		2545	2573	2592	2601	2600	2590	2571	2543	2506	2461		5
5		1769	1863	1955	2044	2128	2207	2280	2347	2408	2461		4
6		0819	0900	0983	1070	1160	1253	1348	1445	1542	1641		3
7		0244	0279	0318	0360	0407	0458	0512	0571	0635	0703		2
8		0042	0051	0060	0071	0083	0097	0014	0132	0153	0176		1
9		0003	0004	0005	0006	0008	0009	0011	0014	0016	0020		0
		59	58	57	56	55	54	53	52	51	50	p	x

(*Continued*)

TABLE I   Binomial Distribution ($n = 10$)

$n = 10$

x	p	01	02	03	04	05	06	07	08	09	10	
0		9044	8171	7374	6648	5987	5386	4840	4344	3894	3487	10
1		0914	1667	2281	2770	3151	3438	3643	3777	3851	3874	9
2		0042	0153	0317	0519	0746	0988	1234	1478	1714	1937	8
3		0001	0008	0026	0058	0105	0168	0248	0343	0452	0574	7
4		0000	0000	0001	0004	0010	0019	0033	0052	0078	0112	6
5		0000	0000	0000	0000	0001	0001	0003	0005	0009	0015	5
6		0000	0000	0000	0000	0000	0000	0000	0000	0001	0001	4
		99	98	97	96	95	94	93	92	91	90	p x

x	p	11	12	13	14	15	16	17	18	19	20	
0		3118	2785	2484	2213	1969	1749	1552	1374	1216	1074	10
1		3854	3798	3712	3603	3474	3331	3178	3017	2852	2684	9
2		2143	2330	2496	2639	2759	2856	2929	2980	3010	3020	8
3		0706	0847	0995	1146	1298	1450	1600	1745	1883	2013	7
4		0153	0202	0260	0326	0401	0483	0573	0670	0773	0881	6
5		0023	0033	0047	0064	0085	0111	0141	0177	0218	0264	5
6		0002	0004	0006	0009	0012	0018	0024	0032	0043	0055	4
7		0000	0000	0000	0001	0001	0002	0003	0004	0006	0008	3
8		0000	0000	0000	0000	0000	0000	0000	0000	0001	0001	2
		89	88	87	86	85	84	83	82	81	80	p x

x	p	21	22	23	24	25	26	27	28	29	30	
0		0947	0834	0733	0643	0563	0492	0430	0374	0326	0282	10
1		2517	2351	2188	2030	1877	1730	1590	1456	1330	1211	9
2		3011	2984	2942	2885	2816	2735	2646	2548	2444	2335	8
3		2134	2244	2343	2429	2503	2563	2609	2642	2662	2668	7
4		0993	1108	1225	1343	1460	1576	1689	1798	1903	2001	6
5		0317	0375	0439	0509	0584	0664	0750	0839	0933	1029	5
6		0070	0088	0109	0134	0162	0195	0231	0272	0317	0368	4
7		0011	0014	0019	0024	0031	0039	0049	0060	0074	0090	3
8		0001	0002	0002	0003	0004	0005	0007	0009	0011	0014	2
9		0000	0000	0000	0000	0000	0000	0001	0001	0001	0001	1
		79	78	77	76	75	74	73	72	71	70	p x

x	p	31	32	33	34	35	36	37	38	39	40	
0		0245	0211	0182	0157	0135	0115	0098	0084	0071	0060	10
1		1099	0995	0898	0808	0725	0649	0578	0514	0456	0430	9
2		2222	2107	1990	1873	1757	1642	1529	1419	1312	1209	8
3		2662	2644	2614	2573	2522	2462	2394	2319	2237	2150	7
4		2093	2177	2253	2320	2377	2424	2461	2487	2503	2508	6
5		1128	1229	1332	1434	1536	1636	1734	1829	1920	2007	5
6		0422	0482	0547	0616	0689	0767	0849	0934	1023	1115	4
7		0108	0130	0154	0181	0212	0247	0285	0327	0374	0425	3
8		0018	0023	0028	0035	0043	0052	0063	0075	0090	0106	2
9		0002	0002	0003	0004	0005	0006	0008	0010	0013	0016	1
10		0000	0000	0000	0000	0000	0000	0000	0001	0001	0001	0
		69	68	67	66	65	64	63	62	61	60	p x

x	p	41	42	43	44	45	46	47	48	49	50	
0		0051	0043	0036	0030	0025	0021	0017	0014	0012	0010	10
1		0355	0312	0273	0238	0207	0180	0155	0133	0114	0098	9
2		1111	1017	0927	0843	0763	0688	0619	0554	0494	0439	8
3		2058	1963	1865	1765	1665	1654	1464	1364	1267	1172	7
4		2503	2488	2462	2427	2384	2331	2271	2204	2130	2051	6
5		2087	2162	2229	2289	2340	2383	2417	2441	2456	2461	5
6		1209	1304	1401	1499	1596	1692	1786	1878	1966	2051	4
7		0480	0540	0604	0673	0746	0824	0905	0991	1080	1172	3
8		0125	0147	0171	0198	0229	0263	0301	0343	0389	0439	2
9		0019	0024	0029	0035	0042	0050	0059	0070	0083	0098	1
10		0001	0002	0002	0003	0003	0004	0005	0006	0008	0010	0
		59	58	57	56	55	54	53	52	51	50	p x

(Continued)

TABLE I Binomial Distribution ($n = 20$)

$n = 20$

x	p	01	02	03	04	05	06	07	08	**09**	**10**		
0		8179	6676	5438	4420	3585	2901	2342	1887	1516	1216		20
1		1652	2725	3364	3683	3774	3703	3526	3282	3000	2702		19
2		0159	0528	0988	1458	1887	2246	2521	2711	2828	2852		18
3		0010	0065	0183	0364	0596	0860	1139	1414	1672	1901		17
4		0000	0006	0024	0065	0133	0233	0364	0523	0703	0898		16
5		0000	0000	0002	0009	0022	0048	0088	0145	0222	0319		15
6		0000	0000	0000	0001	0003	0008	0017	0032	0055	0089		14
7		0000	0000	0000	0000	0000	0001	0002	0005	0011	0020		13
8		0000	0000	0000	0000	0000	0000	0000	0001	0002	0004		12
9		0000	0000	0000	0000	0000	0000	0000	0000	0000	0001		11
		99	98	97	96	95	94	93	92	91	90	p	x

x	p	11	12	13	14	15	16	17	18	19	20		
0		0972	0776	0617	0490	0388	0306	0241	0189	0148	0115		20
1		2403	2115	1844	1595	1368	1165	0986	0829	0693	0576		19
2		2822	2740	2618	2466	2293	2109	1919	1730	1545	1369		18
3		2093	2242	2347	2409	2428	2410	2358	2278	2175	2054		17
4		1099	1299	1491	1666	1821	1951	2053	2125	2168	2182		16
5		0435	0567	0713	0868	1028	1189	1345	1493	1627	1746		15
6		0134	0193	0266	0353	0454	0566	0689	0819	0954	1091		14
7		0033	0053	0080	0115	0160	0216	0282	0360	0448	0545		13
8		0007	0012	0019	0030	0046	0067	0094	0128	0171	0222		12
9		0001	0002	0004	0007	0011	0017	0026	0038	0053	0074		11
10		0000	0000	0001	0001	0002	0004	0006	0009	0014	0020		10
11		0000	0000	0000	0000	0000	0001	0001	0002	0003	0005		9
12		0000	0000	0000	0000	0000	0000	0000	0000	0001	0001		8
		89	88	87	86	85	84	83	82	81	80	p	x

x	p	21	22	23	24	25	26	27	28	29	30		
0		0090	0069	0054	0041	0032	0024	0016	0014	0011	0008		20
1		0477	0392	0321	0261	0211	0170	0137	0109	0087	0068		19
2		1204	1050	0910	0783	0669	0569	0480	0403	0336	0278		18
3		1920	1777	1631	1484	1339	1199	1065	0940	0823	0716		17
4		2169	2131	2070	1991	1897	1790	1675	1553	1429	1304		16
5		1845	1923	1979	2012	2023	2013	1982	1933	1868	1789		15
6		1226	1356	1478	1589	1686	1768	1833	1879	1907	1916		14
7		0652	0765	0883	1003	1124	1242	1356	1462	1558	1643		13
8		0282	0351	0429	0515	0609	0709	0815	0924	1034	1144		12
9		0100	0132	0171	0217	0271	0332	0402	0479	0563	0654		11
10		0029	0041	0056	0075	0099	0128	0163	0205	0253	0308		10
11		0007	0010	0015	0022	0030	0041	0055	0072	0094	0120		9
12		0001	0002	0003	0005	0008	0011	0015	0021	0029	0039		8
13		0000	0000	0001	0001	0002	0002	0003	0005	0007	0010		7
14		0000	0000	0000	0000	0000	0000	0010	0010	0001	0002		6
		79	78	77	76	75	74	73	72	71	70	p	x

(*Continued*)

TABLE I Binomial Distribution ($n = 20$, cont.)

$n = 20$

x	p	31	32	33	34	35	36	37	38	39	40	
0		0006	0004	0003	0002	0002	0001	0001	0001	0001	0000	20
1		0054	0042	0033	0025	0020	0015	0011	0009	0007	0005	19
2		0229	0188	0153	0124	0100	0080	0064	0050	0040	0031	18
3		0619	0531	0453	0383	0323	0270	0224	0185	0152	0123	17
4		1181	1062	0947	0839	0738	0645	0559	0482	0412	0350	16
5		1698	1599	1493	1384	1272	1161	1051	0945	0843	0746	15
6		1907	1881	1839	1782	1712	1632	1543	1447	1347	1244	14
7		1714	1770	1811	1836	1844	1836	1812	1774	1722	1659	13
8		1251	1354	1450	1537	1614	1678	1730	1767	1790	1797	12
9		0750	0849	0952	1056	1158	1259	1354	1444	1526	1597	11
10		0370	0440	0516	0598	0686	0779	0875	0974	1073	1171	10
11		0151	1188	0231	0280	0336	0398	0467	0542	0624	0710	9
12		0051	0066	0085	0108	0136	0168	0206	0249	0299	0355	8
13		0014	0019	0026	0034	0045	0058	0074	0094	0118	0146	7
14		0003	0005	0006	0009	0012	0016	0022	0029	0038	0049	6
15		0001	0001	0001	0002	0003	0004	0005	0007	0010	0013	5
16		0000	0000	0000	0000	0000	0001	0001	0001	0002	0003	4
		69	68	67	66	65	64	63	62	61	60	p	x

x	p	41	42	43	44	45	46	47	48	49	50	
1		0004	0003	0002	0001	0001	0001	0001	0000	0000	0000	19
2		0024	0018	0014	0011	0008	0006	0005	0003	0002	0002	18
3		0100	0080	0064	0051	0040	0031	0024	0019	0014	0011	17
4		0295	0247	0206	0170	0139	0113	0092	0074	0059	0046	16
5		0656	0573	0496	0427	0365	0309	0260	0217	0180	0148	15
6		1140	1037	0936	0839	0746	0658	0577	0501	0432	0370	14
7		1585	1502	1413	1318	1221	1122	1023	0925	0830	0739	13
8		1790	1768	1732	1683	1623	1553	1474	1388	1296	1201	12
9		1658	1707	1742	1763	1771	1763	1742	1708	1661	1602	11
10		1268	1359	1446	1524	1593	1652	1700	1734	1755	1762	10
11		0801	0895	0991	1089	1185	1280	1370	1455	1533	1602	9
12		0417	0486	0561	0642	0727	0818	0911	1007	1105	1201	8
13		0178	0217	0260	0310	0366	0429	0497	0572	0653	0739	7
14		0062	0078	0098	0122	0150	0183	0221	0264	0314	0370	6
15		0017	0023	0030	0038	0049	0062	0078	0098	0121	0148	5
16		0004	0005	0007	0009	0013	0017	0022	0028	0036	0046	4
17		0001	0001	0001	0002	0002	0003	0005	0006	0008	0011	3
18		0000	0000	0000	0000	0000	0000	0001	0001	0001	0002	2
		59	58	57	56	55	54	53	52	51	50	p	x

(*Continued*)

TABLE I Binomial Distribution ($n = 50$)

$n = 50$

x	p	01	02	03	04	05	06	07	08	09	10	
0		6050	3642	2181	1299	0769	0453	0266	0155	0090	0052	50
1		3056	3716	3372	2706	2025	1447	0999	0672	0443	0286	49
2		0756	1858	2555	2762	2611	2262	1843	1433	1073	0779	48
3		0122	0607	1264	1842	2199	2311	2219	1993	1698	1386	47
4		0015	0145	0459	0902	1360	1733	1963	2037	1973	1809	46
5		0001	0027	0131	0346	0658	1018	1359	1629	1795	1849	45
6		0000	0004	0030	0108	0260	0487	0767	1063	1332	1541	44
7		0000	0001	0006	0028	0086	0195	0363	0581	0828	1076	43
8		0000	0000	0001	0006	0024	0067	0147	0271	0440	0643	42
9		0000	0000	0000	0001	0006	0020	0052	0110	0203	0333	41
10		0000	0000	0000	0000	0001	0005	0016	0039	0082	0152	40
11		0000	0000	0000	0000	0000	0001	0004	0012	0030	0061	39
12		0000	0000	0000	0000	0000	0000	0001	0004	0010	0022	38
13		0000	0000	0000	0000	0000	0000	0000	0001	0003	0007	37
14		0000	0000	0000	0000	0000	0000	0000	0000	0001	0002	36
15		0000	0000	0000	0000	0000	0000	0000	0000	0000	0001	35
		99	98	97	96	95	94	93	92	91	90	p	x

x	p	11	12	13	14	15	16	17	18	19	20	
0		0029	0017	0009	0005	0003	0002	0001	0000	0000	0000	50
1		0182	0114	0071	0043	0026	0016	0009	0005	0003	0002	49
2		0552	0382	0259	0172	0113	0073	0046	0029	0018	0011	48
3		1091	0833	0619	0449	0319	0222	0151	0102	0067	0044	47
4		1584	1334	1086	0858	0661	0496	0364	0262	0185	0128	46
5		1801	1674	1493	1286	1072	0869	0687	0530	0400	0295	45
6		1670	1712	1674	1570	1419	1242	1055	0872	0703	0554	44
7		1297	1467	1572	1606	1575	1487	1358	1203	1037	0870	43
8		0862	1075	1262	1406	1493	1523	1495	1420	1307	1169	42
9		0497	0684	0880	1068	1230	1353	1429	1454	1431	1364	41
10		0252	0383	0539	0713	0890	1057	1200	1309	1376	1398	40
11		0113	0190	0293	0422	0571	0732	0894	1045	1174	1271	39
12		0045	0084	0142	0223	0328	0453	0595	0745	0895	1033	38
13		0016	0034	0062	0106	0169	0252	0356	0478	0613	0755	37
14		0005	0012	0025	0046	0079	0127	0193	0277	0380	0499	36
15		0002	0004	0009	0018	0033	0058	0095	0146	0214	0299	35
16		0000	0001	0003	0006	0013	0024	0042	0070	0110	0164	34
17		0000	0000	0001	0002	0005	0009	0017	0031	0052	0082	33
18		0000	0000	0000	0001	0001	0003	0007	0012	0022	0037	32
19		0000	0000	0000	0000	0000	0001	0002	0005	0009	0016	31
20		0000	0000	0000	0000	0000	0000	0001	0002	0003	0006	30
21		0000	0000	0000	0000	0000	0000	0000	0000	0001	0002	29
22		0000	0000	0000	0000	0000	0000	0000	0000	0000	0001	28
		89	88	87	86	85	84	83	82	81	80	p	x

(*Continued*)

Appendix B

TABLE I Binomial Distribution ($n = 50$, cont.)

$n = 50$

x	p	21	22	23	24	25	26	27	28	29	30	
1		0001	0001	0000	0000	0000	0000	0000	0000	0000	0000	49
2		0007	0004	0002	0001	0001	0000	0000	0000	0000	0000	48
3		0028	0018	0011	0007	0004	0002	0001	0001	0000	0000	47
4		0088	0059	0039	0025	0016	0010	0006	0004	0002	0001	46
5		0214	0152	0106	0073	0049	0033	0021	0014	0009	0006	45
6		0427	0322	0238	0173	0123	0087	0060	0040	0027	0018	44
7		0713	0571	0447	0344	0259	0191	0139	0099	0069	0048	43
8		1019	0865	0718	0583	0463	0361	0276	0207	0152	0110	42
9		1263	1139	1001	0859	0721	0592	0476	0375	0290	0220	41
10		1377	1317	1226	1113	0985	0852	0721	0598	0485	0386	40
11		1331	1351	1332	1278	1194	1089	0970	0845	0721	0602	39
12		1150	1238	1293	1311	1294	1244	1166	1068	0957	0838	38
13		0894	1021	1129	1210	1261	1277	1261	1215	1142	1050	37
14		0628	0761	0891	1010	1110	1186	1233	1248	1233	1189	36
15		0400	0515	0639	0766	0888	1000	1094	1165	1209	1223	35
16		0233	0318	0417	0529	0648	0769	0885	0991	1080	1147	34
17		0124	0179	0249	0334	0432	0540	0655	0771	0882	0983	33
18		0060	0093	0137	0193	0264	0348	0444	0550	0661	0772	32
19		0027	0044	0069	0103	0148	0206	0277	0360	0454	0558	31
20		0011	0019	0032	0050	0077	0112	0159	0217	0288	0370	30
21		0004	0008	0014	0023	0036	0056	0084	0121	0168	0227	29
22		0001	0003	0005	0009	0016	0026	0041	0062	0090	0128	28
23		0000	0001	0002	0004	0006	0011	0018	0029	0045	0067	27
24		0000	0000	0001	0001	0002	0004	0008	0013	0021	0032	26
25		0000	0000	0000	0000	0001	0002	0003	0005	0009	0014	25
26		0000	0000	0000	0000	0000	0001	0001	0002	0003	0006	24
27		0000	0000	0000	0000	0000	0000	0000	0001	0001	0002	23
28		0000	0000	0000	0000	0000	0000	0000	0000	0000	0001	22
		79	78	77	76	75	74	73	72	71	70	x

(*Continued*)

TABLE I   Binomial Distribution ($n = 50$, cont.)

$n = 50$

x	p	31	32	33	34	35	36	37	38	39	40	
4		0001	0000	0000	0000	0000	0000	0000	0000	0000	0000	46
5		0003	0002	0001	0001	0000	0000	0000	0000	0000	0000	45
6		0011	0007	0005	0003	0002	0001	0001	0000	0000	0000	44
7		0032	0022	0014	0009	0006	0004	0002	0001	0001	0000	43
8		0078	0055	0037	0025	0017	0011	0007	0004	0003	0002	42
9		0164	0120	0086	0061	0042	0029	0019	0013	0008	0005	41
10		0301	0231	0174	0128	0093	0066	0046	0032	0022	0014	40
11		0493	0395	0311	0240	0182	0136	0099	0071	0050	0035	39
12		0719	0604	0498	0402	0319	0248	0189	0142	0105	0076	38
13		0944	0831	0717	0606	0502	0408	0325	0255	0195	0147	37
14		1121	1034	0933	0825	0714	0607	0505	0412	0330	0260	36
15		1209	1168	1103	1020	0923	0819	0712	0606	0507	0415	35
16		1188	1202	1189	1149	1088	1008	0914	0813	0709	0606	34
17		1068	1132	1171	1184	1171	1133	1074	0997	0906	0808	33
18		0880	0976	1057	1118	1156	1169	1156	1120	1062	0987	32
19		0666	0774	0877	0970	1048	1107	1144	1156	1144	1109	31
20		0463	0564	0670	0775	0875	0956	1041	1098	1134	1146	30
21		0297	0379	0471	0570	0673	0776	0874	0962	1035	1091	29
22		0176	0235	0306	0387	0478	0575	0676	0777	0873	0959	28
23		0096	0135	0183	0243	0313	0394	0484	0580	0679	0778	27
24		0049	0071	0102	0141	0190	0249	0319	0400	0489	0584	26
25		0023	0035	0052	0075	0106	0146	0195	0255	0325	0405	25
26		0010	0016	0025	0037	0055	0079	0110	0150	0200	0259	24
27		0004	0007	0011	0017	0026	0039	0058	0082	0113	0154	23
28		0001	0003	0004	0007	0012	0018	0028	0041	0060	0084	22
29		0000	0001	0002	0003	0005	0008	0012	0019	0029	0043	21
30		0000	0000	0001	0001	0002	0003	0005	0008	0013	0020	20
31		0000	0000	0000	0000	0001	0001	0002	0003	0005	0009	19
32		0000	0000	0000	0000	0000	0000	0001	0001	0002	0003	18
33		0000	0000	0000	0000	0000	0000	0000	0000	0001	0001	17
		69	68	67	66	65	64	63	62	61	60	p	x

(Continued)

TABLE I   Binomial Distribution ($n = 50$, cont.)

$n = 50$

x	p	41	42	43	44	45	46	47	48	49	50	
8		0001	0001	0000	0000	0000	0000	0000	0000	0000	0000	42
9		0083	0002	0001	0001	0000	0000	0000	0000	0000	0000	41
10		0009	0006	0004	0002	0001	0001	0001	0000	0000	0000	40
11		0024	0016	0010	0007	0004	0003	0002	0001	0001	0000	39
12		0054	0037	0026	0017	0011	0007	0005	0003	0002	0001	38
13		0109	0079	0057	0040	0027	0018	0012	0008	0005	0003	37
14		0200	0152	0113	0082	0059	0041	0029	0019	0013	0008	36
15		0334	0264	0204	0155	0116	0085	0061	0043	0030	0020	35
16		0508	0418	0337	0267	0207	0158	0118	0086	0062	0044	34
17		0706	0605	0508	0419	0339	0269	0209	0159	0119	0087	33
18		0899	0803	0703	0604	0508	0420	0340	0270	0210	0160	32
19		1053	0979	0893	0799	0700	0602	0507	0419	0340	0270	31
20		1134	1099	1044	0973	0588	0795	0697	0600	0506	0419	30
21		1126	1137	1126	1092	1030	0967	0884	0791	0695	0598	29
22		1031	1086	1119	1131	1119	1086	1033	0963	0880	0788	28
23		0872	0957	1028	1082	1115	1126	1115	1082	1029	0960	27
24		0682	0780	0872	0956	1026	1079	1112	1124	1112	1080	26
25		0493	0587	0684	0781	0873	0956	1026	1079	1112	1123	25
26		0329	0409	0497	0590	0687	0783	0875	0957	1027	1080	24
27		0203	0263	0333	0412	0500	0593	0690	0786	0877	0960	23
28		0116	0157	0206	0266	0336	0415	0502	0596	0692	0788	22
29		0061	0086	0118	0159	0208	0268	0338	0417	0504	0598	21
30		0030	0044	0062	0087	0119	0160	0210	0270	0339	0419	20
31		0013	0020	0030	0044	0063	0088	0120	0161	0210	0270	19
32		0006	0009	0014	0021	0031	0044	0063	0088	0120	0160	18
33		0002	0003	0006	0009	0014	0021	0031	0044	0063	0087	17
34		0001	0001	0002	0003	0006	0009	0014	0020	0030	0044	16
35		0000	0000	0001	0001	0002	0003	0005	0009	0013	0020	15
36		0000	0000	0000	0000	0001	0001	0002	0003	0005	0006	14
37		0000	0000	0000	0000	0000	0000	0001	0001	0002	0003	13
38		0000	0000	0000	0000	0000	0000	0000	0000	0001	0001	12
		59	58	57	56	55	54	53	52	51	50	p	x

(*Continued*)

TABLE I   Binomial Distribution ($n = 100$)

							$n = 100$						
x	p	01	02	03	04	05	06	07	08	09	10		
0		3660	1326	0476	0169	0059	0021	0007	0002	0001	0000		100
1		3697	2707	1471	0703	0312	0131	0053	0021	0008	0003		99
2		1849	2734	2252	1450	0812	0414	0198	0090	0039	0016		98
3		0610	1823	2275	1973	1396	0864	0486	0254	0125	0059		97
4		0149	0902	1706	1994	1781	1338	0888	0536	0301	0159		96
5		0029	0353	1013	1595	1800	1639	1283	0895	0571	0339		95
6		0005	0114	0496	1052	1500	1657	1529	1233	0895	0596		94
7		0001	0031	0206	0589	1060	1420	1545	1440	1188	0889		93
8		0000	0007	0074	0285	0649	1054	1352	1455	1366	1148		92
9		0000	0002	0023	0121	0349	0687	1040	1293	1381	1304		91
10		0000	0000	0007	0046	0167	0399	0712	1024	1243	1319		90
11		0000	0000	0002	0016	0072	0209	0439	0728	1006	1199		89
12		0000	0000	0000	0005	0028	0099	0245	0470	0738	0988		88
13		0000	0000	0000	0001	0010	0043	0125	0276	0494	0743		87
14		0000	0000	0000	0000	0003	0017	0058	0149	0304	0513		86
15		0000	0000	0000	0000	0001	0006	0025	0074	0172	0327		85
16		0000	0000	0000	0000	0000	0002	0010	0034	0090	0193		84
17		0000	0000	0000	0000	0000	0001	0004	0015	0044	0106		83
18		0000	0000	0000	0000	0000	0000	0001	0006	0020	0054		82
19		0000	0000	0000	0000	0000	0000	0000	0002	0009	0026		81
20		0000	0000	0000	0000	0000	0000	0000	0001	0003	0012		80
21		0000	0000	0000	0000	0000	0000	0000	0000	0001	0005		79
22		0000	0000	0000	0000	0000	0000	0000	0000	0000	0002		78
23		0000	0000	0000	0000	0000	0000	0000	0000	0000	0001		77
		99	98	97	96	95	94	93	92	91	90	p	x

(*Continued*)

TABLE I Binomial Distribution ($n = 100$, cont.)

$n = 100$

x	p	11	12	13	14	15	16	17	18	19	20	
1		0001	0000	0000	0000	0000	0000	0000	0000	0000	0000	99
2		0007	0003	0001	0000	0000	0000	0000	0000	0000	0000	98
3		0027	0012	0005	0002	0001	0000	0000	0000	0000	0000	97
4		0080	0038	0018	0008	0003	0001	0001	0000	0000	0000	96
5		0189	0100	0050	0024	0011	0005	0002	0001	0000	0000	95
6		0369	0215	0119	0063	0031	0015	0007	0003	0001	0001	94
7		0613	0394	0238	0137	0075	0039	0020	0009	0004	0002	93
8		0881	0625	0414	0259	0153	0086	0047	0024	0012	0006	92
9		1112	0871	0632	0430	0276	0168	0098	0054	0029	0015	91
10		1251	1080	0860	0637	0444	0292	0182	0108	0062	0034	90
11		1265	1205	1051	0849	0640	0454	0305	0194	0118	0069	89
12		1160	1219	1165	1025	0838	0642	0463	0316	0206	0128	88
13		0970	1125	1179	1130	1001	0827	0642	0470	0327	0216	87
14		0745	0954	1094	1143	1098	0979	0817	0641	0476	0335	86
15		0528	0745	0938	1067	1111	1070	0960	0807	0640	0481	85
16		0347	0540	0744	0922	1041	1082	1044	0941	0798	0638	84
17		1212	0364	0549	0742	0908	1019	1057	1021	0924	0789	83
18		0121	0229	0379	0557	0739	0895	0998	1033	1000	0909	82
19		0064	0135	0244	0391	0563	0736	0882	0979	1012	0981	81
20		0032	0074	0148	0258	0402	0567	0732	0870	0962	0993	80
21		0015	0039	0084	0160	0270	0412	0571	0728	0859	0946	79
22		0007	0019	0045	0094	0171	0282	0420	0574	0724	0849	78
23		0003	0009	0023	0052	0103	0182	0292	0427	0576	0720	77
24		0001	0004	0011	0027	0058	0111	0192	0301	0433	0577	76
25		0000	0002	0005	0013	0031	0064	0119	0201	0309	0439	75
26		0000	0001	0002	0006	0016	0035	0071	0127	0209	0317	74
27		0000	0000	0001	0003	0008	0018	0040	0076	0134	0217	73
28		0000	0000	0000	0001	0004	0009	0021	0044	0082	0141	72
29		0000	0000	0000	0000	0002	0004	0011	0024	0048	0088	71
30		0000	0000	0000	0000	0001	0002	0005	0012	0027	0052	70
31		0000	0000	0000	0000	0000	0001	0002	0006	0014	0029	69
32		0000	0000	0000	0000	0000	0000	0001	0003	0007	0016	68
33		0000	0000	0000	0000	0000	0000	0000	0001	0003	0008	67
34		0000	0000	0000	0000	0000	0000	0000	0001	0002	0004	66
35		0000	0000	0000	0000	0000	0000	0000	0000	0001	0002	65
36		0000	0000	0000	0000	0000	0000	0000	0000	0000	0001	64
		89	88	87	86	85	84	83	82	81	80	p	x

(Continued)

TABLE I   Binomial Distribution ($n = 100$, cont.)

$n = 100$

x	p	21	22	23	24	25	26	27	28	29	30	
7		0001	0000	0000	0000	0000	0000	0000	0000	0000	0000	93
8		0003	0001	0001	0000	0000	0000	0000	0000	0000	0000	92
9		0007	0003	0002	0001	0000	0000	0000	0000	0000	0000	91
10		0018	0009	0004	0002	0001	0000	0000	0000	0000	0000	90
11		0038	0021	0011	0005	0003	0001	0001	0000	0000	0000	89
12		0076	0043	0024	0012	0006	0003	0001	0001	0000	0000	88
13		0136	0082	0048	0027	0014	0007	0004	0002	0001	0000	87
14		0225	0144	0089	0052	0030	0016	0009	0004	0002	0001	86
15		1343	0233	0152	0095	0057	0033	0018	0010	0005	0002	85
16		0484	0350	0241	0159	0100	0061	0035	0020	0011	0006	84
17		0636	0487	0356	0248	0165	0106	0065	0038	0022	0012	83
18		0780	0634	0490	0361	0254	0171	0111	0069	0041	0024	82
19		0895	0772	0631	0492	0365	0259	0177	0115	0072	0044	81
20		0963	0881	0764	0629	0493	0369	0264	0182	0120	0076	80
21		0975	0947	0869	0756	0626	0494	0373	0269	0186	0124	79
22		0931	0959	0932	0858	0749	0623	0495	0376	0273	0190	78
23		0839	0917	0944	0919	0847	0743	0621	0495	0378	0277	77
24		0716	0830	0905	0931	0906	0837	0736	0618	0496	0380	76
25		0578	0712	0822	0893	0918	0894	0828	0731	0615	0496	75
26		0444	0579	0708	0814	0883	0906	0883	0819	0725	0613	74
27		0323	0448	0580	0704	0806	0873	0896	0873	0812	0720	73
28		0224	0329	0451	0580	0701	0799	0864	0886	0864	0804	72
29		0148	0231	0335	0455	0580	0697	0793	0855	0876	0856	71
30		0093	0154	0237	0340	0458	0580	0694	0787	0847	0868	70
31		0056	0098	0160	0242	0344	0460	0580	0691	0781	0840	69
32		0032	0060	0103	0165	0248	0349	0462	0579	0688	0776	68
33		0018	0035	0063	0107	0170	0252	0352	0464	0579	0685	67
34		0009	0019	0037	0067	0112	0175	0257	0356	0466	0579	66
35		0005	0010	0021	0040	0070	0116	0179	0261	0359	0468	65
36		0002	0005	0011	0023	0042	0073	0120	0183	0265	0362	64
37		0001	0003	0006	0012	0024	0045	0077	0123	0187	0268	63
38		0000	0001	0003	0006	0013	0026	0047	0079	0127	0191	62
39		0000	0001	0001	0003	0007	0015	0028	0049	0082	0130	61
40		0000	0000	0001	0002	0004	0008	0016	0029	0051	0085	60
41		0000	0000	0000	0001	0002	0004	0008	0017	0031	0053	59
42		0000	0000	0000	0000	0001	0002	0004	0009	0018	0032	58
43		0000	0000	0000	0000	0000	0001	0002	0005	0010	0019	57
44		0000	0000	0000	0000	0000	0000	0001	0002	0005	0010	56
45		0000	0000	0000	0000	0000	0000	0000	0001	0003	0005	55
46		0000	0000	0000	0000	0000	0000	0000	0001	0001	0003	54
47		0000	0000	0000	0000	0000	0000	0000	0000	0001	0001	53
48		0000	0000	0000	0000	0000	0000	0000	0000	0000	0001	52
		79	78	77	76	75	74	73	72	71	70	p	x

(*Continued*)

TABLE I   Binomial Distribution ($n = 100$, cont.)

$$n = 100$$

x	p	31	32	33	34	35	36	37	38	39	40	
15		0001	0001	0000	0000	0000	0000	0000	0000	0000	0000	85
16		0003	0001	0001	0000	0000	0000	0000	0000	0000	0000	84
17		0006	0003	0002	0001	0000	0000	0000	0000	0000	0000	83
18		0013	0007	0004	0002	0001	0000	0000	0000	0000	0000	82
19		0025	0014	0008	0004	0002	0001	0000	0000	0000	0000	81
20		0046	0027	0015	0008	0004	0002	0001	0001	0000	0000	80
21		0079	0049	0029	0016	0009	0005	0002	0001	0001	0000	79
22		0127	0082	0051	0030	0017	0010	0005	0003	0001	0001	78
23		0194	0131	0085	0053	0032	0018	0010	0006	0003	0001	77
24		0280	0198	0134	0088	0055	0033	0019	0011	0006	0003	76
25		0382	0283	0201	0137	0090	0057	0035	0020	0012	0006	75
26		0496	0384	0286	0204	0140	0092	0059	0036	0021	0012	74
27		0610	0495	0386	0288	0207	0143	0095	0060	0037	0022	73
28		0715	0608	0495	0387	0290	0209	0145	0097	0062	0038	72
29		0797	0710	0605	0495	0388	0292	0211	0147	0098	0063	71
30		0848	0791	0706	0603	0494	0389	0294	0213	0149	0100	70
31		0860	0840	0785	0702	0601	0494	0389	0295	0215	0151	69
32		0833	0853	0833	0779	0698	0599	0493	0390	0296	0217	68
33		0771	0827	0846	0827	0774	0694	0597	0493	0390	0297	67
34		0683	0767	0821	0840	0821	0769	0691	0595	0492	0391	66
35		0578	0680	0763	0816	0834	0816	0765	0688	0593	0491	65
36		0469	0578	0678	0759	0811	0829	0811	0761	0685	0591	64
37		0365	0471	0578	0676	0755	0806	0824	0807	0757	0682	63
38		0272	0367	0472	0577	0674	0752	0802	0820	0803	0754	62
39		0194	0275	0369	0473	0577	0672	0749	0799	0816	0799	61
40		0133	0197	0277	0372	0474	0577	0671	0746	0795	0812	60
41		0087	0136	0200	0280	0373	0475	0577	0670	0744	0792	59
42		0055	0090	0138	0203	0282	0375	0476	0576	0668	0742	58
43		0033	0057	0092	0141	0205	0285	0377	0477	0576	0667	57
44		0019	0035	0059	0094	0143	0207	0287	0378	0477	0576	56
45		0011	0020	0036	0060	0096	0045	0210	0289	0380	0478	55
46		0006	0011	0021	0037	0062	0098	0147	0211	0290	0381	54
47		0003	0006	0012	0022	0038	0063	0099	0149	0213	0292	53
48		0001	0003	0007	0012	0023	0039	0064	0101	0151	0215	52
49		0001	0002	0003	0007	0013	0023	0040	0066	0102	0152	51
50		0000	0001	0002	0004	0007	0013	0024	0041	0067	0103	50
51		0000	0000	0001	0002	0004	0007	0014	0025	0042	0068	49
52		0000	0000	0000	0001	0002	0004	0008	0014	0025	0042	48
53		0000	0000	0000	0000	0001	0002	0004	0008	0015	0026	47
54		0000	0000	0000	0000	0000	0001	0002	0004	0008	0015	46
55		0000	0000	0000	0000	0000	0000	0001	0002	0004	0008	45
56		0000	0000	0000	0000	0000	0000	0000	0001	0002	0004	44
57		0000	0000	0000	0000	0000	0000	0000	0001	0001	0002	43
58		0000	0000	0000	0000	0000	0000	0000	0000	0001	0001	42
59		0000	0000	0000	0000	0000	0000	0000	0000	0000	0001	41
		69	68	67	66	65	64	63	62	61	60	p	x

(*Continued*)

TABLE I Binomial Distribution ($n = 100$, cont.)

$n = 100$

x	p	41	42	43	44	45	46	47	48	49	50	
23		0001	0000	0000	0000	0000	0000	0000	0000	0000	0000	77
24		0002	0001	0000	0000	0000	0000	0000	0000	0000	0000	76
25		0003	0002	0001	0000	0000	0000	0000	0000	0000	0000	75
26		0007	0003	0002	0001	0000	0000	0000	0000	0000	0000	74
27		0013	0007	0004	0002	0001	0000	0000	0000	0000	0000	73
28		0023	0013	0007	0004	0002	0001	0000	0000	0000	0000	72
29		0039	0024	0014	0008	0004	0002	0001	0000	0000	0000	71
30		0065	0040	0024	0014	0008	0004	0002	0001	0001	0000	70
31		0102	0066	0041	0025	0014	0008	0004	0002	0001	0001	69
32		0152	0103	0067	0042	0025	0015	0008	0004	0002	0001	68
33		0218	0154	0104	0068	0043	0026	0015	0008	0004	0002	67
34		0298	0219	0155	0105	0069	0043	0026	0015	0009	0005	66
35		0391	0299	0220	0156	0106	0069	0044	0026	0015	0009	65
36		0491	0391	0300	0221	0157	0107	0070	0044	0027	0016	64
37		0590	0490	0391	0300	0222	0157	0107	0070	0044	0027	63
38		0680	0588	0489	0391	0301	0222	0158	0108	0071	0045	62
39		0751	0677	0587	0489	0391	0301	0223	0158	0108	0071	61
40		0796	0748	0675	0586	0488	0391	0301	0223	0159	0108	60
41		0809	0793	0745	0673	0584	0487	0391	0301	0223	0159	59
42		0790	0806	0790	0743	0672	0583	0487	0390	0301	0223	58
43		0740	0787	0804	0788	0741	0670	0582	0486	0390	0301	57
44		0666	0739	0785	0802	0786	0739	0669	0581	0485	0390	56
45		0576	0666	0737	0784	0800	0784	0738	0668	0580	0485	55
46		0479	0576	0665	0736	0782	0798	0783	0737	0667	0580	54
47		0382	0480	0576	0065	0736	0781	0797	0781	0736	0666	53
		59	58	57	56	55	54	53	52	51	50	p x

(*Continued*)

Appendix B

TABLE I   Binomial Distribution ($n = 100$, cont.)

$n = 100$

x	p	41	42	43	44	45	46	47	48	49	50	
48		0293	0383	0480	0577	0665	0735	0781	0797	0781	0735	52
49		0216	0295	0384	0481	0577	0664	0735	0780	0796	0780	51
50		0153	0218	0296	0385	0482	0577	0665	0735	0780	0796	50
51		0104	0155	0219	0297	0386	0482	0578	0665	0735	0780	49
52		0068	0105	0156	0220	0298	0387	0483	0578	0665	0735	48
53		0043	0069	0106	0156	0221	0299	0388	0483	0579	0666	47
54		0026	0044	0070	0107	0157	0221	0299	0388	0484	0580	46
55		0015	0026	0044	0070	0108	0158	0222	0300	0389	0485	45
56		0008	0015	0027	0044	0071	0108	0158	0222	0300	0390	44
57		0005	0009	0016	0027	0045	0071	0108	0158	0223	0301	43
58		0002	0005	0009	0016	0027	0045	0071	0108	0159	0223	42
59		0001	0002	0005	0009	0016	0027	0045	0071	0109	0159	41
60		0001	0001	0002	0005	0009	0016	0027	0045	0071	0108	40
61		0000	0001	0001	0002	0005	0009	0016	0027	0045	0071	39
62		0000	0000	0001	0001	0002	0005	0009	0016	0027	0045	38
63		0000	0000	0000	0001	0001	0002	0005	0009	0016	0027	37
64		0000	0000	0000	0000	0001	0001	0002	0005	0009	0016	36
65		0000	0000	0000	0000	0000	0001	0001	0002	0005	0009	35
66		0000	0000	0000	0000	0000	0000	0001	0001	0002	0005	34
67		0000	0000	0000	0000	0000	0000	0000	0001	0001	0002	33
68		0000	0000	0000	0000	0000	0000	0000	0000	0001	0001	32
69		0000	0000	0000	0000	0000	0000	0000	0000	0000	0001	31
		59	58	57	56	55	54	53	52	51	50	p	x

TABLE II   Poisson Distribution ($\lambda = 0.1$ to $\lambda = 2.0$)

From *Handbook of Probability and Statistics* by R. S. Burington and D. C. May, Jr. Copyright 1953 by McGraw-Hill, Inc. Used with permission of McGraw-Hill Book Company.

The following table gives the probability of exactly x successes, for various values of λ, as defined by the Poisson mass function.

$$P(x) = \frac{e^{-\lambda}\lambda^x}{x!}$$

Examples: If $\lambda = 1.5$, then $P(2) = 0.2510$, $P(3) = 0.1255$.

POISSON PROBABILITIES

($\lambda = 0.1$ to $\lambda = 2.0$)

λ

x	0.1	0.2	0.3	0.4	0.5	0.6	0.7	0.8	0.9	1.0
0	.9048	.8187	.7408	.6703	.6065	.5488	.4966	.4493	.4066	.3679
1	.0905	.1637	.2222	.2681	.3033	.3293	.3476	.3595	.3659	.3679
2	.0045	.0164	.0333	.0536	.0758	.0988	.1217	.1438	.1647	.1839
3	.0002	.0011	.0033	.0072	.0126	.0198	.0284	.0383	.0494	.0613
4	.0000	.0001	.0002	.0007	.0016	.0030	.0050	.0077	.0111	.0153
5	.0000	.0000	.0000	.0001	.0002	.0004	.0007	.0012	.0020	.0031
6	.0000	.0000	.0000	.0000	.0000	.0000	.0001	.0002	.0003	.0005
7	.0000	.0000	.0000	.0000	.0000	.0000	.0000	.0000	.0000	.0001

λ

x	1.1	1.2	1.3	1.4	1.5	1.6	1.7	1.8	1.9	2.0
0	.3329	.3012	.2725	.2466	.2231	.2019	.1827	.1653	.1496	.1353
1	.3662	.3614	.3543	.3452	.3347	.3230	.3106	.2975	.2842	.2707
2	.2014	.2169	.2303	.2417	.2510	.2584	.2640	.2678	.2700	.2707
3	.0738	.0867	.0998	.1128	.1255	.1378	.1496	.1607	.1710	.1804
4	.0203	.0260	.0324	.0395	.0471	.0551	.0636	.0723	.0812	.0902
5	.0045	.0062	.0084	.0111	.0141	.0176	.0216	.0260	.0309	.0361
6	.0008	.0012	.0018	.0026	.0035	.0047	.0061	.0078	.0098	.0120
7	.0001	.0002	.0003	.0005	.0008	.0011	.0015	.0020	.0027	.0034
8	.0000	.0000	.0001	.0001	.0001	.0002	.0003	.0005	.0006	.0009
9	.0000	.0000	.0000	.0000	.0000	.0000	.0001	.0001	.0001	.0002

(Continued)

TABLE II   Poisson Distribution ($\lambda = 2.1$ to $\lambda = 4.0$)

x	2.1	2.2	2.3	2.4	2.5	2.6	2.7	2.8	2.9	3.0
0	.1225	.1108	.1003	.0907	.0821	.0743	.0672	.0608	.0550	.0498
1	.2572	.2438	.2306	.2177	.2052	.1931	.1815	.1703	.1596	.1494
2	.2700	.2681	.2652	.2613	.2565	.2510	.2450	.2384	.2314	.2240
3	.1890	.1966	.2033	.2090	.2138	.2176	.2205	.2225	.2237	.2240
4	.0992	.1082	.1169	.1254	.1336	.1414	.1488	.1557	.1622	.1680
5	.0417	.0476	.0538	.0602	.0668	.0735	.0804	.0872	.0940	.1008
6	.0146	.0174	.0206	.0241	.0278	.0319	.0362	.0407	.0455	.0504
7	.0044	.0055	.0068	.0083	.0099	.0118	.0139	.0163	.0188	.0216
8	.0011	.0015	.0019	.0025	.0031	.0038	.0047	.0057	.0068	.0081
9	.0003	.0004	.0005	.0007	.0009	.0011	.0014	.0018	.0022	.0027
10	.0001	.0001	.0001	.0002	.0002	.0003	.0004	.0005	.0006	.0008
11	.0000	.0000	.0000	.0000	.0000	.0001	.0001	.0001	.0002	.0002
12	.0000	.0000	.0000	.0000	.0000	.0000	.0000	.0000	.0000	.0001

λ

x	3.1	3.2	3.3	3.4	3.5	3.6	3.7	3.8	3.9	4.0
0	.0450	.0408	.0369	.0334	.0302	.0273	.0247	.0224	.0202	.0183
1	.1397	.1304	.1217	.1135	.1057	.0984	.0915	.0850	.0789	.0733
2	.2165	.2087	.2008	.1929	.1850	.1771	.1692	.1615	.1539	.1465
3	.2237	.2226	.2209	.2186	.2158	.2125	.2087	.2046	.2001	.1954
4	.1734	.1781	.1823	.1858	.1888	.1912	.1931	.1944	.1951	.1954
5	.1075	.1140	.1203	.1264	.1322	.1377	.1429	.1477	.1522	.1563
6	.0555	.0608	.0662	.0716	.0771	.0826	.0881	.0936	.0989	.1042
7	.0246	.0278	.0312	.0348	.0385	.0425	.0466	.0508	.0551	.0595
8	.0095	.0111	.0129	.0148	.0169	.0191	.0215	.0241	.0269	.0298
9	.0033	.0040	.0047	.0056	.0066	.0076	.0089	.0102	.0116	.0132
10	.0010	.0013	.0016	.0019	.0023	.0028	.0033	.0039	.0045	.0053
11	.0003	.0004	.0005	.0006	.0007	.0009	.0011	.0013	.0016	.0019
12	.0001	.0001	.0001	.0002	.0002	.0003	.0003	.0004	.0005	.0006
13	.0000	.0000	.0000	.0000	.0001	.0001	.0001	.0001	.0002	.0002
14	.0000	.0000	.0000	.0000	.0000	.0000	.0000	.0000	.0000	.0001

(Continued)

TABLE II **Poisson Distribution** ($\lambda = 4.1$ to $\lambda = 6.0$)

x	4.1	4.2	4.3	4.4	4.5	4.6	4.7	4.8	4.9	5.0
0	.0166	.0150	.0136	.0123	.0111	.0101	.0091	.0082	.0074	.0067
1	.0679	.0630	.0583	.0540	.0500	.0462	.0427	.0395	.0365	.0337
2	.1393	.1323	.1254	.1188	.1125	.1063	.1005	.0948	.0894	.0842
3	.1904	.1852	.1798	.1743	.1687	.1631	.1574	.1517	.1460	.1404
4	.1951	.1944	.1933	.1917	.1898	.1875	.1849	.1820	.1789	.1755
5	.1600	.1633	.1662	.1687	.1708	.1725	.1738	.1747	.1753	.1755
6	.1093	.1143	.1191	.1237	.1281	.1323	.1362	.1398	.1432	.1462
7	.0640	.0686	.0732	.0778	.0824	.0869	.0914	.0959	.1002	.1044
8	.0328	.0360	.0393	.0428	.0463	.0500	.0537	.0575	.0614	.0653
9	.0150	.0168	.0188	.0209	.0232	.0255	.0280	.0307	.0334	.0363
10	.0061	.0071	.0081	.0092	.0104	.0118	.0132	.0147	.0164	.0181
11	.0023	.0027	.0032	.0037	.0043	.0049	.0056	.0064	.0073	.0082
12	.0008	.0009	.0011	.0014	.0016	.0019	.0022	.0026	.0030	.0034
13	.0002	.0003	.0004	.0005	.0006	.0007	.0008	.0009	.0011	.0013
14	.0001	.0001	.0001	.0001	.0002	.0002	.0003	.0003	.0004	.0005
15	.0000	.0000	.0000	.0000	.0001	.0001	.0001	.0001	.0001	.0002

x	5.1	5.2	5.3	5.4	5.5	5.6	5.7	5.8	5.9	6.0
0	.0061	.0055	.0050	.0045	.0041	.0037	.0033	.0030	.0027	.0025
1	.0311	.0287	.0265	.0244	.0225	.0207	.0191	.0176	.0162	.0149
2	.0793	.0746	.0701	.0659	.0618	.0580	.0544	.0509	.0477	.0446
3	.1348	.1293	.1239	.1185	.1133	.1082	.1033	.0985	.0938	.0892
4	.1719	.1681	.1641	.1600	.1558	.1515	.1472	.1428	.1383	.1339
5	.1753	.1748	.1740	.1728	.1714	.1697	.1678	.1620	.1632	.1606
6	.1490	.1515	.1537	.1555	.1571	.1584	.1594	.1656	.1605	.1606
7	.1086	.1125	.1163	.1200	.1234	.1267	.1298	.1301	.1353	.1377
8	.0692	.0731	.0771	.0810	.0849	.0887	.0925	.0926	.0998	.1033
9	.0392	.0423	0.454	.0486	.0519	.0552	.0586	.0662	.0654	.0688
10	.0200	.0220	.0241	.0262	.0285	.0309	.0334	.0359	.0386	.0413
11	.0093	.0104	.0116	.0129	.0143	.0157	.0173	.0190	.0207	.0225
12	.0039	.0045	.0051	.0058	.0065	.0073	.0082	.0092	.0102	.0113
13	.0015	.0018	.0021	.0024	.0028	.0032	.0036	.0041	.0046	.0052
14	.0006	.0007	.0008	.0009	.0011	.0013	.0015	.0017	.0019	.0022
15	.0002	.0002	.0003	.0003	.0004	.0005	.0006	.0007	.0008	.0009
16	.0001	.0001	.0001	.0001	.0001	.0002	.0002	.0002	.0003	.0003
17	.0000	.0000	.0000	.0000	.0000	.0001	.0001	.0001	.0001	.0001

(*Continued*)

Appendix B

TABLE II   Poisson Distribution ($\lambda = 6.1$ to $\lambda = 8.0$)

λ

x	6.1	6.2	6.3	6.4	6.5	6.6	6.7	6.8	6.9	7.0
0	.0022	.0020	.0018	.0017	.0015	.0014	.0012	.0011	.0010	.0009
1	.0137	.0126	.0116	.0106	.0098	.0090	.0082	.0076	.0070	.0064
2	.0417	.0390	.0364	.0340	.0318	.0296	.0276	.0258	.0240	.0223
3	.0848	.0806	.0765	.0726	.0688	.0652	.0617	.0584	.0552	.0521
4	.1294	.1249	.1205	.1162	.1118	.1076	.1034	.0992	.0952	.0912
5	.1579	.1549	.1519	.1487	.1454	.1420	.1385	.1349	.1314	.1277
6	.1605	.1601	.1595	.1586	.1575	.1562	.1546	.1529	.1511	.1490
7	.1399	.1418	.1435	.1450	.1462	.1472	.1480	.1486	.1489	.1490
8	.1066	.1099	.1130	.1160	.1188	.1215	.1240	.1263	.1284	.1304
9	.0723	.0757	.0791	.0825	.0858	.0891	.0923	.0954	.0985	.1014
10	.0441	.0469	.0498	.0528	.0558	.0588	.0618	.0649	.0679	.0710
11	.0245	.0265	.0285	.0307	.0330	.0353	.0377	.0401	.0426	.0452
12	.0124	.0137	.0150	.0164	.0179	.0194	.0210	.0227	.0245	.0264
13	.0058	0.065	.0073	.0081	.0089	.0098	.0108	.0119	.0130	.0142
14	.0025	.0029	.0033	.0037	.0041	.0046	.0052	.0058	.0064	.0071
15	.0010	.0012	.0014	.0016	.0018	.0020	.0023	.0026	.0029	.0033
16	.0004	.0005	.0005	.0006	.0007	.0008	.0010	.0011	.0013	.0014
17	.0001	.0002	.0002	.0002	.0003	.0003	.0004	.0004	.0005	.0006
18	.0000	.0001	.0001	.0001	.0001	.0001	.0001	.0002	.0002	.0002
19	.0000	.0000	.0000	.0000	.0000	.0000	.0000	.0001	.0001	.0001

λ

x	7.1	7.2	7.3	7.4	7.5	7.6	7.7	7.8	7.9	8.0
0	.0008	.0007	.0007	.0006	.0006	.0005	.0005	.0004	.0004	.0003
1	.0059	.0054	.0049	.0045	.0041	.0038	.0035	.0032	.0029	.0027
2	.0208	.0194	.0180	.0167	.0156	.0145	.0134	.0125	.0116	.0107
3	.0492	.0464	.0438	.0413	.0389	.0366	.0345	.0324	.0305	.0286
4	.0874	.0836	.0799	.0764	.0729	.0696	.0663	.0632.	.0602	.0573
5	.1241	.1204	.1167	.1130	.1094	.1057	.1021	.0986	.0951	.0916
6	.1468	.1445	.1420	.1394	.1367	.1339	.1311	.1282	.1252	.1221
7	.1489	.1486	.1481	.1474	.1465	.1454	.1442	.1428	.1413	.1396
8	.1321	.1337	.1351	.1363	.1373	.1382	.1388	.1392	.1395	.1396
9	.1042	.1070	.1096	.1121	.1144	.1167	.1187	.1207	.1224	.1241
10	.0740	.0770	.0800	.0829	.0858	.0887	.0914	.0941	.0967	.0993
11	.0478	.0504	.0531	.0558	.0585	.0613	.0640	.0667	.0695	.0722
12	.0283	.0303	.0323	.0344	.0366	.0388	.0411	.0434	.0457	.0481
13	.0154	.0168	.0181	.0196	.0211	.0227	.0243	.0260	.0278	.0296
14	.0078	.0086	.0095	.0104	.0113	.0123	.0134	.0145	.0157	.0169
15	.0037	.0041	.0046	.0051	.0057	.0062	.0069	.0075	.0083	.0090
16	.0016	.0019	.0021	.0024	.0026	.0030	.0033	.0037	.0041	.0045
17	.0007	.0008	.0009	.0010	.0012	.0013	.0015	.0017	.1119	.0021
18	.0003	.0003	.0004	.0004	.0005	.0006	.0006	.0007	.0008	.0009
19	.0001	.0001	.0001	.0002	.0002	.0002	.0003	.0003	.0003	.0004
20	.0000	.0000	.0001	.0001	.0001	.0001	.0001	.0001	.0001	.0002
21	.0000	.0000	.0000	.0000	.0000	.0000	.0000	.0000	.0001	.0001

(*Continued*)

TABLE II Poisson Distribution ($\lambda = 8.1$ to $\lambda = 10$)

λ

x	8.1	8.2	8.3	8.4	8.5	8.6	8.7	8.8	8.9	9.0
0	.0003	.0003	.0002	.0002	.0002	.0002	.0002	.0002	.0001	.0001
1	.0025	.0023	.0021	.0019	.0017	.0016	.0014	.0013	.0012	.0011
2	.0100	.0092	.0086	.0079	.0074	.0068	.0063	.0058	.0054	.0050
3	.0269	.0252	.0237	.0222	.0208	.0195	.0183	.0171	.0160	.0150
4	.0544	.0517	.0491	.0466	.0443	.0420	.0398	.0377	.0357	.0337
5	.0882	.0849	.0816	.0784	.0752	.0722	.0692	.0663	.0635	.0607
6	.1191	.1160	.1128	.1097	.1066	.1034	.1003	.0972	.0941	.0911
7	.1378	.1358	.1338	.1317	.1294	.1271	.1247	.1222	.1197	.1171
8	.1395	.1392	.1388	.1382	.1375	.1366	.1356	.1344	.1332	.1318
9	.1256	.1269	.1280	.1290	.1299	.1306	.1311	.1315	.1317	.1318
10	.1017	.1040	.1063	.1084	.1104	.1123	.1140	.1157	.1172	.1186
11	.0749	.0776	.0802	.0828	.0853	.0878	.0902	.0925	.0948	.0970
12	.0505	.0530	.0555	.0579	.0604	.0629	.0654	.0679	.0703	.0728
13	.0315	.0334	.0354	.0374	.0395	.0416	.0438	.0459	.0481	.0504
14	.0182	.0196	.0210	.0225	.0240	.0256	.0272	.0289	.0306	.0324
15	.0098	.0107	.0116	.0126	.0136	.0147	.0158	.0169	.0182	.0194
16	.0050	.0055	.0060	.0066	.0072	.0079	.0086	.0093	.0101	.0109
17	.0024	.0026	.0029	.0033	.0036	.0040	.0044	.0048	.0053	.0058
18	.0011	.0012	.0014	.0015	.0017	.0019	.0021	.0024	.0026	.0029
19	.0005	.0005	.0006	.0007	.0008	.0009	.0010	.0011	.0012	.0014
20	.0002	.0002	.0002	.0003	.0003	.0004	.0004	.0005	.0005	.0006
21	.0001	.0001	.0001	.0001	.0001	.0002	.0002	.0002	.0002	.0003
22	.0000	.0000	.0000	.0000	.0001	.0001	.0001	.0001	.0001	.0001

λ

x	9.1	9.2	9.3	9.4	9.5	9.6	9.7	9.8	9.9	10
0	.0001	.0001	.0001	.0001	.0001	.0001	.0001	.0001	.0001	.0000
1	.0010	.0009	.0009	.0008	.0007	.0007	.0006	.0005	.0005	.0005
2	.0046	.0043	.0040	.0037	.0034	.0031	.0029	.0027	.0025	.0023
3	.0140	.0131	.0123	.0115	.0107	.0100	.0093	.0087	.0081	.0076
4	.0319	.0302	.0285	.0269	.0254	.0240	.0226	.0213	.0201	.0189
5	.0581	.0555	.0530	.0506	.0483	.0460	.0439	.0418	.0398	.0378
6	.0881	.0851	.0822	.0793	.0764	.0736	.0709	.0682	.0656	.0631
7	.1145	.1118	.1091	.1064	.1037	.1010	.0982	.0955	.0928	.0901
8	.1302	.1286	.1269	.1251	.1232	.1212	.1191	.1170	.1148	.1126
9	.1317	.1315	.1311	.1306	.1300	.1293	.1284	.1274	.1263	.1251
10	.1198	.1210	.1219	.1228	.1235	.1241	.1245	.1249	.1250	.1251
11	.0991	.1012	.1031	.1049	.1067	.1083	.1098	.1112	.1125	.1137
12	.0752	.0776	.0799	.0822	.0844	.0866	.0888	.0908	.0928	.0948
13	.0526	.0549	.0572	.0594	.0617	.0640	.0662	.0685	.0707	.0729
14	.0342	.0361	.0380	.0399	.0419	.0439	.0459	.0479	.0500	.0521
15	.0208	.0221	.0235	.0250	.0265	.0281	.0297	.0313	.0330	.0347
16	.0118	.0127	.0137	.0147	.0157	.0168	.0180	.0192	.0204	.0217
17	.0063	.0069	.0075	.0081	.0088	.0095	.0103	.0111	.0119	.0128
18	.0032	.0035	.0039	.0042	.0046	.0051	.0055	.0060	.0065	.0071
19	.0015	.0017	.0019	.0021	.0023	.0026	.0028	.0031	.0034	.0037
20	.0007	.0008	.0009	.0010	.0011	.0012	.0014	.0015	.0017	.0019
21	.0003	.0003	.0004	.0004	.0005	.0006	.0006	.0007	.0008	.0009
22	.0001	.0001	.0002	.0002	.0002	.0002	.0003	.0003	.0004	.0004
23	.0000	.0001	.0001	.0001	.0001	.0001	.0001	.0001	.0002	.0002
24	.0000	.0000	.0000	.0000	.0000	.0000	.0000	.0001	.0001	.0001

(*Continued*)

Appendix B

TABLE II   Poisson Distribution ($\lambda = 11$ to $\lambda = 20$)

					λ					
x	11	12	13	14	15	16	17	18	19	20
0	.0000	.0000	.0000	.0000	.0000	.0000	.0000	.0000	.0000	.0000
1	.0002	.0001	.0000	.0000	.0000	.0000	.0000	.0000	.0000	.0000
2	.0010	.0004	.0002	.0001	.0000	.0000	.0000	.0000	.0000	.0000
3	.0037	.0018	.0008	.0004	.0002	.0001	.0000	.0000	.0000	.0000
4	.0102	.0053	.0027	.0013	.0006	.0003	.0001	.0001	.0000	.0000
5	.0224	.0127	.0070	.0037	.0019	.0010	.0005	.0002	.0001	.0001
6	.0411	.0255	.0152	.0087	.0048	.0026	.0014	.0007	.0004	.0002
7	.0646	.0437	.0281	.0174	.0104	.0060	.0034	.0018	.0010	.0005
8	.0888	.0655	.0457	.0304	.0194	.0120	.0072	.0042	.0024	.0013
9	.1085	.0874	.0661	.0473	.0324	.0213	.0135	.0083	.0050	.0029
10	.1194	.1048	.0859	.0063	.0486	.0341	.0230	.0150	.0095	.0058
11	.1194	.1144	.1015	.0844	.0663	.0496	.0355	.0245	.0164	.0106
12	.1094	.1144	.1099	.0984	.0829	.0661	.0504	.0368	.0259	.0176
13	.0926	.1056	.1099	.1060	.0956	.0814	.0658	.0509	.0378	.0271
14	.0728	.0905	.1021	.1060	.1024	.0930	.0800	.0655	.0514	.0387
15	.0534	.0724	.0885	.0989	.1024	.0992	.0906	.0786	.0650	.0516
16	.0367	.0543	.0719	.0866	.0960	.0992	.0963	.0884	.0772	.0646
17	.0237	.0383	.0550	.0713	.0847	.0934	.0963	.0936	.0863	.0760
18	.0145	.0256	.0397	.0554	.0706	.0830	.0909	.0936	.0911	.0844
19	.0084	.0161	.0272	.0409	.0557	.0699	.0814	.0887	.0911	.0888
20	.0046	.0097	.0177	.0286	.0418	.0559	.0692	.0798	.0866	.0888
21	.0024	.0055	.0109	.0191	.0299	.0426	.0560	.0684	.0783	.0846
22	.0012	.0030	.0065	.0121	.0204	.0310	.0433	.0560	.0676	.0769
23	.0006	.0016	.0037	.0074	.0133	.0216	.0320	.0438	.0559	.0669
24	.0003	.0008	.0020	.0043	.0083	.0144	.0226	.0328	.0442	.0557
25	.0001	.0004	.0010	.0024	.0050	.0092	.0154	.0237	.0336	.0446
26	.0000	.0002	.0005	.0013	.0029	.0057	.0101	.0164	.0246	.0343
27	.0000	.0001	.0002	.0007	.0016	.0034	.0063	.0109	.0173	.0254
28	.0000	.0000	.0001	.0003	.0009	.0019	.0038	.0070	.0117	.0181
29	.0000	.0000	.0001	.0002	.0004	.0011	.0023	.0044	.0077	.0125
30	.0000	.0000	.0000	.0001	.0002	.0006	.0013	.0026	.0049	.0083
31	.0000	.0000	.0000	.0000	.0001	.0003	.0007	.0015	.0030	.0054
32	.0000	.0000	.0000	.0000	.0001	.0001	.0004	.0009	.0018	.0034
33	.0000	.0000	.0000	.0000	.0000	.0001	.0002	.0005	.0010	.0020
34	.0000	.0000	.0000	.0000	.0000	.0000	.0001	.0002	.0006	.0012
35	.0000	.0000	.0000	.0000	.0000	.0000	.0000	.0001	.0003	.0007
36	.0000	.0000	.0000	.0000	.0000	.0000	.0000	.0001	.0002	.0004
37	.0000	.0000	.0000	.0000	.0000	.0000	.0000	.0000	.0001	.0002
38	.0000	.0000	.0000	.0000	.0000	.0000	.0000	.0000	.0000	.0001
39	.0000	.0000	.0000	.0000	.0000	.0000	.0000	.0000	.0000	.0001

TABLE III Cumulative Normal Distribution

$$F(z) = \int_{-\infty}^{z} \frac{1}{\sqrt{2\pi}} e^{-z^2/2} dz \quad Example:$$

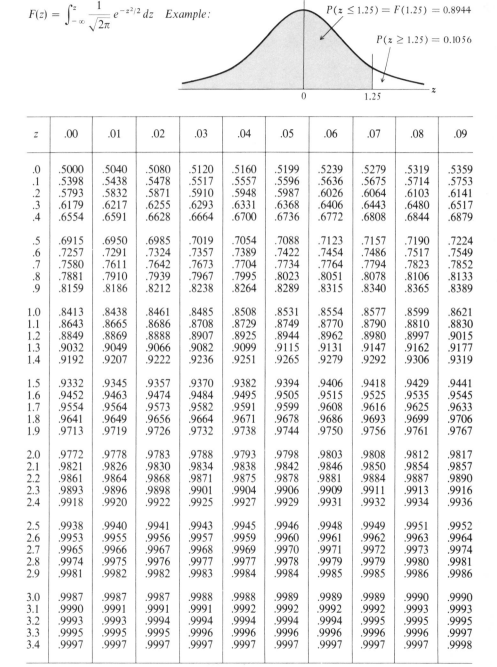

$P(z \le 1.25) = F(1.25) = 0.8944$

$P(z \ge 1.25) = 0.1056$

z	.00	.01	.02	.03	.04	.05	.06	.07	.08	.09
.0	.5000	.5040	.5080	.5120	.5160	.5199	.5239	.5279	.5319	.5359
.1	.5398	.5438	.5478	.5517	.5557	.5596	.5636	.5675	.5714	.5753
.2	.5793	.5832	.5871	.5910	.5948	.5987	.6026	.6064	.6103	.6141
.3	.6179	.6217	.6255	.6293	.6331	.6368	.6406	.6443	.6480	.6517
.4	.6554	.6591	.6628	.6664	.6700	.6736	.6772	.6808	.6844	.6879
.5	.6915	.6950	.6985	.7019	.7054	.7088	.7123	.7157	.7190	.7224
.6	.7257	.7291	.7324	.7357	.7389	.7422	.7454	.7486	.7517	.7549
.7	.7580	.7611	.7642	.7673	.7704	.7734	.7764	.7794	.7823	.7852
.8	.7881	.7910	.7939	.7967	.7995	.8023	.8051	.8078	.8106	.8133
.9	.8159	.8186	.8212	.8238	.8264	.8289	.8315	.8340	.8365	.8389
1.0	.8413	.8438	.8461	.8485	.8508	.8531	.8554	.8577	.8599	.8621
1.1	.8643	.8665	.8686	.8708	.8729	.8749	.8770	.8790	.8810	.8830
1.2	.8849	.8869	.8888	.8907	.8925	.8944	.8962	.8980	.8997	.9015
1.3	.9032	.9049	.9066	.9082	.9099	.9115	.9131	.9147	.9162	.9177
1.4	.9192	.9207	.9222	.9236	.9251	.9265	.9279	.9292	.9306	.9319
1.5	.9332	.9345	.9357	.9370	.9382	.9394	.9406	.9418	.9429	.9441
1.6	.9452	.9463	.9474	.9484	.9495	.9505	.9515	.9525	.9535	.9545
1.7	.9554	.9564	.9573	.9582	.9591	.9599	.9608	.9616	.9625	.9633
1.8	.9641	.9649	.9656	.9664	.9671	.9678	.9686	.9693	.9699	.9706
1.9	.9713	.9719	.9726	.9732	.9738	.9744	.9750	.9756	.9761	.9767
2.0	.9772	.9778	.9783	.9788	.9793	.9798	.9803	.9808	.9812	.9817
2.1	.9821	.9826	.9830	.9834	.9838	.9842	.9846	.9850	.9854	.9857
2.2	.9861	.9864	.9868	.9871	.9875	.9878	.9881	.9884	.9887	.9890
2.3	.9893	.9896	.9898	.9901	.9904	.9906	.9909	.9911	.9913	.9916
2.4	.9918	.9920	.9922	.9925	.9927	.9929	.9931	.9932	.9934	.9936
2.5	.9938	.9940	.9941	.9943	.9945	.9946	.9948	.9949	.9951	.9952
2.6	.9953	.9955	.9956	.9957	.9959	.9960	.9961	.9962	.9963	.9964
2.7	.9965	.9966	.9967	.9968	.9969	.9970	.9971	.9972	.9973	.9974
2.8	.9974	.9975	.9976	.9977	.9977	.9978	.9979	.9979	.9980	.9981
2.9	.9981	.9982	.9982	.9983	.9984	.9984	.9985	.9985	.9986	.9986
3.0	.9987	.9987	.9987	.9988	.9988	.9989	.9989	.9989	.9990	.9990
3.1	.9990	.9991	.9991	.9991	.9992	.9992	.9992	.9992	.9993	.9993
3.2	.9993	.9993	.9994	.9994	.9994	.9994	.9994	.9995	.9995	.9995
3.3	.9995	.9995	.9995	.9996	.9996	.9996	.9996	.9996	.9996	.9997
3.4	.9997	.9997	.9997	.9997	.9997	.9997	.9997	.9997	.9997	.9998

Appendix B

TABLE IV   Exponential Distribution

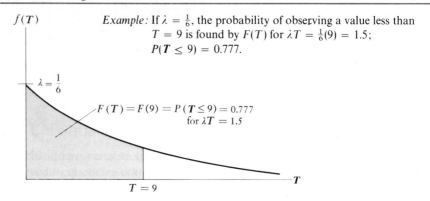

$f(T)$

Example: If $\lambda = \frac{1}{6}$, the probability of observing a value less than $T = 9$ is found by $F(T)$ for $\lambda T = \frac{1}{6}(9) = 1.5$; $P(T \leq 9) = 0.777$.

$\lambda = \frac{1}{6}$

$F(T) = F(9) = P(T \leq 9) = 0.777$ for $\lambda T = 1.5$

$T = 9$

λT	$F(T)$	λT	$F(T)$	λT	$F(T)$	λT	$F(T)$
0.0	0.000	2.5	0.918	5.0	0.9933	7.5	0.99945
0.1	0.095	2.6	0.926	5.1	0.9939	7.6	0.99950
0.2	0.181	2.7	0.933	5.2	0.9945	7.7	0.99955
0.3	0.259	2.8	0.939	5.3	0.9950	7.8	0.99959
0.4	0.330	2.9	0.945	5.4	0.9955	7.9	0.99963
0.5	0.393	3.0	0.950	5.5	0.9959	8.0	0.99966
0.6	0.451	3.1	0.955	5.6	0.9963	8.1	0.99970
0.7	0.503	3.2	0.959	5.7	0.9967	8.2	0.99972
0.8	0.551	3.3	0.963	5.8	0.9970	8.3	0.99975
0.9	0.593	3.4	0.967	5.9	0.9973	8.4	0.99978
1.0	0.632	3.5	0.970	6.0	0.9975	8.5	0.99980
1.1	0.667	3.6	0.973	6.1	0.9978	8.6	0.99982
1.2	0.699	3.7	0.975	6.2	0.9980	8.7	0.99983
1.3	0.727	3.8	0.978	6.3	0.9982	8.8	0.99985
1.4	0.753	3.9	0.980	6.4	0.9983	8.9	0.99986
1.5	0.777	4.0	0.982	6.5	0.9985	9.0	0.99989
1.6	0.798	4.1	0.983	6.6	0.9986	9.1	0.99989
1.7	0.817	4.2	0.985	6.7	0.9988	9.2	0.99990
1.8	0.835	4.3	0.986	6.8	0.9989	9.3	0.99991
1.9	0.850	4.4	0.988	6.9	0.9990	9.4	0.99992
2.0	0.865	4.5	0.989	7.0	0.9991	9.5	0.99992
2.1	0.878	4.6	0.990	7.1	0.9992	9.6	0.99993
2.2	0.889	4.7	0.991	7.2	0.9993	9.7	0.99994
2.3	0.900	4.8	0.992	7.3	0.9993	9.8	0.99994
2.4	0.909	4.9	0.993	7.4	0.9993	9.9	0.99995

TABLE V Critical Values of the χ^2 Distribution

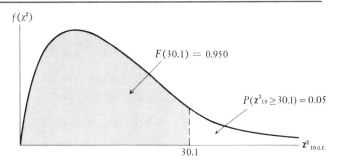

$$F(\chi^2) = \int_0^{\chi^2} \frac{\chi^{(v-2)/2} e^{-\chi/2} \, d\chi}{2^{v/2}[(v-2/2)]}$$

Example: $P(\chi^2_{19} \le 30.1)$ for d.f. $= 19$

$P(\chi^2 \le 30.1) = F(30.1) = 0.950$

$F(30.1) = 0.950$

$P(\chi^2_{19} \ge 30.1) = 0.05$

ν \ F	.005	.010	.025	.050	.100	.900	.950	.975	.990	.995
1	.0⁴393	.0³157	.0³982	.0²393	.0158	2.71	3.84	5.02	6.63	7.88
2	.0100	.0201	.0506	.103	.211	4.61	5.99	7.38	9.21	10.6
3	.0717	.115	.216	.352	.584	6.25	7.81	9.35	11.3	12.8
4	.207	.297	.484	.711	1.06	7.78	9.49	11.1	13.3	14.9
5	.412	.554	.831	1.15	1.61	9.24	11.1	12.8	15.1	16.7
6	.676	.872	1.24	1.64	2.20	10.6	12.6	14.4	16.8	18.5
7	.989	1.24	1.69	2.17	2.83	12.0	14.1	16.0	18.5	20.3
8	1.34	1.65	2.18	2.73	3.49	13.4	15.5	17.5	20.1	22.0
9	1.73	2.09	2.70	3.33	4.17	14.7	16.9	19.0	21.7	23.6
10	2.16	2.56	3.25	3.94	4.87	16.0	18.3	20.5	23.2	25.2
11	2.60	3.05	3.82	4.57	5.58	17.3	19.7	21.9	24.7	26.8
12	3.07	3.57	4.40	5.23	6.30	18.5	21.0	23.3	26.2	28.3
13	3.57	4.11	5.01	5.89	7.04	19.8	22.4	24.7	27.7	29.8
14	4.07	4.66	5.63	6.57	7.79	21.1	23.7	26.1	29.1	31.3
15	4.60	5.23	6.26	7.26	8.55	22.3	25.0	27.5	30.6	32.8
16	5.14	5.81	6.91	7.96	9.31	23.5	26.3	28.8	32.0	34.3
17	5.70	6.41	7.56	8.67	10.1	24.8	27.6	30.2	33.4	35.7
18	6.26	7.01	8.23	9.39	10.9	26.0	28.9	31.5	34.8	37.2
19	6.84	7.63	8.91	10.1	11.7	27.2	30.1	32.9	36.2	38.6
20	7.43	8.26	9.59	10.9	12.4	28.4	31.4	34.2	37.6	40.0
21	8.03	8.90	10.3	11.6	13.2	29.6	32.7	35.5	38.9	41.4
22	8.64	9.54	11.0	12.3	14.0	30.8	33.9	36.8	40.3	42.8
23	9.26	10.2	11.7	13.1	14.8	32.0	35.2	38.1	41.6	44.2
24	9.89	10.9	12.4	13.8	15.7	33.2	36.4	39.4	43.0	45.6
25	10.5	11.5	13.1	14.6	16.5	34.4	37.7	40.6	44.3	46.9
26	11.2	12.2	13.8	15.4	17.3	35.6	38.9	41.9	45.6	48.3
27	11.8	12.9	14.6	16.2	18.1	36.7	40.1	43.2	47.0	49.6
28	12.5	13.6	15.3	16.9	18.9	37.9	41.3	44:5	48.3	51.0
29	13.1	14.3	16.0	17.7	19.8	39.1	42.6	45.7	49.6	52.3
30	13.8	15.0	16.8	18.5	20.6	40.3	43.8	47.0	50.9	53.7
z_α	−2.58	−2.33	−1.96	−1.64	−1.28	+1.28	+1.64	+1.96	+2.33	+2.58

NOTE: For $v > 30$ (i.e., for more than 30 degrees of freedom) take

$$\chi^2 = v\left[1 - \frac{2}{9v} + z_\alpha \sqrt{\frac{2}{9v}}\right]^2 \quad \text{or} \quad \chi^2 = \tfrac{1}{2}[z_\alpha + \sqrt{(2v-1)}]^2$$

according to the degree of accuracy required. z_α is the standardized normal deviate corresponding to the α level of significance, and is shown in the bottom line of the table.

This table is abridged from "Tables of percentage points of the incomplete beta function and of the chi-square distribution," *Biometrika*, Vol. 32 (1941). Reprinted with permission of its author, Catherine M. Thompson, and the editor of *Biometrika*.

Appendix B

TABLE VI   Random Digits

From RAND Corporation, *A Million Random Digits.* By permission.

07018	31172	12572	23968	55216	85366	56223	09300	94564	18172
52444	65625	97918	46794	62370	59344	20149	17596	51669	47429
72161	57299	87521	44351	99981	55008	93371	60620	66662	27036
17918	75071	91057	46829	47992	26797	64423	42379	91676	75127
13623	76165	43195	50205	75736	77473	07268	31330	07337	55901
27426	97534	89707	97453	90836	78967	00704	85734	21776	85764
96039	21338	88169	69530	53300	29895	71507	28517	77761	17244
68282	98888	25545	69406	29470	46476	54562	79373	72993	98998
54262	21477	33097	48125	92982	98382	11265	25366	06636	25349
66290	27544	72780	91384	47296	54892	59168	83951	91075	04724
53348	39044	04072	62210	01209	43999	54952	68699	31912	09317
34482	42758	40128	48436	30254	50029	19016	56837	05206	33851
99268	98715	07545	27317	52459	75366	43688	27460	65145	65429
95342	97178	10401	31615	95784	77026	33087	65961	10056	72834
38556	60373	77935	64608	28949	94764	45312	71171	15400	72182
39159	04795	51163	84475	60722	35268	05044	56420	39214	89822
41786	18169	96649	92406	42773	23672	37333	85734	99886	81200
95627	30768	30607	89023	60730	31519	53462	90489	81693	17849
98738	15548	42263	79489	85118	97073	01574	57310	59375	54417
75214	61575	27805	21930	94726	39454	19616	72239	93791	22610
73904	89123	19271	15792	72675	62175	48746	56084	54029	22296
33329	08896	94662	05781	59187	53284	28024	45421	37956	14252
66364	94799	62211	37539	80172	43269	91133	05562	82385	91760
68349	16984	86532	96186	53893	48268	82821	19526	63257	14288
19193	99621	66899	12351	72438	99839	24228	32079	53517	18558
09237	23489	19172	80439	76263	98918	59330	20121	89779	58862
11007	77008	27646	82072	28048	41589	70883	72035	81800	50296
60622	25875	26446	25738	32962	24266	26814	01194	48587	93319
79973	26895	65304	34978	43053	28951	22676	05303	39725	60054
71080	74487	83196	61939	05045	20405	69324	80823	20905	68727
09923	36773	21247	54735	68996	16937	18134	51873	10973	77090
63094	85087	94186	67793	18178	82224	17069	87880	54945	73489
19806	76028	54285	90845	35464	68076	15868	70063	26794	81386
17295	78454	21700	12301	88832	96796	59341	16136	01803	17537
59338	61051	97260	89829	69121	86547	62195	72492	33536	60137

TABLE VII   Critical Values of the t-Distribution

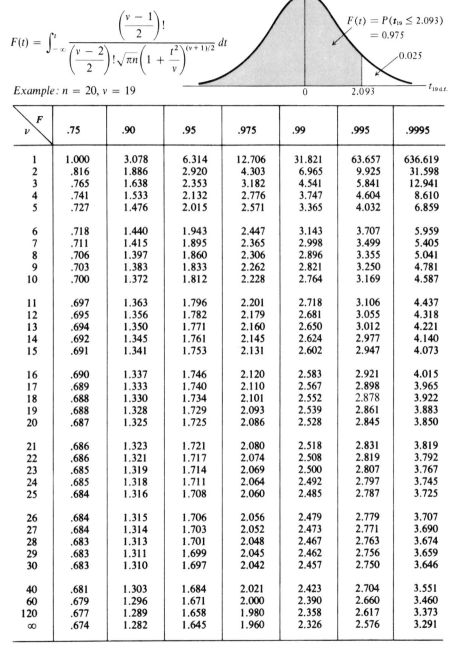

$$F(t) = \int_{-\infty}^{t} \frac{\left(\dfrac{v-1}{2}\right)!}{\left(\dfrac{v-2}{2}\right)!\sqrt{\pi n}\left(1 + \dfrac{t^2}{v}\right)^{(v+1)/2}}\, dt$$

$F(t) = P(t_{19} \leq 2.093)$
$= 0.975$

0.025

Example: $n = 20,\ v = 19$

v \ F	.75	.90	.95	.975	.99	.995	.9995
1	1.000	3.078	6.314	12.706	31.821	63.657	636.619
2	.816	1.886	2.920	4.303	6.965	9.925	31.598
3	.765	1.638	2.353	3.182	4.541	5.841	12.941
4	.741	1.533	2.132	2.776	3.747	4.604	8.610
5	.727	1.476	2.015	2.571	3.365	4.032	6.859
6	.718	1.440	1.943	2.447	3.143	3.707	5.959
7	.711	1.415	1.895	2.365	2.998	3.499	5.405
8	.706	1.397	1.860	2.306	2.896	3.355	5.041
9	.703	1.383	1.833	2.262	2.821	3.250	4.781
10	.700	1.372	1.812	2.228	2.764	3.169	4.587
11	.697	1.363	1.796	2.201	2.718	3.106	4.437
12	.695	1.356	1.782	2.179	2.681	3.055	4.318
13	.694	1.350	1.771	2.160	2.650	3.012	4.221
14	.692	1.345	1.761	2.145	2.624	2.977	4.140
15	.691	1.341	1.753	2.131	2.602	2.947	4.073
16	.690	1.337	1.746	2.120	2.583	2.921	4.015
17	.689	1.333	1.740	2.110	2.567	2.898	3.965
18	.688	1.330	1.734	2.101	2.552	2.878	3.922
19	.688	1.328	1.729	2.093	2.539	2.861	3.883
20	.687	1.325	1.725	2.086	2.528	2.845	3.850
21	.686	1.323	1.721	2.080	2.518	2.831	3.819
22	.686	1.321	1.717	2.074	2.508	2.819	3.792
23	.685	1.319	1.714	2.069	2.500	2.807	3.767
24	.685	1.318	1.711	2.064	2.492	2.797	3.745
25	.684	1.316	1.708	2.060	2.485	2.787	3.725
26	.684	1.315	1.706	2.056	2.479	2.779	3.707
27	.684	1.314	1.703	2.052	2.473	2.771	3.690
28	.683	1.313	1.701	2.048	2.467	2.763	3.674
29	.683	1.311	1.699	2.045	2.462	2.756	3.659
30	.683	1.310	1.697	2.042	2.457	2.750	3.646
40	.681	1.303	1.684	2.021	2.423	2.704	3.551
60	.679	1.296	1.671	2.000	2.390	2.660	3.460
120	.677	1.289	1.658	1.980	2.358	2.617	3.373
∞	.674	1.282	1.645	1.960	2.326	2.576	3.291

This table is abridged from Table III of Fisher & Yates: *Statistical Tables for Biological, Agricultural and Medical Research*, published by Longman Group Ltd. London (previously published by Oliver & Boyd Ltd. Edinburgh) and by permission of the authors and publishers.

Appendix B

TABLE VIII(a)   Critical Values of the F-Distribution (α = 0.05)

Tables VIII(a), (b), and (c) from M. Merrington and C. M. Thompson, "Tables of percentage points of the inverted beta (F) distribution." *Biometrika*, Vol. 33 (1943) by permission of the *Biometrika* Trustees.

The following table gives the critical values of the *F*-distribution for α = 0.05. This probability represents the area exceeding the value of $F_{0.05,\, v_1,\, v_2}$, as shown by the shaded area in the figure below.

Examples: If v_1 = 15 (d.f. for the numerator), and v_2 = 20, then the critical value cutting off 0.05 is 2.20.

$$P(F \geq 2.20) = 0.05,$$
$$P(F \leq 2.20) = 0.95.$$

VALUES OF $F_{0.05,\, v_1,\, v_2}$

v_1 = Degrees of freedom for numerator

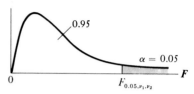

v_2 = Degrees of freedom for denominator

	1	2	3	4	5	6	7	8	9	10	12	15	20	24	30	40	60	120	x
1	161	200	216	225	230	234	237	239	241	242	244	246	248	249	250	251	252	253	254
2	18.5	19.0	19.2	19.2	19.3	19.3	19.4	19.4	19.4	19.4	19.4	19.4	19.4	19.5	19.5	19.5	19.5	19.5	19.5
3	10.1	9.55	9.28	9.12	9.01	8.94	8.89	8.85	8.81	8.79	8.74	8.70	8.66	8.64	8.62	8.59	8.57	8.55	8.53
4	7.71	6.94	6.59	6.39	6.26	6.16	6.09	6.04	6.00	5.96	5.91	5.86	5.80	5.77	5.75	5.72	5.69	5.66	5.63
5	6.61	5.79	5.41	5.19	5.05	4.95	4.88	4.82	4.77	4.74	4.68	4.62	4.56	4.53	4.50	4.46	4.43	4.40	4.37
6	5.99	5.14	4.76	4.53	4.39	4.28	4.21	4.15	4.10	4.06	4.00	3.94	3.87	3.84	3.81	3.77	3.74	3.70	3.67
7	5.59	4.74	4.35	4.12	3.97	3.87	3.79	3.73	3.68	3.64	3.57	3.51	3.44	3.41	3.38	3.34	3.30	3.27	3.23
8	5.32	4.46	4.07	3.84	3.69	3.58	3.50	3.44	3.39	3.35	3.28	3.22	3.15	3.12	3.08	3.04	3.01	2.97	2.93
9	5.12	4.26	3.86	3.63	3.48	3.37	3.29	3.23	3.18	3.14	3.07	3.01	2.94	2.90	2.86	2.83	2.79	2.75	2.71
10	4.96	4.10	3.71	3.48	3.33	3.22	3.14	3.07	3.02	2.98	2.91	2.85	2.77	2.74	2.70	2.66	2.62	2.58	2.54
11	4.84	3.98	3.59	3.36	3.20	3.09	3.01	2.95	2.90	2.85	2.79	2.72	2.65	2.61	2.57	2.53	2.49	2.45	2.40
12	4.75	3.89	3.49	3.26	3.11	3.00	2.91	2.85	2.80	2.75	2.69	2.62	2.54	2.51	2.47	2.43	2.38	2.34	2.30
13	4.67	3.81	3.41	3.18	3.03	2.92	2.83	2.77	2.71	2.67	2.60	2.53	2.46	2.42	2.38	2.34	2.30	2.25	2.21
14	4.60	3.74	3.34	3.11	2.96	2.85	2.76	2.70	2.65	2.60	2.53	2.46	2.39	2.35	2.31	2.27	2.22	2.18	2.13
15	4.54	3.68	3.29	3.06	2.90	2.79	2.71	2.64	2.59	2.54	2.48	2.40	2.33	2.29	2.25	2.20	2.16	2.11	2.07
16	4.49	3.63	3.24	3.01	2.85	2.74	2.66	2.59	2.54	2.49	2.42	2.35	2.28	2.24	2.19	2.15	2.11	2.06	2.01
17	4.45	3.59	3.20	2.96	2.81	2.70	2.61	2.55	2.49	2.45	2.38	2.31	2.23	2.19	2.15	2.10	2.06	2.01	1.96
18	4.41	3.55	3.16	2.93	2.77	2.66	2.58	2.51	2.46	2.41	2.34	2.27	2.19	2.15	2.11	2.06	2.02	1.97	1.92
19	4.38	3.52	3.13	2.90	2.74	2.63	2.54	2.48	2.42	2.38	2.31	2.23	2.16	2.11	2.07	2.03	1.98	1.93	1.88
20	4.35	3.49	3.10	2.87	2.71	2.60	2.51	2.45	2.39	2.35	2.28	2.20	2.12	2.08	2.04	1.99	1.95	1.90	1.84
21	4.32	3.47	3.07	2.84	2.68	2.57	2.49	2.42	2.37	2.32	2.25	2.18	2.10	2.05	2.01	1.96	1.92	1.87	1.81
22	4.30	3.44	3.05	2.82	2.66	2.55	2.46	2.40	2.34	2.30	2.23	2.15	2.07	2.03	1.98	1.94	1.89	1.84	1.78
23	4.28	3.42	3.03	2.80	2.64	2.53	2.44	2.37	2.32	2.27	2.20	2.13	2.05	2.01	1.96	1.91	1.86	1.81	1.76
24	4.26	3.40	3.01	2.78	2.62	2.51	2.42	2.36	2.30	2.25	2.18	2.11	2.03	1.98	1.94	1.89	1.84	1.79	1.73
25	4.24	3.39	2.99	2.76	2.60	2.49	2.40	2.34	2.28	2.24	2.16	2.09	2.01	1.96	1.92	1.87	1.82	1.77	1.71
30	4.17	3.32	2.92	2.69	2.53	2.42	2.33	2.27	2.21	2.16	2.09	2.01	1.93	1.89	1.84	1.79	1.74	1.68	1.62
40	4.08	3.23	2.84	2.61	2.45	2.34	2.25	2.18	2.12	2.08	2.00	1.92	1.84	1.79	1.74	1.69	1.64	1.58	1.51
60	4.00	3.15	2.76	2.53	2.37	2.25	2.17	2.10	2.04	1.99	1.92	1.84	1.75	1.70	1.65	1.59	1.53	1.47	1.39
120	3.92	3.07	2.68	2.45	2.29	2.18	2.09	2.02	1.96	1.91	1.83	1.75	1.66	1.61	1.55	1.50	1.43	1.35	1.25
x	3.84	3.00	2.60	2.37	2.21	2.10	2.01	1.94	1.88	1.83	1.75	1.67	1.57	1.52	1.46	1.39	1.32	1.22	1.00

TABLE VIII(b)   Critical Values of the F-Distribution ($\alpha = 0.025$)

The following table gives the critical values of the F-distribution for $\alpha = 0.025$. This probability represents the area exceeding the value of $F_{0.025,\, v_1,\, v_2}$, as shown by the shaded area in the figure below.

Examples: If $v_1 = 15$ (representing the greater mean square), and $v_2 = 20$, then the critical value for $\alpha = 0.025$ is 2.570.

$$P(F \geq 2.570) = 0.025,$$

$$P(F \leq 2.570) = 0.975.$$

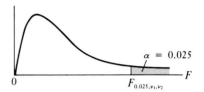

VALUES OF $F_{0.025,\, v_1,\, v_2}$

$v_1 =$ Degrees of freedom for numerator

$v_2 =$ Degrees of freedom for denominator

v_2	1	2	3	4	5	6	7	8	9	10	12	15	20	24	30	40	60	120	∞
1	647.8	799.5	864.2	899.6	921.8	937.1	948.2	956.7	963.3	968.6	976.7	984.9	993.1	997.2	1001	1006	1010	1014	1018
2	38.51	39.00	39.17	39.25	39.30	39.33	39.36	39.37	39.39	39.40	39.41	39.43	39.45	39.46	39.46	39.47	39.48	39.49	39.50
3	17.44	16.04	15.44	15.10	14.88	14.73	14.62	14.54	14.47	14.42	14.34	14.25	14.17	14.12	14.08	14.04	13.99	13.95	13.90
4	12.22	10.65	9.98	9.60	9.36	9.20	9.07	8.98	8.90	8.84	8.75	8.66	8.56	8.51'	8.46	8.41	8.36	8.31	8.26
5	10.01	8.43	7.76	7.39	7.15	6.98	6.85	6.76	6.68	6.62	6.52	6.43	6.33	6.28	6.23	6.18	6.12	6.07	6.02
6	8.81	7.26	6.60	6.23	5.99	5.82	5.70	5.60	5.52	5.46	5.37	5.27	5.17	5.12	5.07	5.01	4.96	4.90	4.85
7	8.07	6.54	5.89	5.52	5.29	5.21	4.99	4.90	4.82	4.76	4.67	4.57	4.47	4.42	4.36	4.31	4.25	4.20	4.14
8	7.57	6.06	5.42	5.05	4.82	4.65	4.53	4.43	4.36	4.30	4.20	4.10	4.00	3.95	3.89	3.84	3.78	3.73	3.67
9	7.21	5.71	5.08	4.72	4.48	4.32	4.20	4.10	4.03	3.96	3.87	3.77	3.67	3.61	3.56	3.51	3.45	3.39	3.33
10	6.94	5.46	4.83	4.47	4.24	4.07	3.95	3.85	3.78	3.72	3.62	3.52	3.42	3.37	3.31	3.26	3.20	3.14	3.08
11	6.72	5.26	4.63	4.28	4.04	3.88	3.76	3.66	3.59	3.53	3.43	3.33	3.23	3.17	3.12	3.06	3.00	2.94	2.88
12	6.55	5.10	4.47	4.12	3.89	3.73	3.61	3.51	3.44	3.37	3.28	3.18	3.07	3.02	2.96	2.91	2.85	2.79	2.72
13	6.41	4.97	4.35	4.00	3.77	3.60	3.48	3.39	3.31	3.25	3.15	3.05	2.95	2.89	2.84	2.78	2.72	2.66	2.60
14	6.30	4.86	4.24	3.89	3.66	3.50	3.38	3.29	3.21	3.15	3.05	2.95	2.84	2.79	2.73	2.67	2.61	2.55	2.49
15	6.20	4.77	4.15	3.80	3.58	3.41	3.29	3.20	3.12	3.06	2.96	2.86	2.76	2.70	2.64	2.59	2.52	2.46	2.40
16	6.12	4.69	4.08	3.73	3.50	3.34	3.22	3.12	3.05	2.99	2.89	2.79	2.68	2.63	2.57	2.51	2.45	2.38	2.32
17	6.04	4.62	4.01	3.66	3.44	3.28	3.16	3.06	2.98	2.92	2.82	2.72	2.62	2.56	2.50	2.44	2.38	2.32	2.25
18	5.98	4.56	3.95	3.61	3.38	3.22	3.10	3.01	2.93	2.87	2.77	2.67	2.56	2.50	2.44	2.38	2.32	2.26	2.19
19	5.92	4.51	3.90	3.56	3.33	3.17	3.05	2.96	2.88	2.82	2.72	2.62	2.51	2.45	2.39	2.33	2.27	2.20	2.13
20	5.87	4.46	3.86	3.51	3.29	3.13	3.01	2.91	2.84	2.77	2.68	2.57	2.46	2.41	2.35	2.29	2.22	2.16	2.09
21	5.83	4.42	3.82	3.48	3.25	3.09	2.97	2.87	2.80	2.73	2.64	2.53	2.42	2.37	2.31	2.25	2.18	2.11	2.04
22	5.79	4.38	3.78	3.44	3.22	3.05	2.93	2.84	2.76	2.70	2.60	2.50	2.39	2.33	2.27	2.21	2.14	2.08	2.00
23	5.75	4.35	3.75	3.41	3.18	3.02	2.90	2.81	2.73	2.67	2.57	2.47	2.36	2.30	2.24	2.18	2.11	2.04	1.97
24	5.72	4.32	3.72	3.38	3.15	2.99	2.87	2.78	2.70	2.54	2.54	2.44	2.33	2.27	2.21	2.15	2.08	2.01	1.94
25	5.69	4.29	3.69	3.35	3.13	2.97	2.85	2.75	2.68	2.61	2.51	2.41	2.30	2.24	2.18	2.12	2.05	1.98	1.91
26	5.66	4.27	3.67	3.33	3.10	2.94	2.82	2.73	2.65	2.59	2.49	2.39	2.28	2.22	2.16	2.09	2.03	1.95	1.88
27	5.63	4.24	3.65	3.31	3.08	2.92	2.80	2.71	2.63	2.57	2.47	2.36	2.25	2.19	2.13	2.07	2.00	1.93	1.85
28	5.61	4.22	3.63	3.29	3.06	2.90	2.78	2.69	2.61	2.55	2.45	2.34	2.23	2.17	2.11	2.05	1.98	1.91	1.83
29	5.59	4.20	3.61	3.27	3.04	2.88	2.76	2.67	2.59	2.53	2.43	2.32	2.21	2.15	2.09	2.03	1.96	1.89	1.81
30	5.57	4.18	3.59	3.25	3.03	2.87	2.75	2.65	2.57	2.51	2.41	2.31	2.20	2.14	2.07	2.01	1.94	1.87	1.79
40	5.42	4.05	3.46	3.13	2.90	2.74	2.62	2.53	2.45	2.39	2.29	2.18	2.07	2.01	1.94	1.88	1.80	1.72	1.64
60	5.29	3.93	3.34	3.01	2.79	2.63	2.51	2.41	2.33	2.27	2.17	2.06	1.94	1.88	1.82	1.74	1.67	1.58	1.48
120	5.15	3.80	3.23	2.89	2.67	2.52	2.39	2.30	2.22	2.16	2.05	1.94	1.82	1.76	1.69	1.61	1.53	1.43	1.31
∞	5.02	3.69	3.12	2.79	2.57	2.41	2.29	2.19	2.11	2.05	1.94	1.83	1.71	1.64	1.57	1.48	1.39	1.27	1.00

TABLE VIII(c)   Critical Values of the F-Distribution ($\alpha = 0.01$)

The following table gives the critical values of the F-distribution for $\alpha = 0.01$. This probability represents the area exceeding the value of $F_{0.01,\,v_1,\,v_2}$, as shown by the shaded area in the figure below.

Examples: If $v_1 = 15$ (representing the greater mean square), and $v_2 = 20$, then the critical value for $\alpha = 0.01$ is 3.09.

$$P(F \geq 3.09) = 0.01,$$
$$P(F \leq 3.09) = 0.99.$$

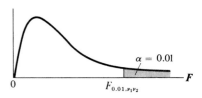

VALUES OF $F_{0.01,\,v_1,\,v_2}$

v_1 = Degrees of freedom for numerator

v_2 = Degrees of freedom for denominator

v_2	1	2	3	4	5	6	7	8	9	10	12	15	20	24	30	40	60	120	x
1	4,052	5,000	5,403	5,625	5,764	5,859	5,928	5,982	6,023	6,056	6,106	6,157	6,209	6,235	6,261	6,287	6,313	6,339	6,366
2	98.5	99.0	99.2	99.2	99.3	99.3	99.4	99.4	99.4	99.4	99.4	99.4	99.4	99.5	99.5	99.5	99.5	99.5	99.5
3	34.1	30.8	29.5	28.7	28.2	27.9	27.7	27.5	27.3	27.2	27.1	26.9	26.7	26.6	26.5	26.4	26.3	26.2	26.1
4	21.2	18.0	16.7	16.0	15.5	15.2	15.0	14.8	14.7	14.5	14.4	14.2	14.0	13.9	13.8	13.7	13.7	13.6	13.5
5	16.3	13.3	12.1	11.4	11.0	10.7	10.5	10.3	10.2	10.1	9.89	9.72	9.55	9.47	9.38	9.29	9.20	9.11	9.02
6	13.7	10.9	9.78	9.15	8.75	8.47	8.26	8.10	7.98	7.87	7.72	7.56	7.40	7.31	7.23	7.14	7.06	6.97	6.88
7	12.2	9.55	8.45	7.85	7.46	7.19	6.99	6.84	6.72	6.62	6.47	6.31	6.16	6.07	5.99	5.91	5.82	5.74	5.65
8	11.3	8.65	7.59	7.01	6.63	6.37	6.18	6.03	5.91	5.81	5.67	5.52	5.36	5.28	5.20	5.12	5.03	4.95	4.86
9	10.6	8.02	6.99	6.42	6.06	5.80	5.61	5.47	5.35	5.26	5.11	4.96	4.81	4.73	4.65	4.57	4.48	4.40	4.31
10	10.0	7.56	6.55	5.99	5.64	5.39	5.20	5.06	4.94	4.85	4.71	4.56	4.41	4.33	4.25	4.17	4.08	4.00	3.91
11	9.65	7.21	6.22	5.67	5.32	5.07	4.89	4.74	4.63	4.54	4.40	4.25	4.10	4.02	3.94	3.86	3.78	3.69	3.60
12	9.33	6.93	5.95	5.41	5.06	4.82	4.64	4.50	4.39	4.30	4.16	4.01	3.86	3.78	3.70	3.62	3.54	3.45	3.36
13	9.07	6.70	5.74	5.21	4.86	4.62	4.44	4.30	4.19	4.10	3.96	3.82	3.66	3.59	3.51	3.43	3.34	3.25	3.17
14	8.86	6.51	5.56	5.04	4.70	4.46	4.28	4.14	4.03	3.94	3.80	3.66	3.51	3.43	3.35	3.27	3.18	3.09	3.00
15	8.68	6.36	5.42	4.89	4.56	4.32	4.14	4.00	3.89	3.80	3.67	3.52	3.37	3.29	3.21	3.13	3.05	2.96	2.87
16	8.53	6.23	5.29	4.77	4.44	4.20	4.03	3.89	3.78	3.69	3.55	3.41	3.26	3.18	3.10	3.02	2.93	2.84	2.75
17	8.40	6.11	5.19	4.67	4.34	4.10	3.93	3.79	3.68	3.59	3.46	3.31	3.16	3.08	3.00	2.92	2.83	2.75	2.65
18	8.29	6.01	5.09	4.58	4.25	4.01	3.84	3.71	3.60	3.51	3.37	3.23	3.08	3.00	2.92	2.84	2.75	2.66	2.57
19	8.19	5.93	5.01	4.50	4.17	3.94	3.77	3.63	3.52	3.43	3.30	3.15	3.00	2.92	2.84	2.76	2.67	2.58	2.49
20	8.10	5.85	4.94	4.43	4.10	3.87	3.70	3.56	3.46	3.37	3.23	3.09	2.94	2.86	2.78	2.69	2.61	2.52	2.42
21	8.02	5.78	4.87	4.37	4.04	3.81	3.64	3.51	3.40	3.31	3.17	3.03	2.88	2.80	2.72	2.64	2.55	2.46	2.36
22	7.95	5.72	4.82	4.31	3.99	3.76	3.59	3.45	3.35	3.26	3.12	2.98	2.83	2.75	2.67	2.58	2.50	2.40	2.31
23	7.88	5.66	4.76	4.26	3.94	3.71	3.54	3.41	3.30	3.21	3.07	2.93	2.78	2.70	2.62	2.54	2.45	2.35	2.26
24	7.82	5.61	4.72	4.22	3.90	3.67	3.50	3.36	3.26	3.17	3.03	2.89	2.74	2.66	2.58	2.49	2.40	2.31	2.21
25	7.77	5.57	4.68	4.18	3.86	3.63	3.46	3.32	3.22	3.13	2.99	2.85	2.70	2.62	2.53	2.45	2.36	2.27	2.17
30	7.56	5.39	4.51	4.02	3.70	3.47	3.30	3.17	3.07	2.98	2.84	2.70	2.55	2.47	2.39	2.30	2.21	2.11	2.01
40	7.31	5.18	4.31	3.83	3.51	3.29	3.12	2.99	2.89	2.80	2.66	2.52	2.37	2.29	2.20	2.11	2.02	1.92	1.80
60	7.08	4.98	4.13	3.65	3.34	3.12	2.95	2.82	2.72	2.63	2.50	2.35	2.20	2.12	2.03	1.94	1.84	1.73	1.60
120	6.85	4.79	3.95	3.48	3.17	2.96	2.79	2.66	2.56	2.47	2.34	2.19	2.03	1.95	1.86	1.76	1.66	1.53	1.38
x	6.63	4.61	3.78	3.32	3.02	2.80	2.64	2.51	2.41	2.32	2.18	2.04	1.88	1.79	1.70	1.59	1.47	1.32	1.00

TABLE IX   Table of Constants for Control Charts

Number of observations in sample	Chart for averages	Chart for ranges			
	Constants for control limits	Constants for central line		Constants for control limits	
n	A_2	d_2	$1/d_2$	D_3	D_4
2	1.880	1.128	0.8865	0	3.276
3	1.023	1.693	0.5907	0	2.575
4	0.729	2.059	0.4857	0	2.282
5	0.577	2.326	0.4299	0	2.115
6	0.483	2.534	0.3946	0	2.004
7	0.419	2.704	0.3698	0.076	1.924
8	0.373	2.847	0.3512	0.136	1.864
9	0.337	2.970	0.3367	0.184	1.816
10	0.308	3.078	0.3249	0.223	1.777
11	0.285	3.173	0.3152	0.256	1.744
12	0.266	3.258	0.3069	0.284	1.719
13	0.249	3.336	0.2998	0.308	1.692
14	0.235	3.407	0.2935	0.329	1.671
15	0.223	3.472	0.2880	0.348	1.652
16	0.212	3.532	0.2831	0.364	1.636
17	0.203	3.588	0.2787	0.379	1.621
18	0.194	3.640	0.2747	0.392	1.608
19	0.187	3.689	0.2711	0.404	1.596
20	0.180	3.735	0.2677	0.414	1.586
21	0.173	3.778	0.2647	0.425	1.575
22	0.167	3.819	0.2617	0.434	1.566
23	0.162	3.858	0.2592	0.443	1.557
24	0.157	3.895	0.2567	0.452	1.548
25	0.153	3.931	0.2544	0.459	1.541

Source: Reproduced by permission from ASTM Manual on Quality Control of Materials, American Society for Testing Materials, Philadelphia, PA, 1951.

Appendix B

TABLE X The Durbin-Watson *d*-Statistic

Significance points of d_L and d_U: 5%

n	$m = 1$ d_L	$m = 1$ d_U	$m = 2$ d_L	$m = 2$ d_U	$m = 3$ d_L	$m = 3$ d_U	$m = 4$ d_L	$m = 4$ d_U	$m = 5$ d_L	$m = 5$ d_U
15	1.08	1.36	0.95	1.54	0.82	1.75	0.69	1.97	0.56	2.21
16	1.10	1.37	0.98	1.54	0.86	1.73	0.74	1.93	0.62	2.15
17	1.13	1.38	1.02	1.54	0.90	1.71	0.78	1.90	0.67	2.10
18	1.16	1.39	1.05	1.53	0.93	1.69	0.82	1.87	0.71	2.06
19	1.18	1.40	1.08	1.53	0.97	1.68	0.86	1.85	0.75	2.02
20	1.20	1.41	1.10	1.54	1.00	1.68	0.90	1.83	0.79	1.99
21	1.22	1.42	1.13	1.54	1.03	1.67	0.93	1.81	0.83	1.96
22	1.24	1.43	1.15	1.54	1.05	1.66	0.96	1.80	0.86	1.94
23	1.26	1.44	1.17	1.54	1.08	1.66	0.99	1.79	0.90	1.92
24	1.27	1.45	1.19	1.55	1.10	1.66	1.01	1.78	0.93	1.90
25	1.29	1.45	1.21	1.55	1.12	1.66	1.04	1.77	0.95	1.89
26	1.30	1.46	1.22	1.55	1.14	1.65	1.06	1.76	0.98	1.88
27	1.32	1.47	1.24	1.56	1.16	1.65	1.08	1.76	1.01	1.86
28	1.33	1.48	1.26	1.56	1.18	1.65	1.10	1.75	1.03	1.85
29	1.34	1.48	1.27	1.56	1.20	1.65	1.12	1.74	1.05	1.84
30	1.35	1.49	1.28	1.57	1.21	1.65	1.14	1.74	1.07	1.83
31	1.36	1.50	1.30	1.57	1.23	1.65	1.16	1.74	1.09	1.83
32	1.37	1.50	1.31	1.57	1.24	1.65	1.18	1.73	1.11	1.82
33	1.38	1.51	1.32	1.58	1.26	1.65	1.19	1.73	1.13	1.81
34	1.39	1.51	1.33	1.58	1.27	1.65	1.21	1.73	1.15	1.81
35	1.40	1.52	1.34	1.58	1.28	1.65	1.22	1.73	1.16	1.80
36	1.41	1.52	1.35	1.59	1.29	1.65	1.24	1.73	1.18	1.80
37	1.42	1.53	1.36	1.59	1.31	1.66	1.25	1.72	1.19	1.80
38	1.43	1.54	1.37	1.59	1.32	1.66	1.26	1.72	1.21	1.79
39	1.43	1.54	1.38	1.60	1.33	1.66	1.27	1.72	1.22	1.79
40	1.44	1.54	1.39	1.60	1.34	1.66	1.29	1.72	1.23	1.79
45	1.48	1.57	1.43	1.62	1.38	1.67	1.34	1.72	1.29	1.78
50	1.50	1.59	1.46	1.63	1.42	1.67	1.38	1.72	1.34	1.77
55	1.53	1.60	1.49	1.64	1.45	1.68	1.41	1.72	1.38	1.77
60	1.55	1.62	1.51	1.65	1.48	1.69	1.44	1.73	1.41	1.77
65	1.57	1.63	1.54	1.66	1.50	1.70	1.47	1.73	1.44	1.77
70	1.58	1.64	1.55	1.67	1.52	1.70	1.49	1.74	1.46	1.77
75	1.60	1.65	1.57	1.68	1.54	1.71	1.51	1.74	1.49	1.77
80	1.61	1.66	1.59	1.69	1.56	1.72	1.53	1.74	1.51	1.77
85	1.62	1.67	1.60	1.70	1.57	1.72	1.55	1.75	1.52	1.77
90	1.63	1.68	1.61	1.70	1.59	1.73	1.57	1.75	1.54	1.78
95	1.64	1.69	1.62	1.71	1.60	1.73	1.58	1.75	1.56	1.78
100	1.65	1.69	1.63	1.72	1.61	1.74	1.59	1.76	1.57	1.78

TABLE X (continued)

Significance points of d_L and d_U: 1%

n	$m = 1$		$m = 2$		$m = 3$		$m = 4$		$m = 5$	
	d_L	d_U	d_L	d_U	d_L	d_U	d_L	d_U	d_L	d_U
15	0.81	1.07	0.70	1.25	0.59	1.46	0.49	1.70	0.39	1.96
16	0.84	1.09	0.74	1.25	0.63	1.44	0.53	1.66	0.44	1.90
17	0.87	1.10	0.77	1.25	0.67	1.43	0.57	1.63	0.48	1.85
18	0.90	1.12	0.80	1.26	0.71	1.42	0.61	1.60	0.52	1.80
19	0.93	1.13	0.83	1.26	0.74	1.41	0.65	1.58	0.56	1.77
20	0.95	1.15	0.86	1.27	0.77	1.41	0.68	1.57	0.60	1.74
21	0.97	1.16	0.89	1.27	0.80	1.41	0.72	1.55	0.63	1.71
22	1.00	1.17	0.91	1.28	0.83	1.40	0.75	1.54	0.66	1.69
23	1.02	1.19	0.94	1.29	0.86	1.40	0.77	1.53	0.70	1.67
24	1.04	1.20	0.96	1.30	0.88	1.41	0.80	1.53	0.72	1.66
25	1.05	1.21	0.98	1.30	0.90	1.41	0.83	1.52	0.75	1.65
26	1.07	1.22	1.00	1.31	0.93	1.41	0.85	1.52	0.78	1.64
27	1.09	1.23	1.02	1.32	0.95	1.41	0.88	1.51	0.81	1.63
28	1.10	1.24	1.04	1.32	0.97	1.41	0.90	1.51	0.83	1.62
29	1.12	1.25	1.05	1.33	0.99	1.42	0.92	1.51	0.85	1.61
30	1.13	1.26	1.07	1.34	1.01	1.42	0.94	1.51	0.88	1.61
31	1.15	1.27	1.08	1.34	1.02	1.42	0.96	1.51	0.90	1.60
32	1.16	1.28	1.10	1.35	1.04	1.43	0.98	1.51	0.92	1.60
33	1.17	1.29	1.11	1.36	1.05	1.43	1.00	1.51	0.94	1.59
34	1.18	1.30	1.13	1.36	1.07	1.43	1.01	1.51	0.95	1.59
35	1.19	1.31	1.14	1.37	1.08	1.44	1.03	1.51	0.97	1.59
36	1.21	1.32	1.15	1.38	1.10	1.44	1.04	1.51	0.99	1.59
37	1.22	1.32	1.16	1.38	1.11	1.45	1.06	1.51	1.00	1.59
38	1.23	1.33	1.18	1.39	1.12	1.45	1.07	1.52	1.02	1.58
39	1.24	1.34	1.19	1.39	1.14	1.45	1.09	1.52	1.03	1.58
40	1.25	1.34	1.20	1.40	1.15	1.46	1.10	1.52	1.05	1.58
45	1.29	1.38	1.24	1.42	1.20	1.48	1.16	1.53	1.11	1.58
50	1.32	1.40	1.28	1.45	1.24	1.49	1.20	1.54	1.16	1.59
55	1.36	1.43	1.32	1.47	1.28	1.51	1.25	1.55	1.21	1.59
60	1.38	1.45	1.35	1.48	1.32	1.52	1.28	1.56	1.25	1.60
65	1.41	1.47	1.38	1.50	1.35	1.53	1.31	1.57	1.28	1.61
70	1.43	1.49	1.40	1.52	1.37	1.55	1.34	1.58	1.31	1.61
75	1.45	1.50	1.42	1.53	1.39	1.56	1.37	1.59	1.34	1.62
80	1.47	1.52	1.44	1.54	1.42	1.57	1.39	1.60	1.36	1.62
85	1.48	1.53	1.46	1.55	1.43	1.58	1.41	1.60	1.39	1.63
90	1.50	1.54	1.47	1.56	1.45	1.59	1.43	1.61	1.41	1.64
95	1.51	1.55	1.49	1.57	1.47	1.60	1.45	1.62	1.42	1.64
100	1.52	1.56	1.50	1.58	1.48	1.60	1.46	1.63	1.44	1.65

SOURCE: Reproduced by permission of the editor and authors, from J. Durbin and G. S. Watson, "Testing for serial correlation in least squares regression, (II)," *Biometrika*, **38**, 1951, pp. 159–178.

TABLE XI   Critical Values of *r* in the Runs Test

Given in the body of Table XI are various critical values of r for various values of n_1 and n_2. For the Wald–Wolfowitz two-sample runs test, any value of r which is equal to or smaller than that shown in Table XI is significant at the 0.05 level.

n_1 \ n_2	2	3	4	5	6	7	8	9	10	11	12	13	14	15	16	17	18	19	20
2											2	2	2	2	2	2	2	2	2
3				2	2	2	2	2	2	2	2	2	2	3	3	3	3	3	3
4			2	2	2	3	3	3	3	3	3	3	3	3	4	4	4	4	4
5		2	2	3	3	3	3	3	4	4	4	4	4	4	4	4	5	5	5
6	2	2	3	3	3	3	4	4	4	4	5	5	5	5	5	5	6	6
7	2	2	3	3	3	4	4	5	5	5	5	5	6	6	6	6	6	6
8	2	3	3	3	4	4	5	5	5	6	6	6	6	6	7	7	7	7
9	2	3	3	4	4	5	5	5	6	6	6	7	7	7	7	8	8	8
10	2	3	3	4	5	5	5	6	6	7	7	7	7	8	8	8	8	9
11	2	3	4	4	5	5	6	6	7	7	7	8	8	8	9	9	9	9
12	2	2	3	4	4	5	6	6	7	7	7	8	8	8	9	9	9	10	10
13	2	2	3	4	5	5	6	6	7	7	8	8	9	9	9	10	10	10	10
14	2	2	3	4	5	5	6	7	7	8	8	9	9	9	10	10	10	11	11
15	2	3	3	4	5	6	6	7	7	8	8	9	9	10	10	11	11	11	12
16	2	3	4	4	5	6	6	7	8	8	9	9	10	10	11	11	11	12	12
17	2	3	4	4	5	6	7	7	8	9	9	10	10	11	11	11	12	12	13
18	2	3	4	5	5	6	7	8	8	9	9	10	10	11	11	12	12	13	13
19	2	3	4	5	6	6	7	8	8	9	10	10	11	11	12	12	13	13	13
20	2	3	4	5	6	6	7	8	9	9	10	10	11	12	12	13	13	13	14

Adapted from Swed, Frieda S., and Eisenhart, C. 1943. Tables for testing randomness of grouping in a sequence of alternatives. *Ann. Math. Statist.*, **14**, 83–86, with the kind permission of the authors and publisher.

**TABLE XII   Critical Values of *T* for the
Wilcoxon Matched-Pairs Signed-Ranks Test**

	Level of significance for one-tailed test		
	.025	.01	.005
n	Level of significance for two-tailed test		
	.05	.02	.01
6	0	—	—
7	2	0	—
8	4	2	0
9	6	3	2
10	8	5	3
11	11	7	5
12	14	10	7
13	17	13	10
14	21	16	13
15	25	20	16
16	30	24	20
17	35	28	23
18	40	33	28
19	46	38	32
20	52	43	38
21	59	49	43
22	66	56	49
23	73	62	55
24	81	69	61
25	89	77	68

Adapted from Table I of Wilcoxon, F. 1949. *Some rapid approximate statistical procedures.* New York: American Cyanamid Company, p. 13, with the kind permission of the author and publisher.

TABLE XIII   Critical Values of *D* in the Kolmogorov–Smirnov One-Sample Test

Sample size (*n*)	Level of significance for $D = \text{maximum} \left| F_i - S_i \right|$				
	.20	.15	.10	.05	.01
1	.900	.925	.950	.975	.995
2	.684	.726	.776	.842	.929
3	.565	.597	.642	.708	.828
4	.494	.525	.564	.624	.733
5	.446	.474	.510	.565	.669
6	.410	.436	.470	.521	.618
7	.381	.405	.438	.486	.577
8	.358	.381	.411	.457	.543
9	.339	.360	.388	.432	.514
10	.322	.342	.368	.410	.490
11	.307	.326	.352	.391	.468
12	.295	.313	.338	.375	.450
13	.284	.302	.325	.361	.433
14	.274	.292	.314	.349	.418
15	.266	.283	.304	.338	.404
16	.258	.274	.295	.328	.392
17	.250	.266	.286	.318	.381
18	.244	.259	.278	.309	.371
19	.237	.252	.272	.301	.363
20	.231	.246	.264	.294	.356
25	.21	.22	.24	.27	.32
30	.19	.20	.22	.24	.29
35	.18	.19	.21	.23	.27
Over 35	$\dfrac{1.07}{\sqrt{n}}$	$\dfrac{1.14}{\sqrt{n}}$	$\dfrac{1.22}{\sqrt{n}}$	$\dfrac{1.36}{\sqrt{n}}$	$\dfrac{1.63}{\sqrt{n}}$

Adapted from Massey, F. J., Jr. 1951. The Kolmogorov–Smirnov test for goodness of fit. *J. Amer. Statist. Ass.*, **46**, 70, with the kind permission of the author and publisher.

Appendix C:
Computer Programmers' Salaries and Experience

APPENDIX C: Computer Programmers' Salaries and Experience

Salaries for Males (1) and Females (0)

	Salary	Experience	Sex		Salary	Experience	Sex
1	$73,500	14	1	34	$61,650	14	1
2	54,990	8	1	35	53,880	13	1
3	58,980	9	1	36	40,710	7	1
4	89,210	22	1	37	60,780	9	1
5	39,800	3	1	38	30,200	1	1
6	49,320	10	1	39	52,500	9	1
7	45,750	11	1	40	48,500	7	1
8	68,430	14	1	41	50,200	6	1
9	78,100	12	1	42	36,000	3	1
10	64,400	8	1	43	43,760	5	1
11	52,560	6	1	44	48,920	7	1
12	57,770	5	1	45	72,310	13	1
13	69,440	8	1	46	55,120	10	1
14	48,200	3	1	47	41,100	5	1
15	45,600	6	1	48	57,380	6	1
16	41,850	4	1	49	52,100	1	1
17	67,100	12	1	50	60,500	8	1
18	98,300	26	1	51	44,990	4	0
19	65,920	16	1	52	68,110	9	0
20	53,380	7	1	53	52,380	6	0
21	41,910	9	1	54	46,640	4	0
22	53,240	8	1	55	60,600	10	0
23	50,670	5	1	56	59,550	8	0
24	59,230	10	1	57	55,630	5	0
25	59,420	8	1	58	42,050	5	0
26	83,900	19	1	59	56,990	6	0
27	60,400	15	1	60	57,700	9	0
28	45,350	7	1	61	54,540	6	0
29	44,100	4	1	62	60,470	12	0
30	51,330	13	1	63	70,880	14	0
31	80,100	21	1	64	62,020	8	0
32	89,520	26	1	65	50,290	5	0
33	94,500	29	1	66	52,140	5	0

APPENDIX C (Continued)

	Salary	Experience	Sex		Salary	Experience	Sex
67	52,850	8	0	84	68,500	10	0
68	61,940	9	0	85	47,000	6	0
69	40,100	3	0	86	46,300	2	0
70	40,000	2	0	87	72,590	17	0
71	49,330	1	0	88	66,930	15	0
72	32,980	1	0	89	46,500	3	0
73	65,930	13	0	90	53,780	7	0
74	78,880	20	0	91	47,100	4	0
75	64,510	7	0	92	44,500	3	0
76	90,400	19	0	93	53,100	6	0
77	60,340	9	0	94	67,220	14	0
78	41,980	1	0	95	36,210	2	0
79	48,770	4	0	96	55,490	8	0
80	47,000	5	0	97	51,240	7	0
81	51,950	4	0	98	53,770	9	0
82	46,910	3	0	99	44,420	5	0
83	63,740	11	0	100	37,440	3	0

References
and
Selected
Bibliography

References and Selected Bibliography

1. Agresti, A., and B. Findlay, *Statistical Methods for the Social Sciences,* 2nd ed. San Francisco: Dellen, 1986.

2. Becker, W. E., and D. L. Harnett, *Business and Economic Statistics: with Computer Applications,* Reading, MA: Addison-Wesley, 1986.

3. Cochran, W. G., *Sampling Techniques,* 2nd ed. New York: Wiley & Sons, Inc. 1963.

4. Conover, W. J., *Practical Nonparametric Statistics,* 2nd ed. New York: Wiley, 1980.

5. Durbin, J., and G. S. Watson, "Testing for Serial Correlation in Least Squares Regression," *Biometrica* 38 (1951): 159–177.

6. Feller, W., *An Introduction to Probability Theory and Its Applications,* 3rd ed., Vol. 1. New York: Wiley, 1968.

7. Ford Motor Company, *Continuing Process Control and Process Capability Improvement.* Internal Training Manual, Ford Motor Company. Dearborn, 1987.

8. Grant, E. L., and R. S. Leavengood, *Statistical Quality Control,* 6th ed. New York: McGraw-Hill, 1988.

9. Kmenta, J., *Elements of Econometrics,* 2nd ed. New York: Macmillan, 1986.

10. McClave, J. T., and P. G. Benson, *Statistics for Business and Economics,* 4th ed. San Francisco: Dellen, 1988.

11. Mendenhall, W., and T. Sincich, *A Second Course in Business Statistics: Regression Analysis,* 3rd ed. San Francisco: Dellen, 1989.

12. Mood, A. M., F. A. Graybill, and D. C. Boss, *Introduction to the Theory of Statistics,* 3rd ed. New York: McGraw-Hill, 1974.

13. Myers, R. H., *Classical and Modern Regression with Applications,* 2nd ed. Boston: PWS-Kent, 1990.

14. Raiffa, H., *Decision Analysis,* Reading, MA: Addison-Wesley, 1968.

15. Rosander, A. C., *Applications of Quality Control in the Service Industries,* New York: Marcel Dekker, 1985.

16. Ryan, T. P., *Statistical Methods for Quality Improvement,* New York: Marcel Dekker, 1989.

17. Schilling, E. G., *Acceptance Sampling in Quality Control,* New York: Marcel Dekker, 1982.

18. S. Siegel and N. J. Castellan, *Nonparametric Statistics for the Behavioral Sciences,* 2nd ed. New York: McGraw-Hill, 1988.

19. Snedecor, G. W., and W. G. Cochran, *Statistical Methods,* 7th ed. Ames, Iowa: Iowa State University Press, 1980.

20. Tanur, J. M., F. Mosteller, W. H. Kruskal, et al., eds. *Statistics, A Guide to the Unknown,* 3rd ed. Pacific Grove, CA: Wadsworth & Brooks/Cole, 1989.

21. Winkler, R. L., *An Introduction to Bayesian Inference and Decision,* New York: Holt, Rinehart and Winston, 1972.

Answers
to
Odd-Numbered
Problems

Answers to Odd-Numbered Problems

Chapter 1

1.7 Mean age is $\mu = 40.17$
Must assume values are evenly distributed throughout the classes, and class marks of 5, 15, etc.

1.9 **a)** Mean: 41,585.50 (1987),   43,235.13 (1988)
b) Methods do not yield the same answer. The average of the percentage column is 4.51%. The average of the totals is 3.97%. In the first case, the eight percentages are all weighted equally. In the second case, the change is in the total, so that the schools are no longer weighted equally.

1.11 Need to assume the midpoint of each class represents the entire class, and then determine these midpoints. The following were used: 10, 60, 300, 2750, and 6000 (an arbitrary choice). Using relative frequencies of 0.901, 0.085, 0.012, 0.002, and 0.0005 (again, an arbitrary choice). These frequencies (which do not quite add to 1) yield a mean of $\mu = 26.21$.

1.13 **a)** Median = 1.0; mode = 0   **b)** Mean = $\mu = 0.8$

1.15 **a)** Median = mode = $50 among the population of 892 winners
b) Mean = $144.28 average among the winners
c) Mean = 12.87 cents among all participants

1.21 Mean = $\mu = 8.5$

1.25 Guess distribution is skewed right.

1.27 They are equal for a symmetrical, unimodal distribution. For a positively skewed distribution they are mean > median > mode. For a negatively skewed distribution, they are mean < median < mode.

1.29 $\sigma^2 = 12064.25$

1.31 a) $\sigma^2 = 0.86$
   b) 80% fall within one standard deviation.
      94% fall within two standard deviations.

1.33 a) $\mu = 10.25$
   b) $\sigma^2 = 28.69$

1.35 a) $\mu = 480, \quad \sigma = 100$
   b) Estimate 68% between 380 and 580.
      Estimate 16% higher than 580.

1.37 a) $\mu = 6.88$
   b) The classes are not of equal sizes, and there are two opened intervals
      (although the first one is really closed at zero).

1.39 $\mu = 81.9063, \quad \sigma^2 = 137.085$

1.41 b) $\mu = 19{,}384.62, \quad$ mode $= 21{,}000$
   c) $\sigma^2 = 65{,}236{,}507 \quad$ (This number is subject to rounding error.)

1.43 a) $\mu = \$28{,}986.50, \quad \sigma = \$4{,}818.14, \quad$ median $= \$27{,}885$
   b) The 10 residents have a smaller mean, but a larger standard deviation.
      The regional income has greater positive skewness because it has a
      greater difference between the mean and the median.

1.49 b) The open-ended category "1000 and over" is not a very satisfactory way
      of summarizing data.
   c) $\mu = 225.25$
   d) $\sigma^2 = 31{,}370$ (subject to rounding error), $\quad \sigma = 177.1$
      Assuming an even distribution throughout each class, 70% fall within one
      standard deviation. 95% fall within two standard deviations (approxi-
      mately).
   e) Median approximately $190
   f) Skewed to the right.

1.51 x (midpoint) f

x (midpoint)	f
0.5	11
1.5	15
2.5	18
3.5	6

   $\mu = 1.88, \quad \sigma^2 = 0.92$ (transformed data)
   $\mu = 1880, \quad \sigma^2 = 920{,}000$ (original data)

1.53 a) $\sigma/\mu = 0.16, \quad \sigma/\mu = 0.185$
      The second has slightly higher variability.
   b) σ/μ: 0.0240 (women) and 0.0327 (men)
      The variability among men is slightly higher.
   c) σ/μ: 0.60 (#1) and 0.50 (#2) and 0.467 (#3)
      Number 1 is the most risky, number 3 the least risky.
      Number 1 has the highest average return.

Chapter 2

2.1 **b)** This probability is subjective.

2.3 **a)** infinite and continuous (as wheat is usually measured)
   b) infinite and discrete
   c) finite and discrete
   d) infinite and continuous
   e) infinite and continuous

2.5 1501/200,000 = 0.007505

2.7 P (face card) = 12/52

2.9 **a)** objective, assuming entries are drawn at random
   b) subjective
   c) subjective unless price changes have been announced

2.11 **a)** P (each sample point) = 1/6

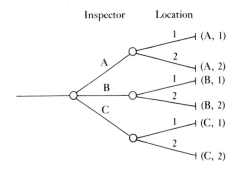

   b) $P(A, 1) + P(B, 2) = 1/6 + 1/6 = 1/3$

2.13 **a)** 0   **b)** $P(A)P(B)$
   c) 0 if A and B are mutually exclusive; otherwise, $P(A|B)$ is unknown

2.15 Formulas (2.4) and (2.5) are the same, except we solve for different probabilities (on the left-hand side).

2.17 **a)** 0.25   **b)** dependence   **c)** $P(S) = 7/16$

   d)

	<30	30–50	>50	
S	1/4	1/16	1/8	7/16
$\bar{S}$	1/4	3/16	1/8	9/16
	1/2	1/4	1/4	

   e) 9/16

2.19 **a)** P (cash adv) = 0.2073, P ($\overline{\text{cash adv}}$) = 0.7927
   b) 0.07   **c)** 0.11   **d)** 1707/10000   **e)** 8305/10000

2.21 (0.01)(0.01)(0.01) = 1/1,000,000
   Since this probability is so low, such "bad luck" is extremely unlikely.

2.23 a) $P(W \text{ or } A) = 0.96,$ $P(W \text{ and } A) = 0.61$
  b) $P(W|A) = 0.777,$ $P(W) = 0.785$
  c) No, $P(W|A) \neq P(W)$
  d) $P(A) = 0.785,$ $P(A \text{ and } W) = 0.610,$ $P(A)P(W) = 0.616$
  Therefore, A and W are not independent.

2.25 a) 0.66 **b)** $P(<50|\text{small}) = 0.19; P(\text{all } 4) = 0.0013$

2.31 a)

	I	II	III	
Very	0.10	0.25	0.15	0.50
Mod.	0.10	0.10	0.10	0.30
Not	0.10	0.05	0.05	0.20
	0.30	0.40	0.30	1.00

  b) 0.50 **c)** 0.50

2.33 a) $P(\text{oil}) = 0.4444,$ $P(\text{gas}) = 0.2540,$ $P(\text{dry}) = 0.3016$
  b) $0.3651 + 0.0317 + 0.0476 = 0.4444$
  c) $P(\text{oil}|1) = 0.6216,$ $P(1|\text{oil}) = 0.8214$
  d) $P(\text{oil}|1) = 0.6216$

2.35 $P(\text{large}|>70) = 0.1874$

2.37 a) $P(\text{cash adv.}) = 0.2073$
  b) $P(<\$100|\text{cash adv.}) = 0.1105$

2.39 a) $P(\text{none}|A3) = 1/3$ **b)** No

2.41 $P(R|H) = 1/3,$ $P(U|H) = 2/3$

2.43 a) $P(>50 \text{ and female}) = 1/4$ **b)** $P(>50|F)/ = 1/2$
  c) $P(F|>50) = 1/3$

Chapter 3

3.1 b) $\mu = 62.6$ hr, $V[x] = 66.24$

3.3 b) $E[x] = 0.0067$
  c) 7,500,000 cards needed

3.7

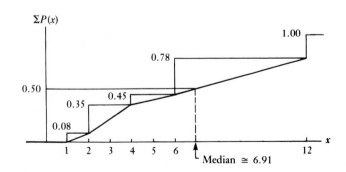

3.9   **a)**

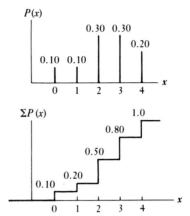

b) $E[x] = 2.4,$ $V[x] = 1.44$
c) $\sigma = 1.2,$ $\mu \pm 1\sigma = 1.2$ to 3.6; includes 60% of the values
       $\mu \pm 2\sigma = 0$ to 4.8; includes 100% of the values

3.11 **a)**

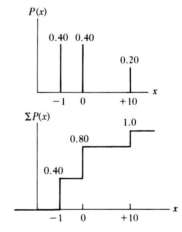

b) $E[x] = 1.6$ **c)** $V[x] = 17.84$

3.13 **a)** Proportion unskilled is $9/14 = 0.643 \, (64.3\%)$

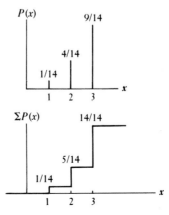

b) $E[x] = 2.57$ $V[x] = 0.3878$

3.15 x = payoff amount for a hit

     x = 0 signifies no hit

x	$P(x)$	
0	0.50	
0.05	0.20	$[= 0.5(0.4)]$
0.10	0.15	
0.25	0.10	
1.00	0.05	

     $E[x] = 0.10,$ $E[\text{return}] = \$25$

3.19 **a)** $E[x] = 2/3$ $V[x] = 1/18$ **b)** Median = 0.707

     c) $\mu \pm 2\sigma$:   0.1952 to 1.138

         $P(0.1952 \le x \le 1) = 0.962$ (using triangles)

3.21 **a)**

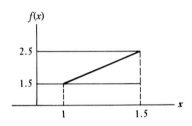

Property 1: $f(x) \ge 0$?   Yes

Property 2:   Area under $f(x) = 1$?   Yes

               Sum of rectangle and triangle under $f(x) = 1.0$

b) $P(5/4 \le x \le 3/2) = 0.5625$ (can be done by triangles)

c) $\mu = 1.2708,$ $V[x] = 0.0205,$ $\sigma = 0.143$

     $\mu \pm 1\sigma$:   1.1278 to 1.4138

     $P(1.1278 \le x \le 1.4138) = 0.584$

     $\mu \pm 2\sigma$:   0.9848 to 1.5568, $P(1 \le x \le 1.5) = 1$

d) $F(x) = x^2 - 0.5x - 0.5$ for $1 \le x \le 1.5$

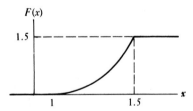

e) $P(5/4 \le x \le 3/2) = 0.5625$

f) $P(1.1278 \le x \le 1.4138) = 0.5839$

     $P(1 \le x \le 1.5) = 1$

3.23 a) Property 1:   all $f(x) > 0$?   Yes
Property 2:   area = 1.0?   Yes

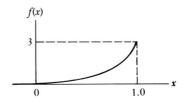

b) $P(x > 1/2) = 0.375$

3.25 a)

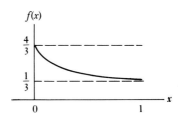

Property 1: $f(x) > 0$?   Yes
Property 2:   area = 1?   Yes

b)
$$F(x) = \begin{cases} 0 & x \leq 0 \\ x^3 & 0 \leq x \leq 1 \\ 1 & x \geq 1 \end{cases}$$
$F(1/4) = 0.0156$

3.27 a) $E[x] = 20{,}000$, $E[y] = 20{,}000$
b) $E[x'] = 2$, $E[x'](10{,}000) = 20{,}000 = E[x]$
$E[y'] = 2$, $E[y'](10{,}000) = 20{,}000 = E[y]$
c) $V[x] = 200{,}000{,}000$
$V[x/10{,}000] = 2$, $V[x]/10{,}000 = 20{,}000$
Relationship between $V[x]$ and $V[x/10{,}000]$ is $(10{,}000)^2$
$V[y] = 66{,}666{,}667$
$V[y/10{,}000] = 2/3$, $V[y]/10{,}000 = 6666.6667$
Relationship between $V[y]$ and $V[y/10{,}000] = (10{,}000)^2$

3.29 a) $E[y] = 4.2$, $V[y] = 2.56$
b) $E[y] = E[x/5 - 15] = 4.2$
$V[y] = V[x/5 - 15] = 2.56$

3.31 a)

x	$P(x)$	
0	.7	$E[x] = 0.30$
1	.3	$V[x] = 0.21$

b) $E[x] = 0(1 - p) + 1(p) = p$, $V[x] = p(1 - p)$

3.33 a) $f(x) = (1/8)x + 1/4$

$$F(x) = \begin{cases} 1 & x \geq 2 \\ 1/16x^2 + 1/4x + 1/4 & -2 \leq x \leq 2 \\ 0 & x \leq -2 \end{cases}$$

$F(-2) = 0; \quad F(0) = 1/4; \quad F(2) = 1$

$P(-1 \leq x \leq 1) = 0.50$

b) $f(x) = e^{-x}$

$$F(x) = \begin{cases} 1 - e^{-x} & x \geq 0 \\ 0 & x \leq 0 \end{cases}$$

$F(0) = 0; \quad F(1) = 0.6321; \quad F(\infty) = 1$

$P(0 \leq x \leq 2) = 0.8647$

3.37 **a)** $P(x, y) = P_x(x)P_y(y)$ for all combinations?   Yes

$E[x, y] = 0.80, \quad E[x] = 2, \quad E[y] = 0.4$

$C[x, y] = 0.8 - 2(0.4) = 0$

b) The fact that $P(x, y) = P_x(x)P_y(y)$ for all combinations does not depend on the numbers used for the variables.

3.39 **a)** $E[x] = 10; V[x] = 9, \quad y = 12 + 2x$

$E[y] = E[12 + 2x] = 32, \quad V[y] = V[12 + 2x] = 36$

b) 1. $E[x \cdot y] = 50, \quad E[13 - 2x] = 3$

2. $V[x - y] = 34, \quad V[x + 2y] = 109$

$V[13 - 2x] = 36$

3. $C[x, y] = 0$ since x and y are independent

3.43 Example: x

1    $V[x] = [(1-2)^2 + (2-2)^2 + (3-2)^2]/3$

2         $= 2/3$

$\dfrac{3}{}$

Mean $= \ \ 2$

$E[x^2] - (E[x])^2 = 4\ 2/3 - 4.0 = 2/3$

3.45 **b)** $E[T] = 1/\lambda \quad V[T] = 1/\lambda^2$

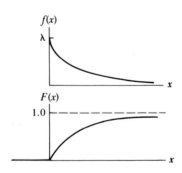

3.47 $C[x, y] = -0.160$

Chapter 4

4.3 **a)** $P(x = 2) = 0.1536$

Independence means the results of one bid have no influence on the results of any other bid.

b) $E[x] = 4.0$; the mean plus or minus three standard deviations is 4 ± 5.4, or (approximately) 0 to 9.

4.5 $P(x = 7) = 0.0079$, $\quad P(x \geq 7) = 0.0086$

4.7 **a)** $E[x] = 5.0$, $\quad V[x] = 4.75$

b) $P(x \leq 1) = 0.0371$

4.9 **a)** Average $= 47.5$ days, $\quad V[x] = 2.375$ days squared

$\sigma = 1.54$ days; using $\mu \pm 3\sigma$: $\quad 42.88$ to 52.12

b) Might be concerned with the assumption that p is a constant at 0.05, and if the events are independent.

4.11 $E[x] = 25$ cars, $\quad 25(\$50) = \$1250$

$V[x] = 18.75$ cars^2, $\quad \sigma = 4.33$ cars

Most number of cars: $\quad \mu + 3\sigma \cong 38$ cars

Highest cost $= \$50(38) = \$1900$ (for 100 cars)

4.13 **a)** $n = 11$, $\quad p = 0.55$

b) $P(x = 5) = 0.19308$; $\quad P(x \geq 5) = 0.82620$

4.15 $P(x \leq 12) = 0.0255$; such a low probability seems to suggest that the hirings were not random with $p = 0.20$. Necessary to assume that hiring is independent from one person to another, with a constant p.

4.17 The number of women in the sample was $500 \, (0.402) = 201$; $P(x \leq 201) = 0.14254$; this probability is not low enough to seriously question the $p = 0.378$ assumption.

4.19 **a)** $P(x \geq 1) = 0.6570$ $\quad$ **b)** $P(x \geq 1) = 0.70833$

4.21 $P(x = 3) = 0.01321$

4.23 $P(x = 3 | n = 20, \quad p = 0.20) = 0.0254$

The probability here differs from 4.21 because now the assumption is that sampling occurs with a constant probability of success (which is really not the case).

4.25 **a)** $P(7D, 1R) = \dfrac{\dfrac{55!}{48! \, (7!)} \dfrac{45!}{44! \, (1!)}}{\dfrac{100!}{92! \, (8!)}}$

b) $P(x = 7) = 0.04907$

c) $P(x \geq 7) = 0.05561$; this probability is not less than the (arbitrary) rule of 0.05, but the Republicans should probably complain anyway.

4.27 $P(x = 1) = 0.44388$

4.31 $P(0 \leq x \leq 1) = 0.40601$

4.33 $P(8 \leq x \leq 12) = 0.57134$

4.45 **a)** $P(x \geq 13) = 0.4241$

4.47 **a)** $P(\text{one specific hand}) = \dfrac{1}{\dfrac{52!}{39!(13!)}} = \dfrac{1}{635,013,559,620}$

    b) The hand in question resulted from the fact that a new deck was put into play and inadvertently not shuffled.

4.49 **a)** $P(n \leq 10) = 0.3668$ **b)** $E[n] = 12.5$ **c)** $V[n] = 18.75$

Chapter 5

5.3 **b)** $P(x \geq 6.00) = 0.0436$, $P(x \leq 0) = 0.1251$

5.5 **a)** $a = 55.74$ **b)** $b = 16.26$
     c) $a = 12.48$, $b = 59.52$

5.7 **b)** $P(x > 1,500,000) = 0.0034$
     $P(x < 500,000) = 0.0838$

5.9 **a)** $P(x \geq 65) = 0.0062$
     $P(x \leq 30) = 0.0301$
     b) $a = 29.32$, $b = 60.68$

5.11 $a = \$49,360$; $b = \$51,120$

5.13 **a)** 0.0516 **b)** 401.4

5.15 **a)** GRE: $z = 1.25$ GMAT: $z = 1.20$
     GRE has the better score.
     b) $a = 375.5$, $b = 704.5$ **c)** 84th percentile

5.17 47 is more than 2 1/2 standard deviations away from 100 $[(47 - 100)/20 = -2.65]$; this will occur infrequently.

5.19 Yes, because the probability is 0.0119

5.21 **a)** height when $x = 100 = \mu$ is 0.126

5.25 **b)** $\mu = 1/3$, $\sigma^2 = 1/9$ **c)** 86.5% and 95.0%

5.27 **a)** $\lambda = 2$ **b)** $\sigma^2 = 1/4$ **c)** 0.865   **d)** 0.018

5.29 **a)** 0.1251   **b)** 0.368   **c)** 0.239

5.31 **b)** 0.369, 0.330, 0.369, 0.301   **c)** mean = 50,   median = 35, $\sigma = 50$

5.33 $a = 0.61$ minutes and $b = 36$ minutes (using a computer).

5.35 0.865,   0.950,   0.982.   Despite the fact that the parent population is not normally distributed, ± 2 and ± 3 standard deviations approximate quite well the normal values expected.

5.37 0.6876,   0.9573,   0.9948
     All three percentages are quite close to normal percentages.

5.39 **a)** $v =$ the degrees of freedom   **b)** $\mu = v$, $\sigma^2 = 2v$

5.41 **a)** $\mu = 24$, $\sigma^2 = 48$
     b) 0.01,   0.100,   0.995

5.43 $n = 27$

5.45 **c)** r/n **d)** positively skewed

5.47 **a)** 0.607

Chapter 6

6.11 $\bar{x} = 3.008$, $s = 1.7609$

6.13 a) $\bar{x} = 0.60$, $s = 0.932$

6.17 a) $\bar{x} = 105$, $s = 2.5820$

b) The sample mean of 105 is considerably larger than the assumed population mean of $\mu = 96$. The sample variance of 2.5820 is considerably less than $\sigma = 4.90$. Assuming $\sigma = 4.90$, the sample mean of 105 is $z = 3.67$ standard deviations above 96.

6.19 a) $\bar{x} = 468,069$ **b)** $\bar{x} = \$6.07$ **c)** $s^2 = 10,006,179$

6.21 The average of the three numbers is 14.3%. But this average assumes the sales of the three companies are weighted equally. A better approach would be to add the sales of all three companies and then determine the overall increase in sales.

6.23 $\bar{x} = 8.545$, $s = 6.999$

6.27 a) $P(x \geq 450) = 0.6915$, $P(x \leq 600) = 0.5987$,
$P(450 \leq x \leq 600) = 0.2902$
b) $P(\bar{x} \leq 560) = 0.6554$, $P(\bar{x} \geq 530) = 0.7881$
$P(540 \leq \bar{x} \leq 560) = 0.3108$

6.31 a) 0.1056 **b)** 0.0594 **c)** 0.0009
d) Conclude that either the sample was not representative of the stated population or (more likely), the assumption of $N(100,256)$ was incorrect.

6.33 a) $\mu = 6$ **b)** $\sigma = 2.516$

6.35 $P(z \geq 7.72) \cong 0$

6.37 a) Possible samples include: (4,4) (4,5) (4,9) (4,10) (5,4)
(5,5) (5,9) (5,10) (9,4) (9,5)
(9,9) (9,10) (10,4) (10,5)
(10,9) (10,10)

$P(\bar{x} = 4.0) = 1/16$, $P(\bar{x} = 4.5) = 2/16$, $P(\bar{x} = 5.0) = 1/16$
$P(\bar{x} = 6.5) = 2/16$, $P(\bar{x} = 7.0) = 4/16$, $P(\bar{x} = 7.5) = 2/16$
$P(\bar{x} = 9.0) = 1/16$, $P(\bar{x} = 9.5) = 2/16$, $P(\bar{x} = 10.0) = 1/16$
b) $E[\bar{x}] = 7.0$, $V[\bar{x}] = 3.25$

6.39 A sample of $n = 2$ is too small for most statistical purposes.
$\bar{x} = 282.5$, $s = 10.61$

6.41 a) normal **b)** neither **c)** t-distribution **d)** neither
e) t-distribution (can be approximated by the normal)
f) t-distribution (approximately)

6.45 $P(t \leq -0.2666) = 0.3960$ (using a computer package)

6.49 a) $P(\chi^2 \geq 38) = 0.0059$ (using a computer package)
b) Because this probability is so low, the suspicion is that the meat content does differ excessively.

6.51 a) $\mu = 24$, $\sigma^2 = 48$
b) $P(\chi^2 \geq 43) = 0.01$, $P(\chi^2 \geq 33.2) = 0.10$, $P(\chi^2 \leq 9.89) = 0.005$

6.55 $P(F \geq 1.818) = 0.0194$ (using a computer package)

6.57 $P(F \geq 3.269) = 0.0033$ (using a computer package)

6.59 $s_M^2 = (2749.3063)^2 \qquad s_F^2 = (2368.5439)^2$

$P(F \geq 1.347) = 0.3426$ (using a computer package)

6.61 $t_\nu = z/\sqrt{\chi^2/\nu}$

6.65 a) nonsampling error

b) A judgment sample does not permit the concepts of probability to be used to make statements about how reliable we think the sample is.

c) One logical approach would be to stratify according to the value of the inventory. Other approaches include the length of time in inventory or the location of the inventory.

Chapter 7

7.5 Sample std dev(median) = 5.3452; Sample std dev ($\bar{x}$) = 3.0862. Since the sample std dev ($\bar{x}$) < sample std dev(median), $\bar{x}$ is a more efficient estimator of μ.

7.7 Both statements are incorrect. A confidence interval is preferred over a point estimate, and $E[\bar{x}] = \mu$.

7.9 a) x/n is unbiased.

b) $V[x/n] = 0.06$ and 0.048. The property of consistency is supported.

7.11 The sample proportion $x/n = 5/100 = 0.05$

7.15 a) 2.576   **b)** 1.96   **c)** 1.645   **d)** 1.282

7.17 a) 95%   **b)** 99%   **c)** 90%   **d)** 80%

7.19 As the $z_{\alpha/2}$ value increases, the confidence interval gets larger.

7.21 As the size of the sample increases, the confidence interval gets smaller.

7.23 $n = 16$

7.25 90% CI: $595.873 \leq \mu \leq 634.127$
      95% CI: $592.210 \leq \mu \leq 637.790$
      99% CI: $585.047 \leq \mu \leq 644.953$

7.27 99% CI: $25{,}355.41 \leq \mu \leq 29{,}344.59$

7.29 $n = 126$

7.31 90% CI: $551.00 \leq \mu \leq 623.50$

7.33 n is approximately 39

7.35 80% CI: $9.234 \leq \sigma^2 \leq 21.468$

7.37 80% CI: $2543.00 \leq \mu \leq 2891.44$

7.39 The 95% CI for candidate A is from 40% to 46%. The 95% CI for candidate B is from 36% to 42%. Since the two CIs overlap, there is no statistical difference between the two candidates.

7.41 a) $\bar{x} = 9.1367, \qquad s = 5.4026$

b) Since $n = 30$, the z-distribution may be used.

c) 95% CI: $7.203 \leq \mu \leq 11.070$

d) $n = 50$

Chapter 8

8.3 The detection approach inspects the final product for defects, whereas the prevention approach monitors the product throughout the process to identify potential problems.

8.5 Variation in line (a) is due to common causes, whereas the variation in line (b) appears to be due to assignable causes. Line (a) is in control.

8.7 Both processes appear to be in control. Process 1, however, has the distribution outside the specification limits.

8.9 Process (a) appears to be in control. Both processes (a) and (b) are out of control. In process (b) two points fall outside the control limits. In process (c) eight points fall on one side of the centerline.

8.11 Both the processes need to be reevaluated since they appear to violate the normality assumptions.

8.13 **a)** $UCL_R = 23.0535$
$LCL_R = 0$
c) The R chart will give us a picture of how the ranges change over time. The R chart is acceptable if the ranges follow a nonrandom pattern and fall within the 3-sigma limits.

8.15 $UCL_{\bar{x}} = 29.089$
$LCL_{\bar{x}} = 16.511$
The process seems to be in control since the data points when plotted all fall within the 3-sigma limits and form a nonrandom pattern.

8.17 **b)** $\bar{R} = 0.0062$; $\quad UCL_R = 0.0160$; $\quad LCL_R = 0$
c) $\bar{\bar{x}} = 0.751$; $\quad UCL_{\bar{x}} = 0.7573$; $\quad LCL_{\bar{x}} = 0.7447$
d) Both charts appear to be in statistical control.
e) The control limits lie within the specified limits.

8.19 **b)** $\bar{R} = 9.40$; $\quad UCL_R = 19.881$; $\quad LCL_R = 0$
c) $\bar{\bar{x}} = 17.18$; $\quad UCL_{\bar{x}} = 22.604$; $\quad LCL_{\bar{x}} = 11.756$
d) Both charts appear to be in statistical control.

8.25 $C_p = 0.5169$; $\quad C_{pk} = 0.3876$
The process is not capable of meeting its specifications since both C_p and C_{pk} are less than 1.

8.27 $C_p = 1.144$; $\quad C_{pk} = 1.097$
The C_{pk} is the better indicator because the specified limits are not centered midway from the process.

8.31 $\bar{p} = 0.083$; $\quad UCL_p = 0.1291$; $\quad LCL_p = 0.0369$

8.33 $\bar{c} = 0.036$; $\quad UCL_c = 0.605$; $\quad LCL_c = 0$

8.35 $\bar{p} = 0.054$; $\quad \bar{n} = 342.87$; $\quad UCL_p = 0.0906$; $\quad LCL_p = 0.0174$
The process appears to be in control.

8.41 **b)** $\bar{R} = 0.00084$; $\quad UCL_R = 0.002$; $\quad LCL_R = 0$
$\bar{\bar{x}} = 6.625$; $\quad UCL_{\bar{x}} = 6.6256$; $\quad LCL_{\bar{x}} = 6.6244$
c) Both the control charts appear to be in statistical control.
d) $C_p = 1.0213$; $\quad C_{pk} = 1.0213$
The process is capable of meeting its specifications.

Chapter 9

9.3 a) The population is all "new customers" who purchased a Ford.
H_0: $p = 0.70$ vs. H_a: $p > 0.70$, a one-sided test.
b) The binomial test for proportions.
c) 0.13904
d) 13.9% chance that 39 or more of 50 customers will be "very pleased" when the population proportion is 0.70.
e) $P(x \geq 41) = 0.0423$, $P(x \geq 40) = 0.07885$; hence $x \geq 41$ is the appropriate C.R.

9.5 1. The population is all cars traveling on highways at a given time.
H_0: $p = 0.20$ vs. H_a: $p > 0.20$.
2. binomial test statistic
3. 0.0368
4. Report 0.0368
5. This is a fairly low p-value, but probably not low enough to withhold federal funds.

9.13 a) Population of U.S. car drivers. H_0: $p = 0.50$ vs. H_a: $p > 0.50$
b) 0.05946
c) C.R. is $x \leq 17$ and $x \geq 33$, as $P(x \leq 17) = P(x \geq 33) = 0.01642$

9.15 H_0: $\mu_R = k$ vs. H_a: $\mu_R \neq k$, where $R = $ returns, and $k = $ previous year's average return. Population is 1989 returns, or at least the first quarter's returns for 1989.

9.19 1. H_0: $p_M - p_F = 0$ vs. H_a: $p_M - p_F \neq 0$
2. Two-sample z-test for proportions
3. $z = -1.946$ p-value $= 0.0516$
4. Report p-value $= 0.0516$
5. If H_0 is rejected, and the conclusion reached that the proportion of males and females differs significantly, there is a 5.16% chance of being wrong.

9.23 1. H_0: $\mu_E - \mu_C = 0$ vs. H_a: $\mu_E - \mu_C \neq 0$
2. Two-sample t-test for matched pairs
3. $t = -0.4905$, p-value $= 0.6256$
4. Report p-value $= 0.6256$
5. If H_0 is rejected, and the conclusion reached that the mean from the experimental and control groups differs significantly, there is a 62.56% chance of being wrong. In this case, H_0 should be accepted.

9.25 1. H_0: $\mu = 0.38$ vs. H_a: $\mu \neq 0.38$
2. One sample t-test
3. $t = 1.168$, p-value $= 0.2430$
4. Report p-value $= 0.2430$
5. Since p-value is relatively large, do not reject H_0, and conclude that the 1990 sample mean does not differ significantly from the 1989 average.

9.27 a) H_0: $\mu = 8.6$ vs. H_a: $\mu \neq 8.6$
$z = 2.00$, p-value $= 0.0456$
If H_0 is rejected, and we conclude that $\mu \neq 8.6$, there is a 4.56% chance of being wrong.
b) $\bar{x} \geq 8.70275$ and $\bar{x} \leq 8.49725$. Accept H_0.

9.29 a) 0.0124 if H_a is two-sided, 0.0062 if H_a is one-sided.

b) 0.0350 if H_a is two-sided, 0.0175 if H_a is one-sided; 1.753 (one-sided) and ± 2.131 (two-sided).

9.31 a) Use H_0: $\mu \leq 70{,}000$. Manufacturer would prefer H_0: $\mu \geq 70{,}001$.
  b) Type I error: concluding the tire lasts more than 70,000 miles when it lasts 70,000 or less.
  Type II error: concluding the tire lasts 70,000 miles or less when it lasts $> 70{,}000$.
  c) 0.1056   **d)** 0.1016

9.33 H_0: $\mu \geq 8.0$ vs. H_a: $\mu < 8.0$
  $t_c = -2.5571$, p-value $= 0.0096$ (using a computer); reject H_0

9.35 a) H_0: $\mu = 85$ vs. H_a: $\mu < 85$
  $t_c = -2.222$, p-value $= 0.0180$
  b) p-value $= 0.0360$

9.37 H_0: $\mu = 31.5$ vs. H_a: $\mu < 31.5$
  $t_c = -3.667$, p-value $= 0.0006$
  Reject H_0 and conclude that the shovel is not performing as well as previously expected.

9.39 a) 1. H_0: $\mu_M - \mu_F = 0$ vs. H_a: $\mu_M - \mu_F \neq 0$
    2. Two-sample z-test
    3. $z_c = 1.310$, p-value $= 0.1902$
    4. Reject H_0
    5. The conclusion is reached that the sample average salaries of the males and the mean females do not differ significantly, recognizing there is a probability of being wrong in accepting H_0.
  b) Critical region is z outside ± 1.96

9.41 1. H_0: $\mu_A - \mu_B \leq 1.00$ vs. H_a: $\mu_A - \mu_B > 1.00$
  2. Two-sample t-test
  3. $t_c = 1.896$, p-value $= 0.0310$
  4. Report p-value $= 0.0310$
  5. The conclusion should be reached that the mean benefits from the two cities differ significantly if $\alpha > 0.0310$.

9.43 1. H_0: $\mu_M - \mu_S = 0$ vs. H_a: $\mu_M - \mu_S \neq 0$
  2. Two-sample t-test
  3. $t_c = 4.819$, p-value $\cong 0$
  4. Report p-value $= 0$
  5. The conclusion should be reached that the mean number of prescriptions from the two sizes of cities differs significantly.

9.45 No, because the pooled estimate is a weighted average of the two sample variances.

9.47 1. H_0: $\mu_A - \mu_B = 0$ vs. H_a: $\mu_A - \mu_B \neq 0$ (this could be a one-sided test).
  2. Two-sample matched pairs t-test
  3. $t_c = 2.367$, p-value $= 0.0288$
  4. Report p-value $= 0.0288$
  5. If $\alpha > 0.0288$, the conclusion should be reached that the mean scores from the two groups differ significantly, recognizing there is a risk, of 2.88%, of being wrong.

9.49 H_0: $p_1 - p_2 = 0$ vs. H_a: $p_1 - p_2 > 0$

$z_c = 4.01$,　　p-value $= 0.00003$
H_0 should be rejected, realizing there is a (small) risk in doing so.

9.53 $\beta = 0.0418$; power $= 1 - \beta = 0.9582$; $\alpha = 0.01$ means that there is a 1% chance the bakery will be judged as selling underweight bread when it is not doing so. $\beta = 0.0418$ means that there is a 4.18% chance that the bakery will be judged as not selling underweight bread when it is, in fact, doing so.

9.55 a) $\beta = 0.1539$　　　**b)** $\beta = 0.1003$,　　$\alpha = 0.0197$

9.57 Optimal C.R. is $x \geq 19$; total cost for $n = 100$ is $30.39

9.59 a) $\alpha = 0.0591$,　　$\beta = 0.0138$
　　b) Type I error:　Conclude that $p = 0.75$ when actually $p = 0.50$;
　　　Make A might falsely advertise the popularity of its car.
　　　Type II error:　Conclude that $p = 0.50$ when actually $p = 0.75$;
　　　Make A might underestimate the popularity of its car.
　　c) No—if the errors are equally serious, then α and β should be approximately the same. Use $x \geq 33$; $\alpha = 0.0815$ and $\beta = 0.0834$.

9.61 Need to assume the parent populations are normally distributed, or that the sample sizes are relatively large.

9.63 a) H_0:　$\sigma_C^2 - \sigma_H^2 = 0$　vs.　H_a:　$\sigma_C^2 - \sigma_H^2 \neq 0$;　use the F-test.
　　b) $F_c = 1.778$; report 0.0438 for $(60, 30)$ d.f.; reject H_0.
　　c) Samples are certainly not random, but your grant would make a great vacation.

9.65 p-value $= 0.1380$; do not reject H_0

9.67 271 people

9.69 a) H_0:　$p = 0.50$　vs.　H_a:　$p > 0.50$;　p-value $= 0.0284$. If $\alpha \geq 0.0284$, conclude that more than 50% save greater than 10%.
　　b) Can't say without comparisons to sample of average income families.

9.71 H_0:　$\mu_1 - \mu_2 \geq -5$　vs.　H_a:　$\mu_1 - \mu_2 < -5$
　　$t_c = -4.08$,　p-value $= 0.0002$
　　Reject the null hypothesis and conclude that the new technique is at least 5 better than the old.

9.73 a) $\alpha = 0.50$,　　$\beta = 0.75$　　**b)** $\alpha = 0.75$,　$\beta = 0.62$
　　c) Second would be more appropriate.

Chapter 10

10.3 No. By the "luck of the draw," you lost $1. This is a bad *outcome*, but that doesn't mean that it was necessarily a bad *decision* to risk this possible loss of $1 for a 50–50 chance at winning $10.

10.9 It is a posterior probability with respect to the new economic figures but a prior probability with respect to the claim from the economic forecaster.

10.11 a) major ad campaign   **b)** no advertising   **c)** EMV (no advertising) = 340,000;   EMV (minor ad campaign) = 420,000;   EMV (major ad campaign) = 440,000.   Choose the major ad campaign.

10.13 If the probability of a recession is larger than 0.3, the company should put the money in the bank.

10.15 a) 0.05   **b)** 0.0087   **c)** 0.1059

10.17 a) 0.0667   **b)** 0.7846   **c)** 0.0219

10.19 a) EMV (perfect information) = 5,   EVPI = 0.50   **b)** usually not

10.23 You should be willing to pay up to $290 for perfect information.

10.25 EMV (Expand) = $6000;   EMV (Buy stocks) = $6400;   EMV (Bank) = $8000;   put money in bank.
EMV (Perfect info.) = $11,600;   EVPI = $3600.

10.27 a)

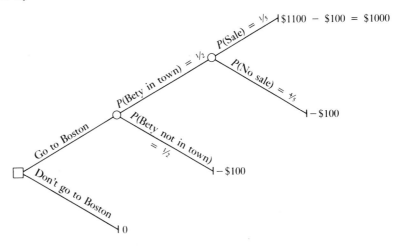

EMV (Go) = $10;   EMV (Don't go) = 0; to maximize, *fly*.
b) Joe values right arm at $50   **c)** EVSI = $26;   ENGS = $16.

10.29 a) EMV (Ship) = 17;   EMV (Repair) = 10
b) Repair coat, EMV = 10   **c)** Ship coat, EMV = 19.28
d) EMV (Sample info.) = 17.70   **e)** EVSI = 0.70;   ENGS = − 0.30.

10.31 P (new product 1|no new plant) = 0.30. If plant is not being built, choose "no advertising." P (new plant) = 0.60.
EMV (Sample info.) = 460,000;   EVSI = 20,000.

10.33 a)

p	Posterior prob.	
0.1	2/26	EMV (Stock 100) = 14.000
0.2	6/26	EMV (Stock 50) = 10.769
0.3	9/26	EMV (Don't Stock) = 0
0.4	4/26	Optimal action: Stock 100
0.5	5/26	

b)

p	Posterior prob.
0.1	18/74
0.2	24/74
0.3	21/74
0.4	6/74
0.5	5/74

EMV (Stock 100) = 4.811
EMV (Stock 50) = 6.757
EMV (Don't Stock) = 0

Optimal action: Stock 50

c) EMV (sample information) = 8.64;   EVSI = 0.84

10.37

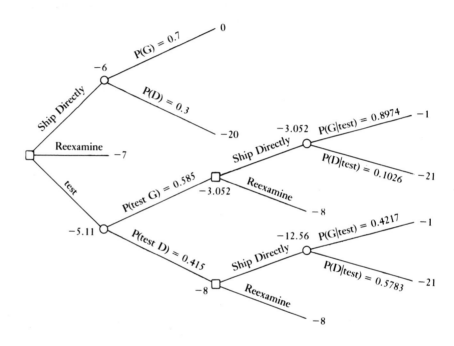

ENGS = 0.89;   EVSI = 1.89

10.41 Below the median

10.45 Normal with mean 109.73, variance 0.267

10.47 1.94

10.49 **a)** (108.76, 111.24), $P(\mu > 110) = 0.50$
b) (108.72, 110.74), $P(\mu > 110) = 0.30$

10.51 123 copies

10.53 7 cars

10.55 The firm should initiate a major ad campaign.

10.57 The probability of a recession has to be at least 0.1935 before the company puts the money in the bank.

10.59

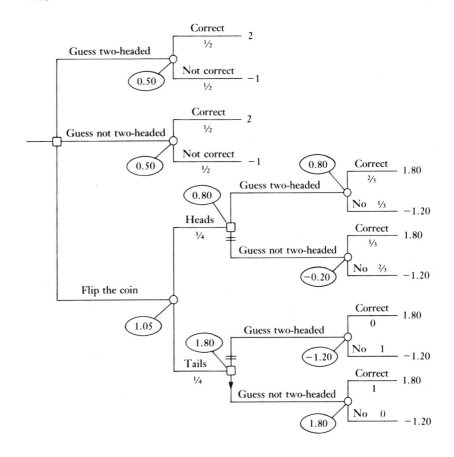

ENGS = 0.55;   EVSI = 0.75

10.63 a) guess 70B–30R   **b)** 3.20   **c)** 0.80   **d)** 1.47

10.67 maximin: either standard or lower bid for airport
maximax: standard bid for dam

10.69 The importer should purchase the scrap iron.

10.71 0.111

10.73 Up to $50,000

10.75 Normal with mean 5.87, variance 0.1829

10.77 11,250 food processors

10.79 a) Take the order without buying the forecast, the insurance, or the futures
contract.
b) Take the order and buy the futures contract.

Chapter 11

11.3 With a positive relationship, the scattergram will be upward sloping. With a negative relationship, the scattergram will be downward sloping.

11.5 **a)** The intercept (43.946) is the point at which the regression line cuts the y-axis at the point $x = 0$. The slope (-0.1068) is the amount by which the mean value of y changes for every 1-unit increase in x.
b) MPG $= 33.9068$
c) The difference in the MPG will be 5.23.

11.7 Fitted values: 3.11, 3.25, 3.28, 3.32, 3.46, 3.51, 3.55, 3.54, 3.62, 3.73.
Residuals: 0.07, 0.01, -0.06, -0.02, 0.04, -0.36, 0.17, 0.06, 0.13, -0.03.

11.9 **b)** $\hat{y} = -314.74 + 80.16x$, where y = total sales and x = number of employees.
c) The slope $(80.16 = \$80.16$ billion$)$ is the amount by which the average yearly sales increase for every 1-unit $(1$ million$)$ increase in the number of employees.
d) Fitted values: 1207.52, 1260.43, 1329.36, 1371.85, 1311.73, 1302.11, 1196.30, 1182.67, 1252.41, 1237.98, 1215.54.
Residuals: 1.48, -12.90, -24.00, -5.65, -1.20, 50.41, 6.22, 25.23, 27.30, -4.47, -62.42.

11.13 **b)** $\hat{y} = -711.286 + 1946.357x$, where y = income and x = years of education.
c) For every additional year of education, the mean income increases by $1946.60.

11.15 **a)** (i) $20,698;   95% CI: $11,520 to $29,876
(ii) $28,484;   95% CI: $19,025 to $37,943
b) It would not be advisable since this value of x ($= 5$) lies outside the range of the historical data.

11.17 The null hypothesis is that the regression line does not improve the estimate of the dependent variable. The hypothesis can be carried out using either the t-test or the F-test.

11.19 **b)** $\hat{y} = 26.105 + 0.058x$, where y = price and x = size.
c) The mean price of a house increases by $58.00 for every 1 square foot increase in size.

11.21 **a)** $F = 142.843$, p-value < 0.0001.   Since the p-value is very small, we can reject the null hypothesis.
b) $t = 11.952$, p-value < 0.0001.

11.23 **a)** SSR $= 588.75$, SSE $= 196.25$, MSR $= 588.75$, MSE $= 9.81$, $F = 60.02$
b) Since $F = 60.02$, reject the null hypothesis at $\alpha = 0.05$.

11.25 **a)** SSR $= 1500$, SSE $= 1000$, MSR $= 1500$, MSE $= 111.11$. $F = 13.5$.
b) Since $F = 13.5$, reject the null hypothesis at $\alpha = 0.05$.
c) p-value < 0.01.

11.27 $S_e = 3.0$. Approximate 95% CI is 42.98 to 54.98.

Approximate 95% CI is 47.87 to 59.87.

11.29 a) $F = 79.638$, p-value < 0.0001

   b) $t = 8.924$, p-value < 0.0001

11.31 a) Set I: $\hat{y} = 3 + 0.5x$
   Set II: $\hat{y} = 3 + 0.5x$
   Set III: $\hat{y} = 3 + 0.5x$
   Set IV: $\hat{y} = 3 + 0.5x$

   c) The graphs show that the same linear regression line can result from quite different data sets.

11.33 (i) The pound: $t = 6.338$, p-value $= 0.0007$
   (ii) The franc: $t = 4.813$, p-value $= 0.0030$

11.35 a) $\hat{y}_g = 4931.63$; 95% CI is 3707.33 to 6155.97

   b) $\hat{y}_g = 4402.93$; 95% CI is 3166.22 to 5639.76

11.37 a) $\hat{y} = \$3,269.67$; 95% CI is $3,173.69 to $3,365.65

   b) 95% CI for $\mu_{y \cdot x_g}$ is $3,209.14 to $3,330.19

11.39 a) cgal $= 47.989 + 2.686$ (cbar)

   b) The price of a gallon of gasoline increases by 2.69 cents for every $1.00 increase in the cost of a barrel of oil.

   c) 91.9%

   d) $s_b = 0.301$; $t = b/s_b = 2.686/0.301 = 8.924$

   e) $F = $ MSR/MSE $= 3717.98/46.68 = 79.638$

11.41 a) vis $= 456.83 + 1832.2$ (mark)

   b) The number of visitors will change by 1832.2 (thousands) for every 1-unit change in the exchange rate for the mark.

   c) $s_b = 533.25$ $s_e = 592.00$

   d) $F = $ MSR/MSE $= 413743/35046.2 = 11.81$; p-value lies between 0.01 and 0.025

   f) 4,121.23

Chapter 12

12.1 a) perfect positive relationship

   b) perfect negative relationship

   c) low negative relationship

   d) moderate positive relationship

   e) no relationship

   f) high negative relationship

12.3 a) The standard error, s_e, gives an indication of the amount of scatter in the data set. The correlation coefficient measures the strength of the relationship between the two variables.

   b) No inferences can be drawn from this correlation. Influences of other variables are not included.

12.7 A high correlation between x and y does not always imply a "cause and effect" relationship because there may be other influences on both variables not accounted for in the analysis.

12.9 **a)** SST = 4687.5;   SSR = 1687.5;   SSE = 3000.0
b) $F = 16.875$.   Reject the null hypothesis at $\alpha = 0.01$.

12.11 **b)** sales = 9209 + 888.59 (coupons)
c) Each additional coupon increases the average sales by $888.59.
d) $r = 0.9709$
e) $t = 9.936$.   Reject the null hypothesis at $\alpha = 0.05$.   The p-value = 0.00006.
f) $r_2 = 0.9427$;   94.27% of the variation in y (sales) is explained by the values of x (number of coupons).

12.13 **a)** $r = 0.7638$; $r^2 = 0.5833$;   58.33% of the variation is explained.
b) $t = 5.80$.   Reject the null hypothesis at $\alpha = 0.05$.   The p-value = 0.000003.

12.15 **a)** A priori, one would find the relationship to be positive.
c) $y = -1.01 + 6.138x$,   where y = percentage of wins and x = team batting average.
d) $r^2 = 0.2948$;   29.48% of the variation is explained by the regression line.

12.17 **a)** $r = 0.9031$
b) $t = 5.9462$.   Reject the null hypothesis at $\alpha = 0.05$.   The p-value = 0.0002.

12.19 **a)** SSR = 4263.16;   SSE = 1000.00;   SST = 5263.16;   MSR = 4263.16;   MSE = 50.00; F-ratio = 85.26
b) $F = 85.26$.   Reject the null hypothesis at $\alpha = 0.05$. The p-value < 0.00001.

12.21 **a)** $r = 0.7884$
b) $t = 3.391$
c) p-value = 0.006

12.23 **a)** $\hat{y} = -5111.62 + 5855.64x$, where y = number of visitors and x = exchange rate.
b) $r = 0.9577$; $r^2 = 0.9172$
c) $t = 8.153$, p-value = 0.00018
d) $\hat{y}_g = 2207.93$; $\hat{y}_g = 2500.71$

12.25 **a)** cosum = $-174.33 + 0.9841$ (pdi)
b) Consumption will increase by $984.1 millions for every $1 billion increase in personal disposable income.
c) $s_b = 0.0554$
d) p-value = 0.00000
e) $r = 0.9830$; p-value = 0.00000

Chapter 13

13.5 **a)** SSR = 3750;   SSE = 1250;   SST = 5000:
MSR = 1250;   MSE = 104.167; $F = 12.00$

b) Since $F = 12.0$, we reject the null hypothesis at $\alpha = 0.01$.

c) p-value $= 0.0012$

13.7 **a)** $m = 4$; $\quad n = 40$

b) $F = 13.125$. Reject the null hypothesis at $\alpha = 0.01$. The p-value $= 0.000002$.

c) $s_e = 5.345$

13.9 **a)** $a = 24.052$; $\quad b_1 = 14.261$; $\quad b_2 = -3.663$ $\quad \hat{y} = 24.052 + 14.261x_1 - 3.663x_2$

b) SSE $= 175.6913$; $\quad$ MSE $= 11.713$; $\quad s_e = 3.422$

c) $F = 37.59$. Reject the null hypothesis at $\alpha = 0.05$. The p-value $= 0.00002$.

d) $t_1 = 10.1429$. Reject the null hypothesis at $\alpha = 0.05$. The p-value $= 0.00002$.

e) $t_2 = -2.718$; $\quad x_1 =$ number of building permits issued is the more important variable.

13.11 **a)** $\hat{y} = 115.625 + 14.752x_1 + 0.013x_2 - 16.873x_3$

b) $F = 54.907$. Reject the null hypothesis at $\alpha = 0.01$.

c) $t_1 = 6.139$. Reject the null hypothesis at $\alpha = 0.05$. The p-value $= 0.00004$.

d) The F-test in part (b) tests for overall regression whereas the t-test in part (c) tests an individual regression coefficient.

13.13 **a)** $t_1 = 3.401$; $\quad t_2 = 11.234$. Reject the null hypothesis for both the t-tests at $\alpha = 0.05$. The p-values are 0.0008 for x_1 and < 0.000001 for x_2.

b) Variable x_2 (the number of persons in the household) is more important of the two since its t-test is more significant.

13.15 **a)** A priori, we would expect the percentage of wins to be higher the higher the team batting average and the lower the team ERA.

b) $\hat{y} = 0.1162 + 3.3723 x_1 - 0.1143x_2$

c) $F = 15.065$. Reject the null hypothesis at $\alpha = 0.01$. The p-value $= 0.0007$.

d) The team ERA is more significant in explaining the percentage of wins.

13.17 **a)** $\hat{y} = 5.3839 + 0.7906x_1 + 0.5324x_2$

b) The regression coefficient b_1 gives the change in the dependent variable for every unit change in x_1 if we keep the effects of variable x_2 constant. With just one independent variable x_1, x_2 does not affect the analysis.

c) $F = 35.003$. Reject the null hypothesis at $\alpha = 0.01$. The p-value is 0.00023.

d) Variable x_1 is more useful in predicting the variation in y.

13.21 **a)** The R^2 value of 0.88 suggests that the model is a good fit to the data. The s_e value by itself does not give an indication of how good the fit may be.

b) $F = 49.8668$. Reject the null hypothesis at $\alpha = 0.05$. The p-value $= 0$.

13.23 **a)** d.f. $= 6$

b) Variable x_3 appears to be the most important.

c) It is not proper to argue about the effects of a single variable when there are three variables in the equation.

13.27 **a)** $R^2_{y \cdot x_1 x_2 x_3} = 0.80$. That is, 80% of the variation in the dependent variable is being explained by these three variables.

   c) SST = 300;   SSE = 60;   SSR = 240;   MSR = 80;
   MSE = 3; F = 26.67; p-value $<$ 0.000001

13.29 a) At α = 0.05, d_L = 1.14 and d_U = 1.65. Since the D-W statistic falls in the range 0 to d_L, the data have positive autocorrelation.

   b) Since there is positive autocorrelation, there is a significant violation of assumption 4.

13.33 a) It appears that it would be possible to have $x1$, $x2$, and $x3$ as independent variables.

   b) Multicollinearity is likely to be a problem since $x1$ and $x2$ are highly correlated.

   c) Variable $x2$ would enter the equation first since it is the most highly correlated with y.

13.35 a) The negative coefficient for the variable 'expr' does not make intuitive sense. We would expect this variable to be positively related with 'sal'.

   b) The test for overall regression is highly significant.

   c) The results of the t-tests are different from the results of the F-test. They are not as significant. The most likely explanation is multicollinearity.

13.37 a) EST. SALES = 114.6938 + 0.1506(POP)

   b) R^2 = 0.3335

   c) t = 2.548, p-value = 0.0121

   d) Variable COMPT will enter the equation next.

   e) After step 2, R^2 will be 0.7826.

   f) s_e = 15.023

   g) F-ratio = 21.598; p-value = 0.0001

Chapter 14

14.3 The simple indexes are 94.3, 96.0, 100.0, 105.0, 108.0, 113.8, 113.6, 115.1, 114.6, 112.7, 113.4, 115.2, 114.6, 116.0

14.5 The simple indexes for the first six months are
P&G—100.00, 104.74, 113.66, 111.57, 118.21, 121.63
Lilly—100.00, 110.09, 138.53, 123.63, 138.99, 148.40
The simple aggregate indexes for the first six months are
100.00, 107.16, 124.92, 117.03, 127.62, 133.75

14.9 The retail sales from 1975 to 1988, adjusted for inflation to 1967 dollars are
364.9, 385.6, 398.1, 411.5, 412.5, 387.9, 384.1, 369.9, 392.5, 417.3, 428.2, 442.9, 443.7, 457.8

14.15 The three-month MA time series for the period Feb 1985 to July 1985 (the first six months) is
132.46, 129.17, 127.38, 126.29, 127.92, 127.85
The five-month MA time series for the period Mar 1985 to Aug 1985 (the first six months) is
130.50, 127.98, 127.45, 127.38, 126.85, 127.10

14.21 c) Linear trend line: $y = 66.393 - 3.056t$ $r^2 = 0.9352$
Exponential curve: $y = 70.133(0.933)^t$ $r^2 = 0.9655$
The exponential curve fits these data better.

14.23 a) Linear trend line: $y = 84280.5 + 1929.23t$
Forecast for 1988 = 113,219
Forecast for 1989 = 115,148

14.29 a) $s_{12} = 82.429$ for $\alpha = 0.2$
Forecasts for Jan 1987 to Dec 1987 are
82.43, 82.06, 82.61, 83.21, 84.15, 85.08, 86.18, 87.37,
88.81, 89.85, 90.50, 90.96
MAD = 0.776,   RSME = 0.864
b) $s_{12} = 77.594$ for $\alpha = 0.4$
Forecasts for Jan 1987 to Dec 1987 are
77.59, 78.80, 81.20, 82.96, 84.94, 86.48, 88.13, 89.72,
91.67, 92.60, 92.80, 92.80.
MAD = 1.321,   RSME = 1.499

14.31 The answers to this problem will depend on the initial estimates of the base value, trend, and seasonal indexes.

14.33 a) There are several different ways to determine these values.
b) The time series appears to be stable with no significant trend. Therefore, low values of the smoothing constants will be more appropriate.

14.35 a) Indexes for the first six months of 1986 are
Franc: 100.00, 106.09, 107.03, 108.65, 111.64, 111.74
Yen: 100.00, 108.64, 111.28, 114.45, 120.44, 130.92
Mark: 100.00, 104.87, 106.55, 107.47, 109.52, 108.98

14.37 b) $y = 41.718 + 0.742t$, where y is the exchange rate for the German mark and t is months.
MAD = 1.821
c) Forecast for Jan = 60.27 (Actual = 60.62)
Forecast for Feb = 61.01 (Actual = 61.01)
Forecast for Mar = 61.75 (Actual = 59.56)

14.39 The seasonal indexes for Jan to Dec are
99.15, 99.26, 99.49, 99.34, 100.29, 101.31, 100.40, 101.05,
100.13, 99.95, 100.00, 99.63

14.41 c) The seasonal indexes for Jan to Dec are
89.88, 88.26, 102.27, 103.69, 111.53, 107.19, 104.74,
105.35, 109.45, 100.38, 88.77, 88.48

14.43 The answers to this problem will depend on the initial estimates of the base value, trend, and the seasonal indexes.

14.45 The answers to this problem will depend on the initial estimates of the base value, trend, and the seasonal indexes.

Chapter 15

15.1 random variation

15.5 The sample means are $\bar{y}_1 = 59/5 = 11.8$, $\bar{y}_2 = 44/5 = 8.8$, $\bar{y}_3 = 61/5 = 12.2$, and $\bar{y}_4 = 43/5 = 8.6$. The grand sample mean is $\bar{y} = 207/20 = 10.35$. The estimated treatment effects are 1.45, -1.55, 1.85, -1.75.

15.7 For the Southeast, $\bar{y}_1 = 893/9 = 99.22$; for the Southwest, $\bar{y}_2 = 1065/10 = 106.50$; for the Northeast, $\bar{y}_3 = 1038/10 = 103.80$; for the Northwest, $\bar{y}_4 = 512/5 = 102.40$; for the Midwest, $\bar{y}_5 = 785/7 = 112.14$; and for the Far West, $\bar{y}_6 = 633/6 = 105.50$. The estimate for the entire United States is the grand sample mean, $\bar{y} = 4926/47 = 104.81$. The estimated treatment effects are $-5.59, 1.69, -1.01, -2.41, 7.33, 0.69$.

15.9

	Case 1	Case 2
SS total	112	112
SS between	0	112
SS within	112	0

These are extreme cases in the sense that SS between is zero in Case 1 and SS within is zero in Case 2.

15.15

Source	Sum of Squares	d.f.	Mean Square	Computed F-value	F-value alpha = .05	p-value
Between groups	54.9500	3	18.3167	7.04	3.24	.003
Error (within groups)	41.6000	16	2.60000			
Total	96.5500	19				

15.17

Source of Variation	SS	d.f.	MS
Between machines	59.2	2	29.6
Within machines	72.6	18	4.0
Total	131.8	20	

$F = \dfrac{29.6}{4.0} = 7.4$. Yes, the manager can reject the hypothesis of equal mean output for the three machines at the $\alpha = 0.05$ level.

15.19 The computed F-value is not significant at the 0.05 level.

15.21 0.0429

15.23

$$1\text{–}2:\quad 0.2 + 1.5 \pm \sqrt{2(6.01)(4.0)\left(\frac{1}{5} + \frac{1}{10}\right)} = 1.7 \pm 3.80 = (-2.10, 5.50)$$

$$1\text{–}3:\quad 0.2 - 2.5 \pm \sqrt{2(6.01)(4.0)\left(\frac{1}{5} + \frac{1}{6}\right)} - 2.3 \pm 4.20 = (-6.50, 1.90)$$

$$2\text{–}3:\quad -1.5 - 2.5 \pm \sqrt{2(6.01)(4.0)\left(\frac{1}{10} + \frac{1}{6}\right)} = -4.0 \pm 3.58 = (-7.58, -0.42)$$

Only the difference between machines 2 and 3 is significant at the 99% confidence level.

15.25 The estimated treatment effects are: $37.25, 21.58, -26.64, -32.20$. The simultaneous confidence intervals are

A–B: $37.25 - 21.58 \pm 27.14 = (-11.47, 42.81)$.

A–C: $37.25 + 26.64 \pm 27.14 = (36.75, 91.03)$.
A–D: $37.25 + 32.20 \pm 27.14 = (42.31, 96.59)$.
B–C: $21.58 + 26.64 \pm 27.14 = (21.08, 75.36)$.
B–D: $21.58 + 32.20 \pm 27.14 = (26.64, 80.92)$.
C–D: $-26.64 + 32.20 \pm 27.14 = (-21.58, 32.70)$.

15.27 Advertising could still have an impact upon sales via interaction effects.

15.29 Over and above their individual effects, putting advertising and type A packaging together reduces sales on average by 2. On the other hand, a synergistic effect is obtained when advertising and type B packaging are put together, resulting in a total effect that is higher (by 7) than the sum of their individual effects.

15.31 a) The means are given in this table:

	A	B	C	
Adv.	36.33	36.33	26.33	33.00
No adv.	32.67	16.33	32.00	27.00
	34.50	26.33	29.17	30.00 = grand sample mean

b) SS Total = 984
SS Columns = 206
SS Rows = 162
SS Error
$$= 17{,}184 - \frac{(109)^2 + (109)^2 + (79)^2 + (98)^2 + (49)^2 + (96)^2}{3} = 109$$
SS Interaction $= 984 - 206 - 162 - 109 = 507$

c) MS Columns $= 206/2 = 103$ MS Rows $= 162/1 = 162$
MS Interaction $= 507/2 = 253.5$ MS Error $= 109/12 = 9.1$

d)

Source of Variation	SS	d.f.	MS	F
Columns	206	2	103.0	11.32
Rows	162	1	162.0	17.80
Interaction	507	2	253.5	27.86
Error	109	12	9.1	
Total	984	17		

e) The tests for nonzero column effects, row effects, and interaction effects (values of F given in c) all yield significant results.

15.33 Adv., A: $(464/10) - (832/20) - (944/30) + (1904/60) = 5.07$
Adv., B: $(302/10) - (680/20) - (944/30) + (1904/60) = -3.53$
Adv., C: $(178/10) - (392/20) - (944/30) + (1904/60) = -1.53$
No adv., A: $(368/10) - (832/20) - (960/30) + (1904/60) = -5.07$
No adv., B: $(378/10) - (680/20) - (960/30) + (1904/60) = 3.53$
No adv., C: $(214/10) - (392/20) - (960/30) + (1904/60) = 1.53$

15.35 None is significant.

15.37 The three F-tests all yield significant results, and the estimated effects are as follows:
Center City $= -0.02$; Lakefront $= 0.05$; West Side $= -0.08$; North suburbs $= 0.07$; Drug Store $= 0.03$; Discount Store $= -0.21$; Grocery

Store = 0.19; Center, Drug = $-$ 0.03; Center, Discount = 0.00; Center, Grocery = 0.01; Lake, Drug = 0.11; Lake, Discount = $-$ 0.03; Lake, Grocery = $-$ 0.08; West, Drug = $-$ 0.08; West, Discount = 0.06; West, Grocery = 0.03; North, Drug = $-$ 0.01; North, Discount = $-$ 0.05; North, Grocery = 0.04

15.45

Source of Variation	SS	d.f.	MS	F
Linear regression	361426.2724	1	361426.2724	315.579
Error	12598.0645	11	1145.2786	
Total	374024.3369	12		

The linear regression effect is significant at the 0.05 level as well as at the 0.01 level.

15.51 **a)** The effects are significant at the 0.05 level.
b) An estimate of σ^2 is MS within = 200.83.
c) Intervals I–II: $-$ 0.67 $-$ 14.33 ± 25.00 = ($-$ 40.00, 10.00)
    II–III: 14.33 + 13.67 ± 25.00 = (3.00, 53.00)
    I–III: $-$ 0.67 + 13.67 ± 25.00 = ($-$ 12.00, 38.00)
Only the difference between II and III is significant.

15.53 **a)** $-$ 0.14, $-$ 1.87,   2.00
b) no
c) The vitamin C group had the fewest days with colds, followed by those taking the placebo. However, the differences are small enough to have occurred by chance.
d) Yes. Knowing one's group could (perhaps subconsciously) have an effect on the reporting of colds.

15.55

Source of Variation	SS	d.f.	MS	F
Hospitals	3450	2	1725.0	107.14
Sex	428	1	428.0	26.58
Interaction	219	2	109.5	6.80
Error	482	30	16.1	
Total	4579	35		

All effects are significant. The estimated effects are as follows:
Hospital A: (382/12) $-$ (698/36) = 12.44
Hospital B: (95/12) $-$ (698/36) = $-$ 11.47
Hospital C: (221/12) $-$ (698/36) = $-$ 0.97
Male: (411/18) $-$ (698/36) = 3.44
Female: (287/18) $-$ (698/36) = $-$ 3.44
A, Male: (199/6) $-$ (382/12) $-$ (411/18) + (698/36) = $-$ 2.11
A, Female: (183/6) $-$ (382/12) $-$ (287/18) + (698/36) = 2.11
B, Male: (60/6) $-$ (95/12) $-$ (411/18) + (698/36) = $-$ 1.36
B, Female: (35/6) $-$ (95/12) $-$ (287/18) + (698/36) = 1.36
C, Male: (152/6) $-$ (221/12) $-$ (411/18) + (698/36) = 3.47
C, Female: (69/6) $-$ (221/12) $-$ (287/18) + (698/36) = $-$ 3.47

15.57 All effects are significant at the 0.05 level. Estimated effects:
Cities: 2.19, 3.69, -5.89; Times: -2.39, -0.89, 3.28;

	1	2	3
9 am	-0.02	2.73	-2.69
12:30 pm	1.73	0.98	-2.69
4 pm	-1.69	-3.69	5.39

15.59 no

15.61 One-factor experiment:

Source of Variation	SS	d.f.	MS	F
Between sweeteners	9.92	2	4.96	4.91
Within sweeteners	300.65	297	1.01	
Total	370.57	299		

The differences are large enough to be attributable to something other than chance (the critical value of F for $\alpha = 0.05$ is 3.00 here).

Combined (two-factor) experiment:

Source of Variation	SS	d.f.	MS	F
Columns (sweeteners)	6.50	2	3.25	1.37
Rows (oil/butter)	143.08	1	143.08	60.12
Interaction	3.95	2	1.98	0.83
Error	699.79	294	2.38	
Total	853.32	299		

The column effects and interaction effects are not even close to being significant, but the row effects are highly significant. Thus, it seems clear that butter should be used, and when butter is used, the average ratings are in the expected neighborhood of 3.5 (3.58 with sugar, 3.61 with corn syrup, and 3.51 with artificial sweetener). It appears that the three sweeteners have about the same acceptance when used with butter. But sugar is considerably more expensive than corn syrup or artificial sweetener, so the firm should choose one of the latter. The final decision should probably depend on the chance of potential problems (government regulation, public opinion, etc.) as well as the relative costs and expected availability of corn syrup and artificial sweetener.

Chapter 16

16.3 **a)** interval **b)** nominal **c)** ratio **d)** nominal

16.5 $E[U] = 800$, $\sigma_U^2 = 10,800$, $\sigma_U = 104$
$z = -4.80$, $P(z \le -4.80) \cong 0$; reject H_0

16.7

X	P(X)	CUMULATIVE PROBABILITY
9	.00977	.00977
10	.00098	.01074

16.9 **a)** The null hypothesis is the two systems have the same median. The alternative hypothesis is the two systems have different medians. Use H_0: $p = 0.50$ *vs.* H_a: $p \neq 0.50$.

X	P(X)	CUMULATIVE PROBABILITY
4	.15625	.15625
5	.03125	.18750

b) $t_c = -1.3093$, p-value $= 0.1303$ (using a computer)

16.11 $P(x \geq 20) = 0.0020$

16.13 **a)** H_0: $p = 0.50$ *vs.* H_a: $p \neq 0.50$

X	P(X)	CUMULATIVE PROBABILITY
7	.07031	.07031
8	.01758	.08789
9	.00195	.08984

b) $T = \min\{4, 41\} = 4$;   reject H_0 if $\alpha \geq 0.02$

16.15 The null hypothesis is that the errors occur at random—i.e., there is no pattern to them. For the errors in Table 14.18, there are $n_1 = 11 +$ signs, $n_2 = 13 -$ signs, and 6 runs. From Table XI, the critical value for the number of runs is 7. Since the number of runs (6) is less than the critical value (7), H_0 should be rejected.

16.17 **a)** There are 12 runs. There does appear to be some pattern to the residuals.
     b) The p-value indicates that H_0 should be rejected if $\alpha > 0.0505$, indicating a possible concern for autocorrelation. There are 15 minus signs, 16 plus signs, and $z = -1.640$ is the standardization of r.

16.19 **a)** nominal   **b)** nominal   **c)** nominal   **d)** ordinal   **e)** ordinal
     f) ordinal   **g)** nominal   **h)** ordinal

16.21 **a)**

CLASS	FREQUENCIES OBSERVED	EXPECTED
1	705.00	696.75
2	224.00	232.25
TOTALS	929.00	929.00

CHI-SQUARE $= 0.391$, p-value $= 0.5319$ (using a computer)
     b) $2P(x \geq 705 | n = 929, p = 0.75) = 0.56$

16.23 Combining cells

	0	1	2	3	≥ 4
O/E	144/139	91/97.3	32/34.1	11/8.0	2/1.6

CHI-SQUARE $= 1.94$; p-value $= 0.2532$ (using a computer)

16.25

	FREQUENCIES	
CLASS	OBSERVED	EXPECTED
1	9.00	10.00
2	21.00	15.00
3	14.00	15.00
4	6.00	10.00
TOTALS	50.00	50.00

CHI-SQUARE $= 4.167$, p-value $= 0.1245$ (using a computer)
Do not reject H_0 if $\alpha < 0.1245$.

16.27 EXPECTED VALUES (Cell format: count/percent: total/percent: row/percent: col/percent)

	1–4 YRS	5–9 YRS	10–14 YRS	>15 YRS	TOTAL
FEMALE	11.50	23.00	9.50	6.00	50.00
	11.50	23.00	9.50	6.00	50.00
	23.00	46.00	19.00	12.00	
	50.00	50.00	50.00	50.00	
MALE	11.50	23.00	9.50	6.00	50.00
	11.50	23.00	9.50	6.00	50.00
	23.00	46.00	19.00	12.00	
	50.00	50.00	50.00	50.00	
TOTAL	23.00	46.00	19.00	12.00	100.00
	23.00	46.00	19.00	12.00	100.00

CHI-SQUARE $= 6.171$, p-value $= 0.1036$

16.29 Max value $|F - S| = 0.0177$, do not reject H_0

16.33 $C = 0.3366$

16.37 Spearman's rho $= 0.2867$
Kendall's tau $= 0.1818$

Index

Index

GLOSSARY OF COMMONLY USED SYMBOLS

$\sum$	summation sign (Greek capital sigma)
∞	infinity
$\cong$	approximately equal to
$|a|$	absolute value of a
$\log_a$	logarithm to base a
$\ln$	natural logarithm (base e)
$\int_a^b$	integral from a to b
μ	mean of a population (Greek mu)
$\overline{x}$	mean of a sample (x-bar)
N	number of values in a population
n	number of values in a sample
σ^2	population variance (Greek sigma squared)
σ	population standard deviation (Greek sigma)
p.m.f.	probability mass function
p.d.f.	probability density function
$E[x]$	expected value of x
$F(x)$	probability that $x \le x$, cumulative function
$C[x, y]$	covariance of x and y
p	probability of success on a binomial trial
λ	Poisson mean and variance (Greek lambda)
z	standardized normal random variable
$N(\mu, \sigma^2)$	normal distribution with mean μ, variance σ^2
T	random variable for exponential distribution
χ^2	random variable for chi-square distribution (Greek chi-square)
s^2	sample variance
s	sample standard deviation
$\mu_{\overline{x}}$	mean of all possible values of $\overline{x}$
$\sigma_{\overline{x}}^2 = V[\overline{x}]$	variance of all possible values of $\overline{x}$
$\sigma_{\overline{x}}$	standard error of the mean ($= \sigma/\sqrt{n}$)
ν	degrees of freedom (Greek nu)
t	random variable for t-distribution
F	random variable for F-distribution
α	probability of making an error (Greek alpha)